W9-BXR-965

Fremantle

Sydney

Leg 4

Auckland

Leg 3

Leg 2

MANAGEMENT

FIFTH EDITION

The Dryden Press Series in Management

MANAGEMENT

FIFTH EDITION

Richard L. Daft
Vanderbilt University

The Dryden Press

A Division of Harcourt College Publishers

Fort Worth Philadelphia San Diego New York Orlando Austin San Antonio
Toronto Montreal London Sydney Tokyo

Publisher *Mike Roche*
Senior Acquisitions Editor *John Weimeister*
Senior Developmental Editor *Tracy Morse*
Project Editor *Becky Dodson*
Art Director *Biatriz Chapa*
Production Manager *Lois West*
Executive Marketing Strategist *Lisé Johnson*
Project Management *Elm Street Publishing Services, Inc.*
Compositor *GTS Graphics, Inc.*

Cover Image *© Marc A. Castelli "Shakedown Sleighride (Chessie)" 1997,
        Watercolor, 22 in. x 30 in. Parker Rockefeller Collection.*

ISBN: 0-03-025967-3
Library of Congress Catalog Card Number:: 99-72430
Copyright © 2000, 1997, 1994, 1991, 1988 by Harcourt, Inc.

All rights reserved. No part of this publication may be reproduced or transmitted in any form or by any means, electronic or mechanical, including photocopy, recording, or any information storage and retrieval system, without permission in writing from the publisher.

Requests for permission to make copies of any part of the work should be mailed to the following address: Permissions Department, Harcourt, Inc., 6277 Sea Harbor Drive, Orlando, FL 32887-6777.

Address for Domestic Orders
Harcourt, Inc., 6277 Sea Harbor Drive, Orlando, FL 32887-6777
800-782-4479

Address for International Orders
International Customer Service
Harcourt, Inc., 6277 Sea Harbor Drive, Orlando, FL 32887-6777
407-345-3800
(fax) 407-345-4060
(e-mail) hbintl@harcourt.com

Address for Editorial Correspondence
Harcourt College Publishers, 301 Commerce Street, Suite 3700, Fort Worth, TX 76102

Web Site Address
http://www.harcourtcollege.com

Printed in the United States of America

0 1 2 3 4 5 6 7   048   9 8 7 6 5 4

Harcourt College Publishers

To the late Martin S. Geisel,
dean, mentor, and friend

DRYDEN

is

Harcourt College Publishers

A Harcourt Higher Learning Company

Now you will find The Dryden Press' distinguished innovation, leadership, and support under a different name . . . a new brand that continues our unsurpassed quality, service, and commitment to education.

We are combining the strengths of our college imprints into one worldwide brand: Harcourt

Our mission is to make learning accessible to anyone, anywhere, anytime—reinforcing our commitment to lifelong learning.

We are now Harcourt College Publishers. Ask for us by name.

One Company
"Where Learning Comes to Life."

www.harcourtcollege.com
www.harcourt.com

Preface

The field of management is undergoing a revolution. Demands on today's managers go well beyond the techniques and ideas traditionally taught in management courses. The traditional management paradigm assumes the purpose of management is to control and limit people, enforce rules and regulations, seek stability and efficiency, design a top-down hierarchy to direct people, and achieve bottom-line results. The emerging paradigm recognizes that today's managers need different skills to engage workers' hearts and minds as well as take advantage of their physical labor. The emerging management paradigm focuses on *leadership,* on harnessing people's creativity and enthusiasm, finding shared vision and values, and sharing information and power. Teamwork, collaboration, participation, and learning are guiding principles that help managers and employees maneuver the difficult terrain of today's complex business environment. Managers focus on developing, not controlling, people to adapt to extraordinary environmental shifts and achieve total corporate effectiveness.

Both the new and the traditional paradigm are guiding management actions in the world today. My vision for the fifth edition of *Management* is to explore the new paradigm in a way that is interesting and valuable to students, while retaining the best of traditional management ideas. To achieve this vision, I have included the most recent management thinking and research, as well as the contemporary application of management ideas in organizations. The combination of established scholarship, new ideas, and real-life applications gives students a taste of the energy, challenge, and adventure inherent in the dynamic field of management. The Dryden Press and I have worked together to provide a textbook better than any other at capturing the excitement of organizational management.

I revised *Management* to provide a book of utmost quality that will create in students both respect for the changing field of management and confidence that they can understand and master it. The textual portion of this book has been enhanced through the engaging, easy-to-understand writing style and the many in-text examples and boxed items that make concepts come alive for students. The graphic component has been enhanced with several new exhibits and a new set of photo essays that illustrate specific management concepts. The well-chosen photographs provide vivid illustrations and intimate glimpses of management scenes, events, and people. The photos are combined with brief essays that explain how a specific management concept looks and feels. Both the textual and the graphic portions of the textbook help students grasp the often abstract and distant world of management.

Focus on the Future

The fifth edition of *Management* is especially focused on the future of management education by identifying and describing emerging elements and examples of the new management paradigm. New materials in the book include the following:

- Chapter 1 introduces the emerging management paradigm, including the growing importance of leadership and new management competencies needed to thrive in today's business world. The chapter also explores the forces affecting today's organizations and managers.

- Chapter 2 has been significantly revised to describe the *learning organization* and examine it as an extension of the historical development of management and organizations.

- The foundations of organizational behavior have been expanded into a new Chapter 15, with topics including personality types, job satisfaction and organizational commitment, the effects of stress, and person-job fit.

- Chapter 21, "Information Systems and Technology," has been completely revised to keep pace with the rapid changes in this area. The chapter includes new or expanded material on such topics as intranets and extranets, geographic information systems, data mining, enterprise resource planning, and knowledge management.

- In recognition of the role of technology in today's world, each chapter of the text integrates coverage of the Internet and emerging technology into the various topics covered in the chapter. In addition, most chapters contain a *Leading the Revolution: Technology* box that features a technologically savvy company or highlights a trend that is impacting today's organizations. Topics include online shopping, push technology that delivers data to desktop PCs, paperless office systems, Internet recruiting, and cross-cultural traps to avoid when building a Web page. The book's technology emphasis is also reflected in new *Surf the Net* exercises at the end of each chapter.

- Each chapter includes a *Leading the Revolution* box that focuses on either *Leadership* or the emerging *Learning Organization*. These examples include leaders at companies such as Interface, Inc., British Petroleum, Hewlett-Packard, Nissan Design International, Monorail, the Girl Scouts, NEXC, Lucent Technologies, Cisco Systems, and the U.S. Army.

- Information on recent trends toward empowerment and participation in organizations has been strengthened in the content of chapters on planning and goal setting, leadership, teamwork, communication, decision making, and motivation, among others

- The chapters on structure have been updated to include more information on innovations such as network and virtual organizations and to compare and contrast characteristics of traditional organizations with those of the emerging learning organization.

- Chapter 8, "Strategy Formulation and Implementation," includes a new discussion of cooperative strategies, reflecting the trend toward collaboration among organizations rather than competition.

- Chapters from the previous edition on "Quality Control" and "Management Control Systems" have been combined to reflect the integration of these topics, resulting in more concise, streamlined coverage highlighting important topics.

- Chapter 22, "Operations and Service Management," has been revised to provide information on supply chain management and the growing importance of logistics.

- A section has been added to the chapter on "Human Resource Management" to examine the changing social contract between people and organizations and the ways it is affecting the nature of careers.

- The chapter, "Managing Diverse Employees," places greater emphasis on the challenges faced by minorities and also includes a discussion of the potential benefits and difficulties of emotional connections in the workplace.

- A brief discussion of personal decision style has been added to the chapter on "Managerial Decision Making" to give students a better understanding of how an individual's style interacts with other factors when managers make decisions.

- Because leadership plays a significant role in the emerging management paradigm, there is a strong emphasis on leadership throughout the entire text. Specific topics include leading the learning organization, changing culture through symbolic leadership, leading change, and using persuasion and influence.

In addition, Dryden has brought together a team of experts to create and coordinate color photographs, video cases, beautiful artwork, and supplementary materials for the best management textbook and package on the market.

Organization

The chapter sequence in *Management* is organized around the management functions of planning, organizing, leading, and controlling. These four functions effectively encompass both management research and real-life characteristics of the manager's job.

Part One introduces the world of management, including the nature of management, the emerging management paradigm, the learning organization, and historical perspectives on management.

Part Two examines the environments of management and organizations. This section includes material on the business environment and corporate culture, the global environment, ethics and social responsibility, the natural environment, and the environment of entrepreneurship and small business management.

Part Three presents three chapters on planning, including organizational goal setting and planning, strategy formulation and implementation, and the decision-making process.

Part Four focuses on organizing processes. These chapters describe dimensions of structural design, the design alternatives managers can use to achieve strategic objectives, structural designs for promoting innovation and change, the design and use of the human resource function, and the ways managing diverse employees are significant to the organizing function.

Part Five is devoted to leadership. This section begins with a chapter on organizational behavior, providing a grounding in understanding people in organizations. This foundation paves the way for subsequent discussions of leadership, motivating employees, communication, and team management.

Part Six describes the controlling function of management, including basic principles of total quality management, the design of control systems, information technology, and techniques for control of operations management.

Special Features

One major goal of this book is to offer better ways of using the textbook medium to convey management knowledge to the reader. To this end, the book includes several special features.

Chapter Outline and Objectives. Each chapter begins with a clear statement of its learning objectives and an outline of its contents. These devices provide an overview of what is to come and can also be used by students to see whether they understand and have retained important points.

Management Problem/Solution. The text portion of each chapter begins with a real-life problem faced by organization managers. The problem pertains to the topic of the chapter and will heighten students' interest in chapter concepts. The questions posed in the Management Problem are resolved in the Chapter Summary at the end of the chapter, where chapter concepts guiding management's actions are highlighted.

Photo Essays. Another feature of the book is the use of photographs accompanied by detailed captions that describe management events and how they relate to chapter material. While the photos are beautiful to look at, they also convey the vividness, immediacy, and concreteness of management events in today's business world.

Contemporary Examples. Every chapter contains a number of written examples of management incidents. They are placed at strategic points in the chapter and are designed to demonstrate the application of concepts to specific companies. These in-text examples—indicated by an icon and shading in the margin—include well-known companies such as McDonald's, General Electric, Hewlett-Packard, and Motorola, as well as less-well-known companies and not-for-profit organizations such as Plastic Lumber Company, Katzinger's Delicatessen, General Stair Corp., and Northwestern Memorial Hospital. These examples put students in touch with the real world of organizations so they can appreciate the value of management concepts.

Leading the Revolution Boxes. These boxes, two in each chapter, illustrate three major themes of the fifth edition: Leadership, Technology, and the Learning Organization. The Technology boxes explore topics of current interest or companies on the cutting edge of today's fast-paced technological business world. Learning Organization boxes examine companies that are using new paradigm ideas to cope with the turbulent environment. The Leadership boxes focus on real-life managers who exemplify the qualities of effective leadership for the 21st century. The book also includes occasional boxes highlighting diversity issues.

Manager's Shoptalk Boxes. These boxes address topics straight from the field of management that are of special interest to students. They may describe a contemporary topic or problem that is relevant to chapter content or they may contain a diagnostic questionnaire or a special example of how managers handle a problem. These boxes will heighten student interest in the subject matter and provide an auxiliary view of management issues not typically available in textbooks.

Video Cases. The six parts of the text conclude with video cases that illustrate the concepts presented in that part. The 22 videos enhance class discussion because students can see the company and more directly apply the management theories they have learned. A detailed description of each video, classroom activities, and discussion questions and answers are provided in the *Instructor's Manual*.

Exhibits. Many aspects of management are research based, and some concepts tend to be abstract and theoretical. To enhance students' awareness and understanding of these concepts, many exhibits have been included throughout the book. These exhibits consolidate key points, indicate relationships among variables, and visually illustrate concepts. They also make effective use of color to enhance their imagery and appeal.

Glossaries. Learning the management vocabulary is essential to understanding contemporary management. This process is facilitated in three ways. First, key concepts are boldfaced and completely defined where they first appear in the text. Second, brief definitions are set out in the margin for easy review and follow-up. Third, a glossary summarizing all key terms and definitions appears at the end of the book for handy reference.

Chapter Summary and Discussion Questions. Each chapter closes with a summary of key points that students should retain. The discussion questions are a complementary learning tool that will enable students to check their understanding of key issues, to think beyond basic concepts, and to determine areas that require further study. The summary and discussion questions help students discriminate between main and supporting points and provide mechanisms for self-teaching.

Management in Practice Exercises. End-of-chapter exercises called "Management in Practice: Experiential Exercise" and "Management in Practice: Ethical Dilemma" provide a self-test for students and an opportunity to experience management issues in a personal way. These exercises take the form of questionnaires, scenarios, and activities, and many also provide an opportunity for students to work in teams.

Surf the Net. Each chapter contains three Internet exercises to involve students in the high-tech world of cyberspace. Students are asked to explore the Web for research into topics related to each chapter. This hands-on experience helps them develop both Internet and management skills.

Case for Critical Analysis. Also appearing at the end of each chapter is a brief but substantive case that provides an opportunity for student analysis and class discussion. Many of these cases are about companies whose names students will recognize; others are based on real management events, but the identities of companies and managers have been disguised. These cases allow students to sharpen their diagnostic skills for management problem solving.

Supplementary Materials—Leading by Example

Another market innovation from Daft, the fifth edition's ancillary package is loaded with powerful resources for students and instructors alike.

Combining the latest technology with proven teaching tools, the package enables students to put chapter concepts into action and gain valuable insight into real-world practices. In addition, an expansive collection of supplemental teaching material offers support to instructors—from the novice to the most seasoned professor.

Completely integrated with the text, this comprehensive package continues to lead the market with its innovation and real-world management application. Many new cutting-edge features have been added to create an unrivaled support system.

- **NEW! Daft Home Page:** *Management,* fifth edition, has crossed the line to online. Students and professors can tap into countless business and education resources with this leading-edge tool.

  Completely integrated with the fifth edition, this interactive Web site gives students hands-on experience using the Internet as a business tool. Through online exercises, students can review chapter material and explore the vast resources available online. A time management section features strategies for avoiding procrastination, getting organized, and setting goals and priorities. A reading room section links users to business journals, daily newspapers, and magazines across the country and around the world.

  An online case library includes an extra collection of cases of varying lengths and levels. In addition, the site links instructors to teaching resources, bibliographies of articles related to text material, ideas on incorporating the Internet into the classroom, and Dryden staff members. Dryden's Teaching Tips Module is also available online, offering insights from instructors nationwide, including teaching tips, cases, exercises, supplemental lecture topics, and more. Most of the resources and Internet-based interactive exercises are organized by chapter.

  This site is a reservoir of management information. In fact, the Daft Web site includes so many resources for each chapter that it could be used as the foundation for a distance-learning course.

- **NEW! Web Instructor's Manual:** Created to help instructors integrate the Daft Web site into the course with ease. Includes detailed outlines of the Daft Web site, instructor's teaching notes for company profiles and exercises, and detailed notes on how the instructor can integrate the Web site into the course.

- **Instructor's Manual:** Designed to provide support for instructors new to the course, as well as innovative materials for more experienced professors, the *Instructor's Manual* (IM) includes detailed "Lecture Outlines" that offer information and examples not in the text, "Class Starter" suggestions, and a "Lecture Illustration File" with real-world examples of management concepts in practice. Annotated learning objectives, changes to the fifth edition, answers to chapter discussion questions, and teaching notes for the end-of-chapter cases and exercises offer additional support to instructors.

  In addition, the video notes are available to help instructors integrate video segments directly with classroom discussion. Support materials include a video outline, references to concepts within the chapter that are discussed in the video, answers to video case discussion questions, individual and group exercises, and a multiple-choice quiz about the video.

- **Computerized Instructor's Manual:** Most elements of the IM are available on disk in a Windows format, enabling instructors to electronically cut and paste custom lecture outlines with ease.

- **Test Bank:** The newest edition—ExaMaster99—is a cross-platform version available on CD-ROM that works with the latest versions of the Macintosh, Windows, and Windows NT operating systems. ExaMaster99 includes online testing capabilities, a grade book, and much more. Scrutinized for accuracy, the *Test Bank* includes more than 2,000 true/false, multiple-choice, short-answer, and essay questions, which have been rated for difficulty and designated as factual or application. The *Test Bank* is available in printed, DOS, Windows, and Macintosh formats.

- **Study Guide:** Packed with real-world examples and additional applications, this learning supplement is an excellent resource for students. For each chapter of the text, the *Study Guide* includes a summary and completion exercise; a review with multiple-choice, true/false, and short-answer questions; a mini-case with multiple-choice questions; management applications; and an experiential exercise that can be assigned as homework or used in class.

- **IMPROVED AND UPDATED! Acetates/Masters:** Created from artwork in the text, as well as outside materials, the full-color acetates and masters are available separately and both include detailed teaching notes.

- **NEW AND UPDATED! Videos:** A complete set of videos featuring the management practices of actual companies and their executives supports the end-of-chapter case materials. Numerous videos have been updated for the fifth edition, and many are new to this edition, such as Hard Candy, Holigan Group, J.C. Penny, Southwest Airlines, Yahoo!, and more.

- **Discovering Your Management Career CD-ROM:** Included free with each new copy of *Management,* fifth edition, by the Dryden Press, is a CD-ROM entitled "Discovering Your Management Career." It contains three programs, each of which may be used in conjunction with your course: *Discovering Your Management Career, Career Design,* and *Management at Sea.*

  Discovering Your Management Career helps students learn about and assess their compatibility with four major management career areas. They were selected not only to represent the diversity of management opportunities available but also for the number of jobs in these fields.

  - Corporate Financial Management
  - Marketing Management
  - Retail Bank Management
  - Store Operations

For each career, students receive broad guidance and practical advice on everything from clarifying the depth of their interest in that management career to preparing and implementing an effective job search strategy.

Also included on the *Discovering Your Management Career* CD-ROM is a free copy of the student version of *Career Design,* the landmark career planning software program that is based on the work of John Crystal, the major contributor to the most widely read career book of all time, *What Color Is Your Parachute?* by Richard N. Bolles. *Career Design* has received worldwide coverage and praise from both the business and computer press, including *BusinessWeek, Fortune, The Wall Street Journal, The Financial Times, The London Times, PC Magazine,* and *PC Computing.* The student version provides general career exercises and a wealth of other resources.

Management at Sea offers students a realistic and exciting view of management in action. Through commentary on actual footage from major sailing races, students will learn how effective management can lead to better results. Sailing is a metaphor for this key theme: If management can make a difference in a sport such as sailing, it can clearly make a difference in the business world where a rapidly changing environment and intense competition are also the norm rather than the exception. Footage of boat construction and race preparation are used to illustrate planning and organizing principles, while videos of sailing races demonstrate leading and controlling.

- **NEW AND IMPROVED! PowerPoint CD-ROM Presentation Software:** This innovative presentation tool enables instructors to customize their own multimedia classroom presentations. The package includes figures and tables from the text, as well as outside materials to supplement chapter concepts. Material is organized by chapter. Instructors can use the material as is or expand and modify it for individual classes. The software is available in two formats: PowerPoint 95 and PowerPoint 97. The PowerPoint 97 version allows instructors to simply click on links to move from the PowerPoint presentation to Web sites. PowerPoint Slides are also saved on the CD in a form without color so that professors can easily print the presentation into Transparency Masters.

- **NEW! Web Support:** The Dryden Press has partnered with WebCT to assist adopters with Web-based education materials. Your local Dryden sales representative can provide you with details.

- **NEW! Performance Module:** In the real world, the bottom line is performance. Employees, managers, top-level executives, entire companies—everything—is evaluated on performance. This unique new module takes an in-depth look at performance issues. It provides insightful material to reinforce class discussions and gives students practice with performance issues.

- **Multicultural Diversity Module:** This module offers an inside look at the broad topic of cultural, ethnic, and gender diversity in today's workplace.

- **Quality Module:** This publication covers the history of the quality movement up to present practices and developments, spotlighting such quality pioneers as W. Edwards Deming, Joseph M. Juran, and Philip Crosby.

- **Management and the Natural Environment Module:** This module addresses issues of the natural environment with each functional management topic. The module includes a separate video, as well as instructor's notes.

The Dryden Press will provide complimentary supplements or supplement packages to those adopters qualified under our adoption policy. Please contact your sales representative to learn how you may qualify. If as an adopter or potential user you receive supplements you do not need, please return them to your sales representative or send them to:

Attn: Returns Department
Troy Warehouse
465 South Lincoln Drive
Troy, MO 63379

Acknowledgments

A gratifying experience for me was working with the Fort Worth team of professionals at The Dryden Press who were committed to the vision of producing the best management text ever. I am grateful to John Weimeister, Senior Acquisitions Editor, whose enthusiasm, creative ideas, and vision kept the book's spirit alive. Lisé Johnson, Executive Marketing Strategist, provided keen market knowledge and innovative ideas for instructional support. Tracy Morse, Senior Developmental Editor, provided superb project coordination and offered excellent ideas and suggestions to help the team meet a demanding and sometimes arduous schedule. Ellen Hostetler, Editorial Assistant, and Marcia Masenda, Marketing Assistant, skillfully pitched in to help keep the project on track. I am also indebted to the team at Elm Street Publishing Services for their production expertise and commitment to producing a quality book. Karen Hill provided extensive assistance on four chapters of the text and also assisted with project coordination. Ingrid Mount and Phyllis Crittenden cheerfully and expertly guided me through the details of the production process. A special thank-you goes out to the entire team at Elm Street. Their careful attention to detail contributed greatly to the quality of the final book.

Here at Vanderbilt, I want to extend special appreciation to my secretary and assistant, Linda Roberts. Linda provided excellent typing and other assistance on a variety of projects that gave me time to write. I also want to acknowledge an intellectual debt to my colleagues, Bruce Barry, Ray Friedman, Barry Gerhart, Tom Mahoney, Rich Oliver, David Owens, and Greg Stewart. Thanks also to the late Dean Marty Geisel who always supported my various projects and maintained a positive scholarly atmosphere in the school.

Another group of people who made a major contribution to this textbook are the management experts who provided advice, reviews, answers to questions, and suggestions for changes, insertions, and clarifications. I want to thank all of these colleagues for their valuable feedback and suggestions:

David C. Adams
Manhattanville College

Erin M. Alexander
University of Houston, Clear Lake

Hal Babson
Columbus State Community College

Reuel Barksdale
Columbus State Community College

Gloria Bemben
Finger Lakes Community College

Art Bethke
Northeast Louisiana University

Thomas Butte
Humboldt State University

Peter Bycio
Xavier University, Ohio

Diane Caggiano
Fitchburg State College

Douglas E. Cathon
St. Augustine's College

Jim Ciminskie
Bay de Noc Community College

Dan Connaughton
University of Florida

Bruce Conwers
Kaskaskia College

Byron L. David
The City College of New York

Richard De Luca
William Paterson University

Robert DeDominic
Montana Tech

Linn Van Dyne
Michigan State University

John C. Edwards
Southern Illinois University at Carbondale

Mary Ann Edwards
College of Mount St. Joseph

Janice M. Feldbauer
Austin Community College

Daryl Fortin
Upper Iowa University

Michael P. Gagnon
New Hampshire Community Technical College

Richard H. Gayor
Antelope Valley College

Dan Geeding
Xavier University, Ohio

James Genseal
Joliet Junior College

Peter Gibson
Becker College

Carol R. Graham
Western Kentucky University

Gary Greene
Manatee Community College

Paul Hayes
Coastal Carolina Community College

Dennis Heaton
Maharishi University of Management, Iowa

Jeffrey D. Hines
Davenport College

Bob Hoerber
Westminster College

James N. Holly
University of Wisconsin–Green Bay

Genelle Jacobson
Ridgewater College

C. Joy Jones
Ohio Valley College

Sheryl Kae
Lynchburg College

Jordan J. Kaplan
Long Island University

J. Michael Keenan
Western Michigan University

Cynthia Krom
Mount St. Mary College

William B. Lamb
Millsaps College

George Lehma
Bluffton College

Janet C. Luke
Georgia Baptist College of Nursing

Jenna Lundburg
Ithaca College

Walter J. Mac Minhaw
Oral Roberts University

Myrna P. Mandell
California State University, Northridge

Daniel B. Marin
Louisiana State University

Dennis W. Meyers
Texas State Technical College

Alan N. Miller
University of Nevada, Las Vegas

Irene A. Miller
Southern Illinois University

Micah Mukabi
Essex County College

David W. Murphy
Madisonville Community College

James L. Moseley
Wayne State University

Nora Nurre
Upper Iowa University

Nelson Ocf
Pacific University

Tomas J. Ogazon
St. Thomas University

Allen Oghenejbo
Mills College

Linda Overstreet
Hillsborough Community College

Ken Peterson
Metropolitan State University

Clifton D. Petty
Drury College

James I. Phillips
Northeastern State University

Kenneth Radig
Medaille College

Gerald D. Ramsey
Indiana University Southeast

Barbara Redmond
Briar Cliff College

William Reisel
St. John's University, New York

Walter F. Rohrs
Wagner College

Marcy Satterwhite
Lake Land College

Don Schreiber
Baylor University

Kilmon Shin
Ferris State University

Daniel G. Spencer
University of Kansas

Gary Spokes
Pace University

M. Sprencz
David N. Meyers College

Shanths Srinivas
California State Polytechnic University, Pomona

Jeffrey Stauffer
Ventura College

William A. Stower
Seton Hall University

Mary Studer
Southwestern Michigan College

James Swenson
Moorhead State University, Minnesota

Irwin Talbot
St. Peter's College

Andrew Timothy
Lourdes College

Frank G. Titlow
St. Petersburg Junior College

John Todd
University of Arkansas

Dennis L. Varin
Southern Oregon University

Gina Vega
Merrimack College

George S. Vozikis
University of Tulsa

Bruce C. Walker
Northeast Louisiana University

Mark Weber
University of Minnesota

Emilia S. Westney
Texas Tech University

Stan Williamson
Northeast Louisiana University

Alla L. Wilson
University of Wisconsin–Green Bay

Ignatius Yacomb
Loma Linda University

Imad Jim Zbib
Ramapo College of New Jersey

Vic Zimmerman
Pima Community College

I would like to extent a personal word of thanks to the many dedicated authors who contributed to the extensive supplement package for the fourth edition. Amit Shah has written a wonderful *Test Bank*. Tom Lloyd has made the *Instructor's Manual* a valuable teaching tool with innovative new features.

Stephen Hiatt has worked hard to ensure that the *Study Guide* reflects the chapter material in the textbook. Charles Beem enhanced the teachability of the *Teaching Acetates and Transparency Masters* with instructive notes. Thanks to Stephen Peters, for his work in creating the PowerPoint Lecture Presentation CD-ROM. Robert Allen wrote the new Performance Teaching Module, and Eric Sandburg, of Career Design Software, designed the CD and Web site. Thanks to them both for these exciting new features.

I'd like to pay special tribute to my editorial associate, Pat Lane. This revision is our fifth project together, and she has spoiled me to the point that I can't imagine how I ever got along on my own. Pat provided truly outstanding help throughout every step of the revision of this text. She skillfully aided in drafting materials for a variety of cases and topics, researched topics when new sources were lacking, and did an absolutely superb job with the copy-edited manuscript and page proofs. Her commitment to this text enabled us to achieve our dream for its excellence.

Finally, I want to acknowledge the love and contributions of my wife, Dorothy Marcic. Dorothy has been very supportive during this revision as we grew in our lives together. I also want to acknowledge my love and support for my five daughters, who make my life special during our precious time together. Thanks also to B.J., Kaitlyn, Kaci, and Matthew for their warmth, silliness, and smiles that brighten my life, especially during our skiing days together.

Richard L. Daft
Nashville, Tennessee
May 1999

About the Author

Richard L. Daft, Ph.D., holds the Ralph Owen Chair of Management in the Owen School of Management at Vanderbilt University, where he specializes in the study of organization theory and leadership. Dr. Daft is a Fellow of the Academy of Management and has served on the editorial boards of *Academy of Management Journal, Administrative Science Quarterly,* and *Journal of Management Education.* He was Associate Editor-in-Chief of *Organization Science* and served for three years as associate editor of *Administrative Science Quarterly.*

Professor Daft has authored or co-authored 11 books, including *Organization Theory and Design* (South-Western College Publishing, 1998), *Leadership. Theory and Practice* (Dryden, 1999), and *What to Study: Generating and Developing Research Questions* (Sage, 1982). He recently published *Fusion Leadership: Unlocking the Subtle Forces That Change People and Organizations* (Berrett-Koehler, 1998, with Robert Lengel). He has also authored dozens of scholarly articles, papers, and chapters. His work has been published in *Administrative Science Quarterly, Academy of Management Journal, Academy of Management Review, Strategic Management Journal, Journal of Management, Accounting Organizations and Society, Management Science, MIS Quarterly, California Management Review,* and *Organizational Behavior Teaching Review.* Professor Daft has been awarded several government research grants to pursue studies of organization design, organizational innovation and change, strategy implementation, and organizational information processing.

Dr. Daft also is an active teacher and consultant. He has taught management, leadership, organizational change, organizational theory, and organizational behavior. He has been involved in management development and consulting for many companies and government organizations, including American Banking Association, Bell Canada, National Transportation Research Board, NL Baroid, Nortel, TVA, Pratt & Whitney, State Farm Insurance, Tenneco, the United States Air Force, the U. S. Army, J.C. Bradford & Co., Central Parking System, Entergy Sales and Service, First American National Bank, and the Vanderbilt University Medical Center.

Brief Contents

Contents

Part Two   THE ENVIRONMENT OF MANAGEMENT   69

Chapter 3   The Environment and Corporate Culture   70

Leading the Revolution:
Technology
Shopping On-Line
Manager's Shoptalk
The New Golden Rule:
   Cooperate!
Leading the Revolution:
The Learning Organization
St. Lukes
Examples
Northern Telecom Ltd.
   (Nortel)
McDonald's

Chapter 4   Managing in a Global Environment   102

Leading the Revolution:
Technology
Cross-Cultural Web Traps
Manager's Shoptalk
Defining Global Ethics
Leading the Revolution:
Leadership
Giving Workers the Freedom
   to Learn
Example
Mercedes-Benz

Part Three   **PLANNING   203**

Chapter 7   **Organizational Planning
and Goal Setting   204**

**Leading the Revolution:
Technology**
Regulating E-mail in the
Workplace
**Leading the Revolution:
The Learning Organization**
Springfield Remanufacturing
Corporation
Examples
Amex Life Assurance
Producers Gas and
Transmission
U.S. Army

Chapter 8   **Strategy Formulation
and Implementation   232**

**Leading the Revolution:
Technology**
Dell Computer
**Leading the Revolution:
The Learning Organization**
Cisco Systems

Chapter 9   Managerial Decision Making   266

Part Five **LEADING 465**

Chapter 15 **Foundations of Behavior in Organizations 466**

Leading the Revolution: Leadership
The Sweet Taste of Success
Manager's Shoptalk
Getting the Right Fit
Leading the Revolution: Technology
Information Warriors
Examples
Microsoft
The Carlson Companies
Wendy's International

Chapter 16 **Leadership in Organizations 500**

Leading the Revolution: Technology
Hunterdon High School
Manager's Shoptalk
Are You a Charismatic Leader?
Leading the Revolution: Leadership
The Girl Scout Way

Examples
PC Connection and Tenneco
Plastic Lumber Company
Business Wire

Chapter 17   Motivation in Organizations   532

Leading the Revolution: Diversity
Motivating Women Workers
   at Ernst & Young
Manager's Shoptalk
The Carrot-and-Stick
   Controversy
Leading the Revolution: The Learning Organization
The Social Experiment at
   Quad/Graphics
Examples
Outback Steakhouse
Katzinger's Delicatessen
Parsons Pine Products
Sequins International, Inc.

Chapter 18   Communicating in Organizations   564

Leading the Revolution: Technology
Creating Community at
   Rykodisc
Leading the Revolution: The Learning Organization
The Friday Morning
   Appointment

Examples
General Electric
Northwestern Memorial
  Hospital

Manager's Shoptalk
How to Run a Great Meeting
**Leading the Revolution:
Technology**
VeriFone's Virtual World
**Leading the Revolution:
Leadership**
Team Leader Qualities
Examples
Whole Foods Market
BP Norge
The Rainbow Warriors

**Leading the Revolution:
Leadership**
A Tale of Two Leaders: One
  Company
**Leading the Revolution:
Technology**
Snowboarding: It's in Control

MANAGEMENT

FIFTH EDITION

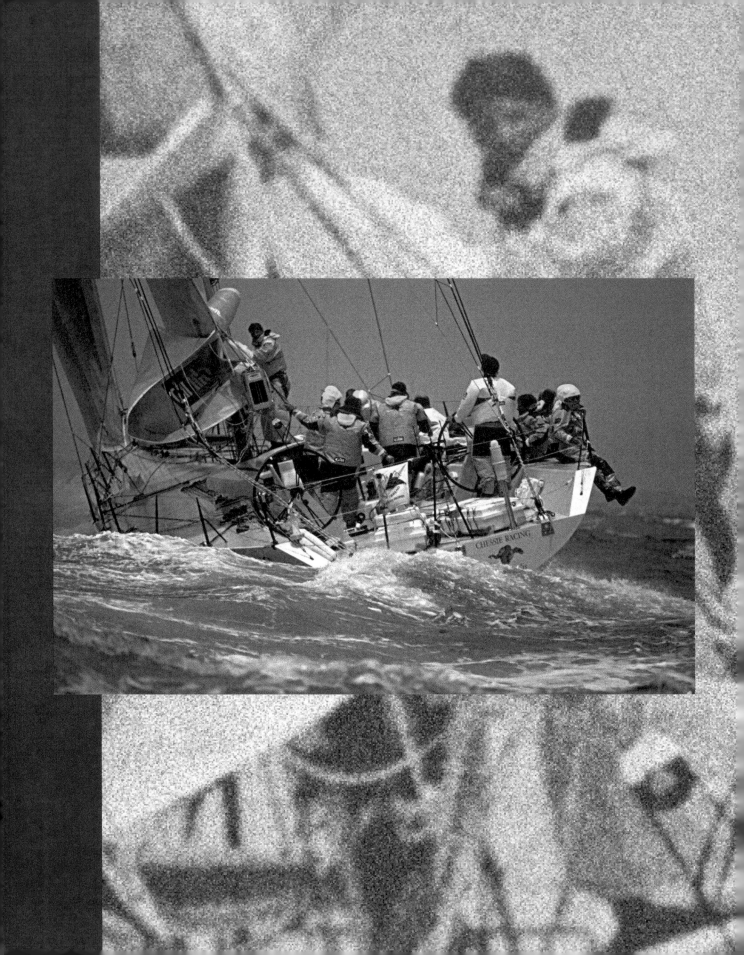

Part One
Introduction to Management

The Whitbread Round the World Race is a punishing test of sailing skill, held every four years since 1973. The most recent race in 1997–1998 began in Southampton, England, and lasted nine months—through nine race legs and a total of 31,600 nautical miles. Boats chased each other and the clock from northern to southern hemisphere and back again with stops in seven countries scattered around the world. As a sporting challenge, it has been compared to scaling Mount Everest.

The Whitbread 60 boats are finely tuned, high-tech machines, with a dozen crew members who have trained together for nearly half a year before the starting signal sounds. They need to draw from the skills they have honed and the teamwork they have learned throughout their journey. The experience and conceptual skills of the skipper can mean the difference between success or failure. The skipper is in charge of coordinating the crew; processing the information from the navigator on shifting wind conditions, ocean currents, and weather forecasts; and charting the course. He or she must also encourage the crew to perform in the worst conditions and to fight together through disasters and setbacks, which are all too common. All members know their roles and need to perform flawlessly when it counts. The stakes are high—a slip in balance could cost you your life. In fact, since the first race in 1973–1974, four sailors have lost their lives and many more have been injured.

The ultimate goal of the crew? Knowing that you endured and beat the competition—the best professional sailors in the world—and capturing the prized Volvo trophy.

In Part One you will learn about the skills and roles of managers and the history and new models of management.

Chapter 1

LEARNING OBJECTIVES

After studying this chapter, you should be able to

☀ Explain the management revolution and how it will affect you as a future manager.

☀ Describe the four management functions and the type of management activity associated with each.

☀ Explain the difference between efficiency and effectiveness and their importance for organizational performance.

☀ Define functional, general, and project managers.

☀ Describe conceptual, human, and technical skills and their relevance for managers and nonmanagers.

☀ Define ten roles that managers perform in organizations.

☀ Describe the new management paradigm and the issues managers must prepare for in the future.

The Changing Paradigm of Management

MANAGEMENT PROBLEM

Liisa Joronen, chairman and owner of SOL, grew up in one of Finland's wealthiest and most prestigious families, but her company competes in one of the world's least glamorous businesses—industrial cleaning. A woman who has never had to sweep a floor a day in her life runs a company of 3,500 employees who scrub hospital floors, sweep grocery aisles, and make hotel beds. The industry is characterized by backbreaking labor, low wages, high turnover, and lousy service. SOL Cleaning Service, however, presents a totally different picture—that of a fast-paced, high-energy, knowledge-driven company whose employees love their jobs. In five years, the company has doubled its number of customers and increased revenues from $35 million to $60 million. Each SOL supervisor leads a team of up to 50 cleaners who cheerfully fan out across Finland wearing bright red-and-yellow jumpsuits. The company headquarters in Helsinki explodes with color, creativity, and chaos. Employees wander the halls talking on bright yellow portable phones and meet in rooms that look more like playgrounds than offices. In Finland, and increasingly across Europe, SOL is known as an icon of what it takes to win in the new world of business.[1]

What management skills and techniques helped Liisa Joronen create one of Northern Europe's most admired companies in such a low-tech industry? If you were a manager at SOL, how would you help workers find satisfaction in hard, low-skilled jobs?

Most students probably have never heard of Liisa Joronen, but the management actions she and other managers perform every day are the key to keeping SOL Cleaning Service healthy, inspired, and productive. Joronen's mantra, "Kill routine before it kills you," is increasingly important to all managers in companies in every industry. Today's companies are struggling to remain competitive in the face of increasingly tough global competition, uncertain environments, cutbacks in personnel and resources, and massive worldwide economic, political, and social shifts. The growing diversity of the workforce brings new challenges: maintaining a strong corporate culture while supporting diversity; balancing work and family concerns; coping with the conflict brought about by the demands of women and ethnic minorities for increased power and responsibility. Workers are asking that managers share rather than hoard power. Organizational structures are becoming flatter, with power and information pushed down and out among fewer layers and with teams of frontline workers playing new roles as decision makers.

Because of these changes a revolution is taking place in the field of management. A new kind of leader is needed who can guide businesses through this turbulence—a strong leader who recognizes the complexity of today's world and realizes there are no perfect answers.[2] The revolution asks managers to do more with less, to engage whole employees, to see change rather than stability as the nature of things, and to create vision and cultural values that allow people to create a truly collaborative workplace. This new management approach is very different from a traditional mindset that emphasizes tight top-down control, employee separation and specialization, and management by impersonal measurements and analysis. Liisa Joronen and SOL Cleaning are excellent examples of a manager and company that are leading this revolution toward a new management paradigm, or way of thinking.

Making a difference as a manager today and tomorrow requires a different approach from yesterday. Successful departments and organizations don't just happen—they are managed to be that way. Managers in every organization today face major challenges and have the opportunity to make a difference.

Lee Iacocca made a difference at Chrysler Corporation when he rescued it from bankruptcy by reducing internal costs, developing new products, and gaining concessions from lenders, the union, and government. Chad Holliday, executive vice president for DuPont, made a difference when he stuck to his decision to recruit local talent to head up DuPont in Japan, despite grumblings by several of the company's top managers. Since Akira Imamichi, who speaks little English, took the reins, earnings have been growing twice as fast, even as the Japanese economy has been in a rut. Likewise, the late Roberto Goizueta made a difference when he shook up the status quo at The Coca-Cola Company. When Goizueta took over as chief executive, the company was mired in a hodgepodge of unrelated businesses, from shrimp farming to winemaking. Its bottling system was badly decayed, with important markets left in the hands of weak operators. Coke's stock had fallen by half and the company was barely making a profit. Perhaps worst of all, there was no strategic vision for the future. Goizueta's actions to solve those problems made Coca-Cola a global powerhouse. From the time he became chief executive until his death in 1997, Coke's sales more than quadrupled, from $4 billion to $18 billion, while its market capitalization ballooned from $4.3 billion to a staggering $180 billion.[3] Chanut Piyaoui made a difference by

The late Roberto C. Goizueta answered an ad for a chemical engineer that appeared in a newspaper in Havana, Cuba. He was hired and twenty-six years later he became Chairman and CEO of The Coca-Cola Company. Managers like Goizueta make a difference for organizations. When his leadership began, creativity at Coke was stifled by a blind adherence to tradition and refusal to accept risk. He gathered his managers together and questioned every assumption they held about the business, preparing them for his vision of the future. Goizueta respected tradition but held nothing sacred except progress.

changing the somewhat unsavory reputation of Thailand hotels as "places of entertainment," as she delicately phrased it. With little initial capital, Chanut's vision and management skills created Thailand's leading hotel chain. Her Dusit Thani Group was ranked by *Asiamoney* magazine as one of the 100 best-managed companies in Asia.[4]

These managers are not unusual. Every day, managers solve difficult problems, turn organizations around, and achieve astonishing performances. To be successful, every organization needs skilled managers.

This textbook introduces and explains the process of management and the changing ways of thinking about and perceiving the world that are becoming increasingly critical for managers of today and tomorrow. By reviewing the actions of some successful and not-so-successful managers, you will learn the fundamentals of management. The challenges Liisa Joronen faces at SOL Cleaning are not unusual for managers. By the end of this chapter, you will already understand how Joronen helps keep SOL on track. By the end of this book, you will understand fundamental management skills for planning, organizing, leading, and controlling a department or an entire organization. In the remainder of this chapter, we will define management and look at the ways in which roles and activities are changing for today's managers. The final section of the chapter talks about the trend toward the learning organization and provides more detail about some of the challenges managers will face in the coming years.

The Definition of Management

What do managers such as Lee Iacocca, Chad Holliday, and Liisa Joronen have in common? They get things done through their organizations. One management scholar, Mary Parker Follett, described management as "the art of getting things done through people."[5] Peter Drucker, a noted management theorist, explains that managers give direction to their organizations, provide leadership, and decide how to use organizational resources to accomplish goals.[6] Getting things done through people and other resources and providing direction and leadership are what managers do. These activities apply not only to top executives such as Liisa Joronen or Roberto Goizueta, but also to a leader of a cleaning crew, a supervisor in a bottling plant, or a director of marketing for Coca-Cola. Moreover, management often is considered universal because it uses organizational resources to accomplish goals and attain high performance in all types of profit and not-for-profit organizations. Thus, our definition of management is as follows:

> **Management** is the attainment of organizational goals in an effective and efficient manner through planning, organizing, leading, and controlling organizational resources.

management
The attainment of organizational goals in an effective and efficient manner through planning, organizing, leading, and controlling organizational resources.

There are two important ideas in this definition: (1) the four functions of planning, organizing, leading, and controlling and (2) the attainment of organizational goals in an effective and efficient manner. Managers use a multitude of skills to perform these functions. Management's conceptual, human, and technical skills are discussed later in the chapter. Exhibit 1.1 illustrates the process of how managers use resources to attain organizational goals. Although some management theorists identify additional management functions, such as staffing, communicating, or decision making, those additional functions will be discussed as subsets of the four primary functions in Exhibit 1.1.

Exhibit *1.1* — *The Process of Management*

Management Functions

Resources
- Human
- Financial
- Raw materials
- Technological
- Information

Planning
Select goals and
ways to attain them

Controlling
Monitor activities
and make corrections

Organizing
Assign
responsibility for task
accomplishment

Leading
Use influence to
motivate employees

Performance
- Attain goals
- Products
- Services
- Efficiency
- Effectiveness

Chapters of this book are devoted to the multiple activities and skills associated with each function, as well as to the environment, global competitiveness, and ethics, which influence how managers perform these functions. The next section begins with a brief overview of the four functions.

The Four Management Functions

Planning

planning
The management function concerned with defining goals for future organizational performance and deciding on the tasks and resource use needed to attain them.

Planning defines where the organization wants to be in the future and how to get there. **Planning** means defining goals for future organizational performance and deciding on the tasks and use of resources needed to attain them. At Komatsu, Japan's leading manufacturer of construction equipment and heavy machinery, president Satoru Anzaki announced a long-range plan called "G"2000, which includes moving the company into high-tech initiatives such as lasers and 3D software, as well as more traditional goals such as advances in heavy machinery and finding more environmentally friendly technologies. Senior managers at Home Depot defined specific plans to increase the number of stores by 25 percent a year and to open 460 new stores in Canada, Mexico, and the United States by 1998.[7]

A lack of planning—or poor planning—can hurt an organization's performance, however. For example, clothing retailer Merry-Go-Round, a once-ubiquitous presence in malls across America, slid into bankruptcy and ultimately disappeared as a result of poor planning. Top managers' lack of vision in perceiving market direction and demographic trends, weak planning efforts regarding acquisitions and growth, and the failure to prepare for management succession helped to kill a 1,500-store, $1-billion nationwide chain.[8]

Organizing

organizing
The management function concerned with assigning tasks, grouping tasks into departments, and allocating resources to departments.

Organizing typically follows planning and reflects how the organization tries to accomplish the plan. **Organizing** involves the assignment of tasks, the grouping of tasks into departments, and the allocation of resources to departments. For example, Hewlett-Packard, Sears Roebuck, Xerox, and Digital Equipment have all undergone structural reorganizations to accommodate their changing plans. Semco, a Brazilian company making industrial pumps, mixers, propellers, and other products, reorganized from a highly structured, autocratic business into a company run on trust, freedom, and democracy. Six people, including one woman, rotate as CEO, each putting in six-month stints. Employees set their own work schedules, organizing themselves to accomplish their tasks. Semco's loose organization has been so successful that Mobil, IBM, and hundreds of other U.S. companies have traveled to São Paulo to see the operation firsthand.[9] Honeywell managers reorganized new product development into "tiger teams" consisting of marketing, engineering, and design employees. The new structural design reduced the time to produce a new thermostat from 4 years to 12 months.[10] Many companies today are following Honeywell's lead by reorganizing into teams that have more responsibility for self-management.

Leading

Providing leadership is becoming an increasingly important management function. **Leading** is the use of influence to motivate employees to achieve organizational goals. Leading means creating a shared culture and values, communicating goals to employees throughout the organization, and infusing employees with the desire to perform at a high level. Leading involves motivating entire departments and divisions as well as those individuals working immediately with the manager. In an era of uncertainty, international competition, and a growing diversity of the workforce, the ability to shape culture, communicate goals, and motivate employees is critical to business success.

Well-known managers such as Lee Iacocca and Jack Welch are exceptional leaders. They are able to communicate their vision throughout the organization and energize employees into action. However, one doesn't have to be well-known to be an exceptional leader. There are many managers working quietly who also provide strong leadership within departments, teams, not-for-profit organizations, and small businesses. For example, Jean Kvasnica excels as a team leader at Hewlett-Packard. According to one team member, Kvasnica succeeds in motivating people because she has "vision and intense commitment to the successful outcome of a project, but the idea that makes it successful could come from anywhere. She's not selfish about it."[11]

At some companies, such as Southwest Airlines, every employee is encouraged to assume leadership responsibility, solve problems, and help motivate others. The philosophy of master leader Herb Kelleher, CEO of Southwest, is that it is the employees on the front lines—not in the front office—who are the heroes of the company. Kelleher has built a strong employee culture based on simple, fundamental principles of giving customers what they want and being happy in the work that one does. Kelleher's leadership has made Southwest's workers the most productive in the industry, and leadership filters down throughout the company. Because workers feel

leading
The management function that involves the use of influence to motivate employees to achieve the organization's goals.

Jean Kvasnica began her career at Hewlett-Packard as a secretary. She is currently head of a multifunctional sales team that competes for sales of computers, meters, and other equipment worth hundreds of millions of dollars. Kvasnica succeeds at leading *partly because she tries to emulate the qualities she responds to in a leader: "...rooted in the ground...not defensive, not egotistical... open minded, able to joke and laugh at themselves. They can take a volatile situation and stay focused."*

valued, they are willing to pitch in wherever needed; for example, pilots might man the boarding gate if necessary, or ticket agents might schlepp luggage. When Southwest acquired tiny Morris Air, hundreds of Southwest employees spontaneously began sending cards, candy, and company T-shirts to Morris workers as a way of welcoming them into the fold.[12]

Of course, poor leadership can have a negative impact on a company. Contrast Kelleher's leadership with that of Frank Lorenzo, former CEO and hatchet man at Continental Airlines. Lorenzo's leadership contributed to employees' *demotivation*. Gregory Brenneman, recruited by new Continental CEO Gordon Bethune to be the airline's chief operating officer, says he was shocked by the demoralized workforce and the degree of rancor that existed between labor and management as a legacy of Lorenzo's reign of terror. The executive suites were kept locked, and top executives' secretaries had buttons under their desks that could be bumped by a knee to call the police. Brenneman and Bethune, who is himself a pilot, are dismantling the destructive culture. They've set up an 800 number for employee complaints, instituted a profit-sharing plan, and started paying bonuses based on the airline's on-time record. Most importantly, Brenneman and Bethune are visiting employees throughout the company, spreading a message of pride and accountability.[13] Their leadership is helping to put Continental back on the right flight path.

Controlling

controlling
The management function concerned with monitoring employees' activities, keeping the organization on track toward its goals, and making corrections as needed.

Controlling is the fourth function in the management process. **Controlling** means monitoring employees' activities, determining whether the organization is on target toward its goals, and making corrections as necessary. Managers must ensure that the organization is moving toward its goals. New trends toward empowerment and trust of employees have led many companies to place less emphasis on top-down control and more emphasis on training employees to monitor and correct themselves. At ISS (International Service System), the Danish company that grew from a local office-cleaning contractor to a $2 billion multinational business, the entire control system is built on the belief that people at all levels will make the right decisions if they are provided with the appropriate information. Front-line employees are thoroughly trained to measure their own performance against company standards and make corrections as needed. Ongoing training programs at Andersen Consulting instill in every employee the company's core values and standards of expected performance, enabling the company to give its employees great freedom without endangering the firm's high standards.[14]

However, managers must realize that what works in one company or one situation may not work in another. C. R. England, a long-haul refrigerated trucking company in Salt Lake City, instituted a strict, computerized control system because the company was losing money and future prospects were dim. The system monitors about 500 procedures a week, and truckers can earn up to $9,000 a year extra if they meet safety and fuel consumption goals. Every employee is graded weekly based on computerized data. Although such strict control opposes recent trends toward trust and empowerment, it brought C. R. England from the brink of destruction to be one of the top five companies in its industry. Although workers don't particularly like such close monitoring, turnover actually dropped when the new system was implemented.[15]

In fact, organization failure can occur when managers are not serious about control or lack control information. Robert Fomon, longtime autocratic chief executive of E. F. Hutton, refused to set up control systems because he wanted to supervise senior management personally. At one time he reviewed the salaries and bonuses of more than 1,000 employees, but Hutton grew too big for his personal supervision. To achieve profit goals, managers got involved in a check-kiting scheme, and the firm pleaded guilty to 2,000 counts of mail and wire fraud. Other schemes exposed were the $900,000 in travel and entertainment expenses for one executive in one year and the listing of women from escort services as temporary secretarial help. The lack of control led to Fomon's demise. E. F. Hutton never fully recovered.[16]

Organizational Performance

The other part of our definition of management is the attainment of organizational goals in an efficient and effective manner. Management is so important because organizations are so important. In an industrialized society where complex technologies dominate, organizations bring together knowledge, people, and raw materials to perform tasks no individual could do alone. Without organizations how could 17,000 airline flights a day be accomplished without an accident, electricity be produced from large dams or nuclear power generators, millions of automobiles be manufactured, or hundreds of films, videos, and compact discs be made available for our entertainment? Organizations pervade our society. Most college students will work in an organization—perhaps Regal Cinemas, Federal Express, or Standard Oil. College students already are members of several organizations, such as a university, junior college, YMCA, church, fraternity, or sorority. College students also deal with organizations every day: to renew a driver's license, be treated in a hospital emergency room, buy food from a supermarket, eat in a restaurant, or buy new clothes. Managers are responsible for these organizations and for seeing that resources are used wisely to attain organizational goals.

Our formal definition of an **organization** is a social entity that is goal directed and deliberately structured. *Social entity* means being made up of two or more people. *Goal directed* means designed to achieve some outcome, such as make a profit (Boeing, Mack Trucks), win pay increases for members (AFL-CIO), meet spiritual needs (Methodist church), or provide social satisfaction (college sorority). *Deliberately structured* means that tasks are divided and responsibility for their performance is assigned to organization members. This definition applies to all organizations, including both profit and not-for-profit. Vickery Stoughton runs Toronto General Hospital and manages a $200 million budget. He endures intense public scrutiny, heavy government regulation, and daily crises of life and death. Hamilton Jordan, formerly President Carter's chief of staff, created a new organization called the Association of Tennis Professionals that has taken control of the professional tennis circuit. John and Marie Bouchard launched a small business called Wild Things that sells goods for outdoor activities. Small, offbeat, and not-for-profit organizations are more numerous than large, visible corporations—and just as important to society.

Based on our definition of management, the manager's responsibility is to coordinate resources in an effective and efficient manner to accomplish the organization's goals. Organizational **effectiveness** is the degree to which the organization achieves a stated goal. It means that the organization succeeds in accomplishing what it tries to do. Organizational effectiveness means

organization
A social entity that is goal directed and deliberately structured.

effectiveness
The degree to which the organization achieves a stated goal.

efficiency
The use of minimal resources—raw materials, money, and people—to produce a desired volume of output.

Leonard Riggio, chief executive of Barnes & Noble Inc., whose book sales total $2.8 billion, is positioning his organization to achieve *high performance. Riggio has set a goal to become the largest retailer for online book sales. After its launch last year, Barnesandnoble.com had sales of $14 million. Sales are planned to reach $100 million this year with a future goal of outselling Amazon.com, whose sales total $400 million.*

performance
The organization's ability to attain its goals by using resources in an efficient and effective manner.

providing a product or service that customers value. Organizational **efficiency** refers to the amount of resources used to achieve an organizational goal. It is based on how much raw materials, money, and people are necessary for producing a given volume of output. Efficiency can be calculated as the amount of resources used to produce a product or service.

Efficiency and effectiveness can both be high in the same organization. For example, Nissan Motor Manufacturing's plant in Smyrna, Tennessee, was ranked as the most productive automaker in North America by the Harbour Report, which tracks productivity and efficiency at 40 auto manufacturing facilities in the United States, Canada, and Mexico. According to consultant James Harbour, "That plant is lean, and its cars are designed for quality and to be assembled with a minimum number of workers." Nissan uses only 2.1 workers and produces more than 400 body panels an hour, about 25 percent better than the average at domestic auto plants. Likewise, management efforts to decentralize decision making and stay on top of technological developments enable Nucor Steel's Crawfordsville, Indiana, plant to produce a ton of flat-rolled steel in less than one worker-hour, compared with an average of four worker-hours elsewhere.[17] In addition to increasing efficiency, managers at Nissan and Nucor improved effectiveness, shown in better product quality, increased revenues, and higher profits.

Managers in other organizations, especially service firms, are improving efficiency and effectiveness, too. Labor shortages in many parts of the United States have prompted managers to find laborsaving tricks. Burger King and Taco Bell restaurants let customers serve themselves drinks. Sleep Inn hotels have a washer and dryer installed behind the desk so that clerks can launder sheets and towels while waiting on customers.[18] Sometimes, however, management efforts to increase efficiency through severe cost-cutting can hurt organizational effectiveness. Delta Airlines has dramatically increased cost efficiency by cutting spending on personnel, food, cleaning, and maintenance. However, it has fallen to last place among major air carriers in on-time performance, and customer complaints about dirty planes and long lines at ticket counters have increased by more than 75 percent.[19]

The ultimate responsibility of managers is to achieve high **performance,** which is the attainment of organizational goals by using resources in an efficient and effective manner. One example of extraordinary performance in the entertainment industry—the Grateful Dead rock band—is described in the Leadership box. Whether managers are responsible for the organization as a whole, such as the Grateful Dead, or for a single department or division, their ultimate responsibility is performance.

Management Skills

A manager's job is complex and multidimensional and, as we shall see throughout this book, requires a range of skills. Although some management theorists propose a long list of skills, the necessary skills for managing a department or an organization can be summarized in three categories: conceptual, human, and technical.[20] As illustrated in Exhibit 1.2, the application of these skills changes as managers move up in the organization. Though the degree of each skill necessary at different levels of an organization may vary, all managers must possess skills in each of these important areas to perform effectively.

Business at the Grateful Dead

News of Jerry Garcia's death in August 1995 stunned the music industry, and millions of Grateful Dead fans mourned the loss of a consummate artist whose words and music spanned generations. Few people remember the other side of Garcia—the leader who helped manage a successful business. Garcia rotated with each band member to share responsibility as chief financial and executive officer of Grateful Dead Productions (GDP). The carefully managed business behind the Grateful Dead was largely responsible for the group's financial success and its almost unmatched 29 years of performing the same program to sellout crowds.

Perhaps the service GDP's customers appreciated most was the band's ticketing business, which distributed nearly half of all Dead concert tickets directly to fans. The group listened to customers and gave them what they wanted. Most rock bands forbid tape-recording at concerts to prevent copyright infringement, yet the Dead would rope off a portion of the concert floor just for "tapeheads."

The band members jointly made major management decisions, but they empowered GDP's 60 or so employees to run the day-to-day business of the group. GDP employees, who earned good salaries and enjoyed extensive benefits, profit sharing, bonuses, and say so, did everything from moving the band from concert to concert to handling catalog merchandising, a publishing company, and a nonprofit foundation. Employees felt like part of the business, and staff turnover was low in an industry known for its instability.

Management counts. The Grateful Dead successfully balanced control and delegation to run a thriving business and keep doing what they loved to do for nearly three decades. They created an organization with a powerful culture, a significant vision, and the motivation of human energy that set a great organization apart from the crowd.

SOURCES: Leslie Brokaw, "The Dead Have Customers, Too," *Inc.*, September 1994, 90–92; David E. Bowen and Caren Siehl, "Sweet Music: Grateful Employees, Grateful Customers. 'Grate' Profits," *Journal of Management Inquiry* (June 1992), 154–156; and Janice C. Simpson, "The Bands of Summer," *Time*, August 3, 1992, 66–67.

Conceptual Skills

Conceptual skill is the cognitive ability to see the organization as a whole and the relationship among its parts. Conceptual skill involves the manager's thinking, information processing, and planning abilities. It involves knowing where one's department fits into the total organization and how the organization fits into the industry, the community, and the broader business and social environment. It means the ability to "think strategically"—to take the broad, long-term view.

Conceptual skills are needed by all managers but are especially important for managers at the top. They must perceive significant elements in a situation and broad, conceptual patterns. For example, Microsoft Corporation, the

conceptual skill
The cognitive ability to see the organization as a whole and the relationship among its parts.

Exhibit **1.2**   *Relationship of Conceptual, Human, and Technical Skills to Management Level*

Management Level
Top Managers

Middle Managers

First-Line Managers

Nonmanagers (Personnel)

Conceptual Skills   Human Skills   Technical Skills

giant software company, reflects the conceptual skills of its founder and chairman, Bill Gates. Overall business goals are clearly stated and effectively communicated throughout the company, contributing to Microsoft's leadership reputation and billion-dollar revenues. While actively participating in and coordinating small units devoted to functional areas such as programming and marketing, Gates spreads his concept for Microsoft by delegating to a cadre of strong managers. As Scott Oki, senior vice-president for U.S. sales and marketing, pointed out, "Each part of the company has a life of its own now, but Bill is the glue that holds it all together."[21]

As managers move up the hierarchy, they must develop conceptual skills or their promotability will be limited. A senior engineering manager who is mired in technical matters rather than thinking strategically will not perform well at the top of the organization. Many of the responsibilities of top managers, such as decision making, resource allocation, and innovation, require a broad view.

Human Skills

human skill

The ability to work with and through other people and to work effectively as a group member.

Human skill is the manager's ability to work with and through other people and to work effectively as a group member. This skill is demonstrated in the way a manager relates to other people, including the ability to motivate, facilitate, coordinate, lead, communicate, and resolve conflicts. A manager with human skills allows subordinates to express themselves without fear of ridicule and encourages participation. As manager of corporate employment for Southwest Airlines, a company that relies heavily on the quality of its people for its success, Rita Bailey uses human skills daily to communicate effectively with other employees in the department as well as to gauge the abilities of applicants to work within Southwest's strong culture. A manager with human skills likes other people and is liked by them. Scott McNealy, CEO of Sun Microsystems, uses humor and hoopla to motivate employees and help them cope with the stress of their demanding jobs. Impromptu high jinks such as an intramural squirt gun war, at which McNealy played general, help bind together and energize employees. Each April Fool's Day, workers play elaborate practical jokes on McNealy and other top managers.[22]

Scott McNealy (left), chief executive of Sun Microsystems Inc., excels at human skills. He works 80-hour weeks and maintains a heavy travel schedule but still finds time to enjoy activities such as this intramural squirt-gun war with employees. As a leader, McNealy is known for his humor and ability to raise a crowd to its feet.

In recent years, awareness of the importance of human skills has increased. Such books as *In Search of Excellence* and *A Passion for Excellence* were among the first to stress the need for managers to take care of the human side of the organization. As globalization, workforce diversity, and competition for highly-skilled knowledge workers increase, human skills become even more crucial. Ken Alvares, who runs worldwide human resources for Sun Microsystems says, "Our goal is to keep people so busy having fun every day that they don't even listen when the headhunters call." It's working—Sun's turnover of hard-to-find engineers is about two-thirds lower than the competition's.[23] A recent survey by *Fortune* magazine found that managers' human skills are important to employee motivation and retention as well as to overall organizational performance. A primary factor in attracting, motivating, and retaining talented workers at companies such as Sun, Intel, Allied Signal, and Southwest Airlines is top management that makes employees feel valued and inspired and promotes close, fun working relationships.[24] Effective managers are cheerleaders, facilitators, coaches, and nurturers. Jack H. Grossman, a professor emeritus at the Kellstadt Graduate School of Business at DePaul University, uses the metaphor of a master gardener to stress the importance of human skills. "What does it take to grow good flowers, fruits, and vegetables?" he asks. "It takes good soil, and that's what a manager tries to create by being sensitive, nurturing, and trying to bring out the best in people."[25]

Technical Skills

Technical skill is the understanding of and proficiency in the performance of specific tasks. Technical skill includes mastery of the methods, techniques, and equipment involved in specific functions such as engineering, manufacturing, or finance. Technical skill also includes specialized knowledge, analytical ability, and the competent use of tools and techniques to solve problems in that specific discipline. Rodney Mott, plant manager at Nucor Corp.'s Hickman, Arkansas, steel mill, needed technical skills to decide on the installation of a new $50 million caster, which turns liquid metal into bands of steel. The move nearly doubled the Hickman plant's capacity, to 36,000 tons a week.[26] Technical skills are particularly important at lower organizational levels. Many managers get promoted to their first management job by having excellent technical skills. However, technical skills become less important than human and conceptual skills as managers move up the hierarchy.

technical skill
The understanding of and proficiency in the performance of specific tasks.

Management Types

Managers use conceptual, human, and technical skills to perform the four management functions of planning, organizing, leading, and controlling in all organizations—large and small, manufacturing and service, profit and not-for-profit. But not all managers' jobs are the same. Managers are responsible for different departments, work at different levels in the hierarchy, and meet different requirements for achieving high performance. For example, Mary Lee Bowen, a middle manager at Rubbermaid, is responsible for teams that create new home organization and bath accessories products. Phillip Knight is chief executive officer for Nike, world leader in sports shoe design and manufacturing.[27] Both are managers, and both must contribute to planning, organizing, leading, and controlling their organizations—but in different amounts and ways.

Vertical Differences

An important determinant of the manager's job is hierarchical level. Three levels in the hierarchy are illustrated in Exhibit 1.3. **Top managers** are at the top of the hierarchy and are responsible for the entire organization. They have such titles as president, chairperson, executive director, chief executive officer (CEO), and executive vice-president. Top managers are responsible for setting organizational goals, defining strategies for achieving them, monitoring

top manager
A manager who is at the top of the organizational hierarchy and is responsible for the entire organization.

Exhibit *1.3*   *Management Levels in the Organizational Hierarchy*

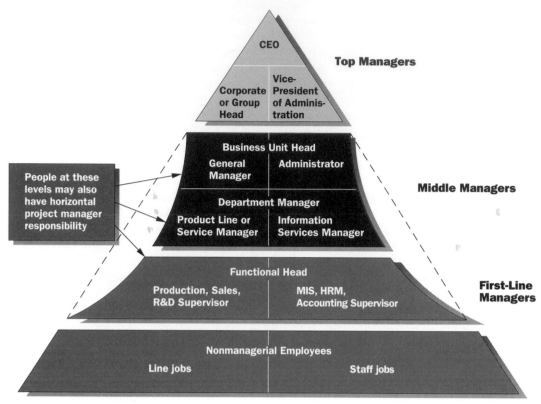

SOURCE: Adapted from Thomas V. Bonoma and Joseph C. Lawler, "Chutes and Ladders: Growing the General Manager," *Sloan Management Review* (Spring 1989), 27–37.

and interpreting the external environment, and making decisions that affect the entire organization. They look to the long-term future and concern themselves with general environmental trends and the organization's overall success. Among the most important responsibilities for top managers are communicating a shared vision for the organization, shaping corporate culture, and nurturing an entrepreneurial spirit that can help the company keep pace with rapid change. Today more than ever before, top managers must engage the unique knowledge, skills, and capabilities of each employee.[28]

middle manager
A manager who works at the middle levels of the organization and is responsible for major departments.

Middle managers work at middle levels of the organization and are responsible for business units and major departments. Examples of middle managers are department head, division head, manager of quality control, and director of the research lab. Middle managers typically have two or more management levels beneath them. They are responsible for implementing the overall strategies and policies defined by top managers. Middle managers generally are concerned with the near future and are expected to establish good relationships with peers around the organization, encourage teamwork, and resolve conflicts.

The middle manager's job has changed dramatically over the past two decades. During the 1980s and early 1990s, many organizations became lean and efficient by laying off middle managers and slashing middle management levels. Traditional pyramidal organization charts were flattened to allow information to flow quickly from top to bottom and decisions to be made with greater speed. The shrinking middle management is illustrated in Exhibit 1.3. For example, Eastman Kodak cut middle management by 30 percent and reduced its middle management levels from seven to three. GE Medical Systems in Milwaukee also went from seven layers of management to three between 1985 and 1995.[29]

However, although middle management levels have been reduced, there is a renewed vitality in the middle manager's job as companies recognize the need for a new type of manager. The Association of Executive Search Consultants reports that searches for middle managers increased 58 percent in 1997.[30] Today's middle manager, rather than managing the flow of information up and down the hierarchy, is responsible for creating a horizontal network, since most work is now organized around teams and projects. Strong project managers are in white-hot demand throughout the corporate world. A **project manager** is responsible for a temporary work project that involves the participation of people from various functions and levels of the organization, and perhaps from outside the company as well. Today's middle manager may work with a variety of projects and teams at the same time, some of which cross geographical and cultural as well as functional boundaries. Dave Galen, an IT manager with Amoco in Chicago, says his work is a series of projects. For one recent project, Galen worked with more than 500 project members who not only crossed company lines but spanned the world.[31] In this environment, middle managers need new skills: the ability to inspire and motivate, negotiating skills; a willingness to listen and ability to communicate clearly; conscientiousness and integrity; and the ability to manage change and conflict.[32]

First-line managers are directly responsible for the production of goods and services. They are the first or second level of management and have such titles as supervisor, line manager, section chief, and office manager. They are responsible for groups of nonmanagement employees. Their primary concern is the application of rules and procedures to achieve efficient production, provide technical assistance, and motivate subordinates. The time horizon at this level is short, with the emphasis on accomplishing day-to-day goals.

Horizontal Differences

The other major difference in management jobs occurs horizontally across the organization. **Functional managers** are responsible for departments that perform a single functional task and have employees with similar training and skills. Functional departments include advertising, sales, finance, human resources, manufacturing, and accounting. Line managers are responsible for the manufacturing and marketing departments that make or sell the product or service. Staff managers are in charge of departments such as finance and human resources that support line departments.

General managers are responsible for several departments that perform different functions. A general manager is responsible for a self-contained division, such as a Dillard's department store, and for all of the functional departments within it. Project managers also have general management responsibility, because they coordinate people across several departments to accomplish a specific project.

Project management is a vital role in today's flatter, delayered organizations and enables middle managers to contribute significantly to corporate success.[33] As executive vice-president William Kelvie, chief information officer for

project manager
A manager responsible for a temporary work project that involves the participation of other people at a similar level in the organization.

first-line manager
A manager who is at the first or second management level and is directly responsible for the production of goods and services.

functional manager
A manager who is responsible for a department that performs a single functional task and has employees with similar training and skills.

general manager
A manager who is responsible for several departments that perform different functions.

the Federal National Mortgage Association (Fannie-Mae), said, "Automation and empowerment take away the need to have managers oversee the day-to-day work. Everything has become projects. This is the way Fannie-Mae does business today."[34] Companies as diverse as consumer products and aerospace firms use project managers to coordinate people from marketing, manufacturing, finance, and production when a new product is developed. As corporations continue to reduce hierarchical levels and move toward flatter, more horizontal structures, more people with project management skills will be needed. Project managers need significant human skills, because they coordinate diverse people to attain project goals.

What Is It Like to Be a Manager?

So far we have described how managers at various levels perform four basic functions that help ensure that organizational resources are used to attain high levels of performance. These tasks require conceptual, human, and technical skills. Unless someone has actually performed managerial work, it is hard to understand exactly what managers do on an hour-by-hour, day-to-day basis. The manager's job is so diverse that a number of studies have been undertaken in an attempt to describe exactly what happens. The question of what managers actually do to plan, organize, lead, and control was answered by Henry Mintzberg, who followed managers around and recorded all their activities.[35] He developed a description of managerial work that included three general characteristics and ten roles. These characteristics and roles have been supported in subsequent research.[36]

Manager Activities

One of the most interesting findings about managerial activities is how busy managers are and how hectic the average workday can be. For Hugh Murphy, operations manager of O'Hare International Airport, the nature of managerial work means he is tossing out litter left on windowsills one minute, then virtually the next minute making complex arrangements for an unexpected landing of Vice President Al Gore in Air Force Two. Immediately after greeting the vice president, Murphy zips back to his office to check his phone messages and return any urgent ones, then consults with computer technicians to make sure a critical malfunction of five security checkpoints has been corrected.[37]

Managerial Activity Is Characterized by Variety, Fragmentation, and Brevity.[38] The manager's involvements are so widespread and voluminous that there is little time for quiet reflection. The average time spent on any one activity is less than nine minutes. Managers shift gears quickly. Significant crises are interspersed with trivial events in no predictable sequence.[39] One example of just two typical hours for general manager, Janet Howard, follows. Note the frequent interruptions and the brevity and variety of tasks.

7:30 A.M.	Janet arrives at work and begins to plan her day.
7:37 A.M.	A subordinate, Morgan Cook, stops in Janet's office to discuss a dinner party the previous night and to review the cost-benefit analysis for a proposed microcomputer.
7:45 A.M.	Janet's secretary, Pat, motions for Janet to pick up the telephone. "Janet, they had serious water damage at the downtown office last

	night. A pipe broke, causing about $50,000 damage. Everything will be back in shape in three days. Thought you should know."
8:00 A.M.	Pat brings in the mail. She also asks instructions for typing a report Janet gave her yesterday.
8:14 A.M.	Janet gets a phone call from the accounting manager, who is returning a call from the day before. They talk about an accounting report.
8:25 A.M.	A Mr. Nance is ushered in. Mr. Nance complains that a sales manager mistreats his employees and something must be done. Janet rearranges her schedule to investigate this claim.
9:00 A.M.	Janet returns to the mail. One letter is from an irate customer. Janet dictates a helpful, restrained reply. Pat brings in phone messages.
9:15 A.M.	Janet receives an urgent phone call from Larry Baldwin. They discuss lost business, unhappy subordinates, and a potential promotion.[40]

The Manager Performs a Great Deal of Work at an Unrelenting Pace.[41] Managers' work is fast paced and requires great energy. The managers observed by Mintzberg processed 36 pieces of mail each day, attended eight meetings, and took a tour through the building or plant. As soon as a manager's daily calendar is set, unexpected disturbances erupt. New meetings are required. During time away from the office, executives catch up on work-related reading and paperwork.

At O'Hare, an unofficial count one October Friday found operations manager Hugh Murphy interacting with about 45 airport employees. In addition, he listened to complaints from local residents about airport noise, met with disgruntled executives of a French firm who built the airport's new $128 million people-mover system, attempted to soothe a Hispanic city alderman who complained that Mexicana Airlines passengers were being singled out by overzealous tow-truck operators, toured the airport's new fire station, and visited the construction site for the new $20 million tower. Hugh Murphy's unrelenting pace is typical for managers.[42] In recent years, many managers' jobs have become even tougher. Management can be rewarding, but it can also be frustrating and stressful, as discussed in the Manager's Shoptalk box.

Manager Roles

Mintzberg's observations and subsequent research indicate that diverse manager activities can be organized into ten roles.[43] A **role** is a set of expectations for a manager's behavior. Exhibit 1.4 provides examples of each of the ten roles. These roles are divided into three conceptual categories: informational (managing by information); interpersonal (managing through people); and decisional (managing through action). Each role represents activities that managers undertake to ultimately accomplish the functions of planning, organizing, leading, and controlling. Although it is necessary to separate the components of the manager's job to understand the different roles and activities of a manager, it is important to remember that the real job of management cannot be practiced as a set of independent parts; all the roles interact in the real world of management. As Mintzberg says, "The manager who only communicates or only conceives never gets anything done, while the manager who only 'does' ends up doing it all alone."[44]

Informational Roles. Informational roles describe the activities used to maintain and develop an information network. General managers spend about 75 percent of their time talking to other people. The *monitor* role

role
A set of expectations for one's behavior.

Do You Really Want to Be a Manager?

The first training course aspiring managers at FedEx take is called "Is Management for Me?" Because people entering the program ask this question first, those who complete it are better managers—happy with their jobs, and capable of dealing with the stress and frustration of management in positive ways. Trent Cobb, an 18-year FedEx veteran who answered yes was eventually promoted to manager of international hub operations in Memphis. "The transition was good from day one," he says. "If you know at the outset how the change is going to affect you, it's much easier to handle."

There are a number of issues would-be managers should consider before deciding they want to pursue a management career:

The increased workload. It isn't unusual for managers to work 70–80 hour weeks, and some work even longer hours. A manager's job always starts before a shift and ends hours after the shift is over. Matt Scott, a software engineer promoted to management at Fore Systems, Inc., found himself frustrated by the increasing paperwork and crowded meeting schedule. Many new managers are surprised by how much of their time is taken up by meetings.

The unrelenting sense of obligation. A manager's work is never done. Nancy Carreon, an associate partner for an architectural firm, sometimes wakes up in the middle of the night thinking about something she needs to do—so she gets up and does it. Argues George Pollard, a senior human resources official at FedEx, "Managers are always on the clock. We're representatives of [the company] even when we're not at work."

The headache of responsibility for other people. A lot of people get into management because they like the idea of having power, but the reality is that many managers feel overwhelmed by the responsibility of supervising and disciplining others. As Mary Smith of FedEx says, "You have to make hard decisions about people, decisions you might not like." Another manager referred to the feeling of constantly being pulled in 15 different directions. In addition, today's managers generally supervise large numbers of people who are spread over different locations and even different continents.

Being caught in the middle. For many people, this is the most difficult aspect of management. Except for those in the top echelons, managers find themselves acting as a backstop, caught between upper management and the work force. A computer software designer explains why she wanted out of management: "I didn't feel comfortable touting the company line in organizational policies and technical decisions I disagreed with. I found it very difficult to fire my team up on something I wasn't fired up about. It was very hard asking folks to do things I wouldn't like to do myself, like put in gobs of overtime or travel at the drop of a hat." Even when managers disagree with the decisions of top executives, they are responsible for implementing them.

For some people, the frustrations aren't worth it. One, who says "there wasn't a single day where I could say I enjoyed myself," left management after only six months. However, for others, management is a fulfilling and satisfying career choice and the emotional rewards can be great. One key to being happy as a manager may be carefully evaluating whether you can answer yes to the question, "Do I really want to be a manager?"

SOURCES: Heath Row, "Is Management for Me? *That* is the Question," *Fast Company,* February–March 1998, 50–52; Timothy D. Schellhardt, "Want to Be a Manager? Many People Say No, Calling Job Miserable," *The Wall Street Journal,* April 4, 1997, A1, A4; Matt Murray, "A Software Engineer Becomes a Manager, with Many Regrets," *The Wall Street Journal,* May 14, 1997, A1, A14; and Hal Lancaster, "Managing Your Career: Nancy Carreon Works Long, Hard Weeks. Does She Need To?" *The Wall Street Journal,* May 13, 1997, B1.

involves seeking current information from many sources. The manager acquires information from others and scans written materials to stay well informed. Lewis Platt, chairman of Hewlett-Packard, spends about 20 percent of his time talking directly with customers, asking what the company is doing right and what it needs to do better.[45] The *disseminator* and *spokesperson* roles are just the opposite: The manager transmits current information to others, both inside and outside the organization, who can use it. With the trend toward empowerment of lower-level employees, many managers are sharing as much information as possible. At Oticon, a $100 million company that has revolutionized the hearing aid industry, CEO Lars Kolind sees the dissemination of knowledge as vital to the company's ability to innovate. For an

Exhibit **1.4**
Ten Manager Roles

Category	Role	Activity
Informational	**Monitor**	Seek and receive information, scan periodicals and reports, maintain personal contacts.
	Disseminator	Forward information to other organization members; send memos and reports, make phone calls.
	Spokesperson	Transmit information to outsiders through speeches, reports, memos.
Interpersonal	**Figurehead**	Perform ceremonial and symbolic duties such as greeting visitors, signing legal documents.
	Leader	Direct and motivate subordinates; train, counsel, and communicate with subordinates.
	Liaison	Maintain information links both inside and outside organization; use mail, phone calls, meetings.
Decisional	**Entrepreneur**	Initiate improvement projects; identify new ideas, delegate idea responsibility to others.
	Disturbance handler	Take corrective action during disputes or crises; resolve conflicts among subordinates; adapt to environmental crises.
	Resource allocator	Decide who gets resources; schedule, budget, set priorities.
	Negotiator	Represent department during negotiation of union contracts, sales, purchases, budgets; represent departmental interests.

SOURCES: Adapted from Henry Mintzberg, *The Nature of Managerial Work* (New York: Harper & Row, 1973), 92–93; and Henry Mintzberg, "Managerial Work: Analysis from Observation," *Management Science* 18 (1971), B97–B110.

interesting example of the spokesperson role, consider the Danish captain of an SAS airplane as "manager" of the flight. Just after takeoff, the plane experienced engine trouble and the crew and passengers spent a harrowing 25 minutes getting safely back on the ground. Captain Ebbe Starcke did something unique: During the descent, acting as spokesperson for the airline and the crew, Starcke never stopped talking to the passengers—in both Danish and English—explaining exactly what was happening and what was being done to solve the problem. By the time the plane landed, Captain Starcke was a hero to a lot of people—some of whom determined to always fly SAS whenever they had a choice.[46]

Interpersonal Roles. Interpersonal roles pertain to relationships with others and are related to the human skills described earlier. The *figurehead* role involves handling ceremonial and symbolic activities for the department or organization. The manager represents the organization in his or her formal managerial capacity as the head of the unit. The presentation of employee awards by a division manager at Taco Bell is an example of the figurehead role. The *leader* role encompasses relationships with subordinates, including motivation, communication, and influence. The *liaison* role pertains to the development of information sources both inside and outside the organization. An example is a face-to-face discussion between a controller and plan supervisor to resolve a misunderstanding about the budget.

John T. Chambers is the leader of Cisco Systems Inc., a San Jose, California company with annual revenues of more than $8 billion. Cisco Systems is the global leader in networking for the Internet. In his inter-personal role as a leader, Chambers says that his vision is simple: "We can change the way people live and work, play and learn." This idealistic vision inspires and motivates Cisco's 13,000-plus employees. In the photo, Chambers attends a company picnic, demonstrating his emphasis on the value of employees.

Decisional Roles. Decisional roles pertain to those events about which the manager must make a choice and take action. These roles often require conceptual as well as human skills. The *entrepreneur* role involves the initiation of change. Managers are constantly thinking about the future and how to get there.[47] Managers become aware of problems and search for improvement projects that will correct them. One manager studied by Mintzberg had 50 improvement projects going simultaneously. The *disturbance handler* role involves resolving conflicts among subordinates or between the manager's department and other departments. For example, the division manager for a large furniture manufacturer got involved in a personal dispute between two section heads. One section head was let go because he did not fit the team. The *resource allocator* role pertains to decisions about how to allocate people, time, equipment, budget, and other resources to attain desired outcomes. The manager must decide which projects receive budget allocations, which of several customer complaints receive priority, and even how to spend his or her own time. The *negotiator* role involves formal negotiations and bargaining to attain outcomes for the manager's unit of responsibility. For example, the manager meets and formally negotiates with others—a supplier about a late delivery, the controller about the need for additional budget resources, or the union about a worker grievance during the normal workday.

Managing in Small Businesses and Not-For-Profit Organizations

Small businesses are growing in importance. Hundreds of small businesses are opened every month by people who have found themselves squeezed out of the corporation due to downsizing or who voluntarily leave the corporate world to seek a slower pace and a healthier balance between work and family life. Many small businesses are opened by women or minorities who found limited opportunities for advancement in large corporations.

As even the smallest businesses become increasingly complicated due to globalization, government regulation, and customer demands for better quality at lower prices, managerial dexterity is critical to success. One survey on trends and future developments in small business found that nearly half of the respondents saw inadequate management skills as a threat to their companies, as compared to less than 25 percent in larger companies.[48]

One interesting finding is that managers in small businesses tend to emphasize roles different from those of managers in large corporations. Managers in small companies often see their most important role as spokesperson, because they must promote the small, growing company to the outside world. The entrepreneur role is also very important in small businesses, because managers must be creative and help their organizations develop new ideas to be competitive. Small-business managers tend to rate lower on the leader role and on information-processing roles compared with counterparts in large corporations.

Not-for-profit organizations also represent a major application of management talent. The Salvation Army, the Girl Scouts, universities, city governments, hospitals, public schools, symphonies, and art museums all require excellent management. Sometimes managers in not-for-profit organizations have been leaders in creating a sense of purpose and mission that motivates employees, empowering workers to try new ideas, and trimming overlong vertical hierarchies.[49] We might expect managers in not-for-profits to place more emphasis on the roles of figurehead (to deal with the public), leader (to motivate employees with fewer financial incentives), and resource allocator (to distribute government resources that often are assigned top down).

As the world of small and not-for-profit organizations becomes increasingly complex, managers should carefully integrate the three categories of roles: They must simultaneously manage by information, manage through people, and manage through action to keep their organizations healthy.

Leading The Management Revolution

How do you learn to be a manager in an uncertain and rapidly changing world? How can a course in management or a college degree in business prepare you to face the challenges of the twenty-first century?

Management is both an art and a science. It is an art because many skills cannot be learned from a textbook. Management takes practice, just like golf, tennis, or skating. Management is a science because a growing body of knowledge and objective facts describes management and how to obtain organizational effectiveness. This knowledge can be conveyed through teaching and textbooks. Becoming a successful manager requires a blend of formal learning and practice, of art and science.

Students today will be leaders tomorrow, leading the management revolution that will change organizations in the twenty-first century. One of the most important contributions a textbook or a management course can make today is to define for students some of the forces that will affect their jobs as managers tomorrow.

The Changing Paradigm of Management

The world of organizations and management is changing. Rapid environmental changes are causing fundamental transformations that have a dramatic impact on the manager's job. These transformations represent a shift from a

paradigm
A mind-set that presents a fundamental way of thinking about, perceiving, and understanding the world.

traditional to a new paradigm, as outlined in Exhibit 1.5. A **paradigm** is a shared mind-set that represents a fundamental way of thinking about, perceiving, and understanding the world. Shifts in ways of thinking are occurring in our society, and these in turn impact organizations, causing shifts in management thinking and behavior.[50] The primary shift is from the traditional vertical organization to something called the learning organization.

The Learning Organization

Traditionally, the most common organizational structure has been one in which activities are grouped by common function from the bottom to the top of the organization. The whole organization is coordinated and controlled through the vertical hierarchy, with decision-making authority residing with upper-level managers. Traditional organizations are characterized by routine, specialized jobs and standardized control procedures. These organizations are very effective in stable times. However, they often do not work well in fast-changing environments. In response, many companies are shifting to a new paradigm and becoming learning organizations.

In the new paradigm, the primary responsibility of managers is not to make decisions, but to create learning capability throughout the organization. Employees on the front lines routinely make decisions rather than passing them up the hierarchy for approval. There is no single model of the *learning organization;* it is a philosophy or attitude about what an organization is and the role of employees. Everyone in the organization participates in identifying and solving problems, enabling the organization to continuously experiment, improve, and increase its capability. In the learning organization, top managers are leaders who create a vision for the future that is widely under-

Exhibit *1.5*

The Changing Paradigm of Management

Forces on Organizations	Old Paradigm Vertical Organization	New Paradigm Learning Organization
Markets	Local, domestic	Global
Workforce	Homogeneous	Diverse
Technology	Mechanical	Electronic
Values	Stability, efficiency	Change, chaos
Management Competencies		
Focus	Profits	Customers, employees
Leadership	Autocratic	Dispersed, empowering
Doing Work	By individuals	By teams
Relationships	Conflict, competition	Collaboration

stood and imprinted throughout the organization. Employees are empowered to identify and solve problems because they understand the vision and long-term goals of the organization.

The traditional top-down hierarchy is giving way to flatter organizations built around self-directed teams collaborating across levels and departments. Lower-level managers serve as team leaders, coaches, and facilitators. Monsanto, a large chemical company, achieved excellent results by tapping the power of teams. Teams of workers at Monsanto's chemical and nylon plant near Pensacola, Florida, were responsible for hiring, purchasing, making job assignments, and producing the product. Management was reduced from seven levels to four, and both profitability and safety increased.[51] However, even though layers of management are reduced, in learning organizations the job of the middle manager has a renewed vitality as a coordinator of teams and projects across levels, departments, and divisions. In addition, the growing trend toward telecommuting and virtual offices brings new challenges for managers.[52] The shift to the learning organization is a result of a number of significant forces impacting today's organizations and managers.

Forces on Organizations

The most striking change now affecting organizations and management is *globalization*. Today, everyone is interconnected in the flow of information, money, or products, and interdependencies are increasing. Between 1987 and 1992, the market value of U.S. investment abroad rose 35 percent to $776 billion, and foreign investment in the United States more than doubled to $692 billion.[53] Some large multinational corporations, including Canada's Northern Telecom, U.S.-based Coca-Cola, Switzerland's Nestlé, and France's Carrefour, all get a large percentage of their sales from outside their home countries. In this global environment, foreign-born people with global experience have been appointed to run such U.S. companies as Ford, Gerber, NCR, and Heinz.[54] However, even the smallest companies are affected by globalization. Taking a global approach has become a necessity for virtually every company and manager. Globalization brings a need for relentless innovation, greater concern for quality, rapid response, enhanced productivity, and new levels of customer service.[55]

Global competition has also triggered a need for new management approaches that emphasize empowerment of workers and involvement of employees. During the 1980s, for example, the success of Japanese firms encouraged U.S. companies to adopt more participatory management practices. A management perspective known as **Theory Z** proposed a hybrid form of management that incorporates techniques from both Japanese and North American management practices. To briefly illustrate Theory Z, consider that traditional Japanese practices emphasize collective resposibility, informal control, and consensual decision making, whereas traditional North American practices encourage individual responsibility, formal control mechanisms, and individual decision making. Theory Z blends the two styles, retaining an emphasis on individual responsibility, but encouraging consensual decision making and more informal control methods.[56]

Today, managers have to understand cross-cultural patterns and often work with team members from many different countries. *Diversity* of the workforce has become a fact of life for all organizations, even those that do not operate globally. Most new entrants to the U.S. labor force are women and minorities

Theory Z
A management perspective that incorporates techniques from both Japanese and North American management practices.

(with half of these being first-generation immigrants), and the workforce in general is growing older, with the median age for U.S. workers now at 45.[57] Studies also project that Asian Americans, African Americans, and Hispanics will make up 85 percent of U.S. population growth and constitute about 30 percent of the total workforce in the twenty-first century.[58] Indeed, diversity is a real advantage in a global marketplace; employees who speak the language and understand the culture of international competitors, customers, and partners can provide a competitive advantage.

Another significant shift is that *technology* is electronic rather than mechanical, as the world is gradually shifting from a workforce that produces material things to one that primarily manages information. Success depends on the intellectual capacity of all employees. Information technology facilitates new ways of working, such as virtual teams and telecommuting, that challenge traditional methods of supervision and control. In addition, technology often leads to greater sharing of information and power throughout the organization.

In the face of these rapid transformations, organizations are learning to value *change* over stability. The fundamental paradigm during much of the twentieth century was a belief that things can be stable and efficient. In contrast, the new paradigm is based on a recognition of change and chaos as the natural order of things.[59] The science of chaos theory suggests that the world is characterized by randomness and uncertainty. Small events often have massive and far-reaching consequences. For example, a seemingly insignificant lawsuit against AT&T some years ago had far-reaching effects, resulting in the emergence of MCI, Sprint, and other long-distance carriers and ultimately creating a whole new world of telecommunications.

The change to the new paradigm of management means that managers now must rethink their approach to organizing, directing, and motivating workers. According to one consultant, many managers trained under the old paradigm complain that workers no longer play by the rules. The consultant's response: "Why should they play by the rules? The rules are dead."[60] Managers who have made a shift to the new paradigm are creating twenty-first century organizations by continuing to break the rules and embrace change. In this new environment, managers give up their command-and-control mind-set and rely on new skills and abilities. The Learning Organization box describes a paradigm shift that is taking place in the United States Army.

New Management Competencies

As discussed earlier in the chapter, not all managers' jobs are the same. Managers rely on varied skills and perform different activities depending on hierarchical level and job responsibilities. For all managers, however, human skills are becoming increasingly important. Critical skills for top-level managers in today's world include the ability to create an exciting and demanding work environment and to inspire confidence in and support for the organization and its leadership. Middle managers have to learn to build relationships, empower others, promote cooperation, and manage conflict. First-line supervisors need the ability to motivate workers on a day-to-day basis and sustain employee energy toward the completion of organizational goals.[61] Thus, although managers at different levels play different roles and rely on different skills, there are some manager competencies that are important to all managers in the new world of organizations.

Nickelodeon, once a cute little children's channel with no ads, has been the top-rated kids cable-TV network since 1995. Herb Scannel, top executive at Nickelodeon, believes in staying connected to customers. He is a thoughtful and soft-spoken manager who keeps the company focused on its major asset, an intimate knowledge of kids, while promoting an inventive, playful company culture. To create a new game show, staffers went off-site to "gamestorm." They spent a day recalling the games and game shows from their childhood, such as capture the flag and "I've Got A Secret," and developed "Figure It Out," a big Nickelodeon hit.

Learning

Guess Who's Shifting Paradigms?

After crushing Iraq's regiments in a one-sided battle, the U.S. Army emerged as the world's premier land force. The army could rest on its laurels and prepare to succeed with a rigid, hierarchical structure. Maybe command and control are the way to go, with remote generals handing down orders to the field.

Nothing could be farther from the truth, however. At the prodding of General Gordon Sullivan, the army has gone through self-examination and self-renewal since the triumph of Desert Storm. Officers on every level are discussing change. The army's environment is highly variable. Since the Gulf War, troops have been sent on dozens of unrelated missions: feeding children in Somalia; purifying water for Rwandan refugees; fighting forest fires; chasing drug lords; and serving police duty in Haiti.

Meeting these demands requires a new way of thinking. Top army officers are choosing change over stability, dispersed control over top management control, transformational over autocratic leadership, and teams over individuals.

Everyone is involved. No other army is so egalitarian. In fact, delegations from other countries come to study the new army. In addition, several of America's most forward-thinking companies, including Motorola and General Electric, study the Army's National Training Center as a source of ideas about leadership and learning. The definitive model at the NTC—which applies to business as well as combat—is learning through failure. All personnel, from enlistees to brigadier generals, go through grueling maneuvers. For fourteen days, at every level, every fiber of the organization is stressed to the breaking point, and some of the fibers inevitably break. Those are the areas leaders hone in on during After Action Reviews—the crux of the learning experience, the place where hardship meets insight, where failure meets growth. The process encourages brutal honesty, enabling individuals and the group to become stronger. Day after day, After Action Reviews stress five key themes: (1) everyone needs to understand the big pic-ture; (2) everyone needs to think all the time; (3) always put yourself in the shoes of an uncooperative opponent; (4) prepare yourself to the point where nothing can surprise you; and (5) put aside hierarchy, foster self-awareness and self-criticism, and learn to work as a team. Nowhere else do senior executives and junior people sit down together and examine how both parties overlooked vital information and made mistakes. Facilitators never lecture, yell, or criticize individual performance, and they continually reinforce the message that the exercise is not about success or failure but about what the experience allows each person to take away. This paradigm fosters continuous learning and growth.

The army continues to grow in technology, too, with new infrared equipment such as goggles and gunsights that enable soldiers to fight at night when the enemy is effectively blind. In the future, army elements will be connected by electronic mail, plus video pictures of battlefield conditions. The E-mail, as in corporations, will further erode the hierarchy and remove communication barriers between units and functions.

And the army believes in personal growth. Two-thirds of the army's officers have advanced degrees, including many with MBAs. The top generals have created brain trusts of dozens of junior officers and enlisted personnel who are challenged to solve the problems of future combat. Eventually lieutenants will see everything that a colonel can see, each person mastering a bigger picture than ever before. High-level officers are told they are preparing for leadership roles in a world that is violent, uncertain, complex, and ambiguous. They are creating a cohesive corporate mission that will be imprinted on every worker or soldier. Believe it or not, the army is way ahead of business in shifting to a paradigm that keeps everyone's eye on the future.

SOURCE: Lee Smith, "New Ideas from the Army (Really)," *Fortune*, September 19, 1994, 203–212; and Brian Smale, "Fight, Learn, Lead," *Fast Company*, August–September 1996, 65–70.

Rather than a single-minded focus on profits, today's managers recognize the importance of staying *connected to customers and employees* on a daily basis. They remain flexible and adaptable, able to respond quickly to customer and employee needs. Rather than simply issuing orders, managers are finding ways to benefit from employees' insight by giving them the freedom to make decisions and solve problems. *Leadership* is dispersed throughout the organization, and managers share rather than hoard power. The model of managers controlling workers no longer applies in a world of rapidly changing technology, diversity, and global competition. Instead, managers act as coaches and facilitators, getting everyone involved and committed. Everyone is given a chance to be a leader. At AES Corporation, a power producer, teams of coal handlers and maintenance workers handle operations, purchasing, human resources, public relations, and even corporate finance. CEO Dennis W. Bakke believes giving workers freedom and responsiblity is the best way to increase the company's brainpower.[62] *Team-building* skills also are crucial for today's managers. Teams of front-line workers who work directly with customers have become the basic building blocks of organizations. In addition, although the CEO of an organization still plays an important role, the focus is more on putting together a diverse, effective top-management team. For today's managers, the ability to build cohesive teams in an environment of diversity and dispersed decision making is paramount.[63]

In other words, success today depends on the strength and quality of *relationships*. New ways of working and managing emphasize cooperation and collaboration across functions and hierarchical levels, as well as with other companies. Some competition can be healthy for a company, but ideas about the nature of competition are changing. Rather than emphasizing the struggle to beat out a competitor, managers direct employees' energy toward being the best that they can be. An environment of teamwork and community that fosters collaboration and mutual support gives employees opportunities to think, learn, and grow.[64]

Indeed, it's an exciting time to be entering the field of management. Throughout this book, you will learn much more about the learning organization and the new and dynamic roles managers are playing in the twenty-first century.

Summary and Management Solution

This chapter introduced a number of important concepts and described the changing nature of management. High performance requires the efficient and effective use of organizational resources through the four management functions of planning, organizing, leading, and controlling. To perform the four functions, managers need three skills—conceptual, human, and technical. Conceptual skills are more important at the top of the hierarchy; human skills are important at all levels; and technical skills are most important for first-line managers.

Two characteristics of managerial work also were explained in the chapter: (1) Managerial activities involve variety, fragmentation, and brevity and (2) Managers perform a great deal of work at an unrelenting pace. Managers also are expected to perform activities associated with ten roles: the informational roles of monitor, disseminator, and spokesperson; the interpersonal roles of figurehead, leader, and liaison; and the decisional roles of entrepreneur, disturbance handler, resource allocator, and negotiator.

These management characteristics are still accurate, but they are being applied in a new world of increasing chaos, diversity, and globalization. A new management paradigm is emerging. New forces affecting organizations include the globalization of the marketplace, increased diversity of the workforce, a shift to electronic information technology, and emphasis on change rather than stability. Today's managers put customers and employees ahead of profits. Leadership is widely dispersed and empowering, and most work is done by teams. Managers give employees opportunities for personal growth and self-fulfillment and emphasize collaboration over competition and conflict. The primary responsibility of managers is to create learning capability, and many companies are becoming learning organizations. Liisa Joronen and SOL Cleaning illustrate this change in managerial perspective. The company has eliminated all perks and status symbols. There are no titles and assigned parking spaces, no secretaries, no individual offices, no set working hours. All work is performed by self-directed teams that create their own budgets, do their own hiring, set their own performance goals, and negotiate their own arrangements with customers. In fact, if a team builds up enough business, it has the right to create its own separate satellite office. SOL's training program would be the envy of a high-tech corporation.

Though it's unlikely that a person growing up would dream of becoming an industrial cleaner, SOL keeps workers motivated and fulfilled by giving them a chance to use their brains as well as their hands. Employees study time management, budgeting, and people and relationship skills. SOL turns cleaners into customer service specialists. Liisa Joronen and the 135 team leaders at SOL perform the traditional functions and roles of management, but within the framework of a learning organization. Joronen's task is more challenging than that of a traditional manager's because it has less structure, more uncertainty, and greater reliance on leadership, human skills, and interpersonal roles. Creating learning organizations is the challenge for future managers.

Discussion Questions

1. Assume you are a research engineer at a petrochemical company, collaborating with a marketing manager on a major product modification. You notice that every memo you receive from her has been copied to senior management. At every company function, she spends time talking to the big shots. You are also aware that sometimes when you are slaving away over the project, she is playing golf with senior managers. What is your evaluation of her behavior?

2. What do you think the text means by a management revolution? Do you expect to be a leader or follower in this revolution? Explain.

3. What similarities do you see among the four management functions of planning, organizing, leading, and controlling? Do you think these functions are related—that is, is a manager who performs well in one function likely to perform well in the others?

4. Why did a top manager such as Frank Lorenzo at Continental fail to motivate employees, while a top manager such as Herb Kelleher at Southwest succeed? Which of the four management functions best explains this difference? Discuss.

5. What is the difference between efficiency and effectiveness? Which is more important for performance? Can an organization succeed in both simultaneously?

6. What changes in management functions and skills occur as one is promoted from a nonmanagement to a management position? How can managers acquire the new skills?

7. If managerial work is characterized by variety, fragmentation, and brevity, how do managers perform basic management functions such as planning, which would seem to require reflection and analysis?

8. A college professor told her students, "The purpose of a management course is to teach students *about* management, not to teach them to be managers." Do you agree or disagree with this statement? Discuss.

9. Describe the characteristics of the new management paradigm. How do these characteristics compare to those of an organization in which you have worked? Would you like to work or manage in a learning organization? Discuss.

10. How could the teaching of management change to prepare future managers to deal with workforce diversity? With empowerment? Do you think diversity and empowerment will have a substantial impact on organizations in the future? Explain.

Management in Practice: Experiential Exercise

Management Aptitude Questionnaire

Rate each of the following questions according to this scale:

5 I always am like this.
4 I often am like this.
3 I sometimes am like this.
2 I rarely am like this.
1 I never am like this.

___ 1. When I have a number of tasks or homework to do, I set priorities and organize the work around the deadlines. C

___ 2. Most people would describe me as a good listener. H

___ 3. When I am deciding on a particular course of action for myself (such as hobbies to pursue, languages to study, which job to take, special projects to be involved in), I typically consider the long-term (three years or more) implications of what I would choose to do. C

___ 4. I prefer technical or quantitative courses rather than those involving literature, psychology, or sociology. T

____ 5. When I have a serious disagreement with someone, I hang in there and talk it out until it is completely resolved. H

____ 6. When I have a project or assignment, I really get into the details rather than the "big picture" issues.* C

____ 7. I would rather sit in front of my computer than spend a lot of time with people. T

____ 8. I try to include others in activities or when there are discussions. H

____ 9. When I take a course, I relate what I am learning to other courses I have taken or concepts I have learned elsewhere. C

____10. When somebody makes a mistake, I want to correct the person and let her or him know the proper answer or approach.* H

____11. I think it is better to be efficient with my time when talking with someone, rather than worry about the other person's needs, so that I can get on with my real work. T

____12. I know my long-term vision for career, family, and other activities and have thought it over carefully. C

____13. When solving problems, I would much rather analyze some data or statistics than meet with a group of people. T

____14. When I am working on a group project and someone doesn't pull a full share of the load, I am more likely to complain to my friends rather than confront the slacker.* H

____15. Talking about ideas or concepts can get me really enthused and excited. C

____16. The type of management course for which this book is used is really a waste of time. T

____17. I think it is better to be polite and not to hurt people's feelings.* H

____18. Data or things interest me more than people. T

Scoring key

Add the total points for the following sections. Note that starred * items are reverse scored, as such:

1 I always am like this.
2 I often am like this.
3 I sometimes am like this.
4 I rarely am like this.
5 I never am like this.

1, 3, 6, 9, 12, 15	**C**onceptual skills total score _____
2, 5, 8, 10, 14, 17	**H**uman skills total score _____
4, 7, 11, 13, 16, 18	**T**echnical skills total score _____

The above skills are three abilities needed to be a good manager. Ideally, a manager should be strong (though not necessarily equal) in all three. Anyone noticeably weaker in any of the skills should take courses and read to build up that skill. For further background on the three skills, please refer to the model in pages 8–11.

*reverse scoring item

NOTE: This exercise was contributed by Dorothy Marcic.

Management in Practice: Ethical Dilemma

Can Management Afford to Look the Other Way?

Harry Rull had been with Shellington Pharmaceuticals for 30 years. After a tour of duty in the various plants and 7 years overseas, Harry was back at headquarters, looking forward to his new role as vice president of U.S. Marketing.

Two weeks into his new job, Harry received some unsettling news about one of the managers under his supervision. Over casual lunch conversation, the director of human resources mentioned that Harry should expect a phone call about Roger Jacobs, Manager of New Product Development. Jacobs had a history of being "pretty horrible" to his subordinates, she said, and one disgruntled employee had asked to speak to someone in senior management. After lunch, Harry did some follow-up work. Jacobs's performance reviews had been stellar, but his personnel file also contained a large number of notes documenting charges of Jacobs's mistreatment of subordinates. The complaints ranged from "inappropriate and derogatory remarks" to subsequently dropped charges of sexual harassment. What was more disturbing was that the amount as well as the severity of complaints had increased with each of Jacobs's ten years with Shellington.

When Harry questioned the company president about the issue, he was told, "Yeah, he's had some problems, but you can't just replace someone with an eye for new products. You're a bottom-line guy; you understand why we let these things slide." Not sure how to handle the situation, Harry met briefly with Jacobs and reminded him to "keep the team's morale up." Just after the meeting, Sally Barton from HR called to let him know the problem she'd mentioned over lunch had been worked out. However, she warned, another employee had now come forward demanding that her complaints be addressed by senior management.

What Do You Do?

1. Ignore the problem. Jacobs's contributions to new product development are too valuable to risk losing him, and the problems over the past ten years have always worked themselves out anyway. No sense starting something that could make you look bad.

2. Launch a full-scale investigation of employee complaints about Jacobs, and make Jacobs aware that the documented history over the past ten years has put him on thin ice.

3. Meet with Jacobs and the employee to try to resolve the current issue, then start working with Sally Barton and other senior managers to develop stronger policies regarding sexual harassment and treatment of employees, including clear-cut procedures for handling complaints.

SOURCE: Based on Doug Wallace, "A Talent for Mismanagement," *What Would You Do? Business Ethics*, Vol II (November–December 1992), 3–4.

Surf the Net

1. **Surfing Skills.** To help you get the most out of the "Surf the Net" exercises throughout this text, visit one of the Web sites listed below. If you're new to the Internet, list three things you learned that will help you develop your "surfing" skills. If you're already a proficient surfer, list three items of information you learned that will help you enhance your level of proficiency.
   www.microsoft.com/magazine/guides/internet/
   **www.zdnet.com/zdhelp/howto_help/websearch/
   search_1.html**
   www.pbs.org/uti/begin.html

2. **Management Career Opportunities.** The Manager's Shoptalk box in this chapter asked you to consider whether you really want to be a manager. To help you explore a future management career, access one of the online career Web sites, such as Career Mosaic or The Monster Board, accessible at **www.100hot.com/jobs/**
   Click on the "job search" feature. You will be asked to enter key search words or select a job title from a list provided. Choose a management career that you are interested in pursuing, such as "sales manager," "financial manager," "human resources manager," or any other field that you want to learn about, then click on the search button. The site will return job postings from many different companies. Select at least three, look at the information, and print out the job descriptions. Compile a list of the education and experience requirements as well as any information about the job that appeals to you. Your instructor may ask you to write a memo on what you found and why you think that a management career will or will not be a good choice for you.

3. **Management Skills.** Use a search engine or try one of the Web addresses listed below to locate information about past or present successful managers, such as Sam Walton, Wal-Mart founder and former CEO; Dave Thomas, of Wendy's Restaurants; Herb Kelleher, CEO of Southwest Airlines, or Jack Welch, CEO of General Electric. As you read about these leaders, identify examples of the conceptual, human, and technical skills exhibited in their work.
   www.wal-mart.com/corporate/wm_story.shtml
   www.wendys.com/dave_history/meet_dave.html
   **http://cgi.pathfinder.com/fortune/careers/1999/01/
   11/interview.html**

Case for Critical Analysis

Electra-Quik

Barbara Russell, a manufacturing vice president, walked into the monthly companywide meeting with a light step and a hopefulness she hadn't felt in a long time. The company's new, dynamic CEO was going to announce a new era of empowerment at Electra-Quik, an 80-year-old publicly held company that had once been a leading manufacturer and retailer of electrical products and supplies. In recent years, the company experienced a host of problems: market share was declining in the face of increased foreign and domestic competition; new product ideas were few and far between; departments such as manufacturing and sales barely spoke to one another; morale was at an all-time low, and many employees were actively seeking other jobs. Everyone needed a dose of hope.

Martin Griffin, who had been hired to revive the failing company, briskly opened the meeting with a challenge: "As we face increasing competition, we need new ideas, new energy, new spirit to make this company great. And the source for this change is you—each one of you." He then went on to explain that under the new empowerment campaign, employees would be getting more information about how the company was run and would be able to work with their fellow employees in new and creative ways. Martin proclaimed a new era of trust and cooperation at Electra-Quik. Barbara felt the excitement stirring within her; but as she looked around the room, she saw many of the other employees, including her friend Harry, rolling their eyes. "Just another pile of corporate crap," Harry said later. "One minute they try downsizing, the next reengineering. Then they dabble in restructuring. Now Martin wants to push empowerment. Garbage like empowerment isn't a substitute for hard work and a little faith in the people who have been with this company for years. We made it great once, and we can do it again. Just get out of our way." Harry had been a manufacturing engineer with Electra-Quik for more than 20 years. Barbara knew he was extremely loyal to the company, but he—and a lot of others like him—were going to be an obstacle to the empowerment efforts.

Top management assigned selected managers to several problem-solving teams to come up with ideas for implementing the empowerment campaign. Barbara loved her assignment as team leader of the manufacturing team, working on ideas to improve how retail stores got the merchandise they needed when they needed it. The team thrived, and trust blossomed among the members. They even spent nights and weekends working to complete their report. They were proud of the ideas they had come up with, which they believed were innovative but easily achievable: permit a manager to follow a product from design through sales to customers; allow salespeople to refund up to $500 worth of merchandise on the spot; make information available to salespeople about future products; and swap sales and manufacturing personnel for short periods to let them get to know one another's jobs.

When the team presented their report to department heads, Martin Griffin was enthusiastic. But shortly into the meeting he had to excuse himself because of a late-breaking deal with a major hardware store chain. With Martin absent, the department heads rapidly formed a wall of resistance. The director of hu-

man resources complained that the ideas for personnel changes would destroy the carefully crafted job categories that had just been completed. The finance department argued that allowing salespeople to make $500 refunds would create a gold mine for unethical customers and salespeople. The legal department warned that providing information to salespeople about future products would invite industrial spying.

The team members were stunned. As Barbara mulled over the latest turn of events, she considered her options: keep her mouth shut; take a chance and confront Martin about her sincerity in making empowerment work; push slowly for reform and work for gradual support from the other teams; or look for another job and leave a company she really cared about. Barbara realized there would be no easy choices and no easy answers.

Questions

1. How might top management have done a better job changing Electra-Quik into a learning organization? What might they do now to get the empowerment process back on track?
2. Can you think of ways Barbara could have avoided the problems her team faced in the meeting with department heads?
3. If you were Barbara Russell, what would you do now? Why?

SOURCE: Based on Lawrence R. Rothstein, "The Empowerment Effort That Came Undone," *Harvard Business Review* (January–February 1995), 20–31.

Endnotes

1. Gina Imperato, "Dirty Business, Bright Ideas," *Fast Company,* February–March 1997, 89–93.
2. Nicholas Imparato and Oren Harari, *Jumping the Curve: Innovation and Strategic Choice in an Age of Transition* (San Francisco: Jossey-Bass Publishers, 1994); Tom Broersma, "In Search of the Future," *Training and Development,* January 1995, 38–43; Rahul Jacob, "The Struggle to Create an Organization for the Twenty-First Century," *Fortune,* April 3, 1995, 90–99; and Charles Handy, *The Age of Paradox* (Boston: Harvard Business School Press, 1994).
3. Justin Martin, "Tomorrow's CEOs," *Fortune,* June 24, 1996, 76–90; David Greising, "I'd Like the World to Buy a Coke," *Business Week,* April 13, 1998, 70–76.
4. Louis Kraar, "Iron Butterflies," *Fortune,* October 7, 1991, 143–154.
5. James A. F. Stoner and R. Edward Freeman, *Management,* 4th ed. (Englewood Cliffs, N.J.: Prentice-Hall, 1989).
6. Peter F. Drucker, *Management Tasks, Responsibilities, Practices* (New York: Harper & Row, 1974).
7. "Komatsu: Getting the Job Done," *Fortune,* August 4, 1997, S-7; David Greising, "Home Depot," in Wendy Zellner, Robert D. Hof, Richard Brandt, Stephen Baker, and David Greising, "Go-Go Goliaths," *Business Week,* February 13, 1995, 64–70.
8. Justin Martin, "The Man Who Boogied Away a Billion," *Fortune,* December 23, 1996, 89–100.
9. Ricardo Semler, *Maverick: The Success Story behind the World's Most Unusual Workplace* (New York: Warner Books, 1993); Ricardo Semler, "All for One, One for All," *Harvard Business Review* (September–October 1989), 76–84; and Fierman, "Winning Ideas from Maverick Managers."
10. John Bussey and Douglas R. Sease, "Manufacturers Strive to Slice Time Needed to Develop Products," *The Wall Street Journal,* February 23, 1988, 1, 13.
11. Stratford Sherman, "How Tomorrow's Best Leaders Are Learning Their Stuff," *Fortune,* November 27, 1995, 90–102.
12. Kenneth Labich, "Is Herb Kelleher America's Best CEO?" *Fortune,* May 2, 1994, 44–52; Brenda Paik Sunoo, "How Fun Flies At Southwest Airlines," *Personnel Journal,* June 1995, 62–73; Kristin Dunlap Godsey, "Slow Climb to New Heights: Combine Strict Discipline with Goofy Antics and Make Billions," *Success,* October 1996, 20–26; and "Southwest Airlines' Herb Kelleher: Unorthodoxy at Work," an inteview with William G. Lee, *Management Review,* January 1995, 9–12.
13. Justin Martin, "Tomorrow's CEOs," *Fortune,* June 24, 1996, 76–90.
14. Christopher A. Bartlett and Sumantra Ghoshal, "Changing the Role of Top Management: Beyond Systems to People," *Harvard Business Review* (May–June 1995), 132–142.
15. Fierman, "Winning Ideas from Maverick Managers."

16. Brett Duval Fromson, "The Slow Death of E. F. Hutton," *Fortune,* February 29, 1988, 82–88.

17. Michael Davis, "Nissan Credits 'Good People' for Efficiency," *The Tennessean,* May 31, 1996, 1E, 4E; Wendy Zellner, Robert D. Hof, Richard Brandt, Stephen Baker, and David Greising, "Go-Go Goliaths," *Business Week,* February 13, 1995, 64–70.

18. David Wessell, "With Labor Scarce, Service Firms Strive to Raise Productivity," *The Wall Street Journal,* June 1, 1989, A1, A8.

19. Martha Brannigan and Eleena De Lisser, "Cost Cutting at Delta Raises the Stock Price But Lowers the Service," *The Wall Street Journal,* June 20, 1996, A1.

20. Robert L. Katz, "Skills of an Effective Administrator," *Harvard Business Review* 52 (September–October 1974), 90–102.

21. Brenton Schlender, "How Bill Gates Keeps the Magic Going," *Fortune,* June 18, 1990, 82–89.

22. Robert D. Hof with Kathy Rebello and Peter Burrows, "Scott McNealy's Rising Sun," *Business Week,* January 22, 1996, 66–73.

23. Anne Fisher, "The 100 Best Companies to Work for in America," *Fortune,* January 12, 1998, 69–70.

24. Anne Fisher "The 100 Best Companies"; Ronald B. Lieber, "Why Employees Love These Companies," *Fortune,* January 12, 1998, 72–74; and Linda Grant, "Happy Workers, High Returns," *Fortune,* January 12, 1998, 81.

25. Jenny C. McCune, "Management's Brave New World," *Management Review,* October 1997, 10–14.

26. Baker, "Nucor," in Zellner et al., "Go-Go Goliaths," 70.

27. Eric Calonius, "Smart Moves by Quality Champs," *Fortune,* special 1991 issue—The New American Century, 24–28.

28. Bartlett and Ghoshal, "Changing the Role of Top Management"; and Sumantra Ghoshal and Christopher A. Bartlett, "Changing the Role of Top Management: Beyond Structure to Processes," *Harvard Business Review* (January–February 1995), 86–96.

29. "Middle Managers Are Back—But Now They're 'High-Impact Players,'" *The Wall Street Journal,* April 14, 1998, B1; and Carol Hymowitz, "When Firms Slash Middle Management, Those Spared Often Bear a Heavy Load," *The Wall Street Journal,* April 5, 1990, B1.

30. "Middle Managers Are Back."

31. Jenny C. McCune, "Management's Brave New World," *Management Review,* October 1997, 10–14.

32. Geoffrey Colvin, "Revenge of the Nerds," *Fortune,* March 2, 1998, 223–224; McCune, "Management's Brave New World," and "Middle Managers Are Back."

33. Steven W. Floyd and Bill Wooldridge, "Dinosaurs or Dynamos? Recognizing Middle Management's Strategic Role," *Academy of Management Executive* 8, no. 4 (1994), 47–57.

34. Thomas A. Stewart, "The Corporate Jungle Spawns a New Species: The Project Manager," *Fortune,* July 10, 1995, 179–180.

35. Henry Mintzberg, *The Nature of Managerial Work* (New York: Harper & Row, 1973); and Mintzberg, "Rounding Out the Manager's Job," *Sloan Management Review* (Fall 1994), 11–26.

36. Robert E. Kaplan, "Trade Routes: The Manager's Network of Relationships," *Organizational Dynamics* (Spring 1984), 37–52; Rosemary Stewart, "The Nature of Management: A Problem for Management Education," *Journal of Management Studies* 21 (1984), 323–330; John P. Kotter, "What Effective General Managers Really Do," *Harvard Business Review* (November–December 1982), 156–167; and Morgan W. McCall, Jr., Ann M. Morrison, and Robert L. Hannan, "Studies of Managerial Work: Results and Methods" (Technical Report No. 9, Center for Creative Leadership, Greensboro, N.C., 1978).

37. Anita Lienert, "A Day in the Life: Airport Manager Extraordinaire," *Management Review,* January 1995, 57–61.

38. Henry Mintzberg, "Managerial Work: Analysis from Observation," *Management Science* 18 (1971), B97–B110.

39. Alan Deutschman, "The CEO's Secret of Managing Time," *Fortune,* June 1, 1992, 135–146.

40. Based on Carol Saunders and Jack William Jones, "Temporal Sequences in Information Acquisition for Decision Making: A Focus on Source and Medium," *Academy of Management Review* 15 (1990), 29–46; Kotter, "What Effective General Managers Really Do"; and Mintzberg, "Managerial Work."

41. Mintzberg, "Managerial Work."

42. Lienert, "A Day in the Life."

43. Lance B. Kurke and Howard E. Aldrich, "Mintzberg Was Right!: A Replication and Extension of *The Nature of Managerial Work,*" *Management Science* 29 (1983), 975–984; Cynthia M. Pavett and Alan W. Lau, "Managerial Work: The Influence of Hierarchical Level and Functional Specialty," *Academy of Management Journal* 26 (1983), 170–177; and Colin P. Hales, "What Do Managers Do? A Critical Review of the Evidence," *Journal of Management Studies* 23 (1986), 88–115.

44. Mintzberg, "Rounding Out the Manager's Job."

45. Shelly Branch, "So Much Work, So Little Time," *Fortune,* February 3, 1997, 115–117.

46. Oren Harari, "Open the Doors, Tell the Truth," *Management Review,* January 1995, 33–35.

47. Harry S. Jonas III, Ronald E. Fry, and Suresh Srivastva, "The Office of the CEO: Understanding the Executive Experience," *Academy of Management Executive* 4 (August 1990), 36–48.

48. Edward O. Welles, "There Are No Simple Businesses Anymore," *The State of Small Business,* 1995, 66–79.

49. John A. Byrne, "Profiting from the Nonprofits," *Business Week,* March 26, 1990, 66–74; and Michael Ryval, "Born-Again Bureaucrats," *Canadian Business,* November 1991, 64–71.

50. The following discussion is based on John A. Byrne, "Paradigms for Postmodern Managers," *Business Week/Reinventing*

America (1992), 62–63; George Land and Beth Jarman, *Breakpoint and Beyond* (New York: Harper Business, 1992); Robert Barner, "Seven Changes That Will Challenge Managers—and Workers," *The Futurist,* March/April, 1996, 33–42; and Lawrence Chimerine, "The New Realities in Business," *Management Review,* January 1997, 12–17.

51. Jeffrey Pfeffer, "Producing Sustainable Competitive Advantage through the Effective Management of People," *Academy of Management Executive* 9, No. 1 (1995), 55–72.

52. Mahlon Apgar, IV, "The Alternative Workplace: Changing How and Where People Work," *Harvard Business Review,* May–June 1998, 121–136; and Jenny C. McCune, "Telecommuting Revisited," *Management Review,* February 1998, 10–16.

53. Toby J. Tetenbaum, "Shifting Paradigms: From Newton to Chaos," *Organizational Dynamics* (Spring 1998), 21–32.

54. Alan Farnham, "Global—or Just Globaloney?" *Fortune,* June 27, 1994, 97–100; William C. Symonds, Brian Bremner, Stewart Toy, and Karen Lowry Miller, "The Globetrotters Take Over," *Business Week,* July 8, 1996, 46–48; Carla Rapoport, "Nestle's Brand Building Machine," *Fortune,* September 19, 1994, 147–156; and "Execs with Global Vision," *USA Today,* International Edition, February 9, 1996, 12B.

55. Lawrence Chimerine, "The New Economic Realities in Business," *Management Review,* January 1997, 12–17; Fred G. Steingraber, "The New Business Realities of the Twenty-First

Century," *Business Horizons,* November–December 1996, 2–5; and Koh Sera, "Corporate Globalizaiton: A New Trend," *Academy of Managment Executive* 6, No. 1 (1992), 89–96.

56. For further information about Theory Z, see William G. Ouchi and Alfred M. Jaeger, "Type Z Organizations: Stability in the Midst of Mobility," *Academy of Management Review* 3 (1978), 308–314; and William G. Ouchi, *Theory Z: How American Business Can Meet the Japanese Challenge* (Reading, Mass.: Addison-Wesley, 1981).

57. Gilbert W. Fairholm, *Leadership and the Culture of Trust,* (Westport, Conn.: Praeger, 1994), 184; and Barner, "Seven Changes That Will Challenge Managers—and Workers."

58. Gilbert W. Fairholm, *Leadership and the Culture of Trust,* (Westport, Conn.: Praeger, 1994), 184.

59. Tetenbaum, "Shifting Paradigms: From Newton to Chaos."

60. Tetenbaum, "Shifting Paradigms: From Newton to Chaos."

61. Christopher A. Bartlett and Sumantra Ghoshal, "The Myth of the Generic Manager: New Personal Competencies for New Management Roles," *California Managmeent Review* 40, No. 1 (Fall 1997), 92–116.

62. Alex Markels, "A Power Producer Is Intent on Giving Power to Its People," *The Wall Street Journal,* July 3, 1995, A1.

63. Barner, "Seven Changes That Will Challenge Managers."

64. Martha H. Peak, "Today's Management Flavor: Plain Vanilla," *Management Review,* July–August 1997, 26–29.

LEARNING OBJECTIVES

After studying this chapter, you should be able to

- Understand how historical forces influence the practice of management

- Describe the learning organization and how it is designed through changes in leadership, structure, empowerment, information sharing, strategy, and culture.

- Identify and explain major developments in the history of management thought.

- Describe the major components of the classical and humanistic management perspectives.

- Discuss the quantitative management perspective.

- Explain the major concepts of systems theory and total quality management.

- Discuss the basic concepts underlying contingency views.

Historical Foundations of the Learning Organization

MANAGEMENT PROBLEM

For most of its 62 years, Mexico's PIPSA (Producer and Importer of Paper S.A.) was a government-owned company with a monopoly in newsprint, the company's only product. PIPSA managers operated in a comfortable, stable environment, but everything changed when PIPSA's monopoly in newsprint was abolished and the Mexican government announced plans to privatize the company. PIPSA rapidly lost nearly 50 percent of its business and revenues plummeted. Managers needed to think fast and move fast to fend off brutal competition. "We're competing with companies 10 times our size," says CEO René Villarreal. "These companies have more money and equipment than we do, so the only way for us to compete is with knowledge." However, while PIPSA's managers are modern, globe-trotting executives, most of the company's 2,000 factory workers have little formal education and still cling to traditional Mexican values. The tradition of oral storytelling is strong, and many workers don't like formal written policies and training manuals. "Creating knowledge workers is easy if you're a software company filled with PhDs," Villarreal laments. "It's more difficult in a company of manual laborers."[1]

If you were René Villarreal, how would you tap the knowledge of PIPSA's 2,000 employees and use it to be more competitive? What advice would you give him for the kind of company he might create?

PIPSA is faced with a situation similar to many companies. Everything is going along fine, and then suddenly the bottom drops out. Unexpected market forces devastated Digital Equipment Corporation, forcing managers to launch an internal revolution as a matter of survival. Behlen, a manufacturer of steel agricultural buildings, lost half its market for grain storage buildings almost overnight when the government stopped subsidizing grain storage. Companies such as LG&E Energy Company and Arizona Public Service Company face a crisis because of increasing deregulation and the growth of small, independent power producers.[2] When everything changes suddenly, managers face a seemingly impossible situation and have to create a new kind of company, one with which they have little experience or skill.

Many organizations succeeded by developing centralized structure and control. These companies use a strict hierarchy to achieve efficiency and profitability. This works fine as long as the world is stable. But the world of the twenty-first century is one of chaos and rapid change. The emerging world is asking far more of managers, which is what this book is about.

Some companies have taken up the challenge of reinventing themselves, of becoming more than status quo companies. For example, Disney's theme parks have become known for people management and creative leadership. Johnsonville Foods and Saturn have moved to self-directed teams and a culture of employee empowerment. Motorola has achieved extraordinary quality. Federal Express achieves excellence through treating its people and customers well. Springfield Remanufacturing has led the way with open-book management, sharing all financial information with every employee. Rubbermaid has excelled by learning to create a flood of new products that are nearly always successful in the marketplace. These companies go beyond the norm to succeed in an increasingly difficult world.[3]

As we discussed in Chapter 1, we are currently experiencing a paradigm shift—the emergence of a new kind of organization and a new approach to management. Managers today face the ultimate paradox: (1) Keep everything running efficiently and profitably, while, at the same time, (2) change everything.[4] It's no longer enough just to learn how to measure and control things. Success accrues to those who learn how to be leaders, to initiate change, and to participate in and even create organizations with fewer managers and less hierarchy that can change quickly.

Management philosophies and organizational forms change over time to meet new needs. We open this chapter by briefly examining the historical forces that influence organizations and the practice of management. The chapter will then discuss a new type of organization for the twenty-first century, called the *learning organization*. After describing the learning organization, we will examine some of the historical trends leading up to it. This foundation of management understanding illustrates that the value of studying management lies not in learning current facts and research but in developing a perspective that will facilitate the broad, long-term view needed for management success.

Management and Organization

A historical perspective on management is important because it gives executives a way of thinking, a way of searching for patterns and understanding trends. A historical perspective provides a context or environment in which to interpret current problems. However, studying history does not mean merely arranging events in chronological order; it means developing an understanding of the impact of societal forces on organizations. Studying history is a way to achieve strategic thinking, see the big picture, and improve conceptual skills. We will start by examining how social, political, and economic forces have influenced organizations and the practice of management.[5]

Social forces refer to those aspects of a culture that guide and influence relationships among people. What do people value? What do people need? What are the standards of behavior among people? These forces shape what is known as the *social contract*, which refers to the unwritten, common rules and perceptions about relationships among people and between employees and management. Expressions such as "a man's as good as his word" and "a day's work for a day's pay" convey such perceptions.

A significant social force affecting organizations today is the changing attitudes, values, and demands of young, highly educated workers. With low unemployment and an aging population, companies are scrambling to attract "knowledge workers"—mostly young people who are smart, educated, creative, and computer literate. Rather than the organization having the power, the power has shifted to the worker, so that the worker can often make outrageous demands. Young college-educated workers don't just want a job; they want a job that's fun and that offers them opportunities for self-discovery and self-fulfillment as well as a top-notch salary.[6] Whereas in the past, many people expected to stay with one company for their entire careers, for today's workers, job-hopping is a way of life.

Political forces refer to the influence of political and legal institutions on people and organizations. Political forces include basic assumptions underlying the political system, such as the desirability of self-government, property rights, contract rights, the definition of justice, and the determination of innocence or guilt of a crime. The end of the Cold War and the spread of capitalism throughout the world are political forces that will dramatically affect business in coming years. Recent moves to establish a free market system in Eastern Europe underscore the growing interdependence among the world's countries. This interdependence requires managers to think in different ways. In addition, the empowerment of citizens throughout the world is a dramatically energetic political force. Power is being diffused both within and among countries as never before.[7] People are demanding empowerment, participation, and responsibility in all areas of their lives, including their work. Managers must learn to share rather than hoard power.

Economic forces pertain to the availability, production, and distribution of resources in a society. Governments, military agencies, churches, schools, and business organizations in every society require resources to achieve their goals, and economic forces influence the allocation of scarce resources. Resources may be human or material, fabricated or natural, physical or conceptual, but over time they are scarce and must be allocated among competing users. Today, finding adequate human resources (good employees) is the biggest problem many companies face. The United States is experiencing a period of economic expansion, which has been going on for so long that most young workers have never experienced a downturn in their working lives. Unemployment is at an all-time low. Economic scarcity may sometimes be the stimulus for technological innovation with which to increase resource availability. For example, the perfection

social forces
The aspects of a culture that guide and influence relationships among people—their values, needs, and standards of behavior.

political forces
The influence of political and legal institutions on people and organizations.

economic forces
Forces that affect the availability, production, and distribution of a society's resources among competing users.

E x h i b i t **2.1**   *Management Perspectives over Time*

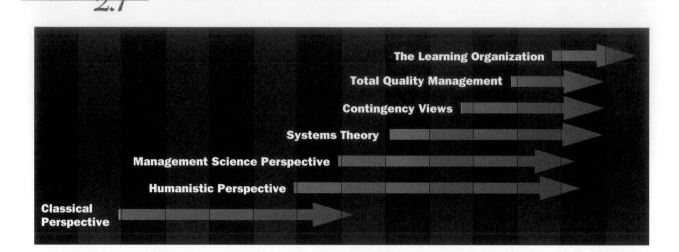

of the moving assembly line at Ford in 1913 cut the number of worker-hours needed for assembling a Model T from 12 to 1.5. Ford doubled its daily pay rate to $5, shortened working hours, and cut the price of Model Ts until its market share reached 57 percent in 1923.

Management practices and perspectives vary over time in response to these social, political, and economic forces in the larger society. Exhibit 2.1 illustrates the evolution of significant management perspectives over time, which have culminated with the learning organization. We will first look at the elements of a learning organization, and then examine each of the other management approaches in Exhibit 2.1.

The Learning Organization

Managers began thinking about the concept of the learning organization after the publication of Peter Senge's book, *The Fifth Discipline: The Art and Practice of Learning Organizations.*[8] Senge described the kind of changes managers needed to undergo to help their organizations adapt to an increasingly chaotic world. These ideas gradually evolved to describe characteristics of the organization itself. There is no single view of what the learning organization looks like. The learning organization is an attitude or philosophy about what an organization can become.

learning organization
An organization in which everyone is engaged in identifying and solving problems, enabling the organization to continuously experiment, improve, and increase its capability.

The **learning organization** can be defined as one in which everyone is engaged in identifying and solving problems, enabling the organization to continuously experiment, change, and improve, thus increasing its capacity to grow, learn, and achieve its purpose. The essential idea is problem solving, in contrast to the traditional organization designed for efficiency. In the learning organization all employees look for problems, such as understanding special customer needs. Employees also solve problems, which means putting things together in unique ways to meet a customer's needs.

Developing a learning organization means making specific changes in the areas of leadership, structure, empowerment, communications/information

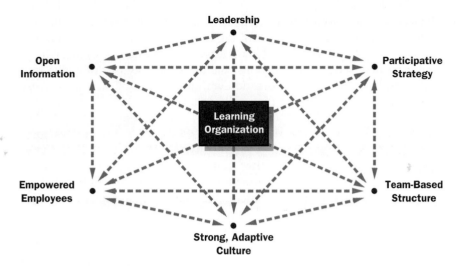

The Web of Interacting Elements in a Learning Organization

sharing, participative strategy, and adaptive culture. These six characteristics are illustrated in Exhibit 2.2, and each is described in the following sections.

Leadership. Leadership is the only means through which a company can change into a learning organization. The traditional view of leaders who set goals, make decisions, and direct the troops reflects an individualistic view. Leadership in learning organizations requires something more. In learning organizations, managers learn to think in terms of "control with" rather than "control over" others. They "control with" others by building relationships based on a shared vision and shaping the culture that can help achieve it. Leaders help people see the whole system, facilitate teamwork, initiate change, and expand the capacity of people to shape the future.[9] Leaders who understand the learning organization can help other people build it.

One of the most important functions of a leader in a learning organization is to *create a shared vision*. The shared vision is a picture of an ideal future for the organization. The vision includes what the organization will look like, performance outcomes, and underlying values. A vision may be created by the leader or with employee participation, but this purpose must be widely understood and imprinted in people's minds. The vision represents desired long-term outcomes; hence, employees are free to identify and solve problems that help achieve that vision. Patricia Gallup, CEO of PC Connection, built a learning organization by spreading her vision of a company that is always thinking about what technology people will need in the future. Her vision, which includes the values of equality, employee empowerment, responsibility, and dedication to serving customers, has created a vibrant organization in which employees use their skills and creative energy to the fullest.[10] Because all employees understand the vision, they can carry it out without direct supervision from the top.

Team-Based Structure. The learning organization breaks down the former vertical structure that separated managers and workers. Self-directed teams are the fundamental unit in a learning organization. These teams are made up of employees with different skills who rotate jobs to produce an entire product or service. They deal directly with customers and make changes and improvements as needed. Team members have the authority to make decisions about new ways of doing things. In learning organizations, bosses practically are eliminated, with team members taking responsibility for training, safety, scheduling vacations, and decisions about work methods, pay and reward systems, and coordination with other teams. Teams are discussed in detail in Chapter 19.

Employee Empowerment. *Empowerment* means giving employees the power, freedom, knowledge, and skills to make decisions and perform effectively. Traditional management tries to limit employees, while empowerment expands their behavior. Empowerment may be reflected in self-directed work teams, quality circles, job enrichment, and employee participation groups as well as through decision-making authority, training, and information so that people can perform jobs without close supervision.

In learning organizations, people are a manager's primary source of strength, not a cost to be minimized. Companies that adopt this perspective believe in treating employees well by providing competitive wages, good working conditions, and opportunities for personal and professional development. In addition, they often provide a sense of employee ownership by sharing gains in productivity and profits.[11]

Open Information.   A learning organization is flooded with information. To identify needs and solve problems, people have to be aware of what's going on. They must understand the whole organization as well as their part in it. Formal data about budgets, profits, and departmental expenses are available to everyone. As organizations work with ideas and information rather than products and things, information sharing reaches extraordinary levels. Like the oil in a car's engine, information is not allowed to get low. Leaders in learning organizations know that too much information is better than too little. Dave Duffield, CEO of PeopleSoft, Inc., puts it this way: "If people don't have total access to information, they have to guess at what they should be doing." Managers at PeopleSoft use information technology

The move to open communication and information sharing usually involves training to bring workers up to speed on company performance. Maytag uses Learning Maps to train employees to understand key business issues and the competitive challenges the company must overcome to remain profitable. During a 26-hour Training Marathon, these employees learn about cash flow challenges through the "Maytag Money Stream." The open-forum nature of Maytag's training sessions allows employees to ask specific questions about the corporation's business decisions as well as provide input on how to improve product quality and overall efficiency.

Lucent Technologies

All day long, Phillip Dailey strings cables inside a steel box the size of a refrigerator—a digital transmitting station for cellular phone systems. But he doesn't get bored, because Dailey is constantly using his brain as well as his hands. Studying a bottleneck along the assembly line one day, Dailey realized a way to increase output by 33 percent. He didn't have to talk to his bosses about his insight; he simply recruited temporary workers from other teams and made it happen.

Lynn Mercer, plant manager at this Lucent Technologies factory in Mount Olive, New Jersey, distributes authority three levels down because she believes those people know the job better than she does. In two years, the factory's self-directed workforce hasn't missed a single delivery deadline, and total labor costs represent an exceedingly low 3 percent of product cost. Teams elect their own leaders to oversee quality, training, scheduling, and coordination with other teams. Each team follows a standard one-page list of "working principles," but teams are continually altering the manufacturing process and even the product design itself. The process is so fluid that none of the manufacturing equipment is bolted to the floor. Engineers and assemblers constantly bat around ideas, and the professional staff cubicles sit right next to the assembly cells to promote constant interaction. According to produc-

tion manager Steve Sherman, "We solve problems in hallways rather than conference rooms."

The factory is flooded with information because Mercer believes that's how any complex system balances itself. Every procedure is written down, but procedures are constantly changing—any worker can propose changing any procedure in the plant, subject to ratification by those whose work it affects. Operating statistics are displayed everywhere, and anyone with a few spare minutes consults an "urgents board" listing orders that are behind schedule, jumping in where they're most needed. Assemblers also work directly with customers by attending trade shows and installation sites as well as giving customer tours of the plant.

Yearly bonuses, based equally on individual achievement and team performance, can be equivalent to 15 percent of regular pay. However, for workers, the greatest motivator is that they have a role in shaping the organization. "This business has been handed to us," says technician Tom Gugqiari. "This business is ours."

www.lucent.com

Source: Thomas Petzinger, Jr., "How Lynn Mercer Manages a Factory That Manages Itself," *The Wall Street Journal*, March 7, 1997, B11.

to create what they call an "infomacracy"—a transparent organization that provides open access to information for all its members. For example, unlike many software companies, which don't allow sales reps or account managers to see what's planned for future release, PeopleSoft lets anyone in the company tap into product development information. Employees have open access to all company databases as well as the ability to communicate electronically with any other person in the company.[12] In a learning organization, a manager's role is to give workers the information they need and the authority to act on it. The Leadership box describes how one manager has used this concept to shift a traditional, machine-based assembly line to a learning system.

Participative Strategy.   Strategy traditionally has been the responsibility of top executives. Strategy is seen as something that is formulated and imposed on the organization. Top managers think about how the company can best respond to competitors, cope with difficult environmental changes, and effectively use available resources. However, in learning organizations, strategy emerges bottom up as well as top down. Top executives shape a vision and direction that all employees support and believe in, but they do not control or direct strategy alone. Everyone helps. When all employees are committed to the vision, their accumulated actions contribute to the development of strategy. Since many employees in a learning organization are linked to customers, suppliers, and new technologies, they identify needs and solutions and participate directly in strategy making. Strategy in learning organizations also may emerge from partnerships with suppliers, customers, and even competitors. Learning organizations have permeable boundaries and often are linked with other companies, giving each organization greater access to information about new strategic needs and directions.[13]

Strong, Adaptive Culture.   Culture is the set of key values, beliefs, and understandings shared by members of the organization. A strong, adaptive organizational culture is the foundation of a learning organization. Equality is one fundamental cultural value in a learning organization. The culture creates a sense of belonging, community, and caring that supports other elements, such as teamwork and participative strategy. Each person is valued and the organization becomes a place for creating a web of relationships that allows people to be wholly engaged and develop to their full potential. Activities that create status differences, such as executive dining rooms and assigned parking spaces, are discarded. The emphasis on treating everyone with care and respect creates a climate of safety and trust that allows experimentation, frequent mistakes, and failures that enable learning.

Another basic value is to question the status quo, the current way of doing things. The culture of a learning organization values risk-taking, improvement, and change. Constant questioning of assumptions opens the gates to creativity and improvement. The culture celebrates and rewards the creators of new ideas, products, and work processes. In addition, the learning organization may also reward failure, to symbolize the importance of taking risks in order to learn and grow. As Marc Sokol, vice president of advanced technology at Computer Associates International, puts it, "Computer Associates tends to reward people who push the envelope. The thing is, if you push the envelope, sometimes it rips."[14]

Although no company represents a perfect example of a learning organization, one that illustrates the spirit of the learning organization is Visa International. Most people have heard of the credit card, but the organization behind it is almost "invisible": it is difficult to answer questions such as who runs the company, who makes the decisions—even where company headquarters are located.

VISA INTERNATIONAL
www.visa.com

Dee Hock, founder of Visa International, believes the better an organization is, the less visible it is. He founded the company more than 25 years ago to be an adaptive, free-flowing, continuously changing system, capable of rapidly responding to new challenges, threats, and opportunities. Visa International works without a hierarchy or rigid organization chart. Unlike the old-style pyramidal organization, Visa is a confederation of companies that virtually organizes itself.

Hock wanted to create an organization based on biological concepts and metaphors, not on the command and control model that had developed to support the industrial revolution. He designed Visa to be highly decentralized, egalitarian, and highly collaborative. Visa is a nonstock, for-profit membership corporation with ownership in the form of nontransferable rights of participation.

Authority, initiative, decision-making, and wealth are pushed out to the periphery of the organization, to the member financial institutions. Members are fierce competitors—they, not Visa, issue the credit cards so they're constantly going after each other's customers. However, members also have to cooperate extensively. It is this harmonious blend of cooperation and competition that has enabled the system to expand worldwide in the face of different currencies, languages, legal codes, cultures, customs, and political philosophies. A "one-best-way" of doing business dictated from headquarters could never have accomplished this. According to Hock, "the organization had to be based on biological concepts to evolve, in effect, to invent and organize itself." Visa, he says, "like the body, the brain, and the biosphere, [is] largely self-organizing."

Hock believes managers should understand that they "work for" those people who are often mislabeled "subordinates." His philosophy is that, to create learning organizations, leaders should lead themselves, lead those with authority over them, and lead their peers, and they should free the people they "work for" to do the same.[15]

Visa International was founded based on concepts that apply to the learning organization. Today, many companies are developing characteristics of learning organizations as a result of the paradigm shift we discussed in Chapter 1. However, these recent innovations were possible, in part, because of the trial and error experiments in organizations during the past century.

Many students wonder why history matters to managers. A historical perspective provides a broader way of thinking, a way of searching for patterns and determining whether they recur across time periods. For example, certain management techniques that seem "modern," such as employee stock ownership programs, have repeatedly gained and lost popularity since the early 20th century because of historical forces.[16]

A study of the past contributes to understanding both the present and the future. It is a way of learning: learning from others' mistakes so as not to repeat them; learning from others' successes so as to repeat them in the appropriate situation; and, most of all, learning to understand why things happen to improve things in the future. The remainder of this chapter will examine a number of management approaches that have led to the development of the learning organization.

Classical Perspective

The practice of management can be traced to 3000 B.C. to the first government organizations developed by the Sumerians and Egyptians, but the formal study of management is relatively recent.[17] The early study of management as we know it today began with what is now called the *classical perspective*.

The **classical perspective** on management emerged during the nineteenth and early twentieth centuries. The factory system that began to appear in the 1800s posed management challenges that earlier organizations had not encountered. Problems arose in tooling the plants, organizing managerial structure, training employees (many of them non-English-speaking immigrants), scheduling complex manufacturing operations, and dealing with increased labor dissatisfaction and resulting strikes.

classical perspective

A management perspective that emerged during the nineteenth and early twentieth centuries that emphasized a rational, scientific approach to the study of management and sought to make organizations efficient operating machines.

In response to the myriad new problems facing management throughout industrial America, managers developed and tested solutions to the mounting challenges. The evolution of modern management, called the classical perspective, thus began. This perspective contains three subfields, each with a slightly different emphasis: scientific management, bureaucratic organizations, and administrative principles.[18]

Scientific Management

Frederick Winslow Taylor (1856–1915) Taylor's theory that labor productivity could be improved by scientifically determined management practices earned him the status of "father of scientific management."

Organizations' somewhat limited success in achieving improvements in labor productivity led a young engineer to suggest that the problem lay more in poor management practices than in labor. Frederick Winslow Taylor (1856–1915) insisted that management itself would have to change and, further, that the manner of change could be determined only by scientific study; hence, the label **scientific management** emerged. Taylor suggested that decisions based on rules of thumb and tradition be replaced with precise procedures developed after careful study of individual situations.[19]

Taylor's approach is illustrated by the unloading of iron from rail cars and reloading finished steel for the Bethlehem Steel plant in 1898. Taylor calculated that with correct movements, tools, and sequencing, each man was capable of loading 47.5 tons per day instead of the typical 12.5 tons. He also worked out an incentive system that paid each man $1.85 a day for meeting the new standard, an increase from the previous rate of $1.15. Productivity at Bethlehem Steel shot up overnight.

Frederick Taylor's scientific management techniques were expanded by automaker Henry Ford, who replaced workers with machines for heavy lifting and moving. One of the first applications of the moving assembly line was the Magneto assembly operation at Ford's Highland Park plant in 1913. Magnetos moved from one worker to the next, reducing production time by one-half. The same principle was applied to total-car assembly, improving efficiency and reducing worker-hours required to produce a Model-T Ford to less than two. Under this system, a Ford rolled off the assembly line every ten seconds.

Although known as the "father of scientific management," Taylor was not alone in this area. Henry Gantt, an associate of Taylor's, developed the *Gantt Chart*—a bar graph that measures planned and completed work along each stage of production by time elapsed. Two other important pioneers in this area were the husband-and-wife team of Frank B. and Lillian M. Gilbreth. Frank B. Gilbreth (1868–1924) pioneered time and motion study and arrived at many of his management techniques independently of Taylor. He stressed efficiency and was known for his quest for the "one best way" to do work. Although Gilbreth is known for his early work with bricklayers, his work had great impact on medical surgery by drastically reducing the time patients spent on the operating table. Surgeons were able to save countless lives through the application of time and motion study. Lillian M. Gilbreth (1878–1972) was more interested in the human aspect of work. When her husband died at the age of 56, she had 12 children ages 2 to 19. The undaunted "first lady of management" went right on with her work. She presented a paper in place of her late husband, continued their seminars and consulting, lectured, and eventually became a professor at Purdue University.[20] She pioneered in the field of industrial psychology and made substantial contributions to human resource management.

Exhibit 2.3
Characteristics of Scientific Management

General Approach
- Developed standard method for performing each job.
- Selected workers with appropriate abilities for each job.
- Trained workers in standard method.
- Supported workers by planning their work and eliminating interruptions.
- Provided wage incentives to workers for increased output.

Contributions
- Demonstrated the importance of compensation for performance.
- Initiated the careful study of tasks and jobs.
- Demonstrated the importance of personnel selection and training.

Criticisms
- Did not appreciate the social context of work and higher needs of workers.
- Did not acknowledge variance among individuals.
- Tended to regard workers as uninformed and ignored their ideas and suggestions.

scientific management
A subfield of the classical management perspective that emphasized scientifically determined changes in management practices as the solution to improving labor productivity.

bureaucratic organizations
A subfield of the classical management perspective that emphasized management on an impersonal, rational basis through such elements as clearly defined authority and responsibility, formal recordkeeping, and separation of management and ownership.

The basic ideas of scientific management are shown in Exhibit 2.3. To use this approach, managers should develop standard methods for doing each job, select workers with the appropriate abilities, train workers in the standard methods, support workers and eliminate interruptions, and provide wage incentives.

Although scientific management improved productivity, its failure to deal with the social context and workers' needs led to increased conflict between managers and employees. Under this system, workers often felt exploited. This was in sharp contrast to the harmony and cooperation that Taylor and his followers had envisioned.

Bureaucratic Organizations

A systematic approach developed in Europe that looked at the organization as a whole is the **bureaucratic organizations** approach, a subfield within the classical perspective. Max Weber (1864–1920), a German theorist, introduced most of the concepts on bureaucratic organizations.[21]

During the late 1800s, many European organizations were managed on a "personal," familylike basis. Employees were loyal to a single individual rather than to the organization or its mission. The dysfunctional consequence of this management practice was that resources were used to realize individual desires rather than organizational goals. Employees in effect owned the organization and used resources for their own gain rather than to serve customers. Weber envisioned organizations that would be managed on an impersonal, rational basis. This form of organization was called a *bureaucracy*. Exhibit 2.4 summarizes the six characteristics of bureaucracy as specified by Weber.

Weber believed that an organization based on rational authority would be more efficient and adaptable to change because continuity is related to formal structure and positions rather than to a particular person, who may leave or die. To Weber, rationality in organizations meant employee selection and advancement based on competence rather than on "whom you know." The organization relies on rules and written records for continuity. The manager depends not on his or her personality for successfully giving orders but on the legal power invested in the managerial position.

Lillian M. Gilbreth (1878–1972) Frank B. Gilbreth (1868–1924)Shown here using a "motion study" device, this husband-and-wife team contributed to the principles of scientific management. His development of time and motion studies and her work in industrial psychology pioneered many of today's management and human resource techniques.

Exhibit *2.4*

Characteristics of Weberian Bureaucracy

Elements of Bureaucracy

1. Labor is divided with clear definitions of authority and responsibility that are legitimized as official duties.
2. Positions are organized in a hierarchy of authority, with each position under the authority of a higher one.
3. All personnel are selected and promoted based on technical qualifications, which are assessed by examination or according to training and experience.
4. Administrative acts and decisions are recorded in writing. Recordkeeping provides organizational memory and continuity over time.
5. Management is separate from the ownership of the organization.
6. Managers are subject to rules and procedures that will ensure reliable, predictable behavior. Rules are impersonal and uniformly applied to all employees.

SOURCE: Adapted from Max Weber, *The Theory of Social and Economic Organizations,* ed. and trans. A. M. Henderson and Talcott Parsons (New York: Free Press, 1947), 328–337.

The term *bureaucracy* has taken on a negative meaning in today's organizations and is associated with endless rules and red tape. We have all been frustrated by waiting in long lines or following seemingly silly procedures. On the other hand, rules and other bureaucratic procedures provide a standard way of dealing with employees. Everyone gets equal treatment, and everyone knows what the rules are. This has enabled many organizations to become extremely efficient. Consider United Parcel Service (UPS), also called the "Brown Giant."

UNITED PARCEL SERVICE

www.ups.com

United Parcel Service took on the U.S. Postal Service at its own game—and won. UPS specializes in the delivery of small packages. Why has the Brown Giant been so successful? One important reason is the concept of bureaucracy. UPS is bound up in rules and regulations. There are safety rules for drivers, loaders, clerks, and managers. Strict dress codes are enforced—no beards; hair cannot touch the collar; mustaches must be trimmed evenly; and no sideburns. Rules specify cleanliness standards for buildings and other properties. No eating or drinking is permitted at employee desks. Every manager is given bound copies of policy books and expected to use them regularly.

UPS also has a well-defined division of labor. Each plant consists of specialized drivers, loaders, clerks, washers, sorters, and maintenance personnel. UPS thrives on written records. Daily worksheets specify performance goals and work output. Daily employee quotas and achievements are reported on a weekly and monthly basis.

Technical qualification is the criterion for hiring and promotion. The UPS policy book says the leader is expected to have the knowledge and capacity to justify the position of leadership. Favoritism is forbidden. The bureaucratic model works just fine at UPS, "the tightest ship in the shipping business."[22]

Administrative Principles

administrative principles
A subfield of the classical management perspective that focused on the total organization rather than the individual worker, delineating the management functions of planning, organizing, commanding, coordinating, and controlling.

Another major subfield within the classical perspective is known as the **administrative principles** approach. Whereas scientific management focused on the productivity of the individual worker, the administrative principles approach focused on the total organization. The contributors to this approach included Henri Fayol, Mary Parker Follett, and Chester I. Barnard.

Henri Fayol (1841–1925) was a French mining engineer who worked his way up to become head of a major mining group known as Comambault.

Comambault survives today as part of Le Creusot-Loire, the largest mining and metallurgical group in central France. In his later years, Fayol wrote down his concepts on administration, based largely on his own management experiences.[23]

In his most significant work, *General and Industrial Management*, Fayol discussed 14 general principles of management, several of which are part of management philosophy today. For example:

- *Unity of command.* Each subordinate receives orders from one—and only one—superior.

- *Division of work.* Managerial and technical work are amenable to specialization to produce more and better work with the same amount of effort.

- *Unity of direction.* Similar activities in an organization should be grouped together under one manager.

- *Scalar chain.* A chain of authority extends from the top to the bottom of the organization and should include every employee.

Fayol felt that these principles could be applied in any organizational setting. He also identified five basic functions or elements of management: planning, organizing, commanding, coordinating, and controlling. These functions underlie much of the general approach to today's management theory.

Mary Parker Follett (1868–1933) was trained in philosophy and political science at what today is Radcliffe College. She applied herself in many fields, including social psychology and management. She wrote of the importance of common superordinate goals for reducing conflict in organizations.[24] Her work was popular with businesspeople of her day but was often overlooked by management scholars.[25] Follett's ideas served as a contrast to scientific management and are reemerging as applicable for modern managers dealing with rapid changes in today's global environment. Her approach to leadership stressed the importance of people rather than engineering techniques. She offered the pithy admonition "Don't Hug Your Blueprints" and analyzed the dynamics of management-organization interactions. Follett addressed issues that are timely today, such as ethics, power, and how to lead in a way that encourages employees to give their best. The concepts of empowerment, facilitating rather than controlling employees, and allowing employees to act depending on the authority of the situation opened new areas for theoretical study by Chester Barnard and others.[26]

Chester I. Barnard (1886–1961) studied economics at Harvard but failed to receive a degree because he lacked a course in laboratory science. He went to work in the statistical department of AT&T and in 1927 became president of New Jersey Bell. One of Barnard's significant contributions was the concept of the informal organization. The *informal organization* occurs in all formal organizations and includes cliques and naturally occurring social groupings. Barnard argued that organizations are not machines and informal relationships are powerful forces that can help the organization if properly managed. Another significant contribution was the *acceptance theory of authority*, which states that people have free will and can choose whether to follow management orders. People typically follow orders because they perceive positive benefit to themselves, but they do have a choice. Managers should treat employees properly because their acceptance of authority may be critical to organization success in important situations.[27]

*Max Weber
(1864–1920)*
The German theorist's concepts on bureaucratic organizations *have contributed to the efficiency of many of today's corporations.*

*Mary Parker Follett
(1868–1933)*
Follett was a major contributor to the administrative principles *approach to management. Her emphasis on worker participation and shared goals among managers was embraced by many businesspeople of the day and has been recently "rediscovered" by corporate America.*

The overall classical perspective as an approach to management was very powerful and gave companies fundamental new skills for establishing high productivity and effective treatment of employees. Indeed, America surged ahead of the world in management techniques, and other countries, especially Japan, borrowed heavily from American ideas.

Humanistic Perspective

humanistic perspective
A management perspective that emerged around the late nineteenth century that emphasized understanding human behavior, needs, and attitudes in the workplace.

Mary Parker Follett and Chester Barnard were early advocates of a more **humanistic perspective** on management that emphasized the importance of understanding human behaviors, needs, and attitudes in the workplace as well as social interactions and group processes.[28] We will discuss three subfields based on the humanistic perspective: the human relations movement, the human resources perspective, and the behavioral sciences approach.

The Human Relations Movement

America has always espoused the spirit of human equality. However, this spirit has not always been translated into practice when it comes to power sharing between managers and workers. The human relations school of thought considers that truly effective control comes from within the individual worker rather than from strict, authoritarian control.[29] This school of thought recognized and directly responded to social pressures for enlightened treatment of employees. The early work on industrial psychology and personnel selection received little attention because of the prominence of scientific management. Then a series of studies at a Chicago electric company, which came to be known as the **Hawthorne studies**, changed all that.

Hawthorne studies
A series of experiments on worker productivity begun in 1924 at the Hawthorne plant of Western Electric Company in Illinois; attributed employees' increased output to managers' better treatment of them during the study.

Beginning about 1895, a struggle developed between manufacturers of gas and electric lighting fixtures for control of the residential and industrial market.[30] By 1909 electric lighting had begun to win, but the increasingly efficient electric fixtures used less total power. The electric companies began a campaign to convince industrial users that they needed more light to get more productivity. When advertising did not work, the industry began using experimental tests to demonstrate their argument. Managers were skeptical about the results, so the Committee on Industrial Lighting (CIL) was set up to run the tests. To further add to the tests' credibility, Thomas Edison was made honorary chairman of the CIL. In one test location—the Hawthorne plant of the Western Electric Company—some interesting events occurred.

This 1914 photograph shows the initiation of a new arrival at a Nebraska planting camp. This initiation was not part of the formal rules and illustrates the significance of the informal organization *described by Barnard. Social values and behaviors were powerful forces that could help or hurt the planting organization depending on how they were managed.*

The major part of this work involved four experimental and three control groups. In all, five different "tests" were conducted. These pointed to the importance of factors *other* than illumination in affecting productivity. To more carefully examine these factors, numerous other experiments were conducted.[31] The results of the most famous study, the first Relay Assembly Test Room (RATR) experiment, were extremely controversial. Under the guidance of two Harvard professors, Elton Mayo and Fritz Roethlisberger, the RATR studies lasted nearly six years (May 10, 1927, to May 4, 1933) and involved 24 separate experimental periods. So many factors were changed and so many unforeseen factors uncontrolled that scholars disagree on the factors that truly contributed to the general increase in performance over that period. Most early interpretations, however, agreed on one thing:

Money was not the cause of the increased output.[32] However, recent reanalyses of the experiments have revealed that a number of factors were different for the workers involved, and some suggest that money may well have been the single most important factor.[33] An interview with one of the original participants revealed that just getting into the experimental group had meant a huge increase in income.[34]

These new data clearly show that money mattered a great deal at Hawthorne, but it was not recognized at the time of the experiments. Then it was felt that the factor that best explained increased output was "human relations." Employees' output increased sharply when managers treated them in a positive manner. These findings were published and started a revolution in worker treatment for improving organizational productivity. To be historically accurate, money was probably the best explanation for increases in output, but at that time experimenters believed the explanation was human relations. Despite the inaccurate interpretation of the data, the findings provided the impetus for the **human relations movement.** That movement shaped management theory and practice for well over a quarter-century, and the belief that human relations is the best approach for increasing productivity persists today. See the Manager's Shoptalk box for a number of management innovations that have become popular over the years.

This is the Relay Room of the Western Electric Hawthorne, Illinois, plant in 1927. Six women worked in this relay assembly test room during the controversial experiments on employee productivity. Professors Mayo and Roethlisberger evaluated conditions such as rest breaks and workday length, physical health, amount of sleep, and diet. Experimental changes were fully discussed with the women and were abandoned if they disapproved. Gradually the researchers began to realize they had created a change in supervisory style and human relations, which they believed was the true cause of the increased productivity.

human relations movement
A movement in management thinking and practice that emphasized satisfaction of employees' basic needs as the key to increased worker productivity.

human resources perspective
A management perspective that suggests jobs should be designed to meet higher-level needs by allowing workers to use their full potential.

The Human Resources Perspective

The human relations movement initially espoused a "dairy farm" view of management—contented cows give more milk, so satisfied workers will give more work. Gradually, views with deeper content began to emerge. The human resources perspective maintained an interest in worker participation and considerate leadership but shifted the emphasis to consider the daily tasks that people perform. The **human resources perspective** combines prescriptions for design of job tasks with theories of motivation.[35] In the human resources view, jobs should be designed so that tasks are not perceived as dehumanizing or demeaning but instead allow workers to use their full potential. Two of the best-known contributors to the human resources perspective were Abraham Maslow and Douglas McGregor.

Abraham Maslow (1908–1970), a practicing psychologist, observed that his patients' problems usually stemmed from an inability to satisfy their needs. Thus, he generalized his work and suggested a hierarchy of needs. Maslow's hierarchy started with physiological needs and progressed to safety, belongingness, esteem, and, finally, self-actualization needs. Chapter 17 discusses his ideas in more detail.

Douglas McGregor (1906–1964) had become frustrated with the early simplistic human relations notions while president of Antioch College in Ohio. He challenged both the classical perspective and the early human

Exhibit
2.5

Theory X and Theory Y

Assumptions of Theory X

- The average human being has an inherent dislike of work and will avoid it if possible....
- Because of the human characteristic of dislike for work, most people must be coerced, controlled, directed, or threatened with punishment to get them to put forth adequate effort toward the achievement of organizational objectives....
- The average human being prefers to be directed, wishes to avoid responsibility, has relatively little ambition, wants security above all.

Assumptions of Theory Y

- The expenditure of physical and mental effort in work is as natural as play or rest. The average human being does not inherently dislike work....
- External control and the threat of punishment are not the only means for bringing about effort toward organizational objectives. A person will exercise self-direction and self-control in the service of objectives to which he or she is committed....
- The average human being learns, under proper conditions, not only to accept but to seek responsibility....
- The capacity to exercise a relatively high degree of imagination, ingenuity, and creativity in the solution of organizational problems is widely, not narrowly, distributed in the population.
- Under the conditions of modern industrial life, the intellectual potentialities of the average human being are only partially utilized.

SOURCE: Douglas McGregor, *The Human Side of Enterprise* (New York: McGraw-Hill, 1960), 33–48.

relations assumptions about human behavior. Based on his experiences as a manager and consultant, his training as a psychologist, and the work of Maslow, McGregor formulated his Theory X and Theory Y, which are explained in Exhibit 2.5.[36] McGregor believed that the classical perspective was based on Theory X assumptions about workers. He also felt that a slightly modified version of Theory X fit early human relations ideas. In other words, human relations ideas did not go far enough. McGregor proposed Theory Y as a more realistic view of workers for guiding management thinking.

The point of Theory Y is that organizations can take advantage of the imagination and intellect of all their employees. Employees will exercise self-control and will contribute to organizational goals when given the opportunity. A few companies today still use Theory X management, but many are trying Theory Y techniques. The Danish company Oticon Holding A/S brings out the creativity and enthusiasm of its employees by operating from Theory Y assumptions.

OTICON HOLDING A/S

www.oticon.com

Lars Kolind, head of the Danish company Oticon Holding A/S, emphasizes that making hearing aids is not the core of what his company is about. "It's about something more fundamental," he says. "It's about the way people perceive work." At Oticon, there are no organization charts, no departments, no functions, no titles, and no permanent desks. Any vestiges of an organizational hierarchy have disappeared. All 150 employees have mobile workstations and are constantly forming and reforming into self-directed teams that work on specific projects. Their desks are wheeled caddies with room for hanging folders, a few binders, and maybe a family photo or two. Everyone has a mobile phone because employees are constantly on the move. Anyone with a compelling idea can become a project leader by competing to attract the people and resources needed to deliver results. Project teams make their own decisions and have almost complete freedom to run the project as they see fit.

Kolind believed the formal organization was getting in the way of allowing employees to use their full potential and find joy in their work. He knew that break-throughs in hearing aid technology required not only science but imagination. Oticon has been so successful at taking advantage of the imagination, creativity, and ability of its employees that it is the fastest-growing hearing aid producer in the world. Within the past five years, Oticon has introduced at least ten major product innovations, including the world's first digital hearing aid. Kolind thinks the organization of the future will liberate employees to grow personally and professionally and to become more creative and action-oriented. At Oticon, the future is now. Says Kolind, "We give people the freedom to do what they want."[37]

The Behavioral Sciences Approach

The **behavioral sciences approach** develops theories about human behavior based on scientific methods and study. Behavioral science draws from sociology, psychology, anthropology, economics, and other disciplines to understand employee behavior and interaction in an organizational setting. The approach can be seen in practically every organization. When General Electric conducts research to determine the best set of tests, interviews, and employee profiles to use when selecting new employees, it is employing behavioral science techniques. Emery Air Freight has utilized reinforcement theory to improve the incentives given to workers and increase the performance of many of its operations. When Westinghouse trains new managers in the techniques of employee motivation, most of the theories and findings are rooted in behavioral science research.

In the behavioral sciences, economics and sociology have significantly influenced the way today's managers approach organizational strategy and structure. Psychology has influenced management approaches to motivation, communication, leadership, and the overall field of human resource management.

All of the remaining chapters of this book contain research findings and applications that can be attributed to the behavioral sciences approach to the study of organizations and management. The Manager's Shoptalk box shows the trend of new management concepts from the behavioral sciences. Note the increase in concepts about 1970 and then again from 1980 until the present. The increasing intensity of global competition has produced great interest in improved behavioral approaches to management. The continued development of new management techniques can be expected in the future.

behavioral sciences approach
A subfield of the humanistic management perspective that applies social science in an organizational context, drawing from economics, psychology, sociology, and other disciplines.

Management Science Perspective

World War II caused many management changes. The massive and complicated problems associated with modern global warfare presented managerial decision makers with the need for more sophisticated tools than ever before. The **management science perspective** emerged to treat those problems. This view is distinguished for its application of mathematics, statistics, and other quantitative techniques to management decision making and problem solving. During World War II, groups of mathematicians, physicists, and other scientists were formed to solve military problems. Because those problems

management science perspective
A management perspective that emerged after World War II and applied mathematics, statistics, and other quantitative techniques to managerial problems.

Ebbs and Flows of Management Innovations, 1950–2000

Over the past 40 years a number of management fashions and fads have appeared. Critics argue that managers adopt quick fixes and that new techniques may not represent permanent solutions. Others feel that managers adopt new techniques because they are working toward continuous improvement in a highly uncertain world.

Most managers are familiar with the innovations listed below. How many can you describe? ∎

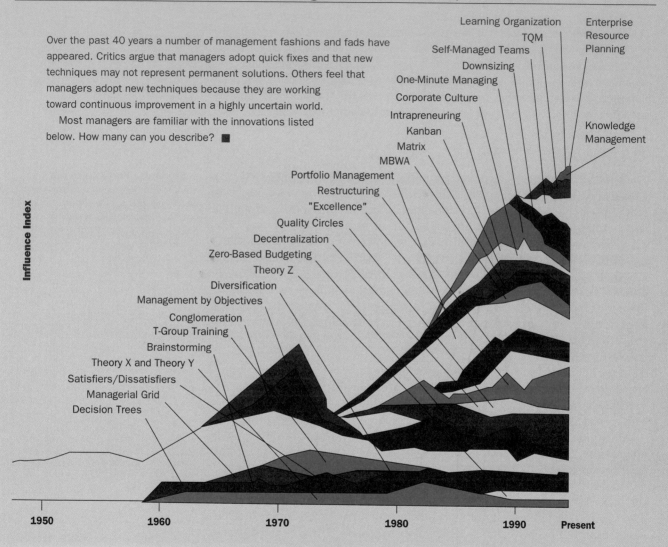

SOURCE: Adapted from Fig. 1.3, Richard Tanner Pascale, *Managing on the Edge* (New York: Touchstone/Simon & Schuster, 1990), 20. Copyright © 1990 by Richard Pascale.

frequently involved moving massive amounts of materials and large numbers of people quickly and efficiently, the techniques had obvious applications to large-scale business firms.[38]

Operations research grew directly out of the World War II groups (called *operational research teams* in Great Britain and *operations research teams* in the

United States).[39] It consists of mathematical model building and other applications of quantitative techniques to managerial problems.

Operations management refers to the field of management that specializes in the physical production of goods or services. Operations management specialists use quantitative techniques to solve manufacturing problems. Some of the commonly used methods are forecasting, inventory modeling, linear and nonlinear programming, queuing theory, scheduling, simulation, and break-even analysis.

Management information systems (MIS) is the most recent subfield of the management science perspective. These systems are designed to provide relevant information to managers in a timely and cost-efficient manner. The advent of the high-speed digital computer opened up the full potential of this area for management.

Many of today's organizations have departments of management science specialists to help solve quantitatively based problems. When Sears used computer models to minimize its inventory costs, it was applying a quantitative approach to management. When AT&T performed network analysis to speed up and control the construction of new facilities and switching systems, it was employing management science tools.

One specific technique used in many organizations is queuing theory. *Queuing theory* uses mathematics to calculate how to provide services that will minimize the waiting time of customers. Queuing theory has been used to analyze the traffic flow through the Lincoln Tunnel and to determine the number of toll booths and traffic officers for a toll road. Queuing theory was used to develop the single waiting line for tellers used in many banks.

Advanced technology gives operations management specialists powerful tools for applying management science techniques. Weirton Steel's Integrated Manufacturing Information System electronically tracks production, while its Logistics and Integrated Scheduling system provides electronic scheduling to all of Weirton's 45 operating units, making it possible to plan production for maximum efficiency, quality, and delivery performance. The new systems provide a competitive edge by giving Weirton managers and employees unprecedented flexibility in adapting to changing customer needs.

Recent Historical Trends

Management is by nature complex and dynamic. Elements of each of the perspectives we have discussed are still in use today. The most prevalent is the humanistic perspective, but even it has been undergoing change in recent years. Three major contemporary extensions of this perspective are systems theory, the contingency view, and total quality management. Examination of each will allow a fuller appreciation of the state of management thinking today.

Systems Theory

A **system** is a set of interrelated parts that function as a whole to achieve a common purpose.[40] A system functions by acquiring inputs from the external environment, transforming them in some way, and discharging outputs back to the environment. Exhibit 2.6 shows the basic **systems theory** of organizations. Here there are five components: inputs, a transformation process, outputs, feedback, and the environment. *Inputs* are the material, human, financial, or information resources used to produce goods or services. The *transformation process* is management's use of production technology to change the inputs into outputs. *Outputs* include the organization's products and services. *Feedback* is knowledge of the results that influence the selection of inputs during the next cycle of the process. The *environment* surrounding the organization includes the social, political, and economic forces noted earlier in this chapter.

system
A set of interrelated parts that function as a whole to achieve a common purpose.

systems theory
An extension of the humanistic perspective that describes organizations as open systems that are characterized by entropy, synergy, and subsystem interdependence.

Organizations can cooperate to achieve synergy, thus accomplishing more together than they could do alone. George Becker, Stephen Yokich, and George Kourpias gathered for a breakfast to symbolize the teaming up of the United Steelworkers of America, the United Auto Workers, and the International Association of Machinists to return clout to the sagging labor movement. The three unions bring varied strengths and skills and give a stronger voice to workers' rights to organize and bargain collectively.

Some ideas in systems theory have had substantial impact on management thinking. These include open and closed systems, entropy, synergy, and subsystem interdependencies.[41]

Open systems must interact with the environment to survive; **closed systems** need not. In the classical and management science perspectives, organizations were frequently thought of as closed systems. In the management science perspective, closed system assumptions—the absence of external disturbances—are sometimes used to simplify problems for quantitative analysis. In reality, however, all organizations are open systems, and the cost of ignoring the environment may be failure.

Entropy is a universal property of systems and refers to their tendency to run down and die. If a system does not receive fresh inputs and energy from its environment, it will eventually cease to exist. Organizations must monitor their environments, adjust to changes, and continuously bring in new inputs in order to survive and prosper. Managers try to design the organization/environment interfaces to reduce entropy.

Synergy means that the whole is greater than the sum of its parts. When an organization is formed, something new comes into the world. Management, coordination, and production that did not exist before are now present. Organizational units working together can accomplish more than those same units working alone. The sales department depends on production and vice versa.

Subsystems are parts of a system that depend on one another. Changes in one part of the organization affect other parts. The organization must be managed as a coordinated whole. Managers who understand subsystem interdependence are reluctant to make changes that do not recognize subsystem impact on the organization as a whole. For example, the adoption of new

Exhibit
2.6

The Systems View of Organizations

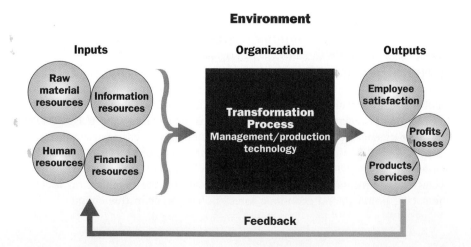

Technology

LEADING THE REVOLUTION: TECHNOLOGY

Buckman Laboratories International

When Bob Buckman took over Buckman Laboratories after the death of his father, he knew he wanted to create a new kind of organization. His father had epitomized the traditional pyramid-style leader, overseeing every decision, sales order, check, or memorandum. Buckman wanted to turn the organization upside down, putting the customer on top and giving front-line workers the information and power to be actively involved in satisfying customer needs. And he knew just where to start: Buckman set a string of transformations in motion by changing how the company manages information. "I realized that if I can give everybody complete access to information about the company, then I don't have to tell them what to do all the time," says Buckman. "The organization starts moving forward of its own initiative."

Today, Buckman Laboratories' knowledge-sharing network, called K'Netix, keeps members of the company's international workforce constantly connected and brings all of the organization's brainpower to bear in serving each customer. Buckman Laboratories, a $270 million company employing 1,200 people in 80 countries, makes more than 1,000 different specialty chemicals in 8 factories around the world. The company competes in a variety of businesses, often with companies three to five times its size. Buckman has an edge because any of its employees can tap into a worldwide knowledge resource—a steady stream of information about products, markets, customers, and opportunities, keeping the company so tuned in to customers that it can anticipate their needs. Companies such as AT&T, 3M, International Paper Company, and USWest have made pilgrimages to this small, Memphis, Tennessee-based company to learn how knowledge can be used as a critical corporate asset.

K'Netix has aided a total cultural transformation at Buckman Labs. The hierarchy has been shattered, teamwork and cooperation are the keys to success, and the customer is king. Buckman admits that getting people to share information in the beginning was difficult because employees had learned to hoard knowledge as a source of power. Now, at Buckman Labs, power comes from being a source of knowledge, sharing whatever you know with others.

www.buckman.com

Source: Glenn Rifkin, "Nothing But 'Net," *Fast Company*, June–July 1996, 118–127.

information technology can have a significant impact on other parts of the organization, as described in the Technology box.

Contingency View

A second contemporary extension to management thinking is the contingency view. The classical perspective assumed a *universalist* view. Management concepts were thought to be universal; that is, whatever worked—leader style, bureaucratic structure—in one organization would work in another. In business education, however, an alternative view exists. This is the *case* view, in which each situation is believed to be unique. There are no universal principles to be found, and one learns about management by experiencing a large number of case problem situations. Managers face the task of determining what methods will work in every new situation.

To integrate these views the **contingency view** has emerged, as illustrated in Exhibit 2.7.[42] Here neither of the other views is seen as entirely correct. Instead, certain contingencies, or variables, exist for helping management identify and understand situations. The contingency view means that a manager's response depends on identifying key contingencies in an organizational situation. For example, a consultant may mistakenly recommend the same management-by-objectives (MBO) system for a manufacturing firm that was successful in a school system. The contingency view tells us that what works

open system
A system that interacts with the external environment.

closed system
A system that does not interact with the external environment.

entropy
The tendency for a system to run down and die.

synergy
The concept that the whole is greater than the sum of its parts.

subsystems
Parts of a system that depend on one another for their functioning.

contingency view
An extension of the humanistic perspective in which the successful resolution of organizational problems is thought to depend on managers' identification of key variables in the situation at hand.

Exhibit **2.7** *The Contingency View of Management*

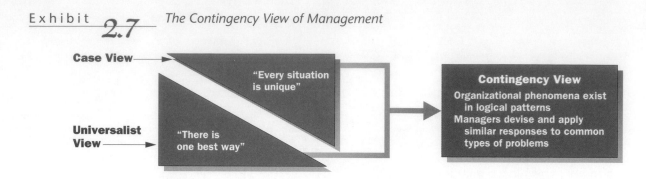

in one setting may not work in another. Management's job is to search for important contingencies. When managers learn to identify important patterns and characteristics of their organizations, they can then fit solutions to those characteristics.

Important contingencies that managers must understand include industry, technology, the environment, and international cultures. Management practice in a rapidly changing industry, for example, will be very different from that in a stable one.

Total Quality Management

The quality movement in Japan emerged partly as a result of American influence after World War II. The ideas of W. Edwards Deming, known as the "father of the quality movement," were initially scoffed at in America, but the Japanese embraced his theories and modified them to help rebuild their industries into world powers.[43] Japanese companies achieved a significant departure from the American model by gradually shifting from an inspection-oriented approach to quality control toward an approach emphasizing employee involvement in the prevention of quality problems.[44]

During the 1980s and into the 1990s, **total quality management (TQM)**, which focuses on managing the total organization to deliver quality to customers, was at the forefront in helping managers deal with global competition. The approach infuses quality values throughout every activity within a company, with front-line workers intimately involved in the process. Four significant elements of quality management are employee involvement, focus on the customer, benchmarking, and continuous improvement.

Employee involvement means that TQM requires companywide participation in quality control. All employees are *focused on the customer;* TQM companies find out what customers want and try to meet their needs and expectations. *Benchmarking* refers to a process whereby companies find out how others do something better than they do and then try to imitate or improve on it. *Continuous improvement* is the implementation of small, incremental improvements in all areas of the organization on an ongoing basis. TQM is not a quick fix, but companies such as Motorola, Procter & Gamble, Xerox, and Du Pont have achieved astonishing results in efficiency, quality, and customer satisfaction through total quality management.[45] TQM, which is still an important part of today's organizations, will be discussed in detail in Chapter 20.

total quality management (TQM)
A concept that focuses on managing the total organization to deliver quality to customers. Four significant elements of TQM are employee involvement, focus on the customer, benchmarking, and continuous improvement.

Summary and Management Solution

This chapter has described the emerging learning organization and examined the historical background leading up to this new approach to management. An understanding of the evolution of management helps present and future managers understand where we are now and continue to progress toward better management.

The three major perspectives on management that have evolved since the late 1800s are the classical perspective, the humanistic perspective, and the management science perspective. Each perspective has several specialized subfields. Recent extensions of management perspectives include systems theory, contingency views, and total quality management. The most recent thinking about organizations has been brought about by the shift to a new management paradigm described in Chapter 1. Many managers are redesigning their companies toward the learning organization, which fully engages all employees in identifying and solving problems. The learning organization is characterized by visionary leadership, a team-based structure, participative strategy, a strong, adaptive culture, empowered employees, and open information. The learning organization represents a substantial departure from the traditional management hierarchy.

Recall from the management problem at the beginning of this chapter that René Villarreal was faced with a sudden shift in the environment of PIPSA, and the company rapidly lost 50 percent of its business. To compete in the new environment, Villarreal took steps toward becoming a learning organization. He created "learning cells" that address particular problems or discuss business issues.

These teams have solved specific problems, such as how to reduce wrinkling on the new bond-paper line, as well as developed ideas for improving service and product quality, increasing market share, and reducing costs. PIPSA's first Chief Learning Officer, Raúl Cicero, believes the best way to create an environment for learning is to link what people learn directly to company performance so employees can see that they are making a difference. In addition, learning extends beyond the factory walls. PIPSA has the most extensive tuition-assistance program in Mexican business, not only covering tuition for its employees but financing private school education for their children as well. PIPSA managers also show respect for different ways of learning and sharing knowledge. For example, rather than using overhead projectors or computer printouts, teams may rely on a *grupo musical,* a group of workers who make a presentation through songs or stories. Villarreal is totally comfortable with these old world traditions, because he knows the importance of getting everyone involved. Villarreal's shift to a new paradigm is paying off. Sales and market share have dramatically increased. The company recently began making paper for telephone directories and is forging alliances with U.S. companies to enter the office-paper market. Villarreal knows that because most of PIPSA's workers have little formal education, it may take his company longer than some others to transform itself into a true learning organization. However, all of PIPSA's workers are learning how to learn, making the company stronger and smarter.[46]

Discussion Questions

1. Why is it important to understand the different perspectives and approaches to management theory that have evolved throughout the history of organizations?
2. How do societal forces influence the practice and theory of management? Do you think management techniques are a response to these forces?
3. A management professor once said that for successful management, studying the present was most important, studying the past was next, and studying the future was least important. Do you agree? Why?
4. Which of the six characteristics of learning organizations do you find most appealing? Which would be hardest for you to adopt?
5. Some experts believe that leadership is more important than ever in a learning organization. Do you agree? Explain.
6. What is the behavioral sciences approach? How does it differ from earlier approaches to management?
7. Explain the basic idea underlying the contingency view and provide an example.
8. Contrast open and closed systems. Can you give an example of each? Can a closed system survive?

9. Why can an event such as the Hawthorne studies be a major turning point in the history of management even if the idea is later shown to be in error? Discuss.

10. Identify the major components of systems theory. Is this perspective primarily internal or external?

11. Do you think management theory will ever be as precise as theories in the fields of physics, chemistry, or experimental psychology? Why or why not?

Management in Practice: Experiential Exercise

Tolerance for Ambiguity Scale

Please read each of the following statements carefully. Then rate each of them in terms of the extent to which you either agree or disagree with the statement using the following scale:

Completely Disagree		Neither Agree nor Disagree				Completely Agree
1	2	3	4	5	6	7

Place the number that best describes your degree of agreement or disagreement in the blank to the left of each statement.

_____ 1. An expert who doesn't come up with a definite answer probably doesn't know too much.

_____ 2. I would like to live in a foreign country for a while.

_____ 3. The sooner we all acquire similar values and ideals the better.

_____ 4. A good teacher is one who makes you wonder about your way of looking at things.

_____ 5. I like parties where I know most of the people more than ones where all or most of the people are complete strangers.

_____ 6. Teachers or supervisors who hand out vague assignments give a chance for one to show initiative and originality.

_____ 7. A person who leads an even, regular life, in which few surprises or unexpected happenings arise, really has a lot to be grateful for.

_____ 8. Many of our most important decisions are based upon insufficient information.

_____ 9. There is really no such thing as a problem that can't be solved.

_____10. People who fit their lives to a schedule probably miss most of the joy of living.

_____11. A good job is one where what is to be done and how it is to be done are always clear.

_____12. It is more fun to tackle a complicated problem than to solve a simple one.

_____13. In the long run, it is possible to get more done by tackling small, simple problems rather than large and complicated ones.

_____14. Often the most interesting and stimulating people are those who don't mind being different and original.

_____15. What we are used to is always preferable to what is unfamiliar.

Scoring:

For odd-numbered questions, add the total points.

For even-numbered questions, use reverse scoring (7 minus the score), and add the total points.

Your score is the total of the even- and odd-numbered questions.

This survey asks 15 questions about personal and work situations with ambiguity. You were asked to rate each situation on a scale of 1 to 7. A perfectly tolerant person would score 15 and a perfectly intolerant person 105. Scores ranging from 20 to 80 have been reported, with a mean of 45. Company managers had an average score of about 45, and nonprofit managers had an average score of about 43, although scores in both groups varied widely.

Typically, people who are highly tolerant of ambiguity (very low score) will be comfortable in organizations characterized by rapid change, unclear authority, empowerment, and movement toward a learning organization. People with low tolerance for ambiguity (high score) are comfortable in more stable, well-defined situations. However, individuals can grow in the opposite direction of their score if they so choose.

SOURCE: Paul C. Nutt, "The Tolerance for Ambiguity and Decision Making," The Ohio State University College of Business Working Paper Series, WP88–291, March 1988. Adapted from Stanley Budner, "Intolerance of Ambiguity as a Personality Variable," *Journal of Personality*, 30:1 (March 1962), table 1, p. 34. Copyright Duke University Press, 1962. Reprinted with permission.

Management in Practice: Ethical Dilemma

The Supervisor

Karen Lowry, manager of a social service agency in a mid-sized city in Illinois, loved to see her employees learn and grow to their full potential. When a rare opening for a supervising clerk occurred, Karen quickly decided to give Charlotte Hines a shot at the job. Charlotte had been with the agency for 17 years and had shown herself to be a true leader. Charlotte worked hard at being a good supervisor, just as she had always worked hard at being a top-notch clerk. She paid attention to the human aspects of employee problems and introduced modern management techniques that strengthened the entire agency.

However, the Civil Service Board decided that a promotional exam should be given to find a permanent placement for the supervising clerk position. For the sake of fairness, the exam was an open competition—anyone, even a new employee, could sign up and take it. The board wanted the candidate with the highest score to get the job but allowed Karen, as manager of the agency, to have the final say-so.

Since she had accepted the provisional opening and proven herself on the job, Charlotte was upset that the entire clerical force was deemed qualified to take the test. When the results came back, she was devastated. Charlotte placed twelfth in the field of candidates, while one of her newly hired clerks placed first. The Civil Service Board, impressed by the new clerk's high

score, is urging Karen to give her the permanent supervisory job. Karen wonders if it's fair to base her decision only on the test results.

What Do You Do?
1. Ignore the test. Charlotte has proven herself and deserves the job.
2. Give the job to the candidate with the highest score. You don't need to make enemies on the Civil Service Board, and, after all, it is an objective way to select a permanent placement.
3. Devise a more comprehensive set of selection criteria— including test results as well as supervisory experience, ability to motivate employees, and knowledge of agency procedures—that can be explained and justified to the board and to employees.

SOURCE: Based on Betty Harrigan, "Career Advice," *Working Woman,* July 1986, 22–24.

Surf the Net

1. **The Learning Organization.** The learning organization guru, Peter Senge, is a senior lecturer at the Massachusetts Institute of Technology (MIT) and director of the Center for Organizational Learning at MIT's Sloan School of Management. Choose one of his articles, such as the one entitled "Learning Organizations," located at
   http://learning.mit.edu/res/kr/index.html
   Be prepared to report in class your findings about the concept of learning organizations.
2. **Culture.** In the April–May 1998 issue of *Fast Company,* Dave Duffield, president and CEO of PeopleSoft, stated: "Our true core competency is our culture... That's what attracts people and keeps them here. It also helps sell customers. Customers want to work with companies that are competent, trustworthy, and fun. Winners like winners." Visit
   www.peoplesoft.com/en/corporate_info/ people_culture/

After reading through the information provided about PeopleSoft's culture, select one of the following options to complete:
OPTION 1: "I think I would fit in with the culture at PeopleSoft and would enjoy working there because of the following characteristics of its culture:"
OPTION 2: "I don't think I would enjoying working at PeopleSoft because of the following characteristics of its culture:"

3. **Quality.** Provide information in response to the following questions: (a) What is the Malcolm Baldrige National Quality Award? (b) What criteria are used to evaluate the companies? (c) What organizations won the award last year? The sites below contain Malcolm Baldrige information.
   www.quality.nist.gov/
   http://www.asqc.org/abtquality/awards/baldrige.html

Case for Critical Analysis
SuperJuice

Luisa de la Cruz sat in her new office thinking about her company's future. After working her way up the corporate ladder for 15 years, she has just been appointed CEO of SuperJuice, a Florida-based company that makes juice and juice drinks that are marketed to high schools and restaurants throughout the Southeast. For nearly two decades, SuperJuice has been the most successful juice drink maker in the region. However, profits haven't risen for four straight years, and several new

competitors continue to steal market share. In fact, one of the new companies was started by two former SuperJuice employees who left the company after top management continually rejected their ideas for new exotic drink mixes or new approaches to marketing. It made Luisa cringe to realize that the hottest selling drink flavors in Florida and several other states had been invented in SuperJuice's own labs but were now being made and sold by a competitor. Competitors were setting up drink carts at outdoor festivals and advertising with jingles and slogans that caught the imaginations of the region's youth. Even Luisa's own 17-year-old son often purchased her competitors' products, saying that "SuperJuice is for kids. This stuff is hot."

SuperJuice management has always prided itself on the company's efficient set of systems, both in the factory and at headquarters. Managers concentrated on making a high-quality product as inexpensively as possible. "SuperJuice is like a well-oiled machine," Luisa told herself with some pride. Most of the company's 200 employees had joined SuperJuice right out of high school or college and liked the way the company operated. They showed up for work on time, performed their jobs efficiently, and rarely complained. The long-standing rules and procedures, combined with an organizational culture that reflected the traditional, family-oriented background of SuperJuice's Cuban-born founder, contributed to a level of politeness and civility in the company that sometimes seemed like a throwback to the 1950s. "SuperJuice is a calm and civilized place to work in the midst of a rapidly changing, chaotic world," Luisa reflected with pleasure.

But her pleasure evaporated as she realized that the company could collapse beneath her if it didn't somehow respond to the changes in the environment. She remembered the scandal that had erupted several years ago when two new employees started "breaking the rules" and pushing for changes in the company. The two worked odd hours, played rock music, and decorated their offices with brightly colored posters, unique photographs, and fanciful "dream catchers" hung from the ceiling. Occasionally, one would tape a note to his door that read, "Gone to the movies to get my creative juices flowing!" Although both workers were highly productive, top management quickly took action to try to bring the two back in line. They worried that this kind of attitude would have a negative impact on the productivity of other employees, who were accustomed to coming to work and putting in their solid eight hours. The previous CEO really blew his stack when the two presented four new drink flavors they had concocted on the sly. He was so angry about the unauthorized use of lab time that he nearly fired both employees on the spot. Luisa remembered finding one of the employees in the lab dejectedly pouring the prototypes down the drain. "You know you can't do anything new in this company," Luisa told her at that time. "It's just not the SuperJuice way." Since that time, SuperJuice has lost a few other young, ambitious employees who have chafed under the tight management control.

Luisa knew she was promoted because she had always followed the rules. But she also realized that continuing to follow the rules could take this company she loved right into bankruptcy. She knows the company has a lot of potential, starting with its loyal, committed workforce. But where should she begin? Can SuperJuice really change itself into a forward-thinking, creative company?

Questions

1. What are some of the social, political, and economic forces affecting SuperJuice and calling for a new approach to management?
2. What do you believe Luisa needs to do first to begin a transformation at SuperJuice?
3. How would you suggest she turn SuperJuice into a learning organization? Think about specific changes she can make to get all employees thinking of new and exciting ways to revitalize the SuperJuice product line and way of doing business.

SOURCE: Based on Suzy Wetlaufer, "What's Stifling the Creativity at CoolBurst?" *Harvard Business Review*, September–October 1997, 36–40.

Endnotes

1. Eric Matson, "You Can Teach This Old Company New Tricks," *Fast Company*, October/November, 1997, 44–46.
2. John Huey, "Managing in the Midst of Chaos," *Fortune*, April 5, 1993, 38–48; Susan Greco, "The Decade-Long Overnight Success," *Inc.*, December 1994, 73–79; Agis Salpukas, "How a Staid Electric Company Becomes a Renegade," *The New York Times*, December 12, 1993, F10; Samuel M. DeMarie and Barbara W. Keats, "Deregulation, Reengineering, and Cultural Transformation at Arizona Public Service Company," *Organizational Dynamics* (winter 1995): 70–76.
3. John A. Byrne, "Management Meccas," *Business Week*, September 18, 1995, 122–132.
4. John Huey, "Managing in the Midst of Chaos," *Fortune*, April 5, 1993, 38–48; and Toby J. Tetenbaum, "Shifting Paradigms: From Newton to Chaos," *Organizational Dynamics* (spring 1998), 21–32.
5. Daniel A. Wren, *The Evolution of Management Thought*, 2d ed. (New York: Wiley, 1979), 6–8. Much of the discussion of these forces comes from Arthur M. Schlesinger, *Political and Social History of the United States, 1829–1925* (New York: Macmillan, 1925); and Homer C. Hockett, *Political and Social History of the United States, 1492–1828* (New York: Macmillan, 1925).
6. Nina Munk, "The New Organization Man," *Fortune*, March 16, 1998, 62–74.
7. Robin Wright and Doyle McManus, *Flashpoints: Promise and Peril in a New World* (New York: Alfred A. Knopf, 1991).
8. Peter Senge, *The Fifth Discipline: The Art and Practice of Learning Organizations* (New York: Doubleday/Currency, 1990).
9. Peter M. Senge, "The Leader's New Work: Building Learning Organizations," *Sloan Management Review* (fall 1990), 7–22.
10. Esther Wachs Book, "Leadership for the Millennium," *Working Woman*, March 1998, 29–34.

11. Jeffrey Pfeffer, "Producing Sustainable Competitive Advantage through the Effective Management of People," *Academy of Management Executive* 9, no. 1 (1995), 55–69.

12. Paul Roberts, "We Are One Company, No Matter Where We Are," *Fast Company,* April–May 1998, 122–128.

13. Marc S. Gerstein and Robert B. Shaw, "Organizational Architectures for the Twenty-First Century," in David A. Nadler, Marc S. Gerstein, Robert B. Shaw, and Associates, eds., *Organizational Architecture: Designs for Changing Organizations* (San Francisco: Jossey-Bass, 1992), 263–274.

14. Jenny C. McCune, "Making Lemonade," *Management Review,* June 1997.

15. M. Mitchell Waldrop, "The Trillion-Dollar Vision of Dee Hock," *Fast Company,* October–November 1996, 75–86; and Alan Webber, "The Best Organization is No Organization," *USA Today,* March 6, 1997, 13A.

16. Eric Abrahamson, "Management Fashion," *Academy of Management Review* 21, no. 1 (January 1996), 254–285. Also see "75 Years of Management Ideas and Practice," a supplement to the *Harvard Business Review,* September–October 1997, for a broad overview of historical trends in management thinking.

17. Daniel A. Wren, "Management History: Issues and Ideas for Teaching and Research," *Journal of Management* 13 (1987), 339–350.

18. The following is based on Wren, *Evolution of Management Thought,* Chapters 4, 5; and Claude S. George, Jr., *The History of Management Thought* (Englewood Cliffs, N.J.: Prentice Hall, 1968), Chapter 4.

19. Charles D. Wrege and Anne Marie Stoka, "Cooke Creates a Classic: The Story behind F. W. Taylor's Principles of Scientific Management," *Academy of Management Review* (October 1978), 736–749; Robert Kanigel, *The One Best Way: Frederick Winslow Taylor and the Enigma of Efficiency* (New York: Viking, 1997); and Alan Farnham, "The Man Who Changed Work Forever," *Fortune* July 21, 1997, 114.

20. Wren, *Evolution of Management Thought,* 171, and George, *History of Management Thought,* 103–104.

21. Max Weber, *General Economic History,* trans. Frank H. Knight (London: Allen & Unwin, 1927); Max Weber, *The Protestant Ethic and the Spirit of Capitalism,* trans. Talcott Parsons (New York: Scribner, 1930); and Max Weber, *The Theory of Social and Economic Organizations,* ed. and trans. A. M. Henderson and Talcott Parsons (New York: Free Press, 1947).

22. "UPS," *The Atlanta Journal and Constitution,* April 26, 1992, H1; Richard L. Daft, *Organization Theory and Design,* 3d ed. (St. Paul, Minn.: West, 1989), 181–182; and Kathy Goode, Betty Hahn, and Cindy Seibert, "United Parcel Service: The Brown Giant" (unpublished manuscript, Texas A&M University, 1981).

23. Henri Fayol, *Industrial and General Administration,* trans. J. A. Coubrough (Geneva: International Management Institute, 1930); Henri Fayol, *General and Industrial Management,* trans. Constance Storrs (London: Pitman and Sons, 1949); and W. J. Arnold and the editors of *Business Week, Milestones in Management* (New York: McGraw-Hill, vol. I, 1965; vol. II, 1966).

24. Mary Parker Follett, *The New State: Group Organization: The Solution of Popular Government* (London: Longmans, Green, 1918); and Mary Parker Follett, *Creative Experience* (London: Longmans, Green, 1924).

25. Henry C. Metcalf and Lyndall Urwick, eds., *Dynamic Administration: The Collected Papers of Mary Parker Follett* (New York: Harper & Row, 1940); Arnold, *Milestones in Management.*

26. Follett, *The New State;* Metcalf and Urwick, *Dynamic Administration* (London: Sir Isaac Pitman, 1941).

27. William B. Wolf, *How to Understand Management: An Introduction to Chester I. Barnard* (Los Angeles: Lucas Brothers, 1968); and David D. Van Fleet, "The Need Hierarchy and Theories of Authority," *Human Relations* 9 (spring 1982), 111–118.

28. Gregory M. Bounds, Gregory H. Dobbins, and Oscar S. Fowler, *Management: A Total Quality Perspective* (Cincinnati: South-Western College Publishing, 1995), 52–53.

29. Curt Tausky, *Work Organizations: Major Theoretical Perspectives* (Itasca, Ill.: F. E. Peacock, 1978), 42.

30. Charles D. Wrege, "Solving Mayo's Mystery: The First Complete Account of the Origin of the Hawthorne Studies—The Forgotten Contributions of Charles E. Snow and Homer Hibarger" (paper presented to the Management History Division of the Academy of Management, August 1976).

31. Ronald G. Greenwood, Alfred A. Bolton, and Regina A. Greenwood, "Hawthorne a Half Century Later: Relay Assembly Participants Remember," *Journal of Management* 9 (fall/winter 1983), 217–231.

32. F. J. Roethlisberger, W. J. Dickson, and H. A. Wright, *Management and the Worker* (Cambridge, Mass.: Harvard University Press, 1939).

33. H. M. Parson, "What Happened at Hawthorne?" *Science* 183 (1974), 922–932; John G. Adair, "The Hawthorne Effect: A Reconsideration of the Methodological Artifact," *Journal of Applied Psychology* 69, No. 2 (1984), 334–345; and Gordon Diaper, "The Hawthorne Effect: A Fresh Examination," *Educational Studies* 16, no. 3 (1990), 261–268.

34. Greenwood, Bolton, and Greenwood, "Hawthorne a Half Century Later," 219–221.

35. Tausky, *Work Organizations: Major Theoretical Perspectives,* 55.

36. Douglas McGregor, *The Human Side of Enterprise* (New York: McGraw-Hill, 1960), 16–18.

37. Polly LaBarre, "This Organization is Disorganization," *Fast Company,* June/July 1996, 110–113.

38. Mansel G. Blackford and K. Austin Kerr, *Business Enterprise in American History* (Boston: Houghton Mifflin, 1986), Chapters 10, 11; and Alex Groner and the editors of *American Heritage* and *Business Week*, *The American Heritage History of American Business and Industry* (New York: American Heritage Publishing, 1972), Chapter 9.

39. Larry M. Austin and James R. Burns, *Management Science* (New York: Macmillan, 1985).

40. Ludwig von Bertalanffy, Carl G. Hempel, Robert E. Bass, and Hans Jonas, "General Systems Theory: A New Approach to Unity of Science," *Human Biology* 23 (December 1951), 302–361; and Kenneth E. Boulding, "General Systems Theory—The Skeleton of Science," *Management Science* 2 (April 1956), 197–208.

41. Fremont E. Kast and James E. Rosenzweig, "General Systems Theory: Applications for Organization and Management," *Academy of Management Journal* (December 1972), 447–465.

42. Fred Luthans, "The Contingency Theory of Management: A Path Out of the Jungle," *Business Horizons* 16 (June 1973), 62–72; and Fremont E. Kast and James E. Rosenzweig, *Contingency Views of Organization and Management* (Chicago: Science Research Associates, 1973).

43. Samuel Greengard, "25 Visionaries Who Shaped Today's Workplace," *Workforce,* January 1997, 50–59.

44. Mauro F. Guillen, "The Age of Eclecticism: Current Organizational Trends and the Evolution of Managerial Models," *Sloan Management Review* (fall 1994), 75–86.

45. Jeremy Main, "How to Steal the Best Ideas Around," *Fortune,* October 19, 1992, 102–106.

46. Matson, "You Can Teach This Old Company New Tricks."

Companies Adopt a New Paradigm of Management

"I would much rather have a company that was bound by love than bound by fear," notes Herb Kelleher, president and CEO of Southwest Airlines. His simple statement speaks volumes about how his company, as well as others you see in this video, has adopted the new paradigm of management that emphasizes change, technology, diversity, and employee empowerment, among other values. As companies strive to remain competitive in the face of tough global competition, uncertain environments, cutbacks in personnel and resources, as well as economic and political shifts around the world, organizational leaders are faced with a management revolution. Their ability to embrace these complex dynamics and skillfully guide and delegate authority to their managers and workers will impact the success of their companies. In this video, you will meet players who are fully engaged in the day-to-day aspects of this revolution, which has led to a new paradigm of management, the learning organization.

At Southwest, the "culture is designed to promote high spirit and avoid complacency," says Libby Sartain, vice president of the People Department. "We have little hierarchy here. Our employees are encouraged to be creative and innovative, to break the rules when they need to in order to provide good service to our customers." Southwest management focuses on customer satisfaction and empowerment of its 20,000 employees, rather than strictly on profits. For skeptics of Southwest's approach, the company is consistently named as one of the Top Ten Best Companies to Work for in America, is the recipient of the Triple Crown Award, and is the world's most profitable airline.

Dineh Mohajer, founder of super hip Hard Candy Cosmetics, agrees with the Southwest approach. "My motto is not to rule with fear, but to rule with empowerment, and to bring people in that are capable and that you can empower, and they can empower you. It's a very mutualistic relationship. That's the only way you can get anywhere." As a manager, Mohajer seems to have wisdom beyond her 26 years. The entrepreneur launched her company when she was a senior at the University of Southern California and sold her homemade sky blue nail polish to the Fred Segal boutique in Santa Monica.

Empowerment, a focus on people, is a recurring value throughout learning organizations. "Good people are very important, obviously, to the success of any company. It's the backbone," says Jeremy Hartley, vice president of operations at La Madeleine French Bakery & Cafes. "We believe in taking care of our guests, obviously. But equally important are the people that work in the company, at any level." David Gatchel, president and CEO of Paradigm Entertainment agrees: "In our business really the value of our company is in the employee base and maintaining good relationships with them."

Collaboration is part of employee empowerment at many of these organizations. Julie Cohn and Linda Finnell, two artists who became entrepreneurs, discovered this as they struggled through the first few years of their company, Two Women Boxing. Both Cohn and Finnell admit that early on they encountered some conflicts with employees. But they found ways to solve these conflicts as their company progressed toward the new paradigm of management. In one instance, they brought in an independent facilitator to help foster communication. They also learned the value of having employees contribute to design ideas. Rather than compete, employees and managers collaborate on designs.

A similar situation presented itself at a much larger, more established organization—Centex Corporation, one of the largest and most geographically diverse home builders in the United States. When top managers discovered that escalating land and construction costs were cutting into the company's profit margin, they turned to employees for help in coming up with innovative ideas. "We conducted a number of focus groups using our own employees to really start to get an idea of how the various trends we saw in society were affecting our own people. It brought people from all over our company together, who then saw they were important to the company—that they were participating in the strategic direction of the company," recalls chairman and CEO Larry Hirsch.

Fossil, like many companies facing the new millennium, is aggressively striving for a global presence, which is also part of the new paradigm of management. Richard Gundy, executive vice president of Fossil, explains, "We were started by a 23 year old who had a vision, who is driven to be successful, who is driven to have a brand that is world dominant." Gundy believes that this global drive meshes well with the young work force at Fossil. "Having young people as management, young people throughout the corporation just gives us a new view on things all the time." Fossil capitalizes on this youth perspective, believing that it keeps the company forward looking all the time. In addition, Fossil leadership, rather than being autocratic as it would be in the old management paradigm, is dispersed and empowering. Tim Hale, vice president of Image notes, "Though there is a structure within the company, I feel like it's a loose structure. It is a tiered structure, but it is a structure that allows for a lot of interaction between very upper management and the very bottom guy that's working in the warehouse. And that openness, I think, is essential to the success of this company."

Finally, there's the issue of diversity, which is very much a part of the learning organization. Charles Brown, vice president and director of Credit at J.C. Penney states, "The J.C. Penney company does place a tremendous value on diversity—understanding diversity, valuing diversity, and certainly embracing it. We see it as having a direct link with our associates, our workforce. We see the demographics. We see what's happening. We see the different consumer mix. We see the consumer becoming more diverse. There are more women in the workplace. There are more minorities in the workplace, more seniors. All those elements are part of our need to understand and value diversity." At Drew Pearson Companies, Ken Shead, partner and president agrees. "We have a multiethnic work force with one common goal. All of our employees are rewarded on an incentive-type basis. What that brings to our corporate culture is a quest to be the best."

As you progress through the text and video series, consider the ways in which each of these companies embraces the new paradigm of management, working toward becoming a learning organization. Note which are more advanced than others and why. Look for organizations where managers can say, as Susan Harmon, vice president of finance at North Texas Public Broadcasting does, "I think you have a sense of mission that is very strong among people who work here. I think it means that they are willing often to work for less money than they could make on the commercial side."

Questions

1. Which of these companies would you like to work for as a manager? Why?

2. Choose one of the companies described here and explain how a manager's conceptual skills, human skills, and technical skills would benefit the company.

3. Choose one of the companies described here and write a memo predicting how you think a manager's role in that company may change in the next ten years.

Continuing Case
Part One: In the Beginning: A Bite Taken from the Apple

On April Fool's Day 1976, Apple Computer was founded by two guys who had been friends in high school, who liked to tinker with electronics, and who had dropped out of college to pursue jobs in the new computer industry in what would later be called the Silicon Valley of California. Apple was no April Fool's joke, although not many people took it seriously at first. Consumers hadn't yet grasped the idea that they could use computers for anything themselves. They saw large mainframes in secluded, air-conditioned rooms at work. But *personal* computers were still unheard of. Even businesses were reluctant to invest in computers for their employees; after all, they had typewriters, and calculators were available for number crunching. But Steve Jobs and Steve Wozniak had a product they thought they could sell: first the Apple I computer, and shortly thereafter the Apple II. They had created the first personal computer in Steve Jobs's garage. The face of business, and daily life, has never been the same.

The Apple computer did sell—in fact, the Apple II sold like crazy, once it gained momentum. Within three years, the Apple II had earned $139 million, representing a 700 percent growth. Consumers were snapping up Apple IIs for writing and calculating as quickly as the company could produce them. With success came further company growth, and the necessity for management. Through the first few years of Apple's existence, Steve Jobs controlled the business side of the company, taking on all of the management functions: planning, organizing, leading, and controlling. He hired a succession of presidents, financial officers, public relations people, and marketing people to handle the company's expanding business. Then there were the product design teams, mid-level managers, and ultimately, more and more investors. Although the atmosphere during the early days was radical—both employees and management liked to foster the counterculture image—as new investors began to take their seats on the board of directors, things changed. These older, more conservative directors insisted that the company be managed in a more traditional fashion. Many of the original employees became disenchanted with the pioneering company they had helped found, and some began to leave. Meanwhile, only five years into the venture, Steve Wozniak was injured in a plane crash and forced to take a leave of absence. Steve Jobs became chairman of Apple at only 26 years old.

As a young manager, Jobs certainly had technical skills. After all, the Apple computer was his brainchild. Although some critics might disagree, he also had conceptual skills: he understood where his organization was and had a vision of where he wanted it to go. But Jobs has never been known for his human skills. Driven toward perfection himself, he expected perfection from his managers and employees. One former employee recalls that Jobs rejected anyone's work the first time he saw it, just on principle. (Employees eventually caught on to this, and deliberately showed him their undeveloped work first, saving their best work for later.) He earned himself a notorious reputation as a manager, one that has followed him to this day.

In 1981, a competitor of goliath proportions emerged: IBM—the powerhouse of mainframe computing—introduced its first personal computer to the marketplace. Jobs, who was essentially an engineer, recognized that he did not have the business or man-

agement skills necessary to take his company to the next level. So, he began to pursue John Sculley, who was then president of Pepsi-Cola. He lured Sculley to Apple with the language of a visionary: "If you stay at Pepsi, five years from now all you'll have accomplished is selling a lot more sugar water to kids . . . If you come to Apple you can change the world." Sculley accepted the challenge.

As the company went public and began to compete with larger organizations like IBM, the people who had originally gone to work for Apple found themselves in a changing environment. Despite Jobs's iron grip, they viewed themselves as a young, hip, innovative group who did things their own way. Even though both Apple founders had dropped out of college, Apple workers were highly educated, creative, and technically skilled. They valued their independence, and most likely chafed under the new "business" orientation. On a larger scale, Apple was charged with changing the way the general public viewed—and ultimately valued—computers. As they introduced new products, it was crucial for consumers to make the connection between the computer and the way it could change their daily work and home environments. Apple was lauded for its product innovations and creativity, and its users became devoted followers.

The economic environment, both inside and outside Apple, was ripe for success. The economic boom of the 1980s meant that people had money to spend. But it also meant that competition, from IBM and other fledgling computer companies, followed closely on Apple's heels. By the early 1980s, Apple management, including new CEO John Sculley (who was a sharp businessman, but who didn't know much about computers), made some costly mistakes. For instance, the Lisa, which was the first mouse-controlled personal computer, was priced at $10,000, far above what the public would accept. No one bought it. And the Apple III was so filled with design flaws that the first 14,000 computers had to be recalled. That computer's image never recovered. Still, many more ups and downs lay ahead for the company as Apple continued to grow and change as an organization.

Questions

1. In what ways did Apple fit the old paradigm of management? In what ways did it fit the new paradigm?
2. From the overview presented in this case, what features of Apple's culture are similar to learning organizations? To bureaucratic organizations? What steps might Apple managers take toward creating—or strengthening—a learning organization?
3. Of the four management functions, which do you think Jobs excelled at? Which was his weakest? Why?
4. What types of roles does a person in Jobs's position at Apple need to perform? List as many informational, interpersonal, and decisional roles that you think apply and explain why you think so.
5. Do you think that you would have liked to be a manager at Apple during its early days? Why or why not?

Sources: Apple Computer Inc. Web site, "Business Summary," "History," and "Steve Paul Jobs" accessed March 23, 1999, at www.apple.com; Brent Schlender and Michael Martin, "Paradise Lost," *Fortune*, February 19, 1996, accessed at www.pathfinder.com. iMac photo: Courtesy of Apple Computer, Inc.

Part Two

The Environment of Management

More than any other factor, the environment profoundly affects the performance of crews and boats during the Whitbread race. The nine boats that completed the race suffered extremes in the external environment—from blistering heat through the tropics, freezing rain and mammoth waves in the "roaring 40s" and "screaming 50s" of the southern hemisphere, close calls with hidden reefs, and icebergs in the North Atlantic. Several boats hit whales at sea, damaging their hulls and keels, and several more were dismasted from the buffeting winds. Through it all, the crews pulled together to overcome obstacles. Forming such a strong group—a culture of cooperation and sharing—from members gathered around the world can be difficult in the best circumstances, but the environment threw its worst at the crew. Add to that food shortages, lack of fresh water, and equipment failures and you can nearly break a crew's will. All was not rosy among some crews; a few members resigned from their boats after differences couldn't be resolved. When boats had setbacks, crew members took individual initiative to fix them: repairing and replacing sails and even diving into frigid waters to examine damage to a hull. Remarkably, only one boat had to withdraw from the race—the tenth boat after leg one due to lack of funding.

In Part Two you'll study the environment of management, the trend toward globalization, the importance of managerial ethics and social responsibility, and entrepreneurship and small business management.

Chapter 3

LEARNING OBJECTIVES

After studying this chapter, you should be able to

◉ Describe the general and task environments and the dimensions of each.

◉ Explain how organizations adapt to an uncertain environment and identify techniques managers use to influence and control the external environment.

◉ Define corporate culture and give organizational examples.

◉ Explain organizational symbols, stories, heroes, slogans, and ceremonies and their relationship to corporate culture.

◉ Describe how corporate culture relates to the environment.

◉ Define a symbolic leader and explain the tools a symbolic leader uses to change corporate culture.

The Environment and Corporate Culture

MANAGEMENT PROBLEM

"Quicken is over!" declared an analyst with William Blair in Chicago. He was discussing the program that remains the undisputed king of personal finance software. On the surface, things look good for Intuit, the company that built its reputation on Quicken. By focusing on consumer needs, Intuit effectively squashed its competition, and Quicken now has about ten million avid users. However, Intuit is learning rapidly that owning a market niche doesn't count for much when new technology comes along and makes your product obsolete. The explosive growth of the Internet is beginning to make Quicken look like a relic of simpler times. Today, customers don't want stand-alone shrink-wrapped software at $50 a pop. Instead, they want to piece together their own customized programs off the Internet. Personal finance tools will be developed by specialists in fields such as banking or real estate and distributed piecemeal via the Internet; customers can pick and choose according to their needs. Further, the new tools will have active links to market updates, bank account information, and other data, so that people won't have to spend hours entering figures. The new technology, combined with market saturation, likely means the analyst is right when he continues his forecast for Quicken: "It's done. It's almost a nonfactor."[1]

How might managers at Intuit anticipate future problems brought about by rapidly changing information technology? If you were a manager at Intuit, how would you control and solve these problems from the environment?

The environment for software companies such as Intuit, as well as other companies operating in the information and communications industry, has changed dramatically since the early 1990s. Rapid advances in technology, increased competition, and growing customer demands mean companies constantly must adapt to the changing environment to remain competitive. The Internet has revolutionized communications and the transmission of data. Now, telecommunications firms around the world are waging war on a new level. But it isn't only high-tech firms that face environmental upheavals. Coke and Pepsi continue to do battle in the cola wars, with PepsiCo recently hauling Coca-Cola's Indian subsidiary into court, accusing Coke of illegal and unethical business practices in India.[2] The environment surprises many companies. In the 1980s, large companies such as Sears, IBM, and General Motors were seriously damaged by competition they didn't anticipate. August Busch III, CEO of Anheuser-Busch, admits that his company was late in recognizing the threat of microbreweries: "If you had asked us ten years ago whether there would be X-hundred little tiny breweries across this country who will end up with 3 percent of the market and 6 percent of the margin pool, we would have said no. . . . We were five years late in recognizing that they were going to take as much market as they did and five years late in recognizing we should have joined them."[3] Anheuser-Busch hasn't been seriously hurt by its tardiness, but consider the case of record store chains such as Camelot Music, Record Giant, Wherehouse Entertainment, and Strawberries, each of which filed for bankruptcy protection within the last few years. The whole nature of the record-selling business changed almost overnight when home electronics behemoth Best Buy started selling CDs for nearly half what they cost in traditional music stores. Today, electronics stores such as Best Buy and Circuit City sell more CDs than Sam Goody's and other record retail chains.[4]

Government actions and red tape also can affect an organization's environment and foment a crisis. Deregulation of the electric utility industry will force a massive restructuring of power companies throughout the United States. Changes in Medicaid are hurting hospitals such as La Rabida, on Chicago's South Side, which is dedicated to serving the poor.[5]

The study of management traditionally has focused on factors within the organization—a closed systems view—such as leading, motivating, and controlling employees. The classical, behavioral, and management science schools described in Chapter 2 focused on internal aspects of organizations over which managers have direct control. These views are accurate but incomplete. Globalization and the trend toward a borderless world affect companies in new ways. Even for those companies that try to operate solely on the domestic stage, events that have greatest impact typically originate in the external environment. To be effective, managers must monitor and respond to the environment—an open systems view.

This chapter explores in detail components of the external environment and how they affect the organization. We will also examine a major part of the organization's internal environment—corporate culture. Corporate culture is shaped by the external environment and is an important part of the context within which managers do their jobs.

The External Environment

The world as we know it is undergoing tremendous and far-reaching change. This change can be understood by defining and examining components of the external environment.

The external **organizational environment** includes all elements existing outside the boundary of the organization that have the potential to affect the organization.[6] The environment includes competitors, resources, technology, and economic conditions that influence the organization. It does not include those events so far removed from the organization that their impact is not perceived.

The organization's external environment can be further conceptualized as having two layers: general and task environments as illustrated in Exhibit 3.1.[7]

The **general environment** is the outer layer that is widely dispersed and affects organizations indirectly. It includes social, demographic, and economic factors that influence all organizations about equally. Increases in the inflation rate or the percentage of dual-career couples in the workforce are part of the organization's general environment. These events do not directly change day-to-day operations, but they do affect all organizations eventually. The **task environment** is closer to the organization and includes the sectors that conduct day-to-day transactions with the organization and directly influence its basic operations and performance. It is generally considered to include competitors, suppliers, and customers.

The organization also has an **internal environment**, which includes the elements within the organization's boundaries. The internal environment is composed of current employees, management, and especially corporate culture, which defines employee behavior in the internal environment and how well the organization will adapt to the external environment.

organizational environment
All elements existing outside the organization's boundaries that have the potential to affect the organization.

general environment
The layer of the external environment that affects the organization indirectly.

task environment
The layer of the external environment that directly influences the organization's operations and performance.

internal environment
The environment within the organization's boundaries.

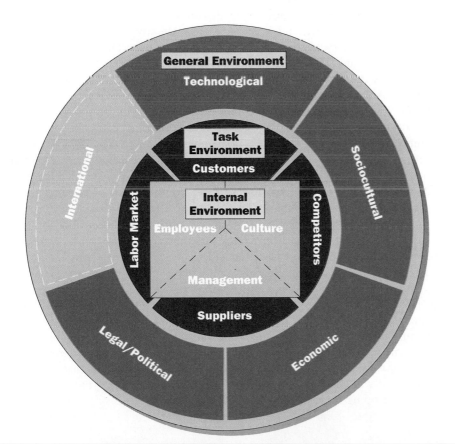

Exhibit **3.1**

Location of the Organization's General, Task, and Internal Environments

Exhibit 3.1 illustrates the relationship among the general, task, and internal environments. As an open system, the organization draws resources from the external environment and releases goods and services back to it. We will now discuss the two layers of the external environment in more detail. Then we will discuss corporate culture, the key element in the internal environment. Other aspects of the internal environment, such as structure and technology, will be covered in Parts IV and V of this book.

General Environment

The general environment represents the outer layer of the environment. These dimensions influence the organization over time but often are not involved in day-to-day transactions with it. The dimensions of the general environment include international, technological, sociocultural, economic, and legal-political.

international dimension
Portion of the external environment that represents events originating in foreign countries as well as opportunities for American companies in other countries.

International.   The **international dimension** of the external environment represents events originating in foreign countries as well as opportunities for American companies in other countries. Note in Exhibit 3.1 that the international dimension represents a context that influences all other aspects of the external environment. The international environment provides new competitors, customers, and suppliers and shapes social, technological, and economic trends, as well.

One study identified 136 U.S. industries—including automobiles, accounting services, entertainment, consumer electronics, and publishing—that will have to compete on a global basis or disappear. The high-quality, low-priced automobiles from Japan and Korea have permanently changed the American automobile industry. Many companies have parts supplied from countries such as Mexico because of low-priced labor. A drop in the dollar's foreign exchange rate lowers the price of U.S. products overseas, increasing export competitiveness. A significant impact of globalization for U.S. business is that it has created an environment of disinflation. For example, companies find it more difficult to raise prices than at virtually any time since World War II. Many companies have had to cut prices to remain competitive in the new global economy. Economic problems in other parts of the world now have a tremendous impact on U.S. companies. Companies such as Coca-Cola, which get a large percentage of sales from Asia, are feeling the pinch of the Asian economic crisis. Russia's economic woes also are affecting U.S. companies. For example, a small distributor of vitamins and sports supplements near Nashville, Tennessee, gets 20 percent of its sales from Russia. The economic turmoil in that country, however, has left U.S.A. Laboratories struggling to get paid and make up for lost orders.[8]

Today, every company must think internationally. Managers who are used to thinking only about the domestic environment must learn new rules to cope with goods, services, and ideas circulating around the globe. For example, products and services exist in a one-world market. A better machine built in Oklahoma City will find buyers from Europe and Asia. Moreover, competitors in a global village come from all over. A company that does not export still will run into competitors in its own marketplace, including some from developing nations.

Chapter 4 describes how today's businesses are operating in an increasingly borderless world and examines in detail how managing in a global environment differs from the management of domestic operations. Perhaps the hardest lesson for managers in the United States to learn is that they do not know best. U.S. decision makers know little about issues and competition in foreign countries. U.S. arrogance is a shortcut to failure. To counter this, Pall Corporation keeps a team of Ph.D.s traveling around the world gathering current information on markets and issues.[9]

The global environment represents an ever changing and uneven playing field compared with the domestic environment. Changes in the international domain can abruptly turn the domestic environment upside down. Consider, for example, the "peace dividend" brought on by the end of the cold war, and the fall of communism. Despite the need for periodic military action in areas such as the Persian Gulf or Bosnia, the peace dividend has increased demand for military cuts, pushing smaller defense contractors out of business and forcing large companies such as McDonnell Douglas, General Dynamics, and Lockheed Martin to convert a significant portion of their operations into nonmilitary production.[10] Top industry scientists and engineers are switching to civilian developments such as high-definition television and new areas of transportation such as electric cars.[11]

Rose Marie Bravo, in her first year as CEO of Burberry, a multinational fashion manufacturer founded in Britain in 1856, is making bold moves to reposition the company within the social, demographic, and economic sectors that influence its general environment. Bravo closed two raincoat factories in Britain, limited distribution of a lower-priced clothing line, and ended all sales to Asia. However, she has made a multimillion dollar investment to update computer and manufacturing systems and hired Roberto Menichetti, right, as creative director to design modern clothes in high performance fabrics. Fashion editors have labeled Menichetti's first Burberry collection a success, but analysts warn that a financial turnaround for the company could take five years, depending on the world economy and the international dimension of the general environment.

Technological. The **technological dimension** includes scientific and technological advancements in a specific industry as well as in society at large. In recent years, the most striking advances have been in the computer industry. A greeting card that plays "Happy Birthday" holds more computing power than existed in the entire world before 1950. Today's home video cameras wield more processing power than the old IBM 360, the wonder machine that launched the age of mainframe computers. Millions of households own personal computers (PCs) and have access to the Internet. Businesses, meanwhile, are demanding ever more sophisticated network technology to support the new global work environment. In addition, computers are being used to aid scientists in understanding the secrets of matter at the level of atoms and to create amazing new materials. For example, "smart gells" that mold to human needs on cue are already on the market, in the soles of golf shoes. When heated by the foot, the shoes conform to the wearer's feet to achieve a perfect fit. High-tech composites, embedded with sensors that enable them to think for themselves, are being used to earthquake-proof bridges and highways as well as build better airplanes and railcars. The emerging "life sciences" industry, which brings together agriculture, biotechnology, and pharmaceuticals, may soon produce grains that taste like meat and cotton that can produce its own color.[12] These and other technological advances can change the rules of the game; thus, every organization must be ready to respond.

technological dimension
The dimension of the general environment that includes scientific and technological advancements in the industry and society at large.

MSNBC, the cable and online television news network, was begun by Microsoft Corp. and General Electric Co.'s NBC unit in recognition of the technological dimension of the companys' general environment. MSNBC positions NBC for a high-tech future where TV and the Internet are combined. With high-tech appeal beamed out of a converted warehouse in hues of metallic orange-tinted blue, and NBC personalities such as Tom Brokaw, Katie Couric, and Jane Pauley, MSNBC draws the affluent 25–54 age group, viewers that advertisers covet. In recent months its primetime household viewership has increased by 144 percent.

sociocultural dimension
The dimension of the general environment representing the demographic characteristics, norms, customs, and values of the population within which the organization operates.

Sociocultural.   The **sociocultural dimension** of the general environment represents the demographic characteristics as well as the norms, customs, and values of the general population. Important sociocultural characteristics are geographical distribution and population density, age, and education levels. Today's demographic profiles are the foundation of tomorrow's workforce and consumers. Forecasters see increased globalization of both consumer markets and the labor supply, with increasing diversity both within organizations and consumer markets.[13] Consider the following key demographic trends in the United States:

1. Minorities, largely African Americans and Hispanics, will make up the majority of the U.S. population by the year 2050.

2. The population and the workforce continue to age with the baby boomers, and some analysts predict a coming shortage of skilled workers.

3. The U.S. will continue to receive a flood of immigrants, largely from Asia and Mexico. Approximately 15 percent of births in recent years were to foreign-born mothers.[14]

Demography also shapes society's norms and values. Recent sociocultural trends that are affecting many companies include the trend toward no smoking, the anticholesterol and reduced fat fervor, the greater purchasing power of young children, and the increased diversity of consumers, with specialized markets for groups such as Hispanics and women over age 30. For example, the *Miami Herald* responded to changes in the sociocultural environment by launching a Spanish-language newspaper, *El Nuevo Herald*, with articles emphasizing Hispanic, Cuban, and Latin American news and sports.[15] This chapter's Technology box illustrates how companies are using new technology to respond to changes in the sociocultural dimension.

economic dimension
The dimension of the general environment representing the overall economic health of the country or region in which the organization functions.

Economic.   The **economic dimension** represents the general economic health of the country or region in which the organization operates. Consumer purchasing power, the unemployment rate, and interest rates are part of an organization's economic environment. Because organizations today are operating in a global environment, the economic dimension has become

LEADING THE REVOLUTION: TECHNOLOGY

Shopping On-Line

Anyone who's ever bought a new car remembers what an ordeal it can be—fending off overly aggressive salespeople, haggling over price, sometimes driving away with the uncomfortable feeling that you've been had. The strain of car shopping, combined with a decrease in leisure time and a demand for convenience, have more and more people turning to the World Wide Web to shop for their dream car. Market researcher J. D. Power & Associates indicates that 16 percent of new-car buyers used the World Wide Web for shopping in 1997, and the number is expected to grow to 50 percent within a few years. Customers can compare prices, check the value of their trade-in, and ask for bids from on-line car-buying services such as Auto-By-Tel, Microsoft CarPoint, and AutoVantage. Daimler Chrysler and General Motors also are experimenting with Web sites to link on-line shoppers with dealers in a handful of regions.

Walter A. Forbes, founder of Comp-U-Card, takes all this as a sign that his 25-year-old dream soon will be a reality. Since the early 1970s, Forbes has envisioned a day when shoppers will buy everything from Cuisinarts to Geo Prizms via their home computers. Forbes recognized that with decreased leisure time, people wanted faster, easier ways to make smart purchasing decisions. So he built CUC International Inc., an operation of two dozen mail-order shopping, travel, auto, entertainment, and financial service clubs with some 68 million members. Now he's taking the next step to make his shopping-club powerhouse an Internet phenomenon. He recently opened netMarket, an electronic superstore offering 250,000 brand-name products, from perfume to furniture. Although on-line shopping malls have a troubled history, Forbes is betting that the convenience, comfort, and savings soon will change that. He predicts that within a few years Internet shopping habits will mimic those in the physical environment, where 80 percent of sales are concentrated in a handful of merchants. Whether Forbes's dream comes true remains to be seen, but it seems clear that Internet shopping will continue to grow.

www.netmarket.com
www.auto-by-tel.com

SOURCES: Larry Armstrong with Kathleen Kerwin, "Downloading Their Dream Cars," *Business Week*, March 9, 1998, 93–94; and Susan Jackson, "Point, Click—and Spend," *Business Week*, September 15, 1997, 74–76.

---

exceedingly complex and creates even more uncertainty for managers. The economies of countries are more closely tied together than ever before. Economic problems in Asia and Russia, for example, have had a significant impact on U.S. companies as well as the stock market.

One significant recent trend in the economic environment is the frequency of mergers and acquisitions. The corporate economic landscape is being altered. In the media industry, Disney and ABC Television negotiated the biggest entertainment merger in history, and Westinghouse acquired CBS Television. In the toy industry, which once was made up of numerous small-to medium-sized companies, the three largest toy makers—Hasbro, Mattel, and Tyco—have gobbled up at least a dozen smaller competitors within the past few years. The impact of these deals on employees can be overwhelming, creating uncertainty about future job security. The merger is just the beginning of employee uncertainty, because about half of the acquired companies are resold.[16]

Legal-Political. The **legal-political dimension** includes government regulations at the local, state, and federal levels as well as political activities designed to influence company behavior. The U.S. political system encourages capitalism, and the government tries not to overregulate business. However, government laws do specify rules of the game. The federal government influences organizations through the Occupational Safety and Health Administration (OSHA), Environmental Protection Agency (EPA), fair trade practices,

legal-political dimension
The dimension of the general environment that includes federal, state, and local government regulations and political activities designed to control company behavior.

libel statutes allowing lawsuits against business, consumer protection legislation, product safety requirements, import and export restrictions, and information and labeling requirements. Although designed to solve problems, government actions often create problems for organizations. For example, with food imports on the rise—and expanding free-trade pacts paving the way for even more—U.S. food processors are facing growing competition. Imported beef from Canada, Mexico, and Argentina has hurt U.S. cattle farmers, and the National Farmers Union is opposing expanded trade agreements.[17]

pressure group
An interest group that works within the legal-political framework to influence companies to behave in socially responsible ways.

Managers must recognize a variety of **pressure groups** that work within the legal-political framework to influence companies to behave in socially responsible ways. Automobile manufacturers, toy makers, and airlines have been targeted by Ralph Nader's Center for Responsive Law. Tobacco companies today are certainly feeling the far-reaching power of antismoking groups. Middle-aged activists who once protested the Vietnam War have gone to battle to keep Wal-Mart from "destroying the quality of small-town life." Some groups have also attacked the giant retailer on environmental issues, which likely will be one of the strongest pressure points in the coming years. Environmental groups put pressure on the lumber industry in the Northwest in the early 1990s because of the industry's threat to the spotted owl, and Greenpeace has managed to make significant changes in the whaling, tuna fishing, and seal fur industries.[18]

Task Environment

As described earlier, the task environment includes those sectors that have a direct working relationship with the organization, among them customers, competitors, suppliers, and the labor market.

customers
People and organizations in the environment who acquire goods or services from the organization.

Customers.   Those people and organizations in the environment who acquire goods or services from the organization are **customers.** As recipients of the organization's output, customers are important because they determine the organization's success. Patients are the customers of hospitals, students the customers of schools, and travelers the customers of airlines. Companies such as AT&T, General Foods, and Beecham Products all have designed special programs and advertising campaigns to court their older customers, who are, with the aging of baby boomers, becoming a larger percentage of their market.[19] To survive in competition with mass merchandisers such as Wal-Mart, small retailers have been forced to come up with new ways to win and keep customers. Baum's, in Morris, Illinois, was started in 1874 as a dry-goods store selling everything from fabrics to grain. Jim Baum, grandson of the founder, has survived by focusing his customer base—he now sells only large-size women's apparel—and investing heavily in advertising and customer service efforts. One of Baum's most-appreciated touches is the comfortable bathrobe in the changing room; shoppers don't have to keep putting their street clothes on to venture onto the shopping floor to select another garment.[20]

competitors
Other organizations in the same industry or type of business that provide goods or services to the same set of customers.

Competitors.   Other organizations in the same industry or type of business that provide goods or services to the same set of customers are referred to as **competitors.** Each industry is characterized by specific competitive issues. The recording industry differs from the steel industry and the pharmaceutical industry. Competition in the steel industry, especially from international producers, caused some companies to go bankrupt. Companies in

Shoptalk

MANAGER'S SHOPTALK

The New Golden Rule: Cooperate!

Worldwide, research and development managers are under pressure as their budgets shrink and technological complexity grows by leaps and bounds. In this new environment, the hottest trend is collaboration—and it's sweeping every field, from autos to aircraft to biotechnology. GM, Ford, and Chrysler are "carpooling" to avoid duplicating R&D efforts. The Big Three have formed 12 consortiums on such projects as electric car batteries and better crash dummies. In biotechnology, an AIDS therapy from a small Quebec company, BioChem Pharma, is being shepherded through clinical trials by Britain's Glaxo Holdings and will be marketed by Burroughs Welcome. The goal of the threesome's deal is to reduce costs, spread risk, and promote cross-fertilization of ideas. Even Hewlett-Packard and Japan's Canon, which compete fiercely in low-priced ink-jet printers, have teamed up on higher-priced laser printers. With technology getting ever more complex, companies realize that no one can do it all alone.

Suppliers also are a part of this new collaborative business world. At Honeywell's factory in Golden Valley, Minnesota, where thermostats and other building controls are made, supplier sales reps have cubicles right next to the factory floor. Some in-plant suppliers do their own research on products

and sales forecasts, are allowed to write sales orders for the company, and look for ways to trim costs. Honeywell's payoff has been inventory levels measured in days rather than weeks or months and 25 percent fewer purchasing agents. Motorola has come to value its suppliers' ingenuity so much that it established a 15-member council of suppliers to rate Motorola's own practices and offer suggestions for improvement. That reduces costs, according to Motorola's procurement chief, Tom Slaninka, "because every time we make an error it takes people at both ends to correct it." While manufacturers win with lower costs, suppliers gain in higher volume, and transaction costs go down for everyone. In the quest for speed and efficiency, collaboration is a trend that's likely to go even further in the coming years.

SOURCES. Peter Coy with Neil Gross, Silvia Sansoni, and Kevin Kelly, "What's the Word in the Lab? Collaborate," *Business Week,* June 27, 1994, 78–80; Fred R. Bleakley, "Some Companies Let Suppliers Work on Site and Even Place Orders," *The Wall Street Journal,* January 13, 1995, A1; Neal Templin and Jeff Cole, "Manufacturers Use Suppliers to Help Them Develop New Products," *The Wall Street Journal,* December 19, 1994, A1; and Myron Magnet, "The New Golden Rule of Business," *Fortune,* February 21, 1994, 60–64.

the pharmaceutical industry are highly profitable because it is difficult for new firms to enter it. Despite the competitive wars being waged worldwide, competitors in some industries are finding that they can cooperate to achieve common goals. For example, Siemens AG of Germany, Toshiba Corporation of Japan, and the U.S. corporation IBM joined together in a project called Triad to develop a revolutionary new memory chip. The Manager's Shoptalk box reveals the extent to which some of today's most competitive companies are cooperating to achieve common goals.

Suppliers.   The raw materials the organization uses to produce its output are provided by **suppliers.** A steel mill requires iron ore, machines, and financial resources. A small, private university may utilize hundreds of suppliers for paper, pencils, cafeteria food, computers, trucks, fuel, electricity, and textbooks. Large companies such as General Motors, Westinghouse, and Exxon depend on as many as 5,000 suppliers. However, many companies are now using fewer suppliers and trying to build good relationships with them so that they will receive high-quality parts at low prices. The relationship between manufacturers and suppliers has traditionally been an adversarial one, but many companies are finding that cooperation is the key to saving money, maintaining quality, and speeding products to market. Cooperation with suppliers is becoming the rule rather than the exception, as discussed in the Manager's Shoptalk box.

suppliers
People and organizations who provide the raw materials the organization uses to produce its output.

labor market
The people available for hire by the organization.

Labor Market.   The **labor market** represents people in the environment who can be hired to work for the organization. Every organization needs a supply of trained, qualified personnel. Unions, employee associations, and the availability of certain classes of employees can influence the organization's labor market. Two labor market factors having an impact on organizations right now are (1) the necessity for continuous investment in human resources through recruitment, education, and training to meet the competitive demands of the borderless world and (2) the effects of international trading blocs, automation, and shifting plant location upon labor dislocations, creating unused labor pools in some areas and labor shortages in others.[21]

Northern Telecom, a Canadian company with multiple U.S. offices, is an example of a complex environment.

NORTHERN TELECOM LTD.

www.nortel.com

The external environment for Northern Telecom Ltd. (Nortel Networks) is illustrated in Exhibit 3.2. The Canadian-based company began in 1895 as a manufacturer of telephones and has reinvented itself many times to keep up with changes in the environment. At various times, Northern Telecom even ventured into consumer products such as refrigerators, televisions, and radios. Now, the company is undergoing another reinvention, changing its brand name to Nortel Networks to reinforce its goal of providing unified network solutions to customers worldwide.

Accustomed to flying high in the high-tech world of global communications, Nortel suddenly tumbled a few years ago. At the end of 1993, the company posted a loss of $848 million, down from earnings of $548 million a year earlier. When Jean Monty stepped in as CEO, things were a real mess, but Monty turned it around by paying attention to the external environment. When he left the company in 1997, Nortel showed record earnings of $812 million. Most of the problems from the environment come from customers, competitors, and changes in technology. One early step Monty took was to repair the rifts that developed between Nortel and some of its largest customers after failures in the company's switching software. Nortel beat its deadline on rewriting and simplifying the code. Monty also instituted a system of surveying customers worldwide once each quarter to find out how they feel about the company, its products, and its competitors.

He sold off unproductive assets and increased the R&D budget to get some new products on the market. By scanning the external environment, Monty saw that the real demand was not for traditional equipment, but for cellular service, which is growing worldwide at 70 percent a year. Today, Nortel Networks is a major force in wireless communications, both in North America and around the world. The R&D department also has been at work on other new products, such as a voice recognition system that will enable people to place calls without ever pressing any buttons.

The big news, though, is the next step in the company's evolution—one initiated by Monty and being continued by his successor, John Roth. Roth wants to transform the Internet into something as ubiquitous, reliable, and easy-to-use as the telephone network. The shift to data-friendly network technology is taking hold around the world, and Nortel Networks intends to be a key player. Early efforts include a system that allows Web users to make a voice connection directly from a Web site. Becoming involved in the Internet brings tremendous new opportunities; however, it also brings with it a larger group of competitors, including Cisco Systems, Inc., the leading Internet equipment maker, which is years ahead of Nortel in this particular game. Nortel is making a series of acquisitions to shore up areas in which it is weak. For example, recently it bought Aptis Communications,

Inc., a maker of extremely high-speed routers (the Internet's version of a switch). The company also is targeting new Web-based products to small, start-up companies that could prove to be major markets in the future.

Internationally, Nortel Networks has made impressive inroads in Taiwan, China, Mexico, Columbia, and Japan. To expand its international presence, Nortel has partnered with companies such as Alcatel and Lagardere Group of France for a joint cellular venture there, and U.S.-based BellSouth to build a cellular network in Israel. Today, Northern Telecom Ltd. competes in more than 100 countries and does more than 40 percent of its business outside of North America.[22]

Exhibit 3.2   *The External Environment of Northern Telecom (Nortel Networks)*

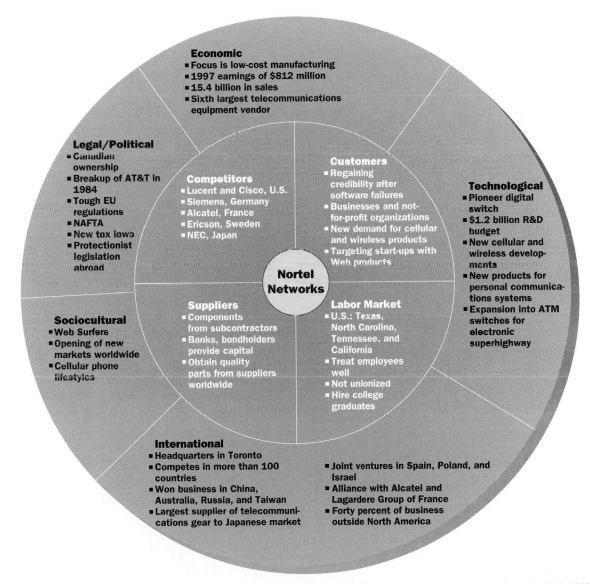

Source: William C. Symonds, J. B. Levine, N. Gross, and P. Coy, "High-Tech Star: Northern Telecom Is Challenging Even AT&T," *Business Week,* July 27, 1992, 54–58; Ian Austen, "Hooked on the Net," *Canadian Business,* June 26–July 10, 1998, 95–103; John Lorinc, "The Death of the Dream?" *Canadian Business,* October 1993, 36–50; Daniel Stoffman, "Mr. Clean," *Canadian Business,* June 1996, 59–65; and Jay Palmer, "A Comeback Coming?" *Barron's,* February 21, 1994, 12–13.

The Organization-Environment Relationship

Why do organizations care so much about factors in the external environment? The reason is that the environment creates uncertainty for organization managers, and they must respond by designing the organization to adapt to the environment or to influence the environment.

Environmental Uncertainty

Organizations must manage environmental uncertainty to be effective. *Uncertainty* means that managers do not have sufficient information about environmental factors to understand and predict environmental needs and changes.[23] As indicated in Exhibit 3.3, environmental characteristics that influence uncertainty are the number of factors that affect the organization and the extent to which those factors change. A large multinational like Northern Telecom has thousands of factors in the external environment creating uncertainty for managers. When external factors change rapidly, the organization experiences very high uncertainty; examples are the electronics and aerospace industries. Firms must make efforts to adapt to these changes. When an organization deals with only a few external factors and these factors are relatively stable, such as for soft-drink bottlers or food processors, managers experience low uncertainty and can devote less attention to external issues.

Two basic strategies for coping with high environmental uncertainty are to adapt the organization to changes in the environment and to influence the environment to make it more compatible with organizational needs.

Adapting to the Environment

If the organization faces increased uncertainty with respect to competition, customers, suppliers, or government regulation, managers can use several strategies to adapt to these changes, including boundary-spanning roles, increased planning and forecasting, a flexible structure, and mergers or joint ventures.

Exhibit **3.3**

The External Environment and Uncertainty

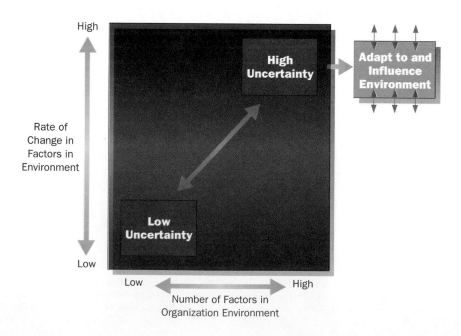

Boundary-Spanning Roles. Departments and **boundary-spanning roles** link and coordinate the organization with key elements in the external environment. Boundary spanners serve two purposes for the organization: They detect and process information about changes in the environment, and they represent the organization's interest to the environment.[24] People in departments such as marketing and purchasing span the boundary to work with customers and suppliers, both face-to-face and through market research. For example, Houston-based Characters, Inc., a prepress company, surveys customers twice a year about the desktop-publishing technology they use or plan to use within the next 12 months. In addition, they recently did a blind survey to determine if the company should enter the growing industry of digital, short-run color printing. Results convinced CEO David Steitz that the $2 million investment in new technology would pay off.[25] Perhaps the largest growth area in boundary spanning is competitive intelligence, also known as snooping and spying. Eighty percent of the *Fortune 1000* companies maintain in-house snoops, also known as *competitive intelligence professionals.* Companies such as Northern Telecom Ltd., Motorola, NutraSweet Co., and Xerox employ competitive intelligence (CI) specialists to scope out their competitors and help managers make better decisions and plans. TELUS Corp., a Canadian telecommunications company in Edmonton, has beefed up its CI team to cope with a tidal wave of competition from rivals in long-distance, data communication, cellular phone, and paging services. NutraSweet's CI professionals helped the company delay a costly advertising campaign when the company learned that a rival sweetener was at least 5 years away from FDA approval. Most CI work is strictly legal, relying on commercial databases, news clippings, help-wanted advertisements, trade publications, product literature, and personal contacts. Computerizing a company's network of intelligence gatherers, as AT&T did several years ago, helps employees learn what they need to know about competitors.[26]

Forecasting and Planning. Forecasting and planning for environmental changes are major activities in many corporations. Planning departments often are created when uncertainty is high.[27] Forecasting is an effort to spot trends that enable managers to predict future events. Forecasting techniques range from quantitative economic models of environmental business activity to newspaper clipping services. One of these services, called Burrelle's Information Services, Inc., monitors 16,000 newspapers and magazines and predicts future trends. Chase investors used information about rapidly multiplying television channels in Western Europe to invest in MCA, Inc., which had a valuable film library.

Control Data, Heinz, United Airlines, and Waste Management Inc. have devised specific management plans for handling crises. Whether the crisis is a hostile takeover attempt or product tampering, an organization that does not have a plan will make mistakes. Planning can soften the adverse effect of rapid shifts in the environment.

Flexible Structure. An organization's structure should enable it to effectively respond to shifts in the environment. Research has found that a loose, flexible structure works best when organizations experience uncertainty created by shifts in the external environment or by innovation within the organization, while a tight structure is most effective in a certain environment.[28]

boundary-spanning roles
Roles assumed by people and/or departments that link and coordinate the organization with key elements in the external environment.

A consumer focus group in Mexico evaluates Campbell's soups, reviewing qualities such as packaging, preparation, appearance, and taste. The passage of NAFTA broadened market opportunities in Mexico, where nearly 9 billion servings of soup are consumed each year. Marketing executives act as boundary spanners to test reactions and assess whether products meet local needs. Boundary spanning provided competitive intelligence that Mexican consumers like convenient dry-soup varieties as well as condensed and ready-to-serve soups.

organic structure
An organizational structure that is free flowing, has few rules and regulations, encourages employee teamwork, and decentralizes decision making to employees doing the job.

The term **organic structure** characterizes an organization that is free flowing, has few rules and regulations, encourages teamwork among employees, and decentralizes decision making to employees doing the job. This type of structure works best when the environment changes rapidly. Dow Chemical and Star-Kist Foods set up "SWAT" teams that can swing into action if an unexpected disaster strikes. These teams include members from multiple departments who can provide the expertise needed for solving an immediate problem, such as a plant explosion. Organic organizations create many teams to handle changes in raw materials, new products, government regulations, or marketing. A **mechanistic structure** is just the opposite, characterized by rigidly defined tasks, many rules and regulations, little teamwork, and centralization of decision making. Although this is fine for a stable environment, few organizations today exist in a stable environment. Organizational structures are shifting toward the image of the networked structure of advanced, worldwide information systems—an organic web rather than a hierarchy.[29]

mechanistic structure
An organizational structure characterized by rigidly defined tasks, many rules and regulations, little teamwork, and centralized decision making.

Mergers and Joint Ventures.   As we discussed, mergers are a major factor in a company's external environment. A merger is also a way to reduce uncertainty. A **merger** occurs when two or more organizations combine to become one. For example, General Host acquired Hickory Farms, a retail chain, to become an outlet for General Host's meat products, thereby reducing uncertainty in the customer sector.

merger
The combination of two or more organizations into one.

A **joint venture** involves a strategic alliance or program by two or more organizations. This typically occurs when the project is too complex, expensive, or uncertain for one firm to do alone. Today, keeping pace with rapid technological change and competing in the global environment have stretched the resources of even the richest companies. Joint ventures are on the rise, particularly between U.S. and Japanese firms. A 50-50 venture between Caterpillar Inc. and Mitsubishi Heavy Industries Ltd. lets Caterpillar manufacture and sell in Japan and helps Mitsubishi expand its export markets.[30] Many small businesses are turning to joint ventures with large firms or with international partners. A larger partner can provide sales staff, distribution channels, financial resources, or a research staff. Small businesses seldom have the expertise to deal internationally, so a company such as Nypro, Inc., a plastic injection-molding manufacturer in Clinton, Massachusetts, joins with overseas experts who are familiar with the local rules. Nypro now does business in four countries.[31]

joint venture
A strategic alliance or program by two or more organizations.

Influencing the Environment

The other major strategy for handling environmental uncertainty is to reach out and change those elements causing problems. Widely used techniques for changing the environment include advertising and public relations, political activity, and trade associations. Exhibit 3.4 summarizes the techniques organizations can use to adapt to and influence the external environment.

Advertising and Public Relations.   Advertising has become a highly successful way to manage demand for a company's products. Companies spend large amounts of money to influence consumer tastes. Hospitals have begun to advertise through billboards, newspapers, and radio commercials to promote special services. Increased competitiveness among CPA firms and law firms has caused them to start advertising for clients, a practice unheard

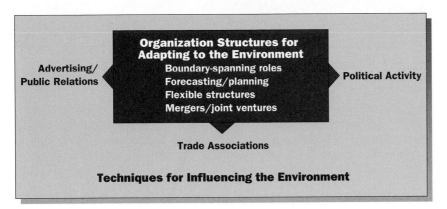

Exhibit 3.4
Organizational Responses to Environmental Changes

of a decade ago. Advertising is an important way to reduce uncertainty about customers. For example, J. C. Penney and Sears have turned their low-priced, house-brand jeans into some of the hottest labels around with hip advertising campaigns that feature rock bands, Web sites, and edgy imagery targeted towards teens.[32]

Public relations is similar to advertising, except that its goal is to influence public opinion about the company itself. Most companies care a great deal about their public image. Each year *Fortune* rates more than 300 companies to see which are the most and least admired in each of 32 industries. Public relations and a good public image are accomplished through advertising as well as speeches and press reports. Companies in the tobacco industry have launched an aggressive public relations campaign touting smokers' rights and freedom of choice in an effort to survive in this antismoking era.[33]

Political Activity. **Political activity** represents organizational attempts to influence government legislation and regulation. GM enlisted political bigwigs in its successful effort to settle a battle with the U.S. Transportation Department over the safety of certain of its pickup trucks. The settlement saved GM the cost of a $1 billion recall, basically allowing the company to buy its way out of the dispute by spending $51 million on safety programs over a five-year period.[34] Many corporations pay lobbyists to express their views to federal and state legislators. Foreign companies are becoming increasingly savvy in U.S. political maneuvering. For example, Japanese companies have placed former key U.S. political insiders on their payrolls as Washington lobbyists and advisers. Under pressure from U.S. companies about government-business collaboration in foreign countries, Washington has warmed to a technology policy that provides government policy support to critical technologies and industry study groups.[35]

Trade Associations. Most organizations join with others having similar interests; the result is a **trade association.** In this way, organizations work together to influence the environment, including federal legislation and regulation. The number and variety of trade associations is staggering. Although many students have heard of the National Rifle Association or the National Association of Manufacturers, few are aware that there is a National Academy of Nannies, a National Coil Coaters Association, or a National Association of Nameplate Manufacturers. One effective association is the National

political activity
Organizational attempts, such as lobbying, to influence government legislation and regulation.

trade association
An association made up of organizations with similar interests for the purpose of influencing the environment.

Bell South's Lynn Holmes, executive director of governmental affairs in North Carolina, attempts to influence the environment through political activity. Holmes worked to get legislation passed that would open North Carolina's local market to competition and change regulatory structures, enabling Bell South to boost earnings if it can market effectively and operate more efficiently in newly competitive markets.

Tooling and Machining Association (NTMA). The NTMA functions primarily as a center of knowledge. In a recent year, NTMA fielded 16,000 queries from members on everything from technical and marketing matters to taxes and labor problems. Since most tooling and machining companies are small, the association lobbies heavily on issues that affect small business, like taxes, health insurance, and government mandates. Recognizing that its members are competing with low-priced competitors in Europe and Japan, the NTMA provides statistics and information to help U.S. companies set competitive prices, and the association has recently committed itself to expanding ties with industry counterparts in Mexico and Canada.[36]

The Internal Environment: Corporate Culture

The internal environment within which managers work includes corporate culture, production technology, organization structure, and physical facilities. Of these, corporate culture has surfaced as extremely important to competitive advantage. The internal culture must fit the needs of the external environment and company strategy. When this fit occurs, highly committed employees create a high-performance organization that is tough to beat.[37]

culture
The set of key values, beliefs, understandings, and norms that members of an organization share.

Culture can be defined as the set of key values, beliefs, understandings, and norms shared by members of an organization.[38] The concept of culture helps managers understand the hidden, complex aspects of organizational life. Culture is a pattern of shared values and assumptions about how things are done within the organization. This pattern is learned by members as they cope with external and internal problems and taught to new members as the correct way to perceive, think, and feel. Culture can be analyzed at three levels, as illustrated in Exhibit 3.5, with each level becoming less obvious.[39] At the surface level are visible artifacts, which include such things as manner of dress, patterns of behavior, physical symbols, organizational ceremonies, and office layout. Visible artifacts are all the things one can see, hear, and observe by watching members of the organization. At a deeper level are the expressed values and beliefs, which are not observable but can be discerned from how people explain and justify what they do. These are values that members of the organization hold at a conscious level. They can be interpreted from the

Exhibit 3.5

Levels of Corporate Culture

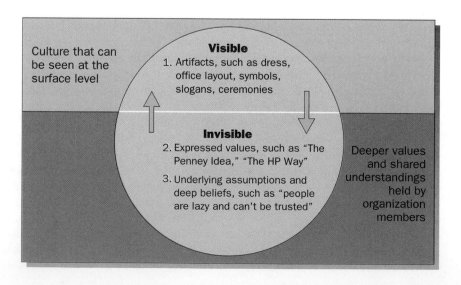

stories, language, and symbols organization members use to represent them. Some values become so deeply embedded in a culture that members are no longer consciously aware of them. These basic, underlying assumptions and beliefs are the essence of culture and subconsciously guide behavior and decisions. In some organizations, a basic assumption might be that people are essentially lazy and will shirk their duties whenever possible; thus, employees are closely supervised and given little freedom, and colleagues are frequently suspicious of one another. More enlightened organizations operate on the basic assumption that people want to do a good job; in these organizations, employees are given more freedom and responsibility, and colleagues trust one another and work cooperatively. Basic assumptions in an organization's culture often begin with strongly held values espoused by a founder or early leader. For example, the founders of St. Luke's, a small advertising agency on the edge of London's Bloomsbury district, created a distinctive culture that provides the company with a competitive advantage, as described in the Learning Organization box.

One of the most important things leaders do is create and influence organizational culture because it has a significant impact on performance. In comparing 18 companies that have experienced long-term success with 18 similar companies that have not done so well, James C. Collins and Jerry I. Porras found the key determining factor in successful companies to be a culture in which employees share such a strong vision that they know in their hearts what is right for the company. Their book, *Built to Last: Successful Habits of Visionary Companies,* describes how companies such as Hewlett-Packard, Walt Disney, and Procter & Gamble have successfully adapted to a changing world without losing sight of the core values that guide the organization. Some companies put values in writing so they can be passed on to new generations of employees. Hewlett-Packard created a list of cultural concepts called "The HP Way." Companies known for their strong, distinctive cultures, such as Southwest Airlines, W. L. Gore, and Hewlett-Packard, regularly show up on *Fortune* magazine's list of the best companies to work for in America.[40]

The fundamental values that characterize cultures at these and other companies can be understood through the visible manifestations of symbols, stories, heroes, slogans, and ceremonies. Any company's culture can be interpreted by observing these factors.

Tom Loutzenheiser, technology president of software company Apexx Technology, appreciates the many positive attributes of the company's Boise Idaho, location, including affordable housing, short commutes, and the opportunity to kayak on the Boise River just minutes away. Employees at Apexx also appreciate the company's corporate culture, which values the individual and believes in giving employees freedom, privacy, and responsibility. Apexx Technology's office layout reflects its cultural values by offering employees more personal space, offices with real windows, and solid walls that rise all the way to the ceiling. "It's not a cube farm," says employee Jennifer Bedford, reflecting her approval.

Symbols

A **symbol** is an object, act, or event that conveys meaning to others. Symbols associated with corporate culture convey the organization's important values. For example, John Thomas, CEO of a mechanical contractor in Andover, Massachusetts, wanted to imprint the value of allowing mistakes and risk taking. He pulled a $450 mistake out of the dumpster, mounted it on a plaque, and named it the "No-Nuts Award" for the missing parts. The award is presented annually and symbolizes the freedom to make mistakes but not to make the same mistake twice.[41] The open office layout at companies such as St. Luke's, described on the next page, and Nickelodeon, the most-watched cable network in the country, symbolize a commitment to values of equality, having fun, and sharing ideas. Randall Larrimore, president of MasterBrand Industries, Inc., wanted to break down the vertical walls that isolated departments and develop a team culture. Faced with skeptical managers who felt incapable of leading such a change process, Larrimore gave a motivational speech and then sym-

symbol
An object, act, or event that conveys meaning to others.

Learning

LEADING THE REVOLUTION: THE LEARNING ORGANIZATION

St. Luke's

An advertising agency seems an unlikely place to find a cultural revolution. That may be why St. Luke's calls itself a communications resource office, not an ad agency. Its mission is to produce honest, ethical advertising that represents a company's "Total Role in Society," which is an evaluation of the organization among the totality of its stakeholders: employees, customers, shareholders, the community, the environment, vendors, competitors, the families of employees, etc. The agency preaches and practices a gospel of total ethics and common ownership. St. Luke's employees own the company—all of it; every employee holds equal shares, from the person who answers the phone to the creative director.

St. Luke's was once the London office of Chiat/Day, the agency known for the Energizer bunny. When communications conglomerate Omnicom bought the struggling agency and announced plans to merge Chiat/Day with a larger agency, Andy Law, managing director, bought the London office and then called in all the employees to let them decide their own future. The employees' response was that they wanted to work for a company that embodied their own personal values. Further, they wanted a concrete mechanism for universal commitment and contribution.

The physical layout of St. Luke's reflects the company's cultural values. Employees have traded desks and personal work spaces for "brand rooms"—large client-specific, glass-enclosed conference rooms where teams meet for each account to generate ideas and store work-in-progress. Between meetings and visits to clients, employees take a seat at any one of dozens of computers that they share communally. Employees eat lunch together, play ping pong, or crawl out the window to enjoy a moment of sunshine on the rooftop. There are no trophies or awards lining the walls and shelves at St. Luke's. The company has never won any advertising awards for the simple reason that they refuse to enter any contests.

After only a year in business, St. Luke's was generating annual billings of around $72 million and was the fastest growing agency in London. In a recent survey asking London's art directors and copywriters where they would most like to work, tiny St. Luke's came in third. Law believes people want to work for a company they can be proud of, and he and his employees have created a distinctive culture at St. Luke's that emphasizes self-motivation, personal growth, and integrity in all actions. "We've created this company to live beyond us," says Law. "We're just renting resources. Remember that we're a collective here—everybody is equal. What's disappeared are ego and greed. . . ."

SOURCE: Stevan Alburty, "The Ad Agency to End All Ad Agencies," *Fast Company*, December–January 1997, 116–124.

---

bolized his message by giving each manager a copy of *Oh, The Places You'll Go*, by Dr. Seuss. The managers now proudly display the book as a symbol of their own pioneering efforts and achievements.[42]

Stories

story
A narrative based on true events that is repeated frequently and shared by organizational employees.

A **story** is a narrative based on true events that is repeated frequently and shared among organizational employees. Stories are told to new employees to keep the organization's primary values alive. Companies such as IBM, Royal Dutch/Shell, Coca-Cola, and U.S. West have sent managers to workshops to learn about the advantages of stories as a way to transmit values and promote change when needed. One of Nordstrom's primary means of emphasizing the importance of customer service is through corporate storytelling. An example is the story about men's clothing salesman Van Mensah, who received a letter explaining that a customer had mistakenly washed his 12 new shirts in hot water, causing the shirts to shrink. The customer wanted to know whether Mensah had any suggestions to help him out of his predicament. Mensah immediately called the customer in Sweden and informed him that a dozen new shirts—in the same size, style, and colors—were being mailed out that day, compliments of the company.[43] Likewise, for years, workers at U.S. Paper Mills Corporation told a story about the company's founder and principal stockholder, Walter Cloud. One morning, when Cloud saw a worker trying to unclog the drain of a blending vat using an extension pole, he quickly climbed over the edge of the vat and reached through the 3-feet-deep slurry of paper fiber to unclog the drain with his hand. As he wiped the muck from his dress pants, Cloud asked the worker, "Now, what are you going to do the next time you need to unclog a drain?" By telling and retelling this story, workers at the mill communicate the importance of jumping in to do whatever needs to be done.[44]

Heroes

A **hero** is a figure who exemplifies the deeds, character, and attributes of a strong culture. Heroes are role models for employees to follow. Sometimes heroes are real, such as Lee Iacocca, who proved the courage of his convictions by working for $1 a year when he first came to Chrysler. Other times they are symbolic, such as the mythical sales representative at Robinson Jewelers who delivered a wedding ring directly to the church because the ring had been ordered late. The deeds of heroes are out of the ordinary, but not so far out as to be unattainable by other employees. Heroes show how to do the right thing in the organization. Companies with strong cultures take advantage of achievements to define heroes who uphold key values.

At Minnesota Mining and Manufacturing (3M), top managers keep alive the heroes who developed projects that were killed by top management. One hero was a vice president who was fired earlier in his career for persisting with a new product even after his boss had told him, "That's a stupid idea. Stop!" After the worker was fired, he would not leave. He stayed in an unused office, working without a salary on the new product idea. Eventually he was rehired, the idea succeeded, and he was promoted to vice president. The lesson of this hero as a major element in 3M's culture is to persist at what you believe in.[45]

hero
A figure who exemplifies the deeds, character, and attributes of a strong corporate culture.

Slogans

A **slogan** is a phrase or sentence that succinctly expresses a key corporate value. Many companies use a slogan or saying to convey special meaning to employees. H. Ross Perot of Electronic Data Systems established the philosophy of hiring the best people he could find and noted how difficult it was to find them. His motto was "Eagles don't flock. You gather them one at a time." At Sequins International, where 80 percent of the employees are Hispanic, words from W. Edwards Deming, "You don't have to please the boss; you have to please the customer," are embroidered in Spanish on the pockets of workers' jackets.[46] Cultural values can also be discerned in written public statements, such as corporate mission statements or other formal statements that express the core values of the organization. Eaton Corporation developed a philosophy statement called "Excellence Through People," which includes a commitment to encouraging employee involvement in all decisions, regular face-to-face communication between executives and employees, promotion from within, and always focusing on the positive behavior of workers.

slogan
A phrase or sentence that succinctly expresses a key corporate value.

Ceremonies

ceremony
A planned activity that makes up a special event and is conducted for the benefit of an audience.

A **ceremony** is a planned activity that makes up a special event and is conducted for the benefit of an audience. Managers hold ceremonies to provide dramatic examples of company values. Ceremonies are special occasions that reinforce valued accomplishments, create a bond among people by allowing them to share an important event, and anoint and celebrate heroes.[47]

The value of a ceremony can be illustrated by the presentation of a major award. Mary Kay Cosmetics Company holds elaborate awards ceremonies, presenting gold and diamond pins, furs, and pink Cadillacs to high-achieving sales consultants. The setting is typically an auditorium, in front of a large, cheering audience, and everyone dresses in glamorous evening clothes. The most successful consultants are introduced by film clips, like the kind used to introduce political nominees or to present award nominees in the entertainment industry. These ceremonies recognize and celebrate high-performing employees and emphasize the rewards for performance.[48] An award can also be bestowed secretly by mailing it to the employee's home or, if a check, by depositing it in a bank. But such procedures would not make the bestowal of rewards a significant organizational event and would be less meaningful to the employee.

In summary, organizational culture represents the values, understandings, and basic assumptions that employees share, and these values are signified by symbols, stories, heroes, slogans, and ceremonies. Managers help define important symbols, stories, and heroes to shape the culture.

Environment and Culture

A big influence on internal corporate culture is the external environment. Cultures can vary widely across organizations; however, organizations within the same industry may often reveal similar cultural characteristics because they are operating in similar environments.[49] The internal culture should embody what it takes to succeed in the environment. If the external environment requires extraordinary customer service, the culture should encourage good service; if it calls for careful technical decision making, cultural values should reinforce managerial decision making.

Adaptive Cultures

Research at Harvard on 207 U.S. firms illustrated the critical relationship between corporate culture and the external environment. The study found that a strong corporate culture alone did not ensure business success unless the culture encouraged healthy adaptation to the external environment. As illustrated in Exhibit 3.6, adaptive corporate cultures have different values and behavior from unadaptive corporate cultures. In adaptive cultures, managers are concerned about customers and those internal people and processes that bring about useful change. In the unadaptive corporate cultures, managers are concerned about themselves, and their values tend to discourage risk taking and change. Thus a strong culture alone is not enough, because an unhealthy culture may encourage the organization to march resolutely in the wrong direction. Healthy cultures help companies

	Adaptive Corporate Cultures	**Unadaptive Corporate Cultures**
Visible Behavior	Managers pay close attention to all their constituencies, especially customers, and initiate change when needed to serve their legitimate interests, even if it entails taking some risks.	Managers tend to behave somewhat insularly, politically, and bureaucratically. As a result, they do not change their strategies quickly to adjust to or take advantage of changes in their business environments.
Expressed Values	Managers care deeply about customers, stockholders, and employees. They also strongly value people and processes that can create useful change (e.g., leadership initiatives up and down the management hierarchy).	Managers care mainly about themselves, their immediate work group, or some product (or technology) associated with that work group. They value the orderly and risk-reducing management process much more highly than leadership initiatives.

Exhibit 3.6

Environmentally Adaptive versus Unadaptive Corporate Cultures

SOURCE: John P. Kotter and James L. Heskett, *Corporate Culture and Performance* (New York, The Free Press, 1992), 51.

adapt to the environment.[50] Managers at McDonald's, for example, are struggling to transform an unadaptive culture before it causes more damage to the giant of fast food.

MCDONALD'S
www.mcdonalds.com

Ray Kroc, founder of McDonald's, once said, "I don't know what we'll be serving in the year 2000, but we'll be serving more of it than anybody." From its founding through the early 1980s, McDonald's changed with America's tastes, seeming to give us what we wanted before we even knew we wanted it. Today, however, Kroc's bold claim doesn't seem so assured. Although McDonald's still has a 42 percent share of the U.S. fast-food market and continues to expand internationally, the company is slipping fast in its ability to recognize and shape popular trends. Its last successful new product was the Chicken McNugget, launched more than 15 years ago, and operating profits haven't even kept pace with inflation.

Some analysts and investors believe the widespread problems with McDonald's are due to the corporation's insular, arrogant culture. The average top executive at McDonald's started working at the company when Richard Nixon was president, and the company has been reluctant to bring in outside leaders to guide management as the environment changes. The board, as well, is made up of close-knit insiders who have done little to agitate for change. As performance declined, top leaders tended to blame others, such as dissident franchisees, news reporters, and Wall Street analysts. "If there were one thing I would change about McDonald's," said Senior Vice President Brad A. Ball, "it would be to correct the misconceptions and misperceptions that have become so pervasive in the last few years."

Now, however, McDonald's is embarking on an effort to reform. Management has been reorganized, and the new head of the domestic division, Jack M. Greenberg, has brought in at least a handful of new managers, including executives from Burger King, Boston Market, and General Electric. He's also dividing up the country into territories, creating smaller companies to recapture some of

McDonald's entrepreneurial zeal. "We are not afraid to do things differently," Greenberg says. Managers are beginning to recognize that, even though McDonald's is still the world's most successful restaurant company, it is far from achieving its potential. They are trying to turn McDonald's back to the healthy adaptive culture of the early years, when it was constantly in touch with the tastes of consumers.[51]

Types of Cultures

One way to think about corporate cultures was suggested by Jeffrey Sonnenfeld and included four types of culture—baseball team, club, academy, and fortress. Each culture has somewhat different potential for supporting a healthy, successful company and has a different impact on the satisfaction and careers of employees.[52]

The *baseball team culture* emerges in an environmental situation with high-risk decision making and fast feedback from the environment. Decision makers quickly learn whether their choice was right or wrong. Talent, innovation, and performance are valued and rewarded. Top performers see themselves as "free agents," and companies scramble for their services. Performers with "low batting averages" are quickly dropped from the lineup. Baseball team cultures are found in fast-paced, high-risk companies involved in areas such as movie production, advertising, and software development where futures are bet on a new product or project.

The *club culture* is characterized by loyalty, commitment, and fitting into the group. This stable, secure environment values age and experience and rewards seniority. As in the case of career military personnel, individuals start young and stay. Club cultures promote from within, and members are expected to progress slowly, proving competence at each level. Individuals tend to be generalists and may have vast experience in a number of organizational functions. Top executives in commercial banks, for example, frequently began as tellers. While many club qualities contribute to flexibility within the organization, they can also contribute to the perception of a closed company, reluctant to change, as we saw in the example of McDonald's.

The *academy culture* also hires young recruits interested in a long-term association and a slow, steady climb up the organization. Unlike the club culture, however, employees rarely cross from one division to another. Each person enters a specific "track" and gains a high level of expertise in that area. Job and technical mastery are the bases for reward and advancement. Many long-established organizations such as universities, Coca-Cola, Ford, and GM maintain strong academy cultures. Although specialization provides job security, this culture may limit broad individual development and interdepartmental collaboration, but it works very well in a stable environment.

The *fortress culture* may emerge in an environmental survival situation. Textile firms and savings and loan organizations are examples of former dominant industries that are now retrenching for survival. The fortress culture offers little job security or opportunity for professional growth while companies restructure and downsize to fit the new environment. This culture is perilous for employees but also offers tremendous turnaround opportunities for individual managers with confidence and love of challenge. Those who succeed, such as Lee Iaccoca (Chrysler) or William Crouse (president of Ortho Diagnostic Systems, Inc.) earn recognition nationally or within their industry.[53]

Shaping Corporate Culture for the Twenty-First Century

Changing and Merging Corporate Cultures

A corporation's culture may not always be in alignment with its needs and environment. Cultural values may reflect what worked in the past. The difference between desired cultural norms and values and actual norms and values is called the **culture gap**.[54]

Culture gaps can be immense, especially in mergers and acquisitions.[55] Despite the popularity of mergers and acquisitions as a corporate strategy, many fail. Almost one-half of acquired companies are sold within five years, and some experts claim that 90 percent of mergers never live up to expectations.[56] One reason for failure is that although managers are able to integrate the acquired firm's financial systems and production technologies, they typically are unable to integrate the unwritten norms and values that have an even greater impact on a company's success.[57] These problems increase in scope and frequency with global companies and cross-cultural mergers and acquisitions. For example, investors cheered at the announcement of a merger between Upjohn Co. of Kalamazoo, Michigan, and Sweden's Pharmacia. The market value of the new Pharmacia & Upjohn, Inc. soared. Eight months later, however, there were clear signs that the merger was in trouble. Cost-cutting was behind schedule, earnings were low, key executives were jumping ship, and morale was lousy. Most agree it's due to the clash of cultures between the two companies. According to Magnus Lundberg, the ex-head of metabolic diseases at P&U, the merger "was like two different species meeting each other." Managers often forget that the human systems of a company are what make or break any change initiative.[58]

Symbolic Leadership

One way managers change norms and values toward what is adaptive to the external environment or for smooth internal integration is through symbolic leadership. Managers can use symbols, stories, slogans, and ceremonies to change corporate culture. Managers literally must overcommunicate to ensure that employees understand the new culture values, and they must signal these values in actions as well as words.

A **symbolic leader** defines and uses signals and symbols to influence corporate culture. Symbolic leaders influence culture in the following manner:

1. *The symbolic leader articulates a vision for the organizational culture that generates excitement and that employees can believe in.* This means the leader defines and communicates central values that employees believe in and will rally around.

2. *The symbolic leader heeds the day-to-day activities that reinforce the cultural vision.* The symbolic leader makes sure that symbols, ceremonies, and slogans match the new values. Even more important, actions speak louder than words. Symbolic leaders "walk their talk."[59]

The reason symbolic leadership works is that executives are watched by employees. Employees learn what is valued most in a company by noting the attitudes and behaviors that managers pay attention to and reward, how they react to organizational crises, and whether the manager's own behavior matches the espoused values.[60] At Levi Strauss, for example, managers' bonus pay,

culture gap
The difference between an organization's desired cultural norms and values and actual norms and values.

symbolic leader
A manager who defines and uses signals and symbols to influence corporate culture.

Symbolic leaders *like Southwest Airlines' chairman, president, and CEO Herb Kelleher shape corporate culture by articulating a clear vision and expressing cultural values through deeds, actions, statements, and ceremonies. Kelleher plays many roles for his employees—inspirational leader, kindly uncle, cheerleader, and clown—to keep spirits high and build a culture where "kindness and the human spirit are nurtured." Through employee videos, Winning Spirit ceremonies, speeches, and everyday personal contact, Kelleher lets Southwest employees know they're the key to the company's success.*

which can be two-thirds of their total compensation, is tied explicitly to how well they follow the corporate aspirations in their daily work. Because leaders at Levi Strauss create linkages between stated values, training, everyday action, and appraisal and reward systems, employees rely on the aspirations as a standard of behavior. Some leaders fail to recognize how carefully they are watched by employees. One senior executive told a story of how employees always knew in advance when someone was about to be laid off in his company. He finally picked up on the pattern. Employees noticed that the executive always dressed in his favorite pink shirt and matching tie when layoffs were to be announced.

Jack Welch transformed General Electric—a huge corporation—by defining a new type of senior manager. His demand was for symbolic leaders, which he described as follows: "Somebody who can develop a vision of what he or she wants their . . . activity to do and be. Somebody who is able to articulate what the business is, and gain through a sharing of the discussion—listening and talking—an acceptance of the vision. And someone who then can relentlessly drive implementation of that vision to a successful conclusion."[61]

Even well-established companies with strong cultures may implement changes through symbolic leadership. When IBM chief Lou Gerstner officially relaxed the company's unofficial straitlaced dress code, he was choosing a common symbol for lightening up a "traditional" business atmosphere. Gerstner has used symbolic leadership in other ways, too. On his first day on the job, Gerstner called a dozen top managers into his office and asked them to write a five-page report that answered such questions as What business are you in? Who are your customers? What are your strengths and weaknesses? He asked for the report in two days. In a company known for meetings steeped in ritual, requiring extensive and elaborate preparations, accompanied by massive reports in blue binders, the message was clear: It was no longer business as usual at Big Blue.[62]

Symbolic leaders search for opportunities. They make public statements, including both oral and written communications, to the organization as a whole. After articulating a vision, symbolic leaders change corporate culture through hundreds of small deeds, actions, statements, and ceremonies. A strong leader who articulated a clear vision accounted for the extraordinary success of Wal-Mart, Disney, Hewlett-Packard, and Levi Strauss. Harold Geneen, former CEO of ITT, captured his corporate value in a few words: "Search for the unshakeable facts." Herb Kelleher of Southwest Airlines has developed a strong, adaptive culture by sticking to the basics: "Do what your customer wants; be happy in your work."[63]

Scott Kohno, managing director of Chaix & Johnson, shocked and revitalized his 30 employees by hauling his desk from a comfortable executive office with 18-foot ceilings to the middle of the work floor. Kohno compared the move to the "difference between being on the basketball floor instead of the bleachers." The increased contact with staff was soon matched by a supercharged employee energy level.[64]

Another story involving a desk illustrates Mars executives' concern for employees and began when Mr. Mars made a midsummer visit to a chocolate factory:

He went up to the third floor, where the biggest chocolate machines were placed. It was hotter than the hinges of hell. He asked the factory manager, "How come you don't have air conditioning up here?" The factory manager replied that it wasn't in his budget, and he darn well had to make the budget. While Mr. Mars allowed that was a fact, he nonetheless went over to the nearby phone and dialed the maintenance people downstairs and asked them to come up immediately. He said, "While we (he and the factory manager) stand here, would you please go downstairs and get all (the factory manager's) furniture and other things from his office and bring them up here? Sit them down next to the big chocolate machine up here, if you don't mind." Mr. Mars told him that once the factory had been air conditioned, he could move back to his office any time he wanted.[65]

Stories such as these can be found in most companies and used to enhance the desired culture. The value of stories depends not on whether they are precisely true but whether they are repeated frequently and convey the correct values.

To summarize, symbolic leaders influence culture through the use of artifacts such as public statements, ceremonies, stories, heroes, symbols, and slogans. When cultural change is needed to adapt to the external environment or to bring about smoother internal integration, managers must become symbolic leaders and learn how to use speech, symbols, and stories to influence underlying cultural assumptions. Changing culture is not easy, but through their words—and particularly their actions—symbolic leaders let other organization members know what really counts in the company.

Summary and Management Solution

This chapter discussed several important ideas about internal and external organizational environments. Events in the external environment are considered important influences on organizational behavior and performance. The external environment consists of two layers: the task environment and the general environment. The task environment includes customers, competitors, suppliers, and the labor market. The general environment includes technological, sociocultural, economic, legal-political, and international dimensions. Management techniques for helping the organization adapt to the environment include boundary-spanning roles, forecasting and planning, a flexible structure, and mergers and joint ventures. Techniques managers can use to influence the external environment include advertising and public relations, political activities, and trade associations.

Companies such as Intuit, described in the chapter opening case, operate in highly uncertain environments because of today's rapid technological change. In an attempt to adapt to this environment, Intuit negotiated a merger with Microsoft, but it was squashed by the Department of Justice on antitrust grounds. Intuit thus was left in a somewhat weaker position than before. The company knows it needs to embrace the Internet, and its goal is to be the best at bringing together all the diverse little financial tools offered on the Net. Now, to attract people to its Web site, Intuit is leaping into strategic alliances with companies such as Excite, the second most popular Internet search engine and directory.

Although it remains to be seen whether Intuit can reinvent itself for the Internet, the company's adaptive culture is a big plus. Corporate culture, a major element of the internal environment, includes the key values, beliefs, understandings, and norms that organization members share. Organizational activities that illustrate corporate culture include symbols, stories, heroes, slogans, and ceremonies. For the organization to be effective, corporate culture should be aligned with the needs of the external environment.

Four types of culture are baseball team, club, academy, and fortress, each of which suits a specific environment. Most companies in the software industry, including Intuit, have a baseball team culture. Strong cultures are effective when they enable the organization to adapt to changes in the external environment.

Symbolic leaders can strengthen or change corporate culture by (1) communicating a vision to employees and (2) reinforcing the vision with day-to-day public statements, ceremonies, slogans, symbols, and stories.

Discussion Questions

1. Some scientists predict major changes in the earth's climate, including a temperature rise of 8°F over the next 60 years. Should any companies be paying attention to this long-range environmental trend? Explain.
2. Would the task environment for a bank contain the same elements as that for a government welfare agency? Discuss.
3. What forces influence organizational uncertainty? Would such forces typically originate in the task environment or the general environment?
4. *In Search of Excellence,* described in Chapter 2, argued that customers were the most important element in the external environment. Are there company situations for which this may not be true?
5. Caterpillar Corporation was thriving until the mid-1980s, when low oil prices, high interest rates, a worldwide recession, a soaring U.S. dollar, and Japanese competition stunned the giant equipment builder. Discuss the type of response Caterpillar's management might take.
6. Define corporate culture and explain its importance for managers.
7. Why are symbols important to a corporate culture? Do stories, heroes, slogans, and ceremonies also have symbolic value? Discuss.
8. Describe the cultural values of a company for which you have worked. Did those values fit the needs of the external environment? Of employees?
9. What type of environmental situation is associated with a baseball team culture? How does this culture differ from the academy culture?
10. Do you think a corporate culture with strong values is better for organizational effectiveness than a culture with weak values? Are there times when a strong culture might reduce effectiveness? Discuss.

Management in Practice: Experiential Exercise

What is a Strong Corporate Culture?

Think about an organization with which you are familiar, such as your school or a company for which you have worked. Answer the questions below based on whether you agree that they describe the organization.

1. Virtually all managers and most employees can describe the company's values, purpose, and customer importance.
2. There is clarity among organization members about how their jobs contribute to organizational goals.
3. It is very seldom that a manager will act in a way contrary to the company's espoused values.
4. Warmth and support of other employees is a valued norm, even across departments.
5. The company and its managers value what's best for the company over the long term more than short-term results.
6. Leaders make it a point to develop and mentor others.
7. Recruiting is taken very seriously, with multiple interviews in an effort to find traits that fit the culture.
8. Recruits are given negative as well as positive information about the company so they can freely choose whether to join.
9. Employees are expected to acquire real knowledge and mastery—not political alliances—before they can be promoted.
10. Company values emphasize what the company must do well to succeed in a changing environment.
11. Conformity to company mission and values is more important than conformity to procedures and dress.

Disagree Strongly			Agree Strongly	
1	2	3	4	5
1	2	3	4	5
1	2	3	4	5
1	2	3	4	5
1	2	3	4	5
1	2	3	4	5
1	2	3	4	5
1	2	3	4	5
1	2	3	4	5
1	2	3	4	5
1	2	3	4	5

12. You have heard stories about the company's leaders or "heroes" who helped make the company great.	1	2	3	4	5
13. Ceremonies and special events are used to recognize and reward individuals who contribute to the company in significant ways.	1	2	3	4	5

Total Score _____

Compute your score. If your total score is 52 or above, your organization has a strong culture, similar to a Procter & Gamble or Hewlett-Packard. A score from 26 to 51 suggests a culture of medium strength, which is positive for the organization, such as for American Airlines, Coca-Cola, and Citibank. A score of 25 or below indicates a weak culture, which is probably not helping the company adapt to the external environment or meet the needs of organization members. Discuss the pros and cons of a strong culture. Does a strong culture mean everyone has to be alike?

SOURCE: Adapted from Richard Pascale, "The Paradox of 'Corporate Culture': Reconciling Ourselves to Socialization," *California Management Review* 27, no. 2 (1985); and David A. Kolb, Joyce S. Osland, and Irwin M. Rubin, *Organizational Behavior: An Experiential Approach,* 6th ed. (Englewood Cliffs, N.J.: Prentice-Hall, 1995), 346–347.

Management in Practice: Ethical Dilemma

Watching Out for Larry

It was the end of the fourth quarter, and Holly Vasquez was completing the profitability statement for her division's regional manager. She was disturbed to see that, for the first time during her tenure as a sales manager for Wallog Computers, her group was not in the top 10 percent of the region. She had watched sales slip during the past year but hoped the fourth quarter might save their numbers. The company was under pressure from stockholders to increase sales. Vasquez was afraid that Wallog would be cutting staff and altering the "people culture" that had kept her there for the past ten years.

As she entered the individual results in the spreadsheet, she saw her main problem: Larry Norris. After 27 years with the company, Norris had more career sales than anyone in the region, but, for the past 3 years, he had not even met his quota. Unlike some of her newer salespeople, Norris was uninformed on new products, and his old-style selling techniques didn't seem to be working. Vasquez had suggested he consult with the "new guys" on technical information and new sales techniques, but Norris was stubborn.

Vasquez knew she had the performance information to move him out of his position, but there was nowhere for him to go at Wallog. At 56, he was too young for retirement but too old to find a job elsewhere at his current salary. Not only was Larry Norris a friend, but also he was well liked in her department, and Vasquez wondered what effect his replacement would have on morale. She didn't want to fire him, but she couldn't risk her team's standing or her own reputation by protecting him anymore.

What do you do?

1. Fire Larry Norris with two-weeks' notice, a generous severance package, and all the help you can provide him in his job hunt.
2. Give him an ultimatum to meet his sales quota or else, and let him find the way. It is his responsibility to stay current and meet his quota.
3. Assign him to study the new products and the sales techniques of the top salespeople—then hope he improves and the others don't slip.

Surf the Net

1. **Sociocultural dimension of general environment.** As stated in this chapter, "Important sociocultural characteristics are geographical distribution and population density, age, and education levels. Today's demographic profiles are the foundation of tomorrow's workforce and consumers." Examine the demographic information available at **http://www.census.gov/**
   For example, among the wealth of information available at this site is a collection of statistics on social and economic conditions in the United States called the *Statistical Abstract of the United States*

   www.census.gov/statab/www/brief.html
   Find six statistics assigned by your instructor or chosen by you, and be prepared to share your findings in the oral or written format assigned by your instructor.

2. **Competitors**. A sector of the task environment is competitors. Select an industry you're interested in researching and write a 1 to 2 page paper about the industry describing who the major players are and identifying competitive information that would be useful for businesses operating in that industry. Try Web sites such as those that follow to gather your information.

www.fuld.com/i3/index.html
www.companiesonline.com/
www.companysleuth.com/
www.corporateinformation.com/
businessdirectory.dowjones.com/

3. **Culture communicated through stories.** David M. Armstrong, CEO of Armstrong International, Inc., has authored three books for the purpose of communicating Armstrong's culture—its key values, beliefs, understandings, and norms shared by members of his organization—

by storytelling. His books are entitled *Managing by Storying Around*; *How to Turn Your Company's Parables into Profit*; and *Once Told, They're Gold*. Go to the Web site listed below and read the stories or watch the video clips that illustrate sample stories from each of his three books. If you choose a video, you will need the Quicktime movie player installed on your computer; the player is available to download from the Armstrong Web site.
www.armintl.com/stories/david-bio.html

Case for Critical Analysis
Society of Equals

Ted Shelby doesn't make very many mistakes, but . . .

"Hey Stanley," says Ted Shelby, leaning in through the door, "you got a minute? I've just restructured my office. Come on and take a look. I've been implementing some great new concepts!"

Stanley is always interested in Ted Shelby's new ideas, for if there is anyone Stanley wants to do as well as, it is Edward W. Shelby IV. Stanley follows Ted back to his office and stops, nonplussed.

Restructured is right! Gone are Ted's size B (Junior Exec.) walnut veneer desk and furniture, and his telephone table. In fact, the room is practically empty save for a large, round, stark white cafeteria table and the half-dozen padded vinyl swivel chairs that surround it.

"Isn't it a beauty! As far as I know, I'm the first executive in the plant to innovate this. The shape is the crucial factor here—no front or rear, no status problems. We can all sit there and communicate more effectively."

We? Communicate? Effectively? Well, it seems that Ted has been attending a series of Executive Development Seminars given by Dr. Faust. The theme of the seminars was—you guessed it—"participative management." Edward W. Shelby IV has always liked to think of himself as a truly democratic person.

"You see, Stanley," says Ted, managing his best sincere/intense attitude, "the main thing wrong with current mainstream management practice is that the principal communication channel is down-the-line oriented. We on the top send our messages down to you people, but we neglect the feedback potential. But just because we have more status and responsibility doesn't mean that we are necessarily (Stanley duly noted the word, "necessarily") better than the people below us. So, as I see the situation, what is needed is a two-way communication network: down-the-line and up-the-line."

"That's what the cafeteria table is for?" Stanley says.

"Yes!" says Ted. "We management people don't have all the answers, and I don't know why I never realized it before that

seminar. Why . . . let's take an extreme example . . . the folks who run those machines out there. I'll bet that any one of them knows a thing or two that I've never thought of. So I've transformed my office into a full-feedback communication net."

"That certainly is an innovation around here," says Stanley.

A few days later Stanley passed by Ted Shelby's office and was surprised that Ted's desk, furniture, and telephone table were back where they used to be.

Stanley, curious about the unrestructuring, went to Bonnie for enlightenment. "What," he asked, "happened to Shelby's round table?"

"That table we were supposed to sit around and input things?" she said. "All I know is, about two days after he had it put in, Mr. Drake came walking through here. He looked in that office, and then he sort of stopped and went back—and he looked in there for a long time. Then he came over to me, and you know how his face sort of gets red when he's really mad? Well, this time he was so mad that his face was absolutely white. And when he talked to me, I don't think he actually opened his mouth; and I could barely hear him, he was talking so low. And he said, 'Have that removed. Now. Have Mr. Shelby's furniture put back in his office. Have Mr. Shelby see me.'"

My, my. You would think Ted would have known better, wouldn't you? But then, by now you should have a pretty firm idea of just why it is those offices are set up as they are.

Questions

1. How would you characterize the culture in this company? What are the dominant values?
2. Why did Ted Shelby's change experiment fail? To what extent did Ted use the appropriate change tools to increase employee communication and participation?
3. What would you recommend Ted do to change his relationship with subordinates? Is it possible for a manager to change cultural values if the rest of the organization, especially top management, does not agree?

SOURCE: R. Richard Ritti and G. Ray Funkhouser, *The Ropes to Skip & The Ropes to Know,* 3d. ed. (New York: Wiley, 1987), 176–177. Reprinted by permission of John Wiley & Sons, Inc.

Endnotes

1. Eryn Brown, "Is Intuit Headed for a Meltdown?" *Fortune,* August 18, 1997, 200–202.

2. Frances Cairncross, *The Death of Distance,* (Boston, Mass.: Harvard Business School Press, 1997); Nikhil Deogun and Jonathan Karp, "Rivals Revive Cola Scuffle," *The Asian Wall Street Journal,* April 27, 1998, 12.

3. Gary Hamel, "Turning Your Business Upside Down," *Fortune,* June 23, 1997, 87–88.

4. Tim Carvell, "The Crazy Record Business: These Prices Really *Are* Insane," *Fortune,* August 4, 1997, 109–115.

5. Peter Coy and Gary McWilliams, "Electricity: The Power Shift Ahead," *Business Week,* December 2, 1996, 78–82; Chuck Hutchcraft, "Fiscal Worries Pain La Rabida in Its 100th Year," *Chicago Tribune,* March 17, 1996, Sec. 5, 1, 6.

6. Richard L. Daft, *Organization Theory and Design,* 5th ed. (St. Paul, Minn.: West, 1995).

7. L. J. Bourgeois, "Strategy and Environment: A Conceptual Integration," *Academy of Management Review* 5 (1980), 25–39.

8. Lawrence Chimerine, "The New Economic Realities in Business," *Management Review,* January 1997, 12–17; Ram Charan, "The Rules Have Changed," *Fortune,* March 16, 1998, 159–162; and Lisa Benavides, "Handful of Tennessee Companies Feel a Pinch," *The Tennessean,* September 5, 1998, 1E, 2E.

9. Richard I. Kirkland, Jr., "Entering a New Age of Boundless Competition," *Fortune,* March 14, 1988, 40–48; and Kenichi Ohmae, "Managing in a Borderless World," *Harvard Business Review* (May–June 1989), 152–161.

10. Nancy J. Perry, "The Arms Makers' Next Battle," *Fortune,* August 27, 1990, 84–88.

11. Eric Schine, Amy Borrus, John Carey, and Geoffery Smith, "The Defense Whizzies Making It in Civvies," *Business Week,* September 7, 1992, 88–90.

12. Gene Bylinsky, "Mutant Materials," *Fortune,* October 13, 1997, 140–147; Richard A. Melcher and Amy Barrett, with Andrew Osterland, "Grains That Taste Like Meat?" *Business Week,* May 25, 1998, 44.

13. William B. Johnston, "Global Work Force 2000: The New World Labor Market," *Harvard Business Review* (March–April 1991), 115–127.

14. *Population Profile of the United States 1995,* United States Department of Commerce, Bureau of the Census, July 1995; Carol D'Amico, *Workforce 2020—Work and Workers in the 21st Century,* Hudson Institute, 1997; and Melinda Beck, "Next Population Bulge Shows Its Might," *The Wall Street Journal,* February 3, 1997, B1, B5.

15. Nicholas Imparato and Oren Harari, *Jumping the Curve: Innovation and Strategic Choice in an Age of Transition* (San Francisco: Jossey-Bass, 1994), 121.

16. David Lieberman, "Keeping up with the Murdochs," *Business Week,* March 20, 1989, 32–34; Don Lee Bohl, ed., *Tying the Corporate Knot* (New York: American Management Association, 1989); and Joseph Pereira, "The Toy Industry, Too, Is Merging Like Crazy to Win Selling Power," *The Wall Street Journal,* October 28, 1994, A1, A13.

17. Paul Magnusson and John Carey, with Elisabeth Malkin, "Eating Scared," *Business Week,* September 8, 1997, 30–32.

18. Linda Himelstein and Laura Zinn, with Maria Mallory, John Carey, Richard S. Dunham, and Joan O'C. Hamilton, "Tobacco: Does It Have a Future?" *Business Week,* July 4, 1994, 24–29; Bob Ortega, "Aging Activists Turn, Turn, Turn Attention to Wal-Mart Protests," *The Wall Street Journal,* October 11, 1994, A1, A8; and Richard L. Daft, *Management,* 3d ed. (Fort Worth, Texas: The Dryden Press, 1994), 44.

19. Walecia Konrad and Gail DeGeorge, "U.S. Companies Go for the Gray," *Business Week,* April 3, 1989, 64–67.

20. Jenny C. McCune, "In the Shadow of Wal-Mart," *Management Review,* December 1994, 10–16.

21. Michael R. Czinkota and Ilkka A. Ronkainen, "Global Marketing 2000: A Marketing Survival Guide," *Marketing Management* (winter 1992), 37–42.

22. Ian Austen, "Hooked on the Net," *Canadian Business,* June 26 July 10, 1998, 95–103; Daniel Stoffman, "Mr. Clean," *Canadian Business,* June 1996, 59–65; and John Lorinc, "The Death of the Dream?" *Canadian Business,* October 1993, 36–50.

23. Robert B. Duncan, "Characteristics of Organizational Environment and Perceived Environmental Uncertainty," *Administrative Science Quarterly* 17 (1972), 313–327; and Daft, *Organization Theory and Design.*

24. David B. Jemison, "The Importance of Boundary Spanning Roles in Strategic Decision-Making," *Journal of Management Studies* 21 (1984), 131–152; and Marc J. Dollinger, "Environmental Boundary Spanning and Information Processing Effects on Organizational Performance," *Academy of Management Journal* 27 (1984), 351–368.

25. David Steitz, "Let the Customer Be Your Guide," *Nation's Business,* March 1995, 4.

26. Brian Dumaine, "Corporate Spies Snoop to Conquer," *Fortune,* November 7, 1988, 68–76; Richard S. Teitelbaum, "The New Race for Intelligence," *Fortune,* November 2, 1992, 104–107; Hugh McBride, "They Snoop to Conquer," *Canadian Business,* July 1997, 45–47; and Stan Crock, Geoffrey Smith, Joseph Weber, Richard A. Melcher, and Linda Himelstein, "They Snoop to Conquer," *Business Week,* October 28, 1996, 172–176.

27. R. T. Lenz and Jack L. Engledow, "Environmental Analysis Units and Strategic Decision-Making: A Field Study of Selected 'Leading Edge' Corporations," *Strategic Management Journal* 7 (1986), 69–89; and Mansour Javidan, "The Impact

of Environmental Uncertainty on Long-Range Planning Practices of the U.S. Savings and Loan Industry," *Strategic Management Journal* 5 (1984), 381–392.

28. Tom Burns and G. M. Stalker, *The Management of Innovation* (London: Tavistock, 1961); J. C. Spender and Eric Kessler, "Managing the Uncertainties of Innovation: Extending Thompson (1967)," *Human Relations* 48, no. 1 (1995), 35–56; and Stephen Ackroyd, "On the Structure and Dynamics of Some Small, UK-Based Information Technology Firms," *Journal of Management Studies* 32, no. 2 (March 1995), 141–161.

29. John Huey, "Waking up to the New Economy," *Fortune,* June 27, 1994, 36–46.

30. Brian Bremner with Zachary Schiller, Tim Smart, and William J. Holstein, "*Keiretsu* Connections," *Business Week,* July 22, 1996, 52–54.

31. James E. Svatko, "Joint Ventures," *Small Business Reports,* December 1988, 65–70; and Joshua Hyatt, "The Partnership Route," *Inc.,* December 1988, 145–148.

32. Ellen Neuborne, "Look Who's Picking Levi's Pocket," *Business Week,* September 8, 1997, 68–69.

33. John Carey, "Big Tobacco's Hidden War," *Business Week,* November 10, 1997, 139–140; and Linda Himelstein, et al., "Tobacco: Does It Have a Future?" *Business Week,* July 4, 1994, 24–29.

34. Daniel Pearl and Gabriella Stern, "How GM Managed to Wring Pickup Pact and Keep on Truckin'," *The Wall Street Journal,* December 5, 1994, A1, A8.

35. Edmund Faltermayer, "The Thaw in Washington," *Fortune* (The New American Century), 1991, 46–51; David B. Yoffie, "How an Industry Builds Political Advantage," *Harvard Business Review* (May–June 1988), 82–89; and Douglas Harbrecht, "How to Win Friends and Influence Lawmakers," *Business Week,* November 7, 1988, 36.

36. David Whitford, "Built by Association," *Inc.,* July 1994, 71–75.

37. Yoash Wiener, "Forms of Value Systems: A Focus on Organizational Effectiveness and Culture Change and Maintenance," *Academy of Management Review* 13 (1988), 534–545; V. Lynne Meek, "Organizational Culture: Origins and Weaknesses," *Organization Studies* 9 (1988), 453–473; John J. Sherwood, "Creating Work Cultures with Competitive Advantage," *Organizational Dynamics* (winter 1988), 5–27; and Andrew D. Brown and Ken Starkey, "The Effect of Organizational Culture on Communication and Information," *Journal of Management Studies* 31, no. 6 (November 1994): 807–828.

38. Ralph H. Kilmann, Mary J. Saxton, and Roy Serpa, "Issues in Understanding and Changing Culture," *California Management Review* 28 (winter 1986), 87–94; and Linda Smircich, "Concepts of Culture and Organizational Analysis," *Administrative Science Quarterly* 28 (1983), 339–358.

39. Based on Edgar H. Schein, *Organizational Culture and Leadership,* 2d ed. (San Francisco: Jossey-Bass, 1992), 3–27.

40. James C. Collins, "Change is Good—But First Know What Should Never Change," *Fortune,* May 29, 1995, 141; and Robert Levering and Milton Moskowitz, "The 100 Best Companies to Work For in America," *Fortune,* January 12, 1998, 84–95.

41. "Make No Mistake," *Inc.,* June 1989, 115.

42. Patrick Flanagan, "The ABCs of Changing Corporate Culture," *Management Review,* July 1995, 57–61.

43. Elizabeth Weil, "Every Leader Tells a Story," *Fast Company,* June–July 1998, 38–39; and Robert Specter, "The Nordstom Way," *Corporate University Review,* May–June 1997, 24–25, 60.

44. Gregory M. Bounds, Gregory H. Dobbins, and Oscar S. Fowler, *Management: A Total Quality Perspective* (Cincinnati: South-Western College Publishing, 1995), 353–354.

45. Terrence E. Deal and Allan A. Kennedy, *Corporate Cultures: The Rites and Rituals of Corporate Life* (Reading, Mass.: Addison-Wesley, 1982).

46. Barbara Ettorre, "Retooling People and Processes," *Management Review,* June 1995, 19–23.

47. Harrison M. Trice and Janice M. Beyer, "Studying Organizational Cultures through Rites and Ceremonials," *Academy of Management Review* 9 (1984), 653–669.

48. Alan Farnham, "Mary Kay's Lessons in Leadership," *Fortune,* September 20, 1993, 68–77.

49. Jennifer A. Chatman and Karen A. Jehn, "Assessing the Relationship Between Industry Characteristics and Organizational Culture: How Different Can You Be?" *Academy of Management Journal* 37, no. 3 (1994): 522–553.

50. John P. Kotter and James L. Heskett, *Corporate Culture and Performance* (New York: The Free Press, 1992).

51. David Leonhardt, "McDonald's: Can It Regain Its Golden Touch?" *Business W46.5 pteek,* March 9, 1998, 70–77.

52. Jeffrey Sonnenfeld, *The Hero's Farewell: What Happens When CEOs Retire* (New York: Oxford University Press, 1988).

53. William A. Schiermann, "Organizational Change: Lessons from a Turnaround," *Management Review,* April 1992, 34–37.

54. Ralph H. Kilmann, Mary J. Saxton, Roy Serpa, and Associates, *Gaining Control of the Corporate Culture* (San Francisco: Jossey-Bass, 1985).

55. Ralph Kilmann, "Corporate Culture," *Psychology Today,* April 1985, 62–68.

56. Morty Lefkoe, "Why So Many Mergers Fail," *Fortune,* June 20, 1987, 113–114.

57. Ibid.; and Afsaneh Nahavandi and Ali R. Malekzadeh, "Acculturation in Mergers and Acquisitions," *Academy of Management Review* 13 (1988), 79–90.

58. Julia Flynn and Keith Naughton with Ariane Sains, "A Drug Giant's Allergic Reaction," *Business Week,* February 3, 1997, 122–125; and Thomas A. Stewart, "Rate Your Readiness to Change," *Fortune,* February 7, 1994, 106–110.

59. Thomas J. Peters and Robert H. Waterman, Jr., *In Search of Excellence* (New York: Warner, 1988).

60. Deanne N. Den Hartog, Jaap J. Van Muijen, and Paul L. Koopman, "Linking Transformational Leadership and Organizational Culture," *The Journal of Leadership Studies* 3, no. 4 (1996): 68–83; and Schein, "Organizational Culture."

61. Russell Mitchell, "Jack Welch: How Good a Manager?" *Business Week,* December 14, 1987, 92–103.

62. Bob Filipczak, "Are We Having Fun Yet?" *Training,* April 1995, 48–56; and Steve Lohr, "On the Road with Chairman Lou," *The New York Times,* June 26, 1994, Section 3, p. 1.

63. "Southwest Airlines' Herb Kelleher: Unorthodoxy at Work," an interview with William G. Lee, *Management Review,* January 1995, 9–12.

64. Ellyn E. Spragins, "Motivation: Out of the Frying Pan," *Inc.,* December 1991, 157.

65. Tom Peters and Nancy Austin, *A Passion for Excellence: The Leadership Difference* (New York: Random House, 1985), 278.

Chapter 4

LEARNING OBJECTIVES

After studying this chapter, you should be able to

◎ Describe the emerging borderless world.

◎ Define international management and explain how it differs from the management of domestic business operations.

◎ Indicate how dissimilarities in the economic, sociocultural, and legal-political environments throughout the world can affect business operations.

◎ Describe market entry strategies that businesses use to develop foreign markets.

◎ Describe the characteristics of a multinational corporation.

◎ Explain the challenges of managing in a global environment.

Managing in a Global Environment

MANAGEMENT PROBLEM

Wal-Mart's first blunder was stocking its shelves with footballs in a country where soccer rules. In the suburbs of São Paulo, Brazil, the highly successful U.S. company is discovering that its merchandise, tactics, and attitudes don't always translate well internationally. With opportunities for growth dwindling at home, Wal-Mart has embarked on a crusade to bring "everyday low prices" to the emerging markets of Brazil, Argentina, China, and Indonesia. But doing business internationally is a learning—and sometimes a losing—process. In its first two years in South America, Wal-Mart lost an estimated $48 million. Part of the difficulty is due to stiff competition from companies such as Brazil's Grupo Pao de Acucar SA and France's Carrefour SA, which have much stronger footholds in the region. However, analysts also blame Wal-Mart. By failing to do its homework, Wal-Mart made mistakes such as stocking footballs instead of soccer balls, live trout instead of sushi, and leaf blowers that are useless in the concrete world of São Paulo. It brought in stock-handling equipment that didn't work with standardized local pallets and installed a computerized bookkeeping system that didn't take Brazil's complicated tax system into account. Perhaps most damaging, the company's insistence on doing things "the Wal-Mart way" has alienated some local suppliers and employees. Wal-Mart CEO David Glass says such missteps are inevitable in entering a new market, however, and he believes Wal-Mart will soon be the dominant retailer in South America. Yet he admits, "You pay a lot of tuition to learn what you need to learn."[1]

Why do you think Wal-Mart has had such difficulty duplicating its U.S. success overseas? What recommendations would you have for Wal-Mart managers as they continue their quest in emerging markets?

Wal-Mart is a well-established company facing enormous challenges in developing a successful international business. Other large, successful U.S. companies, including Federal Express and Nike, also have found that "the rest of the world is not the United States of America," as one FedEx competitor put it. However, all of these companies recognize that international expansion is necessary, despite the risks. Companies such as McDonald's, IBM, Coca-Cola, Kellogg, General Motors, and Caterpillar Tractor all rely on international business for a substantial portion of sales and profits. These companies face special problems in trying to tailor their products and business management to the unique needs of foreign countries—but if they succeed, the whole world is their marketplace.

How important is international business to the study of management? *If you are not thinking international, you are not thinking business management.* It's that serious. As you read this page, ideas, takeover plans, capital investments, business strategies, Reeboks, services, and T-shirts are traveling around the planet by telephone, computer, fax, and overnight mail. A dramatic example of how easy it is for business to cross national borders occurred during the Gulf War. When Iraq first attacked Kuwait, a shrewd Kuwaiti banker began faxing key records to a subsidiary in Bahrain. Even with transmissions being regularly interrupted due to the shooting, by the end of the day all of the bank's key records had been transferred. The next morning, the bank opened as a Bahrain institution, beyond the reach of the Iraqis and not subject to the U.S. freeze on Kuwaiti assets. Essentially, a bank was moved from one country to another via a fax machine.[2]

Rapid advances in technology and communications have made the international dimension an important part of the external environment that is discussed in Chapter 3. Companies can locate different parts of the organization wherever it makes the most business sense—top leadership in one place, technical brainpower and production in other locales. For example, Samsung, the Korean electronics giant, moved its semiconductor-making facilities to the Silicon Valley to be closer to the best scientific brains in the industry. Canada's Northern Telecom selected a location in the southwest of England as its world manufacturing center for a new fixed-access radio product. Siemens of Germany has moved its electronic ultrasound division to the

Fuji Photo Film Co., Kodak's major competitor in the U.S. market, is operating in a global environment with international management. Headquartered in Japan, Fuji has purchased Wal-Mart's six wholesale photo labs (15 percent of the U.S. photo-processing market) and it opened a highly automated $300 million photographic paper plant in Greenwood, S.C. last year. Approximately 31 percent of Fuji's production is outside of Japan, up from 3.5 percent in 1987. In the photo, the Fuji blimp is used as part of a marketing campaign in France.

United States, while the U.S. company DuPont shifted its electronic operations headquarters to Japan.[3]

If you think you are isolated from global influence, think again. Even if you do not budge from your hometown, your company may be purchased tomorrow by the English, Japanese, or Germans. People working for Firestone, Dr. Pepper, Pillsbury, Carnation, Shell Oil, and CBS Records already work for foreign bosses. Further, most American machine tool companies have been foreign-owned for years.

All this means that the environment for companies is becoming extremely complex and extremely competitive. Less-developed countries are challenging mature countries in a number of industries. India has become a major player in software development, and electronics manufacture is rapidly leaving Japan for other countries in Asia.

This chapter introduces basic concepts about the global environment and international management. First, we consider the difficulty managers have operating in an increasingly borderless world. We will address challenges—economic, legal-political, and sociocultural—facing companies within the global business environment. Then we will discuss multinational corporations and touch upon the various types of strategies and techniques needed for entering and succeeding in foreign markets.

A Borderless World

Why do companies such as Wal-Mart, Federal Express, and Nike want to pursue a global strategy, despite failures and losses? They recognize that business is becoming a unified global field as trade barriers fall, communication becomes faster and cheaper, and consumer tastes in everything from clothing to cellular phones converge. Thomas Middelhoff of Germany's Bertelsmann AG, which purchased U.S. publisher Random House, put it this way: "There are no German and American companies. There are only successful and unsuccessful companies."[4]

Companies that think globally have a competitive edge. Consider Hong Kong's Johnson Electric Holdings Ltd., a $195 million producer of micromotors that power hair dryers, blenders, and automobile power windows and door locks. With factories in South China and a research and development lab in Hong Kong, Johnson is thousands of miles away from a leading automaker. Yet the company has cornered the market for electric gizmos for Detroit's Big Three by using new information technology. Via videoconferencing, Johnson design teams meet "face-to-face" for two hours each morning with their customers in the United States and Europe. The company's processes and procedures are so streamlined that Johnson can take a concept and deliver a prototype to the United States in six weeks.[5]

In addition, domestic markets are saturated for many companies. The only potential for significant growth lies overseas. Kimberly-Clark and Procter & Gamble, which spent years slugging it out in the now-flat U.S.

Today's companies operate in a borderless world. Procter & Gamble sales in Southeast Asia are only 3 percent of its worldwide sales, but those numbers are increasing. These shoppers are purchasing P&G's diaper products, Pampers, in Malaysia.

diaper market, are targeting new markets such as China, India, Israel, Russia, and Brazil. The demand for steel in China, India, and Brazil together is expected to grow 10 percent annually in the coming years—three times the U.S. rate. Nucor is opening a minimill in Thailand and partnering with a Brazilian company for a $700 million steel mill in northeastern Brazil. Other steel companies, such as LTV Corp. and North Star Steel, are moving into Asia, Europe, and Australia.[6]

The reality of today's borderless companies also means consumers can no longer tell from which country they're buying. Your Mercury Tracer may have come from Mexico, while a neighbor's Nissan may have been built in Tennessee. A Gap polo shirt may be made from cloth cut in the United States but sewn in Honduras. Eat an all-American Whopper and you've just purchased from a British company.[7]

Corporations can participate in the international arena on a variety of levels, and the process of globalization typically passes through four distinct stages.

1. In the *domestic stage*, market potential is limited to the home country, with all production and marketing facilities located at home. Managers may be aware of the global environment and may want to consider foreign involvement.

2. In the *international stage*, exports increase, and the company usually adopts a *multidomestic* approach, probably using an international division to deal with the marketing of products in several countries individually.

3. In the *multinational stage*, the company has marketing and production facilities located in many countries, with more than one-third of its sales outside the home country. Companies typically have a single home country, although they may opt for a *binational* approach, whereby two parent companies in separate countries maintain ownership and control. Examples are Unilever and the Royal Dutch/Shell Group, both of which are based in the United Kingdom and the Netherlands.

4. Finally, the *global (or stateless) stage* of corporate international development transcends any single home country. These corporations operate in true global fashion, making sales and acquiring resources in whatever country offers the best opportunities and lowest cost. At this stage, ownership, control, and top management tend to be dispersed among several nationalities.[8]

As the number of "stateless" corporations increases, so too the awareness of national borders decreases, as reflected by the frequency of foreign participation at the management level. Rising managers are expected to know a second or third language and to have international experience. The need for global managers is intense. Corporations around the world want the brightest and best candidates for global management, and young managers who want their careers to move forward recognize the importance of global experience. According to Harvard Business School professor Christopher Bartlett, author of *Managing Across Borders*, people should try to get global exposure when they're young in order to start building skills and networks that will grow throughout their careers.[9] Consider the makeup of global companies in today's environment. Nestlé (Switzerland) personifies the stateless corporation with 98 percent of sales and 96 percent of employees outside the home country. Nestlé's CEO is German-born Helmut Maucher, and half of the company's general managers are non-Swiss. Maucher puts strong faith in regional managers who are native to the region and know the local culture. The combination of strong brands and autonomous regional managers has made Nestlé the largest branded food company in Mexico, Brazil, Chile, and Thailand, and the company is on its way to becoming the leader in Vietnam and China as well. U.S. firms also show a growing international flavor. The global media giant News Corporation, owner of Fox Broadcasting Company, is run by Rupert Murdoch, who was born in Australia and educated in Britain and is now an American citizen. At British firm ICI, 40 percent of the top 170 executives are non-British. Meanwhile, German companies such as Hoechst and BASF rely on local managers to run foreign operations.[10]

Both Ford Motor Company and IBM are globalizing their management structures. To aid its efforts, IBM has studied power equipment giant Asea Brown Boveri Ltd. (ABB), a major player in the global game. ABB generates more than $25 billion in revenues and employs 240,000 in Europe, North and South America, Asia, and India. CEO Percy Barnevik points out that ABB has no geographical center. With a Swedish CEO, a Zurich headquarters, a multinational board, and financial results posted in American dollars, ABB is "a company with many homes."[11]

The International Business Environment

International management is the management of business operations conducted in more than one country. The fundamental tasks of business management, including the financing, production, and distribution of products and services, do not change in any substantive way when a firm is transacting business across international borders. The basic management functions of planning, organizing, leading, and controlling are the same whether a company operates domestically or internationally. However, managers will experience greater difficulties and risks when performing these management functions on an international scale. For example:

international management
The management of business operations conducted in more than one country.

- Wal-Mart has encountered difficulties in translating the warehouse club concept to Hong Kong. As a young accountant eyed a 4-pound jar of peanut butter, he said, "The price is right, but where would I put it?"[12]

- When Coors Beer tried to translate a slogan with the phrase "Turn It Loose" into Spanish, it came out as "Drink Coors and Get Diarrhea." Budweiser goofed when its Spanish ad promoted Bud Lite as "Filling, less delicious."

- Nike ran a commercial with people from various countries supposedly saying "Just Do It" in foreign languages, but a Samburu tribesman was actually saying, "I don't want these; give me big shoes."

- United Airlines discovered that even colors can doom a product. The airline handed out white carnations when it started flying from Hong Kong, only to discover that to many Asians such flowers represent death and bad luck.[13]

Although these examples may seem humorous, there's nothing funny about them to managers trying to operate in a competitive global environment. Companies seeking to expand their international presence on the Internet also can run into cross-cultural problems, as discussed in the Technology box. What should managers of emerging global companies look for

Cross-Cultural Web Traps

The World Wide Web is a valuable resource for companies hoping to expand in international markets. However, there are inherent problems with producing a Web site that can easily reach potential customers in over 100 countries. Most Web sites are produced in English, the most widely spoken language in the world. However, most people speak English as a second language and don't understand its nuances. As a result, miscommunications are bound to occur. Web site developers should avoid terms that don't translate well and can be easily misunderstood, such as slang, euphemisms, cliches, proverbs, and military terminology. For example, phrases often used by the U.S. business press, such as "prepare the troops" and "infiltrate," are commonly understood by American readers, but could cause problems or confusion with overseas customers. Cultural misunderstandings also occur through the use of graphics. The thumbs up sign, for example, means approval or encouragement to Americans and Europeans, but in Greece, the gesture is an obscenity. Further, colors may have specific connotations in different countries. For example, while purple is a sign of royalty in some parts of the world, in others it is associated with death.

Experts recommend that whenever possible, companies localize their Web sites, by focusing on select target markets and by providing easily recognizable hotlinks, such as the country's flag, to take surfers to the localized page in the appropriate language. Several companies presently provide services and products to aid in localizing business Web sites. For example, Webtrans (webtrans.com), Weblations (weblations.com), International Communications (intl.com), and Logos Corp. (logos-ca.com) will take a Web site and manually translate the entire site, including graphics. Browser add-ons also are available (try globalink.com) to translate sites written in German, Italian, Spanish, or French into English (or vice versa) so that anyone surfing the Net can browse foreign language sites.

Increasingly, creating a good Web site is becoming an important part of corporate existence. To be sure they're communicating the right message, developers should be guided by principles of clarity, simplicity, and cultural awareness.

SOURCE: Rick Borelli, "A Worldwide Language TRAP," *Management Review*, October 1997, 52–54.

to avoid obvious international mistakes? When they are comparing one country with another, the economic, legal-political, and sociocultural sectors present the greatest difficulties. Key factors to understand in the international environment are summarized in Exhibit 4.1.

The Economic Environment

The economic environment represents the economic conditions in the country where the international organization operates. This part of the environment includes such factors as economic development; infrastructure; resource and product markets; exchange rates; and inflation, interest rates, and economic growth.

Economic Development. Economic development differs widely among the countries and regions of the world. Countries can be categorized as either "developing" or "developed." The developing countries are referred to as *less-developed countries (LDCs)*. The criterion traditionally used to classify countries as developed or developing is *per capita income*, which is the income generated by the nation's production of goods and services divided by total population. The developing countries have low per capita incomes. LDCs generally are located in Asia, Africa, and South America. Developed countries include North America, Europe, and Japan. Today, developing countries in Southeast Asia, Latin America, and Eastern Europe are driving global growth.[14]

Exhibit *4.1*

*Key Factors in the
International Environment*

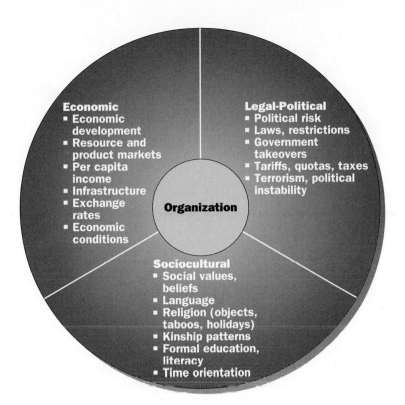

Most international business firms are headquartered in the wealthier, economically advanced countries. However, smart companies are investing heavily in Asia, Eastern Europe, and Latin America. Despite the economic convulsions that have rocked Southeast Asia, large Western companies such as Ford, Procter & Gamble, and Coca-Cola continue to see Asia as the big market of the future. Ford, for example, currently does only 1 percent of its worldwide sales in Southeast Asia, but expects that to expand to 10 percent within the next five years.[15] Although they face risks and challenges today, these companies stand to reap huge benefits in the future. In China, Malaysia, and Brazil, for example, most of the population still is nearly ten years away from their peak buying years.

Infrastructure. A country's physical facilities that support economic activities make up its **infrastructure,** which includes transportation facilities such as airports, highways, and railroads; energy-producing facilities such as utilities and power plants; and communication facilities such as telephone lines and radio stations. Companies operating in LDCs must contend with lower levels of technology and perplexing logistical, distribution, and communication problems. Mike Mazzola, an executive for Reuters Ltd., found that, in Mexico, getting a telephone installed could take up to a year. Even after he got one, he often had to dial several times before the call would go through. Undeveloped infrastructures represent opportunities for some firms, such as United Technologies Corporation, based in Hartford, Connecticut, whose businesses include jet engines, air conditioning and heating systems, and elevators. As countries such as China, Russia, and Vietnam open their markets, new buildings need elevators and air and heat systems; opening remote regions for commerce requires more jet engines and helicopters.[16]

infrastructure
A country's physical facilities that support economic activities.

Projects such as Beijing's fourth ring road, Shenzhen's subway, and, in the photo, the Three Gorges dam project are examples of ongoing megaprojects in China. Analysts expect the Chinese government to boost its spending by 20 percent on public works and other projects to improve the infrastructure *in China.*

Resource and Product Markets.   When operating in another country, company managers must evaluate the market demand for their products. If market demand is high, managers may choose to export products to that country. To develop plants, however, resource markets for providing needed raw materials and labor must also be available. For example, the greatest challenge for McDonald's, which now sells Big Macs on every continent except Antarctica, is to obtain supplies of everything from potatoes to hamburger buns to plastic straws. At McDonald's in Cracow, the burgers come from a Polish plant, partly owned by Chicago-based OSI Industries; the onions come from Fresno, California; the buns come from a production and distribution center near Moscow; and the potatoes come from a plant in Aldrup, Germany. McDonald's tries to contract with local suppliers when possible. In Thailand, McDonald's actually helped farmers cultivate Idaho russet potatoes of sufficient quality to produce their golden french fries.[17]

Exchange Rates.   *Exchange rate* is the rate at which one country's currency is exchanged for another country's. Changes in the exchange rate can have major implications for the profitability of international operations that exchange millions of dollars into other currencies every day.[18] For example, assume that the American dollar is exchanged for 8 French francs. If the dollar increases in value to 10 francs, U.S. goods will be more expensive in France because it will take more francs to buy a dollar's worth of U.S. goods. It will be more difficult to export American goods to France, and profits will be slim. If the dollar drops to a value of 6 francs, on the other hand, U.S. goods will be cheaper in France and can be exported at a profit.

The Legal-Political Environment

Businesses must deal with unfamiliar political systems when they go international, as well as with more government supervision and regulation. Government officials and the general public often view foreign companies as outsiders or even intruders and are suspicious of their impact on economic independence and political sovereignty. Some of the major legal-political concerns affecting international business are political risk, political instability, and laws and regulations.

Political Risk. A company's **political risk** is defined as its risk of loss of assets, earning power, or managerial control due to politically based events or actions by host governments.[19] Political risk includes government takeovers of property and acts of violence directed against a firm's properties or employees. Because such acts are not uncommon, companies must formulate special plans and programs to guard against unexpected losses. For example, Hercules, Inc., a large chemical company, has increased the number of security guards at several of its European plants. Some companies actually buy political risk insurance, especially as they move into high-risk areas such as Eastern Europe, China, and Brazil. Political risk analysis has emerged as a critical component of environmental assessment for multinational organizations.[20]

Political Instability. Another frequently cited problem for international companies is political instability, which includes riots, revolutions, civil disorders, and frequent changes in government. Political instability increases uncertainty. Civil wars and large-scale violence have occurred in Indonesia, Malaysia, Thailand, Sri Lanka (Ceylon), and Myanmar (Burma) in recent decades. Companies moving into former Soviet republics face continued instability because of changing government personnel and political philosophies.

Although most companies would prefer to do business in stable countries, some of the greatest growth opportunities lie in areas characterized by instability. The greatest threat of violence is in countries experiencing political, ethnic, or religious upheaval. In China, for example, political winds have shifted rapidly, and often dangerously. Yet it is the largest potential market in the world for the goods and services of developed countries, and Xerox, AT&T, Motorola, and Kodak are busy making deals there.

U.S. firms or companies linked to the United States often are subject to major threats in countries characterized by political instability. Peruvian revolutionaries have targeted Pizza Hut and Kentucky Fried Chicken. Sixteen foreign managers were murdered in Russia in one recent year, and others working there often hire bodyguards. Even in countries that seem safe, such as Spain and Great Britain, terrorists have bombed tourist attractions.[21]

Laws and Regulations. Government laws and regulations differ from country to country and make manufacturing and sales a true challenge for international firms. Host governments have myriad laws concerning libel statutes, consumer protection, information and labeling, employment and safety, and wages. International companies must learn these rules and regulations and abide by them. For example, French law forbids the use of children in advertising, and Germany prohibits the use of competitive claims.[22] In Mexico City, government inspectors made a surprise visit to Wal-Mart's Supercenter and charged that more than 10,000 of the store's items were improperly labeled or lacked instructions in Spanish. Likewise, Santa Clara, California-based Synergy Semiconductors found its partnership efforts in what used to be East Germany complicated by German labor laws.[23]

The most visible changes in legal-political factors grow out of international trade agreements and the emerging international trade alliance system. Consider,

political risk
A company's risk of loss of assets, earning power, or managerial control due to politically based events or actions by host governments.

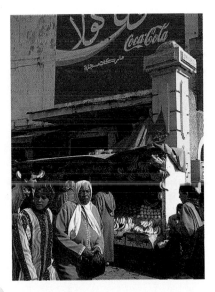

Despite the political risk, political instability, and the local laws and regulations of countries such as Morocco, The Coca-Cola Company earns about 80 percent of its profits from markets outside North America. The soft drink company was named in a recent Fortune *magazine survey as the number 1 company in the world in product quality, attracting and developing new talent, and overall global effectiveness.*

for example, the impact of the General Agreement on Tariffs and Trade (GATT), the European Union (EU), and the North American Free Trade Agreement (NAFTA).

General Agreement on Tariffs and Trade

The General Agreement on Tariffs and Trade (GATT), signed by 23 nations in 1947, started as a set of rules to ensure nondiscrimination, clear procedures, the negotiation of disputes, and the participation of lesser developed countries in international trade. Today, more than 100 member countries abide by the rules of GATT. The primary tools GATT uses to increase trade are tariff concessions, through which member countries agree to limit the level of tariffs they will impose on imports from other GATT members, and the **most favored nation** clause, which calls for each member country to grant to every other member country the most favorable treatment it accords to any country with respect to imports and exports.[24]

GATT has sponsored various rounds of international trade negotiations aimed at reducing trade restrictions. Most recently, the Uruguay Round (the first to be named for a developing country) involved 125 countries and cut more tariffs than ever before. The Round's multilateral trade agreement, which took effect January 1, 1995, is the most comprehensive pact since the original 1947 agreement. Most experts believe the potential benefits for each country far outweigh the temporary costs. The goal of GATT negotiations is to encourage closer relationships among member nations and to help the global marketplace operate more efficiently. The Uruguay Round also boldly moved the world closer to global free trade by calling for the establishment of the World Trade Organization (WTO). The WTO represents the maturation of GATT into a permanent global institution that can monitor international trade and has legal authority to arbitrate disputes on some 400 trade issues.[25]

most favored nation
A term describing a GATT clause that calls for member countries to grant other member countries the most favorable treatment they accord any country concerning imports and exports.

European Union

Formed in 1958 to improve economic and social conditions among its members, the European Economic Community, now called the European Union (EU), has expanded to a 15-nation alliance illustrated in Exhibit 4.2. Countries in Central and Eastern Europe hope economic and political conditions there will stabilize enough for them to begin joining soon.[26]

In the early 1980s, Europeans initiated steps to create a powerful single market system called *Europe '92*. The initiative called for creation of open markets for Europe's 340 million consumers. Europe '92 consisted of 282 directives proposing dramatic reform and deregulation in such areas as banking, insurance, health, safety standards, airlines, telecommunications, auto sales, social policy, and monetary union.

Initially opposed and later embraced by European industry, the increased competition and economies of scale within Europe will enable companies to grow large and efficient, becoming more competitive in U.S. and other world markets. Some observers fear that the EU will become a trade barrier, creating a "fortress Europe" that will be difficult to penetrate by companies in other nations.

The most significant aspect is the EU's monetary revolution and the introduction of the euro. The **euro** is the single European currency that will even-

euro
The single European currency that will replace up to 15 national currencies.

E x h i b i t *4.2*   *The Fifteen Nations within the EU*

tually replace up to 15 national currencies and unify a huge marketplace, creating a competitive $6.4 trillion economy second only to the United States.
In 1999, 11 countries—Germany, France, Spain, Italy, Ireland, the Netherlands, Austria, Belgium, Finland, Portugal, and Luxembourg—formed the
core group setting the exchange rates for adopting the single European currency, with the United Kingdom, Denmark, Greece, and Sweden expected to
join later. The goal is to have the euro replace all national currencies by mid-
2002.[27] The implications of a single European currency are enormous within
as well as outside Europe. As it replaces up to 15 European domestic currencies, the euro will affect legal contracts, financial management, sales and
marketing tactics, manufacturing, distribution, payroll, pensions, training,
taxes, and information management systems. Every corporation that does
business in or with EU countries will feel the impact.[28] In addition, economic
union is likely to speed deregulation, which has already reordered Europe's
corporate and competitive landscape.

There still is much opposition to the idea of economic and monetary union, but it seems likely it will eventually be accomplished. Although building alliances among countries is difficult, the benefits of doing so are overcoming divisions and disagreements. Canada, Mexico, and the United States have established what is expected to be an equally powerful alliance.

North American Free Trade Agreement (NAFTA)

The North American Free Trade Agreement, which went into effect on January 1, 1994, merged the United States, Canada, and Mexico into a megamarket with more than 360 million consumers. The agreement breaks down tariffs and trade restrictions on most agricultural and manufactured products over a 15-year period. The treaty builds upon the 1989 U.S.–Canada agreement and is expected to spur growth and investment, increase exports, and expand jobs in all three nations.[29]

The 14-month negotiations climaxed August 12, 1992, with agreements in a number of key areas.

- *Agriculture.* Immediate removal of tariffs on half of U.S. farm exports to Mexico with phasing out of remaining tariffs over 15 years.

- *Autos.* Immediate 50 percent cut of Mexican tariffs on autos, reaching zero in 10 years. Mandatory 62.5 percent North American content on cars and trucks to qualify for duty-free status.

- *Transport.* U.S. trucking of international cargo allowed in Mexican border area by mid-1990s and throughout Mexico by the end of the decade.

- *Intellectual property.* Mexico's protection for pharmaceutical patents boosted to international standards and North American copyrights safeguarded.

NAFTA has spurred the entry of small businesses into the global arena. Jeff Victor, general manager of Treatment Products, Ltd., which makes car cleaners and waxes, credits NAFTA for his surging export volume. Prior to the pact, Mexican tariffs as high as 20 percent made it impossible for the Chicago-based company to expand its presence south of the border. Similarly, StoneHeart, Inc., of Cheney, Washington, began selling its scooters for people with leg or foot injuries to a distributor in Canada.[30] Although many groups in the United States opposed the agreement, warning of job loss and the potential for industrial "ghost towns," results so far have been positive. Ross Perot once warned of a "giant sucking sound" as Mexico inhaled jobs from America, but today that sound seems to be only an echo. Interviews with workers in various St. Louis area companies recently found not a single person who knew of a colleague, friend, or relative out of work because of international trade.[31] Although criticism of NAFTA continues, many people believe there are important benefits. Experts stress that NAFTA will enable companies in all three countries to compete more effectively with rival Asian and European companies.[32]

Trade Alliances: Promise or Pitfall?

The creation of trading blocs is an increasingly popular part of international business. Plans are underway for the Southeast Asian Nations (ASEAN) free trade agreement, and the future will likely see the creation of a new trade alliance in Central and South America. These developments will provide cheaper Mexican watermelons in the United States, more Israeli shoes in Central Europe, and more Colombian roses in Venezuela. These agreements entail a new future for international companies and pose a range of new questions for international managers.

- Will the creation of multiple trade blocs lead to economic warfare among them?
- Will trade blocs gradually evolve into three powerful trading blocs composed of the American hemisphere, Europe (from Ireland across the former Soviet Union), and the "yen bloc" encompassing the Pacific Rim?
- Will the expansion of global, stateless corporations bypass trading zones and provide economic balance among them?[33]

Only the future will provide answers to these questions. International managers and global corporations will both shape and be shaped by these important trends.

The Sociocultural Environment

A nation's **culture** includes the shared knowledge, beliefs, and values, as well as the common modes of behavior and ways of thinking, among members of a society. Cultural factors are more perplexing than political and economic factors in foreign countries. Culture is intangible, pervasive, and difficult to learn. It is absolutely imperative that international businesses comprehend the significance of local cultures and deal with them effectively.

culture
The shared knowledge, beliefs, values, behaviors, and ways of thinking among members of a society.

Social Values. Research done by Geert Hofstede on 116,000 IBM employees in 40 countries identified four dimensions of national value systems that influence organizational and employee working relationships.[34] Examples of how countries rate on the four dimensions are shown in Exhibit 4.3.

1. *Power distance.* High **power distance** means that people accept inequality in power among institutions, organizations, and people. Low power distance means that people expect equality in power. Countries that value

power distance
The degree to which people accept inequality in power among institutions, organizations, and people.

Country	Power Distance[a]	Uncertainty Avoidance[b]	Individualism[c]	Masculinity[d]
Australia	7	7	2	5
Costa Rica	8 (tie)	2 (tie)	10	9
France	3	2 (tie)	4	7
West Germany	8 (tie)	5	5	3
India	2	9	6	6
Japan	5	1	7	1
Mexico	1	4	8	2
Sweden	10	10	3	10
Thailand	4	6	9	8
United States	6	8	1	4

[a] 1=highest power distance
10=lowest power distance
[b] 1=highest uncertainty avoidance
10=lowest uncertainty avoidance
[c] 1=highest individualism
10=highest collectivisim
[d] 1=highest masculinity
10=highest femininity

Exhibit **4.3**

Rank Orderings of Ten Countries along Four Dimensions of National Value Systems

SOURCE: From Dorothy Marcic, *Organizational Behavior and Cases*, 4th ed. (St. Paul, Minn.: West, 1995). Based on Geert Hofstede, *Culture's Consequences* (London: Sage Publications, 1984); and *Cultures and Organizations: Software of the Mind* (New York: McGraw-Hill, 1991).

uncertainty avoidance
A value characterized by people's intolerance for uncertainty and ambiguity and resulting support for beliefs that promise certainty and conformity.

individualism
A preference for a loosely knit social framework in which individuals are expected to take care of themselves.

collectivism
A preference for a tightly knit social framework in which individuals look after one another and organizations protect their members' interests.

masculinity
A cultural preference for achievement, heroism, assertiveness, work centrality, and material success.

femininity
A cultural preference for cooperation, group decision making, and quality of life.

ethnocentrism
A cultural attitude marked by the tendency to regard one's own culture as superior to others.

high power distance are Malaysia, the Philippines, and Panama. Countries that value low power distance are Denmark, Austria, and Israel.

2. *Uncertainty avoidance.* High **uncertainty avoidance** means that members of a society feel uncomfortable with uncertainty and ambiguity and thus support beliefs that promise certainty and conformity. Low uncertainty avoidance means that people have high tolerance for the unstructured, the unclear, and the unpredictable. High uncertainty avoidance countries include Greece, Portugal, and Uruguay. Countries with low uncertainty avoidance values are Singapore and Jamaica.

3. *Individualism and collectivism.* **Individualism** reflects a value for a loosely knit social framework in which individuals are expected to take care of themselves. **Collectivism** means a preference for a tightly knit social framework in which individuals look after one another and organizations protect their members' interests. Countries with individualist values include the United States, Canada, Great Britain, and Australia. Countries with collectivist values are Guatemala, Ecuador, and Panama.

4. *Masculinity/femininity.* **Masculinity** stands for preference for achievement, heroism, assertiveness, work centrality (with resultant high stress), and material success. **Femininity** reflects the values of relationships, cooperation, group decision making, and quality of life. Societies with strong masculine values are Japan, Austria, Mexico, and Germany. Countries with feminine values are Sweden, Norway, Denmark, and the former Yugoslavia. Both men and women subscribe to the dominant value in masculine and feminine cultures.

Social values influence organizational functioning and management styles. For example, organizations in France and Latin and Mediterranean countries tend to be hierarchical bureaucracies. Germany and other central European countries have organizations that strive to be impersonal, well-oiled machines. In India, Asia, and Africa, organizations are viewed as large families. Effective management styles differ in each country, depending on cultural characteristics.[35]

Other Cultural Characteristics. Other cultural characteristics that influence international organizations are language, religion, attitudes, social organization, and education. Some countries, such as India, are characterized by *linguistic pluralism*, meaning that several languages exist there. Other countries rely heavily on spoken versus written language. Religion includes sacred objects, philosophical attitudes toward life, taboos, and rituals. Attitudes toward achievement, work, and time can all affect organizational productivity. An attitude called **ethnocentrism** means that people have a tendency to regard their own culture as superior and to downgrade other cultures. Ethnocentrism within a country makes it difficult for foreign firms to operate there. Social organization includes status systems, kinship and families, social institutions, and opportunities for social mobility. Education influences the literacy level, the availability of qualified employees, and the predominance of primary or secondary degrees.

Managers in international companies have found that cultural differences cannot be ignored if international operations are to succeed. For example, Coke withdrew its two-liter bottle from the Spanish market after discovering that compartments of Spanish refrigerators were too small for it.[36] McDonald's hasn't even tried to market Egg McMuffins in Brazil because of the deeply ingrained tradition of eating breakfast at home. On the other hand, Kellogg introduced breakfast cereal into Brazil through carefully chosen advertising. Although the traditional breakfast is coffee and a roll, many Brazilians have been won over to the American breakfast and now start their day with Kellogg's Sucrilhos (Frosted Flakes) and Crokinhos (Cocoa Krispies).[37] Organizations that recognize and manage cultural differences report major successes.

When people from different countries work together on a project, managers may find that culture provides more barriers than any other factor to successful collaboration. Consider the Mercedes-Benz plant in Vance, Alabama.

MERCEDES-BENZ
www.mercedes-benz.com

"Here we have created—what's that American phrase of yours?—a melting-pot of styles," says Andreas Renschler, CEO of the Mercedes-Benz plant that sits along Interstate 20 in western Alabama. But he admits that creating it wasn't easy.

For his management team, the native German carefully selected executives from all of the major U.S. and Japanese automakers, originally choosing a perfectly balanced team of four Germans and four Americans. Today, there are six top executives, three of whom are German, two American, and one Canadian. The group was sequestered in Stuttgart, Germany, for a year to finalize the plans for the new U.S. plant. Cultures clashed repeatedly, but a rigid time frame forced the group to negotiate until its members reached compromises. The biggest disagreements were over issues of image and decorum. The Germans were accustomed to private offices and hallways, but the Americans argued for a more open environment. Renschler, at first uncomfortable with the idea of casual attire, eventually embraced the casual "team wear," including sweaters with the Mercedes logo worn by all executives and employees at the plant. However, for months, when executives arrived from Germany, managers at the Alabama plant would quickly don suit coats and ties.

The group also argued over building design and management styles. While the Germans wanted separate structures for the different assembly lines, the Americans felt that separation would work against the team concept of the plant. Eventually, the group decided on an operation that combines the precision of German industrial engineering with an American-style environment of open communications between managers and workers. Most of the team leaders are Alabama natives. Trained in Germany, they were paired with German families for socializing and acculturation. Although some initially found it difficult to adapt to the direct style of German trainers, most eventually came to like the style because it helped them learn faster. Difficulties continued at the plant itself, however. "The Germans are very blunt. . . . " said one worker. "You don't get politeness out of them about work." Most of the Alabamian workers found their bosses to be rigid, formal, even humorless, while the Germans regarded the Americans as lax, too talkative, and somewhat superficial.

Some German executives at Daimler-Benz headquarters derided the American workers, saying "They'll never be able to do it." However, Renschler points out that within a few weeks, Germans and Americans were easily calling upon each other for help when the line was behind schedule. The Vance factory has proven to be a success, and the Mercedes M-Class sport utility vehicle is a hit in the marketplace. Renschler isn't surprised by the success. "We've shown that we can work with another culture."[38] Indeed, learning to do so proved useful in the German company's recent merger with Chrysler Corporation.

Getting Started Internationally

Small and medium-sized companies have a couple of ways to become involved internationally. One is to seek cheaper sources of supply offshore, which is called *outsourcing*. Another is to develop markets for finished products outside their home country, which may include exporting, licensing, and direct investing. These are called **market entry strategies**, because they represent alternative ways to sell products and services in foreign markets. Most firms begin with exporting and work up to direct investment. Exhibit 4.4 shows the strategies companies can use to enter foreign markets.

market entry strategy
An organizational strategy for entering a foreign market.

Outsourcing

global outsourcing
Engaging in the international division of labor so as to obtain the cheapest sources of labor and supplies regardless of country; also called *global sourcing*.

Global outsourcing, sometimes called *global sourcing*, means engaging in the international division of labor so that manufacturing can be done in countries with the cheapest sources of labor and supplies. A company may take away a contract from a domestic supplier and place it with a company in the Far East, 8,000 miles away. With advances in telecommunications, service providers can outsource as well. For example, Citibank taps low-cost skilled labor in India, Hong Kong, Australia, and Singapore to manage data and develop products for its global financial services. M. W. Kellogg, a Houston-based company that builds power and chemical plants around the world, farms out the detailed architectural-engineering work to a partner in Mexico.[39]

A unique variation is the *Maquiladora* industry along the Texas-Mexico border. In the beginning, twin plants were set up, with the U.S. plant manufacturing components with sophisticated machinery and the Mexican plant assembling components using cheap labor. With increasing sophistication in Mexico, new factories with sophisticated equipment are being built farther south of the border, with assembled products imported into the United States at highly competitive prices. The Blue Bird Corporation, a bus manufacturer based in Macon, Georgia, is building a plant in Mexico. The auto industry took advantage of the Maquiladora industry throughout the 1980s to combat the Japanese price challenge. By 1992, more than 100,000 Mexicans were employed by U.S. auto companies in towns such as Hermosillo, giving the area the nickname "Detroit South." The low-cost, high-quality Mexican workforce has also attracted manufacturers from other countries, firms such as Nissan, Renault, and Volkswagen.[40] Asian companies in particular are fast establishing Maquiladoras in Mexican border towns, with more than 30 Japanese companies already assembling there.

exporting
An entry strategy in which the organization maintains its production facilities within its home country and transfers its products for sale in foreign markets.

Daewoo Campus Advisers at U.S. universities? Through exporting, Korea's Daewoo Motor Co. hopes to sell 30,000 vehicles in its first year in the U.S. market. The Campus Advisers, a group of 2,000 college students at some 200 campuses, will run Daewoo events and direct potential buyers to the nearest Daewoo sales showroom. The advisers will receive $300 to $500 per car sold and an all-expense-paid seven-day trip to Korea, plus free use of a car for 3 months and the option to buy it at a discount.

Exporting

With **exporting**, the corporation maintains its production facilities within the home nation and transfers its products for sale in foreign countries.[41] Exporting enables a country to market its products in other countries at modest resource cost and with limited risk. Exporting does entail numerous problems based

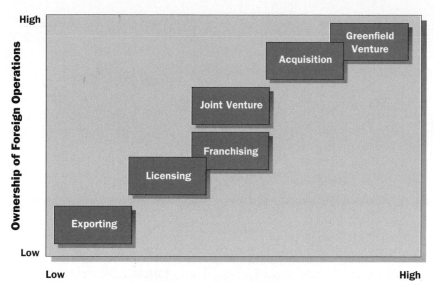

Exhibit 4.4

Strategies for Entering International Markets

on physical distances, government regulations, foreign currencies, and cultural differences, but it is less expensive than committing the firm's own capital to building plants in host countries. For example, a high-tech equipment supplier called Gerber Scientific Inc. prefers not to get involved directly in foreign country operations. Because machinery and machine tools are hot areas of export, executives are happy to ship overseas. U.S. exports are on the rise, and small to mid-size companies are benefiting. Multiplex Co., a St. Louis manufacturer of beverage dispensing equipment for fast-food service, exports about 40 percent of its products. National Graphics, a specialty coater of papers and films, ships 60 percent of its products overseas, and National's CEO believes exports helped to save the company.[42]

A form of exporting to less-developed countries is called **countertrade,** which is the barter of products for products rather than the sale of products for currency. Many less-developed countries have products to exchange but have no foreign currency. An estimated 20 percent of world trade is countertrade.

countertrade
The barter of products for other products rather than their sale for currency.

Licensing

With **licensing,** a corporation (the licensor) in one country makes certain resources available to companies in another country (the licensee). These resources include technology, managerial skills, and/or patent and trademark rights. They enable the licensee to produce and market a product similar to what the licensor has been producing. This arrangement gives the licensor an opportunity to participate in the production and sale of products outside its home country at relatively low cost. Hasbro has licensing agreements with companies in several Latin American countries and Japan. Hasbro builds brand identity and consumer awareness by contracting with toy companies to manufacture products locally. Heineken, which has been called the world's first truly global brand of beer, usually begins by exporting to help boost familiarity with its product; if the market looks enticing enough, Heineken then licenses its brands to a local brewer.

licensing
An entry strategy in which an organization in one country makes certain resources available to companies in another in order to participate in the production and sale of its products abroad.

franchising
A form of licensing in which an organization provides its foreign franchisees with a complete assortment of materials and services.

Franchising is a form of licensing in which the franchisor provides foreign franchisees with a complete package of material and services, including equipment, products, product ingredients, trademark and trade name rights, managerial advice, and a standardized operating system. Some of the best-known international franchisors are the fast-food chains. Kentucky Fried Chicken, Burger King, Wendy's, and McDonald's outlets are found in almost every large city in the world. The story is often told of the Japanese child visiting Los Angeles who excitedly pointed out to his parents, "They have McDonald's in America."

Licensing and franchising offer a business firm relatively easy access to international markets at low cost, but they limit its participation in and control over the development of those markets.

Direct Investing

A higher level of involvement in international trade is direct investment in manufacturing facilities in a foreign country. **Direct investing** means that the company is involved in managing the productive assets, which distinguishes it from other entry strategies that permit less managerial control.

direct investing
An entry strategy in which the organization is involved in managing its production facilities in a foreign country.

joint venture
A variation of direct investment in which an organization shares costs and risks with another firm to build a manufacturing facility, develop new products, or set up a sales and distribution network.

Currently, the most popular type of direct investment is to engage in strategic alliances and partnerships. In a **joint venture,** a company shares costs and risks with another firm, typically in the host country, to develop new products, build a manufacturing facility, or set up a sales and distribution network.[43] A partnership is often the fastest, cheapest, and least risky way to get into the global game. Entrepreneurial companies such as Molex, a manufacturer of connectors, and Nypro, a maker of industrial components, have used partnerships to gain overseas access to several countries. In its quest to become the dominant brand in an expanded European market, Heineken Breweries is teaming up with smaller rivals in Hungary, Poland, and Switzerland. In Asia, Heineken has entered into a joint venture with Singapore's Asia Pacific Breweries, makers of Tiger Beer. Coca-Cola has taken Romania by storm after it entered into a joint venture with that country's largest bottler of soft drinks, Ci-Co S.A. Auburn Farms, a Sacramento, California, manufacturer of all-natural snack foods, recently entered into a joint venture with South Africa's Beacon Sweets & Chocolates.[44] An important consideration for both companies in this venture was that they share similar ethics and policies. As discussed in the Manager's Shoptalk box, business ethics is becoming an increasingly important yet highly complicated consideration for managers as corporations move into developing countries.

wholly owned foreign affiliate
A foreign subsidiary over which an organization has complete control.

The other choice is to have a **wholly owned foreign affiliate,** over which the company has complete control. Direct *acquisition* of an affiliate may provide cost savings over exporting by shortening distribution channels and reducing storage and transportation costs. Local managers also have heightened awareness of economic, cultural, and political conditions. For example, General Electric purchased Hungarian bulbmaker Tungsram in 1990. By 1994 the company was turning a profit, and quality was so good that GE shifted all European lightbulb production there.[45]

greenfield venture
The most risky type of direct investment, whereby a company builds a subsidiary from scratch in a foreign country.

The most costly and risky direct investment is called a **greenfield venture,** which means a company builds a subsidiary from scratch in a foreign country. The advantage is that the subsidiary is exactly what the company wants and has the potential to be highly profitable. The disadvantage is that the company has to acquire all market knowledge, materials, people, and know-how

Shoptalk

MANAGER'S SHOPTALK

Defining Global Ethics

What may seem a cut-and-dried matter of ethics in the United States is never so clear when translated overseas. As companies do more and more business around the globe, managers are walking a moral tightrope, struggling to determine what is right and what is wrong. Dilemmas range from a simple question about the appropriate amount of money to spend on a business gift to complex issues regarding bribery, child labor, and environmental abuse. For example, most people would firmly agree that mistreating children is wrong. However, demonstrating the complexity of the ethical issues, people in different countries may disagree strongly about what constitutes mistreatment. Although Americans consider child labor mistreatment, in some countries it is regarded as a fact of life that is in no way cruel.

Groups such as the Caux Round Table are taking a leadership role in helping managers and organizations deal with the ethical complexity of the global business environment. The Round Table was created in 1986 by Frederik Philips, former president of Philips Electronics, and Olivier Giscard D'Estaing, vice chairman of INSEAD. It brings together leaders from Europe, Japan, and the United States to focus attention on issues of ethics and corporate responsibility. Including such large companies as Siemens AG, Chase Manhattan Bank, ITT Corp., World Bank, Minnesota Mining & Manufacturing, Canon, and Matsushita, the group has developed world standards to measure ethical behavior. These standards are based on two principles: the concept of human dignity, and the Japanese doctrine of *kyosei*—the idea of living and working together for the common good to enable mutual prosperity.

Despite this progress, the international dimensions of business ethics have scarcely been raised, much less adequately addressed. For managers in a borderless world, however, the ethical questions aren't going to disappear.

SOURCE: Charlene Marmer Solomon, "Put Your Ethics To a Global Test," Personnel Journal, January 1996, 66–74.

in a different culture, and mistakes are possible. An example of a greenfield venture is the Mercedes-Benz plant in Vance, Alabama, described earlier. This is the first time the company has built a plant outside Germany. The venture was high risk because the new plant is building a new product (sport utility vehicle) with a new workforce, to be sold in a foreign country.[46]

The Multinational Corporation

The size and volume of international business are so large that they are hard to comprehend. The revenue of General Motors is comparable to the gross domestic product (GDP) of Finland, that of General Electric is comparable in size to Israel's GDP, Toyota revenues to Hong Kong's GDP, and those of the Royal Dutch/Shell Group to the GDP of Norway.[47]

As discussed earlier in this chapter, a large volume of international business is being carried out in a seemingly borderless world by very large international businesses that can be thought of as *global corporations*, *stateless corporations*, or *transnational corporations*. In the business world, these large international firms typically are called *multinational corporations (MNCs)*, which have been the subject of enormous attention and concern. MNCs can move a wealth of assets from country to country and influence national economies, politics, and cultures.

Characteristics of Multinational Corporations

Although there is no precise definition, a **multinational corporation (MNC)** typically receives more than 25 percent of its total sales revenues from

multinational corporation (MNC)
An organization that receives more than 25 percent of its total sales revenues from operations outside the parent company's home country; also called *global corporation* or *transnational corporation*.

Nokia Corp. of Finland is a multinational corporation that manufactures digital cellular phones. This photo was taken in Helsinki, but the variety of features and snazzy design of the Nokia products make them popular worldwide, even in countries as far away as China. Cellular phone subscribers worldwide are expected to double to 550 million by 2001.

operations outside the parent's home country. MNCs also have the following distinctive managerial characteristics:

1. An MNC is managed as an integrated worldwide business system. This means that foreign affiliates act in close alliance and cooperation with one another. Capital, technology, and people are transferred among country affiliates. The MNC can acquire materials and manufacture parts wherever in the world it is most advantageous to do so.

2. An MNC is ultimately controlled by a single management authority that makes key strategic decisions relating to the parent and all affiliates. Although some headquarters are binational, such as the Royal Dutch/Shell Group, some centralization of management is required to maintain worldwide integration and profit maximization for the enterprise as a whole.

3. MNC top managers are presumed to exercise a global perspective. They regard the entire world as one market for strategic decisions, resource acquisition, location of production, advertising, and marketing efficiency.

In a few cases, the MNC management philosophy may differ from that just described. For example, some researchers have distinguished among *ethnocentric companies*, which place emphasis on their home countries, *polycentric companies*, which are oriented toward the markets of individual foreign host countries, and *geocentric companies*, which are truly world oriented and favor no specific country.[48] The truly global companies that transcend national boundaries are growing in number. These companies no longer see themselves as American, Chinese, or German; they are totally globally operating and serve a global market.

Managing in a Global Environment

Managing in a foreign country is particularly challenging. Before undertaking a foreign assignment, managers must understand that they will face great personal challenges. Managers working in foreign countries must be sensitive to cultural subtleties and understand that the ways to provide proper leadership, decision making, motivation, and control vary in different cultures. When companies operate internationally, the need for personal learning and growth is critical.

Personal Challenges for Global Managers

Managers will be most successful in foreign assignments if they are culturally flexible and easily adapt to new situations and ways of doing things. A tendency to be ethnocentric—to believe that your own country's cultural values and ways of doing things are superior—is a natural human condition. Managers can learn to break down those prejudices and appreciate another culture. As one Swedish executive of a large multinational corporation put it, "We Swedes are so content with . . . the Swedish way, that we forget that 99 percent of the rest of the world isn't Swedish."[49] Managers working in foreign countries may never come to understand the local culture like a native; the key is to be sensitive to cultural differences and understand that other ways of thinking and doing are also valid.

Most managers in foreign assignments face a period of homesickness, loneliness, and culture shock from being suddenly immersed in a culture with completely different languages, foods, values, beliefs, and ways of doing things. *Culture shock* refers to the frustration and anxiety that result from constantly being subjected to strange and unfamiliar cues about what to do and how to do it. Even simple, daily events can become sources of stress.[50]

Preparing managers to work in foreign cultures is essential. Some companies try to give future managers exposure to foreign cultures early in their careers. American Express Company's Travel-Related Services unit gives American business-school students summer jobs in which they work outside the United States for up to 10 weeks. Colgate-Palmolive selects 15 recent graduates each year and then provides up to 24 months of training prior to multiple overseas job stints.[51]

Managing Cross-Culturally

To be effective on an international level, managers can first understand their own cultural values and assumptions, as discussed in Chapter 3; then they can interpret the culture of the country and organization in which they are working and develop the sensitivity required to avoid making costly cultural blunders.[52] The following examples illustrate how cultural differences can be significant for foreign managers.

Leading. In relationship-oriented societies such as those in Asia, the Arab world, and Latin America, leaders should use a warm, personalized approach with employees. One of the greatest difficulties American leaders have had doing business in China, for example, is failing to recognize that to the Chinese any relationship is a personal relationship.[53] Managers are expected to have periodic social visits with workers, inquiring about morale and health. Leaders should be especially careful about criticizing others. To Asians, Africans, Arabs, and Latin Americans, the loss of self-respect brings dishonor to themselves and their families. One researcher tells of a Dutch doctor managing a company clinic who had what he considered a "frank discussion" with a Chinese subordinate. The subordinate, who perceived the doctor as a father figure, took the criticism as a "savage indictment" and committed suicide.[54] Though this is an extreme example, the principle of "losing face" is highly important in some cultures.

Decision Making. In America, mid-level managers may discuss a problem and give the boss a recommendation. German managers, on the other hand, expect the boss to issue specific instructions. In Mexico, employees often don't understand participatory decision making. American managers doing business there have been advised to rarely explain a decision, lest workers perceive this as a sign of weakness.[55] In contrast, managers in Arab and African nations are expected to use consultative decision making in the extreme.

Giving Workers the Freedom to Learn

AES Corporation, a producer of electrical power with headquarters in Arlington, Virginia, has become a learning organization by handing power to workers on the front lines. Lots of companies talk about pushing power and responsibility to lower levels, but few have pushed as far as AES. With nearly 6,000 employees (or more than 30,000, counting those working in joint ventures), AES has never established departments for human resources, operations, purchasing, or legal affairs. Fewer than 30 people work at headquarters. All functions—even finance—are handled by decentralized teams that include coal handlers and maintenance workers. For example, two control room operators led the team that raised $350 million to finance a joint venture in Northern Ireland. Teams seek advice from managers or anyone else who may have helpful ideas, but they make their own decisions.

AES disperses power and information so widely because its managers believe that's the only way to keep people thinking and learning. According to co-founder and CEO Dennie Bakke, "If all information about finance goes to the finance department and all information about legal matters goes to the legal department, it's impossible to get well-rounded people who can think about the whole world." AES needs people to think about the whole world as it continues its rapid expansion internationally. The company opened its first plant in 1986. Today, it owns or has an interest in 82 power plants in the United States, Argentina, China, Brazil, Hungary, and other countries. The company has revenues of about $835 million and profits of $125 million. AES also believes in being a good corporate citizen in the countries in which it operates. It has planted 52 million trees in Guatemala, funded medical care in Kazakhstan, organized food banks in Argentina, and built schools in China. Although the company's social responsibility emphasis used to be on environmentalism, it has shifted gears to try to meet the needs of each specific country.

Bakke and co-founder and chairman Roger Sant believe AES has been able to expand so rapidly because giving people on the front lines the power to make decisions has made AES faster and nimbler than competitors. Oscar Prieto, a chemical engineer picked to lead AES's expansion into Brazil, agrees. He'd worked at AES only two years when he was given the challenging assignment, but he'd experienced the power of empowerment and believed it could work crossculturally. He chose Carlos Baldi, a 34-year-old engineer, to manage the plant in Santa Branca, a small facility near São Paolo that had previously been run as a top-heavy bureaucracy. After agreeing on shared goals and expectations, Prieto turned the plant over to Baldi and told him to run it as he saw fit. Now Baldi operates the same way with his people—he gives advice, not approval.

"Power to the people" doesn't always translate so well to other countries, however. For example, managers in Northern Ireland are having a hard time giving up control and operating the AES way. Yet, Bakke and Sant are committed to expanding AES's bottom-up system around the world. The company's mission statement declares that work should be "fun, fulfilling, and exciting." At AES, that means giving workers freedom, challenge, and opportunities to think, learn, grow, and achieve.

SOURCE: Alex Markels, "Power to the People," *Fast Company*, February–March 1998, 155–165.

Motivating. Motivation must fit the incentives within the culture. In Japan, employees are motivated to satisfy the company. A financial bonus for star performance would be humiliating to employees from Japan, China, or the former Yugoslavia. An American executive in Japan offered a holiday trip to the top salesperson, but employees were not interested. After he realized that Japanese are motivated in groups, he changed the reward to a trip for everyone if together they achieved the sales target. They did. Managers in Latin America, Africa, and the Middle East must show respect for employees as individuals with needs and interests outside of work.[56]

Controlling. When things go wrong, managers in foreign countries often are unable to get rid of employees who do not work out. In Europe, Mexico, and Indonesia, to hire and fire on performance seems unnaturally brutal. Workers are protected by strong labor laws and union rules.

In foreign cultures, managers also should not control the wrong things.

A Sears manager in Hong Kong insisted that employees come to work on time instead of 15 minutes late. The employees did exactly as they were told, but they also left on time instead of working into the evening as they had previously. A lot of work was left unfinished. The manager eventually told the employees to go back to their old ways. His attempt at control had a negative effect.

Global Learning

Managing across borders calls for organizations to learn across borders. One reason Japanese companies have been so successful internationally is that their culture encourages learning and adaptability. In Asia generally, teaching and learning are highly regarded, and the role of managers is seen as one of teaching or facilitating—of helping those around them to learn.[57] It is partly this emphasis on continuous learning that has helped Matsushita Electric master markets and diverse cultures in 38 countries, from Malaysia to Brazil, from Austria to China, from Iran to Tanzania. One of Matsushita's top lessons for going global is to be a good corporate citizen in every country, respecting cultures, customs, and languages. In countries with Muslim religious practices, for example, Matsushita provides special prayer rooms and allows two prayer sessions per shift.[58] AES Corporation, an American corporation that encourages continuous learning by giving freedom and power to front-line workers, is now trying to expand its business model internationally, as described in the Learning Organization box.

Summary and Management Solution

This chapter has emphasized the growing importance of an international perspective on management. Successful companies are preparing to expand their business overseas and to withstand domestic competition from foreign competitors. Business in the global arena involves special risks and difficulties because of complicated economic, legal-political, and sociocultural forces. Moreover, the global environment changes rapidly, as illustrated by the emergence of the European Union, the North American Free Trade Agreement, and the shift in Eastern Europe to democratic forms of government. Major alternatives for serving foreign markets are exporting, licensing, franchising, and direct investing through joint ventures or wholly owned subsidiaries.

International markets provide many opportunities but are also fraught with difficulty, as Wal-Mart, described at the beginning of this chapter, discovered. The company has revised its merchandising and changed some of its tactics to better suit local cultures in Brazil and China. In Brazil, for example, it has scaled back the size of stores and moved to midsize cities where competition is less fierce. Wal-Mart is trying to work with local partners who can help the company translate its business cross-culturally. Despite problems, the company plans to open eight stores soon in both Brazil and Argentina, doubling the number now in each country. Bob Martin, Wal-Mart's head of international operations, believes the international market is worth the risks. "The market is ripe and wide open for us."[59]

Much of the growth in international business has been carried out by large businesses called *MNCs*. These large companies exist in an almost borderless world, encouraging the free flow of ideas, products, manufacturing, and marketing among countries to achieve the greatest efficiencies. Managers in MNCs as well as those in much smaller companies doing business internationally face many challenges. Managers often experience culture shock when transferred to foreign countries. They must learn to be sensitive to cultural differences and tailor their management style to the culture. For managers and organizations in an increasingly borderless world, learning across borders is critical.

Discussion Questions

1. Why do you think international businesses traditionally prefer to operate in industrialized countries? Discuss.

2. What considerations in recent years have led international businesses to expand their activities into less-developed countries?

3. What policies or actions would you recommend to an entrepreneurial business wanting to do business in Europe?

4. What steps could a company take to avoid making product design and marketing mistakes when introducing new products into a foreign country?

5. Compare the advantages associated with the foreign-market entry strategies of exporting, licensing, and wholly owned subsidiaries.

6. Should a multinational corporation operate as an integrated, worldwide business system, or would it be more effective to let each subsidiary operate autonomously?

7. What does it mean to say that the world is becoming "borderless"? That large companies are "stateless"?

8. What might managers do to avoid making mistakes concerning control and decision making when operating in a foreign culture?

9. What is meant by the cultural values of individualism and masculinity/femininity? How might these values affect organization design and management processes?

10. How do you think trade alliances such as NAFTA and the EU may affect you as a future manager?

Management in Practice: Experiential Exercise

Test your Global Potential

A global environment requires that American managers learn to deal effectively with people in other countries. The assumption that foreign business leaders behave and negotiate in the same manner as Americans is false. How well prepared are you to live with globalization? Consider the following.

Are you guilty of	Definitely No				Definitely Yes
1. Impatience? Do you think "Time is money" or "Let's get to the point"?	1	2	3	4	5
2. Having a short attention span, bad listening habits, or being uncomfortable with silence?	1	2	3	4	5
3. Being somewhat argumentative, sometimes to the point of belligerence?	1	2	3	4	5
4. Ignorance about the world beyond your borders?	1	2	3	4	5
5. Weakness in foreign languages?	1	2	3	4	5
6. Placing emphasis on short-term success?	1	2	3	4	5
7. Believing that advance preparations are less important than negotiations themselves?	1	2	3	4	5
8. Being legalistic? Of believing "A deal is a deal," regardless of changing circumstances?	1	2	3	4	5
9. Having little interest in seminars on the subject of globalization, failing to browse through libraries or magazines on international topics, not interacting with foreign students or employees?	1	2	3	4	5

Total Score _____

If you scored less than 27, congratulations. You have the temperament and interest to do well in a global company. If you scored more than 27, it's time to consider a change. Regardless of your score, go back over each item and make a plan of action to correct deficiencies indicated by answers of 4 or 5 to any question.

Source: Reprinted by permission of the publisher from Cynthia Barmun and Netasha Wolninsky, "Why Americans Fail at Overseas Negotiations," *Management Review* (October 1989), 55–57, © 1989 American Management Association, New York. All rights reserved.

Management in Practice: Ethical Dilemma

Quality or Closing

On the way home from the launch party celebrating Plaxcor Metals' entrance into the international arena, Donald Fields should have been smiling. He was part of the team that had closed the deal to sell component parts to Asian Business Machine, after his company had spent millions trying to break into this lucrative market. There were several more deals riding on the successful outcome of the first international venture.

The expansion into new markets was critical to Plaxcor's survival. As President Leslie Hanson had put it, "If we aren't global within five years, we may as well close up shop." Fields was tense because of news he learned tonight: Intense bidding for the first sale and several last-minute changes requested by the customer had forced Plaxcor to heavily modify its production process. The production manager had confided that "the product is a mess but still better than most of the competition." He went on to assure him that, although well below normal standards, the variability would "probably not cause any problems" and could be worked out after a few more orders.

Fields had spent the last few months selling Plaxcor on its quality reputation. He knew they could probably get by with the first runs and meet the opening deadline. He was afraid that telling the customer of the potential problems or extending the deadline would risk not only this deal but pending projects as well. But he knew if problems arose with the products, Plaxcor's future in the Asian market would be bleak. Donald Fields wasn't sure Plaxcor could afford to gamble its entrance in the international market on a substandard product.

What Do You Do?

1. Ask the customer for an extension of the deadline, and bring the products up to standard.
2. Gamble on the first runs, and hope the products don't fail.
3. Inform the customer of the problem, and let the customer make the decision.

Surf the Net

1. **Languages on the Web.** According to a recent *Fortune Global 500* listing Hewlett-Packard was ranked as the 47th largest company in the world based on sales revenues. Visit Hewlett-Packard's home page at **www.hp.com** to see how this multinational company provides information for its many customers throughout the world. Check out the links to its pages for countries in the Americas, Asia, and Europe. Compare how other Global 500 companies in the computers and office equipment industry provide access to information for their non-English-speaking customers, for example, IBM **www.ibm.com** and Fujitsu **www.fujitsu.com.** Choose the Web site you thought was most effective in providing multi-language access and explain your choice.

2. **Exchange Rates.** Visit a Web site, such as the CNN Financial Network listed below, to find currency exchange rates. **http://cnnfn.com/markets/currencies** If the Web site provides a currency converter, determine how much $100 in U.S. currency is worth in each of the following currencies:
   Chilean Peso
   Japanese Yen
   Euro
   United Kingdom Pound
   If no currency converter is available, simply list the exchange rate per U.S. dollar for each of the above currencies.

3. **The Multinational Corporation.** To become more knowledgeable about the largest companies in the world, check out the *Fortune Global 500* listing available at **http://pathfinder.com/fortune/global500/500list.html** Answer the following questions: (a) What countries are represented in the top ten? (b) Which country has the most companies represented in the top ten? (c) Select three industries of interest to you, and identify the top three companies and their home countries in each industry. (d) After looking over the information available at this Web site, identify one fact that was particularly interesting to you.

Case for Critical Analysis

Unocal Corporation

Unocal Corporation seems an unlikely candidate for a high-risk global rampage. Consumers everywhere recognize the ubiquitous 76 logo of this quintessential California oil company.

They know it as the nation's 11th largest petroleum retailer, with a prestigious downtown headquarters and important role as a Los Angeles civic booster. Casting aside its reputation as a conservative company with tightly defined domestic markets and focused petroleum interests in California, Unocal has rapidly transformed itself into an international company with major investments in some of the world's least-developed economies. It has also become a prominent topic among political activists, human-rights groups, and President Clinton's foreign policy team. Some observers say that Unocal will become a casualty of its high-risk policies.

In 1995, immediately after becoming chairman of Unocal, Roger Beach began to sell off domestic retail assets and eliminate exploration and refining activities in the United States. Resources shifted to unlikely places where few other major oil producers had risked operations—places such as Myanmar (more commonly known as Burma), Turkmenistan, Uzbekistan, and the strife-ridden Balkans. Beach turned up the heat on company investments in Indonesian oil fields, launched full-service energy subsidiaries through government alliances in Thailand, broadened holdings in Malaysia, and began negotiations for an integrated refining/retailing enterprise in Pakistan. Nearly 40 percent of Unocal's exploration and extraction budget was thrown into these emerging markets, much of it pinpointed for very high risk locations in the former Soviet republics and the Persian subcontinent.

Why take these risks? Beach answers that Unocal, unable to compete head-to-head with the oil industry giants for capital markets, decided to create an extremely attractive strategic package of full-service energy production in countries grasping to develop infrastructure. "What every government likes about Unocal's strategy is one stop shopping; one group able to take the whole project from development to the marketing end," Beach said. "We have become partners in their development and as important to them as they are to us." The Unocal strategy defies normal industry trends based on distributing huge capital investments to tie up oil reserves and mineral rights, then cutting deals for operations. Instead, Unocal comes in the front door with packaged energy services ranging from turning the first spade of dirt on exploration to delivering power to the end user, and that proposal includes oil, gas, or electric power generation.

Beach sees far less risk than industry analysts perceive in the emerging markets. The dangers of war, political upheaval, and currency fluctuations are clear and present, yet the company says it has hedged against these threats by diversifying investments. By 2000, it intends to have nearly 80 percent of its exploration and production capabilities in these underdeveloped areas, and by the end of 1996, it had almost totally abandoned domestic exploration, having sold off nearly $3 billion in assets and oil-field holdings in California. However, according to Beach, success will depend on creating a globally managed company capable of understanding and participating in foreign market environments. Consequently, in 1996, he initiated a major transformation in Unocal's management systems, beginnning by relocating its headquarters from its stately downtown offices to a small, highly efficient suite near the Los Angeles International Airport. Midlevel managers were either repositioned in regional offices, such as Singapore, Istanbul, or

Jakarta, or they left the company. The executive core, which had been distinctly Los Angeleno in character, gained a multicultural character, representing Eastern European and Asian group alliances. Subsidiaries in Jakarta, Thailand and Burma took on local names and corporate identities, shedding their American profiles, and Unocal's many foriegn alliances have made it part of the communities in which it operates.

In Thailand, Unocal has worked on the country's privatization plan to convert its Petroleum Authority of Thailand (PTT) operations into privately owned and operated international oil services. Unocal and the PTT have begun to build pipelines in the Gulf of Thailand linking Unocal's hydrocarbon fields in the nation's rugged peninsula, and a joint venture in Malaysia has begun to open regional energy markets from Burma to the Phillipines. Surface evaluations have hailed this consortium as a master stroke of strategy; however, related activities have exposed Unocal to strong criticism. Unocal became the largest single U.S. investor in Burma as part of the expansion, but Burma's military government has languished in political and economic isolation as a result of U.S legislation aimed at boycotting the country for its unacceptable human-rights practices. Political activists in more than a dozen U.S. states have won passage of legislation barring imports from Burma and outlawing private investments there by U.S. firms. Municipal governments in five states have passed boycott laws, as well, and Unocal, together with PepsiCo and several other American companies operating in Burma, have become major targets for international pressure groups. PepsiCo bowed to the pressure and recently moved out of Burma, but Unocal has flatly refused to budge.

The company's insistence on remaining in Burma, however, is not a vote in support of the country's human-rights record. Indeed, Unocal would find it difficult to withdraw, because it has formed an equity agreement with the giant French petrochemical company Total, which also has substantial pipeline investments with Unocal in the Persian Gulf and southern Asia. Unocal's contracts with Total make it a *de facto* partner of the French government. Moreover, Unocal has invested in public and private interests in Burma that spread to five other major Southeast Asian states. But a Unocal representative cites the importance of the company's role in helping the nation's development. "To withdraw and isolate Burma would have no effect. Questionable human-rights leadership and political practices would continue and perhaps proliferate," she said. "On the other hand, our strength and the fact that we can provide meaningful jobs and ethical international business, encourages changes for the good. Even if every American firm vacated, firms from other nations would welcome the chance to develop Burma without American competition."

That position doesn't relieve the political or financial risk to Unocal. Ethics and U.S. policies aside, Burma lacks a strong track record for keeping its promises. As a closed military state, self-isolated for ideological reasons since the end of World War II, it has few friends anywhere in the world. For years, it was linked to the Soviet Union for aid and military support, and Burma backed insurgent forces in several neighboring civil conflicts. These situations did not endear the government to potential regional economic allies. However, the country is strategically positioned within the Southeast Asian theater, and it has attracted consideration, with much controversy, for membership in ASEAN.

Unocal holds a rather exposed position in the country, as it does in Uzbekistan, Turkmenistan, and the Balkans. An American company without the legal or political support of its home government can expect little help should the host government decide to freeze its assets, bar currency repatriation, or resort to outright expropriation. Meanwhile, Unocal has tied up several billion dollars in the region while maintaining no safety net at home. Indeed, it faces potentially costly threats from home, and if the company is pushed to the wall by legislation, the chairman says, he will take Unocal out of U.S. control.

Questions

1. What market entry strategies has Unocal used, based on the activities described in the case? Would you classify Unocal as a multinational corporation (MNC)? Why or why not?
2. Identify and discuss the various types of risks faced by Unocal in emerging markets (consider the economic, legal-political, and sociocultural environment). Which risks seem most threatening to the company?
3. What do you think of the Unocal representative's statement that "to withdraw and isolate Burma would have no effect" regarding that country's poor human-rights record? Do you believe U.S. companies should stay in such countries in the hope of improving the ethical climate? Discuss.

SOURCE: "Unocal Corporation," from *International Management: Text and Cases*, 143–145, David H. Holt, Copyright © 1998 by Harcourt, Inc., reprinted by permission of the publisher.

Endnotes

1. Jonathan Friedland and Louise Lee, "The Wal-Mart Way Sometimes Gets Lost in Translation Overseas," *The Wall Street Journal*, October 8, 1997, A1, A12.
2. Murray Weidenbaum, "American Isolationism Versus the Global Economy," in *International Business 97/98, Annual Editions*, Fred Maidment, ed., (Guilford, Conn.: Dushkin Publishing Group, 1997), 12–15.
3. Nilly Ostro-Landau and Hugh D. Menzies, "The New World Economics Order," in *International Business 97/98, Annual Editions*, Fred Maidment, ed., (Guilford, Conn.: Dushkin Publishing Group, 1997), 24–30; and Weidenbaum, "American Isolationism Versus the Global Economy."
4. Joseph B. White, "There Are No German or U.S. Companies, Only Successful Ones," *The Wall Street Journal*, May 7, 1998, A1.
5. Pete Engardio, with Robert D. Hof, Elisabeth Malkin, Neil Gross, and Karen Lowry Miller, "High-Tech Jobs All Over the Map," *Business Week/21st Century Capitalism*, November 18, 1994, 112–117.
6. Raju Narisetti and Jonathan Friedland, "Diaper Wars of P&G and Kimberly-Clark Now Heat Up in Brazil," *The Wall Street Journal*, June 4, 1997, and Stephen Baker, "The Bridges Steel is Building," *Business Week*, June 2, 1997, 39.
7. Richard L. Daft, *Management*, 3d ed. (Fort Worth, Texas: The Dryden Press, 1994), 80; James L. Gibson, John M. Ivancevich, and James H. Donnelly, Jr., *Organizations*, 8th ed. (Burr Ridge, Ill.: Irwin, 1994), 54–55.
8. Nancy J. Adler, *International Dimensions of Organizational Behavior* (Boston: PWS-Kent, 1991), 7–8; William Holstein, Stanley Reed, Jonathan Kapstein, Todd Vogel, and Joseph Weber, "The Stateless Corporation," *Business Week*, May 14, 1990, 98–105; and Richard Daft, *Organization Theory and Design* (St. Paul, Minn.: West, 1992).
9. Eric Matson, "How to Globalize Yourself," *Fast Company*, April–May 1997, 133–139; and Gunnar Beeth, "Multicultural Managers Wanted," *Management Review*, May 1997, 17–21.
10. Holstein et al., "The Stateless Corporation"; Carla Rapoport, "Nestlé's Brand Building Machine," *Fortune*, September 19, 1994, 147–156; and Mark Landler, with Joyce Barnathan, Geri Smith, and Gail Edmondson, "Think Globally, Program Locally," *Business Week/21st Century Capitalism*, November 18, 1994, 186–189.
11. William Taylor, "The Logic of Global Business: An Interview with ABB's Percy Barnevik," *Harvard Business Review* (March–April 1991), 91–105; Holstein et al., "The Stateless Corporation"; and John A. Byrne and Kathleen Kerwin, with Amy Cortese and Paula Dwyer, "Borderless Management," *Business Week*, May 23, 1994, 24–26.
12. Carla Rapoport, with Justin Martin, "Retailers Go Global," *Fortune*, February 20, 1995, 102–108.
13. "Slogans Often Lose Something in Translation," *The New Mexican*, July 3, 1994, F1, F2.
14. Louis S. Richman, "Global Growth is on a Tear," in *International Business 97/98, Annual Editions*, Fred Maidment, ed., (Guilford, Conn.: Dushkin Publishing Group, 1997), 6–11.

15. Ronald Henkoff, "Asia: Why Business is Still Bullish," *Fortune,* October 27, 1997, 139–142.

16. Jennifer Farley, "Negotiating the Border," *American Way,* July 1, 1994, 48–51; and Amal Kumar Jaj, "United Technologies Looks Far from Home for Growth," *The Wall Street Journal,* May 26, 1994, B4.

17. Kathleen Deveny, "McWorld?" *Business Week,* October 13, 1986, 78–86; and Andrew E. Serwer, "McDonald's Conquers the World," *Fortune,* October 17, 1994, 103–116.

18. Bruce Kogut, "Designing Global Strategies: Profiting from Operational Flexibility," *Sloan Management Review* 27 (Fall 1985), 27–38.

19. Mark Fitzpatrick, "The Definition and Assessment of Political Risk in International Business: A Review of the Literature," *Academy of Management Review* 8 (1983), 249–254.

20. "Multinational Firms Act to Protect Overseas Workers from Terrorism," *The Wall Street Journal,* April 29, 1986, 31; Robert J. Bowman, "Are You Covered?" *World Trade,* March 1995, 100–104; and Frederick Stapenhurst, "Political Risk Analysis in North American Multinationals: An Empirical Review and Assessment," *The International Executive,* March–April, 1995, 127–145.

21. Patricia Sellers, "Where Killers and Kidnappers Roam," *Fortune,* September 23, 1991, 8; Michael R. Czinkota, Ilkka A. Ronkainen, Michael H. Moffett, and Eugene O. Moynihan, *Global Business* (Fort Worth, Texas: The Dryden Press, 1995); and Paul Hofheinz, "Rising in Russia," *Fortune,* January 24, 1994, 92–97.

22. Laura B. Pincus and James A. Belohlav, "Legal Issues in Multinational Business: To Play the Game, You Have to Know the Rules," *Academy of Management Executive* 10, No. 3 (1996), 52–61; and Rick Borelli, "A Worldwide Language TRAP," *Management Review,* October 1997, 52–54.

23. Geri Smith, "NAFTA: A Green Light for Red Tape," *Business Week,* July 25, 1994, 48; and Ed Fishbein, "Kultur Klash," *World Trade,* March 1995, 53–56.

24. Czinkota et al., *Global Business,* 151; and Robert D. Gatewood, Robert R. Taylor, and O. C. Ferrell, *Management* (Burr Ridge, Ill.: Irwin, 1995), 131–132.

25. "For Richer, for Poorer," *The Economist,* December 1993, 66; Richard Harmsen, "The Uruguay Round: A Boon for the World Economy," *Finance & Development,* March 1995, 24–26; Salil S. Pitroda, "From GATT to WTO: The Institutionalization of World Trade," *Harvard International Review,* Spring 1995, 46–47 and 66–67; and David H. Holt, *International Management: Text and Cases,* (Fort Worth: Dryden, 1998).

26. Mark M. Nelson, "Extra Accommodations," *The Wall Street Journal,* September 30, 1994, R13, R14.

27. Thane Peterson, "The Euro," *Business Week,* April 27, 1998, 90–94.

28. Lynda Radosevich, "New Money," *CIO Enterprise,* Section 2, April 15, 1998, 54–58.

29. Barbara Rudolph, "Megamarket," *Time,* August 10, 1992, 43–44.

30. Amy Barrett, "It's a Small (Business) World," *Business Week,* April 17, 1995, 96–101.

31. Robert S. Greenberger, "As U.S. Exports Rise, More Workers Benefit and Favor Free Trade," *The Wall Street Journal,* September 10, 1997, A1, A10.

32. Amy Borrus, "A Free-Trade Milestone, with Many More Miles to Go," *Business Week,* August 24, 1992, 30–31.

33. Keith Bradsher, "As Global Talks Stall, Regional Trade Pacts Multiply," *The New York Times,* August 23, 1992, F5.

34. Geert Hofstede, "The Interaction between National and Organizational Value Systems," *Journal of Management Studies* 22 (1985), 347–357; and Geert Hofstede, "The Cultural Relativity of the Quality of Life Concept," *Academy of Management Review* 9 (1984), 389–398.

35. Ellen F. Jackofsky, John W. Slocum, Jr., and Sara J. McQuaid, "Cultural Values and the CEO: Alluring Companions?" *Academy of Management Executive* 2 (1988), 39–49.

36. Orla Sheehan, "Managing a Multinational Corporation: Tomorrow's Decision Makers Speak Out," *Fortune,* August 24, 1992, 233.

37. Richard Gibson and Matt Moffett, "Why You Won't Find Any Egg McMuffins for Breakfast in Brazil," *The Wall Street Journal,* October 23, 1997, A1, A8; and Kenneth Labich, "America's International Winners," *Fortune,* April 14, 1986, 34–46.

38. Douglas A. Blackmon, "A Factory in Alabama is the Merger in Microcosm," *The Wall Street Journal,* May 8, 1998, B1; and Justin Martin, "Mercedes: Made in Alabama," *Fortune,* July 7, 1997, 150–158.

39. Engardio et al., "High-Tech Jobs All Over the Map."

40. Gary Jacobson, "The Boom on Mexico's Border," *Management Review* (July 1988), 21–25; Stephen Baker, David Woodruff, and Elizabeth Weiner, "Detroit South," *Business Week,* March 16, 1992, 98–103; "Magic Bus," *World Trade,* March 1995, 106; and James H. Donnelly, Jr., James L. Gibson, and John M. Ivancevich, *Fundamentals of Management,* 9th ed. (Burr Ridge, Ill.: Irwin, 1995), 86.

41. Jean Kerr, "Export Strategies," *Small Business Reports* (May 1989), 20–25.

42. Greenberger, "As U.S. Exports Rise, More Workers Benefit."

43. Kathryn Rudie Harrigan, "Managing Joint Ventures," *Management Review* (February 1987), 24–41; and Therese R. Revesz and Mimi Cauley de Da La Sierra, "Competitive Alliances: Forging Ties Abroad," *Management Review* (March 1987), 57–59.

44. Julia Flynn with Richard A. Melcher, "Heineken's Battle to Stay Top Bottle," *Business Week,* August 1, 1994, 60–62; Nathaniel C. Nash, "Coke's Great Romanian Adventure," *The New York Times,* February 26, 1995, F1; and "Importing Can Help a Firm Expand and Diversify," *Nation's Business,* January 1995, 11.

45. Karen Lowry Miller, with Bill Javetski, Peggy Simpson, and Tim Smart, "Europe: The Push East," *Business Week,* November 7, 1994, 48–49.

46. David Woodruff, with Karen Lowry Miller, "Mercedes' Maverick in Alabama," *Business Week,* September 11, 1995, 64–65; and Michael A. Hitt, R. Duane Ireland, and Robert E. Hoskisson, *Strategic Management: Competitiveness and Globalization* (St. Paul, Minn.: West, 1995).

47. "How Revenues of the Top Ten Global Companies Compare with Some National Economies," *Fortune,* July 27, 1992, 16.

48. Howard V. Perlmutter, "The Tortuous Evolution of the Multinational Corporation," *Columbia Journal of World Business* (January–February 1969), 9–18; and Youram Wind, Susan P. Douglas, and Howard V. Perlmutter, "Guidelines for Developing International Marketing Strategies," *Journal of Marketing* (April 1973), 14–23.

49. Robert T. Moran and John R. Riesenberger, *The Global Challenge* (London: McGraw-Hill, 1994), 260.

50. Gibson et al., *Organizations,* 83.

51. Joann S. Lublin, "Younger Managers Learn Global Skills," *The Wall Street Journal,* March 31, 1992, B1.

52. Moran and Riesenberger, *The Global Challenge,* 251–262.

53. Valerie Frazee, "Keeping Up on Chinese Culture," *Global Workforce,* October 1996, 16–17.

54. Fons Trompenaars, *Riding the Waves of Culture: Understanding Diversity in Global Business* (Burr Ridge, Ill.: Irwin, 1994).

55. Randall S. Schuler, Susan E. Jackson, Ellen Jackofsky, and John W. Slocum, Jr., "Managing Human Resources in Mexico: A Cultural Understanding," *Business Horizons,* May–June 1996, 55–61.

56. Caudron, "Lessons from HR Overseas."

57. Moran and Riesenberger, *The Global Challenge,* 255; and Caudron, "Lessons from HR Overseas."

58. Brenton R. Schlender, "Matsushita Shows How to Go Global," *Fortune,* July 11, 1994, 159–166.

59. Friedland and Lee, "The Wal-Mart Way Sometimes Gets Lost in Translation Overseas."

Chapter 5

LEARNING OBJECTIVES

After studying this chapter, you should be able to

- Define ethics and explain how ethical behavior relates to behavior governed by law and free choice.

- Explain the utilitarian, individualism, moral-rights, and justice approaches for evaluating ethical behavior.

- Describe how both individual and organizational factors shape ethical decision making.

- Define corporate social responsibility and how to evaluate it along economic, legal, ethical, and discretionary criteria.

- Describe four corporate responses to social demands.

- Explain the concept of stakeholder and identify important stakeholders for organizations.

- Describe structures that managers can use to improve their organizations' ethics and social responsiveness.

Managerial Ethics and Corporate Social Responsibility

MANAGEMENT PROBLEM

Coke and Pepsi are battling it out in the soft drink industry. McDonald's and Burger King are waging the burger wars. In the rapidly growing financial-information business, the two giants are Reuters Group PLC and Bloomberg LP. The depth of the rivalry became very clear when Reuters disclosed that a subsidiary was being investigated on charges that it improperly obtained and used information from Bloomberg. What's worse, Reuters is now being accused of further questionable behavior. Executives at nine software houses reported instances in which they thought software or information was improperly copied by the media giant. One tells of demonstrating his new software at Reuters headquarters and then being taken to lunch by Reuters officials. When they returned, the computer—along with the software—was gone. No deal was ever made, and the software executive claims that elements of the program later showed up incorporated into Reuters programs. Another software company says Reuters typically will give a vendor a long list of software changes they want made. Then, while the vendor makes the changes, Reuters is busy making a similar product in-house. Reuters denies all wrongdoing, but most of the complaints are supported by a former Reuters in-house lawyer. He claims that "Reuters has practiced various forms of abuses globally . . . [including] misusing vendor's proprietary information and developing it in-house."[1]

When does a company cross the line between legitimately building on the work of others and improperly taking it without compensation? Do you think Reuters crossed that line? Even if Reuters is found to have behaved legally, do you find their actions ethical?

The situation at Reuters illustrates how difficult ethical issues can be and symbolizes the growing importance of discussing ethics and social responsibility. Corporations are rushing to adopt codes of ethics and develop socially responsible policies: ethics consultants are doing a land-office business. Unfortunately, the trend is necessary. In recent years, numerous companies, including Prudential Insurance, Archer-Daniels-Midland, and Centennial Technology, have been charged with major breaches of ethical or legal standards, including price fixing and insider trading. Columbia/HCA, the largest hospital company in the United States, is under federal investigation for possibly inflating the seriousness of patient illnesses to get larger Medicare and Medicaid payments. A $200 million suit against Baker & Taylor Books alleges that the company deliberately overcharged public libraries for trade books discounted by publishers. It comes as no surprise that in a Gallup poll asking about the perceived trustworthiness of six American institutions, only the United States government scored lower marks than U.S. corporations.[2]

On the other hand, there also is positive news to report. Breadsmith's franchisees provide bread for charity events and disaster victims in their areas, donate all leftovers to food banks, and sponsor at least four charity events a year. Glaxo Wellcome has proposed a plan to slash the price of the AIDS drug AZT for pregnant women in developing nations by as much as 75 percent. Several major manufacturers, including DuPont, Electrolux, S. C. Johnson, and British Petroleum, are embracing environmental goals and developing eco-friendly products. And Eastman Kodak Company took an unprecedented step several years ago by tying a percentage of managers' pay to factors such as how well they treat their employees.[3]

This chapter expands on the ideas about environment, corporate culture, and the international environment discussed in Chapters 3 and 4. We will first focus on specific ethical values that build on the idea of corporate culture. Then we will examine corporate relationships to the external environment as reflected in social responsibility. Ethics and social responsibility are hot topics

The Gap Inc. AIDS Walk reflects the company's commitment to a social responsibility approach to the communities in which it does business. Gap Inc. encourages employees to become involved in volunteer activities, and its Community Action Program, which allows headquarters employees to take paid time off to do so, has involved nearly half of all eligible workers. Gap Inc. also gives approximately 1 percent of pretax profits to organizations addressing social issues, strengthening the company's reputation as a socially responsible business.

in corporate America. This chapter discusses fundamental approaches that help managers think through ethical issues. Understanding ethical approaches helps managers build a solid foundation on which to base future decision making.

What Is Managerial Ethics?

Ethics is difficult to define in a precise way. In a general sense, **ethics** is the code of moral principles and values that govern the behaviors of a person or group with respect to what is right or wrong. Ethics sets standards as to what is good or bad in conduct and decision making.[4] Ethics deals with internal values that are a part of corporate culture and shapes decisions concerning social responsibility with respect to the external environment. An ethical issue is present in a situation when the actions of a person or organization may harm or benefit others.[5]

Ethics can be more clearly understood when compared with behaviors governed by laws and by free choice. Exhibit 5.1 illustrates that human behavior falls into three categories. The first is codified law, in which values and standards are written into the legal system and enforceable in the courts. In this area, lawmakers have ruled that people and corporations must behave in a certain way, such as obtaining licenses for cars or paying corporate taxes. The domain of free choice is at the opposite end of the scale and pertains to behavior about which law has no say and for which an individual or organization enjoys complete freedom. An individual's choice of religion or a corporation's choice of the number of dishwashers to manufacture are examples of free choice.

Between these domains lies the area of ethics. This domain has no specific laws, yet it does have standards of conduct based on shared principles and values about moral conduct that guide an individual or company. In the domain of free choice, obedience is strictly to oneself. In the domain of codified law, obedience is to laws prescribed by the legal system. In the domain of ethical behavior, obedience is to unenforceable norms and standards about which the individual or company is aware. An ethically acceptable decision is both legally and morally acceptable to the larger community.

Many companies and individuals get into trouble with the simplified view that choices are governed by either law or free choice. It leads people to mistakenly assume that "If it's not illegal, it must be ethical," as if there were no third domain.[6] A better option is to recognize the domain of ethics and accept moral values as a powerful force for good that can regulate behaviors both inside and outside corporations. As principles of ethics and social responsibility are more widely recognized, companies can use codes of ethics and their corporate cultures to govern behavior, thereby eliminating the need for additional laws and avoiding the problems of unfettered choice.

ethics
The code of moral principles and values that govern the behaviors of a person or group with respect to what is right or wrong.

E x h i b i t **5.1**

Three Domains of Human Action

ethical dilemma
A situation that arises when all alternative choices or behaviors have been deemed undesirable because of potentially negative ethical consequences, making it difficult to distinguish right from wrong.

Because ethical standards are not codified, disagreements and dilemmas about proper behavior often occur. An **ethical dilemma** arises in a situation when each alternative choice or behavior is undesirable because of potentially harmful ethical consequences. Right or wrong cannot be clearly identified. The individual who must make an ethical choice in an organization is the *moral agent.*[1] Consider the dilemmas facing a moral agent in the following situations:

A top employee at your small company tells you he needs some time off because he has AIDS. You know the employee needs the job as well as the health insurance benefits. Providing health insurance has already stretched the company's budget, and this will send premiums through the roof. You recently read of a case in which federal courts upheld the right of an employer to modify health plans by putting a cap on AIDS benefits. Should you investigate whether this is a legal possibility for your company?

As a sales manager for a major pharmaceuticals company, you've been asked to promote a new drug that costs $2,500 per dose. You've read the reports saying the drug is only 1 percent more effective than an alternate drug that costs less than one-fourth as much. Can you in good conscience aggressively promote the $2,500-per-dose drug? If you don't, could lives be lost that might have been saved with that 1 percent increase in effectiveness?

Your company has been asked to pay a gratuity in India to speed the processing of an import permit. This is standard procedure, and your company will suffer if you do not pay the gratuity. Is this different from tipping a maître d' in a nice restaurant?

You are the accounting manager of a division that is $15,000 below profit targets. Approximately $20,000 of office supplies were delivered on December 21. The accounting rule is to pay expenses when incurred. The division general manager asks you not to record the invoice until February.

Your boss says he cannot give you a raise this year because of budget constraints, but he will look the other way if your expense accounts come in a little high because of your good work this past year.

These are the kinds of dilemmas and issues with which managers must deal that fall squarely in the domain of ethics. Now let's turn to approaches to ethical decision making that provide criteria for understanding and resolving these difficult issues.

Criteria for Ethical Decision Making

Most ethical dilemmas involve a conflict between the needs of the part and the whole—the individual versus the organization or the organization versus society as a whole. For example, should a company install mandatory alcohol and drug testing for employees, which may benefit the organization as a whole but reduce the individual freedom of employees? Or should products that fail to meet tough FDA standards be exported to other countries where government standards are lower, benefiting the company but being potentially harmful to world citizens? Sometimes ethical decisions entail a conflict between two groups. For example, should the potential for local health problems resulting from a company's effluents take precedence over the jobs it creates as the town's leading employer?

Managers faced with these kinds of tough ethical choices often benefit from a normative approach—one based on norms and values—to guide their decision making. Normative ethics uses several approaches to describe values for guiding ethical decision making. Four of these that are relevant to managers are the utilitarian approach, individualism approach, moral-rights approach, and justice approach.[8]

Utilitarian Approach

The **utilitarian approach,** espoused by the nineteenth-century philosophers Jeremy Bentham and John Stuart Mill, holds that moral behavior produces the greatest good for the greatest number. Under this approach, a decision maker is expected to consider the effect of each decision alternative on all parties and select the one that optimizes the satisfaction for the greatest number of people. Because actual computations can be very complex, simplifying them is considered appropriate. For example, a simple economic frame of reference could be used by calculating dollar costs and dollar benefits. Also, a decision could be made that considers only the people who are directly affected by the decision, not those who are indirectly affected. When GM chose to continue operations at its Arlington, Texas, plant while shutting down its Ypsilanti, Michigan, plant, managers justified the decision as producing the greater good for the corporation as a whole. The utilitarian ethic is cited as the basis for the recent trend among companies to police employee personal habits such as alcohol and tobacco consumption on the job, and in some cases after hours as well, because such behavior affects the entire workplace.[9]

The utilitarian ethic was the basis for the state of Oregon's decision to extend Medicaid to 400,000 previously ineligible recipients by refusing to pay for high-cost, high-risk procedures such as liver transplants and bone-marrow transplants. Although a few people needing these procedures have died because the state would not pay, many people have benefited from medical services they would otherwise have had to go without.[10] Critics of the utilitarian ethic fear a developing tendency toward a "Big Brother" approach and question whether the common good is squeezing the life out of the individual. Critics also claim that the Oregon decision does not fully take into account the concept of justice toward the unfortunate victims of life-threatening diseases.[11]

Individualism Approach

The **individualism approach** contends that acts are moral when they promote the individual's best long-term interests. Individual self-direction is paramount, and external forces that restrict self-direction should be severely limited.[12] Individuals calculate the best long-term advantage to themselves as a measure of a decision's goodness. The action that is intended to produce a greater ratio of good to bad for the individual compared with other alternatives is the right one to perform. In theory, with everyone pursuing self-direction, the greater good is ultimately served because people learn to accommodate each other in their own long-term interest. Individualism is believed to lead to honesty and integrity because that works best in the long run. Lying and cheating for immediate self-interest just causes business associates to lie and cheat in return. Thus, individualism ultimately leads to behavior toward others that fits standards of behavior people want toward themselves.[13] One value of understanding this approach is to recognize short-term variations if they are proposed. People might argue for short-term

utilitarian approach
The ethical concept that moral behaviors produce the greatest good for the greatest number.

individualism approach
The ethical concept that acts are moral when they promote the individual's best long-term interests, which ultimately leads to the greater good.

Critics say the forest products industry has behaved unethically for years, according to the moral rights approach, by violating employees' right to life and safety. At Georgia-Pacific, the Atlanta-based company with more than 47,000 employees, you weren't considered a "mill guy" unless you were missing a few fingers. Due to a corporate makeover, safety now comes first. By changing attitudes and behavior regarding safety, G-P now records injuries of 0.7 per 100 workers annually, which according to OSHA is about one-third the injury rate at the average bank.

moral-rights approach
The ethical concept that moral decisions are those that best maintain the rights of those people affected by them.

self-interest based on individualism, but that misses the point. Because individualism is easily misinterpreted to support immediate self-gain, it is not popular in the highly organized and group-oriented society of today. Individualism is closest to the domain of free choice described in Exhibit 5.1.

Moral-Rights Approach

The **moral-rights approach** asserts that human beings have fundamental rights and liberties that cannot be taken away by an individual's decision. Thus an ethically correct decision is one that best maintains the rights of those people affected by it.

Moral rights that could be considered during decision making are

1. The right of free consent—individuals are to be treated only as they knowingly and freely consent to be treated.

2. The right to privacy—individuals can choose to do as they please away from work and have control of information about their private life.

3. The right of freedom of conscience—individuals may refrain from carrying out any order that violates their moral or religious norms.

4. The right of free speech—individuals may criticize truthfully the ethics or legality of actions of others.

5. The right to due process—individuals have a right to an impartial hearing and fair treatment.

6. The right to life and safety—individuals have a right to live without endangerment or violation of their health and safety.

To make ethical decisions, managers need to avoid interfering with the fundamental rights of others. Thus a decision to eavesdrop on employees violates the right to privacy. Sexual harassment is unethical because it violates the right to freedom of conscience. The right of free speech would support whistleblowers who call attention to illegal or inappropriate action within a company.

justice approach
The ethical concept that moral decisions must be based on standards of equity, fairness, and impartiality.

distributive justice
The concept that different treatment of people should not be based on arbitrary characteristics. In the case of substantive differences, people should be treated differently in proportion to the differences among them.

Justice Approach

The **justice approach** holds that moral decisions must be based on standards of equity, fairness, and impartiality. Three types of justice are of concern to managers. **Distributive justice** requires that different treatment of people not be based on arbitrary characteristics. Individuals who are similar in respects relevant to a decision should be treated similarly. Thus men and women should not receive different salaries if they are performing the same job. However, people who differ in a substantive way, such as job skills or job responsibility, can be treated differently in proportion to the differences in skills or responsibility among them. This difference should have a clear relationship to organizational goals and tasks.

Procedural justice requires that rules be administered fairly. Rules should be clearly stated and be consistently and impartially enforced. **Compensatory justice** argues that individuals should be compensated for the cost of their injuries by the party responsible. Moreover, individuals should not be held responsible for matters over which they have no control.

The justice approach is closest to the thinking underlying the domain of law in Exhibit 5.1, because it assumes that justice is applied through rules and regulations. This theory does not require complex calculations such as those demanded by a utilitarian approach, nor does it justify self-interest as the individualism approach does. Managers are expected to define attributes on which different treatment of employees is acceptable. Questions such as how minority workers should be compensated for past discrimination are extremely difficult. However, this approach does justify as ethical behavior efforts to correct past wrongs, playing fair under the rules, and insisting on job-relevant differences as the basis for different levels of pay or promotion opportunities. Most of the laws guiding human resource management (Chapter 13) are based on the justice approach.

These are general principles that managers can recognize as useful in making ethical decisions. However, understanding the approaches is only a first step; managers still have to consider how to apply them.[14] The challenge of applying ethical approaches is illustrated by decisions facing companies in the insurance industry.

procedural justice
The concept that rules should be clearly stated and consistently and impartially enforced.

compensatory justice
The concept that individuals should be compensated for the cost of their injuries by the party responsible and also that individuals should not be held responsible for matters over which they have no control.

When 72-year-old Pok Dong Kim, a Korean-born U.S. citizen, applied for a $10,000 life insurance policy, she and her family never expected the application to be rejected. Yet, a month later, a letter arrived from Northwestern Mutual Life Insurance Co. stating that Kim "did not meet our language requirements for the ability to understand English." Although the company has now dropped the requirement, the family has sued Northwestern for national-origin discrimination.

Insurance companies are increasingly coming under attack for alleged discrimination against minorities and women. Companies often have U.S. citizens with foreign surnames investigated closely, arguing that they could later sue their way out of insurance contracts on grounds that they didn't understand English. In addition, GEICO contends that auto accident rates are 35 percent higher for noncitizens, and until recently the company sold insurance only to U.S. citizens. Insurance companies have also turned down applicants with histories of emergency room visits symptomatic of domestic abuse, prompting outcry from women's organizations.

The companies say they are just making careful business decisions in the best interest of their clients. As a manager at GEICO griped about the recent ruling against them, "Now rates have to go up for everybody." Kenney Shipley of the Florida Insurance Department believes there may often be valid reasons for rejecting applications for race or gender issues. "But," he adds, "we as a society have to say whether or not it's acceptable."[15]

NORTHWESTERN MUTUAL LIFE INSURANCE COMPANY
www.nml.com

Consider for a moment how you think the various ethics approaches support or discredit insurance companies' actions regarding women and minorities.

Factors Affecting Ethical Choices

When managers are accused of lying, cheating, or stealing, the blame is usually placed on the individual or on the company situation. Most people believe that individuals make ethical choices because of individual integrity, which is true, but it is not the whole story. Ethical or unethical business practices usually reflect the values, attitudes, beliefs, and behavior patterns of the organizational culture; thus, ethics is as much an organizational as a personal issue.[16] Let's examine how both the manager and the organization shape ethical decision making.[17]

The Manager

Managers bring specific personality and behavioral traits to the job. Personal needs, family influence, and religious background all shape a manager's value system. Specific personality characteristics, such as ego strength, self-confidence, and a strong sense of independence may enable managers to make ethical decisions.

One important personal trait is the stage of moral development.[18] A simplified version of one model of personal moral development is shown in Exhibit 5.2. At the *preconventional level*, individuals are concerned with external rewards and punishments and obey authority to avoid detrimental personal consequences. In an organizational context, this level may be associated with managers who use an autocratic or coercive leadership style, with employees oriented toward dependable accomplishment of specific tasks. At level two, called the *conventional level*, people learn to conform to the expectations of good behavior as defined by colleagues, family, friends, and society. Meeting social and interpersonal obligations is important. Work group

Exhibit 5.2   *Three Levels of Personal Moral Development*

Level 3: Postconventional

Follows self-chosen principles of justice and right. Aware that people hold different values and seeks creative solutions to ethical dilemmas. Balances concern for individual with concern for common good.

Level 2: Conventional

Lives up to expectations of others. Fulfills duties and obligations of social system. Upholds laws.

Level 1: Preconventional

Follows rules to avoid punishment. Acts in own interest. Obedience for its own sake.

Leadership Style: Autocratic/coercive	Guiding/encouraging, team oriented	Transforming, or servant leadership
Employee Behavior: Task accomplishment	Work group collaboration	Empowered employees, full participation

Sources: Based on L. Kohlberg, "Moral Stages and Moralization: The Cognitive-Developmental Approach," in *Moral Development and Behavior: Theory, Research, and Social Issues,* ed. T. Lickona (New York: Holt, Rinehart, and Winston, 1976) 31–53; and Jill W. Graham, "Leadership, Moral Development and Citizenship Behavior," *Business Ethics Quarterly* 5, no.1 (January 1995), 43–54.

Guidelines for Ethical Decision Making

If Mike Wallace and a "60 Minutes" crew were waiting on your doorstep one morning, would you feel comfortable justifying your actions to the camera? One young manager, when confronted with ethical dilemmas, gives them the "60 Minutes" test. Others say they use such criteria as whether they would be proud to tell their parents or grandparents about their decision or whether they could sleep well at night and face themselves in the mirror in the morning. Managers often rely on their own personal integrity in making ethical decisions. But knowing what to do is not always easy. As a future manager, you will almost surely face ethical dilemmas one day. The following guidelines will not tell you exactly what to do, but, taken in the context of the text discussion, they will help you evaluate the situation more clearly by examining your own values and those of your organization. The answers to these questions will force you to think hard about the social and ethical consequences of your behavior.

1. Is the problem/dilemma really what it appears to be? If you are not sure, *find out.*
2. Is the action you are considering legal? Ethical? If you are not sure, *find out.*
3. Do you understand the position of those who oppose the action you are considering? Is it reasonable?
4. Whom does the action benefit? Harm? How much? How long?
5. Would you be willing to allow everyone to do what you are considering doing?
6. Have you sought the opinion of others who are knowledgeable on the subject and who would be objective?
7. Would your action be embarrassing to you if it were made known to your family, friends, coworkers, or superiors?

There are no correct answers to these questions in an absolute sense. Yet, if you determine that an action is potentially harmful to someone or would be embarrassing to you, or if you do not know the ethical or legal consequences, these guidelines will help you clarify whether the action is socially responsible.

SOURCES: Anthony M. Pagano and Jo Ann Verdin, *The External Environment of Business* (New York: Wiley, 1988), Chapter 5; and Joseph L. Badaracco, Jr., and Allen P. Webb, "Business Ethics: A View from the Trenches," *California Management Review* 37, no. 2 (winter 1995), 8–28.

collaboration is the preferred manner for accomplishment of organizational goals, and managers use a leadership style that encourages interpersonal relationships and cooperation. At the *postconventional,* or *principled* level, individuals are guided by an internal set of values and standards and will even disobey rules or laws that violate these principles. Internal values become more important than the expectations of significant others. For example, when the *USS Indianapolis* sank after being torpedoed during World War II, one Navy pilot disobeyed orders and risked his life to save men who were being picked off by sharks. The pilot was operating from the highest level of moral development in attempting the rescue despite a direct order from superiors. When managers operate from this highest level of development, they use transformative or servant leadership, focusing on the needs of followers and encouraging others to think for themselves and to engage in higher levels of moral reasoning. Employees are empowered and given opportunities for constructive participation in governance of the organization.

The great majority of managers operate at level two. A few have not advanced beyond level one. Only about 20 percent of American adults reach the level-three stage of moral development. People at level three are able to act in an independent, ethical manner regardless of expectations from others inside or outside the organization. Managers at level three of moral development will make ethical decisions whatever the organizational consequences for them. The Manager's Shoptalk box lists some general guidelines to follow for making ethical decisions.

One interesting study indicates that most researchers have failed to account for the different ways in which women view social reality and develop psychologically and have thus consistently classified women as being stuck at lower levels of development. Researcher Carol Gilligan has suggested that the moral domain be enlarged to include responsibility and care in relationships. Women may, in general, perceive moral complexities more astutely than men and make moral decisions based not on a set of absolute rights and wrongs but on principles of not causing harm to others.[19] Women's sense of integrity seems to be entwined with an ethic of care; hence, they may be ideally suited for the servant leadership needed in today's organizations.

One reason higher levels of ethical conduct are increasingly important is the impact of globalization on organizational ethics and corporate culture. As we discussed in Chapter Four, globalization has complicated ethical issues for today's managers. American managers need to develop sensitivity and openness to other systems, as well as mature ethical judgment to work out differences. For example, although tolerance for bribery is waning, it is still an accepted way of doing business in many countries. Foreign managers sometimes resent Americans' "holier-than-thou" attitudes and the stereotypical belief that all foreign managers are corrupt.[20] It is not always easy to resolve international issues. There are, however, increasing calls for the development of global standards for ethical business conduct, which may help managers negotiate the difficult terrain of international ethics. Organizations such as the Caux Round Table, also discussed in the previous chapter, are trying to "identify the transcultural values that we can all salute."[21]

The Organization

The values adopted within the organization are important, especially when we understand that most people are at the level-two stage of moral development, which means they believe their duty is to fulfill obligations and expectations of others. Research has shown that the values of an organization or department strongly influence employee behavior and decision making.[22] In particular, corporate culture serves to let employees know what beliefs and behaviors the company supports and those it will not tolerate. For example, an investigation of thefts and kickbacks in the oil business found that the cause was the historical acceptance of thefts and kickbacks. Employees were socialized into those values and adopted them as appropriate. In most companies, employees believe that if they do not go along with the ethical values expressed, their jobs will be in jeopardy or they will not fit in.[23]

Culture can be examined to see the kinds of ethical signals given to employees. Exhibit 5.3 indicates questions to ask to understand the cultural system. Heroes provide role models that can either support or refute ethical decision making. Founder Sam Walton stood for integrity at Wal-Mart, and his values are ingrained in the organizational culture. With respect to company rituals, high ethical standards are affirmed and communicated through public awards and ceremonies. Myths and stories can reinforce heroic ethical behavior. For example, a story at Johnson & Johnson describes its reaction to the cyanide poisoning of Tylenol capsule users. After seven people in Chicago died, the capsules were removed from the market voluntarily, costing the company more than $100 million. This action was taken against the advice of external agencies—FBI and FDA—but was necessary because of Johnson & Johnson's ethical standards.

Exhibit *5.3*

1. Identify the organization's heroes. What values do they represent? Given an ambiguous ethical dilemma, what decision would they make and why?
2. What are some important organizational rituals? How do they encourage or discourage ethical behavior? Who gets the awards, people of integrity or individuals who use unethical methods to attain success?
3. What are the ethical messages sent to new entrants into the organization—must they obey authority at all costs, or is questioning authority acceptable or even desirable?
4. Does analysis of organizational stories and myths reveal individuals who stand up for what's right, or is conformity the valued characteristic? Do people get fired or promoted in these stories?
5. Does language exist for discussing ethical concerns? Is this language routinely incorporated and encouraged in business decision making?
6. What informal socialization processes exist, and what norms for ethical/unethical behavior do they promote?

Questions for Analyzing a Company's Cultural Impact on Ethics

SOURCES: Linda Klebe Trevino, "A Cultural Perspective on Changing and Developing Organizational Ethics," in *Research in Organizational Change and Development,* ed. R. Woodman and W. Pasmore (Greenwich, Conn.: JAI Press, 1990), 4.

Culture is not the only aspect of an organization that influences ethics, but it is a major force because it defines company values. Other aspects of the organization, such as explicit rules and policies, the reward system, the extent to which the company cares for its people, the selection system, emphasis on legal and professional standards, and leadership and decision processes, can also have an impact on ethical values and manager decision making.[24] At Levi Strauss, for example, the selection system is aimed at promoting diversity of background and thought among workers, a set of "corporate aspirations" written by top management is to guide all major decisions, and one-third of a manager's raise can depend on how well he or she toes the values line.[25]

What Is Social Responsibility?

Now let's turn to the issue of social responsibility. In one sense, the concept of corporate social responsibility, like ethics, is easy to understand: it means distinguishing right from wrong and doing right. It means being a good corporate citizen. The formal definition of **social responsibility** is management's obligation to make choices and take actions that will contribute to the welfare and interests of society as well as the organization.[26]

As straightforward as this definition seems, social responsibility can be a difficult concept to grasp, because different people have different beliefs as to which actions improve society's welfare.[27] To make matters worse, social responsibility covers a range of issues, many of which are ambiguous with respect to right or wrong. For example, if a bank deposits the money from a trust fund into a low-interest account for 90 days, from which it makes a substantial profit, has it been unethical? How about two companies' engaging in intense competition, such as that between Cleveland Electric Illuminating Co. and Cleveland Public Power? Is it socially responsible for the stronger corporation to drive the weaker one into bankruptcy? Or consider companies such as A. H. Robins, maker of the Dalkon shield; Manville Corporation, maker of asbestos; Eastern Airlines; or Texaco, the oil company, all of which declared bankruptcy—which is perfectly legal—to avoid mounting financial obligations to suppliers, labor unions, or competitors. These examples contain moral, legal, and economic considerations that make socially responsible behavior hard to define. A company's environmental impact must also be taken into consideration.

social responsibility
The obligation of organization management to make decisions and take actions that will enhance the welfare and interests of society as well as the organization.

Organizational Stakeholders

One reason for the difficulty understanding social responsibility is that managers must confront the question "responsibility to whom?" Recall from Chapter 3 that the organization's environment consists of several sectors in both the task and general environment. From a social responsibility perspective, enlightened organizations view the internal and external environment as a variety of stakeholders.

stakeholder
Any group within or outside the organization that has a stake in the organization's performance.

A **stakeholder** is any group within or outside the organization that has a stake in the organization's performance. Each stakeholder has a different criterion of responsiveness, because it has a different interest in the organization.[28] For example, Wal-Mart uses aggressive bargaining tactics with suppliers so that it is able to provide low prices for customers. Some stakeholders see this as socially responsible behavior because it benefits customers and forces suppliers to be more efficient. Others, however, argue that the aggressive tactics are an abuse of power and may prevent suppliers from even paying their own employees a decent wage.[29]

Exhibit 5.4 illustrates important stakeholders for an auto manufacturer. Investors and shareholders, employees, customers, and suppliers are considered primary stakeholders, without whom the organization cannot survive. Investors, shareholders, and suppliers' interests are served by managerial efficiency—that is, use of resources to achieve profits. Employees expect work satisfaction, pay, and good supervision. Customers are concerned with decisions about the quality, safety, and availability of goods and services. When any primary stakeholder group becomes seriously dissatisfied, the organization's viability is threatened.[30]

Exhibit **5.4**

Stakeholders Relevant to an Auto Manufacturer

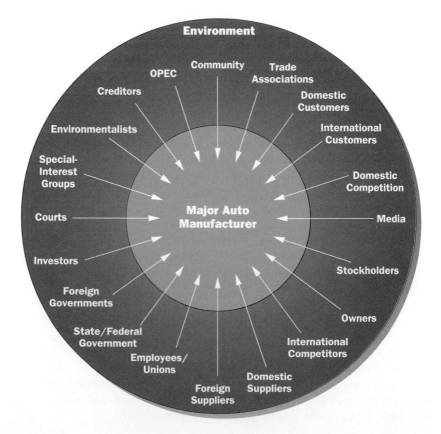

Source: Based on Nancy C. Roberts and Paula J. King, "The Stakeholder Audit Goes Public," *Organizational Dynamics* (winter 1989), 63–79.

Helping Build Healthy Communities

Marketing consultant and real estate developer José de Jesús Legaspi drives more than 250 miles a day in his Toyota Land Cruiser, stopping frequently to get out and walk the streets of south central and east Los Angeles. Some people might see the areas as symbols of urban decay, but Legaspi knows better. Using his knowledge of the Hispanic community and his street smarts, the Mexican-born marketing consultant and real estate developer has brought new life to an amazing variety of retail outlets in the area, including a series of Blockbuster Video stores, a retailer of high-end electronics, and a thriving chain of charbroiled chicken restaurants. In the process, Legaspi has helped to transform decaying urban areas left for dead in the early 1980s.

Legaspi says his vision is built on customer focus rather than do-gooder social consciousness. He wants to bring goods and services to the Hispanic community, and he believes Hispanic customers offer a loyal consumer and strong income base for businesses. He is quick to point out that there are more than 22 million Hispanics in the United States, representing a $220 billion market that still is unserved in many cities. He regularly has successful retail chains asking him, "Why won't they buy from us?" The answer "isn't the competition and it isn't the customer. It's always, always, *you*," says Legaspi. One recent example was Thrifty Drug Stores, which had trouble remaining profitable in areas with high concentrations of Hispanics. Legaspi pointed out that the stores were serving areas with recently arrived immigrants—people who as yet had no bank accounts and no credit cards, but were bringing in steady paychecks. He suggested setting up check-cashing machines inside the stores as well as making it possible for customers to pay utility bills there. After the chain followed Legaspi's advice, Thrifty's sales went up by 20 percent.

Source: Susan Beck, "It Takes Customers to Rebuild the City," *Fast Company*, December–January 1997, 44–45.

Other important stakeholders are the government and the community. Most corporations exist only under the proper charter and licenses and operate within the limits of safety laws, environmental protection requirements, and other laws and regulations in the government sector. The community includes local government, the natural and physical environments, and the quality of life provided for residents. Special-interest groups, still another stakeholder, may include trade associations, political action committees, professional associations, and consumerists. Socially responsible organizations consider the effects of their actions upon all stakeholders.

Enlightened corporations invest in a number of philanthropic causes that benefit stakeholders. Marriott Corp. tries to help build healthy communities through its "Pathways to Independence Program," which targets welfare recipients. The program candidates are put through dozens of hours of rigorous training and then "graduated" to a job in the company.[31] The Diversity box describes how urban entrepreneur José de Jesús Legaspi is helping to rebuild communities in Los Angeles.

Well-meaning companies sometimes run afoul of stakeholders anyway but can take actions to appease them. For example, Fina, Inc., established an oil refinery in Port Arthur, Texas, in 1937. Over the years, subdivisions of attractive ranch-style homes grew up in the shadow of the Fina plant. Homeowners became unhappy with the plant in their midst because of its noise and odor. Residents expected the company to purchase their homes at top market price. Fina made several good faith efforts to resolve problems and then agreed to purchase the homes because the residents had legitimate gripes.[32] Companies such as Fina and Marriott are acting in a socially responsible way by helping stakeholders.

Today, special-interest groups continue to be one of the largest stakeholder concerns that companies face. Environmental responsibility has become a primary issue as both business and the public acknowledge the damage that has been done to our natural environment.

The Natural Environment

When the first Earth Day celebration was held in 1970, environmentalists were considered by most business leaders to be an extremist fringe group, and few managers felt the need to respond to environmental concerns.[33] Today, the world has changed dramatically. Environmental issues have become a hot topic among business leaders, and large corporations as well as small businesses are targeting marketing efforts to woo the environmentally conscious consumer. Companies such as 3M and Baxter International are not only developing less-polluting products and processes but also are helping their customers establish environmental programs. Today, more than a quarter of Baxter's customers, which are mostly hospitals, seek environmental assistance.[34] Jeffrey Hollender built a small business, Seventh Heaven, by targeting the "green" consumer with environmentally friendly products.[35] Companies such as Aveda and John Paul Mitchell are responding to growing concerns for animal welfare by not testing on animals.

The ranks of environmentally conscious consumers are growing, as revealed by a recent study conducted by the New York–based research firm Roper Starch Worldwide, Inc. Roper divides consumers into five categories.[36]

- *True-Blue Greens,* 14 percent of the population, up from 11 percent in 1990, are highly committed and make buying decisions and change their personal behavior to help the natural environment.

- *Greenback Greens,* 6 percent of the population, aren't usually willing to make substantial changes in their purchasing behavior, but they support environmental causes and often vote for pro-environment political candidates.

- *Sprouts,* who shot up from 26 percent in 1990 to 35 percent, make a few environmentally friendly purchases and become involved in environmental causes from time to time.

- *Grousers,* 13 percent, only grudgingly acknowledge environmental mandates.

- *Basic Browns,* 32 percent, are the least environmentally active and generally do not recycle or support governmental regulation designed to help the natural environment.

Although the apathetic Basic Brown group still represents a large percentage of the population, its ranks are thinning. Most observers agree that the direction of society is toward a greater concern for the natural environment and all living things and that managers must be ready for the next "green" wave.[37] Environmentalism has become an integral part of organizational strategy for leading companies. Some companies, including Amoco, Southern California Edison, and Ciba-Geigy, have even begun working collaboratively with environmental groups to determine what is needed to save our environment and what works in practice rather than just in theory. Southern California Edison was intimately involved with the Desert Protection Act, which set aside 7.5 million acres for 70 separate wilderness areas. SCE worked closely with the National Park and Conservation Association, the Sierra Club, and other stakeholders to work out compromises that would preserve the

As part of its "Project Earth" program, A&P Stores urges customers to take an Earth Pledge and get involved in efforts to improve the natural environment. Environmental responsibility *has become a primary issue for businesses. A&P adopted the turtle and frog, which are disappearing all over the world, as the company's mascots to roll out a new program aimed at building environmental awareness. One way A&P contributes directly to conservation efforts is its Energy Conservation System, which monitors and adjusts operating equipment to ensure maximum energy efficiency.*

wilderness area without disrupting SCE's existing infrastructure of pipelines, power lines, telephone lines, etc. Although some adversity still exists between business and environmental groups, there is an increasing emphasis on cooperation.[38] The Natural Step, an international environmental coalition that now has national organizations in Sweden, Australia, the United States, Canada, Japan, and the United Kingdom, is a leader in promoting the idea of cooperation rather than conflict to solve our environmental problems. As founder Karl-Henrik Robèrt describes the process: "First we educate business leaders, politicians, and scientists . . . then we ask them for advice. Instead of telling them what to do, we say, 'How could this be applied in your world?' This sparks creativity and enthusiasm into the process instead of defense mechanisms."[39]

As we've discussed throughout this chapter, companies and managers often walk a fine line in their efforts to do the right thing, make money, and satisfy numerous stakeholders. In the following section, we will look at criteria that can be used to evaluate a company's social performance.

Evaluating Corporate Social Performance

One model for evaluating corporate social performance is presented in Exhibit 5.5. The model indicates that total corporate social responsibility can be subdivided into four criteria—economic, legal, ethical, and discretionary responsibilities.[40] The responsibilities are ordered from bottom to top based on their relative magnitude and the frequency with which managers deal with each issue.

Note the similarity between the categories in Exhibit 5.5 and those in Exhibit 5.1. In both cases, ethical issues are located between the areas of legal and freely discretionary responsibilities. Exhibit 5.5 also has an economic category, because profits are a major reason for corporations' existence.

Total Corporate Social Responsibility

Discretionary Responsibility
Contribute to the community and quality of life.

Ethical Responsibility
Be ethical. Do what is right. Avoid harm.

Legal Responsibility
Obey the law.

Economic Responsibility
Be profitable.

Exhibit **5.5**

Criteria of Corporate Social Performance

SOURCE: Archie B. Carroll, "A Three-Dimensional Conceptual Model of Corporate Performance," *Academy of Management Review* 4 (1979), 499; and "The Pyramid of Corporate Social Responsibility: Toward the Moral Management of Corporate Stakeholders," *Business Horizons* 34 (July-August 1991), 42.

Economic Responsibilities

The first criterion of social responsibility is *economic responsibility*. The business institution is, above all, the basic economic unit of society. Its responsibility is to produce the goods and services that society wants and to maximize profits for its owners and shareholders. Economic responsibility, carried to the extreme, is called the *profit-maximizing view,* advocated by Nobel economist Milton Friedman. This view argues that the corporation should be operated on a profit-oriented basis, with its sole mission to increase its profits so long as it stays within the rules of the game.[41]

The purely profit-maximizing view is no longer considered an adequate criterion of performance in Canada, the United States, and Europe. This approach means that economic gain is the only social responsibility and can lead companies into trouble. A notorious example was Salomon Brothers' attempt to corner the Treasury securities market. Corporate greed, fostered by former chairman John Gutfreund's "win-at-all-costs" culture, resulted in mistakes that led to record penalties of $280 million.[42]

Legal Responsibilities

All modern societies lay down ground rules, laws, and regulations that businesses are expected to follow. *Legal responsibility* defines what society deems as important with respect to appropriate corporate behavior.[43] Businesses are expected to fulfill their economic goals within the legal framework. Legal requirements are imposed by local town councils, state legislators, and federal regulatory agencies.

Organizations that knowingly break the law are poor performers in this category. Intentionally manufacturing defective goods or billing a client for work not done is illegal. An example of the punishment given to one company that broke the law is shown in Exhibit 5.6.

Ethical Responsibilities

Ethical responsibility includes behaviors that are not necessarily codified into law and may not serve the corporation's direct economic interests. As described earlier in this chapter, to be *ethical,* organization decision makers should act with equity, fairness, and impartiality, respect the rights of individuals, and provide different treatment of individuals only when relevant to the organization's goals and tasks.[44] *Unethical* behavior occurs when decisions enable an individual or company to gain at the expense of society. One area that has recently been called into question concerns Internet sites for children set up by companies such as Kellogg, Nabisco, and Frito-Lay. Watchdog groups charge that these companies are acting unethically by using games and other forms of entertainment designed to gather marketing data from children as young as four years old.[45]

On the other hand, Microboard Processing Inc. provides an example of ethical action through its hiring of high-risk employees, from former welfare recipients with little job experience to felons and former drug addicts. CEO Craig T. Hoekenga sees one of his responsibilities to be helping people turn their lives around. Although this approach has caused some problems, Hoekenga attributes the rapid growth of his company to the loyalty and hard work of people who appreciate being given a chance. Hoekenga and his company also make major contributions to charity.[46]

Beatrice E. Rangel, senior vice-president for corporate strategies at Venezuela's largest private conglomerate, the $3.6 billion Cisneros Group, reflects her company's commitment to discretionary responsibility. Rangel is a vocal advocate for Latin America's investment in its people through higher corporate spending on education. Rangel reports that Cisneros spends 8 percent of its corporate budget on training and that via unused channels of Galaxy Latin America, a Cisneros satellite TV venture with Hughes Electronics, the company is launching a broadcast that will reach seven countries to train teachers.

Exhibit *5.6*

*One Company's Punishment
for Breaking the Law*

American Caster Corporation

Dear Businesses & Residents of the City & County of Los Angeles

Pollution of our environment has become a crisis.

Intentional clandestine acts of illegal disposal of hazardous waste, or "midnight dumping" are violent crimes against the community.

Over the past 2 years almost a dozen Chief Executive Officers of both large and small corporations have been sent to jail by the L.A. Toxic Waste Strike Force.

They have also been required to pay huge fines; pay for cleanups; speak in public about their misdeeds; and in some cases place ads publicizing their crime and punishment.

THE RISKS OF BEING CAUGHT ARE TOO HIGH—AND THE CONSEQUENCES IF CAUGHT ARE NOT WORTH IT!

We are paying the price. *TODAY,* while you read this ad our **President and Vice President are serving time in** *JAIL* **and we were forced to place this ad.**

PLEASE TAKE THE LEGAL ALTERNATIVE AND PROTECT OUR ENVIRONMENT.

Very Truly Yours,

American Caster Corporation

141 WEST AVENUE 34
LOS ANGELES, CA 90031

Source: Barry C. Groveman and John L. Segal, "Pollution Police Pursue Chemical Criminals," *Business and Society Review* 55 (fall 1985), 41.

Discretionary Responsibilities

Discretionary responsibility is purely voluntary and guided by a company's desire to make social contributions not mandated by economics, law, or ethics. Discretionary activities include generous philanthropic contributions that offer no payback to the company and are not expected. An example of discretionary behavior occurred when Pittsburgh Brewing Company helped laid-off steelworkers by establishing and contributing to food banks in the Pittsburgh area. Discretionary responsibility is the highest criterion of social responsibility, because it goes beyond societal expectations to contribute to the community's welfare.

discretionary responsibility
Organizational responsibility that is voluntary and guided by the organization's desire to make social contributions not mandated by economics, law, or ethics.

Corporate Actions toward Social Demands

Confronted with a specific social demand, how might a corporation respond? If a stakeholder such as the local government places a demand on the company, what types of corporate action might be taken? Management scholars have developed a scale of response actions that companies use when a social issue confronts them.[47] These actions are obstructive, defensive, accommodative, and proactive and are illustrated on the continuum in Exhibit 5.7.

Obstructive. Companies that adopt **obstructive responses** deny all responsibility, claim that evidence of wrongdoing is misleading or distorted, and place obstacles to delay investigation. During the Watergate years, such

obstructive response
A response to social demands in which the organization denies responsibility, claims that evidence of misconduct is misleading or distorted, and attempts to obstruct investigation.

Exhibit *5.7*

Corporate Responses to Social Demands

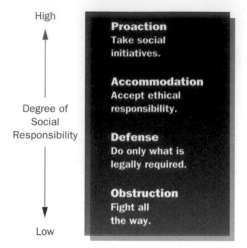

High

Degree of
Social
Responsibility

Low

Proaction
Take social
initiatives.

Accommodation
Accept ethical
responsibility.

Defense
Do only what is
legally required.

Obstruction
Fight all
the way.

obstruction was labeled *stonewalling.* A. H. Robins Company reportedly used obstructive actions when it received warnings about its Dalkon shield, an intrauterine device. The company built a wall around itself. It stood against all evidence and insisted to the public that the product was safe and effective. The company spared no effort to resist investigation. As word about injuries caused by the Dalkon shield kept pouring in, one attorney was told to search the files and destroy all papers pertaining to the product.[48] More recently, during class-action suits against companies in the tobacco industry, the companies were accused of using obstructive measures by hiding the facts of their own research indicating possible health hazards of smoking.

defensive response
A response to social demands in which the organization admits to some errors of commission or omission but does not act obstructively.

Defensive.   The **defensive response** means that the company admits to some errors of omission or commission. The company cuts its losses by defending itself but is not obstructive. Defensive managers generally believe that "these things happen, but they are nobody's fault." Goodyear adopted a defensive strategy by deciding to keep its South Africa plants open and provided an intelligent argument for why that was the proper action.

accommodative response
A response to social demands in which the organization accepts—often under pressure—social responsibility for its actions to comply with the public interest.

Accommodative.   An **accommodative response** means that the company accepts social responsibility for its actions, although it may do so in response to external pressure. Firms that adopt this action try to meet economic, legal, and ethical responsibilities. If outside forces apply pressure, managers agree to curtail ethically questionable activities. Companies often will hire an ethics consultant to help them clean up their act and improve their public image. Both KPMG Peat Marwick and Arthur Andersen & Co. have started ethics consulting units and the field is a booming business.[49] Exxon's decision to clean up the oil spill in Prince William Sound was an accommodative decision based largely on the public's outcry.

proactive response
A response to social demands in which the organization seeks to learn what is in its constituencies' interest and to respond without pressure from them.

Proactive.   The **proactive response** means that firms take the lead in social issues. They seek to learn what is in the public interest and respond without coaxing or pressure from stakeholders. One example of proactive behavior is the Potlatch Corporation. Potlatch makes milk cartons and came up with the idea of printing photographs of missing children on them. The company reported that within days after the Alta-Dena Dairy of Los Angeles placed a missing-kids carton in grocery stores, one of the youngsters returned home.[50] Another proactive response is corporate philanthropy. Many companies, including Miller Brewing, Coca-Cola, and Westinghouse, make generous donations to universities, United Way, and other charitable groups as a way of reaching out and improving society.

These four categories of action are similar to the scale of social performance described in Exhibit 5.5. Obstructiveness tends to occur in firms whose actions are based solely on economic considerations. Defensive organizations are willing to work within the letter of the law. Accommodative organizations respond to ethical pressures. Proactive organizations use discretionary responsibilities to enhance community welfare.

Beech-Nut Nutrition Corporation was accused of unethical and socially irresponsible behavior. How would you evaluate its response?

To Beech-Nut, feeding babies is a sacred trust. Bottles of fruit juice say "100% fruit juice." Yet Beech-Nut was found to have adulterated its best-selling line of apple juice products. A member of the research department became suspicious that the concentrate acquired from suppliers contained nothing more than sugar water and chemicals. When he voiced his concerns, top management accused the employee of not being a team player and wrote in his annual performance review that his judgment was "colored by naivete and impractical ideals." The top managers were not hardened criminals trying to swindle customers. They were honest and well respected but under great financial pressure. The cheap concentrate from the new supplier saved millions of dollars, and managers simply did not want to recognize that they were receiving a poor product. Beech-Nut was running on a shoestring, and enormous financial pressure forced managers to stay with the low-cost supplier.

Beech-Nut learned its lesson the hard way after an FDA investigation. Had the company admitted its error, payment of a fine would have closed the issue. But management stonewalled, and Beech-Nut found itself in the middle of a nightmare as the case changed from civil to criminal. The company's strategy was to stall investigations and avoid publicity until it could unload the diluted apple juice. After 2 years and two criminal trials, Beech-Nut's two top executives were sentenced to 1 year and a day in prison and fined $100,000. The total cost to the company, including fines, legal expenses, and lost sales, was an estimated $25 million.[51]

BEECH-NUT NUTRITION CORPORATION
www.beech-nut.com

Managing Company Ethics and Social Responsibility

Many managers are concerned with improving the ethical climate and social responsiveness of their companies. They do not want to be surprised or be forced into an obstructionist or defensive position. As one expert on the topic of ethics said, "Management is responsible for creating and sustaining conditions in which people are likely to behave themselves."[52] Managers must take active steps to ensure that the company stays on an ethical footing. Management methods for helping organizations be more responsible include leadership by example, codes of ethics, ethical structures, and supporting whistle-blowers.

Leadership by Example.   In a study of ethics policy and practice in successful, ethical companies such as Boeing, Chemical Bank, General Mills, GTE, Xerox, Johnson & Johnson, and Hewlett-Packard, no point emerged

Starbucks Coffee takes a proactive response to social issues by funding programs such as Pied Crow, a children's literary magazine distributed to more than 14,000 primary schools in Kenya. The magazine uses colorful stories and pictures to provide information on health and sanitation, environmental issues, starting a small business, and the prevention of AIDS. Starbucks is North America's leading corporate sponsor of CARE, the international aid and relief organization.

code of ethics
A formal statement of the organization's values regarding ethics and social issues.

more clearly than the crucial role of top managers.[53] Leaders set the tone for an organization's ethics through their own actions. Leaders make a commitment to ethical values and help others throughout the organization embody and reflect those values.[54] The chief executive officer and senior managers need to be openly and strongly committed to ethical conduct. They must give constant leadership in renewing the ethical values of the organization. They must be active in communicating that commitment in speeches, directives, company publications, and especially in actions. The company "grapevine" quickly communicates situations in which top managers chose an expedient action over an ethical one, and subsequent pronouncements of top executives' commitment to ethics count for very little.[55] Top managers set the tone of the organization most clearly by their behavior.

Code of Ethics.   A **code of ethics** is a formal statement of the company's values concerning ethics and social issues; it communicates to employees what the company stands for. Codes of ethics tend to exist in two types: principle-based statements and policy-based statements. *Principle-based statements* are designed to affect corporate culture; they define fundamental values and contain general language about company responsibilities, quality of products, and treatment of employees. General statements of principle are often called *corporate credos.* Examples are GTE's "Vision and Values," Johnson & Johnson's "The Credo," and Hewlett-Packard's "The HP Way."[56]

Policy-based statements generally outline the procedures to be used in specific ethical situations. These situations include marketing practice, conflicts of interest, observance of laws, proprietary information, political gifts, and equal opportunities. Examples of policy-based statements are Boeing's "Business Conduct Guidelines," Chemical Bank's "Code of Ethics," GTE's "Code of Business Ethics" and "Anti-Trust and Conflict of Interest Guidelines," and Norton's "Norton Policy on Business Ethics."[57]

Codes of ethics state the values or behaviors that are expected and those that will not be tolerated, backed up by management's action. A recent study by the Center for Business Ethics found that 90 percent of *Fortune* 500 companies and almost half of all other companies now have codes of ethics. When top management supports and enforces these codes, including rewards for compliance and discipline for violation, ethics codes can uplift a company's ethical climate. When top management doesn't support them, ethics codes are worth little more than the paper on which they're written.[58] The code of ethics at McDonnell Douglas reflects the theme of the company's ethics program: "Always take the high road."

MCDONNELL DOUGLAS
www.boeing.com

At McDonnell Douglas, a short version of the ethics code and an ethical decision-making checklist are printed on cards so that employees may carry them in a pocket or purse. The excerpt printed below indicates that McDonnell Douglas expects its employees to display ethical behavior above that required by law.

> Integrity and ethics exist in the individual or they do not exist at all. They must be upheld by individuals or they are not upheld at all. In order for integrity and ethics to be characteristics of McDonnell Douglas, we who make up the Corporation must strive to be:
>
> • Honest and trustworthy in all our relationships;
> • Reliable in carrying out assignments and responsibilities;

- Truthful and accurate in what we say and write;
- Cooperative and constructive in all work undertaken;
- Fair and considerate in our treatment of fellow employees, customers, and other persons;
- Law abiding in all our activities;
- Dedicated in service to our company and to improvement of the quality of life in the world in which we live.

Integrity and high standards of ethics require hard work, courage, and difficult choices. Integrity and ethics may sometimes require us to forego business opportunities. In the long run, however, we will be better served by doing what is right rather than what is expedient.[59]

An area of growing concern for companies doing business internationally is developing ethics codes that focus on the issue of human rights. Responding to the public outcry against sweatshops, a New York nonprofit organization and a number of influential companies have proposed a set of global labor standards to deal with issues such as child labor, low wages, and unsafe working environments. The group has come up with a scheme called Social Accountability 8000 or SA 8000, which is designed to work like the ISO 9000 quality-auditing system of the International Standards Organization. The SA 8000 is the first auditable social standard in the world. Companies such as Avon and Toys 'R' Us are certifying their factories and requiring their suppliers to do likewise.[60]

Ethical Structures.   Ethical structures represent the various systems, positions, and programs a company can undertake to implement ethical behavior. An **ethics committee** is a group of executives appointed to oversee company ethics. The committee provides rulings on questionable ethical issues. The ethics committee assumes responsibility for disciplining wrongdoers, which is essential if the organization is to directly influence employee behavior. For example, Motorola has an Ethics Compliance Committee that is charged with interpreting, clarifying, and communicating the company's code of ethics and with adjudicating suspected code violations. An **ethics ombudsman** is an official given the responsibility of corporate conscience who hears and investigates ethical complaints and points out potential ethics failures to top management. Pitney Bowes has an ethics ombudsman and offers training seminars and a conduct guide on ethics for employees.

Many organizations today are setting up ethics departments with full-time staff. These offices, such as the one at Northrup Grumman, work as counseling centers more than police departments. They are charged with helping employees deal with day-to-day ethical problems or questions. A toll-free, confidential hot line allows employees to report questionable behavior as well as seek guidance regarding ethical dilemmas. The offices also provide training based on the organization's code of ethics or code of business conduct, so that employees can translate the values into daily behavior.[61] Training programs are an important supplement to a written code of ethics. Texas Instruments developed an eight-hour ethics training course for all employees. In addition, the company incorporates ethics into every course it offers. A computer training class, for example, might include a discussion of the ethical

ethics committee
A group of executives assigned to oversee the organization's ethics by ruling on questionable issues and disciplining violators.

ethics ombudsman
An official given the responsibility of corporate conscience who hears and investigates ethics complaints and points out potential ethical failures to top management.

issues of copying and distributing software. Starbucks Coffee uses new employee training to begin instilling values such as taking personal responsibility, treating everyone with respect, and doing the right thing even if others disagree with you.[62]

A strong ethics program is important, but it is no guarantee against lapses. Dow Corning, whose faulty silicone breast implants shocked the business community, pioneered an ethics program that was looked upon as a model. Established in the mid-1970s, Dow's ambitious ethics program included the Business Conduct committee, training programs, regular reviews and audits to monitor compliance, and reports to the Audit and Social Responsibility committee. What went wrong? The ethics program dealt with the overall environment, but specific programs such as product safety were handled through normal channels—in this case the Medical Device Business Board, which slowed further safety studies.[63] Dow Corning's problems sent a warning to other industries. It is not enough to *have* an impressive ethics program. The ethics program must be merged with day-to-day operations, encouraging ethical decisions to be made throughout the company.

whistle-blowing
The disclosure by an employee of illegal, immoral, or illegitimate practices by the organization.

Whistle-Blowing.   Employee disclosure of illegal, immoral, or illegitimate practices on the employer's part is called **whistle-blowing.**[64] No organization can rely exclusively on codes of conduct and ethical structures to prevent all unethical behavior. Holding organizations accountable depends to some degree on individuals who are willing to blow the whistle if they detect illegal, dangerous, or unethical activities. Whistle-blowers often report wrongdoing to outsiders, such as regulatory agencies, senators, or newspaper reporters. Some firms have instituted innovative programs to encourage and support internal whistle-blowing. For this to be an effective ethical safeguard, however, companies must view whistle-blowing as a benefit to the company and make dedicated efforts to protect whistle-blowers.[65]

When there are no effective protective measures, whistle-blowers suffer. Although whistle-blowing has become widespread in recent years, it is still risky for employees, who can lose their jobs, be ostracized by coworkers, or be transferred to lower-level positions. For example, when Mark Jorgensen exposed fraud in the real-estate funds he managed for Prudential Insurance Company of America, he was shunned by his supervisor and coworkers, accused by company lawyers of breaking the law, and eventually dismissed.[66] Robert A. Bugai, who blew the whistle on unethical college marketing practices, warns that there are considerable costs involved—"mentally, financially, physically, emotionally, and spiritually."[67] It is not enough for top managers to encourage internal whistle-blowing. Managers can be trained to view whistle-blowing as a benefit rather than a threat, and systems can be set up to effectively protect employees who report illegal or unethical activities.

Ethics and the Management Revolution

Many of today's best companies realize that success can be measured in many ways, not all of which show up on the financial statement. However, the relationship of a corporation's ethics and social responsibility to its financial performance concerns both managers and management scholars and has

The Corporation of the Twenty-First Century

Ray Anderson spent most of his life as an environmental glutton. His company, Interface, Inc., an Atlanta-based business with 7,300 employees, turns petrochemicals into textiles. The petroleum the company uses took millions of years to make and is irreplaceable; the carpets that come from it last forever—and most of them end up in landfills after only a decade of use.

But Ray Anderson had a revelation when he came across a book called *The Ecology of Commerce,* by Paul Hawken. As he read about the breadth of toxins accumulating in humans from one generation to the next and the speed at which natural resources were being depleted, the captain of industrial capitalism thought of his grandchildren and wept. Today, Ray Anderson is becoming a radical environmentalist who makes the folks from Greenpeace look timid. He has embraced the concept of sustainability, which calls for mimicking nature—everything's waste is something else's food. Anderson's goal for Interface: create zero waste and consume zero oil while making a healthy profit. It took Anderson a year to convince the rest of his company (the largest maker of commercial carpeting and upholstery for office cubicles) that Interface could save the earth and still make money. Today, however, from the factory floor to the R&D lab, sustainability has become as important a consideration in every business decision as profitability.

Interface's performance shatters the idea that social responsibility and profits can't go hand in hand. From 1995 to 1996, sales grew from $800 million to one billion. During that time, the amount of raw materials used by the company dropped almost 20 percent per dollar of sales. That means,

Anderson points out, "$200 million of sustainable business." Profits have been steadily increasing, and costs keep going down with reduced energy costs, reduced materials, and reduced waste. The company's latest innovation is an "Evergreen Lease," with building owners renting rather than buying carpet. Interface installs, maintains, replaces, carries away, and recycles carpet tiles as they wear out. The old tiles become new carpet. Interface also hopes to soon offer commercial hemp carpet, which can be composted completely when its use is over.

Interface still has a long way to go to reach its goals, but already air pollutants, landfill waste, and use of natural resources have dramatically decreased. The company's simple agenda for the twenty-first century has seven steps: 1) eliminate waste; 2) make emissions benign; 3) shift to renewable energy, gradually moving to solar power; 4) close the loop, using waste as a resource for new textiles; 5) make transportation efficient; 6) teach sustainability to customers, suppliers, and employees; and 7) redesign commerce—shift to cyclic capitalism. Ray Anderson wants to change the world, and ensure that his grandchildren will still have one.

www.interfaceinc.com

SOURCES: Charles Fishman, "I Want to Pioneer the Company of the Next Industrial Revolution," *Fast Company,* April–May 1998, 136–142; Thomas Petzinger, Jr., "Business Achieves Greatest Efficiencies When at Its Greenest," *The Wall Street Journal,* July 11, 1997, B1; and Catherine Arnst with Stanley Reed, Gary McWilliams, and De'Ann Weimer, "When Green Begets Green," *Business Week,* November 10, 1997, 98–106.

generated a lively debate.[68] One concern of managers is whether good citizenship will hurt performance—after all, ethics programs cost money. A number of studies have been undertaken to determine whether heightened ethical and social responsiveness increases or decreases financial performance. Studies have provided varying results but generally have found that there is a small positive relationship between social responsibility and financial performance.[69] For example, James Burke, former CEO of Johnson & Johnson, put together a list of companies known for their high ethical standards, including J&J, Xerox, and Eastman Kodak. In the period from 1950 to 1990, Burke found that the market value of companies that made the list grew at 11.3 percent annually, almost double the 6.2 percent rate achieved by Dow Jones industrials as a group. In addition, the Domini Social Index, created in 1989 to track the stock performance of socially responsible companies, indicates that they perform as well as or better than companies that are not socially responsible. Although results from these studies are not proof, they do provide an indication that use of resources for ethics and

With funding by the Davenport Works division of Alcoa, the world's largest producer of aluminum, college student and commercial fisherman Chad Pregracke is leading a group of volunteers in an attempt to rid the Mississippi River banks of trash and debris in the Quad cities area. Pengracke, who was named the Illinois Wildlife Federation's Environmental Citizen of the Year, has cleared the shores of 30,000 pounds of debris, including 92 metal barrels, 153 tires, three refrigerators, a stove, and a television. By funding such a program, Alcoa enhances its reputation as a socially responsible company.

social responsibility does not hurt companies.[70] Enlightened companies realize that integrity and trust are essential elements in sustaining successful and profitable business relationships. Although doing the right thing may not always be profitable in the short run, it develops a level of trust that money can't buy and that will ultimately benefit the company. McDonald's, for example, credits its strong community involvement for the fact that none of its 31 area restaurants was burned or looted during the 1992 Los Angeles riots.[71]

A related finding is that firms founded on spiritual values usually perform very well. These firms succeed because they have a clear mission, employees seldom have alcohol and drug problems, and a strong family orientation exists. One of the largest and most successful companies is Chick-fil-A, Inc., which refuses to open on Sunday. The Sunday closing costs some sales and has gotten the chain frozen out of some shopping malls, but the policy helps attract excellent workers, and this offsets any disadvantages. When Tom Chappell, co-founder with his wife Kate of Tom's of Maine, became concerned about how to stick to his respect for humanity while keeping his company successful, he went to divinity school. In the writings of the great philosophers, Chappell says he learned that you don't have to sell your soul to make your numbers. Tom's of Maine, a highly successful maker of all-natural personal care products, thrives on spiritual values.[72]

Being ethical and socially responsible does not hurt a firm. Managers and companies can use their discretion to contribute to society's welfare and improve organizational performance at the same time. For Interface, Inc., profitability and social responsibility have become almost synonymous, as described in the Leadership box. The public is tired of unethical and socially irresponsible business practices. Companies that make an uncompromising commitment to maintain integrity may well lead the way to a brighter future for both business and society.

Summary and Management Solution

Ethics and social responsibility are hot topics for today's managers. The ethical domain of behavior pertains to values of right and wrong. Ethical decisions and behavior are typically guided by a value system. Four value-based approaches that serve as criteria for ethical decision making are utilitarian, individualism, moral-rights, and justice. For an individual manager, the ability to make correct ethical choices will depend on both individual and organizational characteristics. An important individual characteristic is level of moral development. Corporate culture is an organizational characteristic that influences ethical behavior.

Corporate social responsibility concerns a company's values toward society. How can organizations be good

corporate citizens? The model for evaluating social performance uses four criteria: economic, legal, ethical, and discretionary. Organizations may use four types of response to specific social pressures: obstructive, defensive, accommodative, and proactive. Evaluating corporate social behavior often requires assessing its impact on organizational stakeholders. Techniques for improving social responsiveness include leadership, codes of ethics, ethical structures, and whistle-blowing. Companies that are socially responsible perform as well as—and often better than—companies that are not socially responsible.

Returning to our management problem, it is not clear if Reuters broke the law. Several lawsuits against the company are pending. However, it does seem clear that Reuters has some ethical problems and that its public image is suffering. Some software vendors say part of the problem is the intimidating corporate culture of Reuters, which encourages strong-arm tactics and threats. So far, the company seems to be taking an obstructive approach, denying responsibility and insisting that any evidence of wrongdoing is misleading or distorted. As knowledge and information, not physical items, increasingly become the primary form of capital for companies, the legal as well as ethical complexities regarding ownership of information likely will increase.

Discussion Questions

1. Dr. Martin Luther King, Jr., said, "As long as there is poverty in the world, I can never be rich. . . . As long as diseases are rampant, I can never be healthy. . . . I can never be what I ought to be until you are what you ought to be." Discuss this quote with respect to the material in this chapter. Would this be true for corporations, too?

2. Environmentalists are trying to pass laws for oil spills that would remove all liability limits for the oil companies. This would punish corporations financially. Is this the best way to influence companies to be socially responsible?

3. Compare and contrast the utilitarian approach with the moral-rights approach to ethical decision making. Which do you believe is the best for managers to follow? Why?

4. Imagine yourself in a situation of being encouraged to inflate your expense account. Do you think your choice would be most affected by your individual moral development or by the cultural values of the company for which you worked? Explain.

5. Is it socially responsible for organizations to undertake political activity or join with others in a trade association to influence the government? Discuss.

6. The criteria of corporate social responsibility suggest that economic responsibilities are of the greatest magnitude, followed by legal, ethical, and discretionary responsibilities. How do these four types of responsibility relate to corporate responses to social demands? Discuss.

7. From where do managers derive ethical values? What can managers do to help define ethical standards for the corporation?

8. Have you ever experienced an ethical dilemma? Evaluate the dilemma with respect to its impact on other people.

9. Lincoln Electric considers customers and employees to be more important stakeholders than shareholders. Is it appropriate for management to define some stakeholders as more important than others? Should all stakeholders be considered equal?

10. Do you think a code of ethics combined with an ethics committee would be more effective than leadership for implementing ethical behavior? Discuss.

Management in Practice: Experiential Exercise

Ethical Work Climates

Answer the following questions by circling the number that best describes an organization for which you have worked.

	Disagree				Agree
1. What is the best for everyone in the company is the major consideration here.	1	2	3	4	5
2. Our major concern is always what is best for the other person.	1	2	3	4	5
3. People are expected to comply with the law and professional standards over and above other considerations.	1	2	3	4	5
4. In this company, the first consideration is whether a decision violates any law	1	2	3	4	5
5. It is very important to follow the company's rules and procedures here.	1	2	3	4	5

6. People in this company strictly obey the company policies.	1	2	3	4	5
7. In this company, people are mostly out for themselves.	1	2	3	4	5
8. People are expected to do anything to further the company's interests, regardless of the consequences.	1	2	3	4	5
9. In this company, people are guided by their own personal ethics.	1	2	3	4	5
10. Each person in this company decides for himself or herself what is right and wrong.	1	2	3	4	5

Total Score _____

Add up your score. These questions measure the dimensions of an organization's ethical climate. Questions 1 and 2 measure caring for people, questions 3 and 4 measure lawfulness, questions 5 and 6 measure rules adherence, questions 7 and 8 measure emphasis on financial and company performance, and questions 9 and 10 measure individual independence. Questions 7 and 8 are reverse scored ($1 = 5$, $2 = 4$, $3 = 3$, $4 = 2$, $5 = 1$). A total score above 40 indicates a very positive ethical climate. A score from 30 to 40 indicates above-average ethical climate. A score from 20 to 30 indicates a below-average ethical climate, and a score below 20 indicates a very poor ethical climate.

Go back over the questions and think about changes that you could have made to improve the ethical climate in the organization. Discuss with other students what you could do as a manager to improve ethics in future companies you work for.

SOURCE: Based on Bart Victor and John B. Cullen, "The Organizational Bases of Ethical Work Climates," *Administrative Science Quarterly* 33 (1988), 101–125.

Management in Practice: Ethical Dilemma

What is Right?

It is often hard for a manager to determine what is "right" and even more difficult to put ethical behavior into practice. A manager's ethical orientation often brings him or her into conflict with people, policies, customers, or bosses. Consider the following dilemmas. How would you handle them?

1. A well-liked member of your staff with an excellent record confides to you that he has Acquired Immune Deficiency Syndrome (AIDS). Although his illness has not affected his performance, you're concerned about his future health and about the reactions of his coworkers. You
   a. tell him to keep you informed about his health and say nothing to his coworkers.
   b. arrange for him to transfer to an area of the organization where he can work alone.
   c. hold a staff meeting to inform his coworkers and ask them how they feel about his continued presence on your team.
   d. consult your human resources officer on how to proceed.

2. During a reorganization, you're told to reduce staff in the department you manage. After analyzing staffing requirements, you realize the job would be a lot easier if two professionals, who both are over age 60, would retire. You
   a. say nothing and determine layoffs based purely on performance and length of service.
   b. schedule a meeting with both employees and ask if they'd consider early retirement.
   c. schedule a meeting with all staff and ask if anyone is interested in severance or early retirement.
   d. lay off the older workers.

3. One of your colleagues has recently experienced two personal tragedies—her husband filed for divorce and her mother died. Although you feel genuine sympathy for her, her work is suffering. A report you completed, based on inaccurate data she provided, has been criticized by management. Your manager asks you for an explanation. You
   a. apologize for the inaccuracies and correct the data.
   b. tell your manager that the data supplied by your colleague was the source of the problem.
   c. say your colleague has a problem and needs support.
   d. tell your manager that because of your work load, you didn't have time to check the figures in the report.

4. Your firm recently hired a new manager who is at the same level you are. You do not like the man personally and consider him a rival professionally. You run into a friend who knows your rival well. You discover this man did not attend Harvard as he stated on his resume and in fact has not graduated from any college. You know his supposed Harvard background was instrumental in getting him hired. You
   a. expose the lie to your superiors.
   b. without naming names, consult your human resources officer on how to proceed.
   c. say nothing. The company obviously failed to check him out, and the lie probably will surface on its own.
   d. confront the man with the information and let him decide what to do.

5. During a changeover in the accounting department, you discover your company has been routinely overcharging members of the public for services provided to them. Your superiors say repayment of charges would wreak havoc on

company profits. Your company is federally regulated, and the oversight commission has not noticed the mistake. Your bosses say the problem will never come to light and they will take steps to correct the problem so it never happens again. You

a. contact the oversight commission.

b. take the matter public, anonymously or otherwise.

c. say nothing. It is now in the hands of the bosses.

d. work with the bosses on a plan to recognize the company's error and set up a schedule of rebates that would not unduly penalize the company.

6. In this morning's mail, you received plans and samples for a promising new product from a competitor's disgruntled employee. You

a. throw the plans away.

b. send the samples to your research department for analysis.

c. notify your competitor about what is going on.

d. call the FBI.

Questions

1. Use the guidelines described in Manager's Shoptalk: "Guidelines for Ethical Decision Making" to determine the appropriate behavior in these cases. Do you have all the information you need to make an ethical decision? How would family or friends react to each alternative if you were in these situations?

2. Which approach to ethical decision making—utilitarian, individualism, justice, or moral-rights—seems most appropriate for handling these situations?

SOURCES: Game developed by Katherine Nelson, "Board Games," *Owen Manager,* spring 1990, 14–16; Craig Dreilinger and Dan Rice, "Office Ethics," *Working Woman,* December 1991, 35–39; and Kevin Kelly and Joseph Weber, "When a Rival's Trade Secret Crosses Your Desk . . . ," *Business Week,* May 20, 1991, 48.

Surf the Net

1. **Social Responsibility.** The Global Business Responsibility Resource Center at **http://www.bsr.org/resourcecenter/** states its mission is "to provide businesses with the information they need to understand and implement more responsible policies and practices, and to promote increased knowledge and collaboration among companies and between business and other sectors." Its goal is "to help companies achieve sustained commercial success in ways that honor high ethical standards and benefit people, communities, and the environment." After registering (free), select a topic and print out a report to submit to your instructor.

2. **Code of Ethics.** Use your search engine to find the codes of ethics for three organizations. One site that contains 850+ codes of ethics is

   http://csep.iit.edu/codes/codes.html

   Compare the three codes to determine the similarities and differences among them in terms of focus, approach, language, and emphases. Provide possible reasons for the similarities and differences you cited. How might you benefit as an employee working for an organization with a code of ethics compared to working for an organization without a code of ethics?

3. **Ethical Structures.** Lockheed Martin is one of the world's leading diversified technology companies. Government and commercial customers around the world purchase its advanced technology systems, products, and services. Its core businesses span aeronautics, electronics, energy, information and services, space, systems integration, and telecommunications. Lockheed Martin provides an excellent example of an organization with a variety of systems, positions, and programs to implement ethical behavior among its employees. Visit the Ethics option available at **www.lockheedmartin.com/about/index.htm.**

   Write a summary of the ethical structures at Lockheed Martin.

Case for Critical Analysis
Colt 45 and the Ad Hoc Group Against Crime

The Ad Hoc Group Against Crime, a Kansas City organization, recently accepted a contribution from Colt 45—the group will get a 25-cent donation for every case of Colt 45 malt liquor sold through participating vendors. In accepting the money, Ad Hoc opened itself to an ethical dilemma that has hounded minority interest groups for decades. Violent crime hits many minority communities hard, and numerous studies have linked crime to alcohol consumption. Studies have also shown that although African Americans have higher rates of abstinence than whites, they still have higher death rates tied to alcohol abuse.

Ad Hoc's president, Alvin Brooks, says the group doesn't see this as encouraging sales of Colt 45. "We are saying to the alcohol companies: 'If you are taking something away from the community, you are going to have to give something back.'" Brooks also notes that Ad Hoc is not in a financial position to turn away viable fund-raising opportunities. Other minority interest groups have long accepted alcohol and tobacco funds for the same reason, and over the years a loyalty has developed—a loyalty that the alcohol and tobacco companies began actively courting decades ago. Studies have shown that billboards advertising tobacco products are placed in black communities four to five times more often than in predominantly white communities and that the number of liquor outlets in proportion to the population is much higher in inner-city neighborhoods.

A spokesperson for Colt 45 said the fund-raiser is simply a way for retailers to show their support for the community. In general, large alcohol and tobacco companies are reluctant to discuss their funding of minority causes. A Philip Morris representative, commenting that the contributions are important in keeping communities economically able to buy products, said, "Their vibrancy is our vibrancy."

Questions

1. Are companies such as Colt 45 and Philip Morris acting in an ethical and socially responsible way? What criteria of social responsibility are these companies following?

2. Is the Ad Hoc Group Against Crime being socially responsible by accepting this money? Should this group take a symbolic stand against alcohol?

3. Can you think of more socially responsible ways Colt 45 might contribute to minority communities?

SOURCE: Based on Mary Sanchez, "When Charity Taps 'Vice' for Money," *The Tennessean,* August 6, 1995, 2D.

Endnotes

1. Debra Sparks, "What the Heck is Going On at Reuters?" *Business Week,* March 16, 1998, 84–85.

2. Del Jones, "Doing the Wrong Thing: 48% of Workers Admit to Unethical or Illegal Acts," *USA Today,* April 4, 1997, 1A, 2A; and William J. Morin, "Silent Sabotage: Mending the Crisis in Corporate Values," *Management Review,* July 1995, 10–14.

3. "Franchise Inc.," *Inc.,* November 1997, 121; Michael Waldholz, "AZT Prize Cut for Third World Mothers-to-Be," *The Wall Street Journal,* March 5, 1998, B1, B12; Catherine Arnst with Stanley Reed, Gary McWilliams and De'Ann Weimer, "When Green Begets Green," *Business Week,* November 10, 1997, 98–106; and Dale Kurschner, "Tying Executive Pay to Social Responsibility," *Business Ethics,* September–October 1995, 47.

4. Gordon F. Shea, *Practical Ethics* (New York: American Management Association, 1988); and Linda K. Trevino, "Ethical Decision Making in Organizations; A Person-Situation Interactionist Model," *Academy of Management Review* 11 (1986), 601–617.

5. Thomas M. Jones, "Ethical Decision Making by Individuals in Organizations: An Issue-Contingent Model," *Academy of Management Review* 16 (1991), 366–395.

6. Rushworth M. Kidder, "The Three Great Domains of Human Action," *Christian Science Monitor,* January 30, 1990.

7. Jones, "Ethical Decision Making."

8. This discussion is based on Gerald F. Cavanagh, Dennis J. Moberg, and Manuel Velasquez, "The Ethics of Organizational Politics," *Academy of Management Review* 6 (1981), 363–374; Justin G. Longenecker, Joseph A. McKinney, and Carlos W. Moore, "Egoism and Independence: Entrepreneurial Ethics," *Organizational Dynamics* (winter 1988), 64–72; and Carolyn Wiley, "The ABCs of Business Ethics: Definitions, Philosophies, and Implementation," *IM,* February 1995, 22–27.

9. Zachary Schiller, Walecia Conrad, and Stephanie Anderson Forest, "If You Light Up on Sunday Don't Come in on Monday," *Business Week,* August 26, 1992, 68–72.

10. Ron Winslow, "Rationing Care," *The Wall Street Journal,* November 13, 1989, R24.

11. Alan Wong and Eugene Beckman, "An Applied Ethical Analysis System in Business," *Journal of Business Ethics* 11 (1992), 173–178.

12. John Kekes, "Self-Direction: The Core of Ethical Individualism," *Organizations and Ethical Individualism,* ed. Konstanian Kolenda (New York: Praeger, 1988), 1–18.

13. Tad Tulega, *Beyond the Bottom Line* (New York: Penguin Books, 1987).

14. Archie B. Carroll, "Principles of Business Ethics: Their Role in Decision Making and Initial Consensus," *Management Decisions* 28, no. 8 (1990), 20–24.

15. Catherine Yang, "Are Life Insurers Biased—Or Just Careful?" *Business Week,* October 16, 1995, 82–85.

16. Lynn Sharp Paine, "Managing for Organizational Integrity," *Harvard Business Review* (March–April 1994), 106–117.

17. This discussion is based on Trevino, "Ethical Decision Making in Organizations."

18. L. Kohlberg, "Moral Stages and Moralization: The Cognitive-Developmental Approach," in *Moral Development and Behavior: Theory, Research, and Social Issues,* ed. T. Lickona (New York: Holt, Rinehart & Winston, 1976) 31–83; L. Kohlberg, "Stage and Sequence: The Cognitive-Developmental Approach to Socialization," in *Handbook of Socialization Theory and Research,* ed. D. A. Goslin (Chicago: Rand McNally, 1969); and Jill W. Graham, "Leadership, Moral Development,

and Citizenship Behavior," *Business Ethics Quarterly* 5, no. 1 (January 1995), 43–54.

19. Carol Gilligan, *In a Different Voice: Psychological Theory and Women's Development* (Cambridge, Mass.: Harvard University Press, 1982).

20. Andrew W. Singer, "Ethics: Are Standards Lower Overseas?" *Across the Board,* September 1991, 31–34; and David Vogel, "Is U.S. Business Obsessed with Ethics?" *Across the Board,* November–December 1993, 31–33.

21. Joe Skelly, "The Caux Round Table Principles for Business: The Rise of International Ethics," *Business Ethics,* March–April 1995 Supplement, 2–5.

22. James Weber, "Influences Upon Organizational Ethical Sub-climates: A Multi-Departmental Analysis of a Single Firm," *Organizational Science* 6, no. 5 (September–October 1995), 509–523.

23. This discussion is based on Linda Klebe Trevino, "A Cultural Perspective on Changing and Developing Organizational Ethics," in *Research and Organizational Change and Development,* ed. R. Woodman and W. Pasmore (Greenwich, Conn.: JAI Press, 1990), 4.

24. Ibid.; John B. Cullen, Bart Victor, and Carroll Stephens, "An Ethical Weather Report: Assessing the Organization's Ethical Climate," *Organizational Dynamics* (autumn 1989), 50–62; and Bart Victor and John B. Cullen, "The Organizational Bases of Ethical Work Climates," *Administrative Science Quarterly* 33 (1988), 101–125.

25. Russell Mitchell with Michael Oneal, "Managing by Values," *Business Week,* August 1, 1994, 46–52; and Alan Farnham, "State Your Values, Hold the Hot Air," *Fortune,* April 19, 1993, 117–124.

26. Eugene W. Szwajkowski, "The Myths and Realities of Research on Organizational Misconduct," in *Research in Corporate Social Performance and Policy,* ed. James E. Post (Greenwich, Conn.: JAI Press, 1986), 9:103–122; and Keith Davis, William C. Frederick, and Robert L. Blostrom, *Business and Society: Concepts and Policy Issues* (New York: McGraw-Hill, 1979).

27. Douglas S. Sherwin, "The Ethical Roots of the Business System," *Harvard Business Review* 61 (November–December 1983), 183–192.

28. Nancy C. Roberts and Paula J. King, "The Stakeholder Audit Goes Public," *Organizational Dynamics* (winter 1989), 63–79; and Thomas Donaldson and Lee E. Preston, "The Stakeholder Theory of the Corporation: Concepts, Evidence, and Implications," *Academy of Management Review* 20, no. 1 (1995), 65–91.

29. Jeffrey S. Harrison and Caron H. St. John, "Managing and Partnering with External Stakeholders," *Academy of Management Executive* 10, no. 2 (1996), 46–60.

30. Max B. E. Clarkson, "A Stakeholder Framework for Analyzing and Evaluating Corporate Social Performance," *Academy of Management Review* 20, no. 1 (1995), 92–117.

31. Jim Collins, "The Foundation for Doing Good," *Inc.,* December 1997, 41–42.

32. Caleb Solomon, "Big Payoff: How a Neighborhood Talked Fina Refinery into Buying It Out," *The Wall Street Journal,* January 10, 1991, A1, A8.

33. Mark A. Cohen, "Management and the Environment," *The Owen Manager* 15, no. 1 (1993), 2–6.

34. Weld F. Royal, "It's Not Easy Being Green," *Sales & Marketing Management,* July 1995, 84–90.

35. Laura M. Litvan, "Going 'Green' in the '90s," *Nation's Business,* February 1995, 30–32; and "Buy Recycled and Save," Environmental Defense Fund and McDonald's Corporation, 1994.

36. Based on Litvan, "Going 'Green' in the '90s," 31.

37. Mark Starik, *Management and the Natural Environment* (Fort Worth, Texas: The Dryden Press, 1994), 1.

38. Gail Dutton, "Green Partnerships," *Management Review,* January 1996, 24–28.

39. "The Natural Step to Sustainability," *Wingspread Journal,* the quarterly publication of The Johnson Foundation, Inc., Spring 1997.

40. Archie B. Carroll, "A Three-Dimensional Conceptual Model of Corporate Performance," *Academy of Management Review* 4 (1979), 497–505. For a discussion of various models for evaluating corporate social performance, also see Diane L. Swanson, "Addressing a Theoretical Problem by Reorienting the Corporate Social Performance Model," *Academy of Management Review* 20, no. 1 (1995), 43–64.

41. Milton Friedman, *Capitalism and Freedom* (Chicago: University of Chicago Press, 1962), 133; and Milton Friedman and Rose Friedman, *Free to Choose* (New York: Harcourt Brace Jovanovich, 1979).

42. Bruce Hager, "What's behind Business' Sudden Fervor for Ethics?" *Business Week,* September 23, 1991, 65.

43. Eugene W. Szwajkowski, "Organizational Illegality: Theoretical Integration and Illustrative Application," *Academy of Management Review* 10 (1985), 558–567.

44. David J. Fritzsche and Helmut Becker, "Linking Management Behavior to Ethical Philosophy—An Empirical Investigation," *Academy of Management Journal* 27 (1984), 165–175.

45. Denise Gellene, "Internet Marketing to Kids Is Seen As a Web of Deceit," *Los Angeles Times,* March 29, 1996, A1, A20.

46. Jeffrey A. Tannenbaum, "Making Risky Hires Into Valued Workers," *The Wall Street Journal,* June 19, 1997, B1, B2.

47. Elizabeth Gatewood and Archie B. Carroll, "The Anatomy of Corporate Social Response: The Rely, Firestone 500, and Pinto Cases," *Business Horizons* 24 (September–October 1981), 9–16.

48. John Kenneth Galbraith, "Behind the Wall," *New York Review of Books,* April 10, 1986, 11–13.

49. "Ethics for Hire," *Business Week,* July 15, 1996, 26–28.

50. Milton R. Moskowitz, "Company Performance Roundup," *Business and Society Review* 53 (spring 1985), 74–77.

51. Chris Welles, "What Led Beech-Nut down the Road to Disgrace," *Business Week,* February 22, 1988, 124–128; Joe Queenan, "Juicemen: Ethics and the Beech-Nut Sentences," *Barron's,* June 20, 1988, 37–38; and Paine, "Managing for Organizational Integrity."

52. Saul W. Gellerman, "Managing Ethics from the Top Down," *Sloan Management Review* (winter 1989), 73–79.

53. "Corporate Ethics: A Prime Business Asset," The Business Roundtable, 200 Park Avenue, Suite 2222, New York, New York, 10166, February 1988.

54. E. Thomas Behr, "Acting From the Center," *Management Review,* March 1998, 51–55; Patrick E. Murphy and George Enderle, "Managerial Ethical Leadership: Do Examples Matter?" *Business Ethics Quarterly* 5, no. 1 (1995), 117–128.

55. Joseph L. Badaracco, Jr., and Allen P. Webb, "Business Ethics: A View from the Trenches, *California Management Review* 37, no. 2 (winter 1995), 8–28.

56. "Corporate Ethics."

57. Ibid.

58. Carolyn Wiley, "The ABC's of Business Ethics: Definitions, Philosophies, and Implementation," *IM,* January–February 1995, 22–27; Badaracco and Webb, "Business Ethics: a View from the Trenches"; and Ronald B. Morgan, "Self- and Co-Worker Perceptions of Ethics and Their Relationships to Leadership and Salary," *Academy of Management Journal* 36, no. 1 (February 1993), 200–214.

59. Patrick E. Murphy, "Implementing Business Ethics," *Business Ethics 95/96,* 7th ed. (Guilford, Conn.: Dushkin Publishing, 1995), 110–118.

60. Aaron Bernstein, "Sweatshop Police," *Business Week,* October 20, 1997, 39; and Louisa Wah, "Treading the Sacred Ground," *Management Review,* July–August, 1998, 18–22.

61. Beverly Geber, "The Right and Wrong of Ethics Offices," *Training,* October 1995, 102–118.

62. Mark Henricks, "Ethics in Action," *Management Review,* January 1995, 53–55; Jennifer Reese, "Starbucks: Inside the Coffee Cult," *Fortune,* December 9, 1996, 190–200.

63. John A. Byrne, "The Best Laid Ethics Programs . . . ," *Business Week,* March 9, 1992, 67–69.

64. Marcia Parmarlee Miceli and Janet P. Near, "The Relationship among Beliefs, Organizational Positions, and Whistle-Blowing Status: A Discriminant Analysis," *Academy of Management Journal* 27 (1984), 687–705.

65. Eugene Garaventa, "*An Enemy of the People* by Henrik Ibsen: The Politics of Whistle-Blowing," *Journal of Management Inquiry* 3, no. 4 (December 1994), 369–374; Marcia P. Miceli and Janet P. Near, "Whistleblowing: Reaping the Benefits," *Academy of Management Executive* 8, no. 3 (1994), 65–74.

66. Kurt Eichenwald, "He Told. He Suffered. Now He's a Hero." *The New York Times,* May 29, 1994, Section 3, 1.

67. Barbara Ettorre, "Whistleblowers: Who's the Real Bad Guy?" *Management Review,* May 1994, 18–23.

68. Philip L. Cochran and Robert A. Wood, "Corporate Social Responsibility and Financial Performance," *Academy of Management Journal* 27 (1984), 42–56.

69. Dale Kurschner, "5 Ways Ethical Business Creates Fatter Profits," *Business Ethics,* March–April 1996, 20–23.

70. Jean B. McGuire, Alison Sundgren, and Thomas Schneeweis, "Corporate Social Responsibility and Firm Financial Performance," *Academy of Management Journal* 31 (1988), 854–872; and Louisa Wah, "Treading the Sacred Ground," *Management Review,* July–August 1998, 18–22.

71. Edmund M. Burke, "Forget the Government, It's the Community That Can Shut You Down," *Business Ethics,* May–June 1997, 11–13.

72. Roger Ricklefs, "Christian-Based Firms Find Following Principles Pays," *The Wall Street Journal,* December 8, 1989, B1; Jo David and Karen File, "Saintly Companies That Make Heavenly Profits," *Working Woman,* October 1989, 122–126, 169–175; and Tom Chappell, "The Soul of a Business," *Executive Female,* January–February 1994, 38–77.

Chapter 6

LEARNING OBJECTIVES

After studying this chapter, you should be able to

Describe the importance of entrepreneurship to the U.S. economy.

Define personality characteristics of a typical entrepreneur.

Describe the planning necessary to undertake a new business venture.

Discuss decision tactics and sources of help that increase chances for new business success.

Describe the five stages of growth for an entrepreneurial company.

Explain how the management functions of planning, organizing, leading, and controlling apply to a growing entrepreneurial company.

Discuss how to facilitate intrapreneurship in established organizations.

The Environment of Entrepreneurship and Small-Business Management

MANAGEMENT PROBLEM

Linda Kesler was one of Salt Lake City's pioneering female entrepreneurs, starting her first business in 1974. She was known as a hard worker who never gave up easily. In the early 1990s, she founded Create-a-Check, Inc., which makes check-printing and electronic payment software. Within a few years, the business was highly successful and growing rapidly. Kesler, exhausted from running three businesses and recently remarried, was ready for a break, so she promoted marketing director Alan Redd to president of Create-a-Check. The transition took place quickly, and although the plan was for the two to talk weekly, they rarely did. After all, everything was running smoothly. Within a few months, though, it became clear that expenses were growing as sales were stagnating. Redd hired telemarketers to generate sales leads, an approach Kesler had opposed. He also brought in new salespeople, who had to wait while the telemarketers struggled to identify contacts. After six months, Kesler realized that the business it had taken her three years to build was rapidly heading toward bankruptcy. By the time she returned to run the firm, Create-a-Check owed about $450,000 to vendors, and lawsuits were pending. In one case, Create-a-Check's failure to show in court meant the company was forced to pay a $10,000 fee from a public relations firm, plus $5,000 in court and lawyers' fees. "I woke up every morning flipping a coin," Kesler recalls. "Either I'd go into bankruptcy or I'd see this thing through. . . . It takes very little time without paying attention to destroy a company."[1]

What advice would you give Linda Kesler? How can she keep Create-a-Check profitable and growing without personally overseeing every aspect of the business?

Many people dream of starting their own business. Entrepreneurship achieved almost cult status in the 1980s and interest continues to grow. At college campuses across the nation, ambitious courses, programs, and centers devoted to entrepreneurship are springing up. In the local bookstore, shelf space devoted to titles such as *How to Run a Small Business* and *Entrepreneurial Life: How to Go for It and How to Get It* continues to expand. Even *Rolling Stone* magazine devotes pages to the subject.[2] Computer technology and the Internet have given big-business power to even the smallest of companies. In addition, the enormous growth of franchising gives beginners an escorted route into a new business.

But Linda Kesler's story represents a fact of life for entrepreneurs. Running a small business is difficult and risky. Two out of three small businesses fail within the first five years. Those that survive the beginning period continue to face tremendous challenges. Despite the risks, Americans are entering the world of entrepreneurship at an unprecedented rate. Small business is booming, and most analysts think the trend is likely to continue.[3]

What Is Entrepreneurship?

Carol Weinstock, a true entrepreneur, recognized a market for multicultural greeting cards and launched EthnoGraphics, creating cards for the African-American, American Indian, Latino, Chinese-American, and Jewish consumer. Weinstock hired artists from the various cultures to create cards that would be true to the lives and feelings of ethnic customers. By filling a niche the major companies left behind, Weinstock found a ready market and is reaping the rewards of entrepreneurship, with EthnoGraphics' revenues tripling each year for three years running.

Entrepreneurship is the process of initiating a business venture, organizing the necessary resources, and assuming the associated risks and rewards.[4] An entrepreneur is someone who engages in entrepreneurship. An **entrepreneur** recognizes a viable idea for a business product or service and carries it out. This means finding and assembling necessary resources—money, people, machinery, location—to undertake the business venture. The entrepreneur also assumes the risks and reaps the rewards of the business. He or she assumes the financial and legal risks of ownership and receives the business's profits.

For example, Mark Moore experienced three business failures by age 22, but then found success doing criminal background checks for employers. With $800 and a leased laptop, Moore started Tenant Information Services (now TIS) to provide landlords with up-to-date eviction information on prospective tenants. When he branched into criminal background checks on job applicants, his business really took off, and Moore expects to soon be doing $3 to $4 million in business a year. When Nancy Friedman started the Telephone Doctor, a company that trains employees in good telephone manners, her first seminar generated a 38-cent profit. Today, the company earns $3 million a year and serves clients on five continents.[5] Moore and Friedman took the risks and are now reaping the rewards of entrepreneurship.

Entrepreneurship as an Option

For decades, half the working population has been confiding secretly to pals and pollsters the desire to leave corporate America and go it alone or with a few partners, but until recently such dreams were often squashed in their infancy by worried parents, friends, and spouses. Clearly, times have changed. After growing steadily since the 1950s, America's largest manufacturers began cutting their payrolls. Downsizing throughout the corporate world forced many employees to consider other options. In addition, many people are beginning to regard entrepreneurship as a better use of their time and skills. They see the opportunity to make more money on their own, while at the same time having more freedom and a better quality of life. Advances in technology have also made it easier than ever for small companies to compete in a global economy.[6]

Women and minorities, who have found their opportunities limited in the corporate world, often are seeing entrepreneurship as the only way to go. Victoria Bondoc, the daughter of Philippine immigrants, is legally blind, but she didn't let that stop her at age 26 from using $1,500 in personal savings to start an information services and facilities management firm. Today, Bondoc's Gemini Industries employs 100 people and operates out of six offices in Massachusetts, New York, Virginia, and the Philippines. William Davis, who lost his job in a downsizing at Occidental Petroleum, started Pulsar Data Systems, the largest black-owned computer firm. In partnership with IBM, Pulsar also has helped incubate other black-owned high-tech companies.[7]

Women are starting businesses today at twice the rate of men. According to the National Foundation for Women Business Owners, women-owned businesses in the United States comprise 36 percent of the business population, and women-owned businesses are a growing economic force throughout the world, with women owning between one-quarter to one-third of all businesses in Australia, Canada, Germany, and Japan. Moreover, businesses owned by minority women are expanding at three times the rate of U.S. business overall.[8]

entrepreneurship
The process of initiating a business venture, organizing the necessary resources, and assuming the associated risks and rewards.

entrepreneur
Someone who recognizes a viable idea for a business product or service and carries it out.

Entrepreneurship and the Environment

Not so long ago, scholars and policymakers were worrying about the potential of small business to survive. Today, entrepreneurship and small business are increasingly important parts of the business world. There are approximately 23 million small businesses in the United States, which account for nearly half the sales of all goods and services. Another interesting finding is that there are more than 20 million Americans who make their living as "solo professionals," often working out of their homes providing services to other companies. One-person offices constitute a $7.5 billion segment of the computer and office equipment markets, and marketing researchers believe solo professionals will continue to be the fastest growing market for phone, fax, and computer makers. Some of the more common businesses for solo professionals are financial services, high-tech marketing, political consultation, and software. As companies continue to downsize, decentralize operations, and outsource more functions, the opportunities for solo professionals will increase.[9]

The long-term trend toward ever-larger companies has reversed itself for a number of reasons.[10]

Economic Changes. Today's economy is fertile soil for entrepreneurs. The economy changes constantly, providing opportunities for new businesses. For example, the demand for services is booming, and 97 percent of service firms are small, with fewer than 100 employees. Since government deregulation in 1980 removed restrictions that inhibited small-business formation, more than 13,000 trucking companies have been started.

Globalization and Increased Competition. Even the largest of companies can no longer dominate their industry in a fast-changing global marketplace. Globalization demands entrepreneurial behavior—companies have to find ways to do things faster, better, and less expensively. Large companies are cutting costs by outsourcing work to smaller businesses or freelancers and selling off extraneous operations. Globalization and increased competition also give an advantage to the flexibility and fast response small business can offer rather than to huge companies with economies of scale.

Technology.   Rapid advances and dropping prices in computer technology have spawned whole new industries as well as entirely new methods of producing goods and delivering services. Unlike technological advances of the past, these are within the reach of companies of all sizes. The explosive growth of the Internet has created tremendous opportunities for entrepreneurs. For example, from a house in Cloverdale, Indiana, Terry Moore's Water Treatment Warehouse pulls in millions annually by selling chemicals via the Internet. Rosalind Resnick runs a popular Web site, LoveSearch.com, out of her Brooklyn brownstone, aiming to capture a chunk of the millions that people spend annually on personals ads and dating services.[11] Although selling products and services via the Internet still is limited, small companies such as A&a Printers are finding many other benefits from the Internet.

A&a PRINTERS AND DIGITAL GRAPHICS

In the early 1990s, customers of A&a Printers interacted with account representatives by phone, by mail, and on a walk-in basis. All that changed when President Robert Hu decided his small company would be one of the first to set up a presence on the World Wide Web. Hu had been looking for a way to give his customers greater involvement in their print jobs, and the Web site seemed promising. Today, customers use the Web site to place orders, track their project's status, and submit questions via E-mail. Clients can even make revisions to their documents on-line; the site's software automatically indicates what changes have been made and by whom. Moreover, A&a's paper supplier checks the company's production schedule daily via the Internet to determine the types and quantity of paper that will be needed for the following day's jobs, meaning A&a no longer has to order paper by phone or store large quantities on site.

Hu says the Internet has dramatically streamlined the way his company does business, while at the same time increasing customer service and satisfaction. He likes the fact that clients now can use A&a Printers as if it were their own in-house printing department rather than an outside contractor. "Publishing and printing have always been a collaborative function," he says. "We saw the Internet as an opportunity to link [the customer and the company] together." Hu also plans to use his site as a tool to team up with other vendors and provide a wider range of services to his clients. Although the Web site has attracted some new customers, Hu sees it primarily as a tool for providing better service.[12]

A&a Printers is among a growing number of small companies using the Internet to improve productivity, communications, and customer service, as well as to obtain information and market products or services. In January of 1997, more than 45 percent of small companies surveyed were using the Internet, compared to only 19 percent just 10 months earlier.[13]

New Opportunities and Market Niches.   Entrepreneurs are taking advantage of the opportunity to meet changing needs in the marketplace. John Erickson founded Senior Campus Living, Inc., which specializes in building and managing communities for middle-income retirees. Taking a cue from colleges,

Senior Campus Living is designed to promote a sense of community and make one's sunset years as socially stimulating as the college years. Recognizing the need for a magazine to serve the United States' estimated 3 million educated, affluent Latina professionals, Anna Maria Arias founded *Latina Style,* a spicy mix of Hispanic cultural, business, and entertainment news.[14]

Few people expected the entrepreneurial explosion, but there's no doubt that it is having a tremendous impact. Before further discussing the impact of small business, we must define what a small business is.

Definition of Small Business

The full definition of "small business" used by the Small Business Administration (SBA) is detailed and complex, taking up 37 pages of SBA regulations. Most people think of a business as small if it has fewer than 500 employees. This general definition works fine, but the SBA further defines it by industry. Exhibit 6.1 gives a few examples of how the SBA defines small business for a sample of industries. It also illustrates the types of businesses most entrepreneurs start—retail, manufacturing, and service. Additional types of new small businesses are construction, agriculture, and wholesaling.

Impact of Entrepreneurial Companies

The impact of entrepreneurial companies on our economy is underscored by the latest figures: approximately 600,000 new businesses are incorporated in the United States each year, and 807,000 new small firms were established in 1995 alone, an all-time record.[15] According to the Internal Revenue Service, approximately 21 million businesses exist, with only 15,000 of those employing more than 500 people. By some estimates, more than half of all U.S. businesses employ fewer than 5 people and almost 90 percent employ fewer than 20 people.[16] Entrepreneurs and small businesses are driving the U.S. economy. The Small Business Administration reports that small businesses employ more than 50 percent of the private workforce in the United States, generate more than half of the nation's gross domestic product, and are responsible for 55 percent of all business innovations. Many recent converts to entrepreneurship are corporate refugees (often middle management victims of corporate layoffs and downsizing) and corporate dropouts (those who prefer the uncertainty of self-employment to the corporate bureaucracy). For example, Candace Kendle Bryan and Christopher C. Bergen founded Kendle International, Inc., now a $44.2 million Cincinnati drug-testing company, when they grew "tired of office politics." In addition, growing numbers of executives are voluntarily leaving their big-company pay and perks at companies such as AT&T, IBM, and American Express to work for small start-up companies, citing the opportunity to do something new, creative, and exciting.[17]

Traditionally, new entrepreneurs most frequently start businesses in the areas of business services and restaurants. Today, inspired by the growth of companies such as Amazon.com, entrepreneurs are flocking to the Internet to start new businesses quickly and inexpensively. Demographic and lifestyle trends have created new opportunities in areas such as environmental services, children's markets, fitness, and home health care. The Leadership box describes an innovative approach to providing home health care to inner-city residents. The entrepreneurship miracle in the United States is an engine for job creation, innovation, and diversity.

Entrepreneurs Chet and Terrie Van Scyoc spotted an opportunity to profit from "shoppertainment," a new trend in today's retailing environment that blends entertainment with tried and true merchandising techniques. Shoppertainment helped the Scyocs build their Sacramento, California hobby store, R/C Country Hobbies, to revenues of approximately $1.2 million. R/C Country Hobbies sells remote-control planes and cars, model-building kits, and other toys to customers who can test a collector train on display or ask an employee to build a model so they can see and feel it. They can even fly a model airplane using a computer program that simulates the event. "This is something our biggest competitors, mail-order catalogs, can't give them," says Terrie. Although small businesses have a tough time competing in an industry where consumers have many options, including discount stores, mail-order, and the Internet, R/C Country Hobbies is a success and customers are loyal.

Exhibit *6.1* *Examples of SBA Definitions of Small Business*

Manufacturing	
Computer terminals and peripheral equipment	Number of employees does not exceed 1,000
Motor vehicle parts and accessories	Number of employees does not exceed 750
Apparel and footwear	Number of employees does not exceed 500
Retail	
Department stores	Average annual receipts do not exceed 20.0 million
Computer and software stores	Average annual receipts do not exceed 6.5 million
Sporting goods stores and bicycle shops	Average annual receipts do not exceed 5.0 million
Services	
Business consulting services	Average annual receipts do not exceed 5.0 million
Architectural services	Average annual receipts do not exceed 2.5 million
Building cleaning and maintenance	Average annual receipts do not exceed 12.0 million
Miscellaneous	
Book, magazine, or newspaper publishing	Number of employees does not exceed 1,000
Banks and credit unions	Has no more than $100 million in assets

Job Creation. Researchers disagree over what percentage of new jobs is created by small business. A dramatic estimate by one method of measuring new job creation indicates that, from 1986 to 1990, large firms created *no* new jobs, while in the smallest businesses (those with fewer than 20 employees), there was a 170 percent increase in new jobs created. According to the U.S. Department of Labor, small business-dominated industries produced about 64 percent of the 2.5 million new jobs created during 1996, the most recent year for which statistics are available.[18] Jobs created by small business give the United States an economic vitality that no other country can claim. Exhibit 6.2 shows how U.S. small business compares to the largest world economies, based on total output.

Innovation. According to Cognetics, Inc., a research firm run by David Birch that traces the employment and sales records of some 9 million companies, new and smaller firms have been responsible for 55 percent of the innovations in 362 different industries and 95 percent of all radical innovations. In addition, fast-growing businesses, which Birch calls "gazelles," produce twice as many product innovations per employee as do larger firms. Among the notable products for which small businesses can be credited are cellophane, the jet engine, and the ballpoint pen. Virtually every new business represents an innovation of some sort, whether a new product or service, how the product is delivered, or how it is made.[19] Entrepreneurial innovation often spurs larger companies to try new things. Lamaur, Inc., created a new shampoo for permanent-waved hair. Soon three giant competitors launched similar products. Small-business innovation keeps U.S. companies competitive, which is especially important in today's global marketplace.

Leadership

LEADING THE REVOLUTION: LEADERSHIP

Hiring from the 'Hood to Serve the 'Hood

Although at first glance Geric Home Health Care looks like a charity organization, founders Gwendolyn and Eric Johnson are hard-driven entrepreneurs. They can claim a growing business with annual sales of $12 million, a spotless report card from Medicare, and expanding operations in Cleveland, Detroit, and Gary, Indiana. Their company specializes in caring for bedridden people in bad neighborhoods—and they hire mostly single welfare mothers to do the work. "We put neighbors to work helping neighbors," says Gwendolyn, a former business teacher and guidance counselor in Cleveland schools. Or, as her son Eric puts it, "We hire from the 'hood to serve the 'hood."

The mother and son team first got the idea for the agency when they experienced firsthand the wariness of many nursing agencies toward black inner-city neighborhoods. Through their anger, frustration, and hurt in trying to find good care for Gwendolyn's mother, the two recognized a business opportunity. They got started by approaching nursing homes, hospitals, and public agencies with an offer few could refuse: "Give us the cases nobody else will take." And boy, did they get them—quadriplegics, MS patients, people on ventilators—many of them young and angry; referrals in rodent-infested and crime-ridden neighborhoods; cases of paralysis or terminal illness exacerbated by the use of drugs or alcohol. As referrals of the "hard cases" soared, many of Geric's nursing aides left, opting for assignments in suburbia. That's when the Johnsons set up a state-certified school for nursing aides and began recruiting from the inner city itself, offering a job to anyone who completed the training.

Although they're careful business people, the Johnsons also are deeply religious and clearly are motivated partly by their spiritual beliefs and desire to help those in need. They are careful to set people up to succeed, not to fail. When the students become employees, their casework is scheduled around child-care constraints and clustered by bus route. Geric gladly advances wages when employees get in a bind over rent or utilities (Eric points out that he has never been burned on an advance). In addition, Geric opened a child-care center for employees and plans to open an elder-care center. The company pays half of the tuition for any employee who enters LPN or RN training, and the Johnsons recognize that they will prosper only by rewarding longevity with career growth.

As the Johnsons expected, workers assigned to their own neighborhoods don't have the same kinds of fears as outsiders, and talk of welfare reform is increasing the number of people interested in Geric's job training program. "The most exciting part is the entrepreneurial spirit," says Alisa Smedley, who is now head of administrative operations for Geric. "We're like Tom Sawyer, lying in the grass, dreaming about what we can do."

www.geric.com

Source: Thomas Petzinger Jr., "Nurse Agency Thrives by Taking Hard Cases in the Inner City," *The Wall Street Journal*, September 26, 1997, B1.

Diversity. Entrepreneurship offers opportunities for individuals who may feel blocked in established corporations. Women-owned and minority-owned businesses may be the emerging growth companies of the next decade. Studies show that in 1997 there were 6.4 million women-owned businesses, which provided jobs for approximately 18.5 million people. Women now own 34 percent of all businesses in the United States. Statistics for minorities also are impressive. Minority-owned businesses now represent 8.9 percent of all businesses and the number is growing. To show the rate of increase, between 1982 and 1987, the number of African American-owned businesses increased 38 percent, Hispanic-owned businesses rose over 80 percent, and Asian/Pacific Islander-owned businesses jumped nearly 90 percent.[20] These firms often provide greater opportunities for minority employees as well. Verle Hammond, the African-American founder of Innolog, a logistics engineering firm, leads an incredibly diverse workforce that includes different races, nationalities, and ages, as well as a growing number of women in what is still a male-dominated field. Hammond sees workforce diversity as both a major challenge and a tremendous resource for today's small companies.[21]

Exhibit *6.2*

Total Output of U.S. Small Business Compared to World's Largest Economies

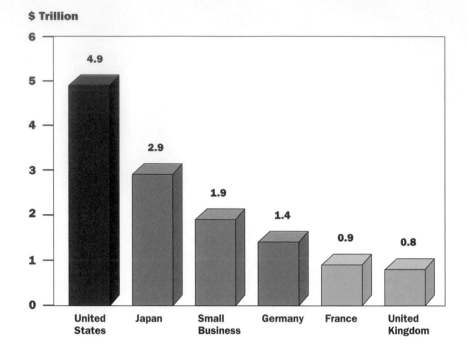

SOURCE: John Case, "The Wonderland Economy," *The State of Small Business,* 1995, 27.

Who Are Entrepreneurs?

The heroes of American business—Ray Kroc, Spike Lee, Henry Ford, Sam Walton, Mary Kay Ash, Bill Gates, Michael Dell—are almost always entrepreneurs. Entrepreneurs start with a vision. Often they are unhappy with their present jobs and see an opportunity to bring together the resources needed for a new venture. However, the image of entrepreneurs as bold pioneers probably is overly romantic. A survey of the CEOs of the nation's fastest-growing small firms found that these entrepreneurs could be best characterized as hardworking and practical, with great familiarity with their market and industry.[22] For example, Bobby Frost worked 22 years in the mirror-manufacturing industry before leaving his employer. He started a mirror and glass fabrication business to use technology that his former employer refused to try and that Frost believed would work. It did. Eight years after its founding, Consolidated Glass & Mirror Corp. had 600 employees and $36 million in sales.

A number of studies have investigated the personality characteristics of entrepreneurs and how they differ from successful managers in established

Exhibit *6.3*

Characteristics of Entrepreneurs

SOURCE: Adapted from Charles R. Kuehl and Peggy A. Lambing, *Small Business: Planning and Management* (Ft. Worth: The Dryden Press, 1994), 45.

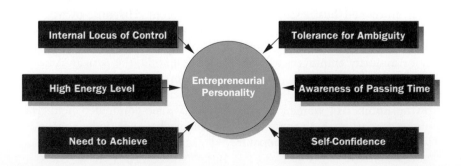

organizations. Some suggest that entrepreneurs in general want something different from life than do traditional managers. Entrepreneurs seem to place high importance on being free to achieve and maximize their potential. For example, Mark Bozzini of Pete's Brewing Company, who traded in his plush office at Seagram Company for a corner of a barn and a desk made out of an old door, says that he wanted "control of my own destiny."[23] Some 40 traits have been identified as associated with entrepreneurship, but 6 have special importance.[24] These characteristics are illustrated in Exhibit 6.3.

Locus of Control.   The task of starting and running a new business requires the belief that you can make things come out the way you want. The entrepreneur not only has a vision but also must be able to plan to achieve that vision and believe it will happen. An **internal locus of control** is the belief by individuals that their future is within their control and that other external forces will have little influence. For entrepreneurs, reaching the future is seen as being in the hands of the individual. Many people, however, feel that the world is highly uncertain and that they are unable to make things come out the way they want. An **external locus of control** is the belief by individuals that their future is not within their control but rather is influenced by external forces. Entrepreneurs are individuals who are convinced they can make the difference between success and failure; hence they are motivated to take the steps needed to achieve the goal of setting up and running a new business.

Energy Level.   A business start-up requires great effort. Most entrepreneurs report struggle and hardship. They persist and work incredibly hard despite traumas and obstacles.[25] A survey of business owners reported that half worked 60 hours or more per week. Another reported that entrepreneurs worked long hours, but that beyond 70 hours little benefit was gained. The data in Exhibit 6.4 show findings from a survey conducted by the National Federation of Independent Business. New business owners work long hours, with only 23 percent working fewer than 50 hours, which is close to a normal workweek for managers in established businesses. For example, Bobby Frost, founder of Consolidated Glass & Mirror, recalls the long hours he and other company officials put in during the early years and provides a shot of small-business work reality: "We'd all be president or whatever during the day and work in the plant at night."[26]

Need to Achieve.   Another human quality closely linked to entrepreneurship is the **need to achieve,** which means that people are motivated to excel and pick situations in which success is likely.[27] People who have high achievement needs like to set their own goals, which are moderately difficult. Easy goals present no challenge; unrealistically difficult goals cannot be achieved. Intermediate goals are challenging and provide great satisfaction when achieved. High achievers also like to pursue goals for which they can obtain feedback about their success.

Self-Confidence.   People who start and run a business must act decisively. They need confidence about their ability to master the day-to-day tasks of the business. They must feel sure about their ability to win customers, handle the technical details, and keep the business moving. Entrepreneurs also have a general feeling of confidence that they can deal with anything in the future; complex, unanticipated problems can be handled as they arise.

John Sculley has been a divisional president of $10 billion PepsiCo, run Apple Computer, worked for yet smaller Spectrum Information Technologies, and in 1995 joined Live Picture, an Internet-imaging start-up with five employees. With Live Picture, Sculley claims he has found true happiness because the small company allows him to express his entrepreneurial spirit. For one thing, it fulfills his need to achieve ("What I have always enjoyed doing is building things," Sculley says). In addition, the work is suited to his tolerance for ambiguity because it allows him to flit from one start-up to another, developing ideas with small teams of creative people, and his internal locus of control because "it means I can design my life the way I want to live it."

internal locus of control
The belief by individuals that their future is within their control and that external forces will have little influence.

external locus of control
The belief by individuals that their future is not within their control but rather is influenced by external forces.

need to achieve
A human quality linked to entrepreneurship in which people are motivated to excel and pick situations in which success is likely.

Exhibit *6.4*   *Reported Hours per Week Worked by Owners of New Businesses*

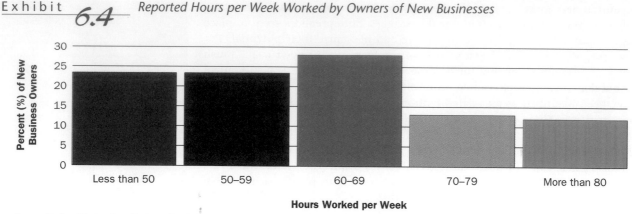

SOURCE: National Federation of Independent Business. Reported in Mark Robichaux, "Business First, Family Second," *The Wall Street Journal,* May 12, 1989, B1.

Awareness of Passing Time.   Entrepreneurs tend to be impatient; they feel a sense of urgency. They want things to progress as if there is no tomorrow. They want things moving immediately and seldom procrastinate. Entrepreneurs "seize the moment."

Tolerance for Ambiguity.   Many people need work situations characterized by clear structure, specific instructions, and complete information. **Tolerance for ambiguity** is the psychological characteristic that allows a person to be untroubled by disorder and uncertainty. This is an important trait, because few situations present more uncertainty than starting a new business. Decisions are made without clear understanding of options or certainty about which option will succeed.

tolerance for ambiguity
The psychological characteristic that allows a person to be untroubled by disorder and uncertainty.

Demographic Factors.   In addition to the six personality traits described so far, entrepreneurs often have background and demographic characteristics that distinguish them from other people. Entrepreneurs are more likely to be the first born within their families, and their parents are more likely to have been entrepreneurs. Children of immigrants also are more likely to be entrepreneurs, as are children for whom the father was absent for at least part of the childhood.[28]

Some research suggests that there are particular times during a person's career life cycle when the opportunities for entrepreneurship are particularly favorable. The two most obvious "windows of opportunity" are when a young person is just beginning a career and when a person is retiring from a career. Other windows present themselves along a continuum as a person grows in experience, industry knowledge, understanding of the marketplace, or financial ability. In addition, unplanned events such as the loss of a job, inheritance, or divorce may create opportunities for entrepreneurship. The important point is that entrepreneurship should be viewed as a career-long process, not something that has to be done at a certain time or age.[29] In the past, most entrepreneurs launched their businesses between the ages of 25 and 40. Today, however, early retirement programs and corporate downsizing have created a whole new class of older entrepreneurs with high-level skills and years of experience. Many of these former managers have decided their chances are better in becoming entrepreneurs than in trying to reenter an overcrowded job market.[30] Today's successful entrepreneurs come in all ages and may have a combination of personality traits. No one should be discouraged from starting a business because he or she doesn't fit a specific profile. Tom Scott and Tom First started their business even before they were out of college. What began as a boat repair and odd-jobs business eventually turned into a juice company; Nantucket Nectars, which originally was made fresh and sold off the owners' boat, is a $50 million-a-year business today. Amy Nye first got the idea for her business at the age of 17, but waited until she had some business experience under her belt before founding AltiTUNES, which sells CDs, tapes, portable electronics, and video games at airport kiosks. Because she uses the "dead space" in airports, Nye's rent is low and she can offer tunes to weary travelers at a reasonable price.[31] Much further along the career life cycle, R. E. Coleberd discovered that you don't have to be young to experience the joys of entrepreneurship.

PACIFIC WEST OIL DATA

Warnings about downsizing, restructuring, and potential layoffs had been circulating for months. Facing uncertain prospects for finding another job, fifty-one-year-old R. E. Coleberd decided to start his own business, reasoning that if he failed it would be his own fault and not the result of poor judgment at the top. His job had given him excellent experience working with petroleum industry statistical data and analysis, and Coleberd thought there might be a market among small firms that didn't have the know-how to work with statistical tables and graphs but that recognized or could be convinced that they needed sophisticated marketing intelligence in an increasingly competitive and complex industry.

On the day he was to leave his place of employment, Coleberd went into a colleague's office and told her, "You and I are going into business." Barbara Saben at first thought he was nuts, but 6 weeks later the two founded Pacific West Oil Data. Their extensive planning and premarketing discussions paid off. The small firms needed data to operate, but most didn't have the staff to handle it. Eventually, even the major players were calling PacWest, saying, "[The data we need] is somewhere in the building, but it takes me two weeks to get it. . . . Sign me up."

Coleberd says he'd pick cotton in Georgia before going back to work for a large corporation. "I have felt like a kid with a new red wagon ever since I started my business."[32]

Starting an Entrepreneurial Firm

Coleberd's story illustrates the first step in pursuing an entrepreneurial dream: Start with a viable idea for the new venture and plan like crazy. Once you have a new idea in mind, a business plan must be drawn and decisions must be made about legal structure, financing, and basic tactics, such as whether to start the business from scratch and whether to pursue international opportunities from the start.

New-Business Idea

To some people, the idea for a new business is the easy part. They do not even consider entrepreneurship until they are inspired by an exciting idea. Other people decide they want to run their own business and set about looking for an idea or opportunity. Exhibit 6.5 shows the most important reasons

Exhibit *6.5* *Sources of Entrepreneurial Motivation and New-Business Ideas*

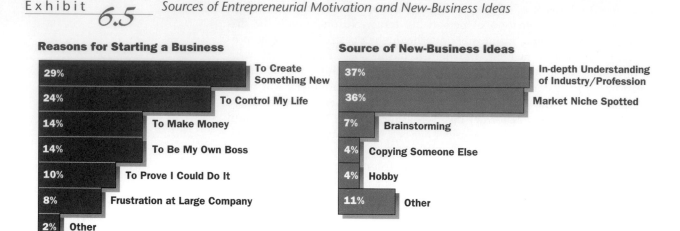

SOURCE: Based on Leslie Brokaw, "How to Start an *Inc.* 500 Company," *Inc. 500,* 1994, 51–65.

people start a new business and the source of new-business ideas, based on a survey of 500 fast-growing firms in the United States. The most important reasons people start new companies are to create something new and to be in control of their own lives. Note that 37 percent of business founders got their idea from an in-depth understanding of the industry, primarily because of past job experience. Interestingly, almost as many—36 percent—spotted a market niche that wasn't being filled.[33] For example, when Michael Kares was doing construction work just out of college, he saw a need for a national, standardized contracting firm to install steel storage systems in warehouses, stores, and factories from coast to coast. Thus, what started as a way to make a few bucks until he found a "real job" turned into a $10 million-a-year business, Coast-To-Coast Installations.[34] As described in the Technology box, Michael Saylor thinks he's spotted a market niche that will enable him to use his skills to build the next billion-dollar software company.

The trick for entrepreneurs is to blend their own skills and experience with a need in the marketplace. Acting strictly on one's own skills may produce something no one wants to buy. On the other hand, finding a market niche that you do not have the ability to fill does not work either. Both personal skill and market need typically must be present.

The Business Plan

business plan
A document specifying the business details prepared by an entrepreneur in preparation for opening a new business.

Once an entrepreneur is inspired by a new-business idea, careful planning is crucial. A **business plan** is a document specifying the business details prepared by an entrepreneur prior to opening a new business. Planning forces the entrepreneur to carefully think through all of the issues and problems associated with starting and developing the business. Most entrepreneurs have to borrow money, and a business plan is absolutely critical to persuading lenders and investors to participate in the business. Studies have shown that small businesses with a carefully thought out, written business plan are much more likely to succeed than those without one.[35]

The details of a business plan may vary, but successful business plans generally share several characteristics:[36]

Microstrategy

Michael Saylor started Microstrategy back in 1989, when he was 24 years old and just out of the Massachusetts Institute of Technology. No one thought the company would amount to much, but Saylor already had the skills and some experience under his belt that told him the market was ripe for his idea. Saylor's radical, long-term vision is to bring all sorts of data directly to the public—to allow the man or woman on the street to wander through the databases of life, finding whatever information he or she needs directly at the source. He believes we will all eventually be able to sit in front of our personal computers and ask complex questions and search for answers in any database around the world. Microstrategy's specialty is relational online analytical processing, or ROLAP, which answers questions by analyzing very large sets of data. Companies have begun to tie their disconnected computer systems into huge networks and at the same time integrate their different databases: customer records, transactions, sales calls, receipts, employee records, and so forth. But all those data are useful only to the extent that they can be accessed and made pertinent to everyone who has a stake in them. Today, using huge databases isn't easy.

Even in large marketing companies, it is difficult to get answers to fairly simple questions, such as how sales of a particular product are doing against the budget in each region. Already, Microstrategy's software is helping companies make their data accessible and useful to all employees as well as suppliers and customers.

The next step is open public access to big databases. Although there are tricky, unresolved questions about privacy and proprietary rights to information, Saylor believes in his vision and believes there are significant economic and social benefits to be gained from open access. He doesn't blink an eye when he talks about building the next billion-dollar software company based on the idea. Saylor doesn't care that some people think he's nuts. With customers such as MCI, S.C. Johnson Wax, Hallmark, and Victoria's Secret, and revenues at $50 million per year and growing, he doesn't have to care. No one ever built a billion-dollar company by thinking small.

www.microstrategy.com

SOURCE: Stewart Alsop, "Now I Know How a Real Visionary Sounds," *Fortune*, September 8, 1997, 161–162; and Lewis Perelman, "Anything, Anywhere, Anytime—Any Questions?" *Fast Company*, April–May 1997, 50–52.

- Demonstrate a clear, compelling vision that creates an air of excitement.
- Provide clear and realistic financial projections.
- Give detailed information about the target market.
- Include detailed information about the industry and competitors.
- Provide evidence of an effective entrepreneurial management team.
- Pay attention to good formatting and clear writing.
- Keep the plan short—no more than 50 pages long.
- Highlight critical risks that may threaten business success.
- Spell out the sources and uses of start-up funds and operating funds.
- Capture the reader's interest with a killer summary.

The business plan should indicate where the product or service fits into the overall industry and should draw on concepts that will be discussed throughout this book. For example, Chapter 8 will describe competitive strategies that entrepreneurs can use. Detailed suggestions for writing a business plan are provided in the Manager's Shoptalk box.

Legal Form

Before entrepreneurs have founded a business, and perhaps again as it expands, they must choose an appropriate legal structure for the company. The three basic choices are proprietorship, partnership, or corporation.

Shoptalk

MANAGER'S SHOPTALK

Helpful Hints for Writing the Business Plan

The Summary

No more than three pages.

This is the most crucial part of your plan because it must capture the reader's interest.

What, how, why, where, etc., must be summarized.

Complete this part *after* the finished business plan has been written.

The Business Description Segment

The name of the business

A background of the industry with history of the company (if any) should be covered here.

The potential of the new venture should be described clearly.

Any unique or distinctive features of the venture should be spelled out.

The Marketing Segment

Convince investors that sales projections and competition can be met.

Market studies should be used and disclosed.

Identify target market, market position, and market share.

Evaluate *all* competition and specifically cover why and how you will be better than the competitors.

Identify all market sources and assistance used for this segment.

Demonstrate pricing strategy, since your price must penetrate and maintain a market share to *produce profits*. Thus the lowest price is *not* necessarily the "best" price.

Identify your advertising plans with cost estimates to validate the proposed strategy.

The Research, Design, and Development Segment

Cover the *extent* of and *costs* involved in needed research, testing, or development.

Explain carefully what has been accomplished *already* (prototype, lab testing, early development).

Mention any research or technical assistance provided for you.

---

proprietorship

An unincorporated business owned by an individual for profit.

Proprietorship. A **proprietorship** is defined as an unincorporated business owned by an individual for profit. Proprietorships make up 70 percent of the 16 million businesses in the United States. This form is popular because it is easy to start and has few legal requirements. A proprietor has total ownership and control of the company and can make all decisions without consulting anyone. However, this type of organization also has drawbacks. The owner has unlimited liability for the business, meaning that if someone sues, the owner's personal as well as business assets are at risk. Also, financing can be harder to obtain because business success rests on one person's shoulders.

partnership

An unincorporated business owned by two or more people.

Partnership. A **partnership** is an unincorporated business owned by two or more people. Partnerships, like proprietorships, are relatively easy to start. Two friends may reach an agreement to start a pet store. To avoid misunderstandings and to make sure the business is well planned, it is wise to draw up and sign a formal partnership agreement with the help of an attorney. The agreement specifies how partners are to share responsibility and resources and how they will contribute their expertise. The disadvantages of partnerships are the unlimited liability of the partners and the disagreements that almost always occur among strong-minded people. A poll by *Inc.* magazine illustrated the volatility of partnerships. Fifty-nine percent of respondents considered partnerships a bad business move, citing reasons such as partner problems and conflicts. Partnerships often dissolve within 5 years. Respondents who liked partnerships pointed to the equality of partners (sharing of workload and emotional and financial burdens) as the key to a successful partnership.[37]

178

The Manufacturing Segment

Provide the advantages of your location (zoning, tax laws, wage rates).

List the production needs in terms of facilities (plant, storage, office space) and equipment (machinery, furnishings, supplies).

Describe the access to transportation (for shipping and receiving).

Explain proximity to your suppliers.

Mention the availability of labor in your location.

Provide estimates of manufacturing costs—be careful; too many entrepreneurs underestimate their costs.

The Management Segment

Provide résumés of all key people in the management of the venture.

Carefully describe the legal structure of the venture (sole proprietorship, partnership, or corporation).

Cover the added assistance (if any) of advisers, consultants, and directors.

Provide information on how everyone is to be compensated (how much, also).

The Critical-Risks Segment

Discuss potential risks *before* investors point them out. Some examples follow:

Price cutting by competitors

Potentially unfavorable industry-wide trends

Design or manufacturing costs in excess of estimates

Sales projections not achieved

Product development schedule not met

Difficulties or long lead times encountered in the procurement of parts or raw materials

Larger-than-expected innovation and development costs to stay competitive

Name alternative courses of action.

The Financial Segment

Provide statements.

Describe the needed sources for your funds and the uses you intend for the money.

Provide a budget.

Create stages of financing for the purpose of allowing evaluation by investors at various points.

The Milestone Schedule Segment

Provide a timetable or chart to demonstrate when each phase of the venture is to be completed. This shows the relationship of events and provides a deadline for accomplishment.

SOURCE: Donald F. Kuratko, Ray V. Montagno, and Frank J. Sabatine, *The Entrepreneurial Decision* (Muncie, IN: The Midwest Entrepreneurial Education Center, Ball State University, 1997), 45–46. Reprinted with permission.

Corporation.   A **corporation** is an artificial entity created by the state and existing apart from its owners. As a separate legal entity, the corporation is liable for its actions and must pay taxes on its income. Unlike other forms of ownership, the corporation has a legal life of its own; it continues to exist regardless of whether the owners live or die. And the corporation, not the owners, is sued in the case of liability. Thus continuity and limits on owners' liability are two principal advantages of forming a corporation. For example, a physician can form a corporation so that liability for malpractice will not affect his or her personal assets. The major disadvantage of the corporation is that it is expensive and complex to do the paperwork required to incorporate the business and to keep the records required by law. When proprietorships and partnerships are successful and grow large, they often incorporate to limit liability and to raise funds through the sale of stock to investors.

corporation
An artificial entity created by the state and existing apart from its owners.

Financial Resources

A crucial concern for entrepreneurs is the financing of the business. An investment usually is required to acquire labor and raw materials and perhaps a building and equipment. The financing decision initially involves two options—whether to obtain loans that must be repaid (debt financing) or whether to share ownership (equity financing). A survey of successful growth businesses asked, "How much money was needed to launch the company?" Approximately one-third were started on less than $10,000, one-third needed from $10,000 to $50,000, and one-third needed more than $50,000.

The primary source of this money was the entrepreneurs' own resources, but they often had to mortgage their home, borrow money from the bank, or give part of the business to a venture capitalist.[38]

Debt Financing.   Borrowing money that has to be repaid at a later date in order to start a business is **debt financing.** One common source of debt financing for a start-up is to borrow from family and friends. Another common source is a bank loan. Banks provide some 25 percent of all financing for small business. Sometimes entrepreneurs can obtain money from a finance company, wealthy individuals, or potential customers.

Another form of loan financing is provided by the Small Business Administration (SBA). The SBA supplies direct loans to some entrepreneurs who are unable to get bank financing because they are considered high risk. The SBA is especially helpful for people without substantial assets, providing an opportunity for single parents, minority group members, and others with a good idea.

Equity Financing.   Any money invested by owners or by those who purchase stock in a corporation is considered equity funds. **Equity financing** consists of funds that are invested in exchange for ownership in the company.

A **venture capital firm** is a group of companies or individuals that invests money in new or expanding businesses for ownership and potential profits. This is a potential form of capital for businesses with high earning and growth possibilities. For example, San Francisco research firm VentureOne reports that in 1997 alone, venture capitalists invested more than $6 billion in about 1,100 "PointCasts," small firms founded by engineers and software gurus that have the potential for rapid growth and high earnings.[39] Venture capital firms want new businesses with an extremely high rate of return, but in return the venture capitalist will provide assistance, advice, and information to help the entrepreneur prosper.

Tactics

There are several ways an aspiring entrepreneur can become a business owner. These include starting a new business from scratch, buying an existing business, or starting a franchise. Other entrepreneurial tactics include participation in a business incubator, being a spin-off of a large corporation, or pursuing international markets from the beginning.

Start a New Business.   One of the most common ways to become an entrepreneur is to start a new business from scratch. This is exciting because the entrepreneur sees a need for a product or service that has not been filled before and then sees the idea or dream become a reality. When Cuban-American Leopoldo Fernández Pujals noticed a growing appetite for fast food in Spain, he invested $80,000 to start a pizza delivery service. Today, TelePizza boasts $260 million in sales and employs some 6,000 workers.[40] The advantage of starting a business is the ability to develop and design the business in the entrepreneur's own way. The entrepreneur is solely responsible for its success. A potential disadvantage is the long time it can take to get the business off the ground and make it profitable. The uphill battle is caused by the lack of established clientele and the many mistakes made by someone new to the business. Moreover, no matter how much planning is done, a start-up is risky; there is no guarantee that the new idea will work.

For Mark Begelman, millionaire and former president of Office Depot, financing his new business, MARS music product stores, involved raising $65 million. However, each of his 11 stores features a stage for impromptu performances, a fully functional recording studio, and music clinics on everything from drums to recording equipment, which raises the cost of opening a store to an estimated $1.2 million. Begelman envisions obtaining the financial resources to have 70 MARS outlets with revenues of more than $500 million by 2003.

debt financing
Borrowing money that has to be repaid at a later date in order to start a business.

equity financing
Financing that consists of funds that are invested in exchange for ownership in the company.

venture capital firm
A group of companies or individuals that invests money in new or expanding businesses for ownership and potential profits.

Buy an Existing Business. Because of the long start-up time and the inevitable mistakes, some entrepreneurs prefer to reduce risk by purchasing an existing business. This offers the advantage of a shorter time to get started and an existing track record. The entrepreneur may get a bargain price if the owner wishes to retire or has other family considerations. Moreover, a new business may overwhelm an entrepreneur with the amount of work to be done and procedures to be determined. An established business already has filing systems, a payroll tax system, and other operating procedures. Potential disadvantages are the need to pay for goodwill that the owner believes exists and the possible existence of ill will toward the business. In addition, the company may have bad habits and procedures or outdated technology, which may be why the business is for sale. Although it is high risk, gutsy entrepreneurs sometimes can achieve great success by taking over a troubled company. Eric Close and Chris Farls, fresh out of graduate school, bought a company that specializes in cleaning, painting, repairing, and inspecting railroad cars. The company (now named ProLine Services, Inc.) had the potential to be a big moneymaker but was in deep trouble, with heavy debt, a load of uncollected accounts receivable, and major operational problems. The two twenty-somethings purchased the company, promptly turned it around, and are well on their way to getting very rich. "Sales just walk through the door," says Close.[41]

Buy a Franchise. Franchising is perhaps the most rapidly growing path to entrepreneurship. Currently, 1 out of every 12 businesses in the United States is franchised, and a new franchise business opens every eight minutes of every business day. Today, franchising employs more than 8 million people.[42] **Franchising** is an arrangement by which the owner of a product or service allows others to purchase the right to distribute the product or service with help from the owner. The franchisee invests his or her money and owns the business but does not have to develop a new product, create a new company, or test the market. The franchisee typically pays a flat fee plus a percentage of gross sales. Franchises exist for weight-loss clinics, pet-sitting services, sports photography, bakeries, janitorial services, auto repair shops, real estate offices, and numerous other types of businesses. Exhibit 6.6 shows examples of some of today's fastest growing franchises in four investment categories. Start-up costs for a franchise can range from less than $5,000, for a business that doesn't require extensive facilities or equipment, to more than $500,000, for a franchise such as McDonald's or Econo Lodge.[43] The powerful advantage of a franchise is that management help is provided by the owner. For example, Burger King does not want a franchisee to fail and will provide the studies necessary to find a good location. The franchisor also provides an established name and national advertising to stimulate demand for the product or service. Potential disadvantages are the lack of control that occurs when franchisors want every business managed in exactly the same way. In some cases, franchisors require that franchise owners use certain contractors or suppliers which may cost more than others would. In addition, franchises can be very expensive, and the high start-up costs are followed with monthly payments to the franchisor that can run from 2 percent to 12 percent of sales.

Entrepreneurs who are considering buying a franchise should investigate the company thoroughly. The prospective franchisee is legally entitled to a

franchising
An arrangement by which the owner of a product or service allows others to purchase the right to distribute the product or service with help from the owner.

Exhibit *6.6*

Today's Winning Franchises

	Company	Product Category	Number of Units
$75,000 or Under	Coldwell Banker Residential Affiliates	Real Estate	2,066
	Money Mailer, Inc.	Business Services	675
	Merry Maids	Maintenance Services	810
$75,001 to $150,000	Blimpie International	Fast Food	966
	GNC Franchising	Retail	2,246
	Snap-On Inc.	Automotive Services	4,963
	Mail Boxes Etc.	Business Services	2,676
$150,001 to $250,000	Glamour Shots Licensing Inc.	Retail	323
	Sir Speedy, Inc.	Printing	887
	ExecuTrain Corp.	Computer-Related Services	135
$250,001 or More	Choice Hotels International	Lodging	3,384
	Dunkin' Donuts	Bakery Goods	3,632
	Hardee's Food Systems	Fast Food	4,060
	Ben Franklin Stores	Retail	912

SOURCE: Adapted from "Winners by Investment," *Success* 42, no. 4 (May 1995), 84.

copy of franchisor disclosure statements, which include information on 20 topics, including litigation and bankruptcy history, identities of the directors and executive officers, financial information, identification of any products the franchisee is required to buy, and from whom those purchases must be made.[44] The entrepreneur also should talk with as many franchise owners as possible, since they are among the best sources of information about how the company really operates. Exhibit 6.7 lists some specific questions entrepreneurs should ask about themselves and the company when considering buying a franchise. Answering such questions may improve the chances for a successful career as a franchisee.

Participate in a Business Incubator.   An attractive innovation for entrepreneurs who want to start a business from scratch is to join a business incubator. The **business incubator** provides shared office space, management support services, and management advice to entrepreneurs. By sharing office space with other entrepreneurs, managers share information about local business, financial aid, and market opportunities.

This innovation arose nearly two decades ago to nurture start-up companies. Business incubators have become a significant segment of the small business economy: the number of incubators nationwide jumped from 385 in 1990 to more than 800 by March 1997, and new ones are opening at about the rate of one a week. Nearly 90 percent of incubators are operated by not-for-profit organizations, including government agencies and universities, to boost the viability of small business and spur job creation. What gives incubators an edge is the expertise of the in-house mentor, who serves an adviser, role model, and cheerleader. This nurturing can be particularly helpful to low-income and minority entrepreneurs. For example, before she entered the Philadelphia Enterprise Center, Donna DuBose Miller still needed food stamps in addition to the income she generated from DuBose

business incubator
An innovation that provides shared office space, management support services, and management advice to entrepreneurs.

Exhibit
6.7   *Sample Questions for Choosing a Franchise*

Questions about the Entrepreneur	Questions about the Franchisor	Before Signing on the Dotted Line
1. Will I enjoy the day-to-day work of this business? 2. Do my background, experience, and goals make this a good choice for me? 3. Am I willing to work within the rules and guidelines established by the franchisor?	1. What assistance does the company provide in terms of: selection of location, set-up costs, and securing credit; day-to-day technical assistance; marketing; and ongoing training and development? 2. How long does it take the typical franchise owner to start making a profit? 3. How many franchises changed ownership within the past year and why?	1. Do I understand the risks associated with this business and am I willing to assume them? 2. Have I had an advisor review the disclosure documents and franchise agreement? 3. Do I understand all the terms of the contract?

SOURCES: Based on Thomas Love, "The Perfect Franchisee," *Nation's Business,* April 1998, 59–65; and Roberta Maynard, "Choosing a Franchise," *Nation's Business,* October 1996, 56–63.

Business Services, which she ran out of her home. Della Clark, president of the Enterprise Center, paired DuBose Miller with a graphic artist to share the $100 rent for a space and coached her in marketing and other business basics. Now, DuBose Miller has put welfare behind her, has hired a part-time employee, and is making enough money to send one of her children to a private school.[45]

Be a Spin-off.   Spin-offs, a unique form of entrepreneurial company, were previously associated with and owe their start-up to another organization. A **spin-off** is an independent company producing a product or service similar to that produced by the entrepreneur's former employer.[46] Spin-offs occur when entrepreneurs with a desire to produce a similar product quit their employers, or in some cases they produce a related product that is purchased by the former employer. The former employer may recognize that it can profit from the idea by selling patents to the spin-off and by investing in it. Employer approval is often the basis for a spin-off, although in some cases entrepreneurs start a new business because they disagree with former employers. Disagreement usually revolves around the failure of the employer to try a new idea that the entrepreneur believes in. A frustrated employee should discuss the possibility of starting a spin-off company with the support of his or her current employer. In this way, the spin-off reduces risk and has a source of management advice. The entrepreneur may also have a guaranteed customer for the spin-off's initial output.

spin-off
An independent company producing a product or service similar to that produced by the entrepreneur's former employer.

Try Globalization.   In today's global economy, no small business can afford to ignore overseas markets. Multiplex Co., a Ballwin, Missouri, maker of beverage-dispensing equipment, now has offices in Germany, France, Taiwan, England, and Canada, with overseas business accounting for about 30 percent of sales. Demetrius Brown, co-owner of Fuci Metals, generated $100 million in sales last year by doing business in Siberia, Turkey, and Africa—markets deemed too small or too risky by most big metals dealers.[47] And small environmental companies, specializing in everything from wastewater treatment gear to landfill management, are finding extensive opportunities in the newly industrialized markets of South Korea, Indonesia, Malaysia, and Taiwan.[48] Many small businesses fail because the entrepreneur thinks provincially, being unaware of overseas markets. Former chief economist for the Small Business Administration, Tom Gray, has estimated that for every dollar of growth in the United States during the next decade, there will be five dollars of growth elsewhere. Although venturing abroad is difficult for small companies, it is increasingly necessary. Many small companies are building overseas operations, and even more are exporting products to foreign markets.

The ability to do business overseas is enhanced by new technology that bypasses former obstacles. Better air travel and better electronic communications help companies establish the connections they need to do business on a global scale. Michael Marks, chairman of Flexitronics International, an electronics company with operations in San Jose and Singapore, says, "I can sit at my computer terminal . . . reading messages from all over the world."[49] Telephone interpreters, software kits, and translation services help bypass language difficulties and make it easier to do business internationally. There are also a growing number of resources for small companies wishing to enter the global arena.

Getting Help

Unlike large corporations, small businesses don't have in-house specialists to help them develop a global presence. Fortunately, assistance is available from a number of sources. The Service Corps of Retired Executives (SCORE) works with the Small Business Administration to match small businesses with mentors who have experience in international business. The Bankers' Association for Foreign Trade, a trade group, runs a program to help small exporters find financing. A good place for small companies to start is the U.S. Commerce Department's hot line, which can provide guidesheets on tricky exporting problems and details about the variety of federal programs designed to help new exporters tap foreign markets.[50] Many government departments offer counseling; research; assistance in finding overseas agents and sales leads; and help with export licensing, loans, export credit insurance, and other services. The Commerce Department has also set up 19 U.S. Export Assistance Centers, or USEACs, around the country. These are one-stop shops designed to help companies get into or expand their exporting operations.[51]

Help also is available to entrepreneurs on issues besides international business. Perhaps the first piece of advice given to new entrepreneurs is to find a good accountant and attorney for help with the financial and legal aspects of the business. For incorporated businesses, a board of directors also can be a good source of knowledge and advice. The U.S. Small Business Administration provides a loan program, described earlier, as well as numerous other assistance programs. The SBA has a Web site (sbaonline.sba.gov) offering information, and the *Directory for Small Business Management* lists all SBA publications and videotapes on management issues. The Service Corps of Retired Executives is an excellent resource for small businesses. These experienced managers can provide advice and assistance on a wide range of issues.

Managing a Growing Business

Once an entrepreneurial business is up and running, how does the owner manage it? Often the traits of self-confidence, creativity, and internal locus of control lead to financial and personal grief as the enterprise grows. A hands-on entrepreneur who gave birth to the organization loves perfecting every detail. But after the start-up, continued growth requires a shift in management style. Those who fail to adjust to a growing business can be the cause of the problems rather than the solution.[52] In this section, we will look at the stages through which entrepreneurial companies move and then consider how managers should carry out their planning, organizing, leading, and controlling.

Stages of Growth

Entrepreneurial businesses go through distinct stages of growth, with each stage requiring different management skills. The five stages are illustrated in Exhibit 6.8.

1. *Existence.* In this stage, the main problems are producing the product or service and obtaining customers. Key issues facing managers are: Can we get enough customers? Will we survive? Do we have enough money?

2. *Survival.* At this stage, the business has demonstrated that it is a workable business entity. It is producing a product or service and has sufficient customers. Concerns here have to do with finances—generating sufficient cash flow to run the business and making sure revenues exceed expenses. The organization will grow in size and profitability during this period.

3. *Success.* At this point, the company is solidly based and profitable. Systems and procedures are in place to allow the owner to slow down if desired. The owner can stay involved or consider turning the business over to professional managers

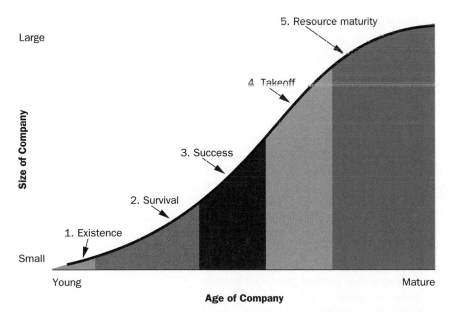

Exhibit
6.8

Five Stages of Growth for an Entrepreneurial Company

Source: Based on Neil C. Churchill and Virginia L. Lewis, "The Five Stages of Small Business Growth," *Harvard Business Review* (May–June 1993), 30–50.

Entrepreneur CEO Jeff Bezos of Amazon.com spent just three years growing his unknown on-line bookstore to the resource maturity stage of growth. The company is projected to have $500 million in sales. Now times are more chaotic with competitors such as Barnesandnoble.com entering Web site competition. Bezos, however, recently refused a partnership offer from the German media giant, Bertelsmann, in favor going it alone—retaining some of the entrepreneurial spirit he had in earlier stages of growth.

4. *Takeoff.* Here the key problem is how to grow rapidly and finance that growth. The owner must learn to delegate, and the company must find sufficient capital to invest in major growth. This is a pivotal period in an entrepreneurial company's life. Properly managed, the company can become a big business. However, another problem for companies at this stage is how to maintain the advantages of "smallness" as the company grows.

5. *Resource maturity.* At this stage, the company has made substantial financial gains, but it may start to lose the advantages of small size, including flexibility and the entrepreneurial spirit. A company in this stage has the staff and financial resources to begin acting like a mature company with detailed planning and control systems.

Planning

In the early stage of existence, formal planning tends to be nonexistent except for the business plan described earlier in this chapter. The primary goal is simply to remain alive. As the organization grows, formal planning usually is not instituted until around the success stage. Recall from Chapter 1 that planning means defining goals and deciding on the tasks and use of resources needed to attain them. Chapters 7, 8, and 9 will describe how entrepreneurs can define goals and implement strategies and plans to meet them. It is important that entrepreneurs view their original business plan as a living document that evolves as the company grows or the market changes. Frontier Cooperative Herbs of Norway, Iowa, founded in 1976, has done formal annual planning since early in its history. However, CEO and co-founder Rick Stewart found that the effectiveness of plans dramatically improved when he established clear accountability for each element of the plan. Now, every annual goal has the name of one person—and one person only—attached to it. Frontier has rapidly grown to a $29.6 million company.[53]

Organizing

In the first two stages of growth, the organization's structure is very informal with all employees reporting to the owner. At about stage 3—success—functional managers often are hired to take over duties performed by the owner. A functional organization structure will begin to evolve with managers in charge of finance, manufacturing, and marketing. During the latter stages of entrepreneurial growth, managers must learn to delegate and decentralize authority. If the business has multiple product lines, the owner may consider creating teams or divisions responsible for each line. The organization must hire competent managers and have sufficient management talent to handle fast growth and eliminate problems caused by increasing size. The latter growth stages also are characterized by greater use of rules, procedures, and written job descriptions.

Some of today's small companies are finding creative ways to stay small but still grow. Barbara Bobo, who turned a stove-top operation making all-natural herbal and floral soaps into a half-million-dollar company, created a network of independent contractors when demand outpaced the company's capabilities. Today, her company, Woodspirits, produces and distributes 300,000 bars of soap annually with just three employees.[54] Chapters 10–14 will discuss organizing in detail.

Leading

The driving force in the early stages of development is the leader's vision. This vision combined with the leader's personality shapes corporate culture. The leader can signal cultural values of service, efficiency, quality, or ethics. Often entrepreneurs do not have good people skills but do have excellent task skills in either manufacturing or marketing. By the success stage of growth, the owner must either learn to motivate employees or bring in managers who can. Rapid takeoff is not likely to happen without employee cooperation.

Stepping from the self-absorption of the early days of a company to the more active communication necessary for growth can be tricky for entrepreneurs. Charles Barnard, the owner of Foot Traffic, a chain of eight specialty sock stores based in Kansas City, Missouri, believes leaders should focus on communication as a company grows. "A lot of the time," Barnard says, "you get to running real fast, and you don't think about the people around you. But you can never get anywhere if you're pulling your staff around behind you all the time."[55] The president of Foreign Candy Company of Hull, Iowa, saw his company grow rapidly when he concentrated more on employee needs and less on financial growth. He made an effort to communicate with employees, conducted surveys to learn how they were feeling about the company, and found ways to involve them in decision making. His leadership style allowed the company to enter the takeoff stage with the right corporate culture and employee attitudes to sustain rapid growth.

Leadership also is important because many small firms are having a hard time hiring qualified employees. Labor shortages often hurt small firms that grow rapidly. A healthy corporate culture can help attract and retain good people.[56] You will learn more about leadership in Chapters 15–19.

Controlling

Financial control is important in each stage of the entrepreneurial firm's growth. In the initial stages, control is exercised by simple accounting records and by personal supervision. By stage 3—success—operational budgets are in place, and the owner should start implementing more structured control systems. During the takeoff stage, the company will need to make greater use of budgets and standard cost systems and perhaps acquire computers to provide statistical reports. These control techniques will become more sophisticated during the resource maturity stage.

Sophisticated accounting software has helped Jay Shrager maintain control at Somerset Farms, a Spring House, Pennsylvania, distributor of food products. Since 1988, when the company entered the profitable niche of providing food products to prisons throughout the country, revenues have grown at the dizzying rate of 40 percent a year. Shrager quickly realized things were moving so fast he couldn't keep up with them. The software program he selected not only keeps the books but also ties accounting to other facets of the business such as ordering, manufacturing, and distribution.[57] Control will be discussed further in Chapters 20–22.

Coping with Chaotic Times

Small businesses operate in the same environment as larger, well-established firms and are affected by the same dramatic changes: increasingly tough global competition, rapid technological change, uncertain environments, the need to do more with less, and new challenges brought about by demographic shifts in the population and workforce. Small companies sometimes are in a better position to weather the chaos because of the speed and flexibility that small-ness provides. However, many entrepreneurs are so focused on day-to-day oper-ations that they fail to take the long-range view necessary for continued growth.

Joel Barker, whose Infinity Ltd. consulting firm has offices in Minneapo-lis and Orlando, says small businesses need to focus on the future in this era of rapid change. Barker advises companies to act now on the predictable changes, such as the growing diversity of the workforce, and prepare them-selves to cope with the unpredictable as the world of business grows ever more turbulent. Taking a long-range view may ensure the survival of a small business in chaotic times.[58]

If a small business does not evolve, it risks failure. Burns & Russell, a family-owned business started in Baltimore in 1775, supplied the bricks for many of the structures around town, including the wharves, the B & O railroad tunnels, and Johns Hopkins Hospital. But Burns & Russell hasn't made a brick for 45 years; today the company has evolved into a high-tech manufacturer of specialty glazes for concrete blocks, along with other specialty chemicals.[59]

Stephen Harper, author of *The McGraw-Hill Guide to Managing Growth in Your Emerging Business,* emphasizes that small businesses can be learning organizations, which in large part means paying attention to signals from the marketplace and changing and adapting to meet customer needs. Harper believes missing those signals is one of the biggest sins of entrepreneurs. "Too many people don't evolve, and the market just passes them by."[60]

Intrapreneurship in a Growing Business

As the entrepreneurial firm grows large, it has a tendency to lose its innova-tive spirit with the implementation of formal control systems and bureaucratic procedures. Established firms often lose innovative ideas to entrepreneurial spin-offs from frustrated employees. The way to keep innovation within the organization is to create conditions in which intrapreneurs can flourish. **Intrapreneurship** is the process whereby an individual sees the need for inno-vation and promotes it within an organization. The goal for managers, who at one time were innovators themselves, is to create a climate that encourages intrapreneurs. Companies such as 3M are known for intrapreneurship. 3M intrapreneur Art Frey invented the Post-it Note as the result of personal frus-tration when his page markers repeatedly fell out of his church hymnal. Even the best ideas need nurturing, support, and financing in a large corporation.

The following rules provide an approach for developing the necessary atmosphere:

1. Encourage action.

2. Use informal meetings whenever possible.

3. Tolerate failure and use it as a learning experience.

4. Be persistent in getting an idea to market.

5. Reward innovation for innovation's sake.

intrapreneurship
The process of recognizing the need for innovation and promoting it within an organization.

Every time she makes a sales pitch or packs a customer order, Linda Desrosiers is running her own company and working for her employer, Pinchot & Co., a consulting and training firm—at the same time. Desrosiers is an intrapreneur, who runs an entrepreneurial operation inside a larger company, selling books written by company founder Gifford Pinchot, who runs Pinchot & Co. with his wife Katherine. The arrangement gives Desrosiers an outlet for her entrepreneurial spirit and creative talents, while allowing Pinchot & Co. to stay focused on its core business yet also move into business areas it otherwise couldn't consider.

6. Plan the physical layout of the firm to encourage informal communication.

7. Encourage clever bootlegging of ideas.

8. Organize people into small teams for future-oriented projects.

9. Strip away rigid procedures and encourage personnel to go around red tape when they find it.

10. Reward and/or promote innovative personnel.[61]

One company that maintains the innovative spirit is Hewlett-Packard.

Charles House is an intrapreneur in Hewlett-Packard's innovative culture. He was assigned to develop a Federal Aviation Agency monitor similar to a television picture tube but with greatly enhanced capacity. It failed to meet government specifications, but House was more interested in other applications. He took a prototype to customers to learn whether it would solve their problems—in violation of HP's rules. He fought for money to support the technology despite its lack of a proven market. Finally, the late Dave Packard himself ordered the project halted. House's immediate superiors still supported him, however, and gave him one more year. House and his team succeeded, generating $10 million in annual sales simply because House persisted and would not give up. House was awarded the Medal of Defiance, shown in Exhibit 6.9. This reward signals Hewlett-Packard's fundamental values in favor of innovation.

In his book *Intrapreneuring*, Gifford Pinchot argues that people like Charles House are needed in organizations. When spotted, intrapreneurs should be encouraged. Characteristics of intrapreneurs include willingness to circumvent orders aimed at stopping their dream; willingness to do any job needed to make the project work; willingness to work underground as long as they can; willingness to be true to their goals; and willingness to remember it is easier to ask for forgiveness than for permission.[62]

HEWLETT-PACKARD
www.hp.com

Exhibit *6.9*

Reward for Intrapreneurship at Hewlett-Packard

Hewlett Packard

MEDAL OF DEFIANCE
CHARLES H. HOUSE

Awarded in recognition of extraordinary contempt and defiance beyond the normal call of engineering duty.

In total defiance of adverse market studies and surveys concluding the existence of a worldwide market of no more than 50 total large screen electrostatic displays, Charles H. House, using all means available — principally pen, tongue, and airplane to extol an unrecognized technical contribution, planted the seeds for a new market resulting in the shipment of 17,769 large screen displays to date.

1 April 1982

SOURCE: Courtesy of Hewlett-Packard Company.

Intrapreneurship is not always successful, however. Many companies, such as Control Data Corporation and Kodak, failed to generate profits from intrapreneur programs and dropped them. A good idea does not guarantee success. Intrapreneurs may be ill-prepared to follow through on their ideas and to make the sacrifice necessary to see the idea reach fruition. Managers may balk at the necessary capital investment or resist making exceptions to corporate policies.[63] As with any strategy, intrapreneurship is only as successful as the planning and support it receives throughout a company.

Summary and Management Solution

This chapter explored entrepreneurship and small-business management. Entrepreneurs start new businesses, and entrepreneurship plays an important role in the economy by stimulating job creation, innovation, and opportunities for minorities and women. An entrepreneurial personality includes the traits of internal locus of control, high energy level, need to achieve, tolerance for ambiguity, awareness of passing time, and self-confidence.

Starting an entrepreneurial firm requires a new-business idea. At that point a comprehensive business plan should be developed and decisions made about legal structure and financing. Tactical decisions for the new venture include whether to start, buy, or franchise, whether to participate in a business incubator, whether to be a company spin-off, and whether to go global. After the business is started, it will typically proceed through five stages of growth—existence, survival, success, takeoff, and resource maturity. The management

functions of planning, organizing, leading, and controlling should be tailored to each stage of growth. Finally, intrapreneurship, a variation of entrepreneurship, is a mechanism for encouraging innovation within a larger firm. Small businesses must continually evolve to cope with changes in the environment and the chaos that characterizes today's business world.

Create-a-Check, described at the beginning of this chapter, illustrates several of the problems entrepreneurs face. Starting any new business requires hard work and long hours, and many small businesses fail. Competition, shifts in the marketplace, new technology, or other elements of the external environment can severely threaten the viability of a new company. However, for fast-growing companies such as Create-a-Check, most of the failures are due to internal problems. Just as her company reached the takeoff stage, Linda Kesler turned it over to someone else so that she could take a break. However, she had not established the control techniques needed to keep the company moving forward smoothly. The transition was made too quickly; Alan Redd was left in charge of a company he wasn't ready to run and without clear guidelines regarding future plans. Kesler eventually got Create-a-Check back on solid ground, but the experience was traumatic for everyone, as she fired Redd and 50 percent of the workforce after she returned to the company. Careful planning, better control systems, and a gradual transition to having someone else manage the company could help prevent a similar situation in the future.

Discussion Questions

1. Dan McKinnon started an airline with one airplane. To do so required filing more than 10,000 pages of manuals, ordering 50,000 luggage tags, buying more than $500 million in insurance, and spending more than $300,000 to train employees. A single inspection test cost $18,000. Evaluate whether you think this is a good entrepreneurial opportunity, and discuss why you think Dan McKinnon undertook it.

2. What do you think are the most important contributions of small business to our economy?

3. Why would small-business ownership have great appeal to immigrants, women, and minorities?

4. Consider the six personality characteristics of entrepreneurs. Which two traits do you think are most like those of managers in large companies? Which two are least like those of managers in large companies?

5. Why is purchasing an existing business or franchise less risky than starting a new business?

6. If you were to start a new business, would you have to search for an idea, or do you already have an idea to try? Explain.

7. Many entrepreneurs say they did little planning, perhaps scratching notes on a legal pad. How is it possible for them to succeed?

8. What is the difference between debt financing and equity financing? What are common sources of each type?

9. How does an entrepreneurial firm in the existence stage differ from one in the success stage?

10. How do the management functions of organizing and controlling differ for the existence and success stages?

11. Explain the difference between entrepreneurship and intrapreneurship. Why would entrepreneurs want intrapreneurship within their companies? Would an entrepreneur's personality tend to inhibit intrapreneurship? Discuss.

Management in Practice: Experiential Exercise

What Is Your Entrepreneurial Quotient?

The following questions are from a test developed by John R. Braun, psychology professor at the University of Bridgeport in Connecticut, and the Northwestern Mutual Life Insurance Company, based in Milwaukee. Simply answer yes or no to each question.

1. Are you a first-generation American?
2. Were you an honor student?
3. Did you enjoy group functions in school—clubs, team sports, even double dates?
4. As a youngster, did you prefer to be alone frequently?
5. As a child, did you have a paper route, a lemonade stand, or some other small enterprise?
6. Were you a stubborn child?
7. Were you a cautious youngster, the last in the neighborhood to try diving off the highboard?
8. Do you worry about what others think of you?
9. Are you in a rut, tired of the same routine day in and day out?
10. Would you be willing to dip deeply into your "nest egg"— and possibly lose all you invested—to go it alone?

11. If your new business should fail, would you get to work immediately on another?
12. Are you an optimist?

Answers:
1. Yes = 1, No = minus 1.
2. Yes = minus 4, No = 4.
3. Yes = minus 1, No = 1.
4. Yes = 1, No = minus 1.
5. Yes = 2, No = minus 2.
6. Yes = 1, No = minus 1.
7. Yes = minus 4, No = 4. If you were a particularly daring child, add another 4 points.
8. Yes = minus 1, No = 1.
9. Yes = 2, No = minus 2.
10. Yes = 2, No = minus 2.
11. Yes = 4, No = minus 4.
12. Yes = 2, No = minus 2.

Now calculate your total score. If you tallied 20 or more points, you have a strong entrepreneurial quotient. The score of 0 to 19 suggests that you have entrepreneurial possibilities. If you scored between 0 and minus 10, your chance of successfully starting an entrepreneurial business is marginal. A score below minus 11 suggests you are not the entrepreneurial type.

Go back over each question, thinking about changes you might make to become more or less entrepreneurial, depending on your career interests.

Source: Peter Lohr, "Should You Be in Business for Yourself?" *Readers Digest*, July 1989, 49–52.

Management in Practice: Ethical Dilemma

To Grow or Not to Grow?

Chuck Campbell is the founder of Expeditions Unlimited, a specialty travel service that researches and arranges trips to unlikely places. He is famous for his unconventional approach to business in everything from his trademark blue jeans and ball caps as working attire to his personal relationships with all clients. He is the type of entrepreneur who makes deep commitments to his employees, with generous educational allowances, family leaves, and profit sharing for all of his staff. The office atmosphere is casual but professional. People dress any way they choose and music plays continually, but everyone works long hours, and customer satisfaction is the ultimate goal. For example, a 24-hour answering service relays messages to agents at home if their clients have emergencies during a booked trip.

Five years ago, Campbell consented to acquiring a computer system when his agents insisted it would help them in their jobs, but he doesn't use it. He pays two receptionists to work full-time, rather than have an automated phone system with voice mail. He believes his clients should be able to talk to a *person* whenever they call. The company has grown steadily, and he knows that at least two of his senior employees are ready to start branches on their own. They want his consent and his supervision, but Campbell isn't sure he wants or can handle such a radical expansion. He knows

he'll need to compromise his level of contact with clients and embrace the new technology to make it work, and he's not sure that he will still enjoy his job after the transition. He also worries that the unique nature of this highly personal business may change with the growth. Campbell says employee satisfaction and growth are important. Does his commitment to employee development demand he expose his business and his personal job satisfaction to the risk of new business arrangements?

What do you do?

1. Refuse to expand your business. Stay within your comfort zone, but give your blessings to the senior employees who want to quit and start their own travel service in other cities.
2. Expand the business in its present location: delegate the bulk of the company and expedition management to the senior agents, with the rest doing the research and arrangements. Step back into a supervisory and client contact position only. Agents receive more responsibility, and you stay in control.
3. Train the senior agents to open branches under your corporate identity, trusting that your long association will insure that they run the branches with the corporate values you instilled. Then let go and give them only as much supervision as you can comfortably afford to give.

Surf the Net

1. **Entrepreneurship.** Go to the "Quiz for Small Business Success" available at the U.S. Small Business Administration Web site. **(http://www.sba.gov/BI/quiz.html)** Assume the role of a small business owner (if you are not one already) and complete the quiz and score your results. Write a paragraph summarizing how your score was interpreted according to the Success Quotient Table. Also, include in your summary whether you think a quiz such as this can be helpful to someone interested in pursuing small business ownership.
2. **Venture capital firms**. Assume you are seeking financing for an entrepreneurial venture and need to check the availability of possible funding in your situation. Visit

America's Business Funding Directory at **http://www.businessfinance.com.** According to the information applicants provide for the search, list the criteria venture capitalists consider when evaluating your capital request. After reviewing the procedure for using this Web site to locate funding sources, examine the tools, references, and resources also available at this site that can help you grow and keep your business strong.

3. **Franchise opportunities.** You will be able to find a great deal of information about franchising opportunities available for entrepreneurs. Use your Internet search engine to locate a site such as "The Franchise Handbook: On-Line" at **http://www.franchise1.com/**

franchise.html or "Business Opportunities Handbook: On-Line" at **http://www.ezines.com.** Select three franchise opportunities that interest you and prepare a table where you will compare information related to each franchise. Across the top of the page list the franchises you've selected; in the left column list information categories provided below. You may add to these categories by using some of the questions from Exhibit 6.7, "Sample Questions for Choosing a Franchise." Fill in the columns with the information related to each franchise.

Franchising since

Number of franchised units

Number of company-owned units

Franchise fee

Capital requirements

Training and support provided

Case for Critical Analysis

I Do Its

Robi Fugate of Birmingham, Alabama, first thought of the idea for her kids' clothing line when she noticed some toddlers whose mismatched duds told her they'd picked out their own outfits. Fugate spotted a niche for a children's clothing line that would allow kids to dress themselves without help—a line of totally coordinated pieces with no defined fronts or backs and no zippers or buttons to fool with. Right then and there she came up with the name "I Do Its," because, she reasoned, "that's what kids say when you try to dress them." However, it was seven years before Fugate got up the courage to leave her $32,000-a-year job managing department store counters for Clinique. She was "scared she'd be chewed up and spit out" in the fashion world, but Fugate felt that too many years had already slipped by and that the time was right for her to start the business. Newly divorced and the mother of an infant, Fugate recruited a partner to invest $120,000, and I Do Its was born.

Fugate commissioned the North River Apparel factory in Berry, Alabama, to manufacture the clothing and contracted with representatives at Cyrilla & Co., an agency whose Atlanta showroom sells to stores from Virginia to Florida, to market the first year's line. I Do Its pulled in $32,000 in sales its first year, and sales quadrupled the following year. More sales representatives signed up in Dallas, Chicago, Los Angeles, and New York, and independent children's stores from around the country began placing orders. Then Fugate suffered the business' first crisis when she didn't have enough cash to deliver the orders. Larry Johnson, owner of North River Apparel, came to the rescue, offering Fugate a line of credit that would be paid off with a 50 percent share of I Do Its' profits. But the problems were just beginning.

Fugate has had a difficult time growing the business because she can't afford a major advertising campaign. Although she's managed to get some free publicity from the *Birmingham Post-Herald* and *Parenting Life,* a local television show, Fugate knows she needs more than local publicity to make I Do Its a success. In addition, she's having a hard time getting retailers to sell her clothing line the way she wants it sold, as matching outfits. She has even visited some stores and found that they had no idea the purpose of the clothing was to allow kids to dress themselves. Although she will ship I Do Its only in matching sets, many stores separate the pieces and mix them in with other labels, making it extremely difficult for parents to put together ensembles, and leaving the stores with mismatched items that have to be marked down at the end of the season.

After three years in business, the I Do Its clothing line is still struggling to catch on. However, despite her frustrations, Fugate believes in her idea and knows the company can be successful. She is particularly excited about launching a catalog next year for disabled kids, as she believes they are natural customers for the I Do Its line. She has also recently invested a modest amount in advertising and is considering how she can get sales reps to promote the I Do Its philosophy so that stores will sell the clothing in sets. I Do Its has many hurdles to cross, but Fugate believes a good idea and a lot of hard work can lead to success.

Questions

1. Of the six personality traits of typical entrepreneurs, which seem most present in Robi Fugate? Which trait do you think is most important for solving the problem of getting stores to sell the clothing in matching sets?
2. Discuss how Fugate should carry out her organizing, leading, and controlling to manage the business for success.
3. Do you believe Fugate will eventually succeed with I Do Its? Why?

Source: Based on: Amanda Walmac, "Getting the Word Out," *Working Woman,* September 1998, 42, 44.

Endnotes

1. Stephanie Gruner, "Death by Unnatural Causes," *Inc. 500,* 1997, 60–65.

2. Marc Ballon, "Campus Inc.," *Inc.,* March 1998, 36–52; and Tom Richman, "Creators of the New Economy," *Inc.—The State of Small Business 1997,* 44–48.

3. Brian O'Reilly, "The New Face of Small Business," *Fortune,* May 2, 1994, 82–88; Richman, "Creators of the New Economy"; and Thomas Petzinger Jr., "The Front Lines: The Rise of the Small and Other Trends to Watch This Year," *The Wall Street Journal,* January 9, 1998, B1.

4. Donald F. Kuratko and Richard M. Hodgetts, *Entrepreneurship: A Contemporary Approach,* 4th ed. (Fort Worth: The Dryden Press, 1998), 30.

5. Mark Richard Moss, "Fourth Time's the Charm," *Nation's Business,* May 1998, 85; "Please, Thank You Still Go a Long Way," *The Tennessean,* April 19, 1998, 2E.

6. O'Reilly, "The New Face of Small Business"; and Richman, "Creators of the New Economy."

7. Harriet Webster, "The 'Expert' Beginner," *Nation's Business,* January 1995, 16; and Shelly Branch, "The New Black Power: The Players," *Fortune,* August 4, 1997, 73.

8. David Whitford, "Taking It to the Street," *Fortune,* August 4, 1997, 48–51; and "Women Entrepreneurs," *Management Review,* May 1997, 6.

9. Richard M. Hodgetts and Donald F. Kuratko, *Effective Small Business Management,* 5th ed. (Fort Worth, Texas: The Dryden Press, 1995), 96–97.

10. This section is based on John Case, "The Wonderland Economy," *The State of Small Business,* 1995, 14–29; and Richard L. Daft, *Management,* 3d ed. (Fort Worth, Texas: The Dryden Press, 1992).

11. Petzinger, "The Front Lines: The Rise of the Small and Other Trends to Watch This Year"; and Alison L. Sprout, "Looking for Love in All the Web Places," *Fortune,* March 3, 1997, 186.

12. Tim McCollum, "Making the Internet Work for You," *Nation's Business,* March 1997, 6–20.

13. McCollum, "Making the Internet Work for You."

14. Jenny C. McCune, "The Entrepreneur Express," *Management Review,* March 1995, 13–19; and Marc Ballon, "Start-up Mambos to Beat of Booming Market," *Inc.,* September 1997, 23.

15. *The State of Small Business: A Report of the President* (Washington, D.C.: Government Printing Office, 1995), 13.

16. Donald F. Kuratko and Richard M. Hodgetts, *Entrepreneurship: A Contemporary Approach,* 4th ed. (Fort Worth: The Dryden Press, 1998), 7–8.

17. Peter Galuskza, "The $44 Million Mom-and-Pop," *Business Week,* June 1, 1998, 74, 76; and Jerry Useem, "The New Entrepreneurial Elite," *Inc.,* December 1997, 50–68.

18. Case, "The Wonderland Economy"; and Kuratko and Hodgetts, *Entrepreneurship: A Contemporary Perspective.*

19. Kuratko and Hodgetts, *Entrepreneurship: A Contemporary Approach,* 4th ed., 11; and "100 Ideas for New Businesses," *Venture,* November 1988, 35–74.

20. Kuratko and Hodgetts, *Entrepreneurship,* 4th ed., 14, 20–21; "Black Entrepreneurship: By the Numbers," *The Wall Street Journal,* April 3, 1992, R4; and "Women-Owned Businesses Outpace All U.S. Firms," *Self-Employed America,* July–August 1995, 7.

21. Sharon Nelton, "Leadership for the New Age," *Nation's Business,* May, 1997, 18–27.

22. John Case, "The Origins of Entrepreneurship," *Inc.,* June 1989, 51–63.

23. Ellen A. Fagenson, "Personal Value Systems of Men and Women Entrepreneurs versus Managers, *Journal of Business Venturing* 8, no. 5 (September 1993), 409–430; and McCune, "The Entrepreneur Express."

24. This discussion is based on Charles R. Kuehl and Peggy A. Lambing, *Small Business: Planning and Management,* 3d ed. (Chicago: The Dryden Press, 1994).

25. Roger Ricklefs and Udayan Gupta, "Traumas of a New Entrepreneur," *The Wall Street Journal,* May 10, 1989, B1.

26. Case, "The Origins of Entrepreneurship."

27. David C. McClelland, *The Achieving Society* (New York: Van Nostrand, 1961).

28. Robert D. Hisrich, "Entrepreneurship-Intrapreneurship," *American Psychologist,* February 1990, 209–222.

29. Michael Harvey and Rodney Evans, "Strategic Windows in the Entrepreneurial Process," *Journal of Business Venturing* 10 (1995), 331–347.

30. "Downsized Chickens Come Home to Roost," *Managing Office Technology,* January 1994, 68.

31. "Two Men and a Bottle," *Inc.: The State of Small Business 1998,* 60–63; and Kristin Dunlap Godsey, "Terminal Velocity," *Success,* October 1997, 12.

32. R. E. Coleberd, "The Business Economist at Work: The Economist as Entrepreneur," *Business Economics,* October 1994, 54–57.

33. Leslie Brokaw, "How to Start an *Inc.* 500 Company," *Inc. 500 1994,* 51–65.

34. "Scared to Be Great," *Success,* August 1998, 88.

35. Paul Reynolds, "The Truth about Start-ups," *Inc.,* February 1995, 23; O'Reilly, "The New Face of Small Business."

36. Based on Linda Elkins, "Tips for Preparing a Business Plan," *Nation's Business,* June 1996, 60R–61R; Carolyn M. Brown, "The Do's and Don'ts of Writing a Winning Business Plan," *Black Enterprise,* April 1996, 114–116; and Kuratko and Hodgetts, *Entrepreneurship,* 4th ed., 295–297.

37. The INC. FAXPOLL, *Inc.*, February 1992, 24.

38. "Venture Capitalists' Criteria," *Management Review* (November 1985), 7–8.

39. Eileen P. Gunn, "Is It Time to Bail from Big-Company Life?" *Fortune,* March 2, 1998, 217–218.

40. Julia Flynn with Heidi Dawley, Stephen Baker, and Gail Edmondson, "Startups to the Rescue," *Business Week,* March 23, 1998, 50–52.

41. Pamela Margoshes, "Basic Training," *Success,* August 1998, 44.

42. Echo Montgomery Garrett, "The Twenty-First-Century Franchise," *Inc.,* January 1995, 79–88.

43. Thomas Love, "The Perfect Franchisee," *Nation's Business,* April 1998, 59–65.

44. Roberta Maynard, "Choosing a Franchise," *Nation's Business,* October 1996, 56–63.

45. Dale Buss, "Bringing New Firms Out of Their Shell," *Nation's Business,* March 1997, 48–50.

46. Thomas S. Bateman and Carl P. Zeithaml, *Management Function and Strategy* (Homewood, Ill.: Irwin, 1990).

47. Jeffrey A. Tannenbaum, "Small Firms, Big Hurdles," *The Wall Street Journal,* September 26, 1995, R21; and Gregory Patterson, "An American in . . . Siberia?" *Fortune,* August 4, 1997, 63.

48. Amy Barrett, "It's a Small (Business) World," *Business Week,* April 17, 1995, 96–101.

49. Tannenbaum, "Small Firms, Big Hurdles."

50. "Want to Go Global? Here's Where to Find Help," *Business Week,* April 17, 1995, 101.

51. Roberta Maynard, "A Simplified Route to Markets Abroad," *Nation's Business,* November 1997, 46–48.

52. Carrie Dolan, "Entrepreneurs Often Fail as Managers," *The Wall Street Journal,* May 15, 1989, B1.

53. "Plan of Attack," *Inc.,* January 1996, 41–44.

54. Barbara Bobo, "Building a Business Using Contractors," *Nation's Business,* June 1995, 6.

55. Michael Barrier, "The Changing Face of Leadership," *Nation's Business,* January 1995, 41–42.

56. Udayan Gupta and Jeffrey A. Tannenbaum, "Labor Shortages Force Changes at Small Firms," *The Wall Street Journal,* May 22, 1989, B1, B2; "Harnessing Employee Productivity," *Small Business Report,* November 1987, 46–49; and Molly Klimas, "How to Recruit a Smart Team," *Nation's Business,* May 1995, 26–27.

57. Tim McCollum, "More Than Just Number Crunchers," *Nation's Business,* April 1998, 46–48.

58. Dale D. Buss, "Coping with Faster Change," *Nation's Business,* March 1995, 27–29.

59. Shu shu Costa, "100 Years and Counting," *American Management Association,* December 1994, 32–34.

60. Minda Zetlin, "Off the Beaten Path," *American Management Association,* December 1994, 28–31.

61. Kuratko and Hodgetts, *Entrepreneurship,* 4th ed., 61.

62. Gifford Pinchot III, *Intrapreneuring* (New York: Harper & Row, 1985).

63. James S. Hirsch, "Kodak Effort at 'Intrapreneurship' Fails," *The Wall Street Journal,* August 17, 1990, B1.

Sweet Talk: Hard Candy's Founder Is Just Like Her Customers

If you're going to start a company, it really helps if you are your own best customer. That way, you'll know the demographics of your market and you'll have a jump on the competition. Chances are, your corporate culture will reflect your own personality and beliefs. You may even be a symbolic leader—providing a vision and helping it become reality. All of this has been true for Dineh Mohajer, the twenty-something entrepreneur who started her own nail polish company when she couldn't find exactly the pale blue shade of polish that she wanted. Since then, Hard Candy has sweetened Mohajer's bank account, now earning $25 million a year in sales and expanding rapidly.

Hard Candy's success isn't sugar-coated; it has come about for a number of solid reasons. First, its founder, Dineh Mohajer, understands the company's external environment and uses it to her advantage. And she has her well-polished nails into the demographics of her market. Her target customers are between the ages of 17 and 25, like to shop in upscale department stores such as Bloomingdale's and Neiman Marcus, and are willing and able to pay $12 for a bottle of their favorite nail polish in hip colors like Trailer Trash (metallic silver) and Sushi (aqua). If those two colors don't appeal to you, you can always try Tantrum, Jailbait, or the more subdued Mint or Sky. How does Mohajer know her customers so well? "I function like an average human being of my age," she explains. "I go to clubs, movies, and watch MTV." Mohajer knows not only whom to sell the polish to but also where to sell it. "I was approached by many stores that were considered low-end, which didn't qualify." By selling her products in trendy shopping areas around Beverly Hills and Los Angeles, Mohajer attracts the type of customers she wants, including celebrities such as Madonna, Winona Ryder, and Alicia Silverstone.

Mohajer is keenly aware of her competitive environment—and the competition is certainly aware of her. Consumers can find $1-per-bottle knockoffs of Hard Candy polishes in drugstores everywhere. "We've been knocked off left and right" by high-end and low-end cosmetic companies, says Mohajer. "It really says something when you're knocked off by Revlon." Being tuned in to the competitive environment is also part of understanding customers. "There's a benefit to being part of your market," explains Mohajer. "I know what I like. Revlon has to do market analysis."

Although still entrepreneurial in spirit, Mohajer is now head of a multimillion-dollar company that has forty employees producing sixty shades of nail polish along with a line of lipsticks, eye color, and even a line of polishes for men called Candy Man (Dennis Rodman likes these). Being head of a rapidly growing company like this means taking on the role of symbolic leader and developing a strong corporate culture, even though it may not seem to be a typical business corporate culture. "It is important to me that the environment that I create for myself and for the people that I employ is one that's creative and open and exciting and very, very much so, like, team spirited," says Mohajer. "You're only as good as your team is. You're only as good as the people that you've empowered to do it for you. . . ." The atmosphere at Hard Candy is, as one employee puts it, "free flowing." Mohajer might conduct an interview with a journalist while sitting cross-legged on the office floor, and employees might be found singing in their offices. Mohajer often asks employees for their opinions on product colors, names, and so forth. "Dineh will ask everybody in the office for their opinions," says one staffer. "It's kind of like a collaborative brainstorm, and everybody gets involved, and I think everybody's input is valuable . . . not only with the creativity but also in terms of management and improving our operations and our systems." Hard Candy's management team is not entirely made up of people Mohajer's age, though. She has peppered it with a few seasoned marketing executives. Both Mohajer and her managers understand that the company and its culture are still constantly changing and growing; in fact, they embrace change as part of creativity. All of these factors, Mohajer believes, are what make Hard Candy such a sweet success.

Questions

1. Dineh Mohajer believes that she has an advantage over her competitors because she is "part of the market." Could this advantage ever turn into a disadvantage? Are there aspects of the organizational environment that she might not be tuned in to?

2. Do you think that Dineh Mohajer is an effective symbolic leader? Why or why not? Describe some specific actions she might take to reinforce her cultural vision for Hard Candy.

3. List some dimensions of Hard Candy's external environment that could contribute to uncertainty and threaten long-term success of the company. Consider sociocultural, economic, and technological dimensions especially in your analysis. What ways could Hard Candy help reduce the uncertainty?

4. Do you think you would be an effective manager at Hard Candy? Why or why not?

SOURCES: Jeffrey Zaslow, "Straight Talk: Dineh Mohajer," *Chicago Sun-Times*, June 26–28, 1998, accessed at www.usaweekend.com; "A Polished Kind of Girl," *Maxi* online magazine accessed March 18, 1999, at www.maximag.com; Ted Rall, "Marketing Madness," *Link, the College Magazine*, September 1997, accessed at www.linkmag.com; "The Best Entrepreneurs: Dineh Mohajer," *Business Week*, February 1998; Jeanne Whalen, "Dineh Mohajer" *Advertising Age's Marketing 100 (1997)*, accessed March 18, 1999 at www.adage.com.

Fossil's Global Reach Makes It Far from Extinct

When Fossil watches first hit jewelry cases in American department stores in the mid-1980s, their appeal was distinctly American. Designed to bring back nostalgic memories of the 1950s, the watches became a fashion accessory instead of a purely functional item. Within a few years, Fossil founders Tom and Kosta Kartsotis had branched into other accessories, including leather goods and sunglasses. Then they decided to go international. Gary Bolinger, senior vice president of international sales and marketing recalls, "It was probably ten years ago Fossil became an international company. We made our first sell, I believe it was into Germany at the time. It was really just the last four to five years that we've concentrated on becoming a global company. And that's where you really take time to become a partner with a given, whether it be a distributor, a sales rep company, our own wholly-owned subsidiaries. You're really involved in the community and the activities of a country, and you're part of the culture."

Clearly, Fossil has quickly come a long way from its initial domestic offerings toward becoming a truly global company, including entering into alliances with foreign organizations. Recently, the company announced a multiyear licensing agreement with Safilo USA, Inc., and Safint B.V. Safilo is one of the world's largest eyewear manufacturers and distributors, and it will design, manufacture, and sell Fossil brand optical frames and sunglasses in Italy. "Safilo provides us the opportunity to extend the Fossil brand into this market and to be represented by one of the largest companies in the eyewear business," says Fossil's Mark Quick.

Going international, then global, can be a complicated process for company managers. Fossil had to have market entry strategies for numerous markets, as well as strategies for dealing with competition. Gary Bollinger explains, "It starts with product. You have to have the right product. Secondly you have to have a marketing package that puts together your story. . . . That has to be uniform and cohesive worldwide. Third, and probably most important, is that [a] business system [must be] in place, the infrastructure, to deliver the product and the marketing to the proper channels and get it where you need it at the right time, the right place." Bolinger also notes the importance of finding the right partners to work with in each country, whether it is for manufacturing, distribution, marketing, or any other business function.

Part of Fossil's strategy for globalization is to acquire companies in the countries where it does business. "We own our own company in Japan," notes Richard Gundy, executive vice president of Fossil. "We own our own company in Italy. We own our own company in Germany, where we can get the management in there that has our vision, shares the passion for the brand, and can commit to the service that our customers demand in those markets." In addition, despite the political and legal uncertainty, Fossil's strongest manufacturing and distribution partners are located in Hong Kong. Gary Bolinger explains that the reason for this is that Hong Kong has both the necessary infrastructure and the cultural attitude that "they can get anything done." After Britain returned Hong Kong to China, China agreed to leave Hong Kong's political system untouched for the next fifty years. Thus far, according to Bolinger, there have been few changes in the regulation of importing and exporting; and those changes have, in fact, been improvements.

The condition of the economic environment is, of course, vital to the success of a globalization effort. In Hong Kong, rents have decreased and salary increases have slowed, which benefits Fossil. In general, Bolinger says, "Currencies can devalue 30 percent in a day and bounce back 50 percent the next day. There's a constant change that goes on that you just have to monitor. . . . We talk with each of our distributors, if not daily, at least weekly with every country we're in around the world."

Fossil lies somewhere between a multinational and a global organization, having achieved this status in a relatively short period of time. Fossil sells over 500 watch styles, leather goods and sunglasses in more than 70 countries worldwide, and that number continues to increase. When asked what the company's ultimate goal is, Gary Bolinger's answer is direct. "We want world domination," he says. His company has no intention of becoming a relic of the past.

Questions

1. What characteristics do you think a Fossil manager would need to be successful in an international business environment?
2. Gary Bolinger notes the importance of infrastructure in doing business in Hong Kong. Name some specific features of infrastructure that you think would be important to Fossil's activities in Hong Kong, and explain why.
3. How do you think the European Union might affect Fossil's efforts in Germany and other European countries?
4. What are the advantages to Fossil of having a licensing agreement with Safilo in Italy?
5. Based on what you know about Fossil's products, consider what types of cultural characteristics Fossil managers might want to consider as they enter new markets around the world, then list questions that managers might ask.

SOURCES: "Fossil Profile," Trade Media Ltd., accessed March 18, 1999, at www.asiansources.com; "The Fossil Story," and Fossil press release, "Fossil & Safilo Enter Licensing Agreement for Optical Frames," accessed at www.fossil.com, March 17, 1999.

Video Case

La Madeleine's Motto: Let Them Eat Bread

"We understand the more we give, the more we receive. That's something we practice every day." Patrick Esquerré might sound like a kindergarten teacher or a preacher. But he's not. He's a successful entrepreneur who understands the importance of corporate responsibility.

Nearly twenty years ago, Esquerré, who spoke little English, opened up a charming little pastry shop on Mockingbird Lane, where customers (whom he calls his "guests") could purchase fabulous French breads and pastries. Soon, La Madeleine, as it was called, became a gathering spot where neighbors could linger over freshly brewed coffee and daily baked treats. Within a few years, Esquerré had opened shops in Fort Worth, Austin, Houston, San Antonio, Atlanta, Chicago, Washington, DC, New Orleans, and Phoenix. Now, La Madeleine is just as well known for its giving back, or "*Merci* marketing" as Esquerré calls it, as it is for its baked delicacies. "*Merci* marketing is something very natural to La Madeleine," explains Esquerré. "It is a way to say thank you even prior to receiving something."

How does Esquerré's company accomplish this? Esquerré practices leadership by example. More than a decade ago, he began to donate food to the local food bank. Now La Madeleine donates both food and money on a regular basis. "We help them by supplying them with fresh food. Not leftover food, but fresh food that is good for them," notes Esquerré. Fresh food includes bread, soup, quiche, and, of course, pastries. La Madeleine's annual contributions to community food banks total nearly $250,000. According to Robert Sank, director of the Dallas Food Bank, "The food bank serves 199 different agencies that operate food pantries, shelters, soup kitchens, programs like that. The on-site feeding programs would serve close to 500,000 meals a month. And without people like Patrick and La Madeleine, we wouldn't be able to supply the food they need to serve those people." In another demonstration of leadership by example, every Saturday morning Esquerré himself takes breakfast to the homeless who gather near Dallas City Hall.

Activities like supporting the food bank illustrate the discretionary responsibility that Esquerré feels his organization should take on. In addition, La Madeleine is a strong fund raiser for public broadcasting. Robert Sank explains, "When public radio conducts their fund raising campaigns, Patrick offers to donate $1 worth of food to the food bank for every $2 donated to public radio." The pitch works. "We help PBS—radio and TV—everywhere we go to raise money for their pledge drive," says Esquerré. And I tell you, there's two weeks per year where every single day, or every single morning, where I'm on PBS just to help them raise money, and it does very, very well."

For an entire organization to be socially responsible, it is important for top leaders like Esquerré to foster the appropriate organizational values among managers and other employees. Esquerré does just that. Managers like Bill Buchanan, a regional manager for La Madeleine, note that Esquerré is key to the success of socially responsible activity within the organization. "Patrick Esquerré is unlike any man that I've ever met in my life. The environment that he provided for everyone to be successful and to care for others to give back to the community in particular has made an impact on my own management style, as well as how I conduct my life. With Patrick, the feeling that you get in your heart is tremendous when you have the freedom to take the food that you bake in your bakery and take it out and feed the homeless. To give it to the children that are sleeping on the sidewalks." Jeremy Hartley, president of La Madeleine, builds on Buchanan's opinion about how socially responsible values are an integral part of the organization's culture. "Our sense of social responsibility, charitable work, all those things—I think it's driven a lot by being very guest oriented, first and foremost." A company that exists to serve its customers can just as easily extend that service to the surrounding community and those who are in need.

All of that service doesn't hurt the bottom line. In fact, it seems to enhance the company's success. Bill Buchanan says, "The most valuable thing for the management that work with me is the fact that they have the special heart and ability to communicate with other people and to build sales."

Questions

1. Can you think of other ways that La Madeleine could practice "*Merci* marketing?" Describe them.
2. How does Patrick Esquerré's vision for La Madeleine illustrate the way he views stakeholders—customers, employees, and the local communities?
3. Describe a firm in your own community that is generally considered to be socially responsible. What types of socially responsible activities does it engage in? Do you think this behavior has increased the organization's success in your community? Why or why not?
4. Could social responsibility be taken too far? Explain why you do or don't think so.
5. Would you like to be a manager in the La Madeleine organization? Why or why not?

SOURCE: La Madeleine French Bakery and Café, at Web site www. lamadeleine.com.

Two Women Boxing: Two Artists-Turned-Entrepreneurs

Linda Finnell and Julie Cohn aren't experts in martial arts; they are experts in design arts who became, almost by accident, entrepreneurs. In 1983, artist Linda Finnell was commissioned by a nonprofit photography gallery to make boxes to be used as artists' portfolios. She asked her best friend and fellow artist, Julie Cohn, to help her fill the order. The two handmade each box in Finnell's living room, then went on to make and sell more boxes, cards, and small books. Julie Cohn recalls sitting on the floor among stacked boxes and joking, "You know, Linda, if we ever have a business, we should call it Two Women Boxing." Thus, Two Women Boxing was born—a new business idea, but without a formal business plan or venture capital (unless you count $400 in start-up cash).

Both Finnell and Cohn had the energy and self-confidence that it takes for entrepreneurs to get their businesses off the ground. Tolerance for ambiguity was also necessary, particularly as their own self-images had to change somewhat as the business took shape. "The transition from artist to businessperson, I think, is an ongoing transformation," observes Julie Cohn. "There's never been a point in 13 years where I've thought, 'OK, now I'm a businessperson.'" In addition, there was no way of knowing what direction the business would take, or how things would work out.

During the first few years, the two entrepreneurs concentrated on selling their products as well as hiring sales representatives who could handle larger geographic regions and go to the trade shows where the company's new products were displayed. "I think a big turning point was when we took our rep on; in terms of our wholesale manufacturing, that was a point in which we had a showroom in the Dallas Trade Center," recalls Cohn. "Probably the next turning point after that was when we took a booth at the New York Stationery Show, and that really, for the first time, put us in sort of a national arena and [we] started taking orders—could we actually accommodate those orders?" In addition, Cohn and Finnell had begun to hire employees to help with production, which meant shaping, gluing, and sewing each item by hand, and eventually a part-time office manager. Two Women Boxing was now moving from the existence stage of growth to the survival stage.

By the early 1990s, the company was grossing nearly half a million dollars each year. Now there was a production manager, but because items were (and still are) made by hand, by about a dozen employees, there was a limit to how much the company could grow. That is still the case. "We are still so primitive in our technique and what we're doing that we again have to look at mechanizing to a certain extent or mechanizing to a certain extent even what we do, because we just can't—and you can't—compete effi-

ciently and effectively with what's being done overseas if you continue to manufacture by hand, especially in the United States," explains Cohn. So Cohn and Finnell have developed what Finnell calls "a real global awareness that is essential to the business. . . . It's having to be aware of everything else that's going on from the flow of retail sales to the price of products that we import, to how we get things in from the Orient in between monsoon seasons. . . ."

Another strategy for growth is the licensing of designs to other companies, including fine china and accessories manufacturer Fitz and Floyd, and specialty publisher Chronicle Books. "It was very exciting to have the opportunities come to us to do the china that we did with Fitz and Floyd, for instance," says Finnell. "Where our designs could be taken completely out of the realm that we had for making things. The work with Chronicle Books has been wonderful in a different way, in that what it's done is really expanded our audience." Of course, not every such venture is without glitches. Cohn explains, "There's been some frustration with the outcome of the product. With Fitz and Floyd there were more compromises to be made because of pricing. And I think that is something that we've actually confronted in all of our licensing situations, is the price of the product. . . . We've overdesigned for the market. We've overdesigned for the price point."

But there have been artistic triumphs that hopefully outshine other problems. "I think probably the biggest high was when the Japanese department store Takashimaya opened in New York, and we were in Takashimaya. That, to me, was the Museum of Modern Art of retailing," says Cohn with pride. "It's one of the most exquisite stores I've ever been in my life, and to have the small selection of product that they do in that store, and to have us be a part of that, it was the equivalent of finally getting in a really good gallery." Proof positive, perhaps, that art and business *do* mix successfully.

Questions

1. What stage of growth do you think Two Women Boxing is at now? What steps might the company take to reach the next stage?
2. Two Women Boxing managed to start up without a formal business plan. But what kind of planning might now help the company succeed as it enters the new millennium?
3. In what ways might Finnell and Cohn promote intrapreneurship in their small company?

Continuing Case

Part Two: From Macintosh to Microsoft

When they founded Apple Computer, Steve Jobs and Steve Wozniak were the kind of entrepreneurs everyone loves to read about. Both college dropouts in their twenties, they developed and built their first product in a family garage in Cupertino, California. When the Apple II took off, so did the personal computing industry. Not only had these two young entrepreneurs changed an industry, but some would argue that they changed history.

Both Jobs and Wozniak had the entrepreneurial characteristics that were crucial to their success. They had the energy and self-confidence necessary to break new ground. By definition, they had to be tolerant of ambiguity in an industry that did not yet exist in the form we know it now. Both had a strong internal locus of control, believing that they could influence the outcomes of their efforts. Finally, they were eager to "seize the moment," recognizing that, if they didn't develop a new type of computer, someone else would. But as the company progressed through its early stages of growth, Jobs and Wozniak diverged in their entrepreneurial styles. Whereas Jobs became market driven, Wozniak backed off, more interested in the technical design of the computers the company built. Eventually, Wozniak left Apple, and he now teaches computer science in the Los Gatos, California, school system. "I'm a private evangelist for the school district in Los Gatos, where I live," said Wozniak in a Web site interview. "I had two goals in life, to be an engineer and to teach fifth grade. For several years I've been teaching computers to not only teachers but also fifth through eighth graders."

Back at Apple, Jobs was about to launch the company's most revolutionary product: the Macintosh. The development of the Macintosh during the early 1980s was a direct response to Apple's competitive and technological environment. IBM had fought back vigorously after Apple's release of its first several computers, coming out with its own PC and surpassing Apple in sales only two years after doing so. In addition, engineers at the Xerox Palo Alto Research Center (known as PARC) were working on a product called Alto, which had a graphical user interface—with elements such as windows, menus, and icons. (Ironically, Xerox never brought the Alto to market because Xerox executives believed that it was too new and probably not usable. But Jobs and his team were allowed to visit PARC and were impressed by what they saw.) Jobs knew that his organization had to adapt quickly to this opportunity in an uncertain environment, so he made two major moves: he hired as president of Apple John Sculley, who was an experienced businessman from Pepsi Cola, and he began development of the new Macintosh product. During this time, to revitalize what was once a pioneering corporate culture, Jobs made efforts to create an environment in which the intelligent, talented, quirky, creative hardware and software designers could thrive. Jobs described his Macintosh team as "well grounded in the philosophical traditions of the last 100 years and the sociological traditions of the '60s." But Jobs drove the team through long hours against impossible deadlines. A reporter who interviewed the team wrote, "The machine's development was, in turn, traumatic, joyful, grueling, lunatic, rewarding, and ultimately the major event in the lives of almost everyone involved." Jobs spoke of the team in public and private as brilliant and committed gladiators. But while he thought we was fostering a spirited, revolutionary culture, in fact workers were exhausted and burned out.

In 1984, the Macintosh was introduced to the world in a dramatic 60-second commercial spot during the Super Bowl. At first, the computer didn't sell well because potential customers perceived it as an expensive toy. But once such products as laser printers and the Pagemaker desktop paging program hit the market, people began to understand how the Macintosh could improve many aspects of the jobs they did. So the Macintosh finally took off about a year after its initial launch. As Macintosh sales increased, so did the size of Apple Computer. Since the computer put more computing power into individual employees' hands, it had mass appeal. The industry was a natural for "boundaryless" corporations, and Apple began to expand around the world until it had an operating territory that included Canada, western and eastern Europe, Asia, South America, Central America, the Caribbean, Scandinavia, South Africa, and the British Isles. Interestingly enough, however, Apple is not yet a truly global organization. Its headquarters are still located in Cupertino, California, and although it has customers, partners, and developers around the world, Apple remains a multinational corporation.

As difficult and driven a manager as Jobs often was, he didn't forget his company's social responsibility. During his tenure, he established several educational projects including Kids Can't Wait, the Apple Education Foundation, and the Apple University Consortium. Currently, the Apple Learning Community has ongoing educational projects from school to university levels.

With all the initiatives Jobs undertook to make Apple a formidable force in the computer industry, his position would seem secure in the company. But eventually, the intense personality of this original entrepreneur became his downfall. In a power struggle with Apple president John Sculley, Steve Jobs was voted out of the company by the board of directors in 1985.

A heated competitive environment can also produce some unsavory results, including companies accusing each other of unethical behaviors such as stealing or hoarding technology. In 1985, John Sculley became immersed in combat with Microsoft's Bill Gates over the introduction of Windows 1.0, whose graphical operating system had technological similarities to Apple's Macintosh operating system. Sculley finally got Gates to agree that Microsoft wouldn't use Mac technology in Windows 1.0, but the signed statement did not include future versions of the Windows interface. Thus, the stage was set for future lawsuits between Apple and Microsoft, which would continue well into the 1990s. More than a decade after the initial tussle, Apple and Microsoft were back in court, with Microsoft being accused of trying to sabotage Apple's multimedia software, Quicktime.

Questions

1. Based on what you've read so far, how do you think Steve Jobs viewed Apple stakeholders?

2. Jobs referred to the Mac team as gladiators. How did this image relate to the Apple corporate culture?
3. What steps might Apple take to become a global corporation?
4. In what ways do you think the entrepreneurs Steve Jobs and Steve Wozniak have been important to the American economy?

Sources: Ryan J. Fass, "Happy Birthday Macintosh," miningco.com, January 25, 1999; Brent Schlender and Michael H. Martin, "Paradise Lost," *Fortune,* February 19, 1996, accessed online at www.pathfinder.com; "Apple in Higher Education," "History," "Steve Paul Jobs," and "Area List," accessed at the Apple Web site, www.apple.com. iMac photo: Courtesy of Apple Computer, Inc.

Part Three

Planning

Planning is a crucial skill in successful racing. In a marathon such as the Whitbread, it is especially critical. From special hull and sail designs, delivery of equipment and supplies to ports, to calculation of onboard food and clothing for the crew, every detail of every leg of the race is plotted, planned, and reexamined to pare costs and boat weight to a minimum. Why? Less weight means more speed. Costs to enter a boat in the Whitbread average around $10 million, with the boat alone taking $2 million of that amount. An average of $10,000 a week is needed to keep the boat, crew, and shore staff supplied and ready.

Race strategy is determined before the race and reviewed before each leg. But once the boat starts, changing weather can shift winds quickly, stranding boats in dead calm or whipping them past their competitors. The navigator's skill in reading satellite weather forecasts and general ocean currents is refined by navigation software to plot the best course—at least for that moment. Skippers use that information to implement their strategy and gain an advantage.

Quick decision making based on experience is also key. Knowledge of the boat's strengths in different conditions enters the equation for success. Which of the seventeen sails on board can give the maximum benefit, what course to set to find the best wind and still minimize the miles to travel, when to tack to pick up a new weather system, how close to come to land to ride on favorable currents—all of these factors must be decided on the spot from general plans made far ahead. Crews that make the best judgments leave the pack behind.

Part Three discusses goal setting and planning, strategy formulation and implementation, and the importance of good managerial decision making.

Chapter 7

LEARNING OBJECTIVES

After studying this chapter, you should be able to

- **Define goals and plans and explain the relationship between them.**

- **Explain the concept of organizational mission and how it influences goal setting and planning.**

- **Describe the types of goals an organization should have and why they resemble a hierarchy.**

- **Define the characteristics of effective goals.**

- **Describe the four essential steps in the MBO process.**

- **Explain the difference between single-use plans and standing plans.**

- **Describe how responsibility can be allocated to accomplish planning and goal setting.**

- **Explain the new planning paradigm and its use in learning organizations.**

Organizational Planning and Goal Setting

MANAGEMENT PROBLEM

Etec Systems, Inc., practically owns the market for pattern generation equipment—expensive machines that use lasers and electron beams to print intricate patterns onto silicon wafers. However, when Stephen Cooper took over as Etec's new president, the company was generating red ink at the rate of $1 million a month. What's worse, politicians and the press were pointing to Etec as a symbol of the decline of U.S. industry. Everyone thought Cooper was crazy when he announced a goal to generate $500 million in revenues by the year 2000. Four years later, Etec was being hailed as one of the most remarkable comebacks in Silicon Valley. Revenues increased by 75 percent and keep going up, while profits also are steadily growing. High-tech industries change so rapidly that many people think it's impossible to plan for the future. At Etec, managers spend most of their time dealing with short-term crises. Yet Cooper turned Etec around by getting back to the basics of planning: "When a company has a clear mission, and people know how their individual mission fits into the big picture, everyone paddles in the same direction," he says. The company is well on its way to reaching Cooper's audacious goal, thanks to a specific, step-by-step plan that helps employees maintain clarity in the face of rapid change. To be successful, Cooper says, people need to understand two fundamental issues: "What's expected of me and how do I accomplish it?"[1]

How did Stephen Cooper get everyone at Etec moving in the same direction? If you were in Cooper's position, how would you help employees who spend most of their time reacting to daily crises keep their eye on the future?

Stephen Cooper knows that one of the primary responsibilities of a leader is to decide where he or she wants the company to be in the future and how to get it there.

In some organizations, typically small ones, planning is informal. In others, managers follow a well-defined planning framework. The company establishes a basic mission and develops formal goals and strategic plans for carrying it out. Shell, IBM, Royal LaPaige, Mazda, and United Way undertake a strategic planning exercise each year—reviewing their missions, goals, and plans to meet environmental changes or the expectations of important stakeholders such as the community, owners, or stockholders.

Of the four management functions—planning, organizing, leading, and controlling—described in Chapter 1, planning is considered the most fundamental. Everything else stems from planning. Yet planning also is the most controversial management function. Planning cannot read an uncertain future. Planning cannot tame a turbulent environment. A statement by General Colin Powell offers a warning for managers: "No battle plan survives contact with the enemy." Consider the following comment by a noted authority on planning:

> Most corporate planning is like a ritual rain dance; it has no effect on the weather that follows, but it makes those who engage in it feel that they are in control. Most discussions of the role of models in planning are directed at improving the dancing, not the weather.[2]

In this chapter, we are going to explore the process of planning and whether it can help bring needed rain.

Special attention is given to goals and goal setting, for that is where planning starts. Then the types of plans organizations can use to achieve those goals are discussed. Finally, we will discuss new approaches to planning that emphasize the involvement of all employees in strategic thinking and execution. Chapter 8 will look at strategic planning in depth and examine a number of strategic options managers can use in a competitive environment. In Chapter 9, we look at management decision making. Proper decision-making techniques are crucial to selecting the organization's goals, plans, and strategic options.

Overview of Goals and Plans

goal
A desired future state that the organization attempts to realize.

plan
A blueprint specifying the resource allocations, schedules, and other actions necessary for attaining goals.

planning
The act of determining the organization's goals and the means for achieving them.

Goals and plans have become general concepts in our society. A **goal** is a desired future state that the organization attempts to realize.[3] Goals are important because organizations exist for a purpose and goals define and state that purpose. A **plan** is a blueprint for goal achievement and specifies the necessary resource allocations, schedules, tasks, and other actions. Goals specify future ends; plans specify today's means. The word **planning** usually incorporates both ideas; it means determining the organization's goals and defining the means for achieving them. Consider Germany's Volkswagen, where chief executive Ferdinand Piëch has set a goal to overtake Toyota Motor Company as the world's Number 3 carmaker, with across-the-board brand recognition. To achieve this outcome, he wants to accomplish the following: purchase the Swedish truckmaker Scania, which would add heavy trucks to the product line; buy Britain's Rolls Royce, to take VW into ultra-luxury cars; and design a V8-powered Volkswagen, to compete directly with Mercedes-Benz. To transform British Airways "from a British airline with a

Exhibit **7.1**

Levels of Goals/Plans and Their Importance

global reach to an airline of the world," CEO Bob Ayling is taking a four-pronged approach: Develop a marketing plan with universal appeal; help employees understand the global vision; benchmark off the mistakes others have made; and select the best partners for joint ventures overseas.[4]

Exhibit 7.1 illustrates the levels of goals and plans in an organization. The planning process starts with a formal mission that defines the basic purpose of the organization, especially for external audiences. The mission is the basis for the strategic (company) level of goals and plans, which in turn shapes the tactical (divisional) level and the operational (departmental) level.[5] Planning at each level supports the other levels.

Goals, Plans, and Performance

The complexity of today's environment and uncertainty about the future overwhelm many managers and lead them to focus on operational issues and short-term results rather than long-term goals and plans. However, planning generally positively affects a company's performance.[6] In addition to improving financial and operational performance, developing explicit goals and plans at each level illustrated in Exhibit 7.1 is important because of the external and internal messages they send. These messages go to both external and internal audiences and provide important benefits for the organization.[7]

Legitimacy. An organization's mission describes what the organization stands for and its reason for existence. It symbolizes legitimacy to external audiences such as investors, customers, and suppliers. The mission helps them and the local community look on the company in a favorable light and, hence, accept its existence. A strong mission also has an impact on employees, enabling them to become committed to the organization because they

MISSION STATEMENT
To be widely recognized for
leadership and accomplishment
as a food processing and
marketing cooperative, by
using all of our member's
and employees' talents.

"To be widely recognized for leadership and accomplishment as a food processing and marketing cooperative, by using all of our members' and employees' talents," is the mission statement *of Pro-Fac Cooperative, an agricultural marketing cooperative, which consists of over 600 members. The cooperative processes fruits, vegetables, and popcorn through its wholly-owned subsidiary, Agrilink Foods, in facilities across the United States. This mission statement, which promotes the talents of employees, opens the annual report and seeks* legitimacy *with external audiences through recognition of Pro-Fac's leadership and accomplishments in food processing.*

can identify with its overall purpose and reason for existence. In *Fortune* magazine's study of the "100 Best Companies to Work for in America," a sense of purpose that employees could believe in and relate to was one of the top three traits cited by employees. For example, at Medtronic, a medical-products company, employees are inspired by the mission of "restoring patients to full life."[8]

Source of Motivation and Commitment.   Goals and plans facilitate employees' identification with the organization and help motivate them by reducing uncertainty and clarifying what they should accomplish. Lack of a clear goal can damage employee motivation and commitment. When Main Street Muffins lost sight of its goal and began branching into new lines of business, morale sank so low that bakers were calling in sick at 3 A.M. or walking off the job with no notice. The company took a nosedive toward bankruptcy before the owners developed a statement to remind everyone that the primary goal of Main Street Muffins was "to profitably improve an organization that overwhelms the food industry with its devotion to high-quality products and services." With the new goal statement as a guide, employee commitment and motivation gradually improved, and the company became profitable again within three months.[9] Whereas a goal provides the "why" of an organization or subunit's existence, a plan tells the "how." A plan lets employees know what actions to undertake to achieve the goal.

Guides to Action.   Goals and plans provide a sense of direction. They focus attention on specific targets and direct employee efforts toward important outcomes. Hartford Technology Services Co., for example, set goals to establish a customer profile database, survey customer satisfaction, and secure service agreements with ten new customers.[10]

Rationale for Decisions.   Through goal setting and planning, managers learn what the organization is trying to accomplish. They can make decisions to ensure that internal policies, roles, performance, structure, products, and expenditures will be made in accordance with desired outcomes. Decisions throughout the organization will be in alignment with the plan.

Standard of Performance.   Because goals define desired outcomes for the organization, they also serve as performance criteria. They provide a standard of assessment. If an organization wishes to grow by 15 percent, and actual growth is 17 percent, managers will have exceeded their prescribed standard. Ed Woolard defined a goal at Du Pont of nurturing high-potential businesses while strengthening old-line businesses to produce an average return on equity of 16 percent. However, formerly fast-growing electronics businesses fell flat, and return on equity plunged to 8.3 percent. Du Pont did not meet its standard of performance for this goal.[11]

The overall planning process prevents managers from thinking merely in terms of day-to-day activities. When organizations drift away from goals and plans, they typically get into trouble. This occurred at Amex Life Assurance, an American Express subsidiary based in San Rafael, California. A new president implemented a strong planning system that illustrates the power of planning to improve organizational performance.

Sarah Nolan knew that the chairman of American Express was a self-professed maniac on quality. But when Nolan arrived as the new president of Amex Life Assurance, she found a paperwork assembly line that served customers at a snail's pace. A simple change of address took two days; sending out a new insurance policy took at least ten. Nolan's primary goal was to get everyone at Amex working together while keeping the focus on the customer. She sent five managers representing different specialties to an empty office park and told them to imagine they were setting up an entirely new business. Nolan gave the group only three rules to follow in their task of planning a new operation:

1. Put the customer first.

2. Don't copy anything we do here.

3. Be ready to process applications yourselves in six months.

When the planning group returned, ten layers of personnel had been collapsed into three, each of which would deal directly with the public. Fewer employees were needed, so more than one-third were transferred to other divisions. Expenses were cut in half and profitability increased sixfold. Nolan used planning to help managers break out of their focus on day-to-day activities and reorient the company toward its strategic goal of customer satisfaction.[12]

AMEX LIFE ASSURANCE

Goals in Organizations

Setting goals starts with top managers. The overall planning process begins with a mission statement and strategic goals for the organization as a whole.

Organizational Mission

At the top of the goal hierarchy is the **mission**—the organization's reason for existence. The mission describes the organization's values, aspirations, and reason for being. A well-defined mission is the basis for development of all subsequent goals and plans. Without a clear mission, goals and plans may be developed haphazardly and not take the organization in the direction it needs to go. Recall that Main Street Muffins found itself being pulled in so many directions it was coming apart until managers began examining whether goals were consistent with the company's mission. By one estimate, more than half of all companies in the United States now have a formal statement of some kind.

The formal **mission statement** is a broadly stated definition of basic business scope and operations that distinguishes the organization from others of a similar type.[13] The content of a mission statement often focuses on the market and customers and identifies desired fields of endeavor. Some mission statements describe company characteristics such as corporate values, product quality, location of facilities, and attitude toward employees. Mission statements often reveal the company's philosophy as well as purpose. One example is the mission statement for Fetzer Vineyards, presented in Exhibit 7.2. Fetzer devised its three-sentence mission statement to express its commitment to ethical considerations as well as good business practices. Fetzer believes its social and environmental commitment contributes directly to the bottom line. For one thing, the statement fosters a positive image for Fetzer in the community. In addition, according to Andy Beckstoffer, one of Fetzer's outside

mission
The organization's reason for existence.

mission statement
A broadly stated definition of the organization's basic business scope and operations that distinguishes it from similar types of organizations.

Exhibit 7.2

Mission Statement for Fetzer Vineyards

Mission Statement for Fetzer Vineyards

We are an environmentally and socially conscious grower, producer, and marketer of wines of the highest quality and value.

Working in harmony and with respect for the human spirit, we are committed to sharing information about the enjoyment of food and wine in a lifestyle of moderation and responsibility.

We are dedicated to the continuous growth and development of our people and business.

Source: From Miriam Schulman "Winery with a Mission," *Issues In Ethics*, Spring 1996, 14–15.

growers, "It's good business to preserve your lands; it's good business to produce a healthy product." Providing employees with opportunities to develop their capabilities strengthens the organization as well. This simple statement makes clear to both employees and customers what Fetzer stands for.[14]

Such short, straightforward mission statements describe basic business activities and purposes as well as the values that guide the company. Another example of this type of mission statement is that of Lunar Productions, a Memphis, Tennessee, corporate-video producer with $800,000 in annual sales. Lunar's president, Geordy Wells, is a spiritual man who wanted to reflect Lunar's commitment to honest, ethical business practices:

Honor God in all we do.

Provide excellent and affordable corporate-video, audio/visual, and broadcast production services to our valued clients.

Communicate with our clients and fellow employees as effectively as we communicate with our audiences.

Make a fair profit.[15]

Because of mission statements such as those of Fetzer Vineyards and Lunar Productions, employees as well as customers, suppliers, and stockholders know the company's stated purpose and values.

Goals and Plans

strategic goals
Broad statements of where the organization wants to be in the future; pertain to the organization as a whole rather than to specific divisions or departments.

Broad statements describing where the organization wants to be in the future are called **strategic goals.** They pertain to the organization as a whole rather than to specific divisions or departments. Strategic goals are often called *official* goals, because they are the stated intentions of what the organization wants to achieve. Several management scholars have suggested that business organizations' goals must encompass more than profits and that businesses actually suffer when profit and shareholder value become the primary goals. Peter Drucker suggests that organizations focus on eight content areas in developing goals: market standing, innovation, productivity, physical and financial resources, profitability, managerial performance and development, worker performance and attitude, and public responsibility.[16]

strategic plans
The action steps by which an organization intends to attain its strategic goals.

Strategic plans define the action steps by which the company intends to attain strategic goals. The strategic plan is the blueprint that defines the organizational activities and resource allocations—in the form of cash, personnel, space, and facilities—required for meeting these targets. Strategic planning tends to be long term and may define organizational action steps from two to five years in the future. The purpose of strategic plans is to turn organizational goals into realities within that time period.

As an example, a small company wanted to improve its market share from 15 percent to 20 percent over the next three years. This strategic goal was pursued through the following strategic plans: (1) allocate resources for the development of new, competitive products with high growth potential; (2) improve production methods to achieve higher output at lower costs; and (3) conduct research to develop alternative uses for current products and services.[17]

The results that major divisions and departments within the organization intend to achieve are defined as **tactical goals.** These goals apply to middle management and describe what major subunits must do in order for the organization to achieve its overall goals. For example, Fetzer Vineyards might have a tactical goal to include English as a Second Language (ESL) classes for its Spanish-speaking workers as part of a comprehensive employee education program. This tactical goal is one part of achieving the strategic goal of contributing to the growth and development of employees.

Tactical plans are designed to help execute major strategic plans and to accomplish a specific part of the company's strategy.[18] Tactical plans typically have a shorter time horizon than strategic plans—over the next year or so. The word *tactical* comes from the military. For example, strategic weapon systems, such as intercontinental ballistic missiles or the B-2 Stealth Bomber, are designed to deliver major blows to the enemy. These weapon systems reflect the country's overall strategic plan. Tactical weapon systems, such as fighter airplanes, are used to achieve just one part of the overall strategic plan. Tactical plans define what the major departments and organizational subunits will do to implement the overall strategic plan. Normally, it is the middle manager's job to take the broad strategic plan and identify specific tactical actions.

The specific results expected from departments, work groups, and individuals are the **operational goals.** They are precise and measurable. "Process 150 sales applications each week," "achieve 90 percent of deliveries on time," "reduce overtime by 10 percent next month," and "develop two new elective courses in accounting" are examples of operational goals.

Operational plans are developed at the lower levels of the organization to specify action steps toward achieving operational goals and to support tactical plans. The operational plan is the department manager's tool for daily and weekly operations. Goals are stated in quantitative terms, and the department plan describes how goals will be achieved. Operational planning specifies plans for supervisors, department managers, and individual employees. For example, Du Pont has a program called Individual Career Management that involves a series of discussions that define what each manager's new goals should be and whether last year's operational goals were met. At Du Pont the goals are set as high as possible to stretch the employee to ensure continued improvement. These year-end discussions also provide the basis for rewards to those who have excelled.[19]

Schedules are an important component of operational planning. Schedules define precise time frames for the completion of each operational goal required for the organization's tactical and strategic goals. Operational planning also must be coordinated with the budget, because resources must be allocated for desired activities. For example, Apogee Enterprises, a window and glass fabricator with 150 small divisions, is fanatical about operational

Look who's helping Owens Corning reach its strategic goal of becoming a $5 billion global company by the year 2000. Owens Corning recently acquired the global rights to the Pink Panther to help the company build a unified marketing campaign around the world. In addition to the target of $5 billion in sales, the company's long-range plan, referred to as OC 2000, sets forth other goals, including achieving 40 percent of sales outside the United States and attracting and maintaining a diverse workforce.

tactical goals
Goals that define the outcomes that major divisions and departments must achieve in order for the organization to reach its overall goals.

tactical plans
Plans designed to help execute major strategic plans and to accomplish a specific part of the company's strategy.

operational goals
Specific, measurable results expected from departments, work groups, and individuals within the organization.

operational plans
Plans developed at the organization's lower levels that specify action steps toward achieving operational goals and that support tactical planning activities.

Exhibit *7.3*   *Hierarchy of Goals for a Manufacturing Organization*

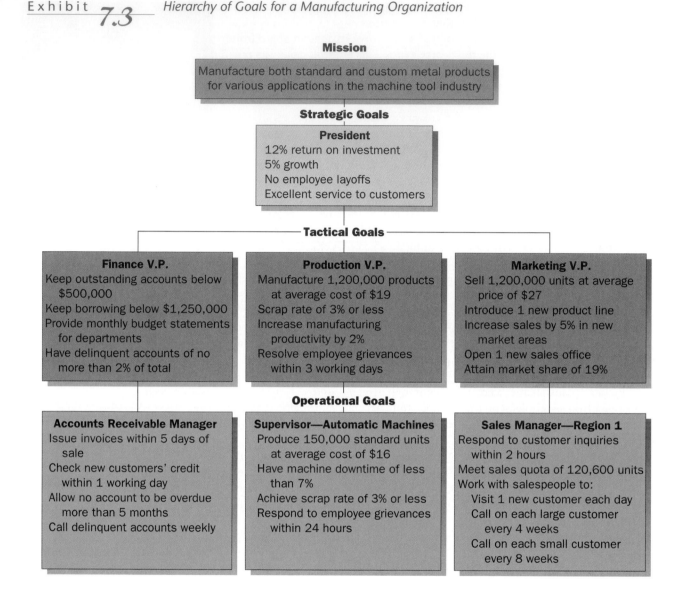

Mission

Manufacture both standard and custom metal products for various applications in the machine tool industry

Strategic Goals

President
12% return on investment
5% growth
No employee layoffs
Excellent service to customers

Tactical Goals

Finance V.P.
Keep outstanding accounts below $500,000
Keep borrowing below $1,250,000
Provide monthly budget statements for departments
Have delinquent accounts of no more than 2% of total

Production V.P.
Manufacture 1,200,000 products at average cost of $19
Scrap rate of 3% or less
Increase manufacturing productivity by 2%
Resolve employee grievances within 3 working days

Marketing V.P.
Sell 1,200,000 units at average price of $27
Introduce 1 new product line
Increase sales by 5% in new market areas
Open 1 new sales office
Attain market share of 19%

Operational Goals

Accounts Receivable Manager
Issue invoices within 5 days of sale
Check new customers' credit within 1 working day
Allow no account to be overdue more than 5 months
Call delinquent accounts weekly

Supervisor—Automatic Machines
Produce 150,000 standard units at average cost of $16
Have machine downtime of less than 7%
Achieve scrap rate of 3% or less
Respond to employee grievances within 24 hours

Sales Manager—Region 1
Respond to customer inquiries within 2 hours
Meet sales quota of 120,600 units
Work with salespeople to:
  Visit 1 new customer each day
  Call on each large customer every 4 weeks
  Call on each small customer every 8 weeks

planning and budgeting. Committees are set up that require inter- as well as intradivisional review and challenge of budgets, profit plans, and proposed capital expenditures. Assigning the dollars makes the operational plan work for everything from hiring new salespeople to increasing travel expenses.

Hierarchy of Goals

Effectively designed organizational goals fit into a hierarchy; that is, the achievement of goals at low levels permits the attainment of high-level goals. This is called a *means-ends chain* because low-level goals lead to accomplishment of high-level goals. Operational goals lead to the achievement of tactical goals, which in turn lead to the attainment of strategic goals. Strategic goals are traditionally considered the responsibility of top management, tactical goals that of middle management, and operational goals that of first-line supervisors and workers. However, as we will discuss later in the chapter, the shrinking of middle management combined with a new emphasis on employee empowerment have led to a greater involvement of all employees in goal setting and planning at each level.

An example of a goal hierarchy is illustrated in Exhibit 7.3. Note how the strategic goal of "excellent service to customers" translates into "Open one new sales office" and "Respond to customer inquiries within two hours" at lower management levels.

Criteria for Effective Goals

To ensure goal-setting benefits for the organization, certain characteristics and guidelines should be adopted. The characteristics of both goals and the goal-setting process are listed in Exhibit 7.4.

Goal Characteristics

The following characteristics pertain to organizational goals at the strategic, tactical, and operational levels.

Specific and Measurable. When possible, goals should be expressed in quantitative terms, such as increasing profits by 2 percent, decreasing scrap by 1 percent, or increasing average teacher effectiveness ratings from 3.5 to 3.7. A team at Sealed Air Corporation, a manufacturer of packaging materials, was motivated by a goal to reduce by two hours the average time needed to change machine settings. The team was spurred to keep going when members could see that their earliest efforts reduced changeover time by a significant amount.[20] Not all goals can be expressed in numerical terms, but vague goals have little motivating power for employees. By necessity, goals are qualitative as well as quantitative, especially at the top of the organization. The important point is that the goals be precisely defined and allow for measurable progress. For example, Liisa Joronen, chairman of SOL Cleaning Service, believes in giving teams the right to set their own performance goals; however, she's a stickler for accountability. "The more we free our people from rules," she says, "the more we need good measurements." Every time SOL lands a contract, the salesperson works at the new customer's site along with the SOL team that will do the future cleaning. Together they establish performance goals. Every month, customers rate the team's performance based on the goals.[21]

Cover Key Result Areas. Goals cannot be set for every aspect of employee behavior or organizational performance; if they were, their sheer number would render them meaningless. Instead, managers should identify a few key result areas—perhaps up to four or five for any organizational department or job. Key result areas are those activities that contribute most to company performance.[22] Robert Hershey, partner in charge of KPMG Peat Marwick's World-Class Finance Practice, recommends that companies as a whole track no more than 20 key result areas in four distinct categories: financial indicators; customer-related indicators; process-related indicators; and future-value indicators (including human resources).[23]

Exhibit **7.4**

Characteristics of Effective Goal Setting

Goal Characteristics
- Specific and measurable
- Cover key result areas
- Challenging but realistic
- Defined time period
- Linked to rewards

3M marketers carefully planned the global launch of Scotch-Brite Never Rust soap pads to maximize sales of the new product. Innovation is the cornerstone of 3M's culture, and the company's challenging but realistic goals have 3M employees turning new ideas into new products faster than ever before. The new goal of achieving 30 percent of sales from products introduced in the past four years was quickly met, thanks to the successful launch of new products such as the soap pads.

Challenging but Realistic.   Goals should be challenging but not unreasonably difficult. One newly hired manager discovered that his staff would have to work 100-hour weeks to accomplish everything expected of them. When goals are unrealistic, they set employees up for failure and lead to decreasing employee morale.[24] However, if goals are too easy, employees may not feel motivated. Tom Peters, coauthor of *In Search of Excellence*, believes that the best quality programs start with extremely ambitious goals, called *stretch goals*, that challenge employees to meet high standards. Companies such as Rubbermaid and 3M bring out the best in their employees by making goals ever more challenging. The CEO of 3M has decreed that 30 percent of sales must come from products introduced in the past four years; the old standard was 25 percent.[25] Managers should, however, make sure that goals are set within the existing resource base, not beyond departments' time, equipment, and financial resources.

Defined Time Period.   Goals should specify the time period over which they will be achieved. A time period is a deadline stating the date on which goal attainment will be measured. A goal of setting up a customer database could have a deadline such as June 30, 2000. If a strategic goal involves a two-to-three-year time horizon, specific dates for achieving parts of it can be set up. For example, strategic sales goals could be established on a three-year time horizon, with a $100 million target in year one, a $129 million target in year two, and a $165 million target in year three.

Linked to Rewards.   The ultimate impact of goals depends on the extent to which salary increases, promotions, and awards are based on goal achievement. People who attain goals should be rewarded. Rewards give meaning and significance to goals and help commit employees to achieving goals. Failure to attain goals often is due to factors outside employees' control. For example, failure to achieve a financial goal may be associated with a drop in market demand due to industry recession; thus, an employee could not be expected to reach it. Nevertheless, a reward may be appropriate if the employee partially achieved goals under difficult circumstances.[26]

Planning Types and Models

Once strategic, tactical, and operational goals have been determined, managers may select a planning approach most appropriate for their situation. Critical to successful planning are *flexibility* and *adaptability* to changing environments. Managers use a number of planning approaches. Among the most popular are management by objectives, single-use plans, standing plans, and contingency (or scenario) plans.

Management by Objectives

management by objectives
A method of management whereby managers and employees define goals for every department, project, and person and use them to monitor subsequent performance.

Management by objectives (MBO) is a method whereby managers and employees define goals for every department, project, and person and use them to monitor subsequent performance.[27] A model of the essential steps of the MBO process is presented in Exhibit 7.5. Four major activities must occur in order for MBO to be successful:[28]

1. *Set goals.* This is the most difficult step in MBO. Setting goals involves employees at all levels and looks beyond day-to-day activities to answer

Exhibit **7.5** *Model of the MBO Process*

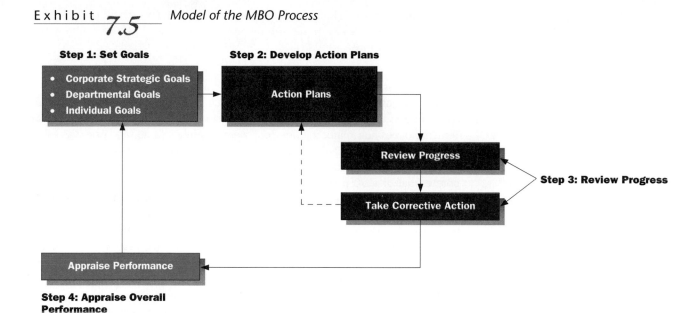

the question "What are we trying to accomplish?" A good goal should be concrete and realistic, provide a specific target and time frame, and assign responsibility. Goals may be quantitative or qualitative, depending on whether outcomes are measurable. Quantitative goals are described in numerical terms, such as "Salesperson Jones will obtain 16 new accounts in December." Qualitative goals use statements such as "Marketing will reduce complaints by improving customer service next year." Goals should be jointly derived. Mutual agreement between employee and supervisor creates the strongest commitment to achieving goals. In the case of teams, all team members may participate in setting goals.

2. *Develop action plans.* An *action plan* defines the course of action needed to achieve the stated goals. Action plans are made for both individuals and departments.

3. *Review progress.* A periodic progress review is important to ensure that action plans are working. These reviews can occur informally between managers and subordinates, where the organization may wish to conduct three-, six-, or nine-month reviews during the year. This periodic checkup allows managers and employees to see whether they are on target or whether corrective action is necessary. Managers and employees should not be locked into predefined behavior and must be willing to take whatever steps are necessary to produce meaningful results. The point of MBO is to achieve goals. The action plan can be changed whenever goals are not being met.

4. *Appraise overall performance.* The final step in MBO is to carefully evaluate whether annual goals have been achieved for both individuals and departments. Success or failure to achieve goals can become part of the performance appraisal system and the designation of salary increases and other rewards. The appraisal of departmental and overall corporate performance shapes goals for the next year. The MBO cycle repeats itself on

an annual basis. The specific application of MBO must fit the needs of each company. An example of how one company used MBO to solve safety problems follows.

PRODUCERS GAS AND TRANSMISSION

Producers Gas and Transmission Company is a medium-sized refinery and distributor of gasoline and other refinery products. A major concern of top management was an unusually high employee accident rate during the previous year. Ten employees had minor injuries, four were severely injured, and one was killed. The company lost 112 employee days of work due to accidents. Top management discussed the accident rate with department heads and decided on a corporate goal of a 50 percent reduction in all accidents for the following year.

Middle managers developed an action plan that included (1) establishing an employee safety training program, (2) creating a company-wide safety committee, and (3) setting up a new system of safety recognition. Also, (4) line supervisors were asked to develop safety training sessions for their departments within 60 days, and (5) middle managers were given 30 days to nominate supervisors to the safety committee. Finally, (6) the safety committee had 30 days in which to design a safety recognition program, including awards.

Progress was reviewed through the compilation of quarterly safety reports measuring percentage of accidents compared to the previous year. The action plan could be revised if obstacles were discovered. The safety committee appraised the safety performance of each department every 90 days and posted the results for all employees to see. Letters of commendation were given to departments that met or exceeded the 50 percent reduction goal.

At the end of the year, an overall performance appraisal was held for individuals, departments, and the corporation as a whole. Departments that had successfully reduced accidents by 50 percent were given awards. Information about safety procedures and accident rates was used to set a new safety goal for the next year. Delinquent departments were given stringent goals. Most important, the company achieved its goal of reducing accidents by 50 percent. The MBO system energized employee actions companywide toward a goal deemed critical by top management. MBO got all employees working toward the same end.[29]

Benefits and Problems with MBO. Many companies, such as Intel, Tenneco, Black & Decker, and Du Pont, have adopted MBO, and most managers believe that MBO is an effective management tool.[30] Managers believe they are better oriented toward goal achievement when MBO is used. Like any system, MBO achieves benefits when used properly but results in problems when used improperly. Benefits and problems are summarized in Exhibit 7.6.

The benefits of the MBO process can be many. Corporate goals are more likely to be achieved when they focus manager and employee efforts. Performance is improved because employees are committed to attaining the goal, are motivated because they help decide what is expected, and are free to be resourceful. Goals at lower levels are aligned with and enable the attainment of goals at top management levels.

Problems with MBO occur when the company faces rapid change. The environment and internal activities must have some stability for performance to be measured and compared against goals. When new goals must be set every few months, there is no time for action plans and appraisal to take effect. Also, poor employer-employee relations reduce effectiveness because there is an element of distrust between managers and workers. Sometimes

Benefits of MBO	Problems with MBO
1. Manager and employee efforts are focused on activities that will lead to goal attainment.	1. Constant change prevents MBO from taking hold.
2. Performance can be improved at all company levels.	2. An environment of poor employer–employee relations reduces MBO effectiveness.
3. Employees are motivated.	3. Strategic goals may be displaced by operational goals.
4. Departmental and individual goals are aligned with company goals.	4. Mechanistic organizations and values that discourage participation can harm the MBO process.
	5. Too much paperwork saps MBO energy.

Exhibit 7.6

MBO Benefits and Problems

goal "displacement" occurs if employees focus exclusively on their operational goals to the detriment of other teams or departments. Overemphasis on operational goals can harm the attainment of overall goals. Another problem arises in mechanistic organizations characterized by rigidly defined tasks and rules that may not be compatible with MBO's emphasis on mutual determination of goals by employee and supervisor. In addition, when participation is discouraged, employees will lack the training and values to jointly set goals with employers. Finally, if MBO becomes a process of filling out annual paperwork rather than energizing employees to achieve goals, it becomes an empty exercise. Once the paperwork is completed, employees forget about the goals, perhaps even resenting the paperwork in the first place.

Single-Use and Standing Plans

Single-use plans are developed to achieve a set of goals that are not likely to be repeated in the future. **Standing plans** are ongoing plans that are used to provide guidance for tasks performed repeatedly within the organization. Exhibit 7.7 outlines the major types of single-use and standing plans. Single-use plans typically include both programs and projects. The primary standing plans are organizational policies, rules, and procedures. Standing plans generally pertain to such matters as employee illness, absences, smoking, discipline, hiring, and dismissal. Many companies are discovering a need to develop standing plans regarding the use of E-mail, as discussed in the Technology box.

single-use plans
Plans that are developed to achieve a set of goals that are unlikely to be repeated in the future.

standing plans
Ongoing plans used to provide guidance for tasks performed repeatedly within the organization.

Quality Planning and the Shewhart Cycle. Many companies have instituted standing plans for quality improvement, often based on W. Edwards Deming's 14 points of quality management. Employees are encouraged to participate in the continuous improvement of product and service quality. TQM (total quality management) will be discussed in more detail in Chapter 20. These companies often use the **Shewhart Cycle** of continuous improvement (sometimes called the PDCA—Plan, Do, Check, Act—Cycle), as illustrated in Exhibit 7.8. Managers first *plan* a test or change in a specific process, then *do* the test or carry out the change, *check* the results, and finally *act* to improve the process based upon what they learn. A number of cycle iterations may be needed before satisfactory results are achieved. The cycle repeats

Shewhart cycle
A planning cycle used in companies that have instituted quality management; also called PDCA—plan, do, check, act—Cycle.

Exhibit **7.7**

Major Types of Single-Use and Standing Plans

Single-Use Plans	Standing Plans
Program • Plans for attaining a one-time organizational goal • Major undertaking that may take several years to complete • Large in scope; may be associated with several projects **Examples:** Boeing's 777 aircraft NASA space station	**Policy** • Broad in scope—a general guide to action • Based on organization's overall goals/strategic plan • Defines boundaries within which to make decisions **Examples:** Drug-free workplace policies Sexual harassment policies Continuous Improvement Shewhart Cycle
Project • Also a set of plans for attaining a one-time goal • Smaller in scope and complexity than a program; shorter time horizon • Often one part of a larger program **Examples:** Development of a rocket booster for NASA space station Development of external shell for NASA space station	**Rule** • Narrow in scope • Describes how a specific action is to be performed • May apply to specific setting **Example:** No-smoking rule in areas of plant where hazardous materials are stored
	Procedure • Sometimes called a standard operating procedure • Defines a precise series of steps to attain certain goals **Examples:** Procedures for issuing refunds Procedures for handling employee grievances

itself continuously, planning is an ongoing activity, and everyone in the organization can learn from experience and help the company improve.[31] An interesting variation of this cycle is used by the U.S. Army at its National Training Center and increasingly is being adopted by corporations.

U.S. ARMY
www.army.mil

At the National Training Center just south of Death Valley, U.S. Army troops engage in a simulated battle: the "enemy" has sent unmanned aerial vehicles (UAVs) to gather targeting data. When troops fire upon the UAVs, they reveal their location to attack helicopters hovering just behind a nearby ridge. After the exercise, unit members and their superiors hold "After-Action Reviews" to review battle plans, discuss what worked and what didn't, and talk about how to do things better. General William Hertzog suggested that inexpensive decoy UAVs might be just the thing to make a distracted enemy reveal his location. The observation amounts to a "lesson learned" for the entire army.

The Army's "lessons-learned" system is a process of identifying and reducing mistakes, of innovating, and of continuously learning from experience. The system has led to lessons such as how to prevent problems leading to friendly fire casualties in the Gulf War and how to avoid minefields and booby traps in Bosnia. The

LEADING THE REVOLUTION: TECHNOLOGY

Regulating E-mail in the Workplace

Top executives around the globe are discovering that casual E-mail messages can come back to haunt them—in court. Messages dashed off years ago by Bill Gates became digital "smoking guns" in the Justice Department's antitrust case against Microsoft. Authorities studied electronic messages by Gates and other top leaders at Microsoft for evidence that the company was out to crush competitors and monopolize access to the Internet.

"E-mail discovery" has companies scrambling to figure out how to avoid getting tripped up by the informal, candid, and sometimes inflammatory messages this new means of communication can foster. People have a tendency to put things in E-mail messages that they wouldn't consider writing in a paper document. Morgan Stanley Dean Witter & Co., for example, recently agreed to settle a discrimination suit based largely on E-mailed jokes playing on stereotypes about African American speech patterns. The growing use of E-mail has made it easier than ever to file lawsuits in cases alleging everything from sexual harassment to stolen trade secrets. Yet companies are just beginning to recognize their E-mail vulnerability. In a 1997 survey, barely half of the companies polled had written policies governing the use of E-mail, and only about a quarter of those

actually enforced the policies. Some worry that monitoring E-mail will trigger complaints of Big Brother in the workplace, while others worry primarily that regulating E-mail stifles creativity.

A few companies are ahead of the game in developing strict E-mail policies. At Prudential Insurance Company, employees are prohibited from using company E-mail to share jokes, photographs, or any kind of nonbusiness information. Merrill Lynch requires all employees to sign off on the company's E-mail policy. Further, some companies are turning to software to help police E-mail. Citibank, Lockheed Martin, and General Electric, for example, have installed electronic shredding programs on thousands of laptops in the field. Hughes Hubbard & Reed LLP, a New York law firm, is developing software called MailCop that uses artificial intelligence to warn workers when they have written or received E-mail that may violate company rules. As problems with electronic mail—and lawsuits—continue to grow, more and more companies are likely to develop strict policies regulating E-mail in the workplace.

SOURCE: Marcia Stepanek, with Steve Hamm, "When the Devil is in the E-mails," *Business Week*, June 8, 1998, 72–74.

Army stockpiles lessons learned and disseminates them throughout the combat force. In Bosnia, a new list of lessons was distributed every 72 hours. The lessons are based not only on simulated battles, but also on real-life experiences of soldiers in the field. The Center for Army Lessons Learned (CALL) sends experts into the field to observe after-action reviews, interview soldiers, and read intelligence reports. In 1994, CALL compiled 26 lessons for replacement troops in Haiti, who actually confronted 23 of those scenarios within their first few months of deployment.

The Army has come to depend greatly on its lessons-learned system for organizational learning and continuous improvement. A case study by the Harvard Business School concluded that the system enables the Army to minimize mistakes and sustain successes efficiently. The lessons-learned system is now getting some attention from corporate America. Black & Veatch, an engineering company based in Kansas City, Missouri, and Steelcase Inc., an office furniture manufacturer in Grand Rapids, Michigan, are among the companies adapting the lessons-learned system to create a process of continuous learning and improvement.[32]

Contingency Plans

When organizations are operating in a highly uncertain environment or dealing with long time horizons, sometimes planning can seem like a waste of time. In fact, strict plans may even hinder rather than help an organization's performance in the face of rapid technological, social, economic, or other environmental change. In these cases, managers can develop multiple future

Exhibit **7.8**

The Shewhart Cycle of Continuous Improvement

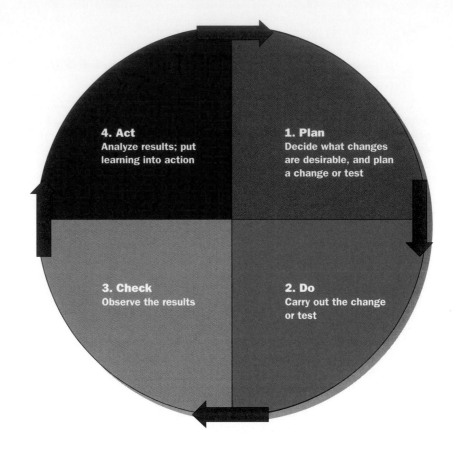

4. Act
Analyze results; put learning into action

1. Plan
Decide what changes are desirable, and plan a change or test

3. Check
Observe the results

2. Do
Carry out the change or test

SOURCE: Based on Thomas F. Rienzo, "Planning Deming Management for Service Organizations" *Business Horizons* 36, no. 3 (May–June 1993), 19–29.

contingency plans
Plans that define company responses to specific situations, such as emergencies, setbacks, or unexpected conditions.

scenarios to help them form more flexible plans. **Contingency plans,** sometimes referred to as *scenarios*, define company responses to be taken in the case of emergencies, setbacks, or unexpected conditions. To develop contingency plans, planners identify uncontrollable factors, such as recession, inflation, technological developments, or safety accidents. To minimize the impact of these potential factors, a planning team can forecast the worst-case scenarios. For example, if sales fall 20 percent and prices drop 8 percent, what will the company do? Contingency plans can then be defined for possible layoffs, emergency budgets, and sales efforts.[33]

Royal Dutch/Shell Oil has used scenario planning since the 1970s and has been consistently better in its oil forecasts than other major oil companies. Several years ago, contingency planning was used at Shell for dealing with a potential drop in oil prices that could be catastrophic. Oil was $28 a barrel and rising, but the planning group challenged Shell managers to consider what they would do in the unlikely event that oil suddenly dropped to $15 a barrel. As it turned out, the price of oil *did* drop to $15 a barrel within a few months, and Shell executives were ready because they had developed contingency plans.[34]

Planning Time Horizon

Organizational goals and plans are associated with specific time horizons. The time horizons are long term, intermediate term, and short term, as illustrated in Exhibit 7.9. *Long-term planning* includes strategic goals and plans and may extend as far as 5 years into the future. *Intermediate-term planning*

Exhibit **7.9** *Planning Time Horizon*

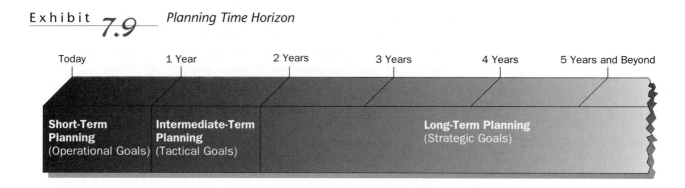

Today | 1 Year | 2 Years | 3 Years | 4 Years | 5 Years and Beyond

Short-Term Planning (Operational Goals)

Intermediate-Term Planning (Tactical Goals)

Long-Term Planning (Strategic Goals)

includes tactical goals and has a time horizon of from 1 to 2 years. *Short-term planning* includes operational goals for specific departments and individuals and has a time horizon of 1 year or less.

One of the major problems in companies today is the emphasis on *short-term results*. Long-term planning is difficult because the world is so uncertain. Moreover, the financial community, including stock analysts and mutual-fund managers, push companies for strong financial results in the short term. This pressure fits the natural inclination of many results-oriented managers, who are concerned with outcomes for today and next week—not next year, and certainly not 5 years out. These pressures tend to reward short-term performance and undercut long-range planning. For example, a Tennessee manufacturer of temperature control devices badly needed new plants and facilities that required massive expenditures. The managers' bonuses were calculated on profits for a 1-year period. In this case, the pressures for short-term results took precedence, and the managers did not invest money in new facilities because short-term profits would suffer.

Focusing too heavily on short-term profitability as a goal has handicapped many U.S. and other Western businesses competing internationally. Japanese companies, by contrast, often take a long-term view and have multiple goals, giving equal weight to market share, profitability, and innovation.[35] Consider Matsushita Electric, the world's largest producer of consumer electronics,

To maintain its position as the premier chain drugstore operator in the United States, Walgreen Co.'s short-term plan includes opening more than a store a day, with its 3,000th store to open in the year 2000. The long-term plan is to operate 6,000 stores across the United States by the year 2010. In the photo is a recently opened Walgreens, its ninth in downtown Chicago. Walgreens is one of the fastest growing retailers in the United States, and it leads the chain drugstore industry in sales and profits.

VCRs, color televisions, and video cameras. Sixty years ago, Konosuke Matsushita foresaw the day when the United States would provide both major markets and manufacturing centers for his company's small appliances. In 1932 he announced an ambitious 250-year plan for the company, perhaps an all-time record for long-range planning.[36] Long-term planning need not resort to such extremes. Today, senior executives are redirecting Matsushita into four areas where future growth is expected: semiconductors, factory automation, office automation, and audiovisual products. These products generate only 13 percent of sales but are expected to do well in the twenty-first century and so today are receiving 70 percent of the company's research expenditures.[37]

Planning in Learning Organizations

The process of planning is changing. Traditionally, strategy and planning have been the domain of top managers. However, in the learning organization, top managers no longer control the planning process; everyone becomes involved. In some companies, planning is being taken out of the executive boardroom and central planning department to become a part of everyday work throughout the organization. We will first discuss traditional, top-down approaches to planning and then examine some of the newer approaches that emphasize bottom-up planning and employee involvement.

Traditional Approaches to Planning

Traditionally, corporate planning has been done entirely by top executives, by consulting firms, or, most commonly, by central planning departments. **Central planning departments** are groups of planning specialists who report directly to the CEO or president, as illustrated in Exhibit 7.10. This approach was popular during the 1970s. Planning specialists were hired to gather data and develop detailed strategic plans for the corporation as a whole. This planning approach was top down because goals and plans were assigned to major divisions and departments from the planning department after approval by the president.

central planning department
A group of planning specialists who develop plans for the organization as a whole and its major divisions and departments and typically report to the president or CEO.

This Corporate Financial Process Team is composed of a blend of AMETEK colleagues from the corporate office and several operating locations. The team developed an integrated financial forecasting program to help automate inventory reporting at AMETEK, a leading manufacturer of electric motors and electronic instruments in North America, Europe, and Asia. For its efforts, this planning task force was awarded the company's annual Dr. John H. Lux Total Quality Accomplishment Award.

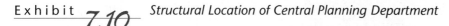

Exhibit 7.10   *Structural Location of Central Planning Department*

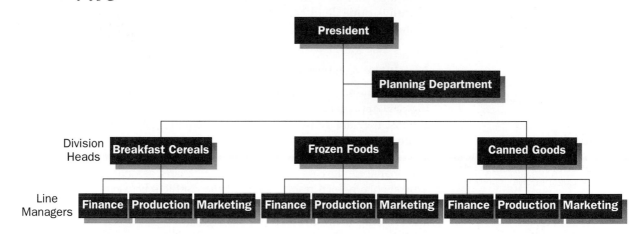

This approach works well in many applications. For example, the Columbia Gas System has a corporate planning department with eight full-time specialists. The department has two sections. The operations analysis section is responsible for acquiring and analyzing economic and other data for use in the strategic planning process. The planning section successfully prepares the strategic plan for the system and also provides guidance to subsidiary companies for strategic planning activities.[38]

Although traditional approaches to planning still are popular with many companies, formal planning increasingly is being criticized as inappropriate for today's fast-paced environment. There are a number of problems with traditional, formal planning:

• *Planners may be out of touch with day-to-day realities.* Central planning departments often are out of touch with the constantly changing realities faced by line managers and front-line workers, who are tuned to the needs of customers. In one case, planners at GE's Major Appliance Business Group made mistakes by relying on abstract data and failing to understand customers. Because families are getting smaller, they reasoned that small appliances were the wave of the future. However, they didn't realize that working women wanted *big* refrigerators in order to cut down on trips to the supermarket.[39]

• *Formal plans may inhibit flexibility.* When plans and goals are set by top executives or a central planning department, managers and workers throughout the organization may be stuck trying to follow a plan that no longer works due to changes in the environment or other factors. A formal annual plan that does not allow for flexibility can lead to disaster in a rapidly changing environment.

• *Formal plans may limit creativity and learning.* When managers and workers follow a set of strict goals and plans outlined by someone else, they have less incentive to think for themselves and come up with creative new business ideas. Motivation and enthusiasm may also suffer. Most new companies, for example, are full of entrepreneurial spirit and energy. When they begin to grow and institute formal, detailed planning systems, they often lose their entrepreneurial edge. Patrick Kelly, founder of Physician Sales and Service, believed telling his managers how to run their business was a surefire way to turn "fast-moving, get-things-done field managers . . . into cover-your-butt manual-reading middle managers."[40]

Modern Approaches to Planning

To overcome some of the problems of traditional planning, managers are trying new approaches. As companies move toward becoming learning organizations, they are getting rid of central planning departments. A more recent approach to planning is the **decentralized planning staff,** which evolved when planning experts were assigned to major departments and divisions to help managers develop their own strategic plans, as indicated in Exhibit 7.11. This change helped resolve some of the conflicts between planners and staff because corporate planners were no longer writing their own strategic plans and handing them down to line managers.

decentralized planning staff
A group of planning specialists assigned to major departments and divisions to help managers develop their own strategic plans.

This approach to planning is evident at Johnson & Johnson, which has mastered the art of decentralized management better than any other organization in the world. J&J runs more than 33 major lines of business, with 180 operating companies in 51 countries. Top executives trust the managers at each business to set their own goals, finding that they often set far more ambitious ones than the top brass would expect. As former CEO Ralph Larsen once said, "The quickest way to destroy morale is to issue edicts from [headquarters]. We do best when we take time to describe the problem and let them come up with a solution."[41]

planning task force
A temporary group consisting of line managers responsible for developing strategic plans.

Larsen also began a process called Frameworks, in which dozens of managers at a time get together to wrestle with specific problems and opportunities and develop strategic plans for handling them. A number of organizations now use such groups, called planning task forces. A **planning task force** is a temporary group of line managers who have the responsibility of developing a strategic plan. A group of line managers thus takes over responsibility for planning. In one study of corporate planning practices, approximately one-third of the companies used an interdepartmental task force to

E x h i b i t *7.11*   *Structural Location of Decentralized Planning Staff*

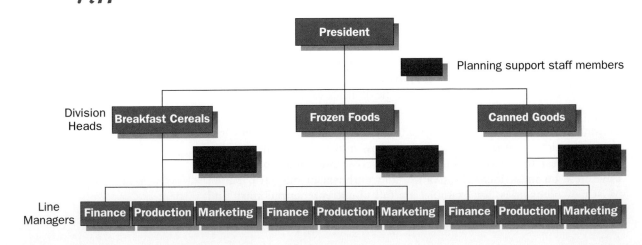

LEADING THE REVOLUTION: THE LEARNING ORGANIZATION

Springfield Remanufacturing Corporation

Jack Stack, chairman and CEO of Springfield Remanufacturing Corp. (SRC), believes companies can thrive by tapping into people's universal desire to win. SRC, which began as a division of International Harvester, is a business Stack calls tough, loud, and dirty—a place "where people work with plugs in their ears and leave the factory every day covered in grease." Stack has built a highly successful company based on the philosophy that "the best, most efficient, most profitable way to operate a business is to give everybody a voice in how the company is run and a stake in the financial outcome, good or bad."

Stack involves every employee in the planning process and uses a bonus system based on hitting the plan's targets. SRC's planning officially kicks off when Stack and other top executives meet with the sales and marketing managers of SRC's 15 divisions in a formal two-day event. But before that meeting, the sales and marketing managers have done their homework by meeting with managers, supervisors, and front-line workers throughout their divisions. If a manager's plan is beyond the plant's capacity, the workers suggest workable alternatives. By the time managers present their plans to the top brass, everyone in the various divisions has had a say and has thus developed a sense of ownership in the plan.

All employees have access to the company's financial data and can compare performance to the plan. SRC has invested heavily in financial education for all workers—everyone learns what's at risk and what's to be gained, and everyone knows how to make a difference. Kevin Dotson, an ex-Marine who works in the Heavy Duty warehouse, says he learns something new about the financial statements every time he goes to a meeting. "It's not like you have just one meeting and learn everything. . . . But you do understand the lines on the statement that you actually affect. That's how you see how you can be more efficient or how we as a small team within a large team can improve so the next group can take the handoff more smoothly. We all have different jobs, but we're all pulling for the same goals."

SOURCE: Jay Finegan, "Everything According to Plan," *Inc.,* March 1995, 78–85.

---

make plans for achieving strategic goals. Each team identified and analyzed alternatives for reaching a specific goal and then outlined the major action steps necessary for achieving it.[42]

The New Planning Paradigm

Today, some companies are taking decentralized planning even farther and involving workers at every level of the organization in the planning process. In this new paradigm, middle managers and planning staff work with line managers and front-line workers to develop dynamic plans that meet the organization's needs. In a complex and competitive business environment, traditional planning done by a select few no longer works. Strategic thinking and execution become the expectation of every employee.[43] For an example of a company that is finding hidden sources of ideas and innovation by involving all its workers in planning, consider Springfield Remanufacturing, described in the Learning Organization box.

Planning comes alive when employees are involved in setting goals and determining the means to reach them. Learning organizations follow six rules of planning.

Start with a Strong Mission. Employee commitment and involvement are critical to helping companies compete in today's rapidly changing world. A compelling mission often serves to increase employee commitment and motivation as well as provide a guide for planning and decision making.[44] In a six-year study of exceptional companies that have stood the test of time, including Wal-Mart, 3M, General Electric, and Johnson & Johnson, James C. Collins and Jerry Porras identified a number of timeless fundamentals that helped make these companies great. They found one of the key factors to be that these companies were guided by a "core ideology"—values and a sense of purpose that go beyond just making money and that provide a guide for behavior. For example, a lot of the faith Johnson & Johnson executives place in decentralized managers can be traced to the well-known Johnson & Johnson Credo, a code of ethics that tells managers what to care about and in what order. Interestingly, in this complex $15 billion organization that has never lost money since going public in 1944, the Credo puts profits dead last on the list of things managers should care about.[45]

Set Stretch Goals.   Stretch goals are highly ambitious goals that are so clear, compelling, and imaginative that they fuel progress. When shifting to a learning organization, top managers can set stretch goals to compel employees to think in new ways. Motorola used stretch goals to improve quality. Leaders first set a goal of a tenfold increase in quality over a two-year period. After this goal was met, they set a new stretch goal of a hundredfold improvement in quality over four years.[46]

Create an Environment that Encourages Learning.   A basic value in learning organizations is to question the status quo. Constant questioning opens the gates to creativity and learning. Companies such as Nucor Steel encourage and reward constant experimentation and risk taking. So much worker experimentation is going on that Larry Roos, manager of the Crawfordsville, Indiana, plant, says "Half the time I don't know who's doing what out there." Although an environment of rampant experimentation can lead to failures, more importantly it leads to flexibility, learning, and improving.[47]

At Textron's Bell Helicopter division, a group of employees meets every day at 7 A.M. to pinpoint and immediately correct production problems. The meetings, which grew from a 1992 all-employee campaign to speed production and cut costs, helped chop 12 months off the time it takes to build a helicopter. Textron has made continuous improvement a way of life; through its Textron 2000 initiative, the company is building a culture in which every organizational member is constantly finding ways to make the company better and faster.

Design New Roles for Planning Staff. Companies transform the conventional planner's job.[48] Planning specialists serve as facilitators and supporters; they do not decide on the substance of goals and plans. Planning experts can be very helpful in gathering data, performing statistical analyses, and doing other specialized tasks. The key difference is that, rather than looking for the "right answers," they supply information in order to broaden the consideration of issues and support strategic thinking.

Make Continuous Improvement a Way of Life. Involving everyone in planning encourages employees to continuously learn and grow, thus helping the organization improve its capability. No plan is set in stone because people are constantly learning and improving. Highly successful companies such as 3M often make their best moves through constant experimentation and improvement. 3M encourages its employees to try just about anything and gives them 15 percent of their work time to do so.

Planning Still Starts and Stops at the Top. Top managers create a mission that is worthy of employees' best efforts and provide a framework for planning and goal setting. Even though planning is decentralized, top managers must show support and commitment to the planning process. Top managers also accept responsibility when planning and goal setting are ineffective, rather than blaming the failure on lower-level managers or workers.

Summary and Management Solution

This chapter focused on organizational planning. Organizational planning involves defining goals and developing a plan with which to achieve them. An organization exists for a single, overriding purpose known as its *mission*—the basis for strategic goals and plans. Goals within the organization are defined in a hierarchical fashion, beginning with strategic goals followed by tactical and operational goals. Plans are defined similarly, with strategic, tactical, and operational plans used to achieve the goals. Other goal concepts include characteristics of effective goals and goal-setting behavior.

Several types of plans were described, including strategic, tactical, operational, single-use, standing, and contingency plans, as well as management by objectives. The Shewhart or PDCA Cycle is used by many companies that have instituted quality management. In the Shewhart Cycle, planning is continuous and everyone can learn and help the company improve. Long-term, intermediate-term, and short-term plans have time horizons of from five years down to six months.

In the past, planning almost always was done entirely by top managers, by consultants, or by central planning departments. More modern approaches are the decentralized planning staff or an interdepartmental task force composed of line managers. Today's learning organizations are pushing decentralization even farther and involving workers at all levels in the planning process. At Etec Systems, described in the chapter opening, all 800 employees are intimately involved in planning. Stephen Cooper, chairman and CEO, wants everyone to understand the mission and to understand how his or her work fits into the big picture. He sets stretch goals that prompt employees to reach for the stars. Each employee develops a personal list of goals and plans that correlate with those of the department and organization. Each person in the company, from shop-floor workers to the CEO, identifies five to seven key goals, creates metrics to track progress, and ranks each goal's importance relative to the others. However, Etec realizes that plans cannot be static. Each week, every employee meets briefly with a direct supervisor to review plans and work together on modifications. The end result of Etec's simple system is that every person in the organization knows what he or she should be doing, how important it is relative to other assignments, and how it relates to the goals of other employees. Etec's system thus enables the company's 800 employees to manage themselves. In a company moving as fast as Etec, says manager Phil Arnold, the system helps you to "keep your eye on the ball."[49]

Discussion Questions

1. What types of planning would have helped Exxon respond more quickly to the oil spill from the Exxon *Valdez* near Alaska?

2. Write a brief mission statement for a local business. Can the purpose and values of a small organization be captured in a written statement?

3. What strategies could the college or university at which you are taking this management course adopt to compete for students in the marketplace? Would these strategies depend on the school's goals?

4. If you were a top manager of a medium-sized real estate sales agency, would you use MBO? If so, give examples of goals you might set for managers and sales agents.

5. A new business venture has to develop a comprehensive business plan to borrow money to get started. Companies such as Federal Express, NIKE, and Rolm Corporation say they did not follow the original plan very closely. Does that mean that developing the plan was a waste of time for these eventually successful companies?

6. A famous management theorist proposed that the time horizons for all strategic plans are becoming shorter because of the rapid changes in organizations' external environments. Do you agree? Would the planning time horizon for IBM or Ford Motor Company be shorter than it was 20 years ago?

7. What are the characteristics of effective goals? Would it be better to have no goals at all than to have goals that do not meet these criteria?

8. What are the advantages and disadvantages of having a central planning department to do an organization's planning compared with having decentralized planning groups provide planning support to line managers?

9. Assume Southern University decides to (1) raise its admission standards and (2) initiate a business fair to which local townspeople will be invited. What types of plans would it use to carry out these two activities?

Management in Practice: Experiential Exercise

Company Crime Wave

Senior managers in your organization are concerned about internal theft. Your department has been assigned the task of writing an ethics policy that defines employee theft and prescribes penalties. Stealing goods is easily classified as theft, but other activities are more ambiguous. Before writing the policy, go through the following list and decide which behaviors should be defined as stealing and whether penalties should apply. Discuss the items with your department members until agreement is reached. Classify each item as an example of (1) theft, (2) acceptable behavior, or (3) in between with respect to written policy. Is it theft when an employee

- Gets paid for overtime not worked?
- Takes a longer lunch or coffee break than authorized?
- Punches a time card for another?

- Comes in late or leaves early?
- Fakes injury to receive workers' compensation?
- Takes care of personal business on company time?
- Occasionally uses company copying machines or makes long-distance telephone calls for personal purposes?
- Takes a few stamps, pens, or other supplies for personal use?
- Takes money from the petty cash drawer?
- Uses company vehicles or tools for own purposes but returns them?
- Damages merchandise so a cohort can purchase it at a discount?
- Accepts a gift from a supplier?

Now consider those items rated "in between." Do these items represent ethical issues as defined in Chapter 5? How should these items be handled in the company's written policy?

Management in Practice: Ethical Dilemma

Repair or Replace?

After only a few months in sales at ComputerSource, a full-service computer business, Sam Nolan realized there were seri-

ous problems in the software department. Most of the complaints from customers were related to the incorrect selection or installation of the software needed to meet their needs. He discussed the problem with his sales manager, who was part-owner and partner with the head of service for ComputerSource. They both were aware of the problem, but they were facing an industry-wide shortage of qualified software engineers.

Nolan received an urgent call from Katherine Perry, operations manager for Ross & Lindsey, a fast-growing financial management firm that was becoming one of his best accounts. She was calling to report that they were having daily network problems that were interfering with her staff's productivity and morale. She needed an immediate solution to the problem. Like many firms, Ross & Lindsey had a hodge-podge of computer equipment and software on their network. They had bought from a series of vendors, with a patchwork approach to problems.

Nolan realized it would take an expert software engineer days or weeks of work to fix all the bugs in their existing system, which ComputerSource could not afford. A costlier alternative was to recommend a system upgrade, replacing the older hardware and loading a newer software version on the entire net-

work. Perry had already confided that she had pushed her bosses as far as they wanted to go on computer expenditures this year, but Nolan knew she was desperate. He didn't want to risk losing her business, but he didn't trust the software engineers to fix the problems. He was also pretty sure Perry would face the same dilemma at any computer retailer in town.

What Do You Do?
1. Gamble on the service department to fix their existing system, within the limits of their budget and their frustration. If it doesn't work, it is their problem.
2. Recommend a system upgrade to correct the problem, even though it will cost the clients more than they want to pay and may jeopardize future sales.
3. Confide in the clients about your perception of the problem, give them the chance to make an informed choice, and risk having them take their business elsewhere.

Surf the Net

1. **Organizational Mission.** As stated in the text, one of the top three traits employees cited in *Fortune* magazine's study of the "100 Best Companies to Work for in America" was a sense of purpose that employees could believe in and relate to. Find three examples of mission statements that you can contribute during a class discussion of mission. If corporate missions are available at a company's Web site, you can usually find them under the "About" option. For example at TDIndustries' home page, click on "About TDIndustries." Listed below are companies that appeared in the top ten of the January 11, 1999, edition of *Fortune's* "100 Best Companies to Work for in America." You may prefer to find mission statements for other organizations in which you have an interest.
   www.tdindustries.com/ (TDIndustries-ranked #2)
   www.hp.com/abouthp/hpway.html (Hewlett-Packard—ranked #10)
   www.synovus.com/infocntr/philosophies.html (Synovus Financial—ranked #1)

2. **Schedules.** Managers must plan for their personal schedules, as well as oversee planning for their areas of responsibility. Among the personal scheduling tools available on the Internet are on-line calendars. Try one of the following such tools and write a review concerning its effectiveness and usefulness. Your review should include a brief description of how the on-line calendar works, its main features, and the advantages and disadvantages of using such a planning tool.
   www.when.com
   www.digital.daytimer.com
   www.anyday.com

3. **Shewhart Cycle.** Use a search engine to find information for a report on Walter A. Shewhart and the Shewhart Cycle. In your report, provide a brief biographical sketch of Shewhart as well as information to supplement what the text provides on his continuous improvement model. Two possible sites are listed below:
   www.miep.org/mqc/news/otm/march_96/toolbox.html
   www.asqc.org/about/history/shewhart.html

Case for Critical Analysis

H.I.D.

Dave Collins, president of H.I.D., sat down at the conference table with his management team members, Karen Setz, Tony Briggs, Dave King, and Art Johnson. H.I.D. owns ten Holiday Inns in

Georgia, eight hotels of different types in Canada, and one property in the Caribbean. It also owns two Quality Inns in Georgia. Dave Collins and his managers got together to define their mission and goals and to set strategic plans. As they began their strategic planning session, the consultant they had hired suggested that each describe what he or she wanted for the company's domestic operations in the next ten years—how many hotels it should own, where to locate them, and who the target market was. Another question he asked them to consider was what the driving force of the company should be—that is, the single characteristic that would separate H.I.D. from other companies.

The team members wrote their answers on flip-charts, and the consultant summarized the results. Dave Collins's goal included 50 hotels in ten years, with the number increasing to 26 or 27 in five years. All the other members saw no more than 20 hotels in ten years and a maximum of 15 or 16 within five years. Clearly there was disagreement among the top managers about long-term goals and the desirable growth rate.

With the consultant's direction, the team members began to critique their growth targets. Dave King, director of operations and development, observed, "We just can't build that many hotels in that time period, certainly not given our current staffing, or any reasonable staffing we could afford. I don't see how we could achieve that goal." Art Johnson, the accountant, agreed. Karen Setz then asked, "Could we build them all in Georgia? You know we've centered on the medium-priced hotel in smaller towns. Do we need to move to bigger towns now, such as Jacksonville, or add another to the one we have in Atlanta?" Dave Collins responded, "We have an opportunity out in California, we may have one in New Jersey, and we are looking at the possibility of going to Jacksonville."

The consultant attempted to refocus the discussion: "Well, how does this all fit with your mission? Where are you willing to locate geographically? Most of your operation is in Georgia. Can you adequately support a national building effort?"

Tony Briggs responded, "Well, you know we have always looked at the smaller-town hotels as being our niche, although we deviated from that for the hotel in Atlanta. But we generally stay in smaller towns where we don't have much competition. Now we are talking about an expensive hotel in California."

Dave Collins suggested, "Maybe it's time we changed our target market, changed our pricing strategy, and went for larger hotels in urban areas across the whole country. Maybe we need to change a lot of factors about our company."

Questions

1. What is H.I.D.'s mission at present? How may this mission change?
2. What do you think H.I.D.'s mission, strategic goals, and strategic plans are likely to be at the end of this planning session? Why?
3. What goal-setting behavior is being used here to reach agreement among H.I.D.'s managers? Do managers typically disagree about the direction of their organization?

SOURCE: This case was provided by James Higgins.

Endnotes

1. Eric Matson, "The Discipline of High-Tech Leaders," *Fast Company,* April–May 1997, 34–36.
2. Russell L. Ackoff, "On the Use of Models in Corporate Planning," *Strategic Management Journal* 2 (1981), 353–359; and Oren Harari, "Good/Bad News about Strategy," *Management Review,* July 1995, 29–31.
3. Amitai Etzioni, *Modern Organizations* (Englewood Cliffs, N.J.: Prentice-Hall, 1984), 6.
4. David Woodruff, "Is VW Revving Too High?" *Business Week,* March 30, 1998, 48–49; and Ronald B. Lieber, "Flying High, Going Global," *Fortune,* July 7, 1997, 195–197.
5. Max D. Richards, *Setting Strategic Goals and Objectives,* 2d ed. (St. Paul, Minn.: West, 1986).
6. C. Chet Miller and Laura B. Cardinal, "Strategic Planning and Firm Performance: A Synthesis of More than Two Decades of Research," *Academy of Management Journal* 37, no. 6 (1994), 1649–1685.
7. This discussion is based on Richard L. Daft and Richard M. Steers, *Organizations: A Micro/Macro Approach* (Glenview, Ill.: Scott, Foresman, 1986), 319–321; Herbert A. Simon, "On the Concept of Organizational Goals," *Administrative Science Quarterly* 9 (1964), 1–22; and Charles B. Saunders and Francis D. Tuggel, "Corporate Goals," *Journal of General Management* 5 (1980), 3–13.
8. Ronald B. Lieber, "Why Employees Love These Companies," *Fortune,* January 12, 1998, 72–74.
9. Steven L. Marks, "Say When," *Inc.,* February 1995, 19–20.
10. David Pearson, "Breaking Away," *CIO,* Section 1, May 1, 1998, 34–46.
11. Joseph Weber, "Du Pont's Trailblazer Wants to Get Out of the Woods," *Business Week,* August 31, 1992, 70–71.
12. Frank Rose, "Now Quality Means Service Too," *Fortune,* April 22, 1991, 99–108.
13. Mary Klemm, Stuart Sanderson, and George Luffman, "Mission Statements: Selling Corporate Values to Employees," *Long-Range Planning* 24, no. 3 (1991), 73–78; John A. Pearce II and Fred David, "Corporate Mission Statements: The Bottom Line," *Academy of Management Executive* (1987), 109–116; Jerome H. Want, "Corporate Mission: The Intangible Contributor to Performance," *Management Review* (August 1986), 46–50; and Alan Farnham, "Brushing Up Your Vision Thing," *Fortune,* May 1, 1995, 129.
14. Miriam Schulman, "Winery with a Mission," *Issues in Ethics,* Spring 1996, 14–15.

15. Sharon Nelton, "Put Your Purpose in Writing," *Nation's Business*, February 1994, 61–64.

16. Peter F. Drucker, *The Practice of Management* (New York: Harper & Brothers, 1954), 65–83; and Peter Doyle, "Setting Business Objectives and Measuring Performance," *Journal of General Management* 20, no. 2 (winter 1994), 1–19.

17. "Strategic Planning: Part 2," *Small Business Report* (March 1983), 28–32.

18. Paul Meising and Joseph Wolfe, "The Art and Science of Planning at the Business Unit Level," *Management Science* 31 (1985), 773–781.

19. Kenneth Labich, "Making Over Middle Managers," *Fortune*, May 8, 1989, 58–64.

20. Mark Fischetti, "Team Doctors, Report to ER!" *Fast Company*, February/March 1998, 170–177.

21. Gina Imperato, "Dirty Business, Bright Ideas," *Fast Company*, February/March, 1997, 89–93.

22. John O. Alexander, "Toward Real Performance: The Circuit-Breaker Technique," *Supervisory Management* (April 1989), 5–12.

23. Cathy Lazere, "All Together Now," *CFO*, February 1998, 29–36.

24. Joy Riggs, "Empowering Workers by Setting Goals," *Nation's Business*, January 1995, 6.

25. A. J. Vogl, "Noble Survivors," *Across the Board*, June 1994, 25–30; and Rahul Jacob, "Corporate Reputations," *Fortune*, March 6, 1995, 54–67.

26. Edwin A. Locke, Garp P. Latham, and Miriam Erez, "The Determinants of Goal Commitment," *Academy of Management Review* 13 (1988), 23–39.

27. George S. Odiorne, "MBO: A Backward Glance," *Business Horizons* 21 (October 1978), 14–24.

28. Jan P. Muczyk and Bernard C. Reimann, "MBO as a Complement to Effective Leadership," *The Academy of Management Executive* 3 (1989), 131–138; and W. Giegold, *Objective Setting and the MBO Process*, vol. 2 (New York: McGraw-Hill, 1978).

29. "Delegation," *Small Business Reports* (July 1986), 71–75; and R. Henry Migliore, Constance A. Pogue, and Jeffrey S. Horvath, "Planning for the Future," *Small Business Reports* (July 1991), 53–63.

30. John Ivancevich, J. Timothy McMahon, J. William Streidl, and Andrew D. Szilagyi, "Goal Setting: The Tenneco Approach to Personnel Development and Management Effectiveness," *Organizational Dynamics* (winter 1978), 48–80.

31. Richard A. Luecke, *Scuttle Your Ships before Advancing* (New York: Oxford University Press, 1994), 64–68; Thomas F. Rienzo, "Planning Deming Management for Service Organizations," *Business Horizons* 36, no. 3 (May–June 1993), 19–29; and Gregory M. Bounds, Gregory H. Dobbins, and Oscar S. Fowler, *Management: A Total Quality Perspective* (Cincinnati: South-Western College Publishing, 1995), 219–220.

32. Thomas E. Ricks, "Army Devises System to Decide What Does, and Does Not, Work," *The Wall Street Journal*, May 23, 1997, A1, A10.

33. "Corporate Planning: Drafting a Blueprint for Success," *Small Business Report* (August 1987), 40–44.

34. Paul J. H. Schoemaker, "Scenario Planning: A Tool for Strategic Thinking," *Sloan Management Review* (winter 1995), 25–40; Christopher Knowlton, "Shell Gets Rich by Beating Risk," *Fortune*, August 21, 1991, 79–82; and Arie P. de Geus, "Planning as Learning," *Harvard Business Review* (March–April 1988), 70–74.

35. Peter Doyle, "Setting Business Objectives and Measuring Performance," *Journal of General Management* 20, no. 2 (winter 1994), 1–19.

36. Anne B. Fisher, "Is Long-Range Planning Worth It?" *Fortune*, April 23, 1990, 281–284.

37. Andrew Tanzer, "We Do Not Take a Short-Term View," *Forbes*, July 13, 1987, 372–374.

38. "Preparing for the Unexpected," *Columbia Today* (winter 1985/86), 2–4.

39. "The New Breed of Strategic Planner," *Business Week*, September 17, 1984, 62–68.

40. Patrick Kelly, "Forget Policy Manuals," *Inc.*, April 1998, 37–38.

41. Brian O'Reilly, "J&J Is on a Roll," *Fortune*, December 26, 1994, 178–191.

42. Daniel H. Gray, "Uses and Misuses of Strategic Planning," *Harvard Business Review* 64 (January–February 1986), 89–97.

43. Harari, "Good News/Bad News about Strategy."

44. Gerald E. Ledford, Jr., Jon R. Wendenhof, and James T. Strahley, "Realizing a Corporate Philosophy," *Organizational Dynamics* (winter 1995), 5–18.

45. James C. Collins, "Building Companies to Last," *The State of Small Business*, 1995, 83–86; James C. Collins and Jerry I. Porras, "Building a Visionary Company," *California Management Review* 37, no. 2 (winter 1995), 80–100; James C. Collins and Jerry I. Porras, "The Ultimate Vision," *Across the Board*, January 1995, 19–23; and O'Reilly, "J&J Is on a Roll."

46. See Kenneth R. Thompson, Wayne A. Hockwarter, and Nicholas J. Mathys, "Stretch Targets: What Makes Them Effective?" *Academy of Management Executive* 11, no. 3 (August 1997), 48.

47. Edward O. Welles, "Bootstrapping for Billions," *Inc.*, September 1994, 78–83; also see Kenneth F. Iverson with Tom Varian, *Plain Talk: Lessons from a Business Maverick*, (John Wiley & Sons, 1997).

48. Henry Mintzberg, "The Fall and Rise of Strategic Planning," *Harvard Business Review*, January–February, 1994, 107–114.

49. Eric Matson, "The Discipline of High-Tech Leaders."

Chapter 8

LEARNING OBJECTIVES

After studying this chapter, you should be able to

- Define the components of strategic management.

- Describe the strategic planning process and SWOT analysis.

- Understand Grand Strategies for domestic and international operations.

- Define corporate-level strategies and explain the portfolio approach.

- Describe business-level strategies, including Porter's competitive forces and strategies and cooperative strategies.

- Explain the major considerations in formulating functional strategies.

- Enumerate the organizational dimensions used for implementing strategy.

Strategy Formulation and Implementation

MANAGEMENT PROBLEM

Blessed with a powerhouse brand name, Kodak was rich, proud, and much admired by consumers. But things haven't been so bright at Kodak lately. Earnings have dropped, the stock took a nosedive, and the company announced its eighth round of layoffs since the mid-1980s. Meanwhile, Kodak's biggest competitor, Japan's Fuji Photo Film Co., is gradually gaining market share, and its stock price has been on a rapid climb. Fuji is already on the brink of overtaking Kodak on a global basis, particularly in Asia, where film sales are growing at about 20 percent a year. Moreover, the Japanese company is creeping up on Kodak's U.S. market at a rate of about 2 percent a year. For the first time in its 118-year history, Kodak can no longer take its home market for granted. In addition to film sales, the two companies are competing in film processing, the manufacture of photographic paper for sale to big photo-processing labs and small retail developers, and digital photography—areas in which Fuji also is gaining an edge. Fuji's current slogan, "You can see the future from here," plays on the desire to differentiate the company from Kodak's nostalgic approach. For Kodak, the future isn't looking too rosy. As one analyst said, if current trends hold, "Kodak will go from being Coke to being Pepsi. That's a very damning thing."[1] The growing strength of Fuji coupled with the problems at Kodak can be attributed to corporate strategy.

How did Fuji CEO Minoru Ohnishi and his managers formulate and implement strategies that have led to the company's current position of strength? If you were George Fisher at Kodak, what strategies might you adopt to regain the competitive edge?

The story of Fuji and Kodak illustrates the importance of strategic planning. When CEO George Fisher took over at Kodak in late 1993, he recognized that the ailing company needed a strategy overhaul. Although conditions have greatly improved for Kodak since that time, the company seems to be out of touch with customers and struggling still to develop a strategic direction for the future. Meanwhile, Fuji's managers have formulated and implemented strategies that have led to significant growth and increased market share for the Japanese company.

Every organization is concerned with strategy. Hershey developed a new strategy of being a fierce product innovator to compete with Mars in the candy wars. Hershey has scored big with the introduction of such products as Hugs, a white-chocolate version of the Hershey's Kiss, and NutRageous, a candy bar.[2] Strategic blunders can hurt a company. Sears suffered in the 1980s by losing sight of what business it was in and what customers it wanted to serve. When Alfred C. Martinez became CEO, he disposed of nonretail assets, closed the catalog division, renovated dowdy stores, upgraded women's apparel, and launched a new, forward-thinking ad campaign. His strategy led to a major turnaround at the department store giant. Now, Sears is positioning itself for growth, particularly through opening a chain of freestanding hardware stores. At Chelsea Milling Co., best known for its pocket-sized, blue-and-white boxes of Jiffy Cake mix, former race-car driver Howard "Howdy" Holmes is leading a total strategic overhaul to help the stagnating family firm compete against giant consumer products companies such as Procter & Gamble, General Mills, and Pillsbury. He's modernizing the factory, revising internal procedures, and expanding the product line to include fruit-flavored muffin mixes, "just-add-water" buttermilk pancake mix, and six-packs of mixes designed to get Jiffy into warehouse clubs such as Sam's.[3]

Both Sears and the Chelsea Milling Co. are involved in strategic management. They are finding ways to respond to competitors, cope with difficult environmental changes, meet changing customer needs, and effectively use available resources. Research has shown that strategic thinking and planning positively affects a firm's performance and financial success.[4] Strategic planning has taken on new importance in today's world of globalization, deregulation, advancing technology, and changing demographics and lifestyles. Managers are responsible for positioning their organizations for success in a world that is constantly changing. Today's top companies thrive by changing the rules of an industry to their advantage or by creating entirely new industries.[5] For example, Champion Enterprises was going broke selling inexpensive factory-built houses. CEO Walter Young Jr. says, "People thought we were in the trailer park business. It was a real perception problem." Young wanted to redraw the rules of the manufactured housing industry. Today, Champion is thriving by building full-size houses in its factories and offering customers such options as porches, skylights, and whirlpool baths.[6]

In this chapter, we focus on the topic of strategic management. First we define components of strategic management and then discuss a model of the strategic management process. Next we examine several models of strategy formulation. Finally, we discuss the tools managers use to implement their strategic plans.

Thinking Strategically

Chapter 7 provided an overview of the types of goals and plans that organizations use. In this chapter, we will explore strategic management, which is considered one specific type of planning. Strategic planning in for-profit business organizations typically pertains to competitive actions in the marketplace. In not-for-profit organizations such as the Red Cross, strategic planning pertains to events in the external environment. Although some companies hire strategic planning experts, the final responsibility for strategic planning rests with line managers. Senior executives at such companies as General Electric, 3M, and Johnson & Johnson want middle- and low-level managers to think strategically. Some companies also are finding ways to get front-line workers involved in strategic thinking and planning. Strategic thinking means to take the long-term view and to see the big picture, including the organization and the competitive environment, and to consider how they fit together. Understanding the strategy concept, the levels of strategy, and strategy formulation versus implementation is an important start toward strategic thinking.

What is Strategic Management?

Strategic management is the set of decisions and actions used to formulate and implement strategies that will provide a competitively superior fit between the organization and its environment so as to achieve organizational goals.[7] Managers ask questions such as "What changes and trends are occurring in the competitive environment? Who are our customers? What products or services should we offer? How can we offer those products and services most efficiently?" Answers to these questions help managers make choices about how to position their organization in the environment with respect to rival companies.[8] Superior organizational performance is not a matter of luck. It is determined by the choices managers make. Top executives use strategic management to define an overall direction for the organization, which is the firm's grand strategy.

Grand Strategy

Grand strategy is the general plan of major action by which a firm intends to achieve its long-term goals.[9] Grand strategies fall into three general categories: growth, stability, and retrenchment. A separate grand strategy can also be defined for global operations.

Growth. *Growth* can be promoted internally by investing in expansion or externally by acquiring additional business divisions. Internal growth can include development of new or changed products, such as Goodyear's development of the Aquatred tire, or expansion of current products into new markets, such as Coors's expansion into the Northeast. External growth typically involves *diversification,* which means the acquisition of businesses that are related to current product lines or that take the corporation into new areas. The number of companies choosing to grow through mergers and acquisitions is astounding, as organizations strive to acquire the size and resources

Every organization must think strategically and the restaurant industry is no exception. ". . . if we aren't seen trying to keep one step ahead, then we'll just end up in the wilderness," states Philip Britten, chef and restauranteur. Britten's restaurant, The Capital, is located in one of London's original small, independent hotels, just around the corner from Harrods. Over the years, Britten's strategic management has caused his menu to go through various stages, from classic French haute cuisine to his current passion for spices that bring a range of nuances to dishes such as scalded lobster with sage pasta.

strategic management
The set of decisions and actions used to formulate and implement strategies that will provide a competitively superior fit between the organization and its environment so as to achieve organizational goals.

grand strategy
The general plan of major action by which an organization intends to achieve its long-term goals.

to compete on a global scale, to invest in new technology, and to control distribution channels and guarantee access to markets. WorldCom (formerly LDDS), once an obscure long-distance carrier, has acquired more than 40 companies in the past decade and expanded into local phone services, data transmission, and Internet traffic. Now WorldCom has forged a deal to buy MCI. Another strategy for international growth is the formation of a joint venture, such as WorldCom's venture with Spanish telecom giant Telefónica, which will extend WorldCom's reach into South America.[10] Consider how a small Montreal-based company with only one major product used diversification to become a global powerhouse.

BOMBARDIER
www.bombardier.com

When CEO Laurent Beaudoin took the reins of Bombardier in 1966 at the age of 27, the company's annual sales of the Ski-Doo snowmobile totaled some $15 million. Today, sales of snowmobiles top $400 million. But Bombardier also is a global force in three industries: aerospace, transportation, and consumer products. Beaudoin turned Bombardier into a premier worldwide manufacturer of transportation equipment by pursuing a strategy of acquiring a string of nearly bankrupt companies and melding them into a competitive whole. Bombardier still makes Ski-Doo snowmobiles, along with Sea-Doo personal watercraft, but today these products account for only 17 percent of sales.

Bombardier's frantic diversification began in 1973, when the energy crisis wiped out all but 4 of the 100 snowmobile manufacturers. Beaudoin's first key deal was a contract to make subway cars for Montreal. Today, Bombardier is building 680 highly automated subway cars for New York City for nearly $1 billion, as well as Amtrak's first high-speed trains, which will carry passengers from Boston to Washington at 150 miles per hour.

Beaudoin's next strategic push was into aerospace. Government-owned Canadair was drowning in debt and had only one viable product, a large business jet. Beaudoin admits "we knew nothing about aerospace," but he knew his company's manufacturing know-how was among the best in the world, and he saw a chance to move into two niches in which his company could excel—business jets and regional aircraft. After acquiring Canadair, Beaudoin snatched up three other ailing plane makers to round out the product line: Boeing's de Havilland unit, business-jet pioneer Lear-jet, and Short Brothers, Northern Ireland's biggest employer.

With 43 percent of sales coming from the United States and Mexico, 41 percent from Europe, 10 percent from Canada, and 6 percent from Asia and the rest of the world, Montreal's Bombardier is one of today's most thoroughly international companies. Although Bombardier has experienced some recent setbacks, many investors believe Beaudoin's continued pursuit of a growth strategy will pull the company out of its stall. To fuel new growth, Beaudoin is counting on a host of new products, including the Global Express, a top-of-the-line executive jet to rival Gulfstream; the electric-powered Neighborhood Vehicle, a souped-up golf cart targeted at gated or retirement communities; and an unmanned hovering aircraft designed to detect buried land mines.[11]

Stability.   *Stability*, sometimes called a *pause strategy*, means that the organization wants to remain the same size or grow slowly and in a controlled fashion. The corporation wants to stay in its current business, such as Allied Tire Stores, whose motto is "We just sell tires." After organizations have undergone a turbulent period of rapid growth, executives often focus on a stability strategy to integrate strategic business units and ensure that the organization is working efficiently.

Retrenchment.   *Retrenchment* means that the organization goes through a period of forced decline by either shrinking current business units or selling off or liquidating entire businesses. The organization may have experienced a precipitous drop in demand for its products or services, prompting managers to order across-the-board cuts in personnel and expenditures. For example, in an effort to pull Continental out of a long stall, CEO Gordon M. Bethune cut nearly 5,000 jobs, grounded 41 planes, slashed capacity by 9 percent, and deferred delivery of new planes.[12] *Liquidation* means selling off a business unit for the cash value of the assets, thus terminating its existence. An example is the liquidation of Minnie Pearl Fried Chicken. *Divestiture* involves the selling off of businesses that no longer seem central to the corporation. After years of frenzied deal making in the entertainment business, giants such as Viacom, Time Warner, and the Walt Disney Company are considering divesting some of their unrelated businesses. Disney has announced it will shed some of the publishing assets acquired in its $19 billion purchase of Capital Cities/ABC, and Viacom recently sold Simon & Schuster. Studies show that between 33 percent and 50 percent of all acquisitions are later divested. When Figgies International Inc. sold 15 of its 22 business divisions, including crown jewel Rawlings Sporting Goods, and when Sears sold its financial services businesses, both corporations were going through periods of retrenchment, also called *downsizing.*[13]

Global Strategy

In addition to the three preceding alternatives—growth, stability, and retrenchment—companies may pursue a separate grand strategy as the focus of global business. In today's global corporations, senior executives try to formulate coherent strategies to provide synergy among worldwide operations for the purpose of fulfilling common goals. A systematic strategic planning process for deciding on the appropriate strategic alternative should be used. The grand strategy of growth is a major motivation for both small and large businesses going international. Each country or region represents a new market with the promise of increased sales and profits.

In the international arena, companies face a strategic dilemma between global integration and national responsiveness. Organizations must decide whether they want each global affiliate to act autonomously or whether activities should be standardized and centralized across countries. This choice leads managers to select a basic grand strategy alternative such as globalization versus multidomestic strategy. Some corporations may seek to achieve both global integration and national responsiveness by using a transnational strategy. The three global strategies are shown in Exhibit 8.1.

Globalization.   When an organization chooses a strategy of **globalization,** it means that its product design and advertising strategies are standardized throughout the world.[14] This approach is based on the assumption that a single global market exists for most consumer and industrial products. The

globalization
The standardization of product design and advertising strategies throughout the world.

Exhibit
8.1
Global Corporate Strategies

SOURCE: Michael A. Hitt, R. Duane Ireland, and
Robert E. Hoskisson, *Strategic Management: Com-
petitiveness and Globalization* (St. Paul, Minn.:
West, 1995), 239.

theory is that people everywhere want to buy the same products and live
the same way. People everywhere want to drink Coca-Cola and wear Levi
blue jeans.[15] For example, the dropping of European customs barriers in
1992 helped make Europe one unified market for standardized manufacturing, packaging, and ads. After acquiring the appliance business of Dutch
consumer-goods giant Philips Electronics, Whirlpool built a coordinated
Europewide organization and shifted manufacturing to common "platforms"
that have European and U.S. appliances sharing technology, design, and suppliers. Using standardized designs and products saves millions of dollars
compared to designing unique models for each country or region.[16]

Globalization enables marketing departments alone to save millions of dollars. For example, Colgate-Palmolive Company sells Colgate toothpaste in
more than 40 countries. For every country where the same commercial runs,
it saves $1 million to $2 million in production costs alone. More millions
have been saved by standardizing the look and packaging of brands.[17]

multidomestic strategy
The modification of product design and
advertising strategies to suit the specific
needs of individual countries.

Multidomestic Strategy.   When an organization chooses a **multidomestic
strategy,** it means that competition in each country is handled independently
of industry competition in other countries. Thus, a multinational company
is present in many countries, but it encourages marketing, advertising, and
product design to be modified and adapted to the specific needs of each country.[18] Many companies reject the idea of a single global market. They have
found that the French do not drink orange juice for breakfast, that laundry
detergent is used to wash dishes in parts of Mexico, and that people in the
Middle East prefer toothpaste that tastes spicy. Parker Pen launched a single

These KitKat candy bars, being stocked by a salesman in a Malaysian shop, are manufactured with locally grown beans—at a price 30 percent below imports. Nestlé, the world's biggest branded food company, rejects the idea of a single global market, opting for a multidomestic strategy that handles competition in each country independently. The Switzerland-based powerhouse is charging across the developing world by hiring people in the region, manipulating ingredients or technology for local conditions, and slapping on one of the company's 8,000 brand names. Of those 8,000 worldwide brands, only 750 are registered in more than one country.

international ad campaign and reduced pen styles from 500 to 100, causing a strategic disaster. New pens and advertising campaigns have now been developed for each market.[19] Du Pont produces customized herbicides for problems with weeds that are unique to countries such as Brazil and Japan. Avon found that its door-to-door sales strategy would not work in Japan and thus customized a soft-sell approach.[20]

Transnational Strategy.   A **transnational strategy** seeks to achieve both global integration and national responsiveness.[21] A true transnational strategy is difficult to achieve, because one goal requires close global coordination while the other goal requires local flexibility. However, many industries are finding that, although increased competition means they must achieve global efficiency, growing pressure to meet local needs demands national responsiveness. One company that is striving to use a transnational strategy to increase its global presence is Citicorp. Citicorp's expansion plans involve constructing a multimillion-dollar global communications network to serve worldwide client investment needs. At the same time, Citicorp is exploring ways to provide detailed, in-depth investment coverage in the growing number of countries in which offices are located.[22] Now Citicorp is merging with Travelers Group to create a megabank that can take advantage of global coordination while distributing a wide variety of financial services products tailored to local tastes. Caterpillar Tractor achieves global efficiencies by designing its products to use many identical components and centralizing manufacturing of components in a few large-scale facilities. However, assembly plants located in each of Caterpillar's major markets add certain product features tailored to meet local needs.[23]

Although most multinational companies want to achieve some degree of global integration to hold costs down, even global products may require some customization to meet government regulations in various countries or some tailoring to fit consumer preferences. In addition, some products are better suited for standardization than others. Most large multinational corporations with diverse products will attempt to use a partial multidomestic strategy for some product lines and global strategies for others.

transnational strategy
A strategy that combines global coordination to attain efficiency with flexibility to meet specific needs in various countries.

Purpose of Strategy

strategy
The plan of action that prescribes resource allocation and other activities for dealing with the environment and helping the organization attain its goals.

Within the overall grand strategy of an organization, executives define an explicit **strategy,** which is the plan of action that describes resource allocation and activities for dealing with the environment and attaining the organization's goals. The essence of strategy is choosing to perform different activities or to execute activities differently than competitors do.[24] For example, Dell Computer succeeded by bypassing the middleman and selling computers directly to the consumer. Today, Dell is finding that electronic commerce is a natural extension of its direct sales approach, as described in the Technology box. Strategy necessarily changes over time to fit environmental conditions, but to remain competitive, companies develop strategies that focus on core competencies, develop synergy, and create value for customers.

core competence
A business activity that an organization does particularly well in comparison to competitors.

Core Competence.   A company's **core competence** is something the organization does especially well in comparison to its competitors. A core competence represents a competitive advantage because the company acquires expertise that competitors do not have. A core competence may be in the area of superior research and development, mastery of a technology, manufacturing efficiency, or customer service.[25] For example, James River Corporation invested in state-of-the-art automation that has given it a core competence of being able to produce paper towels and tissues more cheaply than Scott Paper Company and Procter & Gamble.[26] Wal-Mart has developed core competencies in excellent service to customers and suppliers and streamlined distribution systems that help the company maintain low prices and make the right products available when customers need them. Amgen, a pharmaceuticals company with a 68 percent average annual return over the past decade, succeeds with a core competence of high-quality scientific research. Unlike most drug companies, which start with a disease and work backward, Amgen starts with brilliant science and then finds unique uses for it. For example, the recent discovery of a gene that may hold the key to fighting obesity is the kind of science that could really pay off.[27]

synergy
The condition that exists when the organization's parts interact to produce a joint effect that is greater than the sum of the parts acting alone.

Synergy.   When organizational parts interact to produce a joint effect that is greater than the sum of the parts acting alone, **synergy** occurs. The organization may attain a special advantage with respect to cost, market power, technology, or management skill. When properly managed, synergy can create additional value with existing resources, providing a big boost to the bottom line. Rupert Murdoch's News Corp., for example, is trying to develop synergy between publishing and the movie/television business. News Corp.'s HarperCollins found renewed life after years of losses by bringing out books tied to corporate sibling 20th Century Fox's blockbuster, *Titanic*. There also are books in the works linked to *The Simpsons, Ally McBeal, King of the Hill,* and *The X-Files* movie.[28] Synergy also can be obtained by good relations between suppliers and customers and by strong alliances among companies. Erie Bolt, a small Erie, Pennsylvania, company, teamed up with 14 other area companies to give itself more muscle in tackling competitive markets. Team members share equipment, customer lists, and other information that enables these small companies to go after more business than they ever could have without the team approach.[29] Hammond Enterprises, a seven-employee firm

Dell Computer

For years, Michael Dell has put up with skeptics predicting that direct sales of PCs would never capture more than 15 percent of the market. Today, direct buyers make up a third of the market, and the percentage is growing. Suddenly, everyone wants to be in Dell's position.

Now, the company that invented direct selling of PCs is taking the concept a step further. Dell has become an Internet phenomenon, selling $1 million worth of computers a day on its Web site, and electronic sales are growing 20 percent a month. Dell is making buying over the Internet even more attractive by customizing Web pages for its biggest buyers, including Eastman Chemical, Monsanto, and Wells Fargo, and by developing a new feature that can dash off a digital configuration to customers within five minutes of placing an order. Taking advantage of the Internet is just one more way for Dell to get more bang for its buck—in contrast to the 700 sales reps needed to take orders over the phone, Dell has only 30 people managing Web sales.

Dell's simple secret for turning a classically low-margin mail-order operation into a high-profit business is *speed*. A custom order placed with Dell at 9 A.M. on Monday can be on a delivery truck by 9 P.M. on Tuesday. The company has spent years developing a core competence in speedy delivery by squeezing time lags and inefficiencies out of the manufacturing and assembly process. Now Dell has applied the same brutal standards to the supply chain. Good relationships with key suppliers and precise coordination mean that sometimes Dell can receive parts in fifteen minutes that could take two days to reach IBM or Gateway. Dell also achieves synergy by turning to logistics specialists, such as Caliber Logistics, Inc., to manage supply chains. Speed has enabled Dell to slash inventories and parts costs so low that it can underprice rivals by 10 to 15 percent. Combine all that with electronic sales—the ultimate in low-cost, fast-paced business—and Dell is tough to beat. Now Michael Dell is looking for the next breakthrough. Dell is moving gradually into the $10 billion network server business, exploring ways to combine its PC knowledge with better networking service.

Competitors, having watched as more and more customers turned to Dell, are trying to imitate the company's way of doing business. "In the ideal world," said a Hewlett-Packard marketer, "your customer wants to buy a PC, you source all the parts that day, ship it that day, and get it to the customer that day. . . . Michael Dell is probably as close to that as anybody."

www.dell.com

Sources: Gary McWilliams, "Whirlwind on the Web," *Business Week*, April 7, 1997, 132–136; and David Kirkpatrick, "Now Everybody in PCs Wants to Be Like Mike," *Fortune*, September 8, 1997, 91–92.

in Marietta, Georgia, designs and produces promotional caps, mugs, and T-shirts for major corporations such as Coca-Cola and Lockheed Martin. Synergy develops because Hammond relieves the corporate giants of the hassle of research, paperwork, and design of logo-bearing promotional items, enabling the corporations to obtain the items at less cost than if they produced the items themselves.[30]

Value Creation. Exploiting core competencies and attaining synergy help companies create value for their customers. Value can be defined as the combination of benefits received and costs paid by the customer.[31] A product that is low in cost but does not provide benefits is not a good value. For example, People Express Airlines initially made a splash with ultra-low prices, but travelers couldn't tolerate the airline's consistently late takeoffs at any price.[32] Delivering value to the customer should be at the heart of strategy. Managers need to understand which parts of the company's operation create value and which do not—a company can be profitable only when the value it creates is greater than the cost of resources. When a company does not accurately appraise its value-creating potential, it may become complacent. McDonald's made a thorough study of how to use its core competencies to create better value for customers, resulting in the introduction of "Extra Value Meals" and the decision to open restaurants in different locations, such as inside Wal-Mart and Sears stores.[33]

Levels of Strategy

Another aspect of strategic management concerns the organizational level to which strategic issues apply. Strategic managers normally think in terms of three levels of strategy—corporate, business, and functional—as illustrated in Exhibit 8.2.[34]

Corporate-Level Strategy.   The question *What business are we in?* concerns **corporate-level strategy.** Corporate-level strategy pertains to the organization as a whole and the combination of business units and product lines that make up the corporate entity. Strategic actions at this level usually relate to the acquisition of new businesses; additions or divestments of business units, plants, or product lines; and joint ventures with other corporations in new areas. An example of corporate-level strategy was when the Netherlands-based Philips Electronics sold more than 20 business units, ranging from cable operations to car navigation systems, in order to focus on the core businesses of consumer electronics and semiconductors. Selling off other business units was part of new chairman and president Cor Boonstra's strategy to cut costs, refocus the company, and engineer a turnaround at Europe's largest consumer electronics manufacturer.[35] Using the opposite corporate-level strategy, Bausch & Lomb purchased Miracle Ear (a manufacturer of hearing aids), the maker of the Interplak electric toothbrush, and an array of companies that make implants for dentists, plus started its own lotion and cream business. This strategy redefined Bausch & Lomb from a maker of contact lenses and Ray-Bans to a company serving customer needs for every organ above the neck.[36]

Business-Level Strategy.   The question *How do we compete?* concerns **business-level strategy.** Business-level strategy pertains to each business unit or product line. It focuses on how the business unit competes within its

corporate-level strategy
The level of strategy concerned with the question "What business are we in?" Pertains to the organization as a whole and the combination of business units and product lines that make it up.

business-level strategy
The level of strategy concerned with the question "How do we compete?" Pertains to each business unit or product line within the organization.

Exhibit 8.2   *Three Levels of Strategy in Organizations*

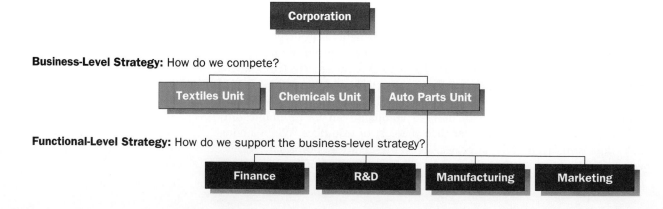

Corporate-Level Strategy: What business are we in?

Corporation

Business-Level Strategy: How do we compete?

Textiles Unit   Chemicals Unit   Auto Parts Unit

Functional-Level Strategy: How do we support the business-level strategy?

Finance   R&D   Manufacturing   Marketing

Merck has a business-level strategy of competing through product innovation. Merck researchers like Amy Cheung and Thomas Rano, using advanced technology, are producing more new compounds in less time than has ever been possible. Merck spends nearly $1.3 billion on research and development and uses every means possible to reduce by months the drug discovery, development, and application processes. Merck maintains a competitive edge by having innovative products in many therapeutic categories for human and animal health.

industry for customers. Strategic decisions at the business level concern amount of advertising, direction and extent of research and development, product changes, new-product development, equipment and facilities, and expansion or contraction of product lines. For example, CEO G. Craig Sullivan has sparked amazing new growth at Clorox with simple product changes and advertising campaigns that make old brands seem new again. Making the household cleaner Pine-Sol smell like lemon and masking the odor of chlorine in Clorox bleach has made sales of these products take off. Sara Lee Corp., in turn, has doubled its advertising budget as part of a business-level strategy to make the brand Sara Lee as pervasive as Coca-Cola. Sears Canada Inc., competing against the recently arrived Wal-Mart, is spending millions to renovate run-down stores, adding big name brands such as Estée Lauder and Liz Claiborne, and upgrading customer service.[37]

Functional-Level Strategy. The question *How do we support the business-level competitive strategy?* concerns **functional-level strategy.** It pertains to the major functional departments within the business unit. Functional strategies involve all of the major functions, including finance, research and development, marketing, and manufacturing. The functional strategy for Sears Canada's marketing department is to target female customers with its new "softer side," a strategy that has been successful for Sears in the United States. At Sherwin-Williams, the marketing department developed advertising aimed

functional-level strategy
The level of strategy concerned with the question "How do we support the business-level strategy?" Pertains to all of the organization's major departments.

at specific markets for its paint. For example, its Dutch Boy paint, touted as "the look that gets the looks," is advertised to do-it-yourselfers who shop the discount chains. The "Ask Sherwin-Williams" advertisements target the professional line of paints. This marketing strategy helped the company increase sales when total industry sales fell.[38]

Strategy Formulation Versus Implementation

The final aspect of strategic management involves the stages of formulation and implementation. **Strategy formulation** includes the planning and decision making that lead to the establishment of the firm's goals and the development of a specific strategic plan.[39] Strategy formulation may include assessing the external environment and internal problems and integrating the results into goals and strategy. This is in contrast to **strategy implementation,** which is the use of managerial and organizational tools to direct resources toward accomplishing strategic results.[40] Strategy implementation is the administration and execution of the strategic plan. Managers may use persuasion, new equipment, changes in organization structure, or a reward system to ensure that employees and resources are used to make formulated strategy a reality.

strategy formulation
The stage of strategic management that involves the planning and decision making that lead to the establishment of the organization's goals and of a specific strategic plan.

strategy implementation
The stage of strategic management that involves the use of managerial and organizational tools to direct resources toward achieving strategic outcomes.

The Strategic Management Process

The overall strategic management process is illustrated in Exhibit 8.3. It begins when executives evaluate their current position with respect to mission, goals, and strategies. They then scan the organization's internal and external environments and identify strategic factors that may require change. Internal or external events may indicate a need to redefine the mission or

E x h i b i t **8.3**   *The Strategic Management Process*

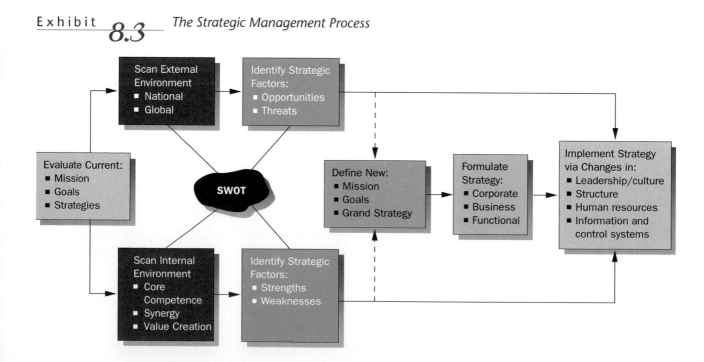

goals or to formulate a new strategy at either the corporate, business, or functional level. The final stage in the strategic management process is implementation of the new strategy.

Situation Analysis

Situation analysis typically includes a search for SWOT—strengths, weaknesses, opportunities, and threats that affect organizational performance. Situation analysis is important to all companies but is crucial to those considering globalization because of the diverse environments in which they will operate. External information about opportunities and threats may be obtained from a variety of sources, including customers, government reports, professional journals, suppliers, bankers, friends in other organizations, consultants, or association meetings. Many firms hire special scanning organizations to provide them with newspaper clippings and analyses of relevant domestic and global trends. Some firms use more subtle techniques to learn about competitors, such as asking potential recruits about their visits to other companies, hiring people away from competitors, debriefing former employees or customers of competitors, taking plant tours posing as "innocent" visitors, and even buying competitors' garbage.[41] In addition, many companies are hiring competitive intelligence professionals to scope out competitors, as we discussed in Chapter 3.

Executives acquire information about internal strengths and weaknesses from a variety of reports, including budgets, financial ratios, profit and loss statements, and surveys of employee attitudes and satisfaction. Managers spend 80 percent of their time giving and receiving information. Through frequent face-to-face discussions and meetings with people at all levels of the hierarchy, executives build an understanding of the company's internal strengths and weaknesses.

Internal Strengths and Weaknesses. *Strengths* are positive internal characteristics that the organization can exploit to achieve its strategic performance goals. *Weaknesses* are internal characteristics that may inhibit or restrict the organization's performance. Some examples of what executives evaluate to interpret strengths and weaknesses are given in Exhibit 8.4. The information sought typically pertains to specific functions such as marketing, finance, production, and R&D. Internal analysis also examines overall organization structure, management competence and quality, and human resource characteristics. Based on their understanding of these areas, managers can determine their strengths or weaknesses vis-à-vis other companies. For example, Marriott Corporation has been able to grow rapidly because of its financial strength. It has a strong financial base, enjoys an excellent reputation with creditors, and has always been able to acquire financing needed to support its strategy of constructing hotels in new locations.[42]

External Opportunities and Threats. *Threats* are characteristics of the external environment that may prevent the organization from achieving its strategic goals. *Opportunities* are characteristics of the external environment that have the potential to help the organization achieve or exceed its strategic goals. Executives evaluate the external environment with information about the nine sectors described in Chapter 3. The task environment sectors are the most relevant to strategic behavior and include the behavior of competitors, customers, suppliers, and the labor supply. The general environment contains those sectors that have an indirect influence on the organization but nevertheless must be

situation analysis
Analysis of the strengths, weaknesses, opportunities, and threats (SWOT) that affect organizational performance.

Bill Gross knows that the primary strengths of his company, idealab!, are creativity and rapid product development. Product innovation keeps idealab! at the forefront of the Net revolution with ventures such as eToys, cooking.com, tickets.com, and the search engine, GoTo.com. Since Gross recognized that he is better at starting companies than at running them, he turned control of the remaining business functions over to his brother, Larry, whom he credits with the company's survival. Bill's most recent innovative idea is an Internet record label, which will sign up artists, pay them huge royalties, and sell their songs as files that can be downloaded on the Internet, cutting out the traditional record companies and distributors.

Exhibit
8.4
Checklist for Analyzing Organizational Strengths and Weaknesses

Management and Organization	Marketing	Human Resources
Management quality	Distribution channels	Employee experience, education
Staff quality	Market share	Union status
Degree of centralization	Advertising efficiency	Turnover, absenteeism
Organization charts	Customer satisfaction	Work satisfaction
Planning, information, control systems	Product quality	Grievances
	Service reputation	
	Sales force turnover	

Finance	Production	Research and Development
Profit margin	Plant location	Basic applied research
Debt-equity ratio	Machinery obsolescence	Laboratory capabilities
Inventory ratio	Purchasing system	Research programs
Return on investment	Quality control	New-product innovations
Credit rating	Productivity/efficiency	Technology innovations

SOURCES: Based on Howard H. Stevenson, "Defining Corporate Strengths and Weaknesses," *Sloan Management Review* 17 (spring 1976), 51–68; and M. L. Kastens, *Long-Range Planning for Your Business* (New York: American Management Association, 1976).

understood and incorporated into strategic behavior. The general environment includes technological developments, the economy, legal-political and international events, and sociocultural changes. Additional areas that might reveal opportunities or threats include pressure groups, interest groups, creditors, natural resources, and potentially competitive industries.

An example of how external analysis can uncover a threat occurred in Kellogg Company's cereal business. Scanning the environment revealed that Kellogg's once-formidable share of the U.S. cold-cereal market had dropped nearly 10 percent. Information from the competitor and customer sectors indicated that major rivals were stepping up new-product innovations and cutting prices. In addition, private-label versions of such standbys as cornflakes were cutting into Kellogg's sales. Kellogg executives used knowledge of this threat as a basis for a strategic response. As a first step, the company boosted national advertising to build its brand names.[43]

The value of situation analysis in helping executives formulate the correct strategy is illustrated by Kinko's.

KINKO'S
www.kinkos.com

When the first Kinko's opened nearly three decades ago in a converted hamburger stand near the University of California, Santa Barbara, it was so small that the one copy machine had to be wheeled out to the sidewalk to make copies. Today, Kinko's is a global powerhouse, with 865 locations in six countries, 23,000 employees, and annual revenues of around $800 million. Kinko's originally catered primarily to college students, locating stores near college campuses and hiring students as part-time workers. Founder and chairman Paul Orfalea shared ownership of stores with investors in different regions, enabling Kinko's to expand rapidly. However, by the mid-1980s, it became clear that Kinko's needed a change to ensure continued success. Orfalea developed a new strategic direction that can be explained with SWOT analysis.

Kinko's had many *strengths,* beginning with the brand name; today, "Kinko's" is to copy centers what "Xerox" is to copy machines. Stores were widespread and all were doing a good business. Local ownership of stores led to more grassroots innovation and a casual, funky corporate culture that contributed to a sense of "community" in Kinko's stores. The greatest *weakness* was the lack of consistency. Stores were painted different colors, followed different marketing plans, kept different hours of operation, and offered different services and inventory. Some partners closed up shop every holiday they could think of, even though customers were asking for longer hours.

The *threats* to Kinko's included increased competition from a growing number of rival low-cost copy centers, shrinking margins, and copyright-infringement lawsuits brought by college textbook companies. However, Kinko's managers also recognized tremendous *opportunities* to grow the business by becoming more than a campus copy center. Just as Kinko's was considering a new strategic direction, corporate America began shedding millions of employees. Suddenly, unemployed middle managers needed well-crafted resumes and portfolios; self-employed consultants and sales reps needed brochures and marketing collateral; freelance artists and designers needed access to scanners, color printers, and other hardware they couldn't afford to buy; and everyone needed a place to check E-mail while they were on the road. Orfalea and other top managers saw a gold mine of unmet needs—a chance to be the home office of "Free Agent Nation."

To capitalize on its strengths and opportunities, Kinko's implemented a business strategy that transformed Kinko's from a decentralized confederation of stores into a unified global enterprise. Customers now found uniform and attractive offices equipped with cutting-edge technology and open all hours. They found employees who could not only operate a copy machine, but could help them discover solutions to their business problems. Kinko's has become more than a place to take care of business; it has become a version of the neighborhood watering hole—a place people can share war stories, gossip, and learn from one another. Although Kinko's has not abandoned the college market, its slogan, "The New Way to Office" signals a shift in strategic direction. With millions of people now operating as self-employed free agents, millions more telecommuting, and still others constantly on the road with little support from the home office, Kinko's fresh strategy fits the new marketplace.[44]

Formulating Corporate-Level Strategy

Portfolio Strategy

Portfolio strategy pertains to the mix of business units and product lines that fit together in a logical way to provide synergy and competitive advantage for the corporation. For example, an individual may wish to diversify in an investment portfolio with some high-risk stocks, some low-risk stocks, some growth stocks, and perhaps a few income bonds. In much the same way, corporations like to have a balanced mix of business divisions called **strategic business units (SBUs)**. An SBU has a unique business mission, product line, competitors, and markets relative to other SBUs in the corporation.[45] Executives in charge of the entire corporation generally define the grand strategy and then bring together a portfolio of strategic business units to carry it out. One useful way to think about portfolio strategy is the BCG matrix.

The BCG Matrix. The BCG (for Boston Consulting Group) matrix is illustrated in Exhibit 8.5. The **BCG matrix** organizes businesses along two dimensions—business growth rate and market share.[46] *Business growth rate*

portfolio strategy
A type of corporate-level strategy that pertains to the organization's mix of SBUs and product lines that fit together in such a way as to provide the corporation with synergy and competitive advantage.

strategic business units (SBUs)
A division of the organization that has a unique business mission, product line, competitors, and markets relative to other SBUs in the same corporation.

BCG matrix
A concept developed by the Boston Consulting Group that evaluates SBUs with respect to the dimensions of business growth rate and market share.

pertains to how rapidly the entire industry is increasing. *Market share* defines whether a business unit has a larger or smaller share than competitors. The combinations of high and low market share and high and low business growth provide four categories for a corporate portfolio.

The *star* has a large market share in a rapidly growing industry. The star is important because it has additional growth potential, and profits should be plowed into this business as investment for future growth and profits. The star is visible and attractive and will generate profits and a positive cash flow even as the industry matures and market growth slows.

The *cash cow* exists in a mature, slow-growth industry but is a dominant business in the industry, with a large market share. Because heavy investments in advertising and plant expansion are no longer required, the corporation earns a positive cash flow. It can milk the cash cow to invest in other, riskier businesses.

The *question mark* exists in a new, rapidly growing industry but has only a small market share. The question mark business is risky: it could become a star, or it could fail. The corporation can invest the cash earned from cash cows in question marks with the goal of nurturing them into future stars.

The *dog* is a poor performer. It has only a small share of a slow-growth market. The dog provides little profit for the corporation and may be targeted for divestment or liquidation if turnaround is not possible.

The circles in Exhibit 8.5 represent the business portfolio for a hypothetical corporation. Circle size represents the relative size of each business in the company's portfolio. Most organizations, such as Gillette, have businesses in more than one quadrant, thereby representing different market shares and growth rates.

Exhibit *8.5*

The BCG Matrix

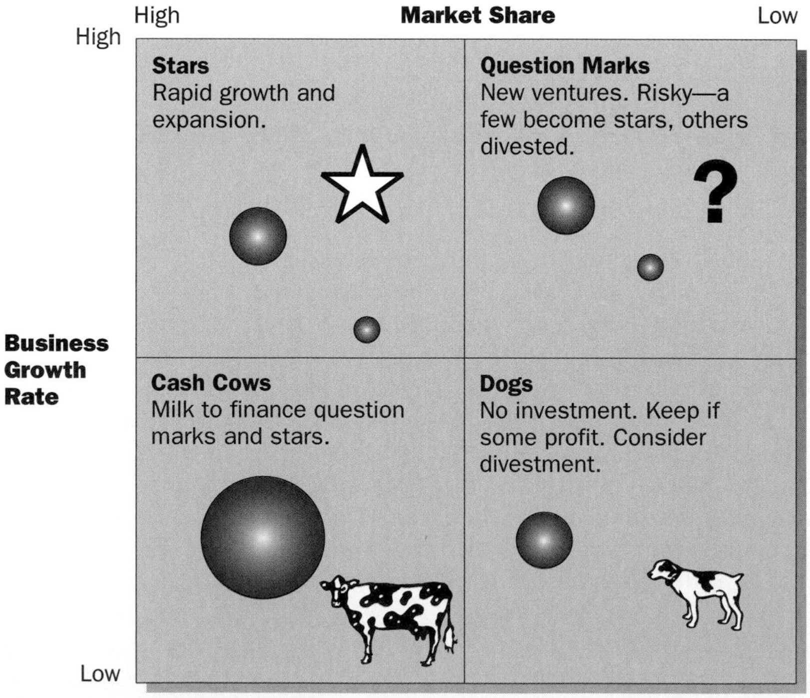

Market Share — High ... Low

Business Growth Rate — High ... Low

Stars
Rapid growth and expansion.

Question Marks
New ventures. Risky—a few become stars, others divested.

Cash Cows
Milk to finance question marks and stars.

Dogs
No investment. Keep if some profit. Consider divestment.

The most famous cash cow in Gillette's portfolio is the shaving division, which accounts for more than half of the company's profits and holds a large share of a stable market. Since 1990, Sensor and Sensor Excel razors have grabbed a leading 27 percent share of the U.S. market, and sales in other countries also are strong. Recently, Gillette rolled out a successor to Sensor—the Mach3, a triple-bladed razor that is expected to generate $1 billion in annual revenues by 2001. The Oral-B division also is a cash cow with its steady stream of new products, such as a new floss made with a proprietary fiber and the top-of-the-line Advantage toothbrush. With the recent purchase of Duracell, the leading producer of alkaline batteries with nearly 50 percent of the U.S. market, Gillette added yet another potential cash cow to its portfolio.

Gillette's Braun subsidiary has star status. Although sales have lagged recently, Gillette believes Braun's growth rate could eventually outpace razors and blades. The company is pumping money into research and development of new electric toothbrushes, personal diagnostic equipment, and other products. The toiletries division is a question mark. A line of women's toiletries aimed at the European market failed, and products such as Right Guard and Soft & Dri deodorant have enjoyed only cyclical success. A new line of men's toiletries, including a gel-based deodorant, a gel shaving cream, and a new body wash, is enjoying some limited success. A bigger question mark for Gillette is the struggling writing instruments division, which includes Parker, Paper-Mate, and Waterman pens. Some critics believe the division is a dog, but Gillette is still trying to come up with some new products to save it from the fate of the Cricket disposable lighter several years ago. Bic dominated the disposable lighter line so completely that Gillette had to recognize Cricket as a dog and put it out of its misery through liquidation. Gillette is investing heavily in its question marks to ensure that its portfolio will continue to include stars and cash cows in the future.[47]

GILLETTE COMPANY
www.gillette.com

Formulating Business-Level Strategy

Now we turn to strategy formulation within the strategic business unit, in which the concern is how to compete. The same three generic strategies—growth, stability, and retrenchment—apply at the business level, but they are accomplished through competitive actions rather than the acquisition or divestment of business divisions. One model for formulating strategy is Porter's competitive strategies, which provides a framework for business unit competitive action.

Porter's Competitive Forces and Strategies

Michael E. Porter studied a number of business organizations and proposed that business-level strategies are the result of five competitive forces in the company's environment.[48]

Five Competitive Forces. Exhibit 8.6 illustrates the competitive forces that exist in a company's environment. These forces help determine a company's position vis-à-vis competitors in the industry environment.

1. *Potential new entrants.* Capital requirements and economies of scale are examples of two potential barriers to entry that can keep out new competitors. It is far more costly to enter the automobile industry, for example, than to start a specialized mail-order business.

Exhibit 8.6   *The Five Forces Affecting Industry Competition*

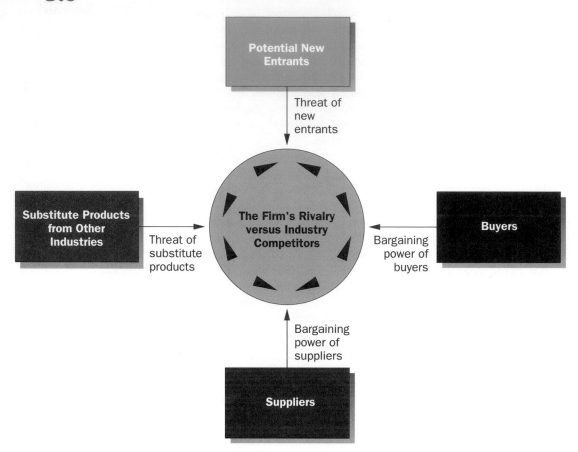

SOURCE: Based on Michael E. Porter, *Competitive Strategy: Techniques for Analyzing Industries and Competitors* (New York: Free Press, 1980).

2. *Bargaining power of buyers.* Informed customers become empowered customers. As advertising and buyer information educate customers about the full range of price and product options available in the marketplace, their influence over a company increases. This is especially true when a company relies on one or two large, powerful customers for the majority of its sales.

3. *Bargaining power of suppliers.* The concentration of suppliers and the availability of substitute suppliers are significant factors in determining supplier power. The sole supplier of engines to a manufacturer of small airplanes will have great power. Other factors include whether a supplier can survive without a particular purchaser, or whether the purchaser can threaten to self-manufacture the needed supplies.

4. *Threat of substitute products.* The power of alternatives and substitutes for a company's product may be affected by cost changes or trends such as increased health consciousness that will deflect buyer loyalty to companies. Companies in the sugar industry suffered from the growth of sugar substitutes; manufacturers of aerosol spray cans lost business as environmentally conscious consumers chose other products.

5. *Rivalry among competitors.* The scrambling and jockeying for position is often exemplified by what Porter called the "advertising slugfest." As illustrated in Exhibit 8.6, these rivalries are influenced by the preceding four forces as well as by cost and product differentiation. A famous example of competitive rivalry is the battle between Pepsi and Coke. Rivalry between Federal Express and United Parcel Service is becoming almost as fierce as the two companies grapple for dominance of the express delivery business. After UPS rolled out an 8:30 A.M. delivery, FedEx introduced its new First Overnight service, promising "earliest morning delivery." When Federal Express introduced FedEx Ship, offering a free PC-based system that lets even the smallest customers order pickups, print shipping labels, and track delivery without ever using a telephone, UPS fired back by unveiling a new alliance to enable customers to book orders through online services.[49]

Competitive Strategies.   In finding its competitive edge within these five forces, Porter suggests that a company can adopt one of three strategies: differentiation, cost leadership, and focus. The organizational characteristics typically associated with each strategy are summarized in Exhibit 8.7.

1. *Differentiation.* The **differentiation** strategy involves an attempt to distinguish the firm's products or services from others in the industry. The organization may use advertising, distinctive product features, exceptional service, or new technology to achieve a product perceived as unique. The differentiation strategy can be profitable because customers are loyal and will pay high prices for the product. Examples of products that have benefited from

differentiation
A type of competitive strategy with which the organization seeks to distinguish its products or services from competitors'.

E x h i b i t   **8.7**   *Organizational Characteristics for Porter's Competitive Strategies*

Strategy	Organizational Characteristics
Differentiation	Acts in a flexible, loosely knit way, with strong coordination among departments
	Strong capability in basic research
	Creative flair, thinks "out-of-the-box"
	Strong marketing abilities
	Rewards employee innovation
	Corporate reputation for quality or technological leadership
Cost Leadership	Strong central authority; tight cost controls
	Maintains standard operating procedures
	Easy-to-use manufacturing technologies
	Highly efficient procurement and distribution systems
	Close supervision; finite employee empowerment
	Frequent, detailed control reports
Focus	May use combination of above policies directed at particular strategic target
	Values and rewards flexibility and customer intimacy
	Measures cost of providing service and maintaining customer loyalty
	Pushes empowerment to employees with customer contact

Sources: Based on Michael E. Porter, *Competitive Strategy: Techniques for Analyzing Industries and Competitors* (New York: The Free Press, 1980); Michael Treacy and Fred Wiersema, "How Market Leaders Keep Their Edge," *Fortune*, February 6, 1995, 88–98; and Michael A. Hitt, R. Duane Ireland, and Robert E. Hoskisson, *Strategic Management* (St. Paul, Minn.: West, 1995), 100–113.

a differentiation strategy include Mercedes-Benz automobiles, Maytag appliances, and Tylenol, all of which are perceived as distinctive in their markets. Companies that pursue a differentiation strategy typically need strong marketing abilities, a creative flair, and a reputation for leadership.[50]

A differentiation strategy can reduce rivalry with competitors if buyers are loyal to a company's brand. For example, successful differentiation reduces the bargaining power of large buyers because other products are less attractive, and this also helps the firm fight off threats of substitute products. Differentiation also erects entry barriers in the form of customer loyalty that a new entrant into the market would have difficulty overcoming.

cost leadership
A type of competitive strategy with which the organization aggressively seeks efficient facilities, cuts costs, and employs tight cost controls to be more efficient than competitors.

2. *Cost Leadership.* With a **cost leadership** strategy, the organization aggressively seeks efficient facilities, pursues cost reductions, and uses tight cost controls to produce products more efficiently than competitors. A low-cost position means that the company can undercut competitors' prices and still offer comparable quality and earn a reasonable profit. Scottish Inns and Motel 6 are low-priced alternatives to Holiday Inn and Ramada Inn. WestJet Airlines Ltd., in Canada, is using a cost-leadership strategy to compete successfully against major carriers such as Air Canada and Canadian Airlines. Chairman and CEO Clive Beddoe analyzed U.S. discount carriers such as Southwest Airlines and saw an opportunity to reap the same kind of rewards in the Canadian market.[51] Dell Computer, described in the Leading the Revolution: Technology box earlier in the chapter, has used a cost-leadership strategy to gain a competitive edge over larger companies.

Being a low-cost producer provides a successful strategy to defend against the five competitive forces in Exhibit 8.6. For example, the most efficient, low-cost company is in the best position to succeed in a price war while still making a profit. Likewise, the low-cost producer is protected from powerful customers and suppliers, because customers cannot find lower prices elsewhere, and other buyers would have less slack for price negotiation with suppliers. If substitute products or potential new entrants occur, the low-cost producer is better positioned than higher-cost rivals to prevent loss of market share. The low price acts as a barrier against new entrants and substitute products.[52]

focus
A type of competitive strategy that emphasizes concentration on a specific regional market or buyer group.

3. *Focus.* With a **focus** strategy, the organization concentrates on a specific regional market or buyer group. The company will use either a differentiation or low-cost approach, but only for a narrow target market. Enterprise Rent-A-Car has made its mark by focusing on a market the major companies such as Hertz and Avis don't even play in—the low-budget insurance replacement market. Drivers whose cars have been wrecked or stolen have one less thing to worry about when Enterprise delivers a car right to their driveway. By using a focus strategy, Enterprise has been able to grow rapidly.[53]

Managers think carefully about which strategy will provide their company with its competitive advantage. Gibson Guitar Corp., famous in the music world for its innovative, high-quality products, found that switching to a low-cost strategy to compete against Japanese rivals such as Yamaha and Ibanez actually hurt the company. When managers realized people wanted Gibson products because of their reputation, not their price, they went back to a differentiation strategy and invested in new technology and marketing.[54] In his studies, Porter found that some businesses did not consciously adopt one of these three strategies and were stuck with no strategic advantage. Without a strategic advantage, businesses earned below-average profits compared with those that used differentiation, cost leadership, or focus strategies.

Cooperative Strategies

So far, we have been discussing strategies that are based on how to compete with other companies. An alternative approach to strategy emphasizes collaboration. In some situations, companies can achieve competitive advantages by cooperating with other firms rather than competing. Cooperative strategies are becoming increasingly popular as firms in all industries join with other organizations to promote innovation, expand markets, and pursue joint goals. Partnering was once a strategy adopted primarily by small firms that needed greater marketing muscle or international access. Today, however, it has become a way of life for most companies, large and small. The question is no longer whether to collaborate, but rather where, how much, and with whom to collaborate.[55] Competition and cooperation often exist at the same time. In New York City, Time Warner refused to carry Fox's twenty-four-hour news channel on its New York City cable systems. The two companies engaged in all-out war that included court lawsuits and front page headlines. This conflict, however, masked a simple fact: the two companies can't live without each other. Fox and Time Warner are wedded to one another in separate business deals around the world. They will never let the local competition in New York upset their larger cooperation on a global scale.[56]

Mutual dependencies and partnerships have become a fact of life, but the degree of collaboration varies. Organizations can choose to build cooperative relationships in many ways, such as through preferred suppliers, strategic business partnering, joint ventures, or mergers and acquisitions. Exhibit 8.8 illustrates these major types of strategic business relationships according to the degree of collaboration involved. With preferred supplier relationships, a company such as Wal-Mart, for example, develops a special relationship with a key supplier such as Procter & Gamble that eliminates middlemen by sharing complete information and reducing the costs of salespeople and distributors. Preferred supplier arrangements provide long-term security for both organizations,

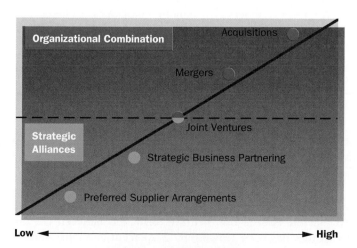

Exhibit 8.8

A Continuum of Cooperative Strategies

Source: Adapted from Roberta Maynard, "Striking the Right Match," *Nation's Business*, May 1996, 18–28.

Cisco Systems

Cisco Systems is transforming itself into a learning organization through strategic partnerships. The pioneer of "Internetworking," Cisco is first or second in all but one of the seven major equipment markets in which it competes. The company is one of the fastest growing companies in Silicon Valley and one of the hottest stocks of the decade. Cisco has achieved its status primarily through strategic relationships.

Cisco Systems was founded in 1984 by a husband-and-wife team who devised a means to connect incompatible computer networks at Stanford University. A series of mergers and acquisitions with start-up companies such as Crescendo Communications, a maker of hubs, and StrataCom, a maker of frame relay devices and switches, turned Cisco into a full-service provider of networking equipment and garnered the technological know-how to keep it on the cutting edge. Just as importantly, Cisco has developed numerous strategic partnerships with other high-tech companies. The company partners with Hewlett-Packard, for example, to develop and sell Internet-based corporate computing systems built with each other's products. Cisco is working with Microsoft to create industry standards for network security. A strategic alliance with MCI means Cisco will deliver premium Internet services via MCI's data-networking infrastructure. Now, Cisco is working with the two giants of computing—Microsoft and Intel—in a joint project called the Networked Multimedia Lab. On the ground floor of the world headquarters of Cisco Systems is a series of rooms in which customers explore how the Internet can deliver voice, video, and interactive multimedia with the clarity and reliability of conventional telephone and cable TV networks.

Cisco CEO John T. Chambers considers picking the right strategic partners to be a key element of his company's strategy. He targets partners who are aggressive, technologically strong, and very customer-focused. Chambers believes his company's partnership with Microsoft and Intel symbolizes that the three will form a triumvirate that will plot the course of the digital revolution. Although that remains to be seen, so far Cisco is playing all its cards right. "We've always known networking is too complex for any one company to tackle—even for MCI, HP, Microsoft, or Intel," says Chambers. "They know it now too. It's better to partner than to compete because . . . it grows the pie bigger for everybody faster."

www.cisco.com

SOURCE: Brent Schlender, "Computing's Next Superpower," *Fortune,* May 12, 1997, 88–101.

but the level of collaboration is relatively low. Strategic business partnering requires a higher level of collaboration. US Order, a software developer in Herndon, Virginia, entered into a partnership with Colonial Data Technologies Corp., of New Milford, Connecticut. US Order had developed a "smart telephone" that sends electronic mail, transmits messages to pagers, and allows for electronic banking and shopping. However, the company had no manufacturing expertise and no distribution channels to telephone companies. Colonial had both, but didn't have the technology or the research and development resources. The two firms entered into a partnership whereby Colonial will manufacture and market the product to phone companies, while US Order will market it to other groups of customers, including banks and paging companies. Each partner will pay the other 10 percent of the profits from products it sells in its respective market.[57] Fast-growing, high-tech companies such as Cisco Systems, described in the Learning Organization box, depend on strategic partnering.

A still higher degree of collaboration is reflected in joint ventures, which are separate entities created with two or more active firms as sponsors. For example, MTV Networks was originally created as a joint venture of Warner Communications and American Express in the late 1970s. In a joint venture, organizations share the risks and costs associated with the new venture. It is estimated that the rate of joint venture formation between U.S. and international companies has been growing by 27 percent annually since 1985. Texas Instruments and Hitachi, for example, formed an international joint venture to produce memory chips. Merck has put together major ventures with such competitors as Johnson & Johnson and AB Astra of Sweden.[58] Mergers and acquisitions represent the ultimate in collaborative relationships. U.S. business is in the midst of the biggest merger and acquisition boom in its history. In 1997 alone, more than 11,000 deals totaled some $908 billion, 47 percent more than the total in 1996, which was itself a record year.[59] The U.S. pharmaceuticals company Upjohn merged with Sweden's Pharmacia. Boeing acquired McDonnell Douglas to form the industry's largest company, and Citicorp and Travelers Group have announced a $70 billion merger that will create a megabank with $700 billion in assets. The two organizations shared a desire to create a fully integrated financial services giant and recognized the synergies they could achieve by merging. Citicorp gains a stronger U.S. direct-sales force to market Citi checking accounts, mutual funds, and credit cards, while Travelers gains greater access to international markets. Reflecting the emphasis on collaboration, John S. Reed of Citicorp and Sanford I. Weill of Travelers will serve as co-CEOs of the new financial services behemoth.[60]

Today's companies simultaneously embrace both competition and cooperation. Few companies can go it alone under a constant onslaught of international competition, changing technology, and new regulations. In this new environment, businesses choose a combination of competitive and cooperative strategies that add to their overall sustainable advantage.[61]

Formulating Functional-Level Strategy

Functional-level strategies are the action plans adopted by major departments to support the execution of business-level strategy. Major organizational functions include marketing, production, finance, human resources, and research and development. Senior managers in these departments adopt strategies that are coordinated with the business-level strategy to achieve the organization's strategic goals.[62]

For example, consider a company that has adopted a differentiation strategy and is introducing new products that are expected to experience rapid growth. The human resources department should adopt a strategy appropriate for growth, which would mean recruiting additional personnel and training middle managers for movement into new positions. The marketing department should undertake test marketing, aggressive advertising campaigns, and consumer product trials. The finance department should adopt plans to borrow money, handle large cash investments, and authorize construction of new production facilities.

A company with mature products or a low-cost strategy will have different functional strategies. The human resources department should develop strategies for retaining and developing a stable workforce, including transfers, advancements, and incentives for efficiency and safety. Marketing should stress brand loyalty and the development of established, reliable distribution channels. Production should maintain long production runs, routinization, and cost reduction. Finance should focus on net cash flows and positive cash balances.

American Trans Air, Inc. uses a focus and differentiation *strategy, targeting the leisure customer with the best value and the most fun in vacation travel. The company recently created a fresh new look and feel, so that from the moment of check-in to arrival at their destination passengers experience a vacation-oriented, fun atmosphere. For example, crew uniforms were redesigned for a casual look, calypso and reggae music welcome passengers aboard, and children's meals are served on souvenir flying saucers.*

Putting Strategy into Action

The final step in the strategic management process is implementation—which is how strategy is put into action. Some people argue that strategy implementation is the most difficult and important part of strategic management.[63] No matter how creative the formulated strategy, the organization will not benefit if it is incorrectly implemented. In today's competitive environment, there is an increasing recognition of the need for more dynamic approaches to formulating as well as implementing strategies. Strategy is not a static, analytical process; it requires vision, intuition, and employee participation.[64] Many organizations are abandoning central planning departments, and strategy is becoming an everyday part of the job for workers at all levels. Strategy implementation involves using several tools—parts of the firm that can be adjusted to put strategy into action—as illustrated in Exhibit 8.9. Once a new strategy is selected, it is implemented through changes in leadership, structure, information and control systems, and human resources.[65]

Leadership

Leadership is the ability to influence organization members to adopt the behaviors needed for strategy implementation. Leadership includes persuasion, motivation, and changes in corporate values and culture. Managers seeking to implement a new strategy may make speeches to employees, issue edicts, build coalitions, and persuade middle managers to go along with their vision for the corporation. If leaders let other employees participate during strategy formulation, implementation will be easier because managers and employees will already understand and be committed to the new strategy. In

E x h i b i t   *8.9*   *Tools for Putting Strategy into Action*

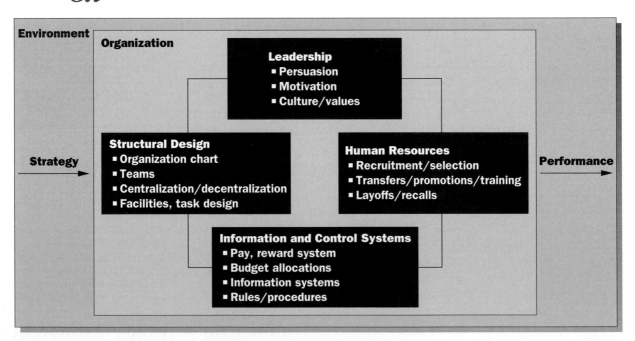

SOURCE: Adapted from Jay R. Galbraith and Robert K. Kazanjian, *Strategy Implementation: Structure, Systems, and Process,* 2d ed. (St. Paul, Minn.: West, 1986), 115. Used with permission.

essence, leadership is used to motivate employees to adopt new behaviors and, for some strategies, to infuse new values and attitudes.

For example, Jürgen Schrempp is using leadership to instill a new culture of responsibility and entrepreneurism at DaimlerChrysler. Whereas previous Daimler chairmen managed from a distance, Schrempp communicates directly with his managers in meetings that can run into the night, fueled by beer and cigars. He personally visits clients and takes an active role in labor negotiations. Schrempp's leadership has turned the formerly stodgy company into an innovative, fast-moving organization.[66]

Structural Design

Structural design typically begins with the organization chart. It pertains to managers' responsibilities, their degree of authority, and the consolidation of facilities, departments, and divisions. Structure also pertains to the degree of decentralization, task design, and production technology. (Structure will be described in Chapter 11.)

Q. T. Wiles used structural changes to implement strategy at MiniScribe Corporation. He reorganized the workforce into small groups, each responsible for a single product, a single customer, or some other narrowly defined target. Each group was an autonomous structural unit with skills and functions necessary to achieve its goals.[67] However, the strategy of merging Uniroyal and Goodrich was unprofitable for the first two years because of implementation problems concerning structural design. Such simple things as the incompatibility of tire molds in the two companies' plants prevented consolidation of equipment and facilities. Blending the marketing and the accounting departments of the two companies proved difficult because of different philosophies and cost accounting systems.[68]

Information and Control Systems

Information and control systems include reward systems, pay incentives, budgets for allocating resources, information systems, and the organization's rules, policies, and procedures. Changes in these systems represent major tools for putting strategy into action. For example, resources can be reassigned from research and development to marketing if a new strategy requires increased advertising but no product innovations. Managers and employees must be rewarded for adhering to the new strategy and making it a success.[69]

At ConAgra, maker of Healthy Choice and Banquet brands, CEO Philip B. Fletcher instituted top-down cost controls in the corporation's 60 operating units and developed new systems for pooling resources to reduce purchasing, warehousing, and transportation costs. To ensure that managers embraced the new strategy of cooperation and efficiency, Fletcher tied 25 percent of their bonuses directly to savings targets. Division heads saved $100 million in the first fiscal year. Fletcher also made changes in information systems by introducing a computerized network to track how much suppliers charge each ConAgra unit.[70] As another example, Outback Steakhouse built one of the nation's hottest restaurant chains by giving managers a significant ownership stake, including 10 percent of their restaurant's cash flow and shares of company stock. Outback's incentive program, believed to be unique among casual-restaurant chains, helped founders Chris Sullivan, Robert Basham, and Timothy Gannon move in only six years from their modest goal of 5 restaurants to more than 200 Outbacks, with revenues of $544 million.[71]

Human Resources

The organization's *human resources* are its employees. The human resource function recruits, selects, trains, transfers, promotes, and lays off employees to achieve strategic goals. For example, training employees can help them understand the purpose and importance of a new strategy or help them develop the necessary specific skills and behaviors. Sometimes employees may have to be let go and replaced. One newspaper shifted its strategy from an evening to a morning paper to compete with a large newspaper from a nearby city. The new strategy fostered resentment and resistance among department heads. In order to implement it, 80 percent of the department heads had to be let go because they refused to cooperate. New people were recruited and placed in those positions, and the morning newspaper strategy was a resounding success.[72]

Mannie Jackson revived the Harlem Globetrotters, an organization on the brink of bankruptcy and irrelevancy, by recruiting new players who could recapture the glory the Globetrotters enjoyed in the 1960s and 1970s. Jackson rates potential players on their skill, charisma, punctuality, and attitude. He wants only top athletes who can promote the Globetrotter brand and are willing to be role models.[73]

Implementing Global Strategies

The difficulty of implementing strategy is greater when a company goes global. In the international arena, flexibility and superb communication emerge as mandatory leadership skills. Likewise, structural design must merge successfully with foreign cultures as well as link foreign operations to the home country. Information and control systems must fit the needs and incentives within local cultures. In a country such as Japan or China, financial bonuses for star performance would be humiliating to an individual, whereas group motivation and reward are acceptable. As in North America, control is typically created through timetables and budgets and by monitoring progress toward desired goals. Finally, the recruitment, training, transfer, promotion, and layoff of international human resources create an array of problems not confronted in North America. Labor laws, guaranteed jobs, and cultural traditions of keeping unproductive employees on the job provide special problems for strategy implementation. Strategy implementation must receive even more attention in the international domain than in the domestic realm.

In summary, strategy implementation is essential for effective strategic management. Managers implement strategy through the tools of leadership, structural design, information and control systems, and human resources. Without effective implementation, even the most creative strategy will fail.

A.J. Peterman Co., the panache-drenched clothing cataloger, recently recruited chief operating officer Arnie Cohen (left) to help implement new strategies through human resources. The 400-employee company, headed by chief executive John Peterman (right), was enjoying notoriety thanks to the TV show, Seinfeld, but was suffering losses and flat sales. Cohen was hired and now the company is extending its brand by opening retail stores and issuing auxiliary catalogs. The goal—to reach $90 million in sales within the year.

Summary and Management Solution

This chapter described important concepts of strategic management. Strategic management begins with an evaluation of the organization's current mission, goals, and strategy. This evaluation is followed by situation analysis (called SWOT analysis), which examines opportunities and threats in the external environment as well as strengths and weaknesses within the organization. Situation analysis leads to the formulation of explicit strategic plans, which then must be implemented.

Strategy formulation takes place at three levels: corporate, business, and functional. Corporate grand strategies include growth, stability, retrenchment, and global. One framework for accomplishing them is the BCG matrix. One approach to business-level strategy is Porter's competitive forces and strategies. An alternative approach to strategic thought emphasizes cooperation rather than competition. Cooperative strategies include preferred supplier arrangements, strategic business partnering, joint ventures, and mergers and acquisitions. Most of today's companies choose a mix of competitive and cooperative strategies. Once business strategies have been formulated, functional strategies for supporting them can be developed.

Even the most creative strategies have no value if they cannot be translated into action. Four organizational tools used for strategy implementation are leadership, structural design, information and control systems, and human resources.

Returning to the opening chapter case, Kodak has long relied on a differentiation strategy, and it has been successful. Indeed, Kodak still is an admired brand in photographic film and equipment. However, Fuji's cost-leadership strategy clearly is cutting into Kodak's sales. Chairman and CEO Minoru Ohnishi is a constant cost-cutter, which gives Fuji more flexibility to cut prices. Fuji also has gained ground through strategic acquisitions. The purchase of Wal-Mart's six wholesale photo labs, for example, gave Fuji 15 percent of the U.S. photo-processing market in one fell swoop. Many analysts believe Kodak needs a new strategy fast to prevent further loss of market share.[74] As George Fisher continues his struggle to turn around the troubled company, he may use SWOT analysis to formulate strategies that build on Kodak's strengths and opportunities. Most importantly, the strategies must be implemented through appropriate changes in leadership, structure, information and control systems, and human resources.

Discussion Questions

1. Assume you are the general manager of a large hotel and have formulated a strategy of renting banquet facilities to corporations for big events. At a monthly management meeting, your sales manager informed the head of food operations that a big reception in one week will require converting a large hall from a meeting room to a banquet facility in only 60 minutes—a difficult but doable operation that will require precise planning and extra help. The food operations manager is furious about not being informed earlier. What is wrong here?

2. Which is more important—strategy formulation or strategy implementation? Do they depend on each other? Is it possible for strategy implementation to occur first?

3. If an organization has hired strategic management professionals to help top managers, during which part of the strategic management process would they play the largest role?

4. Perform a situation (SWOT) analysis for the university you attend. Do you think university administrators consider these factors when devising their strategy?

5. What is meant by the core competence and synergy components of strategy? Give examples.

6. Using Porter's competitive strategies, how would you describe the strategies of Wal-Mart, Bloomingdale's, and Kmart? Do any of these companies also use cooperative strategies? Discuss.

7. Walt Disney Company has four major strategic business units: movies (Touchstone), theme parks, consumer products, and television (primarily cable). Place each of these SBUs on the BCG matrix based on your knowledge of them.

8. As administrator for a medium-sized hospital, you and the board of directors have decided to change to

a drug dependency hospital from a short-term, acute-care facility. Which organizational dimensions would you use to implement this strategy?

9. How would functional strategies in marketing, research and development, and production departments differ if a business changed from a differentiation to a low-cost strategy?

Management in Practice: Experiential Exercise

Developing Strategy for a Small Business

Instructions: Your instructor may ask you to do this exercise individually or as part of a group. Select a local business with which you (or group members) are familiar. Complete the following activities.

Activity 1   Perform a SWOT analysis for the business.

Strengths: _____
_____
_____
_____
_____

Opportunities: _____
_____
_____
_____
_____

Weaknesses: _____
_____
_____
_____
_____

Threats: _____
_____
_____
_____
_____

Activity 2   Write a statement of the business's current strategy.

Activity 3   Decide on a goal you would like the business to achieve in two years, and write a statement of proposed strategy for achieving that goal.

Activity 4   Write a statement describing how the proposed strategy will be implemented.

Activity 5   What have you learned from this exercise?

Management in Practice: Ethical Dilemma

A Great Deal for Whom?

It seemed like a great deal for Kevin Haley, the retired president of a small accounting firm, when he took the job. To sit on the board of Keldine Technologies, all he had to do was listen to some general talk about the company at bi-monthly meetings, vote on operations issues, and collect a nice fee. He didn't worry about his lack of expertise in the company's business of manufacturing transistors, because "nothing ever changed at Keldine."

That was two years ago. Now Keldine Technologies, with 250 employees and ten years in business, was faced with a buyout offer from Graham Industries. Chairman of the Board at

Keldine, Greg Bingham, called the deal a "no-brainer." Graham Industries' offer of $65 a share was high, a great deal for shareholders. The problem for Haley was that he knew Graham Industries was close to bankruptcy, and that it was probably only buying Keldine to leverage some of its debt and hold off creditors. The odds were that both companies would be wiped out within a year if the sale went through. As news of a buyout offer spread, Keldine stock had changed hands rapidly, and speculators in the shareholder ranks were pressuring for a sale. Bingham asserted, "Our mission is to create as much value for shareholders as possible."

He also assured the board that the executives were protected by contingency compensation packages in the event of a "downturn for Keldine." But Haley was torn. The deal was a short-term moneymaker but almost guaranteed disaster for the company's future and the majority of its employees. Haley's commitment to shareholders seemed compromised by the presence of speculators in their ranks. He questioned whether the interests of loyal, long-time employees weren't a higher priority than those of speculators.

What Do You Do?

1. Vote to accept the offer of Graham Industries and assure a short-term profit for the shareholders and executives. They are your first responsibility.
2. Reject the buyout bid. Providing Keldine a future, even if uncertain because of its resistance to change, is more important than accepting what may be the best offer ever received.
3. Pass, and hope a board majority prevails without your vote. You aren't qualified to make a decision on this anyway.

SOURCE: Based on Doug Wallace, "When the Sharks Are Circling," *What Would You Do? Business Ethics,* vol. I (September–October 1991), 42–44.

Surf the Net

1. **Growth through Mergers and Acquisitions.** Use the Internet to identify mergers and acquisitions announced within the past month. One search option is to use Northern Light at **www.northernlight.com**, select "Current News," and type in under "Search for:" "mergers and acquisitions." For each merger or acquisition you identify, give the companies involved, identify the industry, and provide any other interesting information related to the merger or acquisition.

2. **Competitive Intelligence.** The Internet Intelligence Index **www.fuld.com/i3/index.html** is designed to help users gather competitive intelligence information. It contains links to nearly 600 intelligence-related Internet sites, covering everything from macro-economic data to individual patent and stock quote information. Select an industry from the Internet Intelligence Index Web site, such as Apparel, Financial Services, Pharmaceutical/Biotechnology, Travel, or one assigned by your instructor. Based on your research of your industry, prepare a written report in which you identify opportunities and threats to existing firms in that industry.

3. **Competitive Strategies.** Compare the Web sites of companies in the same industry that have adopted different strategies—either differentiation, cost leadership, or focus. For example, you could compare Motel 6 **www.motel6.com** with Holiday Inn **www1.basshotels.com/holiday-inn** and write a list of Web-site indicators of their respective strategies. Other possible comparisons are Enterprise Rent-A-Car **www.erac.com/** and Hertz **www.hertz.com/** or Nordstrom **www.nordstrom.com** and Kmart **www.kmart.com/**.

Case for Critical Analysis

Starbucks Coffee

Beginning with 9 Seattle stores in 1987, Starbucks CEO Howard Schultz has exported the company's chic cafes throughout the country. Service is anything but fast, and the price of a cup of coffee could make the Dunkin' Donuts crowd faint, but each week almost 2 million Americans hit Starbucks to sip skinny lattes or no-whip mochas.

Despite a slowdown in sales from established stores, Starbucks is pursuing rapid expansion. It made its first acquisition in 1994, buying The Coffee Connection Inc., a 23-store Boston rival. With more than 400 stores in place, Schultz plans to open 200 more within a year and has announced plans to team up with foreign partners to open stores in Asia and Europe. In addition, Starbucks has entered into a venture with PepsiCo to develop a new bottled coffee drink. Schultz's strategies are risky, but some analysts think Starbucks has the flexibility and management strength to succeed.

Many of Starbucks's managers have years of experience from such companies as Burger King, Taco Bell, Wendy's, and Blockbuster. Schultz believes a CEO should "hire people smarter than you are and get out of their way." Equally crucial to Starbucks's success are the "baristas" who prepare coffee drinks. Starbucks recruits its workers from colleges and community groups and gives them 24 hours' training in coffeemaking and lore—a key to creating the company's hip image and quality service. To maintain quality control, Starbucks roasts all its coffee in-house. The company also has turned down lucrative alternatives such as franchising and supermarket distribution.

A computer network links the expanding Starbucks empire, and Schultz hired a top information-technology specialist from McDonald's to design a point-of-sale system to enable managers to track sales. Every night, computers from all 400-plus stores send information to headquarters in Seattle so that executives can spot regional buying trends.

For Schultz, a man who has already changed America's coffee-drinking habits, the risks Starbucks is taking are just another challenge.

Questions

1. Which of Porter's competitive strategies is Starbucks using?
2. Discuss how Schultz is using leadership, structure, information and control systems, and human resources to implement strategy at Starbucks.
3. What challenges may Schultz face in trying to expand Starbucks internationally?

SOURCES: Dori Jones Yang, "The Starbucks Enterprise Shifts into Warp Speed," *Business Week,* October 24, 1994, 76; and Michael Treacy, "You Need a Value Discipline—But Which One?" *Fortune,* April 17, 1995, 195.

Endnotes

1. Edward W. Desmond, "What's Ailing Kodak? Fuji," *Fortune,* October 27, 1997, 185–192.

2. Bill Saporito, "The Eclipse of Mars," *Fortune,* November 28, 1994, 82–92.

3. John A. Byrne, "Strategic Planning," *Business Week,* August 26, 1996, 46–52; Gabriella Stern, "Race Car Driver Goes Home, Sets New Course for Bake-Mix Concern," *The Wall Street Journal,* February 19, 1997, A1, A6.

4. C. Chet Miller and Laura B. Cardinal, "Strategic Planning and Firm Performance: A Synthesis of More than Two Decades of Research," *Academy of Management Journal* 37, no. 6 (1994), 1649–1665.

5. Gary Hamel, "Killer Strategies," *Fortune,* June 23, 1997, 70–84; and Costantinos Markides, "Strategic Innovation," *Sloan Management Review,* Spring 1997, 9–23.

6. Hamel, "Killer Strategies."

7. John E. Prescott, "Environments as Moderators of the Relationship between Strategy and Performance," *Academy of Management Journal* 29 (1986), 329–346; John A. Pearce II and Richard B. Robinson, Jr., *Strategic Management: Strategy, Formulation, and Implementation,* 2d ed. (Homewood, Ill.: Irwin, 1985); and David J. Teece, "Economic Analysis and Strategic Management," *California Management Review* 26 (spring 1984), 87–110.

8. Markides, "Strategic Innovation."

9. Kotha Suresh and Daniel Orna, "Generic Manufacturing Strategies: A Conceptual Synthesis," *Strategic Management Journal* 10 (1989), 211–231; and John A. Pearce II, "Selecting among Alternative Grand Strategies," *California Management Review* (spring 1982), 23–31.

10. Andrew Kupfer, "MCI WorldCom: It's the Biggest Merger Ever. Can It Rule Telecom?" *Fortune,* April 27, 1998, 119–128.

11. William C. Symonds, with Farah Nayeri, Geri Smith, and Ted Plafker, "Bombardier's Blitz," *Business Week,* February 6, 1995, 62–66; and Joseph Weber, with Wendy Zellner and Geri Smith, "Loud Noises at Bombardier," *Business Week,* January 26, 1998, 94–95.

12. Wendy Zellner, "Back to Coffee, Tea, or Milk?" *Business Week,* July 3, 1995, 52–56.

13. Laura Landro, "Entertainment Giants Face Pressure to Cut Costs, Get in Focus." *The Wall Street Journal,* February 11, 1997, A1, A10; Terence P. Pare, "The New Merger Boom," *Fortune,* November 28, 1994, 95–106; and Zachary Schiller, "Figgies Turns Over a New Leaf," *Business Week,* February 27, 1995, 94–96.

14. Kenichi Ohmae, "Managing in a Borderless World," *Harvard Business Review* (May–June 1990), 152–161.

15. Theodore Levitt, "The Globalization of Markets," *Harvard Business Review* (May–June 1983), 92–102.

16. Patrick Oster and John Rossant, "Call It WorldPool," *Business Week,* November 28, 1994, 98–99.

17. Joanne Lipman, "Marketers Turn Sour on Global Sales Pitch Harvard Guru Makes," *The Wall Street Journal,* May 12, 1988, 1, 8.

18. Michael E. Porter, "Changing Patterns of International Competition," *California Management Review* 28 (winter 1986), 40.

19. Lipman, "Marketers Turn Sour on Global Sales Pitch."

20. Kenneth Labich, "America's International Winners," *Fortune,* April 14, 1986, 34–46.

21. Based on Michael A. Hitt, R. Duane Ireland, and Robert E. Hoskisson, *Strategic Management: Competitiveness and Globalization* (St. Paul, Minn.: West, 1995), 238.

22. Kathryn M. Bartol and David C. Martin, *Management,* 2d ed. (New York: McGraw-Hill, Inc., 1994), 642.

23. Thomas S. Bateman and Carl P. Zeithaml, *Management: Function and Strategy,* 2d ed. (Homewood, Ill.: Irwin, 1993), 231.

24. Michael E. Porter, "What is Strategy?" *Harvard Business Review,* November–December 1996, 61–78.

25. Arthur A. Thompson, Jr., and A. J. Strickland III, *Strategic Management: Concepts and Cases,* 6th ed. (Homewood, Ill.: Irwin, 1992).

26. Michael Treacy and Fred Wiersema, "How Market Leaders Keep Their Edge," *Fortune,* February 6, 1995, 88–98.

27. Carl Long and Mary Vickers-Koch, "Using Core Capabilities to Create Competitive Advantage," *Organizational Dynamics* 24, no. 1 (summer 1995), 7–22; and Ronald B. Lieber, "Smart Science," *Fortune,* June 23, 1997, 73.

28. Michael Goold and Andrew Campbell, "Desperately Seeking Synergy," *Harvard Business Review,* September–October 1998, 131–143; and Jill Hamburg, "Synergy or Bust," *Working Woman,* September 1998, 15.

29. John S. DeMott, "Company Alliances for Market Muscle," *Nation's Business,* February 1994, 52–53.

30. Bradford McKee, "Ties That Bind Large and Small," *Nation's Business,* February 1992, 24–26.

31. Gregory M. Bounds, Gregory H. Dobbins, and Oscar S. Fowler, *Management: A Total Quality Perspective* (Cincinnati: South-Western College Publishing, 1995), 244.

32. Michael Treacy, "You Need a Value Discipline—But Which One?" *Fortune,* April 17, 1995, 195.

33. Hitt, Ireland, and Hoskisson, *Strategic Management.*

34. Milton Leontiades, *Strategies for Diversification and Change* (Boston: Little, Brown, 1980), 63; and Dan E. Schendel and Charles W. Hofer, eds., *Strategic Management: A New View of Business Policy and Planning* (Boston: Little, Brown, 1979), 11–14.

35. Gail Edmondson, "Ultimatum at Philips," *Business Week,* November 17, 1997, 134–135; and Charles P. Wallace, "Can He Fix Philips?" *Fortune,* March 31, 1997, 98–100.

36. Myron Magnet, "Let's Go for Growth," *Fortune,* March 7, 1994, 60–72.

37. Joan O'C. Hamilton, "Brighter Days at Clorox," *Business Week,* June 16, 1997, 62, 65; David Leonhardt, "Sara Lee: Playing with the Recipe," *Business Week,* April 27, 1998, 114–116; and Sean Silcoff, "The Emporiums Strike Back," *Canadian Business,* September 26, 1997, 53–77.

38. Kathleen Madigan, Julia Flynn, and Joseph Walker, "Masters of the Game," *Business Week,* October 12, 1992, 110, 118.

39. Milton Leontiades, "The Confusing Words of Business Policy," *Academy of Management Review* 7 (1982), 45–48.

40. Lawrence G. Hrebiniak and William F. Joyce, *Implementing Strategy* (New York: Macmillan, 1984).

41. James E. Svatko, "Analyzing the Competition," *Small Business Reports* (January 1989), 21–28; and Brian Dumaine, "Corporate Spies Snoop to Conquer," *Fortune,* November 7, 1988, 68–76.

42. Steve Swartz, "Basic Bedrooms: How Marriott Changes Hotel Design to Tap Mid-Priced Market," *The Wall Street Journal,* September 18, 1985, 1.

43. James B. Treece with Greg Burns, "The Nervous Faces around Kellogg's Breakfast Table," *Business Week,* July 18, 1994, 33.

44. Paul Roberts, "The Free Agent Home Office," *Fast Company,* December–January 1998, 164–179.

45. Frederick W. Gluck, "A Fresh Look at Strategic Management," *Journal of Business Strategy* 6 (fall 1985), 4–19.

46. Thompson and Strickland, *Strategic Management;* and William L. Shanklin and John K. Ryans, Jr., "Is the International Cash Cow Really a Prize Heifer?" *Business Horizons* 24 (1981), 10–16.

47. William C. Symonds, with Carol Matlack, "Gillette's Edge," *Business Week,* January 19, 1998, 70–77; William C. Symonds, "Would You Spend $1.50 for a Razor Blade?" *Business Week,* April 27, 1998, 46; and Barbara Carton, "Gillette Looks Beyond Whiskers to Big Hair and Stretchy Floss," *The Wall Street Journal,* December 14, 1994, B1, B4.

48. Michael E. Porter, *Competitive Strategy* (New York: Free Press, 1980), 36–46; Danny Miller, "Relating Porter's Business Strategies to Environment and Structure: Analysis and Performance Implementations," *Academy of Management Journal* 31 (1988), 280–308; and Michael E. Porter, "From Competitive Advantage to Corporate Strategy," *Harvard Business Review* (May–June 1987), 43–59.

49. David Greising, "Watch Out for Flying Packages," *Business Week,* November 14, 1994, 40.

50. Thomas L. Wheelen and J. David Hunger, *Strategic Management and Business Policy* (Reading, Mass.: Addison-Wesley, 1989).

51. Peter Verburg, "The Little Airline That Could," *Canadian Business,* April, 1997, 34–40.

52. Thompson and Strickland, *Strategic Management.*

53. Greg Burns, "It Only Hertz When Enterprise Laughs," *Business Week,* December 12, 1994, 44.

54. Joshua Rosenbaum, "Guitar Maker Looks for a New Key," *The Wall Street Journal,* February 11, 1998, B1, B5.

55. Based on John Burton, "Composite Strategy: The Combination of Collaboration and Competition," *Journal of General Management* 21, No. 1 (autumn 1995), 1–23; and Roberta Maynard, "Striking the Right Match," *Nation's Business,* May 1996, 18–28.

56. Elizabeth Jensen and Eben Shapiro, "Time Warner's Fight with News Corp. Belies Mutual Dependence," *The Wall Street Journal,* October 28, 1996, A1, A6.

57. Maynard, "Striking the Right Match."

58. Stratford Sherman, "Are Strategic Alliances Working?" *Fortune,* September 21, 1992, 77–78; and David Lei, "Strategies for Global Competition," *Long-Range Planning* 22 (1989), 102–109.

59. James Aley and Matt Siegel, "The Fallout from Merger Mania," *Fortune,* March 2, 1998, 26–27.

60. William Glasgall with John Rossant and Thane Peterson, "Citigroup: Just the Start?" *Business Week,* April 20, 1998, 34–37; and Leah Nathans Spiro, with Debra Sparks, Andrea Mandel-Campbell, Brian Bremmer, and Owen Ullmann, "The 'Coca-Cola of Personal Finance,'" *Business Week,* April 20, 1998, 37–38.

61. Burton, "Composite Strategy: The Combination of Collaboration and Competition."

62. Harold W. Fox, "A Framework for Functional Coordination," *Atlanta Economic Review* (now *Business Magazine*), November–December 1973.

63. L. J. Bourgeois III and David R. Brodwin, "Strategic Implementation: Five Approaches to an Elusive Phenomenon," *Strategic Management Journal* 5 (1984), 241–264; Anil K. Gupta and V. Govindarajan, "Business Unit Strategy, Managerial Characteristics, and Business Unit Effectiveness at Strategy Implementation," *Academy of Management Journal* (1984), 25–41; and Jeffrey G. Covin, Dennis P. Slevin, and Randall L. Schultz, "Implementing Strategic Missions: Effective Strategic, Structural, and Tactical Choices," *Journal of Management Studies* 31, no. 4 (1994), 481–505.

64. Rainer Feurer and Kazem Chaharbaghi, "Dynamic Strategy Formulation and Alignment," *Journal of General Management* 20, no. 3(spring 1995), 76–90; and Henry Mintzberg, *The*

Rise and Fall of Strategic Planning (Toronto: Maxwell Macmillan Canada, 1994).

65. Jay R. Galbraith and Robert K. Kazanjian, *Strategy Implementation: Structure, Systems and Process,* 2d ed. (St. Paul, Minn.: West, 1986); and Paul C. Nutt, "Selecting Tactics to Implement Strategic Plans," *Strategic Management Journal* 10 (1989), 145–161.

66. Alex Taylor III, "Neutron Jurgen Ignites a Revolution at Daimler-Benz," *Fortune,* November 10, 1997, 144–152.

67. Michael W. Miller, "Q. T. Wiles Revives Sick High-Tech Firms with Strong Medicine," *The Wall Street Journal,* June 23, 1986, 1, 12.

68. Zachary Schiller, "What's Deflating Uniroyal Goodrich," *Business Week,* November 30, 1987, 35.

69. Gupta and Govindarajan, "Business Unit Strategy"; and Bourgeois and Brodwin, "Strategic Implementation."

70. Greg Burns, "How a New Boss Got ConAgra Cooking Again," *Business Week,* July 25, 1994, 72–73.

71. Jay Finegan, "Unconventional Wisdom," *Inc.,* December 1994, 44–59.

72. James E. Skivington and Richard L. Daft, "A Study of Organizational 'Framework' and 'Process' Modalities for the Implementation of Business-Level Strategies" (unpublished manuscript, Texas A&M University, 1987).

73. Roger Thurow, "A Sports Icon Regains Its Footing by Using the Moves of the Past," *The Wall Street Journal,* January 21, 1998, A1, A10.

74. Desmond, "What's Ailing Kodak? Fuji."

Chapter 9

LEARNING OBJECTIVES

After studying this chapter, you should be able to

⊛ Explain why decision making is an important component of good management.

⊛ Explain the difference between programmed and nonprogrammed decisions and the decision characteristics of risk, uncertainty, and ambiguity.

⊛ Describe the classical, administrative, and political models of decision making and their applications.

⊛ Identify the six steps used in managerial decision making.

⊛ Explain four personal decision styles used by managers.

⊛ Discuss the advantages and disadvantages of participative decision making.

⊛ Identify guidelines for improving decision-making effectiveness in organizations.

Managerial Decision Making

MANAGEMENT PROBLEM

For most of its 230-year history, the *Encyclopaedia Brittanica* has been viewed as an illustrious repository of cultural and historical knowledge—almost a national treasure. Generations of students and librarians relied on the Britannica to research everything from the Aleutian Islands to the history of zydeco—but that was before CD-ROMs and the Internet became the study tools of choice. Suddenly, the 32-volume collection of encyclopedias seemed destined to fade into history. Britannica was slow to move into electronic media and practically ceded the market to upstarts such as Microsoft's *Encarta*. Managers made a serious blunder in 1993 when they sold the company's Compton unit, a CD-ROM pioneer now being used by millions of consumers. Even when Britannica finally introduced a CD-ROM, it was priced at a staggering $1,200, while Microsoft was offering cut-rate deals or giving *Encarta* away free with personal computers. Now, Swiss-based financier Jacob Safra has bought Britannica and installed new management to help him usher the company into the digital age. He believes Britannica can once again be the quality leader. However, decisions have to be made about how to use the company's venerable name to compete with Microsoft's *Encarta*, Compton's, and IBM's joint venture with *World Book*, as well as with the numerous free or low-cost information options available on the Internet.[1]

If you were a member of the new management team at Britannica, what decisions would you make to successfully compete in today's world? What alternatives would you consider and what course of action would you choose?

Encyclopaedia Brittanica, Inc., is alive and kicking again thanks to early decisions made by new management. Now managers have to sharpen their skills to make important decisions that will affect the future of their business. Every organization grows, prospers, or fails as a result of decisions by its managers.

Managers often are referred to as *decision makers*. Although many of their important decisions are strategic, managers also make decisions about every other aspect of an organization, including structure, control systems, responses to the environment, and human resources. Managers scout for problems, make decisions for solving them, and monitor the consequences to see whether additional decisions are required. Good decision making is a vital part of good management, because decisions determine how the organization solves its problems, allocates resources, and accomplishes its goals.

Decision making is not easy. It must be done amid ever-changing factors, unclear information, and conflicting points of view. For example, during the 1997 Teamster's strike against United Parcel Service, UPS found itself in the middle of a public relations disaster because of a faulty decision. Executives failed to understand the seriousness of the strike, expecting it to last only a day or two. Thus, they decided not to appoint a single UPS spokesperson to handle the media. With as many as a dozen human resources executives answering questions from the press, UPS was unable to tell a clear, unified story, contributing to a loss of public sympathy for the company.[2] Both Mattel and Hasbro, the top U.S. toymakers, passed on the Ninja Turtles idea in the late 1980s, and the action figures went on to sell billions. Coca-Cola pumped some $30 million into developing the BreakMate, a miniature soda fountain, but the product flopped in the marketplace and Break-Mate fountains now sit gathering dust in storage sheds.[3]

The business world is full of evidence of both good and poor decisions. Andy Grove, CEO of Intel Corporation, decided to get out of the DRAM memory-chip business in the mid-1980s and focus relentlessly on microprocessors. The decision was a risky one, and many Intel executives opposed it, but it set Intel on course to become one of the richest and most powerful companies in the world. Now, some observers believe Intel has missed a chance for a second wave of tremendous growth by failing to build simple, fast, inexpensive chips for non-PC devices such as smart identification cards, Internet-ready telephones, hand-held computers, digital cameras, video game players, computers on car dashboards, and other consumer gadgets. As industry watchers talk about the "convergence" of computing and consumer electronics, some warn that Intel's decision to focus on ever-more-powerful processors for PCs will ultimately hurt the company.[4]

Chapters 7 and 8 described strategic planning. This chapter explores the decision process that underlies strategic planning. Plans and strategies are arrived at through decision making; the better the decision making, the better the strategic planning. First we will examine decision characteristics. Then we will look at decision-making models and the steps executives should take when making important decisions. We will also examine participative decision making and discuss techniques for improving decision making in organizations.

Types of Decisions and Problems

decision
A choice made from available alternatives.

A **decision** is a choice made from available alternatives. For example, an accounting manager's selection among Bill, Nancy, and Joan for the position of junior auditor is a decision. Many people assume that making a choice is the major part of decision making, but it is only a part.

Decision making is the process of identifying problems and opportunities and then resolving them.[5] Decision making involves effort both before and after the actual choice. Thus, the decision as to whether to select Bill, Nancy, or Joan requires the accounting manager to ascertain whether a new junior auditor is needed, determine the availability of potential job candidates, interview candidates to acquire necessary information, select one candidate, and follow up with the socialization of the new employee into the organization to ensure the decision's success.

Programmed and Nonprogrammed Decisions

Management decisions typically fall into one of two categories: programmed and nonprogrammed. **Programmed decisions** involve situations that have occurred often enough to enable decision rules to be developed and applied in the future.[6] Programmed decisions are made in response to recurring organizational problems. The decision to reorder paper and other office supplies when inventories drop to a certain level is a programmed decision. Other programmed decisions concern the types of skills required to fill certain jobs, the reorder point for manufacturing inventory, exception reporting for expenditures 10 percent or more over budget, and selection of freight routes for product deliveries. Once managers formulate decision rules, subordinates and others can make the decision, freeing managers for other tasks.

Nonprogrammed decisions are made in response to situations that are unique, are poorly defined and largely unstructured, and have important consequences for the organization. Many nonprogrammed decisions involve strategic planning, because uncertainty is great and decisions are complex. Decisions to build a new factory, develop a new product or service, enter a new geographical market, or relocate headquarters to another city are all nonprogrammed decisions. When AT&T's new CEO C. Michael Armstrong decided to sell two unrelated business units and buy Teleport Communications, a local phone company, he made a nonprogrammed decision. Armstrong and other top managers had to analyze complex problems, evaluate alternatives, and make a choice about how to revive the struggling company. Armstrong's decisions have improved both employee morale and AT&T's flagging stock price.[7]

Certainty, Risk, Uncertainty, and Ambiguity

One primary difference between programmed and nonprogrammed decisions relates to the degree of certainty or uncertainty managers deal with in making the decision. In a perfect world, managers would have all the information necessary for making decisions. In reality, however, some things are unknowable; thus, some decisions will fail to solve the problem or attain the desired outcome. Managers try to obtain information about decision alternatives that will reduce decision uncertainty. Every decision situation can be organized on a scale according to the availability of information and the possibility of failure. The four positions on the scale are certainty, risk, uncertainty, and ambiguity, as illustrated in Exhibit 9.1. Whereas programmed decisions can be made in situations involving certainty, many situations that managers deal with every day involve at least some degree of uncertainty and require nonprogrammed decision making.

---

decision making
The process of identifying problems and opportunities and then resolving them.

programmed decision
A decision made in response to a situation that has occurred often enough to enable decision rules to be developed and applied in the future.

nonprogrammed decision
A decision made in response to a situation that is unique, is poorly defined and largely unstructured, and has important consequences for the organization.

Peter Metcalf feels on top of the world since sales of his company's climbing equipment and backcountry skis have doubled to hit $20 million. As CEO of Salt Lake City, Utah-based Black Diamond Equipment, Ltd., Metcalf made a strategic nonprogrammed decision three years ago to relocate company headquarters from Ventura, California. Real estate prices in Ventura were sky-high, and Black Diamond faced strict regulations, high workers' compensation costs, and rapidly rising health insurance premiums. Yet, relocation would be costly, and there were no guarantees it would pull the company out of its slump. After evaluating alternatives, Metcalf made a decision that proved to be right on target.

certainty
All the information the decision maker needs is fully available.

risk
A decision has clear-cut goals, and good information is available, but the future outcomes associated with each alternative are subject to chance.

uncertainty
Managers know what goal they wish to achieve, but information about alternatives and future events is incomplete.

Certainty.   **Certainty** means that all the information the decision maker needs is fully available.[8] Managers have information on operating conditions, resource costs or constraints, and each course of action and possible outcome. For example, if a company considers a $10,000 investment in new equipment that it knows for certain will yield $4,000 in cost savings per year over the next five years, managers can calculate a before-tax rate of return of about 40 percent. If managers compare this investment with one that will yield only $3,000 per year in cost savings, they can confidently select the 40 percent return. However, few decisions are certain in the real world. Most contain risk or uncertainty.

Risk.   **Risk** means that a decision has clear-cut goals and that good information is available, but the future outcomes associated with each alternative are subject to chance. However, enough information is available to allow the probability of a successful outcome for each alternative to be estimated.[9] Statistical analysis might be used to calculate the probabilities of success or failure. The measure of risk captures the possibility that future events will render the alternative unsuccessful. Some oil companies use a quantitative simulation approach to estimate hydrocarbon reserves, enabling oil executives to evaluate the variation in risk at each stage of exploration and production and make better decisions. McDonald's took a calculated risk and lost with the introduction of its Arch Deluxe sandwich line. McDonald's had information that indicated a line of sandwiches targeted toward adults would be successful, but the Arch Deluxe, introduced at a cost of $100 million, flopped in the marketplace.[10]

Uncertainty.   **Uncertainty** means that managers know which goals they wish to achieve, but information about alternatives and future events is incomplete.[11] Managers do not have enough information to be clear about alternatives or to estimate their risk. Factors that may affect a decision, such as price, production costs, volume, or future interest rates, are difficult to analyze and predict. Managers may have to make assumptions from which to forge the decision even though it will be wrong if the assumptions are incorrect. Managers may have to come up with creative approaches to alternatives and use personal judgment to determine which alternative is best.

For example, Eastman Kodak faced great uncertainty in its decision to invest $500 million a year to develop an array of digital photography products that executives hope will fundamentally change the way people create, store, and view photographs. Microsoft faced uncertainty in deciding to commit major development costs to the Microsoft Network (MSN). At the time, it was not clear whether open networks such as the Internet, or proprietary networks such as MSN, would become the standard. When it became clear that open networks would prevail, Microsoft was able to cut its losses and reorient the MSN concept around the Internet.[12]

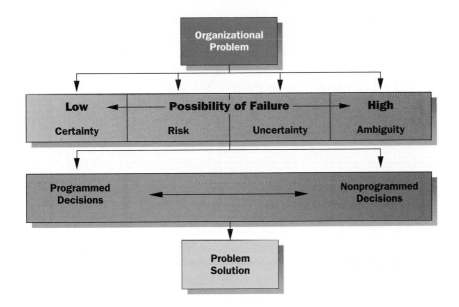

Exhibit *9.1*
Conditions That Affect the Possibility of Decision Failure

Many decisions made under uncertainty do not produce the desired results, but managers face uncertainty every day. They must find creative ways to cope with uncertainty in order to make effective decisions.

Ambiguity. Ambiguity is by far the most difficult decision situation. **Ambiguity** means that the goals to be achieved or the problem to be solved is unclear, alternatives are difficult to define, and information about outcomes is unavailable.[13] Ambiguity is what students would feel if an instructor created student groups, told each group to complete a project, but gave the groups no topic, direction, or guidelines whatsoever. Ambiguity has been called a "wicked" decision problem. Managers have a difficult time coming to grips with the issues. Wicked problems are associated with manager conflicts over goals and decision alternatives, rapidly changing circumstances, fuzzy information, and unclear linkages among decision elements.[14] Sometimes managers will come up with a "solution" only to realize that they hadn't clearly defined the real problem to begin with.[15] Fortunately, most decisions are not characterized by ambiguity. But when they are, managers must conjure up goals and develop reasonable scenarios for decision alternatives in the absence of information. When reports surfaced several years ago that syringes and hypodermic needles had been found in cans of Pepsi, Pepsi-Cola executives faced ambiguity squarely in the face.

ambiguity
The goals to be achieved or the problem to be solved is unclear, alternatives are difficult to define, and information about outcomes is unavailable.

Pepsi-Cola executives faced a truly wicked decision problem when reports began surfacing around the country that syringes and hypodermic needles had been found in cans of Pepsi. Before they could develop decision alternatives, executives first had to identify the problem—could needles have been put in Pepsi at the canning plants, or were the reports a hoax? Information was fuzzy and fast-changing, but executives needed to make a decision quickly.

Pepsi faced a dilemma: Clear evidence of danger would demand a product recall, but such evidence did not exist. A recall would be extremely costly for the company, but loss of consumer trust would be even more expensive in the

PEPSI-COLA
www.pepsico.com

long run. After carefully analyzing the situation, Pepsi's managers believed syringes could not appear in unopened cans of Pepsi. They decided not to issue a recall but rather to respond quickly and openly to consumer fears with a massive public relations and education campaign. Pepsi-Cola's CEO Craig Weatherup himself took to the airwaves to explain how implausible it was that syringes could have been put into Pepsi cans at the plants. At one point, Weatherup appeared on ABC's *Nightline* with FDA Commissioner David Kessler, who did not believe there was evidence of nationwide tampering.

The company took great care to keep bottlers up to speed on fast-breaking developments, and bottlers then passed the information along to every level of the organization—from filling line operators to route salespeople. Nationwide ad campaigns explained the decision and assured consumers that there had been no injuries and not a single confirmed case of a needle found in an unopened can of Pepsi.

By allying itself with the FDA and responding quickly and openly to public fears, Pepsi weathered the syringe-scare crisis with little damage. Pepsi managers made the right decision, believing, based on careful internal analysis, that needles could not possibly have been put into cans of Pepsi at the plants. However, it was a decision that could have backfired if the company were unable to convince consumers that Pepsi products were truly safe.[16]

Decision-Making Models

The approach managers use to make decisions usually falls into one of three types—the classical model, the administrative model, or the political model. The choice of model depends on the manager's personal preference, whether the decision is programmed or nonprogrammed, and the extent to which the decision is characterized by risk, uncertainty, or ambiguity.

Classical Model

classical model
A decision-making model based on the assumption that managers should make logical decisions that will be in the organization's best economic interests.

The **classical model** of decision making is based on economic assumptions. This model has arisen within the management literature because managers are expected to make decisions that are economically sensible and in the organization's best economic interests. The assumptions underlying this model are as follows:

1. The decision maker operates to accomplish goals that are known and agreed upon. Problems are precisely formulated and defined.

2. The decision maker strives for conditions of certainty, gathering complete information. All alternatives and the potential results of each are calculated.

3. Criteria for evaluating alternatives are known. The decision maker selects the alternative that will maximize the economic return to the organization.

4. The decision maker is rational and uses logic to assign values, order preferences, evaluate alternatives, and make the decision that will maximize the attainment of organizational goals.

normative
An approach that defines how a decision maker should make decisions and provides guidelines for reaching an ideal outcome for the organization.

The classical model of decision making is considered to be **normative,** which means it defines how a decision maker *should* make decisions. It does not describe how managers actually make decisions so much as it provides guidelines on how to reach an ideal outcome for the organization. The value of the classical model has been its ability to help decision makers be more rational. For example, many senior managers rely solely on intuition and personal preferences for making decisions.[17] In recent years, the classical approach has been given wider application because of the growth of quantitative decision techniques that use computers. Quantitative techniques (discussed in detail in the appendix) include such things as decision trees, payoff matrices, break-even analysis, linear programming, forecasting, and operations research models. The use of computerized information systems and databases has increased the power of the classical approach.

In many respects, the classical model represents an "ideal" model of decision making that is often unattainable by real people in real organizations. It is most valuable when applied to programmed decisions and to decisions characterized by certainty or risk, because relevant information is available and probabilities can be calculated. One example of the classical approach is the model developed by a Canadian organization for scheduling ambulance services.

URGENCES SANTÉ

Urgences Santé, a public agency responsible for coordinating ambulance service in the Montreal area, schedules vehicle time and working hours for approximately 80 ambulances and 700 technicians. Since Urgences Santé does not own its vehicles or hire technicians but instead rents these from private companies, agency managers wanted to optimize the schedule to avoid unnecessary rental costs.

Two types of calls require ambulance service—emergency calls from the public, which occur randomly throughout the day and require immediate attention, and calls from hospitals, which are concentrated in specific time periods and are generally not urgent. In addition, demand for ambulance service usually is higher in the winter but with more emergency calls on weekends during the summer months. Besides meeting shifting demand, a number of other constraints governed the design of a new schedule.

Urgences Santé applied mathematical formulations and techniques to first build workday schedules for each type of day (weekend or weekday) for each season, then equitably assign workdays to the 15 or so private service companies, and finally build individual schedules for the 700 technicians. More than 85 percent of the individual schedules can now be created automatically. The new system has had two positive effects. First, the agency is able to meet demand while cutting rental hours per week by up to 110 hours, thus saving approximately $250,000 per year. Second, the quality of technicians' schedules has been dramatically improved, leading to a decrease in turnover for the service companies.[18]

Administrative Model

The **administrative model** of decision making describes how managers actually make decisions in difficult situations, such as those characterized by nonprogrammed decisions, uncertainty, and ambiguity. Many management decisions are not sufficiently programmable to lend themselves to any degree of quantification. Managers are unable to make economically rational decisions even if they want to.[19]

administrative model
A decision-making model that describes how managers actually make decisions in situations characterized by nonprogrammed decisions, uncertainty, and ambiguity.

Bounded Rationality and Satisficing. The administrative model of decision making is based on the work of Herbert A. Simon. Simon proposed two concepts that were instrumental in shaping the administrative model:

bounded rationality
The concept that people have the time and cognitive ability to process only a limited amount of information on which to base decisions.

satisfice
To choose the first solution alternative that satisfies minimal decision criteria regardless of whether better solutions are presumed to exist.

bounded rationality and satisficing. **Bounded rationality** means that people have limits, or boundaries, on how rational they can be. The organization is incredibly complex, and managers have the time and ability to process only a limited amount of information with which to make decisions.[20] Because managers do not have the time or cognitive ability to process complete information about complex decisions, they must satisfice. **Satisficing** means that decision makers choose the first solution alternative that satisfies minimal decision criteria. Rather than pursuing all alternatives to identify the single solution that will maximize economic returns, managers will opt for the first solution that appears to solve the problem, even if better solutions are presumed to exist. The decision maker cannot justify the time and expense of obtaining complete information.[21]

An example of both bounded rationality and satisficing occurs when a junior executive on a business trip stains her blouse just before an important meeting. She will run to a nearby clothing store and buy the first satisfactory replacement she finds. Having neither the time nor the opportunity to explore all the blouses in town, she satisfices by choosing a blouse that will solve the immediate problem. In a similar fashion, managers generate alternatives for complex problems only until they find one they believe will work. For example, several years ago then-Disney chairman Ray Watson and chief operating officer Ron Miller attempted to thwart takeover attempts, but they had limited options. They satisficed with a quick decision to acquire Arivda Realty and Gibson Court Company. The acquisition of these companies had the potential to solve the problem at hand; thus, they looked no further for possibly better alternatives.[22]

The administrative model relies on assumptions different from those of the classical model and focuses on organizational factors that influence individual decisions. It is more realistic than the classical model for complex, nonprogrammed decisions. According to the administrative model,

1. Decision goals often are vague, conflicting, and lack consensus among managers. Managers often are unaware of problems or opportunities that exist in the organization.

2. Rational procedures are not always used, and, when they are, they are confined to a simplistic view of the problem that does not capture the complexity of real organizational events.

3. Managers' search for alternatives is limited because of human, information, and resource constraints.

4. Most managers settle for a satisficing rather than a maximizing solution. This is partly because they have limited information and partly because they have only vague criteria for what constitutes a maximizing solution.

The administrative model is considered to be **descriptive,** meaning that it describes how managers actually make decisions in complex situations rather than dictating how they *should* make decisions according to a theoretical ideal. The administrative model recognizes the human and environmental limitations that affect the degree to which managers can pursue a rational decision-making process.

Intuition.   Another aspect of administrative decision making is intuition. **Intuition** represents a quick apprehension of a decision situation based on past experience but without conscious thought.[23] Intuitive decision making

Managers at Hudson Products Corporation, a manufacturer of heat-exchange equipment for the hydrocarbon processing industry, followed the classical model *of decision making to reach their long-term goal to maintain Hudsons's market share in air-cooled heat exchangers while generating income from new products. Hudson just completed one of its best years, with records for bookings, revenues and backlog, and continued high performance toward meeting schedules. Hudson managers have made the decision to participate in alliances with Shell, Dow Chemical, Amoco, Texaco, and Bechtel in order to maintain their strong market share. They also plan to generate income from new products including steam condensers, tank heaters, and a small-footprint gas-oil separator (in the photo) that is particularly suited for offshore platforms.*

is not arbitrary or irrational, because it is based on years of practice and hands-on experience that enable managers to quickly identify solutions without going through painstaking computations. In fact, Michael Ray and Rochelle Myers, in a book called *Creativity in Business*, suggest that intuition really is "recognition." When people build a depth of experience and knowledge in a particular area, the right decision often comes quickly and effortlessly as a recognition of information that has been largely forgotten by the conscious mind. For example, actor and director Jodie Foster is known for making good intuitive decisions at her production company, Egg Pictures. Foster made her movie debut at the age of 8, and her manager-mother involved her in almost all decision making regarding roles, script changes, and so forth. "She understands Hollywood almost mathematically," said one producer.[24] Managers rely on intuition to determine when a problem exists and to synthesize isolated bits of data and experience into an integrated picture. They also use their intuitive understanding to check the results of rational analysis. If the rational analysis does not agree with their intuition, managers may dig further before accepting a proposed alternative.[25]

Intuition helps managers understand situations characterized by uncertainty and ambiguity that have proven impervious to rational analysis. The movie *M*A*S*H* and the television programs "All in the Family," "Hill Street Blues," and "Cheers" would have been squashed in their infancy if producers Robert Altman, Norman Lear, and Stephen Bochco hadn't gone with their gut feelings and pushed the projects.[26]

Political Model

The third model of decision making is useful for making nonprogrammed decisions when conditions are uncertain, information is limited, and there is disagreement among managers about what goals to pursue or what course of action to take. Most organizational decisions involve many managers who are pursuing different goals, and they have to talk with one another to share information and reach an agreement. Managers often engage in coalition building for making complex organizational decisions. A **coalition** is an informal alliance among managers who support a specific goal. *Coalition building* is the process of forming alliances among managers. In other words, a manager who supports a specific alternative, such as increasing the corporation's growth by acquiring another company, talks informally to other executives and tries to persuade them to support the decision. When the outcomes are not predictable, managers gain support through discussion, negotiation, and bargaining. Without a coalition, a powerful individual or group could derail the decision-making process. Coalition building gives several managers an opportunity to contribute to decision making, enhancing their commitment to the alternative that is ultimately adopted.[27]

The political model closely resembles the real environment in which most managers and decision makers operate. Decisions are complex and involve many people, information is often ambiguous, and disagreement and conflict over problems and solutions are normal. The basic assumptions of the political model are:

1. Organizations are made up of groups with diverse interests, goals, and values. Managers disagree about problem priorities and may not understand or share the goals and interests of other managers.

descriptive
An approach that describes how managers actually make decisions rather than how they should.

intuition
The immediate comprehension of a decision situation based on past experience but without conscious thought.

coalition
An informal alliance among managers who support a specific goal.

"*It's a major gut story,*" Bruce Goldsmith says about his decision to open a retail store right in the warehouse of his family's mail-order coffee business. Since Baronet Coffee, Inc.'s warehouse is in an industrial area with little foot traffic, most employees thought the idea was a little wacky, but Goldsmith's intuition told him it was the right thing to do. His years of experience observing customers and a few assumptions about human nature gave him a hunch that people would like the idea of picking up their coffee directly from the source. The hunch was right, and Baronet's retail sales quadrupled Goldsmith's original projections.

Exhibit *9.2*   *Characteristics of Classical, Administrative, and Political Decision-Making Models*

Classical Model	Administrative Model	Political Model
Clear-cut problem and goals	Vague problem and goals	Pluralistic; conflicting goals
Condition of certainty	Condition of uncertainty	Condition of uncertainty/ambiguity
Full information about alternatives and their outcomes	Limited information about alternatives and their outcomes	Inconsistent viewpoints; ambiguous information
Rational choice by individual for maximizing outcomes	Satisficing choice for resolving problem using intuition	Bargaining and discussion among coalition members

2. Information is ambiguous and incomplete. The attempt to be rational is limited by the complexity of many problems as well as personal and organizational constraints.

3. Managers do not have the time, resources, or mental capacity to identify all dimensions of the problem and process all relevant information. Managers talk to each other and exchange viewpoints to gather information and reduce ambiguity.

4. Managers engage in the push and pull of debate to decide goals and discuss alternatives. Decisions are the result of bargaining and discussion among coalition members.

One of the most visible coalition builders of recent years was former president George Bush, who would seek a broad-based coalition at the start of any important decision process. For example, during the decision process for the Persian Gulf War, Bush successfully built a coalition among the heads of several countries by explaining why Saddam Hussein's action threatened each nation's future. He then followed up with constant communication with the head of each country, Congress, and the American public.[28] The inability to build coalitions often makes it difficult or impossible for managers to see their decisions implemented. Hershell Ezrin, president and CEO of Speedy Muffler King, recently left the Canadian-based company in the face of mounting problems. One problem Ezrin faced was that many senior-level executives resented his appointment and he was unable to build a coalition of managers to support his decisions for change.[29]

The key dimensions of the classical, administrative, and political models are listed in Exhibit 9.2. Recent research into decision-making procedures has found rational, classical procedures to be associated with high performance for organizations in stable environments. However, administrative and political decision-making procedures and intuition have been associated with high performance in unstable environments in which decisions must be made rapidly and under more difficult conditions.[30]

Decision-Making Steps

Whether a decision is programmed or nonprogrammed and regardless of managers' choice of the classical, administrative, or political model of decision making, six steps typically are associated with effective decision processes. These are summarized in Exhibit 9.3.

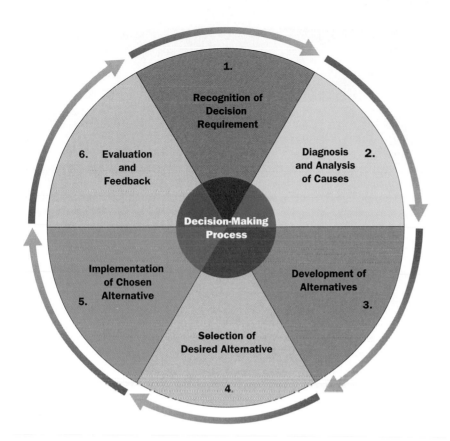

Exhibit *9.3*

Six Steps in the Managerial Decision-Making Process

Recognition of Decision Requirement

Managers confront a decision requirement in the form of either a problem or an opportunity. A **problem** occurs when organizational accomplishment is less than established goals. Some aspect of performance is unsatisfactory. An **opportunity** exists when managers see potential accomplishment that exceeds specified current goals. Managers see the possibility of enhancing performance beyond current levels.

Awareness of a problem or opportunity is the first step in the decision sequence and requires surveillance of the internal and external environment for issues that merit executive attention.[31] This resembles the military concept of gathering intelligence. Managers scan the world around them to determine whether the organization is satisfactorily progressing toward its goals.

Some information comes from periodic accounting reports, MIS reports, and other sources that are designed to discover problems before they become too serious. For example, while reading a routine internal company report, Becky Roloff, a vice-president for IDS Financial Services (now American Express Financial Advisors), noted a high level of employee turnover that was not being addressed by the company. Her discovery of the problem eventually led to a comprehensive redesign of the company, including better training programs, more emphasis on teamwork, and stronger efforts to hire minorities.[32] Managers also take advantage of informal sources. They talk to other managers, gather opinions on how things are going, and seek advice on which problems should be tackled or which opportunities embraced.[33]

problem
A situation in which organizational accomplishments have failed to meet established goals.

opportunity
A situation in which managers see potential organizational accomplishments that exceed current goals.

Gateway is one of the leading direct marketers of personal computers in the world. It develops, markets, manufactures, and supports a broad line of desktop PCs, portable PCs, convergence products that combine the PC with television, home theater and the Internet, and other computer solutions. Until November 1996, all orders were handled by direct purchase, via the telephone, catalog, or World Wide Web. However, Gateway executives, led by Ted Waitt, Chairman and CEO, analyzed all the factors associated with computer buying habits and used diagnosis to decide that ". . . not everyone is comfortable spending $2,500 on a computer over the phone." So, rather than trying to change what makes their customers comfortable, they developed Gateway Country™ stores to meet their needs. The diagnosis and analysis processes that led to the decision to open the stores have apparently been correct. By the end of 1996, for example, 20 percent of their business in Japan was generated by the Tokyo showroom.

Recognizing decision requirements is difficult, because it often means integrating bits and pieces of information in novel ways. Some companies are finding that the World Wide Web can help them translate bits of data into useful information for better decision making, as described in the Technology box.

Diagnosis and Analysis of Causes

Once a problem or opportunity has come to a manager's attention, the understanding of the situation should be refined. **Diagnosis** is the step in the decision-making process in which managers analyze underlying causal factors associated with the decision situation. Managers make a mistake here if they jump right into generating alternatives without first exploring the cause of the problem more deeply.

Kepner and Tregoe, who have conducted extensive studies of manager decision making, recommend that managers ask a series of questions to specify underlying causes, including the following:

- What is the state of disequilibrium affecting us?
- When did it occur?
- Where did it occur?
- How did it occur?
- To whom did it occur?
- What is the urgency of the problem?
- What is the interconnectedness of events?
- What result came from which activity?[34]

Such questions help specify what actually happened and why. Managers at Silicon Graphics, the company whose dazzling three-dimensional graphics computers had a starring role animating the fearsome dinosaurs in *Jurassic Park*, are struggling to diagnose the underlying factors in the computer-maker's declining fortunes. The problem is an urgent one, as sales and stock price have fallen dramatically and SGI is scrambling to stay off technology's

diagnosis
The step in the decision-making process in which managers analyze underlying causal factors associated with the decision situation.

Pushing Key Data to Decision Makers

Some people see "push" technology that delivers data to desktops as overhyped technology. But Pat Brockett, executive vice president of worldwide sales and marketing at National Semiconductor, sees it as a way to boost sales. Brockett believes the technology helped National turn a $2 heat-sensing device into a $100-million-a-year product. The device cools the microprocessors that control multimedia laptops. National tapped into crucial data on its Web site to accurately forecast extraordinary demand for the product and crank up manufacturing.

National's Web site gets 6 million hits a month, mostly from engineers looking for specifications on products or asking questions. The site generates a ton of data, but managers needed a way to make it useful. That's when they discovered Pointcast Network, a Web service that broadcasts news and information to PCs in the form of a screensaver. Users can specify the type of data they want. Allowing National's managers to personalize product reports and select exactly the combination of data they needed thus transformed dry numbers into juicy insights. To get the most from the push technology, National's interactive marketing group added its own channel to Pointcast. Now, instead of plowing through piles of reports

and computer printouts, managers get tailored data and product updates delivered continuously directly to their desktop monitors. They can click through a simple menu to customize the reports, segment data by product lines, and view it in any form they choose.

Brockett is convinced that using the World Wide Web to keep ahead of product demand is essential in today's world of fast-changing technology. "Customers won't wait for us to catch up with their component requirements," he says. "They'll find another supplier." Before Pointcast, National's managers tried to forecast demand using sales and order information, along with market and technical intelligence. That may not have been enough to trigger an increase in development and production of the heat sensors, Brockett says. Adding in the evidence of customer interest on the Web is what tipped the balance toward action—and toward millions of bucks.

www.national.com
www.pointcast.com

SOURCE: Mary J. Cronin, "Using the Web to Push Key Data to Decision Makers," *Fortune*, September 29, 1997, 254.

---

list of has-beens. Managers are looking at the interconnectedness of issues such as the failure to pay attention to the bread-and-butter computer business in favor of dashing into glitzy new markets, the lack of appropriate marketing, inventory management, and quality control systems, missed Internet opportunities, poor coordination between departments, and a corporate culture that encourages a frat-house atmosphere.[35]

Development of Alternatives

Once the problem or opportunity has been recognized and analyzed, decision makers begin to consider taking action. The next stage is to generate possible alternative solutions that will respond to the needs of the situation and correct the underlying causes.

For a programmed decision, feasible alternatives are easy to identify and in fact usually are already available within the organization's rules and procedures. Nonprogrammed decisions, however, require developing new courses of action that will meet the company's needs. For decisions made under conditions of high uncertainty, managers may develop only one or two custom solutions that will satisfice for handling the problem.

Decision alternatives can be thought of as the tools for reducing the difference between the organization's current and desired performance. Consider how Chrysler Corporation, prior to its merger with Daimler Benz, faced the problem of Japanese competition in the automobile industry.

CHRYSLER CORPORATION
www.daimlerchrysler.com

On a hot July afternoon in 1990, Lee Iacocca huddled with a dozen Chrysler engineers to consider a decision that could determine the future of their company—and maybe that of the entire U.S. auto industry. Chrysler hadn't built a subcompact since the Omni and Horizon twins back in 1978, both of which had five safety recalls within the first six months and were blasted by *Consumer Reports* for their high-speed handling.

One alternative was to abandon small cars altogether and try to compete some other way, but Iacocca and other top executives realized how unfeasible that was. They knew that skill in making small cars was crucial for exploiting new opportunities in emerging markets of Asia and Latin America, where auto sales were expected to zoom 50 percent in the next decade. But designing and building small cars had taken Chrysler the same amount of time and money as large cars, although the small ones sold for much less. If the company couldn't make money on small cars, Iacocca knew Chrysler itself could end up on the junk heap. The head of Chrysler's small car team, Robert P. Marcell, built a coalition of managers who believed Chrysler could design and build the car, become the first U.S. company in decades to make a profitable subcompact, and reverse the downward spiral of the U.S. auto industry. This was a risky solution. Chrysler didn't have a reputation for reliability in small cars. If costs weren't rock bottom and quality top-notch, the project would surely fail. But, as Marcell put it, "If we dare to be different, we could be the reason the U.S. auto industry survives."

At the end of the July meeting, Iacocca had been persuaded that Chrysler could do it, and one of the most remarkable development efforts in Detroit's history began. The new Dodge Neon went on sale in January 1994 and, with a base price of $8,600, beat out the Japanese at the game of selling well-equipped small cars at a profit. Developing decision alternatives led to a creative solution that helped Chrysler become more competitive and revived the stagnant U.S. auto industry.[36]

Selection of Desired Alternative

Once feasible alternatives have been developed, one must be selected. The decision choice is the selection of the most promising of several alternative courses of action. The best alternative is one in which the solution best fits the overall goals and values of the organization and achieves the desired results using the fewest resources.[37] The manager tries to select the choice with the least amount of risk and uncertainty. Because some risk is inherent for most nonprogrammed decisions, managers try to gauge prospects for success. Under conditions of uncertainty, they may have to rely on their intuition and experience to estimate whether a given course of action is likely to succeed. Basing choices on overall goals and values can also effectively guide selection of alternatives. Johnson & Johnson's values-based decision making became evident when the company spent $100 million pulling Tylenol from store shelves after cyanide was discovered in some of the capsules. It was an expensive alternative in the short run but one that worked wonders for J&J's image and probably helped save Tylenol as a consumer product.[38]

Making choices depends on managers' personality factors and willingness to accept risk and uncertainty. For example, **risk propensity** is the willingness to undertake risk with the opportunity of gaining an increased payoff. The level of risk a manager is willing to accept will influence the analysis of cost and benefits to be derived from any decision. Consider the situations in Exhibit 9.4. In each situation, which alternative would you choose? A person

risk propensity
The willingness to undertake risk with the opportunity of gaining an increased payoff.

For each of the following decisions, which alternative would you choose?

1. In the final seconds of a game with the college's traditional rival, the coach of a college football team may choose a play that has a 95 percent chance of producing a tie score or one with a 30 percent chance of leading to victory or to sure defeat if it fails.

2. The president of a Canadian company must decide whether to build a new plant within Canada that has a 90 percent chance of producing a modest return on investment or to build it in a foreign country with an unstable political history. The latter alternative has a 40 percent chance of failing, but the returns would be enormous if it succeeded.

3. A college senior with considerable acting talent must choose a career. She has the opportunity to go on to medical school and become a physician, a career in which she is 80 percent likely to succeed. She would rather be an actress but realizes that the opportunity for success is only 20 percent.

Exhibit
9.4

Decision Alternatives with Different Levels of Risk

with a low risk propensity would tend to take assured moderate returns by going for a tie score, building a domestic plant, or pursuing a career as a physician. A risk taker would go for the victory, build a plant in a foreign country, or embark on an acting career. The Manager's Shoptalk box describes biases to avoid when selecting the desired alternative.

Implementation of Chosen Alternative

The **implementation** stage involves the use of managerial, administrative, and persuasive abilities to ensure that the chosen alternative is carried out. This is similar to the idea of strategic implementation described in Chapter 7. The ultimate success of the chosen alternative depends on whether it can be translated into action. Sometimes an alternative never becomes reality because managers lack the resources or energy needed to make things happen. Implementation may require discussion with people affected by the decision. Communication, motivation, and leadership skills must be used to see that the decision is carried out.

One reason Lee Iacocca succeeded in turning Chrysler around was his ability to implement decisions. Iacocca personally hired people from Ford to develop new auto models. He hired people who shared his vision and were eager to carry out his decisions. By contrast, Tandy Corporation's decision to become a major supplier to businesses by setting up 386 computer centers to support a new direct sales force foundered. Tandy had great success selling to consumers through its Radio Shack stores but simply did not know how to sell computers to businesses. The results were disappointing, and many of the computer centers had to be closed. Tandy lacked the ability to implement the decision to go after business customers.[39]

implementation
The step in the decision-making process that involves using managerial, administrative, and persuasive abilities to translate the chosen alternative into action.

Evaluation and Feedback

In the evaluation stage of the decision process, decision makers gather information that tells them how well the decision was implemented and whether it was effective in achieving its goals. For example, Tandy executives' evaluation of and feedback on the decision to open computer centers revealed poor sales performance. Feedback indicated that implementation was unsuccessful, so computer centers were closed and another approach was tried.

Shoptalk
MANAGER'S SHOPTALK

Decision Biases to Avoid

At a time when decision making is so important, many corporate executives do not know how to make a good choice among alternatives. They may rely on computer analyses or personal intuition without realizing that their own cognitive biases affect their judgment. The complexities of modern corporate life make good judgment more critical than ever. Many errors in judgment originate in the human mind's limited capacity and in the natural biases most managers display during decision making. Awareness of the six biases below can help managers make more enlightened choices:

1. *Being influenced by initial impressions.* When considering decisions, the mind often gives disproportionate weight to the first information it receives. These initial impressions, statistics, or estimates act as an anchor to our subsequent thoughts and judgments. Anchors can be as simple as a random comment by a colleague or a statistic read in a newspaper. Past events and trends also act as anchors. For example, in business, managers frequently look at the previous year's sales when estimating sales for the coming year. However, in rapidly changing environments, giving too much weight to the past can lead to poor forecasts and misguided decisions.

2. *Justifying past decisions.* Many people fall into the trap of making choices that justify their past decisions, even if those decisions no longer seem valid. For example, managers may invest tremendous time and energy into improving the performance of a problem employee whom they now realize should never have been hired in the first place. Another example is when investors continue to pour money into failing businesses hoping to turn things around. People are often unwilling to admit they made a mistake, so they continue to make flawed decisions in an effort to correct the past. This tendency to "throw good money after bad" is sometimes called *escalating commitment.*

3. *Seeing what you want to see.* People frequently look for information that supports their existing instinct or point of view and avoid information that contradicts it. This bias affects where managers look for information when considering decisions, as well as how they interpret the information they find. People tend to give too much weight to supporting information and too little to information that

Feedback is important because decision making is a continuous, never-ending process. Decision making is not completed when an executive or board of directors votes yes or no. Feedback provides decision makers with information that can precipitate a new decision cycle. The decision may fail, thus generating a new analysis of the problem, evaluation of alternatives, and selection of a new alternative. Many big problems are solved by trying several alternatives in sequence, each providing modest improvement. Feedback is the part of monitoring that assesses whether a new decision needs to be made.

An illustration of the overall decision-making process, including evaluation and feedback, was the decision to introduce a new deodorant at Tom's of Maine.

TOM'S OF MAINE
www.tomsofmaine.com

Tom's of Maine, known for its all-natural personal hygiene products, saw an opportunity to expand its line with a new natural deodorant. However, the opportunity quickly became a problem when the deodorant worked only half of the time with half of the customers who used it, and its all-recyclable plastic dials were prone to breakage.

The problem of the failed deodorant led founder Tom Chappell and other managers to analyze and diagnose what went wrong. They finally determined that the company's product development process had run amok. The same group of merry product developers was responsible from conception to launch of the product. They were so attached to the product that they failed to test it properly or consider potential problems, becoming instead "a mutual admiration society." Managers

conflicts with their established viewpoints. It is important for managers to be honest with themselves about their motives and to examine all the evidence with equal rigor. Having a devil's advocate to argue against a decision can also help avoid this decision trap.

4. *Perpetuating the status quo.* Managers may base decisions on what has worked in the past and fail to explore new options, dig for additional information, or investigate new technologies. For example, Du Pont clung to its cash cow, nylon, despite growing evidence in the scientific community that a new product, polyester, was superior for tire cords. Celanese, a relatively small competitor, blew Du Pont out of the water by exploiting this new evidence, quickly capturing 75 percent of the tire market.

5. *Being influenced by problem framing.* The decision response of a manager can be influenced by the mere wording of a problem. For example, consider a manager faced with a decision about salvaging the cargo of three barges that sank off the coast of Alaska. If managers are given the option of approving (A) a plan that has a 100 percent chance of saving the cargo of one of the three barges, worth $200,000 or (B) a plan that has a one-third chance of saving the cargo of all three barges, worth $600,000 and a two-thirds chance of saving nothing, most managers choose option A. The same problem with a negative frame would give managers a choice of selecting (C) a plan that has a 100 percent chance of losing two of the three cargoes, worth $400,000 or (D) a plan that has a two-thirds chance of losing all three cargoes but a one-third chance of losing no cargo. With this framing, most managers choose option D. Because both problems are identical, the decision choice depends strictly on how the problem is framed.

6. *Overconfidence.* One of the interesting research findings on decision-making biases is that most people overestimate their ability to predict uncertain outcomes. Before making a decision, managers have unrealistic expectations of their ability to understand the risk and make the right choice. Overconfidence is greatest when answering questions of moderate to extreme difficulty. For example, when people were asked to define quantities about which they had little direct knowledge ("What was the dollar value of Canadian lumber exports in 1997?" "What was the amount of taxes collected by the U.S. Internal Revenue Service in 1990?"), they overestimated their accuracy. Evidence of overconfidence is illustrated in cases in which subjects were so certain of an answer that they assigned odds of 1,000 to 1 of being correct but in fact were correct only about 85 percent of the time. These findings are especially important for strategic decision making, in which uncertainty is high because managers may unrealistically expect that they can successfully predict outcomes and hence select the wrong alternative.

SOURCES: Based on John Hammond, Ralph L. Keeney, and Howard Raiffa, "The Hidden Traps in Decision Making," *Harvard Business Review*, September–October 1998, 47–58; Oren Harari; "The Thomas Lawson Syndrome," *Management Review*, February 1994, 58–61; and Gary Belsky, "Why Smart People Make Major Money Mistakes," *Money*, July 1995, 76–85.

considered several alternatives for solving the problem. The decision to publicly admit the problem and recall the deodorant was an easy one for Chappell, who runs his company on principles of fairness and honesty. Not only did the company apologize to its customers but also listened to their complaints and suggestions. Chappell himself helped answer calls and letters. Even though the recall cost the company $400,000 and led to a stream of negative publicity, it ultimately helped the company improve relationships with customers.

Evaluation and feedback also led Tom's of Maine to set up "acorn groups," from which it hopes mighty oaks of successful products will grow. Acorn groups are cross-departmental teams that will shepherd new products from beginning to end. The cross-functional teams are a mechanism for catching problems— and new opportunities—that ordinarily would be missed. They pass on their ideas and findings to senior managers and the product-development team.

Tom's was able to turn a problem into an opportunity, thanks to evaluation and feedback. Not only did the disaster ultimately help the company solidify relationships with customers, but also it led to a formal mechanism for learning and sharing ideas—something the company did not have before.[40]

Tom's of Maine's decision illustrates all the decision steps, and the process ultimately ended in success. Strategic decisions always contain some risk, but feedback and follow-up decisions can help get companies back on track. By learning from their decision mistakes, managers and companies can turn problems into opportunities.[41]

Personal Decision Framework

Imagine you were a manager at Tom's of Maine, Silicon Graphics, a local movie theater, or the public library. How would you go about making important decisions that may shape the future of your department or company? So far we have discussed a number of factors that affect how managers make decisions. For example, decisions may be programmed or nonprogrammed, situations are characterized by various levels of uncertainty, and managers may use the classical, administrative, or political model of decision making. In addition, there are six recognized steps to take in the decision-making process.

decision style
Differences among people with respect to how they perceive problems and make decisions.

However, not all managers go about making decisions in the same way. In fact, there are significant differences in the ways individual managers may approach problems and make decisions concerning them. These differences can be explained by the concept of personal decision styles. Exhibit 9.5 illustrates the role of personal style in the decision-making process. Personal **decision style** refers to differences among people with respect to how they perceive problems and make decisions. Research has identified four major decision styles: directive, analytical, conceptual, and behavioral.[42]

1. The *directive style* is used by people who prefer simple, clear-cut solutions to problems. Managers who use this style often make decisions quickly because they do not like to deal with a lot of information and may consider only one or two alternatives. People who prefer the directive style generally are efficient and rational and prefer to rely on existing rules or procedures for making decisions.

2. Managers with an *analytical style,* on the other hand, like to consider complex solutions based on as much data as they can gather. These individuals carefully consider alternatives and often base their decisions on objective, rational data from management control systems and other sources. They search for the best possible decision based on the information available.

3. People who tend toward a *conceptual style* also like to consider a broad amount of information. However, they are more socially oriented than those with an analytical style and like to talk to others about the problem and possible alternatives for solving it. Managers using a conceptual style consider many broad alternatives, rely on information from both people and systems, and like to solve problems creatively.

4. The *behavioral style* is often the style adopted by managers having a deep concern for others as individuals. Managers using this style like to talk to people one-on-one and understand their feelings about the problem and

E x h i b i t *9.5*   *Personal Decision Framework*

Situation	Personal Decision Style	Decision Choice
• Programmed/nonprogrammed	• Directive	• Best solution to problem
• Classical, administrative, political	• Analytical	
• Decision steps	• Conceptual	
	• Behavioral	

the effect of a given decision upon them. People with a behavioral style usually are concerned with the personal development of others and may make decisions that help others achieve their goals.

Although most managers have a dominant decision style, frequently they will use several different styles or a combination of styles in making the varied decisions they confront daily. For example, a manager might use a directive style for deciding on which printing company to use for new business cards, yet shift to a more conceptual style when handling an interdepartmental conflict. The most effective managers are able to shift among styles as needed to meet the situation. Being aware of one's dominant decision style can help a manager avoid making critical mistakes when his or her usual style may be inappropriate to the problem at hand.

Increasing Participation in Decision Making

Managers do make some decisions as individuals, but decision makers more often are part of a group. Indeed, major decisions in the business world rarely are made entirely by an individual. Effective decision making often depends on whether managers involve the right people in the right ways in helping them solve problems.[43] Today, many managers are including lower-level employees in the decision-making process whenever possible. In addition, some decisions require a greater degree of subordinate participation. Decisions may be made through a committee, a task group, departmental participation, or an informal coalition. We will begin our discussion of participative decision making with the Vroom-Jago model, which helps identify the correct amount of participation by subordinates in making a particular decision.

Vroom-Jago Model

Victor Vroom and Arthur Jago developed a model of participation in decision making that provides guidance for practicing managers.[44] The **Vroom-Jago model** helps the manager gauge the appropriate amount of participation for subordinates. It has three major components: leader participation styles, a set of diagnostic questions with which to analyze a decision situation, and a series of decision rules.

Vroom-Jago model
A model designed to help managers gauge the amount of subordinate participation in decision making.

Leader Participation Styles. The model employs five levels of subordinate participation in decision making ranging from highly autocratic to highly democratic, as illustrated in Exhibit 9.6. Autocratic leadership styles are represented by AI and AII, consulting styles by CI and CII, and a group decision by G. The five styles fall along a continuum, and the manager should select one style depending on the situation. If the situation warrants, the manager could make the decision alone (AI), share the problem with subordinates individually (CI), or let group members make the decision (G).

Diagnostic Questions. How does a manager decide which of the five decision styles to use? The appropriate degree of decision participation depends on the responses to eight diagnostic questions. These questions deal with the problem, the required level of decision quality, and the importance of having subordinates commit to the decision.

Recognizing that Canada's strong perform-ance in the international seed corn market-place stems from excellent performance in the field, Mike McGuire, president of DEKALB Canada, a division of DEKALB Genetics Corporation, discusses hybrids at a research station in Glanworth, Ontario with Dale Wickersham, associate director of re-search. This participative decision style adds support to managerial decisions.

1. *Quality Requirement* (**QR**): *How important is the quality of this decision?* If a high-quality decision is important for group performance, the leader has to be actively involved.

2. *Commitment Requirement* (**CR**): *How important is subordinate commitment to the decision?* If implementation requires that subordinates commit to the decision, leaders should involve the subordinates in the decision process.

3. *Leader's Information* (**LI**): *Do I have sufficient information to make a high-quality decision?* If the leader does not have sufficient information or expert-ise, the leader should involve subordinates to obtain that information.

4. *Problem Structure* (**ST**): *Is the decision problem well structured?* If the prob-lem is ambiguous and poorly structured, the leader will need to interact with subordinates to clarify the problem and identify possible solutions.

5. *Commitment Probability* (**CP**): *If I were to make the decision by myself, is it reasonably certain that my subordinates would be committed to the decision?* If subordinates typically go along with whatever the leader decides, their involvement in the decision process will be less important.

6. *Goal Congruence* (**GC**): *Do subordinates share the organizational goals to be attained in solving this problem?* If subordinates do not share the goals of the organization, the leader should not allow the group to make the deci-sion alone.

7. *Subordinate Conflict* (**CO**): *Is conflict over preferred solutions likely to occur among subordinates?* Disagreement among subordinates can be resolved by allowing their participation and discussion.

8. *Subordinate Information* (**SI**): *Do subordinates have enough information to make a high-quality decision?* If subordinates have good information, then more responsibility for the decision can be delegated to them.

These questions seem detailed, but they quickly narrow the options available to managers and point to the appropriate level of group participation in the decision.

E x h i b i t   *9.6*   *Five Leader Decision Styles*

	Decision Style	Description
Highly Autocratic	AI	You solve the problem or make the decision yourself using information available to you at that time.
	AII	You obtain the necessary information from your subordinates and then decide on the solution to the problem yourself.
	CI	You share the problem with relevant subordinates individually, getting their ideas and suggestions without bringing them together as a group. Then you make the decision.
	CII	You share the problem with your subordinates as a group, collectively obtaining their ideas and suggestions. Then you make the decision.
Highly Democratic	G	You share a problem with your subordinates as a group. Your role is much like that of chairman. You do not try to influence the group to adopt "your" solution, and you are willing to accept and implement any solution that has the support of the entire group.

Note: A = autocratic; C = consultative; G = group

SOURCE: Reprinted from Victor H. Vroom and Arthur G. Jago, *The New Leadership: Managing Participation in Organizations* (Englewood Cliffs, N.J.: Prentice-Hall, 1988). Copyright 1987 by V. H. Vroom and A. G. Jago. Used with permission of the authors.

Selecting a Decision Style. The decision flowchart in Exhibit 9.7 allows a leader to adopt a participation style by answering the questions in sequence. The leader begins at the left side of the chart with question QR: How important is the quality of the decision? If the answer is high, then the leader proceeds to question CR: How important is subordinate commitment to the decision? If the answer is high, the next question is LI: Do I have sufficient information to make a high-quality decision? If the answer is yes, the leader proceeds to answer question CP because question ST is irrelevant if the leader has sufficient information to make a high-quality decision. Managers can quickly learn to use the basic model to adapt their leadership styles to fit their decision problem and the situation.

Several decision styles are equally acceptable in many situations. When this happens, Vroom and Jago note that the autocratic style saves time without reducing decision quality or acceptance. However, in today's changing workplace, where employees often are demanding more participation, managers should try to involve subordinates in decision making whenever possible.

Exhibit 9.7   *Vroom-Jago Decision Tree for Determining an Appropriate Decision-Making Method—Group Problems*

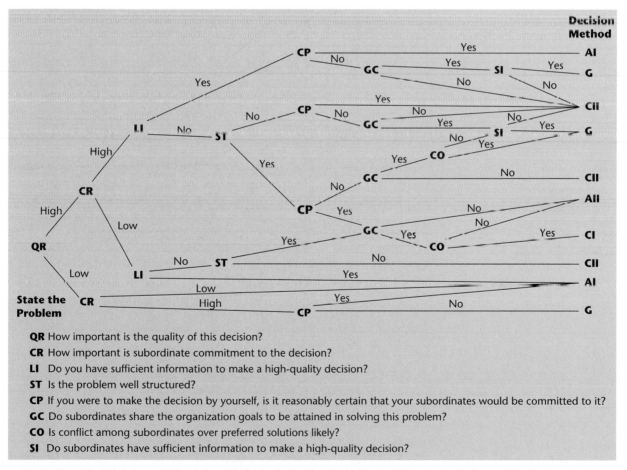

QR How important is the quality of this decision?

CR How important is subordinate commitment to the decision?

LI Do you have sufficient information to make a high-quality decision?

ST Is the problem well structured?

CP If you were to make the decision by yourself, is it reasonably certain that your subordinates would be committed to it?

GC Do subordinates share the organization goals to be attained in solving this problem?

CO Is conflict among subordinates over preferred solutions likely?

SI Do subordinates have sufficient information to make a high-quality decision?

Source: Reprinted from Victor H. Vroom and Arthur G. Jago, *The New Leadership: Managing Participation in Organizations* (Englewood Cliffs, N.J.: Prentice-Hall, 1988). Copyright 1987 by V. H. Vroom and A. G. Jago. Used with permission of the authors.

The decision tree model has been criticized as being less than perfect,[45] but it is useful to decision makers, and the body of supportive research is growing.[46] Managers make timely, high-quality decisions when following the model. One application of the model occurred at Barouh-Eaton Allen Corporation.

KO-REC-TYPE

www.korectype.com

Barouh-Eaton Allen started prospering when owner Vic Barouh noticed that a typist kept a piece of white chalk by her machine. To erase an error, she would lightly rub over it with the chalk. It took several passes, but the correction was neatly made. Barouh's company already made carbon paper, so he tried rubbing chalk on one side of a sheet of paper, putting the paper between the error and typewriter, and striking the same key. Most of the error disappeared under a thin coating of chalk dust. Thus, Ko-Rec-Type was born. Demand for the product was enormous, and the company prospered.

Then IBM invented the self-correcting typewriter. Within two days after IBM's announcement, nearly 40 people told Barouh that the company was in trouble. Nobody was going to buy Ko-Rec-Type again.

Barouh bought a self-correcting typewriter, took it to the plant, called everybody together, and told them what they had to do. To survive, the company had to learn to make this ribbon. They also had to learn to make the cartridge that held the ribbon, because cartridges could not be purchased on the market. They also had to learn to make the spools that held the tape. They had to learn to make the ink, the machine that puts on ink, injection molding to make the spools, and so on. It was an enormous challenge. Barouh got everyone involved regardless of position or education.

To everyone's astonishment, the company produced its first self-correcting ribbon in only six months. Moreover, it was the only company in the world to produce that product. Barouh later learned that it took IBM six years to make its self-correcting ribbon. With the new product, sales remained high, and the company avoided disaster.[47]

The Vroom-Jago model shows that Vic Barouh used the correct decision style. Moving from left to right in Exhibit 9.7, the questions and answers are as follows. (QR) *How important is the quality of this decision?* Definitely high. (CR) *How important is subordinate commitment to the decision?* Importance of commitment is probably low, because subordinates had a great deal of respect for Barouh and would do whatever he asked. (LI) *Did Barouh have sufficient information to make a high-quality decision?* Definitely no. (ST) *Is the problem well structured?* Definitely no. The remaining questions are not relevant because at this point the decision tree leads directly to the CII decision style. Barouh should have used a consultative decision style by having subordinates participate in problem discussions as a group—which he did.

Advantages and Disadvantages of Participative Decision Making

The Vroom-Jago model illustrates that managers can select the degree of group participation in decision making. Managers also can decide whether to bring people together to discuss problems and decision alternatives face-to-face or to consult one-on-one with each member. Research on the Vroom-Jago model indicates that bringing people together as a group leads to more effective decisions than having a manager consult with each member individually.[48]

Increasingly, in today's more empowered workplaces, involving lower-level workers in decision making is the rule rather than the exception. However, managers should remember that group decision making has clear advantages as well as disadvantages compared to individual decision making.[49] Because managers often have a choice between making a decision by themselves or including others, they should understand the advantages and disadvantages of participative decision making, which are summarized in Exhibit 9.8.

Advantages.   Groups have an advantage over individuals because they bring together a broader perspective for defining the problem and diagnosing underlying causes and effects. In addition to enriching problem diagnosis, groups offer more knowledge and facts with which to identify potential solutions and produce more decision alternatives. Moreover, people who participate in decision making are more satisfied with the decision and more likely to support it, thereby facilitating implementation. Group discussion also can help reduce uncertainty for decision makers who may be unwilling to undertake a big risk by themselves. Finally, group discussion enhances member satisfaction and produces support for a possibly risky decision.

Disadvantages.   Group decisions tend to be time-consuming. People must be consulted, and they jointly diagnose problems and discuss solutions. Moreover, groups may reach a compromise solution that is less than optimal for the organization. Another problem is groupthink. **Groupthink** is a phenomenon in which people are so committed to a cohesive in-group that their reluctance to express contrary opinions overrides their motivation to realistically consider alternatives.[50] People do not want to disagree with one another; thus, the group loses the diversity of opinions essential to effective decision making. For example, many of the people involved in making the movie *The Bonfire of the Vanities* had doubts about casting decisions and changes in the story line, but no one was willing to voice these opinions. Director Brian DePalma says he had some reservations as well, but because everyone else seemed to be in agreement, he convinced himself that making the changes was the right decision.[51] One final problem with group decision making is that there is no clear focus of decision responsibility, because the group rather than any single individual makes the decision.

One example of the disadvantages of group decision making occurred when a coalition at Citibank refused to change the practice of "parking"—the bogus transfer of foreign exchange deposits to shift bank profits to countries with low tax rates. The line between illegal and legal activities was hazy,

groupthink
A phenomenon in which group members are so committed to the group that they are reluctant to express contrary opinions.

Advantages	Disadvantages
1. Broader perspective for problem definition and analysis.	1. Time-consuming; wasted resources if used for programmed decisions.
2. More knowledge, facts, and alternatives can be evaluated.	2. Compromise decisions may satisfy no one.
3. Discussion clarifies ambiguous problems and reduces uncertainty about alternatives.	3. Groupthink: Group norms may reduce dissent and opinion diversity.
4. Participation fosters member satisfaction and support for decision.	4. No clear focus for decision responsibility.

Exhibit *9.8*

Advantages and Disadvantages of Participative Decision Making

and groupthink appeared—people were unwilling to disagree with the current practice because group norms supported high profits and reduced taxes. Group members were willing to compromise their values, groupthink reduced dissent, and there was no clear focus of responsibility because everyone had agreed to the potentially illegal practice.[52]

Improving Decision-Making Breadth and Creativity

brainstorming

A decision-making technique in which group members present spontaneous suggestions for problem solution, regardless of their likelihood of implementation, in order to promote freer, more creative thinking within the group.

Springs Specialty Fabrics Group, a leading producer of sheeting fabric, improves decision making breadth and creativity by encouraging all its workers to challenge conventional thinking, "fix things that aren't broken," seek solutions, test ideas, and share results. At the Springs Eureka weaving plant in Chester, South Carolina, these workers implemented changes that resulted in fewer yarn breaks on weaving looms, thus increasing productivity. Guided by the "Springs Quality System," a disciplined approach to quality management, teams at various Springs plants work constantly to improve products, expedite service, and find better and faster ways to operate.

Encouraging employee thinking and participation in solving problems can improve decision quality. Frontline workers who are in touch with the needs and concerns of customers can have a clearer insight into how to solve problems that directly concern those customers. For example, at Chrysler, the team manager for the new Dodge Neon asked for line workers' input regarding specific problems and got more than 4,000 ideas, many of which were implemented.[53]

In today's fast-changing world, decisions often must be made quickly, and an organization's ability to stimulate the creativity and innovativeness of its employees is becoming increasingly important. Competitive pressures are challenging managers to create environments that foster and support creative thinking and sharing of diverse opinions. In addition, the growing use of information technology is making it easier than ever to share information widely and decentralize decision making. An environment in which bosses make all the decisions and hand them down to frontline workers is becoming not only inappropriate but inefficient.[54]

How can managers pursue the advantages of participation and overcome some of the disadvantages? A number of techniques have been developed to help individual managers as well as groups make better decisions. Perhaps the best-known decision aid is brainstorming. **Brainstorming** uses a face-to-face, interactive group to spontaneously suggest ideas for problem solution.[55] Kodak encourages continuous brainstorming and has created a "humor room" where workers can relax and have creative brainstorming sessions. The room is filled with videotapes of comedians, joke books, stress-reducing toys, and software for creative decision making.[56] The brainstorming technique encourages group members to suggest alternatives regardless of their likelihood of being implemented. No critical comments of any kind are allowed until all suggestions have been listed. Members are encouraged to brainstorm possible solutions aloud, and freewheeling is welcomed. The more novel and unusual the idea, the better. The object of brainstorming is to promote freer, more flexible thinking and to enable group members to build on one another's creativity. The typical session begins with a warm-up wherein definitional issues are settled, proceeds through the freewheeling idea-generation stage, and concludes with an evaluation of feasible ideas.[57] At IDEO Product Development, managers use brainstorming to foster organizationwide creativity that has made the

LEADING THE REVOLUTION: THE LEARNING ORGANIZATION

Encouraging Wild Ideas

At IDEO Product Development, managers believe in heavy doses of fun and freedom to encourage creativity and learning. IDEO, the largest product design consulting firm in the United States, has contributed to the development of over 3,000 products, including Crest's Neat Squeeze toothpaste container, Levolor blinds, Nike sunglasses, and a recharger for General Motors electric vehicles. The company averages about 90 new products a year. Where do IDEO's employees, who work in a network of offices stretching from San Francisco to London to Tokyo, come up with so many creative ideas?

IDEO employees are continuously dreaming, experimenting, and sharing ideas. The culture values playfulness, risk-taking, and nonconformity, and a valued company slogan is "fail often to succeed sooner." A "brainstorm" or "brainstormer" is often called at the beginning of a new project or whenever a design team feels stumped, and an invitation goes out by E-mail. Although participation is voluntary, people from a mix of disciplines gladly participate because they want the same participation from others regarding their own projects. Sometimes clients are involved in brainstorms, particularly at the beginning of a project. A project team typically calls several broad brainstorms during the early weeks of a project to generate a range of possible solutions. After that, brainstorms are used sporadically to get fresh ideas when the team gets stale or needs help with a specific problem.

IDEO managers create an environment that encourages brainstorming. The company's brainstorming rooms have whiteboard-covered walls and conference tables covered with butcher paper so people can doodle anywhere, anytime the mood strikes them. The "rules" are posted in several locations so everyone can see them: 1) Defer judgment; 2) Build on the ideas of others; 3) One conversation at a time; 4) Stay focused on the topic; and 5) Encourage wild ideas. Criticism in any form, even negative facial expressions, is discouraged. These rules tend to guide the interaction of employees outside the brainstorming sessions as well. At IDEO, brainstorming is a way of life. Although some people are naturally better at brainstorming than others, IDEO's designers point out that effective brainstorming skills develop over time. By encouraging and supporting brainstorming, IDEO managers help their employees, and their company, get smarter.

www.ideo.com

SOURCE: Tia O'Brien, "Encourage Wild Ideas," *Fast Company*, April–May 1996, 82–88; and Robert I. Sutton and Andrew Hargadon, "Brainstorming Groups in Context: Effectiveness in a Product Design Firm," *Administrative Science Quarterly* 41 (1996), 685–718.

company the world's most celebrated design firm, as described in the Learning Organization box.

Another technique for better group decision making is to assign a **devil's advocate** the role of challenging the assumptions and assertions made by the group.[58] The devil's advocate forces the group to rethink its approach to the problem and to avoid reaching premature consensus or making unreasonable assumptions before proceeding with problem solutions. One management scholar has recommended that companies create "an institutionalized devil's advocate" by appointing teams to act as perpetual challengers of others' ideas and proposals. This forces managers and others to examine and explain the risks associated with a particular decision alternative.[59]

This approach would be similar to **multiple advocacy,** a technique that involves several advocates and multiple points of view. Minority opinions and unpopular viewpoints are assigned to forceful representatives, who then debate before the decision makers. Former president Bush was renowned for using multiple advocacy in his decision making. The proposal for clean-air legislation in 1989 was a textbook case, because White House aides staged debates they called "Scheduled Train Wrecks" to help Bush think through the issue. These were live scrimmages with Bush asking questions back and forth during the debate. The result was a decision based on solid argument and understanding of all perspectives.[60]

devil's advocate
A decision-making technique in which an individual is assigned the role of challenging the assumptions and assertions made by the group to prevent premature consensus.

multiple advocacy
A decision-making technique that involves several advocates and presentation of multiple points of view, including minority and unpopular opinions.

Summary and Management Solution

This chapter made several important points about the process of organizational decision making. The study of decision making is important because it describes how managers make successful strategic and operational decisions. Managers must confront many types of decisions, including programmed and nonprogrammed, and these decisions differ according to the amount of risk, uncertainty, and ambiguity in the environment.

Three decision-making approaches were described: the classical model, the administrative model, and the political model. The classical model explains how managers should make decisions so as to maximize economic efficiency. The administrative model describes how managers actually make nonprogrammed, uncertain decisions with skills that include intuition. The political model relates to making nonprogrammed decisions when conditions are uncertain, information is limited and ambiguous, and there is conflict among managers about what goals to pursue or what course of action to take. Managers have to engage in discussion and coalition building to reach agreement for decisions.

Decision making should involve six basic steps: problem recognition, diagnosis of causes, development of alternatives, choice of an alternative, implementation of the alternative, and feedback and evaluation. Problem recognition at Encyclopaedia Britannica, Inc., described at the beginning of the chapter, was easy: the venerable old company was about to go under. In diagnosing the causes, new owners determined that a major factor was an ossified management culture dominated by book salesmen, leading to years of squabbling over new product development and thus hindering the move into electronic media. One of the first decisions Jacob Safra made was to bring in a new management team. The team then considered various alternatives for reviving the faltering company. Because Britannica was so far behind in the world of electronic media, the new management decided to rush out a series of new products, as well as make prices competitive with *Encarta* and other offerings. Britannica's new products include a revamped, more graphics-intensive CD-ROM package, a complete online subscription service (www.eb.com), and a new Internet search engine (www.eblast.com), which will filter out marginal Web pages and offer consumers what Britannica editors think are the most useful sites. To lure users, Britannica is implementing a multimillion dollar advertising campaign. In addition, to exploit Britannica's wealth of information, the company is developing CD-ROMs on subjects ranging from Shakespeare to black history. The full 32-volume set still is available for those who like the feel of a book in their hands, but Safra decided to do away with the 500-person direct-to-home sales force and strike deals with 300 bookstores and super chains. Managers are now in the process of evaluation and feedback to determine if new decisions need to be made.

Another factor affecting decision making is the manager's personal decision style. The four major decision styles are directive, analytical, conceptual, and behavioral. The chapter also explained the Vroom-Jago model, which managers can use to determine when a decision calls for group participation. As competitive pressures force today's organizations to shift toward forms of decision making that encourage creativity and sharing of diverse views, managers need to maximize the advantages of group decision making and overcome the disadvantages. Useful techniques include devil's advocate, multiple advocacy, and brainstorming. These techniques can help managers and groups define problems and develop more creative solutions.

Discussion Questions

1. You are a busy partner in a legal firm, and an experienced secretary complains of continued headaches, drowsiness, dry throat, and occasional spells of fatigue and flu. She tells you she believes air quality in the building is bad and would like something done. How would you respond?

2. Why is decision making considered a fundamental part of management effectiveness?

3. Explain the difference between risk and ambiguity. How might decision making differ for each situation?

4. Analyze three decisions you made over the past six months. Which of these were programmed and which were nonprogrammed?

5. Why are many decisions made by groups rather than by individuals?

6. The Vroom-Jago model describes five decision styles. How should a manager go about choosing which style to use?

7. What are the major differences between the administrative and political models of decision making?

8. What is meant by *satisficing* and *bounded rationality*? Why do managers not strive to find the economically best solution for many organizational decisions?

9. What techniques could you use to improve your own creativity and effectiveness in decision making?

10. Which of the six steps in the decision-making process do you think is most likely to be ignored by a manager? Explain.

Management in Practice: Experiential Exercise

What's Your Personal Decision Style?
Read each of the following questions and circle the answer that *best* describes you. Think about how you typically act in a work or school situation and mark the answer that first comes to your mind. There are no right or wrong answers.

1. In performing my job or class work, I look for:
   a. practical results
   b. the best solution
   c. creative approaches or ideas
   d. good working conditions
2. I enjoy jobs that:
   a. are technical and well-defined
   b. have a lot of variety
   c. allow me to be independent and creative
   d. involve working closely with others
3. The people I most enjoy working with are:
   a. energetic and ambitious
   b. capable and organized
   c. open to new ideas
   d. agreeable and trusting
4. When I have a problem, I usually:
   a. rely on what has worked in the past
   b. apply careful analysis
   c. consider a variety of creative approaches
   d. seek consensus with others
5. I am especially good at:
   a. remembering dates and facts
   b. solving complex problems
   c. seeing many possible solutions
   d. getting along with others
6. When I don't have much time, I:
   a. make decisions and act quickly
   b. follow established plans or priorities
   c. take my time and refuse to be pressured
   d. ask others for guidance and support
7. In social situations, I generally:
   a. talk to others
   b. think about what's being discussed
   c. observe
   d. listen to the conversation
8. Other people consider me:
   a. aggressive
   b. disciplined
   c. creative
   d. supportive
9. What I dislike most is:
   a. not being in control
   b. doing boring work
   c. following rules
   d. being rejected by others
10. The decisions I make are usually:
   a. direct and practical
   b. systematic or abstract
   c. broad and flexible
   d. sensitive to others' needs

Scoring: Count the number of *a* answers. This is your *directive* score:
Count the number of *b* answers for your *analytical* score:
The number of *c* answers is your *conceptual* score:
The number of *d* answers is your *behavioral* score:

What is your dominant decision style? Are you surprised, or does this reflect the style you thought you used most often?

SOURCE: Adapted from Alan J. Rowe and Richard O. Mason, *Managing with Style: A Guide to Understanding, Assessing, and Improving Decision Making* (San Francisco: Jossey-Bass, 1987), 40–41.

Management in Practice: Ethical Dilemma

The Unhealthy Hospital
When Bruce Reid was hired as Blake Memorial Hospital's new CEO, the mandate had been clear: Improve the quality of care, and set the financial house in order.

As Reid struggled to finalize his budget for approval at next week's board meeting, his attention kept returning to one issue—the future of six off-site clinics. The clinics had been set up six years earlier to provide primary health care to the community's poorer neighborhoods. Although they provided a valuable service, they also diverted funds away from Blake's in-house services, many of which were underfunded. Cutting hospital personnel and freezing salaries could affect Blake's quality of care, which was already slipping. Eliminating the clinics, on the other hand, would save $256,000 without compromising Blake's internal operations.

However, there would be political consequences. Clara Bryant, the recently appointed commissioner of health services, repeatedly argued that the clinics were an essential service for the poor. Closing the clinics could jeopardize Blake's access to city funds. Dr. Susan Russell, the hospital's director of clinics, was equally vocal about Blake's responsibility to the community, although Dr. Winston Lee, chief of surgery, argued forcefully for closing the off-site clinics and having shuttle buses bring patients to the hospital weekly. Dr. Russell argued for an entirely new way of delivering health care—"A hospital is not a building," she said, "it's a service. And wherever the service is needed, that is where the hospital should be." In Blake's case, that meant funding *more* clinics. Russell wanted to create a network of neighborhood-based centers for all the sur-rounding neighborhoods, poor and middle income. Besides improving health care, the network would act as an inpatient referral system for hospital services. Reid considered the proposal: If a clinic network could tap the paying public and generate more inpatient business, it might be worth looking into. Blake's rival hospital, located on the affluent side of town, certainly wasn't doing anything that creative.

What Do You Do?

1. Close the clinics and save a quick $256,000, then move on to tackle the greater problems that threaten Blake's long-term future.

2. Gradually abandon the neighborhood altogether and open free-standing clinics in more affluent suburbs, at the same time opening a minihospital in the poor neighborhood for critical care.

3. Tighten up internal efficiency to deal with immediate financial problems. Keep the clinics open for now, bring Clara Bryant into the decision-making process, and begin working with community groups to explore unmet health-care needs and develop innovative options for meeting them.

SOURCE: Based on Anthony R. Kovner, "The Case of the Unhealthy Hospital," *Harvard Business Review,* September–October 1991, 12–25.

Surf the Net

1. **Creativity.** Using your creative abilities in identifying solutions to problems can be a major asset in the decision-making process. Use your search engine to find Web sites related to creativity, such as the following:
   www.tiac.net/users/seeker/brainlinks.html
   Prepare a summary of your findings and present a 3- to 5-minute report to your classmates summarizing the most useful and interesting ideas you found that relate to creativity in the problem-solving/decision-making process.

2. **Pushing Key Data to Decision Makers.** The Technology box in this chapter made mention of Pointcast Network. In this exercise you will try out this service on your own computer. Go to **www.pointcast.com**, choose "What Is PointCast?" to learn more about what PointCast is and how you can use it to stay informed by having broadcast directly to your computer screen personalized news and information from such sources as CNN, *The Wall Street Journal,* and *The New York Times.* Read how companies are using PointCast's free suite of tools called the PointCast Intranet Broadcast Solution to deploy a news broadcast that keeps employees on top of all the information they need to be competitive. Next, download and install the PointCast Network on your computer. PointCast replaces your screensaver with the latest headline news. Personalize your newscast by selecting which channels you receive as well as the type of information broadcast within each channel. For more information on any headline, try clicking on it to see how PointCast displays the full news story.

3. **Participative Decision Making.** Gather information from the Internet suitable to share in a small-group discussion on participative decision making. This exercise provides an opportunity for you to try a specialized search tool called "Ask Jeeves!" This search tool finds answers to natural-language questions such as "Who won Super Bowl XXV?" Go to **www.ask.com** and type in "What is participative decision making?" Select information from the links that "Ask Jeeves!" provides and be prepared to discuss your findings in class. One particularly interesting article on participative decision making is available at **www.fed.org/leading_companies/oct98/tips.html**

Case for Critical Analysis
Greyhound Lines Inc.

Everyone agreed that Greyhound Lines had problems. The company was operating on paper-thin margins and could not afford to dispatch nearly empty vehicles or have buses and drivers on call to meet surges in demand. In the terminals, employees could be observed making fun of passengers, ignoring them, and handling their baggage haphazardly. To reduce operating costs and improve customer service, Greyhound's top executives put together a reorganization plan that called for massive cuts in personnel, routes, and services, along with the computerization of everything from passenger reservations to fleet scheduling.

However, middle managers disagreed with the plan. Many felt that huge workforce reductions would only exacerbate the company's real problem regarding customer services. Managers in computer programming urged a delay in introducing the computerized reservations system, called Trips, to work out bugs in the highly complex software. The human resources department pointed out that terminal workers often had less than a high school education and would need extensive training before they could be expected to use the system effectively. Terminal managers warned that many of Greyhound's low-income passengers didn't have credit cards or even telephones to use Trips. Despite the disagreements, executives rolled out the new system, emphasizing that the data they had studied showed that Trips would improve customer service, make ticket buying more convenient, and allow customers to reserve space on specific trips. A nightmare resulted. The time Greyhound operators spent responding to phone calls dramatically increased. Many callers couldn't even get through because of problems in

the new switching mechanism. Most passengers arrived to buy their tickets and get on the bus just like they always had, but the computers were so swamped that it sometimes took 45 seconds to respond to a single keystroke and five minutes to print a ticket. The system crashed so often that agents frequently had to hand-write tickets. Customers stood in long lines, were separated from their luggage, missed connections, and were left to sleep in terminals overnight. Discourtesy to customers increased as a downsized workforce struggled to cope with a system they were ill-trained to operate. Ridership plunged sharply, and regional rivals continued to pick off Greyhound's dissatisfied customers.

Questions

1. Was the decision facing Greyhound executives programmed or nonprogrammed?
2. Do you think they should have used the classical, administrative, or political model to make their decision? Which do you believe they used? Discuss.
3. Analyze the Greyhound case in terms of the six steps in the managerial decision making process. Do you think top executives paid adequate attention to all six steps? If you were a Greyhound executive, what would you do now and why?

SOURCE: Robert Tomsho, "How Greyhound Lines Re-Engineered Itself Right Into a Deep Hole," *The Wall Street Journal*, October 30, 1994, A1.

Endnotes

1. Richard A. Melcher, "Dusting Off the *Britannica*," *Business Week*, October 21, 1997, 143, 146.
2. Linda Grant, "How UPS Blew It," *Fortune*, September 29, 1997, 29–30.
3. "Tickling a Child's Fancy," *The Tennessean*, February 6, 1997, 1E, 4E; and John R. Emshwiller and Michael J. McCarthy, "Coke's Soda Fountain for Offices Fizzles, Dashing High Hopes," *The Wall Street Journal*, June 14, 1993, A1, A6.
4. Dean Takahashi, "How the Competition Got Ahead of Intel in Making Cheap Chips," *The Wall Street Journal*, February 12, 1998, A1.
5. Ronald A. Howard, "Decision Analysis: Practice and Promise," *Management Science* 34 (1988), 679–695.
6. Herbert A. Simon, *The New Science of Management* (Englewood Cliffs, N.J.: Prentice-Hall, 1977), 47.
7. Henry Goldblatt, "AT&T Finally Has an Operator," *Fortune*, February 16, 1998, 79–82.
8. Samuel Eilon, "Structuring Unstructured Decisions," *Omega* 13 (1985), 369–377; and Max H. Bazerman, *Judgment in Managerial Decision Making* (New York: Wiley, 1986).
9. James G. March and Zur Shapira, "Managerial Perspectives on Risk and Risk Taking," *Management Science* 33 (1987), 1404–1418; and Inga Skromme Baird and Howard Thomas, "Toward a Contingency Model of Strategic Risk Taking," *Academy of Management Review* 10 (1985), 230–243.
10. J. G. Higgins, "Planning for Risk and Uncertainty in Oil Exploration," *Long Range Planning* 26, no. 1 (February 1993), 111–122; and Bruce Horovitz and Gary Strauss, "Fast-Food Icon Wants Shine Restored to Golden Arches," *USA Today*, May 1, 1998, 1B, 2B.
11. Eilon, "Structuring Unstructured Decisions"; and Philip A. Roussel, "Cutting Down the Guesswork in R&D," *Harvard Business Review* 61 (September–October 1983), 154–160.
12. Hugh Courtney, Jane Kirkland, and Patrick Viguerie, "Strategy Under Uncertainty," *Harvard Business Review*, November–December 1997, 67–79.
13. Michael Masuch and Perry LaPotin, "Beyond Garbage Cans: An AI Model of Organizational Choice," *Administrative Science Quarterly* 34 (1989), 38–67; and Richard L. Daft and Robert H. Lengel, "Organizational Information Requirements, Media Richness and Structural Design," *Management Science* 32 (1986), 554–571.
14. David M. Schweiger, William R. Sandberg, and James W. Ragan, "Group Approaches for Improving Strategic Decision Making: A Comparative Analysis of Dialectical Inquiry, Devil's Advocacy, and Consensus," *Academy of Management Journal* 29 (1986), 51–71; and Richard O. Mason and Ian I. Mitroff, *Challenging Strategic Planning Assumptions* (New York: Wiley Interscience, 1981).

15. Michael Pacanowsky, "Team Tools for Wicked Problems," *Organizational Dynamics* 23, No. 3 (winter 1995), 36–51.

16. Michael J. McCarthy, "Pepsi Faces Problem in Trying to Contain Syringe Scare," *The Wall Street Journal,* June 17, 1993, B1; Elizabeth Lesly and Laura Zinn, "The Right Moves Baby," *Business Week,* July 5, 1993, 30–31; and "The Pepsi Hoax: What Went Right?" The Pepsi-Cola Company Public Affairs Office, 1993.

17. Boris Blai, Jr., "Eight Steps to Successful Problem Solving," *Supervisory Management* (January 1986), 7–9; and Earnest R. Archer, "How to Make a Business Decision: An Analysis of Theory and Practice," *Management Review* 69 (February 1980), 54–61.

18. Jean Aubin, "Scheduling Ambulances," *Interfaces* 22 (March–April 1992), 1–10.

19. Herbert A. Simon, *The New Science of Management Decision* (New York: Harper & Row, 1960), 5–6; and Amitai Etzioni, "Humble Decision Making," *Harvard Business Review* (July–August 1989), 122–126.

20. James G. March and Herbert A. Simon, *Organizations* (New York: Wiley, 1958).

21. Herbert A. Simon, *Models of Man* (New York: Wiley, 1957), 196–205; and Herbert A. Simon, *Administrative Behavior,* 2d ed. (New York: Free Press, 1957).

22. John Taylor, "Project Fantasy: A Behind-the-Scenes Account of Disney's Desperate Battle against the Raiders," *Manhattan* (November 1984).

23. Weston H. Agor, "The Logic of Intuition: How Top Executives Make Important Decisions," *Organizational Dynamics* 14 (winter 1986), 5–18; and Herbert A. Simon, "Making Management Decisions: The Role of Intuition and Emotion," *Academy of Management Executive* 1 (1987), 57–64.

24. Michael L. Ray and Rochelle Myers, *Creativity in Business,* (Garden City, N.Y.: Doubleday, 1986); and Suzanna Andrews, "Calling the Shots," *Working Woman,* November 1995, 30–35, 90.

25. Daniel J. Isenberg, "How Senior Managers Think," *Harvard Business Review* 62 (November–December 1984), 80–90.

26. Annetta Miller and Dody Tsiantar, "A Test for Market Research," *Newsweek,* December 28, 1987, 32–33; Michael Warshaw, "Guts and Glory," *Success,* March 1997, 28–33; and Oren Harari, "The Tarpit of Market Research," *Management Review,* March 1994, 42–44.

27. William B. Stevenson, Jon L. Pierce, and Lyman W. Porter, "The Concept of 'Coalition' in Organization Theory and Research," *Academy of Management Review* 10 (1985), 256–268.

28. Ann Reilly Dowd, "George Bush as Crisis Manager," *Fortune,* September 10, 1990, 55–56; and "How Bush Decided," *Fortune,* February 11, 1991, 45–46.

29. Jonathan Harris, "Why Speedy Got Stuck in Reverse," *Canadian Business,* September 26, 1997, 87–88.

30. James W. Fredrickson, "Effects of Decision Motive and Organizational Performance Level on Strategic Decision Processes," *Academy of Management Journal* 28 (1985), 821–843; James W. Fredrickson, "The Comprehensiveness of Strategic Decision Processes: Extension, Observations, Future Directions," *Academy of Management Journal* 27 (1984), 445–466; James W. Dean, Jr., and Mark P. Sharfman, "Procedural Rationality in the Strategic Decision-Making Process," *Journal of Management Studies* 30, no. 4 (July 1993), 587–610; Nandini Rajagopalan, Abdul M. A. Rasheed, and Deepak K. Datta, "Strategic Decision Processes: Critical Review and Future Directions," *Journal of Management* 19, no. 2 (1993), 349–384; and Paul J. H. Schoemaker, "Strategic Decisions in Organizations: Rational and Behavioral Views," *Journal of Management Studies* 30, no. 1 (January 1993), 107–129.

31. Marjorie A. Lyles and Howard Thomas, "Strategic Problem Formulation: Biases and Assumptions Embedded in Alternative Decision-Making Models," *Journal of Management Studies* 25 (1988), 131–145; and Susan E. Jackson and Jane E. Dutton, "Discerning Threats and Opportunities," *Administrative Science Quarterly* 33 (1988), 370–387.

32. David Greising, "Rethinking IDS from the Bottom Up," *Business Week,* February 8, 1993, 110–112.

33. Richard L. Daft, Juhani Sormumen, and Don Parks, "Chief Executive Scanning, Environmental Characteristics, and Company Performance: An Empirical Study" (unpublished manuscript, Texas A&M University, 1988).

34. C. Kepner and B. Tregoe, *The Rational Manager* (New York: McGraw-Hill, 1965).

35. Robert D. Hof, with Ira Sager and Linda Himelstein, "The Sad Saga of Silicon Graphics," *Business Week,* August 4, 1997, 66–72.

36. David Woodruff with Karen Lowry Miller, "Chrysler's Neon," *Business Week,* May 3, 1993, 116–126.

37. Peter Mayer, "A Surprisingly Simple Way to Make Better Decisions," *Executive Female,* March–April 1995, 13–14; and Ralph L. Keeney, "Creativity in Decision-Making with Value-Focused Thinking," *Sloan Management Review* (summer 1994), 33–41.

38. Brian O'Reilly, "J&J Is on a Roll," *Fortune,* December 26, 1994, 178–191.

39. Todd Mason, "Tandy Finds a Cold, Hard World Outside the Radio Shack," *Business Week,* August 31, 1987, 68–70.

40. Jenny C. McCune, "Making Lemonade," *Management Review,* June 1997, 49–53, 51.

41. McCune, "Making Lemonade."

42. Based on A. J. Rowe, J. D. Boulgaides, and M. R. McGrath, *Managerial Decision Making,* (Chicago: Science Research Associates, 1984); and Alan J. Rowe and Richard O. Mason, *Managing with Style: A Guide to Understanding, Assessing, and Improving Your Decision Making,* (San Francisco: Jossey-Bass, 1987).

43. Victor H. Vroom, "A New Look at Managerial Decision Making," *Organizational Dynamics,* spring 1972, 66–80.

44. V. H. Vroom and Arthur G. Jago, *The New Leadership: Managing Participation in Organizations* (Englewood Cliffs, N.J.: Prentice-Hall, 1988).

45. R. H. G. Field, "A Test of the Vroom-Yetton Normative Model of Leadership," *Journal of Applied Psychology* (October 1982), 523–532; and R. H. G. Field, "A Critique of the Vroom-Yetton Contingency Model of Leadership Behavior," *Academy of Management Review* 4 (1979), 249–257.

46. Jennifer T. Ettling and Arthur G. Jago, "Participation under Conditions of Conflict: More on the Validity of the Vroom-Yetton Model," *Journal of Management Studies* 25 (1988), 73–83; Madeline E. Heilman, Harvey A. Hornstein, Jack H. Cage, and Judith K. Herschlag, "Reactions to Prescribed Leader Behavior as a Function of Role Perspective: The Case of the Vroom-Yetton Model," *Journal of Applied Psychology* (February 1984), 50–60; and Arthur G. Jago and Victor H. Vroom, "Some Differences in the Incidence and Evaluation of Participative Leader Behavior," *Journal of Applied Psychology* (December 1982), 776–783.

47. Tom Richman, "One Man's Family," *Inc.*, November 1983, 151–156.

48. Ettling and Jago, "Participation under Conditions of Conflict."

49. John L. Cotton, David A. Vollarth, Kirk L. Froggatt, Mark L. Lengnick-Hall, and Kenneth R. Jennings, "Employee Participation: Diverse Forms and Different Outcomes," *Academy of Management Review* 13 (1988), 8–22; and Walter C. Swap, "Destructive Effects of Groups on Individuals," in *Group Decision Making,* ed. Walter C. Swap and Associates (Beverly Hills, Calif.: Sage, 1984).

50. Irving L. Janis, *Group Think,* 2d ed. (Boston: Houghton Mifflin, 1982), 9; Glen Whyte, "Groupthink Reconsidered," *Academy of Management Review* 14 (1989), 40–56; and Brian Mullen, Tara Anthony, Eduardo Salas, and James E. Driskell, "Group Cohesiveness and Quality of Decision Making: An Integration of Tests of the Groupthink Hypothesis," *Small Group Research* 25, no. 2, (May 1994), 189–204.

51. Aimee L. Stern, "Why Good Managers Approve Bad Ideas," *Working Woman,* May 1992, 75, 104.

52. Roy Rowan, "The Maverick Who Yelled Foul at Citibank," *Fortune,* January 10, 1983, 46–56.

53. Woodruff with Miller, "Chrysler's Neon."

54. Thomas W. Malone, "Is Empowerment Just a Fad? Control, Decision Making, and IT," *Sloan Management Review,* winter 1997, 23–35.

55. See also, Alex F. Osborn, *Applied Imagination,* 2nd ed. (New York: Scribner, 1957); Robert I. Sutton and Andrew Hargadon, "Brainstorming Groups in Context: Effectiveness in a Product Design Firm," *Administrative Science Quarterly* 41 (1996), 685–718; and "Group Decision Making," *Small Business Report,* July 1988, 30–33.

56. Robert Kreitner and Angelo Kinicki, *Organizational Behavior,* 3d ed. (Chicago: Irwin, 1995), 323.

57. A. Osborn, *Applied Imagination* (New York: Scribner, 1957).

58. David M. Schweiger and William R. Sandberg, "The Utilization of Individual Capabilities in Group Approaches to Strategic Decision-Making," *Strategic Management Journal* 10 (1989), 31–43; and "The Devil's Advocate," *Small Business Report* (December 1987), 38–41.

59. Stern, "Why Good Managers Approve Bad Ideas."

60. Michael Duffy, "Mr. Consensus," *Time,* August 21, 1989, 16–22.

NTBP Broadcasts Good News by Planning

Nonprofit organizations exist in competitive environments just as commercial organizations do. In fact, in some ways a nonprofit organization faces even greater obstacles because it is competing with other nonprofits as well as companies for consumer, corporate, and government dollars, often without being able to promise commensurate products in return. But North Texas Public Broadcasting isn't daunted by this challenge. Instead, the nonprofit broadcasting organization, which operates television stations KERA Channel 13 and KDTN Channel 2, along with radio station KERA 90.1, simply incorporates the challenge into its planning process.

Planning, including effective goal setting, is critical to NTPB's survival. All three stations share the same mission, which is accessible not only to those who work at NTPB but also to the general public on the organization's Web site. The formal mission statement reads:

> The mission of KERA 13, KERA 90.1, and KDTN 2 is to serve their communities by excelling in the production, presentation, and distribution of television and radio programming and related activities that educate, inspire, enrich, inform, and entertain.

NTPB's mission statement influences the organization's strategic goals and plans. It takes money—lots of it—to produce and distribute high-quality programming to the public, and NTPB runs no paid advertising. The organization has an operating budget of $12 million to $14 million per year and must find a way to raise the money to meet that budget. Sylvia Komatsu, vice president of programming explains, "Our ability to raise funds has a direct impact on what we're able to do, on how we're able to meet our mission."

Although NTPB does sell a few promotional products, most of the money raised must come from noncommercial ventures such as several pledge drives for membership per year as well as drives for corporate donations. (Individual memberships make up 50 percent of the annual operating budget.) Strategic, tactical, and operational planning are all connected to the organization's overall goals. "We work in a very competitive marketplace," notes Susan Harmon, vice president of finance and radio. "So when we're planning, even for the next week or the next year or the next three years, we really have to look strategically at what's going on in the marketplace."

Richard Meyer, NTPB's president and CEO, explains further. "Planning goes on every single day. However, we have a budget cycle, and we know, from our records, how much money we raised through various pledge drives, which is only one source of revenue. We have direct mail, we have major gifts, we have underwriting, and so on. So, each year when we prepare the budget, we look at, for example, where the money came from in the past, what the factors are in the coming year, that we can absorb in our own minds to increase the revenue in each of the categories and then we plan how to do that."

Sylvia Komatsu notes the importance of teamwork to all types of planning at NTPB, particularly strategic. "We work together as a team, because we have to know the big picture of the entire station in order to do our individual departmental budgets. . . . We all submit our projects to the business office, which then works with each of us and coordinates with each of us to make sure that we arrive at an overall budget that we think meets the needs of each of the departments that we have at our station."

In addition to ongoing budget planning, NTPB has developed single-use plans for major projects such as the new $8.6 million telecommunications center it recently opened. Overall goal setting and planning for the new facility started at the top, with senior management and a community-based board of directors. Susan Harmon recalls, "We did a very careful year's worth of planning with the board about what the facility would look like, about the budget and how we would go about raising the money. We paid for a feasibility study where somebody went out and interviewed leaders in the community to ask them what they thought about our need for a new facility and what they might give towards it. So, we had an idea going into the campaign that the committee . . . that the leaders in this community perceived we had a need, and that at some level they were going to participate." In the end, more than 1,600 foundations, corporations, and individual donors contributed to NTPB's first capital campaign, which raised complete funding for the facility in a matter of months.

North Texas Public Broadcasting is generally considered one of the top public broadcasting systems in the nation because of its ability to meet its mission and remain in the black financially. NTPB managers believe the organization's success is due to good planning, which has kept NTPB in good shape. "One of the things we've discovered is when we show our balance sheet to foundations, businesses, and wealthy individuals and they see that we operate in a fiscally sound manner, they're more likely to give us money," says Richard Meyer. Proof positive that good planning pays.

Questions

1. In what ways is NTPB's strategic planning different from that of commercial corporations? In what ways is it similar?
2. Describe some operational plans that lower-level managers might make to reach goals at NTPB.
3. Does NTPB sound like a learning organization? Why or why not?
4. What types of responsibilities might a planning task force have had for NTBP's new telecommunications facility?

Source: North Texas Public Broadcasting Web site, "About KERA/KDTN," "Membership," and "Educational Resources," accessed at www.kera.org April 13, 1999.

The Holigan Group: Building the American Dream

In today's fast-paced, high-tech world, most Americans' dream is still very old-fashioned: to own their own home. With the current strong economy, there are now about 1.3 million housing starts each year, but the housing industry is fragmented and highly competitive. Michael Holigan and his father Harold, of Holigan Homes, have simple, old-fashioned goals in this competitive market: "Our ultimate goal is to become the most profitable home builder in the United States," says Michael. "We want to be on the cutting edge of technology. And we want to provide the best jobs for our people." Such grand goals calls for a grand strategy.

Michael and Harold have one—growth. "Mike and I like to expand home building as widely as possible," explains Harold. "Home building to us is creating magazines about home building, TV shows about homebuilding, Web sites about home building, retail centers to help people sell homes . . . unique advertising vehicles to help other people sell homes." In other words, home building to the Holigans is a lot more than sawing boards and banging nails.

The Holigans have already achieved both internal and external growth in a variety of ways. They began their business in land acquisition and manufactured home building, then moved into conventional home building in the early 1990s. Their core competence was a lot like other builders' who were already in conventional home building, so they had to come up with a competitive strategy that created greater value for their customers. They chose a differentiation strategy, focusing on quality, something that many consumers would complain is lacking in current home-building practices. "Mike and I have decided that quality is gonna be the difference between our company and other companies," comments Harold. Michael continues, "We would build our homes a little different. We would use 2-by-6 walls, more efficient insulation, more energy efficient heating and air conditioning units. We would protect them from tornadoes with hurricane straps and tying the frames down to the foundation, things that most builders, volume builders won't do." To get the word out about their superior product, the Holigans made a 30-minute infomercial that was so successful they were about to change their corporate-level strategy.

Michael came up with a novel idea: to create a television show that would educate home buyers about the process of buying and owning a home. Called *Your New House*, the weekly show debuted in Dallas in 1994, was picked up by Home & Garden Television for thirteen episodes, and eventually landed on the Discovery Channel. Now, Michael and Harold were forced to ask themselves, "What business are we in?" Along with the show came a magazine, then a Web site, and the formation of the Holigan Group, whose "total focus was to produce national television shows about home building and then it expanded into other medias," says Michael. So father and son were no longer just building homes; they were creating television shows, publishing a magazine, updating a Web site. This change in corporate strategy, of course, influences business-level strategies, which includes the company's approach to advertising (Holigan not only advertises its own products, it also sells advertising on its Web site to vendors such as car-

pet manufacturers, paint, roof tiles, and so forth), its continued efforts to create value (customers can "design" their own homes right on the Web site), and the development of retail centers for home buyers.

Synergy is an important characteristic of the Holigan organization, between father and son as well as among the different company divisions. Harold notes, "Mike is, without any question, the best long-range planner we have. . . . I, on the other hand, run the day-to-day operations on the home building, the factories that we own and the land development side of the business." In addition, father and son rely on good managers. "We've been extremely fortunate in being able to attract extremely good managers," observes Harold. "It's managers that I have a lot of confidence in." Good relations also exist between workers and management. "The structure of both companies is very, very flat," explains Michael. "My father is the chairman. I'm the president and, I mean, we talk to everybody. It doesn't matter what you do at Holigan, we're there."

Michael speaks specifically about synergy on the media side of the organization. "The media side is a stand-alone and will make millions of dollars on its own side from the home-building company. But again, they're very, very interrelated. Everyone talks about synergy but hardly anyone does anything about it. My role is to make sure that the focus of the show, the magazine, the Internet stays on the same idea, that's to teach people how to buy and build homes."

The Holigans have proved themselves skilled at recognizing opportunities and threats to their business. Indeed, it appears that Michael Holigan will let no opportunity pass his company by. Threats, of course, include changes in interest rates, changes in the economy in general, changes in cost and availability of building materials, changes in the demand for new housing (and thus a change in consumer interest in Holigan's television show, magazine and Web site). But Michael Holigan isn't letting these threats slow him down. "I'm 33 years old and have a great opportunity right now, probably better than anybody in the home building industry. . . . I'm working on the TV show, building the brand through the different types of media. I'm working on the franchising unit, designing it for the next year or so to start selling Michael Holigan Home franchises, the Internet, you know, pushing that to the next level." Indeed, Michael Holigan gives a whole new meaning to the occupation of home builder.

Questions

1. What business do *you* think the Holigan Group is in?
2. List what you think the Holigan Group's strengths and weaknesses are.
3. The Holigans have adopted cooperative strategies through franchising and accepting vendor advertising on its Web site. What other cooperative strategies might help the organization as well?

SOURCE: Michael Holigan Homes, accessed at www.yournewhouse.com March 26, 1999.

Video Case

Good Decisions Are Key to Success

Every day, managers make decisions that may mean life or death to their companies. The programmed decisions are easy: order more paper, renew the office cleaning contract. But the nonprogrammed decisions are the tough ones, and managers who can make them skillfully will help their companies not only survive, but thrive.

Managers at each of the companies in this case have been able to diagnose and analyze problems, recognize opportunities, and deal with risk and uncertainty. They may have different decision making styles, but they all manage to make good decisions for their companies. Jerry Yang and David Filo were graduate students at Stanford University when they began compiling lists of their favorite Web pages and created a free directory called "David's Guide to the World Wide Web." Filo and Yang used a conceptual style of decision making, evaluating a broad amount of information, to come up with a product that eventually revolutionized use of the Internet. "We realized that there weren't really any good tools out there to help you find what you were looking for," recalls Filo. "There was no organization of the Web. And so just for ourselves, we started things." They built a list of sites, continued to classify them, and attracted more users. When their hobby grew bigger than they intended, they transformed it into a search engine called Yahoo! Filo and Yang's intuition, which was really based on recognition, paid off. Today, nearly 2 million users access the Yahoo! site every day, making it one of the most popular sites on the Internet.

Wes Hoffman, Mike Engledinger, and Ron Toupal turned a problem into an opportunity when they were laid off from their software engineering jobs and decided to form their own company, Paradigm Simulation. "Paradigm started out as a company doing very high end simulation for the defense industry," says David Gatchel, president and CEO. But then another problem—and more uncertainty—arose. The defense industry took a slide downhill, and Paradigm was faced with the problem of finding new customers for its simulation software. The company's managers recognized that the price of their product was an obstacle—three-dimensional simulation software cost around $70,000 and the hardware as much as $300,000. They decided to take a risk—if they could reduce the price, they could sell quite a bit more. The move paid off, and Paradigm was already serving a solid client list when Nintendo approached them to create a 3-D game, Pilot Wings 64. The rest, as they say, is computer game history.

Patrick Esquerré faced ambiguity when he emigrated from France to Texas. He barely spoke English, and he vaguely thought he might export professional rodeo back to his homeland. He didn't know what his goals were, what his alternatives were, or what the possible outcomes were. Essentially, he had no idea what he was going to do. "When I came here, I was the 'no'-'no' guy," says Esquerré. I was not a restaurateur. I was not a baker. I was not a Texan. I was not a lawyer. I was not a bunch of things. I was just a guy that I call the 'extra virgin' because I came not knowing anything." At some point, Esquerré thought that introducing French cuisine to Texas might be easier than exporting rodeo. So Esquerré decided to conduct his own, unique market research. Esquerré stopped pedestrians and told them there would be a bakery nearby. When they

asked, "A bakery with a brick oven?" Esquerré said yes. When they asked, "With old beams from the farms in France?" Esquerré replied affirmatively. So it went. "This was in fact the way La Madeleine was built. We tried to tailor the concept of La Madeleine to the way that our guests told us they wanted it to be," explains Esquerré. In his own creative way, Esquerré reduced the uncertainty surrounding his business venture by talking with his future customers. Now, Esquerré's chain of La Madeleine French Bakery and Cafes has a loyal following in several Texas cities, as well as Atlanta, Chicago, Washington, DC, New Orleans, and Phoenix.

Not every decision works out perfectly. Drew Pearson, former wide receiver with the Dallas Cowboys, now an entrepreneur, has fumbled a few. Pearson started a small company manufacturing sports caps and at first sold his products to a wide range of retailers—department stores, discounters, even 7-Eleven convenience stores. JC Penney, who was an early customer of Pearson's, was unhappy with Pearson's expanding distribution because the retailer needed to charge higher prices for its inventory than, say, 7-Eleven. Pearson and his managers needed to sell as many caps as possible, but they also needed to keep their best customers happy. They considered several alternatives, then decided to refine the company's distribution strategy to better serve their clients and obtain a greater market share. "We separate our brands with the more involved looks on our embroidery on our caps," explains Ken Shead, president of Drew Pearson Companies. The more complex designs go to high-end customers; the simpler ones go to the low end of the marketplace. DPC's decision paid off. Today, it is the only headwear company with exclusive rights to market Disney characters worldwide.

The construction business is riddled with uncertainty. Larry Hirsch, chairman and CEO of Centex, the nation's largest and most geographically diverse home builder, is one manager who is undaunted by the uncertainty and risk inherent in his business. He practices a conceptual and participative style of decision making, relying on hard data as well as input from individuals who can help him make a decision. In one instance, "We conducted a number of focus groups using our own employees to really start to get an idea of how the various trends that we saw in society were affecting our own people. It brought people from all over the company together who saw that they were important to the company, that they were participating in the strategic direction of the company." Centex has been responsible for many major public and private building projects, including Disneyland, the Orlando International Airport, and Clorox Company Headquarters.

Questions

1. Choose one of the companies in this case and describe its decision-making process in light of the decision-making model that seems to fit most appropriately.
2. Choose one of the companies in this case and draw a diagram like the one in Exhibit 9.3, filling in each space with information pertinent to that company's decision-making process.
3. Which of these companies would you like to work for? Why?

Continuing Case

Part Three: Apple Managers Decide to Kick, but Miss the Goal

The journey of Apple Computer is one of paths taken and not taken—goals, strategies, and decisions. Some decisions proved to be good moves, others not so great. With both of Apple's founders out of the picture, CEO John Sculley decided to capitalize on one of his company's strengths by pursuing refinement of the Macintosh, one of Apple's most successful products. In 1987, Apple introduced the Mac II, which was designed to be expandable, adapting to the market as technology changed. Customers seemed to fall in love with the Mac all over again, and soon the company was shipping 50,000 computers a month. By 1989, competitor Microsoft's software for PCs looked like it would be a flop in the marketplace, so instead of developing strategies to deal with this potential threat, Apple managers decided to ignore it and concentrate on goals and plans that involved only their own view of personal computing. Meanwhile, the IBM hardware manufacturers were gaining ground.

Within a year, the market was glutted with PC clones, and Apple was the single company selling its Macs. Microsoft then launched Windows 3.0, which was a graphical operating system (like the Mac OS) capable of running on almost all PC clones worldwide. Microsoft had taken a big bite out of Apple's foothold in the software market. Apple's managers were forced to reevaluate the company's goals, plans, and strategies or risk losing everything. Apple management seemed to be rife with conflicting goals and inconsistent viewpoints. The industry environment itself was filled with uncertainty and ambiguity, making decisions difficult—even risky—at every step. But managers came up with the idea to license the Mac OS. Some managers thought that doing so would actually reduce the quality of the Mac and perhaps create even more threats in the form of competition in its own system, but they agreed that Apple simply couldn't design and manufacture both the hardware and the software necessary to control the computer industry. Some managers even proposed the idea of licensing the operating system to run on the new Intel-based machines. But Michael Spindler, Apple's new chief operating officer, vetoed the whole plan. He said it was "too late to license." The strategy was dead, or so it seemed.

Meanwhile, new products were being developed. In 1991, Apple introduced the first generation of PowerBooks, the first laptop computer to offer the kind of power saving and management features we now take for granted; it was an instant success. Backstage, designers were working on the Newton, which John Sculley took on as his pet project and personal goal. But the first Newtons, which relied on handwriting recognition and did not function well at it, sold poorly. Sculley was losing interest in the company, and within the next couple of years he was phased out.

Michael Spindler became the new Apple CEO. With a directive decision-making style, he drove the company to new achievements, which were desperately needed. Personally, he was not approachable and was most likely not keen on participative decision making. But he was extremely goal driven. Spindler entered an alliance with two competitors, Motorola and IBM, to produce the PowerPC chip, which allowed Macs to compete with Intel's speedy new processors. Spindler then reversed his earlier opinion and pursued a licensing strategy, licensing the Mac OS to several companies. But on later evaluation, it appeared that Apple was actually too strict in its licensing agreements, and only a few companies actually licensed the system. In the meantime, the alliance with IBM fell apart.

The mid-1990s were perhaps Apple's lowest point. Although corporate-level strategy continued to include building computers, business-level strategy failed in getting the machines to customers. During one year, Apple had $1 billion in back orders, but lacked the parts needed to build the computers. Apple managers continued to fail in their competitive strategies against unrelenting Microsoft, which launched the powerful Windows 95 in the summer of that year. Finally, Apple made a further strategic mistake by putting more marketing muscle behind its cheaper Performa than the mid-priced PowerMac (containing the PowerPC chip), and consumers weren't interested. The company posted a huge loss that year, and Michael Spindler was asked to resign.

Mike Markkula, a long-time Apple insider and chairman of the board of directors, proposed examining potential alliances with other companies, and at that time, in 1996, a big one was on the table: a potential merger with Sun Microsystems. "This isn't anything new," Markkula claimed. "Since 1986, we held serious discussions with DEC, Kodak, Sony, Sun, Compaq, IBM, and other companies I'd rather not name now. We considered everything from 'Let's trade technology' to 'Let's put the companies together' with each of them." But the merger never went through. Gil Amelio, former head of National Semiconductor, took Spindler's place as CEO. He tried new strategies, but Apple continued to post huge losses, and Amelio was out the door in a year.

Unclear goals and inadequately conceived strategies had pushed Apple from the height of success to the depths of disaster. The company had gone through four top managers, launched several flops, and seemed to be floundering, all because of poor decision making in an admittedly ambiguous environment. But all was not lost. The Macintosh would prove itself to be one of the most innovative, reliable computers available in the marketplace over the years—with a host of loyal followers. Apple was still alive.

Questions

1. It seems that Apple did not have a clear organizational mission during this period of its history. Assume the role of CEO and write a mission statement that you think would have helped the company clarify its goals and plans.

2. Based on what you've read about Apple so far, create a chart showing a SWOT analysis of the company, using one column for each of the following characteristics: strengths, weaknesses, opportunities, threats.

3. Do you think that John Sculley and Michael Spindler were effective managers during their tenure at Apple? Why or why not?

SOURCES: Ryan J. Fass, "Happy 15th Birthday Macintosh," miningco.com, January 25, 1999; Brent Schlender and Michael H. Martin, "Paradise Lost," *Fortune*, February 19, 1996, accessed online at www.pathfinder.com; "History," accessed at the Apple Web site, www.apple.com.
iMac photo: Courtesy of Apple Computer, Inc.

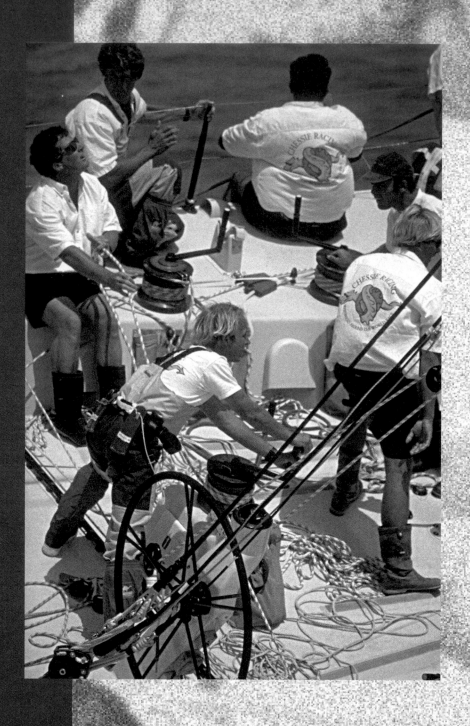

Part Four

Organizing

Clear chains of command are vital for any organization—including a sailboat crew. From the skipper, the navigator, the watch leader, the trimmers, to the riggers authority and responsibility flow throughout a crew. Some boats have co-skippers, sharing duties and trading off when a race leg's demands fit a particular skipper's skills. Crews sometimes change in port to get fresh sailors on board and to rest weary or hurt members. But regardless of the hierarchy on a boat, coordination is key to peak performance. All crew members must know their jobs well and execute them with precision when needed. Whether it's reading a weather forecast, charting a course, changing a sail, or stowing gear, each task contributes to the overall goal of winning the race.

Selecting the right mix of crew members is crucial, and then training them to function as a well-oiled team completes the preparation. In the best-functioning crews, members need to understand the overall strategy and goals not only for the race as a whole but for each race leg. Yet throughout a race, they need to adapt to changing conditions, make decisions, and learn from their mistakes.

Boats in the Whitbread race have diverse crews. Crew members ranged in age from weathered middle-aged veterans to ambitious young newcomers. One boat, EF Education from Sweden, had an all-female crew. Managing such diversity is anything but simple. But all had two things that bound them together—their love of sailing and pride and determination to be the best.

Part Four presents the fundamentals of organizing, the way structure can be used to achieve strategic goals, the role of change and development in organizations, the vital role human resources play, and the challenges of managing diverse employees.

Chapter 10

LEARNING OBJECTIVES

After studying this chapter, you should be able to

⚙ **Explain the fundamental characteristics of organizing, including such concepts as work specialization, chain of command, line and staff, and task forces.**

⚙ **Explain when specific structural characteristics such as centralization, span of management, and formalization should be used within organizations.**

⚙ **Explain the functional approach to structure.**

⚙ **Explain the divisional approach to structure.**

⚙ **Explain the matrix approach to structure and its application to both domestic and international organizations.**

⚙ **Explain the contemporary team and network structures and why they are being adopted by organizations.**

Fundamentals of Organizing

MANAGEMENT PROBLEM

NeoData, the nation's largest fulfillment house, provides delivery and customer service for direct mail products. The undisputed leader in the magazine subscription market, the company gets more than 400 titles into the hands of some 112 million readers every year. In addition, NeoData provides fulfillment for books, financial services, and consumer products. Several years ago, burdened with heavy debt after a leveraged buyout and acquisition binge, NeoData faced an ongoing struggle for cash. In addition, customers were jumping ship because of concerns about rumors, performance problems, and declining service. When Larry Jones came in as NeoData's new CEO, he initiated a massive restructuring to help the company recover. The functional structure had worked well and allowed NeoData to grow to a 5,000-person company with $240 million in revenues. However, NeoData had become so large and departmentalized that an employee at the beginning of the fulfillment process had no idea what was going on at the other stages. The telemarketing operation, lettershop, warehouses, and distribution centers were separated even physically from one another, and clients were beginning to feel that their business was lost in a gigantic shuffle. To stabilize the customer base and build new business, Jones wanted to increase coordination between functions and refocus NeoData on the customer.[1]

What advice would you give Larry Jones about structural design? What structural changes might help NeoData solve its customer service problems?

The problem confronting NeoData is one of structural design. CEO Larry Jones wanted to change the company's structure to help NeoData become more competitive and grow its business.

Every firm wrestles with the problem of how to organize. Reorganization often is necessary to reflect a new strategy, changing market conditions, or innovative production technology. Companies throughout the world are restructuring to become leaner, more efficient, and more nimble in today's highly competitive global environment.

Xerox Corporation has restructured itself from one large, hierarchical company into nine independent product divisions. The new structure allows collaboration within each division that helps provide fast transition of new technology into new products for the marketplace.[2] Eastman Chemical Company replaced its senior vice-presidents for administration, manufacturing, and research and development with self-directed work teams.[3] A growing number of companies operate as network or virtual organizations, limiting themselves to a few core activities and letting outside specialists handle the rest. For example, Super Bakery, Inc., a Pittsburgh-based donut maker majority-owned by former Pittsburgh Steelers running back, Franco Harris, achieved a national presence in a highly competitive industry by using the network approach. Super Bakery concentrates on product development and outsources the selling, manufacturing, and shipping of its products to outside contractors.[4]

organizing
The deployment of organizational resources to achieve strategic goals.

Each of these organizations is using fundamental concepts of organizing. **Organizing** is the deployment of organizational resources to achieve strategic goals. The deployment of resources is reflected in the organization's division of labor into specific departments and jobs, formal lines of authority, and mechanisms for coordinating diverse organization tasks.

Organizing is important because it follows from strategy—the topic of Part 3. Strategy defines *what* to do; organizing defines *how* to do it. Organization structure is a tool that managers use to harness resources for getting things done. Part 4 explains the variety of organizing principles and concepts used by managers. This chapter covers fundamental concepts that apply to all organizations and departments. These ideas are extended in Chapter 11, where we look at how structural designs are tailored to the organization's situation. Chapter 12 discusses how organizations can be structured to facilitate innovation and change. Chapters 13 and 14 examine how to utilize human resources to the best advantage within the organization's structure.

Organizing helps GTE remain competitive in the volatile, worldwide telecommunications industry. GTE Telephone Operations, the largest U.S.-based local telephone company, restructured from an organization based on functions and geographic regions to one focused on markets and customers. Employees in GTE's high-tech Network Operations Center in the Dallas area continuously monitor the company's telephone network nationwide. Replacing 17 smaller network control centers, this facility has improved customer service through more efficient network monitoring while reducing overall costs.

Organizing the Vertical Structure

The organizing process leads to the creation of organization structure, which defines how tasks are divided and resources deployed. **Organization structure** is defined as (1) the set of formal tasks assigned to individuals and departments; (2) formal reporting relationships, including lines of authority, decision responsibility, number of hierarchical levels, and span of managers' control; and (3) the design of systems to ensure effective coordination of employees across departments.[5]

The set of formal tasks and formal reporting relationships provides a framework for vertical control of the organization. The characteristics of vertical structure are portrayed in the **organization chart,** which is the visual representation of an organization's structure.

A sample organization chart for a soda bottling plant is illustrated in Exhibit 10.1. The plant has four major departments—accounting, human resources, production, and marketing. The organization chart delineates the chain of command, indicates departmental tasks and how they fit together, and provides order and logic for the organization. Every employee has an appointed task, line of authority, and decision responsibility. The following sections discuss several important features of vertical structure in more detail.

organization structure
The framework in which the organization defines how tasks are divided, resources are deployed, and departments are coordinated.

organization chart
The visual representation of an organization's structure.

Exhibit **10.1** *Organization Chart for a Soda Bottling Plant*

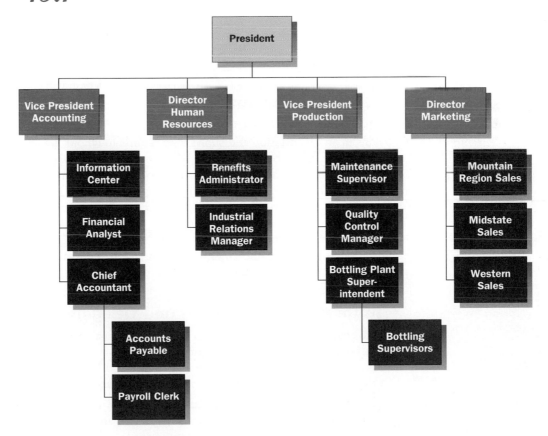

Work Specialization

work specialization
The degree to which organizational tasks are subdivided into individual jobs; also called division of labor.

Organizations perform a wide variety of tasks. A fundamental principle is that work can be performed more efficiently if employees are allowed to specialize.[6] **Work specialization,** sometimes called *division of labor,* is the degree to which organizational tasks are subdivided into separate jobs. Work specialization in Exhibit 10.1 is illustrated by the separation of production tasks into bottling, quality control, and maintenance. Employees within each department perform only the tasks relevant to their specialized function. When work specialization is extensive, employees specialize in a single task. Jobs tend to be small, but they can be performed efficiently. Work specialization is readily visible on an automobile assembly line where each employee performs the same task over and over again. It would not be efficient to have a single employee build the entire automobile or even perform a large number of unrelated jobs.

Despite the apparent advantages of specialization, many organizations are moving away from this principle. With too much specialization, employees are isolated and do only a single, tiny, boring job. Many companies are enlarging jobs to provide greater challenges or assigning teams to tasks so that employees can rotate among the several jobs performed by the team. At Sony Corporation's factory in Kohda, Japan, the assembly line for camcorders has been dismantled and replaced with small, four-person shops, where workers walk through a spiral line and assemble an entire camera themselves, doing everything from soldering to testing. U.S. companies are taking similar paths. Production increased 51 percent after Compaq Computer's Scotland and Texas plants switched from assembly lines to four-worker manufacturing teams.[7] The team approach to organization design will be discussed later in this chapter, and approaches to designing jobs to fit employee needs are described in Chapters 17 and 19.

Chain of Command

chain of command
An unbroken line of authority that links all individuals in the organization and specifies who reports to whom.

The **chain of command** is an unbroken line of authority that links all persons in an organization and shows who reports to whom. It is associated with two underlying principles. *Unity of command* means that each employee is held accountable to only one supervisor. The *scalar principle* refers to a clearly defined line of authority in the organization that includes all employees. Authority and responsibility for different tasks should be distinct. All persons in the organization should know to whom they report as well as the successive management levels all the way to the top. In Exhibit 10.1, the payroll clerk reports to the chief accountant, who in turn reports to the vice president, who in turn reports to the company president.

Authority, Responsibility, and Delegation

authority
The formal and legitimate right of a manager to make decisions, issue orders, and allocate resources to achieve organizationally desired outcomes.

The chain of command illustrates the authority structure of the organization. **Authority** is the formal and legitimate right of a manager to make decisions, issue orders, and allocate resources to achieve organizationally desired outcomes. Authority is distinguished by three characteristics:[8]

1. *Authority is vested in organizational positions, not people.* Managers have authority because of the positions they hold, and other people in the same positions would have the same authority.

2. *Authority is accepted by subordinates.* Although authority flows top down through the organization's hierarchy, subordinates comply because they believe that managers have a legitimate right to issue orders. The *acceptance theory of authority* argues that a manager has authority only if subordinates choose to accept his or her commands. If subordinates refuse to obey because the order is outside their zone of acceptance, a manager's authority disappears.[9] For example, Richard Ferris, the former chairman of United Airlines, resigned because few people accepted his strategy of acquiring hotels, a car rental company, and other organizations to build a travel empire. When key people refused to accept his direction, his authority was lost, and he resigned.

3. *Authority flows down the vertical hierarchy.* Positions at the top of the hierarchy are vested with more formal authority than are positions at the bottom.

Responsibility is the flip side of the authority coin. **Responsibility** is the duty to perform the task or activity an employee has been assigned. Typically, managers are assigned authority commensurate with responsibility. When managers have responsibility for task outcomes but little authority, the job is possible but difficult. They rely on persuasion and luck. When managers have authority exceeding responsibility, they may become tyrants, using authority toward frivolous outcomes.[10]

Accountability is the mechanism through which authority and responsibility are brought into alignment. **Accountability** means that the people with authority and responsibility are subject to reporting and justifying task outcomes to those above them in the chain of command.[11] Subordinates must be aware that they are accountable for a task and accept the responsibility and authority for performing it. Accountability can be built into the organization structure. For example, at Whirlpool incentive programs provide strict accountability. Performance of all managers is monitored, and bonus payments are tied to successful outcomes.

Another concept related to authority is delegation.[12] **Delegation** is the process managers use to transfer authority and responsibility to positions below them in the hierarchy. Most organizations today encourage managers to delegate authority to the lowest possible level to provide maximum flexibility to meet customer needs and adapt to the environment. Managers are encouraged to delegate authority, although they often find it difficult. Techniques for delegation are discussed in the Manager's Shoptalk box. The trend toward increased delegation begins in the chief executive's office in companies such as USX, PPG Industries, Johnsonville Foods, Ford, and General Electric. At Johnsonville, a committee of employees from the shop floor has been delegated authority to formulate the manufacturing budget.

Line and Staff Authority. An important distinction in many organizations is between line authority and staff authority, reflecting whether managers work in line or staff departments in the organization's structure. *Line departments* perform tasks that

responsibility
The duty to perform the task or activity an employee has been assigned.

accountability
The fact that the people with authority and responsibility are subject to reporting and justifying task outcomes to those above them in the chain of command.

delegation
The process managers use to transfer authority and responsibility to positions below them in the hierarchy.

Diane Kerr, standing, is a senior staff geophysicist for Anadarko Petroleum Corporation, one of the world's largest independent oil exploration and production companies. Kerr uses her staff authority to help develop the Alpine Field on Alaska's North Slope. She considers new technology and the strength received from company partnerships to be her most valuable resources on this job which is focused on helping to bring the Alaskan field in production in the year 2000. Diane's co-workers at Anadarko include, from left to right, Glenn Raney, Kevin Stacy, and Valerie Cadden.

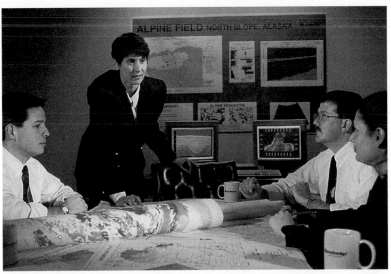

Shoptalk

How to Delegate

The attempt by top management to decentralize decision making often gets bogged down because middle managers are unable to delegate. Managers may cling tightly to their decision-making and task responsibilities. Failure to delegate occurs for a number of reasons: Managers are most comfortable making familiar decisions; they feel they will lose personal status by delegating tasks; they believe they can do a better job themselves; or they have an aversion to risk—they will not take a chance on delegating because performance responsibility ultimately rests with them.

Yet decentralization offers an organization many advantages. Decisions are made at the right level, lower-level employees are motivated, and employees have the opportunity to develop decision-making skills. Overcoming barriers to delegation in order to gain these advantages is a major challenge. The following approach can help each manager delegate more effectively:

1. *Delegate the whole task.* A manager should delegate an entire task to one person rather than dividing it among several people. This gives the individual complete responsibility and increases his or her initiative while giving the manager some control over the results.

2. *Select the right person.* Not all employees have the same capabilities and degree of motivation. Managers must match talent to task if delegation is to be effective. They should identify subordinates who have made independent decisions in the past and have shown a desire for more responsibility.

3. *Ensure that authority equals responsibility.* Merely assigning a task is not effective delegation. Managers often load subordinates with increased responsibility but do not extend their decision-making range. In addition to having responsibility for completing a task, the worker must be given the authority to make decisions about how best to do the job.

4. *Give thorough instruction.* Successful delegation includes information on what, when, why, where, who, and how. The subordinate must clearly understand the task and the expected results. It is a good idea to write down all provisions discussed, including required resources and when and how the results will be reported.

5. *Maintain feedback.* Feedback means keeping open lines of communication with the subordinate to answer questions and provide advice, but without exerting too much control. Open lines of communication make it easier to trust subordinates. Feedback keeps the subordinate on the right track.

6. *Evaluate and reward performance.* Once the task is completed, the manager should evaluate results, not methods. When results do not meet expectations, the manager must assess the consequences. When they do meet expectations, the manager should reward employees for a job well done with praise, financial rewards when appropriate, and delegation of future assignments.

Are You a Positive Delegator?

Positive delegation is the way an organization implements decentralization. Do you help or hinder the decentralization process? If you answer yes to more than three of the following questions, you may have a problem delegating:

- I tend to be a perfectionist.
- My boss expects me to know all the details of my job.
- I don't have the time to explain clearly and concisely how a task should be accomplished.
- I often end up doing tasks myself.
- My subordinates typically are not as committed as I am.
- I get upset when other people don't do the task right.
- I really enjoy doing the details of my job to the best of my ability.
- I like to be in control of task outcomes.

SOURCES: Thomas R. Horton, "Delegation and Team Building: No Solo Acts Please," *Management Review,* September 1992, 58–61; Andrew E. Schwartz, "The Why, What, and to Whom of Delegation," *Management Solutions* (June 1987), 31–38; "Delegation," *Small Business Report* (June 1986), 38–43; and Max E. Douglas, "How to Delegate Safely," *Training and Development Journal,* February 1987, 8.

---

line authority
A form of authority in which individuals in management positions have the formal power to direct and control immediate subordinates.

staff authority
A form of authority granted to staff specialists in their areas of expertise.

reflect the organization's primary goal and mission. In a manufacturing organization, line departments make and sell the product. *Staff departments* include all those that provide specialized skills in support of line departments. Staff departments have an advisory relationship with line departments and typically include marketing, labor relations, research, accounting, and human resources.

Line authority means that people in management positions have formal authority to direct and control immediate subordinates. **Staff authority** is narrower and includes the right to advise, recommend, and counsel in the staff specialists' area of expertise. Staff authority is a communication relationship;

staff specialists advise managers in technical areas. For example, the finance department of a manufacturing firm would have staff authority to coordinate with line departments about which accounting forms to use to facilitate equipment purchases and standardize payroll services.

Span of Management

The **span of management** is the number of employees reporting to a supervisor. Sometimes called the *span of control,* this characteristic of structure determines how closely a supervisor can monitor subordinates. Traditional views of organization design recommended a span of management of about seven subordinates per manager. However, many lean organizations today have spans of management as high as 30, 40, and even higher. Research on the Lockheed Missile and Space Company and other manufacturing companies has suggested that span of management can vary widely and that several factors influence the span.[13] Generally, when supervisors must be closely involved with subordinates, the span should be small, and when supervisors need little involvement with subordinates, it can be large. The following factors are associated with less supervisor involvement and thus larger spans of control:

1. Work performed by subordinates is stable and routine.

2. Subordinates perform similar work tasks.

3. Subordinates are concentrated in a single location.

4. Subordinates are highly trained and need little direction in performing tasks.

5. Rules and procedures defining task activities are available.

6. Support systems and personnel are available for the manager.

7. Little time is required in nonsupervisory activities such as coordination with other departments or planning.

8. Managers' personal preferences and styles favor a large span.

Tall Versus Flat Structure.   The average span of control used in an organization determines whether the structure is tall or flat. A **tall structure** has an overall narrow span and more hierarchical levels. A **flat structure** has a wide span, is horizontally dispersed, and has fewer hierarchical levels.

The trend in recent years has been toward wider spans of control as a way to facilitate delegation.[14] Exhibit 10.2 illustrates how an international metals company was reorganized. The multilevel set of managers shown in panel *a* was replaced with ten operating managers and nine staff specialists reporting directly to the CEO, as shown in panel *b*. The CEO welcomed this wide span of 19 management subordinates because it fit his style, his management team was top quality and needed little supervision, and they were all located on the same floor of an office building.

Centralization and Decentralization

Centralization and decentralization pertain to the hierarchical level at which decisions are made. **Centralization** means that decision authority is located near the top of the organization. With **decentralization,** decision authority is pushed downward to lower organization levels. Organizations may have to experiment to find the correct hierarchical level at which to make decisions.

span of management
The number of employees who report to a supervisor; also called *span of control.*

tall structure
A management structure characterized by an overall narrow span of management and a relatively large number of hierarchical levels.

flat structure
A management structure characterized by an overall broad span of control and relatively few hierarchical levels.

centralization
The location of decision authority near top organizational levels.

decentralization
The location of decision authority near lower organizational levels.

Exhibit *10.2*   *Reorganization to Increase Span of Management for President of an International Metals Company*

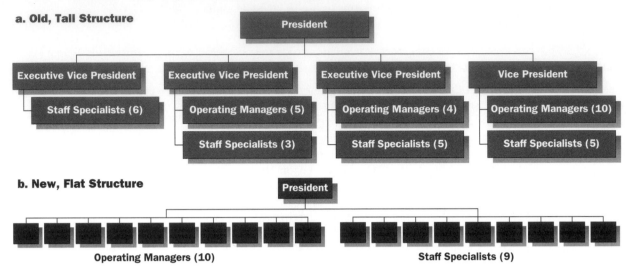

a. Old, Tall Structure

President

Executive Vice President — Staff Specialists (6)

Executive Vice President — Operating Managers (5), Staff Specialists (3)

Executive Vice President — Operating Managers (4), Staff Specialists (5)

Vice President — Operating Managers (10), Staff Specialists (5)

b. New, Flat Structure

President

Operating Managers (10)

Staff Specialists (9)

These employees at CB&T® bank, an affiliate of Synovus Financial Corp.®, have the power to honor the commitment of "Everything You Expect from a Bank. And More." Synovus, a $6.1 billion multifinancial services company, has held fast to a philosophy of decentralization *for more than a century. Each of its 32 affiliate banks retains its own name, management team, board of directors, and decision-making autonomy. Pushing decision authority as close to the customer as possible allows Synovus to take advantage of experienced local teams, making the company one of the highest performers in the financial services industry.*

In the United States and Canada, the trend over the past 30 years has been toward greater decentralization of organizations. Decentralization is believed to relieve the burden on top managers, make greater use of workers' skills and abilities, ensure that decisions are made close to the action by well-informed people, and permit more rapid response to external changes.

However, this trend does not mean that every organization should decentralize all decisions. Managers should diagnose the organizational situation and select the decision-making level that will best meet the organization's needs. Factors that typically influence centralization versus decentralization are as follows:

1. Greater change and uncertainty in the environment are usually associated with decentralization. A good example of how decentralization can help cope with rapid change and uncertainty occurred during Operation Desert Shield, when the highly decentralized U.S. Tactical Air Command deployed double the number of squadrons expected during the first week while other centralized U.S. forces fell behind their deployment schedules.[15] Today, most companies feel greater uncertainty because of intense global competition; hence, many have decentralized.

2. The amount of centralization or decentralization should fit the firm's strategy. For example, Johnson & Johnson gives almost complete authority to its 180 operating companies to develop and market their own products. Decentralization fits the corporate strategy of empowerment that gets each division close to customers so it can speedily adapt to their needs.[16] As new technology and competition changed the banking industry, BancOne Chairman John B. McCoy switched to centralization to cut costs, speed up decision making, and move faster with new products and services.[17]

3. In times of crisis or risk of company failure, authority may be centralized at the top. When Honda could not get agreement among divisions about new car models, President Nobuhiko Kawamoto made the decision himself.[18]

On the Right Track

Nearly everyone has heard stories about the Pentagon's extravagant ways: $250 for a hammer, $600 for a toilet seat. You might think having the Pentagon as a client would be every small contractor's dream. But there are plenty of nightmares, says Rick Lewandowski of MDP Construction, Inc. Winning one of those government contracts means contending with loads of regulations and a mountain of paperwork, as well as dealing with endless scheduling delays caused by bureaucracy. Small contractors are at a decided disadvantage, as the paperwork alone is enough to bury a company with limited personnel.

MDP Construction has learned not only to compete, but to thrive in this bureaucratic system by harnessing the power of information technology. "For the type of construction that we do," says Lewandowski, "we'd normally need maybe eight people in our office just to take care of the correspondence. We have four." Virtually every aspect of Lewandowski's business has been revamped by IT. Every piece of government required paperwork has been scanned into MDP's network so that project supervisors equipped with laptops and modems can access any document they need directly from the construction site. Another benefit of computerization is the ability to coordinate logistics with improved speed and accuracy. A project-management program called SureTrak Project Manager allows MDP to track timelines for the myriad tasks involved in each construction project. Previously, supervisors had to chart all those steps manually, an arduous job consid-

ering many complex construction projects involve well over 1,000 tasks. With SureTrak, managers can oversee a larger number of projects, as well as quickly determine how one "simple" change requested by the client could end up adding months to the schedule. For example, when MDP was building a fire station at Peterson Air Force Base, the government wanted to make a midproject change in wall color. Using SureTrak, Lewandowski was able to show that even this minor adjustment would lead to a delay of 12 weeks in completing the project. Such delays not only waste government dollars but also keep MDP workers idle and tie up company resources that could be used elsewhere.

Lewandowski admits it took some time for MDP's supervisors—all former painters and carpenters—to get the hang of continuously updating SureTrak. Today, however, supervisors in the field use SureTrak to manage their own individual budgets and make better economic decisions. The next step in Lewandowski's revolution is a company Web site that will not only improve internal communication but also smooth the process of exchanging information with the government. Overall, government officials have come to appreciate MDP's streamlined efficiency. For this small construction company, that translates into $12 million in revenues from government contracts.

SOURCE: Christopher Caggiano, "Thriving on Bureaucracy," Inc. Technology, 1997, no. 1, 63–66.

Formalization

Formalization is the written documentation used to direct and control employees. Written documentation includes rule books, policies, procedures, job descriptions, and regulations. These documents complement the organization chart by providing descriptions of tasks, responsibilities, and decision authority. The use of rules, regulations, and written records of decisions is part of the bureaucratic model of organizations described in Chapter 2. As proposed by Max Weber, the bureaucratic model defines the basic organizational characteristics that enable the organization to operate in a logical and rational manner.

Although written documentation is intended to be rational and helpful to the organization, it often creates "red tape" that causes more problems than it solves. Some U.S. government departments are notorious for bureaucratic inefficiency. The Technology box describes how MDP Construction, a small building contractor, harnessed information technology to deal with the mountain of paperwork involved in government construction contracts. As a practical matter, many organizations today are becoming less formal in order to be flexible and responsive to a changing global environment.

formalization
The written documentation used to direct and control employees.

Departmentalization

departmentalization
The basis on which individuals are grouped into departments and departments into total organizations.

Another fundamental characteristic of organization structure is **departmentalization,** which is the basis for grouping positions into departments and departments into the total organization. Managers make choices about how to use the chain of command to group people together to perform their work. There are five approaches to structural design that reflect different uses of the chain of command in departmentalization. The functional, divisional, and matrix are traditional approaches that rely on the chain of command to define departmental groupings and reporting relationships along the hierarchy. Two contemporary approaches are the use of teams and networks. These newer approaches have emerged to meet organizational needs in a highly competitive global environment. A brief illustration of the five structural alternatives is presented in Exhibit 10.3.

1. *Vertical functional approach.* People are grouped together in departments by common skills and work activities, such as in an engineering department and an accounting department.

2. *Divisional approach.* Departments are grouped together into separate, self-contained divisions based on a common product, program, or geographical region. Diverse skills rather than similar skills are the basis of departmentalization.

E x h i b i t **10.3**   *Five Approaches to Structural Design*

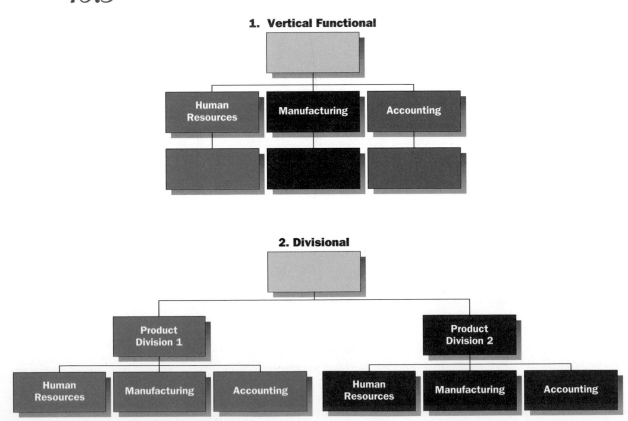

1. Vertical Functional

Human Resources | Manufacturing | Accounting

2. Divisional

Product Division 1 — Human Resources | Manufacturing | Accounting

Product Division 2 — Human Resources | Manufacturing | Accounting

3. *Horizontal matrix approach.* Functional and divisional chains of command are implemented simultaneously and overlay one another in the same departments. Two chains of command exist, and some employees report to two bosses.

4. *Team-based approach.* The organization creates a series of teams to accomplish specific tasks and to coordinate major departments. Teams can exist from the office of the president all the way down to the shop floor.

5. *Network approach.* The organization becomes a small, central hub electronically connected to other organizations that perform vital functions. Departments are independent, contracting services to the central hub for a profit. Departments can be located anywhere in the world.[19]

Each approach to structure serves a distinct purpose for the organization, and each has advantages and disadvantages. The basic difference among structures is the way in which employees are departmentalized and to whom they report. The differences in structure illustrated in Exhibit 10.3 have major consequences for employee goals and motivation. Let us now turn to each of the five structural designs and examine their implications for managers.[20]

E x h i b i t **10.3** *(continued)*

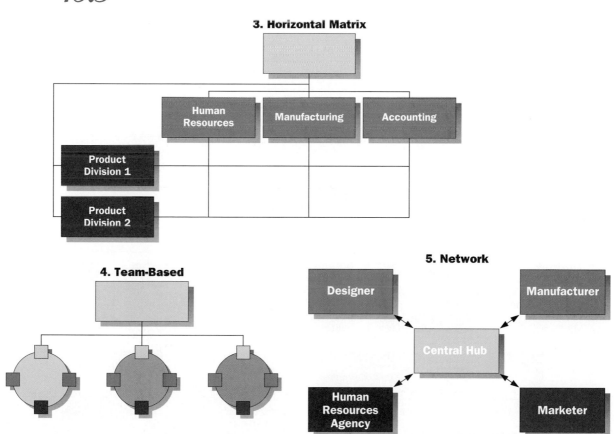

Vertical Functional Approach

Functional structure is the grouping of positions into departments based on similar skills, expertise, and resource use. A functional structure can be thought of as departmentalization by organizational resources, because each type of functional activity—human resources, engineering, manufacturing—represents specific resources for performing the organization's task. People and facilities representing a common organizational resource are grouped into a single department.

An example of a functional structure for American Airlines is presented in Exhibit 10.4. The major departments under the chairman are groupings of similar expertise and resources, such as employee relations, government affairs, operations, information systems, and marketing. Each of the functional departments at American Airlines is concerned with the airline as a whole. The employee relations vice president is concerned with human resources issues for the entire airline, and the marketing department is responsible for all sales and marketing.

Advantages and Disadvantages.   Grouping employees into departments based on similar skills has many advantages for an organization. Employees who perform a common task are grouped so as to permit economies of scale and efficient resource use. At American Airlines, as illustrated in Exhibit 10.4, all information systems people work in the same department. They have the expertise for handling almost any problem within a single, large department. The large functional departments enhance the development of in-depth skills because people work on a variety of problems and are associated with other experts. Career progress is based on functional expertise; thus, employees are motivated to develop their skills. Managers and employees are compatible because of similar training and expertise.

The functional structure also offers a way to centralize decision making and provide unified direction from the top, because the chain of command

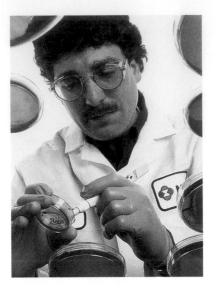

Senior research biochemist, Robert Lobell, Ph.D., is a member of a functional team at Merck & Co., a global research-driven pharmaceutical company, that is using molecular and biochemical methods to develop compounds that inhibit the action of oncogenes (genes that cause abnormal growth). The research conducted by this team of experts is part of Merck's 15-year cancer research initiative that has yielded many new insights, as reflected by Lobell's statement, "My greatest satisfaction is being part of a team that may actually beat cancer."

E x h i b i t **10.4**   *Functional Structure for American Airlines*

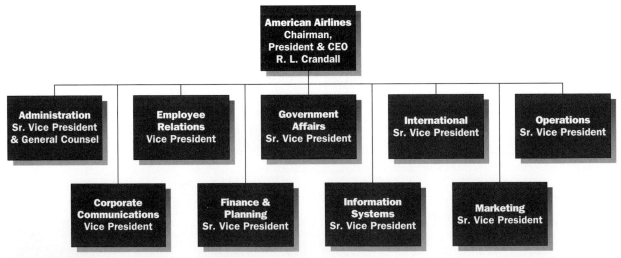

SOURCE: Used with permission of American Airlines.

converges at the top of the organization. Sometimes the functional structure is also associated with wider spans of control because of large departments and common expertise. Communication and coordination among employees within each department are excellent. Finally, functional structure promotes high-quality technical problem solving. Having a pool of well-trained experts, especially those who work with sophisticated technology, motivated toward functional expertise gives the company an important resource.

The disadvantages of functional structure reflect the barriers that exist across departments and a slow response to environmental changes. Because people are separated into distinct departments, communication and coordination across functions are often poor. Poor coordination means a slow response to environmental changes, because innovation and change require involvement of several departments. Because the chains of command are separate beneath the top of the organization, decisions involving more than one department may pile up at the top of the organization and be delayed. The functional structure also stresses work specialization and division of labor, which may produce routine, nonmotivating employee tasks.

The functional structure also creates management problems, such as difficulty in pinpointing problems within departments. In the case of an insurance company, for example, each function works on all products and performs only a part of the task for any product line. Hence, if one life insurance product is not performing well, there is no specific department or group that bears responsibility. In addition, employees tend to focus on the attainment of departmental goals, often to the exclusion of organizational goals. They see only their respective tasks, not the big picture. Because of this narrow task specialization, employees are trained to become experts in their fields, not to manage and coordinate diverse departments. Thus, they fail to become groomed for top management and general management positions.

The advantages and disadvantages of functional structure are summarized in Exhibit 10.5.

Divisional Approach

In contrast to the functional approach, in which people are grouped by common skills and resources, the **divisional structure** occurs when departments are grouped together based on organizational outputs. Functional

functional structure
An organization structure in which positions are grouped into departments based on similar skills, expertise, and resource use.

divisional structure
An organization structure in which departments are grouped based on similar organizational outputs.

Advantages	Disadvantages
• Efficient use of resources, economies of scale	• Poor communication across functional departments
• In-depth skill specialization and development	• Slow response to external changes, lagging innovation
• Career progress within functional departments	• Decisions concentrated at top of hierarchy, creating delay
• Top manager direction and control	• Responsibility for problems is difficult to pinpoint
• Excellent coordination within functions	• Limited view of organizational goals by employees
• High-quality technical problem solving	• Limited general management training for employees

Exhibit **10.5**

Advantages and Disadvantages of Functional Structure

and divisional structures are illustrated in Exhibit 10.6. In the divisional structure, divisions are created as self-contained units for producing a single product. Each functional department resource needed to produce the product is assigned to one division. For example, in a functional structure, all engineers are grouped together and work on all products. In a divisional structure, separate engineering departments are established within each division. Each department is smaller and focuses on a single product line. Departments are duplicated across product lines.

The divisional structure is sometimes called a *product structure, program structure,* or *self-contained unit structure.* Each of these terms means essentially the same thing: Diverse departments are brought together to produce a single organizational output, whether it be a product, a program, or a service to a single customer.

In very large companies, a divisional structure is essential. Most large corporations have separate business divisions that perform different tasks, serve different clients, or use different technologies. When a huge organization produces products for different markets, the divisional structure works because each division is an autonomous business. For example, Time Warner, Inc. uses a divisional structure. Divisions include Warner Brothers, the world's largest record company; HBO, the leading pay cable television channel; *Time* magazine; and Little, Brown, a book publisher. Each of these companies is run as a separate business under the guidance of Time Warner corporate headquarters.

A major difference between divisional and functional structures is that the chain of command from each function converges lower in the hierarchy. In an organization such as the one in Exhibit 10.6, differences of opinion among research and development, marketing, manufacturing, and finance would be resolved at the divisional level rather than by the president. Thus,

Exhibit 10.6 *Functional versus Divisional Structures*

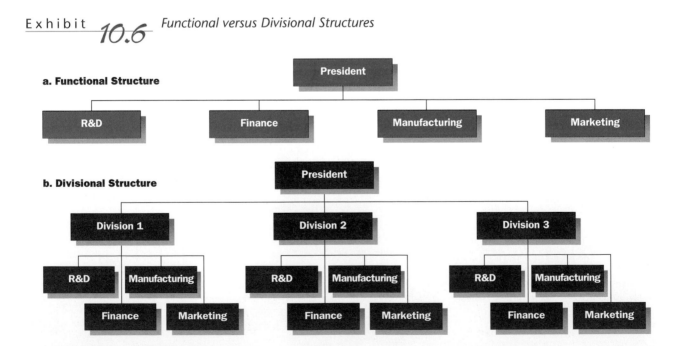

the divisional structure encourages decentralization. Decision making is pushed down at least one level in the hierarchy, freeing the president and other top managers for strategic planning.

Geographic-Based Divisions. An alternative for assigning divisional responsibility is to group company activities by geographic region, as illustrated in Exhibit 10.7. In this structure, all functions in a specific country or region report to the same division manager. This structure focuses company activities on local market conditions. For example, competitive advantage may come from the production or sale of a product adapted to a given country. For example, at LSI Logic Corporation, management's strategy is to divide the world into three geographic markets—Japan, the United States, and Europe. Each division has all the resources to focus on the fierce competition in its part of the world. McDonald's has divided its U.S. operations into five geographic divisions, each with its own staff functions, such as human resources and legal, and its own president. McDonald's CEO Jack Greenberg believes this geographic structure will help speed up decision making, improve communication with franchisees, and enhance innovation.[21]

Advantages and Disadvantages. For medium-sized companies, the choice between functional and divisional structure is difficult because each represents different strengths and weaknesses. The advantages and disadvantages of the divisional structure are listed in Exhibit 10.8. By dividing employees and resources along divisional lines, the organization will be flexible and responsive to change because each unit is small and tuned in to its environment. By having employees working on a single product line, the concern for customers' needs is high. Coordination across functional departments is better because employees are grouped together in a single location and committed to one product line. Great coordination exists within divisions. The divisional structure also enables top management to pinpoint responsibility for performance problems in product lines. Because each division is a self-contained unit, poor performance can be assigned directly to the manager of that unit. Finally, employees' goals typically are directed toward product success rather than toward their own functional

Exhibit **10.7** *Geographic-Based Global Organization Structure*

Exhibit
Exhibit *10.8*

Advantages and Disadvantages of Divisional Structure

Advantages	Disadvantages
• Fast response, flexibility in an unstable environment	• Duplication of resources across divisions
• Fosters concern for customers' needs	• Less technical depth and specialization in divisions
• Excellent coordination across functional departments	• Poor coordination across divisions
• Easy pinpointing of responsibility for product problems	• Less top management control
• Emphasis on overall product and division goals	• Competition for corporate resources
• Development of general management skills	

departments. Employees develop a broader goal orientation that can help them develop into general managers.

The divisional structure also has well-defined disadvantages. The major disadvantage is duplication of resources and the high cost of running separate divisions. Instead of a single research department in which all research people use a single facility, there may be several. The organization loses efficiency and economies of scale. Because departments within each division are small, there is a lack of technical specialization, expertise, and training. The divisional structure fosters excellent coordination *within* divisions, but coordination *across* divisions often is poor. Hewlett-Packard prided itself on the divisional structure that gave autonomy to many small divisions. Problems occurred, however, when these divisions went in opposite directions. The software produced in one division did not fit the hardware produced in another. Thus, the divisional structure was realigned to establish adequate coordination across divisions. Moreover, divisions may feel themselves in competition with one another, especially for resources from corporate headquarters. This can lead to political behavior that is unhealthy for the company as a whole. Because top management control is somewhat weaker under the divisional structure, top managers must assert themselves in order to get divisions to work together.

Many companies must carefully decide whether the divisional or functional structure better suits their needs. It is not uncommon for a company to try one structure and then switch to another as its needs change. One example is Apple Computer, which went to a divisional structure to ensure excellent cooperation within divisions and a rapid response to the external environment. However, a declining market for personal computers made efficiency more important, and Apple reorganized into a functional structure. Then in 1992 Apple reorganized into a product structure, with each division reporting to the CEO.[22]

Horizontal Matrix Approach

matrix approach
An organization structure that utilizes functional and divisional chains of command simultaneously in the same part of the organization.

The **matrix approach** combines aspects of both functional and divisional structures simultaneously in the same part of the organization.[23] The matrix structure evolved as a way to improve horizontal coordination and information sharing. One unique feature of the matrix is that it has dual lines of authority. In Exhibit 10.9, the functional hierarchy of authority runs vertically, and the divisional hierarchy of authority runs horizontally. While the vertical structure provides traditional control within functional departments, the horizontal structure provides coordination across departments. The matrix structure therefore provides a formal chain of command for both functional (vertical) and divisional (horizontal) relationships. As a result of this dual structure, some employees actually report to two supervisors simultaneously.

The matrix structure often is used by global corporations such as Dow Corning or Asea Brown Boveri. The problem for global companies is to achieve simultaneous coordination of various products within each country or region and for each product line. An example of a global matrix structure is illustrated in Exhibit 10.10. The two lines of authority are geographic and product. To see how the matrix works, consider that the geographic boss in Germany coordinates all affiliates in Germany, and the plastics products boss coordinates the manufacturing and sale of plastics products around the world. Managers of local affiliate companies in Germany would report to two superiors, both the country boss and the product boss. The dual authority structure violates the unity-of-command concept described earlier in this chapter but is necessary to give equal emphasis to both functional and divisional lines of authority. Dual lines of authority can be confusing, but after managers learn to use this structure, the matrix provides excellent coordination simultaneously for each geographic region and each product line.

The success of the matrix structure depends on the abilities of people in key matrix roles. **Two-boss employees,** those who report to two supervisors simultaneously, must resolve conflicting demands from the matrix bosses. They must confront senior managers and reach joint decisions. They need excellent human relations skills with which to confront managers and resolve

two-boss employee
An employee who reports to two supervisors simultaneously.

Exhibit **10.9** *Dual-Authority Structure in a Matrix Organization*

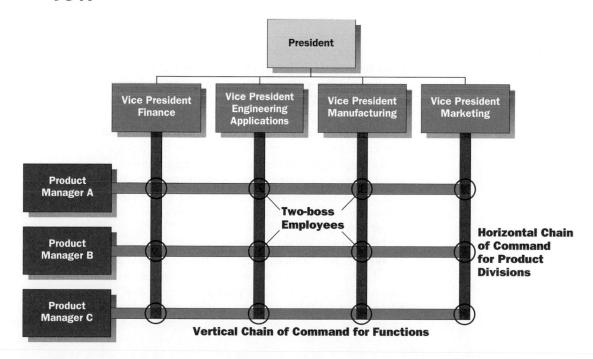

Exhibit *10.10* *Global Matrix Structure*

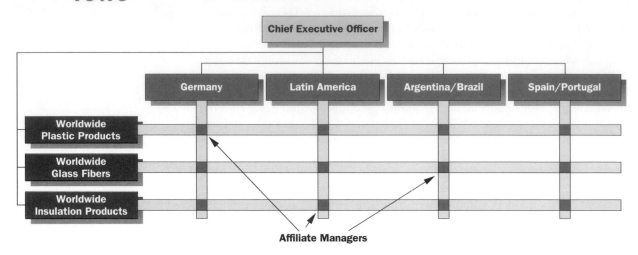

Affiliate Managers

matrix boss
A product or functional boss, responsible for one side of the matrix.

top leader
The overseer of both the product and the functional chains of command, responsible for the entire matrix.

conflicts. The **matrix boss** is the product or functional boss, who is responsible for one side of the matrix. The top leader is responsible for the entire matrix. The **top leader** oversees both the product and functional chains of command. His or her responsibility is to maintain a power balance between the two sides of the matrix. If disputes arise between them, the problem will be kicked upstairs to the top leader.[24]

Advantages and Disadvantages.   The matrix structure is controversial because of the dual chain of command. However, it has been used successfully by companies such as IBM, Unilever, and Ford Motor Company, which have fine-tuned the matrix structure to suit their particular goals and cultures. The matrix can be highly effective in a complex, rapidly changing environment in which the organization needs to be flexible and adaptable.[25] The conflict and frequent meetings generated by the matrix allow new issues to be raised and resolved. The matrix structure makes efficient use of human resources because specialists can be transferred from one division to another. The matrix also provides training for both specialist and general management skills. People within a functional department or within a specific country in a global matrix have access to in-depth training and specialization. At the same time, they coordinate with other programs or divisions, which helps employees develop a general management perspective. Finally, the matrix structure engages the participation of employees in team meetings and in the achievement of divisional goals. Thus, it challenges and motivates employees, giving them a larger task than would be possible in a functional structure.

The matrix structure also has several disadvantages, however. The major problem is the confusion and frustration caused by the dual chain of command. Matrix bosses and two-boss employees have difficulty with the dual reporting relationships. The matrix structure also can generate high conflict because it pits divisional against functional goals in a domestic structure, or product line versus country goals in a global structure. This leads to the third

Advantages	Disadvantages
• More efficient use of resources than single hierarchy	• Frustration and confusion from dual chain of command
• Flexibility, adaptability to changing environment	• High conflict between two sides of matrix
• Development of both general and specialist management skills	• Many meetings, more discussion than action
• Interdisciplinary cooperation, expertise available to all divisions	• Human relations training needed
• Enlarged tasks for employees	• Power dominance by one side of matrix

Exhibit *10.11*

Advantages and Disadvantages of Matrix Structure

disadvantage: time lost to meetings and discussions devoted to resolving this conflict. Often the matrix structure leads to more discussion than action because different goals and points of view are being addressed. For example, Digital Equipment Corp. CEO Robert B. Palmer blames the matrix for delaying for years his company's needed shift from minicomputers to PCs.[26] To survive and perform well in a matrix, employees need human relations training to learn to deal with two bosses, to get by with only "half" of each employee, and to confront and manage conflict. Finally, many organizations find it difficult to maintain the power balances essential for matrix success. The functional and divisional sides of the matrix must have equal power. If one side acquires greater formal authority, the advantages of the matrix structure are lost. The organization then operates like a functional structure with informal lateral relationships.

The advantages and disadvantages of the matrix structure are summarized in Exhibit 10.11.

At General Electric's Lighting division, John Opie created a lean matrix that helped the division cut costs and increase effectiveness.

When Jack Welch hired John Opie to head GE's Lighting division, the business was in serious decline. Opie realized that Lighting needed to radically alter the way it operated to cut costs, simplify and speed decision making, and bring the business closer to its customers. He first organized the three plants into one large operation and then created a matrix structure. Employees are grouped according to functions, such as manufacturing, human resources, and finance. Linking the functions are product managers, each of whom is responsible for a particular product—for example, incandescent lamps. Employees from different functional areas work together in teams, with the product managers serving as team leaders. Lighting workers thus report to both the functional chief and the product manager.

Implementing the matrix structure met with some resistance, but the disruptions the new structure caused were more than compensated for by the efficiencies gained. Overall, the reorganization eliminated 700 white-collar positions and reduced seven layers of management to four. Opie's Lighting team continually looked for ways to simultaneously cut costs and increase effectiveness, and the methods worked. Within two years, GE's Lighting division was producing solid results as sales, profit, market share, and employee productivity dramatically increased.[27]

GENERAL ELECTRIC
www.ge.com

Team Approach

Probably the most widespread trend in departmentalization has been the effort by companies to implement team concepts. The vertical chain of command is a powerful means of control, but passing all decisions up the hierarchy takes too long and keeps responsibility at the top. Today, companies are trying to find ways to delegate authority, push responsibility to low levels, and create participative teams that engage the commitment of workers. This approach enables organizations to be more flexible and responsive in the competitive global environment. Chapter 19 will discuss teams in detail.

Cross-functional teams consist of employees from various functional departments who are responsible to meet as a team and resolve mutual problems. Team members typically still report to their functional departments, but they also report to the team, one member of whom may be the leader. For example, Coca-Cola Fountain Manufacturing's Baltimore Syrup Operation uses cross-functional teams to work on policies for vacation and compensation.[28]

Some organizations have created **permanent teams,** groups of employees who are brought together as a formal department. The permanent-team approach resembles the divisional approach described earlier, except that teams are much smaller. Teams may consist of only 20 to 30 members, each bringing a functional specialty to the team. For example, Kollmorgen Corporation, a manufacturer of electronic circuitry and other goods, divided its organization into teams that average 75 employees.[29] Even at this size, employees think of themselves as a team. Performance jumped dramatically after Kollmorgen shifted to this concept. American Express Financial Advisors implemented teams to improve internal communication and customer service.

cross-functional team
A group of employees assigned to a functional department that meets as a team to resolve mutual problems.

permanent team
A group of participants from several functions who are permanently assigned to solve ongoing problems of common interest.

**AMERICAN EXPRESS
FINANCIAL ADVISORS**
www.americanexpress.com

American Express Financial Advisors sells financial products such as insurance, mutual funds, and investment certificates. But its redesign focuses on *how* the company sells these products, with teams of empowered workers focused on building relationships with customers. The reorganization came about because managers recognized environmental changes that could threaten client-retention. Although AEFA was basking in the glow of 21 percent annual earnings growth, top managers believed stronger horizontal coordination was needed to keep the company successful and competitive. Today, front-line teams set up around core processes are the foundation of the organizational structure.

Leaders also recognized that stronger horizontal coordination was needed in the executive office, as well. Therefore, the position of general sales manager was dropped, and those duties are now shared by seven senior executives. Each has a vertical responsibility, but each also "owns" a process that horizontally spans the organization—for example, client acquisition or account management. Although the organization retains some elements of a functional structure, emphasis is on horizontal collaboration and empowered teams, promoting better and faster communication within the company and with clients.[30]

Many companies reorganize into permanent teams after going through a process called reengineering. **Reengineering** is the radical redesign of business processes to achieve dramatic improvements in cost, quality, service, and speed. Because the focus is on process rather than function, reengineering often leads to a shift away from a vertical structure to one emphasizing teamwork and empowerment.[31]

At Hallmark, reengineering led to a new team approach to greeting-card development. Hallmark used to be organized by functional departments and designed cards in a step-by-step process. Because of delays and rework, it sometimes took the company more than two years to produce a new card. Today, teams of artists, lithographers, writers, designers, and photographers work together, each empowered to develop and make decisions about cards for a particular holiday. Thanks to the power of teams, cycle time for getting new cards to market has been cut in half.[32]

Advantages and Disadvantages.

Designing team relationships often helps overcome shortcomings in a functional, top-down approach to organizing. With cross-functional teams, the organization is able to retain some advantages of a functional structure, such as economies of scale and in-depth training, while gaining the benefits of team relationships. The team concept breaks down barriers across departments. Team members know one another's problems and compromise rather than blindly pursue their own goals. The team concept also allows the organization to more quickly adapt to customer requests and environmental changes and speeds decision making because decisions need not go to the top of the hierarchy for approval. Another big advantage is the morale boost. Employees are enthusiastic about their involvement in bigger projects rather than narrow departmental tasks. Jobs are enriched. The creation of teams also enables responsibility and authority to be pushed down the hierarchy, requiring fewer managers for supervision.

But the team approach has disadvantages as well. Employees may be enthusiastic about team participation, but they may also experience conflicts and dual loyalties. A cross-functional team may make different demands on members than do their department managers, and members who participate in more than one team must resolve these conflicts. A large amount of time is devoted to meetings, thus increasing coordination time. Unless the organization truly needs teams to coordinate complex projects and adapt to the environment, it will lose production efficiency with them. Finally, the team approach may cause too much decentralization. Senior department managers who traditionally made decisions may feel left out when a team moves ahead on its own. Team members often do not see the big picture of the corporation and may make decisions that are good for their group but bad for the organization as a whole. Top management can help keep the team in alignment with corporate goals.

The advantages and disadvantages of the team structure are summarized in Exhibit 10.12.

These members of the Avery Hi-Liter® Ever-Bold™ marker team are part of the North American consumer products division at Avery Dennison Corporation, and collaborated as a cross-functional team to launch a new pen-style highlighter product. Avery Dennison is a company committed to using the team-based approach to maintain and grow their market leadership. The company empowers multi-functional teams of employees to develop and launch new consumer products.

reengineering
The radical redesign of business processes to achieve dramatic improvements in cost, quality, service, and speed.

Exhibit *10.12*
Advantages and Disadvantages of Team Structure

Advantages	Disadvantages
• Some advantages of functional structure	• Dual loyalties and conflict
• Reduced barriers among departments, increased compromise	• Time and resources spent on meetings
• Less response time, quicker decisions	• Unplanned decentralization
• Better morale, enthusiasm from employee involvement	
• Reduced administrative overhead	

Exhibit *10.12*
Advantages and Disadvantages of Team Structure

Network Approach

network structure
An organization structure that disaggregates major functions into separate companies that are brokered by a small headquarters organization.

The most recent approach to departmentalization extends the idea of horizontal coordination and collaboration beyond the boundaries of the organization. The **network structure** means that the firm subcontracts many of its major functions to separate companies and coordinates their activities from a small headquarters organization.[33] The organization may be viewed as a central hub surrounded by a network of outside specialists, as illustrated in Exhibit 10.13. Rather than being housed under one roof, services such as accounting, design, manufacturing, and distribution are outsourced to separate organizations that are connected electronically to the central office.[34] The nature of the network structure means that subcontractors flow into and out of the system when needed. Much like building blocks, parts of the network can be added or taken away to meet changing needs.[35] A further development of the network is the *virtual network organization,* which is a continually evolving group of companies that unite temporarily to exploit specific opportunities or attain strategic advantages and then disband when objectives are met.[36] Data and information are shared electronically among participating companies. Unlike the network structure, in which the hub organization maintains control over work done by various subcontractors, in a virtual organization each independent company gives up some control to temporarily become part of a new, larger organizational system.

Exhibit *10.13* *Network Approach to Departmentalization*

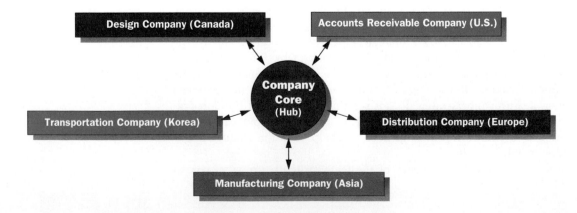

The network approach is revolutionary, because it is difficult to answer the question "Where is the organization?" in traditional terms. For example, a firm may contract for expensive services such as training, transportation, legal, and engineering, so these functions are no longer part of the organization. Or consider a piece of ice hockey equipment that is designed in Scandinavia, engineered in the United States, manufactured in Korea, and distributed in Canada by a Japanese sales organization. These pieces are drawn together contractually and coordinated electronically, creating a new form of organization.

The network approach allows companies to concentrate on what they do best and to outsource the rest. Companies such as Nike and Reebok have succeeded by focusing on their core strengths in design and marketing and contracting all their footwear manufacturing to outside suppliers. Computer firms such as Dell, Gateway, and CompuAdd either purchase their products ready-made or buy all the parts and handle only the final assembly. Sun Microsystems relies so heavily on outside manufacturers and distributors that its own employees never touch one of its computers.[37] Another computer firm thriving with a network approach is Monorail, described in the Learning Organization box.

Small entrepreneurial firms find they can save money and reach a larger market for their products by using outside manufacturers and distributors. For example, Rhoda Makoff started R&D Laboratories, Inc., to develop specialized vitamin and mineral supplements for dialysis patients. She has the products manufactured and packaged by outside pharmaceuticals companies, and about 200 wholesalers handle warehousing and distribution. The network approach has enabled quantum leaps in growth for R&D Labs—as soon as the small company has a promising new product, Makoff can ramp up production and distribution just by making a few phone calls.[38] Tomima Edmark built TopsyTail, Inc., into an $80 million company with only two full-time employees. TopsyTail's production partners include a toolmaker, two injection molders, a package designer, a logo designer, freelance photographers, and a printer. The company also outsources packaging and shipping to three fulfillment houses, television commercials to a video production company, customer mailings to a mailing list firm, and publicity to a public relations firm. Four distributing companies sell TopsyTail products in the United States, Canada, Mexico, the Pacific Rim, Europe, and South Africa.[39]

Advantages and Disadvantages.   The biggest advantage to the network structure seems to be competitiveness on a global scale. Network organizations, even small ones, can be truly global. A network organization can draw on resources worldwide to achieve the best quality and price and can sell its products and services worldwide. A second advantage is workforce flexibility and challenge. Flexibility comes from the ability to hire whatever services are needed, such as engineering design or maintenance, and to change a few months later without constraints from owning plant, equipment, and facilities. The organization can continually redefine itself to fit new product and market opportunities. For those employees who are a permanent part of the organization, the challenge comes from greater job variety and job satisfaction from working within the lean structure. Finally, this structure is perhaps the leanest of all organization forms because little supervision is required. Large teams of staff specialists and administrators are not

The Virtual Computer Company

Monorail, Inc., a fast-growing start-up based in Marietta, Georgia, is succeeding in a competitive industry based on the strength of partnerships. The company has no factories, no warehouses, no credit department, and no help desks or call centers. Yet it is already the 14th leading manufacturer of desktop PCs and is growing at a rate of 50 percent per quarter. Monorail concentrates on product design and marketing and outsources everything else to other organizations. The company was one of the first to offer a computer for less than $1,000, and has designed a remarkably compact PC that takes up only 20 percent of the desk space occupied by a traditional computer.

Monorail founders Doug Johns, David Hocker, and Nicholas Forlenza (all former Compaq managers) point out that relationships are the glue that holds their organization together. Consider how a typical Monorail transaction works. Retailer CompUSA orders a Monorail PC. The order is transmitted electronically through FedEx Logistics Services to one of Monorail's many contract manufacturers. The manufacturer assembles the PC from an inventory of Monorail parts and ships it via FedEx directly to the CompUSA outlet. Meanwhile, FedEx wires an invoice to SunTrust Bank in Atlanta, whose factoring department handles billing and credit approvals for Monorail. Monorail receives payment from SunTrust, which assumes the risk of collecting the funds from CompUSA. Whenever Monorail customers need technical help, they call a service center

that is staffed and run by Sykes Enterprises, Inc., a call-center outsourcing company based in Tampa, Florida. There are only two things Monorail founders believe they can't outsource: world-class management expertise and a knack for partnerships. Monorail's business model depends on seamless integration with its two major partners, FedEx and SunTrust, which play a central role in Monorail's operations. In fact, the unique design feature of Monorail's product line—the compact dimensions of its PC—grew directly out of learning brought about by its partnership with FedEx. Monorail's founders wanted to design a PC that could fit easily into a standard FedEx box.

By using the network approach, Monorail has managed to be one of the leanest and meanest companies in the computer industry. When Doug Johns left Compaq, he was managing 6 million square feet of warehouse and office space. Now, at Monorail, his 50 employees work on a single leased floor of an office building near Atlanta. "We've got the shortest supply lines in the world," he says.

www.monorail.com

SOURCE: Heath Row, "This 'Virtual' Company is for Real," *Fast Company*, December–January, 1998, 48–50; and Evan Ramstad, "A PC Maker's Low-Tech Formula: Start with the Box," *The Wall Street Journal*, December 29, 1997, B1, B8.

needed. A network organization may have only two or three levels of hierarchy compared with ten or more in traditional organizations.[40] These advantages of a network structure, along with the disadvantages, are summarized in Exhibit 10.14.

One of the major disadvantages is lack of hands-on control.[41] Managers do not have all operations under one roof and must rely on contracts, coordination, negotiation, and electronic messages to hold things together. A problem of equal importance is the possibility of losing an organizational part. If a subcontractor fails to deliver, goes out of business, or has a plant burn down, the headquarters organization can be put out of business. Uncertainty is higher because necessary services are not under one roof and under direct management control. Finally, in this type of organization, employee loyalty can

Exhibit **10.14**

Advantages and Disadvantages of Network Structure

Advantages	Disadvantages
• Global competitiveness	• No hands-on control
• Workforce flexibility/challenge	• Can lose organizational part
• Reduced administrative overhead	• Employee loyalty weakened

weaken. Employees may feel they can be replaced by contract services. A cohesive corporate culture is less likely to develop, and turnover tends to be higher because emotional commitment between organization and employee is weak. With changing products and markets, the organization may need to reshuffle employees at any time to acquire the correct mix of skills.

Summary and Management Solution

This chapter introduced a number of important organizing concepts. Fundamental characteristics of organization structure include work specialization, chain of command, authority and responsibility, span of management, and centralization and decentralization. These dimensions of organization represent the vertical hierarchy and indicate how authority and responsibility are distributed along the hierarchy.

The other major concept is departmentalization, which describes how organization employees are grouped. Three traditional approaches are functional, divisional, and matrix; contemporary approaches are team and network structures. The functional approach groups employees by common skills and tasks. The opposite structure is divisional, which groups people by organizational output such that each division has a mix of functional skills and tasks. The matrix structure uses two chains of command simultaneously, and some employees have two bosses. The two chains of command in a domestic organization typically are functional and product division, and, for international firms, the two chains of command typically are product and geographic regions. The team approach uses permanent teams and cross-functional teams to achieve better coordination and employee commitment than is possible with a pure functional structure. The network approach represents the newest form of organization structure. With the network approach, a firm concentrates on what it does best and subcontracts other functions to separate organizations that are connected to the headquarters electronically. Each organization form has advantages and disadvantages and can be used by managers to meet the needs of the competitive situation.

At NeoData, described at the beginning of the chapter, a new CEO wanted to increase horizontal coordination and improve the company's customer service. His solution was to shift to a divisional structure, as well as use teams to improve customer service. Jones first set up six Customer Service Centers. At each center, all of the services performed for one large client or several small clients were brought together under one roof. People are part of a team effort to produce a complete service, rather than being committed only to lettershop or printing, for example. Some clients who had been planning to leave NeoData decided to stay because of the improved service brought about by the shift to Customer Service Centers. Next, NeoData was restructured into three operating units, divided according to the type of industries they serve. The Publishing Division focuses on books and magazines, as well as on-line publishing. The Consumer Products Division deals with consumer products companies, most notably Philip Morris. The Services Division offers fulfillment for the telecommunications, financial services, utility, and health care industries. In addition, a new international division in Limerick, Ireland, handles overseas clients. By having Customer Service teams that are focused on getting to know and understand the need of a particular industry, NeoData is transforming its relationships with clients and improving its financial health.

Discussion Questions

1. Sonny Holt, manager of Electronics Assembly, asked Hector Cruz, his senior technician, to handle things in the department while Sonny worked on the budget. Sonny needed peace and quiet for at least a week to complete his figures. After ten days, Sonny discovered that Hector had hired a senior secretary, not realizing that Sonny had promised interviews to two other people. Evaluate Sonny's approach to delegation.

2. Many experts note that organizations have been making greater use of teams in recent years. What factors might account for this trend?

3. Contrast centralization with span of management. Would you expect these characteristics to affect each other in organizations? Why?
4. An organizational consultant was heard to say, "Some aspect of functional structure appears in every organization." Do you agree? Explain.
5. The divisional structure is often considered almost the opposite of a functional structure. Do you agree? Briefly explain the major differences in these two approaches to departmentalization.
6. Some people argue that the matrix structure should be adopted only as a last resort because the dual chains of command can create more problems than they solve. Do you agree or disagree? Why?

7. What is the network approach to structure? Is the use of authority and responsibility different compared with other forms of departmentalization? Explain.
8. Why are divisional structures frequently used in large corporations? Does it make sense for a huge corporation such as American Airlines to stay in a functional structure?
9. An international matrix structure tends to be organized by product divisions and geographic regions. Why would these two chains of command be used rather than product and function as in domestic companies? Explain.

Management in Practice: Experiential Exercise

Family Business

You are the parent of ten children and have just used your inheritance to acquire a medium-sized pharmaceutical company. Last year's sales were down 18 percent from the previous year. In fact, the last three years have been real losers. You want to clean house of current managers over the next ten years and bring your children into the business. Being a loving parent, you agree to send your children to college to educate each of them in one functional specialty. The ten children are actually five sets of twins exactly one year apart. The first set will begin college this fall, followed by the remaining sets the next four years. The big decision is which specialty each child should study. You want to have the most important functions taken over by your children as soon as possible, so you will ask the older children to study the most important areas.

Your task right now is to rank in order of priority the functions to which your children will be assigned and develop reasons for your ranking.

The ten functions follow:

____ Distribution
____ Manufacturing
____ Market Research
____ New-Product Development
____ Human Resources
____ Product Promotion
____ Quality Assurance
____ Sales
____ Legal and Governmental Affairs
____ Office of the Controller

Analyze your reasons for how functional priority relates to the company's environmental/strategic needs. Now rank the functions as part of a group. Discuss the problem until group members agree on a single ranking. How does the group's reasoning and ranking differ from your original thinking?

Management in Practice: Ethical Dilemma

Caught in the Middle

Tom Harrington loved his job as an assistant quality control officer for Rockingham Toys. After six months of unemployment, he was anxious to make a good impression on his boss, Frank Golopolus. One of the responsibilities of his boss was ensuring that new product lines met federal safety guidelines. Rockingham had made several manufacturing changes over the past year. Golopolus and the rest of the quality control team had been working 60-hour weeks to troubleshoot the new production process.

While sorting incoming mail during the past weeks, Harrington had become aware of numerous changes in product

safety guidelines that he knew would impact the new Rockingham toys. Golopolus was taking no action to implement new guidelines, and he didn't seem to understand or care about them. Harrington, who avoided the questions he received from the floor to cover for his boss, was beginning to wonder if Rockingham would have time to make changes with the Christmas season rapidly approaching.

Harrington knew it was not his job to order the changes, and he didn't want to alienate Golopolus by interfering, but he was beginning to worry what might happen if he didn't act. Rockingham had a fine product safety reputation and was rarely challenged on matters of quality. He felt loyalty to Golopolus for giving him a job, but he worried Golopolus was in over his head.

What Do You Do?

1. Prepare a memo to Golopolus, summarizing the new safety guidelines that affect the Rockingham product line and recommending implementation.

2. Mind your own business. You do not have authority to monitor the federal regulations. Besides, you've been unemployed and need this job.

3. Send copies of the reports anonymously to the operations manager, who is Golopolus's boss.

SOURCE: Based on Doug Wallace, "The Man Who Knew Too Much," *What Would You Do? Business Ethics,* vol. II (March–April 1993), 7–8.

Surf the Net

1. **Examples of Organizational Structure.** Visit the Web sites for several companies to find two examples of organization charts or organizational structure descriptors that you can print out and bring to class. These examples can be analyzed by you and your classmates to determine what approach to structure the organization has used. For example, does the chart or description illustrate the functional, divisional, matrix, contemporary team, or network approach to structure?

   Two examples are listed below. When you're looking for a company's organizational structure, you can often find it under a heading such as "Company Overview," "About Us," "Corporate Profile," or other such descriptors. Sometimes, the organizational structure is verbally described (as the Microsoft example below), and other times, a literal organization chart is provided (as the Xerox example below).
   www.xerox.com/factbook/1998/orgchart.htm
   www.microsoft.com/presspass/cpOrg.htm

2. **Divisional Structure.** Examine the divisional structure illustrated by PepsiCo. Visit **www.pepsico.com,** select "Corporate Information" and then "Corporate Structure." Write a brief summary describing the PepsiCo divisions and examples of products in each division.

3. **The Virtual Network.** After reading the information in this chapter's Learning Organization box on the virtual computer company, Monorail, Inc., visit the company's Web site at **www.monorail.com.** Write a 2 to 3 paragraph description of your impressions of this company from a consumer perspective. If you hadn't had the textbook background before going to the site, would you have known this is a virtual company? What clues did you get from the Web site alone that this is a virtual company? Also list reasons why you would or would not consider purchasing a computer made by one of this company's contract manufacturers.

Case for Critical Analysis
Tucker Company

In 1978 the Tucker Company underwent an extensive reorganization that divided the company into three major divisions. These new divisions represented Tucker's three principal product lines. Mr. Harnett, Tucker's president, explained the basis for the new organization in a memo to the board of directors as follows:

> The diversity of our products requires that we reorganize along our major product lines. Toward this end I have established three new divisions: commercial jet engines, military jet engines, and utility turbines. Each division will be headed by a new vice president who will report directly to me. I believe that this new approach will enhance our performance through the commitment of individual managers. It should also help us to identify unprofitable areas where the special attention of management may be required.

For the most part, each division will be able to operate independently. That is, each will have its own engineering, manufacturing, accounting departments, etc. In some cases, however, it will be necessary for a division to utilize the services of other divisions or departments. This is necessary because the complete servicing with individual divisional staffs would result in unjustifiable additional staffing and facilities.

The old companywide laboratory was one such service department. Functionally, it continued to support all of the major divisions. Administratively, however, the manager of the laboratory reported to the manager of manufacturing in the military jet engine division.

From the time the new organization was initiated until February 1988, when the laboratory manager Mr. Garfield retired, there was little evidence of interdepartmental or interdivisional conflict. His replacement, Mr. Hodge, unlike Mr. Garfield, was always eager to gain the attention of management. Many of Hodge's peers perceived him as an empire builder who was interested in his own advancement rather than the company's well-being. After about six months in the new position, Hodge became involved in several interdepartmental conflicts over work that was being conducted in his laboratory.

Historically, the engineering departments had used the laboratory as a testing facility to determine the properties of materials selected by the design engineers. Hodge felt that the laboratory should be more involved in the selection of these materials and in the design of experiments and subsequent evaluations of the experimental data. Hodge discussed this with Mr. Franklin of the engineering department of the utility turbine division. Franklin offered to consult with Hodge but stated that the final responsibility for the selection of materials was charged to his department.

In the months that followed, Hodge and Franklin had several disagreements over the implementation of the results. Franklin told Hodge that, because of his position at the testing lab, he was unable to appreciate the detailed design considerations that affected the final decision on materials selection. Hodge claimed that Franklin lacked the materials expertise that he, as a metallurgist, had.

Franklin also noted that the handling of his requests, which had been prompt under Garfield's management, was taking longer and longer under Hodge's management. Hodge explained that military jet engine divisional problems had to be assigned first priority because of his administrative reporting structure. He also said that if he were more involved in Franklin's problems, he could perhaps appreciate when a true sense of urgency existed and could revise priorities.

The tensions between Franklin and Hodge reached a peak when one of Franklin's critical projects failed to receive the scheduling that he considered necessary. Franklin phoned Hodge to discuss the need for a schedule change. Hodge suggested that they have a meeting to review the need for the work. Franklin then told Hodge that this was not a matter of his concern and that his function was merely to perform the tests as requested. He further stated that he was not satisfied with the low-priority rating that his division's work received. Hodge reminded Franklin that when Hodge had suggested a means for resolving this problem, Franklin was not receptive. At this point, Franklin lost his temper and hung up on Hodge.

Questions

1. Sketch out a simple organization chart showing Tucker Company's three divisions, including the location of the laboratory. Why would the laboratory be located in the military jet engine division?

2. Analyze the conflict between Mr. Hodge and Mr. Franklin. Do you think the conflict is based on personalities or on the way in which the organization is structured?

3. Sketch out a new organization chart showing how you would restructure Tucker Company so that the laboratory would provide equal services to all divisions. What advantages and disadvantages do you see in the new structure compared to the previous one?

SOURCE: Reprinted with permission of Macmillan Publishing Company from "The Laboratory," *Organizational Behavior: Readings and Cases,* 2d ed., 385–387, by L. Katz, prepared under the supervision of Theodore T. Herbert. Copyright© 1981 by Theodore T. Herbert.

Endnotes

1. Minda Zetlin, "From Fulfillment House to Strategic Partner," *Management Review,* October 1996, 33–37.

2. Lisa Driscoll, "The New, New Thinking at Xerox," *Business Week,* June 22, 1992.

3. John A. Byrne, "The Horizontal Corporation," *Business Week,* December 20, 1993, 76–81.

4. Tim R. V. Davis and Bruce L. Darling, "How Virtual Corporations Manage the Performance of Contractors: The Super Bakery Case," *Organizational Dynamics* 26, no. 1 (summer 1995), 70–75.

5. John Child, *Organization: A Guide to Problems and Practice,* 2d ed. (London: Harper & Row, 1984).

6. Adam Smith, *The Wealth of Nations* (New York: Modern Library, 1937).

7. Michael Williams, "Some Plants Tear Out Long Assembly Lines, Switch to Craft Work," *The Wall Street Journal,* October 24, 1994, A1, A6.

8. This discussion is based on Richard L. Daft, *Organization Theory and Design,* 4th ed. (St. Paul, Minn.: West, 1992), 387–388.

9. C. I. Barnard, *The Functions of the Executive* (Cambridge, Mass.: Harvard University Press, 1938).

10. Thomas A. Stewart, "CEOs See Clout Shifting," *Fortune,* November 6, 1989, 66.

11. Michael G. O'Loughlin, "What Is Bureaucratic Accountability and How Can We Measure It?" *Administration & Society* 22, no. 3 (November 1990), 275–302.

12. Carrie R. Leana, "Predictors and Consequences of Delegation," *Academy of Management Journal* 29 (1986), 754–774.

13. Paul D. Collins and Frank Hull, "Technology and Span of Control: Woodward Revisited," *Journal of Management Studies* 23 (March 1986), 143–164; David D. Van Fleet and Arthur G. Bedeian, "A History of the Span of Management," *Academy of Management Review* 2 (1977), 356–372; and

C. W. Barkdull, "Span of Control—A Method of Evaluation," *Michigan Business Review* 15 (May 1963), 25–32.

14. Brian Dumaine, "What the Leaders of Tomorrow See," *Fortune,* July 3, 1989, 48–62.

15. James Kitfield, "Superior Command," *Government Executive,* October 1993, 18–23.

16. Brian O'Reilly, "J&J Is on a Roll," *Fortune,* December 26, 1994, 178–191; and Joseph Weber, "A Big Company That Works," *Business Week,* May 4, 1992, 124–132.

17. Saul Hansell, "Banc One Lives Up to Its Name," *The New York Times,* May 12, 1995, C1, C4.

18. Clay Chandler and Paul Ingrassia, "Just as U.S. Firms Try Japanese Management, Honda Is Centralizing," *The Wall Street Journal,* April 11, 1991, A1, A10.

19. Raymond E. Miles, "Adapting to Technology and Competition: A New Industrial Relation System for the Twenty-First Century," *California Management Review* (winter 1989), 9–28.

20. The following discussion of structural alternatives draws heavily on Jay R. Galbraith, *Designing Complex Organizations* (Reading, Mass.: Addison-Wesley, 1973); Jay R. Galbraith, *Organization Design* (Reading, Mass.: Addison-Wesley, 1977), Robert Duncan, "What Is the Right Organization Structure?" *Organizational Dynamics* (winter 1979), 59–80; and J. McCann and Jay R. Galbraith, "Interdepartmental Relations," in *Handbook of Organizational Design,* ed. P. Nystrom and W. Starbuck (New York: Oxford University Press, 1981), 60–84.

21. Mike Tharp, "LSI Logic Corp. Does as the Japanese Do," *The Wall Street Journal,* April 17, 1986, 6; and Shelly Branch, "What's Eating McDonald's?" *Fortune,* October 13, 1997, 122–125.

22. Kathy Rebello, "Apple's Daring Leap into the All-Digital Future," *Business Week,* May 25, 1992, 120–122.

23. Lawton R. Burns, "Matrix Management in Hospitals: Testing Theories of Matrix Structure and Development," *Administrative Science Quarterly* 34 (1989), 349–368.

24. Stanley M. Davis and Paul R. Lawrence, *Matrix* (Reading, Mass.: Addison-Wesley, 1977).

25. Robert C. Ford and W. Alan Randolph, "Cross-Functional Structures: A Review and Integration of Matrix Organization and Project Management," *Journal of Management* 18, no. 2 (1992), 267–294; and Paula Dwyer with Pete Engardio, Zachary Schiller, and Stanley Reed, "Tearing Up Today's Organization Chart," *Business Week/Twenty-first Century Capitalism,* 80–90.

26. Dwyer et al., "Tearing Up Today's Organization Chart."

27. Noel M. Tichy and Stratford Sherman, *Control Your Destiny or Someone Else Will* (New York: Currency Doubleday, 1993), 176–178.

28. Sandra N. Phillips, "Team Training Puts Fizz in Coke Plant's Future," *Personnel Journal,* January 1996, 87–92.

29. Lucien Rhodes, "The Passion of Robert Swiggett," *Inc.,* April 1984, 121–140.

30. Rahul Jacob, "The Struggle to Create an Organization for the 21st Century," *Fortune,* April 3, 1995, 90–99.

31. Michael Hammer with Steven Stanton, "The Art of Change," *Success,* April 1995, 44A–44H; and Byrne, "The Horizontal Corporation."

32. John Hillkirk, "Challenging Status Quo Now in Vogue," *USA Today,* November 9, 1993; and Thomas A. Stewart, "The Search for the Organization of Tomorrow," *Fortune,* May 18, 1992, 92–98.

33. Raymond E. Miles and Charles C. Snow, "The New Network Firm: A Spherical Structure Built on a Human Investment Philosophy," *Organizational Dynamics,* (spring 1995), 5–18; and Raymond E. Miles, Charles C. Snow, John A. Matthews, Grant Miles, and Henry J. Coleman, Jr., "Organizing in the Knowledge Age: Anticipating the Cellular Form," *Academy of Management Executive* 11, no. 4 (1997), 7–24.

34. Raymond E. Miles and Charles C. Snow, "Organizations: New Concepts for New Forms," *California Management Review* 28 (spring 1986), 62–73; and "Now, The Post-Industrial Corporation," *Business Week,* March 3, 1986, 64–74.

35. Gregory G. Dess, Abdul M. A. Rasheed, Kevin J. McLaughlin, and Richard L. Priem, "The New Corporate Architecture," *Academy of Management Executive* 9, no. 3 (1995), 7–20.

36. John Byrne, "The Virtual Corporation," *Business Week,* February 8, 1993, 99–103; and Dess et al., "The New Corporate Architecture."

37. Gianni Lorenzoni and Charles Baden-Fuller, "Creating a Strategic Center to Manage a Web of Partners," *California Management Review* 37, no. 3 (spring 1995), 146–163; Shawn Tully, "You'll Never Guess Who Really Makes . . . ," *Fortune,* October 3, 1994, 124–128; and G. Pascal Zachary, "High-Tech Firms Find It's Good to Line Up Outside Contractors," *The Wall Street Journal,* July 29, 1992, A1, A5.

38. John Case, "The Age of the Specialist," *Inc.,* August 1995, 15–16.

39. Echo Montgomery Garrett, "Innovation + Outsourcing = Big Success," *Management Review,* September 1994, 17–20; and Tom Field, "The Personal Touch," *CIO,* August 1, 1998, 18.

40. Miles, "Adapting to Technology and Competition," and Miles and Snow, "The New Network Firm."

41. Dess et al., "The New Corporate Architecture."

Chapter 11

LEARNING OBJECTIVES

After studying this chapter, you should be able to

⚙ **Explain why organizations need coordination across departments and hierarchical levels.**

⚙ **Describe mechanisms for achieving coordination and when they may be applied.**

⚙ **Explain the major differences between traditional vertical organizations and learning organizations.**

⚙ **Describe how structure can be used to achieve an organization's strategic goals.**

⚙ **Describe how organization structure can be designed to fit environmental uncertainty.**

⚙ **Define production technology (manufacturing and service) and explain how it influences organization structure.**

⚙ **Explain the types of departmental interdependence and how structure can be used to accommodate them.**

Using Structural Design to Achieve Strategic Goals

MANAGEMENT PROBLEM

Frank Fulkerson was watching the business his grandfather founded 50 years earlier slowly fall apart. Vortex Industries of Costa Mesa, California, is a 130-employee family-owned business that repairs and replaces warehouse doors. By the early 1990s, high costs and stagnant sales were threatening the company's viability. New commercial construction was down sharply due to the deepening recession, and companies that might once have been installing warehouse doors were now repairing them, in direct competition with Vortex. Although the company served customers in six counties, most of its people and equipment were bunched at one location near downtown Los Angeles. Work specialization meant that each employee handled a single, specific task. Vortex's bureaucratic procedures, combined with its high prices, had customers turning to competitors for cheaper and faster service. Employee morale was sinking with the company's fortunes, because employees felt their individual actions made little difference. Fulkerson was faced with a desperate situation. He knew that for Vortex to survive, it had to cut costs and prices, build employee morale, and serve customers better and faster.[1]

If you were Frank Fulkerson, how would you transform Vortex to serve customers faster with lower prices? What advice would you give him about using organization structure to achieve this goal?

Managers in companies like Vortex frequently must rethink structure and may reorganize to meet new competitive conditions in the environment. In Chapter 10, we examined the fundamentals of structure that apply to all organizations. In this chapter, we focus more precisely on structure as a tool, especially on how managers can use such concepts as departmentalization and chain of command to achieve specific goals. In recent years, many corporations, including American Express, Apple, IBM, Amex Corporation, and Bausch & Lomb, have realigned departmental groupings, chains of command, and teams and task forces to attain new strategic goals. Structure is a powerful tool for reaching strategic goals, and a strategy's success often is determined by its fit with organization structure. By the end of this chapter, the problem at Vortex will be easily identified as a mismatch of Vortex's structure with its technology and competitive situation. Frank Fulkerson's solution to achieve better coordination called for a new structural approach.

The Horizontal Organization

Many companies are recognizing that traditional vertical organization structures are ineffective in today's fast-shifting environment. Managers are working to transform their organizations into more flexible systems that emphasize rapid response and customer focus. In general, the trend is toward breaking down barriers between departments, and many companies are moving toward horizontal structures based on work processes rather than departmental functions.[2] Regardless of the type of structure, all organizations need mechanisms for horizontal coordination.

The Need for Coordination

As organizations grow and evolve, two things happen. First, new positions and departments are added to deal with factors in the external environment or with new strategic needs.[3] For example, Raytheon established a new-products center to facilitate innovation in its various divisions. Korbel Champagne Cellars created a Department of Romance, Weddings, and Entertaining to enhance the linkage between romance and champagne consumption among potential customers. Exhibit 11.1 shows an ad for Korbel's Director of Romance that generated more than 800 applications.[4] Many companies, including Federal Express and American Airlines, have created a position for Chief Information Officer (CIO) to manage the growing amount of technology-based information and help them seize new competitive advantages. CIOs manage the infrastructure that gets necessary information to the right people at the right time.[5] As companies add positions and departments to meet changing needs, they grow more complex, with hundreds of positions and departments performing incredibly diverse activities.

Second, senior managers have to find a way to tie all of these departments together. The formal chain of command and the supervision it provides is effective, but it is not enough. The organization needs systems to process information and enable communication among people in different departments and at different levels. **Coordination** refers to the quality of collaboration across departments. Without coordination, a company's left hand will not act in concert with the right hand, causing problems and conflicts. Coordination is required regardless of whether the organization has a functional, divisional, or team structure. Employees identify with their immediate

coordination
The quality of collaboration across departments.

DIRECTOR OF ROMANCE

Korbel Champagne Cellars, California-based producer of America's best-selling premium champagne, seeks dynamic individual for one-of-a-kind corporate position as Director of Romance for the winery's Department of Romance, Weddings & Entertaining. Position involves:

- reporting to media on lighthearted romance surveys commissioned by Korbel
- researching the latest news and information on the romance front
- writing articles on romance-related subjects
- appearing on television and radio programs to discuss the subject of romance

Ideal candidate will have published books or articles on the subject of romance, possess a degree in a related field such as psychology and/or personify romance in some highly visible or glamorous way. Previous media experience preferred. Individuals and spokesperson search firm applicants welcome. No phone calls please. An equal opportunity employer. Send resume to:

FRANK DE FALCO
KORBEL CHAMPAGNE CELLARS
13250 RIVER ROAD
GUERNEVILLE, CA 95446

Exhibit *11.1*

Example of a Position Created to Deal with Environment and Strategy

SOURCE: Courtesy of Korbel Champagne Cellars.

department or team, taking its interest to heart, and may not want to compromise with other units for the good of the organization as a whole.

Without a major effort at coordination, an organization may be like Chrysler Corporation when Lee Iacocca took over:

> What I found at Chrysler were 35 vice presidents, each with his own turf. . . . I couldn't believe, for example, that the guy running engineering departments wasn't in constant touch with his counterpart in manufacturing. But that's how it was. Everybody worked independently. I took one look at that system and I almost threw up. That's when I knew I was in really deep trouble.
>
> I'd call in a guy from engineering, and he'd stand there dumbfounded when I'd explain to him that we had a design problem or some other hitch in the engineering-manufacturing relationship. He might have the ability to invent a brilliant piece of engineering that would save us a lot of money. He might come up with a terrific new design. There was only one problem: he didn't know that the manufacturing people couldn't build it. Why? Because he had never talked to them about it. Nobody at Chrysler seemed to understand that interaction among the different functions in a company is absolutely critical. People in engineering and manufacturing almost have to be sleeping together. These guys weren't even flirting![6]

If one thing changed at Chrysler in the years before Iacocca retired, it was improved coordination. Cooperation among engineering, marketing, and manufacturing enabled the design and production of the stunning line of new LH automobiles in only three years, compared with the five years of development previously required.

In the international arena, coordination is especially important. How can managers ensure that needed coordination will take place in their company, both domestically and globally? Coordination is the outcome of information and cooperation. Managers can design systems and structures to promote horizontal coordination. Exhibit 11.2 illustrates the evolution of organizational structures, with a growing emphasis on horizontal coordination and communication. The vertical functional structure, discussed in the previous chapter,

E x h i b i t *11.2* *Evolution of Organization Structures*

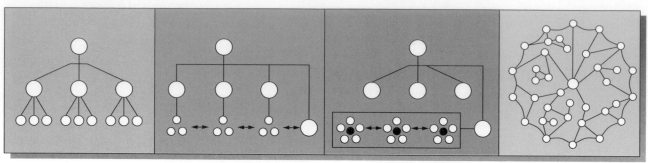

| **Traditional Vertical Structure** | **Teams and Project Managers for Horizontal Coordination** | **Reengineering to Horizontal Processes** | **The Learning Organization** |

dates back nearly a century and was the first to be widely used by large organizations.[7] Although the structure is effective in stable environments, it does not provide the horizontal coordination needed in times of rapid change. Innovations such as teams, task forces, and project managers work within the vertical structure but provide a means to increase cross-functional communication and cooperation. The next stage involves reengineering to structure the organization around horizontal processes rather than vertical functions. The vertical hierarchy is flattened, with perhaps only a few senior executives in traditional support functions such as finance and human resources. Some organizations have taken a further step to the learning organization, doing away with all vestiges of an organizational hierarchy. The learning organization represents the ultimate in horizontal coordination. The following sections examine in more detail these methods for achieving horizontal coordination.

Task Forces, Teams, and Project Management

task force
A temporary team or committee formed to solve a specific short-term problem involving several departments.

A **task force** is a temporary team or committee designed to solve a short-term problem involving several departments.[8] Task force members represent their departments and share information that enables coordination.

For example, the Shawmut National Corporation created two task forces in the human resources department to consolidate all employment services into a single area. The task force looked at job banks, referral programs, employment procedures, and applicant tracking systems; found ways to perform these functions for all Shawmut's divisions in one human resource department; and then disbanded.[9] General Motors uses task forces to solve temporary problems in its manufacturing plants. When a shipment of car doors arrived from a fabricating plant with surface imperfections, the plant manager immediately created a task force to solve the problem. He got everybody together on the factory floor to examine the part that was causing the trouble, and the task force resolved the problem in about two hours.[10]

team
A group of participants from several departments who meet regularly to solve ongoing problems of common interest.

In addition to creating task forces, companies also set up teams. As used for coordination, a **team** is a group of participants from several departments who meet regularly to solve ongoing problems of common interest.[11] The permanent team is similar to a task force except that it works with continuing rather than temporary problems and may exist for several years. Teams used for coordination are like the cross-functional teams described in Chapter 10. For example, to improve coordination at Simplicity Pattern Company, CEO Louis Morris set up a Creative Committee, made up of the heads of the sales, finance, marketing, and creative departments. Snap-On Tools gained a competitive edge by creating engineering teams to work with marketing and customer-focus groups to discuss ideas and define new products. Team cooperation helps new-product projects sail smoothly through the design and development cycle.[12]

Companies also use project managers to increase coordination between functional departments. A **project manager** is a person who is responsible for coordinating the activities of several departments for the completion of a specific project.[13] Project managers may be working on several different projects at one time. The distinctive feature of the project manager position is that the person is not a member of one of the departments being coordinated. The project manager position may also have a title such as product manager, program manager, or branch manager. The coordinator is assigned to coordinate departments on a full-time basis to achieve desired project or product outcomes.

General Mills, Procter & Gamble, and General Foods all use product managers to coordinate their product lines. A manager is assigned to each line, such as Cheerios, Bisquick, and Hamburger Helper. Product managers set budget goals, marketing targets, and strategies and obtain the cooperation from advertising, production, and sales personnel needed for implementing product strategy.

In some organizations, project managers are included on the organization chart, as illustrated in Exhibit 11.3. The project manager is drawn to one side of the chart to indicate authority over the project but not over the people assigned to it. Dashed lines to the project manager indicate responsibility for coordination and communication with assigned team members, but department managers retain line authority over functional employees.

project manager
A person responsible for coordinating the activities of several departments on a full-time basis for the completion of a specific project.

Reengineering

One of the most popular management concepts sweeping corporate America is reengineering, introduced in the previous chapter. Sometimes called *business process reengineering*, this approach involves a complete rethinking and

E x h i b i t   *11.3*   *Example of Project Manager Relationships to Other Departments*

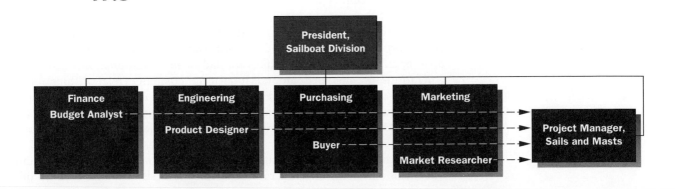

U.S. Department of Defense

The Pentagon can act quickly to move thousands of tons of humanitarian aid material or hundreds of thousands of troops, but sending employees on routine travel has been a different story. Before Pentagon travelers could even board a bus, they had to secure numerous approvals and fill out reams of paperwork. Coming home wasn't any easier—the average traveler spent six hours preparing vouchers for reimbursement following a trip.

The Department of Defense set up a task force to reengineer the cumbersome travel system, aiming to make it cheaper, more efficient, and more customer friendly. The reengineered system reduces the steps in the pretravel process from an astounding 13 to only 4, as shown in the exhibit. Travel budgets and authority to approve travel requests and vouchers, which have traditionally rested in the budget channels of the various service commands, will be transferred to local supervisors. Travelers will make all their arrangements through a commercial travel office, which will prepare a "should-cost" estimate for each trip. This document will be all a traveler needs before, during, and after a trip: With a supervisor's signature, it becomes a travel authorization; during travel, it serves as an itinerary; after amendments to reflect variations from plans, it becomes an expense report. Other travel expenses and needed cash or travelers' checks will be charged to a government-issued travel card, with payment made directly to the travel card company through electronic funds transfer.

A second task force has been created to implement the reengineering recommendations. "Tiger teams," bringing together employees from across previously isolated functional departments, have been set up to tackle specific issues, such as how to simplify the Defense Department's travel regulations. Within three months, 230 pages of regulations had been reduced to a 16-page pamphlet.

In reengineering travel, says Gerry Kauvar, deputy director of the Defense Performance Review, the Defense Department "is linking authority, responsibility, and accountability at the local level." If the reengineered travel system is successful, it could serve as a management model that can be duplicated in other areas.

www.defenselink.mil

SOURCE: Richard Koonce, "Reengineering the Travel Game," *Government Executive*, May 1995, 28–34, 69–70.

---

transformation of key business processes, leading to strong horizontal coordination and greater flexibility in responding to changes in the environment.[14] Because work is organized around process rather than function, reengineering often involves a shift to a horizontal structure based on teams. For example, BellSouth Telecommunications cast aside the traditional, functional hierarchy in favor of teams of employees focused on serving customers in specific geographic regions.[15] One survey found that 21 percent of companies of all sizes reported being involved in corporatewide reengineering.[16] Union Carbide, Pacific Bell, Chemical Bank, and J. P. Morgan all have achieved breakthroughs in speed, flexibility, innovation, and quality through reengineering.

Reengineering basically means starting over, throwing out all the notions of how work *was* done and deciding how it can best be done now. It requires identifying customer needs and then designing processes and aligning people to meet those needs. Liquid Carbonic Industries, an Oak Brook, Illinois, industrial gas company, reengineered to improve customer service. The two-year effort dramatically changed the company, transforming it into an enterprise operating along process lines instead of the traditional business units. Operations are mapped around long-term customer relationships; sales employees, who once competed with one other, now cooperate to sell a range of products rather than specialize in one product.[17] As described in the Learning Organization box, reengineering also can squeeze out the dead space and time lags in work flows.

Organizing around key business processes also may lead to redesigning information systems to cut across departmental lines. Managers are finding

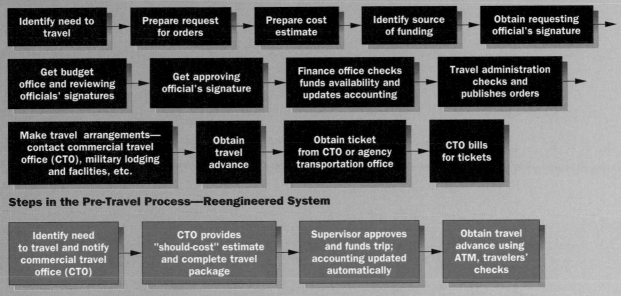

Steps in the Pre-Travel Process—Old System

| Identify need to travel | → | Prepare request for orders | → | Prepare cost estimate | → | Identify source of funding | → | Obtain requesting official's signature | → |

| Get budget office and reviewing officials' signatures | → | Get approving official's signature | → | Finance office checks funds availability and updates accounting | → | Travel administration checks and publishes orders | → |

| Make travel arrangements—contact commercial travel office (CTO), military lodging and faclities, etc. | → | Obtain travel advance | → | Obtain ticket from CTO or agency transportation office | → | CTO bills for tickets |

Steps in the Pre-Travel Process—Reengineered System

| Identify need to travel and notify commercial travel office (CTO) | → | CTO provides "should-cost" estimate and complete travel package | → | Supervisor approves and funds trip; accounting updated automatically | → | Obtain travel advance using ATM, travelers' checks |

ways to share information throughout the organization to make their companies more competitive and more responsive to customers. To speed up order cycle time and improve service to giant customers such as Wal-Mart,

The Engineering Division of Rohm and Haas Company used business process reengineering to achieve radical goals of building new plants faster and with dramatically lower costs. At one critical stage, existing processes were "mapped" using symbols so that inefficiencies could be identified and eliminated. Rohm and Haas, long recognized as an innovative leader in the specialty chemicals business, has committed itself to reanalyzing its work processes so the company can meet the higher expectations of today's customers, employees, and shareholders.

the Gillette Company of Boston changed from a mainframe computer to a client-server system that can draw information from around the company and be accessed by any team member who needs it. Bow Valley Energy redesigned its computer information system so that geologists, geophysicists, production engineers, and contract managers can now consolidate information and share data worldwide.[18]

Reengineering can lead to stunning results, but, like all business ideas, it has its drawbacks. Simply defining the organization's key business processes can be mind-boggling. AT&T's Network Systems division started with a list of 130 processes and then began working to pare them down to 13 core ones.[19] According to some estimates, 70 percent of reengineering efforts fail to reach their intended goals.[20] Because reengineering is expensive, time consuming, and usually painful, it seems best suited to companies that are facing serious competitive threats.

Traditional versus Learning Organizations

Recall that the purpose of structure is to organize resources to accomplish organizational goals. Elements of structure such as chain of command, centralization/decentralization, formal authority, teams, and coordination devices fit together to form an overall structural approach. In some organizations, the formal, vertical hierarchy is emphasized as the way to achieve control and coordination. In other organizations, decision making is decentralized, cross-functional teams are implemented, and employees are given great freedom to pursue their tasks as they see fit.

The increasing shift toward more horizontal versus vertical structures reflects the trend toward greater employee empowerment, broad information sharing, and decentralized decision making. At the apex of this movement is a type of organization called the *learning organization*. There is no single view of what the learning organization looks like. It is an attitude or philosophy about what an organization can become. Exhibit 11.4 compares characteristics of the learning organization with the traditional vertical organization.

In the traditional organization, the vertical structure predominates, with few task forces, teams, or project managers for horizontal coordination. Information is formally communicated up and down the organizational hierarchy and is not widely shared. In addition, jobs are broken down into narrow, specialized tasks, and employees generally have little say over how they do their work. The culture is rigid and does not encourage risk taking and change, and decision making is centralized. At the opposite end of the scale is the learning organization. The **learning organization** can be defined as one in which everyone is engaged in identifying and solving problems, enabling the organization to continuously experiment, change, and improve, thus increasing its capacity to grow, learn, and achieve its purpose. The learning organization is characterized by a horizontal team-based structure, open information, decentralized decision making, empowered employees, and a strong adaptive culture.

learning organization
An organization in which everyone is engaged in identifying and solving problems, enabling the organization to continuously experiment, improve, and increase its capability.

Team-Based Structure.   In the learning organization, the vertical structure that created distance between the top and bottom of the organization is disbanded. Self-directed teams are the fundamental unit in a learning organization. Self-directed teams are made up of employees with different skills

Exhibit 11.4 *Differences in Traditional versus Learning Organizations*

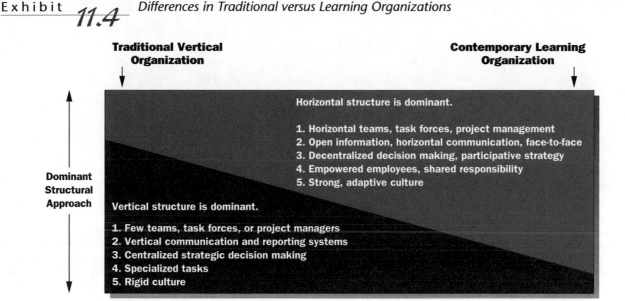

Traditional Vertical Organization

Contemporary Learning Organization

Dominant Structural Approach

Horizontal structure is dominant.

1. Horizontal teams, task forces, project management
2. Open information, horizontal communication, face-to-face
3. Decentralized decision making, participative strategy
4. Empowered employees, shared responsibility
5. Strong, adaptive culture

Vertical structure is dominant.

1. Few teams, task forces, or project managers
2. Vertical communication and reporting systems
3. Centralized strategic decision making
4. Specialized tasks
5. Rigid culture

who rotate jobs to produce an entire product or service, and they deal directly with customers, making changes and improvements as they go along. Team members have the authority to make decisions about new ways of doing things. In learning organizations, bosses are practically eliminated, with team members taking responsibility for training, safety, scheduling vacations, and decisions about work methods, pay and reward systems, and coordination with other teams. Teams are discussed in detail in Chapter 19.

The learning organization also uses other recent ideas to increase collaboration within and between organizations, such as virtual teams, alliances, and concepts such as the network organization. The Technology box describes how information technology supports collaboration at British Petroleum Company.

Open Information.   In a learning organization, information is widely shared. To identify needs and solve problems, people have to be aware of what's going on. They must understand the whole organization as well as their part in it. Formal data about budgets, profits, and departmental expenses are available to everyone. This approach, which will be described in Chapter 20, is called open-book management. Every employee is free to look at the books and exchange information with anyone in the company. At PeopleSoft, everyone has access to all company information, including product development information and financial data. Employees have open access to all company databases as well as the ability to communicate electronically with any other person in the company.[21]

Electronic communication is essential to information sharing in today's learning organization. However, the learning organization also emphasizes the importance of getting people communicating face-to-face, with the emphasis on listening. Some companies are using *dialogue,* which takes people away from work in groups of 30 or 40 to communicate deeply and honestly. Open communication and information sharing will be discussed in detail in Chapters 18 and 21.

Collaborating Around the World

British Petroleum CEO John Browne believes transforming to a learning organization helped save his company. Whereas a decade ago BP was a mediocre performer, today it is the most profitable of the major oil companies. Debt has been slashed; finding and development costs are among the lowest in the industry; and output is growing at about 5 percent a year.

Today, BP is a horizontal, decentralized global corporation based on teams and informal networks in which people eagerly share knowledge. There are no layers of management between the business units and the top executive committee. The people closest to the customer are given the autonomy to run their business as they see fit. However, with 53,000 employees and some 90 business units that span the globe, BP needed a way to share knowledge across business units. That's where the corporation's *virtual team network* comes in—it makes it easy for people to work cooperatively and share knowledge quickly and easily regardless of time, distance, and organizational boundaries. The network is a rapidly growing system of personal computers that boast videoconferencing capability, electronic blackboards, scanners, faxes, and groupware. In addition, everyone is connected to a company intranet. BP spent about $4 million training people to work in a virtual environment, and the results have paid

off. The company estimates that the virtual team network produced at least $30 million in value in its first year alone. Benefits include a drop in the person-hours needed to solve problems, a decrease in the number of helicopter trips needed to offshore oil platforms, and a reduction in rework during construction projects because designers, fabricators, construction workers, and operations people can collaborate more effectively through the virtual network.

Now, BP is extending the virtual team network to outside organizations. For example, it uses the virtual team approach to improve how it works with partners such as Shell Oil in the Gulf of Mexico, and with contractors such as Brown & Root in the North Sea. John Browne believes you build an enduring business by building relationships. British Petroleum's virtual team network helps build and support those relationships around the world, enabling rich exchanges of knowledge without the constraints of formal structures.

www.bp.com

SOURCE: Steven E. Prokesch, "Unleashing the Power of Learning: An Interview with British Petroleum's John Browne," *Harvard Business Review*, September–October 1997, 147–168.

Decentralized Decision Making and Participative Strategy.   In traditional organizations, decisions are passed up the hierarchy for approval. In a learning organization, the people closest to the problem are given the authority and responsibility for decision making. Because people at all levels are intimately involved in making decisions, this allows strategy to emerge bottom up as well as top down. In traditional vertical organizations, top executives are responsible for strategy because only they have the big picture, knowledge, and expertise to direct the corporation. In the learning organization, leaders still influence overall vision and direction, but they do not control or direct strategy alone. Everyone helps. Information is gathered by employees who work directly with customers, suppliers, and other organizations. Perhaps thousands of people are in touch with the environment, providing data about external changes in technology and customer needs. They are the ones to identify needs and solutions, passing these ideas into the organization for discussion.[22]

Participative strategy relies on an experimental mind-set. People are encouraged to try new things, and failure is accepted. Problems and decisions are a series of learning opportunities. For example, Ralph Stayer, CEO of Johnsonville Foods, did not make the decision to accept an invitation to make products to be sold under a grocery store chain's own label. He turned the decision over to employees, who met in teams for an entire day to investigate every aspect of this opportunity. The employees determined it would be beneficial to the company. They decided strategy.[23] Strategy in learning organizations also may emerge from partnerships with suppliers, customers, and even competitors. Learning organizations have permeable boundaries and often are linked with other companies, giving each organization greater access to information about new strategic needs and directions.[24]

Empowered Employees and Shared Responsibility.   Learning organizations empower employees to an extraordinary degree, giving them the authority and responsibility to use their own discretion and ability to achieve an outcome. *Empowerment* means giving employees the power, freedom, knowledge, and skills to make decisions and perform effectively. Rather than dividing jobs into rigidly defined, specialized tasks, learning organizations allow people the freedom and opportunity to react quickly to changing conditions. There are few rules and procedures, and knowledge and control of tasks are located with workers rather than top managers. Individuals are encouraged to experiment, learn, and solve problems within the team. How do companies implement empowerment? It starts by promoting the decentralization of decision making and broader worker participation. For example, there are very few rules for teams at SEI Investments. Teams have as few as 2 members or as many as 30, and the various teams are structured differently. The teams themselves make the decisions about what roles each worker plays, how the team will operate, when it's time to disband, and so forth. The company's CEO calls it "fluid leadership."[25]

In learning organizations, people are considered a primary source of strength, not a cost to be minimized. Firms that adopt this perspective often employ the following practices: Treat employees well. Provide employment security and good wages. Provide a sense of employee ownership by sharing gains in productivity and profits. Commit to education for all members' growth and development. Help employees become world-renowned experts. Cross-train to help people acquire multiple skills. Promote from within.[26]

Strong, Adaptive Culture.   *Corporate culture* is the set of key values, beliefs, understandings, and norms shared by members of the organization. The culture is the foundation of a learning organization. The culture of a learning organization is strong and typically includes strong values in the following three areas:

1. *The whole is more important than the part, and boundaries between parts are minimized.*[27] People in the learning organization are aware of the whole system and how parts fit together. The emphasis on the whole reduces boundaries. People no longer hoard information or ideas for themselves. The move toward a "boundaryless organization" means reducing barriers among departments, divisions, and external organizations. The free flow of people, ideas, and information allows coordinated action to occur in an uncertain and changing environment.

2. *The culture is egalitarian.* The culture of a learning organization creates a sense of community, compassion, and caring for one another. People count. Every person has value. The learning organization becomes a place for creating a web of relationships that nurtures and develops each person to his or her maximum potential. Executive perks such as private dining rooms or reserved parking spots are eliminated. Everyone gets the

In the past two years, over 300 software engineers have immigrated to Barbados from all over the world. Doug Mellinger, CEO of PRT, a custom-software engineering company, has created a high-tech nation, an egalitarian culture on a tropical island. Workers are provided with their own state-of-the-art computer platforms and a workspace designed to the specs of the international banking industry. They work directly with managers who can teach and challenge them while working on projects considered "the good stuff." On the island, employees' bills are paid, transportation is free, and their savings pile up in the bank. Mellinger likes to say, "I don't want them to have to think about anything but having fun and writing killer code."

same amount of vacation regardless of position. Everyone may share in stock options or performance bonuses, too. The orientation toward people provides safety for experimentation, frequent mistakes, and failures that enable learning. People are treated with respect and thereby contribute their best to the company.

3. *The culture values improvement and adaptation.* A basic value is to question the status quo, the current way of doing things. Can we do this any better? Why do we do this job that way? Constant questioning of assumptions and challenging the status quo open the gates to creativity and improvement. The organization learns to do things faster and to improve everything on an ongoing basis. An adaptive culture means that people care about important stakeholders, including employees, customers, and stockholders. Managers pay close attention to stakeholders and initiate change when needed. The culture also celebrates and rewards the creators of new ideas, products, and work processes.

In the learning organization, the culture encourages openness, boundarylessness, equality, continuous improvement, and change. The learning organization is always moving forward. Although no company represents a perfect example of a learning organization, one excellent example is Chaparral Steel, which has been called a learning laboratory.

CHAPARRAL STEEL
www.chaparralsteel.com

The tenth-largest U.S. steel producer, Chaparral Steel has won international recognition for quality and productivity. Chaparral produces 1,100 tons of steel each year compared to the U.S. average of 350 tons. Started nearly 20 years ago, it has become an experimental laboratory for the latest techniques of learning organizations.

What makes Chaparral so effective? Managers articulate a clear vision—to lead the world in the low-cost, safe production of high-quality steel—along with the cultural values of egalitarianism and respect for the individual. Everyone participates. Everyone is empowered to solve problems. When a cooling hose burst, a group of operators—a welder, a foreman, and a buyer—all responded because they saw the problem. There is no assumption that other people are expected to do a job. Since employees know the vision and values, supervisors do not micromanage. Chaparral has few supervisors, and only two levels of hierarchy separate the CEO from operators in the rolling mill.

Employees are rewarded for learning new skills and for performance. Ideas are contributed by just about everyone. Employees are paid a salary rather than an hourly wage—hence, everyone acts like an owner and a manager. People are also rewarded with bonuses from company profits, which are shared with everyone, including janitors and secretaries.

All employees contribute to sharing information and knowledge. A steel plant is deliberately held to fewer than 1,000 employees so that people can communicate easily. An employee experimenting with new equipment will tell other people how it works. Employees who visit a competitor's plant will explain to others what they learned. There are no staff people and no boundaries among departments because there are few departments. Everyone is considered a salesperson and is free to communicate with customers and potential customers. There is no research and development department because employees on the line are responsible for innovation in new techniques and products. To reinforce continuous learning, employees are encouraged to attend school, and many are teachers of other employees in formal classes. The culture values ideas that benefit the whole company rather than individual ownership of ideas, so new knowledge is shared liberally.

Experimentation is rampant. The cultural value is: If you have an idea, try it. First-level managers can authorize thousands of dollars for employee experiments. Everyone is encouraged to push beyond current knowledge. This involves risk, which is another cultural value. Employees tolerate, even welcome, risk on a production line that is very expensive to shut down.

Strategy emerges from employee contacts outside the organization. Employees travel constantly, scanning for new ideas at trade shows and other companies. Teams of employees that include vice-presidents and shop people travel together to investigate a new technology.

Chaparral is so good at what it does that it welcomes competitors to visit the plant. A competitor can be shown everything Chaparral does and yet take away nothing, because a learning organization is created by leadership, culture, and empowered people. Most other steelmakers have been unable to achieve this, because they don't have the commitment or the vision.[28]

Chaparral Steel is becoming a true learning organization. The leadership provides a flat, team-based design, a shared vision, and an attitude of serving employees. The culture stresses egalitarian values, providing support for risk taking. There are no boundaries separating departments. People are empowered to the point where no one has to take orders if he or she feels the order is wrong. The strategy emerges through the experiences of employees who work with customers and new technologies. Chaparral is flooded with information from experiments and travel, which is liberally shared.

Factors Affecting Structure

How do managers know whether to design a structure that emphasizes the formal, vertical hierarchy or one with an emphasis on horizontal communication and collaboration? The answer lies in the contingency factors that influence organization structure. Recall from Chapter 2 that *contingency* pertains to those factors on which structure depends. Research on organization structure shows that the emphasis given to a rigid or flexible structure depends on the contingency factors of strategy, environment, production technology, and departmental interdependence. The right structure is designed to "fit" the contingency factors as illustrated in Exhibit 11.5. Let us look at the relationship between each contingency factor and organization structure in more detail to see how structure should be designed.

Contingency Factor: Strategic Goals

In Chapter 8, we discussed several strategies that business firms can adopt. Two strategies proposed by Porter are differentiation and cost leadership.[29] With a differentiation strategy, the organization attempts to develop innovative products unique to the market. With a cost leadership strategy, the organization strives for internal efficiency. The strategies of cost leadership versus differentiation typically require different structural approaches, so managers try to pick strategies and structures that are congruent.

Exhibit
11.5

Contingency Factors That Influence Organization Structure

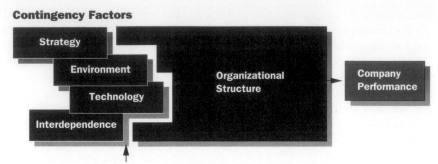

Contingency Factors

The right mix of vertical/horizontal structure fits the contingency factors.

Exhibit 11.6 shows a simplified continuum that illustrates how structural approaches are associated with strategic goals. The pure functional structure is appropriate for achieving internal efficiency goals. The vertical functional structure uses task specialization and a strict chain of command to gain efficient use of scarce resources, but it does not enable the organization to be flexible or innovative. In contrast, the learning organization is appropriate when the primary goal is innovation and flexibility. Each team is small, is able to be responsive, and has the people and resources necessary for performing its task. The flexible horizontal structure enables organizations to differentiate themselves and respond quickly to the demands of a shifting environment but at the expense of efficient resource use. Changing strategy and environmental conditions also shape structure in government organizations. For example, under financial pressure to cut costs and political pressure to keep customers happy, Departments of Motor Vehicles in some states are farming out DMV business whenever possible, moving toward a network structure. In Illinois and Oregon, auto dealers register new cars on site when they're sold.[30]

Exhibit 11.6 also illustrates how other forms of structure described in Chapter 10—decentralized with horizontal coordination, divisional, and team—represent intermediate steps on the organization's path to efficiency and/or innovation. The functional structure with horizontal teams and integrating managers provides greater coordination and flexibility than the pure

Exhibit
11.6   *Relationship of Strategic Goals to Structural Approach*

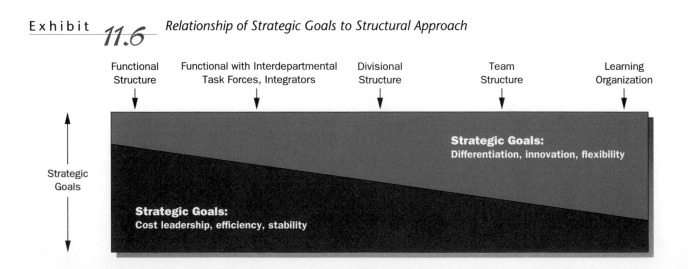

functional structure. The divisional structure promotes differentiation because each division can focus on specific products and customers, although divisions tend to be larger and less flexible than small teams. Exhibit 11.6 does not include all possible structures, but it illustrates how structures can be used to facilitate the strategic goals of cost leadership or differentiation. For example, Polaroid changed its structure as it changed its strategy.

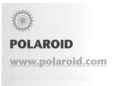

POLAROID
www.polaroid.com

Polaroid president I. M. Booth used a scale similar to the one in Exhibit 11.6 to describe his efforts to tear down internal barriers, decentralize decisions, and achieve coordination across functional departments. He defined a structural scale of 1 to 10. A 10 is a structure made up of autonomous teams, each with its own marketing, engineering, and management people. A 1 is a totally functional structure, with a single manufacturing division for the whole company, a single marketing division, and so on. Booth claims that Polaroid was a 1 for many years. Its departments were uncoordinated, and little things were being neglected. Booth's goal was to break up Polaroid's vertical functional structure by creating separate divisions for three businesses: magnetics, consumer products, and industrial photography products. Booth felt that the right amount of flexibility and innovation would put Polaroid at a 6 or 7 on the structural scale, and he planned to continue pushing until it neared the high end of the scale.[31]

Contingency Factor: The Environment

In Chapter 3, we discussed the nature of environmental uncertainty. Environmental uncertainty means that decision makers have difficulty acquiring good information and predicting external changes. Uncertainty occurs when the external environment is rapidly changing and complex. An uncertain environment causes three things to happen within an organization.

1. *Increased differences occur among departments.* In an uncertain environment, each major department—marketing, manufacturing, research and development—focuses on the task and environmental sectors for which it is responsible and hence distinguishes itself from the others with respect to goals, task orientation, and time horizon.[32] Departments work autonomously. These factors create barriers among departments.

2. *The organization needs increased coordination to keep departments working together.* Additional differences require more emphasis on horizontal coordination to link departments and overcome differences in departmental goals and orientations.

3. *The organization must adapt to change.* The organization must maintain a flexible, responsive posture toward the environment. Changes in products and technology require cooperation among departments, which means additional emphasis on coordination through the use of teams, task forces, and horizontal information processing.[33]

The contingency relationship between environmental uncertainty and structural approach is illustrated in Exhibit 11.7. When the external environment is more stable, the organization should have a traditional structure that emphasizes vertical control. There is little need for change, flexibility, or intense coordination. The structure can emphasize specialization, centralized decision making, and wide spans of control. When environmental uncertainty is high, a horizontal structure that emphasizes lateral relationships such as

CEO David Biegler admits the restructuring of Lone Star Gas Company, the natural gas distribution business of ENSERCH Corporation, was painful, but the company needed a more flexible structure to cope with environmental uncertainty. The reorganization reduced layers of management, eliminated obsolete jobs, and realigned jobs to serve customers better and faster. The new structure makes Lone Star more efficient and flexible, able to adapt quickly as the gas industry continues to evolve.

Exhibit *11.7* *Relationship Between Environment and Structure*

STRUCTURE

	Vertical	Horizontal
Uncertain (Unstable)	**Incorrect Fit:** Vertical structure in uncertain environment — Structure too tight	**Correct Fit:** Horizontal structure in uncertain environment
Certain (Stable)	**Correct Fit:** Vertical structure in certain environment	**Incorrect Fit:** Horizontal structure in certain environment — Structure too loose

ENVIRONMENT (row label on left)

teams and task forces is appropriate. Vertical structure characteristics such as specialization, centralization, and formalized procedures should be downplayed. In an uncertain environment, the organization figures things out as it goes along, departments must cooperate, and decisions should be decentralized to the teams and task forces working on specific problems.

When managers use the wrong structure for the environment, reduced performance results. A rigid, vertical structure in an uncertain environment prevents the organization from adapting to change. Likewise, a loose, horizontal structure in a stable environment is inefficient. Too many resources are devoted to meetings and discussions when employees could be more productive focusing on specialized tasks.

Many companies are forced to alter their structures as the environment changes. Consider the case of Zeneca Agricultural Products.

ZENECA AGRICULTURAL PRODUCTS

www.zeneca.com

Top executives of the North American agrochemicals business of Britain's Imperial Chemical Industries met to consider the company's future. Profits were down, and inventories were out of control. Matching a competitor's price cut had just cost $25 million. It seemed things couldn't get any worse—but they did. Executives learned that the company would be part of a huge deconglomeration when ICI spun off its pharmaceutical, agrochemical, and specialty-chemical lines. They knew that, unless things turned around fast, their business might not survive the whirlwind.

Zeneca was a traditional functional organization in which managers were fiercely loyal to their own departments. CEO Bob Woods knew that an immediate, full-scale reorganization would arouse opposition and take time and money Zeneca didn't have. However, everyone agreed the cash problem had to be solved, and that's where Woods found his opening. He first reached below the department managers, creating cross-functional teams of midlevel managers charged with getting working capital under control. Those teams later became the model for the larger transformation, as Zeneca Ag converted from a business laid out along product lines to one structured by customers; for example, corn and soybean farmers. Again, Woods created teams from the middle, who soon became heroes in the organization as profits and customer satisfaction increased.

Although some top managers squawked, many eventually wanted to join the teams, thus enabling Woods to gradually restructure the entire company.

The transformation was a success. Zeneca entered 1995 with profits up 68 percent, head count down just 10 percent, and a leadership team poised for rapid response to further environmental changes.[34]

Contingency Factor: Manufacturing and Service Technologies

Technology includes the knowledge, tools, techniques, and activities used to transform organizational inputs into outputs.[35] Technology includes machinery, employee skills, and work procedures. A useful way to think about technology is as "work flow." The production work flow may be to produce steel castings, television programs, or computer software.

Production technology is significant because it has direct influence on the organization structure. Structure must be designed to fit the technology as well as to accommodate the external environment. Technologies vary between manufacturing and service organizations. In the following paragraphs, we discuss each characteristic of technology and the structure that best fits it.

Woodward's Manufacturing Technology. The most influential research into the relationship between manufacturing technology and organization structure was conducted by Joan Woodward, a British industrial sociologist.[36] She gathered data from 100 British firms to determine whether basic structural characteristics, such as administrative overhead, span of control, centralization, and formalization, were different across firms. She found that manufacturing firms could be categorized according to three basic types of work flow technology.

1. *Small batch and unit production.* **Small batch production** firms produce goods in batches of one or a few products designed to customer specification. Each customer orders a unique product. This technology also is used to make large, one-of-a-kind products, such as computer-controlled machines. Small batch manufacturing is close to traditional skilled-craft work, because human beings are a large part of the process; they run machines to make the product. Examples of items produced through small batch manufacturing include custom clothing, special-order machine tools, space capsules, satellites, and submarines.

2. *Large batch and mass production.* **Mass production** technology is distinguished by standardized production runs. A large volume of products is produced, and all customers receive the same product. Standard products go into inventory for sale as customers need them. This technology makes greater use of machines than does small batch production. Machines are designed to do most of the physical work, and employees complement the machinery. Examples of mass production are automobile assembly lines and the large batch techniques used to produce computers, tobacco products, and textiles.

3. *Continuous process production.* In **continuous process production,** the entire work flow is mechanized. This is the most sophisticated and complex form of production technology. Because the process runs continuously, there is no starting and stopping. Human operators are not part of actual

technology
The knowledge, tools, techniques, and activities used to transform the organization's inputs into outputs.

small batch production
A type of technology that involves the production of goods in batches of one or a few products designed to customer specifications.

mass production
A type of technology characterized by the production of a large volume of products with the same specifications.

continuous process production
A type of technology involving mechanization of the entire work flow and nonstop production.

Computer companies such as IBM, Compaq, and Hewlett-Packard are initiating new small batch production *methods in order to compete with Dell Computer's low-cost strategy. Unlike Dell, which builds PCs only after they have been ordered and sends them directly to customers, IBM, Compaq, and H-P have previously employed* mass production techniques—*building, testing, inspecting, boxing, and storing large volumes before shipping products to resellers. In the photo, Mike Rust unpacks the case of an IBM PC for Entex, a reseller that IBM has delegated to complete assembly of its computers in smaller batches as they are ordered.*

technical complexity
The degree to which complex machinery is involved in the production process to the exclusion of people.

flexible manufacturing
A manufacturing technology using computers to automate and integrate manufacturing components such as robots, machines, product design, and engineering analysis.

production because machinery does all of the work. Human operators simply read dials, fix machines that break down, and manage the production process. Examples of continuous process technologies are chemical plants, distilleries, petroleum refineries, and nuclear power plants.

The difference among the three manufacturing technologies is called technical complexity. **Technical complexity** means the degree to which machinery is involved in the production to the exclusion of people. With a complex technology, employees are hardly needed except to monitor the machines.

The structural characteristics associated with each type of manufacturing technology are illustrated in Exhibit 11.8. Note that formalization and centralization are high for mass production technology and low for continuous process. Unlike small batch and continuous process, standardized mass production machinery requires centralized decision making and well-defined rules and procedures. The administrative ratio and the percentage of indirect labor required also increase with technological complexity. Because the production process is nonroutine, closer supervision is needed. More indirect labor in the form of maintenance people is required because of the machinery's complexity; thus, the indirect/direct labor ratio is high. Span of control for first-line supervisors is greatest for mass production. On an assembly line, jobs are so routinized that a supervisor can handle an average of 48 employees. The number of employees per supervisor in small batch and continuous process production is lower because closer supervision is needed. Overall, small batch and continuous process firms have somewhat loose, flexible structures, and mass production firms have tight, vertical structures.

The important conclusion about manufacturing technology was described by Woodward as follows: "Different technologies impose different kinds of demands on individuals and organizations, and these demands have to be met through an appropriate structure."[37] Woodward found that the relationship between structure and technology was directly related to company performance. Low-performing firms tended to deviate from the preferred structural form, often adopting a structure appropriate for another type of technology. High-performing organizations had characteristics very similar to those listed in Exhibit 11.8.

Flexible Manufacturing.   The most recent development in manufacturing technology is called **flexible manufacturing,** which uses computers to automate and integrate manufacturing components such as robots, machines, product design, and engineering analysis. Companies such as Deere, General Motors, Intel, and Illinois Tool Works use flexible manufacturing in a single manufacturing plant to do small batch and mass production operations *at the same time*. Bar codes enable machines to make instantaneous changes—such as putting a larger screw in a different location—as different batches flow down the automated assembly line. Sunrise Medical uses flexible manufacturing to make wheelchairs tailored to an individual customer's exact specifications.[38] Taken to its ultimate, flexible manufacturing allows for *mass customization,* producing products in large batches but with each product tailored to customer specification. Levi Strauss has experimented with mass producing custom-made jeans through its Personal Pair program. At Custom Foot stores, customers browse through the store, mixing and matching design components such as style, color, and leather type. A high-tech electronic scanner measures the customer's foot, and the complete order is zapped by modem to Custom Foot's headquarters in

	Manufacturing Technology		
	Small Batch	Mass Production	Continuous Process
Technical Complexity of Production Technology	Low	Medium	High
Organization structure:			
Formalization	Low	High	Low
Centralization	Low	High	Low
Top administrator ratio	Low	Medium	High
Indirect/direct labor ratio	1/9	1/4	1/1
Supervisor span of control	23	48	15
Communication:			
Written (vertical)	Low	High	Low
Verbal (horizontal)	High	Low	High
Overall structure	Flexible	Rigid	Flexible

Exhibit *11.8*

Relationship Between Manufacturing Technology and Organization Structure

Source: Based on Joan Woodward, *Industrial Organizations: Theory and Practice* (London: Oxford University Press, 1965).

Florence, Italy. Shoes generally are ready in about three weeks and often cost slightly less than many premium brands sold off the shelf.[39] Flexible manufacturing and mass customization are considered to be at a higher level of technical complexity than the three manufacturing technologies studied by Woodward. The structures associated with the new technology tend to have few rules, decentralization, a small ratio of administrators to workers, face-to-face horizontal communication, and a team-oriented, flexible approach.[40]

Service Technology. Service organizations are becoming increasingly important in North America. Since 1982, more employees have been employed in service organizations than in manufacturing organizations. Thus, new research has been undertaken to understand the structural characteristics of

"Our position as a global technology leader gives us tremendous potential as an engine systems supplier," states Chuck McNamara, President, of the Engine Components Group at Dana Corporation. The technical complexity that enables the Group to attain $1.8 billion in sales, however, requires the skillful maintenance assistance of employees such as Janet Duncan, who has worked for the company for 20 years. In the photo, Duncan installs a cam cover into an automated assembly system at the Dana plant in Paris, Tennessee.

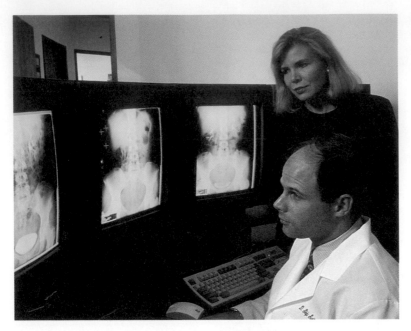

Skip Sallee and Susan Hinson of Team Radiology in Durham, North Carolina, use "telemedicine" to relieve hospitals of the costly administrative burdens associated with radiology. By connecting to Team Radiology over a computer network, small rural hospitals can offer radiology services previously not financially feasible. Advanced information technology has revolutionized service technology, allowing the creation of structures that couldn't have existed before. New computerized forms of communication and cooperation support the informal, flexible, and decentralized structure needed in many service organizations.

service technology
Technology characterized by intangible outputs and direct contact between employees and customers.

service organizations. **Service technology** can be defined as follows:

1. *Intangible output.* The output of a service firm is intangible. Services are perishable and, unlike physical products, cannot be stored in inventory. The service is either consumed immediately or lost forever. Manufactured products are produced at one point in time and can be stored until sold at another time.

2. *Direct contact with customers.* Employees and customers interact directly to provide and purchase the service. Production and consumption are simultaneous. Service firm employees have direct contact with customers. In a manufacturing firm, technical employees are separated from customers, and hence no direct interactions occur.[41]

The output of service organizations is frequently intangible; that of manufacturing organizations is tangible. Examples of service firms include consulting companies, law firms, brokerage houses, airlines, hotels, advertising firms, public relations firms, amusement parks, and educational organizations. Service technology also characterizes many departments in large corporations, even manufacturing firms. In a manufacturing organization such as Ford Motor Company, the legal, human resources, finance, and market research departments provide service. Thus, the structure and design of each of these departments reflect its own service technology rather than the manufacturing plant's technology. Service technology concepts therefore can be used to structure both service organizations and the many large service departments within manufacturing organizations.

One distinct feature of service technology that directly influences structure is the need for employees to be close to the customer.[42] Structural characteristics are similar to those for continuous manufacturing technology, shown in Exhibit 11.8. Service firms tend to be flexible, informal, and decentralized. Horizontal communication is high because employees must share information and resources to serve customers and solve problems. Some Taco Bell restaurants operate with no manager on the premises. Self-directed teams manage inventory, schedule work, order supplies, and train new employees. Services also are dispersed; hence each unit is often small and located geographically close to customers. For example, banks, hotels, fast-food franchises, and doctors' offices disperse their facilities into regional and local offices.

Although service firms in general tend to be more flexible and decentralized, some, such as McDonald's, develop set rules and procedures for customer service. When services can be standardized, a tight, centralized structure can be very effective, as revealed by the Marriott Corporation.

MARRIOTT CORPORATION
www.marriott.com

Marriott Corporation's success has come from two strategies: Put hotels where the customers are and provide excellent service. Putting hotels where the customers are means building hotels downtown and at airports. Convention centers, such as

Atlantic City, are another target. Marriott also searches for new niches. The Court-yard is a new type of garden apartment hotel aimed at the moderate-priced seg-ment of the market. Courtyards are scattered around major metropolitan areas.

At Marriott, the hotel itself is the main service, and a mind-boggling sys-tem is used to make the right impression every time. Top managers make no apologies for the tightly centralized system of policies, procedures, and con-trols for operational details. Room attendants have 66 things to do in clean-ing a room, from dusting the tops of pictures (number 7) to keeping the tele-phone book and Bibles in a neat condition (number 37). President Bill Marriott says, "The more the system works like the Army, the better." The cooks have 6,000 recipes available to them, and they are not allowed to deviate. One rule for chefs says, "Deviations from the standard written specifications may not be made without prior approval and written consent of the vice president of food and beverages."

Marriott Corporation plans to add new hotels each year. It routinizes the serv-ice and builds luxury into the physical structure to ensure that guests are treated the same way every time. One recent program is First 10, which focuses on making a lasting impression of great service on customers during the first ten minutes of their hotel stay. Marriott was rated as one of the five best-managed companies, and Bill Marriott and four executive vice-presidents spend half the year on the road visiting company facilities. The close, personal supervision and careful reading of customer suggestions help Bill Marriott give business travel-ers the service they expect and deserve.[43]

The managers at Marriott designed the structure and procedures to fit a service where work can be broken down into a series of explicit steps for employees to follow in serving customers. The many rules and procedures, centralized decision making, and refined division of labor provide a structure that is suited to the underlying technology. However, this structure would not work in a service such as a doctor's office, where new problems are encountered every day and employees must develop creative solutions for solving problems and serving customers.

Contingency Factor: Departmental Interdependence

The final characteristic of the organization's situation that influences struc-ture is called *interdependence*. **Interdependence** means the extent to which departments depend on each other for resources or materials to accomplish their tasks. A low level of interdependence means that departments do their work independently and have little need for interaction, coordination, or exchange of materials. A high level of interdependence means that depart-ments must constantly exchange information and resources. Three types of interdependence that influence organization structure are illustrated in Exhibit 11.9.[44]

interdependence
The extent to which departments depend on each other for resources or materials to accomplish their tasks.

Pooled Interdependence. *Pooled interdependence* means that each department is part of the organization and contributes to the common good, but each department is relatively independent because work does not flow between units. Citibank branch banks or Wendy's restaurants are examples of pooled interdependence. They share financial resources from a common pool but do not interact with each other.

Exhibit **11.9**

Types of Interdependence and Required Coordination

Form of Inter-dependence	Type of Coordination Required
1. Pooled (bank) Clients	▪ Chain of command ▪ Standardization of procedures ▪ Rules and regulations
2. Sequential (assembly line) Client	▪ Plans and schedules ▪ Scheduled meetings ▪ Liaison roles
3. Reciprocal (hospital) Client	▪ Unscheduled meetings ▪ Teams ▪ Task forces ▪ Project managers

Sequential Interdependence. *Sequential interdependence* means that parts or outputs of one department become inputs to another department in serial fashion. The first department must perform correctly so that the second department can perform correctly. An example is assembly line technology, such as in the automobile industry. This is greater interdependence than with the pooled type, because departments exchange resources and depend on others to perform well.

Reciprocal Interdependence. The highest level is *reciprocal interdependence,* which means that the output of operation A is the input to operation B, and the output of operation B is the input back again to operation A. Departmental outputs influence other departments in reciprocal fashion. For example, hospitals must coordinate services to patients, such as when a patient moves back and forth among the surgery, physical therapy, and X-ray departments.

Structural Implications. When interdependence among departments is pooled, coordination is relatively easy. Managers can develop standardized procedures, rules, and regulations that ensure similar performance in all branches. For sequential interdependence, coordination is somewhat more difficult, requiring future planning and scheduling so that the flow of outputs and resources is coordinated to the benefit of all departments. Moreover, scheduled meetings and face-to-face discussions are used for day-to-day coordination among departments. Reciprocal interdependence is the most difficult. These departments should be located physically close together in the organization so that communication is facilitated. Structural mechanisms for coordination include teams, task forces, unscheduled meetings, and perhaps project managers to ensure that departments are working out coordination problems on a daily basis.[45]

Exhibit **11.10**   *Product Development, Product Delivery, and Customer Service Interdependencies*

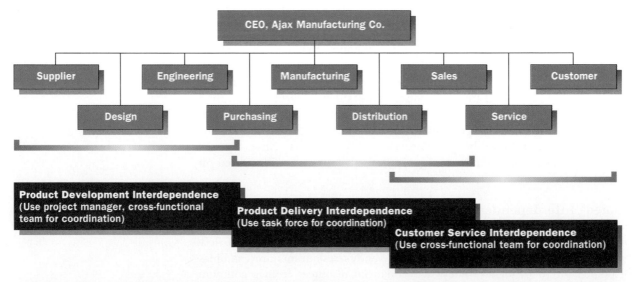

SOURCE: Based on John F. Rockart and James E. Short, "IT in the 1990s: Managing Organizational Interdependence," *Sloan Management Review* (winter 1989), 7–17.

Within most organizations, interdependence will be high (reciprocal) for some departmental activities and low (pooled) for others. For example, Exhibit 11.10 illustrates how reciprocal interdependence among sets of departments exists for the tasks of product development, product delivery, and customer service. The design and purchasing departments can work independently on many tasks, but for product development, they must be coordinated, perhaps with a team or task force. Purchasing must be coordinated with distribution for the delivery of products. Suppliers and customers also are a part of the interdependence and in some organizations may be included as part of a team.

Summary and Management Solution

This chapter introduced a number of important organizing concepts. As organizations grow, they add new departments, functions, and hierarchical levels. A major problem confronting management is how to tie the whole organization together. Structural characteristics such as chain of command, work specialization, and departmentalization are valuable organization concepts but often are not sufficient to coordinate far-flung departments. Horizontal coordination mechanisms provide coordination across departments and include reengineering, task forces, teams, and project managers.

There is an increasing shift toward more horizontal versus vertical structures, which reflects the trend toward greater employee involvement and participation. At the apex of this movement is a type of organization called the learning organization. The learning organization is characterized by a horizontal structure, open information, decentralized decision making, empowered employees, and a strong, adaptive culture. Contingency factors of strategy, environment, production technology, and departmental interdependence influence the correct structural approach. When a firm's strategy is to differentiate the firm's product from competitors, a flexible structural approach using teams, decentralization, and empowered employees is appropriate. When environmental uncertainty is high, horizontal coordination is important, and the organization should have a looser, flexible structure, such as in a learning organization.

Other factors that influence structure are technology and interdependence. For manufacturing firms, small batch, continuous process, and flexible manufacturing technologies tend to be structured loosely, whereas a tighter vertical structure is appropriate for mass production. Service technologies are people oriented, and firms are located geographically close to dispersed customers. Some services can be broken down into explicit steps where employees follow objective, standardized procedures for serving customers and solving problems, and these may be controlled with a vertical structure. However, in general, services tend to have more flexible, horizontal structures, with decentralized decision making.

Finally, departmental interdependence also determines the form of structure. An organization with a low level of interdependence, such as the pooled type, can be controlled mainly with the vertical chain of command and standardization of procedures, rules, and regulations. When interdependence is high, such as for new-product introductions, then horizontal coordination mechanisms such as unscheduled meetings, teams, and project managers are required, or the organization may place the interdependent groups into separate, self-contained units.

At Vortex Industries, described at the beginning of the chapter, the highly centralized, vertical structure was preventing the company from providing the level of customer service needed to fend off new competition. High overhead costs meant the company had to charge higher prices. Vortex also suffered because its services were not located geographically close to customers. Frank Fulkerson set out to reengineer his company, although he didn't call it by that name. As an experiment, he split off one branch of the company in one of the six counties Vortex served and rearranged the duties of everyone who worked there. The branch manager served as team leader and handled several functions that had previously been divided among people in rigid categories at the central office. To encourage team spirit, Fulkerson set up a profit-sharing plan. Business at the branch went through the roof, so Fulkerson reorganized the company into six independent branches, with only a lightly staffed home office. Fulkerson also flipped the organization chart, from a pyramid with him at the top to a cone with him at the bottom. Now, he sees his job as helping the staff at the home office. In turn, their job is to help the field teams, whose job is to help the customers. Employees mastered several skills instead of just one. Fulkerson's structural changes set Vortex on the right path and led to a $1.5 million increase in sales. The company has expanded to ten branches in Southern California and one in Denver.[46]

Discussion Questions

1. Carnival Cruise Lines provides pleasure cruises to the masses. Carnival has several ships and works on high volume/low price rather than offering luxury cruises. What would you predict about the organization structure of a Carnival Cruise ship?

2. Why is structure different depending on whether a firm's strategy is low cost or differentiation?

3. The chapter suggested that structure should be designed to fit strategy. Some theorists argue that strategy should be designed to fit the organization's structure. With which theory do you agree? Explain.

4. Explain the three levels of departmental interdependence and give an example of each.

5. Some experts argue that interdependence within organizations is greater now than 15 years ago because of rapid changes in the global environment. If so, what does this mean for the present structure of organizations compared with that of 15 years ago?

6. What is the difference between a task force and a project manager? Which would be more effective in achieving coordination?

7. Discuss why an organization in an uncertain environment requires more horizontal relationships than one in a certain environment.

8. Why are empowered employees, open information, and cultural values of minimal boundaries and equality important in a learning organization as opposed to a traditional, vertical organization?

9. What is the difference between manufacturing and service technology? How would you classify a university, a local discount store, a nursery school? How would you expect the structure of a service organization to differ from that of a manufacturing organization?

10. Flexible manufacturing systems combine elements of both small batch and mass production. What effect might this new form of technology have on organization structure? Explain.

Management in Practice: Experiential Exercise

Loose versus Tight Organization Structure

Interview an employee at your university, such as a department head or secretary. Have the employee answer the following thirteen questions about his or her job and organizational conditions.

	Disagree Strongly				Agree Strongly
1. Your work would be considered routine.	5	4	3	2	1
2. There is a clearly known way to do the major tasks you encounter.	5	4	3	2	1
3. Your work has high variety and frequent exceptions.	1	2	3	4	5
4. Communications from above consist of information and advice rather than instructions and directions.	1	2	3	4	5
5. You have the support of peers and supervisor to do your job well.	1	2	3	4	5
6. You seldom exchange ideas or information with people doing other kinds of jobs.	5	4	3	2	1
7. Decisions relevant to your work are made above you and passed down.	5	4	3	2	1
8. People at your level frequently have to figure out for themselves what their jobs are for the day.	1	2	3	4	5
9. Lines of authority are clear and precisely defined.	5	4	3	2	1
10. Leadership tends to be democratic rather than autocratic in style.	1	2	3	4	5
11. Job descriptions are written and up-to-date for each job.	5	4	3	2	1
12. People understand each other's jobs and often do different tasks.	1	2	3	4	5
13. A manual of policies and procedures is available to use when a problem arises.	5	4	3	2	1

Total Score _____

A score of 52 or above suggests that the employee is working in a "loosely structured" organization. The score reflects a flexible structure that is often associated with uncertain environments and small-batch technology. People working in this structure feel empowered. Many organizations today are moving in the direction of flexible structures and empowerment.

A score of 26 or below suggests a "tight structure." This structure utilizes traditional control and functional specialization, which often occurs in a certain environment, a stable organiza-tion, and routine or mass-production technology. People in this structure may feel controlled and constrained.

Discuss the pros and cons of loose versus tight structure. Does the structure of the employee you interviewed fit the na-ture of the organization's environment, strategic goals, and technology? How might you redesign the structure to make the work organization more effective?

Management in Practice: Ethical Dilemma

A Matter of Giving

Renee Washington was proud to have been recruited out of college to work at Standol Corporation. In addition to a spot-less reputation in environmental responsibility, Standol was fa-mous for its active part in supporting various civic and cultural organizations in the community. When the opportunity came to participate in the Helping Hands drive, Washington quickly volunteered. She soon had reason to regret her decision.

A memo was issued to the volunteer coordinator in each de-partment, indicating the expected donation from each em-ployee. It was Washington's job to collect a "pledge" to be with-drawn from each payroll check, or a lump sum payment. The memo indicated Standol expected each volunteer coordinator to collect the suggested amount or make up the difference out of their own pockets. Washington found herself listening to countless hard-luck stories as she applied pressure to fellow employees for their contributions. As she enlisted the aid of managers in the coercion, Washington felt her pride and ex-citement in the project diminishing.

She began to question whether a sterling reputation in com-munity charities was worth the embarrassment and resentment it caused Standol employees. She wondered if people might give more freely if they felt they weren't being ordered to give at levels set by top management. She wanted to make sugges-tions for changes but feared doing so would threaten her future at Standol.

What Do You Do?

1. Comply with the traditional fund-raising approach, blaming the company for putting you in the position of the bad guy.
2. Collect only the funds that are genuinely donated, without making up the difference out of pocket. If you are criticized, expose the coercive practices to Helping Hands officials and the press.
3. Propose changes for coordinating fund-raising across de-partments that emphasize teamwork and come from within the organization, rather than from the top down.

SOURCE: Based on Doug Wallace, "A Twisted Arm," *What Would You Do? Business Ethics,* vol. II (January–February 1994), 17–18.

Surf the Net

1. **Project Management.** This exercise will broaden your understanding of the many responsibilities of a project manager. Go to the Project Management Institute's Web site at **www.pmi.org**. At this site you will find a link to a free download called *A Guide to the Project Manage-ment Body of Knowledge.* Go through the steps required to download the document. You will need the Adobe Acrobat Reader, available at this Web site, to view the *Guide.* After reading through the contents page, go to page 13 and print Figure 1-1: Overview of Project Man-agement Knowledge Areas and Project Management Processes.

2. **Production Technology.** See how a Saturn vehicle is man-ufactured at **www.gm.com/about/info/overview/gmnao.html**. The video you view at this site requires the RealPlayerJ plug-in, which is free and can be accessed from this site. Next, go on a tour of Nissan's Smyrna, Tennessee plant by visiting **www.nissan-na.com/smyrna/index.html**. Write a brief description of what you learned about the manufacturing process at each of Nissan's main plant areas: (a) Stamping, (b) Body Assembly, (c) Component Assembly, (d) Paint, and (e) Trim & Chassis.

Case for Critical Analysis

Malard Manufacturing Company

Malard Manufacturing Company produces control valves that regulate flows through natural gas pipelines. Malard has approximately 1,400 employees and has successfully produced a standard line of control valves that are price competitive in the industry. However, whenever the production of a new control valve is required, problems arise. Developments in electronics, metallurgy, and flow control theory require the introduction of new products every year or two. These new products have been associated with interdepartmental conflict and disagreement.

Consider the CV305, which is in process. As usual, the research and development group developed the basic design, and the engineering department converted it into a prototype control valve. Now the materials department must acquire parts for the prototype and make plans for obtaining parts needed for production runs. The production department is to manufacture and assemble the product, and marketing is responsible for sales.

Department heads believe that future work on the CV305 should be done simultaneously instead of sequentially. Marketing wants to provide input to research and development so that the design will meet customer needs. Production insists that the design fit machine limitations and be cost efficient to manufacture—indeed, it wants to speed up development of the final plans so that it can acquire tooling and be ready for standard production. Engineering, on the other hand, wants to slow down development to ensure that specifications are correct and have been thoroughly tested.

All of these controversies with the CV305 exist right now. Department managers are frustrated and becoming uncommunicative. The research and development and engineering departments are keeping their developmental plans secret, causing frustration for the other departments. Moreover, several department managers are new and inexperienced in new-product development. Ms. Crandell, the executive vice president, likes to keep tight control over the organization. Department managers must check with her before making major decisions. However, with the CV305, she has been unable to keep things running smoothly. The span of control is so large that Crandell has no time to personally shepherd the CV305 through the system.

On November 1, Crandell received a memo from the marketing department head. It said, in part,

> The CV305 must go to market immediately. This is urgent. It is needed now because it provides the precision control our competitors' products already have. Three of our salespeople reported that loyal customers are about to place orders with competitors. We can keep this business if we have the CV305 ready for production in 30 days.

Questions

1. What is the balance between vertical and horizontal structure in Malard Manufacturing? Is it appropriate that department managers always turn to the executive vice-president for help rather than to one another?
2. If you were Ms. Crandell, how would you resolve this problem? What could you do to facilitate production of the CV305 over the next 30 days?
3. What structural changes would you recommend to prevent these problems in future new-product developments? Would a smaller span of control help? A project manager with responsibility for coordinating the CV305? A task force?

Endnotes

1. Michael Barrier, "Re-engineering Your Company," *Nation's Business,* February 1994, 16–22.
2. Laurie P. O'Leary, "Curing the Monday Blues: A U.S. Navy Guide for Structuring Cross-Functional Teams," *National Productivity Review,* spring 1996, 43–51; and Alan Hurwitz, "Organizational Structures for the 'New World Order,'" *Business Horizons,* May–June 1996, 5–14.
3. Richard L. Daft, *Organization Theory and Design,* 5th ed. (St. Paul, Minn.: West, 1995).
4. Bruce Buursma, "Wanted: Romance Executive," *Chicago Tribune,* July 19, 1989.
5. E. Esterson, "Hail to the Chiefs," *Inc. Tech,* 1998, no. 2, 65; and E. Wakin, "Multifaceted CIO," *Beyond Computing,* May 1995, 37–40.
6. Lee Iacocca with William Novak, *Iacocca: An Autobiography* (New York: Phantom Books, 1984), 152–153.
7. Alan Webber, "The Best Organization is No Organization," *USA Today,* March 6, 1997, 13A.
8. William J. Altier, "Task Forces: An Effective Management Tool," *Management Review* (February 1987), 52–57.
9. "Task Forces Tackle Consolidation of Employment Services," *Shawmut News,* Shawmut National Corp., May 3, 1989, 2.
10. Michael Brody, "Can GM Manage It All?" *Fortune,* July 8, 1985, 22–28.
11. Henry Mintzberg, *The Structure of Organizations* (Englewood Cliffs, N.J.: Prentice-Hall, 1979).
12. Barbara Ettorre, "Simplicity Cuts a New Pattern," *Management Review* (December 1993), 25–29; and Joyce Hoffman, ed., *Reflections,* vol. 10 (1989), 12–15.
13. Paul R. Lawrence and Jay W. Lorsch, "New Managerial Job: The Integrator," *Harvard Business Review* (November–December 1967), 142–151.

14. This discussion is based on Richard L. Daft, *Organization Theory and Design,* 5th ed. (Minneapolis, Minn.: West Publishing Company, 1995), 238; Raymond L. Manganelli and Mark M. Klein, "A Framework for Reengineering," *Management Review,* June 1994, 9–16; and Barbara Ettorre, "Reengineering Tales from the Front," *Management Review,* January 1995, 13–18.

15. "Plugging in Change," *Across the Board,* October 1995, 24–31.

16. L. Calabro, "The Numbers Don't Lie," *CFO,* October 1994, 15.

17. Ettorre, "Reengineering Tales from the Front."

18. Bob Lindgren, "Going Horizontal," *Enterprise,* April 1994, 20–25.

19. John A. Byrne, "The Horizontal Corporation," *Business Week,* December 20, 1993, 76–81.

20. Erik Brynjolfsson, Amy Austin Renshaw, and Marshall Van Alstyne, "The Matrix of Change," *Sloan Management Review,* (winter 1997), 37–54.

21. Paul Roberts, "We Are One Company, No Matter Where We Are," *Fast Company,* April–May 1998, 122–128.

22. E. C. Nevis, A. J. DiBella, and J. M. Gould, "Understanding Organizations as Learning Systems," *Sloan Management Review,* (winter 1995), 73–85; and G. Hamel, "Strategy as Revolution," *Harvard Business Review,* July–August 1996, 69–82.

23. Myron Magnet, "Meet the New Revolutionaries," *Fortune,* February 24, 1992, 94–101.

24. Marc S. Gerstein and Robert B. Shaw, "Organizational Architectures for the Twenty-First Century," in David A. Nadler, Marc S. Gerstein, Robert B. Shaw and Associates, eds., *Organizational Architecture: Designs for Changing Organizations* (San Francisco: Jossey-Bass, 1992), 263–274.

25. Scott Kirsner, "Every Day, It's a New Place," *Fast Company,* April–May 1998, 130–134.

26. Jeffrey Pfeffer, "Producing Sustainable Competitive Advantage Through the Effective Management of People," *Academy of Management Executive* 9, no. 1 (1995), 55–69.

27. Mary Anne Devanna and Noel Tichy, "Creating the Competitive Organization of the Twenty-First Century: The Boundaryless Corporation," *Human Resource Management* 29 (winter 1990), 455–471; and Fred Kofman and Peter M. Senge, "Communities of Commitment: The Heart of Learning Organizations," *Organizational Dynamics* (autumn 1993), 4–23.

28. Dorothy Leonard-Barton, "The Factory as a Learning Laboratory," *Sloan Management Review* (fall 1992), 23–38.

29. Michael E. Porter, *Competitive Strategy* (New York: Free Press, 1980), 36–46.

30. Pam Black, "Finally, Human Rights for Motorists," *Business Week,* May 1, 1995, 45.

31. Clem Morgello, "Booth: Creating a New Polaroid," *Dun's Business Month,* August 1985, 51–52.

32. Paul R. Lawrence and Jay W. Lorsch, *Organization and Environment* (Homewood, Ill.: Irwin, 1969).

33. Robert B. Duncan, "Characteristics of Organizational Environments and Perceived Environmental Uncertainty," *Administrative Science Quarterly* 17 (1972), 313–327; W. Alan Randolph and Gregory G. Dess, "The Congruence Perspective of Organization Design: A Conceptual Model and Multivariate Research Approach," *Academy of Management Review* 9 (1984), 114–127; and Masoud Yasai-Ardekani, "Structural Adaptations to Environments," *Academy of Management Review* 11 (1986), 9–21.

34. Thomas A. Stewart, "How to Lead a Revolution," *Fortune,* November 28, 1994, 48–61.

35. Denise M. Rousseau and Robert A. Cooke, "Technology and Structure: The Concrete, Abstract, and Activity Systems of Organizations," *Journal of Management* 10 (1984), 345–361; Charles Perrow, "A Framework for the Comparative Analysis of Organizations," *American Sociological Review* 32 (1967), 194–208; and Denise M. Rousseau, "Assessment of Technology in Organizations: Closed versus Open Systems Approaches," *Academy of Management Review* 4 (1979), 531–542.

36. Joan Woodward, *Industrial Organizations: Theory and Practice* (London: Oxford University Press, 1965); and Joan Woodward, *Management and Technology* (London: Her Majesty's Stationery Office, 1958).

37. Woodward, *Industrial Organizations,* vi.

38. Barrier, "Re-engineering Your Company."

39. Justin Martin, "Give 'Em *Exactly* What They Want," *Fortune,* November 10, 1997, 283, 285.

40. R. Parthasarthy and S. B. Sethi, "The Impact of Flexible Automation on Business Strategy and Organizational Structure," *Academy of Management Review* 17 (1992), 86–111; P. L. Nemetz and L. W. Fry, "Flexible Manufacturing Organizations: Implementation for Strategy Formulation and Organization Design," *Academy of Management Review* 13 (1988), 627–638; and P. S. Adler, "Managing Flexible Automation," *California Management Review* (spring 1988), 34–56.

41. Peter K. Mills and Thomas Kurk, "A Preliminary Investigation into the Influence of Customer-Firm Interface on Information Processing and Task Activity in Service Organizations," *Journal of Management* 12 (1986), 91–104; Peter K. Mills and Dennis J. Moberg, "Perspectives on the Technology of Service Operations," *Academy of Management Review* 7 (1982), 467–478; and Roger W. Schmenner, "How Can Service Businesses Survive and Prosper?" *Sloan Management Review* 27 (spring 1986), 21–32.

42. Richard B. Chase and David A. Tansik, "The Customer Contact Model for Organization Design," *Management Science* 29 (1983), 1037–1050; and Gregory B. Northcraft and Richard B. Chase, "Managing Service Demand at the Point of Delivery," *Academy of Management Review* 10 (1985), 66–75.

43. Maryfran Johnson, "Marriott Rests on RS/6000," *Computerworld,* October 5, 1992, 6; and Thomas Moore, "Marriott Grabs for More Rooms," *Fortune,* October 31, 1983, 107–122.

44. James Thompson, *Organizations in Action* (New York: McGraw-Hill, 1967).

45. Jack K. Ito and Richard B. Peterson, "Effects of Task Difficulty and Interdependence on Information Processing Systems," *Academy of Management Journal* 29 (1986), 139–149; and Andrew H. Van de Ven, Andre Delbecq, and Richard Koenig, "Determinants of Coordination Modes within Organizations," *American Sociological Review* 41 (1976), 322–338.

46. Barrier, "Re-engineering Your Company."

LEARNING OBJECTIVES

After studying this chapter, you should be able to

- Define organizational change and explain the forces for change.

- Describe the sequence of four change activities that must be performed in order for change to be successful.

- Explain the techniques managers can use to facilitate the initiation of change in organizations, including idea champions and new-venture teams.

- Define sources of resistance to change.

- Explain force field analysis and other implementation tactics that can be used to overcome resistance to change.

- Explain the difference among technology, product, structure, and culture/people changes.

- Explain the change process—bottom up, top down, horizontal—associated with each type of change.

- Define organizational development and large-group interventions.

Change and Development

MANAGEMENT PROBLEM

Several years ago, Midwest Contract Furnishings, Inc., a small firm that designs and furnishes hotel interiors, faced a crisis that left employees reeling. The company's biggest customer, Renaissance Hotels International, was sold to Marriott International, which was unlikely to need Midwest's services. Even though Midwest had only 20 employees and had been in business for only five years, it had landed a showcase project in Orlando that brought it to the attention of Renaissance. So, for two years, Midwest had been focusing much of its energies on serving the huge Renaissance account. Now, since Marriott did most of that kind of work in-house, Midwest faced the loss of at least 80 percent of its revenues. Midwest owner Christopher Cogan needed to reshape his company immediately, and he needed the full commitment of employees to do it. However, everyone—including Cogan—was devastated by the loss of the Renaissance account. "I wanted to crawl under a rock and not show up for work for a couple of months," he said. Employees were fearful of losing their jobs and didn't feel much motivation to come to work either. Cogan pushed aside his own fears and developed a plan for taking Midwest in a new direction. Then he asked himself a tough question: How could he implement the changes in such a way that employees would be motivated to help the company emerge from this crisis?[1]

If you were Christopher Cogan, how would you handle this situation? What approaches can he take to help employees adapt to the changes he has in mind for Midwest?

Christopher Cogan and Midwest Contract Furnishings are not alone. Every organization goes through periods of change that can cause stress and uncertainty. Sometimes, changes are brought about by forces outside the organization, as in the case at Midwest. Other times, managers within the company want to initiate major changes but don't know how. Lack of innovation from within is widely recognized as one of the critical problems facing business today in the United States and Canada. To be successful, organizations must embrace many types of change. Businesses must develop improved production technologies, create new products desired in the marketplace, implement new administrative systems, and upgrade employees' skills. Companies such as Westinghouse, Black & Decker, and Merck implement all of these changes and more.

How important is organizational change? Consider this: The parents of today's college students grew up without digital cameras, E-mail, personal computers, VCRs, electronic games, CDs, cellular phones, video stores, or laser checkout systems in supermarkets. Companies that produce the new products have prospered, but many companies caught with outdated products and technologies have failed. Today's successful companies are constantly striving to come up with new products and services. For example, automakers such as DaimlerChrysler, General Motors, and Toyota are investing heavily to develop fuel-cell power systems that could make today's noisy, polluting piston engines as obsolete as the steam locomotive. Colt's Manufacturing is working on a computerized "smart gun" that can be fired only by the owner. Pharmaceutical companies around the world are searching for new drugs and vaccines to fight diseases such as AIDS and cancer.[2] Organizations that change successfully, such as General Electric, Hewlett-Packard, and Motorola, are both profitable and admired.

organizational change
The adoption of a new idea or behavior by an organization.

Organizational change is defined as the adoption of a new idea or behavior by an organization.[3] In this chapter, we will look at how organizations can be designed to respond to the environment through internal change and development. First we will examine the basic forces for organizational change. Then we will look closely at how managers facilitate two change requirements: initiation and implementation. Finally, we will discuss the four major types of change—technology, new product, structure, and culture/people—and how the organization can be designed to facilitate each.

The Learning Organization

In today's highly complex world, organizations need to continuously adapt to new situations if they are to survive and prosper. The current trend is toward development of the *learning organization,* which is the epitome of continuous organizational change and growth. As we have discussed in previous chapters, the learning organization engages everyone in problem solving and continuous improvement based on the lessons of experience.[4]

The interacting systems that make up the learning organization, as discussed in Chapter 2, resemble a web in which each element responds to and influences every other element toward change. For example, *leadership* provides vision for development of new strategies and serves as a crucial support function for empowerment of employees and the extent of openness in information sharing. *Empowerment* liberates employees but also places upon them the added responsibilities of working collaboratively, initiating changes, and participating in strategy to benefit the entire organization. Redefining *culture* demands the rethinking of roles, processes, and values, breaking down barriers that have separated departments so that everyone shares information and works together. *Information sharing* requires adjustments on the part of managers for the inclusion of employees, suppliers, and customers, often necessitating cultural and structural changes. *Strategy* is likewise linked to structure and culture as the organization changes its fundamental way of doing business and allows change initiatives to flow bottom up as well as top down. The *horizontal structure,* which replaces the familiar hierarchical pyramid, incorporates empowerment and information sharing and relies on employees as team members and managers as facilitators.

The learning organization simultaneously embraces two types of planned change: *operational change,* based on organizational efforts to improve basic work and organizational processes in different areas of the business; and *transformational change,* which involves redesign and renewal of the total organization.[5]

Model of Planned Organizational Change

Change can be managed. By observing external trends, patterns, and needs, managers use planned change to help the organization adapt to external problems and opportunities.[6] When organizations are caught flat-footed, failing to anticipate or respond to new needs, management is at fault.

An overall model for planned change is presented in Exhibit 12.1. Four events make up the change sequence: (1) Internal and external forces for change exist; (2) organization managers monitor these forces and become aware of a need for change; and (3) the perceived need triggers the initiation of change, which (4) is then implemented. How each of these activities is handled depends on the organization and managers' styles.

We now turn to a brief discussion of the specific activities associated with the first two events—forces for change and the perceived need for the organization to respond.

Forces for Change

Forces for organizational change exist both in the external environment and within the organization.

Exhibit *12.1* *Model of Change Sequence of Events*

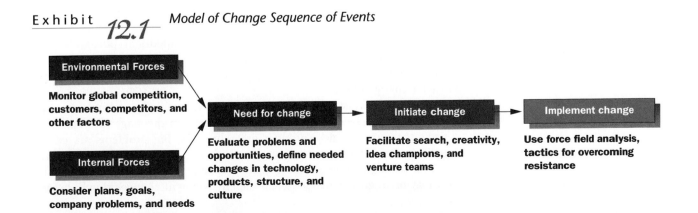

Environmental Forces.   As described in Chapters 3 and 4, external forces originate in all environmental sectors, including customers, competitors, technology, economic forces, and the international arena. For example, many North American companies have been blindsided by global competition. Consider General Electric, which built a new factory to produce microwave ovens. As GE's plans were being made, Yun Soo Chu was working 80 hours per week for Samsung in Korea to perfect a microwave oven. About the time the GE plant came on stream, Samsung started exporting thousands of microwaves to the United States at one-third the cost of GE microwaves. Today, Samsung has 25 percent of the U.S. market, and GE is one of its best customers. GE closed its microwave plant, preferring to buy the cheaper Samsung ovens to sell under the GE label.[7] After three engineers started Ensoniq Corporation to produce home computers, they experienced an external force of low consumer demand and switched product lines to electronic keyboards. Using innovative technologies, Ensoniq's founders produced an affordable Mirage keyboard, enabling people with various musical talents as well as the untalented to make music. Ensoniq responded to other environmental needs by producing the Sound Selector hearing aid, which is programmable to meet the particular needs of each individual.[8]

Internal Forces.   Internal forces for change arise from internal activities and decisions. If top managers select a goal of rapid company growth, internal actions will have to be changed to meet that growth. New departments or technologies will be created. General Motors' senior management, frustrated by poor internal efficiency, designed the Saturn manufacturing plant to solve this internal need. Demands by employees, labor unions, and production inefficiencies all can generate a force to which management must respond with change.

Need for Change

As indicated in Exhibit 12.1, external or internal forces translate into a perceived need for change within the organization.[9] Managers sense a need for change when there is a **performance gap**—a disparity between existing and desired performance levels. The performance gap may occur because current procedures are not up to standard or because a new idea or technology could improve current performance. Managers try to establish a sense of urgency so that others will understand the need for change. Sometimes a crisis, such as the one described in the opening example of Midwest, provides an undoubted sense of urgency. In many cases, however, there is no obvious crisis and managers have to recognize and then make others aware of the need for change.[10] Recall from Chapter 8 that management's responsibility is to monitor threats and opportunities in the external environment as well as strengths and weaknesses within the organization to determine whether a need for change exists.

Managers in every company must be alert to problems and opportunities, because the perceived need for change is what sets the stage for subsequent actions that create a new product or technology. Big problems are easy to spot. Sensitive monitoring systems are needed to detect gradual changes that can fool managers into thinking their company is doing fine. An organization may be in greater danger when the environment changes slowly, because

performance gap
A disparity between existing and desired performance levels.

managers may fail to trigger an organizational response. Failing to use planned change to meet small needs can place the organization in hot water, as illustrated in the following passage:

> When frogs are placed in a boiling pail of water, they jump out—they don't want to boil to death. However, when frogs are placed in a cold pail of water, and the pail is placed on a stove with the heat turned very low, over time the frogs will boil to death.[11]

search
The process of learning about current developments inside or outside the organization that can be used to meet a perceived need for change.

creativity
The generation of novel ideas that may meet perceived needs or offer opportunities for the organization.

Initiating Change

After the need for change has been perceived and communicated the next part of the change process is initiating change, a truly critical aspect of change management. This is where the ideas that solve perceived needs are developed. Responses that an organization can make are to search for or create a change to adopt.

Search

Search is the process of learning about current developments inside or outside the organization that can be used to meet the perceived need for change. Search typically uncovers existing knowledge that can be applied or adopted within the organization. Managers talk to friends and colleagues, read professional reports, or hire consultants to learn about ideas used elsewhere.

Many needs, however, cannot be resolved through existing knowledge but require that the organization develop a new response. Initiating a new response means that managers must design the organization so as to facilitate creativity of both individuals and departments, encourage innovative people to initiate new ideas, or create new-venture departments. These techniques have been adopted by such corporations as GE and Apple with great success.

Creativity

Creativity is the generation of novel ideas that may meet perceived needs or respond to opportunities for the organization. Creativity is the essential first step in innovation, which is vital to long-term organizational success.[12] People noted for their creativity include Edwin Land, who invented the Polaroid camera; Frederick Smith, who came up with the idea for Federal Express's overnight delivery service during an undergraduate class at Yale; and Swiss engineer George de Mestral, who created Velcro after noticing the tiny hooks on the burrs caught on his wool socks. Each of these people saw unique and creative opportunities in a familiar situation.

Each of us has the capacity to be creative. Characteristics of highly creative people are illustrated in the left-hand column of Exhibit 12.2. Creative people often are known for originality, open-mindedness, curiosity, a focused approach to problem solving, persistence, a relaxed and playful attitude, and receptivity to new ideas.[13]

Creativity can also be designed into organizations. Companies or departments within companies can be organized to be creative and initiate changes. Most companies want more highly creative employees and often seek to hire creative individuals. However, the individual is only part of the story, and everyone has

CEO Robert Benmosche is initiating change at Metropolitan Life Insurance Co. His search discovered the need to change the company that had operated as a mutual company since 1915 and led to a plan to go public, or "demutualize." Employees play an intrinsic role in his plan, which includes energizing the company culture. Benmosche is known to be at his best when mixing with the troops, as in the photo taken at a corporate retreat in Puerto Rico. Recently he spent four hours at a conference center encouraging the creativity of some 40 branch managers to find solutions for company problems. Benmosche has boosted productivity per MetLife sales agent from $19,000 to $23,000, while sales practice and service complaints are down 50 percent from their peak in 1994.

Technological creativity is not new to Charles Schwab. The company's Pocketerm, a chunky hand-held device that downloads stock quotes, dates back to 1982. But Schwab's latest creative venture into cutting-edge technology is its investing Web site, www.schwab.com, which invented a new kind of brokerage and reshaped the firm. The Web site is responsible for more than $4 billion worth of security trades each week. It was designed by Hyo Yeon and Arun Bordoloi (of Razorfish, a web site design firm in New York), whose creativity gave the site a consistent look and made it easy to navigate.

some potential for creativity. Managers are responsible for creating a work environment that allows creativity to flourish.[14] The characteristics of creative organizations correspond to those of individuals, as illustrated in the right-hand column of Exhibit 12.2. Creative organizations are loosely structured. People find themselves in a situation of ambiguity, assignments are vague, territories overlap, tasks are poorly defined, and much work is done through teams.[15] Creative organizations have an internal culture of playfulness, freedom, challenge, and grass-roots participation.[16] They harness all potential sources of new ideas from within. Many participative management programs are born out of the desire to enhance creativity for initiating changes. People are not stuck in the rhythm of routine jobs.

The most creative companies embrace risk and encourage employees to make mistakes. Jim Read, president of the Read Corporation, says, "When my employees make mistakes trying to improve something, I give them a round of applause. No mistakes mean no new products. If they ever become afraid to make one, my company is doomed."[17]

Open channels of communication, overlapping jobs, discretionary resources, decentralization, and employees' freedom to choose problems and make mistakes can generate unexpected benefits for companies. Creative organizational conditions such as those described in Exhibit 12.2 enable more than 200 new products a year to bubble up from 3M's research labs.

The same creative conditions enabled the project team working on the NASA/Jet Propulsion Laboratory's Mars Pathfinder to find better, faster, and cheaper ways of doing things. When the Pathfinder landed on July 4, 1997,

Exhibit
12.2

Characteristics of Creative People and Organizations

SOURCE: Based on Gary A. Steiner, ed., *The Creative Organization* (Chicago: University of Chicago Press, 1965), 16–18; Rosabeth Moss Kanter, "The Middle Manager as Innovator," *Harvard Business Review* (July–August 1982), 104–105; and James Brian Quinn, "Managing Innovation: Controlled Chaos," *Harvard Business Review* 63 (May–June 1985), 73–84.

The Creative Individual	The Creative Organization or Department

1. Conceptual fluency
   Open-mindedness
	1. Open channels of communication
	   Contact with outside sources
	   Overlapping territories
	   Suggestion systems, brainstorming, group techniques

2. Originality	2. Assignment of nonspecialists to problems
	   Eccentricity allowed
	   Use of teams

3. Less authority
   Independence
	3. Decentralization, loosely defined positions, loose control
	   Acceptance of mistakes
	   Risk-taking norms

4. Playfulness
   Undisciplined exploration
   Curiosity
	4. Freedom to choose and pursue problems
	   Not a tight ship, playful culture
	   Freedom to discuss ideas, long time horizon

5. Persistence
   Commitment
   Focused approach
	5. Resources allocated to creative personnel and projects without immediate payoff
	   Reward system encourages innovation
	   Absolution of peripheral responsibilities

Making Creative Sparks Fly

Jerry Hirshberg argues that sometimes the right person for the job is two people. Hirshberg's world-renowned design studio, Nissan Design International, hires people in what he calls *divergent pairs*—people who see the world in totally different ways. Consider Tom Semple and Allan Flowers. Semple searches for "artistic intuition" when he starts to work on the design of a new car. He likes to clear away all traces of earlier projects, start with a blank piece of paper, and invent entirely new forms. Flowers, on the other hand, worries about nuts and bolts. He conducts a methodical assessment of components and materials, schedules and priorities. Semple and Flowers are one of about two dozen odd couples creating the vehicles of the future at NDI. Teaming people with widely different perspectives produces what Hirshberg calls "creative abrasion," a kind of friction that produces wildly creative sparks. Those sparks have been flying at NDI for more than 20 years, producing such trendsetting innovations as the Nissan Pathfinder and the Infiniti series.

Hirshberg's ideas about hiring in divergent pairs began by accident. After Nissan recruited him from General Motors in the late 1970s to create its first design studio in the United States, he needed to find great designers to work with him. Semple and Flowers agreed to join the firm—but that's about the only thing they did agree on. "They were spectacularly gifted but utterly different," Hirshberg says. "They were from different solar systems." However, Hirshberg noticed that the creative tension between the two spawned a vitality that quickly began paying off in good ideas. Today, hiring in divergent pairs has become an organizing principle of NDI, which has grown to about 50 design professionals. Whereas one divergent pair sets off sparks, Hirshberg believes that 25 such pairs create an organization with unlimited potential for creativity.

SOURCE: Katharine Mieszkowski, "Opposites Attract," *Fast Company*, December–January 1998, 42, 44.

millions watched as the Sojourner rover explored the rocky planet for clues to the evolution of Mars and hints to whether life could have existed there. The project took only 44 months from start to touchdown, compared to the seven years it had taken to complete the 1976 Viking mission to Mars. In addition to saving time and money, the Pathfinder team achieved innovative engineering feats and scientific breakthroughs by fostering conditions that allowed creativity to flourish. The team set ambitious goals, made a commitment to extensive communication and information sharing, and encouraged eccentricity and diverse perspectives.[18] The Leadership box describes a unique approach to sparking creativity by teaming people with dramatically different perspectives.

Idea Champions and New-Venture Teams

If creative conditions are successful, new ideas will be generated that must be carried forward for acceptance and implementation. This is where idea champions come in. The formal definition of an **idea champion** is a person who sees the need for and champions productive change within the organization. For example, Bonnie McKeever of Federal Express championed the idea of a coalition of companies to combat mounting medical fees. The Memphis Business Group on Health was created, saving its members an estimated tens of millions of dollars through competitive bidding and discounts.[19] Wendy Black of Best Western International championed the idea of coordinating the corporate mailings to the company's 2,800 hoteliers into a single packet every two weeks. Some hotels were receiving three special mailings a day from different departments. Her idea saved $600,000 a year for five years in postage alone.[20]

idea champion
A person who sees the need for and champions productive change within the organization.

Remember: Change does not occur by itself. Personal energy and effort are required to successfully promote a new idea. Often a new idea is rejected by management. Champions are passionately committed to a new product or idea despite rejection by others.

Championing an idea successfully requires roles in organizations, as illustrated in Exhibit 12.3. Sometimes a single person may play two or more of these roles, but successful innovation in most companies involves an interplay of different people, each adopting one role. The *inventor* develops a new idea and understands its technical value but has neither the ability nor the interest to promote it for acceptance within the organization. The *champion* believes in the idea, confronts the organizational realities of costs and benefits, and gains the political and financial support needed to bring it to reality. The *sponsor* is a high-level manager who approves the idea, protects the idea, and removes major organizational barriers to acceptance. The *critic* counterbalances the zeal of the champion by challenging the concept and providing a reality test against hard-nosed criteria. The critic prevents people in the other roles from adopting a bad idea.[21]

Managers can directly influence whether champions will flourish. When Texas Instruments studied 50 of its new-product introductions, a surprising fact emerged: Without exception, every new product that had failed had lacked a zealous champion. In contrast, most of the new products that succeeded had a champion. Texas Instruments' managers made an immediate decision: No new product would be approved unless someone championed it.

new-venture team
A unit separate from the mainstream of the organization that is responsible for developing and initiating innovations.

A recent idea for facilitating corporate innovation is known as a new-venture team. A **new-venture team** is a unit separate from the rest of the organization and is responsible for developing and initiating a major innovation.[22] New-venture teams give free reign to members' creativity because their separate facilities and location free them from organizational rules and procedures. These teams typically are small, loosely structured, and flexible, reflecting the characteristics of creative organizations described in Exhibit 12.2. Peter Drucker advises organizations that wish to innovate to use a separate team or department:

Exhibit **12.3**   *Four Roles in Organizational Change*

Inventor	Champion	Sponsor	Critic
Develops and understands technical aspects of idea Does not know how to win support for the idea or make a business of it	Believes in idea Visualizes benefits Confronts organizational realities of cost, benefits Obtains financial and political support Overcomes obstacles	High-level manager who removes organizational barriers Approves and protects idea within organization	Provides reality test Looks for shortcomings Defines hard-nosed criteria that idea must pass

SOURCES: Based on Harold L. Angle and Andrew H. Van de Ven, "Suggestions for Managing the Innovation Journey," in *Research in the Management of Innovation: The Minnesota Studies,* ed. A. H. Van de Ven, H. L. Angle, and Marshall Scott Poole (Cambridge, Mass.: Ballinger/Harper & Row, 1989); and Jay R. Galbraith, "Designing the Innovating Organization," *Organizational Dynamics* (winter 1982), 5–25.

For the existing business to be capable of innovation, it has to create a structure that allows people to be entrepreneurial.... This means, first, that the entrepreneurial, the new, has to be organized separately from the old and the existing. Whenever we have tried to make an existing unit the carrier of the entrepreneurial project, we have failed.[23]

The new-venture team is quite different from the horizontal relationships or the matrix structure described in Chapter 10. In those structures, employees remain members of their everyday departments and simply work on a project part-time while reporting to their regular boss. Under the new-venture team concept, employees no longer report through the normal structure.[24] New-venture teams are kept small and separate to ensure that no bureaucracy will intrude.

Xerox Corporation's Palo Alto Research Center (PARC) is responsible for hatching new ideas that are either used by Xerox or spun off into separate ventures. New entrepreneurial ventures under the Xerox New Enterprises umbrella include Documentum, a family of open client-server programs that organize corporate knowledge so that it can be reused easily, and Dpix, which produces flat-panel displays that generate graphics and text almost as clear as a printed page.[25] Other companies that have created new-venture units are Monsanto, Levi Strauss, and Exxon. 3M utilizes action teams to create new products. The action team concept allows individuals with new product ideas to recruit team members from throughout the company. These people may end up running the newly created division if the idea is successful.[26]

One variation of new-venture teams is the **new-venture fund,** which provides resources from which individuals and groups can draw to develop new ideas, products, or businesses. For example, Lockheed-Martin has discovered that it's better to tap into rather than resist its employees' entrepreneurial urges. Employees can take two years of unpaid leave to explore new ideas, using the company's labs and paying company rates for health insurance. If the idea is successful, Lockheed-Martin's venture-capital group invests about $250,000 in the start-up company. One successful start-up is Genase, which creates and sells an enzyme that "stonewashes" denim.[27]

new-venture fund
A fund providing resources from which individuals and groups draw to develop new ideas, products, or businesses.

Implementing Change

Creative culture, idea champions, and new-venture teams are ways to facilitate the initiation of new ideas. The other step to be managed in the change process is implementation. A new, creative idea will not benefit the organization until it is in place and being fully utilized. One frustration for managers is that employees often seem to resist change for no apparent reason. To effectively manage the implementation process, managers should be aware of the reasons for employee resistance and be prepared to use techniques for obtaining employee cooperation. Major, corporate-wide changes can be particularly difficult, as discussed in the Manager's Shoptalk box.

Resistance to Change

Idea champions often discover that other employees are unenthusiastic about their new ideas. Members of a new-venture group may be surprised when managers in the regular organization do not support or approve their innovations.

Making Change Stick

Employees are not always receptive to change. A combination of factors can lead to rejection of, or even outright rebellion against, management's "new and better ideas."

Land's End, Inc., of Dodgeville, Wisconsin, began as a small mail-order business specializing in sailing gear. Employees enjoyed the family-like atmosphere and uncomplicated work environment. By 1994, the company had mushroomed into a $1 billion company with several overseas outlets and had passed giant L. L. Bean as number one in specialty catalog sales in the United States.

Such success encouraged founder and chairman Gary Comer to embark on a dramatic management experiment incorporating many of today's trends—teams, 401k plans, peer reviews, and the elimination of guards and time clocks. Comer brought in top talent, including former L. L. Bean executive William T. End as CEO, to implement the changes.

But employees balked. Weekly production meetings became a nuisance to workers. "We spent so much time in meetings that we were getting away from the basic stuff of taking care of business," says one employee. Even a much-ballyhooed new mission statement seemed "pushy." One long-time employee complained that "we don't need anything hanging over our heads telling us to do something we're already doing."

Confusion and frustration reigned at Land's End and was reflected in an earnings drop of 17 percent. By the end of December 1994, End was forced out, and a new CEO initiated a return to the familiar "Land's End Way" of doing things. Teams were disbanded and many of the once-promising initiatives shelved as workers embraced what was familiar and uncomplicated.

The inability of people to adapt to change is not new. Neither is the failure of management to sufficiently lay the groundwork to prepare employees for change. Harvard professor John P. Kotter established an eight-step plan for implementing change that can provide a greater potential for successful transformation of a company:

1. Establish a sense of urgency through careful examination of the market and identification of opportunities and potential crises.
2. Form a powerful coalition of managers able to lead the change.
3. Create a vision to direct the change and the strategies for achieving that vision.
4. Communicate the vision throughout the organization.
5. Empower others to act on the vision by removing barriers, changing systems, and encouraging risk taking.
6. Plan for visible, short-term performance improvements and create those improvements.
7. Consolidate improvements, reassess changes, and make necessary adjustments in the new programs.
8. Articulate the relationship between new behaviors and organizational success.

Major change efforts can be messy and full of surprises, but following these guidelines can break down resistance and mean the difference between success and failure.

SOURCES: Gregory A. Patterson, "Land's End Kicks Out Modern New Managers, Rejecting a Makeover," *The Wall Street Journal,* April 3, 1995, A1, A6; and John P. Kotter, "Leading Changes: Why Transformation Efforts Fail," *Harvard Business Review* (March–April 1995), 59–67.

Managers and employees not involved in an innovation often seem to prefer the status quo. Employees appear to resist change for several reasons, and understanding them helps managers implement change more effectively.

Self-Interest.   Employees typically resist a change they believe will take away something of value. A proposed change in job design, structure, or technology may lead to a perceived loss of power, prestige, pay, or company benefits. The fear of personal loss is perhaps the biggest obstacle to organizational change.[28] When Mesa Oil Corporation tried to buy Phillips Petroleum, Phillips employees started a campaign to prevent the takeover. Employees believed that Mesa would not treat them well and that they would lose financial benefits. Their resistance to change was so effective that the merger failed to take place.

Lack of Understanding and Trust.   Employees often do not understand the intended purpose of a change or distrust the intentions behind it.

If previous working relationships with an idea champion have been negative, resistance may occur. One manager had a habit of initiating a change in the financial reporting system about every 12 months and then losing interest and not following through. After the third time, employees no longer went along with the change because they did not trust the manager's intention to follow through to their benefit.

Uncertainty. *Uncertainty* is the lack of information about future events. It represents a fear of the unknown. Uncertainty is especially threatening for employees who have a low tolerance for change and fear the novel and unusual. They do not know how a change will affect them and worry about whether they will be able to meet the demands of a new procedure or technology.[29] Union leaders at General Motors' Steering Gear Division in Saginaw, Michigan, resisted the introduction of employee participation programs. They were uncertain about how the program would affect their status and thus initially opposed it.

Different Assessments and Goals. Another reason for resistance to change is that people who will be affected by innovation may assess the situation differently from an idea champion or new-venture group. Often critics voice legitimate disagreements over the proposed benefits of a change. Managers in each department pursue different goals, and an innovation may detract from performance and goal achievement for some departments. For example, if marketing gets the new product it wants for its customers, the cost of manufacturing may increase, and the manufacturing superintendent thus will resist. Resistance may call attention to problems with the innovation. At a consumer products company in Racine, Wisconsin, middle managers resisted the introduction of a new employee program that turned out to be a bad idea. The managers truly believed that the program would do more harm than good. One manager bluntly told his boss, "I've been here longer than you, and I'll be here after you've gone, so don't tell me what really counts at this company."[30]

These reasons for resistance are legitimate in the eyes of employees affected by the change. The best procedure for managers is not to ignore resistance but to diagnose the reasons and design strategies to gain acceptance by users.[31] Strategies for overcoming resistance to change typically involve two approaches: the analysis of resistance through the force field technique and the use of selective implementation tactics to overcome resistance.

Force Field Analysis

Force field analysis grew from the work of Kurt Lewin, who proposed that change was a result of the competition between *driving* and *restraining* forces.[32] When a change is introduced, some forces drive it and other forces resist it. To implement a change, management should analyze the change forces. By selectively removing forces that restrain change, the driving forces will be strong enough to enable implementation, as illustrated by the move from A to B in Exhibit 12.4. As restraining forces are reduced or removed, behavior will shift to incorporate the desired changes.

Just-in-time (JIT) inventory control systems schedule materials to arrive at a company just as they are needed on the production line. In an Ohio

force field analysis
The process of determining which forces drive and which resist a proposed change.

Exhibit

Exhibit **12.4** *Using Force Field Analysis to Change from Traditional to Just-in-Time Inventory System*

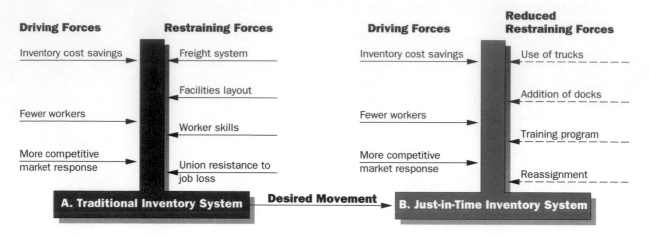

manufacturing company, management's analysis showed that the driving forces associated with the implementation of JIT were (1) the large cost savings from reduced inventories, (2) savings from needing fewer workers to handle the inventory, and (3) a quicker, more competitive market response for the company. Restraining forces discovered by managers were (1) a freight system that was too slow to deliver inventory on time, (2) a facility layout that emphasized inventory maintenance over new deliveries, (3) worker skills inappropriate for handling rapid inventory deployment, and (4) union resistance to loss of jobs. The driving forces were not sufficient to overcome the restraining forces.

To shift the behavior to JIT, managers attacked the restraining forces. An analysis of the freight system showed that delivery by truck provided the flexibility and quickness needed to schedule inventory arrival at a specific time each day. The problem with facility layout was met by adding four new loading docks. Inappropriate worker skills were attacked with a training program to instruct workers in JIT methods and in assembling products with uninspected parts. Union resistance was overcome by agreeing to reassign workers no longer needed for maintaining inventory to jobs in another plant. With the restraining forces reduced, the driving forces were sufficient to allow the JIT system to be implemented.

Implementation Tactics

The other approach to managing implementation is to adopt specific tactics to overcome employee resistance. For example, resistance to change may be overcome by educating employees or inviting them to participate in implementing the change. Methods for dealing with resistance to change have been studied by researchers. The following five tactics, summarized in Exhibit 12.5, have proven successful.[33]

Communication and Education. *Communication* and *education* are used when solid information about the change is needed by users and others who may resist implementation. Education is especially important when

Approach	When to Use
Communication, education	• Change is technical. • Users need accurate information and analysis to understand change.
Participation	• Users need to feel involved. • Design requires information from others. • Users have power to resist.
Negotiation	• Group has power over implementation. • Group will lose out in the change.
Coercion	• A crisis exists. • Initiators clearly have power. • Other implementation techniques have failed.
Top management support	• Change involves multiple departments or reallocation of resources. • Users doubt legitimacy of change.

Exhibit 12.5

Tactics for Overcoming Resistance to Change

Source: Based on J. P. Kotter and L. A. Schlesinger, "Choosing Strategies for Change," *Harvard Business Review* 57 (March–April 1979), 106–114.

the change involves new technical knowledge or users are unfamiliar with the idea. Canadian Airlines International spent a year and a half preparing and training employees before changing its entire reservations, airport, cargo, and financial systems as part of a new "Service Quality" strategy. Smooth implementation resulted from this intensive training and communications effort, which involved 50,000 tasks, 12,000 people, and 26 classrooms around the world.[34]

Participation. *Participation* involves users and potential resisters in designing the change. This approach is time-consuming, but it pays off because users understand and become committed to the change. Participation also helps managers determine potential problems and understand the differences in perceptions of change among employees.[35] When General Motors tried to implement a new management appraisal system for supervisors in its Adrian, Michigan, plant, it met with immediate resistance. Rebuffed by the lack of cooperation, top managers proceeded more slowly, involving supervisors in the design of the new appraisal system. Through participation in system design, managers understood what the new approach was all about and dropped their resistance to it.

Negotiation. Negotiation is a more formal means of achieving cooperation. *Negotiation* uses formal bargaining to win acceptance and approval of a desired change. For example, if the marketing department fears losing power if a new management structure is implemented, top managers may negotiate with marketing to reach a resolution. General Motors, General Electric, and other companies that have strong unions frequently must formally negotiate change with the unions. The change may become part of the union contract reflecting the agreement of both parties.

Coercion. *Coercion* means that managers use formal power to force employees to change. Resisters are told to accept the change or lose rewards or even their jobs. In most cases, this approach should not be used because employees feel like victims, are angry at change managers, and may even sabotage the changes. However, coercion may be necessary in crisis situations when a rapid response is urgent. When middle managers at TRW, Inc.'s Valve

Herman Wright, PruCare of Austin's director of sales and marketing, shown here with his sales and service staff, knows that top management support is essential to overcoming resistance to change. In PruCare's thrust toward customer satisfaction, Wright used the implementation tactics of communication and participation. He communicated his desire to build customer relationships based on trust and then pushed responsibility down to everyone in the organization: "We stopped telling people what to do and started listening."

Division in Cleveland refused to go along with a new employee involvement program, top management reassigned several first-line supervisors and managers. The new jobs did not involve supervisory responsibility. Further, other TRW managers were told that future pay increases depended on their adoption of the new procedures. The coercive techniques were used as a last resort because managers refused to go along with the change any other way.[36]

Top Management Support.   The visible support of top management also helps overcome resistance to change. *Top management support* symbolizes to all employees that the change is important for the organization. Top management support is especially important when a change involves multiple departments or when resources are being reallocated among departments. Without top management support, these changes can get bogged down in squabbling among departments. Moreover, when top managers fail to support a project, they can inadvertently undercut it by issuing contradictory orders. This happened at Flying Tiger Lines before it was acquired by Federal Express. The airborne freight hauler came up with a plan to eliminate excessive paperwork by changing the layout of offices so that two agents rather than four could handle each shipment. No sooner had part of the change been implemented than top management ordered another system; thus, the office layout was changed again. The new layout was not as efficient, but it was the one that top management supported. Had middle managers informed top managers and obtained their support earlier, the initial change would not have been defeated by a new priority.[37]

The following example illustrates how smart implementation techniques can smooth the change process.

GENERAL STAIR CORPORATION

General Stair Corp., a maker of prefabricated stairs and railings, was facing a desperate situation in the mid-1990s. Competition was increasing, and General Stair's profit and market share were declining. The company found itself dealing with a constant price war. Founder Saby Behar wanted to find a way to keep his customers less focused on price. To distinguish his company from the competition, Behar decided General Stair should start offering a money-back delivery guarantee, something he knew his customers (who often worked on 30 or more buildings at a time) would appreciate. However, managers and other employees were aghast at the suggestion. Workers weren't sure they could meet the requirements for such a guarantee and were concerned that it might require more overtime. Managers worried about the cost of upgrading communications systems for field reps to stay in touch with headquarters as well as builders and contractors.

Implementation of the change involved several steps. To combat the initial resistance among his managers, Behar held several meetings explaining his reasons for making the change and answering managers' questions. This at least got people talking about whether and how such a guarantee could actually work. Next, managers brought in the rest of the employees to discuss the proposed change and how to put it into action. They knew they had to revamp communications, but discussions with employees led them to realize other systems, such as distribution and compensation, needed to change as well. In addition, rather than a complete money-back guarantee, the group eventually settled on a fine of $50 per day for late deliveries. Although the company already had a good on-time delivery record, employees were trained in new procedures that would help assure consistent performance.

Because top management involved employees from the early stages, the changes went smoothly. Labor costs were slashed by 30 percent, even though employees were earning up to 60 percent more money because of a new piece-rate system. Productivity was up 300 percent. And, within the first year, the company had to pay out only a few $50 vouchers for late deliveries. General Stair's market share and profits are once again looking healthy.[38]

Types of Planned Change

Now that we have explored how the initiation and implementation of change can be carried out, let us look at the different types of change that occur in organizations. We will address two issues: what parts of the organization can be changed and how managers can apply the initiation and implementation ideas to each type of change.

The types of organizational change are strategy, technology, products, structure, and culture/people, as illustrated in Exhibit 12.6. Organizations may innovate in one or more areas, depending on internal and external forces for change. In the rapidly changing toy industry, a manufacturer has to introduce new products frequently. In a mature, competitive industry, production technology changes are adopted to improve efficiency. The arrows connecting the types of change in Exhibit 12.6 show that a change in one part may affect other parts of the organization: A new product may require changes in technology, and a new technology may require new people skills or a new

Exhibit *12.6*

Types of Organizational Change

SOURCE: Based on Harold J. Leavitt, "Applied Organizational Change in Industry: Structural, Technical, and Human Approaches," in *New Perspectives in Organization Research,* ed. W. W. Cooper, H. J. Leavitt, and M. W. Shelly II (New York: Wiley, 1964), 55–74.

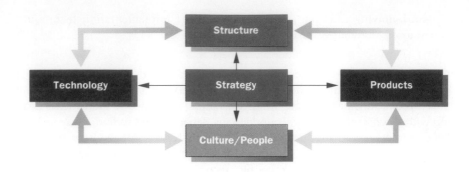

structure. For example, when Shenandoah Life Insurance Company computerized processing and claims operations, the structure had to be decentralized, employees required intensive training, and a more participative culture was needed. Related changes were required for the new technology to increase efficiency.

Technology Changes

technology change
A change that pertains to the organization's production process.

Technology changes *in computers and aircraft design allow Boeing Company aircraft designers to skip the paper drawings and work in teams with input from the airlines, mechanics, and marketers. These Boeing designers working on the 777 wide-body, twin-jet program can use the new technology to reduce errors through digital design and preassembly. A three-dimensional digital mechanic can crawl through on-screen aircraft images to locate defects. This technology allows designers to test innovative ideas without the cost of building a full mock-up.*

A **technology change** is related to the organization's production process—how the organization does its work. Technology changes are designed to make the production of a product or service more efficient. For example, the adoption of robotics to improve production efficiency at General Motors is an example of a technology change, as is the adoption of laser-scanning checkout systems at supermarkets. At IBM's manufacturing plant in Charlotte, North Carolina, an automated miniload storage and retrieval system was installed to handle production parts. This change provided an efficient method for handling small-parts inventory and changed the technology of the IBM plant.

How can managers encourage technology change? The general rule is that technology change is bottom up.[39] The *bottom-up approach* means that ideas are initiated at lower organization levels and channeled upward for approval. Lower-level technical experts act as idea champions—they invent and champion technological changes. Employees at lower levels understand the technology and have the expertise needed to propose changes. For example, at Dana Corporation's Elizabethtown, Kentucky, plant, two workers came up with an idea for automatically loading steel sheets into a forming press. This technology change saves the auto-parts maker $250,000 a year.[40]

Managers can facilitate the bottom-up approach by designing creative departments as described earlier in this chapter. A loose, flexible, decentralized structure provides employees with the freedom and opportunity to initiate continuous improvements. A rigid, centralized, standardized structure stifles technology innovation. Anything managers can do to involve the grass roots of the organization—the people who are experts in their parts of the production process—will increase technology change. Great Harvest Bread Company encourages bottom-up change among its franchisees by giving them almost complete freedom to run their businesses as they see fit. This freedom inspires new and better ways of doing things that quickly spread to other stores by phone, fax, and E-mail. "Innovation happens overnight in our company," says co-founder Laura Wakeman.[41]

A *top-down approach* to technology change usually does not work.[42] Top managers are not close to the production process and lack expertise in technological developments. Mandating technology change from the top produces fewer rather than more technology innovations. The spark for a creative new idea comes from people close to the technology. The rationale behind Motorola's "participative management program," Data General's "pride teams," and Honeywell's "positive action teams" is to encourage new technology ideas from people at lower levels of the organization.

New-Product Changes

A **product change** is a change in the organization's product or service output. New-product innovations have major implications for an organization, because they often are an outcome of a new strategy and may define a new market.[43] In addition, product life cycles are getting shorter, so that companies need to continuously come up with innovative ideas for new products and services that meet needs in the marketplace. Product innovation is the primary way in which many organizations adapt to changes in markets, technologies, and competition.[44] Examples of new products include Frappuccino, a bottled drink from Starbuck's, Apple Computer's new iMac, and Gillette's MACH3 triple-bladed razor.

product change
A change in the organization's product or service output.

Introducing a new product is not easy, but hundreds of new products are introduced every day. Even though the cost of successfully launching a new product is $20 million to $50 million, approximately 25,000 new products appeared in 1997 alone. The majority of those products will fail in the marketplace—the most optimistic estimate is that one in five launches will succeed, while the most pessimistic forecast is for one out of 671. Consider such flops as Gerber's "Singles" meals for adults, which looked like jars of baby food, or Nestea's launch of a yellowish carbonated beverage called Tea Whiz.[45] Product development is a risky, high-stakes game for organizations. Companies that successfully develop new products usually have the following characteristics:

1. People in marketing have a good understanding of customer needs.

2. Technical specialists are aware of recent technological developments and make effective use of new technology.

3. Members from key departments—research, manufacturing, marketing—cooperate in the development of the new product.[46]

These findings mean that the ideas for new products typically originate at the lower levels of the organization just as they do for technology changes. The difference is that new-product ideas flow horizontally among departments. Product innovation requires expertise from several departments simultaneously. A new-product failure is often the result of failed cooperation.[47]

One approach to successful new-product innovation is called the **horizontal linkage model,** which is illustrated in Exhibit 12.7.[48] The model shows that research, manufacturing, and marketing must simultaneously develop new products. People from these departments meet frequently in teams and task forces to share ideas and solve problems. Research people inform marketing of new technical developments to learn whether they will be useful to customers. Marketing people pass customer complaints to research to use in the design of new products. Manufacturing informs other

horizontal linkage model
An approach to product change that emphasizes shared development of innovations among several departments.

E x h i b i t *12.7*

Horizontal Linkage Model for
New-Product Innovation

departments whether a product idea can be manufactured within cost limits. When the horizontal linkage model is used, the decision to develop a new product is a joint one.

Today's increasingly sophisticated consumer is demanding an ever increasing role in product development and marketing. Empowerment in today's competitive environment goes beyond employees to include suppliers and customers in the product development process. Entire industries, such as automakers, are actively soliciting consumer feedback for new products and are including consumer participation from the beginning of the design process. Marketing departments have been surveying customers for years to determine what they want and need. A new approach is to actually *observe* customers using products or services in their normal, everyday routines in order to gather information about unarticulated customer desires. For example, after visiting the homes of customers, Kimberly-Clark recognized the emotional appeal of pull-on diapers and invented Huggies Pull-Ups. By the time competitors caught on, the company was selling $400 million worth of the product annually.[49] This type of consumer research requires creative interaction among many departments, which is characteristic of the horizontal linkage model.

Horizontal linkages are being adopted in the computer industry to overcome new-product problems. For example, at Convergent Technologies, Workslate, a portable computer, received accolades when it was introduced. One year later, Workslate was dead. Production problems with the new product had not been worked out. Marketing people had not fully analyzed customer needs. The idea had been pushed through without sufficient consultation among research, manufacturing, and marketing. IBM PC Company changed its approach to new product development to reduce development time. New products are now created by teams of workers from research, design, procurement, logistics, marketing, and manufacturing—all working side-by-side in one location rather than being spread out across the country as they were before.[50]

Innovation is becoming a major strategic weapon in the global marketplace. One example of innovation is the use of **time-based competition,** which means delivering products and services faster than competitors, giving companies a significant strategic advantage. For example, Hewlett-Packard reduced the time to develop a new printer from 4.5 years to 22 months. Lenscrafters jumped from 3 to 300 stores based on its ability to provide quality eyeglasses in one hour. Dillard's department stores went to an automatic reorder system that replenishes stocks in 12 days rather than 30, providing retail goods to customers more quickly.[51] Sprinting to market with a new product requires a *parallel approach,* or *simultaneous linkage* among departments. This is similar to a rugby match wherein players run together,

time-based competition
A strategy of competition based on the ability to deliver products and services faster than competitors.

passing the ball back and forth as they move downfield. The teamwork required for the horizontal linkage model is a major component of using rapid innovation to beat the competition with speed.[52]

Structural Changes

Structural changes involve the hierarchy of authority, goals, structural characteristics, administrative procedures, and management systems.[53] Almost any change in how the organization is managed falls under the category of structural change. For example, to turn things around at Owens Corning, CEO Glen Hiner completely revamped how the company sells and services products, implemented a new information-management system that connects all the information that flows through the company in a single system, and radically restructured human resources and compensation plans.[54] IBM's change from a functional to a product structure was a structural change. The implementation of a no-smoking policy usually is considered a structural or an administrative change.

Successful structural change is accomplished through a top-down approach, which is distinct from technology change (bottom up) and new products (horizontal).[55] Structural change is top down because the expertise for administrative improvements originates at the middle and upper levels of the organization. The champions for structural change are middle and top managers. Lower-level technical specialists have little interest or expertise in administrative procedures. If organization structure causes negative consequences for lower-level employees, complaints and dissatisfaction alert managers to a problem. Employee dissatisfaction is an internal force for change. The need for change is perceived by higher managers, who then take the initiative to propose and implement it.

The top-down process does not mean that coercion is the best implementation tactic. Implementation tactics include education, participation, and negotiation with employees. Unless there is an emergency, managers should not force structural change on employees. They may hit a resistance wall, and the change will fail. This is exactly what happened at the company for which Mary Kay Ash worked before she started her own cosmetics business. The owner learned that even a top-down change in commission rate needs to incorporate education and participation to succeed:

> I worked for a company whose owner decided to revise the commission schedule paid to his sales managers. . . . To an audience of 50 sales managers he announced that the 2 percent override they were presently earning on their units' sales production was to be reduced to 1 percent. "However," he said, "in lieu of that 1 percent, you will receive a very nice gift for each new person you recruit and train."
>
> At that point a sales manager stood up and let him have it with both barrels. "How dare you do this to us? Why, even 2 percent wasn't enough. But cutting our overrides in half and offering us a crummy gift for appeasement insults our intelligence." With that she stormed out of the room. And every other sales manager for that state followed her—all 50 of them. In one fell swoop the owner had lost his entire sales organization in that region—the best in the country. I had never seen such an overwhelming rejection of a change of this kind in my entire life![56]

Top-down change means that initiation of the idea occurs at upper levels and is implemented downward. It does not mean that lower-level employees

structural change
Any change in the way in which the organization is designed and managed.

Jim Chesterton admits some painful cultural changes are needed at AW Chesterton, a Stoneham, Massachusetts, producer of mechanical seals, pumps, and other flow-control products. A cozy, close-knit company culture exists. Jim hosts a yearly Christmas party and employee birthday celebrations, and he believes in keeping employees on the payroll even when, as one employee put it, "there was nothing to do but sweep up the parking lot." However, the culture is hurting the company's ability to compete against four rivals which recently merged into two large companies, making them better able to serve the needs of Chesterton customers seeking single suppliers. Today, Chesterton employees are going through a people/culture change to help the company respond to the increased competition. One step was when Chesterton suspended the all-expenses-paid employee and spouse vacations to Disney World and Las Vegas.

The Paperless Office

One summer morning, Dan Caulfield stormed through the headquarters of his company, Hire Quality, Inc., carrying a large waste barrel. Employees laughed at first as he snatched yellow Post-it notes off of computer monitors, crumpled up spreadsheets, and tossed out reports. However, they were stunned when he soaked the trash heap with lighter fluid and set it ablaze. Some employees saw a month of their work go up in flames. Workers were definitely not amused, and one employee quit the company because of the incident.

Caulfield now realizes his method of implementing a change to a totally paperless office may have been counterproductive. But he felt that he needed to do something dramatic to get people to stop using paper and start taking advantage of the $400,000 worth of information technology systems he had installed. Caulfield believes paper is nothing but trouble when you're in a field that's as driven by speed and high volume as his job-placement firm. A former lieutenant in the U.S. Marine Corps, Caulfield started Hire Quality to place honorably discharged military personnel in mostly blue-collar and service-technician jobs. It's not unusual for the company to screen about 35,000 candidates and send out at least 3,000 resumes each month. There's no way his company could afford the number of staff it would take to handle everything on a paper-only basis.

Hire Quality has a massive database that can store information on up to 200,000 job candidates and be searched by more than 150 possible fields, making it much easier to match candidates with potential jobs. Caulfield also instituted a policy of allowing candidates to register only electronically and he asks clients such as Fed Ex and Bell Atlantic to send job descriptions electronically. Practically every employee's desk has a scanner so that any paper that does infiltrate the office can automatically be converted to an electronic file. To eliminate paper calendars and schedule books, he issued Hewlett-Packard 200LX Palmtop PCs to employees who had been with the firm at least six months.

Caulfield's mistake was that he didn't educate employees and allow them to participate in the change. For example, to get them to stop using paper, he instituted a penalty system, enacting a fine of $1 for using the fax machine and 25 cents per page for printing any resume. Employees rebelled against the harsh tactics and Hire Quality has not yet reaped the expected benefits from the new technology. However, Caulfield still believes his goal of a totally paperless office is a wise one, and many experts agree that there are major advantages to paperless office systems. Caulfield is trying to tone down his brutal implementation and work gradually to change employee attitudes.

SOURCE: Joshua Macht, "Pulp Addiction," *Inc. Technology*, no. 1, 1997, 43–46.

are not educated about the change or allowed to participate in it. Dan Caulfield, founder of Hire Quality, Inc., discovered this when he tried to switch to a "paperless" office, as described in the Technology box.

Culture/People Changes

culture/people change
A change in employees' values, norms, attitudes, beliefs, and behavior.

A **culture/people change** refers to a change in employees' values, norms, attitudes, beliefs, and behavior. Changes in culture and people pertain to how employees think; these are changes in mind-set rather than technology, structure, or products. People change pertains to just a few employees, such as when a handful of middle managers is sent to a training course to improve their leadership skills. Culture change pertains to the organization as a whole, such as when Union Pacific Railroad changed its basic mind-set by becoming less bureaucratic and focusing employees on customer service and quality through teamwork and employee participation.[57] Training is the most frequently used tool for changing the organization's mind-set. A company may offer training programs to large blocks of employees on subjects such as teamwork, listening skills, quality circles, and participative management. Training programs will be discussed further in Chapter 13 on human resource management.

Another major approach to changing people and culture is organizational development. This has evolved as a separate field that is devoted to large-scale organizational change.

Organizational Development

Organizational development (OD) is the application of behavioral science knowledge to improve an organization's health and effectiveness through its ability to cope with environmental changes, improve internal relationships, and increase problem-solving capabilities.[58] Organizational development ...ves working relationships among employees.

...he following are three types of current problems that OD can help man-...ers address.[59]

1. *Mergers/acquisitions.* The disappointing financial results of many mergers and acquisitions are caused by the failure of executives to determine whether the administrative style and corporate culture of the two companies "fit." Executives may concentrate on potential synergies in technology, products, marketing, and control systems but fail to recognize that two firms may have widely different values, beliefs, and practices. These differences create stress and anxiety for employees, and these negative emotions affect future performance. Cultural differences should be evaluated during the acquisition process, and OD experts can be used to smooth the integration of two firms.

2. *Organizational decline/revitalization.* Organizations undergoing a period of decline and revitalization experience a variety of problems, including a low level of trust, lack of innovation, high turnover, and high levels of conflict and stress. The period of transition requires opposite behaviors, including confronting stress, creating open communication, and fostering creative innovation to emerge with high levels of productivity. OD techniques can contribute greatly to cultural revitalization by managing conflicts, fostering commitment, and facilitating communication.

3. *Conflict management.* Conflict can occur at any time and place within a healthy organization. For example, a product team for the introduction of a new software package was formed at a computer company. Made up of strong-willed individuals, the team made little progress because members would not agree on project goals. At a manufacturing firm, salespeople promised delivery dates to customers that were in conflict with shop supervisor priorities for assembling customer orders. In a publishing company, two managers disliked each other intensely. They argued at meetings, lobbied politically against each other, and hurt the achievement of both departments. Organizational development efforts can help solve these kinds of conflicts.

organizational development (OD)
The application of behavioral science techniques to improve an organization's health and effectiveness through its ability to cope with environmental changes, improve internal relationships, and increase problem-solving capabilities.

Each year thousands of business managers have visited Lincoln Electric in Cleveland, Ohio to study one of the oldest and most radical pay-for-performance incentive programs in the country. The Lincoln Electric system paid employees up to 100 percent of their wages in annual performance-linked bonuses. Recently, due to global competition and an increase in institutional shareholders, workers' bonuses have decreased while revenues reached $1 billion. Workers were disgruntled when a two-tier wage system was attempted (and later withdrawn), and others were concerned that recent pay raises would cause future bonus reductions. As Lincoln Electric managers struggle to halt organizational decline and revitalize the company, they may choose to use organizational development techniques to adapt to current conditions without sacrificing employee goodwill.

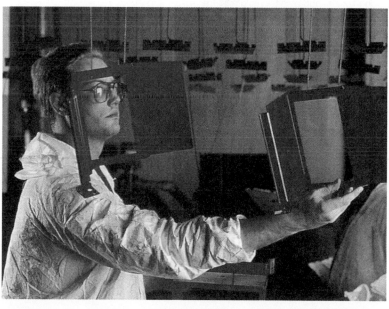

Organizational development can be used to solve the types of problems just described and many others. However, to be truly valuable to companies and employees, organizational development practitioners go beyond looking at ways to solve specific problems. Instead, they become involved in broader issues that contribute to improving organizational life, such as encouraging a sense of community, pushing for an organizational climate of openness and trust, and making sure the company provides employees with opportunities for personal growth and development.[60] Specialized techniques have been developed to help meet OD goals.

OD Activities.   A number of OD activities have emerged in recent years. Some of the most popular and effective are as follows.

1. *Team-building activities.* **Team building** enhances the cohesiveness and success of organizational groups and teams. For example, a series of OD exercises can be used with members of cross-departmental teams to help them learn to act and function as a team. An OD expert can work with team members to increase their communication skills, facilitate their ability to confront one another, and accept common goals.

2. *Survey-feedback activities.* **Survey feedback** begins with a questionnaire distributed to employees on values, climate, participation, leadership, and group cohesion within their organization.[61] After the survey is completed, an OD consultant meets with groups of employees to provide feedback about their responses and the problems identified.[62] Employees are engaged in problem solving based on the data.

3. *Large-Group Interventions.* In recent years, there has been a growing interest in applications of OD techniques to large group settings, which are more attuned to bringing about fundamental organizational change in today's complex, fast-changing world.[63] The **large-group intervention** approach brings together participants from all parts of the organization—often including key stakeholders from outside the organization as well—to discuss problems or opportunities and plan for change. A large-group intervention might involve 50–500 people and last several days. The idea is to include everyone who has a stake in the change, gather perspectives from all parts of the system, and enable people to create a collective future through sustained, guided conversation and dialogue.

Large-group interventions reflect a significant shift in the approach to organizational change from earlier OD concepts and approaches. Exhibit 12.8 lists the primary differences between the traditional OD model and the large-scale intervention model of organizational change.[64] In the newer approach, the focus is on the entire system, which takes into account the organization's interaction with its environment. The source of information for discussion is expanded to include customers, suppliers, community members, even competitors, and this information is shared widely so that everyone has the same picture of the organization and its environment. The acceleration of change when the entire system is involved can be remarkable. In addition, learning occurs across all parts of the organization simultaneously, rather than in individuals, small groups, or business units. The end result is that the large-group approach offers greater possibilities for fundamental, radical transformation of the entire culture, whereas the traditional approach creates incremental change in a few individuals or small groups at a time.

team building
A type of OD intervention that enhances the cohesiveness of departments by helping members learn to function as a team.

survey feedback
A type of OD intervention in which questionnaires on organizational climate and other factors are distributed among employees and the results reported back to them by a change agent.

large-group intervention
An approach that brings together participants from all parts of the organization (and may include key outside stakeholders as well) to discuss problems or opportunities and plan for major change.

	Traditional Organizational Development Model	Large-Group Intervention Model
Focus for action:	Specific problem or group	Entire system
Information Source:	Organization	Organization and environment
Distribution:	Limited	Widely shared
Time frame:	Gradual	Fast
Learning:	Individual, small group	Whole organization

Change process:	Incremental change	Rapid transformation

Exhibit 12.8
OD Approaches to Culture Change

SOURCE: Adapted from Barbara Benedict Bunker and Billie T. Alban, "Conclusion: What Makes Large Group Interventions Effective," *The Journal of Applied Behavioral Science* 28, no. 4 (December 1992), 579–591.

Large-group interventions represent a significant shift in the way leaders think about change and reflect an increasing awareness of the importance of dealing with the entire system, including external stakeholders, in any significant change effort.

OD Steps.   Consider the cultural change at Westinghouse Canada's manufacturing facility at Airdrie, Alberta. Cycle time for made-to-order motor-controlled devices was reduced from 17 weeks to 1 week. One major requirement for reducing the time was to change the mind-set of both managers and workers to give workers more discretion. Instead of waiting for approval from superiors, production employees now talk directly with customers and suppliers to solve their problems.[65]

Organizational development experts acknowledge that corporate culture and human behavior are relatively stable and that company-wide changes, such as those at Westinghouse Canada, require major effort. The theory underlying organizational development proposes three distinct steps for achieving behavioral and attitudinal change: (1) unfreezing, (2) changing, and (3) refreezing.[66]

In the first step, **unfreezing,** participants must be made aware of problems and be willing to change. This step is often associated with *diagnosis,* which uses an outside expert called a *change agent.* The **change agent** is an OD specialist who performs a systematic diagnosis of the organization and identifies work-related problems. He or she gathers and analyzes data through personal interviews, questionnaires, and observations of meetings. The diagnosis helps determine the extent of organizational problems and helps unfreeze managers by making them aware of problems in their behavior.

The second step, **changing,** occurs when individuals experiment with new behavior and learn new skills to be used in the workplace. This is sometimes known as *intervention,* during which the change agent implements a specific plan for training managers and employees.

The third step, **refreezing,** occurs when individuals acquire new attitudes or values and are rewarded for them by the organization. The impact of new behaviors is evaluated and reinforced. The change agent supplies new data that show positive changes in performance. Senior executives can reward positive behavioral changes by employees. Managers and employees also participate in refresher courses to maintain and reinforce the new behaviors.

unfreezing
A step in the diagnosis stage of organizational development in which participants are made aware of problems in order to increase their willingness to change their behavior.

change agent
An OD specialist who contracts with an organization to facilitate change.

changing
A step in the intervention stage of organizational development in which individuals experiment with new workplace behavior.

refreezing
A step in the reinforcement stage of organizational development in which individuals acquire a desired new skill or attitude and are rewarded for it by the organization.

The spirit of what OD tries to accomplish with culture/people change is illustrated by General Electric's Work Out Program, which provides an excellent example of the large-group intervention approach.

GENERAL ELECTRIC
www.ge.com

The Work Out program is one of the ways Jack Welch has reshaped General Electric for renewed productivity and growth. The program was created out of Welch's desire to reach and motivate 300,000 employees and his insistence that the people on the front lines, where change had to happen, be empowered to create the change.

GE's Work Out began in large-scale off-site meetings facilitated by a combination of top leaders, outside consultants, and human resources specialists. In each business unit, the basic pattern was the same. Hourly and salaried workers came together from many different parts of the organization in an informal 3-day meeting to discuss and solve problems. Gradually, the Work Out events began to include external stakeholders such as suppliers and customers as well as employees. Today, Work Out is not an event, but a process of how work is done and problems are solved at GE.

The format for Work Out includes seven steps:

1. Choose a work process or problem for discussion.

2. Select an appropriate cross-functional team, to include external stakeholders.

3. Assign a "champion" to follow through on recommendations.

4. Meet for several days and come up with recommendations to improve processes or solve problems.

5. Meet with leaders, who are required to respond to recommendations on the spot.

6. Hold additional meetings as needed to pursue the recommendations.

7. Start the process all over again with a new process or problem.

GE's Work Out process not only solves problems and improves productivity for the company but also gives employees the experience of openly and honestly interacting with one another without regard to vertical or horizontal boundaries. By doing so, the process has helped to create what Welch calls a "culture of boundarylessness" that is critical for continuous learning and improvement.[67]

Summary and Management Solution

Change is inevitable in organizations. This chapter discussed the techniques available for managing the change process. The trend today is toward the learning organization, which embraces continuous learning and change. Managers should think of change as having four elements—the forces for change, the perceived need for change, the initiation of change, and the implementation of change. Forces for change can originate either within or outside the firm, and managers are responsible for monitoring events that may require a planned organizational response. Techniques for initiating changes include designing the organization for creativity, encouraging change agents, and establishing new-venture teams. The final step is implementation. Force field analysis is one technique for diagnosing restraining forces, which often can be removed. Managers also should draw on the implementation tactics of communication, participation, negotiation, coercion, or top management support.

At Midwest Contract Furnishings, discussed in the chapter opening, a crisis caused by the loss of a major customer made managers and employees acutely aware of a need for change. However, owner Christopher Cogan knew he needed to implement changes carefully in order to raise employee motivation to the level it would take to survive this crisis. Because he was devastated by the situation, Cogan says this was a time when communicating was especially difficult for him, but he realized he needed to communicate clearly and openly with employees about the situation. After breaking the bad news, Cogan spent a few hours going over every detail of his plan to take the company in a new direction. He also knew that, even though it would cost him, he had to keep all employees on the payroll in order to maintain trust and commitment to the change process. Midwest also implemented programs that encourage continuous learning and change on a small scale so that employees will be more prepared when larger changes are needed. Teams of workers regularly look for ways to cut costs or do things better. Midwest's new business approach, Hotel Co-op, an online source for hotel products, is up and running smoothly. In addition, the company has won several major new contracts, including two projects for Marriott. Because Cogan carefully managed the change process, Midwest weathered the crisis and has even begun hiring new people.

This chapter also discussed specific types of change. Technology changes are accomplished through a bottom-up approach that utilizes experts close to the technology. Successful new-product introduction requires horizontal linkage among marketing, research and development, manufacturing, and perhaps other departments. Structural changes tend to be initiated in a top-down fashion, because upper managers are the administrative experts and champion these ideas for approval and implementation. Culture/people change pertains to the skills, behaviors, and attitudes of employees. Organizational development is an important approach to changes in people's mind-set and corporate culture. The OD process entails three steps—unfreezing (diagnosis of the problem), the actual change (intervention), and refreezing (reinforcement of new attitudes and behaviors). Popular OD techniques include team building, survey feedback, and large-group interventions.

Discussion Questions

1. A manager of an international chemical company said that very few new products in her company were successful. What would you advise the manager to do to help increase the company's success rate?

2. What are internal and external forces for change? Which force do you think is the major cause of organizational change?

3. Carefully planned change often is assumed to be effective. Do you think unplanned change can sometimes be beneficial to an organization? Discuss.

4. Why do organizations experience resistance to change? What techniques can managers use to overcome resistance?

5. Explain force field analysis. Analyze the driving and restraining forces for a change with which you have been associated.

6. Define the roles associated with an idea champion. Why are idea champions so essential to the initiation of change?

7. To what extent would changes in technology affect products and vice versa? Compare the process for changing technology and that for product change.

8. Given that structural change is often made top down, should coercive implementation techniques be used?

9. Do the underlying values of organizational development differ from assumptions associated with other types of change? Discuss.

10. How do large-group interventions differ from OD techniques such as team-building and survey feedback?

Management in Practice: Experiential Exercise

Is Your Company Creative?

An effective way to assess the creative climate of an organization for which you have worked is to fill out the questionnaire below. Answer each question based on your work experience in that firm. Discuss the results with members of your group, and talk about whether changing the firm along the dimensions in the questions would make it more creative.

Instructions: Answer each of the following questions using the five-point scale. (*Note there is no rating of 4*):0, we never do this; 1, we rarely do this; 2, we sometimes do this; 3, we frequently do this; and 5, we always do this.)

_____ We are encouraged to seek help anywhere inside or outside the organization with new ideas for our work unit.

_____ Assistance is provided to develop ideas into proposals for management review.

_____ Our performance reviews encourage risky, creative efforts, ideas, and actions.

_____ We are encouraged to fill our minds with new information by attending professional meetings and trade fairs, visiting customers, and so on.

_____ Our meetings are designed to allow people to free-wheel, brainstorm, and generate ideas.

_____ All members contribute ideas during meetings.

_____ During meetings, there is much spontaneity and humor.

_____ We discuss how company structure and our actions help or spoil creativity within our work unit.

_____ During meetings, the chair is rotated among members.

_____ Everyone in the work unit receives training in creativity techniques and maintaining a creative climate.

To measure how effectively your organization fosters creativity, use the following scale:

Highly effective: 35–50
Moderately effective: 20–34
Moderately ineffective: 10–19
Ineffective: 0–9

SOURCE: Adapted from Edward Glassman, *Creativity Handbook: Idea Triggers and Sparks That Work* (Chapel Hill, N.C.: LCS Press, 1990). Used by permission. (919/967–2015)

Management in Practice: Ethical Dilemma

Research for Sale

Lucinda Jackson walked slowly back to R&D Laboratory 4 at Reed Pharmaceuticals. She was stunned. Top management was planning to sell her entire team project to Trichem Industries in an effort to raise the capital Reed needed to buy a small, competing drug company. Two years ago, when she was named project administrator for the cancer treatment program, Jackson was assured that the program was the highest priority at Reed. She was allowed to recruit the best and the brightest in the research center in their hunt for an effective drug to treat lung cancer. There had been press releases and personal appearances at stockholder meetings.

When she first approached a colleague, Len Rosen, to become head chemist on the project, he asked her whether Reed was in cancer research for the long haul or if they were just grabbing headlines. Based on what she had been told by the vice president in charge of R&D, Jackson assured him that their project was protected for as long as it took. Now, a short two years later, she learned that not only was Reed backing out but also that the project was being sold as a package to an out-of-state firm. There were no jobs at Reed being offered as alternatives for the team. They were only guaranteed jobs if they moved with the project to Trichem.

Jackson felt betrayed, but she knew it was nothing compared to what the other team members would feel. Rosen was a ten-year veteran at Reed, and his wife and family had deep roots in the local community. A move would be devastating to them. Jackson had a few friends in top management, but she didn't know if any would back her if she fought the planned sale.

What Do You Do?

1. Approach top management with the alternative of selling the project and sending the team temporarily to train staff at Trichem but allowing them to return to different projects at Reed after the transition. After all, they promised a commitment to the project.

2. Wait for the announcement of the sale of the project and then try to secure as much support as possible for the staff and families in their relocation: moving expense reimbursement, job placement for spouses, etc.

3. Tell a few people, such as Rosen, and then combine forces with them and threaten to quit if the project is sold. Make attempts to scuttle the sale to Trichem before it happens, and perhaps even leak the news to the press. Perhaps the threat of negative publicity will cause top management to reconsider.

SOURCE: Adapted from Doug Wallace, "Promises Made, Promises Broken," *What Would You Do? Business Ethics* 1 (March–April 1990), 16–18. Reprinted with permission from *Business Ethics*, P.O. Box 8439, Minneapolis, MN 55408, (612) 879-0695.

Surf the Net

1. **The Learning Organization.** Released in March 1999, the learning organization guru, Peter Senge, authored *The Dance of Change: The Challenges of Sustaining Momentum in Learning Organizations.* Use your search engine to find a book review of this work and write a summary of this find-ings. One place to find book reviews is **www.amazon.com**.

2. **New-Venture Team.** Xerox Corporation's Palo Alto Research Center (PARC) was mentioned in the text as an example of an organization with new-venture teams. Visit PARC at **www.parc.xerox.com/parc-go.html** to find an-

swers to the following questions: (a) What are the strategic themes of PARC's research agenda? (b) Which one of PARC's inventions (available under the "History" section) do you think is most useful, and why? (c) Which one of the current PARC projects did you find most intriguing, and why?

3. **Survey feedback.** One of the OD activities mentioned in the chapter is survey feedback. One leading company in the field of employee attitude surveys is Stanard and Associates, Chicago, Illinois. Go to their Web site at **www5.interaccess.com/stanard** to learn more about the attitude survey instrument and to respond to the survey questions on-line so you can see how the procedure would work in an organizational setting. If your instructor asks you to do so, you may also want to print out the sample survey to refer to during the classroom discussion on this topic.

Case for Critical Analysis
Southern Discomfort

Jim Malesckowski remembers the call of two weeks ago as if he just put down the telephone receiver. "I just read your analysis and I want you to get down to Mexico right away," Jack Ripon, his boss and chief executive officer, had blurted in his ear. "You know we can't make the plant in Oconomo work anymore—the costs are just too high. So go down there, check out what our operational costs would be if we move, and report back to me in a week."

At that moment, Jim felt as if a shiv had been stuck in his side, just below the rib cage. As president of the Wisconsin Specialty Products Division of Lamprey, Inc., he knew quite well the challenge of dealing with high-cost labor in a third-generation, unionized U.S. manufacturing plant. And although he had done the analysis that led to his boss's knee-jerk response, the call still stunned him. There were 520 people who made a living at Lamprey's Oconomo facility, and if it closed, most of them wouldn't have a journeyman's prayer of finding another job in the town of 9,000 people.

Instead of the $16-per-hour average wage paid at the Oconomo plant, the wages paid to the Mexican workers—who lived in a town without sanitation and with an unbelievably toxic effluent from industrial pollution—would amount to about $1.60 an hour on average. That's a savings of nearly $15 million a year for Lamprey, to be offset in part by increased costs for training, transportation, and other matters.

After two days of talking with Mexican government representatives and managers of other companies in the town, Jim had enough information to develop a set of comparative figures of production and shipping costs. On the way home, he started to outline the report, knowing full well that unless some miracle occurred, he would be ushering in a blizzard of pink slips for people he had come to appreciate.

The plant in Oconomo had been in operation since 1921, making special apparel for persons suffering injuries and other medical conditions. Jim had often talked with employees who would recount stories about their fathers or grandfathers working in the same Lamprey company plant—the last of the original manufacturing operations in town.

But friendship aside, competitors had already edged past Lamprey in terms of price and were dangerously close to overtaking it in product quality. Although both Jim and the plant manager had tried to convince the union to accept lower wages, union leaders resisted. In fact, on one occasion when Jim and the plant manager tried to discuss a cell manufacturing approach, which would cross-train employees to perform up to three different jobs, local union leaders could barely restrain their anger. Yet probing beyond the fray, Jim sensed the fear that lurked under the union reps' gruff exterior. He sensed their vulnerability, but could not break through the reactionary bark that protected it.

A week has passed and Jim just submitted his report to his boss. Although he didn't specifically bring up the point, it was apparent that Lamprey could put its investment dollars in a bank and receive a better return than what its Oconomo operation is currently producing.

Tomorrow, he'll discuss the report with the CEO. Jim doesn't want to be responsible for the plant's dismantling, an act he personally believes would be wrong as long as there's a chance its costs can be lowered. "But Ripon's right," he says to himself. "The costs are too high, the union's unwilling to cooperate, and the company needs to make a better return on its investment if it's to continue at all. It sounds right but feels wrong. What should I do?"

Questions

1. Assume you want to lead the change to save the Oconomo plant. Describe how you would proceed, using the four stages of the change process described in the chapter—forces, need, initiation, and implementation.
2. What is the primary type of change needed—technology, product, structure, or people/culture? To what extent will the primary change have secondary effects on other types of change at the Oconomo factory?
3. What techniques would you use to overcome union resistance and implement change?

SOURCE: Doug Wallace, "What Would You Do?" *Business Ethics,* March/April 1996, 52–53. Reprinted with permission.

Endnotes

1. Michael Barrier, "Managing Workers in Times of Change," *Nation's Business,* May 1998, 31, 34.

2. Stuart F. Brown, "The Automaker's Big-Time Bet on Fuel Cells," *Fortune,* March 30, 1998, 122(B)–122(D); and "'Smart' Idea Comes Up for Gun Control," *The Tennessean,* October 22, 1998, 1A.

3. Richard L. Daft, "Bureaucratic vs. Nonbureaucratic Structure in the Process of Innovation and Change," in *Perspectives in Organizational Sociology: Theory and Research,* ed. Samuel B. Bacharach (Greenwich, Conn.: JAI Press, 1982), 129–166.

4. This discussion is based on Richard L. Daft, *Organization Theory and Design,* 5th ed. (St. Paul, Minn.: West, 1995); and Don Hellriegel and John W. Slocum, Jr., *Management,* 7th ed. (South-Western, 1996).

5. Tom Broersma, "In Search of the Future," *Training and Development,* January 1995, 38–43.

6. Andre L. Delbecq and Peter K. Mills, "Managerial Practices That Enhance Innovation," *Organizational Dynamics* 14 (summer 1985), 24–34.

7. Ira Magaziner and Mark Tatinkin, *The Silent War: Inside the Global Business Battles Shaping America's Future* (New York: Random House, 1989).

8. S. Nelton, "How a Pennsylvania Company Makes the Sweet Sounds of Innovation," *Nation's Business,* Dec. 1991, 16.

9. A. H. Van de Ven, H. Angle, and M. S. Poole, *Research on the Management of Innovation* (Cambridge, Mass.: Ballinger, 1989).

10. John P. Kotter, *Leading Change* (Boston: Harvard University Press, 1996), 20–25; and "Leading Change: Why Transformation Efforts Fail," *Harvard Business Review,* March–April, 1995, 59–67.

11. Attributed to Gregory Bateson in Andrew H. Van de Ven, "Central Problems in the Management of Innovation," *Management Science* 32 (1986), 595.

12. Teresa M. Amabile, "Motivating Creativity in Organizations: On Doing What You Love and Loving What You Do," *California Management Review* 40, No. 1 (fall 1997), 39–58; and Timothy A. Matherly and Ronald E. Goldsmith, "The Two Faces of Creativity," *Business Horizons,* September/October 1985, 8.

13. Gordon Vessels, "The Creative Process: An Open-Systems Conceptualization," *Journal of Creative Behavior* 16 (1982), 185–196; and Pearlman, "A Theoretical Model."

14. Robert J. Sternberg, Linda A. O'Hara, and Todd I. Lubart, "Creativity as Investment," *California Management Review* 40, no. 1 (fall 1997), 8–21; Teresa M. Amabile, "Motivating Creativity in Organizations"; and Ken Lizotte, "A Creative State of Mind," *Management Review,* May 1998, 15–17.

15. James Brian Quinn, "Managing Innovation: Controlled Chaos," *Harvard Business Review* 63 (May–June 1985),

73–84; Howard H. Stevenson and David E. Gumpert, "The Heart of Entrepreneurship," *Harvard Business Review* 63 (March–April 1985), 85–94; and Marsha Sinetar, "Entrepreneurs, Chaos, and Creativity—Can Creative People Really Survive Large Company Structure?" *Sloan Management Review* 6 (winter 1985), 57–62.

16. Cynthia Browne, "Jest for Success," *Moonbeams,* August 1989, 3–5; and Rosabeth Moss Kanter, *The Change Masters* (New York: Simon and Schuster, 1983).

17. "Hands On: A Manager's Notebook," *Inc.,* January 1989, 106.

18. Price Pritchett and Brian Muirhead, *The Mars Pathfinder Approach to 'Faster-Beter-Cheaper'* (Dallas: Pritchett & Associates, Inc., 1998).

19. Bonnie McKeever, "How I Did It: Teaming Up to Cut Medical Costs," *Working Woman,* July 1992, 23–24.

20. Katy Koontz, "How to Stand Out from the Crowd," *Working Woman,* January 1988, 74–76.

21. Harold L. Angle and Andrew H. Van de Ven, "Suggestions for Managing the Innovation Journey," in *Research in the Management of Innovation: The Minnesota Studies,* ed. A. H. Van de Ven, H. L. Angle, and Marshall Scott Poole (Cambridge, Mass.: Ballinger/Harper & Row, 1989).

22. C. K. Bart, "New Venture Units: Use Them Wisely to Manage Innovation," *Sloan Management Review* (summer 1988), 35–43.

23. Peter F. Drucker, *Innovation and Entrepreneurship* (New York: Harper & Row, 1985).

24. Michael Tushman and David Nadler, "Organizing for Innovation," *California Management Review* 28 (spring 1986), 74–92.

25. Otis Port, "Xerox Won't Duplicate Past Errors," *Business Week,* September 29, 1997, 98.

26. Russell Mitchell, "Masters of Innovation: How 3M Keeps Its New Products Coming," *Business Week,* April 10, 1989, 58–63.

27. Phaedra Hise, "New Recruitment Strategy: Ask Your Best Employees to Leave," *Inc.,* July 1997, 2.

28. J. P. Kotter and L. A. Schlesinger, "Choosing Strategies for Change," *Harvard Business Review* 57 (March–April 1979), 106–114.

29. G. Zaltman and Robert B. Duncan, *Strategies for Planned Change* (New York: Wiley Interscience, 1977).

30. Leonard M. Apcar, "Middle Managers and Supervisors Resist Moves to More Participatory Management," *The Wall Street Journal,* September 16, 1985, 25.

31. Dorothy Leonard-Barton and Isabelle Deschamps, "Managerial Influence in the Implementation of New Technology," *Management Science* 34 (1988), 1252–1265.

32. Kurt Lewin, *Field Theory in Social Science: Selected Theoretical Papers* (New York: Harper & Brothers, 1951).

33. Paul C. Nutt, "Tactics of Implementation," *Academy of Management Journal* 29 (1986), 230–261; Kotter and Schlesinger, "Choosing Strategies"; R. L. Daft and S. Becker, *Innovation in Organizations: Innovation Adoption in School Organizations*

(New York: Elsevier, 1978); and R. Beckhard, *Organization Development: Strategies and Models* (Reading, Mass.: Addison-Wesley, 1969).

34. Rob Muller, "Training for Change," *Canadian Business Review,* (spring 1995), 16–19.

35. Taggart F. Frost, "Creating a Teamwork-Based Culture within a Manufacturing Setting," *IM,* May–June 1994, 17–20.

36. Apcar, "Middle Managers."

37. Jeremy Main, "The Trouble with Managing Japanese-Style," *Fortune,* April 2, 1984, 50–56.

38. J. Hyatt, "Guaranteed Growth," *Inc.,* Sept. 1995, 69–78.

39. Daft, *Organization Theory and Design;* and Tom Burns and G. M. Stalker, *The Management of Innovation* (London: Tavistock Publications, 1961).

40. Richard Teitelbaum, "How to Harness Gray Matter," *Fortune,* June 9, 1997, 168.

41. Thomas Petzinger, Jr., "The Front Lines: Bread Store Chain Tells Its Franchisees: Do Your Own Thing," *The Wall Street Journal,* November 21, 1997, B1.

42. Richard L. Daft, "A Dual-Core Model of Organizational Innovation," *Academy of Management Journal* 21 (1978), 193–210; and Kanter, *The Change Masters.*

43. Harold J. Leavitt, "Applied Organizational Change in Industry: Structural, Technical, and Human Approaches," in *New Perspectives in Organization Research,* ed. W. W. Cooper, H. J. Leavitt, and M. W. Shelly II (New York: Wiley, 1964), 55–74.

44. Glenn Rifkin, "Competing through Innovation: The Case of Broderbund," *Strategy & Business* Issue 11, Second Quarter, 1998, 48–58; and Deborah Dougherty and Cynthia Hardy, "Sustained Product Innovation in Large, Mature Organizations: Overcoming Innovation-to-Organization Problems," *Academy of Management Journal* 39, no. 5 (1996), 1120–1153.

45. Paul Lukas, "The Ghastliest Product Launches," *Fortune,* March 16, 1998, 44; and Robert McMath, *What Were They Thinking? Marketing Lessons I've Learned from Over 80,000 New-Product Innovations and Idiocies,* (New York: Times Business, 1998).

46. Andrew H. Van de Ven, "Central Problems in the Management of Innovation," *Management Science* 32 (1986), 590–607; Daft, *Organization Theory;* and Science Policy Research Unit, University of Sussex, *Success and Failure in Industrial Innovation* (London: Centre for the Study of Industrial Innovation, 1972).

47. William L. Shanklin and John K. Ryans, Jr., "Organizing for High-Tech Marketing," *Harvard Business Review* 62 (November–December 1984), 164–171; and Arnold O. Putnam, "A Redesign for Engineering," *Harvard Business Review* 63 (May–June 1985), 139–144.

48. Daft, *Organization Theory.*

49. Dorothy Leonard and Jeffrey F. Rayport, "Spark Innovation through Empathic Design," *Harvard Business Review,* November–December 1997, 102–113.

50. Ira Sager, "The Man Who's Rebooting IBM's PC Business," *Business Week,* July 24, 1995, 68–72.

51. Susan Caminiti, "A Quiet Superstar Rises in Retailing," *Fortune,* October 23, 1989, 167–174.

52. Brian Dumaine, "How Managers Can Succeed through Speed," *Fortune,* February 13, 1989, 54–59; and George Stalk, Jr., "Time—The Next Source of Competitive Advantage," *Harvard Business Review* (July–August 1988), 41–51.

53. Fariborz Damanpour, "The Adoption of Technological, Administrative, and Ancillary Innovations: Impact of Organizational Factors," *Journal of Management* 13 (1987), 675–688.

54. Thomas A. Stewart, "Owens Corning: Back from the Dead," *Fortune,* May 26, 1997, 118–126.

55. Daft, "Bureaucratic vs. Nonbureaucratic Structure."

56. Mary Kay Ash, *Mary Kay on People Management* (New York: Warner, 1984), 75.

57. E. H. Schein, "Organizational Culture," *American Psychologist* 45 (Feb. 1990), 109–119; and A. Kupfer, "An Outsider Fires Up a Railroad," *Fortune,* Dec. 18, 1989, 133–146.

58. M. Sashkin and W. W. Burke, "Organization Development in the 1980s," *General Management* 13 (1987), 393–417; and E. F. Huse and T. G. Cummings, *Organization Development and Change,* 3d ed. (St. Paul, Minn.: West, 1985).

59. Paul F. Buller, "For Successful Strategic Change: Blend OD Practices with Strategic Management," *Organizational Dynamics* (winter 1988), 42–55; and Robert M. Fulmer and Roderick Gilkey, "Blending Corporate Families: Management and Organization Development in a Postmerger Environment," *The Academy of Management Executive* 2 (1988), 275–283.

60. W. Warner Burke, "The New Agenda for Organizational Development," *Organizational Dynamics,* Summer 1997, 7–19.

61. David A. Nadler, *Feedback and Organizational Development: Using Data-Based Methods* (Reading, Mass.: Addison-Wesley, 1977).

62. Wendell L. French and Cecil H. Bell, Jr., *Organization Development: Behavioral Science Interventions for Organization Improvement,* 3d ed. (Englewood Cliffs, N.J.: Prentice-Hall, 1984).

63. This discussion is based on Kathleen D. Dannemiller and Robert W. Jacobs, "Changing the Way Organizations Change: A Revolution of Common Sense," *The Journal of Applied Behavioral Science* 28, no. 4 (December 1992), 480–498; and Barbara Benedict Bunker and Billie T. Alban, "Conclusion: What Makes Large Group Interventions Effective?" *The Journal of Applied Behavioral Science* 28, no. 4 (December 1992), 570–591.

64. Bunker and Alban, "What Makes Large Group Interventions Effective?"

65. Buller, "For Successful Strategic Change."

66. Kurt Lewin, "Frontiers in Group Dynamics: Concepts, Method, and Reality in Social Science," *Human Relations* 1 (1947), 5–41; and Huse and Cummings, *Organization Development.*

67. J. Quinn, "What a Work-Out!" *Performance,* November 1994, 58–63; and B. B. Bunker and B. T. Alban, "Conclusion: What Makes Large Group Interventions Effective?" *The Journal of Applied Behavioral Science* 28, no. 4 (December 1992), 572–591.

Chapter 13

LEARNING OBJECTIVES

After studying this chapter, you should be able to

✸ Explain the role of human resource management in organizational strategic planning.

✸ Describe federal legislation and societal trends that influence human resource management.

✸ Explain what the changing social contract between organizations and employees means for workers and human resource managers.

✸ Explain how organizations determine their future staffing needs through human resource planning.

✸ Describe the tools managers use to recruit and select employees.

✸ Describe how organizations develop an effective workforce through training and performance appraisal.

✸ Explain how organizations maintain a workforce through the administration of wages and salaries, benefits, and terminations.

Human Resource Management

MANAGEMENT PROBLEM

When Jim McCann took over as president of 800-Flowers, the company was burdened by debt and had less than $1 million in annual revenues. To effectively meet customers' floral delivery needs, 800-Flowers needed dedicated order takers and customer service representatives. Yet it was in these departments that employee enthusiasm was lowest and turnover highest. The problem was compounded by the seasonal ebb and flow of the floral business, which meant that the company needed around 2,400 employees during peak seasons, such as Valentine's Day or Mother's Day, and only 900 workers during slow periods. To regain competitiveness, McCann needed a strategy to deal with this fluctuating demand for workers. In addition, to build and maintain a reputation for quality service, the company needed to retain good employees in the high-pressure order-taking and customer service departments.[1]

How can McCann find and keep a core group of high-quality employees and cope with seasonal demands for additional workers? Can human resource management be part of the strategy to restore 800-Flowers to competitiveness?

Walgreens Co., the leader in the chain drugstore industry in both sales and profits, recognizes the strategic role of human resource management. In its Annual Report, the company states, "Well-trained pharmacy technicians like Celeste Burgess (photo) are pivotal to both patient service and the efficient operation of Walgreens Intercom Plus workflow system. Approximately 2,000 technicians passed a national certification exam during 1998, enhancing their pay and pharmacy knowledge."

human resource management (HRM)
Activities undertaken to attract, develop, and maintain an effective workforce within an organization.

Jim McCann's problem at 800-Flowers illustrates the need for managing human resources. McCann and his management team must develop the company's ability to recruit, train, and keep first-quality employees, as well as its ability to train and motivate seasonal workers. Without effective human resource management, company growth will be restricted and performance will continue to suffer. The term **human resource management (HRM)** refers to activities undertaken to attract, develop, and maintain an effective workforce within an organization. Companies such as General Electric and Hewlett-Packard have become famous for their philosophy about human resource management, which is the foundation of their success. HRM is equally important for not-for-profit organizations. For example, the Catholic church must address the crisis of the sharply declining number of priests. Unless the church can find ways to attract and keep priests, a mere 17,000 priests will be serving 75 million U.S. Catholics by the year 2005.[2]

Over the past decade, human resource management has shed its old "personnel" image and gained recognition as a vital player in corporate strategy. Research has found that effective human resource management has a positive impact on organizational performance, including higher employee productivity and stronger financial performance.[3] Especially in today's tight labor market, the ability to attract and retain quality employees can be a powerful strategic weapon. Small businesses in particular report that finding and keeping good workers is the biggest problem they face.[4] With unemployment in the late 1990s at a 25-year low, many businesses had to develop creative ways to attract and keep workers. Steve Jacobus moved his company, Olson Warehouse & Distribution, from the suburbs to inner-city Milwaukee in order to tap into the larger pool of unemployed workers. To keep talented workers at Booz, Allen & Hamilton Inc., the New York consulting firm recently started a job rotation plan to help employees cope with a consultant's grueling schedule.[5]

Despite its importance, many managers still do not understand the value of human resources activities. In addition, company employees often do not understand the full range of HRM functions. For example, at Transamerica surveys indicated employees were not aware of the full range of human resource services or their access to those services. Effective education about HRM functions is essential.[6]

Human resource management consists of three parts. First, all managers are human resource managers. For example, at IBM every manager is expected to pay attention to the development and satisfaction of subordinates. Line managers use surveys, career planning, performance appraisal, and compensation to encourage commitment to IBM.[7] Second, employees are viewed as assets. Employees, not buildings and machinery, give a company a competitive advantage. In today's brutally competitive business environment, how a company manages its workforce may be the single most important factor in sustained competitive success.[8] Third, human resource management is a matching process, integrating the organization's goals with employees' needs. Employees should receive satisfaction equal to that of the company.

The Strategic Role of HRM

In this chapter, we will examine the three primary goals of HRM as illustrated in Exhibit 13.1. These goals, which take place within the organizational environment, include competitive strategy, federal legislation, and societal trends. The three goals are to attract an effective workforce to the organization, develop the workforce to its potential, and maintain the workforce over the long term.[9] Achieving these goals requires skills in planning, training, performance appraisal, wage and salary administration, benefit programs, and even termination. Each of the activities in Exhibit 13.1 will be discussed in this chapter. Most organizations employ human resource professionals to perform these functions. *Human resource specialists* focus on one of the HRM areas, such as recruitment of employees or administration of wage or benefit programs. *Human resource generalists* have responsibility in more than one HRM area.

Environmental Influences on HRM

"Our strength is the quality of our people."

"Our people are our most important resource."

These often-repeated statements by executives emphasize the importance of HRM. Human resource managers must find, recruit, train, nurture, and retain the best people. Human resource programs are designed to fit organizational needs, core values, and strategic goals. HRM is more important today than ever before.[10] A mix of economic, demographic, and social factors has led to an excessively tight labor market in most areas of the United States. In addition, an era of downsizing, restructuring, and reengineering has left many employees with decreased morale and little loyalty to their employers. In this environment, more managers are recognizing the value of paying attention to human resources issues. Without the proper personnel,

E x h i b i t 13.1 *Human Resource Management Goals*

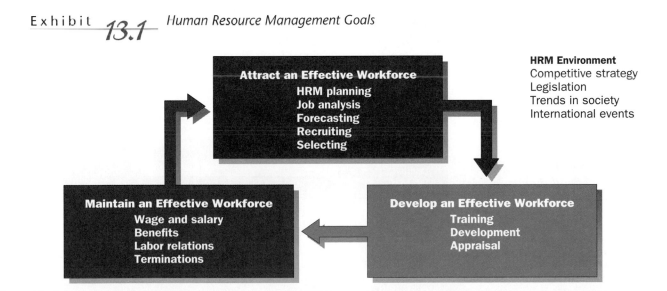

HRM Environment
Competitive strategy
Legislation
Trends in society
International events

Attract an Effective Workforce
HRM planning
Job analysis
Forecasting
Recruiting
Selecting

Develop an Effective Workforce
Training
Development
Appraisal

Maintain an Effective Workforce
Wage and salary
Benefits
Labor relations
Terminations

the brightest idea or management trend—whether teams, quality circles, telecommuting, or flexible compensation—is doomed to failure. In addition, when employees don't feel valued, usually they are not willing to give their best to the company and often leave to find a more supportive work environment. For these reasons, it is important that human resource executives be involved in competitive strategy. Human resource executives also interpret federal legislation and respond to the changing nature of careers and work relationships.

Competitive Strategy

HRM helps companies find the right mix of people and skills they need to meet organizational goals. HRM contributes directly to the bottom line through its appreciation that it is the organization's human assets—its people—that meet or fail to meet strategic goals. Judy Lyles of DET Distributing Company in Nashville, Tennessee, which delivers for Adolph Coors and Miller Brewing Company, reports what her boss told her when he hired her as human resources manager: "Any good manager will tell you that a company's greatest asset is its employees, but employees show up as a liability on a profit-and-loss statement. Yet our trucks are an asset. So, we've got all these mechanics to work on the fleet, but we don't have anyone working on our greatest asset, which is our people." Lyles sees herself as the human mechanic and head cheerleader for DET workers. She considers the human resources department not just as the keeper of the rules but as the "keeper of workers' hearts—the keeper of why they want to come to work every day."[11]

The human resource management function has changed enormously over the years. In the 1920s, HRM was a low-level position charged with ensuring that procedures were developed for hiring and firing employees and with implementing benefit plans. By the 1950s unions were a major force, and the HRM manager was elevated to a senior position as chief negotiator. During the 1980s, unions began to decline, and top HRM managers became directly involved in corporate strategic management.[12]

Exhibit 13.2 illustrates the interdependence between company and human resource strategy. Human resource strategy is designed to provide the correct mix of employees and skills needed to meet competitive conditions. The Louis Harris Laborforce 2000 survey of 400 American-based corporations found that the top strategic issues of concern to managers were to become more competitive on a global basis, to cut costs and improve efficiency, and to improve quality, productivity, and customer service. An organization's competitive strategy may also include mergers and acquisitions, reengineering, or

Exhibit *13.2*

Interdependence of Organizational and Human Resource Strategy

SOURCE: Adapted from Cynthia A. Lengnick-Hall and Mark L. Lengnick-Hall, "Strategic Human Resources Management: A Review of the Literature and a Proposed Typology," *Academy of Management Review* 13 (1988), 454–470.

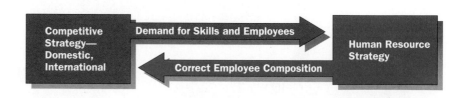

the acquisition of automated production technology.[13] All of these strategic decisions determine the company's need for skills and employees. It is the role of HRM strategy to include the correct employee composition to implement the organization's competitive strategy.

Today more than ever, strategic decisions are related to human resource considerations. For example, the shift to the *learning organization,* where everyone is engaged in making decisions and solving problems, requires a different mix of workers and skills than what is needed in a traditional vertical organization where most decisions are made by top managers. Learning companies look for people who are open-minded, curious, and willing to break the rules. One staffing director at a computer company that emphasizes autonomy, informality, and learning reports that, "we look for people's passions, what they've done with their lives: the guy who took a year off after his MBA to play the violin or travel the world."[14]

As another example, the introduction of flexible manufacturing systems such as those described in Chapter 11 have dramatically changed the need for workforce skill. These new machines require a highly skilled workforce, including interpersonal skills and the ability to work as a team. To make the strategic change to automated technology, the HRM department must upgrade the skills of shop machine operators and recruit new employees who have human skills as well as technical skills.[15] Chrysler spent a million hours training workers, many without a high school education, to run its highly automated Detroit plant using self-directed work teams. As aging factory workers retire, the company is recruiting workers with more education to replace them. Today, most companies want workers who can learn new skills quickly and require less supervision.[16]

Federal Legislation

Over the past 30 years, several federal laws have been passed to ensure equal employment opportunity (EEO). Some of the most significant legislation and executive orders are summarized in Exhibit 13.3. The point of the laws is to stop discriminatory practices that are unfair to specific groups and to define enforcement agencies for these laws. EEO legislation attempts to balance the pay given to men and women; provide employment opportunities without regard to race, religion, national origin, and sex; ensure fair treatment for employees of all ages; and avoid discrimination against disabled individuals.

The Equal Employment Opportunity Commission (EEOC) created by the Civil Rights Act of 1964 initiates investigations in response to complaints concerning discrimination. The EEOC is the major agency involved with employment discrimination. **Discrimination** occurs when some applicants are hired or promoted based on criteria that are not job relevant. For example, refusing to hire a black applicant for a job he is qualified to fill or paying a woman a lower wage than a man for the same work are discriminatory acts. When discrimination is found, remedies include providing back pay and taking affirmative action. **Affirmative action** requires that an employer take positive steps to guarantee equal employment opportunities for people within protected groups. An affirmative action plan is a formal document that can be reviewed by employees and enforcement agencies. The goal of organizational affirmative action is to reduce or eliminate internal inequities among affected employee groups.

discrimination
The hiring or promoting of applicants based on criteria that are not job relevant.

affirmative action
A policy requiring employers to take positive steps to guarantee equal employment opportunities for people within protected groups.

Exhibit 13.3   *Major Federal Laws Related to Human Resource Management*

Federal Law	Year	Provisions
Equal Opportunity/Discrimination Laws		
Civil Rights Act	1991	Provides for possible compensatory and punitive damages plus traditional back pay for cases of intentional discrimination brought under Title VII of the 1964 Civil Rights Act. Shifts the burden of proof to the employer.
Americans with Disabilities Act	1990	Prohibits discrimination against qualified individuals by employers on the basis of disability and demands that "reasonable accommodations" be provided for the disabled to allow performance of duties.
Vocational Rehabilitation Act	1973	Prohibits discrimination based on physical or mental disability and requires that employees be informed about affirmative action plans.
Age Discrimination in Employment Act (ADEA)	1967 (amended 1978, 1986)	Prohibits age discrimination and restricts mandatory retirement.
Civil Rights Act, Title VII	1964	Prohibits discrimination in employment on the basis of race, religion, color, sex, or national origin.
Compensation/Benefits Laws		
Family and Medical Leave Act	1993	Requires employers to provide up to 12 weeks unpaid leave for childbirth, adoption, or family emergencies.
Equal Pay Act	1963	Prohibits sex differences in pay for substantially equal work.
Health/Safety Laws		
Consolidated Omnibus Budget Reconciliation Act (COBRA)	1985	Requires continued health insurance coverage (paid by employee) following termination.
Occupational Safety and Health Act (OSHA)	1970	Establishes mandatory safety and health standards in organizations.

However, in recent years, the perception of affirmative action as a means for "leveling the playing field" has been replaced by complaints of the program as a way of imposing quotas. Even the intended beneficiaries of affirmative action are divided on the need for continuation. For example, a 1995 poll revealed that 49 percent of women favor continuation of affirmative action while 41 percent oppose it.[17]

Failure to comply with equal employment opportunity legislation can result in substantial fines and penalties for employers. For example, Shoney's was accused of discrimination against black employees and job applicants.

The class-action suit charged that company policy conspired to limit the number of black employees working in public areas of the restaurant. In 1992 the company agreed to pay $105 million to victims of its hiring, promotion, and firing policies, dating back to 1985.[18] Suits for discriminatory practices can cover a broad range of employee complaints.

One thing concerning human resource legislation is clear: The scope of equal employment opportunity legislation is increasing at federal, state, and municipal levels. The working rights and conditions of women, minorities, older employees, and the disabled will receive increasing legislative attention in the future. Also, most cases in the past have concerned low-level jobs, but increasing attention is being given to equal employment opportunity in upper-level management positions.

The Changing Nature of Careers

One issue of growing concern to organizations and human resource managers is the changing nature of careers. HRM can benefit employees and organizations by responding to recent changes in the relationship between employers and employees and new ways of working, such as telecommuting and job sharing.

The Changing Social Contract

In the old social contract between organization and employee, the employee could contribute ability, education, loyalty, and commitment and expect in return the company would provide wages and benefits, work, advancement, and training throughout the employee's working life. But the volatile changes in the environment have disrupted this contract. Many organizations have been downsized, eliminating many employees. Employees who are left may feel little stability. In a fast-moving company, a person is hired and assigned to a project. The project changes over time, as do the person's tasks. Then the person is assigned to another project and then to still another. These new projects require working with different groups and leaders and schedules. Workers often have no place to call their own.[19] Careers no longer progress up a vertical hierarchy but move across jobs horizontally. People succeed only if the organization succeeds, and they may lose their jobs. Particularly in learning organizations, everyone is expected to be a self-motivated worker who has excellent interpersonal relationships and is continuously acquiring new skills.

Exhibit 13.4 lists some elements of the new social contract. The new contract is based on the concept of employability rather than lifetime employment.

	New Contract	Old Contract
Employee	Employability, personal responsibility	Job security
	Partner in business improvement	A cog in the machine
	Learning	Knowing
Employer	Continuous learning, lateral career movement, incentive compensation	Traditional compensation package
	Creative development opportunities	Standard training programs
	Challenging assignments	Routine jobs
	Information and resources	Limited information

E x h i b i t *13.4*

The Changing Social Contract

Source: Based on Louisa Wah, "The New Workplace Paradox," *Management Review*, January 1998, 7; and Douglas T. Hall and Jonathan E. Moss, "The New Protean Career Contract: Helping Organizations and Employees Adapt," *Organizational Dynamics*, winter 1998, 22–37.

Individuals manage their own careers; the organization no longer takes care of them or guarantees employment. Companies agree to pay somewhat higher wages and invest in creative training and development opportunities so that people will be more employable when the company no longer needs their services. Employees take more responsibility and control in their jobs, becoming partners in business improvement rather than cogs in a machine. In return, the organization provides challenging work assignments as well as information and resources to enable workers to continuously learn new skills. The new contract can provide many opportunities for employees to be more involved and express new aspects of themselves.

However, many employees are not prepared for new levels of cooperation or responsibility on the job. Employment insecurity is stressful for most employees, and it is harder than it was in the past to gain an employee's full commitment and enthusiasm. In addition, one study found that while most workers today feel they are contributing to their companies' success, they are increasingly skeptical that their hard work is being fully recognized.[20] Some companies are discovering they went overboard with downsizing efforts in the 1990s and are now finding it difficult to keep good workers because employee trust has been destroyed. Many employees feel little loyalty to their employers. To respond to these problems, HRM departments can help organizations develop a mix of training, career development opportunities, compensation packages, and rewards and incentives. They can provide career information and assessment, combined with career coaching, to help employees determine new career directions.[21]

New Ways of Working

On the eve of the 21st century, America's largest employer is a temporary agency, Manpower, Inc. More companies are turning to interim or contingency workers to save money and avoid layoffs in the future. People in these temporary jobs do everything from typing to becoming the temporary CEO. In addition, organizational transformation is taking place on a global scale.[22]

The rapid changes affecting today's companies have brought about a change in the nature of careers. Organizations no longer offer lifetime employment; workers, instead, must maintain lifelong employability. Raychem Corporation is creatively confronting these changes in the workplace by helping its workers continually reinvent themselves. Raychem's career center is designed to create a "career-resilient workforce," helping workers move into other jobs within or outside the company. At Raychem, nothing is guaranteed except the chance for self-improvement and the promise that breadth of skill and experience are valued.

Not since the advent of mass production and modern organizations has a redefinition of work and career been so profound. In the new image, each person must take care of herself or himself.

Companies undergoing rapid change no longer offer certain employment. Instead, it's the individual's responsibility to maintain lifelong employability. The employer's obligation is to provide opportunity for self-improvement. It is up to the individual, however, to take charge of his or her own career.

Career paths in the twenty-first century will be a mix of the old and the new. There still will be traditional managers in traditional hierarchies, but many careers will be less linear and less secure than before. People can look for niches that suit their talents and ways of working that suit their needs. One of the biggest trends is telecommuting. **Telecommuting** means using computers and telecommunications equipment to do work without going to an office. The U.S. Department of Transportation has predicted that the number of telecommuters will increase to 15 million workers by the year 2002.[23] These "virtual" workers and managers live wherever they want, untethered to any office or city. At PeopleSoft, for example, all 6,000 employees work from remote locations at some time during their employment. Weekly meetings sometimes are conducted in person and sometimes online. AT&T has 35,000 telecommuters, who E-mail a list of weekly goals on Monday and follow up on Friday.[24]

The advent of teams is another significant trend in careers. People who used to work alone on the shop floor, in the advertising department, or in middle management are now thrown into teams and succeed as part of a group. Each member of the team acts like a manager, becoming responsible for quality standards, scheduling, and even hiring and firing other team workers. At an empowered Frito-Lay plant in Lubbock, Texas, the number of managers dropped from 38 to 13 while the hourly workforce grew by more than 20 percent to about 220.[25] With less supervision the plant has improved quality, productivity, and profits. But people on the teams lose some of their autonomy and must develop excellent skills of communication and a positive attitude. They also must learn several jobs; they won't be doing just one thing.

Sometimes, people looking for a new career direction decide to start their own businesses. Often, employees who are laid off during company downsizing do not want to return. Other people never want to join a large corporation, preferring the challenge and autonomy of running their own businesses. People who become freelancers or virtual workers often can create their own enterprise, hiring their own employees to provide services to larger companies. As corporations try to reduce costs, they hire outside services to meet their needs. This is called *outsourcing.* Entrepreneurship is challenging and exciting, and if you fit the criteria described in Chapter 6 or if you desire the autonomy and challenge of your own business, this may be an effective career path for you.

Within the context of new trends in careers and working relationships, human resource managers must achieve the three primary goals described earlier in this chapter: attracting, developing, and maintaining an effective workforce for the organization. Let us now review some of the established techniques for accomplishing these goals.

telecommuting
Using computers and telecommunications equipment to perform work from home or another remote location.

Betty Ford has launched City Boxers, an online retailer of hand-tailored boxer shorts. The product fills an attractive niche geared toward the Net's large male audience. She founded her company to seek her fortune on the Web and also, according to Ford, because its virtual reality is helpful to black and other minority entrepreneurs like herself, allowing shoppers to "make their decision on what the boxer shorts will look like, not on who's selling them."

Attracting an Effective Workforce

The first goal of HRM is to attract individuals who show signs of becoming valued, productive, and satisfied employees. The first step in attracting an effective workforce involves human resource planning, in which managers or

HRM professionals predict the need for new employees based on the types of vacancies that exist, as illustrated in Exhibit 13.5. The second step is to use recruiting procedures to communicate with potential applicants. The third step is to select from the applicants those persons believed to be the best potential contributors to the organization. Finally, the new employee is welcomed into the organization.

Underlying the organization's effort to attract employees is a matching model. With the **matching model,** the organization and the individual attempt to match the needs, interests, and values that they offer each other. The organization offers "inducements," and the employee offers "contributions."[26] HRM professionals attempt to identify a correct match. For example, a small software developer may require long hours from creative, technically skilled employees. In return, it can offer freedom from bureaucracy, tolerance of idiosyncrasies, and potentially high pay. A large manufacturer can offer employment security and stability, but it may have more rules and regulations and require greater skills for "getting approval from the higher-ups." The individual who would thrive working for the software developer might feel stymied and unhappy working for a large manufacturer. Both the company and the employee are interested in finding a good match.

matching model
An employee selection approach in which the organization and the applicant attempt to match each other's needs, interests, and values.

Human Resource Planning

human resource planning
The forecasting of human resource needs and the projected matching of individuals with expected job vacancies.

Human resource planning is the forecasting of human resource needs and the projected matching of individuals with expected vacancies. Human resource planning begins with several questions:

- What new technologies are emerging, and how will these affect the work system?
- What is the volume of the business likely to be in the next five to ten years?
- What is the turnover rate, and how much, if any, is avoidable?

The responses to these questions are used to formulate specific questions pertaining to HRM activities, such as the following:

E x h i b i t   *13.5*   *Attracting an Effective Workforce*

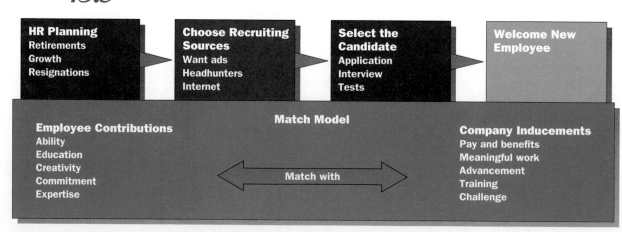

- How many senior managers will we need during this time period?

- What types of engineers will we need, and how many?

- Are persons with adequate computer skills available for meeting our projected needs?

- How many administrative personnel—technicians, secretaries—will we need to support the additional managers and engineers?[27]

Answers to these questions help define the direction for the organization's HRM strategy. For example, if forecasting suggests that there will be a strong need for more technically trained individuals, the organization can (1) define the jobs and skills needed in some detail, (2) hire and train recruiters to look for the specified skills, and/or (3) provide new training for existing employees. By anticipating future HRM needs, the organization can prepare itself to meet competitive challenges more effectively than organizations that react to problems only as they arise.

One of the most successful applications of human resource planning is the Tennessee Valley Authority's development of an eight-step system.

TVA
www.tva.com

In the confusion and uncertainty following a period of reorganization and downsizing, a crucial role for HRM is balancing the need for future workforce planning with the creation of a climate of stability for the remaining workers. TVA created an eight-step plan that can serve as a model for companies in assessing future HR needs and formulating actions to meet those needs. The first step is laying the groundwork for later implementation of the program by creating planning and oversight teams within each business unit. Step two involves assessing processes and functions that can be benchmarked. Step three involves the projection of skills and employee numbers (demand data) necessary to reach goals within each business unit. Once these numbers are in place, step four involves projection of the current employee numbers (supply data) over the "planning horizon" without new hires and taking into consideration the normal attrition of staff through death, retirement, resignation, and so forth. Comparison of the difference between supply and demand (step five) gives the "future gap" or "surplus situation." This knowledge enables HR to develop strategies and operational plans (step six). Step seven involves communication of the action plan to employees. The final step is to periodically evaluate and update the plan as the organization's needs change.

Although, in a small organization, developing demand and supply data could be handled with a pad and a calculator, TVA uses a sophisticated automated system to update and revise the plan as needed to meet new competitive situations. Determining skills-gap and surplus information (step five) helped TVA develop a workforce plan to implement cross-organizational placement and retraining as alternatives to further employee cutbacks in the individual business units, thereby providing a greater sense of stability for workers. If needs change and TVA faces a demand for additional employees, this process will enable the company to recruit workers with the skills needed to help meet organizational goals.[28]

Recruiting

Recruiting is defined as "activities or practices that define the characteristics of applicants to whom selection procedures are ultimately applied."[29] Although we frequently think of campus recruiting as a typical recruiting

recruiting
The activities or practices that define the desired characteristics of applicants for specific jobs.

Craig Johnson (standing, with some of his recruits) is the founder of Venture Law Group, a firm that redefined what a law firm can do by seizing a unique niche for itself. The firm helps launch successful start-up companies using services that include external recruiting. Joseph Grundfest, a Stanford University professor, called Johnson with the vaguest glimmer of a business idea. Johnson recognized the elements of a successful start-up and used his expertise to get the business off the ground. "What we needed was somebody who could act as a coach and a team builder, who could bring to the table the right mix of people early on," comments Grundfest, who compares Johnson's role in Silicon Valley to that of a talent agent in Hollywood.

activity, many organizations use *internal recruiting,* or "promote-from-within" policies, to fill their high-level positions.[30] At Mellon Bank, for example, current employees are given preference when a position opens. Open positions are listed in Mellon's career opportunity bulletins, which are distributed to employees. Internal recruiting has several advantages: It is less costly than an external search, and it generates higher employee commitment, development, and satisfaction, because it offers opportunities for career advancement to employees rather than outsiders.

Frequently, however, *external recruiting*—recruiting newcomers from outside the organization—is advantageous. Applicants are provided by a variety of outside sources including advertising, state employment services, private employment agencies ("headhunters"), job fairs, and employee referrals. Some employers even provide cash awards for employees who submit names of people who subsequently accept employment, because referral is one of the cheapest and most reliable methods for external recruiting.[31]

realistic job preview (RJP)
A recruiting approach that gives applicants all pertinent and realistic information about the job and the organization.

Realistic Job Previews.   One approach to enhancing recruiting effectiveness is called a *realistic job preview.* A **realistic job preview (RJP)** gives applicants all pertinent and realistic information—positive and negative—about the job and the organization.[32] RJPs enhance employee satisfaction and reduce turnover, because they facilitate matching individuals, jobs, and organizations. Individuals have a better basis on which to determine their suitability to the organization and "self-select" into or out of positions based on full information. When employees choose positions without RJPs, unmet expectations may cause initial job dissatisfaction and increased turnover. For example, Linda McDermott left a good position in an accounting firm to become an executive vice-president of a new management consulting company. She was told she would have a major role in helping the business grow. As it turned out, her boss relegated her to administrative duties, so she quit after a few months, causing the company to initiate another lengthy search and sidetracking her career for a year or two.[33]

Legal Considerations.   Organizations must ensure that their recruiting practices conform to the law. As discussed earlier in this chapter, equal employment opportunity (EEO) laws stipulate that recruiting and hiring decisions cannot discriminate on the basis of race, national origin, religion, or sex. *Affirmative action* refers to the use of goals, timetables, or other methods in recruiting to promote the hiring, development, and retention of "protected groups"—persons historically underrepresented in the workplace. For example, companies adopting an affirmative action policy may recruit at colleges with large enrollments of black students. A city may establish a goal of recruiting one black firefighter for every white firefighter until the proportion of black firefighters is commensurate with the black population in the community.

Most large companies try to comply with affirmative action and EEO guidelines. Prudential Insurance Company's policy is presented in Exhibit 13.6. Prudential actively recruits employees and takes affirmative action steps to recruit individuals from all walks of life.

Another legal consideration is company liability in connection with hiring employees who later commit crimes in the workplace, such as an employee who goes berserk and shoots fellow workers. An increasing number of court cases cite employer negligence in hiring people without careful background checks. As a result, HR departments are increasingly looking beyond personal references and personnel records to investigate prospective employees through past immediate supervisors, credit bureaus, criminal court records, and driver's license records. Careful hiring practices are important, but they must be implemented without discriminating against applicants or violating the individual's right to privacy.[34]

New Approaches to Recruiting.   In today's tight labor market, many companies are having a difficult time finding good workers. However, human resource managers have new tools to use for recruiting. The World Wide Web enables companies to cast a wide net in search of employees. Internet recruiting is increasingly being used by both large and small companies. Systems West Computer Resources in Salt Lake City first tried online recruiting in 1994, when few companies had moved into this new area. Although the company's first attempts were not very successful, within two years Systems West was receiving about 40 percent of incoming resumes online.[35]

Exhibit *13.6*   *Prudential's Corporate Recruiting Policy*

An Equal Opportunity Employer

Prudential recruits, hires, trains, promotes, and compensates individuals without regard to race, color, religion or creed, age, sex, marital status, national origin, ancestry, liability for service in the armed forces of the United States, status as a special disabled veteran or veteran of the Vietnam era, or physical or mental handicap.

This is official company policy because: • we believe it is right
• it makes good business sense
• it is the law

We are also committed to an ongoing program of affirmative action in which members of under-represented groups are actively sought out and employed for opportunities in all parts and at all levels of the company. In employing people from all walks of life, Prudential gains access to the full experience of our diverse society.

SOURCE: Prudential Insurance Company.

"Welcome. Would You Like a Job?"

For Cisco Systems, effective recruiting has become a powerful strategic weapon. The company's rapid growth has meant it had to double its workforce in 18 months while hiring only the highest caliber workers. Cisco's human resources team identified exactly the kind of people they wanted and then figured out the best methods for recruiting. One key element is the World Wide Web.

Cisco still uses newspaper help-wanted ads, but with a difference. Rather than listing specific job openings, Cisco runs ads featuring an Internet address and an invitation to apply for work at Cisco. Cisco's Web site has become a turbo-charged recruiting tool. It allows the company to post hundreds of job openings with specific information about each one. The company also advertises its site in cyberspace, which helps to reach a self-selected set of candidates (people who can easily navigate the Internet) from around the globe. People looking for a job can search by keyword to match their skills with job openings at the company. Then, they're able to file a resume or fill out a resume form online using Cisco's resume builder program. Most importantly, the site pairs each applicant with a volunteer "friend" inside the company. This friend will teach you about Cisco, introduce you to important people, and lead you through the hiring process.

The real power of Cisco's Web site is that it targets "passive" job-seekers—people who are happy and successful in their current jobs. Cisco advertises its site at places where its kind of people hang out. For example, the company has linked to the Dilbert Web page, which attracts a large audience of programmers. One of Cisco's best sources of employees is its competitors. Since many prospects visit Cisco's Web site from their jobs, Cisco can even tell where they work and pull some sneaky tricks. For example, anyone who visits the site from archrival 3Com is greeted with the following message: "Welcome to Cisco. Would you like a job?"

www.cisco.com

Source: Patricia Nakache, "Cisco's Recruiting Edge," *Fortune*, September 29, 1997, 275–276; Bill Birchard, "Hire Great People Fast," *Fast Company*, August–September 1997, 132–143.

The Technology box describes how Cisco Systems has used new methods to gain an edge in recruitment. Another innovative approach to recruiting workers in a tight labor market is to turn to nontraditional sources of employees. Arte Nathan, vice president for human resources at Mirage Resorts in Las Vegas, targets nonviolent first offenders who were sentenced to a Marine-style boot camp rather than a prison. Nathan works closely with parole officers and other court representatives to identify graduates who will make good employees. United Parcel Service recruits welfare recipients and arranges transportation and on-the-job assistance that will keep them working. A test program in Philadelphia showed that UPS retained 88 percent of its welfare employees and saw no decline in productivity.[36]

Whatever methods are used, recruiting is an important responsibility for HRM. Perhaps no company does it better than McDonald's, where one out of every eight Americans has worked at some time in their careers.

MCDONALD'S

www.mcdonalds.com

The fast-food business is known for high turnover, so recruiting is a never-ending job. However, McDonald's has some unique recruiting strategies that help the company lure a larger number of job applicants than most other fast-food restaurants. McDonald's emphasizes alternative labor sources. It has long been one of the nation's largest employers of young people, and the company makes effective use of internal recruiting to move some of these workers into management jobs rather than losing them after they graduate from school. In addition, two highly successful programs target groups that have proven to be loyal workers: older people and people who have physical or mental challenges.

A program called ReHIREment has recruited more than 40,000 older employees to serve McDonald's customers. Each older person is assigned a "buddy" who works alongside the new employee for the training period. Older workers appreciate McDonald's flexibility in scheduling and they are able to set the number of hours they work so as not to jeopardize Social Security benefits. The McJobs program was founded to assist in recruiting employees with physical or mental disabilities. Each recruit is paired with a job coach, who may be a specially trained McDonald's worker or a state agency counselor, for a period of six to eight weeks. So far, more than 9,000 workers have gone through the McJobs program. As a result of these two innovative recruiting programs, an entire pool of workers that often goes untapped is now successfully working for McDonald's rather than its competitors.[37]

Selecting

The next step for managers is to select desired employees from the pool of recruited applicants. In the **selection** process, employers attempt to determine the skills, abilities, and other attributes a person needs to perform a particular job. Then they assess applicants' characteristics in an attempt to determine the "fit" between the job and applicant characteristics.

selection
The process of determining the skills, abilities, and other attributes a person needs to perform a particular job.

Job Descriptions. A good place to start in making a selection decision is the job description. Human resource professionals or line managers who make selection decisions may have little direct experience with the job to be filled. If these persons are to make a good match between job and candidate, they should read the job description before they review applications.

A **job description** typically lists job duties as well as desirable qualifications for a particular job. For internal recruiting, companies may come up with lists of skills and abilities they want candidates to have. For example, Sara Lee Corp. identified six functional areas and 24 significant skills that it wants its finance executives to develop, as illustrated in Exhibit 13.7. Financial officers are tracked on their development and moved into other positions to help them acquire needed skills. Sara Lee believes that by developing talent in-house, it will rarely have to recruit top managers from outside the company.[38]

job description
A listing of duties as well as desirable qualifications for a particular job.

Selection Devices. Several devices are used for assessing applicant qualifications. The most frequently used are the application form, interview, paper-and-pencil test, and assessment center. Human resource professionals may use a combination of these devices to obtain a valid prediction of employee job performance. **Validity** refers to the relationship between one's score on a selection device and one's future job performance. A valid selection procedure will provide high scores that correspond to subsequent high job performance.

validity
The relationship between an applicant's score on a selection device and his or her future job performance.

Application Form. The **application form** is used to collect information about the applicant's education, previous job experience, and other background characteristics. Research in the life insurance industry shows that biographical information inventories can validly predict future job success.[39]

One pitfall to be avoided is the inclusion of questions that are irrelevant to job success. In line with affirmative action, the application form should not ask questions that will create an adverse impact on "protected groups"

application form
A device for collecting information about an applicant's education, previous job experience, and other background characteristics.

The Right Way to Interview a Job Applicant

A so-so interview usually nets a so-so employee. Many hiring mistakes can be prevented during the interview. The following techniques will ensure a successful interview:

1. *Know what you want.* Before the interview, prepare questions based on your knowledge of the job to be filled. If you do not have a thorough knowledge of the job, read a job description. If possible, call one or more jobholders, and ask them about the job duties and what is required to succeed. Another idea is to make up a list of traits and qualifications for the ideal candidate. Be specific about what it will take to get the job done.

2. *Prepare a road map.* Develop questions that will reveal whether the candidate has the correct background and qualifications. The questions should focus on previous experiences that are relevant to the current job. If the job requires creativity and innovation, ask a question such as "What do you do differently from other sales reps?"

3. *Use open-ended questions in which the right answer is not obvious.* Ask the applicant to give specific examples of previous work experiences. For example, don't ask, "Are you a hard worker?" or "Tell me about yourself." Instead ask, "Can you give me examples from your previous work history that reflect your level of motivation?" or "How did you go about getting your current job?"

4. *Do not ask questions that are irrelevant to the job.* This is particularly important when the irrelevant questions might adversely affect minorities or women. Questions that are considered objectionable are the same as those considered objectionable on application forms.

5. *Listen; don't talk.* You should spend most of the interview listening. If you talk too much, the focus will shift to you, and you may miss important cues. One expert actually recommends laying out all your questions right at the beginning

unless the questions are clearly related to the job.[40] For example, employers should not ask whether the applicant rents or owns his or her own home because (1) an applicant's response might adversely affect his or her chances

Exhibit
13.7

Sara Lee's Required Skills for Finance Executives

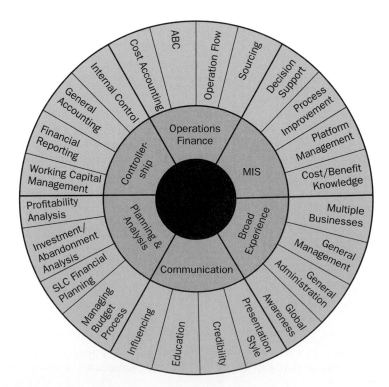

SOURCE: Victoria Griffith, "When Only Internal Expertise Will Do," *CFO*, (October 1998), 95–96, 102.

of the interview and following up with only brief reminders. This forces you to sit back and listen and also gives you a chance to watch a candidate's behavior and body language.

6. *Allow enough time so that the interview will not be rushed.* Leave time for the candidate to ask questions about the job. The types of questions the candidate asks can be an important clue to his or her interest in the job. Try to delay forming an opinion about the applicant until after the entire interview has been completed.

7. *Avoid reliance on your memory.* Request the applicant's permission to take notes; then do so unobtrusively during the interview or immediately after. If several applicants are interviewed, notes are essential for remembering what they said and the impressions they made.

Even a well-planned interview may be disrupted by the unexpected. Robert Half asked vice presidents and human resource directors at 100 major American corporations to describe the most unusual thing that they were aware of ever happening during a job interview. Various applicants reportedly:

- "Wore a Walkman and said she could listen to me and the music at the same time."
- "Announced she hadn't had lunch and proceeded to eat a hamburger and french fries in the interviewer's office."

- "Wore a jogging suit to interview for a position as a vice-president."
- "He said he was so well-qualified that if he didn't get the job, it would prove that the company's management was incompetent."
- "A balding candidate abruptly excused himself. He returned to the office a few minutes later wearing a hairpiece."
- "Not only did he ignore the 'No Smoking' sign in my office, he lit up the wrong end of several filter-tip cigarettes."
- "She chewed bubble gum and constantly blew bubbles."
- "Job applicant challenged the interviewer to arm wrestle."
- "He stretched out on the floor to fill out the job application."
- "He interrupted to telephone his therapist for advice on answering specific interview questions."
- "He dozed off and started snoring during the interview."
- "He said that if he were hired, he would demonstrate his loyalty by having the corporate logo tattooed on his forearm."

SOURCES: James M. Jenks and Brian L. P. Zevnik, "ABCs of Job Interviewing," *Harvard Business Review* (July–August 1989), 38–42; Dr. Pierre Mornell, "Zero Defect Hiring," *Inc.,* March 1998, 75–83; and Martha H. Peak, "What Color Is Your Bumbershoot?" Reprinted by permission of publisher from *Management Review* (October 1989), 63, ©1989. American Management Association, New York. All rights reserved.

at the job, (2) minorities and women may be less likely to own a home, and (3) home ownership is probably unrelated to job performance. On the other hand, the CPA exam is relevant to job performance in a CPA firm; thus, it is appropriate to ask whether an applicant for employment has passed the CPA exam even if only one-half of all female or minority applicants have done so versus nine-tenths of male applicants.

Interview. The interview is used in the hiring process in almost every job category in virtually every organization. The *interview* serves as a two-way communication channel that allows both the organization and the applicant to collect information that would otherwise be difficult to obtain.

Although widely used, the interview as generally practiced is not a valid predictor of later job performance. Interviews are more likely to test how well someone interviews than to test how well they will actually perform on the job. Most interviews follow a rather predictable series of steps, and candidates can prepare and practice their answers. Less predictable interviews help give a better idea of how a person actually will perform.[41] The Manager's Shoptalk discusses several ideas for effective interviewing, as well as some unusual interview experiences.

Paper-and-Pencil Test. Many companies use **paper-and-pencil tests** such as intelligence tests, aptitude and ability tests, and personality inventories, particularly those shown to be valid predictors.[42] Many companies today are particularly interested in personality inventories that measure such characteristics as openness to learning, initiative, responsibility, creativity, and emotional stability. One of the newest types of testing is an emotional intelligence quotient scale, designed by Multi-Health Systems in Toronto. The idea

paper-and-pencil test
A written test designed to measure a particular attribute such as intelligence or aptitude.

is that measuring a candidate's emotional intelligence, including such things as self-awareness, ability to empathize with others, and the capacity to build positive relationships, can give clues as to how well the person will do in his or her professional as well as personal life. Both the U.S. Air Force and Canada Life, a large insurance company, have used the EQ test.[43]

Assessment Center.   First developed by psychologists at AT&T, assessment centers are used to select individuals with high potential for managerial careers by such organizations as AT&T, IBM, General Electric, and JCPenney.[44] **Assessment centers** present a series of managerial situations to groups of applicants over, say, a two- or three-day period. One technique is the "in-basket" simulation, which requires the applicant to play the role of a manager who must decide how to respond to ten memos in his or her in-basket within a two-hour period. Panels of two or three trained judges observe the applicant's decisions and assess the extent to which they reflect interpersonal, communication, and problem-solving skills.

Assessment centers have proven to be valid predictors of managerial success, and some organizations now use them for hiring technical workers.[45] Nucor Steel uses a variation of the assessment center idea. It evaluates people by watching how they actually perform on their current jobs. One of Nucor's best sources of new steelworkers are the *construction* workers who build its plants. Nucor managers monitor their construction sites and keep close tabs on the moods, competence, and diligence of the people building them. Besides making sure the project is done on time and within budget, this gives managers time to look for carpenters, plumbers, electricians, and crane operators who demonstrate the values and work behaviors Nucor wants in its workers. These people are then offered employment as steelworkers in the plant they're building.[46]

assessment center
A technique for selecting individuals with high managerial potential based on their performance on a series of simulated managerial tasks.

Developing an Effective Workforce

Following selection, the major goal of HRM is to develop employees into an effective workforce. Development includes training and performance appraisal.

Training and Development

Training and development represent a planned effort by an organization to facilitate employees' learning of job-related behaviors.[47] Some authors distinguish the two forms of intervention by noting that the term *training* usually refers to teaching low-level or technical employees how to do their present jobs, whereas *development* refers to teaching managers and professionals the skills needed for both present and future jobs. For simplicity, we will refer to both interventions as *training.*

Organizations spend nearly $100 billion each year on training. Training may occur in a variety of forms. The most common method is on-the-job training. In **on-the-job training (OJT),** an experienced employee is asked to take a new employee "under his or her wing" and show the newcomer how to perform job duties. OJT has many advantages, such as few out-of-pocket costs for training facilities, materials, or instructor fees and easy transfer of learning back to the job. The learning site is the work site.

on-the-job training (OJT)
A type of training in which an experienced employee "adopts" a new employee to teach him or her how to perform job duties.

Other frequently used training methods include:

- *Orientation training,* in which newcomers are introduced to the organization's "culture," standards, and goals.
- *Classroom training,* including lectures, films, audiovisual techniques, and simulations.
- *Programmed and computer-assisted instruction,* in which the employee works at his or her own pace to learn material from a text that includes exercises and quizzes to enhance learning.
- *Conference and case discussion groups,* in which participants analyze cases or discuss topics assisted by a training leader.

We have developed our own proprietary interactive software programs that use touch-screen technology to teach transaction processing to our sales associates. They can learn at their own pace, and the system eliminates the need for one-on-one training by another staff member.

Dillard's, one of the most successful retail chains in the United States, takes advantage of information technology for training and developing an effective workforce. Interactive software programs use touch-screen technology to teach computerized transaction processing to new sales associates. The system eliminates the need for one-on-one training and allows employees to learn at their own pace. Dillard's further develops sales associates' skills through training programs regularly broadcast over the company's private satellite network. The high-tech approach allows employees to instantaneously receive the latest information on products and key company developments.

When Advanced Microelectronics, Inc., a fast-growing computer services company, let its training programs lapse, productivity sagged and turnover soared. Departing employees told CEO Steve Burkhart they were leaving because they felt they were getting "out of date" or "not keeping up with changes." Burkhart responded by reinstating the training program and expanding it to include bookkeepers and administrative workers as well as computer-repair and network-service technicians.[48] Companies as well as employees are increasingly appreciating the importance of training programs as they expect workers not only to have skills related to specific tasks but also to demonstrate the ability to think critically and solve problems.

Most companies are increasing training budgets. In addition, they are experimenting with a variety of new training approaches. One of the most popular is "cross-training," which teaches employees multiple skills so they can perform a number of different jobs, thus providing variety for employees and enabling companies to quickly adjust to changes in staffing needs. Another approach, "integrative learning," uses team exercises to establish and reinforce effective teamwork habits.[49]

Promotion from Within. Promotion from within helps companies retain and develop productive employees. It provides challenging assignments, prescribes new responsibilities, and helps employees grow by developing their abilities.

One approach to promotion from within is *job posting,* which means that positions are announced on bulletin boards or in company publications as openings occur. Interested employees notify the human resource department, which then helps make the fit between employees and positions.

Another approach is the *employee resource chart,* which is designed to identify likely successors for each management position. The chart looks like a typical organization chart with every employee listed. Every key position includes the names of top candidates to move into that position when it becomes vacant. Candidates are rated on a five-point scale reflecting whether they are ready for immediate promotion or need additional experience. These charts show the potential flow of employees up through the hierarchy and provide motivation to employees who have an opportunity for promotion.

Performance Appraisal

Performance appraisal is another important technique for developing an effective workforce. **Performance appraisal** comprises the steps of observing and assessing employee performance, recording the assessment, and providing feedback to the employee. Managers use performance appraisal to describe and evaluate the employees' performances. During performance appraisal, skillful managers give feedback and praise concerning the acceptable elements of the employee's performance. They also describe performance areas that need improvement. Employees can use this information to change their job performance.

Performance appraisal can also reward high performers with merit pay, recognition, and other rewards. However, the most recent thinking is that linking performance appraisal to rewards has unintended consequences. The idea is that performance appraisal should be ongoing, not something that is done once a year as part of a consideration of raises. Kelly Allan, senior associate of Kelly Allen Associates, Ltd., a consulting firm based in Columbus,

performance appraisal
The process of observing and evaluating an employee's performance, recording the assessment, and providing feedback to the employee.

To rehearse for the complex and rapidly changing real world, the United States Army puts everyone from PFCs to brigadier generals through maneuvers that stress them to the breaking point and then subjects them to a rigorous performance appraisal in public. The army is way ahead of most corporations in designing a bottom-up process that allows subordinates to appraise the performance of their bosses. In the After Action Review process, a colonel may question the actions of a subordinate, but junior officers can question the judgment of superiors as well. In this photo, a captain leads his tank platoon in a review following a mock battle at Fort Polk, Louisiana.

Ohio, puts it this way: "A raise is a transaction about how much money you or I can get. Feedback is a conversation about how much *meaning* you and I can create." At Allan's company, associates meet weekly to discuss performance on their current projects. The firm schedules formal sessions monthly or quarterly to discuss the past, present, and future of each person's work. These conversations never include discussions of pay; pay raises are considered totally separately.[50]

Generally, HRM professionals concentrate on two things to make performance appraisal a positive force in their organization: (1) the accurate assessment of performance through the development and application of assessment systems such as rating scales and (2) training managers to effectively use the performance appraisal interview, so managers can provide feedback that will reinforce good performance and motivate employee development.

Assessing Performance Accurately.   To obtain an accurate performance rating, managers must acknowledge that jobs are multidimensional and performance thus may be multidimensional as well. For example, a sports broadcaster may perform well on the job-knowledge dimension; that is, she or he may be able to report facts and figures about the players and describe which rule applies when there is a questionable play on the field. But the same sports broadcaster may not perform as well on another dimension, such as communication. She or he may be unable to express the information in a colorful way that interests the audience or may interrupt the other broadcasters.

If performance is to be rated accurately, the performance appraisal system should require the rater—usually the supervisor—to assess each relevant performance dimension. A multidimensional form increases the usefulness of the performance appraisal and facilitates employee growth and development.

A recent trend in performance appraisal is called "**360-degree feedback,**" a process that uses multiple raters, including self-rating, as a way to increase awareness of strengths and weaknesses and guide employee development. Members of the appraisal group may include supervisors, coworkers, and customers, as well as the individual, thus providing appraisal of the employee

360-degree feedback
A process that uses multiple raters, including self-rating, to appraise employee performance and guide development.

Con-Way's Team Improvement Review

Most work in companies that are shifting to a learning organization is performed by empowered teams of workers. Yet performance reviews in many cases are handled the same way they always have been—in one-on-one sessions between a manager and the individuals who report directly to him or her. The Information Systems department at Con-Way Transportation Services knew there had to be a better way.

Now, teams in Con-Way's IS department evaluate *themselves* through a process called the Team Improvement Review (TIR). The department wanted to avoid the terms "performance review" or "appraisal" because they conjure up the old image of a boss judging a subordinate. The TIR process takes a more positive approach by having teams look at what they're doing that's working, what they're doing that's not working, and ways to improve. The TIR process has three core features. First, it separates feedback sessions from salary reviews. Debbie Blanchard, a senior systems analyst, points out that people are much more open when they know that whatever they say is not going to affect their own or another team member's salary.

The TIR also guarantees that feedback takes place in a "safe" environment. Managers usually are not present for sessions; instead, the team brings in a neutral facilitator to lead the discussions. Last, the TIR provides a formal process about once every three months by which team members can offer feedback. Prior to a session, participants rate team performance on a 1 to 5 scale for 31 different criteria. In the group meeting, people discuss the team's overall performance as well as individual performance in the context of the team. One technique for making individual reviews easier is called the Round Robin. Each team member creates two columns on a sheet of paper, one headed "Strengths" and the other headed "Something to Work On." People almost always list something that other team members believe they need to improve, so it gives the team an opportunity to coach the individual rather than criticize.

www.con-way.com

SOURCE: Gina Imperato, "How to Give Good Feedback," *Fast Company*, September 1998, 144–156.

---

from a variety of perspectives.[51] With the advent of empowered teams and learning organizations, the appraisal and feedback process is changing. Parkview Medical Center in Pueblo, Colorado, did away with its top-down performance appraisal process. There's still an annual review, but it consists of employees telling managers what they can do to help the worker better perform his or her job. The review process is called APOP (Annual Piece of Paper) because the only form used is a piece of paper signed and dated by both parties that records that the conversation occurred. There are no scores, written reviews, or lists of goals for the coming year. Performance feedback is handled on a daily basis between employees and managers, not once a year in an appraisal meeting.[52] The Learning Organization box describes another innovative approach to performance appraisal.

Although we would like to believe that every manager carefully assesses employees' performances, researchers have identified several rating problems.[53] For example, **halo error** occurs when an employee receives the same rating on all dimensions even if his or her performance is good on some dimensions and poor on others. **Homogeneity** occurs when a rater gives all employees a similar rating even if their performances are not equally good.

One approach to overcome management performance evaluation errors is to use a behavior-based rating technique, such as the behaviorally anchored rating scale. The **behaviorally anchored rating scale (BARS)** is developed from critical incidents pertaining to job performance. Each job performance scale is anchored with specific behavioral statements that describe varying degrees of performance. By relating employee performance to specific incidents, raters can more accurately evaluate an employee's performance.[54]

halo error
A type of rating error that occurs when an employee receives the same rating on all dimensions regardless of his or her performance on individual ones.

homogeneity
A type of rating error that occurs when a rater gives all employees a similar rating regardless of their individual performances.

behaviorally anchored rating scale (BARS)
A rating technique that relates an employee's performance to specific job-related incidents.

Exhibit **13.8** *Example of a Behaviorally Anchored Rating Scale*

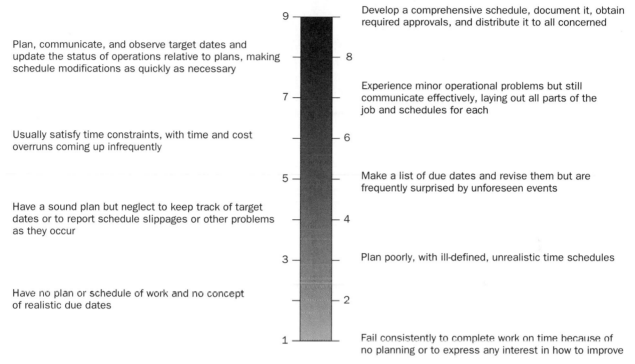

Job: Production Line Supervisor
Work Dimension: Work Scheduling

9 — Develop a comprehensive schedule, document it, obtain required approvals, and distribute it to all concerned

Plan, communicate, and observe target dates and update the status of operations relative to plans, making schedule modifications as quickly as necessary — 8

7 — Experience minor operational problems but still communicate effectively, laying out all parts of the job and schedules for each

Usually satisfy time constraints, with time and cost overruns coming up infrequently — 6

5 — Make a list of due dates and revise them but are frequently surprised by unforeseen events

Have a sound plan but neglect to keep track of target dates or to report schedule slippages or other problems as they occur — 4

3 — Plan poorly, with ill-defined, unrealistic time schedules

Have no plan or schedule of work and no concept of realistic due dates — 2

1 — Fail consistently to complete work on time because of no planning or to express any interest in how to improve

SOURCES: Based on J. P. Campbell, M. D. Dunnette, R. D. Arvey, and L. V. Hellervik, "The Development and Evaluation of Behaviorally Based Rating Scales," *Journal of Applied Psychology* 57 (1973), 15–22; and Francine Alexander, "Performance Appraisals," *Small Business Reports* (March 1989), 20–29.

Exhibit 13.8 illustrates the BARS method for evaluating a production line supervisor. The production supervisor's job can be broken down into several dimensions, such as equipment maintenance, employee training, or work scheduling. A behaviorally anchored rating scale should be developed for each dimension. The dimension in Exhibit 13.8 is work scheduling. Good performance is represented by a 7, 8, or 9 on the scale and unacceptable performance as a 1, 2, or 3. If a production supervisor's job has eight dimensions, the total performance evaluation will be the sum of the scores for each of eight scales.[55]

Maintaining an Effective Workforce

Now we turn to the topic of how managers and HRM professionals maintain a workforce that has been recruited and developed. Maintenance of the current workforce involves compensation, wage and salary structure, benefits, and occasional terminations.

Compensation

The term **compensation** refers to (1) all monetary payments and (2) all goods or commodities used in lieu of money to reward employees.[56] An organization's compensation structure includes wages and/or salaries and benefits

compensation
Monetary payments (wages, salaries) and nonmonetary goods/commodities (benefits, vacations) used to reward employees.

such as health insurance, paid vacations, or employee fitness centers. Developing an effective compensation system is an important part of human resource management because it helps to attract and retain talented workers. In addition, a company's compensation system has an impact on strategic performance.[57] Human resource managers design the pay and benefits systems to fit company strategy and to provide compensation equity.

Wage and Salary Systems.   Ideally, management's strategy for the organization should be a critical determinant of the features and operations of the pay system.[58] For example, managers may have the goal of maintaining or improving profitability or market share by stimulating employee performance. Thus, they should design and use a merit pay system rather than a system based on other criteria such as seniority. As another example, managers may have the goal of attracting and retaining desirable employees. Here they can use a pay survey to determine competitive wages in comparable companies and adjust pay rates to meet or exceed the going rates.

Skill-based pay systems are becoming increasingly popular in both large and small companies, including Nortel, au Bon Pain, and Quaker Oats. Employees with higher skill levels receive higher pay than those with lower skill levels. At Quaker Oats pet food plant in Topeka, Kansas, for example, employees start at $8.75 per hour but can reach a top hourly rate of $14.50 when they master a series of skills.[59] Also called *competency-based pay,* skill-based pay systems encourage employees to develop their skills and competencies, thus making them more valuable to the organization as well as more employable if they leave their present job. Thus, these systems work well within the context of the changing nature of careers and working relationships discussed earlier in this chapter. In addition, skill-based pay helps the organization be more flexible and adaptable to changing needs from the environment.

Another approach to establishing wage or salary rates, which has been widely used in the past, is *job-based pay.* With job-based pay, compensation is linked to the specific tasks that an employee performs. Although job-based pay systems still are used by some companies, they do present some problems. For one thing, job-based pay may fail to reward the type of learning behavior needed for the organization to adapt and survive in today's rapidly changing environment. In addition, these systems reinforce an emphasis on organizational hierarchy and centralized decision making and control, which are inconsistent with the growing emphasis on employee participation and increased responsibility.[60]

Compensation Equity.   Whether the organization uses job-based pay or skill-based pay, managers strive to maintain a sense of fairness and equity within the pay structure and thereby fortify employee morale. **Job evaluation** refers to the process of determining the value or worth of jobs within an organization through an examination of job content. Job evaluation techniques enable managers to compare similar and dissimilar jobs and to determine internally equitable pay rates—that is, pay rates that employees believe are fair compared with those for other jobs in the organization. Managers also may want to provide income security so that their employees need not be overly concerned with the financial consequences of disability or retirement.

Incentive Pay.   Another approach increasingly used is *incentive pay,* which links some portion of an employee's pay beyond base wage or salary to job performance. Incentives are aligned with the behaviors needed to help the

job evaluation
The process of determining the value of jobs within an organization through an examination of job content.

organization achieve its strategic goals. Employees have an incentive to make the company more efficient and profitable because if goals are not met, no bonuses are paid. Duke Power Company gives cash awards to employees in thirty different business units based on the company's achieving its targeted return on equity and the business unit realizing its goals.[61] Incentive pay systems may also be designed as a form of profit sharing to reward employees when the company meets its overall profitability goals.

Designing a Wage and Salary Structure

Large organizations typically employ HRM compensation specialists to establish and maintain a pay structure. They may also hire outside consultants, such as the Hay Group or PAQ (Position Analysis Questionnaire) Associates, whose pay systems have been adopted by many companies and government organizations. The majority of large public- and private-sector U.S. employers use some formal process of job evaluation.[62]

The most commonly used job evaluation system is the **point system.**[63] First, compensation specialists must ensure that job descriptions are complete, up-to-date, and accurate. Next, top managers select compensable job factors (such as skill, effort, and responsibility) and decide how each factor will be weighed in establishing job worth. These factors are described in a point manual, which is used to assign point values to each job. For example, the characteristic of "responsibility" could receive from 0 to 5 points depending on whether job responsibility is "routine work performed under close supervision" (0 points) or "complete discretion with errors having extreme consequences to the organization and public safety" (5 points).

The compensation specialist then compares each job factor in a given job description to that specified in the point manual. This process is repeated until the job has been evaluated on all factors. Then the compensation specialist evaluates a second job and repeats the process until all jobs have been evaluated.

The job evaluation process can establish an internal hierarchy of job worth. However, to determine competitive market pay rates, most organizations obtain one or more pay surveys. **Pay surveys** show what other organizations pay incumbents in jobs that match a sample of "key" jobs selected by the organization. Pay surveys are available from many sources, including consulting firms and the U.S. Bureau of Labor Statistics.

The compensation specialist then compares the survey pay rates for key jobs with their job evaluation points by plotting them on a graph as illustrated in Exhibit 13.9. The **pay-trend line** shows the relationship between pay and total point values. The compensation specialist can use the pay-trend line to determine the pay values of all jobs for which point values have been calculated. Ranges of pay for each job class are established, enabling a newcomer or low performer to be paid less than other people in the same job class. The organization must then specify how individuals in the same job class can advance from the low to the high end of the range. For example, the organization can reward merit, seniority, or a combination of both.

Benefits

The best human resource managers know that a compensation package requires more than money. Although wage and salary is an important component, it is only a part. Equally important are the benefits offered by the

point system
A job evaluation system that assigns a predetermined point value to each compensable job factor in order to determine the worth of a given job.

pay survey
A study of what other companies pay employees in jobs that correspond to a sample of key positions selected by the organization.

pay-trend line
A graph that shows the relationship between pay and total job point values for determining the worth of a given job.

Exhibit *13.9*

Pay-Trend Line

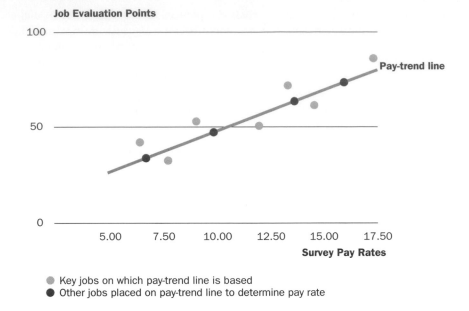

Key jobs on which pay-trend line is based
Other jobs placed on pay-trend line to determine pay rate

organization. Benefits were once called "fringe" benefits, but this term is no longer accurate because they are now a central rather than peripheral part of the pay structure. A U.S. Chamber of Commerce survey has revealed that benefits in general compose more than one-third of labor costs and in some industries nearly two-thirds.[64]

Some benefits are required by law, such as social security, unemployment compensation, and worker's compensation. In addition, companies with 50 or more employees are required by the Family and Medical Leave Act of 1993 to give up to twelve weeks of unpaid leave for such things as the birth or adoption of a child, the serious illness of a spouse or family member, or an employee's serious illness. Other types of benefits, such as health insurance, vacations, and such things as on-site fitness centers are not required by law but are provided by organizations to maintain an effective workforce.

One reason that benefits make up such a large portion of the compensation package is that health-care costs have been increasing so quickly. Because employers frequently provide health-care insurance as an employee benefit, these costs are important in the management of benefits. Between 1983 and 1993, annual corporate spending on health care tripled to $225 billion.[65] The federal government has been struggling to reform health care, and many companies are reviewing health plans.

Organizations that want to provide cost-effective benefits should be sensitive to changes in employee lifestyles. Two decades ago, benefits were based on the assumption that the typical worker was a married man with a dependent wife and two school-age children. The benefits packages provided life insurance coverage for the worker, health insurance coverage for all family members, and no assistance with child-care expenses. But today fewer than 10 percent of American workers fit the description of the so-called typical worker.[66] Increased workforce diversity means that far more workers are single; in addition, both spouses in most families are working. These workers are not likely to value the traditional benefits package. In response, some companies are establishing *cafeteria-plan benefits packages* that allow employees to select the benefits of greatest value to them.[67] Other companies use surveys to determine which combination of fixed benefits is most desirable. The benefits packages provided by large companies attempt to meet the needs of all employees.

At Whole Foods Markets, employees get "flexible credit dollars" to buy the benefits they most need. One employee might buy health insurance for her children while another might put all her credit dollars into a 401(K). All 13,000 Whole Foods employees are eligible for the program, and the longer they work for the company the more credit dollars they receive. The company also provides innovative benefits to lure and keep talented workers. For example, every employee who's been with the company for three years is eligible for a six-week sabbatical. The software company SAS Institute provides its employees with subsidized child care and a health center staffed by two primary care doctors and six nurse practitioners. SAS headquarters also boasts basketball and racquetball courts, a soccer field, and a fitness center. In an industry with an average turnover rate of 20 percent, SAS has managed to keep turnover to only 3 percent.[68]

Termination

Despite the best efforts of line managers and HRM professionals, the organization will lose employees. Some will retire, others will depart voluntarily for other jobs, and still others will be forced out through mergers and cutbacks or for poor performance. The value of termination for maintaining an effective workforce is twofold. First, employees who are poor performers can be dismissed. Productive employees often resent disruptive, low-performing employees who are allowed to stay with the company and receive pay and benefits comparable to theirs. Second, employers can use exit interviews. An **exit interview** is an interview conducted with departing employees to determine why they are leaving.[69] The value of the exit interview is to provide an excellent and inexpensive tool for learning about pockets of dissatisfaction within the organization and hence for reducing future turnover.

When companies experience downsizing through mergers or because of global competition, often a large number of managers and workers are terminated at the same time. In these cases, enlightened companies try to find a smooth transition for departing employees. For example, General Electric laid off 900 employees in three gradual steps. It also set up a reemployment center to assist employees in finding new jobs or in learning new skills. It provided counseling in how to write a résumé and conduct a job search. An additional step General Electric took was to place an advertisement in local newspapers saying that these employees were available.[70]

Downsizing is not as big an issue today as it has been in recent decades, and many companies are having a hard time finding good workers. Chevron Corp., however, found that it had too many workers in some operating units and not enough in others. To avoid massive layoffs, Chevron set up a special program to rematch and train employees to job-hop to other units. A petroleum engineer might be trained to fill in for a chemical engineering position. Employees scheduled for termination were generally given a six-month grace period to find an intracompany job. The company also provided training and job-hunting assistance for employees who couldn't find an intracompany job or who chose to leave rather than move to a different unit. In addition, an educational assistance program reimbursed 75 percent of tuition,

exit interview
An interview conducted with departing employees to determine the reasons for their termination.

books, and fees for up to two years after termination for former employees who took courses that would enhance their opportunities for finding a job outside the company.[71] By showing genuine concern in helping place laid-off employees, a company communicates the value of human resources and helps maintain a positive corporate culture.

Summary and Management Solution

This chapter described several important points about human resource management in organizations. All managers are responsible for human resources, and most organizations have a human resource department that works with line managers to ensure a productive workforce. The human resource department is responsible for interpreting and responding to the large human resource environment. The HR department must be part of the organization's competitive strategy, implement procedures to reflect federal and state legislation, and respond to changes in working relationships and career directions. The old social contract of the employee being loyal to the company and the company taking care of the employee until retirement no longer holds. Employees are responsible for managing their own careers. While many people still follow a traditional management career path, others look for new opportunities as telecommuters, team players, and entrepreneurs.

The HR department strives to achieve three goals for the organization. The first goal of the human resource department is to attract an effective workforce through human resource planning, recruiting, and employee selection. The second is to develop an effective workforce. Newcomers are introduced to the organization and to their jobs through orientation and training programs. Moreover, employees are evaluated through performance appraisal programs. The third goal is to maintain an effective workforce. Human resource managers retain employees with wage and salary systems, benefits packages, and termination procedures.

At 800-Flowers, Jim McCann used a new approach to training that helped him motivate workers, reduce bureaucracy, and adjust to fluctuating labor demands. 800-Flowers cross-trains employees so they can switch to different jobs as departmental needs change. Employees in the fast-paced order-taking and customer service departments traditionally burn out quickly, so as a reward for their hard work they may be transferred to one of the company's retail stores or to a job in headquarters. During the peak season, regular order takers become supervisors to train and assist temporary workers. Switching jobs helps keep employee enthusiasm high and revitalizes the business as employees bring fresh perspectives to each new job they do. To symbolize their cross-training in what McCann calls the "Reebok System," each participant gets a new pair of sneakers. The Reebok System has helped McCann turn the debt-ridden company into a blockbuster with more than $100 million in revenues. Effectively managing human resources enables 800-Flowers to do more with fewer workers, retain quality employees, and be more responsive and efficient in satisfying customers.[72]

Discussion Questions

1. It is the year 2010. In your company, central planning has given way to frontline decision making, and bureaucracy has given way to teamwork. Shop floor workers use computers and robots. There is a labor shortage for many job openings, and the few applicants lack skills to work in teams, make decisions, or use sophisticated technology. As vice-president of human resource management since 1990, what did you do to prepare for this problem?
2. If you were asked to advise a private company about its equal employment opportunity responsibilities, what two points would you emphasize as most important?
3. How can the human resource activities of planning, recruiting, performance appraisal, and compensation be related to corporate strategy?
4. Think back to your own job experience. What human resource management activities described in this chapter were performed for the job you filled? Which ones were absent?

5. How might the changing social contract affect the ways human resource departments recruit, develop, and retain workers?

6. How "valid" do you think the information obtained from a personal interview versus a paper-and-pencil test versus an assessment center would be for predicting effective job performance for a college professor? An assembly-line worker in a team-oriented plant? Discuss.

7. What techniques can managers adopt to improve their recruiting and interviewing practices?

8. How does affirmative action differ from equal employment opportunity in recruiting and selection?

9. How can exit interviews be used to maintain an effective workforce?

10. Describe the procedure used to build a wage and salary structure for an organization.

Management in Practice: Experiential Exercise

Test Your Human Resources Knowledge

This quiz will test your knowledge of human resources issues affecting today's workplace. The quiz was designed by the Council on Education in Management, a Walnut Creek, California, firm that conducts human resources and employment law seminars nationwide.

1. If you receive an unsolicited résumé in the mail, you must keep it for two years.   T   F

2. Time management principles are pretty much the same in any administrative job.   T   F

3. Regardless of the type of business or the various laws that may apply, there is a core of common practices for keeping personnel records and files that makes sense for almost any organization.   T   F

4. Every employer must have an affirmative action plan.   T   F

5. An employer must investigate an allegation of sexual harassment even if the victim asks to remain anonymous.   T   F

6. An employer is not obligated to pay overtime to a nonexempt employee who works more than 40 hours in a week after being asked not to put in overtime.   T   F

7. If your company is found guilty of discrimination, the Equal Employment Opportunity Commission will be more lenient if your records show that the violation was unintentional.   T   F

8. Americans with Disabilities Act regulations require companies to maintain written job descriptions.   T   F

9. Reference checking is an important procedure, despite the fact that many companies won't release this information.   T   F

10. Your employee orientation and handbook should help assure new employees that they will be a part of the team as long as they do a good job.   T   F

Answers: 1. F; 2. F; 3. T; 4. F; 5. T; 6. F; 7. F; 8. F; 9. T; 10. F.

Management in Practice: Ethical Dilemma

A Conflict of Responsibilities

As director of human resources, Tess Danville was asked to negotiate a severance deal with Terry Winston, the Midwest regional sales manager for Cyn-Com Systems. Winston's problems with drugs and alcohol had become severe enough to precipitate his dismissal. His customers were devoted to him, but top management was reluctant to continue gambling on his reliability. Lives depended on his work as the salesman and installer of Cyn-Com's respiratory diagnostic technology. Winston had been warned twice to clean up his act, but had never succeeded. Only his unique blend of technical knowledge and high-powered sales ability had saved him before.

But now the vice-president of sales asked Danville to offer Winston the option of resigning rather than be fired if he would sign a noncompete agreement and agree to go into rehabilitation. Cyn-Com would also extend a guarantee of confidentiality on the abuse issue and a good work reference as thanks for the millions of dollars of business that Winston had brought to Cyn-Com. Winston agreed to take the deal. After his departure, a series of near disasters was uncovered as a result of Winston's mismanagement. Some of his maneuvers to cover up his mistakes bordered on fraud.

Today Danville received a message to call the human resources director at a cardiopulmonary technology company to give a personal reference on Terry Winston. From the area code, Danville could see that he was not in violation of the noncompete agreement. She had also heard that Winston had completed a 30-day treatment program as promised. Danville knew she was expected to honor the confidentiality agreement, but she also knew that if his shady dealings had been discovered before his departure, he would have been fired without any agreement. Now she was being asked to give Winston a reference for another medical sales position.

What Do You Do?

1. Honor the agreement, trusting Winston's rehabilitation is complete on all levels and that he is now ready for a responsible position. Give a good recommendation.

2. Contact the vice-president of sales and ask him to release you from the agreement or to give the reference himself. After all, he made the agreement. You don't want to lie.

3. Without mentioning specifics, give Winston such an unenthusiastic reference that you hope the other human resources director can read between the lines and believe that Winston will be a poor choice.

Surf the Net

1. **Equal Employment Opportunity**. Andrea Kingston, a small business owner with 35 employees, has hired you as a human resources consultant. One area you are working on is making sure your client is in compliance with the federal laws related to her employees. The first step in the process is educating Andrea on what is required of her because her level of knowledge in this area is very minimal. Go to "Small Business Information" at the U.S. Equal Employment Opportunity Commission's home page **(www.eeoc.gov)** to gather information for Andrea. Write an outline of the information you will cover in that meeting.

2. **Recruiting.** Just as you get impressions about companies based on how you are treated when you visit their human resources departments to inquire about job openings or to ask for a job application form, you also get impressions based on how companies present themselves on the Internet. Go to several online human resources departments at companies you might like to work for someday, or check out those listed below, and record your impressions—things you liked and didn't like—as you conduct your on-line job search:

   Federal Express **(http://www.fedex.com/us/careers)**
   Intel **(www.intel.com/intel/oppty/index.htm)**
   Cisco Systems **(www.cisco.com/jobs)**

3. **Benefits.** The Employee Benefit Research Institute (EBRI) at **www.ebri.org/ebrilinks.htm** provides access to a number of sites that deal with benefits issues. Assuming the human resources consultant role described in problem 1, prepare a recommended benefits checklist for Andrea so that she can compare her current benefits package with the benefits appropriate for a small business to offer its employees.

Case for Critical Analysis
Waterway Industries

Waterway Industries was founded in the early 1960s as a small manufacturer of high-quality canoes. Based in Lake Placid, New York, the company quickly gained a solid reputation throughout the Northeast and began building a customer base in the Pacific Northwest as well. By the early 1980s, Waterway was comfortably ensconced in the canoe market nationwide. Although earnings growth was fairly steady up until 1990, CEO Cyrus Maher was persuaded by a friend to venture into kayaks. After Waterway began selling its own line of compact, inexpensive kayaks in 1992, Maher quickly learned that the decision was a good one. Most of Waterway's existing canoe customers placed sizable kayak orders, and a number of private-label companies also began contacting Maher about making kayaks for their companies. When Lee Carter was hired to establish a formal marketing department at Waterway, things really took off. Carter began bringing in so many large orders that the company had to contract with other manufacturers to keep up.

For the most part, Waterway's 45 or so employees adjusted well to the faster pace at the company. The expanded business didn't seem to change the company's relaxed, informal working atmosphere. Most employees were outdoor enthusiasts, and on days when the weather was good Maher knew that the building would be almost empty by 4:00 pm. He also knew, however, that employees enjoyed their jobs, got their work completed on time, and were always speaking out with new ideas and suggestions. However, Lee Carter, unlike other employees, seemed totally focused on her work. She traveled constantly and worked so hard that she barely had time to get to know the rest of the staff. She came in on weekends to catch up on paperwork. She had even missed the Waterway picnic, along with two of her direct reports, because the three were on the road trying to nail down a large order. Maher likes the dedication but wonders if this approach could eventually have a negative effect on the company's culture.

Turnover at Waterway has always been low, and Maher believes most employees are happy working at the company. However, within the past year, both of Waterway's designers have approached Maher to request salary adjustments. Each suggested they would be interested in equity in the company, whereby they would receive a share of the profits if their designs did well. Maher's response was to give the senior designer a modest pay raise and extra vacation and to increase the bonuses for both designers. Both seemed satisfied with the new arrangement. Waterway's CFO, on the other hand, recently left the company to take a position with a power boat manufacturer after Maher twice refused his request for a redesigned compensation package to include equity. Now, on a trip to the cafeteria to get a cup of coffee, Maher has just overheard Lee Carter discussing a possible job opportunity with another company. He is well aware of the lucrative packages being offered to sales and marketing managers in the sporting goods industry, and he doesn't want to lose Carter. Even though he suspects she will eventually leave the company anyway, especially if the market for kayaks falls flat, he would like to find a way to recognize her hard work and keep her at Waterway for at least a few more years.

Maher has asked you, the company's sole human resource manager, for advice about changing the company's compensation system. In the past, he has handled things informally, giving employees annual salary increases and bonuses, and dealing with employees one-on-one (as he did with the designers) when they have concerns about their current compensation. Now, Maher is wondering if his company has grown to the point where he needs to establish some kind of formal compensation system that can recognize employees who make outstanding contributions to the company's success.

Questions

1. What impact, positive or negative, do you think a formal compensation system might have on Waterway?
2. What type of compensation approach would you suggest Maher implement?
3. How can nonfinancial incentives play a role in helping Waterway retain aggressive, ambitious employees like Lee Carter?

SOURCE: Based on Robert D. Nicoson, "Growing Pains," *Harvard Business Review,* July–August 1996, 20–36.

Endnotes

1. Jenny C. McCune, "On the Train Gang," *Management Review,* October 1994, 57–60.
2. R. Gustav Niebuhr, "Mass Shortage: Catholic Church Faces Crisis as Priests Quit and Recruiting Falls," *The Wall Street Journal,* November 13, 1990, A1, A13.
3. Mark A. Huselid, Susan E. Jackson, and Randall S. Schuler, "Technical and Strategic Human Resource Management Effectiveness as Determinants of Firm Performance," *Academy of Management Journal* 40, no. 1 (1997), 171–188; and John T. Delaney and Mark A. Huselid, "The Impact of Human Resource Management Practices on Perceptions of Organizational Performance," *Academy of Management Journal* 39, no. 4 (1996), 949–969.
4. Dale D. Buss, "Help Wanted Desperately," *Nation's Business,* April 1996, 16–23.
5. Buss, "Help Wanted Desperately,"; and Aaron Bernstein, "We Want You to Stay. Really," *Business Week,* June 22, 1998, 67–72.
6. David E. Bowen and Edward E. Lawler III, "Total Quality-Oriented Human Resource Management," *Organizational Dynamics* (spring 1992), 29–41.
7. D. Kneale, "Working at IBM: Intense Loyalty in a Rigid Culture," *The Wall Street Journal,* April 7, 1986, 17.
8. Jeffrey Pfeffer, "Producing Sustainable Competitive Advantage through the Effective Management of People," *Academy of Management Executive* 9, no. 1 (1995), 55–72.
9. Cynthia D. Fisher, "Current and Recurrent Challenges in HRM," *Journal of Management* 15 (1989), 157–180.
10. See Dave Ulrich, "A New Mandate for Human Resources," *Harvard Business Review,* January–February 1998, 124–134; Jennifer J. Laabs, "It's OK to Focus on Heart and Soul," *Workforce,* January 1997, 60–69; and Philip H. Mirvis, "Human Resource Management: Leaders, Laggards, and Followers," *Academy of Management Executive* 11, no. 2 (1997), 43–56.
11. Jennifer J. Laabs, "It's OK to Focus on Heart and Soul," *Workforce,* January 1997, 60–69.
12. Cynthia A. Lengnick-Hall and Mark L. Lengnick-Hall, "Strategic Human Resources Management: A Review of the Literature and a Proposed Typology," *Academy of Management Review* 13 (1988), 454–470; and "Human Resources Managers Aren't Corporate Nobodies Any More," *Business Week,* December 2, 1985, 58–59.
13. Philip H. Mirvis, "Human Resource Management: Leaders, Laggards, and Followers," *Academy of Management Executive* 11, no. 2 (1997), 43–56.
14. Peter Carbonara, "Hire for Attitude, Train for Skill," *Fast Company,* August–September 1996, 73–81.
15. Richard E. Walton and Gerald I. Susman, "People Policies for the New Machines," *Harvard Business Review* 87 (March–April 1987), 98–106; and Randall S. Schuler and Susan E. Jackson, "Linking Competitive Strategies with Human Resource Management Practices," *The Academy of Management Executive* 1 (1987), 207–219.
16. Neal Templin, "Auto Plants, Hiring Again, Are Demanding Higher-Skilled Labor," *The Wall Street Journal,* March 11, 1994, A1, A4.
17. Joanne L. Symons, "Is Affirmative Action in America's Interest?" *Executive Female,* May–June 1995, 52; and David M. Alpern, "Why Women Are Divided on Affirmative Action," *Working Woman,* July 1995, 18.

18. Deidre A. Depke, "Picking Up the Tab for Bias at Shoney's," *Business Week,* November 6, 1992, 50.

19. Charles F. Falk and Kathleen A. Carlson, "Newer Patterns in Management for the Post–Social Contract Era," *Midwest Management Society Proceedings* (1995), 45–52.

20. Richard Pascale, "The False Security of 'Employability,'" *Fast Company,* April–May 1996, 62, 64; and Louisa Wah, "The New Workplace Paradox," *Management Review,* January 1998, 7.

21. Douglas T. Hall and Jonathan E. Moss, "The New Protean Career Contract: Helping Organizations and Employees Adapt," *Organizational Dynamics,* winter 1998, 22–37.

22. Hall and Moss, "The New Protean Career Contract."

23. Richard W. Judy and Carol D'Amico, *Workforce 2020: Work and Workers in the 21st Century,* (Indianapolis, Ind.: The Hudson Institute, 1997). For information on telecommuting and its impact, see Mahlon Apgar, IV, "The Alternative Workplace: Changing Where and How People Work, *Harvard Business Review,* May–June 1998, 121–133; and Jenny C. McCune, "Telecommuting Revisited," *Management Review,* February 1998, 10–16.

24. Carol A. L. Dannhauser, "The Invisible Worker," *Working Woman,* November 1998, 38.

25. Wendy Zellner, "Team Player: No More 'Same-ol'-same-ol'," *Business Week,* October 17, 1994, 95–96.

26. James G. March and Herbert A. Simon, *Organizations* (New York: Wiley, 1958).

27. Dennis J. Kravetz, *The Human Resources Revolution* (San Francisco, Calif.: Jossey-Bass, 1989).

28. David E. Ripley, "How to Determine Future Workforce Needs," *Personnel Journal,* January 1995, 83–89.

29. J. W. Boudreau and S. L. Rynes, "Role of Recruitment in Staffing Utility Analysis," *Journal of Applied Psychology* 70 (1985), 354–366.

30. Brian Dumaine, "The New Art of Hiring Smart," *Fortune,* August 17, 1987, 78–81.

31. P. Farish, "HRM Update: Referral Results," *Personnel Administrator* 31 (1986), 22.

32. J. P. Wanous, *Organizational Entry* (Reading, Mass.: Addison-Wesley, 1980).

33. Larry Reibstein, "Crushed Hopes: When a New Job Proves to Be Something Different," *The Wall Street Journal,* June 10, 1987, 25.

34. Jacquelyn Denalli, "Negligent Hiring: Are You Liable When Employees Do Wrong?" *Self-Employed America,* January–February 1995, 10–11; and William S. Saling, "The Worth of Another's Words," *Self-Employed America,* January–February 1995, 11.

35. Thomas Love, "Smart Tactics for Finding Workers," *Nation's Business,* January 1998, 20; and Shannon Peters Talbott, "How to Recruit Online," *Recruitment Staffing Sourcebook,* supplement to *Personnel Journal,* March 1996, 14–17.

36. Love, "Smart Tactics for Finding Workers"; and Roy Furchgott, "UPS's Package Deal for Workers," *Business Week,* June 1, 1998, 104.

37. Gillian Flynn, "Can't Get This Big Without HR Deluxe," *Personnel Journal,* December 1996, 47–53.

38. Victoria Griffith, "When Only Internal Expertise Will Do," *CFO,* October 1998, 95–96, 102.

39. P. W. Thayer, "Somethings Old, Somethings New," *Personnel Psychology* 30 (1977), 513–524.

40. J. Ledvinka, *Federal Regulation of Personnel and Human Resource Management* (Boston: Kent, 1982); and Civil Rights Act, Title VII, 42 U.S.C. Section 2000e et seq. (1964).

41. Pierre Mornell, "Zero Defect Hiring," *Inc.,* March 1998, 75–83.

42. A. Brown, "Employment Tests: Issues without Clear Answers," *Personnel Administrator* 30 (1985), 43–56.

43. Lorie Parch, "Testing . . . 1, 2, 3," *Working Woman,* October 1997, 74–78.

44. "Assessment Centers: Identifying Leadership through Testing," *Small Business Report* (June 1987), 22–24; and W. C. Byham, "Assessment Centers for Spotting Future Managers," *Harvard Business Review* (July–August 1970), 150–167.

45. G. F. Dreher and P. R. Sackett, "Commentary: A Critical Look at Some Beliefs about Assessment Centers," in *Perspectives on Employee Staffing and Selection,* ed. G. F. Dreher and P. R. Sackett (Homewood, Ill.: Irwin, 1983), 258–265.

46. Peter Carbonara, "Hire for Attitude, Train for Skill," *Fast Company,* August–September 1996, 73–81.

47. Bernard Keys and Joseph Wolfe, "Management Education and Development: Current Issues and Emerging Trends," *Journal of Management* 14 (1988), 205–229.

48. Steve Bates, "Building Better Workers," *Nation's Business,* June 1998, 18–27.

49. Pfeffer, "Producing Sustainable Competitive Advantage"; McCune, "On the Train Gang"; Max Messmar, "Cross-Discipline Training: A Strategic Method to Do More with Less," *Management Review* (May 1992), 26–28; and Robert Cournoyer, "Integrative Learning Speeds Teamwork," *Management Review* (December 1991), 43–44.

50. Gina Imperato, "How to Give Good Feedback," *Fast Company,* September 1998, 144–156.

51. Walter W. Tornow, "Editor's Note: Introduction to Special Issue on 360-Degree Feedback," *Human Resource Management* 32, no. 2/3 (summer/fall 1993), 211–219; and Brian O'Reilly, "360 Feedback Can Change Your Life," *Fortune,* October 17, 1994, 93–100.

52. Imperato, "How to Give Good Feedback."

53. V. R. Buzzotta, "Improve Your Performance Appraisals," *Management Review* (August 1988), 40–43; and H. J. Bernardin and R. W. Beatty, *Performance Appraisal: Assessing Human Behavior at Work* (Boston: Kent, 1984).

54. Ibid.

55. Francine Alexander, "Performance Appraisals," *Small Business Reports* (March 1989), 20–29.

56. Richard I. Henderson, *Compensation Management: Rewarding Performance,* 4th ed. (Reston, Va.: Reston, 1985).

57. L. R. Gomez-Mejia, "Structure and Process Diversification, Compensation Strategy, and Firm Performance," *Strategic Management Journal* 13 (1992), 381–397; and E. Montemayor, "Congruence Between Pay Policy and Competitive Strategy in High-Performing Firms," *Journal of Management* 22, no. 6 (1996), 889–908.

58. Renée F. Broderick and George T. Milkovich, "Pay Planning, Organization Strategy, Structure and 'Fit': A Prescriptive Model of Pay" (paper presented at the 45th Annual Meeting of the Academy of Management, San Diego, August 1985).

59. L. Wiener, "No New Skills? No Raise," *U.S. News and World Report,* October 26, 1992, 78.

60. E. E. Lawler, III, *Strategic Pay: Aligning Organizational Strategies and Pay Systems,* (San Francisco: Jossey-Bass, 1990); and R. J. Greene, "Person-Focused Pay: Should It Replace Job-Based Pay?" *Compensation and Benefits Management* 9, no. 4 (1993), 46–55.

61. Don Hellriegel, Susan E. Jackson, and John W. Slocum, Jr., *Management,* 8th edition, (Cincinnati: South-Western College Publishing, 1999), 417.

62. L. R. Burgess, *Wage and Salary Administration* (Columbus, Ohio: Merrill, 1984); and E. J. McCormick, *Job Analysis: Methods and Applications* (New York: AMACOM, 1979).

63. B. M. Bass and G. V. Barrett, *People, Work, and Organizations: An Introduction to Industrial and Organizational Psychology,* 2d ed. (Boston: Allyn & Bacon, 1981); and D. Doverspike, A. M. Carlisi, G. V. Barrett, and R. A. Alexander, "Generalizability Analysis of a Point-Method Job Evaluation Instrument," *Journal of Applied Psychology* 68 (1983), 476–483.

64. U.S. Chamber of Commerce, *Employee Benefits 1983* (Washington, D.C.: U.S. Chamber of Commerce, 1984).

65. Christopher Farrell, Paul Magnusson, and Wendy Zellner, "The Scary Math of New Hires," *Business Week,* February 22, 1993, 70–71.

66. J. A. Haslinger, "Flexible Compensation: Getting a Return on Benefit Dollars," *Personnel Administrator* 30 (1985), 39–46, 224.

67. Robert S. Catapano-Friedman, "Cafeteria Plans: New Menu for the '90s," *Management Review* (November 1991), 25–29.

68. Carol A. L. Dannhauser, "Beyond the Paycheck," *Working Woman,* October 1998, 40.

69. "Exit Interviews: An Overlooked Information Source," *Small Business Report* (July 1986), 52–55.

70. Yvette Debow, "GE: Easing the Pain of Layoffs," *Management Review,* September 1997, 15–18.

71. Gillian Flynn, "New Skills Equal New Opportunities," *Personnel Journal,* June 1996, 77–79.

72. McCune, "On the Train Gang."

Chapter 14

LEARNING OBJECTIVES

After studying this chapter, you should be able to

- Explain the dimensions of employee diversity and why ethnorelativism is the appropriate attitude for today's corporations.

- Discuss the changing workplace and the management activities required for a culturally diverse workforce.

- Understand the challenges minority employees face daily.

- Explain affirmative action and why factors such as the glass ceiling have kept it from being more successful.

- Describe how to change the corporate culture, structure, and policies and how to use diversity awareness training to meet the needs of diverse employees.

- Explain the importance of addressing sexual harassment in the workplace.

- Describe benefits that accrue to companies that value diversity.

Managing Diverse Employees

MANAGEMENT PROBLEM

After paying $275,000 to settle a class-action lawsuit alleging racial discrimination at one of its facilities, Chicago's R. R. Donnelley & Sons initiated a companywide diversity training program. Since 1993, Donnelley has spent millions on diversity training, believing it would promote understanding and defuse tensions between workers of diverse backgrounds. However, the program backfired, leading to even more charges of discrimination and harassment. Employees say the diversity program is nothing but window dressing and that top managers have failed to address the real concerns of minority employees. They point out, for example, that black employment actually fell from 8 percent to 6.6 percent in the two years after the program began. There were so few minority workers at Donnelley that some were asked to attend training sessions multiple times in order to ensure diverse participation. One employee, who spoke out in a diversity session about how hard it was to work in a place that was insensitive to women and minorities, claims she was later denied a customer service position because she was "too direct and too honest." Although a group of minority employees asked for a review of hiring and compensation policies, they say company officials failed to include the request in a list of issues to be addressed by the corporate diversity council.[1]

Why has R. R. Donnelley's diversity program led to more problems than solutions? What advice would you give top managers to get the diversity program back on track?

R. R. Donnelley & Sons is not the only company that has faced difficulties with issues of diversity. Diversity in the population, the workforce, and the marketplace is a fact of life no manager can afford to ignore today. All managers daily face the challenge of managing employee diversity. The management of employee diversity entails recruiting, training, and fully utilizing workers who reflect the broad spectrum of society in all areas—gender, race, age, disability, ethnicity, religion, sexual orientation, education, and economic level.

Companies such as American Express, Monsanto, Avon, Hoechst Celanese, and Hewlett-Packard all have established programs for increasing diversity. These programs teach current employees to value ethnic, racial, and gender differences, direct their recruiting efforts, and provide development training for females and minorities. These companies value diversity and are enforcing this value in day-to-day recruitment and promotion decisions.

Companies are beginning to reflect the U.S. image as a melting pot, but with a difference. In the past, the United States was a place where people of different national origins, ethnicities, races, and religions came together and blended to resemble one another. Opportunities for advancement were limited to those workers who fit easily into the mainstream of the larger culture. Some immigrants chose desperate measures to fit in, such as abandoning their native language, changing their last name, and sacrificing their own unique cultures. In essence, everyone in workplace organizations was encouraged to share similar beliefs, values, and lifestyles despite differences in gender, race, and ethnicity.[2]

Now organizations recognize that everyone is not the same and that the differences people bring to the workplace are valuable.[3] Rather than expecting all employees to adopt similar attitudes and values, companies are learning that these differences enable them to compete globally and to acquire rich sources of new talent. Although diversity in North America has been a reality for some time, genuine efforts to accept and *manage* diverse people began only in recent years.

This chapter introduces the topic of diversity, its causes and consequences. Ways to deal with workforce diversity are discussed, and organizational responses to diversity are explored. Further, the benefits of successfully maintaining a diverse workforce are discussed.

Valuing Diversity

At 3Com Corporation's sprawling modem factory near Chicago, 65 different national flags are displayed, each representing the origin of at least one person who has worked at the plant. The 1,200 employees at 3Com speak more than 20 different languages, including Tagalog, Gujarati, and Chinese. Most instructions are in the form of big color-coded drawings that hang over each workstation to illustrate the procedure to be followed. At Rotoflow, a small southern California factory that manufactures giant turbines used in the natural gas industry, president Frank Van Gogh counts 30 nationalities among only 200 employees.[4] Such astonishing diversity is becoming typical in many companies.

Most managers, from any ethnic background, are ill-prepared to handle these multicultural differences. Many Americans attended segregated schools, lived in racially unmixed neighborhoods, and were unexposed to people substantially different from themselves.[5] A typical manager, schooled in traditional management training, easily could make the following mistakes.[6]

In college, Ken Chenault spent endless hours arguing that the Afro-American cause was best served in the long run by rising to power within the Establishment instead of assailing it from the outside. Today he is president and chief operating officer of American Express Co., a $19 billion company that he and CEO Harvey Golub helped bring back from the brink. Together they raised earnings per share by 12 percent to 15 percent annually while maintaining a return to equity of 20 percent. Chenault has been conspicuous at AmEx not only for his accomplishments but also for the workforce diversity he brings to the company. Minorities at AmEx now make up 17 percent of the company's managers. "His ambition is to become CEO, not the best African-American CEO," says John Utendahl, founder and CEO of Utendahl Capital Partners, Wall Street's largest black-owned investment bank.

- To reward a Vietnamese employee's high performance, her manager promoted her, placing her at the same level as her husband, who also worked at the factory. Rather than being pleased, the worker became upset and declined the promotion because Vietnamese husbands are expected to have a higher status than their wives.

- A manager, having learned that a friendly pat on the arm or back would make workers feel good, took every chance to touch his subordinates. His Asian employees hated being touched and thus started avoiding him, and several asked for transfers.

- A manager declined a gift offered by a new employee, an immigrant who wanted to show gratitude for her job. He was concerned about ethics and explained the company's policy about not accepting gifts. The employee was so insulted she quit.

These issues related to cultural diversity are difficult and real. But before discussing how companies handle them, let's define *diversity* and explore people's attitudes toward it.

Dimensions of Diversity

Workforce diversity means the hiring and inclusion of people with different human qualities or who belong to various cultural groups. From the perspective of individuals, diversity means including people different from themselves along dimensions such as age, ethnicity, gender, or race.

Several important dimensions of diversity are illustrated in Exhibit 14.1. This "diversity wheel" shows the multiple combinations of traits that make up diversity. The inside wheel represents primary dimensions of diversity, which include inborn differences or differences that have an impact throughout one's life.[7] Primary dimensions are core elements through which people shape their self-image and world view. These dimensions include age, race, ethnicity, gender, mental or physical abilities, and sexual orientation. Turn the wheel and these primary characteristics match up with various secondary dimensions of diversity.

workforce diversity
Hiring people with different human qualities who belong to various cultural groups.

Exhibit *14.1*

The Diversity Wheel

SOURCE: Marilyn Loden, *Implementing Diversity* (Homewood, IL: Irwin, 1996). Used with permission.

Secondary dimensions can be acquired or changed throughout one's lifetime. These dimensions tend to have less impact than those of the core but nevertheless affect a person's self-definition and world view and have an impact on how the person is viewed by others. For example, Vietnam veterans may have been profoundly affected by their military experience and may be perceived differently from other people. An employee living in a public housing project will certainly be perceived differently from one who lives in an affluent part of town. Secondary dimensions such as work style, communication style, and educational or skill level are particularly relevant in the organizational setting.[8] The challenge for today's managers is to recognize that each person can bring value and strengths to the workplace based on his or her own unique combination of diversity characteristics.

Attitudes toward Diversity

Valuing diversity by welcoming, recognizing, and cultivating differences among people so they can develop their unique talents and be effective organizational members is difficult to achieve. **Ethnocentrism** is the belief that one's own group and subculture are inherently superior to other groups and cultures. Ethnocentrism makes it difficult to value diversity. Viewing one's own culture as the best culture is a natural tendency among most people.[9] Moreover, the business world tends to reflect the values, behaviors, and assumptions based on the experiences of a rather homogeneous, white, middle-class, male workforce.[10] Indeed, most theories of management presume that workers share similar values, beliefs, motivations, and attitudes about work and life in general. As discussed in the Manager's Shoptalk box, this is a false supposition, even when dealing with workers who share the same cultural background. These theories presume there is one set of behaviors that best help an organization to be productive and effective and therefore should be adopted by all employees.[11] This one-best-way approach explains why a manager may cause a problem by touching Asian employees or by not knowing how to handle a gift from an immigrant.

Ethnocentric viewpoints and a standard set of cultural practices produce a **monoculture,** a culture that accepts only one way of doing things and one set of values and beliefs, which can cause problems for minority employees. People of color, women, gay people, the disabled, the elderly, and other diverse employees may feel undue pressure to conform, may be victims of

ethnocentrism
The belief that one's own group or subculture is inherently superior to other groups or cultures.

monoculture
A culture that accepts only one way of doing things and one set of values and beliefs.

Shoptalk

MANAGER'S SHOPTALK

Do Women and Men Communicate Differently?

In recent years, researchers and writers have captured the public imagination with descriptions of gender differences in communication and moral development. Carol Gilligan's *In a Different Voice* describes how women's sense of morality and right versus wrong is different (though not necessarily better or worse) than men's. In decision making, then, men are more concerned with abstract concepts, rules, and hierarchy, while women focus on connections with other human beings and the quality of relationships. Similarly, Deborah Tannen's *You Just Don't Understand* identified the tendency for women to be more relationship oriented. Hence, they tend to be better communicators and try to be supportive and inclusive without offending others. Men, on the other hand, have a more competitive communication style that is outcome oriented. In relationships, women often want to share and process, while men want to give advice and offer solutions.

It should be pointed out that no one is ever purely a "male" or "female" style. However, the following chart shows some basic gender differences in communication.

Male style	Female style
Emphasis is on	**Emphasis is on**
Superiority or uniqueness	Understanding
Work accomplishments	Personal needs of self or others
Content	Process
Asking directly for needs	Hinting about needs
Acting businesslike with others at work	Making others feel comfortable and included
Raising voice	Speaking politely
Rules, procedures, and techniques to solve problems	Relying on the strength of relationships to resolve issues
Showing power with position in organization	Showing power with respect to others

Gilligan found that the differences begin early in life. Young boys tend to play games with elaborate rules and a lot of competition; when there is a problem, the rules are used to solve it. Girls' games, on the other hand, are more relationship oriented and have few rules, being designed to make other players feel included. When they have problems, girls often end the game rather than jeopardize the friendship. Gilligan believes adult male and female style differences are based on these early divergent approaches.

As to where these differences come from, the debate over whether boys and girls are born different or socialized to be different rages on. As shown in the following chart from an actual kindergarten class, girls are often taught different values, motivations, and attitudes at an early age and carry these into adulthood.

Chart of Kindergarten Awards

Boys' Awards	Girls' Awards
Very best thinker	All-around sweetheart
Most eager learner	Sweetest personality
Most imaginative	Cutest personality
Most enthusiastic	Best sharer
Most scientific	Best artist
Best friend	Biggest heart
Mr. Personality	Best manners
Hardest worker	Best helper
Best sense of humor	Most creative

SOURCES: Carol Gilligan, *In a Different Voice* (Cambridge, Mass.: Harvard University Press, 1982); Deborah Tannen, *You Just Don't Understand* (New York: Morrow Books, 1990); Nancy Langton, "Gender Difference in Communication," in *Organizational Behavior: Experiences and Cases*, ed. Dorothy Marcic, 4th ed. (St. Paul, Minn.: West, 1995), 265–268; and Kathleen Deveny, "Chart of Kindergarten Awards," *The Wall Street Journal*, December 5, 1994, B1.

stereotyping attitudes, and may be presumed deficient because they are different. White, heterosexual men, many of whom themselves do not fit the notions of the "ideal" employee, may also feel uncomfortable with the monoculture and resent stereotypes that label all white males as racists and sexists. Valuing diversity means ensuring that *all* people are given equal opportunities in the workplace.[12]

The goal for organizations seeking cultural diversity is pluralism rather than a monoculture and ethnorelativism rather than ethnocentrism. **Ethnorelativism** is the belief that groups and subcultures are inherently equal. **Pluralism** means that an organization accommodates several subcultures. Movement toward pluralism seeks to fully integrate into the organization the employees who otherwise would feel isolated and ignored. As the workforce changes, organizations will come to resemble a global village.

ethnorelativism
The belief that groups and subcultures are inherently equal.

pluralism
The organization accommodates several subcultures, including employees who would otherwise feel isolated and ignored.

Most organizations must undertake conscious efforts to shift from a monoculture perspective to one of pluralism. Employees in a monoculture may not be aware of culture differences, or they may have acquired negative stereotypes toward other cultural values and assume that their own culture is superior. Through effective training, employees can be helped to accept different ways of thinking and behaving, the first step away from narrow, ethnocentric thinking. Ultimately, employees are able to integrate diverse cultures, which means that judgments of appropriateness, goodness, badness, and morality are no longer applied to cultural differences. Cultural differences are experienced as essential, natural, and joyful, enabling an organization to enjoy true pluralism and take advantage of diverse human resources.[13]

For example, UNUM Life Insurance Company of America has made a firm commitment to break out of monoculture thinking. Senior managers, most of whom were white males, began meeting regularly with representatives of minority groups and were shocked to hear how "out of place" many minorities felt in the workplace. Since then, UNUM has implemented a widespread diversity program, including a three-day diversity workshop to help employees develop "cultural competence," a newsletter covering diversity topics, and "Lunch and Learn" talks that help employees understand different cultures and perspectives. Most importantly, a diversity board made up of members from each minority group represented at the company meets monthly with UNUM's president to discuss systematic changes in policies and procedures to encourage and support diversity.[14] By helping all employees, beginning with senior managers, develop greater sensitivity and acceptance of cultural differences, UNUM moves away from an ethnocentric attitude and is able to accept and integrate people from diverse backgrounds.

The Changing Workplace

The importance of cultural diversity and employee attitudes that welcome cultural differences will result from the inevitable changes taking place in the workplace, in our society, and in the economic environment. These changes include globalization and the changing workforce.[15] Earlier chapters described the impact of global competition on business in North America. Competition is intense. About 70 percent of all U.S. businesses are engaged directly in competition with companies overseas. Companies that succeed in this environment need to adopt radical new ways of doing business, with sensitivity toward the needs of different cultural practices. For example, approximately 18 car companies, especially those from Japan and Germany, have established design centers in Los Angeles. Southern California is viewed as a melting pot, an Anglo-Afro-Latino-Asian ethnic mix. Companies that need to sell cars all over the world love the diverse values in this multicultural proving ground.[16]

The single biggest challenge facing companies is the changing composition of the workforce. The average worker is older now, and many more women, people of color, and immigrants are entering the workforce. Indeed, immigration accounted for nearly half of the increase in the labor force in the 1990s and immigrants likely will constitute an increasing share of workers in the twenty-first century.[17] Studies also project that in the twenty-first century Asian Americans, African Americans, and Hispanics will make up 85 percent of U.S. population growth and constitute about 30 percent of the total workforce.[18] So far, the ability of organizations to manage diversity has not kept pace with the changing workforce, which has created a number of significant challenges for minority workers and managers.

Challenges Minorities Face

The one-best-way approach discussed in the previous section leads to a mind-set that views difference as deficiency or dysfunction. For many career women and minorities, their experience suggests that no matter how many college degrees they earn, how many hours they work, how they dress, or how much effort and enthusiasm they invest, they are never perceived as "having the right stuff." A recent Gallup poll found that 45 percent of blacks surveyed believe that blacks are treated less fairly than whites on the job.[19] A Hispanic executive, in discussing the animosity he experienced in one job, said, "The fact that I graduated first in my class didn't make as much difference as the fact that I looked different."[20] If the standard of quality were based, for instance, on being white and male, anything else would be seen as deficient. This dilemma often is difficult for white men to understand because most of them are not intentionally racist and sexist. Many men feel extremely uncomfortable with the prevailing attitudes and stereotypes, but don't know how to change them. These attitudes are deeply rooted in our society as well as in our organizations. The Technology box describes how the Internet is leveling the playing field for many minority entrepreneurs.

Another problem is that many minority workers feel they have to become bicultural in order to succeed. **Biculturalism** can be defined as the sociocultural skills and attitudes used by racial minorities as they move back and forth between the dominant culture and their own ethnic or racial culture.[21] Research on differences between whites and blacks has focused on issues of biculturalism and how it affects employees' access to information, level of respect and appreciation, and relation to superiors and subordinates. In general, African Americans, as well as other racial minorities, feel less accepted in their organizations, perceive themselves to have less discretion on their jobs, receive lower ratings on job performance, experience lower levels of job satisfaction, and reach career plateaus earlier than whites.

Racism in the workplace often shows up in subtle ways—the disregard by a subordinate for an assigned chore; a lack of urgency in completing an important assignment; the ignoring of comments or suggestions made at a meeting. Black managers often struggle daily with the problem of delegating authority and responsibility to employees who show them little respect. They find themselves striving to adopt behaviors and attitudes that will help them be successful in the white-dominated corporate world while at the same time maintaining their ties to the black community and culture.

Other minority groups struggle with biculturalism as well. J. D. Hokoyama started a nonprofit organization, Leadership Education for Asian Pacifics, Inc., to teach Asian Americans how to be bicultural. Asian Americans who aspire to management positions are often frustrated by the stereotype that they are hard workers but not executive material because they are too quiet or not assertive enough. Hokoyama's workshops alert Asian Americans to the ways in which their communication style may hold them back in the American workplace. Participants are taught to use more eye contact, start more sentences with "I,"

biculturalism
The sociocultural skills and attitudes used by racial minorities to move back and forth between the dominant culture and their own ethnic or racial culture.

Leveling the Playing Field

Betty Ford is used to having customers approach the white sales clerk at her company, Mailbox Haven, and assume he is the manager of her suburban Seattle package-delivery business. Ford, who is African-American, deals constantly with a subtle racism that still pervades much of American society. Ford says other customers have been more blatant—she recalls one who warned her, "I'm going to watch you wrap my package." Although Ford's business is thriving, she's selling out to focus all her energy on her new business, City Boxers, an online retailer of hand-tailored boxer shorts.

On the Internet, Ford says, customers "make their decision on what the boxer shorts look like, not on who's selling them." Ford isn't the only person who appreciates the "color-blindness" of the Internet. Many other minority entrepreneurs are bypassing the real-life racial tensions of the workplace by doing business on the World Wide Web, where they can succeed or not based on their own merits. Roosevelt Gist, a 51-year-old former car salesman, launched an online forum

for buying, selling, and researching cars. His site attracts 40,000 visitors a month and collects about $200,000 a year in advertising revenue. Gist recalls his days working at a large Virginia dealership, where white customers would frequently ask to speak to another salesman when Gist approached them.

Working in the anonymity of cyberspace has psychological benefits for minority entrepreneurs, but there are other advantages too. For one thing, launching and running an online business is much less expensive than starting a traditional business. For minority entrepreneurs who may have a hard time getting financing, that's a big plus. While the online world of business is no answer to the real problem of racism, it does level the playing field for many minority entrepreneurs.

www.cityboxers.com

SOURCE: Roger O. Crockett, "Invisible—And Loving It," *Business Week*, October 5, 1998, 124, 128.

and use more assertive body language. Many Asian Americans are offended by the implication that they should abandon their cultural values to succeed. Hokoyama, however, looks at this as a way to help more Asian Americans adjust their style so they can move into management positions.[22] The workshops offered by Leadership Education for Asian Pacifics, Inc., are a sad commentary on the opportunities for minorities in America's organizations. Many minorities feel they have a chance for career advancement only by becoming bicultural or by abandoning their native cultures altogether. Culturally sensitive managers can work to remove these barriers.

Management Activities for a Diverse Workforce

Exhibit 14.2 illustrates the management activities required for dealing with a culturally diverse workforce. For example, consider the increased career involvement of women. By the year 2020, it is estimated that women will comprise fully half of the total U.S. workforce.[23] This change represents an enormous opportunity to organizations, but it also means that organizations must deal with issues such as work-family conflicts, dual-career couples, and sexual harassment. Since seven of ten women in the labor force have children, organizations should prepare to take more of the responsibility for child care.

Moreover, can human resource management systems operate bias free, dropping the perception of a middle-aged, white male as the ideal employee? People of African, Asian, and Hispanic descent are expected to make up about 35 percent of the U.S. population by 2020. Already more than 30 percent of

Exhibit **14.2** *Management Activities for a Culturally Diverse Workforce*

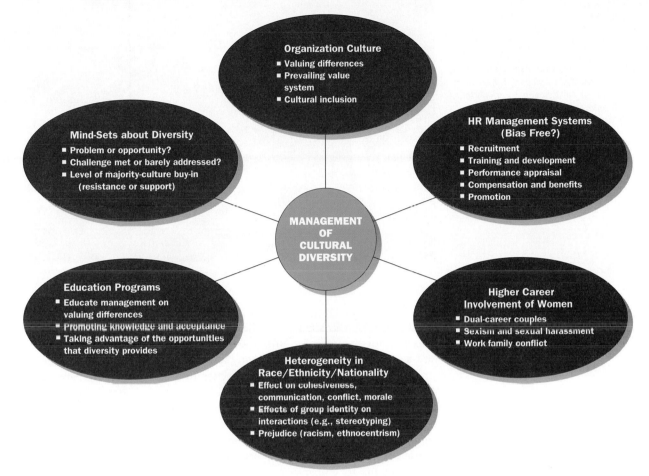

Source: Taylor H. Cox and Stacy Blake, "Managing Cultural Diversity: Implications for Organizational Competitiveness," *Academy of Management Executive* 5, no. 3 (1991), 45–56.

New York City's residents are foreign born. Miami is two-thirds Hispanic-American; Detroit is two-thirds African-American; and San Francisco is one-third Asian-American.[24] Whereas in previous generations most foreign-born immigrants came from Western Europe, 84 percent of recent immigrants come from Asia and Latin America.[25] These immigrants come to the United States with a wide range of backgrounds, often without adequate skills in using English. Organizations must face not only the issues of dealing with race, ethnicity, and nationality to provide a prejudice-free workplace but also develop sufficient educational programs to help immigrants acquire the technical and customer service skills required in a service economy.

Top managers can help shape organizational values and employee mind-sets about cultural differences. In addition, training programs can promote knowledge and acceptance of diverse cultures and educate managers on valuing the differences. Allstate Insurance Company takes a further step by actually rating its managers on how well they handle diversity.

At AT&T, former Chairman Robert Allen helped shape organizational values to meet the company's goal of creating "a work environment that sets the world-class standard for valuing diversity." Pictured here are representatives of AT&T's seven caucuses that represent African-American, Latino, Native-American, Asian, gay, female, and disabled employees. Following outrage over a 1993 company cartoon that many employees and customers considered racist, Allen implemented an accelerated diversity plan, including a call for top officers to increase their direct interaction with employee caucuses. In 1994, 35 percent of new management hires were women and 28 percent were minorities. Representation in top management ranks also is rising.

ALLSTATE INSURANCE COMPANY

www.allstate.com

Allstate Insurance doesn't just talk about the importance of diversity; the company actually tracks support for diversity at every level of management. As the largest property insurer for African-Americans and Hispanics, Allstate made diversity a priority in 1993. The company already had a working affirmative action program and had tried several approaches to diversity training. However, Jerry Choate, CEO, and Carlton Yearwood, director of Allstate's diversity team, believed the company needed a way to track its success on supporting diversity. Its new system gives top executives feedback that they can use continually to make the workplace more comfortable and satisfying for all employees. Today, Allstate surveys all 50,000 workers each quarter on how well it's meeting its commitments to employees and customers, including recruiting, developing, and promoting employees regardless of race or gender. A "diversity index" probes how well workers feel their managers "walk the talk" about bias-free service, respect for the individual, and a culturally sensitive workplace. Performance on these indexes determines 25 percent of a manager's bonus pay.

Overall, Allstate is doing pretty well on the diversity index. Some 21 percent of executives and managers are minorities, compared to a national average of around 10 percent. An African-American who worked his way up through the system holds the company's top sales position. Allstate believes the tracking system contributes to a more productive work environment, where all employees feel valued.[26]

Affirmative Action

Since 1964, civil legislation has prohibited discrimination in hiring based on race, religion, sex, or national origin. As described in Chapter 13 of the text, these policies were designed to facilitate recruitment, retention, and promotion of minorities and women. To some extent, these policies have been successful, opening organization doors to women and minorities. However, despite the job opportunities, women and minorities have not succeeded in getting into top management posts.

Current Debates about Affirmative Action

Affirmative action was developed in response to conditions 30 years ago. Adult white males dominated the workforce, and economic conditions were stable and improving. Because of widespread prejudice and discrimination, legal and social coercion were necessary to allow women, people of color, immigrants, and other minorities to become part of the economic system.[27]

Today, the situation has changed. More than half the U.S. workforce consists of women and minorities; the economic situation is changing rapidly as a result of international competition.

Within this fluid situation, many companies actively recruited women and minorities to comply with affirmative action guidelines. Companies often succeeded in identifying a few select individuals who were recruited, trained, and given special consideration. These people carried great expectations and pressure. They were highly visible role models for the newly recruited groups. It was generally expected that these individuals would march right to the top of the corporate ladder.

Within a few years, it became clear that few of these people would reach the top. Management typically was frustrated and upset because of the money poured into the affirmative action programs. The individuals were disillusioned about how difficult it was to achieve and felt frustrated and alienated. Managers were unhappy with the program failures and may have doubted the qualifications of people they recruited. Did they deserve the jobs at all? Were women and minority candidates to blame for the failure of the affirmative action program? Should companies be required to meet federally mandated minority-hiring targets?

In recent years, outspoken opponents of affirmative action have brought the debate into the public consciousness. Affirmative action has been hotly debated in the states, Congress, the Supreme Court, and corporate America. National Republican leaders have made statements strongly opposing racial hiring preferences, and hiring and college admissions practices targeting minorities have been dismantled in several states. For the first time since its inception, President Bill Clinton ordered an internal review of affirmative action, signaling a less-than-firm commitment on the part of Democratic leaders, as well.[28] Even the intended beneficiaries of affirmative action programs often disagree as to their value, and some believe these programs do more harm than good. One reason for this may be the "stigma of incompetence" that often is associated with affirmative action hires. One study found that both working managers and students consistently rated people portrayed as affirmative action hires as less competent and recommended lower salary increases than for those not associated with affirmative action.[29]

Some companies are arguing the need for broader diversity strategies intended to foster a bias-free workplace, rather than strict head counts of women or minorities hired. Social justice activists, on the other hand, argue that this is just a way for companies to put on a show of virtue without having to do anything concrete about affirmative action issues. Al Jackson, director of diversity and staff development at *Scholastic Magazine,* echoes the sentiments of many when he notes that most firms do not hire and promote women and minorities as readily as they do white males, no matter how much they talk about valuing diversity.[30]

Ultimately, the problem with affirmative action boils down to an unspoken and often unintended sexism and racism in organizations. While it is rare to hear or see blatant expressions of racism and sexism in corporate America today, many minorities believe a more subtle but just as dangerous form has replaced them. For instance, many whites believe racial discrimination is in the past and that blacks are pushing too hard and moving too fast. These "new racists" often see affirmative action programs as unfair.[31] In addition, top managers often find it hard to understand just how white and male their corporate culture is and how forbidding it seems to those who are obviously different.[32] The affirmative action cycle fails when women, people of color, and immigrants are brought into a monoculture system and the burden of adaptation falls on the candidates coming through the system rather than on the organization itself. Part of the reason for the failure may be attributed to what is called the *glass ceiling*.

The Glass Ceiling

glass ceiling
Invisible barrier that separates women and minorities from top management positions.

The **glass ceiling** is an invisible barrier that separates women and minorities from top management positions. They can look up through the ceiling and see top management, but prevailing attitudes are invisible obstacles to their own advancement. A recent study suggested the additional existence of "glass walls," which serve as invisible barriers to important lateral movement within the organization. Glass walls bar experience in areas such as line supervisor positions that would enable women and minorities to advance vertically.[33]

Evidence of the glass ceiling is the distribution of women and minorities, who are clustered at the bottom levels of the corporate hierarchy. A recent study shows that 97 percent of the top managers in the United States are white, and at least 95 percent of them are male.[34] Women and minorities also earn substantially less. As shown in Exhibit 14.3, black, male employees earn 24 percent to 27 percent less than their white counterparts earn, even when educational levels are similar. Women earn considerably less than their male peers, with black women earning the least. As women move up the career ladder, the wage gap widens; at the level of vice president, a woman's average salary is 42 percent less than her male counterpart.[35]

In particular, women who leave the corporate world to care for young children have a difficult time moving up the hierarchy when they return. One term used to describe this is the *mommy track*, which implies that women's commitment to their children limits their commitment to the company or their ability to handle the rigors of corporate management. These women risk being treated as beginners when they return, no matter how vast their skills and experience, and they continue to lag behind in salary, title, and responsibility.[36]

Another current issue related to the glass ceiling is homosexuals in the workplace. Many gay men and lesbians believe they will not be accepted as they are and risk losing their jobs or their chances for advancement. The director of human resources for a large Midwestern hospital would like to be honest about her lesbianism but says she knows of almost no one at her level of the corporate hierarchy who has taken that step—"It's just not done here."[37] Thus, gays and lesbians often fabricate heterosexual identities to keep their jobs or avoid running into the glass ceiling they see other employees encounter.

Why does the glass ceiling persist? The monoculture at top levels is the most frequent explanation. Top-level corporate culture evolves around white, heterosexual, American males, who tend to hire and promote people who look, act, and think like them. Compatibility in thought and behavior plays

E x h i b i t **14.3** *The Wage Gap*

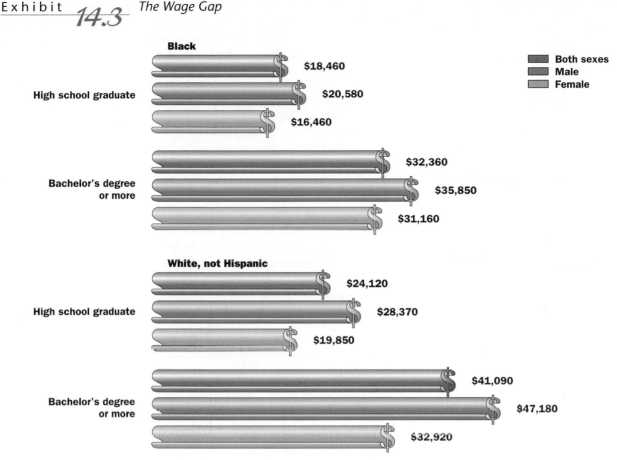

Black

High school graduate
- $18,460
- $20,580
- $16,460

Bachelor's degree or more
- $32,360
- $35,850
- $31,160

White, not Hispanic

High school graduate
- $24,120
- $28,370
- $19,850

Bachelor's degree or more
- $41,090
- $47,180
- $32,920

Legend:
- Both sexes
- Male
- Female

SOURCE: *Population Profile of the United States 1995*, U.S. Department of Commerce, Bureau of the Census, July 1995.

an important role at higher levels of organizations.[38] For example, in a survey of women who have managed to break through the glass ceiling, fully 96 percent said adapting to a predominantly white male culture was an important factor in their success.[39]

Another reason for the persistent glass ceiling is the relegation of women and minorities to less visible positions and projects so that their work fails to come to the attention of top executives. Stereotyping by male middle managers may lead to the assumption that a woman's family life will interfere with her work or that minorities lack competence for important assignments. Women and minorities often believe that they must work harder and perform at higher levels than their white male counterparts in order to be noticed, recognized, fully accepted, and promoted.

New Responses to Cultural Diversity

Affirmative action opened the doors of organizations in this country to women and minorities. However, the path toward promotion to top ranks has remained closed for the most part, with many women and minorities hitting the glass ceiling.[40] Although the federal government responded to this problem with the Civil Rights Act of 1991 to amend and strengthen the Civil

Although corporate cultures are not conducive to including women and minorities in important decision-making processes, women such as Susannah Swihart, chief financial officer and vice chairman of the $71.4 billion (in assets) BankBoston Corp. are becoming more common. In 1995, only 10 women held the CFO post at a Fortune 500 company, but recently there were 23 women holding that position—a 130 percent increase.

Rights Act of 1964, affirmative action currently is under attack. As the debate over affirmative action continues, companies need to find new ways to deal with the obstacles that prevent women and minorities from advancing to senior management positions in the future.

How can managers prepare their organizations to accommodate diversity in the future? First, organization leaders and managers must come to terms with their own definitions of diversity and should be encouraged to think beyond race and gender issues to consider such factors as education, background, and personality differences.

Once a vision for a diverse workplace has been created and defined, the organization can analyze and assess the current culture and systems within the organization. This assessment is followed by a willingness to change the status quo in order to modify current systems and ways of thinking. Throughout this process, people need support in dealing with the many challenges and inevitable conflicts they will face. Training and support are important for the people in pioneering roles. Finally, managers should not de-emphasize affirmative action programs, because these are critical for giving minorities and women access to jobs in the organization.

Once managers accept the need for a program to develop a truly diverse workplace, action can begin. A program to implement such a change involves three major steps: (1) building a corporate culture that values diversity; (2) changing structures, policies, and systems to support diversity; and (3) providing diversity awareness training. For each of these efforts to succeed, top management support is critical, as well as holding all managerial ranks accountable for increasing diversity.

Changing the Corporate Culture

For the most part, today's corporate cultures reflect the white male model of doing business. These cultures are not conducive to including women and minorities in important decision-making processes or enabling them to go high in the corporate hierarchy. The result of this mismatch between the dominant culture and the growing employee population of minorities and women is that many employees' talents will be underutilized, and the corporation will be less competitive.

Chapters 3 and 12 describe approaches for changing corporate culture. Managers can start by actively using symbols for the new values, such as encouraging and celebrating the promotion of minorities. To promote positive change, executives must change their own assumptions and recognize that employee diversity is real, is good, and must be valued. Executives must lead the way in changing from a white male monoculture to a multiculture in which differences among people are valued.

To accomplish this, managers can examine the unwritten rules and assumptions. What are the myths about minorities? What are the values that exemplify the existing culture? Are unwritten rules communicated from one person to another in a way that excludes women and minorities? For example, many men may not discuss unwritten rules with women and minorities because they assume everyone is aware of them and they do not want to seem patronizing.[41]

Companies are addressing the issue of changing culture in a variety of ways. Some are using surveys, interviews, and focus groups to identify how the cultural values affect minorities and women. Others have set up structured networks of people of color, women, and other minority groups to explore the issues they face in the workplace and to recommend changes to senior management. Corning, Inc., appointed a task force to tackle the problem of how to recruit, retain, and develop talented minority workers.

CORNING, INC.

In the mid-1980s, Corning was losing female and African-American professionals at twice the rate of white males. As part of a corporatewide total quality effort, top management appointed a task force to examine the problem of how to retain and develop talented women and African Americans. The task force was part of a top-down initiative with the goal of ensuring that each employee had the opportunity "to participate fully, to grow professionally, and to develop to his or her highest potential." The task force study led to the following interventions:

- Race and gender awareness training, in which aspects of corporate culture that inhibit flexibility and diversity are addressed. One outcome is that new employees are no longer encouraged to adopt the dress, style, and social activities of the white male culture.

- Company child-care services and expanded family-care leaves for all workers who need them.

- Career-planning seminars for all employees, plus more widely disseminated information about the processes for promotion.

- Community projects that make the geographical area more attractive to minority families.

- Incorporation of workplace flexibility and diversity issues into management performance reviews.

Since Corning began making these changes, the recruitment, retention, and advancement of women and African Americans have all improved, and the company is now turning its attention to other minority groups. Corning's culture has gradually begun to change; diverse styles are seen as a strength that helps the company relate to the varied styles of its customers.[42]

Many companies have discovered, as did Corning, that people will choose companies that are accepting, inviting, and friendly and that help them meet personal goals.[43] Successful companies, such as Corning, carefully assess their cultures and make changes from the top down because the key to productivity is a loyal, trained, capable workforce. New cultural values mean that the exclusionary practices of the past must come to an end.

Texaco learned this the hard way, paying more than $175 million to settle a racial discrimination suit. Following a public scandal related to the suit, which included reports of executives using racial slurs, top managers greatly expanded the company's diversity efforts. Prior to the suit, Texaco's diversity program was a routine workshop giving top executives practical tips for managing a diverse workforce. Today, all 20,000 Texaco employees are required to attend a two-day diversity "learning experience." Part of the experience includes learning what it feels like to be excluded. One employee leaves the room while the others form a circle, holding hands and standing shoulder to shoulder. When the person returns to the room, the people in the circle totally ignore him or her, laughing and joking among themselves.[44] Texaco also uses a number of other exercises to develop employees' sensitivity to others as well as their skills for interacting with diverse coworkers. These programs

Exhibit **14.4**

Major Elements of Texaco's Culture Change Initiatives

SOURCE: Don Hellriegel, Susan E. Jackson, and John W. Slocum, Jr., *Management,* 8th ed. (Cincinnati, OH; South-Western College Publishing, 1999). Used with permission. Originally adapted from V. C. Smith, "Texaco outlines comprehensive initiatives," *Human Resource Executive.* February 1997, 13; A. Bryant, "How much has Texaco changed? A mixed report card on anti-bias efforts," *New York Times,* November 2, 1997, 3–1, 3–16, 3–17; and "Texaco's workforce diversity plan," as reprinted in *Workforce,* March 1997 (suppl.).

Recruitment and Hiring

- Ask search firms to identify wider arrays of candidates
- Enhance the interviewing, selection, and hiring skills of managers
- Expand college recruitment at historically minority colleges

Identifying and Developing Talent

- From a partnership with INROADS, a nationwide internship program that targets minority students for management careers
- Establish a mentoring process
- Refine the company's global succession planning system to improve identification of talent
- Improve the selection and development of managers and leaders to help ensure that they are capable of maximizing team performance

Ensuring Fair Treatment

- Conduct extensive diversity training
- Implement an alternative dispute resolution process
- Include women and minorities on all human resources committees throughout the company

Holding Managers Accountable

- Link managers' compensation to their success in creating "openness and inclusion in the workplace"
- Implement 360-degree feedback for all managers and supervisors
- Redesign the company's employee attitude survey and begin using it annually to monitor employee attitudes

Improve Relationships with External Stakeholders

- Broaden the company's base of vendors and suppliers to incorporate more minority- and women-owned businesses
- Increase banking, investment, and insurance business with minority- and women-owned firms
- Add more independent, minority retailers and increase the number of minority managers in company-owned gas stations and Xpress Lube outlets

are part of a widespread culture change effort at Texaco. Exhibit 14.4 outlines major components of Texaco's initiatives, which illustrate that valuing diversity goes far beyond a few diversity workshops.

Changing Structures and Policies

Many policies within organizations originally were designed to fit the stereotypical male employee. Now leading companies are changing structures and policies to facilitate the recruitment and career advancement of diverse employee groups.

Recruitment. A good way to revitalize the recruiting process is for the company to examine employee demographics, the composition of the labor pool in the area, and the composition of the customer base. Managers then can work toward a workforce composition that reflects the labor pool and the customer base. Moreover, the company can look at dimensions of diversity other than race and gender, including age, ethnicity, physical abilities, and sexual orientation. For example, workers age 55 and over are the fastest growing segment of America's labor force, and concern over age discrimination is an increasingly important issue.[45]

For many organizations, a new approach to recruitment will mean recruiting more effectively than today. This could mean making better use of formal recruiting strategies, offering internship programs to give people opportunities, and developing creative ways to draw upon previously unused labor markets.

Career Advancement. The successful advancement of diverse group members means that organizations must find ways to eliminate the glass ceiling. One of the most successful structures to accomplish this is the mentoring relationship. A mentor is a higher ranking, senior organizational member who is committed to providing upward mobility and support to a protégé's professional career.[46] Mentoring provides minorities and women with direct training and inside information on the norms and expectations of the organization. A mentor also acts as a friend or counselor, enabling the employee to feel more confident and capable.

Research indicates that women and minorities are less likely than men to develop mentoring relationships.[47] In the workplace where people's backgrounds are diverse, forging these relationships may be more difficult. Women often do not seek mentors because they feel job competency is enough to succeed, or they may fear that initiating a mentoring relationship could be misunderstood as a romantic overture. Male mentors may feel uncomfortable with minority male protégés. Their backgrounds and interests may differ, leaving them with nothing but work in common. Male mentors may stereotype women as mothers, wives, or sisters rather than as executive material. The few minorities and women who have reached the upper ranks often are overwhelmed with mentoring requests from people like themselves, and they may feel uncomfortable in highly visible minority-minority or female-female mentoring relationships, which isolate them from the white male status quo.

The solution is for organizations to overcome some of the barriers to mentor relationships between white males and minorities. When organizations can institutionalize the value of white males actively seeking women and minority protégés, the benefits will mean that women and minorities will be steered into pivotal jobs and positions critical to advancement. Mentoring programs also are consistent with the Civil Rights Act of 1991 that requires the diversification of middle and upper management.

Accommodating Special Needs. Many people have special needs of which top managers are unaware. For example, if a number of people entering the organization at the lower level are single parents, the company can reassess job scheduling and opportunities for child care. If a substantial labor pool is non-English-speaking, training materials and information packets can be provided in another language.

In many families today, both parents work, which means that the company may provide structures to deal with child care, maternity or paternity leave, flexible work schedules, home-based employment, and perhaps part-time employment or seasonal hours that reflect the school year. The key to attracting and keeping elderly or disabled workers may include long-term-care insurance and special health or life benefits. Alternative work scheduling also may be important for these groups of workers.

In the United States, racial/ethnic minorities and immigrants have fewer educational opportunities than most other groups. Many companies have

Colgate-Palmolive is an example of a company that facilitates the recruitment and career advancement of diverse employee groups. Its Code of Conduct states that its "commitment to caring for people is manifested in the workplace through a variety of programs designed to promote and reward individual and team achievement." It further states that in matters of employment, their policy is "to select, place, and pay employees on the basis of qualifications for the work to be performed and without discrimination on the basis of race, religion, national origin, color, sex, age, citizenship, sexual preference, veteran status, marital status or a disability unrelated to the requirements of the position."

started working with high schools to provide fundamental skills in literacy and arithmetic, or they provide these skills within the company to upgrade employees to appropriate educational levels. The movement toward increasing educational services for employees can be expected to increase for immigrants and the economically disadvantaged in the years to come.

Diversity Awareness Training

diversity awareness training
Special training designed to make people aware of their own prejudices and stereotypes.

Many organizations, including Monsanto, Xerox, and Mobil Oil, provide special training, called **diversity awareness training**, to help people become aware of their own cultural boundaries, their prejudices and stereotypes, so

Exhibit *14.5*　*Stages of Diversity Awareness*

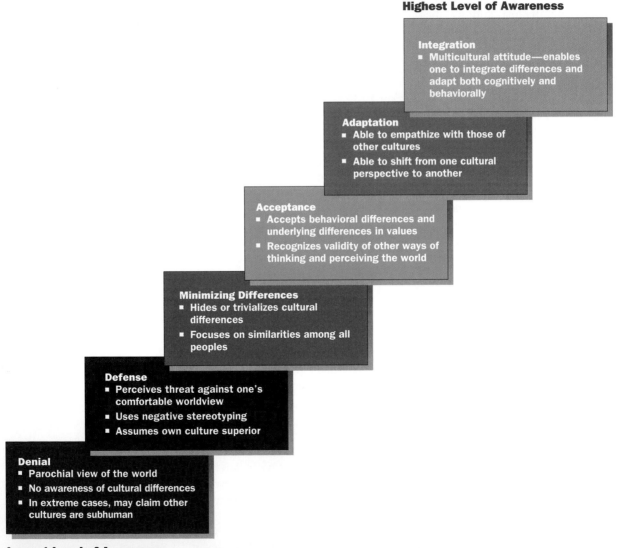

Highest Level of Awareness

Integration
- Multicultural attitude—enables one to integrate differences and adapt both cognitively and behaviorally

Adaptation
- Able to empathize with those of other cultures
- Able to shift from one cultural perspective to another

Acceptance
- Accepts behavioral differences and underlying differences in values
- Recognizes validity of other ways of thinking and perceiving the world

Minimizing Differences
- Hides or trivializes cultural differences
- Focuses on similarities among all peoples

Defense
- Perceives threat against one's comfortable worldview
- Uses negative stereotyping
- Assumes own culture superior

Denial
- Parochial view of the world
- No awareness of cultural differences
- In extreme cases, may claim other cultures are subhuman

Lowest Level of Awareness

SOURCE: Based on M. Bennett, "A Developmental Approach to Training for Intercultural Sensitivity," *International Journal of Intercultural Relations* 10 (1986), 179–196.

they can learn to work and live together. Working or living within a multi-cultural context requires a person to use interaction skills that transcend the skills typically effective when dealing with others from one's own in-group.[48] Diversity awareness programs help people learn how to handle conflict in a constructive manner, which tends to reduce stress and negative energy in diverse work teams.

People vary in their sensitivity and openness to other cultures. Exhibit 14.5 shows a model of six stages of diversity awareness. The continuum ranges from a total lack of awareness to a complete understanding and acceptance of people's differences. This model is useful in helping diversity awareness trainers assess participants' openness to change. People at different stages may require different kinds of training. A basic aim of awareness training is to help people recognize that hidden and overt biases direct their thinking about specific individuals and groups. If people can come away from a training session recognizing that they prejudge people and that this needs to be consciously addressed in communications with and treatment of others, an important goal of diversity awareness training has been reached.

Many diversity awareness programs used today are designed to help people of varying backgrounds communicate effectively with one another and to understand the language and context used in dealing with people from other groups. The point of this training is to help people be more flexible in their communications with others, to treat each person as an individual, and not to rely on stereotypes. Effective programs move people toward being open in their relationships with others. For example, if you were a part of such a program, it would help you develop an explicit awareness of your own cultural values, your own cultural boundaries, and your own cultural behaviors. Then you would be provided the same information about other groups, and you would be given the opportunity to learn about and communicate with people from other groups. One of the most important elements in diversity training is to bring together people of differing perspectives so that they can engage in learning new interpersonal communication skills with one another.

Defining New Relationships in Organizations

One outcome of diversity is an increased incidence of close personal relationships in the workplace, which can have both positive and negative results for employees as well as the organization. Two issues of concern are emotional intimacy and sexual harassment.

Emotional Intimacy

Close relationships between men and women often have been discouraged in companies for fear that they would disrupt the balance of power and threaten organizational stability.[49] This opinion grew out of the assumption that organizations are designed for rationality and efficiency, which were best achieved in a nonemotional environment. Close relationships between men and women could become romantic or sexual in nature, upsetting the stable working relationships.

A recent study of friendships in organizations sheds interesting light on this issue.[50] Managers and workers responded to a survey about emotionally intimate relationships with both male and female coworkers. Many men and women reported having close relationships with an opposite-sex coworker.

Called "nonromantic love relationships," the friendships resulted in trust, respect, constructive feedback, and support in achieving work goals. Intimate friendships did not necessarily become romantic, and they affected each person's job and career in a positive way. Rather than causing problems, nonromantic love relationships, according to the study, affected work teams in a positive manner because conflict was reduced. Indeed, men reported somewhat greater benefit than women from these relationships, perhaps because the men had fewer close relationships outside the workplace upon which to depend.

However, when such relationships *do* become romantic or sexual in nature real problems can result. Office romance is on the rise, with more than 30 percent of employees reporting they have been involved with a coworker at some time in their careers. Although not all office romances lead to trouble, usually they create difficulties for managers. Such relationships disrupt productivity and distract coworkers. According to Dorothy Light, president of Alden Enterprises, a consulting business in Minneapolis, office romances are the biggest productivity disrupters next to mergers and downsizing. One of the most difficult dilemmas is how to deal with other staff members who may be jealous, intrigued, or embarrassed by the relationship or may spend their time gossiping about the involvement of their coworkers.[51] There is a growing recognition that companies can't ban office romance, but it is an important issue that should be managed carefully.

Romances that require the most attention from managers are those that arise between a supervisor and a subordinate. These relationships often lead to morale problems among other staff members, complaints of favoritism, and questions about the supervisor's intentions or judgment. Although few companies have written policies about workplace romance in general, 70 percent of companies recently surveyed have policies prohibiting romantic relationships between a superior and a subordinate.[52] At IBM, training programs and written policies emphasize that a manager can become romantically involved with a subordinate only if he or she agrees to stop supervising the subordinate. If a manager wants to pursue a relationship with a subordinate, the company requests that he or she step forward and transfer to another job within or outside the company. The onus is on the manager rather than the subordinate to take action.[53] The most difficult part of an office romance often is when it comes to an end. At worst, such failed relationships can lead to claims of sexual harassment—one of the most troubling people issues managers face today.

Sexual Harassment

While psychological closeness between men and women in the workplace may be a positive experience, sexual harassment is not. Sexual harassment is illegal. As a form of sexual discrimination, sexual harassment in the workplace is a violation of Title VII of the 1964 Civil Rights Act. Sexual harassment in the classroom is a violation of Title VIII of the Education Amendment of 1972. The following categorize various forms of sexual harassment as defined by one university:

• *Generalized.* This form involves sexual remarks and actions that are not intended to lead to sexual activity but that are directed toward a coworker based solely on gender and reflect on the entire group.

- *Inappropriate/offensive.* Though not sexually threatening, it causes discomfort in a coworker, whose reaction in avoiding the harasser may limit his or her freedom and ability to function in the workplace.

- *Solicitation with promise of reward.* This action treads a fine line as an attempt to "purchase" sex, with the potential for criminal prosecution.

- *Coercion with threat of punishment.* The harasser coerces a coworker into sexual activity by using the threat of power (through recommendations, grades, promotions, and so on) to jeopardize the victim's career.

- *Sexual crimes and misdemeanors.* The highest level of sexual harassment, these acts would, if reported to the police, be considered felony crimes and misdemeanors.[54]

Ever since Anita Hill confronted Clarence Thomas on national television nearly a decade ago, the number of sexual harassment claims filed annually in the United States has more than doubled. Nearly 16,000 claims were filed in 1997 alone.[55] For example, during that year, Mitsubishi Motor Corp. agreed to pay $9.5 million to settle with 27 female employees who claimed they were regularly groped and grabbed by male coworkers at the company's factory in Normal, Illinois. Some women said they had to agree to sex to win jobs. Mitsubishi has since sent the factory's 4,000 workers through an eight-hour course in sexual harassment awareness and has created a special unit to investigate all sexual harassment claims, as well.[56]

Recently, a decision handed down by the U.S. Supreme Court broadened the definition of sexual harassment to include same sex harassment as well as harassment of men by female coworkers. In the suit that prompted the Court's decision, a male oil-rig worker claimed he was singled out by other members of the all-male crew for crude sex play, unwanted touching, and threats of rape.[57] Eight men, former employees of Jenny Craig Inc., have sued the company charging that female bosses made lewd comments or that they were denied promotions because of their sex. A male worker at a hot tub manufacturer won a $1 million court decision after claiming that his female boss made sexual overtures to him almost daily. These are among a growing number of men urging recognition that sexual harassment is not just a woman's problem.[58]

Because the corporate world is dominated by a male culture, however, sexual harassment affects women to a much greater extent. Women who are moving up the corporate hierarchy by entering male-dominated industries report a high frequency of harassment. Surveys report an increase in sexual harassment programs, but female employees also report a lack of prompt and just action by executives to incidents of sexual harassment. However, companies are discovering that "an ounce of prevention really is worth a pound of cure." Top executives are seeking to address problems of harassment through company diversity programs, revised complaint systems and grievance procedures, written policy statements, workshops, lectures, and role-playing exercises to increase employee sensitivity and awareness to the issue.[59]

Global Diversity

Globalization is a reality for today's companies. As stated in a recent report from the Hudson Institute, *Workforce 2020,* "The rest of the world matters to a degree that it never did in the past."[60] Even small companies that do not do business in other countries are affected by global diversity issues. However, large multinational companies that hire employees in many countries face tremendous challenges because they must apply diversity management across a broader stage than North America. Managers must develop new skills and awareness to handle the unique challenges of global diversity: cross-cultural understanding, the ability to build networks, and the understanding of geopolitical forces. Two significant aspects of global diversity programs involve employee selection and training and the understanding of the communication context.

Selection and Training

expatriates
Employees who live and work in a country other than their own.

Expatriates are employees who live and work in a country other than their own. Careful screening, selection, and training of employees to serve overseas increase the potential for corporate global success. Human resource managers consider global skills in the selection process. In addition, expatriates receive cross-cultural training that develops language skills and cultural and historical orientation. Career-path counseling often is available.[61] General Motors has a variety of exchange programs that provide opportunities for its employees around the world to learn about different cultures. According to Cindy Gier, diversity manager at GM Powertrain Division, such experiences "expose people to cultures other than their own, providing them with new insights while changing their perceptions of the world and equipping them with global management skills."[62]

Equally important, however, is honest self-analysis by overseas candidates and their families. Before seeking or accepting an assignment in another country, a candidate should ask himself or herself such questions as the following:

- Is your spouse interrupting his or her own career path to support your career? Is that acceptable to both of you?

- Is family separation for long periods involved?

- Can you initiate social contacts in a foreign culture?

The children in this Avezzano, Italy, school share cultures and learn firsthand the dynamics of global diversity. The school was established by Texas Instruments for the families of U.S. and Japanese employees involved in T.I.'s six-nation team that is building Europe's largest semiconductor. Such efforts, along with Minority Procurement programs, demonstrate T.I.'s commitment to a diverse, multinational corporate environment.

- Can you adjust well to different environments and changes in personal comfort or quality of living, such as the lack of television, gasoline at $5 per gallon, limited hot water, varied cuisine, national phone strikes, and *warm* beer?

- Can you manage your future reentry into the job market by networking and maintaining contacts in your home country?[63]

Employees working overseas must adjust to all of these conditions. Managers going global may find that their own management "style" needs adjustment to succeed in a foreign country. One aspect of this adjustment is learning the communication context of a foreign location.

Communication Differences

People from some cultures tend to pay more attention to the social context (social setting, nonverbal behavior, social status) of their verbal communication than Americans do. For example, General Norman Schwarzkopf soon realized that social context was of considerable importance to leaders of Saudi Arabia. During the initial buildup for the Persian Gulf War, he suppressed his own tendency toward impatience and devoted hours to "philosophizing" with members of the Saudi royal family. Schwarzkopf realized it was *their* way of making decisions.[64]

Exhibit 14.6 indicates how the emphasis on social context varies among countries. In a **high-context culture,** people are sensitive to circumstances surrounding social exchanges. People use communication primarily to build personal social relationships; meaning is derived from context—setting, status, nonverbal behavior—more than from explicit words; relationships and trust are more important than business; and the welfare and harmony of the group are valued. In a **low-context culture,** people use communication primarily to exchange facts and information; meaning is derived primarily from words; business transactions are more important than building relationships and trust; and individual welfare and achievement are more important than the group.[65]

To understand how differences in cultural context affect communications, consider the U.S. expression "The squeaky wheel gets the oil." It means that the loudest person will get the most attention, and attention is assumed to be favorable. Equivalent sayings in China and Japan are "Quacking ducks get shot" and "The nail that sticks up gets hammered down," respectively. Standing out as an individual in these cultures clearly merits unfavorable attention.

High-context cultures include Asian and Arab countries. Low-context cultures tend to be American and Northern European. Even within North America, cultural subgroups vary in the extent to which context counts, explaining why differences among groups make successful communication difficult. White females, Native Americans, and African Americans all tend to prefer higher context communication than do white males. A high-context interaction requires more time because a relationship has to be developed, and trust and friendship must be established. Furthermore, most male managers and most people doing the hiring in organizations are from low-context cultures, which conflicts with people entering the organization from a background in a higher context culture. Overcoming these differences in communication is a major goal of diversity awareness training.

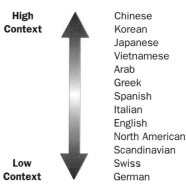

Exhibit 14.6

Arrangement of High- and Low-Context Cultures

High Context

Low Context

Chinese
Korean
Japanese
Vietnamese
Arab
Greek
Spanish
Italian
English
North American
Scandinavian
Swiss
German

Sources: Edward T. Hall, *Beyond Culture* (Garden City, N.Y.: Anchor Press/Doubleday, 1976); and J. Kennedy and A. Everest, "Put Diversity in Context," *Personnel Journal* (September 1991), 50–54.

high-context culture
A culture in which communication is used to enhance personal relationships.

low-context culture
A culture in which communication is used to exchange facts and information.

Benefits of Valuing Diversity

As a rule, organizations have not been highly successful in managing women and minorities, as evidenced by higher turnover rates, higher absenteeism, lower job satisfaction, and general frustration over career development for these groups. Moreover, the fact that women and minorities are clustered at lower organization levels indicates they are not progressing as far as they might and are not developing their full potential.[66]

Diversity in the workplace is inevitable and provides many benefits for organizations. Organizations need internal diversity to help them meet the needs of an increasingly diverse marketplace. With the growing diversity of the U.S. population, formerly small market niches, such as African Americans,

For Michele Luna, president of Atlas Headwear, Inc., a Phoenix company that manufactures military and sports hats, managing diversity is just good business. Luna has built a diverse management team that includes Freddy Torres, left, and Alfredo Luna, her husband. Ninety-four percent of Atlas's employees are Asian and Hispanic, and many of them are immigrants. Bilingual employees help bridge the communication gap with employees who do not speak English, and weekly meetings are held to facilitate mutual understanding among workers. For Luna, rising revenues and a committed workforce reflect the benefits of valuing diversity.

Asian Americans, and Hispanics, are becoming major ones that many companies want to pursue. Avon Company and Maybelline are successfully marketing cosmetics to African Americans and Hispanics by hiring representatives of these minority groups as marketing managers. DuPont recently leveraged the cultural understanding of its African-American workers in opening up promising new markets for its agricultural products.[67] In addition, when companies compete on a global scale, ethnic and cultural diversity can pay significant benefits. At Metasys, Inc., a transportation software company, owner Patrick Thean, himself an immigrant from Singapore, believes his multicultural staff makes his company more competitive. For example, when Roy Thorpe, who grew up in Wales, reviewed the company's software for the first time, he noted that it was "Americanized." For one thing, the zip code field was designed for the standard U.S. five-digit code. Metasys is now globalizing its software so the company can serve large shipping clients with international needs.[68]

Another benefit from valuing diversity is the opportunity to develop employee and organizational potential. This means higher morale, because people feel valued for what they bring to the organization. It also produces better relationships at work, because people acquire the skills to recognize, understand, and accept cultural differences. Developing employee skills and valuing diversity have become a bottom-line business issue.

In addition, companies that treat women and racial/ethnic minorities well will be able to recruit the best employees, both those new to the workforce and experienced employees from other organizations. Retaining these employees means a qualified, trained workforce for the future. Demographics tell us that the labor market is slowly tightening, and those organizations that boast a healthy environment for women and minorities will be in the best competitive position to attract and retain scarce employees. When women and minorities experience prejudice and nonacceptance, reduced individual and organizational productivity occurs because people do not feel valued and are not willing to take risks for the organization.

The Strength of Diversity

Creating a diverse, inclusive workforce is a continuous process at Hewlett-Packard, where managers see diversity as an opportunity to tap a broad range of human potential and use it to keep learning, changing, and growing. H-P's commitment to diversity began years before equal employment opportunity or affirmative action guidelines required it. It is an outgrowth of the company's founding values of treating each employee with dignity and respect.

However, after a survey revealed that many women and employees of color did not feel they had equal opportunities at Hewlett-Packard, company managers involved all employees in a complete examination of H-P's work environment. By involving all employees, managers avoided the problem of issuing a "diversity directive" that did not have the support of line managers. In addition, participation ensured that the real needs of employees were addressed. Today, Hewlett-Packard's diversity strategy recognizes many aspects of diversity, including race, gender, culture, age, economic status, sexual orientation, and physical ability. The emphasis on employee involvement has continued, with the formation of employee network groups that represent various minority groups in the organization. Workers also are involved in discussing diversity issues at coffee talks, task forces, diversity councils, conferences, and regular team meetings. Supporting diversity is ingrained in the culture at H-P. Managers and other workers are encouraged to challenge norms and biases and address inappropriate language or behavior. Often, those who do so are rewarded by the company for being "diversity champions."

Another key to a successful diversity program at Hewlett-Packard is ensuring management leadership and involvement. Senior managers representing all of H-P's businesses develop and drive diversity initiatives worldwide. However, top managers then cascade responsibility and accountability for diversity success to all managers and employees through performance plans and evaluations. Diversity objectives are of major importance in staffing activities and decisions. When hiring new people, a diverse interviewing team is considered equally as important as a diverse slate of candidates. This helps to ensure that minority candidates have equal opportunities to move into higher management positions. In addition, H-P sponsors a unique mentoring program to make sure "supporting diversity" is more than talk. The program matches minority employees with higher-level managers, who are evaluated on their mentee's progress. Many participants in the program move into higher-level jobs in the company. The company also supports and funds a number of other employee development and job enrichment opportunities and assignments for minority employees. As a learning organization, Hewlett-Packard is continually striving to create an environment where everyone feels valued and included.

www.hewlett-packard.com

SOURCE: Michael L. Wheeler, "Global Diversity: Reality, Opportunity, and Challenge," *Business Week*, December 1, 1997, Special Advertising Section.

Minority employees often leave the company out of frustration if they feel their opportunities for career advancement are blocked.

Finally, diversity within the organization provides a broader and deeper base of experience for problem solving, creativity, and innovation. For example, research shows that heterogeneous teams produce more innovative solutions to problems than do homogeneous teams. One reason is that people with diverse backgrounds bring different perspectives to problem solving. In addition, when allowed an active role, minority employees can help organizations grow and improve by challenging basic assumptions about how the organization works. African Americans, women, Hispanics, Native Americans, Asian Americans, and others outside the mainstream of corporate America can help managers and organizations break out of status quo thinking.[69]

Diversity is essential to the *learning organization*, in which teams of workers that cross functional boundaries are engaged regularly in identifying and solving problems. Employees in learning organizations are encouraged to think, express divergent opinions, and be creative in order to help the organization learn and change; a diverse mix of employees is a real plus in this environment. One study found that companies that rate highly on creativity and innovation have a higher percentage of women and nonwhite male employees than less innovative companies.[70] Hewlett-Packard, a company long known for innovation, makes a strong commitment to diversity, as discussed in the Learning Organization box. Competitive pressures are challenging all managers to create organizational environments that support diversity.

As one senior executive said, "In a country seeking competitive advantage in a global economy, the goal of managing diversity is to develop our capacity to accept, incorporate, and empower the diverse human talents of the most diverse nation on earth. It is our reality. We need to make it our strength."[71]

Summary and Management Solution

Several important ideas pertain to workforce diversity, which is the inclusion of people with different human qualities and from different cultural groups. Dimensions of diversity are both primary, such as age, gender, and race, and secondary, such as education, marital status, and income. Ethnocentric attitudes generally produce a monoculture that accepts only one way of doing things and one set of values and beliefs, thereby excluding nontraditional employees from full participation. Minority employees face several significant challenges in the workplace.

Acceptance of workforce diversity is becoming especially important because of sociocultural changes and the changing workforce. Diversity in the workplace reflects diversity in the larger environment. Innovative companies are initiating a variety of programs to take advantage of the diverse workforce.

Affirmative action programs have been successful in gaining employment for women and minorities, but the glass ceiling has kept many women and minorities from obtaining top management positions. The Civil Rights Act of 1991 amends and strengthens the Civil Rights Act of 1964.

Breaking down the glass ceiling ultimately means changing the corporate culture within organizations; changing internal structures and policies toward employees, including accommodating special needs; and providing diversity awareness training to help people become aware of their own cultural boundaries and prejudices. This training also helps employees learn to communicate with people from other cultural contexts.

The increased diversity in organizations has provided opportunities for emotional intimacy and friendship between men and women that are beneficial to all parties. However, when these relationships become romantic or sexual, they can present problems for managers. Increasing diversity also means that organizations must develop programs to deal with global as well as domestic diversity and with potential conflicts, such as sexual harassment, that arise.

Valuing diversity has many benefits, such as developing employees to their full potential and allowing successful interaction with diverse clients in the marketplace. Diversity also provides a broader and deeper base of experience for problem solving, creativity, and innovation.

Although diversity training programs are important, they can backfire if they are not combined with real and substantive changes in policies and structures to support the inclusion and advancement of minority members. For diversity efforts to be successful, they should be integrated into the organization's culture and strategy. At R. R. Donnelley & Sons, described in the opening chapter case, diversity training backfired because employees felt the programs were only window dressing. Donnelley managers now understand that supporting diversity means linking diversity training to concrete hiring and promotion goals for minorities. The first step the company took was to retain a consultant to examine hiring, pay, and promotion policies, which minority employees had earlier requested. In addition, R. R. Donnelley is undergoing an overall culture change effort that includes diversity and inclusion initiatives. R. R. Donnelley is on the right track, but only time will tell if managers can make the necessary changes in culture, structure, and policies to help the company reap the benefits of a diverse workforce.

Discussion Questions

1. If you were a senior manager at a company such as R. R. Donnelley, Allstate Insurance, or Texaco, how would you address the challenges faced by minority employees?

2. Some people argue that social class is a major source of cultural differences, yet social class is not listed as a primary or secondary dimension in Exhibit 14.1. Discuss reasons for this.

3. Have you been associated with an organization that made assumptions associated with a monoculture? Describe the culture.

4. Do you think any organization can successfully resist diversity today? Discuss.

5. What is the glass ceiling, and why do you think it has proved to be such a barrier to women and minorities?

6. In preparing an organization to accept diversity, do you think it is more important to change the corporate culture or to change structures and policies? Explain.

7. If a North American corporation could choose either high-context or low-context communications, which do you think would be best for the company's long-term health? Discuss.

8. What do you think the impact on an organization would be for diversity within its own country versus international diversity? Discuss.

9. Many single people meet and date people from their work organization because the organization provides a context within which to know and trust another person. How do you think this practice affects the potential for emotional intimacy? Sexual harassment?

10. How might diversity within the organization ultimately lead to better problem solving and greater creativity?

Management in Practice: Experiential Exercise

How Tolerant Are You?

For each of the following questions circle the answer that best describes you.

1. Most of your friends
   a. are very similar to you
   b. are very different from you and from each other
   c. are like you in some respects but different in others

2. When someone does something you disapprove of, you
   a. break off the relationship
   b. tell how you feel but keep in touch
   c. tell yourself it matters little and behave as you always have

3. Which virtue is most important to you?
   a. kindness
   b. objectivity
   c. obedience

4. When it comes to beliefs, you
   a. do all you can to make others see things the same way you do
   b. actively advance your point of view but stop short of argument
   c. keep your feelings to yourself

5. Would you hire a person who has had emotional problems?
   a. no
   b. yes, provided there is evidence of complete recovery
   c. yes, if the person is suitable for the job

6. Do you voluntarily read material that supports views different from your own?
   a. never
   b. sometimes
   c. often

7. You react to old people with
   a. patience
   b. annoyance
   c. sometimes a, sometimes b

8. Do you agree with the statement, "What is right and wrong depends upon the time, place, and circumstance?"
   a. strongly agree
   b. agree to a point
   c. strongly disagree

9. Would you marry someone from a different race?
   a. yes
   b. no
   c. probably not

10. If someone in your family were homosexual, you would
    a. view this as a problem and try to change the person to a heterosexual orientation
    b. accept the person as a homosexual with no change in feelings or treatment
    c. avoid or reject the person

11. You react to little children with
    a. patience
    b. annoyance
    c. sometimes a, sometimes b

12. Other people's personal habits annoy you
    a. often
    b. not at all
    c. only if extreme

13. If you stay in a household run differently from yours (cleanliness, manners, meals, and other customs), you
    a. adapt readily
    b. quickly become uncomfortable and irritated
    c. adjust for a while, but not for long
14. Which statement do you agree with most?
    a. We should avoid judging others because no one can fully understand the motives of another person.
    b. People are responsible for their actions and have to accept the consequences.
    c. Both motives and actions are important when considering questions of right and wrong.

Circle your score for each of the answers below and total the scores:

1. a = 4; b = 0; c = 2
2. a = 4; b = 2; c = 0
3. a = 0; b = 2; c = 4
4. a = 4; b = 2; c = 0
5. a = 4; b = 2; c = 0
6. a = 4; b = 2; c = 0
7. a = 0; b = 4; c = 2
8. a = 0; b = 2; c = 4
9. a = 0; b = 4; c = 2
10. a = 2; b = 0; c = 4
11. a = 0; b = 4; c = 2
12. a = 4; b = 0; c = 2
13. a = 0; b = 4; c = 2
14. a = 0; b = 4; c = 2

Total Score:

0–14: If you score 14 or below, you are a very tolerant person and dealing with diversity comes easily to you.

15–28: You are basically a tolerant person and others think of you as tolerant. In general, diversity presents few problems for you, but you may be broad minded in some areas and have less tolerant ideas in other areas of life, such as attitudes toward older people or male-female social roles.

29–42: You are less tolerant than most people and should work on developing greater tolerance of people different from you. Your low tolerance level could affect your business or personal relationships.

43–56: You have a very low tolerance for diversity. The only people you are likely to respect are those with beliefs similar to your own. You reflect a level of intolerance that could cause difficulties in today's multicultural business environment.

SOURCE: Adapted from the Tolerance Scale by Maria Heiselman, Naomi Miller, and Bob Schlorman, Northern Kentucky University, 1982, in George Manning, Kent Curtis, and Steve McMillen, *Building Community: The Human Side of Work,* (Cincinnati, Ohio: Thomson Executive Press, 1996), 272–277.

Management in Practice: Ethical Dilemma

Promotion or Not?

You are the president of CrownCutters, Inc. You have worked closely with Bill Smith for several years now. In many situations, he has served as your *de facto* right-hand person.

Due to a retirement, you have an opening in the position of executive vice president. Bill is the natural choice—and this is obvious to the other mid- and senior-level managers at Crown-Cutters. Bill is popular with most of the managers in the company. Of course, he also has his share of detractors.

Prior to announcing the appointment of Bill Smith, you receive a memo from Jane Jones, your controller. Jane's memo indicates that she was subjected to sporadic sexual harassment by Bill starting ten years ago when she first joined the company and was working for him. Her memo indicates that the harassment essentially stopped six years ago when she moved to a position in which Bill was no longer her superior. She requests that this information be kept totally confidential.

You have never heard of any allegations like this about Bill before.

What Do You Do?

1. Move ahead with the promotion because, even if true, this is an isolated incident that is a part of Bill's past and is not his current behavior.
2. Stop the promotion because Bill is not the type of person who should help lead the company and shape its values.
3. Put the promotion on hold until you can discuss the situation extensively with Bill and Jane, although this means the accusation probably will become public knowledge.

SOURCE: This case was provided by Professor David Scheffman, Owen Graduate School of Management, Vanderbilt University, Nashville, Tennessee.

Surf the Net

1. **The Glass Ceiling.** In order to learn more about the glass ceiling, visit **www.ilr.cornell.edu/library/e_archive/ glassceiling**. You will need to have the Acrobat Reader, available as a free download from this site, installed on your computer. Select the "Recommendations of the Glass Ceiling Commission," and answer these two questions: (a) What was the mission of the Glass Ceiling Commission? (b) What are the eight recommendations the Commission made for business?

2. **Diversity Awareness Training.** Use a search engine keying in the words "diversity awareness training," and compare the content and focus of 3 to 4 different training pro-

grams in this area. Recommend the training program you think would do the best job of improving employees' diversity awareness. Sample sites are included below:

www.adl.org/frames/front_awod.html

chrissy-jackson.com/diversity.html

www.corcommunications.com

www.dnai.com/~mail/daw.html

3. **Sexual Harassment.** Go to **www.capstn.com** and find the sexual harassment quiz prepared by Capstone Communications. Take the quiz, print out a copy after you have selected your answers, and bring the completed quiz to class. Your instructor may wish to use this quiz to determine how well the class understands sexual harassment.

Case for Critical Analysis
Draper Manufacturing

You have just been hired as a diversity consultant by Draper Manufacturing. Ralph Draper, chairman and CEO, and other top managers feel a need to resolve some racial issues that have been growing over the past several years at their plant in Nashville, Tennessee. Draper Manufacturing is a small, family-owned company that manufactures mattresses. It employs 90 people full-time, including African Americans, Asians, and Hispanics. About 75 percent of the workforce is female. The company also occasionally hires part-time workers, most of whom are Hispanic women. Most of these part-timers are hired for periods of a few months at a time, when production is falling behind schedule.

To begin your orientation to the company, Draper has asked his production manager, Wallace Burns, to take you around the plant. As Burns points out the various areas responsible for each stage of the production process, you overhear several different languages being spoken. In the shipping and receiving department, you notice that most workers are black men. Burns confirms that 90 percent of the workers in shipping and receiving are African American and points out that the manager of that department, Adam Fox, is also African American.

Later in the afternoon you attend a regular meeting of top managers to meet everyone and get a feel for the organizational culture. Draper introduces you as a diversity consultant and notes that several of his managers have expressed concerns about festering racial tensions in the company. He notes that "Each of the minority groups sticks together. The blacks and Orientals rarely mix, and most of the Mexicans stick together and speak only in Spanish. It seems that some of our workers are just downright lazy sometimes. We keep falling behind in our production schedule and having to hire part-time workers, but then we generally have to fire two or three of those a month

for goofing off on the job." He closes his introduction by saying that you have been hired to help the company solve their growing diversity problems.

Draper then turns toward the management committee's routine daily business. The others present are the general manager, human resources manager (the only woman), sales manager, quality control manager, plant manager (Wallace Burns), and shipping and receiving manager (Adam Fox, the only non-white manager). Soon an angry debate begins between Fox and the sales manager. The sales manager says that orders are not being shipped on time, and several complaints have been received about the quality of the product. Fox argues that he needs more workers in shipping and receiving to do the job right, and he adds that the quality of incoming supplies is lousy. While this debate continues, the other managers remain silent and seem quite uncomfortable. Finally, the quality control manager attempts to calm things down with a joke about his wife. Most of the men in the group laugh loudly, and the conversation shifts to other topics on the agenda.

Questions
1. What suggestions would you make to Draper's managers to help them move toward successfully managing diversity issues?
2. If you were the shipping and receiving or human resources manager, how do you think you would feel about working at Draper? What are some of the challenges you might face at this company?
3. Based on the information in the case, at what stage of diversity awareness (Exhibit 14.5) do managers at Draper Manufacturing seem to be? Discuss.

SOURCE: Based on "Northern Industries," a case prepared by Rae Andre of Northeastern University.

Endnotes

1. Alex Markels, "A Diversity Program Can Prove Divisive," *The Wall Street Journal,* January 30, 1997, B1, B2.
2. M. Fine, F. Johnson, and M. S. Ryan, "Cultural Diversity in the Workforce," *Public Personnel Management* 19 (1990), 305–319.
3. Taylor H. Cox, "Managing Cultural Diversity: Implications for Organizational Competitiveness," *Academy of Management Executive* 5, no. 3 (1991), 45–56; and Faye Rice, "How to Make Diversity Pay," *Fortune,* August 8, 1994, 78–86.

4. Timothy Aeppel, "A 3Com Factory Hires a Lot of Immigrants, Gets Mix of Languages," *The Wall Street Journal,* March 30, 1998, A1; and Louis Uchitelle, "The New Faces of U.S. Manufacturing," *The New York Times,* July 3, 1994, Sec. 3, 1, 6.

5. Lennie Copeland, "Valuing Diversity, Part I: Making the Most of Cultural Differences at the Workplace," *Personnel,* June 1988, 52–60.

6. Lennie Copeland, "Learning to Manage a Multicultural Workforce," *Training,* May 25, 1988, 48–56; and D. Farid Elashmawi, "Culture Clashes: Barriers to Business," *Managing Diversity* 2, no. 11 (August 1993), 1–3.

7. Marilyn Loden and Judy B. Rosener, *Workforce America!* (Homewood, Ill.: Business One Irwin, 1991); and Marilyn Loden, *Implementing Diversity* (Homewood, Ill.: Irwin, 1996).

8. Frances J. Milliken and Luis I. Martins, "Searching for Common Threads: Understanding the Multiple Effects of Diversity in Organizational Groups," *Academy of Management Review* 21, no. 2 (1996), 402–433.

9. G. Haight, "Managing Diversity," *Across the Board* 27, no. 3 (1990), 22–29.

10. Songer, "Workforce Diversity," *B&E Review,* April–June 1991, 3–6.

11. Robert Doktor, Rosalie Tung, and Mary Ann von Glinow, "Future Directions for Management Theory Development," *Academy of Management Review* 16 (1991), 362–365; and Mary Munter, "Cross-Cultural Communication for Managers," *Business Horizons,* May–June 1993, 69–78.

12. Renee Blank and Sandra Slipp, "The White Male: An Endangered Species?" *Management Review,* September 1994, 27–32; Michael S. Kimmel, "What Do Men Want?" *Harvard Business Review,* November–December 1993, 50–63; and Sharon Nelton, "Nurturing Diversity," *Nation's Business,* June 1995, 25–27.

13. M. Bennett, "A Developmental Approach to Training for Intercultural Sensitivity," *International Journal of Intercultural Relations* 10 (1986), 179–196.

14. Jenny C. McCune, "Diversity Training: A Competitive Weapon," *Management Review,* June 1996, 25–28.

15. C. Keen, "Human Resource Management Issues in the '90s," *Vital Speeches* 56, no. 24 (1990), 752–754.

16. Kurt Anderson, "California Dreamin'," *Time,* September 23, 1991, 38–42.

17. Richard W. Judy and Carol D'Amico, *Workforce 2020: Work and Workers in the 21st Century* (Indianapolis, IN: Hudson Institute, 1997).

18. Gilbert W. Fairholm, *Leadership and the Culture of Trust* (Westport, Conn.: Praeger, 1994), 184.

19. Judy Rosener, *America's Competitive Secret: Women Managers* (New York: Oxford University Press, 1997), 33–34; and Susan Garland, "Going Beyond Rhetoric on Race Relations," *Business Week,* June 23, 1997, 40.

20. Ann Morrison, *The New Leaders: Guidelines on Leadership Diversity in America* (San Francisco: Jossey-Bass, 1992), 37.

21. Robert Hooijberg and Nancy DeTomaso, "Leadership In and Of Demographically Diverse Organizations," *Leadership Quarterly* 7, no. 1 (1996): 1–19.

22. Vivian Louie, "For Asian-Americans, A Way to Fight a Maddening Stereotype," *The New York Times,* 8 August 1993, 9.

23. Judy and D'Amico, *Workforce 2020.*

24. Copeland, "Valuing Diversity, Part I: Making the Most of Cultural Differences at the Workplace"; and Judy and D'Amico, *Workforce 2020.*

25. S. Hutchins, Jr., "Preparing for Diversity: The Year 2000," *Quality Process* 22, no. 10 (1989), 66–68.

26. Leon E. Wynter, "Allstate Rates Managers on Handling Diversity," *The Wall Street Journal* (Business and Race column), October 1, 1997, B1.

27. Roosevelt Thomas, Jr., "From Affirmative Action to Affirming Diversity," *Harvard Business Review* (March–April 1990), 107–117; and Nicholas Lemann, "Taking Affirmative Action Apart," *The New York Times Magazine,* July 11, 1995, 36–43.

28. Catherine Yang, Maria Mallory, and Alice Cuneo, "A 'Race-Neutral' Helping Hand?" *Business Week,* February 27, 1995, 120–121; and Lemann, "Taking Affirmative Action Apart."

29. Madeline E. Heilman, Caryn J. Block, and Peter Stathatos, "The Affirmative Action Stigma of Incompetence: Effects of Performance Information Ambiguity," *Academy of Management Journal* 40, no. 1 (1997), 603–625.

30. Jack Gordon, "Different from What? Diversity as a Performance Issue," *Training,* May 1995, 25–33; and Leon E. Wynter, "Diversity Is Often All Talk, No Affirmative Action," *The Wall Street Journal,* December 21, 1994, B1.

31. Arthur P. Brief, Robert T. Buttram, Robin M. Reizenstein, S. Douglas Pugh, Jodi D. Callahan, Richard L. McCline, and Joel B. Vaslow, "Beyond Good Intentions: The Next Steps Toward Racial Equality in the American Workplace," *Academy of Management Executive* 11, no. 4 (1997), 59–72.

32. B. Geber, "Managing Diversity," *Training* 27, no. 7 (1990), 23–30.

33. Julie Amparano Lopez, "Study Says Women Face Glass Walls as Well as Ceilings," *The Wall Street Journal,* March 3, 1992, B1, B2; and Ida L. Castro, "Q: Should Women Be Worried About the Glass Ceiling in the Workplace?" *Insight,* February 10, 1997, 24–27.

34. Nelton, "Nurturing Diversity."

35. C. Soloman, "Careers under Glass," *Personnel Journal* 69, no. 4 (1990), 96–105.

36. Deborah L. Jacobs, "Back from the Mommy Track," *The New York Times,* October 9, 1994, F1, F6.

37. Barbara Presley Noble, "A Quiet Liberation for Gay and Lesbian Employees," *The New York Times,* June 13, 1993, F4.

38. Soloman, "Careers under Glass."

39. Belle Rose Ragins, Bickley Townsend, and Mary Mattis, "Gender Gap in the Executive Suite: CEOs and Female Executives Report on Breaking the Glass Ceiling," *Academy of Management Executive* 12, no. 1 (1998), 28–42.

40. Anne B. Fisher, "When Will Women Get to the Top?" *Fortune,* September 21, 1992, 44–56.

41. Copeland, "Learning to Manage a Multicultural Workforce."

42. Douglas T. Hall and Victoria A. Parker, "The Role of Workplace Flexibility in Managing Diversity," *Organizational Dynamics* (summer 1993), 5–18.

43. Geber, "Managing Diversity."

44. Hanna Rosin, "Cultural Revolution at Texaco," *The New Republic,* February 2, 1998, 15–18.

45. Loden and Rosener, *Workforce America!;* (Homewood, IL: Business One Irwin, 1991); and Genevieve Capowski, "Ageism: The New Diversity Issue," *Management Review,* October 1994, 10–15.

46. B. Ragins, "Barriers to Mentoring: The Female Manager's Dilemma," *Human Relations* 42, no. 1 (1989), 1–22; and Ragins et al., Gender Gap in the Executive Suite."

47. Mary Zey, "A Mentor for All," *Personnel Journal,* January 1988, 46–51.

48. J. Black and M. Mendenhall, "Cross-Cultural Training Effectiveness: A Review and a Theoretical Framework for Future Research," *Academy of Management Review* 15 (1990), 113–136.

49. E. G. Collins, "Managers and Lovers," *Harvard Business Review* 61 (1983), 142–153.

50. Sharon A. Lobel, Robert E. Quinn, Lynda St. Clair, and Andrea Warfield, "Love without Sex: The Impact of Psychological Intimacy between Men and Women at Work," *Organizational Dynamics* (summer 1994), 5–16.

51. Carol Hymowitz, "Drawing the Line on Budding Romances in Your Workplace," *The Wall Street Journal* (Managing Your Career column), November 18, 1997, B1.

52. William C. Symonds with Steve Hamm and Gail DeGeorge, "Sex on the Job," *Business Week,* February 16, 1998, 30–31.

53. Carol Hymowitz and Ellen Joan Pollock, "The One Clear Line in Interoffice Romance Has Become Blurred," *The Wall Street Journal,* February 4, 1998, A1, A8.

54. "Sexual Harassment: Vanderbilt University Policy" (Nashville: Vanderbilt University, 1993).

55. Jack Corcoran, "Of Nice and Men," *Success,* June 1998, 65–67.

56. De'Ann Weimer with Emily Thornton, "Slow Healing at Mitsubishi," *Business Week,* September 22, 1997, 74.

57. Corcoran, "Of Nice and Men."

58. Barbara Carton, "At Jenny Craig, Men Are Ones Who Claim Sex Discrimination," *The Wall Street Journal,* November 29, 1994, A1, A11.

59. Jennifer J. Laabs, "Sexual Harassment: HR Puts Its Questions on the Line," *Personnel Journal,* February 1995, 35–45; Sharon Nelton, "Sexual Harassment: Reducing the Risks," *Nation's Business,* March 1995, 24–26; and Gary Baseman, "Sexual Harassment: The Inside Story," *Working Woman,* June 1992, 47–51, 78.

60. Judy and D'Amico, *Workforce 2020.*

61. Joann S. Lublin, "Companies Use Cross-Cultural Training to Help Their Employees Adjust Abroad," *The Wall Street Journal,* August 4, 1992, B1, B9.

62. Michael L. Wheeler, "Global Diversity: Reality, Opportunity, and Challenge," *Business Week,* December 1, 1997, Special Advertising Section.

63. Gilbert Fuchsberg, "As Costs of Overseas Assignments Climb, Firms Select Expatriates More Carefully," *The Wall Street Journal,* January 9, 1992, B3, B4.

64. Brian Dumaine, "Management Lessons from the General," *Fortune,* November 2, 1992, 143.

65. J. Kennedy and A. Everest, "Put Diversity in Context," *Personnel Journal,* September 1991, 50–54.

66. Cox, "Managing Cultural Diversity."

67. Gail Robinson and Kathleen Dechant, "Building a Business Case for Diversity," *Academy of Management Executive* 11, no. 3 (1997), 21–31.

68. K. D. G., "Master of Mixology," *Success,* October 1997, 27.

69. Robinson and Dechant, "Building a Business Case for Diversity"; and David A. Thomas and Robin J. Ely, "Making Differences Matter: A New Paradigm for Managing Diversity," *Harvard Business Review,* September–October 1996, 79–90.

70. Taylor H. Cox, *Cultural Diversity in Organizations* (San Francisco: Berrett-Koehler, 1994).

71. Thomas, "From Affirmative Action to Affirming Diversity."

$\mathcal{V}ideo\ \mathcal{C}ase$

Hard Candy: From Cosmic Chaos to Cosmetic Order

Dineh Mohajer admits it herself: she had no intention of founding her own company. She just wanted a certain shade of pale blue nail polish that didn't exist, so she made her own. Several high-end department stores such as Bloomingdale's and Neiman Marcus picked up on it, and five years later she was running a multimillion dollar company with 40 employees producing 60 shades of nail polish with such catchy names as Tantrum and Sushi. Ben Einstein, Mohajer's boyfriend and co-founder recalls simply, "The idea started as way to make a little bit of extra money over the summer." Mohajer echoes that memory, perhaps still in shock over how quickly it all happened: "Basically what happened in the beginning of Hard Candy was it turned into this company overnight."

Success is sweet, but it comes at a price. In this case, Mohajer and Einstein didn't have a chance to build their company slowly, from the ground up. So, even though they had some basic strategies, the company lacked organization. Of course, decision making was centralized—but there were only two people managing the company and responding to demands from customers. Problems stemming from lack of organizational structure arose almost immediately. For instance, Hard Candy simply couldn't produce enough bottles of polish, in enough shades, to satisfy customers because the polish had become so popular so quickly. "It just got bigger and worse and badder and more insane every day," recalls Mohajer. "Every day that went by as we grew and this monster, like, took over my house and took over my bathroom and took over my relationship . . . it was too much." In addition to explosive growth, Hard Candy, whose initial strategy had been to target certain types of high-end customers and stores, began to sell everywhere, which ultimately could have hurt its relationship with the customers it truly wanted to attract. Jeanne Chavez, who is now vice president of sales, explains that the polishes were going to "salons and beauty supply stores, and that really doesn't mesh well with being in Neiman Marcus or Bloomingdale's in New York City. So we had to really clean it up." As Mohajer puts it, Hard Candy was being run by "crisis management."

Another enterpreneur might have given up, sold the company, or gone under. But Dineh Mohajer decided to get organized for the long haul. "It came to the point where if there's not formal structure implemented into this organization, there's no way that this company can get to the next level," says Pooneh Mohajer, Dineh's sister. "We decided that the company needed a seasoned businessperson to come and help lead the growth." So the young entrepreneurs hired Ernst & Young to find them a temporary CEO who immediately helped implement accounting systems, began inventory tracking systems, and formed a management team. Now Hard Candy has an organizational chart that looks a little top heavy, but that's because Dineh, Pooneh, and Ben share the position of CEO. There is also a chief operating officer who, according to Dineh, is "primarily focused on financial information and inventory systems." At the next level, "some of the first steps we took in strategic planning were hiring department heads," explains Chavez. "We hired a marketing manager, a production manager,

sales managers throughout the country and overseas. We hired some in-house PR people and basically each of us focus[ed] on our departments." The company also has an outside management consultant "for the likeness and image, and developing the brand and making strategic choices about what the right things are for the brand."

The company seems to have the organizational chart of a very traditional, departmentalized company. It does—except for those three CEOs at the top. The founders recognized that in order to move their strategy forward, they needed to organize the structure of the company. And they adapted a vertical structure to suit their own needs. They are glad they did. "Getting, you know, good people to help with different . . . parts of the operation definitely was a relief," admits Ben Einstein.

Dineh Mohajer is also sold on the effectiveness of teams, both cross-functional and permanent. She uses them at Hard Candy whenever she can. "What I have now is a team of people," she explains. "That's what I've always looked for . . . worked for . . . worked towards, was assembling the right team, a team that can work together and grow a company." With her co-CEOs, she even forms a team at the top. "There's a core team that drives the growth of the company," she says. "The three owners, I guess, I guess you could coin them as CEOs, but collectively." They each have different talents and perspectives—Ben is the strategist, Pooneh focuses on the bottom line, and Dineh is the creative force behind product development. "It's nice because we kind of really balance each other out," says Pooneh. And balance is, after all, the ideal of any organizational structure.

Questions

1. Describe a specific situation in which Dineh Mohajer might form a cross-functional team, including who might be on it (representatives from which departments) and what goal they might be striving to accomplish.
2. Do you think that Hard Candy places emphasis on work specialization? Why or why not?
3. Do you think that Hard Candy will become increasingly decentralized as the company grows? Why or why not?
4. Do you think that having a team of CEOs will be effective in the long run? Why or why not? If not, what might be some alternative solutions?

SOURCES: Jeffrey Zaslow, "Straight Talk: Dineh Mohajer," *Chicago Sun-Times*, June 26–28, 1998, accessed at www.usaweekend.com; "A Polished Kind of Girl," *Maxi* online magazine accessed March 18, 1999, at www.maximag.com; Ted Rall, "Marketing Madness," *Link, the College Magazine*, September 1997, accessed at www.linkmag.com; "The Best Entrepreneurs: Dineh Mohajer," *Business Week*, February 1998; Jeanne Whalen, "Dineh Mohajer," *Advertising Age's Marketing 100* (1997), accessed March 18, 1999 at www.adage.com.

Paradigm Simulation Inc.: Virtual Groundbreakers

Change, for better or for worse, is inevitable for all organizations. All kinds of forces, environmental and internal, drive this change. Outside the organization, customers may demand new products or lower prices, regulations may tighten or loosen, new technology may develop, competition may increase. Inside the organization, top managers may set a goal of rapid growth, employees may request better benefits, production may increase or decline. A decade ago, three young software engineers who were laid off from their jobs responded to the change in their environment by forming their own company, Paradigm Simulation. Mike Engledinger, Wes Hoffman, and Ron Toupal saw a coming change in computer technology that their former employer did not—and they bet their careers on it. "That company did simulation and training applications, but they didn't see the computer graphics side as being all that important," recalls Engledinger, Paradigm vice president of engineering. "They didn't think there was much of a future in it. As it turns out, there is, and we knew there was."

The three partners figured out a way to develop and produce three-dimensional simulation software at a price that was accessible. (Before Paradigm came along, 3-D simulation software products cost upwards of $80,000 and the hardware could run as much as $300,000. Paradigm was able to drop the price to $5,000.) Their core product was a tool called Vega—software that enabled both programmers and nonprogrammers to build interactive, 3-D simulations and virtual reality applications, meaning that average managers could use the product without knowing how to write computer code. At first, Paradigm focused on developing high-end simulation products for the defense industry. Next, it began to develop a client list that included Chrysler, Silicon Graphics, and BMW. Then Nintendo came along.

Paradigm was founded as a creative organization, by creative people. They had seen an opportunity for that their former employer had missed and seized it. Now they had another chance. Nintendo approached Paradigm about creating a 3-D game to launch their Nintendo 64 console system, and Paradigm accepted. It came up with Pilot Wings 64. When the game sold more than a million copies, Paradigm's founders decided to re-evaluate its original vision, with an eye toward a possible change in direction. They knew technology changes would be continual in their business to keep current. But they had to decide whether a product change would benefit the company. "Technology has always been a core strength for us," says David Gatchel, executive vice president of entertainment. "That's how we've distinguished ourselves initially and that's something that we continue to try to emphasize. We have an R&D (research and development) staff that continues to try to come up with innovative technologies that we can use to develop our products and stay on the leading edge of what's currently out in the market, as far as hardware or delivery platforms."

All of the signs of successful new product development were there: Paradigm managers understood what their customers wanted; software developers were working on state-of-the-art

technology; all key employees were on board with the new direction. So Paradigm shifted its focus from defense to entertainment. The company began conservatively. "We started off really doing technical production," says Gatchel. "And as we've learned more about the business, we've understood that there's a lot of opportunities there if we begin to do full production and control the creative side. So we've adapted to that and we've brought on new staff to try to accomplish those things."

Although Paradigm values its creative side, the company is systematic in the way it makes changes. Formal goals are set and new product ideas are fully researched in an organization that illustrates the horizontal linkage model (even if its founders wouldn't call it that) by fully integrating research, manufacturing, and marketing. "Normally we try to come up with corporate objectives each year," explains Gatchel. "One [objective] that we wanted to become stronger in is character animation and that was clearly a weakness we had. If we could improve on that we'd become much more competitive and we would have increased opportunities."

In a single decade, Paradigm has become a leader in the race to develop 3-D real-time software technology, but company managers are not content to rest on their laurels. Recently, organization executives announced another major change: a merger agreement with MultiGen Inc., whose products are different from, but complementary to, Paradigm's. "The synergy represented by this merger is phenomenal," exclaims Ron Toupal, one of Paradigm's founders. "While the benefits to both companies are obvious, the true beneficiaries will be our customers. Together we will find efficient and innovative ways to deliver ground-breaking solutions to customers in a wide variety of markets worldwide." Merging products and organizational cultures will be perhaps the biggest change—and challenge—the company has yet faced. But so far, these leaders of the virtual world have proved themselves up to the task.

Questions

1. Does Paradigm Simulation appear to be a learning organization? Why or why not?
2. The last change described, the merger with MultiGen, may not be accomplished as easily as some of the others. Why not?
3. In what ways might Paradigm and MultiGen managers use OD activities to complete a successful merger of the two organizations?

SOURCES: "MultiGen Inc. and Paradigm Simulation Inc. Sign Definitive Merger Agreement," press release, September 3, 1998, accessed at www.paradigmsim.com, March 26, 1999.

Yahoo! Manages its Human Resources

When Jerry Yang and David Filo, two engineering graduate students at Stanford University, first created their directory to Internet Web sites, they did it for themselves. But the directory soon became so popular that they formed a company called Yahoo! to market and expand their search engine. Forming a company meant hiring people and managing them. The company grew so fast in the first five years that if human resource management had not been addressed, it could have fallen apart. But the two did address the issue, and although everyone who works for Yahoo! likes to think that the organization is nontraditional, funky, and maverick, it still has a management structure, and it has a human resource department. "I consider Yahoo! a flat organization," notes Beth Haba, human resource manager. "It's an organization where, you know, your executive management is a team of about four or five people and functionally there's about three functional areas. You've got sales and marketing. You've got engineering and operation type roles and then you've got finance administration." And, there is human resources.

At Yahoo! the link between human resource management and organizational strategic planning appears right in the job description. "As the position acts as an important pivot between the strategic objectives of the corporation and the outstanding professionals who work there, the HR manager must be capable of developing partnerships with management while also serving as a resource/ombudsman for the employee populations," says the description for the position of human resource manager—international. The same statement appears in the description for the human resource generalist. Human resource professionals at Yahoo! work directly with managers to accomplish the company's goals. "Must be effective at influencing management, exhibit superior communication skills, work well in a quickly changing environment, and be able to prioritize and demonstrate initiative. Experience in integrating employee growth through mergers and acquisitions desired," continues the job description for human resource generalist. In addition, as Yahoo! expands from its Santa Clara, California, headquarters to worldwide operations, its human resource professionals must be familiar with legislative and societal trends overseas. "This includes ensuring compliance with local laws and regulations," explains the job description. "In addition, will work with Manager of Worldwide Compensation and Benefits to establish and manage competitive compensation and benefits programs in these regions."

Yahoo! uses various methods of recruitment, from in-house human resource managers to its Web site, where potential candidates can review the company's job listings and learn a little more about the company's policies. What kind of employees does Yahoo! want to attract? "Our workforce is a very young workforce and that kind of lends towards the spontaneity and creativity that we have around here," says Beth Haba. "We prefer to hire obviously people that have . . . business degrees or engineering degrees. It's not necessarily required for every position. We obviously feel that a college graduate carries with them a certain level of maturity within the organization. . . ." On the Yahoo! Web site, candidates will find these remarks: "We're always interested in intelligent, adventurous people with backgrounds in software engineering, marketing, sales, finance, and information systems. And, honestly, that's just the be-

ginning. The way we're growing, we're constantly expanding in new directions."

As a young company, Yahoo! embraces the new social contract between company and employees in a variety of ways. Part of this is a flexible work schedule. Beth Haba observes, "This really, truly is a flexible environment in the sense that for the most part people can come in to work anywhere between . . . 8:00 A.M. and about 11:30 or 12:00, and some people choose to work a later hour because that's when they're creative." Haba notes that Yahoo! does have an employee handbook that spells out more of the contract, but "we tried to add a positive, fun spin on it." On its Web site, Yahoo! describes the work environment. "From our highly creative (and highly casual) work environment, to the fact that we celebrate just about every success with a party. . . . Not to mention our funky yellow and purple color scheme. . . . At Yahoo! we have a corporate culture unlike any other. And that's a good thing." What does Yahoo! expect in return? People who are willing to contribute to the "behind the scenes" action at the company; people who are willing to learn and to take responsibility for their contributions to the organization. "Show us what you're good at; we'll see if there's a place for you at Yahoo!" proclaims the company.

Part of the new social contract includes benefits. Yahoo! has some traditional benefits and some less traditional ones. "Compensation at Yahoo! and in startup environments is typically, you'll have a base salary and you'll have stock options," explains Beth Haba. "In Yahoo!'s case now we're a public company and to some regards that is a big incentive because you know that the stock has value. . . . Stock options at Yahoo! are offered to every regular full-time hire that has benefits, which is a very, very neat thing." As for salaries, Haba notes that "basically we base all of our salaries on market wages and internal equity to make sure that we're, you know, compensating people fairly internally so that you don't have problems from an internal standpoint." Other employee benefits include a 401(k) plan; vacation time; medical, dental, vision, and life insurance benefits; education reimbursement; domestic partner coverage; sick days and paid holidays; a catered lunch program; and membership at an upscale health club. "Everyone here puts their all into everything they do, and we reward them with a generous compensation package," claims the company on its Web site. According to the new contract, much is expected of every employee—but employees are valued and rewarded for their contributions to the organization. Yahoo! illustrates how a young, creative, aggressive company can use human resource management to help the organization grow and remain competitive in a rapidly changing, highly competitive environment.

Questions

1. What questions might Yahoo! human resource managers ask in order to forecast human resource needs for the next five years?
2. What types of selection devices would be most appropriate for design or engineering job candidates at Yahoo? What types of selection devices would be most appropriate for marketing and sales candidates? For customer care candidates?
3. Would you call Yahoo! a learning organization? Why or why not?

SOURCE: **Yahoo! Web site, accessed April 25, 1999, at www.yahoo.com.**

J.C. Penney: Practicing the Golden Rule

When James Cash Penney opened his first retail store in Kemmerer, Wyoming, in 1902, he called it "The Golden Rule." Penney promised that he would treat his customers as he would wish to be treated—with courtesy and respect, offering high-quality merchandise and low prices. The golden rule also applied to employees, whom Penney referred to as associates. "If there is a secret of good management in the business of living, it lies in the partnerships we make," explained Penney in a speech before a gathering of associates to celebrate the company's fortieth anniversary. "For no man is sufficient unto himself. I say partners because we believe that all our associates work together as partners. We make our selection of partners according to the character qualities that best fit into our business. That builds rapidly into the principles of our business. . . . Honor, Confidence, Service and Cooperation." Whether or not he realized it at the beginning, James Cash Penney had planted the seeds of a corporate culture that would nourish diversity in a changing population.

Nearly a century after its opening, the name of that original store has taken on more meaning, as the J.C. Penney organization strives to manage an increasingly diverse workforce and serve an increasingly diverse customer base. Today, there are more than 1,200 J.C. Penney department stores in 50 states, Puerto Rico, and Santiago, Chile. Nearly 200,000 Penney associates serve 98 million customers each year. Penney's may be the country's largest department store, but its founder's philosophy of partnership and the golden rule still lies at the core of the organization's culture. During the last decade, the company has launched an aggressive initiative to support diversity and nurture ethnorelativism throughout the organization. The initiative includes a formal diversity awareness training program. "We have in place at J.C. Penney a Valuing Cultural Differences program," says Mary Rostad, vice president of human resources. "It is a one-and-a-half day workshop designed to develop and to create an awareness for each and every associate in our company." In another move to meet the needs of diverse employees, "We've instituted two internal advisory teams—a minority advisory team and a women's advisory team," continues Rostad.

Penney's supports its training programs with a formal policy statement that applies to the organization as a whole. "We participated in the development of a diversity positioning statement, which for the first time established the company's position relative to diversity," notes Charles Brown, former chair of the minority advisory team. "And more importantly, what that did was we took that position statement and we put it in the hands of every associate in the J.C. Penney Company so that they clearly understand that it's a commitment that the company has made to diversity. They clearly understand that it is everyone's responsibility to embrace diversity in this company." When the policy was finalized, it was introduced to employees in a video message from company chairman W.R. Howell. "I want to talk with you about a topic that is very important to me and to our company . . . valuing diversity," the message began. "Each of us is a one-of-a-kind combination of physical characteristics, personality, gender, race, religion, skills, and ethnic and cultural background. This uniqueness of individu-

als is what we call diversity. Valuing diversity means respecting individual differences and appreciating the advantages our diversity offers. The golden rule asks us to respect each other regardless of our differences and to look beyond the differences to see what we have in common."

To carry out the policy statement, the advisory teams continued their work, including establishing a mentor program to provide positive role models for minority employees. Charles Brown explains that the mentor program was designed to help minority employees understand the corporate culture and thus be their most effective within it. In addition, the advisory teams assisted minority workers in developing career paths within the organization, making certain that employees had equal opportunities for career planning and advancement. The teams also assisted the human resources department in its recruitment of top minority job candidates. Finally, the teams addressed the problem of the glass ceiling that women have traditionally faced. With Howell's support, the organization established a formal policy of accelerating the representation of women at all levels of the company, but particularly at upper management levels, including the executive committee. Recognizing that policies and goals are ineffective without accountability and measurement, Penney's made sure to follow through. "I think the important thing to remember with any goal is that if it isn't measured it doesn't matter," says Cathy Mills, vice president of corporate communications. "And so, measurements were established—accountability measurements—where all members of the organization were challenged and held accountable for their efforts, not only women, but with the minority population."

J.C. Penney recognizes that if it can meet some of the special needs of its diverse employees, the employees will be more productive and more likely to stick with the organization. Mary Rostad notes, "Here in our home office we have on-site child care, and we also have flexible work arrangements throughout our company, part-time employment positions, telecommuting, and a fitness center here in the home office." Cathy Mills observes, "We're finding more and more that initiatives that began in response to the needs of women are serving the whole population phase."

All of these programs and policies are terrific for associates, but how do they benefit the J.C. Penney organization from a business standpoint? CEO Howell answers very clearly. "Our diversity gives us a real competitive advantage. So we must use this tremendous resource to the fullest. . . . This way we will ensure our continued success." Mary Rostad addresses the bottom line. "Certainly if we have a workforce that mirrors our customer base, that will bring in sales and profits."

Questions

1. In addition to those mentioned by W.R. Howell and Mary Rostad, in what other ways might the J.C. Penney organization benefit from its diversity programs?
2. Based on its corporate culture, do you think that J.C. Penney is properly positioned to expand globally? Why or why not?

What further steps might the organization have to take to manage diversity overseas?

3. Do you think a formal affirmative action program is necessary in an organization like J.C. Penney? Why or why not?

Continuing Case

Part Four: The Apple Motto—Think Different

Think Different. The new Apple motto implies—and invites—change. "'Think different' isn't just advice we dispense to our customers: it's the ethic that guides everything we do," says the Apple Web site. By the mid-1990s, it seemed that Apple had been through as much organizational change as it could stand, most from the top down. Even changes that were designed to solve problems or increase the company's competitiveness caused more chaos, leading to more changes. Gil Amelio, Apple CEO for a little more than a year, instituted grand changes in the organizational structure, including breaking Apple into seven separate divisions, each responsible for its own profits and losses. In late 1997, another major change shook the company: Steve Jobs returned, in an agreement acquiring the company he had formed after leaving Apple, called NeXTstep. Immediately, Jobs (who was being touted as "interim CEO") declared yet more changes in Apple's organizational structure, including a new board of directors, an aggressive ad campaign, and upcoming new versions of the Mac. But the most shocking change was yet to come: Jobs's announcement of an alliance with Microsoft, in which Microsoft invested $150 million in Apple.

With the infusion of cash from Microsoft, Jobs turned to even more structural changes designed to achieve new strategic goals. In late 1997, Apple began selling its computers directly to consumers, both over the Web and by phone. The Web site, called The Apple Store, was an instant success. Within its first week, it had become the third largest e-commerce site on the Web. Apple began to show profits again. Over the next few years, Apple shifted back to its beginnings, focusing once again on its core competencies and developing an organizational structure that reflected clear strategic goals. This included laying off employees and creating new types of jobs positions that were better "aligned with our new technical directions, customer needs and in identifying new markets."

All these changes raise the issue of managing human resources at Apple. Steve Jobs began to call the new Apple "a really well-funded start-up." What did he mean? Probably that the environment is lively, creative, hectic, and pioneering. "We've gone back to our roots," says the employment section of the company's Web site. "And though we're proud of our past, we live in the future." Apple began actively recruiting employees via its Web site, where potential job candidates can take a virtual tour of company facilities, have basic employment questions answered, review company benefits, read about the company's training programs, and e-mail resumes directly to the human resource department. "We employ and hire the very best in the industry; our high standards are what separates us from our competitors," says the company. "If you want to work with intelligent and talented people, come to Apple."

Apple is a prime example of the new social contract with workers, who are expected to be employable, take personal responsibility for their performance, continue to learn, and act as partners in business improvement. In return, Apple offers creative development opportunities, continuous learning (including an education reimbursement program), challenging assignments, and necessary resources. "You have the freedom to do your best work at Apple because there are varied skillsets and many different kinds of thinking that we value inside our culture," says the company. "You are directly or indirectly working on cutting edge technology. We have a focus inside Apple these days that makes it clear what you are working on, when it is due, and how you can make a difference."

Benefits at Apple are both tangible and intangible, designed to attract and keep the best workers. Compensation includes salaries, bonuses, stock purchases, and a 401(k) plan. Apple also now has a program called FlexBenefits, which is designed to allow employees to choose the benefits package that best suits them. The company allocates what it calls "FlexDollars" to purchase basic insurance benefits such as medical, dental, vision care, and life insurance. Then, if employees choose not to purchase any more benefits, they increase their take-home pay or deposit the remaining Flex-Dollars in their 401(k) account. If they choose to purchase additional benefits, say, for family members, they can use their Flex-Dollars to do so. In addition, Apple has a health and fitness program that includes exercise programs, health education, and preventive care.

Apple relies heavily on training to continue to develop an effective workforce. Training programs not only provide workers with new knowledge and skills but also help reduce environmental uncertainty in an industry that is based almost entirely on cutting-edge knowledge and technology. The company has a number of formal training programs, including the Apple Learn & Earn Program, which is available to employees in the United States, Canada, and Asia/Pacific region, and is designed to help employees stay abreast of the many developments in Apple strategies, products, technologies, and solutions. In other words, Apple wants its workers to continue to "think different."

Questions

1. Do you think that the number of structural changes presented a unique challenge to human resource managers at Apple over the years? If so, what types of challenges can you think of?
2. How are culture/people changes related to technology/product changes at Apple?
3. Do you think the functional, divisional, or matrix approach to structure would work best for Apple as it faces the future?

SOURCES: Apple Web site accessed April 27, 1999, at www.apple.com; Guy Kawasaki, "Steve Jobs to Return as Apple CEO," *Macworld*, November 1994, accessed March 9, 1999, at macworld.zdnet.com; Sean Silverthorne, "Steve Jobs, Interim CEO—Now and Forever?" ZDNet news, September 16, 1997, accessed March 9, 1999, at www.zdnet.com.

Part Five

Leadership

What does it take to lead and motivate a group of individuals to perform at their peak? The nine skippers of the Whitbread race know—and so do their crews. Their personalities vary from crusty and abrasive, to determined and driven, to energetic and likable. But all are considered tops in their sport and worthy of piloting a $2 million boat around the world—with a dozen people's lives in their hands. Personal expertise as a sailor, confidence in their abilities, competitiveness to win, intensity, and, above all, professionalism are characteristics they share.

Skippers varied in their approaches to accomplishing their goals of building teamwork and coming in first. Despite the stresses of a long and physically uncomfortable voyage, the Dutch crew aboard BrunelSunenergy dubbed itself the "Happy Crew" and was described as having good humor, drive, spirit, and nerve. Christine Guillou, the skipper of the all-female crew of EF Education, said, "It was a great experience, especially discovering . . . what you can do with a good team and good spirit." The winning skipper, Paul Cayard of EF Language, attributed his win to his crew and their professionalism, saying that "maximizing the use of every minute I have at my disposal, and my team's mentality being the same, was the key factor for us to win"—high praise at the end of the grueling months at sea.

In Part Five, you'll learn about behavior in organizations, the ways leadership, motivation, and communication can be powerful influences on performance, and the importance of teamwork in today's competitive world.

Chapter 15

LEARNING OBJECTIVES

After studying this chapter, you should be able to

◉ Define *attitudes*, including their major components, and explain their relationship to behavior.

◉ Discuss the importance of work-related attitudes.

◉ Identify major personality traits and describe how personality can influence workplace attitudes and behaviors.

◉ Summarize the steps in the perception process and perceptual biases.

◉ Explain how people learn in general and in terms of individual learning styles.

◉ Discuss the effects of stress and how individuals differ in their responses to stress.

◉ Identify ways organizations and individuals can manage stress.

Foundations of Behavior in Organizations

MANAGEMENT PROBLEM

Running an airline isn't an easy job, as Rakesh Gangwal, CEO of US Airways, knows. Gangwal has had to make a number of quick, difficult decisions in his quest to turn the nearly bankrupt airline into a moneymaker. A quiet, disciplined man, Gangwal readily admits that he is "driven to succeed," but says he doesn't want his drive to become an issue of personal grandiosity. Others describe Gangwal as a quick thinker, a leader who is demanding and acts with authority. Gangwal spends his days poring over facts and figures, as well as talking to other people, to learn what he needs to know to solve tough problems fast. Gangwal has impressed the aviation industry with his role in the quick turnaround at US Airways. Now, he and his longtime mentor, Stephen M. Wolf (now chairman of the parent company US Airways Group), face new challenges. At one recent meeting, Gangwal pondered a potentially disastrous problem—a growing number of passengers have been complaining about rude service, particularly at the airline's international terminal in Philadelphia, where part-time employees make up 42 percent of the workforce. A broader challenge is figuring out how to establish a strong global presence for US Airways, which is necessary for the airline to survive and grow. With customer service, global expansion, and overall profitability problems waiting to be solved, Gangwal must act quickly for the sake of the organization.[1]

If you were Gangwal, what would you do to solve such diverse problems as unprofessional behavior by terminal staff and the need for global expansion? What personality traits and problem-solving styles might be useful to a manager wrestling with these problems?

People differ in many ways. At work, these differences influence how they interpret an assignment, whether they like to be told what to do, and how they handle challenges. Managers' personalities and attitudes can also profoundly affect the workplace, as Rakesh Gangwal's story illustrates. People are an organization's most valuable resource—and the source of some of the most difficult problems. People problems can be particularly challenging due to the complex and unique qualities that people bring to the workplace. Three basic leadership skills are at the core of identifying and solving people problems: (1) diagnosing, or gaining insight into the situation a manager is trying to influence; (2) adapting individual behavior and resources to meet the needs of the situation; and (3) communicating in a way that others can understand and accept. Thus, managers need insight about individual differences to understand what a behavioral situation is now and what it may be in the future.

To handle this responsibility, managers need to understand the principles of organizational behavior—that is, the ways individuals and groups tend to act in organizations. By increasing their knowledge of individual differences in the areas of attitudes, personality, perception, learning, and stress management, managers can understand and lead employees and colleagues through many workplace challenges. This chapter introduces basic principles of organizational behavior in each of these areas.

Organizational Behavior

organizational behavior
An interdisciplinary field dedicated to the study of how individuals and groups tend to act in organizations.

Organizational behavior, commonly called OB, is an interdisciplinary field dedicated to the study of human attitudes, behavior, and performance in organizations. OB draws concepts from many disciplines, including psychology, sociology, cultural anthropology, industrial engineering, economics, ethics, and vocational counseling, as well as the discipline of management. The concepts and principles of organizational behavior are important to managers because in every organization human beings ultimately make the decisions that control how the organization will acquire and use resources. Those people may cooperate with, compete with, support, or undermine one another. Their beliefs and feelings about themselves, their coworkers, and the organization shape what they do and how well they do it. People can distract the organization from its strategy by engaging in conflict and misunderstandings, or they can pool their diverse talents and perspectives to accomplish much more as a group than they could ever do as individuals.

By understanding what causes people to behave as they do, managers can exercise leadership to achieve positive outcomes. They can foster behaviors such as **organizational citizenship,** that is, work behavior that goes beyond job requirements and contributes as needed to the organization's success. An employee demonstrates organizational citizenship by being helpful to coworkers and customers, doing extra work when necessary, and looking for ways to improve products and procedures. Managers can encourage organizational citizenship by applying their knowledge of human behavior in many ways, such as selecting people with positive attitudes and personalities, helping them see how they can contribute, and enabling them to learn from and cope with workplace challenges.

organizational citizenship
Work behavior that goes beyond job requirements and contributes as needed to the organization's success.

Attitudes

Managers observe that some people show up at work eager to get started, whereas others appear to wish they were elsewhere. Some employees tackle problems with the expectation that they and their coworkers will cooperate to find a solution; others grumble or panic. These different kinds of behavior partly reflect variations in employee attitudes. Defined formally, an **attitude** is an evaluation that predisposes a person to act in a certain way. A person who has the attitude "I love my work; it's challenging and fun" probably will tackle work-related problems cheerfully, while one who comes to work with the attitude "I hate my job" is not likely to exhibit much enthusiasm or commitment to solving problems.

attitude
A cognitive and affective evaluation that predisposes a person to act in a certain way.

Components of Attitudes

Behavioral scientists consider attitudes to have three components: cognitions (thoughts), affect (feelings), and behavior.[2] The cognitive component of an attitude includes the beliefs, opinions, and information the person has about the object of the attitude, such as knowledge of what a job entails and opinions about personal abilities. The affective component is the person's emotions or feelings about the object of the attitude, such as enjoying or hating a job. The behavioral component of an attitude is the person's intention to behave toward the object of the attitude in a certain way. Exhibit 15.1 illustrates the three components of a positive attitude toward one's job. The cognitive element is the conscious thought that "my job is interesting and challenging." The affective element is the feeling that "I love this job." These, in turn, are related to the behavioral component—an employee might choose to arrive at work early because he or she is happy with the job.

Often, when we think about attitudes, we focus on the cognitive component. However, it is important for managers to remember the other components as well. When people feel strongly about something, the affective component may predispose them to act, no matter what someone does to change their opinions. For example, if an employee is passionate about a new idea, that employee may go to great lengths to implement it. Likewise, an employee who is furious about being asked to work overtime on his birthday may act on that anger—by failing to cooperate, lashing out at coworkers, or even quitting—no matter what arguments the employee's manager presents about the need to work. In cases such as these, effective leadership includes addressing the affect (emotions) associated with the attitude. Are employees so excited that their judgment may be clouded, or so discouraged that they have given up trying? If nothing else, the manager probably needs to be aware of situations that involve strong emotions and give employees a chance to vent their feelings safely.

Recognizing components of attitudes also is useful for managers when they want to change an attitude. As a general rule, changing one component of an attitude—cognitions, affect, or behavior—can contribute to an overall change in attitude. Suppose a manager concludes that some employees have the attitude that the manager should make all the decisions affecting the department, but the manager prefers that employees assume more decision-making responsibility. To change the underlying attitude, the manager would consider whether to educate employees about the areas in which

The Chicago-based retailer, Sears Roebuck & Co., has been re-examining its principles of organizational behavior. In a 5-year period, 510,000 Americans, who had declared bankruptcy, signed reaffirmations pledging to pay Sears debts that totaled $412 million. Because the company did not file the signed reaffirmations with a court so a judge could review whether debtors could handle the new payment, the company's actions were a serious breach of law. Upon discovery of the scandal, at a meeting of Sears' top 200 executives, Chairman Arthur C. Martinez told every executive to spend the next half hour at his or her desk doing nothing but thinking about his or her own operation. ". . . to fundamentally rethink—Is what I do, the direction I give, the body language I use, creating an environment where something like this could happen?"

Exhibit *15.1*

Components of an Attitude

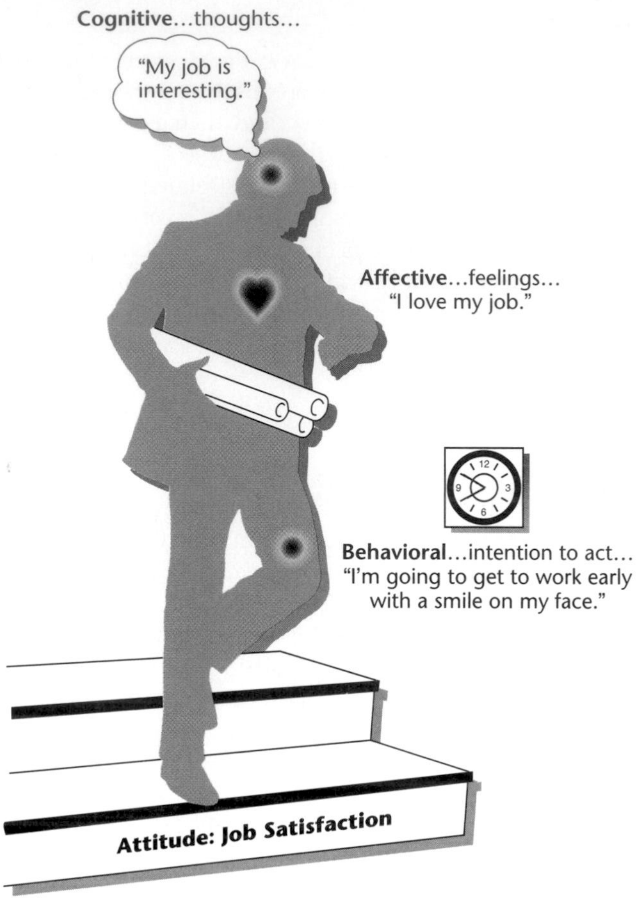

Cognitive...thoughts...

"My job is interesting."

Affective...feelings...
"I love my job."

Behavioral...intention to act...
"I'm going to get to work early with a smile on my face."

Attitude: Job Satisfaction

they can make good decisions (changing the cognitive component), build enthusiasm with pep talks about the satisfaction of employee empowerment (changing the affective component), or simply insist that employees make their own decisions (behavioral component) with the expectation that, once they experience the advantages of decision-making authority, they will begin to like it.

Work-Related Attitudes

The attitudes of most interest to managers are those related to work, especially attitudes that influence how well employees perform. To lead employees effectively, managers logically seek to cultivate the kinds of attitudes that are associated with high performance. Two attitudes that may relate to high performance are satisfaction with one's job and commitment to the organization.

job satisfaction
A positive attitude toward one's job.

Job Satisfaction.   A positive attitude toward one's job is called **job satisfaction.** In general, people experience this attitude when their work matches their needs and interests, when working conditions and rewards (such as pay) are satisfactory, and when the employees like their co-workers. In the Emergent Solutions Group of accounting and consulting giant

PricewaterhouseCoopers, a group of talented programmers and systems designers are developing an advanced computer system that models complex human behavior, such as the way people interact in stores. Employees often labor long hours, because they are excited to be working on ground-breaking technology. Their attitude toward participation in pioneering work underlies a high degree of job satisfaction.[3]

Many managers believe job satisfaction is important because they think satisfied employees will do better work. In fact, research shows that the link between satisfaction and performance is generally small and is affected by other factors.[4] The importance of satisfaction varies according to the amount of control the employee has; an employee doing routine tasks may produce about the same output no matter how he or she feels about the job. But, there are reasons managers should care about job satisfaction. When unemployment rates are low and workers can easily find jobs elsewhere, managers want their productive employees to be happy enough to stay with the organization. In addition, as human beings, managers may simply want employees to feel good about their work—and they may prefer to work with people who have a positive outlook.

Organizational Commitment. Another important attitude is **organizational commitment**, which is loyalty to and heavy involvement in the organization. An employee with a high degree of organizational commitment is likely to say "we" when talking about the organization. Such a person tries to contribute to the organization's success and wishes to remain with the organization. This attitude is common at the A. W. Chesterton Company, a Massachusetts company that produces mechanical seals and pumps. CEO James D. Chesterton takes a personal interest in his employees, and they in turn are very loyal to him and to the organization. When two Chesterton pumps that supply water on Navy ship *USS John F. Kennedy* failed on a Saturday night just before the ship's scheduled departure, Todd Robinson, the leader of the team that produces the seals, swung into action. He and his fiancèe, who also works for Chesterton, worked through the night to make new seals and deliver them to be installed before the ship left port.[5]

Most managers want to enjoy the benefits of loyal, committed employees, including low turnover and willingness to do more than the job's basic requirements. Organizational commitment has become especially important in recent years, because a tight labor market has forced employers to compete harder to attract and keep good workers in many fields. Adding to the challenge, past downsizing and restructuring have made many employees distrustful of their employers. As shown in Exhibit 15.2, a survey of 450,000 employees found that although most executives believe employees respect management, their employees' attitudes are in fact quite different.[6] The percentage of workers who say management is respected by employees has been steadily declining since 1991. In the most recent available year of the survey (1997), about 50

Set designer Anne Larlarb's job satisfaction is high. She is one of a new breed of global workers whose attitude toward work has led them to go anywhere for an interesting job. After college graduation two years ago, Larlarb arrived in London on a student visa to assist a famous set designer. Now she is in Thailand where she is apprenticing in the art workshop for a major motion picture, working 14 hour days, living out of three suitcases at a hotel, and using e-mail as her only address. But Larlarb thinks it's worth it—the exposure to new cultures has been invaluable research for her design work. She displays her attitude with a one-word comment as she pages through her journal: "Wow!"

organizational commitment
Loyalty to and heavy involvement in one's organization.

Exhibit *15.2*

Changing Attitudes: Employees' Respect for Management

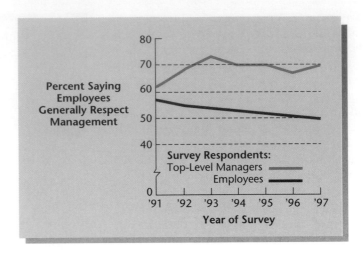

SOURCE: Adapted from Aaron Bernstein, "We Want You to Stay. Really," *Business Week,* June 22, 1998, 67–68+ (citing data from an annual survey of 450,000 employees and managers by the International Survey Research Corporation).

percent of employees reported that management generally is respected, as compared with about 70 percent of top managers who believed that. Managers can take action to promote organizational commitment by keeping employees informed, giving them a say in decisions, providing the necessary training and other resources that enable them to succeed, treating them fairly, and offering rewards they value. Microsoft keeps turnover for its technical support staff exceedingly low by fostering organizational commitment.

MICROSOFT

www.microsoft.com

If you've ever called technical support for help with your computer and had trouble getting through, part of the problem is likely due to the difficulty high-tech companies have in keeping their help desks well staffed. For many companies, the nature of the job means that help-desk help is hard to keep. Listening on a phone to problems all day eventually wears a person down. In addition, technical support people generally feel they are stuck in dead-end jobs and have few career paths open to them. No wonder the average turnover rate for help-desk engineers is 65 percent.

Microsoft, however, beats the odds; turnover for technical support staff is just 7 percent. Microsoft goes to great lengths to foster organizational commitment. In hiring support engineers, it looks for people with intelligence and drive, not just technical skills. Then the company provides them with an ample amount of training that allows them to grow and feel that they're constantly learning. Microsoft not only provides instructions about the company's products but offers training in areas such as customer satisfaction, customer relations, handling sensitive customer issues, and even communications skills such as writing or developing effective presentations.

Microsoft also offers technical support people a variety of career paths so they can see that their training is leading them somewhere. For example, there's a management path for engineers whose goal is to become managers and a technical path for those who want to specialize in one area, such as operating systems or end-user applications. A mentoring path gives engineers a chance to take on the added responsibility of helping other support staff solve problems. Other career paths are a training path and a product-preparation path. Managers play a big role in helping keep support staff committed by actively listening to them and understanding their career development concerns.[7]

Conflicts Among Attitudes

Sometimes a person may discover that his or her attitudes conflict with one another or are not reflected in his or her behavior. For example, a person's high level of organizational commitment may conflict with that person's commitment to family members. If employees routinely work evenings and weekends, their long hours and dedication to the job may conflict with their belief that family ties are important. This can create a state of **cognitive dissonance**, a psychological discomfort that occurs when individuals recognize inconsistencies in their own attitudes and behaviors.[8] The theory of cognitive dissonance, developed by social psychologist Leon Festinger in the 1950s, says that people want to behave in accordance with their attitudes and usually will take corrective action to alleviate the dissonance and achieve balance.

cognitive dissonance
A condition in which two attitudes or a behavior and an attitude conflict.

In the case of working overtime, a person who feels in control of her hours might restructure her responsibilities so that she has time for both work and family. In contrast, another individual who is unable to restructure his workload might change his attitude toward his employer, reducing his organizational commitment. He might resolve his dissonance by saying he loves his children but has to work long hours because his unreasonable employer demands it.

Personality

In the workplace, we find people whose behavior is consistently pleasant or aggressive or stubborn in a variety of situations. To explain that behavior, we may say, "He has a pleasant personality" or "She has an aggressive personality." An individual's **personality** is the set of characteristics that underlie a relatively stable pattern of behavior in response to ideas, objects, or people in the environment. Understanding an individual's personality can help managers predict how that person will act in a particular situation. Managers who appreciate the ways their employees' personalities differ have insight into what kinds of leadership behavior will be most influential.

personality
The set of characteristics that underlie a relatively stable pattern of behavior in response to ideas, objects, or people in the environment.

Personality Traits

In common usage, people think of personality in terms of traits, or relatively stable characteristics of a person. Researchers have investigated whether any traits stand up to scientific scrutiny. Although investigators have examined thousands of traits over the years, their findings have been distilled into five general dimensions that describe personality. These often are called the "Big Five" personality factors, as illustrated in Exhibit 15.3.[9] Each factor may contain a wide range of specific traits. The **Big Five personality factors** describe an individual's extroversion, agreeableness, conscientiousness, emotional stability, and openness to experience. Each of these qualities is defined below:

Big Five personality factors
Dimensions that describe an individual's extroversion, agreeableness, conscientiousness, emotional stability, and openness to experience.

1. Extroversion—the degree to which a person is sociable, talkative, assertive, and comfortable with interpersonal relationships.

2. Agreeableness—the degree to which a person is able to get along with others by being good-natured, cooperative, forgiving, understanding, and trusting.

3. Conscientiousness—the degree to which a person is focused on a few goals, thus behaving in ways that are responsible, dependable, persistent, and achievement oriented.

Exhibit *15.3*

The "Big Five" Personality Factors

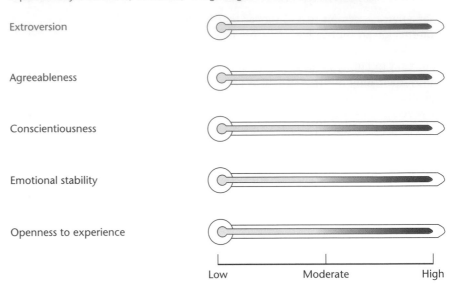

A person may have a low, moderate, or high degree of each of these factors:

Extroversion

Agreeableness

Conscientiousness

Emotional stability

Openness to experience

Low   Moderate   High

4. Emotional stability—the degree to which a person is calm, enthusiastic, and secure, rather than tense, nervous, depressed, moody, or insecure.

5. Openness to experience—the degree to which a person has a broad range of interests and is imaginative, creative, artistically sensitive, and willing to consider new ideas.

James Oxedine has no boss worries, a reasonable income, a home office with a view, and a high internal locus of control. He works as a free agent, helping neighborhoods, banks, and bureaucrats get along during revitalization projects in cities such as Spartanburg, South Carolina and Atlanta, Georgia. Oxedine feels that independence means you never have to say you're bored.

As illustrated in the exhibit, these factors represent a continuum. That is, any individual may exhibit a low, moderate, or high degree of each quality. A person who has an extremely high degree of agreeableness would likely be described as warm, friendly, and good natured, while one at the opposite extreme might be described as cold, rude, or hard to get along with. In general, having a moderate-to-high degree of each of the personality factors is considered desirable for a wide range of employees. In addition, certain factors may be particularly important for specific kinds of work. For example, many successful entrepreneurs, such as Robert Steinberg and John Scharffenberger, profiled in the Leadership box, display a high degree of creativity (openness to ideas) and conscientiousness. As another example, when Stacey Kanzler was watching coverage of disaster relief for the flood-stricken Midwest, she was amazed to see that sandbags were filled by hand. She applied her experience in working at an earth-moving business to develop the idea for a machine that could automate the work, eventually turning the idea into a $2 million company. In the case of FUBU The Collection, its four founders showed extraordinary conscientiousness. They sought financing at over 20 banks, but none were interested in backing a company selling urban fashions and owned by four young black men. Still they persisted, and one owner mortgaged his home. With publicity from rap artist LL Cool J, the company eventually began bringing in millions of dollars in revenues.[10]

Despite the logic and even the validity of the Big Five personality factors, they can be difficult to measure precisely. Furthermore, research has been mostly limited to subjects in the United States, so this theory is difficult to apply in an international context.

The Sweet Taste of Success

Entrepreneurs are, by their very nature, open to new experiences, even if they are trying to reinvent the wheel. John Scharffenberger and Robert Steinberg share a willingness to try new ideas—and a passion for chocolate, which they now manufacture and sell under the name Scharffen Berger. Chocolate has been around for centuries, but until these two came along, only a handful of chocolate makers actually imported, roasted, and ground their own cacao beans, and none of the other makers was independent. Before venturing into candy making, Scharffenberger had already launched a successful sparkling wine business; his wine was used by Reagan and Gorbachev to toast the end of the Cold War. His goal was, as he put it, "to bring joy and innovation to the world of food." Steinberg, on the other hand, is a former physician who sold his practice to follow his interest in cooking when he was diagnosed with an incurable lymphoma. Both are creative men, willing to take chances on new experiences. "What they've done is really unusual," says Alice Medrich, a chocolate chef. "No one just starts a factory. It's too tricky." Steinberg puts it modestly: "Naiveté has worked well for me."

Scharffenberger and Steinberg also are extroverts who love to talk about their sweet passion. Most mass-market chocolates are mainly sugar, says Steinberg. "But chocolate really is a whole possibility of flavors." Scharffenberger claims, "People bite into our chocolate and go 'Wow'!" Both men are conscientious, dividing responsibilities according to their talents and interests. Steinberg has become a cacao expert and Scharffenberger handles the marketing. They now have ten employees at their San Francisco factory, which produces 10,000 pounds of chocolate each month. In addition, Steinberg volunteers at a medical clinic, where he is fond of handing out free chocolate to patients.

What does the public think about the new chocolate? "It's like the beginnings of the gourmet coffee craze," observes Andrea Marcum, manager of Angeli Caffe in West Hollywood, where the rich, tasty chocolate bars sell out frequently. "A lot of our customers are heavily addicted to Scharffen Berger." Charlene Reis, a pastry chef at Chez Panisse in Berkeley comments, "It's rich and roasty and has a lot of flavor. It's an intense taste." Those are sweet words to two entrepreneurs with a taste for culinary adventure.

SOURCE: Alex Tresniowski and Ron Arias, "Misters Bean," *People,* November 9, 1998, 69–70.

Attitudes and Behaviors Influenced by Personality

An individual's personality influences a wide variety of work-related attitudes and behaviors. Among those that are of particular interest to managers are locus of control, authoritarianism, Machiavellianism, and problem-solving styles.

Locus of Control.   People differ in terms of what they tend to attribute as the cause of their success or failure. Their **locus of control** defines whether they place the primary responsibility within themselves or on outside forces.[11] Some people believe that their actions can strongly influence what happens to them. They feel in control of their own fate. These individuals have a high *internal* locus of control. Other people believe that events in their lives occur because of chance, luck, or outside people and events. They feel more like pawns of their fate. These individuals have a high *external* locus of control. An example of someone with a high internal locus of control is Gail Lieberman, chief financial officer at Thomson Financial & Professional Publishing Group, who says obstacles to career advancement really are just invitations for people to think creatively and thus determine their own success: "People have asked me, 'How did you do it? Who helped you?' And I say, 'No one ever helped me. I did it myself.'"[12]

Research on locus of control has shown real differences in behavior across a wide range of settings. People with an internal locus of control are easier to motivate because they believe the rewards are the result of their behavior.

locus of control
The tendency to place the primary responsibility for one's success or failure either within oneself (internally) or on outside forces (externally).

They are better able to handle complex information and problem solving, are more achievement oriented, but are also more independent and therefore more difficult to lead. On the other hand, people with an external locus of control are harder to motivate, less involved in their jobs, more likely to blame others when faced with a poor performance evaluation, but more compliant and conforming and, therefore, easier to lead.[13]

Do you believe luck plays an important role in your life, or do you feel that you control your own fate? To find out more about your locus of control, read the instructions and complete the questionnaire in Exhibit 15.4.

authoritarianism
The belief that power and status differences *should* exist within the organization.

Authoritarianism.   **Authoritarianism** is the belief that power and status differences *should* exist within the organization.[14] Individuals high in authoritarianism tend to be concerned with power and toughness, obey recognized authority above them, stick to conventional values, critically judge others, and oppose the use of subjective feelings. The degree to which managers possess authoritarianism will influence how they wield and share power. The degree to which employees possess authoritarianism will influence how they react to their managers. If a manager and employees differ in their degree of

E x h i b i t   *15.4*   *Measuring Locus of Control*

The questionnaire below is designed to measure locus-of-control beliefs. Researchers using this questionnaire in a recent study of college students found a mean of 51.8 for men and 52.2 for women, with a standard deviation of 6 for each. The higher your score on this questionnaire, the more you tend to believe that you are generally responsible for what happens to you; in other words, higher scores are associated with internal locus of control. Low scores are associated with external locus of control. Scoring low indicates that you tend to believe that forces beyond your control, such as powerful other people, fate, or chance, are responsible for what happens to you.

For each of these ten questions, indicate the extent to which you agree or disagree using the following scale:
1. = strongly disagree   5. = slightly agree
2. = disagree   6. = agree
3. = slightly disagree   7. = strongly agree
4. = neither disagree nor agree

———   1. When I get what I want, it's usually because I worked hard for it.
———   2. When I make plans, I am almost certain to make them work.
———   3. I prefer games involving some luck over games requiring pure skill.
———   4. I can learn almost anything if I set my mind to it.
———   5. My major accomplishments are entirely due to my hard work and ability.
———   6. I usually don't set goals, because I have a hard time following through on them.
———   7. Competition discourages excellence.
———   8. Often people get ahead just by being lucky.
———   9. On any sort of exam or competition, I like to know how well I do relative to everyone else.
——— 10. It's pointless to keep working on something that's too difficult for me.

To determine your score, reverse the values you selected for questions 3, 6, 7, 8, and 10 (1 = 7, 2 = 6, 3 = 5, 4 = 4, 5 = 3, 6 = 2, 7 =1). For example, if you strongly disagreed with the statement in question 3, you would have given it a value of 1. Change this value to a 7. Reverse the scores in a similar manner for questions 6, 7, 8, and 10. Now add the point values from all ten questions together.

Your score: _____

SOURCE: Adapted from J. M. Burger, *Personality: Theory and Research* (Belmont, Calif.: Wadsworth, 1986), 400–401, cited in D. Hellriegel, J. W. Slocum, Jr., and R. W. Woodman, *Organizational Behavior*, 6th ed. (St. Paul, Minn.: West, 1992), 97–100. Original Source: "Sphere-Specific Measures of Perceived Control" by D. L. Paulhus, *Journal of Personality and Social Psychology, 44*, 1253–1265.

authoritarianism, the manager may have difficulty leading effectively. The following example illustrates how authoritarianism can have both positive and negative impacts on an organization.

THE CARLSON COMPANIES
www.carlson.com

The late Curtis L. Carlson built the Carlson Companies into one of the world's largest private companies, including the Radisson hotel chain and T.G.I. Friday's restaurants. His authoritarian style marked the company during his tenure as CEO and continued even in his retirement. Until his death in 1999, Carlson retained voting control over the family-owned company's stock. He ran the company with an iron fist for six decades and had trouble giving up power to allow someone else to take the reins. A decade ago, he appointed a son-in-law, Edwin C. "Skip" Gage as CEO, but the two fought bitterly over decisions and Gage left the company after a few years. Next, Carlson tapped an outsider to run things, but he also left when Carlson insisted on micromanaging his affairs. The bitter fights left the family empire in turmoil.

A few years before his death, Carlson put his daughter, Marilyn Carlson Nelson, in charge of the company, and Nelson is still struggling to transform the culture to fit her own less authoritarian style. "I want to lead with love, not fear," she says. Although Carlson kept close tabs on all his daughter's decisions and the two had strong disagreements, Nelson was able to implement new benefits and profit-sharing plans, introduce flex-time and a day care center, and recruit outside directors. Today she is continuing her efforts to make the Carlson Companies' culture less authoritarian.[15]

Machiavellianism. Another personality dimension that is helpful in understanding work behavior is **Machiavellianism**, which is characterized by the acquisition of power and the manipulation of other people for purely personal gain. Machiavellianism is named after Niccolo Machiavelli, a sixteenth-century author who wrote *The Prince,* a book for noblemen of the day on how to acquire and use power.[16] Psychologists have developed instruments to measure a person's Machiavellianism (Mach) orientation.[17] Research shows that high Machs are predisposed to being pragmatic, capable of lying to achieve personal goals, more likely to win in win-lose situations, and more likely to persuade than be persuaded.[18] In contrast, Kathryn Gould, general partner of Foundation Capital, sounds like a low Mach: "To enjoy 'power' is to enjoy control—especially over other people. I suppose I could wield that kind of power, but I choose not to. I'd rather persuade people with my powers of reasoning than dictate to them from a higher position."[19]

Different situations may require people who exhibit one or the other type of behavior. In loosely structured situations, high Machs actively take control, while low Machs accept the direction given by others. Low Machs thrive in highly structured situations, while high Machs perform in a detached, disinterested way. High Machs are particularly good in jobs that require bargaining skills or that involve substantial rewards for winning.[20]

Machiavellianism
The tendency to direct much of one's behavior toward the acquisition of power and the manipulation of others for personal gain.

Problem-Solving Styles. Managers also need to understand that individuals differ in the way they go about gathering and evaluating information for problem solving and decision making. Psychologist Carl Jung has identified four functions related to this process: sensation, intuition, thinking, and feeling.[21] According to Jung, gathering information and evaluating information are separate activities. People gather information either by *sensation* or *intuition,* but not by both simultaneously. Sensation-type people would rather work with known facts and hard data and prefer routine and order in gathering information. Intuitive-type people would rather look for possibilities than work with facts and prefer solving new problems and using abstract concepts.

Information evaluation involves making judgments about the information a person has gathered. People evaluate information by *thinking* or *feeling*. These represent the extremes in orientation. Thinking-type individuals base their judgments on impersonal analysis, using reason and logic rather than personal values or emotional aspects of the situation. Feeling-type individuals base their judgments more on personal feelings such as harmony and tend to make decisions that result in approval from others.

According to Jung, only one of the four functions—sensation, intuition, thinking, or feeling—is dominant in an individual. However, the dominant function usually is backed up by one of the functions from the other set of paired opposites. Exhibit 15.5 shows the four problem-solving styles that result from these matchups, as well as occupations that people with each style tend to prefer.

Studies show that the sensation-thinking combination characterizes many managers in Western industrialized societies. A case in point is James C. Curvey, president of Fidelity Investments. Describing him, Fred K. Foulkes, a professor who serves as a consultant to Fidelity, says Curvey focuses on setting goals and achieving them, rather than on pondering more abstract interpersonal and intergroup issues.[22] However, as shown in Exhibit 15.5, the intuitive-thinking style is useful for top executives who have to deal with many complex problems and make fast decisions.

E x h i b i t *15.5*   *Four Problem-Solving Styles*

Personal Style	Action Tendencies	Likely Occupations
Sensation–thinking	• Emphasizes details, facts, certainty • Is decisive, applied thinker • Focuses on short-term, realistic goals • Develops rules and regulations for judging performance	• Accounting • Production • Computer programming • Market research • Engineering
Intuitive–thinking	• Prefers dealing with theoretical or technical problems • Is creative, progressive, perceptive thinker • Focuses on possibilities using impersonal analysis • Is able to consider a number of options and problems simultaneously	• Systems design • Systems analysis • Law • Middle/Top management • Teaching business, economics
Sensation–feeling	• Shows concern for current, real-life human problems • Is pragmatic, analytical, methodical, and conscientious • Emphasizes detailed facts about people rather than tasks • Focuses on structuring organizations for the benefit of people	• Directing supervisor • Counseling • Negotiating • Selling • Interviewing
Intuitive–feeling	• Avoids specifics • Is charismatic, participative, people oriented, and helpful • Focuses on general views, broad themes, and feelings • Decentralizes decision making, develops few rules and regulations	• Public relations • Advertising • Personnel • Politics • Customer services

Getting the Right Fit

One of the most important parts of a manager's job is getting the right person-job fit. Bruce M. Hubby, chairman and founder of Professional Dynamic Programs, is a consultant who has designed surveys to help managers determine which candidates are right for which jobs. In the past two decades, he has helped more than 5,000 companies match people to jobs, and jobs to people. Here are some of his tips:

1. *People do best when they can use their natural strengths.* Look for employees' strongest traits and create an environment that enhances them. When people act naturally, they are the most productive; when they are forced to act against their nature, they become stressed and less productive.

2. *Learn which of the four basic traits is most prominent in a person.* Hubby identifies dominance, extroversion, patience, and conformity as the four basic personality traits that describe most people. Dominant people are innovative and confident, and they like to be in control. Extroverted people are outgoing and social. Patient people know how to pace themselves; they are focused but adaptable. Conforming people have a strong sense of right and wrong; they are structured and quality oriented. Learning which basic trait is most prevalent (and how the other three factor in) will help managers determine who is right for a job.

3. *Resist the urge to hire someone who is exactly like you.* We naturally gravitate toward people who are like us, so a manager may hire someone who has the same natural strengths or personality traits, even if those strengths and traits are not right for the job.

4. *Reshape the job, not the person.* If an employee is struggling with a job because of poor person-job fit, it's much easier to reshape the job—or move the employee to another job—than it is to reshape the employee's personality. Usually, there's no need to let that worker go.

SOURCE: David Beardsley, "These Tests Will Give You Fits," *Fast Company,* November 1998, 88, 90.

Person-Job Fit

Given the wide variation among personalities and among jobs, an important responsibility of managers is to try to match employee and job characteristics so that work is done by people who are well suited to do it. This requires that managers be clear about what they expect employees to do. They should have a sense of the kinds of people who would succeed at the work that must be done. The extent to which a person's ability and personality match the requirements of a job is called **person-job fit.** When hiring and leading employees, managers should try to achieve person-job fit, so that employees are more likely to contribute and be satisfied.[23] The Manager's Shoptalk box lists some tips to help managers put the right people in the right jobs.

person-job fit
The extent to which a person's ability and personality match the requirements of a job.

Dennis Brozak, owner of Design Basics, was meticulous about person-job fit when it came time to pick a successor. The person he selected was Linda Reimer, whom Brozak had first hired as a part-timer to photocopy blueprints. Over the years, Brozak added to her responsibilities as he discovered she was eager to learn the business, had financial acumen, cared about design and construction, and shared core values such as the idea that all work is honorable. To test her management skills, Brozak made Reimer human resources director, put her in charge of a product, made her an operations director, and then promoted her to a position of vice president charged with product development. In each position, Reimer boosted the company's performance, so Brozak appointed her company president, a decision that has paid off in double-digit growth. Although a person toiling at the photocopier might not have seemed to be a candidate for company president just a few years later, Brozak's focus on abilities rather than job titles enabled him to achieve a good person-job fit for the company's top position.[24]

An understanding of personality also is important when managers want to change the nature of the work, because such changes may affect person-job fit. How flexible are employees? Will they be likely to voice their questions and concerns? Will the new work structure require a level of responsibility with which the employees will be comfortable? Personality does not lend itself to change. When person-job fit is poor, the manager may have to restructure tasks or replace employees.

Perception

perception
The process people use to make sense of the environment by selecting, organizing, and interpreting information from the environment.

People often approach an assignment differently because one person "sees" the assignment differently from others. "Seeing" things differently is an inevitable outcome of **perception**—the process people use to make sense out of the environment by selecting, organizing, and interpreting information from the environment. Because of individual differences in what people perceive and how they organize and interpret it, perceptions vary among people and differ from objective reality. Recognizing the difference between what is perceived and what is real is a key element in diagnosing a situation.

We can think of perception as a step-by-step process, as shown in Exhibit 15.6. First, we observe information (sensory data) from the environment through our senses: taste, smell, hear, see, and touch. Next, our mind screens the data and will select only the items we will process further. Third, we organize the selected data into meaningful patterns for interpretation and response. Most differences in perception among people at work are related to how they select and organize sensory data.

Perceptual Selectivity

We all are aware of our environment, but not everything in it is equally important to our perception of it. We tune in to some data (e.g., a familiar voice off in the distance) and tune out other data (e.g., paper shuffling next to us). People are bombarded by so much sensory data that it is impossible to process it all. The brain's solution is to run the data through a perceptual filter that retains some parts (selective attention) and eliminates others. **Perceptual selectivity** is the process by which individuals screen and select the various objects and stimuli that vie for their attention. Certain stimuli catch their attention, and others do not.

perceptual selectivity
The process by which individuals screen and select the various stimuli that vie for their attention.

Exactly what a person screens and selects depends on a number of factors. These relate either to the stimuli being perceived or characteristics of the perceiver.

Exhibit *15.6*

The Perception Process

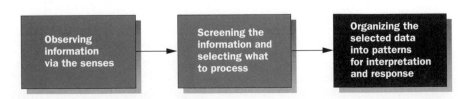

Observing information via the senses → Screening the information and selecting what to process → Organizing the selected data into patterns for interpretation and response

Characteristics of the Stimuli. The following characteristics of the stimuli can enhance the chance it will be selected:

- Contrast—People notice a stimulus more if it stands out from background stimuli. Examples include a loud noise in a quiet room or bold type on a white page.

- Novelty—A stimulus that is new or different from stimuli previously perceived may attract more attention.

- Familiarity—People tend to perceive stimuli that are known or familiar.

- Intensity—People are more inclined to notice a stimulus that is intense in some way, for example, by being loud or bright.

- Motion—Objects that move a lot tend to be noticed more.

- Repetition—Repeated stimuli tend to attract more attention.

- Size—A larger object generally receives more attention than a smaller object.

The influence of stimuli characteristics on the perceptual process comes into play in an employment interview. In evaluating a job applicant, interviewers may notice particular characteristics that are either novel or comfortingly familiar. In addition, if a candidate repeatedly refers to some qualification, the interviewer is likely to pay more attention to that piece of information.

Contrast and novelty also influence how people are perceived in many situations. People who differ in some way—by race, sex, or disability status, for example—receive more than their share of scrutiny. Jessica Bibliowicz, president and chief operating officer of investment adviser John A. Levin & Company, found this worked to her advantage early in her career. When she made presentations to clients, they were surprised to see a woman, so they took note of her and remembered her when they saw her again.[25]

Characteristics of the Perceiver. Several characteristics of the perceiver also can influence the selection of sensory data:

- Needs and motivation—People tend to notice stimuli that provide a way to satisfy their needs.

- Values and beliefs—People tend to pay the most attention to stimuli that are consistent with their values and beliefs.

- Personality—People pay the most attention to stimuli that reinforce their personality.

- Learning—Experience with similar stimuli teaches people what it is important for them to pay attention to.

- Primacy—People pay relatively greater attention to stimuli near the beginning of an event.

- Recency—People pay relatively greater attention to stimuli toward the end of an event.

The impact of *primacy* on perceptual selectivity supports the old truism that first impressions are important. It really is important to look your best when you meet someone in a job interview or at a meeting. The primacy characteristic can cause people to form impressions quickly and then to pay less attention to later behavior, even though it could contradict that first impression. Unfortunately, early impressions can lead to perceptual errors.

Applications of Perceptual Selectivity.   As these examples show, perceptual selectivity is not a simple process of reducing data to an amount that is easy to perceive. It is a complex filtering process that determines which sensory data will receive attention. Managers can use these principles of selective perception to obtain clues about why one person "sees" things differently from others, and they can apply the principles to their own communications, especially when they want to attract or focus attention. At a meeting to develop a statement of the vision for a new high school, the School for Environmental Studies in Apple Valley, Minnesota, the challenge was how to keep people's attention focused on the ideas that best reflected the group's views. As people suggested ideas, someone wrote them on index cards and posted them on the wall. Then participants moved to the display of cards and used colored-dot stickers to indicate their favorite ideas. The bright dots were an attention-getting way for the participants to focus the remainder of their attention on the cards with the most dots.[26]

An obvious application of selective perception is advertising; organizations want to use the factors that enhance perception to create ads that grab attention. Columbia Sportswear, for example, wanted to distinguish itself from its competitors, which invariably advertised by showing images of their high-tech gear worn by obviously fit models. Columbia, in contrast, began running a series of ads featuring the company's chairwoman, Gert Boyle, as a "tough mother," determined that her products would meet her high standards. The ploy worked; sales soon skyrocketed.[27]

Perceptual Organization

Once people have selected the sensory data to be perceived, they begin grouping the data into recognizable patterns. **Perceptual organization** is the process by which people organize or categorize stimuli according to their frame of reference. Individuals learn to simplify and make sense out of their perceptions through a gradual process of organizing sensory data from their experiences. The process begins early in life with experiences about how to interpret facial expressions and what objects we can safely and pleasurably eat (bread is good, sand is not). This process continues throughout our lives. In the workplace, the process of organizing sensory data is affected by our experiences in meetings, performance appraisals, interaction with our bosses and co-workers, and so forth.

Several factors in perceptual organization contribute to individual differences among people in the work setting. These include perceptual grouping, figure-ground, and perceptual distortions.

Perceptual Grouping.   To make sense of a highly complex world, people engage in **perceptual grouping,** or the organizing of sensory data into patterns. This process is beneficial when it leads to conclusions that accurately reflect objective reality. Mechanisms for perceptual grouping include closure, continuity, proximity, and similarity.

Closure is the tendency to perceive incomplete data in its whole, complete form. What do you see in part *a* of Exhibit 15.7? Most people see this series of spots as a dog. Through closure, the brain imagines the missing details.

Continuity is the tendency to perceive sensory data in continuous patterns, even if they are not actually continuous. Read aloud the message in part *b*

perceptual organization
The process by which people organize or categorize stimuli according to their frame of reference.

perceptual grouping
The organizing of sensory data into patterns.

Exhibit 15.7 *What Do You See?*

(a)

(c)

(b)
Read this sentence out loud.

A BIRD IN THE
THE HAND IS WORTHLESS.

of Exhibit 15.7. Did you notice that the word *the* appears twice—at the end of the first line and again at the beginning of the second line? Many people read this as a continuous sentence with only one *the*. Because people tend to organize messages in a way that makes sense to them, managers must be extremely careful in how they communicate messages that may be unexpected or difficult to understand.

Proximity is the tendency to perceive sensory data as related because of close physical location. For example, people working on the same floor of a large office building may be perceived as a unit even though they represent portions of several departments of the company. Likewise, discussing performance appraisals and salary reviews at the same meeting signals that decisions about performance and salary are related.

Similarity is the tendency to group sensory data because they are alike in some way. For example, a manager might use the mental category "scientific research" for research reports he considers valid and reliable. He might tend to assign reports to this group whenever they contain a lot of numerical data or a large number of respondents. However, for perceptions to be accurate, it is important to examine the criteria for assigning a stimulus to a particular group. In this example, not every survey with a lot of data or a large sample will be objectively "scientific." When a report is significant to the manager, he should therefore examine its conclusions carefully before relying on it.

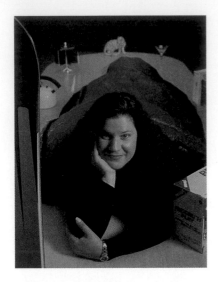

Stereotyping *Michelle Breiner as a ruthless, disloyal jobhopper—typical generalizations attributed to her generation—would be easy. At 30, she's already worked in five industries, from CD-Rom development to Web page design to e-commerce. Today, she's creative director at the Internet Shopping Network. But Breiner sees herself positively as a nomad, knowing how to spot the next trend and find a job at a company poised to exploit it. She works hard and stays focused on preparing for new challenges. In five years she will be "possibly running or starting a company," she says, "I'm guessing it will involve a technology that's not here yet."*

figure-ground
The tendency to perceive the sensory data one is most attentive to as standing out against the background of other sensory data.

perceptual distortions
Errors in perceptual judgment that arise from inaccuracies in any part of the perception process.

stereotyping
The tendency to assign an individual to a group or broad category and then attribute generalizations about the group to the individual.

halo effect
An overall impression of a person or situation based on one attribute, either favorable or unfavorable.

projection
The tendency to see one's own personal traits in other people.

Figure-Ground.   Another factor in perceptual organization is **figure-ground**—people's tendency to perceive the sensory data they are most attentive to as standing out against the background of sensory data to which they are less attentive. Look at part *c* of Exhibit 15.7. How many blocks do you see, six or seven? Some people have to turn the figure upside down before they can see seven blocks. Although this is just a reversible figure-ground pattern, it shows us that once we have "seen" something one way, it can be difficult for us to "see" it differently. Managers who want to change their own or others' perceptions must be patient and try showing the new interpretation from more than one angle.

Perceptual Distortions.   Errors in perceptual judgment, called **perceptual distortions,** can arise from inaccuracies in any part of the perception process. Some types of errors are so common that managers should become familiar with them. These include stereotyping, the halo effect, projection, and perceptual defense. Managers who recognize these perceptual distortions can better adjust their perceptions to more closely match objective reality.

Stereotyping is the tendency to assign an individual to a group or broad category (e.g., female, black, elderly or male, white, disabled) and then to attribute widely held generalizations about the group to the individual. Thus, someone meets a new colleague, sees he is in a wheelchair, assigns him to the category "physically disabled," and attributes to this colleague generalizations she believes about people with disabilities, which may include a belief that he is less able than other co-workers. However, the person's inability to walk should not be seen as indicative of lesser abilities in other areas. Indeed, the assumption of limitations may not only offend him, it also prevents the person making the stereotypical judgment from benefiting from the many ways in which this person can contribute. Because stereotyping clouds individual differences, it prevents people from truly knowing those they classify in this way. In addition, negative stereotypes can prevent talented people from advancing in an organization and fully contributing their talents to the organization's success.

The **halo effect** occurs when the perceiver develops an overall impression of a person or situation based on one attribute, either favorable or unfavorable. In other words, a halo blinds the perceiver to other attributes that should be used in generating a more complete assessment. The halo effect can play a significant role in performance appraisal. For example, a person with an outstanding attendance record may be assessed as responsible, industrious, and highly productive; another person with less-than-average attendance may be assessed as a poor performer. Either assessment may be true, but it is the manager's job to be sure the assessment is based on complete information about all job-related attributes and not just his or her preferences for good attendance.

Projection is the tendency of perceivers to see their own personal traits in other people; that is, they project their own needs, feelings, values, and attitudes into their judgment of others. For example, a manager who is achievement oriented may assume that her subordinates are as well. This may cause her to restructure jobs in her department to be less routine and more challenging, without regard for her employees' actual satisfaction. The best guards against errors based on projection are self-awareness and empathy. *Empathy* means being able to put yourself in someone else's shoes, to recognize what others are feeling without them needing to tell you.

Perceptual defense is the tendency of perceivers to protect themselves against ideas, objects, or people that are threatening. People perceive things that are satisfying and pleasant but tend to disregard things that are disturbing and unpleasant. In essence, people develop blind spots in the perceptual process so that negative sensory data do not hurt them. For example, in the early years of her career, Darlene Mann, now a venture partner with Onset Ventures in Menlo Park, California, tried to help an entrepreneur by offering advice (but not funding). She later learned that he said she was overly critical and liked telling people what was wrong with their ideas. Mann's original response was anger based on the belief that the entrepreneur would not have said that about a man. She then reevaluated her reaction and concluded that she had been mistaken to offer advice the entrepreneur did not ask for.[28] As Mann did, recognizing perceptual blind spots will help people develop a clearer picture of reality.

perceptual defense
The tendency of perceivers to protect themselves by disregarding ideas, objects, or people that are threatening to them.

Attributions

As people organize what they perceive, they often draw conclusions about the stimuli. For example, stereotyping involves assigning a number of traits to a person. Among the judgments people make as part of the perceptual process are attributions. **Attributions** are judgments about what caused a person's behavior—something about the person or something about the situation. An *internal attribution* says characteristics of the person led to the behavior ("My boss yelled at me because he's impatient and doesn't listen"). An *external attribution* says something about the situation caused the person's behavior ("My boss yelled at me because I missed the deadline and the customer is upset"). Attributions are important because they help people decide how to handle a situation. In the case of the boss yelling, a person who blames the yelling on the boss's personality will view the boss as the problem and might cope by avoiding the boss. In contrast, someone who blames the yelling on the situation might try to help prevent such situations in the future.

attributions
Judgments about what caused a person's behavior—either characteristics of the person or of the situation.

Social scientists have studied the attributions people make and identified three factors that influence whether an attribution will be external or internal.[29] These three factors are illustrated in Exhibit 15.8:

1. *Distinctiveness*—Whether the behavior is unusual for that person (in contrast to a person displaying the same kind of behavior in many situations). If the behavior is distinctive, the perceiver probably will make an *external* attribution.

2. *Consensus*—Whether other people tend to respond to similar situations in the same way. A person who has observed others handle similar situations in the same way will likely make an *external* attribution; that is, it will seem that the situation produces the type of behavior observed.

3. *Consistency*—Whether the person being observed has a history of behaving in the same way. People generally make *internal* attributions about consistent behavior.

In addition to these general rules, people tend to have biases that they apply when making attributions. When evaluating others, we tend to underestimate the influence of external factors and overestimate the influence of internal factors. This tendency is called the **fundamental attribution error.** For example, when someone has been promoted to chief executive officer, people generally consider the characteristics of the person that allowed him

fundamental attribution error
The tendency to underestimate the influence of external factors on another's behavior and to overestimate the influence of internal factors.

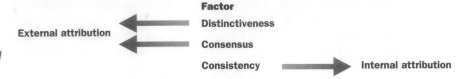

or her to achieve the promotion. In reality, however, the selection of that person may have been heavily influenced by external factors, such as business conditions creating a need for someone with a strong financial or marketing background at that particular time.

Another bias that distorts attributions involves attributions we make about our own behavior. People tend to overestimate the contribution of internal factors to their successes and overestimate the contribution of external factors to their failures. This tendency, called the **self-serving bias,** means people give themselves too much credit for what they do well and give external forces too much blame when they fail. Thus, if your manager says you don't communicate well enough, and you think your manager doesn't listen well enough, the truth may actually lie somewhere in between.

self-serving bias
The tendency to overestimate the contribution of internal factors to one's successes and the contribution of external factors to one's failures.

Learning

Years of schooling have conditioned many of us to think that learning is something students do in response to teachers in a classroom. With this view, in the managerial world of time deadlines and concrete action, learning seems remote—even irrelevant. However, today's successful managers need specific knowledge and skills as well as the ability to adapt to changes in the world around them. Managers have to learn.

Learning is a change in behavior or performance that occurs as the result of experience. Experience may take the form of observing others, reading or listening to sources of information, or experiencing the consequences of one's own behavior. This important way of adapting to events is linked to perception, because learning depends on the way a person perceives sensory data.

learning
A change in behavior or performance as a result of experience.

Two individuals who undergo similar experiences—for example, a business transfer to a foreign country—probably will differ in how they adapt their behaviors to (that is, learn from) the experience. In other words, there are individual differences in the learning process.

The Learning Process

One model of the learning process, shown in Exhibit 15.9 depicts learning as a four-stage cycle.[30] First, a person encounters a concrete experience. This is followed by thinking and reflective observation, which lead to abstract conceptualization and, in turn, to active experimentation. The results of the experimentation generate new experiences, and the cycle repeats.

The Best Buy chain of consumer electronics superstores owes its birth to the learning process of its founder, Richard M. Schulze. In the 1960s, Schulze built a stereo store called Sound of Music into a chain of nine stores in and near St. Paul, Minnesota. However, a tornado destroyed his largest and most profitable store, so he held a massive clearance sale in the parking lot. So many shoppers descended on the lot that they caused traffic to back up for

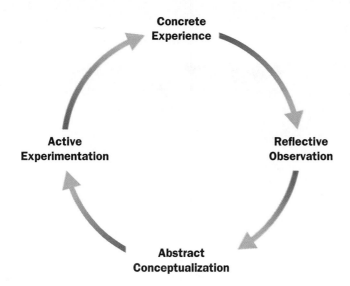

E x h i b i t
15.9
Experiential Learning Cycle

two miles. Reflecting on this experience, Schulze decided there was great demand for a store featuring large selection and low prices, backed by heavy advertising. He tried out his idea by launching his first Best Buy superstore. Today there are more than 280 Best Buy outlets, and the chain's profits are in the billions of dollars.[31]

The arrows in the model of the learning process imply that this process is a recurring cycle. People continually test their conceptualizations and adapt them as a result of their personal reflections and observations about their experiences.

Learning Styles

Individuals develop personal learning styles that vary in terms of how much they emphasize each stage of the learning cycle. These differences occur because the learning process is directed by individual needs and goals. For example, an engineer may place greater emphasis on abstract concepts, while a salesperson may emphasize concrete experiences. Because of these preferences, personal learning styles typically have strong and weak points.

To assess a person's strong and weak points as a learner in the learning cycle, questionnaires have been developed to measure the relative emphasis the person places on each of the four learning stages shown in Exhibit 15.9: concrete experience, reflective observation, abstract conceptualization, and active experimentation. Some people have a tendency to overemphasize one stage of the learning process, or to avoid some aspects of learning. Not many people have totally balanced profiles, but the key to effective learning is competence in each of the four stages when it is needed.

Each person's learning style is a combination of the emphasis placed on the four stages. Researchers have identified four fundamental learning styles that combine elements of the four stages.[32] Exhibit 15.10 summarizes the characteristics and dominant learning abilities of these four learning styles, labeled Diverger, Assimilator, Converger, and Accommodator. The exhibit also lists occupations that frequently attract individuals with each of the learning styles. For example, people whose dominant style is Accommodator often are drawn

Exhibit *15.10* *Learning Style Types*

Learning Style Type	Dominant Learning Abilities	Learning Characteristics	Likely Occupations
Diverger	• Concrete experience • Reflective observation	• Is good at generating ideas, seeing a situation from multiple perspectives, and being aware of meaning and value • Tends to be interested in people, culture, and the arts	• Human resource management • Counseling • Organization development specialist
Assimilator	• Abstract conceptualization • Reflective observation	• Is good at inductive reasoning, creating theoretical models, and combining disparate observations into an integrated explanation • Tends to be less concerned with people than ideas and abstract concepts	• Research • Strategic planning
Converger	• Abstract conceptualization • Active experimentation	• Is good at decisiveness, practical application of ideas, and hypothetical deductive reasoning • Prefers dealing with technical tasks rather than interpersonal issues	• Engineering • Production
Accommodator	• Concrete experience • Active experimentation	• Is good at implementing decisions, carrying out plans, and getting involved in new experiences • Tends to be at ease with people but may be seen as impatient or pushy	• Marketing • Sales

to sales and marketing. An illustration of the Accommodator style is Steve Ballmer, who joined Microsoft to handle its sales and customer support. Now Microsoft's president, Ballmer is known for responsiveness to customer needs. When ABC, a Microsoft customer, asked Microsoft to make a change in its licensing agreement, Ballmer immediately called a meeting and resolved the concern by the next day. A former Microsoft executive describes Ballmer's approach to problem solving as "Don't have an elegant plan. Do the smart, obvious thing. Then fix it as you go." Ballmer even embodies some of the shortcomings of the Accommodator style. He is known for making statements that are more impulsive than diplomatic. For example, when the Justice Department launched its antitrust lawsuit against Microsoft, Ballmer publicly said, "To heck with [Attorney General] Janet Reno!"[33]

Through awareness of their learning style, managers can understand how they approach problems and issues, their learning strengths and weaknesses, and how they react to employees or co-workers who have different learning styles.

Continuous Learning

To thrive or even to survive in today's fast-changing business climate, individuals and organizations must be continuous learners. For individuals, continuous learning entails looking for opportunities to learn from classes, reading, and talking to others, as well as looking for the lessons in life's experiences. For organizations, continuous learning involves the processes and systems through which the organization enables its people to learn, share their growing knowledge, and apply it to their work. In an organization in which continuous learning is taking place, employees actively apply comments from customers, news about competitors, training programs, and more to increase their knowledge and improve the organization's practices.

Someone who embodies the spirit of continuous learning is Dr. Ben Carson, a respected pediatric neurosurgeon. Carson notes that the medical community has learned more about the human brain in the past two decades than it knew in total before that. He expects that pattern to repeat itself, as researchers gain knowledge at an exponential rate. This humbling realization of what he has yet to learn inspires Carson to keep his mind open to new information. If a patient improved as a result of another doctor's surgery, Carson contacts that doctor to see if he can learn anything to apply when it is his turn to operate. He also builds on the knowledge gained from experience. For example, he found that patients were taking a long time to regain consciousness following a radical brain operation called a hemispherectomy. He evaluated the circumstances and revised how the procedure is performed so that the patient's brain stem would not be disturbed.[34]

Managers can foster continuous learning by consciously stopping from time to time and asking, "What can we learn from this experience?" They can allow employees time to attend training and reflect on their experiences. Recognizing that experience can be the best teacher, managers should focus on how they and their employees can learn from mistakes, rather than fostering a climate in which employees hide mistakes because they fear being punished for them. Managers also can encourage organizational learning by establishing information systems that enable employees to share knowledge and learn in new ways. The Technology box describes how managers at organizations such as Oracle, IBM, and Kodak are learning new approaches to business by attending "virtual reality school" at the U.S. Army's National Defense University. Information technology will be discussed in detail in Chapter 21. As individuals, managers can help themselves and set an example for their employees by being continuous learners, listening to others, reading widely, and reflecting on what they observe.

Maytag Corporation, a manufacturer of home and commercial appliances, joins with the state of Iowa to advertise the benefits of their continuous learning style. Maytag makes the following claims in their ad: "We have partnered successfully with the state and our community on education and training alliances and infrastructure improvements that advance our commitment to profitable growth."

Stress and Stress Management

Just as organizations can support or discourage learning, many other organizational characteristics interact with individual differences to influence behavior in the organization. In every organization, these characteristics include sources of stress. Formally defined, **stress** is an individual's physiological and emotional response to stimuli that place physical or psychological demands on the individual and create uncertainty and lack of personal control when important outcomes are at stake.[35] These stimuli, called stressors, produce some combination of frustration (the inability to achieve a goal, such as the inability to meet a deadline because of inadequate resources) and anxiety (such as the fear of being disciplined for not meeting deadlines).

People's responses to stressors vary according to their personality, the resources available to help them cope, and the context in which the stress occurs. Thus, a looming deadline will feel different depending on the degree

stress
A physiological and emotional response to stimuli that place physical or psychological demands on an individual.

Information Warriors

Recently, Steve Knode steered an open-air rig across treacherous terrain. The dusty red soil swallowed the truck's tires. The temperature was 200 degrees below zero. Knode was navigating the surface of Mars in the DRiViR's seat (Decision Room Incorporating Virtual Reality) at the National Defense University (NDU).

Knode and his colleagues are thinking about war in a world in which the battlefield has shifted from air, land, and sea to the realm of cyberspace. And they're writing lesson plans that are designed to shape the future of business competition as well as combat. Students from companies across America regularly travel to NDU's Washington, D.C., campus to attend the Advanced Management Program (AMP), a three-and-a-half-month boot camp. During the program, they learn how digital technology is changing the nature of war, business, and even society itself. Every aspect of the AMP integrates the new realities of 21st-century combat with the new logic of business, and the students come from both worlds. Oracle, Corning, IBM, and Eastman Kodak all have sent managers through the program, where they take courses such as Virtual Reality for Managers and Innovative Thinking for the Information Age.

Students at NDU learn two different ways—they spend time in the classroom talking about big ideas such as strategy and the future of work, but they also venture into the real world, visiting innovative companies to see ideas in action. NDU encourages teamwork and group problem solving. Each student is issued a laptop stuffed with groupware and hooked up to a wireless communications network, so they can collaborate on projects and brainstorm solutions to case studies.

Jack North of GTE (the telecommunications giant) was one of the first nongovernmental students to graduate from the program, which he says "made me rethink much of what we do here [at GTE]." Inspired by what he learned, North returned to GTE and quickly installed groupware applications and desktop videoconferencing to promote collaboration and continuous learning at the health systems division he runs. "The program produces a whole group of managers who are ready to go back and become change agents," North says. "There's a lot of down-and-dirty *practical* reality."

SOURCE: Based on Daniel H. Pink, "Hey, Your CEO Wears Combat Boots!" *Fast Company*, June–July 1997, 46, 48.

---

to which you enjoy a challenge, the willingness of coworkers to team up and help each other succeed, and family members' understanding of your need to work extra hours, among other factors.

When the level of stress is low relative to a person's coping resources, stress can be a positive force, stimulating desirable change and achievement. However, too much stress is associated with many negative consequences, including sleep disturbances, drug and alcohol abuse, headaches, ulcers, high blood pressure, and heart disease. People who are experiencing the ill effects of too much stress may withdraw from interactions with their coworkers, take time off for illnesses, and look for less stressful jobs elsewhere. They may become so irritable that they cannot work constructively with others; some employees may even explode in tantrums or violence. Clearly, too much stress is harmful to employees as well as the organization.

In biological terms, the stress response follows a pattern known as the General Adaptation Syndrome. The **General Adaptation Syndrome (GAS)** is a physiological response to a stressor, which begins with an alarm response, continues to resistance, and may end in exhaustion if the stressor continues beyond a person's ability to cope.[36] As shown in Exhibit 15.11, the GAS begins when an individual first experiences a source of stress (called a stressor). The stressor triggers an alarm response; the person may feel panic and helplessness, wondering how to cope with the stressor. Occasionally, people simply give up, but more often they move to the next stage of the stress response, called resistance. At this stage, the person gathers

General Adaptation Syndrome (GAS)
The physiological response to a stressor, beginning with an alarm response, continuing to resistance, and sometimes ending in exhaustion if the stressor continues beyond the person's ability to cope.

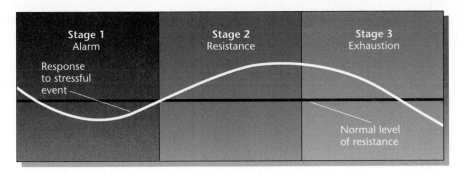

Exhibit *15.11*
The Stress Response: General Adaptation Syndrome

strength and begins to decide how to cope. If exposure to the stressor continues past the person's ability to maintain resistance, the person enters the third stage: exhaustion.

Type A and Type B Behavior

Researchers have observed that some people seem to be more vulnerable than others to the ill effects of stress. From studies of stress-related heart disease, they have categorized people as having behavior patterns called Type A and Type B.[37] The **Type A behavior** pattern includes extreme competitiveness, impatience, aggressiveness, and devotion to work. In contrast, people with a **Type B behavior** pattern exhibit less of these behaviors. They consequently experience less conflict with other people and a more balanced, relaxed lifestyle. Type A people tend to experience more stress-related illness than Type B people.

David L. House, chief executive of Bay Networks, exhibits many Type A characteristics. He proudly told a *Business Week* reporter that on one business trip he led seven meetings in nine hours, handled business on his car phone, and attended a dinner. At his former employer, Intel, co-workers gave him a T-shirt with the message "Captain Adrenaline," reflecting his high-energy, driven style. His drive and discipline carry over to activities outside the workplace. He schedules early-morning exercise five days a week, and his aggressive play at racquetball has reportedly caused several opponents to require stitches. House admits that his behavior has consequences; he says his intense schedule is a reason his two marriages ended in divorce.[38]

By pacing themselves and learning control and intelligent use of their natural high-energy tendencies, Type A individuals can be powerful forces for innovation and leadership within their organizations. However, many Type A personalities cause stress-related problems for themselves, and sometimes for those around them. Type-B individuals typically live with less stress unless they are in high-stress situations. There are a number of factors that can cause stress in the workplace, even for people who are not naturally prone to high stress.

Causes of Work Stress

Most people have a general idea of what a stressful job is like: difficult, uncomfortable, exhausting, even frightening. Managers can better cope with their own stress and establish ways for the organization to help employees cope if they define the conditions that tend to produce work stress. One way

Type A behavior
Behavior pattern characterized by extreme competitiveness, impatience, aggressiveness, and devotion to work.

Type B behavior
Behavior pattern that lacks Type A characteristics and includes a more balanced, relaxed lifestyle.

to identify work stressors is to place them in four categories: demands associated with job tasks, physical conditions, roles (sets of expected behaviors), and interpersonal pressures and conflicts.

Task demands are stressors arising from the tasks required of a person holding a particular job. Some kinds of decisions are inherently stressful: those made under time pressure, those that have serious consequences, and those that must be made with incomplete information. For example, emergency room doctors are under tremendous stress as a result of the task demands of their jobs. They regularly have to make quick decisions, based on limited information, that may determine whether a patient lives or dies. Although not as extreme, many other jobs have task demands that lead to stress. Recall from Chapter 9 that managers frequently have to make *nonprogrammed decisions*—decisions that are characterized by incomplete information and have important consequences for the organization. Managers also experience stress from other factors, such as the responsibility of supervising or disciplining other people. Federal Express found that 10 percent of employees promoted to their first management job left the company within a year or so. The company learned that many didn't realize the difficulty of the task demands facing managers: longer hours, the commitment of representing the company even outside work, and the consequences of having responsibility for others.[39]

Physical demands are stressors associated with the setting in which an individual works. Some people must cope with work in a poorly designed setting, such as an office with inadequate lighting or little privacy. Some employees must maneuver in a cramped workspace; some have too little or too much heat for comfort. Some workplaces even present safety and health hazards, from greasy floors to polluted air. Work that involves repetitive movements, such as poultry processing or extensive computer work, also can lead to injury; thus this type of work intensifies stress for employees.

Role demands are challenges associated with a role—that is, the set of behaviors expected of a person because of that person's position in the group. Some people encounter **role ambiguity,** meaning they are uncertain about what behaviors are expected of them. For example, one clinical psychologist who specializes in executive stress says that many upper-level executives, who grew up at a time when norms were different, do not understand what diversity requires of them—such as what women in the workplace view as appropriate conduct. Consequently, some are fearful of inadvertently doing something that a woman will regard as sexual harassment.[40]

Role ambiguity results in many complications in the workplace, as some employees of Wendy's International experienced personally. Role ambiguity was the norm at Wendy's when the hamburger chain began rapid expansion during the 1970s.

role ambiguity
Uncertainty about what behaviors are expected of a person in a particular role.

WENDY'S INTERNATIONAL
www.wendysintl.com

Wendy's top executive, Dave Thomas, says his biggest mistake was not completing high school. Thomas, who knew he wanted to be in the restaurant business, dropped out of school because he thought he could learn more by working. One thing he learned was that quitting school made his business life a lot harder. Thomas found that a lot of people would talk down to him, and he had to work twice as hard to get people to treat him as an equal. Further, when Thomas started building his business, he felt insecure and uncomfortable about his lack of a formal education (he finally returned to school and earned his GED in the 1990s).

Thomas believed that because of his lack of education, he needed to delegate extensively. Unfortunately, Wendy's was growing so fast that Thomas delegated more and more decision-making authority without providing the managers and crew with the training they needed to make good work decisions. The result? People didn't understand what they were supposed to do, didn't know what top management expected from them, felt tremendous stress and anxiety, and eventually became frustrated, some to the point of exhaustion. As soon as Thomas and other top managers realized what was happening, they took immediate action to provide employees with the clear guidelines and training they needed. Today, Wendy's managers work hard to make sure all employees feel empowered—not stressed out.[41]

Although role ambiguity can be stressful, people who experience *role conflict* can feel as if they are being torn apart by conflicting expectations. **Role conflict** occurs when an individual perceives incompatible demands from others. Managers often feel role conflict because the demands of their superiors conflict with those of the employees in their department. For example, they may be expected to support employees and provide them with opportunities to experiment and be creative, while at the same time top executives are demanding a consistent level of output that leaves little time for creativity and experimentation. In a company whose philosophy is "We're one big family," a manager who has to lay off employees would likely feel that this role conflicts with the expectation that she care about employees. These types of role conflict can create a high level of stress. Role conflict may also be experienced when a person's internalized values and beliefs collide with the expectations of others. For example, a manager who believes in being honest and ethical in all his relationships may be told by a superior to "fudge a little" on quality control reports in order to meet an important deadline. This role conflict leaves the manager with the choice of either being disloyal to his superior or acting unethically, according to his personal values.[42]

Interpersonal demands are stressors associated with relationships in the organization. Although in some cases interpersonal relationships can alleviate stress, they also can be a source of stress when the group puts pressure on an individual or when there are conflicts. Interpersonal conflict occurs when two or more individuals perceive that their attitudes or goals are in opposition. Managers can work to resolve many interpersonal and intergroup conflicts, using techniques discussed in Chapter 19. A particularly challenging stressor is the personality clash. A personality clash occurs when two people simply cannot get along and do not see eye-to-eye on any issue. This type of conflict can be exceedingly difficult to resolve, and many managers have found that it is best to separate the two people so that they do not have to interact with one another.

> **role conflict**
> Incompatible demands of different roles.

Stress Management

Organizations that want to challenge their employees and stay competitive in a fast-changing environment will never be stress-free. But because many consequences of stress are negative, managers need to participate in stress management for themselves and for their employees. They can do so by

Stress management is very important for nonfamily managers who work for a family business. Outsiders are concerned about such issues as how much decision-making responsibility they'll have and what the job growth potential is in a family-run enterprise. Family in-fighting can be particularly stressful for nonfamily employees. Rhonda and Glenn Shaw, president and general manager (standing) of Trinity Valley Erectors, an Emory, Texas, provider of passenger boarding bridges and baggage carriers for airports, managed potential stress when hiring Judy Luckett as the company's bookkeeper. "They warned me that sometimes when they don't agree it could get loud. I assured them that as long as they don't yell or drag me into their disagreements, it was okay," Luckett says. "They never have."

identifying the major sources of stress, including the task, physical, role, and interpersonal demands of the job and organization. Does the overall level of these demands match the employee's taste for challenge and his or her coping resources? If so, the level of stress may be part of a successful person-job fit. If not, the organization and its employees should look for ways to reduce the stressors and increase employees' coping skills. Organizations can provide training or clearer directions so that employees feel able to handle their responsibilities. They can make the work environment safer and more comfortable. Individuals also can act on their own initiative to develop their knowledge and skills.

A variety of techniques help individuals manage stress. Among the most basic strategies are those that help people stay healthy: exercising regularly, getting plenty of rest, and eating a healthful diet. Organizations can support these good habits through wellness programs that, for example, provide access to nutrition counseling and exercise facilities. Relaxation and meditation also help people cope with stress. Organizations can support these stress management techniques by encouraging employees to take regular breaks and vacations. The time off is a valuable investment when it allows employees to approach their tasks with renewed energy and a fresh perspective when they return to work.

Nan K. Chase faced a challenge peculiar to business owners: taking time off for herself. Chase, a consultant and freelance writer, loved her work so much that she was neglecting her family life. She found the solution in her Jewish roots: the Sabbath, a weekly day of rest. She began organizing her time so that she could treat each Sabbath day as a minivacation, refusing even to discuss work with her husband. As a result, not only did Chase rejuvenate her family relationships, but her more focused work efforts allowed her to double her income within a year.[43]

Most people cope with stress more effectively if they lead balanced lives and are part of a network of people who support and encourage them. Family, relationships, friendships, and memberships in nonwork groups such as community or religious organizations are helpful for stress management, as well as for other benefits. Managers in today's hectic, highly competitive work environment may sometimes think of these activities as luxuries. The study of organizational behavior, however, offers a reminder that employees are *human* resources with human needs.

Summary and Management Solution

The principles of organizational behavior describe how people as individuals and groups behave and affect the performance of the organization as a whole. Attitudes are evaluations that predispose people to behave in certain ways. Desirable work-related attitudes include job satisfaction and organizational commitment. Conflicts among attitudes create a state of cognitive dissonance, which people try to alleviate by shifting attitudes or behaviors. Personality, the set of characteristics that underlie a relatively stable pattern of behavior, contributes to shaping attitudes and behaviors. When an individual's

personality and abilities match the requirements of a particular job, the individual and organization enjoy a good person-job fit.

Work-related attitudes and behaviors of particular interest to managers are locus of control, authoritarianism, Machiavellianism, and problem-solving styles. Four problem-solving styles are sensation-thinking, intuitive-thinking, sensation-feeling, and intuitive-feeling. Rakesh Gangwal, described in the opening case, demonstrates the intuitive-thinking style, which is a useful style for top managers who have to deal with many complex problems and make decisions quickly. As he describes his philosophy, "Life for me is about learning, touching, reading minds, understanding dynamics. You can't boil it down to a number." In solving the problem of rude behavior by airline terminal employees, Gangwal knew intuitively that part of the problem was due to a lack of organizational commitment from the part-time workers. After pondering the problem for only a short time, he quickly decreed, "Take the number of full-time workers up to 70 percent." Gangwal believes full-time workers will have greater job satisfaction and organizational commitment and will therefore provide better service to customers. He and Wolf also are combining their thinking and problem-solving styles to tackle the problem of global expansion. One way to enter the European market before actually sending jets to Europe is to team up with another carrier—in this case, American Airlines. Gangwal has immersed himself in learning all the technical details of combining frequent flier miles. To improve profitability, he has launched a low-cost shuttle, signed a pilot's contract that saved the company $88 million, and shut down money-losing routes. In one recent year, earning increased four-fold, to $1 billion.

This chapter also discussed the perception process, which includes perceptual selectivity (screening and selecting the stimuli to pay attention to) and perceptual organization (categorizing the stimuli according to the individual's frame of reference). Individuals often make errors in perceptual judgment, called perceptual distortions. These include stereotyping, the halo effect, projection, and perceptual defense. Attributions are judgments individuals make about whether a person's behavior was caused by internal or external factors.

Learning is a change in behavior or performance that occurs as a result of experience. The learning process goes through a four-stage cycle, and individual learning styles differ. Four learning styles are Diverger, Assimilator, Converger, and Accommodator. Today's rapidly changing business environment requires a commitment to continuous learning by both individuals and organizations. Rapid changes in today's marketplace may create more than the need for ongoing learning, however. It may also create greater stress for many of today's workers. Stress is a person's response to a stimulus that places a demand on that person. Physiologically, the stress response follows a pattern known as the General Adaptation Syndrome. The causes of work stress include task demands, physical demands, role demands, and interpersonal demands. Individuals and organizations can alleviate the negative effects of stress by engaging in a variety of techniques for stress management.

Discussion Questions

1. What are the three basic leadership skills that lie at the core of identifying and solving people problems? Why is it important for managers to develop these skills?

2. In what ways might the cognitive and affective components of attitude influence the behavior of employees who are faced with learning an entirely new set of computer-related skills in order to retain their jobs at a manufacturing facility?

3. What steps might managers at a company that is about to be merged with another company take to promote organizational commitment among employees?

4. Think about an important event in your life. Do you believe that the success or failure of the event was your responsibility (internal locus of control) or the responsibility of outside forces or people (external locus of control)? Has your belief changed since the event took place? How does your locus of control affect the way you now view the event?

5. In the Big Five personality factors, extroversion is considered a "good" quality to have. Why might introversion be an equally positive quality?

6. Review Exhibit 15.5. According to the chart, which type of problem-solving style do you prefer? Describe briefly a decision you have made using this style.

7. Why is it important for managers to achieve person-job fit when they are hiring employees?

8. How might a design manager use a combination of novelty, familiarity, and repetition in the presentation of a new product idea to the company's financial managers?

9. What characteristics of perceivers might influence the attendees of a human resources seminar on employee benefits (such as retirement planning, health care insurance, vacation, and the like)?

10. Describe a situation in which you learned how to do something—use a computer or ride a snowboard. In your description, identify the four stages of the learning cycle.

11. Do you think that a Type A person or a Type B person would be better suited to managing a health care facility? Why?

Management in Practice: Experiential Exercise

High Five: How Many of the "Big Five" Personality Traits Are Yours?

Each individual's collection of personality traits is different; it's what makes us unique. But, although each *collection* of traits varies, we all share many common traits. To find out which are your most prominent traits, mark "yes" or "no" after each of the following statements. Then, for fun, compare your responses with classmates.

1. I love meeting and talking with new people at parties. _____

2. I try not to hold grudges against others. _____

3. I am focused on graduating from college and finding a good job in my field. _____

4. I enjoy performing under pressure—for example, in a big athletic event. _____

5. When I finish school, I want to travel around the world. _____

6. Final exams don't really bother me because I prepare well for them. _____

7. I like to take part in group projects. _____

8. I don't mind giving oral presentations in class. _____

9. Just for fun, I would sign up to take a course in a discipline completely outside my field. _____

10. I work summers in order to fund as much of my own education as I can. _____

Statements 1 and 8 deal with extroversion; statements 2 and 7 deal with agreeableness; statements 3, 6, and 10 deal with conscientiousness; statements 4 and 6 deal with emotional stability; statements 5 and 9 deal with openness to new experiences.

Management in Practice: Ethical Dilemma

Should I Fudge the Numbers?

Sara MacIntosh recently joined MicroPhone, a large telecommunications company with headquarters in Denver, to take over the implementation of a massive customer service training project. The program was created by Kristin Cole, head of human resources and Sara's new boss. According to the grapevine, Kristin was hoping this project alone would give her the "star quality" she needed to earn a promotion she'd been longing for. Industry competition was heating up, and MicroPhone's strategy called for being the very best at customer service. That meant having the most highly trained people in the industry, especially those who would work directly with customers. Kristin had put together a crash team to develop the new training program, which called for an average of one full week of intense customer service training for each of three thousand people and had a price tag in the neighborhood of $40 million. Kristin's team, made up of several staffers who already felt overwhelmed with their day-to-day workload, rushed to put the proposal together. It was scheduled to go to the board of directors next month.

Kristin knew she needed someone well qualified and dedicated to manage and implement the project, and Sara, with eight years of experience, a long list of accomplishments, and advanced degrees in finance and organizational behavior, was perfect for the job. When Sara agreed to come aboard, Kristin expressed great relief and confidence in Sara's ability to make the program work. However, during a thorough review of the proposal, Sara discovered some assumptions built into the formulas of the proposal that raised red flags. She approached Dan Sotal, the team's coordinator, about her concerns, but the more Dan tried to explain how the financial projections were derived, the more Sara realized that Kristin's proposal was seriously flawed. No matter how she tried to work them out, the most that could be squeezed out of the $40 million budget was 20 hours of training a week, not the 40 hours everyone expected for such a high price tag.

Sara knew that, although the proposal had been largely developed before she came on board, it would bear her signature. As she carefully described the problems with the proposal to Kristin and outlined the potentially devastating consequences, Kristin impatiently tapped her pencil on the marble tabletop. Finally, she stood up, leaned forward, and interrupted Sara, quietly saying, "Sara, make the numbers work so that it adds up to forty hours and stays within the $40 million budget." Sara glanced up and replied, "I don't think it can be done unless we either change the number of employees who are to be trained or the cost figure . . . ." Kristin's smile froze on her face and her eyes began to snap as she again interrupted. "I don't think you understand what I'm saying. We have too much at stake here. *Make the previous numbers work.*" Stunned, Sara belatedly began to realize that Kristin was ordering her to fudge the numbers. She felt an anxiety attack coming on as she wondered what she should do.

What Do You Do?

1. Make the previous numbers work. Kristin and the entire team have put massive amounts of time into the project and they all expect you to be a team player. You don't want to let them down. Besides, this is a great opportunity for you in a highly visible position.

2. Stick to your ethical principles and refuse to fudge the numbers. Tell Kristin you will work overtime to help develop an alternate proposal that stays within the budget by providing

more training to employees who work directly with customers and fewer training hours for those who don't have direct customer contact.

3. Go to the team and tell them what you've been asked to do. If they refuse to support you, threaten to reveal the true numbers to the CEO and board members.

SOURCE: Adapted from Doug Wallace, "Fudge the Numbers or Leave," *Business Ethics*, May–June, 1996, 58–59. Adapted with permission.

Surf the Net

1. **Authoritarianism.** The textbook example of authoritarianism is Carlson Companies, one of the largest privately held corporations in the United States, with operations in more than 140 countries and 147,000 people employed under its brands. Go to the corporate Web site at **www.carlson.com** and find information for the following items: (a) Name two of Carlson Companies' brands not mentioned in the chapter. (b) Besides the fact that Curtis Carlson graduated from the University of Minnesota's School of Management, what other connection is there between the two?

2. **Perceptual Organization.** Using the keyword "perception" in your Web browser, locate other interesting perceptual images that could supplement those in Exhibit 15.7 in this chapter. The following sites provide excellent examples. Select your favorite perceptual image; print it out, and bring it to class to contribute during a class discussion on this topic.

valley.uml.edu/landrigan/illusion.html
www.illusionworks.com
www.exploratorium.edu/exhibits (NOTE: Many of the Exploratorium on-line exhibits at this site require plug-ins, such as Shockwave, RealAudio, or QuickTime)

3. **Learning Styles.** Many approaches exist for analyzing personal learning styles. For example, at **www.hcc.hawaii. edu/intranet/committees/FacDevCom/guidebk/ teachtip/lernstyle.htm,** you can access a learning styles instrument that will categorize you as a visual, auditory, or tactile learner. Other sites at which you can get feedback on your learning styles are **www.dc.peachnet.edu/ ~jgutliph/Books/learning styles/the form.html www.fln.vcu.edu/Intensive/chronotope.html mumnt1.mid.muohio.edu/phy/inventory/invent.htm** Choose and take an on-line learning styles instrument, print out the results, and submit a copy of both the instrument and the results to your instructor.

Case for Critical Analysis
Volkswagen's Ferdinand Piëch

While many of today's organizations are shifting toward more democratic, participative types of management, one is not: Volkswagen. In fact, Volkswagen's chief executive, Ferdinand Piëch, rules his realm with an iron hand. After a long executive career at such prestigious automakers as Audi and Porsche (Piëch's maternal grandfather was Ferdinand Porsche), Piëch took over as Volkswagen's CEO in 1993. He immediately centralized power in the organization, firing managers who questioned his ideas or who didn't follow his lead. He dove into engineering projects himself, proposing new projects, tinkering with designs. He presided over meetings with the demeanor of an autocrat, with the occasional result that "critical questions aren't asked, because people know things can rapidly get uncomfortable," notes one former executive.

Piëch had—and still has—a reason for ruling supreme over his company. He isn't satisfied that VW is Europe's leading mass-market auto manufacturer; he wants to turn it into the most powerful, most respected carmaker in the world. He won't settle for less. "We're trying to redefine the status game," explains Jens Neumann, a member of Volkswagen's management board and supporter of Piëch. After creating successes at both Porsche and Audi, such as the Quattro all-wheel drive, Piëch is intent on doing even more at VW. "He is the most brilliant and forward-looking CEO in the business today," claims an analyst for a major VW investor. Indeed, in the first five years at the wheel, Piëch turned around several languishing auto models, increased the company's lead in Europe, and created a comeback in the United States market. His most famous project perhaps is his reintroduction of the beloved VW Beetle. Despite warnings by market experts, Piëch pushed the bug ahead—redesigned so it's a little larger than its predecessor and with all the necessary technological bells and whistles—to a warm welcome from U.S. customers.

Perhaps one reason Piëch is so successful in his method of management is his extensive knowledge of and passion for the cars themselves. From his days as an automotive engineering student at Zurich's Swiss Federal Institute of Technology, through his stint at Porsche, where he helped create world-class race cars, to his development of Audi's Quattro and now the launch of the VW Beetle, Piëch has been found under the hood, tinkering. Thus, he knows his product and his customers and how to fit them together better than anyone else in the industry.

Critics charge that Piëch has too tight a hold over his company. "At VW, nothing happens without Piëch," notes a former colleague. One-person rule can result in massive mistakes. For instance, several years ago, Piëch pushed for the purchase of Rolls-Royce Motors from its parent, Vickers PLC. But in a botched deal, he lost the rights to the Rolls-Royce brand name, which actually belongs to Rolls-Royce PLC, the aerospace manufacturer. Critics also point out that Piëch's fanatical grip on VW has more to do with his personal insecurity than a philosophy of management. "He wants to prove that he has been underestimated for years," muses one former VW executive. But with Piëch in the lead, VW now is reporting over $2 billion a year in earnings, over 100 percent more than before he took the driver's seat.

Questions

1. What personality traits do you think Ferdinand Piëch exhibits? Do you think these contribute to a good person-job fit? Why or why not?

2. Hardly anyone would argue that Piëch is an authoritarian executive. Do you sense that he is Machiavellian as well? Do you think these characteristics have a positive or negative impact on the way Volkswagen is run? Explain your answer.

3. Imagine that you are a manager at Volkswagen, and you are experiencing some cognitive dissonance about being asked to work long hours on one of Piëch's pet projects—a new car model whose success you have doubts about. How might you resolve your dissonance?

SOURCE: David Woodruff and Keith Naughton, "Hard-Driving Boss," *Business Week,* October 5, 1998, 82–87.

Endnotes

1. Lorraine Woellert and David Leonhardt, "Pulling US Airways Out of a Dive," *Business Week,* September 14, 1998, 131–132.

2. S. J. Breckler, "Empirical Validation of Affect, Behavior, and Cognition as Distinct Components of Attitude," *Journal of Personality and Social Psychology,* May 1984, 1191–1205; and J. M. Olson and M. P. Zanna, "Attitudes and Attitude Change," *Annual Review of Psychology* 44 (1993), 117–154.

3. John A. Byrne, "Virtual Management," *Business Week,* September 21, 1998, 80–82.

4. M. T. Iaffaldano and P. M. Muchinsky, "Job Satisfaction and Job Performance: A Meta-Analysis," *Psychological Bulletin,* March 1985, 251–273; C. Ostroff, "The Relationship between Satisfaction, Attitudes, and Performance: An Organizational Level Analysis," *Journal of Applied Psychology,* December 1992, 963–974; and M. M. Petty, G. W. McGee, and J. W. Cavender, "A Meta-Analysis of the Relationship between Individual Job Satisfaction and Individual Performance," *Academy of Management Review,* October 1984, 712–721.

5. William C. Symonds, "Where Paternalism Equals Good Business," *Business Week,* July 20, 1998, 16E4, 16E6.

6. Aaron Bernstein, "We Want You to Stay. Really," *Business Week,* June 22, 1998, 67–68+.

7. John P. Mello, "Good Help Is Hard to Keep," *Inside Technology Training,* November 1998, 20–22, 24.

8. For a discussion of cognitive dissonance theory, see Leon A. Festinger, *Theory of Cognitive Dissonance* (Stanford, California.: Stanford University Press, 1957).

9. See J. M. Digman, "Personality Structure: Emergence of the Five-Factor Model," *Annual Review of Psychology* 41 (1990), 417–440; M. R. Barrick and M. K. Mount, "Autonomy as a Moderator of the Relationships Between the Big Five Personality Dimensions and Job Performance," *Journal of Applied Psychology,* February 1993, 111–118; and J. S. Wiggins and A. L. Pincus, "Personality: Structure and Assessment," *Annual Review of Psychology* 43 (1992), 473–504.

10. Debra Phillips, G. David Doran, Elaine W. Teague, and Laura Tiffany, "Young Millionaires," *Entrepreneur,* November 1998, 118–126.

11. J. B. Rotter, "Generalized Expectancies for Internal versus External Control of Reinforcement," *Psychological Monographs* 80, no. 609 (1966).

12. Julie C. Dalton, "More Room at the Top," *CFO,* August 1998, 30–38.

13. See P. E. Spector, "Behavior in Organizations as a Function of Employee's Locus of Control," *Psychological Bulletin* (May 1982), 482–497.

14. T. W. Adorno, E. Frenkel-Brunswick, D. J. Levinson, and R. N. Sanford, *The Authoritarian Personality* (New York: Harper & Row, 1950).

15. De' Ann Weimer, "'I Want to Lead with Love, Not Fear,'" *Business Week,* August 17, 1998, 52–53.

16. Niccolo Machiavelli, *The Prince,* trans. George Bull (Middlesex: Penguin, 1961).

17. Richard Christie and Florence Geis, *Studies in Machiavellianism* (New York: Academic Press, 1970).

18. R. G. Vleeming, "Machiavellianism: A Preliminary Review," *Psychological Reports,* February 1979, 295–310.

19. Anna Muoio, "Women and Men, Work and Power," *Fast Company,* February/March 1998, 71–72+.

20. Christie and Geis, *Studies in Machiavellianism.*

21. Carl Jung, *Psychological Types* (London: Routledge and Kegan Paul, 1923).

22. Geoffrey Smith, "'The Executioner' Takes Charge," *Business Week,* September 14, 1998, 188.

23. Charles A. O'Reilly III, Jennifer Chatman, and David F. Caldwell, "People and Organizational Culture: A Profile Comparison Approach to Assessing Person-Organization Fit," *Academy of Management Journal* 34(3), 1991, 487–516.

24. Mike Hofman, "The Leader Within," *Inc.,* September 1998, 127.

25. Anna Muoio, "Women and Men, Work and Power," *Fast Company,* February/March 1998, 71–72+.

26. John Grossmann, "We've Got to Start Meeting Like This," *Inc.,* April 1998, 70–72, 74.

27. Stephanie Gruner, "Our Company, Ourselves," *Inc.,* April 1998, 127–128.

28. Muoio, "Women and Men, Work and Power," 82.

29. H. H. Kelley, "Attribution in Social Interaction," in E. Jones et al. (Eds.), *Attribution: Perceiving the Causes of Behavior* (Morristown, N.J.: General Learning Press, 1972).

30. David A. Kolb, "Management and the Learning Process," *California Management Review* 18, no. 3 (spring 1976), 21–31.

31. De' Ann Weimer, "The Houdini of Consumer Electronics," *Business Week,* June 22, 1998, 88, 92.

32. See David. A. Kolb, I. M. Rubin, and J. M. McIntyre, *Organizational Psychology. An Experimental Approach,* 3rd ed. (Englewood Cliffs, N.J.: Prentice-Hall, 1984), 27–54.

33. Steve Hamm, "Bill's Co-Pilot," *Business Week,* September 14, 1998, 76–78+.

34. Chuck Salter, "This Is Brain Surgery," *Fast Company,* February/March 1998, 147–150.

35. T. A. Beehr and R. S. Bhagat, *Human Stress and Cognition in Organizations: An Integrated Perspective* (New York: Wiley, 1985).

36. Hans Selye, *The Stress of Life* (New York: McGraw-Hill, 1976).

37. M. Friedman and R. Rosenman, *Type A Behavior and Your Heart* (New York: Knopf, 1974).

38. Andy Reinhardt, "Mr. House Finds His Fixer-Upper," *Business Week,* February 2, 1998, 66–68.

39. Heath Row, "Is Management for Me? *That* Is the Question," *Fast Company,* February/March 1998, 50, 52.

40. Anne Fisher, "Why Are You So Paranoid?" *Fortune,* September 8, 1997, 171–172.

41. Dave Thomas, "My Biggest Mistake," *Inc.,* September 1998, 129.

42. Robert Kreitner and Angelo Kinicki, *Organizational Behavior,* 4th ed. (Boston, Mass.: Irwin/McGraw-Hill, 1998), 293.

43. Nan K. Chase, "The One-Day Rest Cure," *Inc.,* August 1998, 106.

Chapter 16

LEARNING OBJECTIVES

After studying this chapter, you should be able to

◉ **Define leadership and explain its importance for organizations.**

◉ **Identify personal characteristics associated with effective leaders.**

◉ **Explain the five sources of power and how each causes different subordinate behavior.**

◉ **Describe the leader behaviors of initiating structure and consideration and when they should be used.**

◉ **Describe Hersey and Blanchard's situational theory and its application to subordinate participation.**

◉ **Explain the path-goal model of leadership.**

◉ **Explain how leadership fits the organizational situation and how organizational characteristics can substitute for leadership behaviors.**

◉ **Describe transformational leadership and when it should be used.**

◉ **Explain the role of leaders in learning organizations.**

Leadership in Organizations

MANAGEMENT PROBLEM

When Mary Ann Byrnes took over as CEO of Corsair Communications, she was faced with a group of complacent employees who were accustomed to working what one called a "10-percent-of-the-day kind of job." These government-contract engineers, all men, had spent most of their careers working for defense contractor TRW, which had just jettisoned them and their project. Byrnes needed to find a way to turn this dispassionate group into a team of quick-thinking, fast-moving entrepreneurs. Like big defense contractors everywhere, California-based TRW was forced to find commercial applications for many of its products. One good prospect, developed by the top-secret ESL division, was a technology that could identify the specific source of electronic transmissions. The technology was useful to the military because it could identify such things as which particular Soviet submarine emitted a transmission. It also had significant commercial potential for inhibiting fraudulent cellular-telephone use, since no two cellular phones—like no two military devices—emit the same electronic finger-print. Corsair Communications was created as a spin-off company, owned 20 percent by TRW, 60 percent by venture capitalists, and 20 percent by its employees. When Byrnes was hired, Corsair already had a product (although it was far from perfected), a multimillion dollar con-tract with a cellular carrier, and a group of first-rate engineers. Everything was in place to build the new business—except the glue that would hold it together.[1]

How does a leader inspire employees to give their best to the organization? What leadership style would you recommend Byrnes use to turn complacent workers into a team of entrepreneurial thinkers pulling together to serve the customer?

Mary Ann Byrnes is a leader at one of today's thriving high-tech companies, and her leadership style may differ from another successful leader in a different situation. Contrast the leadership style of Warnaco CEO Linda Wachner with that of Jan Carlzon, president and CEO of Scandinavian Airline Systems Group (SAS). Wachner is known for her tough leadership style and "Do It Now" philosophy, which energizes the entire workforce to achieve her vision of becoming the Coca-Cola of the intimate apparel business. Carlzon, on the other hand, used caring and compassion, listening, and connecting to employees on a personal basis to turn SAS around in an era of brutal competition.[2] Carlzon and Wachner use very different leadership styles, and yet both are highly successful leaders who have helped their organizations thrive. Many styles of leadership can be effective, depending on the leader and the situation. Today, many executives of global companies study the multinational leadership techniques used by Irish pop star Bob Geldof, who mobilized aid for Ethiopia's famine-stricken population in the 1980s. Geldof threaded together diverse international forces to create historical music events, Band Aid and Live Aid. Alternatively stroking, coaxing, and prodding, Geldof successfully coordinated communication technology and delicate star egos into a "collective individualism."[3]

This chapter explores one of the most widely discussed and researched topics in management—leadership. Here we will define leadership, explore the differences between a leader and a manager, and discuss the sources of leader power. We will examine trait, behavioral, and contingency theories of leadership effectiveness. We will also discuss new leadership styles, such as transformational and charismatic approaches. The chapter closes with a discussion of leadership for learning organizations. Chapters 17 through 19 deal with many of the functions of leadership, including employee motivation, communication, and leading groups.

The Nature of Leadership

There is probably no topic more important to business success today than leadership. The concept of leadership continues to evolve as the needs of organizations change. Among all the ideas and writings about leadership, three aspects stand out—people, influence, and goals. Leadership occurs among people, involves the use of influence, and is used to attain goals.[4] *Influence* means that the relationship among people is not passive. Moreover, influence is designed to achieve some end or goal. Thus, **leadership** as defined here is the ability to influence people toward the attainment of goals. This definition captures the idea that leaders are involved with other people in the achievement of goals.

leadership
The ability to influence people toward the attainment of organizational goals.

Leadership is reciprocal, occurring *among* people.[5] Leadership is a "people" activity, distinct from administrative paper shuffling or problem-solving activities. Leadership is dynamic and involves the use of power.

Leadership versus Management

Much has been written in recent years about the difference between management and leadership. Management and leadership are both important to organizations. Because management power comes from organizational structure, it promotes stability, order, and problem solving within the structure. Leadership power, on the other hand, comes from personal sources that are not as invested in the organization, such as personal interests, goals, and values. Leadership power promotes vision, creativity, and change in the organization. Exhibit 16.1 illustrates the different qualities attributed to leaders and managers, although it is important to remember that some people can exhibit a combination of leader/manager qualities.

One of the major differences between the leader and the manager relates to their source of power and the level of compliance it engenders within followers. **Power** is the potential ability to influence the behavior of others.[6] Power represents the resources with which a leader effects changes in employee behavior. Within organizations, there are typically five sources of power: legitimate, reward, coercive, expert, and referent.[7] Sometimes power comes from a person's position in the organization, while other sources of power are based on personal characteristics.

power
The potential ability to influence others' behavior.

Position Power

The traditional manager's power comes from the organization. The manager's position gives him or her the power to reward or punish subordinates in order to influence their behavior. Legitimate power, reward power, and coercive power are all forms of position power used by managers to change employee behavior.

Legitimate Power.   Power coming from a formal management position in an organization and the authority granted to it is called **legitimate power.** For example, once a person has been selected as a supervisor, most workers understand that they are obligated to follow his or her direction with respect to work activities. Subordinates accept this source of power as legitimate, which is why they comply.

legitimate power
Power that stems from a formal management position in an organization and the authority granted to it.

LEADER

SOUL
Visionary
Passionate
Creative
Flexible
Inspiring
Innovative
Courageous
Imaginative
Experimental
Initiates change
Personal power

MANAGER

MIND
Rational
Consulting
Persistent
Problem solving
Tough-minded
Analytical
Structured
Deliberate
Authoritative
Stabilizing
Position power

E x h i b i t **16.1**
Leader versus Manager Qualities

SOURCE: Genevieve Capowski, "Anatomy of a Leader: Where Are the Leaders of Tomorrow?" *Management Review,* March 1994, 12.

reward power
Power that results from the authority to reward others.

coercive power
Power that stems from the authority to punish or recommend punishment.

Reward Power. Another kind of power, **reward power,** stems from the authority to bestow rewards on other people. Managers may have access to formal rewards, such as pay increases or promotions. They also have at their disposal such rewards as praise, attention, and recognition. Managers can use rewards to influence subordinates' behavior.

Coercive Power. The opposite of reward power is **coercive power:** It refers to the authority to punish or recommend punishment. Managers have coercive power when they have the right to fire or demote employees, criticize, or withdraw pay increases. For example, if Paul, a salesman, does not perform as expected, his supervisor has the coercive power to criticize him, reprimand him, put a negative letter in his file, and hurt his chance for a raise.

Different types of position power elicit different responses in followers.[8] Legitimate power and reward power are most likely to generate follower compliance. *Compliance* means that workers will obey orders and carry out instructions, although they may personally disagree with them and may not be enthusiastic. Coercive power most often generates resistance. *Resistance* means that workers will deliberately try to avoid carrying out instructions or will attempt to disobey orders.

Thomas C. Graham, chairman of AK Steel, is a believer in position power. Unimpressed with new ideas about empowering workers, he prefers a military-style management, where cost cutting is rewarded and mistakes are quickly disciplined. His blunt views suggest that management in the steel industry has failed to push people and equipment hard enough. Graham's tough hierarchical approach has resulted in turnarounds for mills at LTV, U.S. Steel, and Washington Steel, but has also caused him to be ousted or passed over for promotion in the midst of his successes.[9]

Personal Power

In contrast to the external sources of position power, personal power most often comes from internal sources, such as a person's special knowledge or personality characteristics. Personal power is the tool of the leader. Subordi-

Jill E. Barad, the chairman and chief executive of the toy company, Mattel, Inc., is one of the most powerful, highest-paid women in corporate America. Her power sources include legitimate power *stemming from her formal management position at Mattel, and* expert power *because she is known to be a fierce competitor with an eye for trends and a keen sense of style, packaging, and consumer tastes.*

nates follow a leader because of the respect, admiration, or caring they feel for the individual and his or her ideas. Personal power is becoming increasingly important as more businesses are run by teams of workers who are less tolerant of authoritarian management.[10] Two types of personal power are expert power and referent power.

Expert Power. Power resulting from a leader's special knowledge or skill regarding the tasks performed by followers is referred to as **expert power.** When the leader is a true expert, subordinates go along with recommendations because of his or her superior knowledge. Leaders at supervisory levels often have experience in the production process that gains them promotion. At top management levels, however, leaders may lack expert power because subordinates know more about technical details than they do.

Referent Power. The last kind of power, **referent power,** comes from leader personality characteristics that command subordinates' identification, respect, and admiration so they wish to emulate the leader. When workers admire a supervisor because of the way she deals with them, the influence is based on referent power. Referent power depends on the leader's personal characteristics rather than on a formal title or position and is most visible in the area of charismatic leadership, which will be discussed later in this chapter.

The follower reaction most often generated by expert power and referent power is commitment.[11] *Commitment* means that workers will share the leader's point of view and enthusiastically carry out instructions. Needless to say, commitment is preferred to compliance or resistance. It is particularly important when change is the desired outcome of a leader's instructions, because change carries risk or uncertainty. Commitment assists the follower in overcoming fear of change.

An example of expert power is Rachel Hubka, owner of Rachel's Bus Company (formerly Stewart Bus Company) in Chicago. When Rachel joined Stewart Bus Company as a dispatcher, she wanted to learn every job in the business. She mastered the complex routing systems, hired and trained drivers, developed and implemented a safety program, scrubbed floors, and did numerous other tasks. After she bought the company, employees respected Rachel's leadership because of her intimate knowledge of the company's operations. Rachel also demonstrates referent power. She often hires people with marginal employment histories, gives them extensive training, and treats them like professionals. She is known as a great listener who is able to engage others in meaningful conversation. Rachel takes pride when employees leave her company to start their own businesses.[12]

Empowerment

A significant recent trend in corporate America is for top executives to *empower* lower employees. Fully 74 percent of executives in a survey claimed that they are more participatory, more concerned with consensus building, and more reliant on communication than on command compared with the past. Executives no longer hoard power.

Empowering employees works because total power in the organization seems to increase. Everyone has more say and hence contributes more to organizational goals. The goal of senior executives in many corporations today is not simply to wield power but also to give it away to people who can get jobs done.[13] For example, when Robin Landew Silverman and her

expert power
Power that stems from special knowledge of or skill in the tasks performed by subordinates.

referent power
Power that results from characteristics that command subordinates' identification with, respect and admiration for, and desire to emulate the leader.

husband made the decision to move their clothing store from downtown Grand Forks, North Dakota, to a suburban location, they knew they would need the full commitment of their staff. The Silvermans had been accustomed to calling the shots, but a new approach was needed to successfully accomplish the difficult transition. By giving up control of the operation, the Silvermans gave their employees opportunities to apply themselves in new ways. "Skills emerged that we didn't know people had," says Robin. For example, a timid secretary became a dynamic bid researcher, and a marketing manager showed a talent for interior design.[14]

Leadership Traits

traits
Distinguishing personal characteristics, such as intelligence, values, and appearance.

Early efforts to understand leadership success focused on the leader's personal characteristics or traits. **Traits** are the distinguishing personal characteristics of a leader, such as intelligence, values, and appearance. The early research focused on leaders who had achieved a level of greatness and hence was referred to as the *great man* approach. The idea was relatively simple: Find out what made these people great, and select future leaders who already exhibited the same traits or could be trained to develop them. Generally, research found only a weak relationship between personal traits and leader success.[15] For example, football coaches Steve Spurrier at Florida and Joe Paterno at Penn State have different personality traits, but both are successful leaders of their football programs.

In addition to personality traits, physical, social, and work-related characteristics of leaders have been studied. Exhibit 16.2 summarizes the physical, social, and personal leadership characteristics that have received the greatest research support.[16] However, these characteristics do not stand alone. The appropriateness of a trait or set of traits depends on the leadership situation. The same traits do not apply to every organization or situation.

John Reed, chairman of Citicorp, and Sanford E. Weill, chairman of Travellers Group Inc., are involved in an $83 billion merger and plan to run the new firm as coleaders. Both have been successful leaders of their organizations, but they exhibit very different traits. Weill is a highly ambitious, "let's-get-it-done" kind of manager. He acts instinctively, sometimes even impulsively, and keeps a neon sign in his office that blinks "The Chairman is Not Happy." Reed, on the other hand, is quiet, reserved, and clinical. He likes to

Exhibit **16.2**   *Personal Characteristics of Leaders*

Physical characteristics Activity Energy **Social background** Mobility **Intelligence and ability** Judgment, decisiveness Knowledge Fluency of speech	**Personality** Alertness Originality, creativity Personal integrity, ethical conduct Self-confidence **Work-related characteristics** Achievement drive, desire to excel Drive for responsibility Responsibility in pursuit of goals Task orientation	**Social characteristics** Ability to enlist cooperation Cooperativeness Popularity, prestige Sociability, interpersonal skills Social participation Tact, diplomacy

SOURCE: Adapted from Bernard M. Bass, *Stogdill's Handbook of Leadership,* rev. ed. (New York: Free Press, 1981), 75–76. This adaptation appeared in R. Albanese and D. D. Van Fleet, *Organizational Behavior: A Managerial Viewpoint* (Hinsdale, Ill.: The Dryden Press, 1983).

think things out, gather all the facts, and consider all the angles of a decision. The two will try to merge their varied personal traits to provide the best leadership for the new company, Citigroup, Inc.[17]

Further studies have expanded the understanding of leadership beyond the personal traits of the individual to focus on the dynamics of the relationship between leaders and followers.

Autocratic versus Democratic Leaders

One way to approach leader characteristics is to examine autocratic and democratic leaders. An **autocratic leader** is one who tends to centralize authority and rely on legitimate, reward, and coercive power. A **democratic leader** delegates authority to others, encourages participation, and relies on expert and referent power to influence subordinates.

The first studies on these leadership characteristics were conducted at Iowa State University by Kurt Lewin and his associates.[18] These studies compared autocratic and democratic leaders and produced some interesting findings. The groups with autocratic leaders performed highly so long as the leader was present to supervise them. However, group members were displeased with the close, autocratic style of leadership, and feelings of hostility frequently arose. The performance of groups who were assigned democratic leaders was almost as good, and these were characterized by positive feelings rather than hostility. In addition, under the democratic style of leadership, group members performed well even when the leader was absent and left the group on its own.[19] The participative techniques and majority rule decision making used by the democratic leader trained and involved group members such that they performed well with or without the leader present. These characteristics of democratic leadership explain why the empowerment of lower employees is a popular trend in companies today.

This early work suggested that leaders were either autocratic or democratic in their approach. However, further work by Tannenbaum and Schmidt indicated that leadership could be a continuum reflecting different amounts of employee participation.[20] Thus, one leader might be autocratic (boss centered), another democratic (subordinate centered), and a third a mix of the two styles. The leadership continuum is illustrated in Exhibit 16.3.

Leaders may adjust their styles depending on the situation. Recall the Vroom-Jago model from Chapter 8, which assists the leader in determining the appropriate participation level of subordinates in the decision-making process. Tannenbaum and Schmidt also suggested that the extent to which leadership is boss centered or subordinate centered depends on organizational circumstances. For example, if there is time pressure on a leader or if it takes too long for subordinates to learn how to make decisions, the leader will tend to use an autocratic style. When subordinates are able to learn decision-making skills readily, a participative style can be used. Another situational factor is the skill difference between subordinates and the leader. The greater the skill difference, the more autocratic the leader approach, because it is difficult to bring subordinates up to the leader's expertise level.[21]

For example, John B. McCoy built Banc One into the nation's seventh largest bank using a democratic leadership style. He let the chairmen of local banks run their own show and prided himself on having a friendly, informal relationship with employees throughout the company. However, when Banc One's profits and stock price took a sharp dive in late 1994, McCoy shifted

autocratic leader
A leader who tends to centralize authority and rely on legitimate, reward, and coercive power to manage subordinates.

democratic leader
A leader who delegates authority to others, encourages participation, and relies on expert and referent power to manage subordinates.

No longer leading a basketball team, Magic Johnson is now an entrepreneurial business leader. In 1995, Johnson, in partnership with Sony Retail Entertainment, opened the very successful Magic Johnson Theatres. The Baldwin Hills/Crenshaw, California theater complex is one of the highest-grossing theaters in the nation. Johnson describes his winning business leadership style as autocratic and centralized, "I've got a team of people who work for me and advise me. But I call my own shots. . .The team I built taught me how to get into business, how to run a business. They gave me the knowledge I needed to have. But now I'm on my own. . .Everybody knows they have to deal with me."

Exhibit *16.3* *Leadership Continuum*

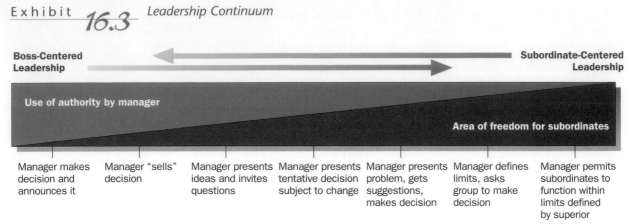

SOURCE: Reprinted by permission of *Harvard Business Review*. An exhibit from Robert Tannenbaum and Warren Schmidt, "How to Choose a Leadership Pattern" (May–June 1973). Copyright © 1973 by the president and Fellows of Harvard College, all rights reserved.

to an autocratic style to try to get things back on track. He began issuing directives from headquarters, stripped local bank chiefs of much of their power, and toned down his gung-ho informality and bantering with employees. McCoy believes the organization's current situation demands a more autocratic style of leadership. Dorothy Roberts, CEO of Echo Scarves, uses a participative style of leadership to keep her company competitive in the tough fashion industry. She shows employees respect and courtesy, shares decision making, and creates an environment of openness and trust. Roberts's leadership creates satisfied employees who, in turn, create satisfied customers, which may be more difficult with an autocratic style.[22] The Technology box describes how a school superintendent used participative leadership to launch a technological and educational revolution.

Behavioral Approaches

The autocratic and democratic styles suggest that it is the "behavior" of the leader rather than a personality trait that determines leadership effectiveness. Perhaps any leader can adopt the correct behavior with appropriate training. The focus of recent research has shifted from leader personality traits toward the behaviors successful leaders display. Important research programs on leadership behavior were conducted at Ohio State University, the University of Michigan, and the University of Texas.

Ohio State Studies

consideration
A type of leader behavior that describes the extent to which a leader is sensitive to subordinates, respects their ideas and feelings, and establishes mutual trust.

initiating structure
A type of leader behavior that describes the extent to which a leader is task oriented and directs subordinates' work activities toward goal achievement.

Researchers at Ohio State University surveyed leaders to study hundreds of dimensions of leader behavior.[23] They identified two major behaviors, called *consideration* and *initiating structure*.

Consideration is the extent to which the leader is mindful of subordinates, respects their ideas and feelings, and establishes mutual trust. Considerate leaders are friendly, provide open communication, develop teamwork, and are oriented toward their subordinates' welfare.

Initiating structure is the extent to which the leader is task oriented and directs subordinate work activities toward goal attainment. Leaders with this

Hunterdon High School

According to Ray Farley, "Once you put people in charge of their own destiny and say, 'Here's where you need to go if you want to be ready for the future,' the rest just happens." Farley has turned some of the traditional power of a school superintendent over to teams of students, teachers, and parents. Now, they decide what gets taught, who gets hired, and what the school calendar looks like.

One of the most important outcomes of this participative leadership has been a technological revolution at Hunterdon High School. The school's team found a way to equip the school with PCs, video facilities, ISDN lines, fiber-optic cables—the works—for $40,000 per classroom. Hunterdon also has a student-run FM radio station, a television studio, a telephone in every classroom, and a state-of-the-art instructional media center. Each classroom is linked to the school library, to the Internet, and to a host of other databases. The technology has led to a sort of virtual busing that links suburban, mostly white Hunterdon to four inner-city, mostly black New Jersey schools. Students at Hunterdon collaborate, for example, with their counterparts at Asbury Park to produce a poetry magazine in real time. With just a mouse-click, a teacher can drop in and participate in the teamwork going on. Now, Asbury Park is increasing its technological edge as well. According to Dan Murphy, Asbury Park's principal, "One year ago we had two computers hooked up to the Internet. Right now, technicians are setting up 200 computers, providing them all with access. . . . And all of this is just the tip of the iceberg. It's unbelievable."

"Kids today live in a nanosecond world," Farley says. "You have to make available all the technology you can get your hands on. And then you have to do one more thing—you have to trust them."

www.hcrhs.hunterdon.k12.nj.us

SOURCE: Nicholas Morgan, "Fast Times at Hunterdon High," *Fast Company*, February/March 1998, 42, 44.

style typically give instructions, spend time planning, emphasize deadlines, and provide explicit schedules of work activities.

Consideration and initiating structure are independent of each other, which means that a leader with a high degree of consideration may be either high or low on initiating structure. A leader may have any of four styles: high initiating structure–low consideration, high initiating structure–high consideration, low initiating structure–low consideration, or low initiating structure–high consideration. The Ohio State research found that the high consideration–high initiating structure style achieved better performance and greater satisfaction than the other leader styles. However, new research has found that effective leaders may be high on consideration and low on initiating structure or low on consideration and high on initiating structure, depending on the situation. Thus, the "high-high" style is not always the best.[24]

Michigan Studies

Studies at the University of Michigan at about the same time took a different approach by comparing the behavior of effective and ineffective supervisors.[25] The most effective supervisors were those who focused on the subordinates' human needs in order to "build effective work groups with high performance goals." The Michigan researchers used the term *employee-centered leaders* for leaders who established high performance goals and displayed supportive behavior toward subordinates. The less effective leaders were called *job-centered leaders*; these tended to be less concerned with goal achievement and human needs in favor of meeting schedules, keeping costs low, and achieving production efficiency.

Exhibit
16.4

The Leadership Grid® Figure

SOURCE: The Leadership Grid® Figure from Robert R. Blake and Anne Adams McCanse, *Leadership Dilemmas—Grid Solutions* (Houston: Gulf, 1991), 29. Copyright © 1991, by Scientific Methods, Inc. Reproduced by permission of the owners.

High

9   **1,9**
    Country Club Management
    Thoughtful attention to the
    needs of people for satisfying
8   relationships leads to a
    comfortable, friendly organization
    atmosphere and work tempo.
7

                                        9,9
                                        Team Management
                                        Work accomplishment is
                                        from committed people;
                                        interdependence through
                                        a "common stake" in
                                        organization purpose
                                        leads to relationships of
                                        trust and respect.

6

5   **5,5**
                            Middle-of-the-Road Management
                            Adequate organization performance is
4   possible through balancing the necessity
                            to get out work with maintaining morale of
                            people at a satisfactory level.

3   **Authority-Compliance**
    Impoverished Management   Efficiency in operations
    Exertion of minimum effort   results from arranging
2   to get required work done   conditions of work in
    is appropriate to sustain   such a way that human
    organization membership.   elements interfere to a
1   **1,1**   minimum degree.   **9,1**

Low

    1   2   3   4   5   6   7   8   9

Low   **Concern for Production**   **High**

Concern for People (vertical axis)

The Leadership Grid

leadership grid
A two-dimensional leadership theory that
measures a leader's concern for people and
concern for production.

Blake and Mouton of the University of Texas proposed a two-dimensional leadership theory called **leadership grid** that builds on the work of the Ohio State and Michigan studies.[26] The two-dimensional model and five of its seven major management styles are depicted in Exhibit 16.4. Each axis on the grid is a 9-point scale, with 1 meaning low concern and 9 high concern.

Team management (9,9) often is considered the most effective style and is recommended for managers because organization members work together to accomplish tasks. *Country club management* (1,9) occurs when primary emphasis is given to people rather than to work outputs. *Authority-compliance management* (9,1) occurs when efficiency in operations is the dominant orientation. *Middle-of-the-road management* (5,5) reflects a moderate amount of concern for both people and production. *Impoverished management* (1,1) means the absence of a management philosophy; managers exert little effort toward interpersonal relationships or work accomplishment. Consider these examples.

PC CONNECTION AND TENNECO

www.pcconnection.com
www.tenneco.com

"Employees are customers, too," says PC Connection CEO Patricia Gallup, "so we have to exceed their expectations." Gallup uses a friendly, open, and accessible style of leadership. Even with more than 800 employees, she knows most of them by name and communicates directly with many of them on a daily basis. Anyone who wants to talk about a problem can simply walk into her office. PC Connection offers full health benefits, even for part-timers. The company also offers 26 weeks of pregnancy leave and pays for child care when employees have to attend industry conferences. Any worker can take a one-month leave for any reason. Gallup has also come up with some offbeat perks, such as free turkeys for Thanksgiving, ski jaunts, casino nights, and hiking trips. She has been known to send employees who come through in a crunch on all-expenses-paid vacations to the Bahamas. Gallup thinks meeting employee needs is an important part of running a successful business. At PC Connection, it's clear her style is working.

Compare the style of Gallup to that of former West Point professor Dana G. Mead, CEO of Tenneco. His motto, adapted from General George Patton, is "Plan deliberately; execute violently." Mead's hard-driving management style includes setting virtually unattainable targets for division presidents on everything from return on capital investments to workplace safety. He requires each of the five division managers to give monthly presentations about their performance relative to the targets in an open forum. Before they prevailed upon him to remove it, Mead had a noose hanging in his office. "The first division president that walks in here and hasn't made his numbers is going to try it on for size," he used to say. Mead's style builds enormous pressure on the division managers, but he says it works—division presidents generally meet the highly ambitious goals.[27]

The leadership style of Gallup is characterized by high people concern and moderate concern for production. Dana Mead, in contrast, is high on concern for costs and production and low on concern for people. Both styles are successful because of the different situations. The next group of theories builds on the leader-follower relationship of behavioral approaches to explore how organizational situations affect the leader's approach.

Contingency Approaches

Several models of leadership that explain the relationship between leadership styles and specific situations have been developed. These are termed **contingency approaches** and include the leadership model developed by Fiedler and his associates, the situational theory of Hersey and Blanchard, the path-goal theory presented by Evans and House, and the substitutes-for-leadership concept.

contingency approach
A model of leadership that describes the relationship between leadership styles and specific organizational situations.

Fiedler's Contingency Theory

An early, extensive effort to combine leadership style and organizational situation into a comprehensive theory of leadership was made by Fiedler and his associates.[28] The basic idea is simple: Match the leader's style with the situation most favorable for his or her success. By diagnosing leadership style and the organizational situation, the correct fit can be arranged.

Leadership Style. The cornerstone of Fiedler's contingency theory is the extent to which the leader's style is relationship oriented or task oriented. A *relationship-oriented leader* is concerned with people, as in the consideration style described earlier. A *task-oriented leader* is primarily motivated by task accomplishment, which is similar to the initiating structure style described earlier.

Leadership style was measured with a questionnaire known as the least preferred coworker (LPC) scale. The **LPC scale** has a set of 16 bipolar adjectives

LPC scale
A questionnaire designed to measure relationship-oriented versus task-oriented leadership style according to the leader's choice of adjectives for describing the "least preferred coworker."

along an 8-point scale. Examples of the bipolar adjectives used by Fiedler on the LPC scale follow:

open	—	—	—	—	—	—	—	—	guarded
quarrelsome	—	—	—	—	—	—	—	—	harmonious
efficient	—	—	—	—	—	—	—	—	inefficient
self-assured	—	—	—	—	—	—	—	—	hesitant
gloomy	—	—	—	—	—	—	—	—	cheerful

If the leader describes the least preferred coworker using positive concepts, he or she is considered relationship oriented, that is, a leader who cares about and is sensitive to other people's feelings. Conversely, if a leader uses negative concepts to describe the least preferred coworker, he or she is considered task oriented that is, a leader who sees other people in negative terms and places greater value on task activities than on people.

Situation. Leadership situations can be analyzed in terms of three elements: the quality of leader-member relationships, task structure, and position power.[29] Each of these elements can be described as either favorable or unfavorable for the leader.

1. *Leader-member relations* refers to group atmosphere and members' attitude toward and acceptance of the leader. When subordinates trust, respect, and have confidence in the leader, leader-member relations are considered good. When subordinates distrust, do not respect, and have little confidence in the leader, leader-member relations are poor.

2. *Task structure* refers to the extent to which tasks performed by the group are defined, involve specific procedures, and have clear, explicit goals. Routine, well-defined tasks, such as those of assembly-line workers, have a high degree of structure. Creative, ill-defined tasks, such as research and development or strategic planning, have a low degree of task structure. When task structure is high, the situation is considered favorable to the leader; when low, the situation is less favorable.

3. *Position power* is the extent to which the leader has formal authority over subordinates. Position power is high when the leader has the power to plan and direct the work of subordinates, evaluate it, and reward or punish them. Position power is low when the leader has little authority over subordinates and cannot evaluate their work or reward them. When position power is high, the situation is considered favorable for the leader; when low, the situation is unfavorable.

Combining the three situational characteristics yields a list of eight leadership situations, which are illustrated in Exhibit 16.5. Situation I is most favorable to the leader because leader-member relations are good, task structure is high, and leader position power is strong. Situation VIII is most unfavorable to the leader because leader-member relations are poor, task structure is low, and leader position power is weak. All other octants represent intermediate degrees of favorableness for the leader.

Contingency Theory. When Fiedler examined the relationships among leadership style, situational favorability, and group task performance, he found the pattern shown in Exhibit 16.6. Task-oriented leaders are more

Minoru Nakamura, president of the $16 billion Nissan North America, Inc., demonstrated high initiating structure–low consideration when he pushed aside five top executives and stepped in as head of Nissan's U.S. sales. Nakamura disbanded the sales department and folded it into Nissan North America. Using centralized authority, he stopped a $200 million brand advertising campaign, dropped two sporty cars from the Nissan line, trimmed customer and dealer cash incentives, and closed the Smyrna, Tennessee Nissan factory on Fridays. Nakamura is using his leadership power in an attempt to overcome a $787 million sales loss by focusing on quality and long-term profits instead of U.S. sales volume.

Exhibit *16.5* *Fiedler's Classification of Situation Favorableness*

	Very Favorable		Intermediate				Very Unfavorable	
Leader-Member Relations	Good	Good	Good	Good	Poor	Poor	Poor	Poor
Task Structure	High		Low		High		Low	
Leader Position Power	Strong	Weak	Strong	Weak	Strong	Weak	Strong	Weak
Situations	I	II	III	IV	V	VI	VII	VIII

SOURCE: Fred E. Fiedler, "The Effects of Leadership Training and Experience: A Contingency Model Interpretation," *Administrative Science Quarterly* 17 (1972), 455. Reprinted by permission of *Administrative Science Quarterly*.

effective when the situation is either highly favorable or highly unfavorable. Relationship-oriented leaders are more effective in situations of moderate favorability.

The task-oriented leader excels in the favorable situation because everyone gets along, the task is clear, and the leader has power; all that is needed is for someone to take charge and provide direction. Similarly, if the situation is highly unfavorable to the leader, a great deal of structure and task direction is needed. A strong leader defines task structure and can establish authority over subordinates. Because leader-member relations are poor anyway, a strong task orientation will make no difference in the leader's popularity.

The relationship-oriented leader performs better in situations of intermediate favorability because human relations skills are important in achieving high group performance. In these situations, the leader may be moderately well liked, have some power, and supervise jobs that contain some ambiguity. A leader with good interpersonal skills can create a positive group atmosphere that will improve relationships, clarify task structure, and establish position power.

Exhibit *16.6* *How Leader Style Fits the Situation*

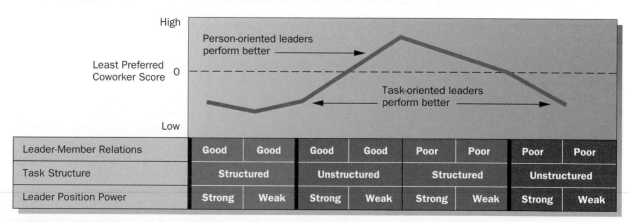

Leader-Member Relations	Good	Good	Good	Good	Poor	Poor	Poor	Poor
Task Structure	Structured		Unstructured		Structured		Unstructured	
Leader Position Power	Strong	Weak	Strong	Weak	Strong	Weak	Strong	Weak

SOURCE: Fred E. Fiedler, "The Effects of Leadership Training and Experience: A Contingency Model Interpretation," *Administrative Science Quarterly* 17 (1972), 455. Reprinted by permission of *Administrative Science Quarterly*.

A leader, then, needs to know two things in order to use Fiedler's contingency theory. First, the leader should know whether he or she has a relationship- or task-oriented style. Second, the leader should diagnose the situation and determine whether leader-member relations, task structure, and position power are favorable or unfavorable.

Fitting leader style to the situation can yield big dividends in profits and efficiency.[30] On the other hand, using an incorrect style for the situation can cause problems, as Alan Robbins discovered at Plastic Lumber Company.

PLASTIC LUMBER COMPANY
www.plasticlumber.com

Alan Robbins intentionally put his factory in a gritty downtown neighborhood in Akron, Ohio. He considers himself an enlightened employer who wants to give people—even those who have made serious missteps—a chance to prove themselves. Plastic Lumber Company, which converts old plastic milk and soda bottles into fake lumber, employs about 50 workers.

When he started the company, Robbins wanted to be both a boss and a friend to his workers. He would sometimes serve cold beers for everyone at the end of a shift or grant personal loans to employees in a financial bind. He stressed teamwork and spent lots of time running ideas by workers on the factory floor. He resisted the idea of drug testing, partly because of the expense and partly because it showed distrust. Besides, he couldn't imagine workers would show up drunk or on drugs when they knew they'd be operating dangerous machinery.

He was wrong. Robbins's relationship-oriented style didn't work in the situation in which he was operating. The low-skilled workers, many from low-income, drug-infested neighborhoods, weren't ready for the type of freedom Robbins granted them. Workers were frequently absent or late without calling, showed up under the influence, and started fights on the factory floor. The turning point came for Robbins when one worker was roaming the factory with an iron pipe in his hand, looking for a fight. Today, Robbins has given up his ideals of being a pal. "I'm too busy just trying to make sure they show up," he says.[31]

Robbins's leadership at Plastic Lumber was unsuccessful because he used a relationship-oriented style in an unfavorable situation. Because of their life circumstances, many of the employees he hired were naturally distrustful, thus leader-member relations were poor. Although Robbins had high formal power, many workers had poor work ethics and little respect for authority. In their view, Robbins's failure to provide rules, guidelines, and direction weakened his authority. In the early days, workers believed they could get away with anything because of Robbins's easygoing style. Today, Robbins is developing a more task-oriented style, including putting together a comprehensive rules and policy manual and requiring drug tests of all new workers.

An important contribution of Fiedler's research is that it goes beyond the notion of leadership styles to show how styles fit the situation to improve organizational effectiveness. On the other hand, the model has also been criticized.[32] Using the LPC score as a measure of relationship- or task-oriented behavior seems simplistic, and how the model works over time is unclear. For example, if a task-oriented leader is matched with an unfavorable situation and is successful, the organizational situation is likely to improve and become more favorable to the leader. Thus, the leader might have to adjust his or her style or go to a new situation. For example, at Plastic Lumber Company, Alan Robbins is trying to shift to a task-oriented style, even though his natural inclination is to be a relationship-oriented leader.

Hersey and Blanchard's Situational Theory

The **situational theory** of leadership is an interesting extension of the behavioral theories described earlier and summarized in the leadership grid (Exhibit 16.4). More than previous theories, Hersey and Blanchard's approach focuses a great deal of attention on the characteristics of employees in determining appropriate leadership behavior. The point of Hersey and Blanchard is that subordinates vary in readiness level. People low in task readiness, because of little ability or training, or insecurity, need a different leadership style than those who are high in readiness and have good ability, skills, confidence, and willingness to work.[33]

The relationships between leader style and follower readiness are summarized in Exhibit 16.7. The upper part of the exhibit indicates style of leader, which is based on a combination of relationship behavior and task behavior. The bell-shaped curve is called a prescriptive curve, because it indicates when each leader style should be used. The four styles—telling (S1), selling (S2), participating (S3), and delegating (S4)—depend on the readiness of followers, indicated in the lower part of Exhibit 16.7. R1 is low readiness and R4 represents high readiness. The telling style is for low-readiness subordinates, because people are unable and unwilling to take responsibility for their own task behavior. The selling and participating styles work for followers with moderate readiness, and delegating is appropriate for employees with high readiness.

situational theory
A contingency approach to leadership that links the leader's behavioral style with the task readiness of subordinates.

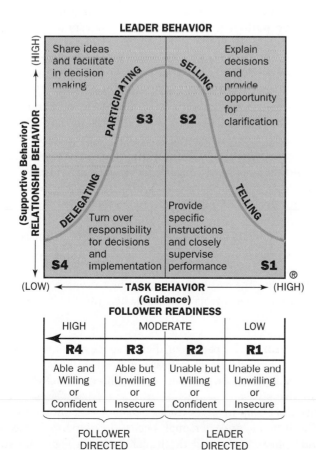

E x h i b i t *16.7*

The Situational Theory of Leadership

SOURCE: Paul Hersey, *Situational Selling* (Escondido, CA, Center for Leadership Studies, Inc., 1985) Copyrighted material. Used by permission. All rights reserved.

This contingency model is easier to understand than Fiedler's model, but it incorporates only the characteristics of followers, not those of the situation. The leader should evaluate subordinates and adopt whichever style is needed. If one or more followers are at low levels of readiness, the leader must be very specific, telling them exactly what to do, how to do it, and when. For followers high in readiness, the leader provides a general goal and sufficient authority to do the task as the followers see fit. Leaders must carefully diagnose the readiness level of followers and then tell, sell, participate, or delegate.

Phil Hagans is a leader who understands how follower readiness determines leadership style. As the owner of two McDonald's franchises in northeast Houston, Hagans gives many of his young employees their first job as well as an introduction to the culture of work as he received it, moving up through the ranks. Starting with instruction on every detail of the job from how to dress to how to clean the grill, he coaches them through their first days. As they grow in ability and confidence, he uses a more participatory style but continues to mentor them with financial planning and educational assistance. Because many of his employees have never held a job before, Hagans knows to guide them through each level of readiness.[34] A leader would need to use a different style with a part-time worker who was retired after 40 years in the business world.

Path-Goal Theory

path-goal theory
A contingency approach to leadership specifying that the leader's responsibility is to increase subordinates' motivation by clarifying the behaviors necessary for task accomplishment and rewards.

Another contingency approach to leadership is called the path-goal theory.[35] According to the **path-goal theory**, the leader's responsibility is to increase subordinates' motivation to attain personal and organizational goals. As illustrated in Exhibit 16.8, the leader increases their motivation by either (1) clarifying the subordinates' path to the rewards that are available or (2) increasing the rewards that the subordinates value and desire. Path clarification means that the leader works with subordinates to help them identify and learn the behaviors that will lead to successful task accomplishment and organizational rewards. Increasing rewards means that the leader talks with subordinates to learn which rewards are important to them—that is, whether they desire intrinsic rewards from the work itself or extrinsic rewards such as raises or promotions. The leader's job is to increase personal payoffs to subordinates for goal attainment and to make the paths to these payoffs clear and easy to travel.[36]

This model is called a contingency theory because it consists of three sets of contingencies—leader behavior and style, situational contingencies, and the use of rewards to meet subordinates' needs.[37] Whereas in the Fiedler theory described earlier the assumption would be to switch leaders as situations change, in the path-goal theory leaders switch their behaviors to match the situation.

Leader Behavior.   The path-goal theory suggests a fourfold classification of leader behaviors.[38] These classifications are the types of leader behavior the leader can adopt and include supportive, directive, achievement-oriented, and participative styles.

Supportive leadership involves leader behavior that shows concern for subordinates' well-being and personal needs. Leadership behavior is open, friendly, and approachable, and the leader creates a team climate and treats

Exhibit
16.8 *Leader Roles in the Path-Goal Model*

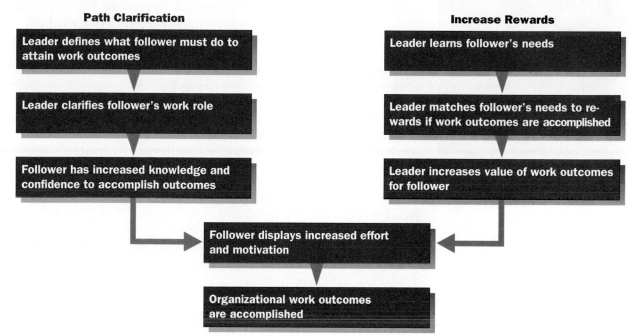

SOURCE: Based on Bernard M. Bass, "Leadership: Good, Better, Best," *Organizational Dynamics* 13 (Winter 1985), 26–40.

subordinates as equals. Supportive leadership is similar to the consideration leadership described earlier.

Directive leadership occurs when the leader tells subordinates exactly what they are supposed to do. Leader behavior includes planning, making schedules, setting performance goals and behavior standards, and stressing adherence to rules and regulations. Directive leadership behavior is similar to the initiating-structure leadership style described earlier.

Participative leadership means that the leader consults with his or her subordinates about decisions. Leader behavior includes asking for opinions and suggestions, encouraging participation in decision making, and meeting with subordinates in their workplaces. The participative leader encourages group discussion and written suggestions.

Achievement-oriented leadership occurs when the leader sets clear and challenging goals for subordinates. Leader behavior stresses high-quality performance and improvement over current performance. Achievement-oriented leaders also show confidence in subordinates and assist them in learning how to achieve high goals.

The four types of leader behavior are not considered ingrained personality traits as in the Fiedler theory; rather, they reflect types of behavior that every leader is able to adopt, depending on the situation.

Situational Contingencies. The two important situational contingencies in the path-goal theory are (1) the personal characteristics of group members and (2) the work environment. Personal characteristics of subordinates are similar to Hersey and Blanchard's readiness level and include such factors as ability, skills, needs, and motivations. For example, if an employee has a low

"Nothing can quite compare with the Marine Corps training and combat service to stretch your leadership skills," states Phillip Rooney, vice-chairman of the building and maintenance service company, ServiceMaster. Marines demonstrate participative leadership. The colonel, or Marine form of CEO (the general is similar to a board member) has absolute authority, but is trained in making team decisions. For example, if a group receives a humanitarian mission order, such as the one in the photo, the team determines the issues such as potential strengths and weaknesses, and the information requirements, targets, key questions for clarification, etc. The team draws the detailed mission plans and if they are lucky, the members of the participative leadership team will get a few hours sleep before they execute their plans.

level of ability or skill, the leader may need to provide additional training or coaching in order for the worker to improve performance. If a subordinate is self-centered, the leader must use rewards to motivate him or her. Subordinates who want clear direction and authority require a directive leader who will tell them exactly what to do. Craftworkers and professionals, however, may want more freedom and autonomy and work best under a participative leadership style.

The work environment contingencies include the degree of task structure, the nature of the formal authority system, and the work group itself. The task structure is similar to the same concept described in Fiedler's contingency theory; it includes the extent to which tasks are defined and have explicit job descriptions and work procedures. The formal authority system includes the amount of legitimate power used by managers and the extent to which policies and rules constrain employees' behavior. Work group characteristics are the educational level of subordinates and the quality of relationships among them.

Use of Rewards.   Recall that the leader's responsibility is to clarify the path to rewards for subordinates or to increase the amount of rewards to enhance satisfaction and job performance. In some situations, the leader works with subordinates to help them acquire the skills and confidence needed to perform tasks and achieve rewards already available. In others, the leader may develop new rewards to meet the specific needs of a subordinate.

Exhibit 16.9 illustrates four examples of how leadership behavior is tailored to the situation. In the first situation, the subordinate lacks confidence; thus, the supportive leadership style provides the social support with which to encourage the subordinate to undertake the behavior needed to do the work and receive the rewards. In the second situation, the job is ambiguous, and the employee is not performing effectively. Directive leadership behavior is used to give instructions and clarify the task so that the follower will know

E x h i b i t **16.9**   *Path-Goal Situations and Preferred Leader Behaviors*

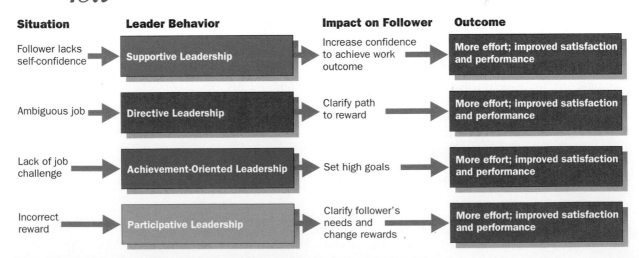

Situation	Leader Behavior	Impact on Follower	Outcome
Follower lacks self-confidence	**Supportive Leadership**	Increase confidence to achieve work outcome	**More effort; improved satisfaction and performance**
Ambiguous job	**Directive Leadership**	Clarify path to reward	**More effort; improved satisfaction and performance**
Lack of job challenge	**Achievement-Oriented Leadership**	Set high goals	**More effort; improved satisfaction and performance**
Incorrect reward	**Participative Leadership**	Clarify follower's needs and change rewards	**More effort; improved satisfaction and performance**

SOURCE: Adapted from Gary A. Yukl, *Leadership in Organizations* (Englewood Cliffs, N.J.: Prentice-Hall, 1981), 146–152.

how to accomplish it and receive rewards. In the third situation, the subordinate is unchallenged by the task; thus, an achievement-oriented behavior is used to set higher goals. This clarifies the path to rewards for the employee. In the fourth situation, an incorrect reward is given to a subordinate, and the participative leadership style is used to change this. By discussing the subordinate's needs, the leader is able to identify the correct reward for task accomplishment. In all four cases, the outcome of fitting the leadership behavior to the situation produces greater employee effort by either clarifying how subordinates can receive rewards or changing the rewards to fit their needs.

Lorry Lokey, founder and president of San Francisco-based Business Wire, uses a participative style to understand the rewards that motivate highly skilled professionals.

BUSINESS WIRE
www.businesswire.com

Lorry Lokey believes in trying to do everything he can to hold on to valued employees. Business Wire was founded over 35 years ago to transmit corporate press releases to the news media. Lokey attributes the success of his company to highly committed long-time employees. He quickly realized he couldn't keep talented workers by rewarding them with salary alone—they could easily be lured away by higher offers. So he started listening to what employees really wanted: benefits that would improve the quality of their lives. Lokey has used a state-of-the-art benefits package to build a cadre of talented people who stay with the company rather than taking their knowledge elsewhere.

Business Wire's benefits package includes not only medical/dental/optical insurance, three weeks of vacation, and a 401(K) contribution, but also an educational allotment, health club allotment, savings-trust donation, and occasional bonuses that can amount to more than $8,000 per year. Business Wire's 20 key people also get a $500,000 annuity, which highly motivates them to keep their knowledge and expertise with the company. Terry Vitorelo, who began her work with Business Wire as an entry-level editor, puts it this way: "[I can] retire at age 55, and once all my benefits from Business Wire get factored together, for the rest of my life I'll earn more money than I do now, working. That's surreal! When Lorry Lokey told me the way the annuity would work, I just laughed and laughed."

The most important aspect of Lokey's leadership is that he listens to what employees want so that the benefits package can keep changing to meet their needs. For example, when one employee wanted to bring her baby to the office, he converted a spare conference room into a nursery. Today, the nursery is run like a parents' cooperative, with parents bringing in toys and supplies and staffing it round-robin style. As employee needs change, Lokey is willing to consider creative new additions to his comprehensive benefits package. He says he has only one rule: "You can't stand still."[39]

Path-goal theorizing can be complex, but much of the research on it has been encouraging.[40] Using the model to specify precise relationships and make exact predictions about employee outcomes may be difficult, but the four types of leader behavior and the ideas for fitting them to situational contingencies provide a useful way for leaders to think about motivating subordinates.

Substitutes for Leadership

The contingency leadership approaches considered so far have focused on the leaders' style, the subordinates' nature, and the situation's characteristics. The final contingency approach suggests that situational variables can be so powerful that they actually substitute for or neutralize the need for leadership.[41] This approach outlines those organizational settings in which a leadership style is unimportant or unnecessary.

Exhibit 16.10 shows the situational variables that tend to substitute for or neutralize leadership characteristics. A **substitute** for leadership makes the leadership style unnecessary or redundant. For example, highly professional subordinates who know how to do their tasks do not need a leader who initiates structure for them and tells them what to do. A **neutralizer** counteracts the leadership style and prevents the leader from displaying certain behaviors. For example, if a leader has absolutely no position power or is physically removed from subordinates, the leader's ability to give directions to subordinates is greatly reduced.

Situational variables in Exhibit 16.10 include characteristics of the group, the task, and the organization itself. For example, when subordinates are highly professional and experienced, both leadership styles are less important. The employees do not need much direction or consideration. With respect to task characteristics, highly structured tasks substitute for a task-oriented style, and a satisfying task substitutes for a people-oriented style. With respect to the organization itself, group cohesiveness substitutes for both leader styles. Formalized rules and procedures substitute for leader task orientation. Physical separation of leader and subordinate neutralizes both leadership styles.

The value of the situations described in Exhibit 16.10 is that they help leaders avoid leadership overkill. Leaders should adopt a style with which to complement the organizational situation. For example, the work situation for bank tellers provides a high level of formalization, little flexibility, and a highly structured task. The head teller should not adopt a task-oriented style, because the organization already provides structure and direction. The head teller should concentrate on a people-oriented style. In other organizations, if group cohesiveness or previous training meet employees' social needs, the

substitute
A situational variable that makes a leadership style redundant or unnecessary.

neutralizer
A situational variable that counteracts a leadership style and prevents the leader from displaying certain behaviors.

Exhibit **16.10** *Substitutes and Neutralizers for Leadership*

Variable		Task-Oriented Leadership	People-Oriented Leadership
Organizational variables:	Group cohesiveness	Substitutes for	Substitutes for
	Formalization	Substitutes for	No effect on
	Inflexibility	Neutralizes	No effect on
	Low positional power	Neutralizes	Neutralizes
	Physical separation	Neutralizes	Neutralizes
Task characteristics:	Highly structured task	Substitutes for	No effect on
	Automatic feedback	Substitutes for	No effect on
	Intrinsic satisfaction	No effect on	Substitutes for
Group characteristics:	Professionalism	Substitutes for	Substitutes for
	Training/experience	Substitutes for	No effect on

leader is free to concentrate on task-oriented behaviors. The leader can adopt a style complementary to the organizational situation to ensure that both task needs and people needs of the work group will be met.

New Leadership for Learning Organizations

In Chapter 1, we defined management to include the functions of leading, planning, organizing, and controlling. But recent work on leadership has begun to distinguish leadership as something more: a quality that inspires and motivates people beyond their normal levels of performance. Leadership is particularly important in companies trying to make the shift to a learning organization. Research has found that some leadership approaches are more effective than others for bringing about change in organizations.

Change Leadership

What kind of people can lead an organization through major changes? Two types of leadership that can have a substantial impact are charismatic and transformational. These types of leadership are best understood in comparison to transactional leadership.

Transactional Leaders. The traditional management function of leading has been called *transactional leadership*.[42] **Transactional leaders** clarify the role and task requirements of subordinates, initiate structure, provide appropriate rewards, and try to be considerate to and meet the social needs of subordinates. The transactional leader's ability to satisfy subordinates may improve productivity. Transactional leaders excel at management functions. They are hardworking, tolerant, and fair minded. They take pride in keeping things running smoothly and efficiently. Transactional leaders often stress the impersonal aspects of performance, such as plans, schedules, and budgets. They have a sense of commitment to the organization and conform to organizational norms and values.

transactional leader
A leader who clarifies subordinates' role and task requirements, initiates structure, provides rewards, and displays consideration for subordinates.

Charismatic Leaders. Charismatic leadership goes beyond transactional leadership techniques. Charisma has been referred to as "a fire that ignites followers' energy and commitment, producing results above and beyond the call of duty."[43] The **charismatic leader** has the ability to inspire and motivate people to do more than they would normally do, despite obstacles and personal sacrifice. Followers transcend their own self-interests for the sake of the department or organization. The impact of charismatic leaders is normally from (1) stating a lofty vision of an imagined future that employees identify with, (2) shaping a corporate value system for which everyone stands, and (3) trusting subordinates and earning their complete trust in return.[44] Charismatic leaders tend to be less predictable than transactional leaders. They create an atmosphere of change, and they may be obsessed by visionary ideas that excite, stimulate, and drive other people to work hard. Charismatic leaders have an emotional impact on subordinates. They stand for something, have a vision of the future, are able to communicate that vision to subordinates, and motivate them to realize it.[45] The Manager's Shoptalk box provides a short quiz to help you determine whether you have the potential to be a charismatic leader.

charismatic leader
A leader who has the ability to motivate subordinates to transcend their expected performance.

Are You a Charismatic Leader?

If you were the head of a major department in a corporation, how important would each of the following activities be to you? Answer yes or no to indicate whether you would strive to perform each activity.

1. Help subordinates clarify goals and how to reach them.

2. Give people a sense of mission and overall purpose.

3. Help get jobs out on time.

4. Look for the new product or service opportunities.

5. Use policies and procedures as guides for problem solving.

6. Promote unconventional beliefs and values.

7. Give monetary rewards in exchange for high performance from subordinates.

8. Command respect from everyone in the department.

9. Work alone to accomplish important tasks.

10. Suggest new and unique ways of doing things.

11. Give credit to people who do their jobs well.

12. Inspire loyalty to yourself and to the organization.

13. Establish procedures to help the department operate smoothly.

14. Use ideas to motivate others.

15. Set reasonable limits on new approaches.

16. Demonstrate social nonconformity.

The even-numbered items represent behaviors and activities of charismatic leaders. Charismatic leaders are personally involved in shaping ideas, goals, and direction of change. They use an intuitive approach to develop fresh ideas for old problems and seek new directions for the department or organization. The odd-numbered items are considered more traditional management activities, or what would be called *transactional leadership*. Managers respond to organizational problems in an impersonal way, make rational decisions, and coordinate and facilitate the work of others. If you answered yes to more even-numbered than odd-numbered items, you may be a potential charismatic leader.

SOURCES: Based on Bernard M. Bass, *Leadership and Performance beyond Expectations* (New York: Free Press, 1985); and Lawton R. Burns and Selwyn W. Becker, "Leadership and Managership," in *Health Care Management*, ed. S. Shortell and A. Kaluzny (New York: Wiley, 1986).

Charismatic leaders include Mother Theresa, Martin Luther King, Jr., Adolf Hitler, and Charles Manson. Charisma can be used for positive outcomes that benefit the group, but it can also be used for self-serving purposes that lead to deception, manipulation, and exploitation of others. When charismatic leaders respond to organizational problems in terms of the needs of the entire group rather than their own emotional needs, they can have a powerful, positive influence on organizational performance.[46] Herb Kelleher, CEO of Southwest Airlines, is an example of a business leader with charisma. Kelleher inspires his employees to break the rules, maintain their individuality, and have fun. In general, leaders who genuinely love what they do exhibit an element of charisma.

transformational leader

A leader distinguished by a special ability to bring about innovation and change.

Transformational Leaders. **Transformational leaders** are similar to charismatic leaders, but are distinguished by their special ability to bring about innovation and change. Transformational leaders create significant change in both followers and the organization.[47] They have the ability to lead changes in the organization's mission, strategy, structure, and culture, as well as to promote innovation in products and technologies. Transformational leaders do not rely solely on tangible rules and incentives to control specific transactions with followers. They focus on intangible qualities such as vision, shared values, and ideas to build relationships, give larger meaning to diverse activities, and find common ground to enlist followers in the change process.[48]

Percy Barnevik is a transformational leader who transformed two rather sleepy engineering firms (ASEA, a Swedish engineering group, and Brown Boveri, a Swiss competitor) into the world's top engineering giant. Barnevik had a vision of a new type of organization for a new Europe without boundaries. He wanted ABB to be a transnational company operating freely across borders, one that combined global scale and world class technology with small company dynamism and deep roots in the local community. Barnevik pushed authority, responsibility, and accountability down to the lowest levels of the organization and empowered employees throughout the company to help him achieve his vision for the new Asea Brown Boveri.[49]

Co-chairmen of California Pizza Kitchen Inc. (CPK) restaurants, Rick Rosenfield and Larry Flax are leading their company through major changes. After PepsiCo Inc. bought 67 percent of CPK, the two leaders stayed as co-CEOs, managing a Pepsi-financed expansion that tripled the company's size to 90 restaurants. When Pepsi sold its restaurant business, Rosenfield and Flax bought their chain back at a profit. Now the co-leaders are sharpening their transformational leadership skills as they execute their vision to add 15 outlets a year and introduce frozen supermarket pizzas. "We always believed we could surpass Pizza Hut [a $4.7 billion chain]," says Flax, "We still believe we will."

Leading the Learning Organization

Leadership is the only means by which a company can change into a learning organization. The view of leaders who set goals, make decisions, and direct the troops reflects an individualistic approach. In learning organizations, managers learn to think in terms of "control with" rather than "control over" others. To "control with" others, leaders build relationships based on a shared vision and shape the culture that can help achieve it. In learning organizations, leaders help people see the whole system, facilitate teamwork, initiate change, and expand the capacity of people to shape the future.[50] Leaders in a learning organization have three distinct roles.

1. *Create a shared vision.* The shared vision is a picture of an ideal future for the organizaton. The vision includes what the organization will look like, performance outcomes, and underlying values. A vision may be created by the leader or with employee participation, but this purpose must be widely understood and imprinted in people's minds. The vision represents desired long-term outcomes; hence, employees are free to identify and solve problems that help achieve that vision. Without a shared vision, employee action may not add to the whole because decisions are fragmented and take people in different directions.

   Alfred P. West, Jr., founder and CEO of SEI Investments, transformed his company into a learning organization by spreading his vision of a new kind of financial services company. The vision included abolishing the old organization chart and assigning all work to self-directed teams who work directly with customers. West's vision includes the values of equality, freedom, responsibility, and dedication to serving customers.[51] Because all employees understand the vision, they can carry it out without direct supervision from the top.

2. *Design structure.* The leader puts in place an organization structure, including policies, strategies, and formats that support the learning organization. The learning organization takes advantage of horizontal relationships, including teams, task forces, and frequent meetings that involve cross-sections

The Girl Scout Way

Frances Hesselbein currently runs the Drucker Foundation, a small organization dedicated to sharing the leadership thinking of Peter Drucker. But she got her start more than 40 years ago as a volunteer Scout leader. She eventually rose to CEO of the Girl Scouts, inheriting a troubled organzation of 680,000 people, only one percent of whom were paid employees. By the time she retired in 1990, Hesselbein had turned around declining membership, dramatically increased participation by minorities, and replaced a brittle hierarchy with one of the most vibrant organizations in the nonprofit or business world.

How did she do it? By developing a leadership philosophy that emphasizes helping other people meet their needs. Hesselbein describes how she works with others as a circle in which everyone is included. Business and nonprofit leaders learn from Hesselbein's leadership style. George Sparks, manager of Hewlett-Packard's measuring-equipment business, says the time he spent following Hesselbein around was "the best two days of my career." As Sparks observed Hesselbein in action, he noted her ability to sense people's needs on an emotional level. Hesselbein listens carefully and then links people with matching needs and skills so that their personal needs are met at the same time they are serving the needs of the organization. She recognizes that the only way to achieve high performance is through the work of others, and she consistently

treats people with care and respect. Hesselbein doesn't believe in forcing change on others. She draws her power from moral values, not from her position. For example, when she proposed that five-year-old girls from single-parent households be included as Girl Scout members (the minimum age was six), most of the councils opposed the plan. Even though the change was important because it would expand the Girl Scouts' reach into the minority community, Hesselbein didn't impose the change. She began working with the few councils who agreed with her and let the others continue their own way. Within a year, two-thirds of the councils had adopted the new age limit.

Hesselbein says her definition of leadership was "very hard to arrive at, very painful. . . . [It] is not a basket of tricks or skills. It is the quality and character and courage of the person who is the leader. It's a matter of ethics and moral compass, the willingness to remain highly vulnerable." To Frances Hesselbein, leadership means serving others, helping employees meet their personal needs at the same time they serve the organization.

SOURCE: Stratford Sherman, "How Tomorrow's Best Leaders Are Learning Their Stuff," *Fortune*, September 27, 1995, 90–102; and James O'Toole, *Leading Change: The Argument for Values-Based Leadership*, (San Francisco: Jossey-Bass Publishers, 1995).

of employees. The structure works toward boundarylessness, with people reaching out to each other across departments rather than competing. The leader also helps people understand that reorganization is continuous, with people taking on new roles and learning new skills. At some learning organizations, all workers have mobile workstations because teams are continuously reorganizing as needed to solve problems. Employees at Xerox Business Services (XBS) are constantly switching jobs and learning new skills to keep up with rapid change and growth. Chris Turner, XBS's "Chief Learning Person," says her main job is to "disturb the system" and turn the company's 15,000 workers into a community of inquirers and learners.[52]

3. *Servant leadership.* Learning organizations are built by servant leaders who devote themselves to others and to the organization's mission. Servant leadership operates from the assumption that work exists for the development of the worker as much as the worker exists to do the work.[53] **Servant leaders** operate on two levels: for the fulfillment of their subordinates' goals and needs and for the realization of the larger purpose or mission of their organization. Servant leaders give things away—power, ideas, information, recognition, credit for accomplishments. They truly value other people, encourage participation, share power, enhance others'

servant leader
A leader who works to fulfill subordinates' needs and goals as well as to achieve the organization's larger mission.

self-worth, and unleash people's creativity, full commitment, and natural impulse to learn.[54] Frances Hesselbein, former CEO of the Girl Scouts, exhibits many of the qualities of a servant leader, as described in the Leadership box. Servant leaders bring the follower's higher motives to the work and connect them to the organizational mission and goals. They are devoted to building the

organization rather than acquiring things for themselves. The leader who wants to be a single actor, a hero seeking personal recognition and resources, cannot build a learning organization.

Terri Bowersock, Entrepreneur *magazine's entrepreneurial Woman of the Year, runs a successful furniture company with a franchised chain of 12 superstores in five states and annual sales of $15 million. Bowersock practices* servant leadership. *She demonstrates her value for her workers, encourages their participation, and shares the leadership power. "I talk to my employees," Bowersock says. "I get out there with them so I know what works...There are key employees who've worked as hard as I have." Bowersock also mentors other women entrepreneurs.*

Summary and Management Solution

This chapter covered several important ideas about leadership. The early research on leadership focused on personal traits such as intelligence, energy, and appearance. Later, research attention shifted to leadership behaviors that are appropriate to the organizational situation. Behavioral approaches dominated the early work in this area; consideration and initiating structure were suggested as behaviors that lead work groups toward high performance. The Ohio State and Michigan approaches and the managerial grid are in this category. Contingency approaches include Fiedler's theory, Hersey and Blanchard's situational theory, the path-goal model, and the substitutes-for-leadership concept.

Leadership concepts have evolved from the transactional approach to charismatic and transformational leadership behaviors. Charismatic leadership is the ability to articulate a vision and motivate followers to make it a reality. Transformational leadership extends charismatic qualities to guide and foster dramatic organizational change. Leadership is particularly important in companies trying to make the shift to a learning organization. Leaders in learning organizations have three distinct roles: to create a shared vision; to design an appropriate horizontal structure to help achieve the vision; and to act as servant leaders. Servant leadership facilitates the growth, goals, and empowerment of followers first in order to liberate their best qualities in pursuing organizational goals.

Mary Ann Byrnes is a transformational leader who is turning Corsair Communications into a learning organization. Byrnes's first step was to visualize the kind of place she wanted Corsair to be and to instill enthusiasm throughout the company. She wanted to create a culture that communicated a sense of shared responsibility and destiny—of everyone pulling together to serve the customer, sharing in the success or failure of their collaborative efforts. She started by allowing workers to make the decisions they would have to live with—for example, Byrnes had to narrow a group of 60 engineers down to 30, so she allowed the engineers themselves to decide who would stay and who would go. Later, she let those who stayed select the new vice president of engineering. She set up cross-functional teams that work face-to-face with customers and began sharing all company information with employees. Company-wide pizza lunches enhance information sharing as well as team spirit. Byrnes fields questions about whatever's on employees' minds, and she asks them how things are going and how she can help. And, when a big check comes in, employees don't just hear about it—the check gets passed around so everyone can see it, touch it, and realize they had a part in it. Today, Corsair is thriving and growing rapidly, and most agree it is due to Byrnes's leadership. Corsair's culture has become its major competitive weapon. By trusting her workers and not making all the decisions herself, Byrnes has created an environment that motivates the engineers and helps them to get the job done.

Discussion Questions

1. Rob Martin became manager of a forklift assembly plant and believed in participative management, even when one supervisor used Rob's delegation to replace two competent line managers with his own friends. What would you say to Rob about his leadership style in this situation?
2. Suggest some personal traits that you believe would be useful to a leader. Are these traits more valuable in some situations than in others?
3. What is the difference between trait theories and behavioral theories of leadership?
4. Suggest the sources of power that would be available to a leader of a student government organization. To be effective, should student leaders keep power to themselves or delegate power to other students?
5. Would you prefer working for a leader who has a consideration or an initiating-structure leadership style? Discuss the reasons for your answer.
6. Consider Fiedler's theory as illustrated in Exhibit 16.5. How often do very favorable, intermediate, or very unfavorable situations occur in real life? Discuss.
7. What is transformational leadership? Differentiate between transformational leadership and transactional leadership. Give an example of each.
8. Some experts believe that leadership is more important than ever in a learning organization. Do you agree? Explain.
9. What is meant by "servant leadership"? Have you ever known a servant leader? Discuss.
10. Do you think leadership style is fixed and unchangeable for a leader or flexible and adaptable? Discuss.
11. Consider the leadership position of a senior partner in a law firm. What task, subordinate, and organizational factors might serve as substitutes for leadership in this situation?

Management in Practice: Experiential Exercise

T–P Leadership Questionnaire:
An Assessment of Style

Some leaders deal with general directions, leaving details to subordinates. Other leaders focus on specific details with the expectation that subordinates will carry out orders. Depending on the situation, both approaches may be effective. The important issue is the ability to identify relevant dimensions of the situation and behave accordingly. Through this questionnaire, you can identify your relative emphasis on two dimensions of leadership: task orientation (T) and people orientation (P). These are not opposite approaches, and an individual can rate high or low on either or both.

Directions: The following items describe aspects of leadership behavior. Respond to each item according to the way you would most likely act if you were the leader of a work group. Circle whether you would most likely behave in the described way: always (A), frequently (F), occasionally (O), seldom (S), or never (N).

1. I would most likely act as the spokesperson of the group.   A F O S N
2. I would encourage overtime work.   A F O S N
3. I would allow members complete freedom in their work.   A F O S N
4. I would encourage the use of uniform procedures.   A F O S N
5. I would permit members to use their own judgment in solving problems.   A F O S N
6. I would stress being ahead of competing groups.   A F O S N
7. I would speak as a representative of the group.   A F O S N
8. I would needle members for greater effort.   A F O S N
9. I would try out my ideas in the group.   A F O S N
10. I would let members do their work the way they think best.   A F O S N
11. I would be working hard for a promotion.   A F O S N
12. I would tolerate postponement and uncertainty.   A F O S N
13. I would speak for the group if there were visitors present.   A F O S N
14. I would keep the work moving at a rapid pace.   A F O S N
15. I would turn the members loose on a job and let them go to it.   A F O S N
16. I would settle conflicts when they occur in the group.   A F O S N
17. I would get swamped by details.   A F O S N
18. I would represent the group at outside meetings.   A F O S N
19. I would be reluctant to allow the members any freedom of action.   A F O S N

20. I would decide what should be done and how it should be done.   A F O S N
21. I would push for increased production.   A F O S N
22. I would let some members have authority which I could keep.   A F O S N
23. Things would usually turn out as I had predicted.   A F O S N
24. I would allow the group a high degree of initiative.   A F O S N
25. I would assign group members to particular tasks.   A F O S N
26. I would be willing to make changes.   A F O S N
27. I would ask the members to work harder.   A F O S N
28. I would trust the group members to exercise good judgment.   A F O S N
29. I would schedule the work to be done.   A F O S N
30. I would refuse to explain my actions.   A F O S N
31. I would persuade others that my ideas are to their advantage.   A F O S N
32. I would permit the group to set its own pace.   A F O S N
33. I would urge the group to beat its previous record.   A F O S N

34. I would act without consulting the group.   A F O S N
35. I would ask that group members follow standard rules and regulations.   A F O S N
T _____ P _____

The T–P Leadership Questionnaire is scored as follows:

a. Circle the item number for items 8, 12, 17, 18, 19, 30, 34, and 35.
b. Write the number 1 in front of a *circled item number* if you responded S (seldom) or N (never) to that item.
c. Also write a number 1 in front of *item numbers not circled* if you responded A (always) or F (frequently).
d. Circle the number 1s that you have written in front of the following items: 3, 5, 8, 10, 15, 18, 19, 22, 24, 26, 28, 30, 32, 34, and 35.
e. *Count the circled number 1s.* This is your score for concern for people. Record the score in the blank following the letter P at the end of the questionnaire.
f. *Count uncircled number 1s.* This is your score for concern for task. Record this number in the blank following the letter T.

SOURCE: The T–P Leadership Questionnaire was adapted by J. B. Ritchie and P. Thompson in *Organization and People* (New York: West, 1984). Copyright 1969 by the American Educational Research Association. Adapted by permission of the publisher.

Management in Practice: Ethical Dilemma

Does Wage Reform Start at the Top?

Paula Smith has just been offered the opportunity of a lifetime. The chairman of the board of Resitronic Corporation has just called to ask her to take the job as director of the troubled audio equipment manufacturing subsidiary. The first question Smith asked was "Will the board give me the autonomy to turn this company around?" The answer was yes. Resitronic's problems were so severe that the board was desperate for change and ready to give Smith whatever it took to save the company.

Smith knows that cost cutting is the first place she needs to focus. Labor expenses are too high, and product quality and production times are below industry standards. She sees that labor and management at Resitronic are two armed camps, but she needs cooperation at all levels to achieve a turnaround. Smith is energized. She knows she finally has the autonomy to try out her theories about an empowered workforce. Smith knows she must ask managers and workers to take a serious pay cut, with the promise of incentives to share in any improvements they might make. She also knows that everyone will be looking at her own salary as an indication of whether she walks her talk.

Smith is torn. She realizes she faces a year or two of complete hell, with long hours, little time for her family or outside interests, bitter resistance in subordinates, and no guarantees of success. Even if she comes in at the current director's salary, she will be taking a cut in pay. But if she takes a bigger cut coming in, with the promise of bonuses and stock options tied to her own performance, she sends a strong message to the entire subsidiary that they rise or fall together. She wonders what might happen if she fails. Many influences on the audio equipment subsidiary are beyond her control. Resitronic itself is in trouble. From her current vantage point, Smith believes she can turn things around, but what will she discover when she gets inside? What if the board undercuts her? Doesn't she owe it to herself and her family to be compensated at the highest possible level for the stress and risk they will be enduring? Can she afford to risk her own security to send a message of commitment to the plan she is asking others to follow?

What Do You Do?

1. Take the same salary as the current director for one year. Circulate the information that although you are taking a cut to come to Resitronic, you are confident that you can make a difference. Build in pay incentive bonuses for the following years if the subsidiary succeeds.

2. Take a bigger cut in pay with generous incentive bonuses. Ask the board and the entire workforce to do the same. Open the books and let the whole company know exactly where they stand.

3. Ask for the same salary you are making now. You know you are going to be worth it, and you don't want to ask your family to suffer monetarily as well as in their quality of life during this transition.

Surf the Net

1. **Leadership Style.** Test your leadership style with a questionnaire available at **www.leaderx.com**. After you complete the assessment, select the "Submit to Tabulate Your Score" button, and receive a customized report on your leadership style. Print out your report so that you may evaluate it. Write a 1 to 2 paragraph statement regarding what you agree/disagree with in the report, whether anything surprised you in the report, and what you've learned from the report. Submit both the printout and your comments to your instructor.

2. **Leadership Training.** As stated at its Web site, Ninth House Network **www.ninthhouse.com** is the "only online learning network, Ninth House delivers personalized, interactive strategic business skills training to the desktop on demand." Further, Ninth House Network was "established to offer companies an innovative, entertaining, and cost-effective way for employees to develop business skills that will enable them to perform their jobs with greater confidence, competence, and efficiency." Through an innovative combination of proven training techniques, captivating storytelling, and universally adopted technology, the Ninth House Network provides business skills learning in areas that corporations consider most critical to their success, including leadership, communication, the basics of good business, managing, team building and project management. Download and watch the nearly 3-minute video at this Web site (video player instructions are provided at the Web site) to become familiar with this leadership training tool.

3. **Leadership Research.** The Leadership-Development.com Web site offers insight and information on leadership for executives, CEOs, and other leaders. Visit the site at **www.leadership-development.com**, select a leadership topic of interest to you, and print out the information you can use during a small-group discussion of your topic.

Case for Critical Analysis
DGL International

When DGL International, a manufacturer of refinery equipment, brought in John Terrill to manage its Technical Services division, company executives informed him of the urgent situation. Technical Services, with 20 engineers, was the highest-paid, best-educated, and least-productive division in the company. The instructions to Terill: Turn it around. Terrill called a meeting of the engineers. He showed great concern for their personal welfare and asked point blank: "What's the problem? Why can't we produce? Why does this division have such turnover?"

Without hesitation, employees launched a hail of complaints. "I was hired as an engineer, not a pencil pusher." "We spend over half our time writing asinine reports in triplicate for top management, and no one reads the reports."

After a two-hour discussion, Terrill concluded he had to get top management off the engineers' backs. He promised the engineers, "My job is to stay out of your way so you can do your work, and I'll try to keep top management off your backs too." He called for the day's reports and issued an order effective immediately that the originals be turned in daily to his office rather than mailed to headquarters. For three weeks, technical reports piled up on his desk. By month's end, the stack was nearly three feet high. During that time no one called for the reports. When other managers entered his office and saw the stack, they usually asked, "What's all this?" Terrill answered, "Technical reports." No one asked to read them.

Finally, at month's end, a secretary from finance called and asked for the monthly travel and expense report. Terrill responded, "Meet me in the president's office tomorrow morning."

The next morning the engineers cheered as Terrill walked through the department pushing a cart loaded with the enormous stack of reports. They knew the showdown had come.

Terrill entered the president's office and placed the stack of reports on his desk. The president and the other senior executives looked bewildered.

"This," Terrill announced, "is the reason for the lack of productivity in the Technical Services division. These are the reports you people require every month. The fact that they sat on my desk all month shows that no one reads this material. I suggest that the engineers' time could be used in a more productive manner, and that one brief monthly report from my office will satisfy the needs of other departments."

Questions

1. What leadership style did John Terrill use? What do you think was his primary source of power?
2. Based on the Hersey-Blanchard theory, should Terrill have been less participative? Should he have initiated more task structure for the engineers? Explain.
3. What leadership approach would you have taken in this situation?

Endnotes

1. Alessandra Bianchi, "Mission Improbable," *Inc.* September 1996, 69–75.

2. Charles Pappas, "The Top 20 Best-Paid Women in Corporate America," *Working Woman*, February 1998, 26–39; Sharon Nelton, "Men, Women, and Leadership," *Nation's Business*, May 1991, 16–22; and George Gendron and Stephen D. Solomon, "The Art of Loving," inteview with Jan Carlzon, *Inc.*, May 1989, 35–46.

3. David C. Limerick, "Managers of Meaning: From Bob Geldof's Band Aid to Australian CEOs," *Organizational Dynamics* (Spring 1990), 22–23.

4. Gary Yukl, "Managerial Leadership: A Review of Theory and Research," *Journal of Management* 15 (1989), 251–289.

5. James M. Kouzes and Barry Z. Posner, "The Credibility Factor: What Followers Expect from Their Leaders," *Management Review,* January 1990, 29–33.

6. Henry Mintzberg, *Power In and Around Organizations* (Englewood Cliffs, N.J.: Prentice-Hall, 1983); and Jeffrey Pfeffer, *Power in Organizations* (Marshfield, Mass.: Pitman, 1981).

7. J. R. P. French, Jr., and B. Raven, "The Bases of Social Power," in *Group Dynamics*, ed. D. Cartwright and Alvin F. Zander (Evanston, Ill.: Row, Peterson, 1960), 607–623.

8. G. A. Yukl and T. Taber, "The Effective Use of Managerial Power," *Personnel* (March–April 1983), 37–44.

9. Erle Norton, "Chairman of AK Steel Tries to Shake Off Tag of 'Operating Man,'" *The Wall Street Journal,* November 25, 1994, A1, A5.

10. Jay A. Conger, "The Necessary Art of Persuasion," *Harvard Business Review*, May–June 1998, 84–95.

11. Yukl and Taber, "The Effective Use of Managerial Power."

12. Michael E. McGill and John W. Slocum, Jr., "A *Little* Leadership, Please?" *Organizational Dynamics*, Winter 1998, 39–49.

13. Thomas A. Stewart, "New Ways to Exercise Power," *Fortune,* November 6, 1989, 52–64; and Thomas A. Stewart, "CEOs See Clout Shifting," *Fortune,* November 6, 1989, 66.

14. Robin Landew Silverman, "A Moving Experience," *Inc.*, August 1996, 23–24.

15. G. A. Yukl, *Leadership in Organizations* (Englewood Cliffs, N.J.: Prentice-Hall, 1981); and S. C. Kohs and K. W. Irle, "Prophesying Army Promotion," *Journal of Applied Psychology* 4 (1920), 73–87.

16. R. Albanese and D. D. Van Fleet, *Organizational Behavior: A Managerial Viewpoint* (Hinsdale, Ill.: The Dryden Press, 1983).

17. Leslie Scism, Anita Raghavan, and Stephen E. Frank, "Weill and Reed Merge Their Firms; Can They Also Merge Their Egos?" *The Wall Street Journal*, April 7, 1998, A1.

18. K. Lewin, "Field Theory and Experiment in Social Psychology: Concepts and Methods," *American Journal of Sociology* 44 (1939), 868–896; K. Lewin and R. Lippitt, "An Experimental Approach to the Study of Autocracy and Democracy: A Preliminary Note," *Sociometry* 1 (1938), 292–300; and K. Lewin, R. Lippitt, and R. K. White, "Patterns of Aggressive Behavior in Experimentally Created Social Climates," *Journal of Social Psychology* 10 (1939), 271–301.

19. R. K. White and R. Lippitt, *Autocracy and Democracy: An Experimental Inquiry* (New York: Harper, 1960).

20. R. Tannenbaum and W. H. Schmidt, "How to Choose a Leadership Pattern," *Harvard Business Review* 36 (1958), 95–101.

21. F. A. Heller and G. A. Yukl, "Participation, Managerial Decision Making and Situational Variables," *Organizational Behavior and Human Performance* 4 (1969), 227–241.

22. Matt Murray, "After Long Overhaul, Banc One Now Faces Pressure to Perform," *The Wall Street Journal*, March 10, 1998, A1; and Patricia O'Toole, "How Do You Build a $44 Million Company? By Saying 'Please'," *Working Woman*, April 1990, 88–92.

23. C. A. Schriesheim and B. J. Bird, "Contributions of the Ohio State Studies to the Field of Leadership," *Journal of Management* 5 (1979), 135–145; and C. L. Shartle, "Early Years of the Ohio State University Leadership Studies," *Journal of Management* 5 (1979), 126–134.

24. P. C. Nystrom, "Managers and the High-High Leader Myth," *Academy of Management Journal* 21 (1978), 325–331; and L. L. Larson, J. G. Hunt, and Richard N. Osborn, "The Great High-High Leader Behavior Myth: A Lesson from Occam's Razor," *Academy of Management Journal* 19 (1976), 628–641.

25. R. Likert, "From Production- and Employee-Centeredness to Systems 1–4," *Journal of Management* 5 (1979), 147–156.

26. Robert R. Blake and Jane S. Mouton, *The Managerial Grid III* (Houston: Gulf, 1985).

27. Esther Wachs Book, "Leadership for the Millennium," *Working Woman*, March 1998, 29–34; Allen R. Myerson, "West Pointer Commands Tenneco," *The New York Times*, May 15, 1994, F4; and Charles M. Farkas and Suzy Wetlaufer, "The

Ways Chief Executive Officers Lead," *Harvard Business Review*, May–June 1996, 110–122.

28. Fred E. Fiedler, "Assumed Similarity Measures as Predictors of Team Effectiveness," *Journal of Abnormal and Social Psychology* 49 (1954), 381–388; F. E. Fiedler, *Leader Attitudes and Group Effectiveness* (Urbana, Ill.: University of Illinois Press, 1958); and F. E. Fiedler, *A Theory of Leadership Effectiveness* (New York: McGraw-Hill, 1967).

29. Fred E. Fiedler and M. M. Chemers, *Leadership and Effective Management* (Glenview, Ill.: Scott, Foresman, 1974).

30. Fred E. Fiedler, "Engineer the Job to Fit the Manager," *Harvard Business Review* 43 (1965), 115–122; and F. E. Fiedler, M. M. Chemers, and L. Mahar, *Improving Leadership Effectiveness: The Leader Match Concept* (New York: Wiley, 1976).

31. Timothy Aeppel, "Personnel Disorders Sap a Factory Owner of His Early Idealism," *The Wall Street Journal*, January 14, 1998, A1, A14.

32. R. Singh, "Leadership Style and Reward Allocation: Does Least Preferred Coworker Scale Measure Tasks and Relation Orientation?" *Organizational Behavior and Human Performance* 27 (1983), 178–197; and D. Hosking, "A Critical Evaluation of Fiedler's Contingency Hypotheses," *Progress in Applied Psychology* 1 (1981), 103–154.

33. Paul Hersey and Kenneth H. Blanchard, *Management of Organizational Behavior: Utilizing Human Resources,* 4th ed. (Englewood Cliffs, N.J.: Prentice-Hall, 1982).

34. Jonathon Kaufman, "A McDonald's Owner Becomes a Role Model for Black Teenagers," *The Wall Street Journal,* August 23, 1995, A1, A6.

35. M. G. Evans, "The Effects of Supervisory Behavior on the Path-Goal Relationship," *Organizational Behavior and Human Performance* 5 (1970), 277–298; M. G. Evans, "Leadership and Motivation: A Core Concept," *Academy of Management Journal* 13 (1970), 91–102; and B. S. Georgopoulos, G. M. Mahoney, and N. W. Jones, "A Path-Goal Approach to Productivity," *Journal of Applied Psychology* 41 (1957), 345–353.

36. Robert J. House, "A Path-Goal Theory of Leader Effectiveness," *Administrative Science Quarterly* 16 (1971), 321–338.

37. M. G. Evans, "Leadership," in *Organizational Behavior,* ed. S. Kerr (Columbus, Ohio: Grid, 1974), 230–233.

38. Robert J. House and Terrence R. Mitchell, "Path-Goal Theory of Leadership," *Journal of Contemporary Business* (Autumn 1974), 81–97.

39. Jill Andresky Fraser, "'Tis Better to Give and Receive," *Inc.*, February, 1995, 84–90.

40. Charles Greene, "Questions of Causation in the Path-Goal Theory of Leadership," *Academy of Management Journal* 22 (March 1979), 22–41; and C. A. Schriesheim and Mary Ann von Glinow, "The Path-Goal Theory of Leadership: A Theoretical and Empirical Analysis," *Academy of Management Journal* 20 (1977), 398–405.

41. S. Kerr and J. M. Jermier, "Substitutes for Leadership: Their Meaning and Measurement," *Organizational Behavior and Human Performance* 22 (1978), 375–403; and Jon P. Howell and Peter W. Dorfman, "Leadership and Substitutes for Leadership among Professional and Nonprofessional Workers," *Journal of Applied Behavioral Science* 22 (1986), 29–46.

42. The terms *transactional* and *transformational* come from James M. Burns, *Leadership* (New York: Harper & Row, 1978); and Bernard M. Bass, "Leadership: Good, Better, Best," *Organizational Dynamics* 13 (Winter 1985), 26–40.

43. Katherine J. Klein and Robert J. House, "On Fire: Charismatic Leadership and Levels of Analysis," *Leadership Quarterly* 6, No. 2 (1995), 183–198.

44. Jay A. Conger and Rabindra N. Kanungo, "Toward a Behavioral Theory of Charismatic Leadership in Organizational Settings," *Academy of Management Review* 12 (1987), 637–647; Walter Kiechel III, "A Hard Look at Executive Vision," *Fortune,* October 23, 1989, 207–211; and William L. Gardner and Bruce J. Avolio, "The Charismatic Relationship: A Dramaturgical Perspective," *Academy of Management Review* 23, No. 1 (1998), 32–58.

45. Robert J. House, "Research Contrasting the Behavior and Effects of Reputed Charismatic vs. Reputed Non-Charismatic Leaders" (paper presented as part of a symposium, "Charismatic Leadership: Theory and Evidence," Academy of Management, San Diego, 1985).

46. Robert J. House and Jane M. Howell, "Personality and Charismatic Leadership," *Leadership Quarterly* 3, No. 2 (1992), 81–108; and Jennifer O'Connor, Michael D. Mumford, Timothy C. Clifton, Theodore L. Gessner, and Mary Shane Connelly, "Charismatic Leaders and Destructiveness: A Historiometric Study," *Leadership Quarterly* 6, No. 4 (1995), 529–555.

47. Bernard M. Bass, "Theory of Transformational Leadership Redux," *Leadership Quarterly* 6, No. 4 (1995), 463–478; Noel M. Tichy and Mary Anne Devanna, *The Transformational Leader* (New York: John Wiley & Sons, 1986); and Badrinarayan Shankar Pawar and Kenneth K. Eastman, "The Nature and Implications of Contextual Influences on Transformational Leadership: A Conceptual Examination," *Academy of Management Review* 22, No. 1 (1997) 80–109.

48. Richard L. Daft and Robert H. Lengel, *Fusion Leadership: Unlocking the Subtle Forces that Change People and Organizations*, (San Francisco: Berrett-Koehler, 1998).

49. Manfred F. R. Kets De Vries, "Charisma in Action: The Transformational Abilities of Virgin's Richard Branson and ABB's Percy Barnevik," *Organizational Dynamics*, Winter 1998, 7–21.

50. Peter M. Senge, "The Leader's New Work: Building Learning Organizations," *Sloan Management Review*, (Fall 1990), 7–22.

51. Scott Kirsner, "Every Day, It's a New Place," *Fast Company*, April–May 1998, 130–134.

52. Kirsner, "Every Day, It's a New Place"; Polly LaBarre, "This Organization is Disorganization," *Fast Company*, June–July 1996, 110–113; Alan M. Webber, "XBS Learns to Grow," *Fast Company*, August–September 1996, 44–51.

53. Daft and Lengel, *Fusion Leadership*.

54. Senge, "The Leader's New Work."

Chapter 17

LEARNING OBJECTIVES

After studying this chapter, you should be able to

- Define *motivation* and explain the difference between current approaches and traditional approaches to motivation.

- Identify and describe content theories of motivation based on employee needs.

- Identify and explain process theories of motivation.

- Describe reinforcement theory and how it can be used to motivate employees.

- Discuss major approaches to job design and how job design influences motivation.

- Discuss how empowerment heightens employee motivation.

Motivation In Organizations

After 13 years at Sandstrom Products, a manufacturer of paints and coatings, Leo Henkelman was thinking about quitting. He'd started as a paint runner, the lowest job in the plant, and worked his way up to a mill operator position. Henkelman spent his days mixing paints in a giant blender, following formulas supplied by the lab. As he gained knowledge and experience, he came up with a lot of good ideas for improving formulas; yet the guys in the lab continually ignored his suggestions. "It was like they hired me from the neck down," he said. "Warm body, strong back, weak mind." Increasing pressure from quality-conscious customers multiplied the frustration he shared with most of the operators, who felt powerless to change anything. Some workers, including Henkelman, just stopped caring. Finding no challenge at work, he would show up with a hangover and just put in time until he could clock out and hit the bottle again. Top management knew the company had problems—for one thing, Sandstrom was hemorrhaging cash, losing money for the third year out of the last five. Things had to change or Sandstrom would go broke.[1]

If you were the president of Sandstrom Products, how would you motivate employees like Leo Henkelman to give their all to the company? Is high motivation even possible in this kind of routine manufacturing operation?

The problem for Sandstrom Products is that unmotivated employees do the minimum amount of work, causing product quality to suffer and the company to lose its competitive edge. One secret for success in small and medium-sized businesses is motivated and enthusiastic employees. The challenge for Sandstrom Products and other companies is to keep employee motivation consistent with organizational goals. Motivation is a challenge for managers because motivation arises from within employees and typically differs for each employee. For example, Janice Rennie makes a staggering $350,000 a year selling residential real estate in Toronto; she attributes her success to the fact that she likes to listen carefully to clients and then find a house to meet their needs. Greg Storey is a skilled machinist who is challenged by writing programs for numerically controlled machines. After dropping out of college, he swept floors in a machine shop and was motivated to learn to run the machines. Frances Blais sells *World Book Encyclopedia.* She is a top salesperson, but she does not care about the $50,000-plus commissions: "I'm not even thinking money when I'm selling. I'm really on a crusade to help children read well." In stark contrast, Rob Michaels gets sick to his stomach before he goes to work. Rob is a telephone salesperson who spends all day trying to get people to buy products they do not need, and the rejections are painful. His motivation is money; he earned $120,000 in the past year and cannot make nearly that much doing anything else.[2]

Rob is motivated by money, Janice by her love of listening and problem solving, Frances by the desire to help children read, and Greg by the challenge of mastering numerically controlled machinery. Each person is motivated to perform, yet each has different reasons for performing. With such diverse motivations, it is a challenge for managers to motivate employees toward common organizational goals.

This chapter reviews theories and models of employee motivation. First we will review several perspectives on motivation and cover models that describe the employee needs and processes associated with motivation. Then, we will discuss how *job design*—changing the structure of the work itself—can affect employee satisfaction and productivity. Finally, we will examine the trend of *empowerment,* where authority and decision making are delegated to subordinates to increase employee motivation.

The Concept of Motivation

motivation
The arousal, direction, and persistence of behavior.

Most of us get up in the morning, go to school or work, and behave in ways that are predictably our own. We respond to our environment and the people in it with little thought as to why we work hard, enjoy certain classes, or find some recreational activities so much fun. Yet all these behaviors are motivated by something. **Motivation** refers to the forces either within or external to a person that arouse enthusiasm and persistence to pursue a certain course of action. Employee motivation affects productivity, and part of a manager's job is to channel motivation toward the accomplishment of organizational goals.[3] The study of motivation helps managers understand what prompts people to initiate action, what influences their choice of action, and why they persist in that action over time.

A simple model of human motivation is illustrated in Exhibit 17.1. People have basic *needs,* such as for food, achievement, or monetary gain, that translate into an internal tension that motivates specific behaviors with

Some employees at software developer SAS Institute in Cary, North Carolina, are motivated by the top-quality day care that is available for $250 per month for their young children. Other SAS employees are motivated by offerings such as a 35-hour week, a free on-site medical clinic, or 12 holidays a year plus a paid week off between Christmas and New Year's. These extrinsic rewards that help employees maintain a balance between work and personal life earned SAS third-place honors in Fortune *magazine's list of the 100 best companies to work for in America.*

which to fulfill the need. To the extent that the behavior is successful, the person is rewarded in the sense that the need is satisfied. The reward also informs the person that the behavior was appropriate and can be used again in the future.

Rewards are of two types: intrinsic and extrinsic. **Intrinsic rewards** are the satisfactions a person receives in the process of performing a particular action. The completion of a complex task may bestow a pleasant feeling of accomplishment, or solving a problem that benefits others may fulfill a personal mission. For example, Frances Blais sells encyclopedias for the intrinsic reward of helping children read well. **Extrinsic rewards** are given by another person, typically a manager, and include promotions and pay increases. They originate externally, as a result of pleasing others. Rob Michaels, who hates his sales job, nevertheless is motivated by the extrinsic reward of high pay.

The importance of motivation as illustrated in Exhibit 17.1 is that it can lead to behaviors that reflect high performance within organizations. One recent study found that high employee motivation goes hand-in-hand with

intrinsic reward
The satisfaction received in the process of performing an action.

extrinsic reward
A reward given by another person.

Exhibit 17.1 *A Simple Model of Motivation*

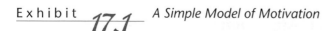

NEED Creates desire to fulfill needs (food, friendship, recognition, achievement) → **BEHAVIOR** Results in actions to fulfill needs → **REWARDS** Satisfy needs; intrinsic or extrinsic rewards

FEEDBACK Reward informs person whether behavior was appropriate and should be used again.

high organizational performance and profits.[4] Managers can use motivation theory to help satisfy employees' needs and simultaneously encourage high work performance. Particularly in today's era of low unemployment, with many companies scrambling to find and keep qualified workers, managers are searching for the right combination of motivational techniques and rewards to keep workers happy and productive. Workers at many of today's leading companies say they are motivated by factors such as a fun, challenging work environment; flexibility that provides a balance between work and personal life; and the potential to learn, grow, and be creative in their jobs.[5] The Diversity box describes how one company is rethinking work to keep female employees productive and motivated.

Foundations of Motivation

A manager's assumptions about employee motivation and use of rewards depend on his or her perspective on motivation. Three distinct perspectives on employee motivation that have evolved are the traditional approach, the human relations approach, and the human resources approach.[6] The most recent theories about motivation represent a fourth perspective called *contemporary approaches*.

Traditional Approach

The study of employee motivation really began with the work of Frederick W. Taylor on scientific management. Recall from Chapter 2 that scientific management pertains to the systematic analysis of an employee's job for the purpose of increasing efficiency. Economic rewards are provided to employees for high performance. The emphasis on pay evolved into the perception of workers as *economic people*—people who would work harder for higher pay. This approach led to the development of incentive pay systems, in which people were paid strictly on the quantity and quality of their work outputs.

Human Relations Approach

The economic man was gradually replaced by a more sociable employee in managers' minds. Beginning with the landmark Hawthorne studies at a Western Electric plant, as described in Chapter 2, noneconomic rewards, such as congenial work groups who met social needs, seemed more important than money as a motivator of work behavior.[7] For the first time, workers were studied as people, and the concept of *social man* was born.

Human Resource Approach

The human resource approach carries the concepts of economic man and social man farther to introduce the concept of the *whole person*. Human resource theory suggests that employees are complex and motivated by many factors. For example, the work by McGregor on Theory X and Theory Y described in Chapter 2 argued that people want to do a good job and that work is as natural and healthy as play. Proponents of the human resource approach believed that earlier approaches had tried to manipulate employees

LEADING THE REVOLUTION: DIVERSITY

Motivating Women Workers at Ernst & Young

Ernst & Young managers are trying to change the way the firm operates to improve female professionals' motivation and decrease turnover. To begin with, workers are told not to check their E-mail or voice mail on weekends and holidays. But what if a report is delayed or a client has to wait for an important piece of information? Top managers say, "So be it." It is one small step in a widespread effort to lessen the demands on Ernst & Young's professional employees. Although the intense work environment—with long hours and constant travel—affects men as well as women, top executives believe women generally feel a greater strain because of greater commitments outside of work. They decided that only a complete overhaul of how people think about work could decrease the strain on female employees and root out systemic biases toward men at the company.

The company's efforts to rethink work grew out of a 1996 critique by Catalyst, a research group on corporate women, that underscored the firm's gender-related problems. Although Ernst & Young hired male and female entry-level professionals in equal numbers, only 8 percent of the firm's partners were women. In addition, only 27 percent of E & Y's women staffers reported that becoming partner was a "realistic goal," compared to 59 percent of their male counterparts. The company was losing 22 percent of its female professionals annually, costing around $150,000 per job to hire and train replacements.

E & Y Chairman Philip A. Laskaway created an "Office of Retention" and hired Deborah K. Holmes, the young lawyer who had headed the Catalyst study, to find ways to turn things around. One of the first problems Holmes and her team identified was that biases toward men served to demotivate female employees. One woman, for example, had her expense report rejected after she took a client for a manicure. If it had been a golf game or one of a few other traditionally male diversions, it would have readily been approved. To solve the problem, a task force worked on broadening the range of acceptable entertaining activities for clients, including family-friendly activities such as picnics and baseball games.

The firm also is developing ways to avoid forcing employees to compromise their personal lives in order to meet preformed business expectations, including incorporating elements such as a casual-dress policy and flexible work schedules. In addition, there are efforts to hire more administrative staff who can assume some of the duties once handled by professionals. One unique program is called "client triage." Partners now routinely consider the demands on their employees in assessing a client's profitability to the firm. They work with each client before a project begins to come to clear, mutual expectations about what will be required of staff members. A "utilization committee," made up of employees from all levels, meets regularly to reconcile client demands with employees' personal needs.

Most partners at Ernst & Young support the new ideas, but Holmes knows the company has a long way to go in changing attitudes and structures to provide greater motivation and job satisfaction for female professionals. "There's no silver bullet for work-life balance," she says. Maybe telecommunications-free weekends are a good place to start.

www.ey.com

Source: Keith H. Hammonds with Gabrielle Saveri, "Accountants Have Lives, Too, You Know," *Business Week,* February 23, 1998, 88, 90.

through economic or social rewards. By assuming that employees are competent and able to make major contributions, managers can enhance organizational performance. The human resource approach laid the groundwork for contemporary perspectives on employee motivation.

Contemporary Approaches

Contemporary approaches to employee motivation are dominated by three types of theories, each of which will be discussed in the following sections. The first are *content theories,* which stress the analysis of underlying human needs. Content theories provide insight into the needs of people in organizations and help managers understand how needs can be satisfied in the workplace. *Process theories* concern the thought processes that influence behavior. They focus on how employees seek rewards in work circumstances. *Reinforcement theories* focus on employee learning of desired work behaviors. In Exhibit 17.1, content theories focus on the concepts in the first box, process theories on those in the second, and reinforcement theories on those in the third.

Content Perspectives on Motivation

content theories
A group of theories that emphasize the needs that motivate people.

hierarchy of needs theory
A content theory that proposes that people are motivated by five categories of needs—physiological, safety, belongingness, esteem, and self-actualization—that exist in a hierarchical order.

Content theories emphasize the needs that motivate people. At any point in time, people have basic needs such as those for food, achievement, or monetary reward. These needs translate into an internal drive that motivates specific behaviors in an attempt to fulfill the needs. An individual's needs are like a hidden catalog of the things he or she wants and will work to get. To the extent that managers understand worker needs, the organization's reward systems can be designed to meet them and reinforce employees for directing energies and priorities toward attainment of organizational goals.

Hierarchy of Needs Theory

Probably the most famous content theory was developed by Abraham Maslow.[8] Maslow's **hierarchy of needs theory** proposes that humans are motivated by multiple needs and that these needs exist in a hierarchical order as illustrated in Exhibit 17.2. Maslow identified five general types of motivating needs in order of ascendance:

1. *Physiological needs.* These are the most basic human physical needs, including food, water, and sex. In the organizational setting, these are reflected in the needs for adequate heat, air, and base salary to ensure survival.

2. *Safety needs.* These are the needs for a safe and secure physical and emotional environment and freedom from threats—that is, for freedom from violence and for an orderly society. In an organizational workplace, safety needs reflect the needs for safe jobs, fringe benefits, and job security.

3. *Belongingness needs.* These needs reflect the desire to be accepted by one's peers, have friendships, be part of a group, and be loved. In the organization, these needs influence the desire for good relationships with coworkers, participation in a work group, and a positive relationship with supervisors.

4. *Esteem needs.* These needs relate to the desire for a positive self-image and to receive attention, recognition, and appreciation from others. Within organizations, esteem needs reflect a motivation for recognition, an increase in responsibility, high status, and credit for contributions to the organization.

5. *Self-actualization needs.* These represent the need for self-fulfillment, which is the highest need category. They concern developing one's full potential, increasing one's competence, and becoming a better person. Self-actualization needs can be met in the organization by providing people with opportunities to grow, be creative, and acquire training for challenging assignments and advancement.

A group called WashTech is trying to unionize Microsoft's 6,000 temporary employees (permatemps) and independent contractors. After working two years as a temporary software test engineer, Marcus Courtney (left) quit Microsoft to organize WashTech. The group claims Microsoft is not meeting the basic or higher-level needs of temporary workers. Although temps often do the same work as regular employees, they receive no benefits or stock options (safety needs). In addition, temps say they feel like second-class citizens—a feeling reinforced by their orange badges versus blue ones for regular employees and the fact that temps are not allowed to attend company picnics or parties, use Microsoft sports fields, or play on company teams (belongingness and esteem needs).

According to Maslow's theory, low-order needs take priority—they must be satisfied before higher-order needs are activated. The needs are satisfied in sequence: Physiological needs come before safety needs, safety needs before social needs, and so on. A person desiring physical safety will devote his or her efforts to securing a safer environment and will not be concerned

Exhibit 17.2 *Maslow's Hierarchy of Needs*

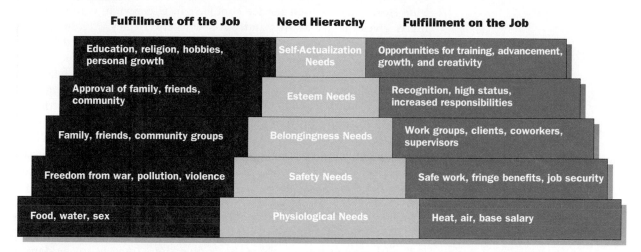

Fulfillment off the Job	Need Hierarchy	Fulfillment on the Job
Education, religion, hobbies, personal growth	Self-Actualization Needs	Opportunities for training, advancement, growth, and creativity
Approval of family, friends, community	Esteem Needs	Recognition, high status, increased responsibilities
Family, friends, community groups	Belongingness Needs	Work groups, clients, coworkers, supervisors
Freedom from war, pollution, violence	Safety Needs	Safe work, fringe benefits, job security
Food, water, sex	Physiological Needs	Heat, air, base salary

with esteem needs or self-actualization needs. Once a need is satisfied, it declines in importance and the next higher need is activated. At All Metro Health Care in Lynbrook, New York, CEO Irving Edwards set up a special "customer service" department for his home health aides to help meet their basic needs, such as applying for food stamps and finding transportation and child care. Three employees are available solely to help workers with these issues. Once these lower-level needs are met, employees desire to have higher-level needs met in the workplace, so Irving developed programs such as an award for caregiver of the year, essay contests with prizes, and special recognition for high scoring on quarterly training exercises.[9]

ERG Theory. Clayton Alderfer proposed a modification of Maslow's theory in an effort to simplify it and respond to criticisms of its lack of empirical verification.[10] His **ERG theory** identified three categories of needs:

1. *Existence needs.* These are the needs for physical well-being.

2. *Relatedness needs.* These pertain to the need for satisfactory relationships with others.

3. *Growth needs.* These focus on the development of human potential and the desire for personal growth and increased competence.

The ERG model and Maslow's need hierarchy are similar because both are in hierarchical form and presume that individuals move up the hierarchy one step at a time. However, Alderfer reduced the number of need categories to three and proposed that movement up the hierarchy is more complex, reflecting a **frustration-regression principle,** namely, that failure to meet a high-order need may trigger a regression to an already fulfilled lower-order need. Thus, a worker who cannot fulfill a need for personal growth may revert to a lower-order need and redirect his or her efforts toward making a lot of money. The ERG model therefore is less rigid than Maslow's need hierarchy, suggesting that individuals may move down as well as up the hierarchy, depending on their ability to satisfy needs.

ERG theory
A modification of the needs hierarchy theory that proposes three categories of needs: existence, relatedness, and growth.

frustration-regression principle
The idea that failure to meet a high-order need may cause a regression to an already satisfied lower-order need.

Need hierarchy theory helps explain why organizations find ways to recognize employees and encourage their participation in decision making. Fine Host Corp., a food service company in Greenwich, Connecticut, regularly gives quality awards and posts workers' names in company buildings to recognize their good work. Employees receive framed certificates when they complete training courses. According to president and CEO Richard Kerley, "Though there may be economic restraints on what we pay them, there are no restraints on the recognition we give them."[11] The importance of filling higher-level belongingness and esteem needs on the job was illustrated by a young manager who said, "If I had to tell you in one sentence why I am motivated by my job, it is because when I know what is going on and how I fit into the overall picture, it makes me feel important." Many companies are finding that "fun" is also a great, high-level motivator, particularly for today's young, well-educated, computer-savvy workers who are in high demand and can command high salaries wherever they go. At Vantage One Communications Group, a marketing firm in Cleveland, Ohio, employees regularly take breaks by playing foosball in the company's rec room. Such diversions lighten up the daily routine and create a feeling of belongingness and community. An employee of GoldMine Software, a Pacific Palisades, California, company where the refrigerator is regularly stocked with Sierra Nevada and Pete's Wicked Ale, puts it this way: "It's like the coolest house I lived in at college; everyone has this weird, wacky thing about them—everyone's totally different—but we all get along so well."[12]

Two-Factor Theory

Frederick Herzberg developed another popular theory of motivation called the *two-factor theory*.[13] Herzberg interviewed hundreds of workers about times when they were highly motivated to work and other times when they were dissatisfied and unmotivated at work. His findings suggested that the work characteristics associated with dissatisfaction were quite different from those pertaining to satisfaction, which prompted the notion that two factors influence work motivation.

The two-factor theory is illustrated in Exhibit 17.3. The center of the scale is neutral, meaning that workers are neither satisfied nor dissatisfied. Herzberg believed that two entirely separate dimensions contribute to an employee's behavior at work. The first, called **hygiene factors,** involves the presence or absence of job dissatisfiers, such as working conditions, pay, company policies, and interpersonal relationships. When hygiene factors are poor, work is dissatisfying. However, good hygiene factors simply remove the dissatisfaction; they do not in themselves cause people to become highly satisfied and motivated in their work.

The second set of factors does influence job satisfaction. **Motivators** are high-level needs and include achievement, recognition, responsibility, and opportunity for growth. Herzberg believed that when motivators are absent, workers are neutral toward work, but when motivators are present, workers are highly motivated and satisfied. Thus, hygiene factors and motivators represent two distinct factors that influence motivation. Hygiene factors work only in the area of dissatisfaction. Unsafe working conditions or a noisy work environment will cause people to be dissatisfied; their correction will not lead

hygiene factors
Factors that involve the presence or absence of job dissatisfiers, including working conditions, pay, company policies, and interpersonal relationships.

motivators
Factors that influence job satisfaction based on fulfillment of high-level needs such as achievement, recognition, responsibility, and opportunity for growth.

Highly
Satisfied

Area of Satisfaction

Motivators

Achievement
Recognition
Responsibility
Work itself
Personal growth

Motivators
influence level
of satisfaction.

Neither
Satisfied nor
Dissatisfied

Area of Dissatisfaction

**Hygiene
Factors**

Working conditions
Pay and security
Company policies
Supervisors
Interpersonal
relationships

Hygiene factors
influence level of
dissatisfaction.

Highly
Dissatisfied

Exhibit **17.3**

Herzberg's Two-Factor Theory

to a high level of motivation and satisfaction. Motivators such as challenge, responsibility, and recognition must be in place before employees will be highly motivated to excel at their work.

The implication of the two-factor theory for managers is clear. Providing hygiene factors will eliminate employee dissatisfaction but will not motivate workers to high achievement levels. On the other hand, recognition, challenge, and opportunities for personal growth are powerful motivators and will promote high satisfaction and performance. The manager's role is to remove dissatisfiers—that is, to provide hygiene factors sufficient to meet basic needs—and then use motivators to meet higher-level needs and propel employees toward greater achievement and satisfaction. Consider the manager's role at Outback Steakhouse.

With their years of experience in the restaurant business, Robert Basham, Timothy Gannon, and Chris Sullivan, founders of Outback Steakhouse, were acutely aware of the hygiene factors in the food-service industry. While the average restaurant is designed to maximize the number of customers at the expense of the food preparation area, Outback puts the emphasis on providing the best possible spaces for servers and kitchen staff to do their jobs effectively, even at peak business times. Outback's dinner-only policy and maximum five-day workweek give managers and staff time for a life outside the restaurant, which cuts down on employee turnover. Each server handles only three tables at a time, ensuring first-class service to customers and higher tips for servers.

To motivate managers, Outback provides ownership. After making a $25,000 investment and signing a five-year contract, Outback managers receive 10 percent of the earnings of their restaurants each month. This provides the average

OUTBACK STEAKHOUSE
www.outback.com

manager with a total income of about \$118,600 per year, far above the rest of the industry. In addition, managers receive about 4,000 shares of stock that are vested at the end of five years. Hourly staff also participate in a stock ownership plan.

Managers are further motivated by the level of responsibility Outback bestows on them. Restaurant managers have the authority to make their own decisions rather than merely implement decisions dictated by headquarters.

Has Outback's motivational approach worked? In December 1994, six years after its launch, there were 210 Outbacks, with revenues estimated at \$544 million, up from \$347.5 million the year before. As Timothy Gannon put it, "We believe if you treat employees as if you were one of them and give them the right environment, they will blow you away with their performance."[14]

Acquired Needs Theory

The final content theory was developed by David McClelland. The *acquired needs theory* proposes that certain types of needs are acquired during the individual's lifetime. In other words, people are not born with these needs but may learn them through their life experiences.[15] The three needs most frequently studied are these:

1. *Need for achievement:* the desire to accomplish something difficult, attain a high standard of success, master complex tasks, and surpass others.

2. *Need for affiliation:* the desire to form close personal relationships, avoid conflict, and establish warm friendships.

3. *Need for power:* the desire to influence or control others, be responsible for others, and have authority over others.

Early life experiences determine whether people acquire these needs. If children are encouraged to do things for themselves and receive reinforcement, they will acquire a need to achieve. If they are reinforced for forming warm human relationships, they will develop a need for affiliation. If they get satisfaction from controlling others, they will acquire a need for power.

For more than 20 years, McClelland studied human needs and their implication for management. People with a high need for achievement tend to be entrepreneurs. They like to do something better than competitors and take sensible business risks. On the other hand, people who have a high need for affiliation are successful "integrators," whose job is to coordinate the work of several departments in an organization.[16] Integrators include brand managers and project managers who must have excellent people skills. People high in need for affiliation are able to establish positive working relationships with others.

A high need for power often is associated with successful attainment of top levels in the organizational hierarchy. For example, McClelland studied managers at AT&T for 16 years and found that those with a high need for power were more likely to follow a path of continued promotion over time. More than half of the employees at the top levels had a high need for power. In contrast, managers with a high need for achievement but a low need for power tended to peak earlier in their careers and at a lower level. The reason is that achievement needs can be met through the task itself, but power needs can be met only by ascending to a level at which a person has power over others.

In summary, content theories focus on people's underlying needs and label those particular needs that motivate people to behave. The hierarchy of needs theory, the ERG theory, the two-factor theory, and the acquired needs theory all help managers understand what motivates people. In this way, managers can design work to meet needs and hence elicit appropriate and successful work behaviors.

Process Perspectives on Motivation

Process theories explain how workers select behavioral actions to meet their needs and determine whether their choices were successful. There are two basic process theories: equity theory and expectancy theory.

Equity Theory

Equity theory focuses on individuals' perceptions of how fairly they are treated compared with others. Developed by J. Stacy Adams, equity theory proposes that people are motivated to seek social equity in the rewards they expect for performance.[17]

According to equity theory, if people perceive their compensation as equal to what others receive for similar contributions, they will believe that their treatment is fair and equitable. People evaluate equity by a ratio of inputs to outcomes. Inputs to a job include education, experience, effort, and ability. Outcomes from a job include pay, recognition, benefits, and promotions. The input-to-outcome ratio may be compared to another person in the work group or to a perceived group average. A state of **equity** exists whenever the ratio of one person's outcomes to inputs equals the ratio of another's outcomes to inputs.

Inequity occurs when the input/outcome ratios are out of balance, such as when a person with a high level of education or experience receives the same salary as a new, less educated employee. Perceived inequity also occurs in the other direction. Thus, if an employee discovers she is making more money than other people who contribute the same inputs to the company, she may feel the need to correct the inequity by working harder, getting more education, or considering lower pay. Perceived inequity creates tensions within individuals that motivate them to bring equity into balance.[18]

The most common methods for reducing a perceived inequity are these:

- *Change inputs.* A person may choose to increase or decrease his or her inputs to the organization. For example, underpaid individuals may reduce their level of effort or increase their absenteeism. Overpaid people may increase effort on the job.

- *Change outcomes.* A person may change his or her outcomes. An underpaid person may request a salary increase or a bigger office. A union may try to improve wages and working conditions in order to be consistent with a comparable union whose members make more money.

- *Distort perceptions.* Research suggests that people may distort perceptions of equity if they are unable to change inputs or outcomes. They

process theories
A group of theories that explain how employees select behaviors with which to meet their needs and determine whether their choices were successful.

equity theory
A process theory that focuses on individuals' perceptions of how fairly they are treated relative to others.

equity
A situation that exists when the ratio of one person's outcomes to inputs equals that of another's.

At Georgia Pacific's Philomath, Oregon, sawmill, employees know they'll get a fair chance at any available job because their peers, such as Curtis Chilcote and Ben Garcia shown here, will make the selection. Georgia Pacific values its employees and fosters an environment in which workers feel secure, challenged, committed to common goals, and treated fairly in line with equity theory. Job openings are posted internally for 48 hours, and interested workers submit a bid to a volunteer committee made up of one salaried and four hourly workers. Crew members appreciate the system because it allows those closest to the job to make hiring and transfer decisions.

may artificially increase the status attached to their jobs or distort others' perceived rewards to bring equity into balance.

- *Leave the job.* People who feel inequitably treated may decide to leave their jobs rather than suffer the inequity of being under- or overpaid. In their new jobs, they expect to find a more favorable balance of rewards.

The implication of equity theory for managers is that employees indeed evaluate the perceived equity of their rewards compared to others'. An increase in salary or a promotion will have no motivational effect if it is perceived as inequitable relative to that of other employees. Some organizations, for example, have created a two-tier wage system to reduce wage rates. New employees make far less than experienced ones, which creates a basis for inequity. Flight attendants at American Airlines are determined to topple the two-tier structure under which they are paid. Chris Boschert, who sorts packages for United Parcel Service, was hired after the two-tier wage system took effect. "It makes me mad," Boschert said. "I get $9.68 an hour, and the guy working next to me makes $13.99 doing exactly the same job."[19] Inequitable pay puts pressure on employees that is sometimes almost too great to bear. They attempt to change their work habits, try to change the system, or leave the job.[20]

Smart managers try to keep feelings of equity in balance in order to keep their workforces motivated.

Expectancy Theory

expectancy theory
A process theory that proposes that motivation depends on individuals' expectations about their ability to perform tasks and receive desired rewards.

E → P expectancy
Expectancy that putting effort into a given task will lead to high performance.

Expectancy theory suggests that motivation depends on individuals' expectations about their ability to perform tasks and receive desired rewards. Expectancy theory is associated with the work of Victor Vroom, although a number of scholars have made contributions in this area.[21] Expectancy theory is concerned not with identifying types of needs but with the thinking process that individuals use to achieve rewards. Consider Bill Bradley, a university student with a strong desire for a B in his accounting course. Bill has a C+ average and one more exam to take. Bill's motivation to study for that last exam will be influenced by (1) the expectation that hard study will lead to an A on the exam and (2) the expectation that an A on the exam will result in a B for the course. If Bill believes he cannot get an A on the exam or that receiving an A will not lead to a B for the course, he will not be motivated to study exceptionally hard.

Expectancy theory is based on the relationship among the individual's *effort,* the individual's *performance,* and the desirability of *outcomes* associated with high performance. These elements and the relationships among them are illustrated in Exhibit 17.4. The keys to expectancy theory are the expectancies for the relationships among effort, performance, and outcomes with the value of the outcomes to the individual.

E → P expectancy involves whether putting effort into a task will lead to high performance. For this expectancy to be high, the individual must have the ability, previous experience, and necessary machinery, tools, and opportunity to perform. For Bill Bradley to get a B in the accounting course, the E → P expectancy is high if Bill truly believes that with hard work, he can get an A on the final exam. If Bill believes he has neither the ability nor the opportunity to achieve high performance, the expectancy will be low, and so will be his motivation.

Circuit City managers are using ex-pectancy theory principles to help meet employees' needs while attaining organizational goals. By creating an incentive program that is a commission-based plan designed to provide the highest compensation to sales counselors who are committed to serving every customer, Circuit City achieves its volume and profitability objectives. The incentive program is also used in other areas such as distribution, where employees are recognized for accomplishments in safety, productivity, and attendance.

Exhibit **17.4** *Major Elements of Expectancy Theory*

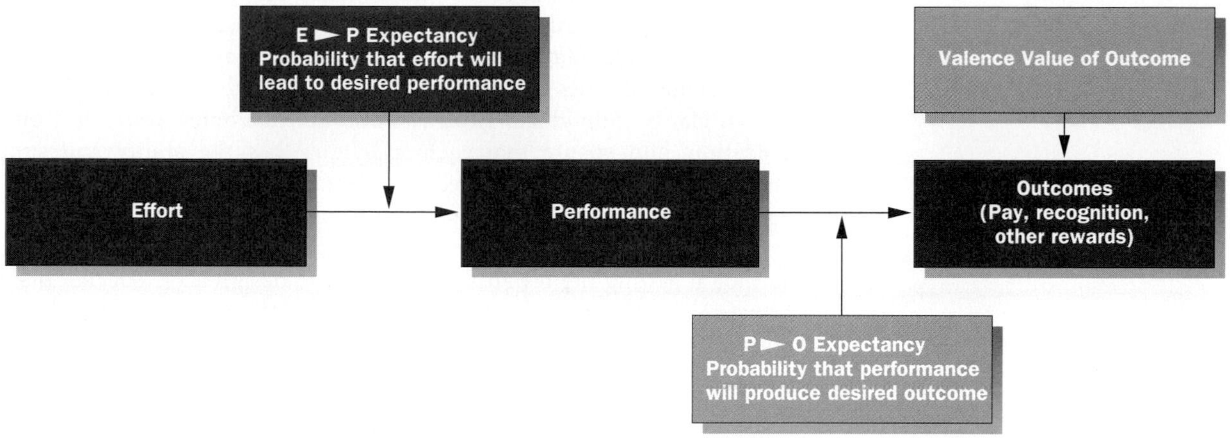

P → O **expectancy** involves whether successful performance will lead to the desired outcome. In the case of a person who is motivated to win a job-related award, this expectancy concerns the belief that high perform-ance will truly lead to the award. If the P → O expectancy is high, the indi-vidual will be more highly motivated. If the expectancy is that high per-formance will not produce the desired outcome, motivation will be lower. If an A on the final exam is likely to produce a B in the accounting course, Bill Bradley's P → O expectancy will be high. Bill may talk to the profes-sor to see whether an A will be sufficient to earn him the B in the course. If not, he will be less motivated to study hard for the final exam.

Valence is the value of outcomes, or attraction for outcomes, for the indi-vidual. If the outcomes that are available from high effort and good per-formance are not valued by employees, motivation will be low. Likewise, if outcomes have a high value, motivation will be higher.

Expectancy theory attempts not to define specific types of needs or rewards but only to establish that they exist and may be different for every individual. One employee may want to be promoted to a position of increased responsibility, and another may have high valence for good relationships with peers. Consequently, the first person will be motivated to work hard for a promotion and the second for the opportunity for a team position that will keep him or her associated with a group.

A simple sales department example will explain how the expectancy model in Exhibit 17.4 works. If Jane Anderson, a salesperson at the Diamond Gift Shop, believes that increased selling effort will lead to higher personal sales, we can say that she has a high E → P expectancy. Moreover, if Jane also believes that higher personal sales will lead to a promotion or pay raise, we can say that she has a high P → O expectancy. Finally, if Jane places a high value on the promotion or pay raise, valence is high and Jane will have a high motivational force. On the other hand, if either the E → P or P → O expectancy is low, or if the money or promotion has low valence for Jane, the overall motivational force will be low. For an employee to be highly moti-vated, all three factors in the expectancy model must be high.[22]

P → O expectancy
Expectancy that successful performance of a task will lead to the desired outcome.

valence
The value or attraction an individual has for an outcome.

Implications for Managers.   The expectancy theory of motivation is similar to the path-goal theory of leadership described in Chapter 16. Both theories are personalized to subordinates' needs and goals. Managers' responsibility is to help subordinates meet their needs and at the same time attain organizational goals. Managers must try to find a match between a subordinate's skills and abilities and the job demands. To increase motivation, managers can clarify individuals' needs, define the outcomes available from the organization, and ensure that each individual has the ability and support (namely, time and equipment) needed to attain outcomes.

Some companies use expectancy theory principles by designing incentive systems that identify desired organizational outcomes and give everyone the same shot at getting the rewards. The trick is to design a system that fits with employees' abilities and needs. Consider the following example from the restaurant industry.

KATZINGER'S DELICATESSEN

When Steve and Diane Warren, co-owners of Katzinger's Delicatessen in Columbus, Ohio, instituted open-book management, they hoped it would help them cut costs and save money. The Warrens trained employees in how to read the financials and told them Katzinger's would share the rewards with employees if financial performance improved. However, because most of their workers were young and mobile, not committed to a long-term career with the company, the vague long-range goals and rewards did not provide a high degree of motivation. Many of them felt that they could do little to improve overall performance and that doing so was the job of managers anyway. Thus, both E → P expectancy and P → O expectancy were low. The Warrens needed a simple, short-term goal as a way to energize their young workers. They proposed a simple plan: if workers would help reduce food costs to below 35 percent of sales without sacrificing food quality or service, they would be rewarded with half the savings.

Katzinger's workers were well-trained and knew they had the skills and ability to meet the goal if they all worked together; thus, the E → P expectancy was high. Workers immediately began proposing ideas to reduce waste, such as matching perishable food orders more closely to expected sales. The P → O expectancy was also high because of the level of trust at the company; workers were highly motivated to cooperate to decrease food costs because they knew everyone would benefit from the savings. Since anyone could look at the financials, workers could actually track their progress toward meeting the goal. At the end of the first month, food costs had fallen nearly 2 percent and employees took home about $40 each from the savings. Later monthly payouts were as high as $95 per employee. By the end of the year, food consistency and service had improved and Katzinger's had indeed reduced its food costs to below 35 percent of total sales, saving the company $30,000. The Warrens gladly distributed $15,000 of that amount to their workers for helping to meet the goal. Now, the Warrens are working out a similar plan to increase sales at Katzinger's.[23]

Reinforcement Perspective on Motivation

reinforcement theory
A motivation theory based on the relationship between a given behavior and its consequences.

The reinforcement approach to employee motivation sidesteps the issues of employee needs and thinking processes described in the content and process theories. **Reinforcement theory** simply looks at the relationship between behavior and its consequences. It focuses on changing or modifying the employees' on-the-job behavior through the appropriate use of immediate rewards and punishments.

Reinforcement Tools

Behavior modification is the name given to the set of techniques by which reinforcement theory is used to modify human behavior.[24] The basic assumption underlying behavior modification is the **law of effect,** which states that behavior that is positively reinforced tends to be repeated, and behavior that is not reinforced tends not to be repeated. **Reinforcement** is defined as anything that causes a certain behavior to be repeated or inhibited. The four reinforcement tools are positive reinforcement, avoidance learning, punishment, and extinction. Each type of reinforcement is a consequence of either a pleasant or unpleasant event being applied or withdrawn following a person's behavior. The four types of reinforcement are summarized in Exhibit 17.5.

Positive Reinforcement. *Positive reinforcement* is the administration of a pleasant and rewarding consequence following a desired behavior. A good example of positive reinforcement is immediate praise for an employee who arrives on time or does a little extra in his or her work. The pleasant consequence will increase the likelihood of the excellent work behavior occurring again. As another example, Frank Bohac, CEO of Computer Systems Development in Albuquerque, New Mexico, has rewarded his employees with computers, vacations, and even horses for meeting personal as well as organizational goals.[25] Studies have shown that positive reinforcement does help to improve organizational performance. In addition, nonfinancial rewards, such as positive feedback, often are as effective as financial incentives.[26]

behavior modification
The set of techniques by which reinforcement theory is used to modify human behavior.

law of effect
The assumption that positively reinforced behavior tends to be repeated and unreinforced or negatively reinforced behavior tends to be inhibited.

reinforcement
Anything that causes a given behavior to be repeated or inhibited.

Exhibit **17.5** *Changing Behavior with Reinforcement*

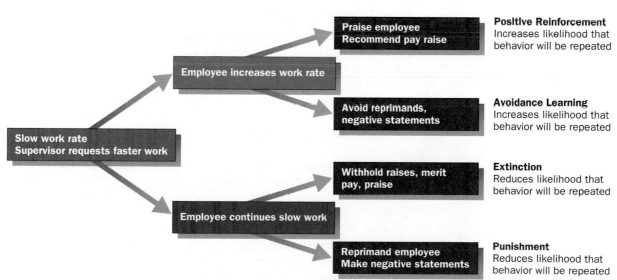

SOURCE: Based on Richard L. Daft and Richard M. Steers, *Organizations: A Micro/Macro Approach* (Glenview, Ill.: Scott, Foresman, 1986), 109.

Avoidance Learning.   *Avoidance learning* is the removal of an unpleasant consequence following a desired behavior. Avoidance learning is sometimes called *negative reinforcement*. Employees learn to do the right thing by avoiding unpleasant situations. Avoidance learning occurs when a supervisor stops criticizing or reprimanding an employee once the incorrect behavior has stopped.

Punishment.   *Punishment* is the imposition of unpleasant outcomes on an employee. Punishment typically occurs following undesirable behavior. For example, a supervisor may berate an employee for performing a task incorrectly. The supervisor expects that the negative outcome will serve as a punishment and reduce the likelihood of the behavior recurring. The use of punishment in organizations is controversial and often criticized because it fails to indicate the correct behavior. However, almost all managers report finding it necessary to occasionally impose forms of punishment ranging from verbal reprimands to employee suspensions or firings.[27]

Extinction.   *Extinction* is the withdrawal of a positive reward, meaning that behavior is no longer reinforced and hence is less likely to occur in the future. If a perpetually tardy employee fails to receive praise and pay raises, he or she will begin to realize that the behavior is not producing desired outcomes. The behavior will gradually disappear if it is continually nonreinforced.

Some executives use reinforcement theory very effectively to shape employees' behavior. Jack Welch, chairman of General Electric, always made it a point to reinforce behavior. As an up-and-coming group executive, Welch reinforced purchasing agents by having someone telephone him whenever an agent got a price concession from a vendor. Welch would stop whatever he was doing and call the agent to say, "That's wonderful news; you just knocked a nickel a ton off the price of steel." He would also sit down and scribble out a congratulatory note to the agent. The effective use of positive reinforcement and the heightened motivation of purchasing employees marked Jack Welch as executive material in the organization.[28]

Schedules of Reinforcement

A great deal of research into reinforcement theory suggests that the timing of reinforcement has an impact on the speed of employee learning. **Schedules of reinforcement** pertain to the frequency with which and intervals over which reinforcement occurs. A reinforcement schedule can be selected to have maximum impact on employees' job behavior. There are five basic types of reinforcement schedules, which include continuous and four types of partial reinforcement.

schedule of reinforcement
The frequency with which and intervals over which reinforcement occurs.

Continuous Reinforcement.   With a **continuous reinforcement schedule,** every occurrence of the desired behavior is reinforced. This schedule can be very effective in the early stages of learning new types of behavior, because every attempt has a pleasant consequence.

continuous reinforcement schedule
A schedule in which every occurrence of the desired behavior is reinforced.

Partial Reinforcement.   However, in the real world of organizations, it is often impossible to reinforce every correct behavior. With a **partial reinforcement schedule,** the reinforcement is administered only after some occurrences of the correct behavior. There are four types of partial reinforcement schedules: fixed interval, fixed ratio, variable interval, and variable ratio.

partial reinforcement schedule
A schedule in which only some occurrences of the desired behavior are reinforced.

Fixed-Interval Schedule. The *fixed-interval schedule* rewards employees at specified time intervals. If an employee displays the correct behavior each day, reinforcement may occur every week. Regular paychecks or quarterly bonuses are examples of a fixed-interval reinforcement. At Leone Ackerly's Mini Maid franchise in Marietta, Georgia, workers are rewarded with an attendance bonus each pay period if they have gone to work every day on time and in uniform.[29]

Fixed-Ratio Schedule. With a *fixed-ratio schedule,* reinforcement occurs after a specified number of desired responses, say, after every fifth. For example, paying a field hand $1.50 for picking ten pounds of peppers is a fixed-ratio schedule. Most piece-rate pay systems are considered fixed-ratio schedules.

Variable-Interval Schedule. With a *variable-interval schedule,* reinforcement is administered at random times that cannot be predicted by the employee. An example would be a random inspection by the manufacturing superintendent of the production floor, at which time he or she commends employees on their good behavior.

Variable-Ratio Schedule. The *variable-ratio schedule* is based on a random number of desired behaviors rather than on variable time periods. Reinforcement may occur sometimes after 5, 10, 15, or 20 displays of behavior. One example is the attraction of slot machines for gamblers. People anticipate that the machine will pay a jackpot after a certain number of plays, but the exact number of plays is variable.

The schedules of reinforcement available to managers are illustrated in Exhibit 17.6. Continuous reinforcement is most effective for establishing new learning, but behavior is vulnerable to extinction. Partial reinforcement schedules are more effective for maintaining behavior over extended time periods. The most powerful is the variable-ratio schedule, because employee behavior will persist for a long time due to the administration of reinforcement only after a long interval.[30]

Exhibit **17.6** *Schedules of Reinforcement*

Schedule of Reinforcement	Nature of Reinforcement	Effect on Behavior When Applied	Effect on Behavior When Withdrawn	Example
Continuous	Reward given after each desired behavior	Leads to fast learning of new behavior	Rapid extinction	Praise
Fixed-interval	Reward given at fixed time intervals	Leads to average and irregular performance	Rapid extinction	Weekly paycheck
Fixed-ratio	Reward given at fixed amounts of output	Quickly leads to very high and stable performance	Rapid extinction	Piece-rate pay system
Variable-interval	Reward given at variable times	Leads to moderately high and stable performance	Slow extinction	Performance appraisal and awards given at random times each month
Variable-ratio	Reward given at variable amounts of output	Leads to very high performance	Slow extinction	Sales bonus tied to number of sales calls, with random checks

Shoptalk
MANAGER'S SHOPTALK

The Carrot-and-Stick Controversy

Everybody thought Rob Rodin was crazy when he decided to wipe out all individual incentives for his sales force at Marshall Industries, a large distributor of electronic components based in El Monte, California. He did away with all bonuses, commissions, vacations, and other awards and rewards. All salespeople would receive a base salary plus the opportunity for profit sharing, which would be the same percent of salary for everyone, based on the entire company's performance. Six years later, Rodin says productivity per person has tripled at the company, but still he gets questions and criticism about his decision.

Rodin is standing right in the middle of a big controversy in modern management. Do financial and other rewards really motivate the kind of behavior organizations want and need? A growing number of critics say no, arguing that carrot-and-stick approaches are a holdover from the Industrial Age and are inappropriate and ineffective in today's economy. Today's workplace demands innovation and creativity from everyone—behaviors that rarely are inspired by money or other financial incentives. Reasons for criticism of carrot-and-stick approaches include the following:

1. *Extrinsic rewards diminish intrinsic rewards.* When people are motivated to seek an extrinsic reward, whether it be a bonus, an award, or the approval of a supervisor, generally they focus on the reward rather than on the work they do to achieve it. Thus, the intrinsic satisfaction people receive from performing their jobs actually declines. When people lack intrinsic rewards in their work, their performance stays just adequate to achieve the reward offered. In the worst case, employees may cover up mistakes, such as hiding an on-the-job accident in order to win a safety award.

2. *Extrinsic rewards are temporary.* Offering outside incentives may ensure short-term success, but not long-term high performance. When employees are focused only on the reward, they lose interest in their work. Without personal interest, the potential for exploration, creativity, and innovation disappears. While the current deadline or goal may be met, better ways of working will not be discovered.

3. *Extrinsic rewards assume people are driven by lower-level needs.* Rewards such as bonuses, pay increases, and even praise presume that the primary reason people initiate and persist in behavior is to satisfy lower-level needs. However, particularly among today's knowledge workers, behavior also is based on yearnings for self-expression, and on feelings of self-esteem and self-worth. Offers of an extrinsic reward do not encourage the myriad behaviors that are motivated by people's need to express themselves and realize their higher needs for growth and fulfillment.

As Rob Rodin discovered at Marshall Industries, today's organizations need employees who are motivated to think, experiment, and continuously search for ways to solve new problems. Alfie Kohn, one of the most vocal critics of carrot-and-stick approaches, offers the following advice to managers regarding how to pay employees: "Pay well, pay fairly, and then do everything you can to get money off people's minds." Indeed there is some evidence that money is not primarily what people work for. Managers should understand the limits of extrinsic motivators and work to satisfy employees' higher, as well as lower, needs. To be motivated, employees need jobs that offer self-satisfaction in addition to a yearly pay raise.

SOURCE: Alfie Kohn, "Incentives Can Be Bad for Business," *Inc.,* January 1998, 93–94; A. J. Vogl, "Carrots, Sticks, and Self-Deception" (an interview with Alfie Kohn), *Across the Board,* January 1994, 39–44; and Geoffrey Colvin, "What Money Makes You Do," *Fortune,* August 17, 1998, 213–214.

One example of a small business that successfully uses reinforcement theory is Parsons Pine Products.

PARSONS PINE PRODUCTS

Parsons Pine Products has only 75 employees, but it is the world's largest manufacturer of slats for louvered doors and shutters. Managers have developed a positive reinforcement scheme for motivating and rewarding workers. The plan includes the following:

1. *Safety pay.* Every employee who goes for a month without a lost-time accident receives a bonus equal to four hours' pay.

2. *Retro pay.* If the company saves money when its worker's compensation premiums go down because of a lower accident rate, the savings are distributed among employees.

3. *Well pay.* Employees receive monthly well pay equal to eight hours' wages if they have been neither absent nor tardy.

4. *Profit pay.* All company earnings above 4 percent after taxes go into a bonus pool, which is shared among employees.

The plan for reinforcing correct behaviors has been extraordinarily effective. Parsons's previous accident rate had been 86 percent above the state average; today it is 32 percent below it. Turnover and tardiness are minimal, and absenteeism has dropped to almost nothing. The plan works because the reinforcement schedules are strictly applied, with no exceptions. Owner James Parsons has said, "One woman called to say that a tree had fallen, and she couldn't get her car out. She wanted me to make an exception. If I did that, I'd be doing it all the time."[31]

Reinforcement also works at such organizations as Campbell Soup Co., Emery Air Freight, Michigan Bell, and General Electric, because managers reward appropriate behavior. They tell employees what they can do to receive reinforcement, tell them what they are doing wrong, distribute rewards equitably, tailor rewards to behaviors, and keep in mind that failure to reward deserving behavior has an equally powerful impact on employees.

Reward and punishment motivational practices dominate organizations, with as many as 94 percent of companies in the United States reporting that they use practices that reward performance or merit with pay.[32] However, despite the testimonies of numerous organizations that enjoy successful incentive programs, there is growing criticism of these so-called carrot-and-stick methods, as discussed in the Manager's Shoptalk box.

Job Design for Motivation

A *job* in an organization is a unit of work that a single employee is responsible for performing. A job could include writing tickets for parking violators in New York City or doing long-range planning for ABC television. Jobs are important because performance of their components may provide rewards that meet employees' needs. An assembly line worker may install the same bolt over and over, whereas an emergency room physician may provide each trauma victim with a unique treatment package. Managers need to know what aspects of a job provide motivation as well as how to compensate for routine tasks that have little inherent satisfaction. **Job design** is the application of motivational theories to the structure of work for improving productivity and satisfaction. Approaches to job design are generally classified as job simplification, job rotation, job enlargement, and job enrichment.

job design
The application of motivational theories to the structure of work for improving productivity and satisfaction.

Job Simplification

Job simplification pursues task efficiency by reducing the number of tasks one person must do. Job simplification is based on principles drawn from scientific management and industrial engineering. Tasks are designed to be simple, repetitive, and standardized. As complexity is stripped from a job, the worker has more time to concentrate on doing more of the same routine task. Workers with low skill requirements can perform the job, and the organization achieves a high level of efficiency. Indeed, workers are interchangeable, because they need little training or skill and exercise little judgment. As a motivational technique, however, job simplification has failed. People dislike

job simplification
A job design whose purpose is to improve task efficiency by reducing the number of tasks a single person must perform.

At the Frito-Lay plant in Lubbock, Texas, Julia Garcia used to just pack bags of chips into cardboard cartons. Today, she's interviewing new hires, refusing products that don't meet quality standards, and sending home excess workers if machines shut down. Hourly workers have been enjoying the benefits of job enlargement *and* job enrichment *since Frito-Lay introduced work teams four years ago. Garcia's 11-member potato chip team is responsible for everything from potato processing to equipment maintenance. Says Garcia of the new job design: "It's more fun. It used to be it was just the same ol'—same ol', [but] now there are more things happening."*

job rotation
A job design that systematically moves employees from one job to another to provide them with variety and stimulation.

job enlargement
A job design that combines a series of tasks into one new, broader job to give employees variety and challenge.

routine and boring jobs and react in a number of negative ways, including sabotage, absenteeism, and unionization. Job simplification is compared with job rotation and job enlargement in Exhibit 17.7.

Job Rotation

Job rotation systematically moves employees from one job to another, thereby increasing the number of different tasks an employee performs without increasing the complexity of any one job. For example, an autoworker may install windshields one week and front bumpers the next. Job rotation still takes advantage of engineering efficiencies, but it provides variety and stimulation for employees. Although employees may find the new job interesting at first, the novelty soon wears off as the repetitive work is mastered.

Companies such as National Steel, Motorola, and Dayton Hudson have built on the notion of job rotation to train a flexible workforce. As companies break away from ossified job categories, workers can perform several jobs, thereby reducing labor costs. One employee might shift among the jobs of drill operator, punch operator, and assembler, depending on the company's need at the moment. Some unions have resisted the idea, but many now go along, realizing that it helps the company be more competitive.[33]

Job Enlargement

Job enlargement combines a series of tasks into one new, broader job. This is a response to the dissatisfaction of employees with oversimplified jobs. Instead of only one job, an employee may be responsible for three or four and will have more time to do them. Job enlargement provides job variety and a greater challenge for employees. At Maytag, jobs were enlarged when work was redesigned such that workers assembled an entire water pump rather than doing each part as it reached them on the assembly line. In General Motors' new assembly plants, the assembly line is gone. In its place is a freewheeling, motorized carrier that transports each car independently through the assembly process. The carrier moves to a workstation, where it stops for a group of workers to perform a coordinated block of tasks, such as installing an engine and its accessories. Thus the workers perform an enlarged job on a stationary automobile, rather than a single task on a series of automobiles moving past them.

E x h i b i t   17.7   *Types of Job Design*

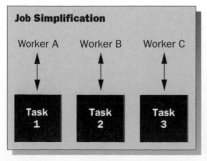
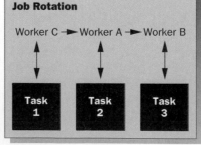
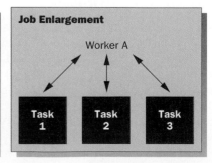

LEADING THE REVOLUTION: THE LEARNING ORGANIZATION

The Social Experiment at Quad/Graphics

Harry V. Quadracci, founder of the $600 million printing giant Quad/Graphics in Peewaukee, Wisconsin, has been called revolutionary because he wanted to help his employees, mostly high school graduates, "become something more than what they ever hoped to be." Quad/Graphics doesn't use organizational charts, strategic plans, or even budgets. Top executives run the company with a minimum of rules and a maximum of indoctrination with values. For example, Quadracci believed organizational charts limit people's responsibility, and thus their motivation and job satisfaction. At Quad/Graphics, if you see something that needs to be done, you do it. There is no separation between management and labor. There are supervisors, but they wear the same uniform as their charges and do the same work. People and relationships are highly valued.

Quadracci once said that all of business is an experiment: "You try something and if it works, it works. If it doesn't work, you try something else. Quad Graphics is a social experiment because we've . . . just tried to experiment with the way we can interact in the workplace as individuals and as responsible citizens." Quad/Graphics managers may do things differently, but their approach has enabled the company to boast average annual growth rates near 40 percent in an industry that is struggling to maintain double-digit growth.

The Quad/Graphics system takes a lot of trust, but managers agree with Quadracci's belief that "if you trust your employees, they'll trust you, and they'll rise to your level of belief in them." Managers celebrate employee mistakes, particularly what Quadracci called "perfect failures." An example of a perfect failure is when two technicians spent a year and almost $800,000 developing a paper folding machine that didn't work. The company celebrated afterward, and even gave the workers a bonus for having the courage to try. Quad/Graphics top managers believe that when employees are afraid to make mistakes, the business is doomed. This belief has made Quad/Graphics a certifiable success, racing ahead of its competitors. Managers continue to look for ways to give employees opportunities to grow financially and personally, to continue to "become something more than what they ever hoped to be."

SOURCE: "Harry V. Quadracci," an interview with Craig Cox, *Business Ethics*, May/June 1993, 19–21.

Job Enrichment

Recall the discussion of Maslow's need hierarchy and Herzberg's two-factor theory. Rather than just changing the number and frequency of tasks a worker performs, **job enrichment** incorporates high-level motivators into the work, including job responsibility, recognition, and opportunities for growth, learning, and achievement. In an enriched job, employees have control over the resources necessary for performing it, make decisions on how to do the work, experience personal growth, and set their own work pace. Many companies, including AT&T, Procter & Gamble, and Motorola, have undertaken job enrichment programs to increase employees' motivation and job satisfaction. At Quad/Graphics, described in the Learning Organization box, managers have incorporated job enrichment ideas to help meet employees' higher-level needs.

job enrichment
A job design that incorporates achievement, recognition, and other high-level motivators into the work.

Job Characteristics Model

One significant approach to job design is the job characteristics model developed by Richard Hackman and Greg Oldham.[34] Hackman and Oldham's research concerned **work redesign**, which is defined as altering jobs to increase both the quality of employees' work experience and their productivity. Hackman and Oldham's research into the design of hundreds of jobs yielded the **job characteristics model**, which is illustrated in Exhibit 17.8. The model consists of three major parts: core job dimensions, critical psychological states, and employee growth-need strength.

work redesign
The altering of jobs to increase both the quality of employees' work experience and their productivity.

job characteristics model
A model of job design that comprises core job dimensions, critical psychological states, and employee growth-need strength.

Exhibit *17.8*   *The Job Characteristics Model*

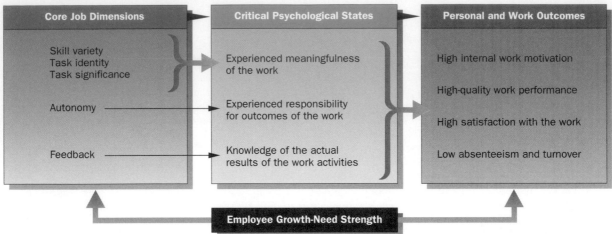

SOURCE: Adapted from J. Richard Hackman and G. R. Oldham, "Motivation through the Design of Work: Test of a Theory," *Organizational Behavior and Human Performance* 16 (1976), 256.

Core Job Dimensions.   Hackman and Oldham identified five dimensions that determine a job's motivational potential:

1. *Skill variety* is the number of diverse activities that compose a job and the number of skills used to perform it. A routine, repetitive, assembly line job is low in variety, whereas an applied research position that entails working on new problems every day is high in variety.

2. *Task identity* is the degree to which an employee performs a total job with a recognizable beginning and ending. A chef who prepares an entire meal has more task identity than a worker on a cafeteria line who ladles mashed potatoes.

3. *Task significance* is the degree to which the job is perceived as important and having impact on the company or consumers. People who distribute penicillin and other medical supplies during times of emergencies would feel they have significant jobs.

4. *Autonomy* is the degree to which the worker has freedom, discretion, and self-determination in planning and carrying out tasks. A house painter can determine how to paint the house; a paint sprayer on an assembly line has little autonomy.

5. *Feedback* is the extent to which doing the job provides information back to the employee about his or her performance. Jobs vary in their ability to let workers see the outcomes of their efforts. A football coach knows whether the team won or lost, but a basic research scientist may have to wait years to learn whether a research project was successful.

The job characteristics model says that the more these five core characteristics can be designed into the job, the more the employees will be motivated and the higher will be performance quality and satisfaction.

Critical Psychological States.   The model posits that core job dimensions are more rewarding when individuals experience three psychological states in response to job design. In Exhibit 17.8, skill variety, task identity, and task significance tend to influence the employee's psychological state of *experienced meaningfulness of work*. The work itself is satisfying and provides intrinsic rewards for the worker. The job characteristic of autonomy influences the worker's *experienced responsibility*. The job characteristic of feedback provides the worker with *knowledge of actual results*. The employee thus knows how he or she is doing and can change work performance to increase desired outcomes.

Personal and Work Outcomes.   The impact of the five job characteristics on the psychological states of experienced meaningfulness, responsibility, and knowledge of actual results leads to the personal and work outcomes of high work motivation, high work performance, high satisfaction, and low absenteeism and turnover.

Employee Growth-Need Strength.   The final component of the job characteristics model is called *employee growth-need strength*, which means that people have different needs for growth and development. If a person wants to satisfy low-level needs, such as safety and belongingness, the job characteristics model has less effect. When a person has a high need for growth and development, including the desire for personal challenge, achievement, and challenging work, the model is especially effective. People with a high need to grow and expand their abilities respond very favorably to the application of the model and to improvements in core job dimensions.

One application of the job characteristics model that worked extremely well took place at Sequins International Inc.

Workers at the Alexander Doll Company in Harlem manufacture Madame Alexander dolls, which cost from $40 to $600 apiece and have hand-painted faces and elaborate costumes. Employees work in teams of seven or eight, with each team being responsible for completing about 300 dolls or wardrobe assemblies a day. Their work provides skill variety because the costumes alone contain 20 or more separate items that have to go through as many as 30 production steps. Workers also experience task identity because each team performs the complete job of manufacturing dolls that are ready for consumers.

Sequins International Inc., based in Woodside, N.Y., faces tough global competition, particularly from factories in China and India, where women and children hand sew sequins for meager wages, producing $100 million in wholesale goods annually. To compete, U.S. manufacturers use machines that were first developed in the 1940s. The machines save labor but create other problems: The repetitive motions used in the process produce an array of muscle pains as well as mind-numbing boredom. With funding from the Ergonomics Project, administered by the International Ladies Garment Workers Union, Sequins International redesigned the machines to reduce the physical stresses experienced by sequin makers. At the same time, skill variety was increased, as inspection jobs that were once performed separately were integrated into the manufacturing process. This gave workers increased task identity and a greater stake in quality control.

Because Sequins's workforce is 80 percent Hispanic and many workers have poor English skills, the company offers English lessons during lunch hours three times a week. Classes in mathematics and statistical process control are also available to train workers for a variety of new tasks. Two teams, one for product satisfaction and the other for customer support, monitor quality control and machine maintenance as part of the production process, as well as provide operators with ongoing feedback and training.

SEQUINS INTERNATIONAL INC.
www.sequins.com

These improvements in job design and motivation dramatically increased worker satisfaction. As a result, absenteeism is down two and one-half times in some areas. In addition, Sequins International has reduced the cost of producing a unit of goods by 30 percent and realized 30 percent cuts in cycle time, inventory, and overhead.[35]

Empowerment and Other Motivational Programs

Despite the controversy over carrot-and-stick motivational practices discussed in the Manager's Shoptalk box earlier in this chapter, many organizations continue to use various types of incentive compensation as a way to motivate employees to higher levels of performance. Exhibit 17.9 summarizes several methods of incentive pay. These programs can be effective if they are used appropriately and combined with motivational ideas that provide employees with intrinsic rewards and meet higher-level needs. Effective organizations do not use incentive pay plans as the sole basis of motivation.

empowerment
The delegation of power and authority to subordinates.

The newest trend in motivation is **empowerment,** the delegation of power or authority to subordinates in an organization.[36] Increasing employee power heightens motivation for task accomplishment because people improve their own effectiveness, choosing how to do a task and using their creativity.[37] Most people come into an organization with the desire to do a good job, and empowerment releases the motivation that is already there.

Ralph Stayer, CEO of Johnsonville Foods, believes a manager's strongest power comes from committed and motivated employees: "Real power comes from giving it up to others who are in a better position to do things than you are."[38] The manager who shares power with employees receives motivation and creativity in return.

Empowering employees means giving them four elements that enable them to act more freely to accomplish their jobs: information, knowledge, power, and rewards.[39]

Employees receive information about company performance. In companies where employees are fully empowered, such as Com-Corp Industries, no information is secret. At Com-Corp, every employee has access to all financial information, including executive salaries.

Employees have knowledge and skills to contribute to company goals. Companies use training programs to help employees acquire the knowledge and skills they need to contribute to organizational performance. At Tellabs, Inc., a maker of sophisticated telephone equipment, CEO Grace Pastiak personally leads workshops for about a dozen factory workers each month, enabling them to solve problems and make quality improvements on their own.[40]

Employees have the power to make substantive decisions. Workers have the authority to directly influence work procedures and organizational performance, often through quality circles or self-directed work teams. At Compaq Computer, salespeople now work out of their homes and set their own schedules. The company provides a fully equipped networked computer so workers can share information with colleagues and access comprehensive databases. Under the new system, Compaq's sales force has set new records for productivity.[41]

Program Name	Purpose
Pay for Performance	Rewards individual employees in proportion to their performance contributions. Also called merit pay.
Gain Sharing	Rewards all employees and managers within a business unit when predetermined performance targets are met. Encourages teamwork.
Employee Stock Ownership Plan (ESOP)	Gives employees part ownership of the organization, enabling them to share in improved profit performance.
Lump-Sum Bonuses	Rewards employees with a one-time cash payment based on performance.
Pay for Knowledge	Links employee salary with the number of task skills acquired. Workers are motivated to learn the skills for many jobs, thus increasing company flexibility and efficiency.
Flexible Work Schedule	Flextime allows workers to set their own hours. Job sharing allows two or more part-time workers to jointly cover one job. Telecommuting, sometimes called flex-place, allows employees to work from home or an alternate workspace.
Team-based Compensation	Rewards employees for behavior and activities that benefit the team, such as cooperation, listening, and empowering others.

Exhibit *17.9*

New Motivational Compensation Programs

Employees are rewarded based on company performance. Organizations that empower workers often reward them based on the results shown in the company's bottom line. Johnsonville Foods instituted a "company performance share," a fixed percentage of pretax profits to be divided every six months among employees. Individual shares are based on a performance appraisal system designed and administered by a volunteer team of line workers.[42] Organizations may also use other motivational programs described in Exhibit 17.9 to tie employee efforts to company performance.

Many of today's organizations are implementing empowerment programs, but they are empowering workers to varying degrees. At some companies, empowerment means encouraging workers' ideas while managers retain final authority for decisions; at others it means giving employees almost complete freedom and power to make decisions and exercise initiative and imagination.[43] Current methods of empowerment fall along a continuum, as illustrated in Exhibit 17.10. The continuum runs from a situation in which front-line workers have almost no discretion, such as on a traditional assembly line, to full empowerment, where workers even participate in formulating organizational strategy. An example of full empowerment is when self-directed teams are given the authority to hire, discipline, and dismiss team members and to set compensation rates. Few companies have moved to this level of empowerment. One that has W. L. Gore and Associates, which operates with no titles, hierarchy, or any of the conventional structures associated with a company of its size. Gore's culture emphasizes teamwork, mutual support, freedom, intrinsic motivation, independent effort, and commitment to the total organization rather than to narrow jobs or departments. With empowerment, workers are motivated because they are intellectually challenged, provided with opportunities to use their minds and imaginations, and given the power to make decisions that affect their

Exhibit *17.10* *A Continuum of Empowerment*

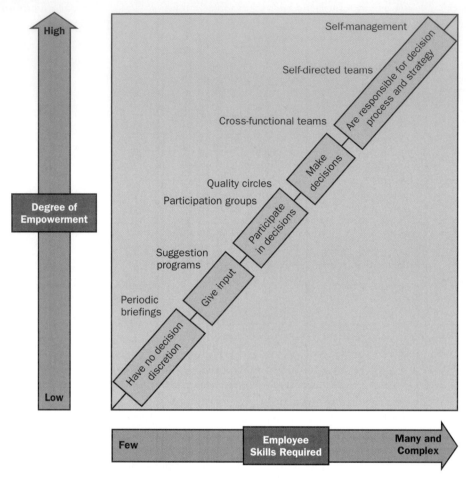

SOURCES: Based on Robert C. Ford and Myron D. Fottler, "Empowerment: A Matter of Degree," *Academy of Management Executive* 9, no. 3 (1995), 21–31; Lawrence Holpp, "Applied Empowerment," *Training* (February 1994), 39–44; and David P. McCaffrey, Sue R. Faerman, and David W. Hart, "The Appeal and Difficulties of Participative Systems," *Organization Science* 6, no. 6 (November–December 1995), 603–627.

work. Research indicates that most people have a need for self-efficacy, which is the capacity to produce results or outcomes, to feel that they are effective.[44] By meeting higher-level needs, empowerment can provide powerful motivation.

Summary and Management Solution

This chapter introduced a number of important ideas about the motivation of people in organizations. The content theories of motivation focus on the nature of underlying employee needs. Maslow's hierarchy of needs, Alderfer's ERG theory, Herzberg's two-factor theory, and McClelland's acquired needs theory all suggest that people are motivated to meet a range of needs. Process theories examine how people go about selecting rewards with which to meet needs. Equity theory says that people compare their contributions and outcomes with others' and are motivated to maintain a feeling of equity. Expectancy theory suggests that people calculate the probability of achieving certain outcomes. Managers can increase motivation by treating employees fairly and by clarifying employee paths toward meeting their needs. Still another motivational approach is reinforcement theory, which says that employees learn to behave in certain ways based on the availability of reinforcements.

The application of motivational ideas is illustrated in job design and other motivational programs. Job design approaches include job simplification, job rotation, job enlargement, job enrichment, and the job characteristics model. Managers can change the structure of work to meet employees' high-level needs. The recent trend toward empowerment motivates by giving employees more information and authority to make decisions in their work while connecting compensation to the results. Other motivational programs include pay for performance, gain sharing, ESOPs, lump-sum bonuses, pay for knowledge, flexible work schedules, and team-based compensation. A highly successful application of motivational ideas occurred for factory workers at Sandstrom Products.

Recall from the chapter opening case that Leo Henkelman was an alienated mill operator considering quitting. When top management empowered workers by implementing open-book management, Henkelman was given the opportunity to take on more responsibility, learn new skills, and make improvements. He learned his own strengths and limitations in the process. While serving as a temporary plant manager, he found that delegation was not his strength—doing was. When a technician job opened up in the lab, he applied. Although he lacked the educational background normally required, the lab director gave him a chance. Now, using his experience, Henkelman guides the manufacturing process from beginning to end, working with customers to develop new products and refine old ones. As his skills and responsibilities increased, so did his pay, thanks to a proficiency pay system that based his pay on his skills and accomplishments and a gain-sharing plan that allowed him to share in the company's profits. By trusting and empowering workers, Sandstrom gave them a reason to care about the company and the knowledge and power to make personal contributions to organizational performance. Results were staggering as Sandstrom rebounded from a loss of $100,000 to earnings of almost $800,000 two years later. Surprisingly, the turnaround occurred while sales stayed the same, without new product lines or new customers. It was cost cutting and improvements instituted by an empowered workforce that made the difference.[45]

Discussion Questions

1. Low-paid service workers represent a motivational problem for many companies. Consider the ill-trained and poorly motivated X-ray machine operators trying to detect weapons in airports. How might these people be motivated to reduce boredom and increase their vigilance?

2. One small company recognizes an employee of the month, who is given a parking spot next to the president's space near the front door. What theories would explain the positive motivation associated with this policy?

3. Campbell Soup Company reduces accidents with a lottery. Each worker who works 30 days or more without losing a day for a job-related accident is eligible to win prizes in a raffle drawing. Why has this program been successful?

4. One executive argues that managers have too much safety because of benefit and retirement plans. He rewards his managers for taking risks and has removed many guaranteed benefits. Would this approach motivate managers? Why?

5. If an experienced secretary discovered that she made less money than a newly hired janitor, how would she react? What inputs and outcomes might she evaluate to make this comparison?

6. Would you rather work for a supervisor high in need for achievement, need for affiliation, or need for power? Why? What are the advantages and disadvantages of each?

7. A survey of teachers found that two of the most important rewards were the belief that their work was important and a feeling of accomplishment. Is this consistent with Hackman and Oldham's job characteristics model?

8. The teachers in question 7 also reported that pay and benefits were poor, yet they continued to teach. Use Herzberg's two-factor theory to explain this finding.

9. Many organizations use sales contests and motivational speakers to motivate salespeople to overcome frequent rejections and turndowns. How would these devices help motivate salespeople?

10. What characteristics of individuals determine the extent to which work redesign will have a positive impact on work satisfaction and work effectiveness?

11. Do you think an empowerment program of increased employee authority and responsibility would succeed without being tied to a motivational compensation program, such as gain sharing or ESOPs? Discuss.

Management in Practice: Experiential Exercise

What Motivates You?

You are to indicate how important each characteristic is to you. Answer according to your feelings about the most recent job you had or about the job you currently hold. Circle the number on the scale that represents your feeling—1 (very unimportant) to 7 (very important).

When you have completed the questionnaire, score it as follows:

Rating for question 5 = ___. Divide by 1 = ___ security.
Rating for questions 9 and 13 = ___. Divide by 2 = ___ social.

Rating for questions 1, 3, and 7 = ___. Divide by 3 = ___ esteem.
Rating for questions 4, 10, 11, and 12 = ___. Divide by 4 = ___ autonomy.
Rating for questions 2, 6, and 8 = ___. Divide by 3 = ___ self-actualization.

The instructor has national norm scores for presidents, vice-presidents, and upper middle-level, lower middle-level, and lower-level managers with which you can compare your *mean* importance scores. How do your scores compare with the scores of managers working in organizations?

1. The feeling of self-esteem a person gets from being in that job	1	2	3	4	5	6	7
2. The opportunity for personal growth and development in that job	1	2	3	4	5	6	7
3. The prestige of the job inside the company (that is, regard received from others in the company)	1	2	3	4	5	6	7
4. The opportunity for independent thought and action in that job	1	2	3	4	5	6	7
5. The feeling of security in that job	1	2	3	4	5	6	7
6. The feeling of self-fulfillment a person gets from being in that position (that is, the feeling of being able to use one's own unique capabilities, realizing one's potential)	1	2	3	4	5	6	7
7. The prestige of the job outside the company (that is, the regard received from others not in the company)	1	2	3	4	5	6	7
8. The feeling of worthwhile accomplishment in that job	1	2	3	4	5	6	7
9. The opportunity in that job to give help to other people	1	2	3	4	5	6	7
10. The opportunity in that job for participation in the setting of goals	1	2	3	4	5	6	7
11. The opportunity in that job for participation in the determination of methods and procedures	1	2	3	4	5	6	7
12. The authority connected with the job	1	2	3	4	5	6	7
13. The opportunity to develop close friendships in the job	1	2	3	4	5	6	7

SOURCE: Lyman W. Porter, *Organizational Patterns of Managerial Job Attitudes* (New York: American Foundation for Management Research, 1964), 17, 19.

Management in Practice: Ethical Dilemma

Compensation Showdown

When Suzanne Lebeau, human resources manager, received a call from Bert Wilkes, comptroller of Farley Glass Works, she anticipated hearing good news to share with the Wage and Bonus Committee. She had already seen numbers to indicate that the year-end bonus plan, which was instituted by her committee in lieu of the traditional guaranteed raises of the past, was going to exceed expectations. It was a real relief to her, because the plan, devised by a committee representing all levels of the workforce, had taken eleven months to complete. It had

also been a real boost to morale at a low point in the company's history. Workers at the glass shower production plant were bringing new effort and energy to their jobs, and Lebeau wanted to see them rewarded.

She was shocked to see Wilkes's face so grim when she arrived for her meeting. "We have a serious problem, Suzanne," Wilkes said to open the meeting. "We ran the numbers from third quarter to project our end-of-the-year figures and discovered that the executive bonus objectives, which are based on net operating profit, would not be met if we paid out the employee bonuses first. The executive bonuses are a major source of their income. We can't ask them to do without their salary to insure a bonus for the workers."

Lebeau felt her temper rising. After all their hard work, she was not going to sit by and watch the employees be disappointed because the accounting department had not structured the employee bonus plan to work with the executive plan. She was afraid they would undo all the good that the bonus plan had done in motivating the plant workers. They had kept their end of the bargain, and the company's high profits were common knowledge in the plant.

What Do You Do?

1. Ask to appear before the executive committee to argue that the year-end bonus plan for workers be honored. Executives could defer their bonuses until the problem in the structure of the compensation plan is resolved.
2. Go along with the comptroller. It isn't fair for the executives to lose so much money. Begin to prepare the workers to not expect much this first year of the plan.
3. Go to the board of directors and ask for a compromise plan that splits the bonuses between the executives and the workers.

SOURCE: Based on Doug Wallace, "Promises to Keep," *What Would You Do?* (reprinted from *Business Ethics*), vol. II (July–August 1993), 11–12. Reprinted with permission from *Business Ethics Magazine*, P.O. Box 8439, Minneapolis, MN 55408 (612) 879-0695.

Surf the Net

1. **Motivation.** Go to **www.recognition-plus.com/motivati. htm** and print out the page "Motivation: Fact vs. Fallacy." For each of the ten points, think of a personal or work-related example that illustrates the point being made. If you disagree with any of the ten points, be prepared to give your reasons during a class discussion on motivation.
2. **Employee Rewards and Recognition.** Bob Nelson, author of two best-selling books on motivation, *1001 Ways to Reward Employees* and *1001 Ways to Energize Employees* provides many excellent resources at his Web site **(www.nelson-motivation.com).** Check out the page titled "Bob Nelson's Guide to the Best Employee Rewards and Recognition Sites on the Web." After checking out several

sites, write a 1 to 2 page summary of what you learned about rewarding and recognizing employees that you believe would be most useful for managers.
3. **Motivational Compensation Programs.** The Foundation for Economic Development **(www.fed.org)** provides a 10-question quiz that allows you to test your knowledge of employee ownership as a means of motivating employees. After completing and scoring the quiz, explore the links provided to learn more about employee ownership. In addition, check out the links on the main page that provide articles, case studies, and research on such topics as "Employee Motivation and Empowerment" and "Trends in Employee Ownership."

Case for Critical Analysis
Bloomingdale's

Bloomingdale's is at the forefront of a quiet revolution sweeping department store retailing. Thousands of hourly sales employees are being converted to commission pay. Bloomingdale's hopes to use commissions to motivate employees to work harder, to attract better salespeople, and to enable them to earn more money. For example, under the old plan, a Bloomingdale's salesclerk in women's wear would earn about $16,000 a year, based on $7 per hour and 0.5 percent commission on $500,000 sales. Under the new plan, the annual pay would be $25,000 based on 5 percent commission on $500,000 sales.

John Palmerio, who works in the men's shoe salon, is enthusiastic about the changeover. His pay has increased an average of $175 per week. But in women's lingerie, employees are less enthusiastic. A target of $1,600 in sales per week is difficult to achieve but is necessary for salespeople to earn their previous

salary and even to keep their jobs. In previous years, the practice of commission pay was limited to big-ticket items such as furniture, appliances, and men's suits, where extra sales skill pays off. The move into small-item purchases may not work as well, but Bloomingdale's and other stores are trying anyway.

One question is whether Bloomingdale's can create more customer-oriented salespeople when they work on commission. They may be reluctant to handle complaints, make returns, and clean shelves, preferring instead to chase customers. Moreover, it cost Bloomingdale's about $1 million per store to install the commission system because of training programs, computer changes, and increased pay in many departments. If the overall impact on service is negative, the increased efficiency may not seem worthwhile.

Questions

1. What theories about motivation underlie the switch from salary to commission pay?
2. Are high-level needs met under the commission system?
3. As a customer, would you prefer to shop where employees are motivated to make commissions?

SOURCES: Based on Francine Schwadel, "Chain Finds Incentives a Hard Sell," *The Wall Street Journal,* July 5, 1990, B4; and Amy Dunkin, "Now Salespeople Really Must Sell for Their Supper," *Business Week,* July 31, 1989, 50–52.

Endnotes

1. David Whitford, "Before & After," *Inc.,* June 1995, 44–50.
2. David Silburt, "Secrets of the Super Sellers," *Canadian Business,* January 1987, 54–59; "Meet the Savvy Supersalesmen," *Fortune,* February 4, 1985, 56–62; Michael Brody, "Meet Today's Young American Worker," *Fortune,* November 11, 1985, 90–98; and Tom Richman, "Meet the Masters. They Could Sell You Anything . . . ," *Inc.,* March 1985, 79–86.
3. Richard M. Steers and Lyman W. Porter, eds., *Motivation and Work Behavior,* 3d ed. (New York: McGraw-Hill, 1983); Don Hellriegel, John W. Slocum, Jr., and Richard W. Woodman, *Organizational Behavior,* 7th ed. (St. Paul, Minn.: West, 1995), 170; and Jerry L. Gray and Frederick A. Starke, *Organizational Behavior: Concepts and Applications,* 4th ed. (New York: Macmillan, 1988), 104–105.
4. Linda Grant, "Happy Workers, High Returns," *Fortune,* January 12, 1998, 81.
5. Anne Fisher, "The 100 Best Companies to Work for in America," *Fortune,* January 12, 1998, 69–70.
6. Steers and Porter, *Motivation.*
7. J. F. Rothlisberger and W. J. Dickson, *Management and the Worker* (Cambridge, Mass.: Harvard University Press, 1939).
8. Abraham F. Maslow, "A Theory of Human Motivation," *Psychological Review* 50 (1943), 370–396.
9. Roberta Maynard, "How to Motivate Low-Wage Workers," *Nation's Business,* May 1997, 35–39.
10. Clayton Alderfer, *Existence, Relatedness and Growth* (New York: Free Press, 1972).
11. Roberta Maynard, "How to Motivate Low-Wage Workers."
12. Nina Munk, "The New Organization Man," *Fortune,* March 16, 1998, 62–74.
13. Frederick Herzberg, "One More Time: How Do You Motivate Employees?" *Harvard Business Review* (January–February 1968), 53–62.
14. Jay Finegan, "Unconventional Wisdom," *Inc.,* December 1994, 44–58.
15. David C. McClelland, *Human Motivation* (Glenview, Ill.: Scott, Foresman, 1985).
16. David C. McClelland, "The Two Faces of Power," in *Organizational Psychology,* ed. D. A. Colb, I. M. Rubin, and J. M. McIntyre (Englewood Cliffs, N.J.: Prentice-Hall, 1971), 73–86.
17. J. Stacy Adams, "Injustice in Social Exchange," in *Advances in Experimental Social Psychology,* 2d ed., ed. L. Berkowitz (New York: Academic Press, 1965); and J. Stacy Adams, "Toward an Understanding of Inequity," *Journal of Abnormal and Social Psychology* (November 1963), 422–436.
18. Ray V. Montagno, "The Effects of Comparison to Others and Primary Experience on Responses to Task Design," *Academy of Management Journal* 28 (1985), 491–498; and Robert P. Vecchio, "Predicting Worker Performance in Inequitable Settings," *Academy of Management Review* 7 (1982), 103–110.
19. "The Double Standard That's Setting Worker against Worker," *Business Week,* April 8, 1985, 70–71.
20. James E. Martin and Melanie M. Peterson, "Two-Tier Wage Structures: Implications for Equity Theory," *Academy of Management Journal* 30 (1987), 297–315.
21. Victor H. Vroom, *Work and Motivation* (New York: Wiley, 1964); B. S. Gorgopoulos, G. M. Mahoney, and N. Jones, "A Path-Goal Approach to Productivity," *Journal of Applied Psychology* 41 (1957), 345–353; and E. E. Lawler III, *Pay and Organizational Effectiveness: A Psychological View* (New York: McGraw-Hill, 1981).
22. Richard L. Daft and Richard M. Steers, *Organizations: A Micro/Macro Approach* (Glenview, Ill.: Scott, Foresman, 1986).
23. Mike Hofman, "Everyone's a Cost Cutter," *Inc.,* July 1998, 117; and Abby Livingston, "Gain-Sharing Encourages Productivity," *Nation's Business,* January 1998, 21–22.
24. Alexander D. Stajkovic and Fred Luthans, "A Meta-Analysis of the Effects of Organizational Behavior Modification on Task Performance, 1975–95," *Academy of Management Journal,* October 1997, 1122–1149; H. Richlin, *Modern Behaviorism* (San Francisco: Freeman, 1970); and B. F. Skinner, *Science and Human Behavior* (New York: Macmillan, 1953).
25. Fred Goodman, "Suite Smarts," *Success,* January, 1998, 11.
26. Stajkovic and Luthans, "A Meta-Analysis of the Effects of Organizational Behavior Modification on Task Performance, 1975–95."
27. Kenneth D. Butterfield and Linda Klebe Trevino, "Punishment from the Manager's Perspective: A Grounded Investigation and Inductive Model," *Academy of Management Journal* 39, no. 6 (December 1996), 1479–1512; and Andrea Casey,

"Voices from the Firing Line: Managers Discuss Punishment in the Workplace," *Academy of Management Executive* 11, no. 3 (1997), 93–94.

28. Tom Peters and Nancy Austin, *A Passion for Excellence: The Leadership Difference* (New York: Random House, 1985), 267.

29. Roberta Maynard, "How to Motivate Low-Wage Workers."

30. L. M. Sarri and G. P. Latham, "Employee Reaction to Continuous and Variable Ratio Reinforcement Schedules Involving a Monetary Incentive," *Journal of Applied Psychology* 67 (1982), 506–508; and R. D. Pritchard, J. Hollenback, and P. J. DeLeo, "The Effects of Continuous and Partial Schedules of Reinforcement on Effort, Performance, and Satisfaction," *Organizational Behavior and Human Performance* 25 (1980), 336–353.

31. "Creating Incentives for Hourly Workers," *Inc.,* July 1986, 89–90.

32. A. J. Vogl, "Carrots, Sticks, and Self-Deception" (an interview with Alfie Kohn), *Across the Board,* January 1994, 39–44.

33. Norm Alster, "What Flexible Workers Can Do," *Fortune,* February 13, 1989, 62–66.

34. J. Richard Hackman and Greg R. Oldham, *Work Redesign* (Reading, Mass.: Addison-Wesley 1980); and J. Richard Hackman and Greg Oldham, "Motivation through the Design of Work: Test of a Theory," *Organizational Behavior and Human Performance* 16 (1976), 250–279.

35. Barbara Ettorre, "Retooling People and Processes," *Management Review,* June 1995, 19–23.

36. Edwin P. Hollander and Lynn R. Offermann, "Power and Leadership in Organizations," *American Psychologist* 45 (February 1990), 179–189.

37. Jay A. Conger and Rabindra N. Kanungo, "The Empowerment Process: Integrating Theory and Practice," *Academy of Management Review* 13 (1988), 471–482.

38. Thomas A. Stewart, "New Ways to Exercise Power," *Fortune* 6 (November 1989), 52–64.

39. David E. Bowen and Edward E. Lawler III, "The Empowerment of Service Workers: What, Why, How, and When," *Sloan Management Review* (spring 1992), 31–39; and Ray W. Coye and James A. Belohav, "An Exploratory Analysis of Employee Participation," *Group and Organization Management* 20, no. 1, (March 1995), 4–17.

40. John Holusha, "Grace Pastiak's 'Web of Inclusion,'" *The New York Times,* May 5, 1991, F1, F6.

41. Arno Penzias, "New Paths to Success," *Fortune,* June 12, 1995, 90–94.

42. Ralph Stayer, "How I Learned to Let My Workers Lead," *Harvard Business Review,* November–December 1990, 66–83.

43. This discussion is based on Robert C. Ford and Myron D. Fottler, "Empowerment: A Matter of Degree," *Academy of Management Executive* 9, no. 3 (1995), 21–31.

44. Jay A. Conger and Rabindra N. Kanungo, "The Empowerment Process: Integrating Theory and Practice," *Academy of Management Review* 13 (1998), 471–482.

45. Whitford, "Before & After."

Chapter 18

LEARNING OBJECTIVES

After studying this chapter, you should be able to

❋ **Explain why communication is essential for effective management and describe how nonverbal behavior and listening affect communication among people.**

❋ **Explain how managers use communication to persuade and influence others.**

❋ **Describe the concept of channel richness, and explain how communication channels influence the quality of communication among managers.**

❋ **Explain the difference between formal and informal organizational communications and the importance of each for organization management.**

❋ **Describe team communication and how structure influences communication outcomes.**

❋ **Discuss how open communication and dialogue can enhance team spirit and effectiveness.**

❋ **Describe barriers to organizational communication, and suggest ways to avoid or overcome them.**

Communicating in Organizations

MANAGEMENT PROBLEM

For over a quarter of a century, Childress Buick/Kia Co. had served the Phoenix area, gaining a reputation as a top Buick dealer. The family-owned dealership prided itself on good communication and quality service, and its customer retention rate was 40 percent higher than the industry average. Founder and president George Ray Childress, affectionately known as "Mr. C," constantly looked for ways to help his employees reach their personal and professional potential, and he jumped at the chance to add computer technology to the business. By the time Childress discovered that the computer system was inadequate, system snafus were creating long lines of disgruntled customers and a workforce of bickering, stressed-out employees. Sales were falling, and the dealership's CSI (customer service index) plummeted. Mr. C. pulled his son Rusty from head of marketing to take over a new role—owner-relations manager. His assignment was not to fix the computer but to fix organizational communications, with the goal of improving customer and employee satisfaction.[1]

If you were Rusty Childress, how would you improve communications at Childress Buick? What steps do you think he took to enhance communications and pull people together?

Managers at E-commerce companies strive to maintain effective communications with employees, customers, and even competitors to keep up with rapid changes in the industry. Even though they're competitors, the CEOs of Internet start-up companies often sit on each other's boards, invest in each other's companies, and ask for each other's advice. This cross-company communication provides a form of insurance for managers such as Techwave CEO Dwayne Walker, who sits on the board of Accountingnet. In the photo, Walker and Accountingnet CEO Derek Doke share advice.

The management at Childress Buick/Kia believed in communication but faced problems in breaking down communication barriers. In today's intensely competitive environment, top managers at many companies are trying to improve communication. Jim Chesterton, CEO of A. W. Chesterton Co., holds quarterly meetings at which employees can ask him about anything and everything. Similarly, at Cisco Systems, every year during their birthday month employees get an invitation to a birthday breakfast with CEO John Chambers, where they can put their toughest questions directly to the top executive.[2] It isn't always easy when workers confront top managers with difficult questions or challenge them regarding management failings, but getting candid feedback from employees helps executives spot problems or recognize opportunities that might otherwise be missed.

These executives are interested in staying connected with employees and customers and with shaping company direction. To do so, they must be in touch; hence they excel at personal communications. Nonmanagers often are amazed at how much energy successful executives put into communication. Consider the comment about Robert Strauss, former chairman of the Democratic National Committee and former ambassador to Russia:

> One of his friends says, "His network is everywhere. It ranges from bookies to bank presidents. . . ."
> He seems to find time to make innumerable phone calls to "keep in touch"; he cultivates secretaries as well as senators; he will befriend a middle-level White House aide whom other important officials won't bother with. Every few months, he sends candy to the White House switchboard operators.[3]

This chapter explains why executives such as Robert Strauss, Jim Chesterton, and John Chambers are effective communicators. First we will see how managers' jobs require communication. Next, we will define *communication* and describe a model of the communication process. Then we will consider the interpersonal aspects of communication, including communication channels, persuasion, and listening skills, that affect managers' ability to communicate. After, we will look at the organization as a whole and consider formal upward and downward communications as well as informal communications. Finally, we will examine barriers to communication and how managers can overcome them.

Communication and the Manager's Job

How important is communication? Consider this: Managers spend at least 80 percent of every working day in direct communication with others. In other words, 48 minutes of every hour is spent in meetings, on the telephone, or talking informally while walking around. The other 20 percent of a typical manager's time is spent doing desk work, most of which is also communication in the form of reading and writing.[4] Exhibit 18.1 illustrates the crucial position of management in the information network. Managers gather

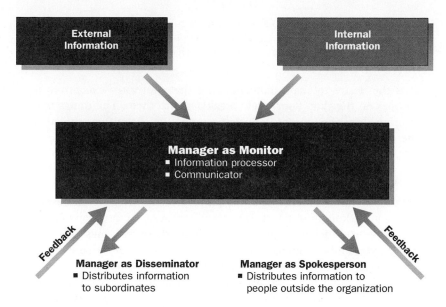

Exhibit 18.1
The Manager as Information Nerve Center

SOURCE: Adapted from Henry Mintzberg, *The Nature of Managerial Work* (New York: Harper & Row, 1973), 72.

important information from both inside and outside the organization and then distribute appropriate information to others who need it.

Communication permeates every management function described in Chapter 1.[5] For example, when managers perform the planning function, they gather information; write letters, memos, and reports; and then meet with other managers to explain the plan. When managers lead, they communicate to share a vision of what the organization can be and motivate employees to help achieve it. When managers organize, they gather information about the state of the organization and communicate a new structure to others. Communication skills are a fundamental part of every managerial activity.

What Is Communication?

Before going farther, let us determine what communication is. A professor at Harvard once asked a class to define communication by drawing pictures. Most students drew a manager speaking or writing. Some placed "speech balloons" next to their characters; others showed pages flying from a typewriter. "No," the professor told the class, "none of you has captured the essence of communication." He went on to explain that communication means "to share"—not "to speak" or "to write."

Communication thus can be defined as the process by which information is exchanged and understood by two or more people, usually with the intent to motivate or influence behavior. Communication is not just sending information. This distinction between *sharing* and *proclaiming* is crucial for successful management. A manager who does not listen is like a used-car salesperson who claims, "I sold a car—they just did not buy it." Management communication is a two-way street that includes listening and other forms of feedback. Effective communication, in the words of one expert, is as follows:

> When two people interact, they put themselves into each other's shoes, try to perceive the world as the other person perceives it, try to predict how the other

communication

The process by which information is exchanged and understood by two or more people, usually with the intent to motivate or influence behavior.

will respond. Interaction involves reciprocal role-taking, the mutual employment of empathetic skills. The goal of interaction is the merger of self and other,
a complete ability to anticipate, predict, and behave in accordance with the joint
needs of self and other.[6]

It is the desire to share understanding that motivates executives to visit
employees on the shop floor or eat breakfast with them. The things managers
learn from direct communication with employees shape their understanding
of the corporation.

The Communication Process

Many people think communication is simple because they communicate without conscious thought or effort. However, communication usually is complex,
and the opportunities for sending or receiving the wrong messages are innu-
merable. No doubt, you have heard someone say, "But that's not what I
meant!" Have you ever received directions you thought were clear and yet still
got lost? How often have you wasted time on misunderstood instructions?

To more fully understand the complexity of the communication process,
note the key elements outlined in Exhibit 18.2. Two common elements in
every communication situation are the sender and the receiver. The *sender* is
anyone who wishes to convey an idea or concept to others, to seek information, or to express a thought or emotion. The *receiver* is the person to
whom the message is sent. The sender **encodes** the idea by selecting symbols with which to compose a message. The **message** is the tangible formulation of the idea that is sent to the receiver. The message is sent through a
channel, which is the communication carrier. The channel can be a formal
report, a telephone call, or a face-to-face meeting. The receiver **decodes** the
symbols to interpret the meaning of the message. Encoding and decoding are
potential sources for communication errors, because knowledge, attitudes,
and background act as filters and create "noise" when translating from symbols to meaning. Finally, **feedback** occurs when the receiver responds to the
sender's communication with a return message. Without feedback, the communication is *one-way;* with feedback, it is *two-way.* Feedback is a powerful
aid to communication effectiveness, because it enables the sender to determine whether the receiver correctly interpreted the message.

Managers who are effective communicators understand and use the circu-
lar nature of communication. For example, James Treybig of Tandem Computers, Inc., widened the open-door policy in order to communicate with
employees. Treybig appears on a monthly television program broadcast over
the company's in-house television station. Employees around the world watch
the show and call in their questions and comments. The television is the
channel through which Treybig sends his encoded message. Employees
decode and interpret the message and encode their feedback, which is sent
through the channel of the telephone hookup. The communication circuit is
complete. At Graphic Solutions, a custom printer in Burr Ridge, Illinois, owners Suzanne Zaccone and her brother Bob maintain communication channels
by meeting monthly with a few workers from each department. Workers'
questions and comments range from daily workplace concerns to the company's long-range plans.[7] Jim Treybig and the Zaccones understand the elements of communication and have developed systems that work.

encode
To select symbols with which to compose a message.

message
The tangible formulation of an idea to be sent to a receiver.

channel
The carrier of a communication.

decode
To translate the symbols used in a message for the purpose of interpreting its meaning.

feedback
A response by the receiver to the sender's communication.

Communicating among People

The communication model in Exhibit 18.2 illustrates the components that must be mastered for effective communication. Communications can break down if sender and receiver do not encode or decode language in the same way.[8] The selection of communication channels can determine whether the message is distorted by noise and interference. The listening skills of both parties can determine whether a message is truly shared. Thus, for managers to be effective communicators, they must understand how interpersonal factors such as communication channels, nonverbal behavior, and listening all work to enhance or detract from communication.

Communication Channels

Managers have a choice of many channels through which to communicate to other managers or employees. A manager may discuss a problem face-to-face, use the telephone, send an electronic message, write a memo or letter, or put an item in a newsletter, depending on the nature of the message. Recent research has attempted to explain how managers select communication channels to enhance communication effectiveness.[9] The research has found that channels differ in their capacity to convey information. Just as a pipeline's physical characteristics limit the kind and amount of liquid that can be pumped through it, a communication channel's physical characteristics limit the kind and amount of information that can be conveyed among managers. The channels available to managers can be classified into a hierarchy based on information richness. **Channel richness** is the amount of information that can be transmitted during a communication episode. The hierarchy of channel richness is illustrated in Exhibit 18.3.

    The capacity of an information channel is influenced by three characteristics: (1) the ability to handle multiple cues simultaneously; (2) the ability to facilitate rapid, two-way feedback; and (3) the ability to establish a personal focus for the communication. Face-to-face discussion is the richest medium, because it permits direct experience, multiple information cues,

channel richness
The amount of information that can be transmitted during a communication episode.

Exhibit **18.2**   *A Model of the Communication Process*

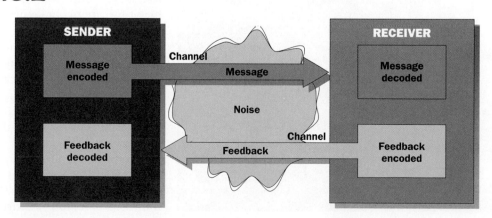

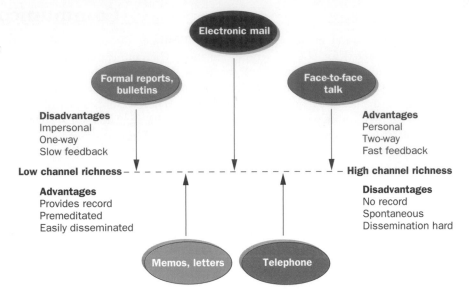

Exhibit *18.3*

A Continuum of Channel Richness

Electronic mail

Formal reports, bulletins

Face-to-face talk

Disadvantages
Impersonal
One-way
Slow feedback

Advantages
Personal
Two-way
Fast feedback

Low channel richness — — — — — — — — — — — — — — — High channel richness

Advantages
Provides record
Premeditated
Easily disseminated

Disadvantages
No record
Spontaneous
Dissemination hard

Memos, letters   **Telephone**

Live town-hall meetings helped Ford employees communicate directly with former Chairman and CEO Alex Trotman and Ford Automotive Operations President Ed Hagenlocker. The meetings were part of Ford's efforts to help employees face the challenges of a rapidly changing world with flexibility and a willingness to become leaders. Ford executives selected a rich channel to communicate a nonroutine message and give employees a chance to ask questions. This televised meeting was based in Dearborn, Michigan, but was simultaneously broadcast in five languages, with live, two-way satellite links, to employee audiences around the world.

immediate feedback, and personal focus. Face-to-face discussions facilitate the assimilation of broad cues and deep, emotional understanding of the situation. For example, Tony Burns, CEO of Ryder Systems, Inc., likes to handle things face-to-face: "You can look someone in the eyes, and you can tell by the look in his eyes or the inflection in his voice what the real problem or question or answer is."[10] Telephone conversations and interactive electronic media, such as voice mail and electronic mail, while increasing the *speed* of communication, lack the element of "being there." Eye contact, gaze, blush, posture, and body language cues are eliminated. In recognition of the need for channel richness, interactive communication is taking on the immediacy of "being there" through increased use of video conferencing. Written media that are personalized, such as memos, notes, and letters, can be personally focused, but they convey only the cues written on paper and are slow to provide feedback. Impersonal written media, including fliers, bulletins, and standard computer reports, are the lowest in richness. These channels are not focused on a single receiver, use limited information cues, and do not permit feedback.

It is important for managers to understand that each communication channel has advantages and disadvantages, and that each can be an effective means of communication in the appropriate circumstances.[11] Channel selection depends on whether the message is routine or nonroutine. *Nonroutine messages* typically are ambiguous, concern novel events, and impose great potential for misunderstanding. Nonroutine messages often are characterized by time pressure and surprise. Managers can communicate nonroutine messages effectively only by selecting rich channels. On the other hand, routine communications are simple and straightforward. *Routine messages* convey data or statistics or simply put into words what managers already agree on and understand. Routine messages can be efficiently communicated through a channel lower in richness. Written communications also should be used when the audience is widely dispersed or when the communication is "official" and a permanent record is required.[12]

Consider a CEO trying to work out a press release with public relations people about a plant explosion that injured 15 employees. If the press release must be ready in three hours, the communication is truly nonroutine and forces a rich information exchange. The group will meet face-to-face, brainstorm ideas, and provide rapid feedback to resolve disagreement and convey the correct information. If the CEO has three days to prepare the release, less information capacity is needed. The CEO and public relations people might begin developing the press release with an exchange of memos and telephone calls.

The key is to select a channel to fit the message. One successful manager who understands channel selection is Jack Welch, chairman and CEO of General Electric.

GENERAL ELECTRIC
www.ge.com

For more than 17 years, Jack Welch has led General Electric to one revenue and earnings record after another and helped increase the market share of GE from $12 billion in 1981 to about $280 billion today. Welch, a master at communication, spends more than half his time on what he calls "people issues." He has created a sense of informality and sharing that is rare for a huge company such as GE. His preferred form of communication typically is personal notes accompanied by a phone call. He is well known for dashing off handwritten notes to people throughout the company to congratulate them for a job well done or to explain a controversial decision. For example, when Welch vetoed the idea of buying AT&T Universal Card, he sent a note to the manager at GE Capital who had spent hundreds of hours studying the proposed acquisition. He wanted her to know that despite his decision, he had been impressed with her analysis and presentation. There are no forms letters or memos from Welch—not to employees, managers, top executives, or even board members. Everything is handled with personal notes, phone calls, or face-to-face communication.

Welch kicks off each year for GE with a session in Boca Raton, Florida, for the top 500 executives. The meeting gives Welch a chance to set the agenda for the year and to celebrate the company's newest heroes. Managers from the various businesses can exchange ideas with their counterparts. Informal chat sessions may last until 2 or 3 A.M., with Welch himself participating. His wrap-up talk at the end of the meeting is videotaped, translated into eight different languages, and dispatched to GE locations around the world, where managers use it to spark communication with their own teams about the issues GE will face in the coming year. Other formal means of communication are the Corporate Executive Council sessions held each quarter, at which GE's top 30 officers track progress and swap ideas. These meetings have earned descriptions from executives such as "food fights" or "free-for-alls" because all information—good and bad—is shared openly. At these sessions Welch gets unfiltered information.

One of the most important forms of communication for Welch is the informal, unscheduled communication in which he participates almost daily. Every week, there are unexpected visits to plants and offices, during which Welch talks directly with GE people at all levels. He regularly schedules impromptu luncheons with managers several layers below him to get their ideas and perspectives. Indeed, in an average year, Welch directly meets and talks with several thousand General Electric employees. He uses a metaphor of the company as an old-fashioned grocery store, where he can mentally roll up his sleeves, get behind the counter, and get to know employees and customers intimately.[13]

Jack Welch's communication skills have helped him wield enormous influence over the most far-flung, complex organization in American business. Leaders such as Welch understand that, in addition to the message content, the choice of communication channel can convey a symbolic meaning to the receiver. Welch's decision to communicate through personal notes, phone calls, and face-to-face meetings rather than by form letters and memos signals to employees that he cares about them as individuals.

Persuasion and Influence

Communication is used not only to convey information, but to persuade and influence people. Managers use communication to sell employees on the vision for the organization and influence them to behave in such a way as to accomplish the vision. While communication skills have always been important to managers, the ability to persuade and influence others is more critical today than ever before. The command-and-control mindset of managers telling workers what to do and how to do it is gone. Businesses are run largely by cross-functional teams who are actively involved in making decisions. Issuing directives is no longer an appropriate or effective way to get things done.[14] Therefore, managers should understand how communication can be used to persuade and influence others.

Managers can enrich their communication encounters by paying attention to the language they use as well as the channels of communication they select to convey their messages. To persuade and influence, managers connect with others on an emotional level by using symbols, metaphors, and stories to express their messages. Patrick Kelly, founder of Physician Sales & Service (now PSS/World Medical Inc.), believes in the power of storytelling to keep people unified and focused on shared goals. "We've never had a policy manual," Kelly says. "The way we pass along our values is to sit around the campfire and share stories." In the early days of founding PSS, Kelly spent much of his time visiting various company locations and telling stories about his own life, as well as discussing challenges facing the company.[15] David Armstrong, president of Armstrong International, wrote *Management by Storying Around* after he noticed the way people listened to his minister's stories each Sunday.[16] Even when people had heard a story many times, their attention perked up. Armstrong saw that people loved to hear stories and decided to use that to enhance his management and communication skills. He began using stories to replace rules and regulations. For example, he told a story about an executive traveling for the company who spent money just the way he did at home. This story gradually replaced Armstrong International's travel and entertainment expense rulebook. Stories eventually replaced the entire policy manual.

Using symbols and stories also helps managers make sense of a fast-changing environment in ways that members throughout the organization can understand. Managers help inspire desirable behaviors for change by tapping into the imaginations of their subordinates. If we think back to our early school years, we may remember that the most effective lessons often were couched in stories. Consider the meaning conveyed by a manager telling the following story: "Every morning in Africa, a gazelle wakes up. It knows it must outrun the fastest lion or it will be killed. Every morning in Africa, a lion wakes up. It knows it must run faster than the slowest gazelle or it will starve. It doesn't matter whether you're a lion or a gazelle—when the sun comes up, you'd better be running."[17]

Presenting hard facts and figures rarely has the same power as telling vivid stories. Evidence of the compatibility of stories with human thinking was demonstrated by a study at Stanford Business School.[18] The point was to convince MBA students that a company practiced a policy of avoiding layoffs. For some students, only a story was used. For others, statistical data were provided that showed little turnover compared to competitors. For other students, statistics and stories were combined, and yet other students were shown the company's official policy statements. Of all these approaches, the students presented with a vivid story alone were most convinced that the company truly practiced a policy of avoiding layoffs.

Nonverbal Communication

Managers also use symbols to communicate what is important. Managers are watched, and their behavior, appearance, actions, and attitudes are symbolic of what they value and expect of others.

Nonverbal communication refers to messages sent through human actions and behaviors rather than through words.[19] Although most nonverbal communication is unconscious or subconscious on our part, it represents a major portion of the messages we send and receive. Most managers are astonished to learn that words themselves carry little meaning. Major parts of the shared understanding from communication come from the nonverbal messages of facial expression, voice, mannerisms, posture, and dress.

Nonverbal communication occurs mostly face-to-face. One researcher found three sources of communication cues during face-to-face communication: the verbal, which are the actual spoken words; the vocal, which include the pitch, tone, and timbre of a person's voice; and facial expressions. According to this study, the relative weights of these three factors in message interpretation are as follows: verbal impact, 7 percent; vocal impact, 38 percent; and facial impact, 55 percent.[20]

This research strongly implies that "it's not what you say but how you say it." A manager's tone of voice or glint in the eye may signal something entirely different from his or her words. Nonverbal messages convey thoughts and feelings with greater force than do our most carefully selected words. Body language often communicates our real feelings eloquently. Thus, while the conscious mind may be formulating vocal messages such as "I'm happy" or "Congratulations on your promotion," the body language may be signaling true feelings through blushing, perspiring, glancing, crying, or avoiding eye contact. When the verbal and nonverbal messages are contradictory, the receiver may be confused and usually will give more weight to behavioral actions than to verbal messages.[21]

nonverbal communication
A communication transmitted through actions and behaviors rather than through words.

A manager's office also sends powerful nonverbal cues. For example, what do the following seating arrangements mean if used by your supervisor? (1) She stays behind her desk, and you sit in a straight chair on the opposite side. (2) The two of you sit in straight chairs away from her desk, perhaps at a table. (3) The two of you sit in a seating arrangement consisting of a sofa and easy chair. To most people, the first arrangement indicates "I'm the boss here" or "I'm in authority." The second arrangement indicates "This is serious business." The third indicates a more casual and friendly "Let's get to know each other."[22] Nonverbal messages can be a powerful asset to communication if they complement and support verbal messages. Managers should pay close attention to nonverbal behavior when communicating. They must learn to coordinate their verbal and nonverbal messages and at the same time be sensitive to what their peers, subordinates, and supervisors are saying nonverbally.

Listening

listening
The skill of receiving messages to accurately grasp facts and feelings to interpret the genuine meaning.

One of the most important tools of manager communication is listening, both to employees and customers. Most managers now recognize that important information flows from the bottom up, not the top down, and managers had better be tuned in.[23] In the communication model in Exhibit 18.2, the listener is responsible for message reception, which is a vital link in the communication process. **Listening** involves the skill of grasping both facts and feelings to interpret a message's genuine meaning. Only then can the manager provide the appropriate response. Listening requires attention, energy, and skill. Lt. General William G. Pagonis, who led the U.S. Army's 22nd Support Command for the Persian Gulf War, believes that one of the keys to effective leadership in war or business is to develop effective listening skills and put them into practice. He recalls a wise commanding officer once telling him, "Never pass up the opportunity to remain silent."[24]

Many people do not listen effectively. They concentrate on formulating what they are going to say next rather than on what is being said to them. Our listening efficiency, as measured by the amount of material understood and remembered by subjects 48 hours after listening to a 10-minute message, is, on average, no better than 25 percent.[25]

What constitutes good listening? Exhibit 18.4 gives ten keys to effective listening and illustrates a number of ways to distinguish a bad from a good listener. A good listener finds areas of interest, is flexible, works hard at listening, and uses thought speed to mentally summarize, weigh, and anticipate what the speaker says.

Merrill Lynch superbroker Richard F. Green explained the importance of listening to organizational success: "If you talk, you'll like me. If I talk, I'll like you—but if I do the talking, my business will not be served. Green builds long-term relationships with his clients by listening. Rick Pitino, coach of the Boston Celtics, also believes in the power of listening. His rule for improving your communication skills is to listen four times as much as you speak. Pitino tells a story of how, as coach of the University of Kentucky Wildcats, he failed to recruit a hot prospect because he spent the entire time talking, impressing the player and his family with the greatness of the Wildcats, the team's half-million-dollar weight room and private plane, and the thrill of playing before Kentucky's worshipful fans. Having learned his lesson, Pitino took a different approach with prospect Tony Delk, a player thought unlikely

Exhibit 18.4 *Ten Keys to Effective Listening*

Keys	Poor Listener	Good Listener
1. Listen actively	Is passive, laid back	Asks questions, paraphrases what is said
2. Find areas of interest	Tunes out dry subjects	Looks for opportunities, new learning
3. Resist distractions	Is easily distracted	Fights or avoids distractions; tolerates bad habits; knows how to concentrate
4. Capitalize on the fact that thought is faster than speech	Tends to daydream with slow speakers	Challenges, anticipates, mentally summarizes; weighs the evidence; listens between the lines to tone of voice
5. Be responsive	Is minimally involved	Nods; shows interest, give and take, positive feedback
6. Judge content, not delivery	Tunes out if delivery is poor	Judges content; skips over delivery errors
7. Hold one's fire	Has preconceptions, starts to argue	Does not judge until comprehension is complete
8. Listen for ideas	Listens for facts	Listens to central themes
9. Work at listening	Shows no energy output; faked attention	Works hard, exhibits active body state, eye contact
10. Exercise one's mind	Resists difficult material in favor of light, recreational material	Uses heavier material as exercise for the mind

SOURCES: Adapted from Sherman K. Okum, "How to Be a Better Listener," *Nation's Business* (August 1975), 62; and Philip Morgan and Kent Baker, "Building a Professional Image: Improving Listening Behavior," *Supervisory Management* (November 1985), 34–38.

to choose the University of Kentucky. When he met with Delk and his parents, Pitino didn't do much talking. Instead he asked a lot of questions—what Delk wanted from a coach; what the parents wanted for their son in a college. For nearly an hour, Pitino only asked questions and listened to the answers. Not only did Pitino successfully recruit Delk, but four years later the star player helped lead Kentucky to its sixth national championship. It's a story Pitino says he likes to tell business groups because "it illustrates how important it is to listen to people."[26]

Organizational Communication

Another aspect of management communication concerns the organization as a whole. Organization-wide communications typically flow in three directions—downward, upward, and horizontally. Managers are responsible for establishing and maintaining formal channels of communication in these three directions. Managers also use informal channels, which means they get out of their offices and mingle with employees.

Formal Communication Channels

Formal communication channels are those that flow within the chain of command or task responsibility defined by the organization. The three formal channels and the types of information conveyed in each are illustrated in Exhibit 18.5.[27] Downward and upward communication are the primary forms of communication used in most traditional, vertically organized companies. The learning organization, in contrast, emphasizes horizontal communication, with people constantly sharing information across departments and levels. The Technology box discusses how one company shares

formal communication channel
A communication channel that flows within the chain of command or task responsibility defined by the organization.

Exhibit **18.5** — *Downward, Upward, and Horizontal Communication in Organizations*

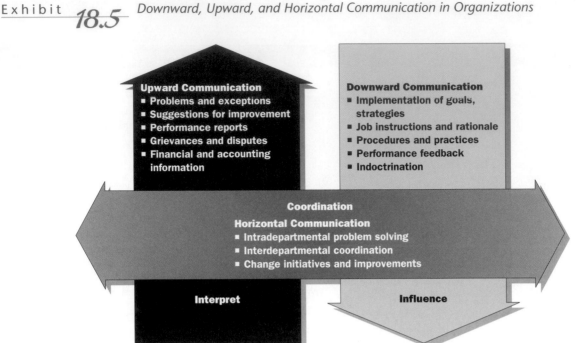

SOURCE: Adapted from Richard L. Daft and Richard M. Steers, *Organizations: A Micro/Macro Approach,* 538. Copyright © 1986 by Scott, Foresman and Company. Used by permission.

information across time and space as well as across functional departments. Electronic communications, such as E-mail, have made it easier than ever for information to flow in all directions. For example, when used appropriately and in the right organizational environment, E-mail can improve upward communication flow because employees can contact managers at any time to ask questions or offer ideas, without having to wait for a meeting. Suzanne Zaccone of Graphic Solutions prefers face-to-face communication with her 65 employees, but when she's on the road, she encourages them to communicate with her through electronic mail.[28]

Downward Communication. The most familiar and obvious flow of formal communication, **downward communication,** refers to the messages and information sent from top management to subordinates in a downward direction. For example, Mike Olson, plant manager at Ryerson Midwest Coil Processing, holds monthly meetings to discuss financial data and performance analyses with all employees. He also uses other forms of communication. Because workers were continuously dropping expensive power tools, Olson hung price tags on the tools to show the replacement cost; workers solved the problem by finding a way to hook up the tools so they wouldn't be dropped. Olson's communication helps workers see how their actions affect the entire company and creates a climate of working *together* for solutions.[29] Top managers at Cincinnati Milacron also found a creative approach to downward communication. Several years ago, Alan Shaffer and two other vice presidents dressed as the actors in the comedy-horror movie *Ghostbusters* to address a room full of 500 salespeople. To stress the need for a new way of thinking, the vice presidents jumped on stage, shouted, "We don't know what causes

downward communication
Messages sent from top management down to subordinates.

Creating Community At Rykodisc

Rykodisc, Inc., the largest independent record label in the United States, was first outlined on the back of a napkin in 1983, when the four founders decided to kick around ideas about U.S. production of compact discs, which at that time were produced solely in Japan and Germany. The biggest problem was that the partners were spread all over the country—from Los Angeles to Philadelphia, from Minneapolis to Salem, Massachusetts—and no one intended to move.

The solution from the beginning was constant information sharing as the cornerstone of the organizational culture. The founders attribute Rykodisc's success to the company's obsession with keeping every type of information constantly flowing among all employees, no matter where they're situated geographically, functionally, or hierarchically. All Rykodisc employees, from the mailroom clerk to the chief financial officer, write and circulate short weekly memos, so that everyone knows what everyone else in the company is doing. Armed with information, Rykodisc employees consistently outproduce larger competitors. The founders and department heads also hold weekly conference calls to talk about specific problems or opportunities.

At first, Rykodisc built its communications primarily around phone calls, faxes, and airline schedules, avoiding networks and E-mail because of a fear that less personal communications might erode the sense of community. Yet it was new technology that led to the birth of Rykodisc, and the founders soon realized that technology could serve as another tool to keep far-flung employees communicating. "Technology itself is a cool medium," says founder Dan Rose, "[but] the way we use it we make it a warm process." He's found that some employees are more comfortable leaving an E-mail message than walking into his office or calling him on the phone. Rose answers all internal E-mail personally and now corresponds regularly with some employees he'd had little interaction with before the company networked.

Rykodisc turned to its own employees rather than to outside talent to make sure its high-tech systems are developed and used in a way that brings people together rather than keeping them apart. One highly motivated employee, Lars Murray, is now responsible for maintaining the Rykodisc Web page. Visitors to the site can download art and listen to music samples from the Rykodisc catalog. The company is gearing up for the day when music will be distributed online. Rykodisc knows that connection to the customer is a vital part of information flow.

For a company intent on sharing information as broadly as possible, high technology is another tool to maintain a sense of community and keep employees working toward the common goal of "delivering music to the customer."

www.rykodisc.com

SOURCE: Hal Plotkin, "Spin Doctors," *Inc. Technology* 2 (1995), 60–61.

paradigms, but we got 'em in the room," and then started shooting with their laser guns. The managers busted an outmoded paradigm that day in a fun-filled way. Within five years, those 500 salespeople had helped Cincinnati Milacron evolve from a seller of machine tools into a leading global supplier of industrial products, machinery for plastics goods, and machinery systems used to make everything from backhoes to airplanes.[30]

Managers can communicate downward to employees in many ways. Some of the most common are through speeches, messages in company newsletters, electronic mail, information leaflets tucked into pay envelopes, material on bulletin boards, and policy and procedure manuals. At Veri-Fone Inc., managers believe there's no such thing as giving employees too much information. They flood employees' home mailboxes with newsletters, total-compensation updates, benefit-program descriptions, and stock option plans. Since VeriFone is largely a "virtual" company, in which geographical dispersion is the operating principle, the company also makes extensive use of electronic mail. CEO Hatim Tyabji distributes E-mail about leadership and invites employees to challenge him if he is not living up to his own precepts.[31]

Downward communication in an organization usually encompasses the following topics:

1. *Implementation of goals and strategies.* Communicating new strategies and goals provides information about specific targets and expected behaviors. It gives direction for lower levels of the organization. Example: "The new quality campaign is for real. We must improve product quality if we are to survive."

2. *Job instructions and rationale.* These are directives on how to do a specific task and how the job relates to other organizational activities. Example: "Purchasing should order the bricks now so the work crew can begin construction of the building in two weeks."

3. *Procedures and practices.* These are messages defining the organization's policies, rules, regulations, benefits, and structural arrangements. Example: "After your first 90 days of employment, you are eligible to enroll in our company-sponsored savings plan."

4. *Performance feedback.* These messages appraise how well individuals and departments are doing their jobs. Example: "Joe, your work on the computer network has greatly improved the efficiency of our ordering process."

5. *Indoctrination.* These messages are designed to motivate employees to adopt the company's mission and cultural values and to participate in special ceremonies, such as picnics and United Way campaigns. Example: "The company thinks of its employees as family and would like to invite everyone to attend the annual picnic and fair on March 3."

The major problem with downward communication is *drop off,* the distortion or loss of message content. Although formal communications are a powerful way to reach all employees, much information gets lost—25 percent or so each time a message is passed from one person to the next. In addition, the message can be distorted if it travels a great distance from its originating source to the ultimate receiver. A tragic example is the following:

> A reporter was present at a hamlet burned down by the U.S. Army 1st Air Cavalry Division in 1967. Investigations showed that the order from the Division headquarters to the brigade was: "On no occasion must hamlets be burned down."
> The brigade radioed the battalion: "Do not burn down any hamlets unless you are absolutely convinced that the Viet Cong are in them."
> The battalion radioed the infantry company at the scene: "If you think there are any Viet Cong in the hamlet, burn it down."
> The company commander ordered his troops: "Burn down that hamlet."[32]

Information drop off cannot be completely avoided, but the techniques described in the previous sections can reduce it substantially. Using the right communication channel, consistency between verbal and nonverbal messages and active listening can maintain communication accuracy as it moves down the organization.

upward communication

Messages transmitted from the lower to the higher level in the organization's hierarchy.

Upward Communication.   Formal **upward communication** includes messages that flow from the lower to the higher levels in the organization's hierarchy. Most organizations take pains to build in healthy channels for upward communication. Employees need to air grievances, report progress, and provide feedback on management initiatives. Coupling a healthy flow of upward and downward communication ensures that the communication circuit between managers and employees is complete.[33] Five types of information communicated upward are the following:

1. *Problems and exceptions.* These messages describe serious problems with and exceptions to routine performance in order to make senior managers aware of difficulties. Example: "The printer has been out of operation for two days, and it will be at least a week before a new one arrives."

2. *Suggestions for improvement.* These messages are ideas for improving task-related procedures to increase quality or efficiency. Example: "I think we should eliminate step 2 in the audit procedure because it takes a lot of time and produces no results."

3. *Performance reports.* These messages include periodic reports that inform management how individuals and departments are performing. Example: "We completed the audit report for Smith & Smith on schedule but are one week behind on the Jackson report."

4. *Grievances and disputes.* These messages are employee complaints and conflicts that travel up the hierarchy for a hearing and possible resolution. Example: "The manager of operations research cannot get the cooperation of the Lincoln plant for the study of machine utilization."

5. *Financial and accounting information.* These messages pertain to costs, accounts receivable, sales volume, anticipated profits, return on investment, and other matters of interest to senior managers. Example: "Costs are 2 percent over budget, but sales are 10 percent ahead of target, so the profit picture for the third quarter is excellent."

Managers at the plumbing and air-conditioning contractor company, TDINDUSTRIES, facilitate upward communication through their commitment to the philosophy of "servant leadership." Upward communication and active listening allow managers to respect the interests and heed the preferences of workers. Apprentices, such as those in the photo being taught to install plumbing systems, look forward to being part of the company's democratic system in addition to enjoying ownership of part of the 75 percent of the company's stock that is owned by lower-level employees.

Many organizations make a great effort to facilitate upward communication. Mechanisms include suggestion boxes, employee surveys, open-door policies, management information system reports, and face-to-face conversations between workers and executives.

William J. O'Brien, CEO of Hanover Insurance Company, points out: "The fundamental movement in business in the next 25 years will be in the dispersing of power, to give meaning and fulfillment to employees in a way that avoids chaos and disorder." Power sharing means inviting upward communication. At Pacific Gas & Electric, CEO Richard A. Clark keeps employee communication lines open with employee surveys, biannual video presentations, and monthly brown-bag lunches to hear questions and complaints.[34]

Despite these efforts, however, barriers to accurate upward communication exist. Managers may resist hearing about employee problems, or employees may not trust managers sufficiently to push information upward.[35] Innovative companies search for ways to ensure that information gets to top managers without distortion. IBM's respected Speak Up program consists of anonymous employee letters or E-mails regularly channeled to management for action. Top managers at Golden Corral, a restaurant chain with headquarters in Raleigh, North Carolina, spend at least one weekend a year in the trenches—cutting steaks, rolling silverware, setting tables, and taking out the trash. This gives managers a better understanding of the needs of both employees and customers. For example, while taking out the trash at the restaurant, executives discovered that the narrow dimensions of the trash disposal area made it almost impossible for two workers to lift the heavy cans into a large trash container. It was a situation that was not only inefficient but also ripe for employee injury—and one that managers would not have known about without the innovative program. By understanding the daily routines and challenges of waiters, chefs, and other employees at their restaurants, Golden Corral executives increase their awareness of how management actions affect others.[36]

horizontal communication
The lateral or diagonal exchange of messages among peers or coworkers.

Horizontal Communication.   **Horizontal communication** is the lateral or diagonal exchange of messages among peers or coworkers. It may occur within or across departments. The purpose of horizontal communication is not only to inform but also to request support and coordinate activities. Horizontal communication falls into one of three categories:

1. *Intradepartmental problem solving.* These messages take place among members of the same department and concern task accomplishment. Example: "Betty, can you help us figure out how to complete this medical expense report form?"

2. *Interdepartmental coordination.* Interdepartmental messages facilitate the accomplishment of joint projects or tasks. Example: "Bob, please contact marketing and production and arrange a meeting to discuss the specifications for the new subassembly. It looks like we may not be able to meet their requirements."

3. *Change Initiatives and Improvements.* These messages are designed to share information among teams and departments that can help the organization change, grow, and improve. Example: We are streamlining the company travel procedures and would like to discuss them with your department.

Horizontal communication is particularly important in learning organizations, where teams of workers are continuously solving problems and searching for new ways of doing things. Recall from Chapters 10 and 11 that many organizations build in horizontal communications in the form of task forces, committees, or even a matrix structure to encourage coordination. At Chicago's Northwestern Memorial Hospital, two doctors created a horizontal task force to solve a serious patient health problem.

NORTHWESTERN MEMORIAL HOSPITAL

We've all heard of it happening—a patient checks into the hospital for a routine procedure and ends up getting sicker instead of better. Hospital-borne infections afflict about two million patients—and kill nearly 100,000—each year. Greater antibiotic use only causes the germs to develop greater resistance. The infection epidemic is growing worse worldwide, but a task force at Northwestern Memorial Hospital has reversed the trend by breaking down communication barriers.

When a cancer patient became Northwestern's first victim of a new strain of deadly bacteria, infectious-disease specialists Lance Peterson and Gary Noskin realized it would take everyone's help to defeat the insidious enemy. As infection spread throughout the hospital, they launched a regular Monday morning meeting to plot countermoves. Although some physicians and staff members were offended at having their procedures questioned, the goal of preventing needless deaths overrode their concerns. Absolute candor was the rule at the Monday morning meetings, which involved not only doctors and nurses, but also lab technicians, pharmacists, computer technicians, and admissions representatives. One pharmacist, for example, recognized that antibiotics act as fertilizer for many bacteria, which encouraged physicians to decrease their use of antibiotics in favor of alternative treatments. Computer representatives and admissions people got together to develop software to identify which returning patients might pose a threat for bringing infection back into the hospital. Eventually, the task force even included maintenance staff when studies showed that a shortage of sinks was inhibiting hand-washing.

Increasing horizontal communication paid off at Northwestern, saving millions in annual medical costs and at least a few lives. Over three years, Northwestern's rate of hospital-borne infections plunged 22 percent. In the last fiscal year, such infections totaled 5.1 per 1,000 patients, roughly half the national average.[37]

Informal Communication Channels

Informal communication channels exist outside the formally authorized channels and do not adhere to the organization's hierarchy of authority. Informal communications coexist with formal communications but may skip hierarchical levels, cutting across vertical chains of command to connect virtually anyone in the organization. For example, to improve communications at SafeCard Services of Jacksonville, Florida, Paul Kahn propped open the door to the executive wing, made the "executives-only" fitness center available to all employees, and began scheduling regular breakfasts and lunches for employees and managers to get together in a relaxed, informal atmosphere. Providing greater opportunities for informal communications helped Kahn turn the struggling company around.[38] An illustration of both formal and informal communications is given in Exhibit 18.6. Note how formal communications can be vertical or horizontal, depending on task assignments and coordination responsibilities.

Two types of informal channels used in many organizations are "management by wandering around" and the "grapevine."

informal communication channel
A communication channel that exists outside formally authorized channels without regard for the organization's hierarchy of authority.

Valassis Communication, Inc.'s "On the M.O.V.E." committee (which stands for Motivate Our Valassis Employees) researches and implements programs such as flexible hours, job sharing, and suggestion review systems, as well as plans a variety of "lighten up" events that contribute to high employee morale and a strong corporate culture. Valassis formed the committee to improve horizontal communication and create positive energy across the entire organization. It's one of many techniques VCI uses to stimulate new ideas, promote teamwork, and encourage ongoing communication.

Exhibit *18.6*

Formal and Informal Organizational Communication Channels

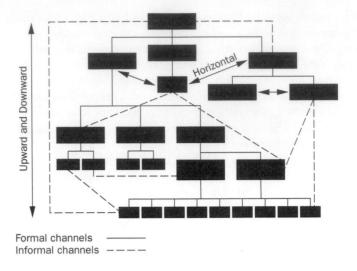

Formal channels ————
Informal channels – – – –

management by wandering around (MBWA)
A communication technique in which managers interact directly with workers to exchange information.

Management by Wandering Around.   The communication technique known as **management by wandering around (MBWA)** was made famous by the books *In Search of Excellence* and *A Passion for Excellence*.[39] These books describe executives who talk directly with employees to learn what is going on. MBWA works for managers at all levels. They mingle and develop positive relationships with employees and learn directly from them about their department, division, or organization. For example, the president of ARCO had a habit of visiting a district field office. Rather than schedule a big strategic meeting with the district supervisor, he would come in unannounced and chat with the lowest-level employees. Andy Pearson of PepsiCo started his tours from the bottom up: He went directly to a junior assistant brand manager and asked, "What's up?" In any organization, both upward and downward communication are enhanced with MBWA. Managers have a chance to describe key ideas and values to employees and in turn learn about the problems and issues confronting employees.

When managers fail to take advantage of MBWA, they become aloof and isolated from employees. For example, Peter Anderson, president of Ztel, Inc., a maker of television switching systems, preferred not to personally communicate with employees. He managed at arm's length. As one manager said, "I don't know how many times I asked Peter to come to the lab, but he stayed in his office. He wasn't that visible to the troops." This formal management style contributed to Ztel's troubles and eventual bankruptcy.[40]

grapevine
An informal, person-to-person communication network of employees that is not officially sanctioned by the organization.

The Grapevine.   The **grapevine** is an informal, person-to-person communication network of employees that is not officially sanctioned by the organization.[41] The grapevine links employees in all directions, ranging from the president through middle management, support staff, and line employees. The grapevine will always exist in an organization, but it can become a dominant force when formal channels are closed. In such cases, the grapevine is actually a service because the information it provides helps makes sense of an unclear or uncertain situation. Employees use grapevine rumors to fill in information gaps and clarify management decisions. The grapevine tends to be more active during periods of change, excitement, anxiety, and sagging economic conditions. For example, when Jel, Inc., an auto supply firm, was under great pressure from Ford and GM to increase quality, rumors circulated on the shop floor about the company's possible demise. Management changes to improve quality—learning statistical process control, introducing a new compensation system, buying a fancy new screw machine from Germany—all started out as rumors, circulating days ahead of the actual announcements, and were generally accurate.[42]

Research suggests that a few people are primarily responsible for the grapevine's success. Exhibit 18.7 illustrates the two most typical grapevines.[43] In the *gossip chain,* a single individual conveys a piece of news to many other people. In a *cluster chain,* a few individuals each convey information to several others. Having only a few people conveying information may account for the accuracy of grapevines. If every person told one other person in sequence, distortions would be greater.

Surprising aspects of the grapevine are its accuracy and its relevance to the organization. About 80 percent of grapevine communications pertain to business-related topics rather than personal, vicious gossip. Moreover, from 70 to 90 percent of the details passed through a grapevine are accurate.[44] Many managers would like the grapevine to be destroyed because they consider its rumors to be untrue, malicious, and harmful to personnel. Typically this is not the case; however, managers should be aware that almost five of every six important messages are carried to some extent by the grapevine rather than through official channels. In a recent survey of 22,000 shift workers in varied industries, 55 percent said they get most of their information via the grapevine.[45] Some experts recommend that managers accept and use the grapevine to their advantage, sharing information with people they know will spread it to others. Smart managers understand the company's grapevine. They recognize who's connected to whom and which employees are key players in the informal spread of information. However, one interesting finding is that in today's workplace young people tend to participate in the grapevine much less than older workers. Young workers generally don't plan to stay with a company for more than a few years, so they are less involved in the rumor mill.[46] In all cases, but particularly in times of crisis, executives need to manage communications effectively so that the grapevine is not the only source of information.

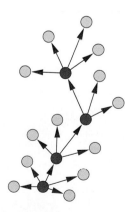

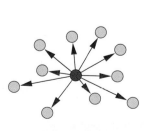

Gossip Chain
(One tells many)

Cluster Chain
(A few tell selected others)

Exhibit 18.7

Two Grapevine Chains in Organizations

Source: Based on Keith Davis and John W. Newstrom, *Human Behavior at Work: Organizational Behavior,* 7th ed. (New York: McGraw-Hill, 1985).

Communicating in Teams

ATI Technologies Inc. in suburban Toronto is the most successful 3-D chipmaker in the industry, with Dell, Compaq, and IBM among its biggest customers. In the fast-moving chip industry, product-cycle turnaround is critical. Kwok Yuen Ho, Chinese émigré to Canada and the head of ATI, has been able to cut ATI's product turnaround time in half (to under nine months) by double-teaming engineers to keep a steady stream of innovations moving through the pipeline. A decentralized network *of communications between ATI engineers helps teams continuously solve problems, helping to provide profits that are expected to rise by 15 percent to $125 million. ATI's latest chip, Rage 128, gives amazing reality to such games as* Quake II *and* Half-Life, *and plans to release the next generation version are already forming.*

The importance of teamwork in organizations, discussed in more detail in Chapter 19, emphasizes the need for team communication. Team members work together to accomplish tasks, and the team's communication structure influences both team performance and employee satisfaction. Three aspects of team communication are networks, open communication, and dialogue.

Networks.   Research into team communication has focused on two characteristics: the extent to which team communications are centralized and the nature of the team's task.[47] The relationship between these characteristics is illustrated in Exhibit 18.8. In a **centralized network,** team members must communicate through one individual to solve problems or make decisions. In a **decentralized network,** individuals can communicate freely with other team members. Members process information equally among themselves until all agree on a decision.[48]

In laboratory experiments, centralized communication networks achieved faster solutions for simple problems. Members could simply pass relevant information to a central person for a decision. Decentralized communications were slower for simple problems because information was passed among individuals until someone finally put the pieces together and solved the problem. However, for more complex problems, the decentralized communication network was faster. Because all necessary information was not restricted to one person, a pooling of information through widespread communications provided greater input into the decision. Similarly, the accuracy of problem solving was related to problem complexity. The centralized networks made fewer errors on simple problems but more errors on complex ones. Decentralized networks were less accurate for simple problems but more accurate for complex ones.[49]

The implication for organizations is as follows: In a highly competitive global environment, organizations use teams to deal with complex problems. When team activities are complex and difficult, all members should share information in a decentralized structure to solve problems. Teams need a free flow of communication in all directions.[50] At Microsoft, for example, teams hold "triage" meetings in the final months of a software development cycle. Everyone jumps in with their ideas and opinions and then "negotiates" to a decision.[51] However, teams who perform routine tasks spend less

E x h i b i t **18.8**

Effectiveness of Team Communication Network

SOURCES: Adapted from A. Bavelas and D. Barrett, "An Experimental Approach to Organization Communication," *Personnel* 27 (1951), 366–371; M. E. Shaw, *Group Dynamics: The Psychology of Small Group Behavior* (New York: McGraw-Hill, 1976); and E. M. Rogers and R. A. Rogers, *Communication in Organizations* (New York: Free Press, 1976).

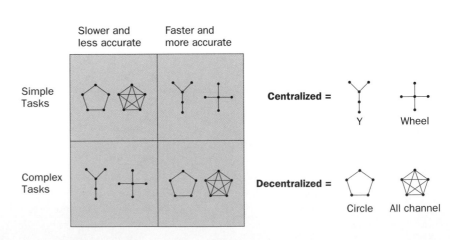

LEADING THE REVOLUTION: THE LEARNING ORGANIZATION

The Friday Morning Appointment

From the outside, everything looked fine at NECX, the world's leading independent distributor of semiconductors and other computer products. The company was highly successful and growing fast—its workforce had swelled from 100 to 250 in just a few years. However, from the inside, Henry Bertolon, cofounder and CEO, could see that NECX was coming apart at the seams. "We'd have meetings that just melted down," he says. "Everyone would scream at each other and then leave."

Bertolon's first plan was to hire a management consultant to help solve the company's communication problems. However, most consultants he interviewed came in and told the company what its problems were rather than listening to managers and employees. So Bertolon took an unusual approach: he hired Wil Calmas, a Boston psychologist with an MBA, to be the organizational shrink. Calmas set up a one-day-a-week program to get people talking—and listening—to one another on a new and deeper level. The day begins at 8 A.M. with a 90 minute meeting of the company's top executives. There is never a formal agenda for the meetings—executives are encouraged to express fear, hostility, frustration, secret wishes, whatever feelings are affecting their lives and work. The early-morning meeting is just the first of a day-long series of dialogues among NECX employees from all ranks and departments. The sales department has become so adept at dialogue that they now meet on their own, without Calmas's guidance.

Bertolon is convinced that the sessions are having a positive impact on NECX's people and performance. When Calmas first began his work, Bertolon asked managers to rate, on a scale of 1 to 10, how much they agreed with statements such as "All the managers help one another" and "My staff finds it easy to talk to me about everything." The average score was 1.5. When the test was given again recently, the average score had jumped to 7.5. Bertolon also believes those results have driven other important numbers, such as revenues, which have jumped from $62 million in 1992 to almost $400 million in 1996. Employee turnover has dropped from 42 percent to 20 percent.

In a fast-growing business, Bertolon believes that getting people communicating in a way that builds common understanding is critical to success. The dialogue sessions create a safe environment for people to reveal their feelings, voice their opinions, and build common ground. It also keeps them loose, flexible, and open to new ideas—ready to respond to rapid changes taking place all around them.

www.necx.com

SOURCE: Scott Kirsner, "Want to Grow? Hire a Shrink!" *Fast Company*, December–January 1998, 68, 70.

---

time processing information, and thus communications can be centralized. Data can be channeled to a supervisor for decisions, freeing workers to spend a greater percentage of time on task activities.

Open Communication. A recent trend that reflects management's increased emphasis on empowering employees and enhancing team productivity is open communication. **Open communication** means sharing all types of information throughout the company, across functional and hierarchical levels. Many companies, such as Springfield Remanufacturing Corporation, Johnsonville Foods, and Quad/Graphics, are opening the financial books to workers at all levels so they understand how and why the company operates as it does. Team approaches that bring together people from different departments require broader information sharing. Wabash National Corporation, one of the nation's leading truck-trailer manufacturers, has employees complete several hours of business training and then holds regular meetings on the shop floor to review the company's financial performance. AES Corporation, a power producer, shares so much financial data with its 2,000 employees that it has declared them all insiders for stock-trading purposes.[52] At Cypress Semiconductor, CEO T. J. Rodgers says information of all types is collected and shared in so much detail that the corporation can be considered "transparent."[53]

centralized network
A team communication structure in which team members communicate through a single individual to solve problems or make decisions.

decentralized network
A team communication structure in which team members freely communicate with one another and arrive at decisions together.

open communication
Sharing all types of information throughout the company, across functional and hierarchical levels.

dialogue
A group communication process aimed at creating a culture based on collaboration, fluidity, trust, and commitment to shared goals.

Dialogue.   Another means of creating team spirit is through dialogue. The "roots of dialogue" are *dia* and *logos*, which can be thought of as "stream of meaning." **Dialogue** is a group communication process in which people together create a stream of shared meaning that enables them to understand each other and share a view of the world.[54] People may start out at polar opposites, but by talking openly to one another, they discover common ground, common issues, and shared goals on which they can build a better future.

A useful way to describe dialogue is to contrast it with discussion. Exhibit 18.9 illustrates the differences between dialogue and discussion. The intent of discussion, generally, is to deliver one's point of view and persuade others to adopt it. A discussion is often resolved by logic or "beating down" opponents. Dialogue, on the other hand, asks that participants suspend their attachments to a particular viewpoint so that a deeper level of listening, synthesis, and meaning can evolve from the group. A dialogue's focus is to reveal feelings and build common ground. As described in the Learning Organization box, one company even hired a psychologist to help employees engage in dialogue and cope with rapid change. Both forms of communication, dialogue and discussion, can result in change. However, the result of discussion is limited to the topic being deliberated, whereas the result of dialogue is characterized by group unity, shared meaning, and transformed mindsets. As new and deeper solutions are developed, a trusting relationship is built among team members.[55]

E x h i b i t **18.9**   *Dialogue and Discussion: The Differences*

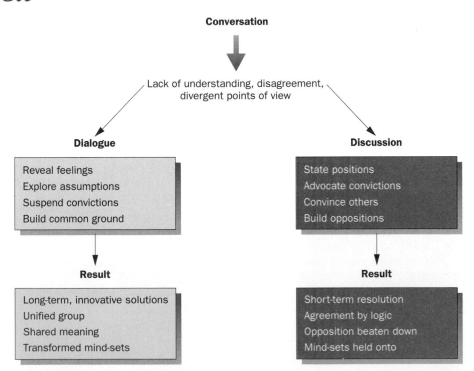

Source: Adapted from Edgar Schein, "On Dialogue, Culture, and Organization Learning," *Organizational Dynamics* (Autumn 1993), 46.

Managing Organizational Communication

Many of the ideas described in this chapter pertain to barriers to communication and how to overcome them. Barriers can be categorized as those that exist at the individual level and those that exist at the organizational level. First we will examine communication barriers; then we will look at techniques for overcoming them. These barriers and techniques are summarized in Exhibit 18.10.

Barriers to Communication

Barriers to communication can exist within the individual or as part of the organization.

Individual Barriers.   First, there are interpersonal barriers; these include problems with emotions and perceptions held by employees. For example, rigid perceptual labeling or categorizing of others prevents modification or alteration of opinions. If a person's mind is made up before the communication starts, communication will fail. Moreover, people with different backgrounds or knowledge may interpret a communication in different ways.

Second, selecting the wrong channel or medium for sending a communication can be a problem. For example, when a message is emotional, it is better to transmit it face-to-face rather than in writing. On the other hand, writing works best for routine messages but lacks the capacity for rapid feedback and multiple cues needed for difficult messages.

Third, semantics often causes communication problems. **Semantics** pertains to the meaning of words and the way they are used. A word such as *effectiveness* may mean achieving high production to a factory superintendent and employee satisfaction to a human resources staff specialist. Many common words have an average of 28 definitions; thus, communicators must take care to select the words that will accurately encode ideas.[56]

Fourth, sending inconsistent cues between verbal and nonverbal communications will confuse the receiver. If one's facial expression does not reflect one's words, the communication will contain noise and uncertainty. The tone of voice and body language should be consistent with the words, and actions should not contradict words.

semantics
The meaning of words and the way they are used.

Barriers	How to Overcome
Individual	
Interpersonal dynamics	Active listening
Channels and media	Selection of appropriate channel
Semantics	Knowledge of other's perspective
Inconsistent cues	MBWA
Organizational	
Status and power differences	Climate of trust
Departmental needs and goals	Development and use of formal channels
Communication network unsuited to task	Changing organization or group structure to fit communication needs
Lack of formal channels	Encouragement of multiple channels, formal and informal

Exhibit **18.10**

Communication Barriers and Ways to Overcome Them

Organizational Barriers.   Organizational barriers pertain to factors for the organization as a whole. First is the problem of status and power differences. Low-power people may be reluctant to pass bad news up the hierarchy, thus giving the wrong impression to upper levels.[57] High-power people may not pay attention or may feel that low-status people have little to contribute.

Second, differences across departments in terms of needs and goals interfere with communications. Each department perceives problems in its own terms. The production department is concerned with production efficiency and may not fully understand the marketing department's need to get the product to the customer in a hurry.

Third, the communication flow may not fit the team's or organization's task. If a centralized communication structure is used for nonroutine tasks, there will not be enough information circulated to solve problems. The organization, department, or team is most efficient when the amount of communication flowing among employees fits the task.

Fourth, the absence of formal channels reduces communication effectiveness. Organizations must provide adequate upward, downward, and horizontal communication in the form of employee surveys, open-door policies, newsletters, memos, task forces, and liaison personnel. Without these formal channels, the organization cannot communicate as a whole.

Overcoming Communication Barriers

Managers can design the organization so as to encourage positive, effective communication. Designing involves both individual skills and organizational actions.

Individual Skills.   Perhaps the most important individual skill is active listening. Active listening means asking questions, showing interest, and occasionally paraphrasing what the speaker has said to ensure that one is interpreting accurately. Active listening also means providing feedback to the sender to complete the communication loop.

Second, individuals should select the appropriate channel for the message. A complicated message should be sent through a rich channel, such as face-to-face discussion or telephone. Routine messages and data can be sent through memos, letters, or electronic mail, because there is little chance of misunderstanding.

Third, senders and receivers should make a special effort to understand each other's perspective. Managers can sensitize themselves to the information receiver so that they will be better able to target the message, detect bias, and clarify missed interpretations. By communicators understanding others' perspectives, semantics can be clarified, perceptions understood, and objectivity maintained.

The fourth individual skill is management by wandering around. Managers must be willing to get out of the office and check communications with others. For example, John McDonnell of McDonnell Douglas always eats in the employee cafeteria when he visits far-flung facilities. Through direct observation and face-to-face meetings, managers develop an understanding of the organization and are able to communicate important ideas and values directly to others.

Organizational Actions. Perhaps the most important thing managers can do for the organization is to create a climate of trust and openness. This will encourage people to communicate honestly with one another. Subordinates will feel free to transmit negative as well as positive messages without fear of retribution. Efforts to develop interpersonal skills among employees can be made to foster openness, honesty, and trust.

Second, managers should develop and use formal information channels in all directions. Scandinavian Design uses two newsletters to reach employees. GM's Packard Electric plant is designed to share all pertinent information—financial, future plans, quality, performance—with employees. Dana Corporation has developed innovative programs such as the "Here's a Thought" board—called a HAT rack—to get ideas and feedback from workers. Other techniques include direct mail, bulletin boards, and employee surveys.

Third, managers should encourage the use of multiple channels, including both formal and informal communications. Multiple communication channels include written directives, face-to-face discussions, MBWA, and the grapevine. For example, managers at GM's Packard Electric plant use multimedia, including a monthly newspaper, frequent meetings of employee teams, and an electronic news display in the cafeteria. Sending messages through multiple channels increases the likelihood that they will be properly received.

Fourth, the structure should fit communication needs. For example, Harrah's created the Communication Team as part of its structure at the Casino/Holiday Inn in Las Vegas. The team includes one member from each department. It deals with urgent company problems and helps people think beyond the scope of their own departments to communicate with anyone and everyone to solve those problems. An organization can be designed to use teams, task forces, project managers, or a matrix structure as needed to facilitate the horizontal flow of information for coordination and problem solving. Structure should also reflect information needs. When team or department tasks are difficult, a decentralized structure should be implemented to encourage discussion and participation. Dialogue can help team members arrive at collective solutions to complex problems.

The scoreboard at Colonial Mills, Inc., a $7 million specialty-rug manufacturer in Pawtucket, Rhode Island, overcomes communication barriers by helping all employees get involved in business targets and results. The board stretches 30 feet and covers most of the lunchroom wall. A big gold rocket ship in the middle shows the year-to-date company profit. Columns for winding, braiding, and the other production departments show monthly output—cans filled, square feet braided, etc.—all compared with the company's plan. The Colonial Mills scoreboard is a unique communication channel that encourages upward, downward, and horizontal communication. "Our targets aren't the powers-that-be coming down and saying, 'This shall be the number,'" says Colonial Mills CEO Don Scarlata. "They're numbers everybody has discussed and signed off on."

Summary and Management Solution

This chapter described several important points about communicating in organizations. Communication takes up 80 percent of a manager's time. Communication is a process of encoding an idea into a message, which is sent through a channel and decoded by a receiver. Communication among people can be affected by communication channels, nonverbal communication, and listening skills. Important aspects of management communication include persuasion and influence. Managers use communication to sell people on the vision for the organization and to influence them to behave in such a way as to accomplish the vision. To influence others, managers connect with people on an emotional level by using symbols, metaphors, and stories to communicate their messages.

At the organizational level, managers are concerned with managing formal communications in a downward, upward, and horizontal direction. Informal communications also are important, especially management by wandering around and the grapevine. Moreover, research shows that communication structures in teams and departments should reflect the underlying tasks. Open communication and dialogue can develop a sense of trust and team spirit.

Finally, several barriers to communication were described. These barriers can be overcome by active listening, selecting appropriate channels, engaging in MBWA, developing a climate of trust, using formal channels, and designing the correct structure to fit communication needs.

At Childress Buick/Kia Company, Rusty Childress used a variety of tools to harness employee brainpower and break down communication barriers. Customers as well as employees were frustrated and dissatisfied, and Rusty knew the company needed to open the lines of communication fast to remain competitive in the volatile car dealership business. A new employee manual emphasizing the importance of active listening skills, together with a seven-week orientation program, refocused organizational efforts on service through communication. Upward as well as downward communications were strengthened with regular meetings, such as "Donuts and Dialogue," town-hall-style get-togethers for all employees, and "Take 5" meetings between a manager and five employees to brainstorm about problems or opportunities. Committees were set up to encourage cross-functional communication and understanding. In addition, a monthly newsletter, employee mailboxes, a computer-based "Suggestion Connection," a telephone hot line, and a weekly E-mail update keep information flowing across departmental lines to assure better and faster customer service. Today, information flows throughout the company in all directions, and an employee-run team is charged with continuous improvement in internal communications. Childress's customer service indexes are regularly above 95 percent for overall customer satisfaction, and employee turnover is among the lowest in the industry. The company boasts a wall full of "Best in Class" awards from General Motors, and Childress regularly hosts visitors from other organizations that use the dealership as a benchmark for customer service.[58]

Discussion Questions

1. ATI Medical, Inc., has a "no-memo" policy. The 300 employees must interact directly for all communications. What impact do you think this policy would have on the organization?

2. Describe the elements of the communication process. Give an example of each part of the model as it exists in the classroom during communication between teacher and students.

3. Why do you think stories are more effective than hard facts and figures in persuading others?

4. Should the grapevine be eliminated? How might managers control information that is processed through the grapevine?

5. What do you think are the major barriers to upward communication in organizations? Discuss.

6. What is the relationship between group communication and group task? For example, how should communications differ in a strategic planning group and a group of employees who stock shelves in a grocery store?

7. Some senior managers believe they should rely on written information and computer reports because these yield more accurate data than do face-to-face communications. Do you agree?

8. Why is management by wandering around considered effective communication? Consider channel richness and nonverbal communications in formulating your answer.

9. Is speaking accurately or listening actively the more important communication skill for managers? Discuss.

10. Assume that you have been asked to design a training program to help managers become better communicators. What would you include in the program?

Management in Practice: Experiential Exercise

Listening Self-Assessment

Instructions: Choose one response for each of the items below. Base your choice on what you usually do, not on what you think a person *should* do.

1. When you are going to lunch with a friend, you:
   a. Focus your attention on the menu and then on the service provided

   b. Ask about events in your friend's life and pay attention to what's said
   c. Exchange summaries of what is happening to each of you while focusing attention on the meal

2. When someone talks nonstop, you:
   a. Ask questions at an appropriate time in an attempt to help the person focus on the issue

b. Make an excuse to end the conversation

c. Try to be patient and understand what you are being told

3. If a group member complains about a fellow employee who, you believe, is disrupting the group, you:

a. Pay attention and withhold your opinions

b. Share your own experiences and feelings about that employee

c. Acknowledge the group member's feelings and ask the group member what options he or she has

4. If someone is critical of you, you:

a. Try not to react or get upset

b. Automatically become curious and attempt to learn more

c. Listen attentively and then back up your position

5. You are having a very busy day and someone tells you to change the way you are completing a task. You believe the person is wrong, so you:

a. Thank her or him for the input and keep doing what you were doing

b. Try to find out why she or he thinks you should change

c. Acknowledge that the other may be right, tell her or him you are very busy, and agree to follow up later

6. When you are ready to respond to someone else, you:

a. Sometimes will interrupt the person if you believe it is necessary

b. Almost always speak before the other is completely finished talking

c. Rarely offer your response until you believe the other has finished

7. After a big argument with someone you have to work with every day, you:

a. Settle yourself and then try to understand the other's point of view before stating your side again

b. Just try to go forward and let bygones be bygones

c. Continue to press your position

8. A colleague calls to tell you that he is upset about getting assigned to a new job. You decide to:

a. Ask him if he can think of options to help him deal with the situation

b. Assure him that he is good at what he does and that these things have a way of working out for the best

c. Let him know you have heard how badly he feels

9. If a friend always complains about her problems but never asks about yours, you:

a. Try to identify areas of common interest

b. Remain understanding and attentive, even if it becomes tedious

c. Support her complaints and mention your own complaints

10. The best way to remain calm in an argument is to:

a. Continue to repeat your position in a firm but even manner

b. Repeat what you believe is the other person's position

c. Tell the other person that you are willing to discuss the matter again when you are both calmer

Score each item of your Listening Self-Assessment

	(a)	(b)	(c)
1.	0	10	5
2.	10	0	5
3.	5	0	5
4.	5	10	0
5.	0	10	5
6.	5	0	10
7.	10	5	0
8.	5	5	10
9.	0	10	5
10.	0	10	5

Add up your total score

80–100 You are an active, excellent listener. You achieve a good balance between listening and asking questions, and you strive to understand others.

50–75 You are an adequate-to-good listener. You listen well, although you may sometimes react too quickly to others before they are finished speaking.

25–45 You have some listening skills but need to improve them. You may often become impatient when trying to listen to others, hoping they will finish talking so you can talk.

0–20 You listen to others very infrequently. You may prefer to do all of the talking and experience extreme frustration while waiting for others to make their point.

SOURCE: Richard G. Weaver and John D. Farrell, *Managers As Facilitators: A Practical Guide to Getting Work Done in a Changing Workplace* (San Francisco: Berrett-Koehler Publishers, 1997), 134–136. Used with permission.

Management in Practice: Ethical Dilemma

The Voice of Authority

When Gehan Rasinghe was hired as an account assistant at Werner and Thompson, a business and financial management firm, he was very relieved. He was overqualified for the job with his degree in accounting, but the combination of his accented English and his quiet manner had prevented him from securing any other position. Beatrice Werner, one of the managing partners of the firm, was impressed by his educational credentials and his courtly manner. She assured him he had advancement potential with the firm, but the account assistant position was the only one available. After months of rejections in his job hunt, Rasinghe accepted the position. He was committed to making his new job work at all costs.

Account Manager Cathy Putnam was Rasinghe's immediate superior. Putnam spoke with a heavy Boston accent, speaking at a lightning pace to match her enormous workload. She indicated to Rasinghe that he would need to get up to speed as quickly as possible to succeed in working with her. It was soon apparent that Putnam and Rasinghe were at odds. She resented having to repeat directions more than once to teach him his responsibilities. He also seemed resistant to making the many phone calls asking for copies of invoices, disputing charges on credit cards, and following up with clients' staff to get the information necessary to do his job. His accounting work was impeccable, but the public contact part of his job was in bad shape. Even his quiet answer of "No problem" to all her requests was starting to wear thin on Putnam. Before giving Rasinghe his three-month review, Putnam appealed to Beatrice Werner for help. Putnam was frustrated at their communication problems and didn't know what to do.

Werner had seen the problem coming. Although she had found Rasinghe's bank reconciliations and financial report

preparations to be first-rate, she knew that phone work and client contact were a big part of any job in the firm. But as the daughter of German immigrants, Werner also knew that language and cultural barriers could be overcome with persistence and patience. Diversity was one of her ideals for her company, and it was not always easy to achieve. She felt sure that Rasinghe could become an asset to the firm in time. She worried that the time it would take was more than they could afford to give him.

What Do You Do?

1. Give Rasinghe his notice, with the understanding that a job that is primarily paperwork would be a better fit for him. Make the break now rather than later.

2. Place him with an account manager who has more time to help him develop his assertiveness and telephone skills and appreciates his knowledge of accounting.

3. Create a new position for him, where he could do the reports and reconciliations for several account managers, while their assistants concentrated on the public contact work. He would have little chance of future promotion, however.

Surf the Net

1. **E-mail.** E-mail is a common communication channel used in organizations. The Internet provides much advice on how to effectively use e-mail. Visit one of the sites below and prepare a 2 to 3 paragraph summary of the ideas that you found most helpful to you in improving your skill at using this communication channel.
   www.webfoot.com/advice/email.top.html
   www.augsburg.edu/library/aib/mailmanners.html
   www.cappyscove.com/bobf/e-mail/index.html
   www.ucc.ie/info/net/acronyms/acro.html
   http://netconference.miningco.com/msub6.htm

2. **Group Presentations.** Another common communication channel, particularly for managers, is speaking before groups both inside and outside the organization. Go to **www.leaderx.com** and test your presentation style. After completing and submitting your test for scoring, you will

get a customized report with valuable feedback on important presentation pointers. Print out and read your report, highlighting the most valuable idea you received from the report. Submit the printout to your instructor.

3. **Listening.** A communication skill development area from which nearly everyone can benefit is improving listening skills. Use your search engine to find helpful information on being a better listener (one example is provided below). After reading through the materials you locate, select one specific area that you will work to improve. Use every listening opportunity you have for the next 24 hours to apply what you have learned. Then write a 2 to 3 paragraph summary of what you practiced to become a better listener and the results you experienced.
   www.thepargroup.com/articles.html

Case for Critical Analysis
Inter-City Manufacturing, Inc.

The president of Inter-City Manufacturing Inc., Rich Langston, wanted to facilitate upward communication. He believed an open-door policy was a good place to start. He announced that his own door was open to all employees and encouraged senior managers to do the same. He felt this would give him a way to

get early warning signals that would not be filtered or redirected through the formal chain of command. Langston found that many employees who used the open-door policy had been with the company for years and were comfortable talking to the president. Sometimes messages came through about inadequate policies and procedures. Langston would raise these issues and explain any changes at the next senior managers' meeting.

The most difficult complaints to handle were those from people who were not getting along with their bosses. One employee, Leroy, complained bitterly that his manager had overcommitted the department and put everyone under too much pressure. Leroy argued that long hours and low morale were major problems. But he would not allow Rich Langston to bring the manager into the discussion nor to seek out other employees to confirm the complaint. Although Langston suspected that Leroy might be right, he could not let the matter sit and blurted out, "Have you considered leaving the company?" This made Leroy realize that a meeting with his immediate boss was unavoidable.

Before the three-party meeting, Langston contacted Leroy's manager and explained what was going on. He insisted that the manager come to the meeting willing to listen and without hostility toward Leroy. During the meeting, Leroy's manager listened actively and displayed no ill will. He learned the problem from Leroy's perspective and realized he was over his head in his new job. After the meeting, the manager said he was relieved. He had been promoted into the job from a technical position just a few months earlier and had no management or planning experience. He welcomed Rich Langston's offer to help him do a better job of planning.

Questions

1. What techniques increased Rich Langston's communication effectiveness? Discuss.
2. Do you think that an open-door policy was the right way to improve upward communications? What other techniques would you suggest?
3. What problems do you think an open-door policy creates? Do you think many employees are reluctant to use it? Why?

SOURCE: Based on Everett T. Suters, "Hazards of an Open-Door Policy," *Inc.,* January 1987, 99–102.

Endnotes

1. Jean Kerr, "The Informers," *Inc.,* March 1995, 50–61.
2. Jenny C. McCune, "That Elusive Thing Called Trust," *Management Review,* July–August 1998, 10–16; and Matt Goldberg, "Cisco's Most Important Meal of the Day," *Fast Company,* February–March 1998, 56.
3. Elizabeth B. Drew, "Profile: Robert Strauss," *The New Yorker,* May 7, 1979, 55–70.
4. Henry Mintzberg, *The Nature of Managerial Work* (New York: Harper & Row, 1973).
5. Fred Luthans and Janet K. Larsen, "How Managers Really Communicate," *Human Relations* 39 (1986), 161–178; and Larry E. Penley and Brian Hawkins, "Studying Interpersonal Communication in Organizations: A Leadership Application," *Academy of Management Journal* 28 (1985), 309–326.
6. D. K. Berlo, *The Process of Communication* (New York: Holt, Rinehart and Winston, 1960), 24.
7. Nelson W. Aldrich, Jr., "Lines of Communication," *Inc.,* June 1986, 140–144; and Roberta Maynard, "Back to Basics, From the Top," *Nation's Business,* December 1996, 38–39.
8. Bruce K. Blaylock, "Cognitive Style and the Usefulness of Information," *Decision Sciences* 15 (winter 1984), 74–91.
9. Robert H. Lengel and Richard L. Daft, "The Selection of Communication Media as an Executive Skill," *Academy of Management Executive* 2 (August 1988), 225–232; Richard L. Daft and Robert H. Lengel, "Organizational Information Requirements, Media Richness and Structural Design," *Managerial Science* 32 (May 1986), 554–572; and Jane Webster and Linda Klebe Trevino, "Rational and Social Theories as Complementary Explanations of Communication Media Choices: Two Policy-Capturing Studies," *Academy of Management Journal* 38, no. 6 (1995), 1544–1572.
10. Ford S. Worthy, "How CEOs Manage Their Time," *Fortune,* January 18, 1988, 88–97.
11. Ronald E. Rice, "Task Analyzability, Use of New Media, and Effectiveness: A Multi-Site Exploration of Media Richness," *Organizational Science* 3, no. 4 (November 1992), 475–500; and M. Lynne Markus, "Electronic Mail as the Medium of Managerial Choice," *Organizational Science* 5, no. 4 (November 1994), 502–527.
12. Richard L. Daft, Robert H. Lengel, and Linda Klebe Trevino, "Message Equivocality, Media Selection and Manager Performance: Implication for Information Systems," *MIS Quarterly* 11 (1987), 355–368.
13. John A. Byrne, "Special Report: Jack," *Business Week,* June 8, 1998, 91–106.
14. Jay A. Conger, "The Necessary Art of Persuasion," *Harvard Business Review,* May–June 1998, 84–95.
15. Elizabeth Weil, "Every Leader Tells a Story," *Fast Company,* June–July 1998, 38, 40.
16. David Armstrong, *Management by Storying Around: A New Method of Leadership* (New York: Doubleday Currency, 1992).
17. Nancy K. Austin, "Just Do It," *Working Woman,* April 1990, 78–80, 126.
18. J. Martin and M. Powers, "Organizational Stories: More Vivid and Persuasive than Quantitative Data," in B. M. Staw, ed., *Psychological Foundations of Organizational Behavior* (Glenview, Illinois: Scott Foresman, 1982), 161–168.

19. I. Thomas Sheppard, "Silent Signals," *Supervisory Management* (March 1986), 31–33.

20. Albert Mehrabian, *Silent Messages* (Belmont, Calif.: Wadsworth, 1971); and Albert Mehrabian, "Communicating without Words," *Psychology Today,* September 1968, 53–55.

21. Sheppard, "Silent Signals."

22. Arthur H. Bell, *The Complete Manager's Guide to Interviewing* (Homewood, Ill.: Richard D. Irwin, 1989).

23. C. Glenn Pearce, "Doing Something about Your Listening Ability," *Supervisory Management* (March 1989), 29–34; and Tom Peters, "Learning to Listen," *Hyatt Magazine* (spring 1988), 16–21.

24. Lt. General William G. Pagonis with Jeffrey L. Cruikshank, *Moving Mountains: Lessons In Leadership and Logistics from the Gulf War* (Boston, Mass.: Harvard Business School Press, 1992).

25. Gerald M. Goldhaber, *Organizational Communication,* 4th ed. (Dubuque, Iowa: Wm. C. Brown, 1980), 189.

26. Monci Jo Williams, "America's Best Salesman," *Fortune,* October 26, 1987, 122–134; and David Carnoy, "Rick Pitino," *Success,* October 1998, 68–71, 82.

27. Daft and Steers, *Organizations;* and Daniel Katz and Robert Kahn, *The Social Psychology of Organizations,* 2d ed. (New York: Wiley, 1978).

28. Roberta Maynard, "Back to Basics, From the Top."

29. Roberta Maynard, "It Can Pay to Show Employees the Big Picture," *Nation's Business,* December 1994, 10.

30. Anita Lienert, "Of Wolfpacks, Jedi Masters and Paradigm Busters," *Management Review,* March 1998, 10–16.

31. William C. Taylor, "At VeriFone, It's a Dog's Life (And They Love It)," *Fast Company,* November 1995, 12–15; and William R. Pape, "Relative Merits," *Inc. Technology* 1998, no. 1, 23.

32. J. G. Miller, "Living Systems: The Organization," *Behavioral Science* 17 (1972), 69.

33. Michael J. Glauser, "Upward Information Flow in Organizations: Review and Conceptual Analysis," *Human Relations* 37 (1984), 613–643; and "Upward/Downward Communication: Critical Information Channels," *Small Business Report* (October 1985), 85–88.

34. Anne B. Fisher, "CEO's Think That Morale Is Dandy," *Fortune,* November 18, 1991, 83–84.

35. Mary P. Rowe and Michael Baker, "Are You Hearing Enough Employee Concerns?" *Harvard Business Review* 62 (May–June 1984), 127–135; W. H. Read, "Upward Communication in Industrial Hierarchies," *Human Relations* 15 (February 1962), 3–15; and Daft and Steers, *Organizations.*

36. Barbara Ettorre, "The Unvarnished Truth," *Management Review,* June 1997, 54–57; and Roberta Maynard, "Back to Basics, From the Top."

37. Thomas Petzinger, "A Hospital Applies Teamwork to Thwart An Insidious Enemy," *The Wall Street Journal,* May 8, 1998, B1.

38. Nancy K. Austin, "The Skill Every Manager Must Master," *Working Woman,* May 1995, 29–30.

39. Thomas J. Peters and Robert H. Waterman Jr., *In Search of Excellence* (New York: Harper & Row, 1982); and Tom Peters and Nancy Austin, *A Passion for Excellence: The Leadership Difference* (New York: Random House, 1985).

40. Lois Therrien, "How Ztel Went from Riches to Rags," *Business Week,* June 17, 1985, 97–100.

41. Keith Davis and John W. Newstrom, *Human Behavior at Work: Organizational Behavior,* 7th ed. (New York: McGraw-Hill, 1985).

42. Joshua Hyatt, "The Last Shift," *Inc.,* February 1989, 74–80.

43. Goldhaber, *Organizational Communication;* and Philip V. Louis, *Organizational Communication,* 3d ed. (New York: Wiley, 1987).

44. Donald B. Simmons, "The Nature of the Organizational Grapevine," *Supervisory Management* (November 1985), 39–42; and Davis and Newstrom, *Human Behavior.*

45. Barbara Ettorre, "Hellooo. Anybody Listening?" *Management Review,* November 1997, 9.

46. "They Hear It Through the Grapevine," in Michael Warshaw, "The Good Guy's Guide to Office Politics," *Fast Company,* April–May 1998, 157–178 (page 160); Carol Hildebrand, "Mapping the Invisible Workplace," *CIO Enterprise,* Section 2, July 15, 1998, 18–20; and David I. Bradford and Allan R. Cohen, *Power Up: Transforming Organizations Through Shared Leadership* (John Wiley & Sons, 1998).

47. E. M. Rogers and R. A. Rogers, *Communication in Organizations* (New York: Free Press, 1976); and A. Bavelas and D. Barrett, "An Experimental Approach to Organization Communication," *Personnel* 27 (1951), 366–371.

48. This discussion is based on Daft and Steers, *Organizations.*

49. Bavelas and Barrett, "An Experimental Approach"; and M. E. Shaw, *Group Dynamics: The Psychology of Small Group Behavior* (New York: McGraw-Hill, 1976).

50. Richard L. Daft and Norman B. Macintosh, "A Tentative Exploration into the Amount and Equivocality of Information Processing in Organizational Work Units," *Administrative Science Quarterly* 26 (1981), 207–224.

51. Matt Goldberg, "Microsoft Knows How to Operate—*Fast,*" *Fast Company,* April–May 1998, 76.

52. John Case, "Opening the Books," *Harvard Business Review,* March–April 1997, 118–127.

53. D. Keith Denton, "Open Communication," *Business Horizons,* September–October 1993, 64–69.

54. David Bohm, *On Dialogue* (Ojai, Calif.: David Bohm Seminars, 1989).

55. The discussion is based on Glenna Gerard and Linda Teurfs, "Dialogue and Organizational Transformation," in *Community Building: Renewing Spirit and Learning in Business,* ed. Kazinierz Gozdz (New Leaders Press, 1995), 142–153; and Edgar H. Schein, "On Dialogue, Culture, and Organizational Learning," *Organizational Dynamics* (autumn 1993), 40–51.

56. James A. F. Stoner and R. Edward Freeman, *Management,* 4th ed. (Englewood Cliffs, N.J.: Prentice-Hall, 1989).

57. Janet Fulk and Sirish Mani, "Distortion of Communication in Hierarchical Relationships," in *Communication Yearbook,* vol. 9, ed. M. L. McLaughlin (Beverly Hills, Calif.: Sage, 1986), 483–510.

58. Jean Kerr, "The Informers."

LEARNING OBJECTIVES

After studying this chapter, you should be able to

✺ **Identify the types of teams in organizations.**

✺ **Discuss new applications of teams to facilitate employee involvement.**

✺ **Identify roles within teams and the type of role you could play to help a team be effective.**

✺ **Explain the general stages of team development.**

✺ **Explain the concepts of team cohesiveness and team norms and their relationship to team performance.**

✺ **Understand the causes of conflict within and among teams and how to reduce conflict.**

✺ **Discuss the assets and liabilities of organizational teams.**

Teamwork in Organizations

MANAGEMENT PROBLEM

Roberts Express, the largest expedited freight carrier in North America, has moved it all—lighting equipment for Oprah Winfrey's show in the Texas town where she was battling cattle ranchers in a lawsuit; equipment to the set of Titanic in Nova Scotia; Christmas cards to the White House. Roberts picks up most shipments within 90 minutes of receiving an order and delivers more than half of them on the *same day*. Most of Roberts's shipments have to get there fast—or else. Joe Greulich, manager of management information systems, says the company is the "ambulance service for industrial freight." Moving freight by truck more quickly and cheaply than air freight gave Roberts a competitive edge when the company started in the early 1980s. Roberts served customers in a limited regional area, and agents and dispatchers knew most of their customers and drivers by name. The company rapidly expanded nationwide and was eventually making more than 200,000 deliveries a year. Success came at a price, however. Agents, unaware of which trucks or drivers were available, took orders and then passed them on to dispatchers, who scrambled to cover the deliveries. Service began to suffer. In addition, customers missed the intimacy of the old Roberts, where they could deal with an agent who knew their names and their company's needs. Roberts needed a way to serve each customer with the responsiveness and personal attention that the company had started out with.[1]

What would you recommend to recapture the responsiveness and customer intimacy of the "old Roberts"? How might the formation of teams help solve this problem?

The problems facing Roberts Express also confront many other companies. How can they be more flexible and responsive in an increasingly competitive environment? A quiet revolution has been taking place in organizations across the country and around the world as companies respond by using employee teams. From the assembly line to the executive office, from large corporations such as British Petroleum and 3M to government agencies such as the United States Information Agency, teams are becoming the basic building block of organizations. One survey found that, within three years, the number of *Fortune* 1000 companies using work teams increased by almost 20 percent, and teamwork has become the most frequent topic taught in company training programs. Similarly, a study of 109 Canadian organizations found that 42 percent report "widespread team-based activity" and only 13 percent report little or no team activity.[2]

Teams are popping up in the most unexpected places. An electromechanical assembly plant found that both quality and productivity increased after it abandoned the traditional production line in favor of work teams.[3] At Mattel, a team of artists, toy designers, computer experts, and automobile designers slashed 13 months from the usual toy design process, creating Top Speed toy cars in only 5 months. Hecla Mining Company uses teams for company goal setting; a major telecommunications company uses teams of salespeople to deal with big customers with complex purchasing requirements; and Lassiter Middle School in Jefferson County, Kentucky, uses teams of teachers to prepare daily schedules and handle student discipline problems. Multinational corporations are now using international teams composed of managers from different countries. Ford uses teams to spot quality problems and improve efficiency, and other manufacturers use teams to master sophisticated new production technologies.[4] And as we saw in Chapter 9, teams often are used to make important decisions, and many organizations are now run by top management teams under the title of Office of the CEO.

As we will see in this chapter, teams have emerged as a powerful management tool, because they involve and empower employees. Teams can cut across organizations in unusual ways. Hence workers are more satisfied, and higher productivity and product quality typically result. Moreover, managers discover a more flexible organization in which workers are not stuck in narrow jobs.

This chapter focuses on teams and their new applications within organizations. We will define various types of teams, explore their stages of development, and examine such characteristics as size, cohesiveness, and norms. We will discuss how individuals can make contributions to teams and review the benefits and costs associated with teamwork. Teams are an important aspect of organizational life, and the ability to manage them is an important component of manager and organization success.

Teams at Work

In this section, we will first define teams and then discuss a model of team effectiveness that summarizes the important concepts.

What Is a Team?

team
A unit of two or more people who interact and coordinate their work to accomplish a specific goal.

A **team** is a unit of 2 or more people who interact and coordinate their work to accomplish a specific goal.[5] This definition has three components. First, 2 or more people are required. Teams can be quite large, although most have fewer than 15 people. Second, people in a team have regular interaction. People who do not interact, such as when standing in line at a lunch counter or riding in an elevator, do not compose a team. Third, people in a team share a performance goal, whether it be to design a new hand-held computer, build a car, or write a textbook. Students often are assigned to teams to do classwork assignments, in which case the purpose is to perform the assignment and receive an acceptable grade.

Although a team is a group of people, the two terms are not interchangeable. An employer, a teacher, or a coach can put together a *group* of people and never build a *team*. The team concept implies a sense of shared mission and collective responsibility. Exhibit 19.1 lists the primary differences between groups and teams. When the University of Kentucky Wildcats won the 1998 national basketball championship, coaches and commentators noted that the team had less individual talent and fewer stars than some other teams but achieved a high level of success through excellent teamwork—shared leadership, purpose, and responsibility by all members working toward a common goal.

Teams are emerging as a powerful management tool and are popping up in the most unexpected places, such as this manufacturing cell at TRINOVA'S Aeroquip Inoac facility in Fremont, Ohio. The facility uses more than 40 teams that cross operations and job functions, helping the company eliminate non-value-added activities, lower costs, improve customer responsiveness, and increase quality. Toyota recently selected the Fremont facility, a joint venture between Aeroquip and Japan's Inoac Corporation, to participate in its prestigious Toyota Production System Strategic Program.

Model of Work Team Effectiveness

Some of the factors associated with team effectiveness are illustrated in Exhibit 19.2. Work team effectiveness is based on two outcomes—productive output and personal satisfaction.[6] *Satisfaction* pertains to the team's ability to meet the personal needs of its members and hence maintain their membership and commitment. *Productive output* pertains to the quality and quantity of task outputs as defined by team goals.

The factors that influence team effectiveness begin with the organizational context.[7] The organizational context in which the group operates is described in other chapters and includes such factors as structure, strategy, environment, culture, and reward systems. Within that context, managers define teams. Important team characteristics are the type of team, the team structure, and

Group	Team
Has a designated strong leader	Shares or rotates leadership roles
Individual accountability	Individual and mutual accountability (accountable to each other)
Identical purpose for group and organization	Specific team vision or purpose
Individual work products	Collective work products
Runs efficient meetings	Meetings encourage open-ended discussion and problem solving
Effectiveness measured indirectly by influence on business (such as financial performance)	Effectiveness measured directly by assessing collective work
Discusses, decides, delegates work to individuals	Discusses, decides, shares work

Exhibit **19.1**

Differences between Groups and Teams

Source: Adapted from Jon R. Katzenbach and Douglas K. Smith, "The Discipline of Teams," *Harvard Business Review* (March–April 1995), 111–120.

Exhibit *19.2*   *Work Team Effectiveness Model*

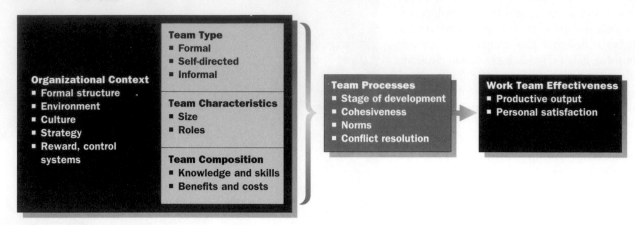

team composition. Factors such as the diversity of the team in terms of gender and race, as well as knowledge, skills, and attitudes, can have a tremendous impact on team processes and effectivenss.[8] Managers must decide when to create permanent teams within the formal structure and when to use a temporary task team. Team size and roles also are important. Managers must also consider whether a team is the best way to do a task. If costs outweigh benefits, managers may wish to assign an individual employee to the task.

These team characteristics influence processes internal to the team, which in turn affect output and satisfaction. Leaders must understand and manage stages of development, cohesiveness, norms, and conflict in order to establish an effective team. These processes are influenced by team and organizational characteristics and by the ability of members and leaders to direct these processes in a positive manner.

The model of team performance in Exhibit 19.2 is the basis for this chapter. In the following sections, we will examine types of organizational teams, team structure, internal processes, and team benefits and costs.

Types of Teams

Many types of teams can exist within organizations. The easiest way to classify teams is in terms of those created as part of the organization's formal structure and those created to increase employee participation.

Formal Teams

formal team
A team created by the organization as part of the formal organization structure.

Formal teams are created by the organization as part of the formal organization structure. Two common types of formal teams are vertical and horizontal, which typically represent vertical and horizontal structural relationships, as described in Chapters 10 and 11. These two types of teams are illustrated in Exhibit 19.3. A third type of formal team is the special-purpose team.

vertical team
A formal team composed of a manager and his or her subordinates in the organization's formal chain of command.

Vertical Team.   A **vertical team** is composed of a manager and his or her subordinates in the formal chain of command. Sometimes called a *functional team* or a *command team*, the vertical team may in some cases include

Exhibit 19.3 *Horizontal and Vertical Teams in an Organization*

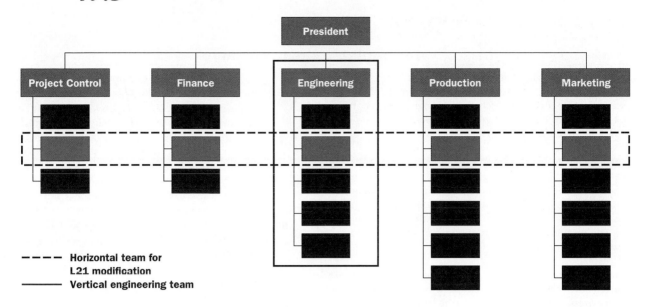

--- Horizontal team for
L21 modification

——— Vertical engineering team

three or four levels of hierarchy within a functional department. Typically, the vertical team includes a single department in an organization. The third-shift nursing team on the second floor of St. Luke's Hospital is a vertical team that includes nurses and a supervisor. A financial analysis department, a quality control department, an accounting department, and a human resource department are all command teams. Each is created by the organization to attain specific goals through members' joint activities and interactions.

Horizontal Team. A **horizontal team** is composed of employees from about the same hierarchical level but from different areas of expertise.[9] A horizontal team is drawn from several departments, is given a specific task, and may be disbanded after the task is completed. The two most common types of horizontal teams are task forces and committees.

As described in Chapter 11, a *task force* is a group of employees from different departments formed to deal with a specific activity and existing only until the task is completed. Sometimes called a *cross-functional team,* the task force might be used to create a new product in a manufacturing organization or a new history curriculum in a university. Several departments are involved, and many views have to be considered, so these tasks are best served with a horizontal team. US Airways set up a task force made up of mechanics, flight attendants, dispatchers, aircraft cleaners, ramp workers, luggage attendants, reservations agents, and others to design and start a low-fare airline to compete with the expansion of Southwest Airlines into the East. The task force spent several months pricing peanuts, conducting focus groups, studying the competition, and developing a plan to present to senior management for a new low-fare airline, MetroJet.[10] At Hallmark Cards, a cross-functional team made up of artists, writers, lithographers, designers, and photographers is set up to develop new greeting cards for each major holiday.

horizontal team

A formal team composed of employees from about the same hierarchical level but from different areas of expertise.

How to Run a Great Meeting

Many executives believe that meetings are a waste of time. Busy executives may spend up to 70 percent of their time in meetings at which participants doodle, drink coffee, and think about what they could be doing back in their offices.

Meetings need not be unproductive. Most meetings are called to process important information or to solve a problem. The key to success is what the chairperson does. Most of the chairperson's contributions are made before the meeting begins. He or she should make sure discussion flows freely and follow up the meeting with agreed-upon actions. The success of a meeting depends on what is done in advance of, during, and after it.

Prepare in Advance. Advance preparation is the single most important tool for running an efficient, productive meeting. Advance preparation should include the following:

1. *Define the purpose.* The chairperson should be very explicit in setting goals and expressing them concisely and meaningfully. If the purpose of the meeting is to "discuss the reduction of the 1999 research and development budget," then say so explicitly in the memo sent out to members.

2. *Circulate background papers.* Any reading materials relevant to the discussion should be given to each member in advance. Make sure members know their assignments and have background materials.

3. *Prepare an agenda.* The agenda is a simple list of the topics to be discussed. It is important because it lets people know what to expect and keeps the meeting on track. The agenda provides order and logic and gives the chairperson a means of control during the meeting if the discussion starts to wander.

4. *Issue invitations selectively.* If the group gets too big, the meeting will not be productive. If everyone is expected to participate, keep membership between 4 and 12.

5. *Set a time limit.* A formal meeting should have a specified amount of time. The ending time should be announced in advance, and the agenda should require the meeting to move along at a reasonable pace.

During the Meeting. If the chairperson is prepared in advance, the meeting will go smoothly. Moreover, certain techniques will bring out the best in people and make the meeting even more productive:

6. *Start on time.* This sounds obvious—but do not keep busy people waiting. Starting on time has symbolic value, because it tells people that the topic is important.

---

committee

A long-lasting, sometimes permanent team in the organization structure created to deal with tasks that recur regularly.

A **committee** generally is long-lived and may be a permanent part of the organization's structure. Membership on a committee usually is decided by a person's title or position rather than by personal expertise. A committee often needs official representation, compared with selection for a task force, which is based on personal qualifications for solving a problem. Committees typically are formed to deal with tasks that recur regularly. For example, a grievance committee handles employee grievances; an advisory committee makes recommendations in the areas of employee compensation and work practices; a worker-management committee may be concerned with work rules, job design changes, and suggestions for work improvement.[11]

As part of the horizontal structure of the organization, task forces and committees offer several advantages: (1) They allow organization members to exchange information; (2) they generate suggestions for coordinating the organizational units that are represented; (3) they develop new ideas and solutions for existing organizational problems; and (4) they assist in the development of new organizational practices and policies.

special-purpose team

A team created outside the formal organization to undertake a project of special importance or creativity.

Special-Purpose Team.
Special-purpose teams are created outside the formal organization structure to undertake a project of special importance or creativity. McDonald's created a special team to create the Chicken

7. *State the purpose and review the agenda.* The chairperson should start the meeting by stating the explicit purpose and clarifying what should be accomplished by the time the meeting is over.

8. *Encourage participation.* Good meetings contain lots of discussion. If the chairperson merely wants to present one-way information to members, he or she should send a memo. A few subtle techniques go a long way toward increasing participation:

   a) *Draw out the silent.* This means saying, "Bob, what do you think of Nancy's idea?"

   b) *Control the talkative.* Some people overdo it and dominate the discussion. The chairperson's job is to redirect the discussion toward other people. One organization has a rule called NOSTUESO (No one speaks twice until everyone speaks once).

   c) *Encourage the clash of ideas.* A good meeting is not a series of dialogues but a crosscurrent of discussion and debate. The chairperson guides, mediates, stimulates, and summarizes this discussion.

   d) *Call on the most senior people last.* Sometimes junior people are reluctant to disagree with senior people, so it is best to get the junior people's ideas on the table first. This will provide wider views and ideas.

   e) *Give credit.* Make sure that people who suggest ideas get the credit, because people often make someone else's ideas their own. Giving due credit encourages continued participation.

f) *Listen.* The chairperson should not preach or engage in one-on-one dialogue with group members. The point is to listen and to facilitate discussion.

9. *Stick to the purpose.* Encouraging a free flow of ideas does not mean allowing participants to sidetrack the meeting into discussions of issues not on the agenda. This can waste valuable time and prevent the group from reaching its goals.

After the meeting. The actions following the meeting are designed to summarize and implement agreed-upon points. Postmeeting activities are set in motion by a call to action.

10. *End with a call to action.* The last item of the meeting's agenda is to summarize the main points and make sure everyone understands his or her assignments.

11. *Follow-up.* Mail minutes of the meeting to members. Use this memorandum to summarize the key accomplishments of the meeting, suggest schedules for agreed-upon activities, and start the ball rolling in preparation for the next meeting.

SOURCES: Based on Edward Michaels, "Business Meetings," *Small Business Reports* (February 1989), 82–88; Daniel Stoffman, "Waking Up to Great Meetings," *Canadian Business*, November 1986, 75–79; Antoney Jay, "How to Run a Meeting," *Harvard Business Review* (March–April 1976), 120–134; Jana Kemp, "Avoiding Agenda Overstack," *Corporate University Review*, May–June 1997, 42–43; and John Grossman, "We've Got to Start Meeting Like This," *Inc.*, April 1998, 70–74.

McNugget. E. J. (Bud) Sweeney was asked to head up a team to bring bits of batter-covered chicken to the marketplace. The McNugget team needed breathing room and was separated from the formal corporate structure to give it the autonomy to perform successfully. A special-purpose team still is part of the formal organization and has its own reporting structure, but members perceive themselves as a separate entity.[12]

The formal teams described here must be skillfully managed to accomplish their purpose. One important skill, knowing how to run a team meeting, is described in the Manager's Shoptalk box.

Self-Directed Teams

Employee involvement through teams is designed to increase the participation of low-level workers in decision making and the conduct of their jobs, with the goal of improving performance. Employee involvement represents a revolution in business prompted by the success of teamwork in Japanese companies. Hundreds of companies, large and small, are jumping aboard the bandwagon, including DaimlerChrysler, Cummins Engine, Wilson Golf Ball, and Edy's Grand Ice Cream. Employee involvement started out simply with techniques such as information sharing with employees or asking employees

Highsmith Inc., a Fort Atkinson, Wisconsin company, is the country's leading mail-order supplier of equipment such as book displays, audio-video tools, and educational software for schools and libraries. The company's employees work in a flat organization in which self-directed teams, along with a continuous-learning program and flextime, are manifest. According to CEO Duncan Highsmith, "We have a limited labor market, so I wanted to make the most of the people we had by helping them become decision makers, by providing them with information and the context to make good decisions." In the photo is a team of librarians (left to right, Oma Dixon, Lisa Guedea Carreño, and Genevieve Mecherly) who facilitate the culture of autonomy at Highsmith. "We're here to help people integrate information into their jobs as seamlessly as possible," says Carreño. "That way, they can keep doing their jobs."

problem-solving team
Typically 5 to 12 hourly employees from the same department who meet to discuss ways of improving quality, efficiency, and the work environment.

self-directed team
A team consisting of 5 to 20 multiskilled workers who rotate jobs to produce an entire product or service, often supervised by an elected member.

for suggestions about improving the work. Gradually, companies moved toward greater autonomy for employees, which led first to problem-solving teams and then to self-directed teams.[13]

Problem-solving teams typically consist of 5 to 12 hourly employees from the same department who voluntarily meet to discuss ways of improving quality, efficiency, and the work environment. Recommendations are proposed to management for approval. Problem-solving teams usually are the first step in a company's move toward greater employee participation. The most widely known application is quality circles, initiated by the Japanese, in which employees focus on ways to improve quality in the production process. USX has adopted this approach in several of its steel mills, recognizing that quality takes a team effort. Under the title All Product Excellence program (APEX), USX set up 40 APEX teams of up to 12 employees at its plant in West Mifflin, Pennsylvania. These teams meet several times a month to solve quality problems. The APEX teams have since spread to mills in Indiana, Ohio, and California.[14]

As a company matures, problem-solving teams can gradually evolve into self-directed teams, which represent a fundamental change in how employee work is organized. Self-directed teams enable employees to feel challenged, find their work meaningful, and develop a strong sense of identity with the company.[15] **Self-directed teams** typically consist of 5 to 20 multiskilled workers who rotate jobs to produce an entire product or service or at least one complete aspect or portion of a product or service (e.g., engine assembly, insurance claim processing). The central idea is that the teams themselves, rather than managers or supervisors, take responsibility for their work, make decisions, monitor their own performance, and alter their work behavior as needed to solve problems, meet goals, and adapt to changing conditions.[16] Self-directed teams are permanent teams that typically include the following elements:

- The team includes employees with several skills and functions, and the combined skills are sufficient to perform a major organizational task. A team may include members from the foundry, machining, grinding, fabrication,

VeriFone's Virtual World

VeriFone, an equipment supplier for credit card verification and automated payments, started out as a virtual company over 15 years ago and today uses virtual teams in every aspect of its business. Teams of facility managers work together to determine how to reduce toxins in their offices. Marketing and development groups brainstorm new products. Sales reps pool information and customer testimonials.

VeriFone's concept of virtual teams is highly flexible. Some teams may include only VeriFone employees while others include outsiders, such as the employees of a customer or partner. Some are permanent, such as operational teams that run their companies virtually, while others are temporary. Any employee can organize a temporary virtual team to work on a specific problem. For example, one sales rep sent out an SOS when he saw a major sales prospect in Greece falling apart. Overnight, a team made up of sales, marketing, and technical-support staff from around the world came together to provide data and testimonials that eventually helped the Greek representative make the sale.

Despite all this flexibility, VeriFone has some pretty strict "rules" to ensure that teams are not formed haphazardly. Employees complete a 40-hour training program in which they learn how to create a successful virtual team. In addition, leaders of virtual teams follow written procedures put together by the company's senior managers. VeriFone offers the following guidelines for successful virtual teams:

1. *Define the purpose.* A VeriFone team always starts by putting its purpose in writing. This keeps everyone on track and prevents misunderstandings.

2. *Recruit team members.* Most virtual teams should be between three and seven members. Also, the team should include people who represent a diversity of views and experiences. Selecting members in different time zones means productive work can be going on around the clock.

3. *Determine the duration of the team.* Decide whether the purpose and goals call for a short-term task force or problem-solving team or for a long-term operational team.

4. *Select the communications technology.* All VeriFone staffers are not only well-trained in *how* to use communications tools but also in *when* to use them. General guidelines are that for keeping in contact remotely, teams use beepers, cell phones, and voice mail; for disseminating information, fax, E-mail, and application sharing over the network. For brainstorming, discussion, and decision making, teams use E-mail, conference calls, and videoconferencing. Selecting the right tool is critical to the success of the virtual team.

VeriFone employees also are trained to understand the psychological pitfalls of communicating virtually. Some subtleties of meaning are always lost and misunderstandings are more common than when teams work face-to-face. E-mail in particular can lead to misunderstandings, so team members communicate by phone or videoconference on sensitive or complicated issues.

www.verifone.com

SOURCE: William R. Pape, "Group Insurance," *Inc. Technology* 1997, no. 2, 29, 31.

---

and sales departments, with each member cross-trained to perform one another's jobs. The team eliminates barriers among departments, enabling excellent coordination to produce a product or service.

- The team is given access to resources such as information, equipment, machinery, and supplies needed to perform the complete task.

- The team is empowered with decision-making authority, which means that members have the freedom to select new members, solve problems, spend money, monitor results, and plan for the future.[17]

In a self-directed team, team members take over managerial duties such as scheduling work or vacations or ordering materials. They work with minimum supervision, perhaps electing one of their own as supervisor, who may change each year. Teams at Corning work without shift supervisors and work closely with other plant divisions to solve production-line problems and coordinate deadlines and deliveries. Teams have the authority to make and implement decisions, complete projects, and solve problems.[18]

Self-directed teams can be highly effective. Service companies such as Federal Express and IDS have boosted productivity up to 40 percent by adopting self-directed teams. Volvo uses self-directed teams of 7 to 10 hourly workers to assemble four cars per shift. However, there still is a reluctance among management to entrust workers with managerial responsibilities and duties. A survey conducted by the University of Southern California's Center for Effective Organizations found that, although 68 percent of *Fortune* 1000 companies report using self-directed teams, only 10 percent of workers are involved.[19]

virtual team
A team that uses computer technology and groupware so that geographically distant members can collaborate on projects and reach common goals.

One type of self-directed team, the virtual team, has resulted from globalization and advances in technology. **Virtual teams** use computer technology and groupware to tie together geographically distant members working toward a common goal. Virtual teams can be formed within an organization whose plants and offices are scattered across the nation or around the world. A company may also use virtual teams in partnership with suppliers or, in many cases, with competitors to pull together the best minds to complete a project or speed a new product to market. Leadership among team members is shared or altered, depending on the area of expertise needed at each point in the project. The success of virtual teams is dependent upon several crucial elements, including careful selection of partners and team members, strong management support of the team and its goals, clear goals, utilization of the best communications tools and procedures, the development of trust among all members, and information sharing.[20] VeriFone, described in the Technology box, uses virtual teams in every aspect of its business.

Companies are trying to integrate a variety of team approaches into their operations. For example, Whole Foods Market, the largest natural foods grocer in the United States, has turned teamwork into a highly profitable business model.

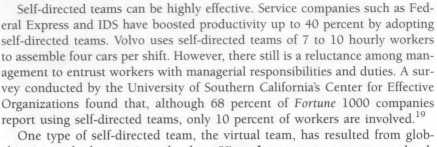

WHOLE FOODS MARKET
www.wholefoods.com

As recently as 1991, Whole Foods Market had barely a dozen stores in three states. Today, it has the clout of a nationwide chain, with stores in ten states and net profits that are typically double the national average.

The Whole Foods culture is based on decentralized teamwork. Each store is an autonomous profit center made up of an average of 10 self-directed teams—grocery, produce, and so forth. Teams—and only teams—have the power to approve new hires for full-time jobs. Store leaders screen candidates and recommend them for a job on a specific team, but it takes a two-thirds vote of the team to approve the hire.

The company believes the first prerequisite of teamwork is trust. That trust starts with the hiring vote. In addition, Whole Foods supports teamwork with wide-open information on financial and operations systems. Sensitive figures on store sales, team sales, profit margins, and even yearly salaries and bonuses are available to any employee. Executive salaries are limited to no more than eight times the average wage. According to CEO John Mackey, open information keeps everyone "aligned to the vision of shared fate. . . .If you're trying to create a high-trust organization, an organization where people are all-for-one and one-for-all, you can't have secrets."[21]

Work Team Characteristics

Teams in organizations take on characteristics that are important to internal processes and team performance. Two characteristics of concern to managers are team size and member roles.

Size

The ideal size of work teams often is thought to be 7, although variations of from 5 to 12 typically are associated with good team performance. These teams are large enough to take advantage of diverse skills, enable members to express good and bad feelings, and aggressively solve problems. They also are small enough to permit members to feel an intimate part of the group.

In general, as a team increases in size, it becomes harder for each member to interact with and influence the others. A summary of research on group size suggests the following:

1. Small teams (2 to 4 members) show more agreement, ask more questions, and exchange more opinions. Members want to get along with one another. Small teams report more satisfaction and enter into more personal discussions. They tend to be informal and make few demands on team leaders.

2. Large teams (12 or more) tend to have more disagreements and differences of opinion. Subgroups often form, and conflicts among them occur, ranging from protection of "turf" to trivial matters such as "what kind of coffee is brewing in the pot." Demands on leaders are greater because there is more centralized decision making and less member participation. Large teams also tend to be less friendly. Turnover and absenteeism are higher in a large team, especially for blue-collar workers. Because less satisfaction is associated with specialized tasks and poor communication, team members have fewer opportunities to participate and feel an intimate part of the group.[22]

As a general rule, large teams make need satisfaction for individuals more difficult; thus, there is less reason for people to remain committed to their goals. Teams of from 5 to 12 seem to work best. If a team grows larger than 20, managers should divide it into subgroups, each with its own members and goals.

Member Roles

For a team to be successful over the long run, it must be structured so as to both maintain its members' social well-being and accomplish its task. In successful teams, the requirements for task performance and social satisfaction are met by the emergence of two types of roles: task specialist and socioemotional.[23]

People who play the **task specialist role** spend time and energy helping the team reach its goal. They often display the following behaviors:

task specialist role
A role in which the individual devotes personal time and energy to helping the team accomplish its task.

- *Initiation:* Propose new solutions to team problems.

- *Give opinions:* Offer opinions on task solutions; give candid feedback on others' suggestions.

- *Seek information:* Ask for task-relevant facts.

- *Summarize:* Relate various ideas to the problem at hand; pull ideas together into a summary perspective.

- *Energize:* Stimulate the team into action when interest drops.[24]

People who adopt a **socioemotional role** support team members' emotional needs and help strengthen the social entity. They display the following behaviors:

socioemotional role
A role in which the individual provides support for team members' emotional needs and social unity.

- *Encourage:* Are warm and receptive to others' ideas; praise and encourage others to draw forth their contributions.

- *Harmonize:* Reconcile group conflicts; help disagreeing parties reach agreement.

- *Reduce tension:* May tell jokes or in other ways draw off emotions when group atmosphere is tense.

- *Follow:* Go along with the team; agree to other team members' ideas.

- *Compromise:* Will shift own opinions to maintain team harmony.[25]

Exhibit 19.4 illustrates task specialist and socioemotional roles in teams. When most individuals in a team play a social role, the team is socially oriented. Members do not criticize or disagree with one another and do not forcefully offer opinions or try to accomplish team tasks, because their primary interest is to keep the team happy. Teams with mostly socioemotional roles can be very satisfying, but they also can be unproductive. At the other extreme, a team made up primarily of task specialists will tend to have a singular concern for task accomplishment. This team will be effective for a short period of time but will not be satisfying for members over the long run. Task specialists convey little emotional concern for one another, are unsupportive, and ignore team members' social and emotional needs. The task-oriented team can be humorless and unsatisfying.

As Exhibit 19.4 illustrates, some team members may play a dual role. People with **dual roles** both contribute to the task and meet members' emotional needs. Such people may become team leaders because they satisfy both types of needs and are looked up to by other members. Exhibit 19.4 also shows the final type of role, called the *nonparticipator role.* People in the **nonparticipator role** contribute little to either the task or the social needs of team members. They typically are held in low esteem by the team.

The important thing for managers to remember is that effective teams must have people in both task specialist and socioemotional roles. Humor and social concern are as important to team effectiveness as are facts and problem solving. Managers also should remember that some people perform better in one type of role; some are inclined toward social concerns and others

dual role
A role in which the individual both contributes to the team's task and supports members' emotional needs.

nonparticipator role
A role in which the individual contributes little to either the task or members' socioemotional needs.

Exhibit **19.4**   *Team Member Roles*

	Member Social Behavior	
High	**Task Specialist Role** Focuses on task accomplishment over human needs — Important role, but if adopted by everyone, team's social needs won't be met	**Dual Role** Focuses on task and people — May be a team leader — Important role, but not essential if members adopt task specialist and socioemotional roles
Member Task Behavior	**Nonparticipator Role** Contributes little to either task or people needs of team — Not an important role—if adopted by too many members, team will disband	**Socioemotional Role** Focuses on people needs of team over task — Important role, but if adopted by everyone, team's tasks won't be accomplished
Low	Low	High

toward task concerns. A well-balanced team will do best over the long term because it will be personally satisfying for team members and permit the accomplishment of team tasks.

Team Processes

Now we turn our attention to internal team processes. Team processes pertain to those dynamics that change over time and can be influenced by team leaders. In this section, we will discuss the team processes of stages of development, cohesiveness, and norms. The fourth type of team process, conflict, will be covered in the next section.

forming
The stage of team development characterized by orientation and acquaintance.

storming
The stage of team development in which individual personalities and roles, and resulting conflicts, emerge.

Stages of Team Development

After a team has been created, there are distinct stages through which it develops.[26] New teams are different from mature teams. Recall a time when you were a member of a new team, such as a fraternity or sorority pledge class, a committee, or a small team formed to do a class assignment. Over time the team changed. In the beginning, team members had to get to know one another, establish roles and norms, divide the labor, and clarify the team's task. In this way, members became parts of a smoothly operating team. The challenge for leaders is to understand the stage of the team's development and take action that will help the group improve its functioning.

Research findings suggest that team development is not random but evolves over definitive stages. Several models describing these stages exist; one useful model is shown in Exhibit 19.5. The five stages typically occur in sequence. In teams that are under time pressure or that will exist for only a few days, the stages may occur rapidly. Each stage confronts team leaders and members with unique problems and challenges.[27]

Exhibit 19.5

Five Stages of Team Development

Forming. The **forming** stage of development is a period of orientation and getting acquainted. Members break the ice and test one another for friendship possibilities and task orientation. Team members find which behaviors are acceptable to others. Uncertainty is high during this stage, and members usually accept whatever power or authority is offered by either formal or informal leaders. Members are dependent on the team until they find out what the ground rules are and what is expected of them. During this initial stage, members are concerned about such things as "What is expected of me?" "What is acceptable?" "Will I fit in?" During the forming stage, the team leader should provide time for members to get acquainted with one another and encourage them to engage in informal social discussions.

Storming. During the **storming** stage, individual personalities emerge. People become more assertive in clarifying their roles and what is expected of them. This stage is marked by conflict and disagreement. People may disagree over their perceptions of the team's mission. Members may jockey for positions, and coalitions or subgroups based on common interests may form. One subgroup may disagree with another over the total team's goals or how to achieve them. The team is not yet cohesive and may be characterized by a general lack of unity. Unless teams can successfully move beyond this stage, they may get bogged down and never achieve high performance. During the storming stage, the team leader should encourage participation by each team member. Members should propose ideas, disagree with one another, and work through the uncertainties and conflicting perceptions about team tasks and goals.

norming
The stage of team development in which conflicts developed during the storming stage are resolved and team harmony and unity emerge.

Norming.   During the **norming** stage, conflict is resolved, and team harmony and unity emerge. Consensus develops on who has the power, who is the leader, and members' roles. Members come to accept and understand one another. Differences are resolved, and members develop a sense of team cohesion. This stage typically is of short duration. During the norming stage, the team leader should emphasize oneness within the team and help clarify team norms and values.

performing
The stage of team development in which members focus on problem solving and accomplishing the team's assigned task.

Performing.   During the **performing** stage, the major emphasis is on problem solving and accomplishing the assigned task. Members are committed to the team's mission. They are coordinated with one another and handle disagreements in a mature way. They confront and resolve problems in the interest of task accomplishment. They interact frequently and direct discussion and influence toward achieving team goals. During this stage, the leader should concentrate on managing high task performance. Both socioemotional and task specialists should contribute.

adjourning
The stage of team development in which members prepare for the team's disbandment.

Adjourning.   The **adjourning** stage occurs in committees, task forces, and teams that have a limited task to perform and are disbanded afterward. During this stage, the emphasis is on wrapping up and gearing down. Task performance is no longer a top priority. Members may feel heightened emotionality, strong cohesiveness, and depression or even regret over the team's disbandment. They may feel happy about mission accomplishment and sad about the loss of friendship and associations. At this point, the leader may wish to signify the team's disbanding with a ritual or ceremony, perhaps giving out plaques and awards to signify closure and completeness.

Excite, the number 2 search engine company after Yahoo, was founded through teamwork. The Excite team, made up of members, whose nicknames are (from left to right), Okmo, Koenig, Foopee, Mister Swiss, Picklock, and Tsar, met at Stanford University. During their team's forming stage, they engaged in informal social discussions while developing a plan to protect themselves from injury. "Well, when we played at Cal, the students used to throw frozen fruit at us. It would really hurt if you got hit, so one year we got golf clubs—three woods, I think they were—and we whaled those oranges right back in the crowd. It was great." Genius comes in many forms, and today the company's revenues exceed $50.2 million dollars.

The stages of team development are illustrated by the formation of self-directed teams at BP Norge, the Norwegian arm of British Petroleum.

BP NORGE
www.bp.no

Early efforts to introduce self-directed teams at BP Norge failed, leaving employees disillusioned and skeptical. Managers needed a way to work through barriers of resistance and negativity, reenergize the work force, and help the existing work groups develop into true self-directed teams.

The solution was to hold a series of workshops and meetings to discuss the self-directed team concept and educate employees about the stages of team development. At BP Norge, the stages of team development were called denial, resistance, exploration, and commitment. In the *denial* stage (similar to forming), employees idealized the past, resisted mutual accountability, and gradually began to surface their skepticism, confusion, and uncertainty. Relationships were characterized by politeness as people explored what was expected of them in their new roles. The *resistance* stage (storming) was marked by anxiety, anger, depression, apathy, and conflict. BP Norge's *exploration* stage straddles the storming and the norming stages in our model. There still is some confusion, but teams are letting go of old values and ideas and incorporating new ones. Conflict is resolved and team roles and expectations are defined. The final stage, *commitment,* is analogous to the performing stage in our model. The focus here is on a common purpose and approach and the complete movement from "I" to "we." Team members accept the concept of mutual responsibility and accountability and are focused on performance and task accomplishment.

Because workers understood the stages of team development, they were able to recognize what was happening as normal and take a nonjudgmental "this is where we are in the process" attitude rather than a "this will never work" attitude. Thus, each member was able to approach the development of teams as a natural process that involved self-discovery, exploration of new ideas, and the opportunity to grow and develop.[28]

Team Cohesiveness

Another important aspect of the team process is cohesiveness. **Team cohesiveness** is defined as the extent to which members are attracted to the team and motivated to remain in it.[29] Members of highly cohesive teams are committed to team activities, attend meetings, and are happy when the team succeeds. Members of less cohesive teams are less concerned about the team's welfare. High cohesiveness is normally considered an attractive feature of teams.

team cohesiveness
The extent to which team members are attracted to the team and motivated to remain in it.

Determinants of Team Cohesiveness.   Characteristics of team structure and context influence cohesiveness. First is *team interaction.* The greater the amount of contact among team members and the more time spent together, the more cohesive the team. Through frequent interactions, members get to know one another and become more devoted to the team.[30] Second is the concept of *shared goals.* If team members agree on goals, they will be more cohesive. Agreeing on purpose and direction binds the team together. Third is *personal attraction to the team*, meaning that members have similar attitudes and values and enjoy being together.

Two factors in the team's context also influence group cohesiveness. The first is the presence of competition. When a team is in moderate competition

This "trust fall" during a team-building session at Gilbane Building Company helps strengthen team cohesiveness by leading to increased communication, trust, and a friendly team atmosphere. High team cohesiveness has almost uniformly good effects on the satisfaction and morale of team members. Team building and project partnering are major components of Gilbane's culture, and the company is now extending the team concept to include clients, customers, and subcontractors.

with other teams, its cohesiveness increases as it strives to win. Whether competition is among sales teams to attain the top sales volume or among manufacturing departments to reduce rejects, competition increases team solidarity and cohesiveness.[31] Finally, team success and the favorable evaluation of the team by outsiders add to cohesiveness. When a team succeeds in its task and others in the organization recognize the success, members feel good, and their commitment to the team will be high.

Chaparral Steel, an amazingly successful steel company in Midlothian, Texas, encourages team cohesiveness through promotion of the "Chaparral Process." The steelmaker strives to create super teams in which each member sees his or her job in relation to the entire organization and its goals. Commitment to cohesiveness and efficiency enables Chaparral teams to perform amazing tasks. The purchase and installation of new mill equipment is a highly complicated task for any steel company, and calibrating and finetuning the steelmaking process can take years. However, a Chaparral team of four completed the worldwide search, purchase negotiations, shipment, and installation in one year.[32]

Consequences of Team Cohesiveness.   The outcome of team cohesiveness can fall into two categories—morale and productivity. As a general rule, morale is higher in cohesive teams because of increased communication among members, a friendly team climate, maintenance of membership because of commitment to the team, loyalty, and member participation in team decisions and activities. High cohesiveness has almost uniformly good effects on the satisfaction and morale of team members.[33]

With respect to team performance, research findings are mixed, but cohesiveness may have several effects.[34] First, in a cohesive team, members' productivity tends to be more uniform. Productivity differences among members are small because the team exerts pressure toward conformity. Noncohesive teams do not have this control over member behavior and therefore tend to have wider variation in member productivity.

With respect to the productivity of the team as a whole, research findings suggest that cohesive teams have the potential to be productive, but the degree of productivity depends on the relationship between management and the working team. Thus, team cohesiveness does not necessarily lead to higher team productivity. One study surveyed more than 200 work teams and correlated job performance with their cohesiveness.[35] Highly cohesive teams were more productive when team members felt management support and less productive when they sensed management hostility and negativism. Management hostility led to team norms and goals of low performance, and the highly cohesive teams performed poorly, in accordance with their norms and goals.

The relationship between performance outcomes and cohesiveness is illustrated in Exhibit 19.6. The highest productivity occurs when the team is cohesive and also has a high performance norm, which is a result of its positive relationship with management. Moderate productivity occurs when cohesiveness is low, because team members are less committed to performance norms. The lowest productivity occurs when cohesiveness is high and the team's performance norm is low. Thus, cohesive teams are able to attain their goals and enforce their norms, which can lead to either very high or very low productivity. For an excellent example of team cohesiveness

Exhibit 19.6   *Relationship among Team Cohesiveness, Performance Norms, and Productivity*

High	**Moderate Productivity** Weak norms in alignment with organization goals	**High Productivity** Strong norms in alignment with organization goals
Team Performance Norms		
Low	**Low/Moderate Productivity** Weak norms in opposition to organization goals	**Low Productivity** Strong norms in opposition to organization goals
	Low **Team Cohesiveness**	High

combined with a high performance norm, consider the "Rainbow Warriors," the pit crew that helped lead NASCAR driver Jeff Gordon from anonymity to unprecedented success.

Jeff Gordon, at age 24 the youngest-ever winner of the Winston Cup Championship, has become a "superstar," showing up on late-night talk shows and *People* magazine's 50 Most Beautiful People list. But he gives much of the credit for his success to his pit crew, led by Ray Evernham, widely considered the premier pit crew chief in NASCAR (the National Association for Stock Car Auto Racing). Evernham has spoken to groups of executives from DuPont, Digital, and Ingersoll Rand on how to win in the game of business as well as auto racing. Both Evernham and Gordon support the pit crew and push them to be the best in the business. When Gordon's car wins, everybody shares in the prize money. In addition, Evernham puts a percentage of his own bonus into the team account. Whenever he gets a personal service contract and is paid to speak or sign autographs, the team gets a share of what he earns. Evernham and Gordon constantly strive to make sure team members know that every success belongs to the team.

Evernham promotes team cohesiveness in a number of ways. Crew members wear rainbow-striped jumpsuits and call themselves the Rainbow Warriors. When they meet, they put their chairs in a circle to symbolize the "circle of strength," that they are stronger as a team than on their own. Evernham even hired a coach to train and rehearse the crew with exercises to build trust and cohesiveness. "I'm sure that it all looked funny," Evernham says, "but it worked. Typically we pit in 17 seconds or less—about a second faster than other teams do. In one second, a car going 200 mph travels nearly 300 feet. So right there, we gain 300 feet on the competition."[36]

THE RAINBOW WARRIORS
www.nascar.com

Team Norms

A team **norm** is a standard of conduct that is shared by team members and guides their behavior.[37] Norms are informal. They are not written down as are rules and procedures. Norms are valuable because they define boundaries of acceptable behavior. They make life easier for team members by providing a frame of reference for what is right and wrong. Norms identify key values, clarify role expectations, and facilitate team survival. For example, union members may develop a norm of not cooperating with management because they do not trust management's motives. In this way, norms protect the group and express key values.

norm
A standard of conduct that is shared by team members and guides their behavior.

Norms begin to develop in the first interactions among members of a new team.[38] Norms that apply to both day-to-day behavior and employee output and performance gradually evolve. Norms thus tell members what is acceptable and direct members' actions toward acceptable productivity or performance. Four common ways in which norms develop for controlling and directing behavior are illustrated in Exhibit 19.7.[39]

Critical Events. Often *critical events* in a team's history establish an important precedent. One example occurred when Arthur Schlesinger, despite his serious reservations about the Bay of Pigs invasion, was pressured by Attorney General Robert Kennedy not to raise his objections to President Kennedy. This critical incident helped create a norm in which team members refrained from expressing disagreement with the president.

Any critical event can lead to the creation of a norm. In one organization, a department head invited the entire staff to his house for dinner. The next day people discovered that no one had attended, and this resulted in a norm prohibiting outside entertaining.[40]

Primacy. *Primacy* means that the first behaviors that occur in a team often set a precedent for later team expectations. For example, at one company a team leader began his first meeting by raising an issue and then "leading" team members until he got the solution he wanted. The pattern became ingrained so quickly into an unproductive team norm that team members dubbed meetings the "Guess What I Think" game.[41]

Carryover Behaviors. *Carryover behaviors* bring norms into the team from outside. One current example is the strong norm against smoking in many management teams. Some team members sneak around, gargling with mouthwash, and fear expulsion because the team culture believes everyone should kick the habit. At such companies as Johnson & Johnson, Dow Chemical, and Aetna Life & Casualty, the norm is "If you want to advance, don't

Exhibit *19.7*
Four Ways Team Norms Develop

smoke."[42] Carryover behavior also influences small teams of college students assigned by instructors to do class work. Norms brought into the team from outside suggest that students should participate equally and help members get a reasonable grade.

Explicit Statements. With *explicit statements,* leaders or team members can initiate norms by articulating them to the team. Explicit statements symbolize what counts and thus have considerable impact. Making explicit statements is probably the most effective way for managers to change norms in an established team. For example, Richard Boyle of Honeywell wrote a memo relaxing the company's excessive formality and creating a new norm. Called "Loosening Up the Tie," the memo said in part:

> I wish to announce a relaxed wearing apparel policy, and loosen my tie for the summer. Let's try it starting on May 15th and tentatively ending on September 15th. Since departments vary in customer contact and, depending on location, may even vary slightly in temperature, Department Heads are hereby given authority to allow variations. . . .
>
>   This change requires each of us to use good judgment. On the one extreme it means you do not have to wear a tie; on the other, tennis shoes, shorts, and a t-shirt is too relaxed. Have a comfortable, enjoyable summer. I hope to.[43]

The tie memo helped demonstrate management's interest in developing a relaxed, more casual atmosphere at Honeywell.

Managing Team Conflict

The final characteristic of team process is conflict. Of all the skills required for effective team management, none is more important than handling the conflicts that inevitably arise among members. Whenever people work together in teams, some conflict is inevitable. Conflict can arise among members within a team or between one team and another. **Conflict** refers to antagonistic interaction in which one party attempts to block the intentions or goals of another.[44] Competition, which is rivalry among individuals or teams, can have a healthy impact because it energizes people toward higher performance.[45] In addition, some conflict within teams may lead to better decision making because multiple viewpoints are considered. There is some research evidence that low conflict in top management teams is associated with poor decision making. Team members just go along with the strongest opinion, which often is that of the CEO, rather than consider alternate ideas and solutions.[46] However, too much conflict can be destructive, tear relationships apart, and interfere with the healthy exchange of ideas and information.[47]

conflict
Antagonistic interaction in which one party attempts to thwart the intentions or goals of another.

Causes of Conflict

Several factors can cause people to engage in conflict:[48]

Scarce Resources. Resources include money, information, and supplies. In their desire to achieve goals, individuals may wish to increase their resources, which throws them into conflict. Whenever individuals or teams must compete for scarce or declining resources, conflict is almost inevitable. At the Levi Strauss blue jeans plant near Knoxville, Tennessee, a change in pay systems—in which employees were paid based on team output rather than on the old individual piecework system—led to severe conflict because some employees felt that slower team members hurt their pocketbooks. One worker says her hourly pay dropped nearly $2, while slower team members realized an increase over what they earned on the piecework system.[49]

Jurisdictional Ambiguities.   Conflicts also emerge when job boundaries and responsibilities are unclear. When task responsibilities are well defined and predictable, people know where they stand. When they are unclear, people may disagree about who has responsibility for specific tasks or who has a claim on resources. A conflict emerged between the two sides of Andersen Worldwide—Andersen Consulting (management consulting) and Arthur Andersen (accounting services)—because both sides are suddenly going after the same business. Jurisdictional ambiguities have led to a global brawl that threatens to tear apart the giant company.[50]

Communication Breakdown.   Communication, as described in Chapter 18, sometimes is faulty. The potential for communication breakdown is even greater with virtual teams and global teams made up of members from different countries and cultures. Poor communications result in misperceptions and misunderstandings of other people and teams. In some cases, information may be intentionally withheld, which can jeopardize trust among teams and lead to long-lasting conflict.

Personality Clashes.   A personality clash occurs when people simply do not get along with one another and do not see eye-to-eye on any issue. Personality clashes are caused by basic differences in personality, values, and attitudes. Often it's a good idea to simply separate the parties so that they need not interact with one another.

Power and Status Differences.   Power and status differences occur when one party has disputable influence over another. Low-prestige individuals or departments may resist their low status. People may engage in conflict to increase their power and influence in the team or organization.

Goal Differences.   Conflict often occurs simply because people are pursuing conflicting goals. Goal differences are natural in organizations. Individual salespeople's targets may put them in conflict with one another or with the sales manager. Moreover, the sales department may have goals that conflict with those of manufacturing. One conflict emerged within the United Auto Workers (UAW) because one subgroup is against teamwork, believing that it exploits workers and does nothing but make them work harder. Other factions in the UAW believe it is beneficial for both workers and the organization. These opposing goals are causing major clashes among these UAW subgroups.[51]

Styles to Handle Conflict

Teams as well as individuals develop specific styles for dealing with conflict, based on the desire to satisfy their own concern versus the other party's concern. A model that describes five styles of handling conflict is in Exhibit 19.8. The two major dimensions are the extent to which an individual is assertive versus cooperative in his or her approach to conflict.

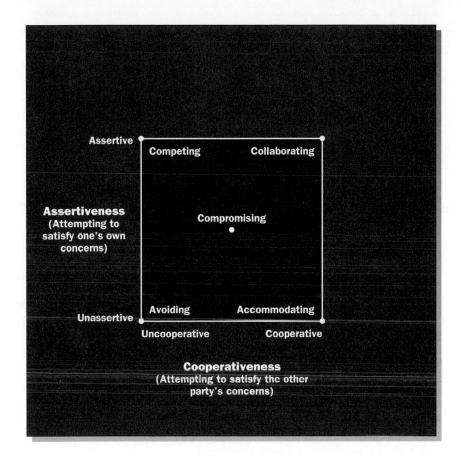

Exhibit **19.8**

A Model of Styles to Handle Conflict

SOURCE: Adapted from Kenneth Thomas, "Conflict and Conflict Management," in *Handbook of Industrial and Organizational Behavior,* ed. M. D. Dunnette (New York: John Wiley, 1976), 900.

Effective team members vary their style of handling conflict to fit a specific situation. Each style is appropriate in certain cases.

1. The *competing style,* which reflects assertiveness to get one's own way, should be used when quick, decisive action is vital on important issues or unpopular actions, such as during emergencies or urgent cost cutting.

2. The *avoiding style,* which reflects neither assertiveness nor cooperativeness, is appropriate when an issue is trivial, when there is no chance of winning, when a delay to gather more information is needed, or when a disruption would be very costly.

3. The *compromising style* reflects a moderate amount of both assertiveness and cooperativeness. It is appropriate when the goals on both sides are equally important, when opponents have equal power and both sides want to split the difference, or when people need to arrive at temporary or expedient solutions under time pressure.

4. The *accommodating style* reflects a high degree of cooperativeness, which works best when people realize that they are wrong, when an issue is more important to others than to oneself, when building social credits for use in later discussions, and when maintaining harmony is especially important.

5. The *collaborating style* reflects both a high degree of assertiveness and cooperativeness. The collaborating style enables both parties to win, although it may require substantial bargaining and negotiation. The collaborating

style is important when both sets of concerns are too important to be compromised, when insights from different people need to be merged into an overall solution, and when the commitment of both sides is needed for a consensus.[52]

The various styles of handling conflict can be used when an individual disagrees with others. But what does a manager or team member do when a conflict erupts among others within a team or among teams for which the manager is responsible? Research suggests that several techniques can be used as strategies for resolving conflicts among people or departments. These techniques might also be used when conflict is formalized, such as between a union and management.

superordinate goal
A goal that cannot be reached by a single party.

mediation
The process of using a third party to settle a dispute.

Lloyd Ward is the head of Maytag Corporation's large appliance division, which is responsible for more than 50 percent of the company's approximately $4 billion in revenues. A former Michigan State basketball star, Ward has earned a reputation as a team builder who excels at revving up the troops. Using team strategy to focus employees on a superordinate goal, he has astounded skeptics and revived this once-faltering unit. His strategies helped Maytag shares to soar more than 60 percent in 1998. Profits are expected to increase 50 percent to $271 million.

Superordinate Goals.   The larger mission that cannot be attained by a single party is identified as a **superordinate goal.**[53] This is similar to the concept of *vision*. A powerful vision of where the organization wants to be in the future often compels employees to overcome conflicts and cooperate for the greater good. Similarly, a superordinate goal requires the cooperation of conflicting team members for achievement. People must pull together. To the extent that employees can be focused on team or organization goals, the conflict will decrease because they see the big picture and realize they must work together to achieve it.

Bargaining/Negotiation.   Bargaining and negotiation mean that the parties engage one another in an attempt to systematically reach a solution. They attempt logical problem solving to identify and correct the conflict. This approach works well if the individuals can set aside personal animosities and deal with the conflict in a businesslike way.

Mediation.   Using a third party to settle a dispute involves **mediation.** A mediator could be a supervisor, higher-level manager, or someone from the human resource department. The mediator can discuss the conflict with each party and work toward a solution. If a solution satisfactory to both sides cannot be reached, the parties may be willing to turn the conflict over to the mediator and abide by his or her solution.

Facilitating Communication.   Managers can facilitate communication to ensure that conflicting parties hold accurate perceptions. Providing opportunities for the disputants to get together and exchange information reduces conflict. As they learn more about one another, suspicions diminish and improved teamwork becomes possible.

Facilitating communication is one important responsibility of a team leader. The Leadership box describes the changing

Team Leader Qualities

"We're going to be implementing teams, and each of you will serve as facilitator for your team."

Those words can send traditional managers into near panic. Few understand what the transition to teams involves. In addition, managers are confused about their role as coach and facilitator rather than supervisor and are leery of broadly sharing information and power with lower-level workers. Many are suspicious that the move to teams is simply a fancy way to eliminate their jobs.

In the traditional hierarchical structure, career paths were clear, and the ambitious moved from shop floor to line supervisor and, potentially, into management by developing clearly defined skills. But under the team concept, a new set of skills is called for—the so-called soft skills, such as communication, conflict resolution, motivation, sharing, and trust building.

Development of successful teams begins with development of confident team leaders; companies should not merely toss the ball to managers and expect them to automatically become experts in team leadership. Training can help managers define and learn how to be effective team leaders. There are a number of points team leaders should remember:

1. Team leaders don't have to know everything. This can be especially daunting in leading cross-functional teams. The leader should determine his or her own strengths and how those strengths can benefit the entire group.

2. Team leaders embrace the concept of teamwork in deeds as well as words. That means sharing power and information in order to empower team members and reach goals.

3. Team leaders enable members to find answers for themselves by asking questions and encouraging balanced participation.

4. Team leaders coordinate team activities and avoid wasting time on details that can be better handled through transfer of responsibility to the team.

5. Team leaders accept the concept of continuous, on-the-job learning.

Following these guidelines can help you become an effective team leader. For example, after seven years as a manufacturing engineer, Boeing's Bruce Moravec knew he had mastered his technical discipline, but when he was appointed to lead the 757 Stretch Program team, he had to lead people who worked in areas he knew little about. Moravec knew better than to pretend he had all the answers. "That dooms you to failure. I tell all my people we have different roles. My job is to pull things together. They're the experts." Boeing has a series of training programs, from workshops to an intranet site offering instructional materials and diagnostic tools, to teach people how to be effective team leaders. Phil Polizatto leads a workshop that has a waiting list of 340 eager team leaders who understand the importance of their new roles. "Just as a flight crew is dependent on the captain's behavior," Polizatto says, "the work of a team is dependent on its leader's behavior."

www.boeing.com

SOURCES: Susan Caminiti, "What Team Leaders Need to Know," *Fortune*, February 20, 1995, 93–100; Lawrence Holpp, "New Roles for Leaders: An HRD Reporter's Inquiry," *Training & Development*, March 1995, 46–50; and Eric Matson, "Congratulations, You're Promoted," *Fast Company*, June–July 1997, 116–130.

role of leadership in companies shifting to teamwork. Four guidelines can help facilitate communication and keep teams focused on substantive issues rather than interpersonal conflicts.[54]

• *Focus on facts.* Keep team discussions focused on issues, not personalities. Working with more data and information rather than less can help keep team members focused on facts and prevent meetings from degenerating into pointless debates over opinions. At Star Electronics, the top management team meets daily, weekly, and monthly to examine a wide variety of specific operating measures. Looking at the details helps team members debate critical issues and avoid useless arguments.

• *Develop multiple alternatives.* Teams that deliberately develop many alternatives, sometimes considering four or five options at once, have a lower incidence of interpersonal conflict. Having a multitude of options to consider concentrates team members' energy on solving problems. In addition, the process of generating multiple choices is fun and creative, which sets a positive tone for the meeting and reduces the chance for conflict.

- *Maintain a balance of power.* Managers and team leaders should accept the team's decision as fair, even if they do not agree with it. Fairness requires a balance of power within the team. When the team that designed a low-fare airline for US Airways first came together, everyone was asking about other team members' job titles to figure out the "pecking order." The team leader quickly made it clear that their was no hierarchy—everyone would have an equal voice and an equal vote.

- *Never force a consensus.* There will naturally be conflict over some issues, which managers find a way to resolve without forcing a consensus. When there are persistent differences of opinion, the team leader sometimes has to make a decision guided by input from other team members. At Androm-eda Processing, the CEO insisted on consensus from his top management team, causing a debate to rage on for months. Eventually, most of the managers just wanted a decision, no matter whether it was the one they agreed with or not. Conflict and frustration mounted to the point where some top managers left the company. The group achieved consensus only at the price of losing several key managers.

Benefits and Costs of Teams

In deciding whether to use teams to perform specific tasks, managers must consider both benefits and costs. Teams may have positive impact on both the output productivity and satisfaction of members. On the other hand, teams may also create a situation in which motivation and performance actually are decreased.

Potential Benefits of Teams

Teams come closest to achieving their full potential when they enhance individual productivity through increased member effort, members' personal satisfaction, integration of diverse abilities and skills, and increased organizational flexibility.

Level of Effort.   Employee teams often unleash enormous energy and creativity from workers who like the idea of using their brains as well as their bodies on the job. Companies such as Kimberly-Clark have noticed this change in effort among employees as they switched to team approaches.[55] The shift to a team approach is an important component of the evolution to the learning organization as described in Chapter 2 and Chapter 11. To facilitate learning and problem solving, organizations are breaking down barriers, empowering workers, and encouraging employees to use their brains and creativity. Research has found that working in a team increases an individual's motivation and performance. **Social facilitation** refers to the tendency for the presence of others to enhance an individual's motivation and performance. Simply being in the presence of other people has an energizing effect.[56]

social facilitation
The tendency for the presence of others to influence an individual's motivation and performance.

Satisfaction of Members.   As described in Chapter 17, employees have needs for belongingness and affiliation. Working in teams can help meet these needs. Participative teams reduce boredom and often increase employees' feeling of dignity and self-worth because the whole person is employed. People who have a satisfying team environment cope better with stress and enjoy their jobs.

Expanded Job Knowledge and Skills.   The third major benefit of using teams is the empowerment of employees to bring greater knowledge and ability to the task. For one thing, multiskilled employees learn all of the jobs that the team performs. Teams gain the intellectual resources of several members who can suggest shortcuts and offer alternative points of view for team decisions.

Organizational Flexibility.   Traditional organizations are structured so that each worker does only one specific job. But when employee teams are used, from 5 to 15 people work next to one another and are able to exchange jobs. Work can be reorganized and workers reallocated as needed to produce products and services with great flexibility. The organization is able to be responsive to rapidly changing customer needs.

Cooper Industries' Bussmann division has firsthand knowledge of the benefits of teams. Angelina Bernardi, Steve Goble, Ed Haworth, and Lynne Sanick worked on Bussmann's first experimental team to develop the new line of Optima overcurrent protection modules, which combine a fuse and fuseholder in a single, easy-to-use power protection system. The team introduced the line in 10 months compared to the average 24-month cycle time. The enhanced flexibility and rapid response to customer needs led Bussmann to create Rapid Development Teams for each of its major markets segments. The teams consistently cut new-product development time in half.

Potential Costs of Teams

When managers decide whether to use teams, they must assess certain costs or liabilities associated with teamwork. When teams do not work very well, the major reasons usually are power realignment, free riding, coordination costs, or legal hassles.

Power Realignment.   When companies form shop workers into teams, the major losers are low- and middle-level managers. These managers are reluctant to give up power. Indeed, when teams are successful, fewer supervisors are needed. This is especially true for self-directed teams, because workers take over supervisory responsibility. The adjustment is difficult for managers who fear the loss of status or even their job and who have to learn new, people-oriented skills to survive.[57]

Free Riding.   The term **free rider** refers to a team member who attains benefit from team membership but does not do a proportionate share of the work.[58] Free riding sometimes is called *social loafing,* because members do not exert equal effort. In large teams, some people are likely to work less. For example, research found that the pull exerted on a rope was greater by individuals working alone than by individuals in a group. Similarly, people who were asked to clap and make noise made more noise on a per person basis when working alone or in small groups than they did in a large group.[59] The problem of free riding has been experienced by people who have participated in student project groups. Some students put more effort into the group project than others, and often it seems that no members work as hard for the group as they do for their individual grades.

free rider
A person who benefits from team membership but does not make a proportionate contribution to the team's work.

Coordination Costs.   The time and energy required to coordinate the activities of a group to enable it to perform its task are called **coordination costs.** Groups must spend time getting ready to do work and lose productive time in

coordination costs
The time and energy needed to coordinate the activities of a team to enable it to perform its task.

deciding who is to do what and when.[60] Once again, student project groups illustrate coordination costs. Members must meet after class just to decide when they can meet to perform the task. Schedules must be checked, telephone calls made, and meeting times arranged in order to get down to business. Hours may be devoted to the administration and coordination of the group. Students often feel they could do the same project by themselves in less time.

Legal Hassles.   As more companies utilize teams, new questions of legality surface. A 1990 National Labor Relations Board judgment against management's use of union-member teams at Electromation, Inc., set a confusing precedent. The Wagner Act of 1935 was enacted to prevent companies from forming organizations or employee committees to undercut legitimate unions. Union leaders today support the formation of problem-solving teams but may balk when management takes an active role in the formation and direction of such teams. As union membership and power decline, increasingly vocal critics charge that the team concept is a management ploy to kill unions. Autoworkers especially are challenging team approaches because union jobs continue to disappear despite repeated concessions. Although few experts expect the courts to halt teams altogether, most believe that strict new guidelines will be implemented to control the formation and use of teams.[61]

Summary and Management Solution

Several important concepts about teams were described in this chapter. Organizations use teams both to achieve coordination as part of the formal structure and to encourage employee involvement. Formal teams include vertical teams along the chain of command and horizontal teams such as cross-functional task forces and committees. Special-purpose teams are used for special, large-scale, creative organization projects. Employee involvement via teams is designed to bring low-level employees into decision processes to improve quality, efficiency, and satisfaction. Companies typically start with problem-solving teams, which may evolve into self-directed teams that take on responsibility for management activities.

At Roberts Express, described at the beginning of this chapter, managers decided to reorganize into teams to help the growing company operate more quickly yet still serve customers as if it were a small, regional shipping service. Roberts "shrunk" itself by dividing into several self-directed Customer Assistance Teams (CATs). Each CAT is assigned to a specific geographic region, and the company's phone system automatically routes calls accordingly. To regular customers, Roberts seems no bigger than a particular CAT—when a call comes through from a customer in New Jersey, they hear the same familiar voices and are usually rerouted to the dispatcher or agent they worked with the previous time. In addition,

having agents, dispatchers, and other employees all working together to serve a particular region increases both the quality and speed of service. The team approach, combined with new information technology that helps Roberts employees always know where their drivers and trucks are located, guarantees that Roberts can continue its tradition of delivering hot, last-minute shipments right on time.

Most teams go through systematic stages of development: forming, storming, norming, performing, and adjourning. Team characteristics that can influence organizational effectiveness are size, cohesiveness, norms, and members' roles. All teams experience some conflict because of scarce resources, ambiguous responsibility, communication breakdown, personality clashes, power and status differences, and goal conflicts. Techniques for resolving these conflicts include superordinate goals, bargaining, mediation, and communication. Techniques for facilitating team communication to minimize conflict are to focus on facts, develop multiple alternatives, maintain a balance of power, and never force a consensus. Advantages of using teams include increased motivation, diverse knowledge and skills, satisfaction of team members, organizational flexibility, and learning. Potential costs of using teams are power realignment, free riding, coordination costs, and legal hassles.

Discussion Questions

1. Volvo went to self-directed teams to assemble cars because of the need to attract and keep workers in Sweden, where pay raises are not a motivator (high taxes) and many other jobs are available. Is this a good reason for using a team approach? Discuss.
2. During your own work experience, have you been part of a formal vertical team? A task force? A committee? An employee involvement team? How did your work experience differ in each type of team?
3. What are the five stages of team development? What happens during each stage?
4. How would you explain the emergence of problem-solving and self-directed teams in companies throughout North America? Do you think implementation of the team concept is difficult in these companies? Discuss.
5. Assume that you are part of a student project team and one member is not doing his or her share. Which conflict resolution strategy would you use? Why?
6. Do you think a moderate level of conflict might be healthy for an organization? Discuss.
7. When you are a member of a team, do you adopt a task specialist or socioemotional role? Which role is more important for a team's effectiveness? Discuss.
8. What is the relationship between team cohesiveness and team performance?
9. Describe the advantages and disadvantages of teams. In what situations might the disadvantages outweigh the advantages?
10. What is a team norm? What norms have developed in teams to which you have belonged?
11. One company had 40 percent of its workers and 20 percent of its managers resign during the first year after reorganizing into teams. What might account for this dramatic turnover? How might managers ensure a smooth transition to teams?

Management in Practice: Experiential Exercise

Is Your Group a Cohesive Team?

Think about a student group with which you have worked. Answer the questions below as they pertain to the functioning of that group.

	Disagree Strongly			Agree Strongly	
1. Group meetings were held regularly and everyone attended.	1	2	3	4	5
2. We talked about and shared the same goals for group work and grade.	1	2	3	4	5
3. We spent most of our meeting time talking business, but discussions were open-ended and active.	1	2	3	4	5
4. We talked through any conflicts and disagreements until they were resolved.	1	2	3	4	5
5. Group members listened carefully to one another.	1	2	3	4	5
6. We really trusted each other, speaking personally about what we really felt.	1	2	3	4	5
7. Leadership roles were rotated and shared, with people taking initiative at appropriate times for the good of the group.	1	2	3	4	5
8. Each member found a way to contribute to the final work product.	1	2	3	4	5
9. I was really satisfied being a member of the group.	1	2	3	4	5
10. We freely gave each other credit for jobs well done.	1	2	3	4	5
11. Group members gave and received feedback to help the group do even better.	1	2	3	4	5
12. We held each other accountable; each member was accountable to the group.	1	2	3	4	5
13. Group members really liked and respected each other.	1	2	3	4	5

Total Score _____

The questions here are about team cohesion. If you scored 52 or greater, your group experienced authentic teamwork. Congratulations. If you scored between 39 and 51, there was a positive group identity that might have been developed even further. If you scored between 26 and 38, group identity was weak and probably not very satisfying. If you scored below 26, it was hardly a group at all, resembling a loose collection of individuals.

Remember, teamwork doesn't happen by itself. Individuals like you have to understand what a team is and then work to make it happen. What can you do to make a student group more like a team? Do you have the courage to take the initiative?

Management in Practice: Ethical Dilemma

Consumer Safety or Team Commitment?

Nancy was part of a pharmaceutical team developing a product called loperamide, a liquid treatment for diarrhea for people unable to take solid medicine, namely infants, children, and the elderly. Loperamide contained 44 times the amount of saccharin allowed by the FDA in a 12-ounce soft drink, but there were no regulations governing saccharin content in medication.

Nancy was the only medical member of the seven-person project team. The team made a unanimous decision to reduce the saccharin content before marketing loperamide, so the team initiated a three-month effort for reformulation. In the meantime, management was pressuring the team to allow human testing with the original formula until the new formula became available. After a heated team debate, all the team members except Nancy voted to begin testing with the current formula.

Nancy believed it was unethical to test on old people and children a drug she considered potentially dangerous. As the only medical member of the team, she had to sign the forms allowing testing. She refused and was told that unless she signed, she would be removed from the project, demoted, and seen as a poor team player, nonpromotable, lacking in judgment, and unable to work with marketing people. Nancy was aware that no proof existed that high saccharin would be directly harmful to potential users of loperamide.

What Do You Do?

1. Refuse to sign. As a medical doctor, Nancy must stand up for what she believes is right.
2. Resign. There is no reason to stay in this company and be punished for ethically correct behavior. Testing the drug will become someone else's responsibility.
3. Sign the form. The judgment of other team members cannot be all wrong. The loperamide testing is not illegal and will move ahead anyway, so it would preserve team unity and company effectiveness to sign.

SOURCE: Based on Tom L. Beauchamp, *Ethical Theory and Business*, 2d ed. (Englewood Cliffs, N.J.: Prentice-Hall, 1983).

Surf the Net

1. **Self-Directed Work Teams.** Use your search engine to find a site such as **www.oeg.net/tmb.html** that will provide information on the team-building process. Another good site can be found at **http://users.ids.net/~brim/sdwth.html,** where you can click on "Sites on Team Basics" and read several of the linked features (most of them are fairly short). Select three ideas that you could apply to improve the performance of a team that you are currently a member of—an employee group, an athletic team, a campus or community organization, etc. Report to your class the ideas you implemented and what impact they had on your team's performance.

2. **Team Meetings.** The communication process used frequently in the team environment is group meetings. Productive meetings don't just automatically happen. One Web site loaded with excellent links to information about improving the meeting process can be found at **www.infoteam.com/nonprofit/nica/meeting.html.** Find information on the following issues: (a) What can the team leader do to facilitate the meeting? (b) What common characteristics do the best meeting facilitators possess? (c) What are some techniques for managing conflicts that arise during meetings?

3. **Team Performance.** Something very evident among athletic teams is the importance of keeping the team members motivated to achieve their goal of winning the game. Assume the role of "chief motivator" for a work team and design a one-page flyer to be given to each team member in which you include the best advice you can find for enhancing team performance. A good starting point for finding information for your flyer is **http://pw1.netcom.com/~spritex/frames.html** (select the heading of "Teamwork"). You can copy and paste those items from this site or other sites into your word processing program to create your flyer.

Case for Critical Analysis

Acme Minerals Extraction Company

Several years ago, Acme Minerals Extraction Company introduced teams in an effort to solve morale and productivity problems at its Wichita plant. Acme used highly sophisticated technology, employing geologists, geophysicists, and engineers on what was referred to as the "brains" side of the business, as well as skilled and semi-skilled labor on the "brawn" side to run the company's underground extracting operations. The two sides regularly clashed, and when some engineers locked several operations workers out of the office in 100-degree heat, the local press had a field day. Suzanne Howard was hired to develop a program that would improve productivity and morale at the Wichita plant, with the idea that it would then be implemented at other Acme sites.

Howard had a stroke of luck in the form of Donald Peterson, a long-time Acme employee who was highly respected at the Wichita plant and was looking for one final, challenging project before he retired. Peterson had served in just about every possible line and staff position at Acme over his 39-year career, and he understood the problems workers faced on both the "brains" and the "brawn" sides of the business. Howard was pleased when Peterson agreed to serve as leader for the Wichita pilot project. There were three functional groups at the Wichita plant: operations, made up primarily of hourly workers who operated and maintained the extracting equipment; the "below ground" group, consisting of engineers, geologists, and geophysicists who determined where and how to drill; and the "above ground" group of engineers in charge of cursory refinement and transportation of the minerals. Howard and Peterson decided the first step was to get these different groups talking to one another and sharing ideas. They instituted a monthly "problem chat," an optional meeting to which all employees were invited to discuss unresolved problems. At the first meeting, Howard and Peterson were the only two people who showed up. However, people gradually began to attend the meetings, and after about six months they had become lively problem-solving discussions that led to many improvements.

Next, Howard and Peterson introduced teams to "select a problem and implement a tailored solution," or SPITS. These were ad hoc groups made up of members from each of the three functional areas. They were formed to work on a specific problem identified in a chat meeting and were disbanded when the problem was solved. SPITS were given the authority to address problems without seeking management approval. There were some rocky moments, as engineers resented working with operations personnel and vice versa. However, over time, and with the strong leadership of Peterson, the groups began to come together and focus on the issues rather than spending most of their time arguing. Eventually, workers in Wichita were organized into permanent cross-functional teams that were empowered to make their own decisions and elect their own leaders. After a year and a half, things were really humming. The different groups weren't just working together; they had also started socializing together. At one of the problem chats, an operations worker jokingly suggested that the brains and the brawn should duke it out once a week to get rid of the tensions so they could focus all their energy on the job to be done. Several others joined in the joking, and eventually, the group decided to square off in a weekly softball game. Peterson had T-shirts printed up that said BRAINS AND BRAWN. The softball games were well attended, and both sides usually ended up having a few beers together at a local bar afterward. Productivity and morale soared at the Wichita plant, and costs continued to decline.

Top executives believed the lessons learned at Wichita should make implementing the program at other sites less costly and time-consuming. However, when Howard and her team attempted to implement the program at the Lubbock plant, things didn't go well. They felt under immense pressure from top management to get the team-based productivity project running smoothly at Lubbock. Because people weren't showing up for the problem chat meetings, attendance was made mandatory. However, the meetings still produced few valuable ideas or suggestions. Although a few of the SPITS teams solved important problems, none of them showed the kind of commitment and enthusiasm Howard had seen in Wichita. In addition, the Lubbock workers refused to participate in the softball games and other team-building exercises that Howard's team developed for them. Howard finally convinced some workers to join in the softball games by bribing them with free food and beer. "If I just had a Donald Peterson in Lubbock, things would go a lot more smoothly," Howard thought. "These workers don't trust us the way workers in Wichita trusted him." It seemed that no matter how hard Howard and her team tried to make the project work in Lubbock, morale continued to decline and conflicts between the different groups of workers actually seemed to increase.

Questions

1. What types of teams described in the chapter are represented in this case?
2. Why do you think the team project succeeded at Wichita but isn't working in Lubbock?
3. What advice would you give Suzanne Howard and her team for improving the employee involvement climate at the Lubbock plant?

SOURCE: Based on Michael C. Beers, "The Strategy That Wouldn't Travel," *Harvard Business Review*, November–December 1996, 18–31.

Endnotes

1. Chuck Salter, "Roberts Rules of the Road," *Fast Company*, September 1998, 114–128.

2. Susan G. Cohen, Gerald E. Ledford, Jr., and Gretchen M. Spreitzer, "A Predictive Model of Self-Managing Work Team Effectiveness," *Human Relations* 49, no. 5 (1996), 643–676; "Training in the 1990s," *The Wall Street Journal*, March 1, 1990, B1; and Patricia Booth, "Embracing the Team Concept," *Canadian Business Review*, Autumn 1994, 10–13.

3. Rajiv D. Banker, Joy M. Field, Roger G. Schroeder, and Kingshuk K. Sinha, "Impact of Work Teams on Manufacturing Performance: A Longitudinal Field Study," *Academy of Management Journal* 39, no. 4 (1996), 867–890.

4. Eric Schine, "Mattel's Wild Race to Market," *Business Week*, February 21, 1994, 62–63; Frank V. Cespedes, Stephen X. Dole, and Robert J. Freedman, "Teamwork for Today's Selling," *Harvard Business Review* (March–April 1989), 44–55; Victoria J. Marsick, Ernie Turner, and Lars Cederholm, "International Managers as Team Leaders," *Management Review* (March 1989), 46–49; and "Team Goal-Setting," *Small Business Report*, January 1988, 76–77.

5. Carl E. Larson and Frank M. J. LaFasto, *TeamWork* (Newbury Park, Calif.: Sage, 1989).

6. Eric Sundstrom, Kenneth P. De Meuse, and David Futrell, "Work Teams," *American Psychologist* 45 (February 1990), 120–133.

7. Deborah L. Gladstein, "Groups in Context: A Model of Task Group Effectiveness," *Administrative Science Quarterly* 29 (1984), 499–517.

8. Dora C. Lau and J. Keith Murnighan, "Demographic Diversity and Faultlines: The Compositional Dynamics of Organizational Groups," *Academy of Management Review* 23, no. 2 (1998), 325–340.

9. Thomas Owens, "Business Teams," *Small Business Report*, January 1989, 50–58.

10. Susan Carey, "US Air 'Peon' Team Pilots Start-Up of Low-Fare Airline," *The Wall Street Journal*, March 24, 1998, B1.

11. "Participation Teams," *Small Business Report*, September 1987, 38–41.

12. Larson and LaFasto, *TeamWork*.

13. James H. Shonk, *Team-Based Organizations* (Homewood, Ill.: Business One Irwin, 1992); and John Hoerr, "The Payoff from Teamwork," *Business Week*, July 10, 1989, 56–62.

14. Gregory L. Miles, "Suddenly, USX Is Playing Mr. Nice Guy," *Business Week*, June 26, 1989, 151–152.

15. Jeanne M. Wilson, Jill George, and Richard S. Wellings, with William C. Byham, *Leadership Trapeze: Strategies for Leadership in Team-Based Organizations* (San Francisco: Jossey-Bass, 1994).

16. Ruth Wageman, "Critical Success Factors for Creating Superb Self-Managing Teams," *Organizational Dynamics*, summer 1997, 49–61.

17. Thomas Owens, "The Self-Managing Work Team," *Small Business Report*, February 1991, 53–65.

18. Mary Cianni and Donna Wnuck, "Individual Growth and Team Enhancement: Moving Toward a New Model of Career Development," *Academy of Management Executive* 11, no. 1 (1997), 105–115.

19. Brian Dumaine, "The Trouble with Teams," *Fortune*, September 5, 1994, 86–92; and Brian Dumaine, "Who Needs a Boss?" *Fortune*, May 7, 1990, 52–60.

20. Dumaine, "The Trouble with Teams"; and Beverly Geber, "Virtual Teams," *Training*, April 1995, 36–40.

21. Charles Fishman, "Whole Foods is All Teams," *Fast Company*, April–May 1996, 102–109.

22. For research findings on group size, see M. E. Shaw, *Group Dynamics*, 3d ed. (New York: McGraw-Hill, 1981); and G. Manners, "Another Look at Group Size, Group Problem-Solving and Member Consensus," *Academy of Management Journal* 18 (1975), 715–724.

23. George Prince, "Recognizing Genuine Teamwork," *Supervisory Management* (April 1989), 25–36; K. D. Benne and P. Sheats, "Functional Roles of Group Members," *Journal of Social Issues* 4 (1948), 41–49; and R. F. Bales, *SYMOLOG Case Study Kit* (New York: Free Press, 1980).

24. Robert A. Baron, *Behavior in Organizations*, 2d ed. (Boston: Allyn & Bacon, 1986).

25. Ibid.

26. Kenneth G. Koehler, "Effective Team Management," *Small Business Report*, July 19, 1989, 14–16; and Connie J. G. Gersick, "Time and Transition in Work Teams: Toward a New Model of Group Development," *Academy of Management Journal* 31 (1988), 9–41.

27. Bruce W. Tuckman and Mary Ann C. Jensen, "Stages of Small-Group Development Revisited," *Group and Organizational Studies* 2 (1977), 419–427; and Bruce W. Tuckman, "Developmental Sequences in Small Groups," *Psychological Bulletin* 63 (1965), 384–399. See also Linda N. Jewell and H. Joseph Reitz, *Group Effectiveness in Organizations* (Glenview, Ill.: Scott, Foresman, 1981).

28. Milan Moravec, Odd Jan Johannessen, and Thor A. Hjelmas, "Thumbs Up for Self-Managed Teams," *Management Review*, July–August 1997, 42–47.

29. Shaw, *Group Dynamics*.

30. Daniel C. Feldman and Hugh J. Arnold, *Managing Individual and Group Behavior in Organizations* (New York: McGraw-Hill, 1983).

31. Ricky W. Griffin, *Management* (Boston: Houghton Mifflin, 1990).

32. Dumaine, "Who Needs a Boss?"

33. Dorwin Cartwright and Alvin Zander, *Group Dynamics: Research and Theory*, 3d ed. (New York: Harper & Row, 1968);

and Elliot Aronson, *The Social Animal* (San Francisco: W. H. Freeman, 1976).

34. Peter E. Mudrack, "Group Cohesiveness and Productivity: A Closer Look," *Human Relations* 42 (1989), 771–785. Also see Miriam Erez and Anit Somech, "Is Group Productivity Loss the Rule or the Exception? Effects of Culture and Group-Based Motivation," *Academy of Management Journal* 39, no. 6 (1996), 1513–1537.

35. Stanley E. Seashore, *Group Cohesiveness in the Industrial Work Group* (Ann Arbor, Mich.: Institute for Social Research, 1954).

36. Chuck Salter, "Life in the Fast Lane," *Fast Company,* October 1998, 172–178.

37. J. Richard Hackman, "Group Influences on Individuals," in *Handbook of Industrial and Organizational Psychology,* ed. M. Dunnette (Chicago: Rand McNally, 1976).

38. Kenneth Bettenhausen and J. Keith Murnighan, "The Emergence of Norms in Competitive Decision-Making Groups," *Administrative Science Quarterly* 30 (1985), 350–372.

39. The following discussion is based on Daniel C. Feldman, "The Development and Enforcement of Group Norms," *Academy of Management Review* 9 (1984), 47–53.

40. Hugh J. Arnold and Daniel C. Feldman, *Organizational Behavior* (New York: McGraw-Hill, 1986).

41. Wilson, et al., *Leadership Trapeze,* 12.

42. Alix M. Freedman, "Cigarette Smoking Is Growing Hazardous to Career in Business," *The Wall Street Journal,* April 23, 1987, 1, 14.

43. Reprinted by permission of the *Harvard Business Review.* Excerpts from "Wrestling with Jellyfish" by Richard J. Boyle (January–February 1984). Copyright © 1984 by the president and Fellows of Harvard College; all rights reserved.

44. Stephen P. Robbins, *Managing Organizational Conflict: A Nontraditional Approach* (Englewood Cliffs, N.J.: Prentice-Hall, 1974).

45. Daniel Robey, Dana L. Farrow, and Charles R. Franz, "Group Process and Conflict in System Development," *Management Science* 35 (1989), 1172–1191.

46. Kathleen M. Eisenhardt, Jean L. Kahwajy, and L. J. Bourgeois III, "Conflict and Strategic Choice: How Top Management Teams Disagree," *California Management Review* 39, no. 2 (Winter 1997), 42–62.

47. Koehler, "Effective Team Management"; and Dean Tjosvold, "Making Conflict Productive," *Personnel Administrator* 29 (June 1984), 121.

48. This discussion is based in part on Richard L. Daft, *Organization Theory and Design* (St. Paul, Minn.: West, 1992), Chapter 13; and Paul M. Terry, "Conflict Management," *The Journal of Leadership Studies* 3, no. 2 (1996), 3–21.

49. Ralph T. King, Jr., "Levi's Factory Workers Are Assigned to Teams, And Morale Takes a Hit," *The Wall Street Journal,* May 20, 1998, A1.

50. David Whitford, "Arthur, Arthur," *Fortune,* November 10, 1997, 169–178; and Elizabeth MacDonald and Joseph B. White, "How Consulting Issue Is Threatening to Rend Andersen Worldwide," *The Wall Street Journal,* February 4, 1998, A1, A10.

51. Wendy Zeller, "The UAW Rebels Teaming Up against Teamwork," *Business Week,* March 27, 1989, 110–114; and Wendy Zeller, "Suddenly, the UAW Is Raising Its Voice at GM," *Business Week,* November 6, 1989, 96–100.

52. This discussion was based on K. W. Thomas, "Towards Multidimensional Values in Teaching: The Example of Conflict Behaviors," *Academy of Management Review* 2 (1977), 487.

53. Robbins, *Managing Organizational Conflict.*

54. Based on Kathleen M. Eisenhardt, Jean L. Kahwajy, and L. J. Bourgeois III, "How Management Teams Can Have a Good Fight," *Harvard Business Review,* July–August 1997, 77–85.

55. Gary Jacobson, "A Teamwork Ultimatum Puts Kimberly-Clark's Mill Back on the Map," *Management Review* (July 1989), 28–31.

56. R. B. Zajonc, "Social Facilitation," *Science* 149 (1965), 269–274; and Erez and Somech, "Is Group Productivity Loss the Rule or the Exception?"

57. Aaron Bernstein, "Detroit vs. the UAW: At Odds over Teamwork," *Business Week,* August 24, 1987, 54–55.

58. Robert Albanese and David D. Van Fleet, "Rational Behavior in Groups: The Free-Riding Tendency," *Academy of Management Review* 10 (1985), 244–255.

59. Baron, *Behavior in Organizations.*

60. Harvey J. Brightman, *Group Problem Solving: An Improved Managerial Approach* (Atlanta: Georgia State University, 1988).

61. Aaron Bernstein, "Putting a Damper on That Old Team Spirit," *Business Week,* May 4, 1992, 60; and Hoerr, "Is Teamwork a Management Plot? Mostly Not," 70.

Video Case

Southwest Airlines Flies High on the Wings of Its Leader

Launching a new airline requires leadership from someone who's gutsy, determined, a maverick. Herb Kelleher, CEO of Southwest Airlines, is all of those things—and more. Twenty-five years ago, when the first Southwest Airlines plane taxied down the runway at Dallas's Love field, industry experts were certain the company would skid out of control before it ever got off the ground. Company founder Herb Kelleher wasn't just trying to start up a conventional airline; he was trying to start up a whole new type: a short-haul, low-fare, high-frequency, point-to-point carrier. Today, Southwest Airlines is proud to be the most profitable commercial airline in the world.

Everyone, including business experts and Southwest employees, credit Kelleher with Southwest's success. A true leader rather than simply a good manager, Kelleher began with a vision and had the ability to use his position power as founder and head of the company to influence employees at all levels to do everything they could to attain the organization's goals. His own traits were reflected in the corporate culture. One business writer describes Kelleher as "commonsensical, down-to-earth and pragmatic, with an underpinning of zaniness." She continues by cataloging Kelleher's many roles at Southwest: "coach, quarterback, cheerleader, sage, father figure, huggy bear, entertainer, friend, and legend." Kelleher's zaniness is what gets most people's attention. He's not afraid to dress up as Elvis Presley in public to make a point; he rides a Harley-Davidson; he's known for giving employees big bear hugs when he meets them in the hallway. Kelleher is more reserved and modest in his description of necessary leadership traits. "Tolerance, patience, and respect are very important to leadership," he counsels.

Kelleher calls himself a charismatic leader, and no one would dispute that. When asked in an interview why Southwest Airlines employees treat their customers so well, he answers, "Well, I'll tell you, I could give you a short assessment of that: I think it's the charisma of the Chief Executive." By necessity, he has also been a transformational leader. Not only has he brought about change and innovation within his own organization, but he has done the same to the entire airline industry. Noticeably, he credits his workers as much as—or more than—himself. Inscribed on a lobby wall at corporate headquarters is this tribute: "Our people transformed an idea into a legend. That legend will continue to grow only so long as it is nourished by our people's indomitable spirit, boundless energy, immense goodwill, and burning desire to excel." This description of Southwest's workforce is indistinguishable from many people's description of Kelleher.

Kelleher is very achievement oriented, stressing high-quality performance and improvement. When Kelleher first became CEO, he realized that the information systems department was spinning its wheels. "There were no programs or applications coming out," he says. "Just constant demands for more people and more machines." So Kelleher took action, creating a new corporate services department and focusing the department on serving internal customers as well as the entire company focused on external ones. He also recognizes that, in many cases, achievement requires participative leadership behavior. Recently, Southwest employees were engaged in a training exercise in which they were required to work as a team to create a structure that could hold a raw egg intact when the egg was dropped. What looked like fun and games was really training in meeting goals with limited time and resources. When the exercise was over, the instructor announced to participants, "It didn't matter if your egg broke or stayed intact. . . . My goals were met when you guys took this seemingly impossible task with limited resources and limited time, and nobody threw up their hands and said it was impossible"—a lesson in determination that all could apply to daily work.

Kelleher's views on both participative and supportive leadership are evident in his comments. "Our employees are encouraged to be creative and innovative, to break rules when they need to, in order to provide good service to our customers." In other words, they are empowered to make decisions based on their knowledge and good judgment. Once, when Kelleher stumbled on a technological problem, he learned that a team of technical and business employees had already begun planning the solution—an improvement that was later proved to be revolutionary in the industry—ticketless reservations. "We don't view leaders as just being top leadership. And in fact, our culture allows no elitism at all. We feel like we're all one big team. We work together as a team. And so we start with employees from the minute they're hired in training them to be good leaders." Participative leadership dovetails with supportive leadership. "If you create the type of environment that a person really feels valued and they felt that they make a difference, then they're going to be motivated," muses Kelleher. Those are high-flying words.

Questions

1. Do you think that referent power is a factor in Kelleher's success with his employees? Why or why not?
2. Is Kelleher an autocratic leader or a democratic leader? Explain your choice.
3. Where would you plot Southwest Airlines on the Blake and Mouton leadership grid? Why?
4. Would you describe each of the three elements of the Southwest leadership situation (leader-member relations, task structure, and leader position power) as favorable or unfavorable for Herb Kelleher? Why?

Sources: Kathleen Melymuka, "Sky King," *Computerworld,* September 28, 1998, accessed at www.computerworld.com; John Huey and Geoffrey Colvin, "Staying Smart," *Fortune,* January 11, 1999, accessed at cgi.pathfinder.com/fortune.

Video Case

Treating Employees Right

In the early 1900s, employers didn't think much about what motivated employees. They expected people to show up at work on time, do their jobs, and go home. Working conditions in many industrial environments were sometimes harsh and hours were long, but no one complained. In fact, it may never have occurred to them to complain. Employees were happy just to have a job. Early studies of motivation, such as scientific management, were really designed to find out how to get more out of workers in less time. Punishment was not unusual, and rewards were extrinsic rather than intrinsic. Today, things have changed radically in the work environment. Treating employees right has become an integral part of the way companies do business in order to remain competitive. The companies in this case illustrate a new order in the approach to motivation.

Both extrinsic and intrinsic rewards are used by these companies, but the extrinsic rewards have a distinctly different flavor than they did nearly a century ago. Southwest Airlines, a company that is well known for its focus on people, uses the extrinsic reward of stock purchases. "Because every employee who comes in is a stockholder, they do focus on costs. We're the low-cost airline. That relates to the bottom line for them as well as for the company because when Southwest makes money, all of our people make money," explains Sherry Phelps, director of employment. Michael Holigan, president of Holigan Companies, describes the extrinsic reward system at his organization. "Motivation of employees really depends on which side you're talking to. When you're with the home building side and you're talking to the superintendents, the motivation is a bonus structure according to how quickly they get a home done, and how few callbacks they have on warranties. On the sales side, it's totally a money deal, and it's also some patting on the back—having Salesperson of the Month. Seeing how much money they made, and encouraging them to get to that next level. We want everyone to become rich, and we're going to give them the tools to help them do that."

Most of these companies also focus on intrinsic rewards, satisfaction in a job well done. These rewards dovetail with employees' needs for relatedness and growth. "I want to put a broadcast schedule together that literally can give somebody the opportunity to learn a little bit more about themselves or the world around them," says Michael Seymour, vice president of broadcasting at North Texas Public Broadcasting. Susan Harmon, vice president of finance for the same organization notes, "I think it means that [employees] are willing often to work for less money than they could make on the commercial side. I think people want to work here primarily because they want to make a difference." Managers at Fossil Watch are clear that the company combines extrinsic and intrinsic rewards. "The way we motivate is we are very performance driven. We have a shipping goal every month," says Gary Bolinger, senior vice president of international sales and marketing. But Tim Hale, vice president of image, observes, "The thing that really keeps people motivated is when they see their idea gets put into play and makes an impact. . . . When people see those kinds of rewards, it fuels an energy."

Reinforcement at these companies tends to be positive whenever possible. "I think it's important to recognize when people do well. To recognize them with words and appreciation financially," notes Dineh Mohajer, founder and president of Hard Candy. Promotion—also a reward—is perhaps the ultimate positive reinforcement. "Whenever possible, we believe in promoting from within," comments Patrick Esquerré, founder and CEO of La Madeline.

Meeting various types of employee needs is an important goal of human resource managers at these organizations. On Maslow's hierarchy, the physiological and safety needs (as they relate to employment) include good pay, job security, and fringe benefits. David Gatchel, president and CEO of Paradigm Entertainment, talks about a corporate environment that mirrors the "safety" of home. "People can relax as far as they are dressed. The hours are flexible. We provide free soft drinks and snacks and distractions for people when they want to take a break . . . activities where the employees can relax a little bit, forget about a problem they're working on for a few minutes, and take a little bit of time off, and then refocus and get back to it." Yahoo! has a similar philosophy about meeting employees' needs by providing a flexible working environment that "lends towards people that do have obligations at home," explains Beth Haba, human resources manager. "You know, if they've got kids they need to be picking up later in the day, they'll come in earlier." In other words, these organizations strive to provide a worry-free environment so that workers can concentrate on their jobs. Other needs include those of belongingness and esteem. "We want people here at the Drew Pearson Companies to feel that they are a part of this team—that what they do on a daily basis is the reason why we're here," says Drew Pearson, founder and CEO of his own company. "And if we can continue to impress the importance of each and every individual to the organization, then I think we can have a chance to continue to be successful."

The issue of equity gained increasing importance among organizations during the last half of the twentieth century, particularly in regard to women and racial or ethnic minorities, as more and more members of these groups entered the workforce. Linda Finnell, co-founder of Two Women Boxing, notes , "We have an incredible number of women who have worked for us, who come back and talk to us about what it was like to work here, and they say it was one of the most wonderful work experiences they've ever had, as far as being able to flex their own hours and interject ideas into a design business." J.C. Penney, a much larger organization, has formal programs in place designed to promote equity. The move makes sense: since 80 percent of all purchases at the company's stores are made by women, the company has focused on moving women into higher positions within the company. Charles Brown, vice president of credit and finance, describes the team set up to encourage advancement by minorities. "The team, early on, established really three priorities. One was to establish a mentor program. . . . The second priority we had was what we call career pathing. . . . And the third priority that we established was one of recruiting."

Questions

1. How do the issues of motivation discussed in the case relate to the concept of the learning organization?

2. Choose one of the companies discussed and describe how you would apply Herzberg's two-factor theory in order to motivate employees.

3. Assume the role of manager at one of these companies and describe how you would use empowerment to motivate your employees.

Video Case

Centex Is Committed to Communication

Since its founding in 1950 in Dallas, Texas, Centex Corporation has become the largest builder of single-family, detached homes in the United States. A Fortune 500 company, Centex not only builds homes but provides customers with security monitoring, pest-control services, lawn care, financial services, and construction products. Managing all of these activities effectively requires superior communication throughout the organization. Recognizing the importance of communication, Sheila Gallagher, vice president of corporate communications notes, "I think in any company, the communications philosophy has to come from the top."

Formal communication at Centex isn't just a phrase, and it isn't always that formal. Organization executives and managers look for all kinds of ways to use formal communication to disseminate as much information as possible to employees, customers, and stockholders. They also strive for channel richness in every communication event. For instance, when the organization when through a major restructuring, managers recognized that the change could create anxiety among employees and that information would help reduce that anxiety. "So what we have done is put together a slide show to tell everybody what the plan is . . . and we've gone around the country and met with each of [the] groups to try to answer any of their questions, tell them what the game plan is, help them understand why we needed to make the changes. . . . Our CEO of the parent company went with us on every one of these trips," explains Mike Albright, vice president of finance and controller. When the company acquired Vista Properties, "we also covered that in employee meetings and put out a press release to the media, which was received by . . . analysts, shareholders, and others," reports David Quinn, vice chairman and CFO.

Perhaps a company's most formal communication document is its annual report, which is usually distributed to top managers and stockholders. But Centex executives believe that everyone in the company should have access to this information. So a copy is mailed to each Centex employee at home. "We want it to go to the homes so that the families of the people who work here have a sense of what the company's about and how important our employees are to us," explains Sheila Gallagher.

Centex understands the value of stories and other informal ways of communicating—even if they appear in formal disguise. The company has put together a video called *The Movie*, "which gives a very good picture of the company and our operations," says Sheila Gallagher. "Another means of communicating here is the corporate newsletter called *Some Times* . . . so named because it only comes out sometimes. And in that publication, we capture all kinds of information about the company, what's going on financially, new products we may be building, new markets we may be going into."

Because of the organization's large size, much communication is decentralized, conducted face to face. "We get together in a very casual and relaxed atmosphere and have a lot of green-light discussion, and it can be very energetic," comments John Lile, vice president of Centex Homes. Face-to-face communication also takes place between top managers and employees. "Centex executives get together with the employees several times a year," remarks Mike Albright. "We generally try to do it for one of two reasons. We either try to impart information to them or we try to solicit their views on various topics."

The importance of listening to communication is hard to overstate. Although Centex seems to be continually finding ways to disseminate information, managers go to great lengths to listen. "We went out in the field and met with twenty different offices throughout the United States and asked them what they wanted from their healthcare benefits, what was important to them," recalls Mike Albright. "We also have a very successful series of meetings called fishbowl luncheons where one of the executives . . . has luncheon with ten or fifteen of the employees who just put their names in a hat and are selected on a random basis and [the executive] tells something about himself or herself and has an opportunity to answer questions," says Larry Hirsch, chairman and CEO.

The Centex organization's commitment to communication with and among its 1,000 employees in 800 offices (and job sites) has paid off in its ability to continue growing in an extremely uncertain business environment. Centex now has annual revenues approaching $4 billion. "We're very fortunate that our senior management is very committed to internal communication because of the way we feel about our employees," notes Sheila Gallagher. "We do feel like they're the heart and soul of the company." Centex management has learned how to listen—and make it count.

Questions

1. If you were an entry-level employee at Centex, would you feel comfortable approaching one of the top managers with an idea? Why or why not?
2. How might managers at Centex make positive use of the grapevine?
3. Do you think Centex senior managers chose the best channel and medium for informing employees about the company restructuring? Why or why not?

SOURCES: Trish Brennan, "Centex Homes Building Intelligent Homes in Houston," Centex press release, Business Wire, March 11, 1999; "Centex Homes and Its Chief Executive Named National Builder of the Year," Centex press release, PR Newswire, January 26, 1999; "About Centex Corp," accessed March 26, 1999, at www.centex.com.

Video Case

Southwest Teams Up from Top to Bottom

Teamwork is part the organizational culture at Southwest Airlines, which is the most profitable commercial airline in the world. Employees even sing and dance about teams as part of a company video. "What a team," they exclaim. "What a family. From the top to the bottom, we're a fun factory."

If singing and dancing about teamwork is hard to imagine, then imagine this. At a Southwest orientation seminar, an instructor stands before a group of new employees and outlines their assignment. They will break into teams and work together to create a device (using straws and tape) that will protect a raw egg from cracking when the contraption (containing the egg) is dropped from a height of eight feet. How important is the assignment? Very. These employees are learning how to function as special-purpose teams within the organization, brought together to undertake a particularly important or creative new project. In another teamwork training exercise, employees work together to create an airline report card, discussing qualities of an excellent airline. At the conclusion of the assignment the orientation instructor explains, "No matter how impossible the task is, if you put your mind to it, and if you put your collective minds to it, you can do whatever it takes to keep this airline on top." Collaboration and creative problem solving are the keys to Southwest's success—what it calls "positively outrageous service."

Training employees to become effective team members is a vital part of Southwest's organizational strategy. "We feel like we're all one big team," notes Libby Sartain, vice president of people. "We work together as a team. And so we start with employees from the minute they're hired in training them to be good leaders." The company also recruits and hires people who show potential as good team members. "We hire people who show a high degree of commitment to team work," continues Sartain, "and a high interest in being part of the company. When someone joins the company, we have a continuous learning process and they go to training."

How does teamwork training translate to results at Southwest? One special-purpose team consisting of technical and business employees identified problems in the reservations system and began immediately to plan a new innovation—ticketless reservations—without the nod from CEO Herb Kelleher. They simply recognized a problem and went to work. Ticketless reservations quickly became a revolution in the airline industry. "We were really forced into it," Kelleher now recalls. "It grew out of necessity, and

our people did a fabulous job. All of a sudden, the whole United States airline industry had to go ticketless because people liked it so much." One reason the team was so effective was that it was able to move quickly as a special-purpose team—something like entrepreneurs within the larger organization. Satisfaction and productive output were high. "I tell our people to try to preserve that entrepreneurial quickness and alertness," says Kelleher. Still another team developed Southwest's Web site, complete with company home page (the first in the airline industry). "It was done all inside by our own people," boasts Kelleher. "No consultants whatsoever. And everybody loves the Web page." Joyce Rogge, vice president of marketing, describes how Kelleher empowers his teams. "He sets the blueprint and clears the decks and makes room [for the group] to let this explode. But we don't sit around waiting for Herb to tell us what to do. He hires good people and gives them the freedom to do their job."

Formal horizontal teams also exist at Southwest. Joint steering committees identify technology projects and prioritize them based on potential business benefits to the company. Kelleher allows these committees to function autonomously. "It's much too labyrinthian and complex a process to go through," he objects, with a hint of humor. "But I have seen them taking claw hammers into their meetings."

If a family is an example of a successfully functioning team, Kelleher views his company as family—and he says so. "Southwest Airlines is not a company in my opinion. It is a family with everybody well loved, well regarded, well thought of, and very important, likes each other personally." Of course, it doesn't hurt that this team-family is considered by many to be the best in the world.

Questions

1. Based on what you've read about Southwest's teams, what might be some of the norms for teamwork at Southwest?
2. Assume the role of a Southwest manager and describe how you would set up a self-directed team to improve productivity in your department.
3. All Southwest employees own stock in the company. How does this help form teamwork? What factors other than financial reward seem to be the key to Southwest teamwork success?

SOURCE: Kathleen Melymuka, "Sky King," *Computerworld*, September 28, 1998, accessed at www.computerworld.com.

Continuing Case

Part Five: The Leader Returns

Perhaps Steve Jobs is forever destined to be linked with Apple. Even though he already had a job—CEO at Pixar Animation Studios—Jobs continued to serve as Apple's "interim" CEO through the late 1990s. By 1999, industry observers began to predict that Jobs's interim status would become permanent, although Jobs himself refused to make a commitment. But Jobs's leadership skills were credited with turning the company around, and neither Jobs nor the Apple board of directors wanted to let go. "The board doesn't even talk about it," said Bill Campbell, chief executive of Intuit and an Apple board member. "I can't imagine anyone who would have better managed their company in the last two years than Steve Jobs." With both position power as top executive and personal power (as co-founder of the company and an expert in the field), Jobs couldn't lose. He appeared to be at the top of his game.

Jobs has always exhibited strong leadership traits—self-confidence, intelligence, energy, creativity, and achievement drive to name a few. Many people also consider him to be charismatic. "Steve's a pied piper," says Wes Richards, a managing partner at the executive recruitment firm Heidrick & Struggles. "People want to work for him. One of the great attributes that few executives have is that ability to recruit—which is usually dependent on the name of the company or on its brand." Jean-Louis Gassee, a former chief technology officer at Apple and now CEO at Be Inc., credits Jobs with using his leadership personality to turn the company around. "Steve is the ultimate salesman. And, he commands a level of respect that keeps his people focused and keeps them on target. This was critical to Apple's turnaround." But Jobs has not always received such high praise as a leader. In fact, his achievement drive actually caused him to alienate employees during earlier days with the company. But workers eventually began to concede that Jobs was trying harder to become a consensus manager.

Even though the company is now considered to be back on track (the return of Jobs and the introduction of the new iMac have probably been the two greatest contributing factors), management continues to seek ways to attract and motivate employees. One way it does this is by recognizing and meeting employees' needs, at several levels. A progressive compensation and benefits package, including competitive salaries, stock purchase opportunities, and retirement plans, as well as a variety of insurances and a health and fitness program, takes care of existence needs. An environment that fosters teamwork and good relationships among employees (including informal opportunities to play basketball, volleyball, and billiards on site) addresses relatedness needs. And opportunities to take part in innovative projects covers growth needs. "If you want to take on a project that is going to make an impact in the computer industry, you can do that here at Apple," boasts the employment section of the Apple Web site. Informal communication is encouraged at Apple and is actually used as a motivational tool. At the headquarters alone, there are places to play games, cafes where employees can eat and chat, and a fitness center where staffers can socialize as they work out. "If laughing in the halls is an important part of your day, humor is most certainly present here at Apple," says the Web site. Thus, the grapevine flourishes at Apple.

Apple products are almost always developed and marketed by teams, so the company recruits people who are team players. The company relies on all kinds of teams, from self-directed to special projects. "If you want to become part of a team that builds great products, or part of a new advertising campaign that is getting the word out, or a new marketing team that is talking with customers and connecting with engineering, or if you're interested in manufacturing those products and shipping them, come to Apple and make a difference," encourages the Web site. Jobs himself recognizes the importance of teams at all levels in the company. He put together a strong management team to carry out the company's objectives, and industry writers have noticed that teamwork is now a priority among top executives, rather than the "intrigue and back stabbing" that characterized the management of earlier years. However, Jobs is well known for making life difficult for executives who disagree with him, and it may be that some managers go along with the team spirit in order to get along.

In two decades, Apple has enjoyed the highest highs and survived the lowest lows. And while the media have focused on the company's products, stock prices, and management upheaval, not much attention has been paid to the stresses that Apple employees have undergone. Long hours, nearly impossible deadlines, and uncertainty about the future are just a few of the stresses that workers have endured. Recognizing this, and the fact that employees need ways to manage their stress, Apple has put a number of programs in place that function as stress management techniques, including the fitness center, the open areas on campus where colleagues are encouraged to relax and chat with each other, and the various on-site informal eateries. In addition, the company tries to emphasize having fun in the workplace as a way to reduce stress. The formula of leadership, motivation, teamwork, and stress management seems to be working as Apple prepares to meet the challenges of the new millennium. "I love coming to work in the morning, and when I leave, I know that I helped contribute to our success," says employee Tammy Taylor. "There is strong leadership at every organizational level."

Questions

1. How will work related attitudes among employees be important to Apple as it faces new challenges?
2. Do you think that Steve Jobs's leadership style has helped or hindered Apple's progression toward becoming a learning organization? Explain your answer.
3. Do you think that empowerment is a key to employee motivation at Apple? Why or why not?
4. What might be some barriers to organizational communication at Apple?

SOURCES: Charles Cooper, "Steve Jobs' Job for Life (or the Interim)," ZDNN Tech News Now, April 27, 1999, accessed at www.zdnet.com; Sean Silverthorne, "Steve Jobs, Interim CEO—Now and Forever?" ZDNN, September 16, 1997, accessed at www.zdnet.com; "About Apple—Employment," accessed March 1999 at www.apple.com.
iMac photo: Courtesy of Apple Computer, Inc.

Part Six

Controlling

Innovative use of technology played a big part in the seventh Whitbread Round the World Race. For starters, the boats' locations and speed were relayed via satellite to the race office every six hours. And since the boats rely on wind currents for motion, world weather modeling forecasts and satellite picture analysis of pressure systems were relayed to crews to help them plan and revise their strategies. Navigators used weather routing software and databases to calculate the optimal routes to take and then refined them based on the crews' knowledge of the boat's general design and the speed it could achieve with various sail configurations. So, with all the technology available, did the crews put the boats on autopilot? No—the combination of technology and human know-how gave the race its thrills—and race rules wouldn't allow it.

In addition to the technology used to plot and track the race, several other pieces of high-tech equipment kept the boat and crew running: water desalinators for drinking water, Kevlar sails, not to mention laptop computers. Modems and other communications technology kept the race crew in touch with their shore team and the world—24 hours a day—via the Internet. Through satellite transmitters, the boats were linked directly to the Whitbread Race Office, where a mainframe computer processed and delivered E-mail, images, and audio from the crews. The race was broadcast on TV to a worldwide audience, and the first-time Internet hookups allowed couch sailors to track the race whenever they wanted.

Technology plays a major role in controlling organizations as well as sailboats. Part Six discusses the importance of quality control and productivity, information systems and technology, and operations and service management to managerial excellence.

Chapter 20

LEARNING OBJECTIVES

After studying this chapter, you should be able to

⊛ Define organizational control and explain why it is a key management function.

⊛ Describe differences in control focus, including feedforward, concurrent, and feedback control.

⊛ Explain the four steps in the control process.

⊛ Discuss the use of financial statements, financial analysis, and budgeting as management controls.

⊛ Contrast the bureaucratic and decentralized control approaches.

⊛ Describe the concept of total quality management and major TQM techniques.

⊛ Identify current trends in control and discuss their impact on organizations.

⊛ Summarize the characteristics of an effective control system.

Foundations of Quality Control

MANAGEMENT PROBLEM

Michael Dell was nineteen years old when he started his computer company from his dorm room at the University of Texas more than fifteen years ago. He had no way to push his computers through traditional distribution channels, so he took $1,000 of his personal savings and advertised in various publications that he was selling computer components through the mail. Dell's success is now legendary in selling made-to-order PCs directly to consumers. At the beginning, Dell focused on growth—wooing large corporate customers by offering an unprecedented level of service for the PC industry and taking its direct-sales model global. But within a few years, the company was in trouble because top management had failed to implement effective control systems. Most of Dell's managers did not have experience running a large company, and top executives soon learned that a single minded focus on growth, and the failure to measure other performance indicators, was hurting profitability. For example, the company had expanded its product line to include notebook computers on the assumption that any growth was good, but it wound up with poorly designed, unreliable machines that had to be withdrawn from the market. Dell also experimented with selling through retail stores such as CompUSA and Wal-Mart. Although sales grew to $2.8 billion in one year, Dell actually suffered a net loss of $36 million. "Any one strength used to excess becomes a weakness," notes Thomas J. Meredith, Dell's chief financial officer, who joined the company from Sun Microsystems in 1993. Meredith needed to work with Michael Dell to implement an effective overall control system that could keep Dell both growing *and* profitable.[1]

If you were a consultant to Dell, what would you recommend to top managers? How can the company broaden its control strategies to strengthen its position in the computer industry?

A Tale of Two Leaders, One Company

If a manager understands the best types of controls to implement in his or her company, the company can be successful, but if the controls don't fit the company, it can hit bottom. Both things happened to Viewpoint DataLabs International Inc. in the span of a few years.

John Wright started Viewpoint with a unique idea. While working at a previous job, he noticed that lawyers used customized, computer-generated renderings of auto accidents in courtroom cases involving car accidents. Instead of throwing away each model when the case was over, he thought, why not build a library of the computerized images and license them? Thus, Viewpoint was launched. Wright hired graphic artists, salespeople, and other staff. But soon, he had run through all the venture capital, as well as all of Viewpoint's revenues. When he had a new idea, he pulled artists off an existing project and assigned them immediately to the fledgling project. Once he sent engineers to the Indianapolis 500 just to measure cars, at a cost of several hundred thousand dollars, without investigating whether there was a market for the images. Another time he decided to completely restructure the company from a decentralized, egalitarian environment to one with a hierarchical bureaucracy, with layers of managers. To cut costs, he fired all his in-house artists and outsourced all the art, until he was convinced by managers that his artists were his only source of revenue. There were no quantifiable standards of performance; people in the same job earned vastly different salaries for no apparent reason. "There were no rules," recalls one former employee. "No development plans." Although Wright was considered a visionary, his company was out of control.

Wright recognized that Viewpoint needed someone with the skills to develop and implement control systems, so in stepped Eliot Jacobsen, a young alumnus from Harvard Business School and Boston's Bain & Co. When he took the job as CFO of Viewpoint, Jacobsen had no clear idea of the state of the company. But he soon discovered how badly stretched Viewpoint's finances were and the tumultuous state of the employees. He had to turn things around. With a short-term infusion of cash from the outside, Jacobsen began to repair shop. First, he changed marketing and sales from a reactive force to a proactive force by initiating a product line called Collections and Libraries—bundles of models that could be sold as discrete entities "so we could proactively turn ourselves into a product business." Then he established standards of performance so that employees' work could be appraised fairly. Now each assignment that comes in to Viewpoint is evaluated in terms of time and skill required; in-house artists bid for the job. Every model generates the same pay, but the artists who are more experienced or faster can move on to the next assignment more quickly, thus earning more money. This method of control has increased productivity tremendously because Jacobsen understands how artists want to work. "Our new meritocracy is a practice people trust. Creative people want to control their own destiny. It changed from a 40-hour week to a 55-hour week . . . ; you see them here at 2:00 in the morning." Finally, Viewpoint's prime source of revenue was truly invested in the success of the company.

Viewpoint is now a leader in the three-dimensional modeling market, with 90 happy employees, productivity up 60 percent, and revenue per employee leaping from $40,000 to $100,000. Its digitized models now appear in TV commercials for Oldsmobile and Dodge, Reebok and Nike, and other highly visible products. Jacobsen remains modest about his role. "I wouldn't call it a turnaround," he demurs. "It was more a restart, like a computer. If a business crashes, you load the programs in a different order and, sometimes, it works."

www.viewpoint.com

SOURCE: Robert A. Mamis, "Change of Viewpoint," *CFO,* February 1998, 54–58.

Control is an issue facing every manager in every organization today. Dell managers continually look for new ways to improve customer satisfaction, maintain relationships with suppliers, cut inventory costs, and develop the right products. Other businesses face similar challenges, such as minimizing the time needed to resupply merchandise in stores, the time that customers must wait in checkout lines, and the number of steps to process and package a roll of film. Control, including quality control, also involves office productivity, such as improved customer service, elimination of bottlenecks, and reduction in paperwork mistakes. In addition, every organization needs basic systems for allocating financial resources, developing human resources, analyzing financial performance, and evaluating overall profitability.

This chapter introduces basic mechanisms for controlling the organization. It begins by summarizing the basic structure and objectives of the control process. Then it discusses controlling financial performance, including the use of budgets. The next sections of the chapter examine relatively recent perspectives on control, including the changing philosophy of control, the use of total quality management, and recent trends such as open-book management and international standards for quality control. The chapter concludes by identifying qualities of effective control systems.

organizational control
The systematic process through which managers regulate organizational activities to make them consistent with expectations established in plans, targets, and standards of performance.

The Importance of Control

Here is a true story: Ken Jones, president of the Ontario Centre for Advanced Manufacturing, said that once when IBM Canada Ltd. ordered some parts from a new supplier in Japan, it specified that acceptable quality would be 1.5 percent defects—a high standard in North America at that time. The Japanese supplier sent the parts, with a few packaged separately in plastic. An accompanying letter said, "We don't know why you want 1.5 percent defective parts, but for your convenience we have packaged them separately."[2]

These radically different perceptions of acceptable quality dramatize what happens when management is complacent and slow to learn or to encourage employees to improve. North American managers were unnerved by this realization two decades ago, and they began to adopt a new control philosophy. As we saw in the chapters on leadership, structure, motivation, and teams, they began including low-level employees in control decisions.

Organizational control is the systematic process of regulating organizational activities to make them consistent with the expectations established in plans, targets, and standards of performance. In a classic article on the control function, Douglas S. Sherwin summarizes this concept as follows: "The essence of control is action which adjusts operations to predetermined standards, and its basis is information in the hands of managers."[3] Thus, effectively controlling an organization requires information about performance standards and actual performance, as well as actions taken to correct any deviations from the standards. Managers need to decide what information is essential, how they will obtain that information (and share it with employees), and how they can and should respond to it. The Leadership box demonstrates the importance that control plays in an organization's survival.

For Netpreneurs like Matthew Glickman (left) and Mark Selcow control *means learning to strike a balance between their dual roles as chief technologists and CEOs. According to a recent study by Pricewaterhouse Coopers LLP, the main control issue of concern, as reported by two-thirds of the CEOs polled, was lack of qualified workers. Other control issues included concern over market demand (43 percent), legislative and regulatory pressures (32 percent), competition from foreign markets (13 percent), and their own ability to manage or reorganize (26 percent).*

Organizational Control Focus

Control can focus on events before, during, or after a process. For example, a local automobile dealer can focus on activities before, during, or after sales of new cars. Careful inspection of new cars and cautious selection of sales employees are ways to ensure high quality or profitable sales even before those sales take place. Monitoring how salespeople act with customers would be considered control during the sales task. Counting the number of new cars sold during the month or telephoning buyers about their satisfaction with sales transactions would constitute control after sales have occurred. These three types of control are formally called *feedforward, concurrent,* and *feedback* and are illustrated in Exhibit 20.1.

Feedforward Control

feedforward control
Control that focuses on human, material, and financial resources flowing into the organization; also called *preliminary* or *preventive control.*

Control that attempts to identify and prevent deviations before they occur is called **feedforward control.** Sometimes called *preliminary* or *preventive control,* it focuses on human, material, and financial resources that flow into the organization. Its purpose is to ensure that input quality is high enough to prevent problems when the organization performs its tasks.

Feedforward controls are evident in the selection and hiring of new employees. Organizations attempt to improve the likelihood that employees will perform up to standards by identifying the necessary skills and using tests and other screening devices to hire people who have those skills. Many organizations also conduct drug screening to ensure that job candidates or

E x h i b i t 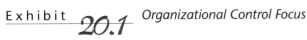 *Organizational Control Focus*

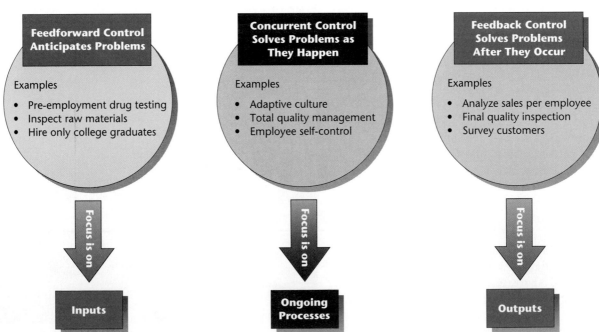

Feedforward Control Anticipates Problems

Examples
- Pre-employment drug testing
- Inspect raw materials
- Hire only college graduates

Focus is on

Inputs

Concurrent Control Solves Problems as They Happen

Examples
- Adaptive culture
- Total quality management
- Employee self-control

Focus is on

Ongoing Processes

Feedback Control Solves Problems After They Occur

Examples
- Analyze sales per employee
- Final quality inspection
- Survey customers

Focus is on

Outputs

employees do not impair their ability to work safely and effectively. Another example is the requirement that professional football, basketball, and baseball players pass a physical exam before their contracts are validated. All of these kinds of testing are feedforward controls because they are intended to prevent deviations from acceptable performance.

Another type of feedforward control is to identify and manage risks. The large accounting firms have recognized that they can offer value to their clients by looking for risks the clients have knowingly or unknowingly taken on, rather than merely evaluating their financial performance after the fact. The firms have developed methods, such as Arthur Andersen's Business Audit, to study a client's industry, strategy, and operations to identify key business risks not shown on typical financial statements. In conducting such an audit for an Asian client, Arthur Andersen learned that the company was preparing to enter a contract to buy natural gas futures without sufficiently protecting itself against sudden shifts in the price of natural gas. A sudden change in gas prices could have forced the company to buy at an excessive price, costing it as much as a year's earnings. Because the problem was identified ahead of time, the client was able to protect itself from this potential loss.[4]

Concurrent Control

Control that monitors ongoing employee activities to ensure they are consistent with quality standards is called **concurrent control.** Concurrent control assesses current work activities, relies on performance standards, and includes rules and regulations for guiding employee tasks and behaviors. Its intent is to ensure that work activities produce the correct results. It includes self-control, through which individuals impose concurrent controls on their own behavior.

Many manufacturing operations include devices that measure whether the items being produced meet quality standards. Employees monitor the measurements; if they see that standards are not met in some area, they make a correction themselves or signal the appropriate person that a problem is occurring. Technology advancements are adding to the possibilities for concurrent control in services as well. For example, nearly three-fourths of major U.S. trucking companies use computers to help plan their routes for efficiency. And almost two-thirds employ electronic devices that monitor truckers' activities, using satellites to beam data back to headquarters. The trucks of Covenant Transport are equipped with antennas that transmit data indicating their position at all times to monitor the status of deliveries. In addition, electronic engines save fuel by automatically shutting off if the engine idles longer than a preset period, and they promote safety by preventing the truck from going faster than 68 miles per hour.[5]

Other concurrent controls involve the ways in which organizations influence employees. An organization's cultural norms and values influence employee behavior, as do the norms of an employee's peers or work group. As explained later in this chapter, an organization that adopts a philosophy of total quality management establishes the norm that employees will seek ways to continuously improve the organization's activities. Employees who accept that norm will look for ways to improve quality, thus contributing to the standard of continuous improvement.

Pyramidal systems, in which top managers control everything, are giving way to a new philosophy about organizational control that involves lower-level workers in management and control decisions. At the Honeywell Industrial Automation and Control facility in Phoenix, employees' quality-control decisions cut defect rates by 70 percent, inventory by 46 percent, and customer lead times by an average of 75 percent. Their efforts were recognized when Industry Week magazine named the facility one of America's ten best plants.

concurrent control
Control that consists of monitoring ongoing activities to ensure they are consistent with standards.

Feedback Control

feedback control
Control that focuses on the organization's outputs; also called *postaction* or *output control.*

Sometimes called *postaction* or *output control,* **feedback control** focuses on the organization's outputs—in particular, the quality of an end product or service. An example of feedback control in a manufacturing department is an intensive final inspection of a refrigerator at a General Electric assembly plant. In Kentucky, school administrators conduct feedback control by evaluating each school's performance every other year. They review reports of students' scores on an annual test featuring essay questions about core subjects, as well as the school's dropout and attendance rates. The state rewards schools with rising scores and brings in consultants to work with schools whose scores have fallen.[6]

Besides producing high-quality products and services, businesses need to earn a profit, and even nonprofit organizations need to operate efficiently to carry out their mission. Therefore, many feedback controls focus on financial measurements. As discussed later in this chapter, managers evaluate whether they have operated within their budget targets, whether they have generated sufficient sales and profits, and so on.

Feedback Control Model

All well-designed control systems involve the use of feedback to determine whether performance meets established standards. Managers set up control systems that consist of the four key steps illustrated in Exhibit 20.2: establish standards, measure performance, compare performance to standards, and make corrections as necessary. The Technology box describes how EZRider, a snowboard business, uses computerized systems to carry out these control functions.

Establish Standards of Performance. Within the organization's overall strategic plan, managers define goals for organizational departments in specific, operational terms that include a *standard of performance* against which to compare organizational activities. A standard of performance could include "reducing the reject rate from 15 to 3 percent," "increasing

Exhibit **20.2** *Feedback Control Model*

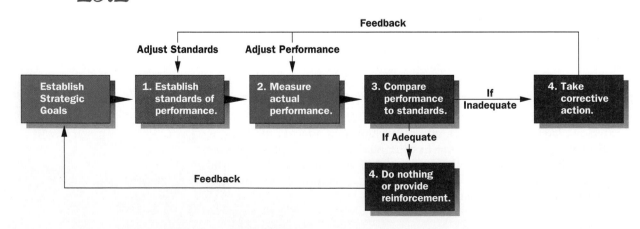

Snowboarding: It's in Control

Snowboarding has come of age during a high-tech era, so it's no surprise that Anthony Scaturro, owner of EZRider, a retail and mail-order snowboard business, embraces the use of information systems to collect feedback on the business's performance. The generation gap is evident, however, in the fact that Anthony's father, Nick Scaturro, runs a ski shop and records every bit of data—from inventory to payroll—with pen and paper.

Upon opening his shop, the younger Scaturro dreamed of a global mail-order business and quickly realized that the only way he could achieve his dream was by using computer systems to collect and analyze the right data. Anthony knew that he needed to track his day-to-day operations, measuring performance, comparing performance to standards, and making corrections in various areas—for example, inventory. He also needed to be able to plan for the future. So he invested $25,000 in an integrated system that has seven point-of-sale terminals, a customer database, and integrated modules for point-of-sale, inventory control, purchase orders, accounts payable and receivable, and general ledger. A year later, he plunked down another $10,000 on all the equipment he needed to produce his own print ads and catalogs in-house, saving him layout and design costs. Then he launched a Web site (www.ezrider.com), which he is hyperlinking to other vendor sites that he hopes will steer business in his company's direction.

Scaturro explains that, while it takes his dad hours each pay period to calculate his salespeople's commissions, he can do it in about 30 seconds. While his dad counts inventory manually, Anthony can monitor his by simply keying in item descriptions. During buying season, Anthony can contact vendors to ask them to ship products early if he needs them or hold shipments if he's slow or overloaded, which means that he finishes the season with less inventory, "the kind that eats up profits," he comments. "That gives me more control." Anthony uses his information system to break down sales by period so that he can determine when his busiest times are and staff his shop accordingly. "That means no more paying staff to sit around when business is slow," he says. He loves having everything from marketing expenses to discounts a keystroke away so that he can compare actual numbers against forecasts and be "proactive if I'm not where I want to be."

Anthony wishes his dad would venture into computer technology to provide feedback control not only to make his job easier but also, ultimately, to make his ski shop more profitable. But sometimes the generation gap is unbridgeable, and sometimes skiers and snowboarders just get in each other's way as they slide down the same snowy slope.

www.ezrider.com

SOURCE: Anthony Scaturro, "All In the Family," *Inc. Tech*, no. 1, 1998, 25–26.

the corporation's return on investment to 7 percent," or "reducing the number of accidents to one per each 100,000 hours of labor."

Managers should carefully assess what they will measure and how they will define it. Especially when the organization will reward employees for the achievement of standards, these standards should reflect activities that contribute to the organization's overall strategy in a significant way. Standards should be defined precisely so that managers and workers can determine whether activities are on target. In addition, the people responsible for achieving standards must be able to understand them. An example of an organization that exercises this type of care in establishing performance standards is Texaco.

Texaco's management has emphasized carefully defining meaningful standards of performance. First, the company sought to avoid information overload by consolidating the categories of expenses that executives monitor, shrinking the number from 400 to fewer than 200; eventually, management hopes to simplify budgets to 75 or fewer line items. The objective is to state expenses

TEXACO INC.
www.texaco.com

in terms of a limited number of categories so that executives can really watch all the critical budget lines.

In addition to reducing the number of financial standards employees must monitor, Texaco has formally reviewed the terminology used in each of its business units and developed common terms for the entire range of company activities. That way, everyone understands exactly what is being measured. Simple as that sounds, few large companies take this basic step to ensure that everyone in the organization understands what a standard really means.

Finally, the company has identified financial measures that actually drive the company's long-term profitability, such as expenses per barrel of oil. The next step is to establish clear standards of performance for nonfinancial operational factors, such as worker safety, and tie them to employee compensation. Managers admit that establishing standards for these intangible factors is more difficult than the financial measures. However, they are committed to clearly defining meaningful standards that all employees can understand and work toward.[7]

Measure Actual Performance. Most organizations prepare formal reports of quantitative performance measurements that managers review daily, weekly, or monthly. These measurements should be related to the standards set in the first step of the control process. For example, if sales growth is a target, the organization should have a means of gathering and reporting sales data. If the organization has identified appropriate measurements, regular review of these reports helps managers stay aware of whether the organization is doing what it should be.

In most companies, managers do not rely exclusively on quantitative measures. They get out into the organization to see how things are going, especially for such goals as increasing employee participation and learning. Managers have to observe for themselves whether employees are participating in decision making and have opportunities to add to and share their knowledge.

Compare Performance to Standards. The third step in the control process is comparing actual activities to performance standards. When managers read computer reports or walk through the plant, they identify whether actual performance meets, exceeds, or falls short of standards. Typically, performance reports simplify such comparisons by placing the performance standards for the reporting period alongside the actual performance for the same period and by computing the variance, that is, the difference between each actual amount and the associated standard.

To correct the problems that most require attention, managers focus on variances. For example, the increase in Medicare spending for home health care is steep. Expenditures for home health care rose 30 percent a year on average during the 1990s, and the average number of visits per year to a home health care patient almost quadrupled. The unusual growth rate has drawn the attention of government officials. Furthermore, Medicare spending for home health care in Louisiana is twice the national average. Medicare administrators therefore launched an investigation targeting the 50 top-billing companies in that state.[8]

When performance deviates from a standard, managers must interpret the deviation. They are expected to dig beneath the surface and find the cause of the problem. If the sales goal is to increase the number of sales calls by 10 percent and a salesperson achieved an increase of 8 percent, where did she fail to achieve her goal? Perhaps several businesses on her route closed, additional salespeople were assigned to her area by competitors, or she needs training in making cold sales calls more effectively. Managers should take an inquiring approach to deviations in order to gain a broad understanding of factors that influenced performance. Effective management control involves subjective judgment and employee discussions as well as objective analysis of performance data.

Take Corrective Action. When performance deviates from standards, managers must determine what changes, if any, are necessary. In the previous example of Medicare payments for home health care, corrective actions the federal government has taken or considered include prosecuting companies that bill the government fraudulently, charging a copayment for home health care, and paying agencies by the case instead of by the visit.[9] In a traditional top-down approach to control, managers exercise their formal authority to make necessary changes. Managers may encourage employees to work harder, redesign the production process, or fire employees. In contrast, managers using a participative control approach collaborate with employees to determine the corrective action necessary.

Knowing when and how to take corrective action requires good judgment, and even experienced managers make mistakes. The directors of Prudential Insurance Company of America demonstrated poor judgment when allegations of fraud by its agents began to surface. Some Prudential customers complained that their agents tricked them into using up the cash value in their policies to buy new, larger policies on the false promise that those new policies wouldn't cost them anything. Internal audits conducted for the company reported "major irregularities," but the company's directors treated the problem as a series of isolated incidents, rather than instituting significant changes to prevent the problems from continuing. Eventually, state insurance regulators formed a task force that investigated the company, determined the problem was widespread and that managers should have known about it, and

Baldor Electric Company designs, manufactures, and markets a broad line of energy-efficient motors and adjustable-speed drives. AC motors from 20 to 300 HP, which are manufactured in Baldor's Columbus, Mississippi plant, are one of the fastest growing segments of their motor business. Company managers credit the Columbus plant employees' commitment to continuous improvement *as one of the reasons for that* growth. *For two years in a row, Baldor's District Sales Managers awarded the Columbus plant with their annual "Quality Award" in recognition of their efforts—providing* positive reinforcement *for a job well done!*

fined Prudential $35 million. The company also settled a class-action lawsuit for over $400 million.[10]

In some cases, managers may take corrective action to change performance standards. They may realize that standards are too high or too low if departments continually fail to meet or routinely exceed standards. If contingency factors that influence organizational performance change, performance standards may need to be altered to make them realistic and provide continued motivation for employees.

Managers may wish to provide positive reinforcement when performance meets or exceeds targets. They may reward a department that has exceeded its planned goals or congratulate employees for a job well done. Managers should not ignore high-performing departments at the expense of taking corrective actions elsewhere.

Budget and Financial Controls

In every organization, managers need to watch how well the organization is performing financially. Not only do budget and financial controls tell whether the organization is on sound financial footing, but they can be useful indicators of other kinds of performance problems. For example, a sales decline may signal problems with products, customer service, or sales force effectiveness. Likewise, if maintenance expenses routinely exceed the amount budgeted, the organization might investigate whether equipment is too old or whether employees know how to use it properly.

Financial Analysis

Managers need to be able to evaluate financial reports that compare their organization's performance with earlier data or industry norms. These comparisons enable them to see whether the organization is improving and whether it is competitive with others in the industry. The most common financial analysis focuses on ratios, statistics that express the relationships between performance indicators such as profits and assets, sales and inventory. Ratios are stated as a fraction or proportion; Exhibit 20.3 summarizes some financial ratios, which are measures of an organization's liquidity, activity, profitability, and leverage. These are among the most common ratios, but many measures are used. Managers decide which ratios reveal the most important relationships for their business.

liquidity ratio
A financial ratio that indicates the organization's ability to meet its current debt obligations.

Liquidity Ratios.   A **liquidity ratio** indicates an organization's ability to meet its current debt obligations. For example, the *current ratio* (current assets divided by current liabilities) tells whether there are sufficient assets to convert into cash to pay off debts, if needed. If a hypothetical company, Oceanographics, Inc., has current assets of $600,000 and current liabilities of $250,000, the current ratio is 2.4, meaning it has sufficient funds to pay off immediate debts 2.4 times. This is normally considered a satisfactory margin of safety.

activity ratio
A financial ratio that measures the organization's internal performance with respect to key activities defined by management.

Activity Ratios.   An **activity ratio** measures internal performance with respect to key activities defined by management. For example, *inventory turnover* is calculated by dividing total sales by average inventory. This ratio

Exhibit 20.3

Common Financial Ratios

Liquidity Ratios	
Current ratio	Current assets/Current liabilities
Activity Ratios	
Inventory turnover	Total sales/Average inventory
Conversion ratio	Purchase orders/Customer inquiries
Profitability Ratios	
Profit margin on sales	Net income/Sales
Gross margin	Gross income/Sales
Return on assets (ROA)	Net income/Total assets
Leverage Ratios	
Debt ratio	Total debt/Total assets

tells how many times the inventory is used up to meet the total sales figure. If inventory sits too long, money is wasted. Dell Computer Corporation, described at the beginning of the chapter, has achieved a strategic advantage by minimizing its inventory costs. Dell produces computers to order, using just a 12-day inventory of parts. Dividing Dell's annual sales of over $10 billion by its small inventory generates a very high figure for inventory turnover. Dell's managers use inventory levels as a key performance indicator, which makes sense in the computer business. Prices of computer components tend to fall rather than rise over time, so keeping a large inventory entails the added cost of buying components at a higher price than if the company waits until the last minute.[11] Another type of activity ratio, the *conversion ratio*, is purchase orders divided by customer inquiries. This ratio is an indicator of a company's effectiveness in converting inquiries into sales.

Profitability Ratios. Managers analyze a company's profits by studying **profitability ratios,** which state profits relative to a source of profits, such as sales or assets. One important profitability ratio is the *profit margin on sales,* which is calculated as net income divided by sales. Similarly, *gross margin* is the gross (before-tax) profit divided by total sales. Entrepreneur Norm Brodsky helped the owner of a cosmetics accessories business use gross margin to identify why her business always seemed to be short of cash. Brodsky had her record the gross margin for each type of product and each customer at the end of every month; the business owner quickly realized that certain products and customers were unprofitable. She was able to save her business by raising prices and cutting costs on some items, as well as adding more profitable items to her product mix.[12]

Another profitability measure is *return on total assets (ROA),* which is a percentage representing what a company earned from its assets, computed as net income divided by total assets. ROA is a valuable yardstick for comparing a company's ability to generate earnings with other investment opportunities. In basic terms, the company should be able to earn more by using its assets to operate the business than it could by putting the same investment in the bank. Caterpillar Inc., which produces construction and mining equipment, uses return on assets as its main measure of performance. It sets ROA standards for each area of its business and uses variances from the standards to identify problems with how efficiently it is operating and whether it is fully using its assets. Since it began using ROA standards, Caterpillar has enjoyed double-digit returns.[13]

profitability ratio
A financial ratio that describes the firm's profits in terms of a source of profits (for example, sales or total assets).

Leverage Ratios.   Leverage refers to funding activities with borrowed money. A company can use leverage to make its assets produce more than they could on their own. However, too much borrowing can put the organization at risk such that it will be unable to keep up with repayment of its debt. Managers therefore track their *debt ratio,* or total debt divided by total assets, to make sure it does not exceed a level they consider acceptable. Lenders may consider a company with a debt ratio above 1.0 to be a poor credit risk.

Budgeting

responsibility center
An organizational unit under the supervision of a single person who is responsible for its activity.

expense budget
A budget that outlines the anticipated and actual expenses for a responsibility center.

revenue budget
A budget that identifies the forecasted and actual revenues of the organization.

Entrepreneurs, as well as large corporations, use leveraged funds to finance their companies. Joshua Silver, a physics professor at England's Oxford University, needs $8 million for the manufacture and marketing of his glasses, which are the world's first adjustable-prescription specs. At a cost of ony $10 per pair, the glasses could be a boon for the one-sixth of the world's population who are vision-impaired and can't afford regular glasses. However, having already invested $650,000 in his idea, Silver has an immense sum of money yet to borrow before he and the world can profit from his invention.

Budgets are a useful tool for planning an organization's expenditures. When managers use budgets to ensure they are meeting their plans, budgets also are a control technique. The Manager's Shoptalk box lists tips for effective budgeting. As a control device, budgets are reports that list planned and actual expenditures for cash, assets, raw materials, salaries, and other resources. In addition, budget reports usually list the variance between the budgeted and actual amounts for each item.

A budget is created for every division or department within an organization, no matter how small, so long as it performs a distinct project, program, or function. The fundamental unit of analysis for a budget control system is called a responsibility center. A **responsibility center** is defined as any organizational department or unit under the supervision of a single person who is responsible for its activity.[14] Top managers use budgets for the company as a whole, and middle managers traditionally focus on the budget performance of their department or division. Examples of types of budgets managers use are expense budgets, revenue budgets, cash budgets, and capital budgets.

Expense Budget.   An **expense budget** includes anticipated and actual expenses for each responsibility center and for the total organization. An expense budget may show all types of expenses or may focus on a particular category, such as materials or research and development expenses. When actual expenses exceed budgeted amounts, the difference signals the need for managers to identify whether a problem exists. The difference may arise from inefficiency, or expenses may be higher because the organization's sales are growing faster than anticipated. Conversely, expenses below budget may signal exceptional efficiency or failure to meet some other standards, such as a desired level of sales or quality of service. Either way, expense budgets can help identify the need for further investigation but do not substitute for it.

Revenue Budget.   A **revenue budget** lists forecasted and actual revenues of the organization. In general, revenues below the budgeted amount signal a need to investigate the problem to see whether the organization can improve revenues. In contrast, revenues above budget would require determining whether the organization can obtain the necessary resources to meet the higher-than-expected demand for its products.

Budgeting Is a People Thing

It's easy to think of budgeting as a money thing, a numbers thing—even a computer thing. And that's the problem with budgeting processes in many companies, say some experts. Lawrence B. Serven, a manager at Deloitte & Touche Consulting Group, notes that, while many managers may agree that their budgeting process needs an overhaul to be effective, all the time, money, and technology in the world won't help if people aren't involved in the budgeting process and if they can't make the connection between budgets and their own jobs. "The real issues are not process related or systems related; they are people related." Holly Snyder, director of planning and management reporting at Nationwide Financial Services (NFS) agrees. She says today's budgets often fail to be effective because they are designed simply to please corporate headquarters. "People don't take ownership of the process," she explains. Here is some advice from the experts for managers who want their budgets to be effective:

1. *Involve the team.* In other words, make sure the budget has input from people in all divisions and functions within the company. If possible, establish a formal team to develop a budget.

2. *Limit data requests to those that are necessary to strategic objectives.* Stick to the subject. Don't digress.

3. *Use technology as a tool, but don't rely on it to resolve everything.* Data must be well defined, and there must not be too much data, for the planning process to succeed.

4. *Link budget forecasting to activity-based management.* Spell out clear definitions of processes and other factors that affect your projections. Be sure to take into account the expense side of sales and operations.

5. *Don't fall prey to trendy procedures.* Stick to proven procedures, or ones that you are reasonably certain will be effective and valuable. Otherwise, your time and effort may be wasted.

6. *Be a business partner.* Budgeting and other financial processes need to be linked in partnership to the overall business process.

SOURCE: Cathy Lazere, "All Together Now," *CFO*, February 1998, 28–36.

Cash Budget. The **cash budget** estimates receipts and expenditures of money on a daily or weekly basis to ensure that an organization has sufficient cash to meet its obligations. The cash budget shows the level of funds flowing through the organization and the nature of cash disbursements. If the cash budget shows that the firm has more cash than necessary to meet short-term needs, the company can arrange to invest the excess to earn interest income. In contrast, if the cash budget shows a payroll expenditure of $20,000 coming at the end of the week but only $10,000 in the bank, the organization must borrow cash to meet the payroll.

cash budget
A budget that estimates and reports cash flows on a daily or weekly basis to ensure that the company has sufficient cash to meet its obligations.

Capital Budget. The **capital budget** lists planned investments in major assets such as buildings, trucks, and heavy machinery, often involving expenditures over more than a year. Capital expenditures not only have a large impact on future expenses, they are investments designed to enhance profits. Therefore, a capital budget is necessary to plan the impact of these expenditures on cash flow and profitability. Controlling involves not only monitoring the amount of capital expenditures but evaluating whether the assumptions made about the return on the investments are holding true. Managers should evaluate whether continuing investment in particular projects is advisable, as well as whether their procedures for making capital expenditure decisions are adequate. Some companies, including Boeing, Merck, Shell, United Technologies, and Whirlpool, evaluate capital projects at several stages to determine whether they still are in line with the company's strategy.[15]

capital budget
A budget that plans and reports investments in major assets to be depreciated over several years.

Large corporations such as Navistar, Scott Paper, and Joseph E. Seagram & Sons assign financial analysts to work exclusively on developing capital budgets and monitoring whether actual capital expenditures and returns are going according to plan. These analysts can provide important expertise for assessing risks and forecasting returns, but their advice will not be worth as much if managers primarily view their analysis as a hurdle to cross to obtain approval for projects they wish to carry out. In contrast, if the people providing information for capital budgeting decisions view themselves as partners with those who analyze the information, the quality of information will be much higher.[16]

top-down budgeting
A budgeting process in which middle and lower-level managers set departmental budget targets in accordance with overall company revenues and expenditures specified by top management.

Budgeting is an important part of organizational planning and control. Many traditional companies use **top-down budgeting,** which means that the budgeted amounts for the coming year are literally imposed on middle and lower-level managers.[17] These managers set departmental budget targets in accordance with overall company revenues and expenditures specified by top executives. Although there are some advantages to the top-down process, the movement toward employee empowerment, participation, and learning means that many organizations are adopting **bottom-up budgeting,** a process in which lower-level managers anticipate their departments' resource needs and pass them up to top management for approval.[18]

bottom-up budgeting
A budgeting process in which lower-level managers budget their departments' resource needs and pass them up to top management for approval.

The differences in top-down or bottom-up budgeting reflect a distinction between *bureaucratic control* and *decentralized control*. With many organizations moving toward participation and employee empowerment, managers must choose between a traditional bureaucratic approach to control or a contemporary decentralized approach.

The Changing Philosophy of Control

Bureaucratic control and decentralized control represent different philosophies of corporate culture, which was discussed in Chapter 3. Most organizations display some aspects of both bureaucratic and decentralized control, but managers generally emphasize one or the other, depending on the organizational culture and their own beliefs about control. In general, today's organizations are moving away from strict, hierarchical control toward greater decentralization, information sharing, and empowerment of employees.

bureaucratic control
The use of rules, policies, hierarchy of authority, reward systems, and other formal devices to influence employee behavior and assess performance.

Bureaucratic control involves monitoring and influencing employee behavior through extensive use of rules, policies, hierarchy of authority, written documentation, reward systems, and other formal mechanisms.[19] In contrast, **decentralized control** relies on cultural values, traditions, shared beliefs, and trust to foster compliance with organizational goals. Managers operate on the assumption that employees are trustworthy and willing to perform effectively without extensive rules and close supervision.

decentralized control
The use of organizational culture, group norms, and a focus on goals, rather than rules and procedures, to foster compliance with organizational goals.

Exhibit 20.4 contrasts the use of bureaucratic and decentralized methods of control. Bureaucratic methods define explicit rules, policies, and procedures for employee behavior. Control relies on centralized authority, the formal hierarchy, and close personal supervision. Responsibility for quality control rests with quality control inspectors and supervisors rather than with employees. Job descriptions generally are very specific and task related, and managers define minimal standards for acceptable employee performance. In exchange for meeting the standards, individual employees are given extrinsic rewards such as wages, benefits, and possibly promotions up the hierarchy. Employees rarely participate in the control process, with any participation being for-

Exhibit **20.4**

Bureaucratic and Decentralized Methods of Control

SOURCE: Based on Richard E. Walton, "From Control to Commitment in the Workplace," *Harvard Business Review,* (March-April 1985), 76–84; and Don Hellriegel, Susan E. Jackson, and John W. Slocum, Jr. *Management,* 8th ed. (Cincinnati, OH: South-Western College Publishing, 1999), 663.

Bureaucratic Control	Decentralized Control
Uses detailed rules and procedures; formal control systems	Limited use of rules; relies on values, group and self-control, selection and socialization
Top-down authority, formal hierarchy, position power, quality control inspectors	Flexible authority, flat structure, expert power, everyone monitors quality
Task-related job descriptions; measurable standards define minimum performance	Results-based job descriptions; emphasis on goals to be achieved
Emphasis on extrinsic rewards (pay, benefits, status)	Extrinsic and intrinsic rewards (meaningful work, opportunities for growth)
Rewards given for meeting individual performance standards	Rewards individual and team; emphasis on equity across employees
Limited, formalized employee participation (e.g., grievance procedures)	Broad employee participation, including quality control, system design, and organizational governance
Rigid organizational culture; distrust of cultural norms as means of control	Adaptive culture; culture recognized as means for uniting individual, team, and organizational goals for overall control

malized through mechanisms such as grievance procedures. With bureaucratic control, the organizational culture is somewhat rigid, and managers do not consider culture a useful means of controlling employees and the organization. Technology often is used to control the flow and pace of work or to monitor employees, such as by measuring how long employees spend on phone calls or how many keystrokes they make at the computer.

Bureaucratic control techniques can enhance organizational efficiency and effectiveness. Many employees appreciate a system that clarifies what is expected of them, and they may be motivated by challenging, but achievable, goals.[20] However, although many managers effectively use bureaucratic control, too much control can backfire. Employees resent being watched too closely, and they may try to sabotage the control system. Veteran truck driver Clink Satterlund expressed his unhappiness with electronic monitoring to a *Wall Street Journal* reporter investigating the use of devices that monitor truck locations. According to Satterlund, "It's getting worse and worse all the time. Pretty soon they'll want to put a chip in the drivers' ears and make them robots." He added that he occasionally escapes the relentless monitoring by parking under an overpass to take a needed nap out of the range of the surveillance satellites.[21]

Decentralized control is based on values and assumptions that are almost opposite to those of bureaucratic control. Rules and procedures are used only when necessary. Managers rely instead on shared goals and values to control employee behavior. The organization places great emphasis on the selection and socialization of employees to ensure that workers have the appropriate values needed to influence behavior toward meeting company goals. No organization can control employees 100 percent of the time, and self-discipline and self-control are what keep workers performing their jobs up to standard. Empowerment of employees, effective socialization, and training all can contribute to internal standards that provide self-control.

With decentralized control, power is more dispersed and is based on knowledge and experience as much as position. The organizational structure

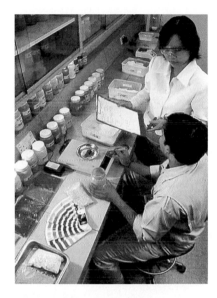

For more than a decade, managers at General Electric have been dedicated to decentralized control *through a program called "Work Out." Work Out is an ongoing effort to achieve what Jack Welch has called "boundaryless behavior"—behavior that, as stated in the GE Annual Report, "ends all barriers of rank, function, geography, and bureaucracy in an endless pursuit of the best idea." With boundaries diminished, GE launched "Six Sigma," a disciplined methodology that focuses on quality for every process that affects the GE customer. Cindy Lee and S. Mani were part of a Six Sigma team at the color lab of the GE Plastics plant in Singapore. The team reduced the lead time for matching colors of GE resins to customer requirements by 85 percent, providing a distinct competitive advantage in the fast-paced global market for plastics.*

is flat and horizontal, as discussed in Chapter 11, with flexible authority and teams of workers solving problems and making improvements. Everyone is involved in quality control on an ongoing basis. Job descriptions generally are results-based, with an emphasis more on the outcomes to be achieved than on the specific tasks to be performed. Managers use not only extrinsic rewards such as pay, but the intrinsic rewards of meaningful work and the opportunity to learn and grow. Technology is used to empower employees by giving them the information they need to make effective decisions, work together, and solve problems. People are rewarded for team and organizational success as well as their individual performance, and there is an emphasis on equity among employees. Employees participate in a wide range of areas, including setting goals, determining standards of performance, governing quality, and designing control systems. For example, at Neilsen Manufacturing, Inc., which produces sheet metal parts and assemblies to order, teams of employees prepare budgets for each area of operations. The company posts monthly budget-versus-actual performance figures so that all employees can track how well they're doing. Their participation gives employees a sense of responsibility and an understanding of how their actions help the company either meet or fall short of its goals.[22]

With decentralized control, the culture is adaptive, and managers recognize the importance of organizational culture for uniting individual, team, and organizational goals for greater overall control. Ideally, with decentralized control, employees will pool their areas of expertise to arrive at procedures better than managers working alone. In this way, the decentralized approach to control supports efforts to build and maintain a learning organization—that is, an organization whose members continually add to and share their knowledge. One organization that has reaped benefits from decentralized control is CompuWorks, a computer software company based in Pittsfield, Massachusetts.

COMPUWORKS
www.cwsite.com

Decentralized control is the rule at CompuWorks, which develops, installs, and trains people to use software that integrates a company's computer systems. Through a series of strategic planning sessions, the company created profit goals, specifying the revenues and profits that each department was to contribute to the company's overall goals. Each department then takes responsibility for determining how to meet its goals and how to track its progress.

The departments assembled teams of employees to identify what measurements were most significant and how to display those numbers. The group that develops custom software designed a scoreboard resembling the yellow brick road from the *Wizard of Oz*. A wizard in a balloon floats upward as sales dollars grow, and to track the source of those dollars, Dorothy moves along the chart to show the number of billable hours—preferably trailed, not led, by a witch representing internal (i.e., nonbillable) time. Similarly, the sales department designed its own chart to measure sales, profits, and expenses. The training department created a vase with paper flowers—when certain targets for billable hours or students trained are reached, the department adds a flower to the vase. Every department set targets by month, quarter, and year, and each department has a small budget for rewards if it reaches its goals. A big green scoreboard tracks the company's overall progress. CompuWorks's president, Alan Bauman, says, "People don't necessarily feel they can change the big board directly. What they do feel they can do is change *their* numbers."[23]

Although decentralized control utilizes methods different from those of bureaucratic control, it is a mistake to assume that decentralized control is weak or represents the absence of control simply because visible rules, procedures, and supervision are absent. Indeed, some people believe that the decentralized approach is the stronger form of control because it engages employees' commitment and involvement. Spurred by this belief, a growing number of organizations are adopting decentralized control as part of a strong corporate culture that encourages employee involvement and commitment to quality.

Total Quality Management

Driven by stiff international competition and rising customer expectations, beginning in the 1980s U.S. organizations identified quality improvement as the route to competitiveness. Many adopted an approach called **total quality management (TQM),** an organizationwide effort to infuse quality into every activity in a company through continuous improvement. TQM was attractive because it had been successfully implemented by Japanese companies that were gaining market share—and an international reputation for high quality. The Japanese system was based on the work of such U.S. researchers and consultants as Deming, Juran, and Feigenbaum, whose ideas attracted U.S. executives after the methods were tested overseas.[24]

total quality management (TQM)
An organizationwide commitment to infusing quality into every activity through continuous improvement.

The TQM philosophy focuses on teamwork, increasing customer satisfaction, and lowering costs. Organizations implement TQM by encouraging managers and employees to collaborate across functions and departments, as well as with customers and suppliers, to identify areas for improvement, no matter how small. Teams of workers are trained and empowered to make decisions that help the organization achieve high standards of quality. Organizations shift responsibility for quality control from specialized departments to all employees. Thus, total quality management means a shift from a bureaucratic to a decentralized approach to control.

Companywide participation in quality control requires a major change from the Western notion of achieving an "acceptable quality level," which by definition allows a certain percentage of defects. Total quality management not only engages the participation of all employees to improve quality, it has a target of zero defects. Each quality improvement is a step toward perfection, and quality control is part of the day-to-day business of every employee.

The implementation of total quality management is similar to that of other decentralized control methods. Feedforward controls include training employees to think in terms of prevention, not detection, of problems and giving them the responsibility and power to correct errors, expose problems, and contribute to solutions. Concurrent controls include an organizational culture and employee commitment that favor total quality and employee participation. Feedback controls include targets for employee involvement and for zero defects.

TQM Techniques

The implementation of total quality management involves the use of many techniques. Most companies that have adopted TQM have incorporated quality circles, empowerment, benchmarking, outsourcing, standards for reduced cycle time, and continuous improvement.

quality circle
A group of 6 to 12 volunteer employees who meet regularly to discuss and solve problems affecting the quality of their work.

Quality Circles. One approach to implementing the decentralized approach of TQM is to use quality circles. A **quality circle** is a group of 6 to 12 volunteer employees who meet regularly to discuss and solve problems affecting the quality of their work.[25] At a set time during the workweek, the members of the quality circle meet, identify problems, and try to find solutions. Circle members are free to collect data and take surveys. Many companies train team members in team building, problem solving, and statistical quality control. The reason for using quality circles is to push decision making to an organization level at which recommendations can be made by the people who do the job and know it better than anyone else. The quality circle process as used in most U.S. companies is illustrated in Exhibit 20.5, which begins with a selected problem and ends with a decision given back to the team.

The quality circle concept spread to the United States and Canada from Japan. It had been developed by Japanese companies as a method of gaining employee commitment to high standards. The success of quality circles impressed executives visiting Japan from Lockheed, the first U.S. company to adopt this practice. Many other North American companies, including Westinghouse and Baltimore Gas & Electric Company, have since adopted quality circles. In several of these companies, managers attest to the improved performance and cost savings.

Empowerment. TQM relies on the empowerment of employees, as well as the contributions of suppliers and customers in the decision-making process. Input from all these groups is essential to continuous improvement. Furthermore, as companies reduce staff and layers of management, or shift tasks to suppliers or outside organizations, managers need to share information and collaborate with customers and suppliers. As customers increase their product sophistication and demands for higher quality, organizations need to include them in the information loop by providing product and service information and developing relationships with them.

Exhibit *20.5*   *The Quality Circle Process*

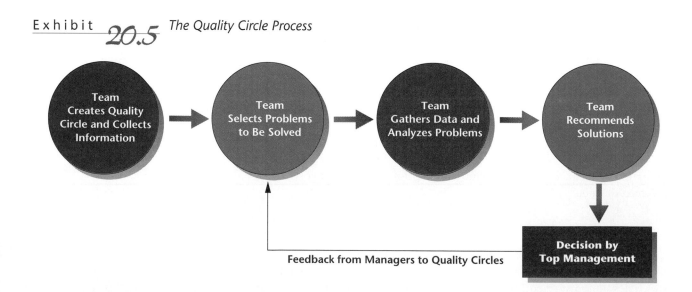

Benchmarking. Introduced by Xerox in 1979, benchmarking is now a major TQM component. **Benchmarking** is defined by Xerox as "the continuous process of measuring products, services, and practices against the toughest competitors or those companies recognized as industry leaders."[26] The key to successful benchmarking lies in analysis. Starting with its own mission statement, a company should honestly analyze its current procedures and determine areas for improvement. As a second step, a company *carefully* selects competitors worthy of copying. For example, Xerox studied the order fulfillment techniques of L. L. Bean and learned ways to reduce warehouse costs by 10 percent. Companies can emulate internal processes and procedures of competitors, but must take care to select companies whose methods are compatible. Once a strong, compatible program is found and analyzed, the benchmarking company can then devise a strategy for implementing a new program.

Outsourcing. Although it is not necessarily a part of TQM, an organization can improve quality through **outsourcing**, the contracting out of a company's in-house function to a preferred vendor with a high-quality level in the particular task area. Outsourcing is one of the fastest-growing trends in U.S. business. Companies such as B. F. Goodrich and J. C. Penney have latched on to outsourcing as a route to almost immediate savings and quality improvement. By farming out activities in which they do not have a specialty, such as human resource or inventory management, organizations can save costs on employee benefits and free existing personnel for other duties. Manufacturing companies have outsourced the designing of new plants, and service organizations have outsourced mailrooms, warehousing, and delivery services. Outsourcing also has become a viable option for city and state governments trying to slash costs and improve efficiency. In Scottsdale, Arizona, Rural/Metro Company contracts with the city to run fire departments and emergency medical services and is able to provide better service at a fraction of the cost of traditional government-run services.[27]

Outsourcing does not eliminate the need for control. Rather, managers must identify how they will ensure that the quality of the outsourced function is acceptable. Feedforward controls include carefully selecting the operations that can be accomplished with greater quality elsewhere and finding the best outsourcing partners. Concurrent controls include maintaining good relationships and communications with the partners. Feedback controls include regular reports on the outsourced activities and associated costs.

Reduced Cycle Time. In the book *Quality Alone Is Not Enough,* the authors refer to cycle time as the "drivers of improvement." **Cycle time** refers to the steps taken to complete a company process, such as teaching a class, publishing a textbook, or designing a new car. The simplification of work cycles, including the dropping of barriers between work steps and among departments and the removal of worthless steps in the process, is what enables a TQM program to succeed. Even if an organization decides not to use quality circles, substantial improvement is possible by focusing on improved responsiveness and acceleration of activities into a shorter time. Reduction in cycle time improves overall company performance as well as quality.[28]

The sprockets in this photo have been manufactured for Harley-Davidson motorcycles. They were produced, however, by an outside supplier. The manufacturer is Emerson Electric Co.'s Emerson Power Transmission division, which produces the complete assemblies at its Browning plant in Kentucky. According to Emerson's annual report, "Browning's commitment to total quality and manufacturing consistency . . . are key factors" in the company's selection as an outsource supplier to Harley-Davidson.

benchmarking
The continuous process of measuring products, services, and practices against major competitors or industry leaders.

outsourcing
The contracting out of a company's in-house function to a preferred vendor.

cycle time
The steps taken to complete a company process.

For example, L. L. Bean, Inc., the Freeport, Maine, mail-order firm, is a recognized leader in cycle time control. Workers have used flowcharts to track their movements and pinpoint wasted motions. They also completely redesigned the order-fulfillment process. A computerized system breaks down an order based on the geographic area of the warehouse in which items are stored. Items are placed on conveyor belts, where electronic sensors re-sort the items for individual orders. After orders are packed, they are sent to a FedEx facility on site. Improvements such as these have enabled L. L. Bean to process most orders within two hours after the order is received.[29]

Continuous Improvement.   In North America, crash programs and designs have traditionally been the preferred method of innovation. Managers measure the expected benefits of a change and favor the ideas with the biggest payoffs. In contrast, Japanese companies have realized extraordinary success from making a series of mostly small improvements. This approach, called **continuous improvement,** is the implementation of a large number of small, incremental improvements in all areas of the organization on an ongoing basis. In a successful TQM program, all employees learn that they are expected to contribute by initiating changes in their own job activities. The basic philosophy is that improving things a little bit at a time, all the time, has the highest probability of success. Innovations can start simple, and employees can build on their success in this unending process.

The continuous improvement concept applies to all departments, products, services, and activities throughout an organization. At South Carolina Baptist Hospital in Columbia, South Carolina, 2,500 employees have been trained in continuous improvement techniques. Managers learn a coaching role, empowering employees to recognize and act on their contributions. Baptist has learned that countless improvements require a long-term approach to building quality into the very fiber of the organization. Over time, project by project, human activity by human activity, quality through continuous improvement has become the way the hospital's employees do their work.[30]

continuous improvement
The implementation of a large number of small, incremental improvements in all areas of the organization on an ongoing basis.

TQM Success Factors

Despite its promise, total quality management does not always work. A few firms have had disappointing results. Many contingency factors (listed in Exhibit 20.6) can influence the success of a TQM program. For example,

E x h i b i t *20.6*
Quality Program Success Factors

Positive Factors	Negative Factors
• Tasks make high skill demands on employees.	• Management expectations are unrealistically high.
• TQM serves to enrich jobs and motivate employees.	• Middle managers are dissatisfied about loss of authority.
• Problem-solving skills are improved for all employees.	• Workers are dissatisfied with other aspects of organizational life.
• Participation and teamwork are used to tackle significant problems.	• Union leaders are left out of QC discussions.
• Continuous improvement is a way of life.	• Managers wait for big, dramatic innovations.

quality circles are most beneficial when employees have challenging jobs; participation in a quality circle can contribute to productivity because it enables employees to pool their knowledge and solve interesting problems. TQM also tends to be most successful when it enriches jobs and improves employee motivation. In addition, when participating in the quality program improves workers' problem-solving skills, productivity is likely to increase. Finally, a quality program has the greatest chance of success in a corporate culture that values quality and stresses continuous improvement as a way of life.

Trends in Quality and Financial Control

As noted earlier, changing organizational structures and the resulting management methods that emphasize information sharing, employee participation, and teamwork have required changes in organizational control. More stringent quality demands from customers, together with the need to cut costs while improving products and services, also require new approaches to financial control. Today, companies are responding to changing economic realities and global competition by reassessing organizational management and processes—including control mechanisms. Some of the major trends in controls include international quality standards, open-book management, economic value-added (EVA) systems, and activity-based costing (ABC).

International Quality Standards

One impetus for total quality management in the United States is the increasing significance of the global economy. Many countries have endorsed a universal framework for quality assurance called **ISO 9000**, a set of international standards for quality management adopted in the late 1900s by more than 50 nations, including the United States. These standards, established by the International Standards Organization (a federation of 130 national standards bodies based in Geneva, Switzerland), set uniform guidelines defining what manufacturing and service organizations should do to ensure that their products conform to high quality requirements.[31] These standards do not detail the inputs (such as materials) that will be used for particular products or the outputs (specifications for products) but rather assume that when a company has a quality management system, it can successfully negotiate and meet the desired specifications. For example, such a system would include subsystems for ensuring that testing is carried out and that employees have adequate training. Organizations whose facilities pass an independent audit may obtain a certificate showing they have complied with ISO 9000 standards.

By the mid-1990s, as international corporations increasingly required ISO registration from their suppliers, over 90,000 sites became registered worldwide. U.S. companies initially lagged behind as the world rushed to meet the rigid standards, but pressure to meet international competition prompted a surge of applications, to more than 8,000 by the mid-1990s. Ford, General Motors, and Chrysler (now DaimlerChrysler) together established their own QS9000 standard, which combines ISO 9000 standards with other criteria that are specific to the auto industry. Beginning in 1997, all parts suppliers to these three companies had to comply with QS9000.[32]

ISO 9000
A set of international standards for quality management, setting uniform guidelines for processes to ensure that products conform to customer requirements.

The process of application and certification for ISO 9000 is expensive and time-consuming, but participants benefit from the rigorous analysis of their manufacturing and service processes. Such areas as design, training, marketing, testing, packaging, and record-keeping gain from the refining of processes and the elimination of repetition and waste. In addition, for companies doing business on a global scale, including Exxon, Federal Express, GE, and Xerox, ISO 9000 certification is an important indicator of world-class quality.

Open-Book Management

open-book management
Sharing financial information and results with all employees in the organization.

In an organizational environment that touts information sharing, teamwork, and the role of managers as facilitators, executives cannot hoard financial data. They must admit employees throughout the organization into the loop of financial control and responsibility to encourage active participation and commitment to organizational goals. A growing number of managers are opting for full disclosure in the form of **open-book management.** Open-book management allows employees to see for themselves—through charts, computer printouts, meetings, and so forth—the financial condition of the company. Second, open-book management shows the individual employee how his or her job fits into the big picture and affects the financial future of the organization. Finally, open-book management ties employee rewards to the company's overall success. With training in interpreting the financial data, employees can see the interdependence and importance of each function. If they are rewarded according to performance, they become motivated to take responsibility for their entire team or function, rather than merely their individual jobs.[33] Cross-functional communication and cooperation are also enhanced.

The goal of open-book management is to get every employee thinking and acting like a business owner rather than like a hired hand. To get employees to think like owners, management provides them with the same information owners have: what money is coming in and where it is going. Open-book management helps employees appreciate why efficiency is important to the organization's success.

Economic Value Added (EVA) Systems

economic value added (EVA) system
A control system that measures performance in terms of after-tax profits minus the cost of capital invested in tangible assets.

Hundreds of companies, including AT&T, Quaker Oats, the Coca-Cola Company, and Philips Petroleum Company, have set up **economic value added (EVA)** measurement systems as a new way to gauge financial performance. EVA can be defined as a company's net (after-tax) operating profit minus the cost of capital invested in the company's tangible assets.[34] Measuring performance in terms of EVA is intended to capture all the things a company can do to add value from its activities, such as run the business more efficiently, satisfy customers, and reward shareholders. Each job, department, or process in the organization is measured by the value added.

In practice, the use of EVA is complicated. Firms must select from more than 150 possible accounting adjustments to bring EVA measures into line with the company's real-world performance. For example, the Whirlpool Corporation considered using 140 adjustments, then decided to use the ones thought to make the most difference, including goodwill, capitalized leases, and minority (less than 50 percent) interests in investments.[35] EVA can be particularly difficult to adapt to companies in certain kinds of industries. In particular, natural resource companies invest a lot of capital in acquiring resources, which they must then manage carefully. A basic EVA measure would reward these companies for using up their inventories as fast as they can, which might be disastrous in the long run; the companies could sell at low prices when supplies are large, then at some point have nothing to sell (at a potentially better price) to meet the demand for these resources. Philips Petroleum has attempted to overcome this obstacle by crediting managers for the value of petroleum as soon as the company has a funded development plan for an oil field, rather than when the oil is sold.[36]

One problem with EVA is that, because of the differences in ways companies adjust EVA measurements, the technique is not very useful for comparing the performance of different companies. However, when used correctly, EVA systems can effectively measure and help control a company's financial performance. To be successful, EVA should be central to the financial management system and integrated throughout company policies and procedures. Employees throughout the organization should be trained to understand this control measure, because even the smallest jobs can help create value.

Activity-Based Costing (ABC)

A basic objective of controlling is to ensure that the organization's activities are profitable. Managers measure the cost of producing goods and services so that they can be sure they are selling these products for more than the cost to produce them. The traditional approach to costing has assumed that most production costs involve the materials and labor used to manufacture the products. These costs are measured precisely, and other costs—such as selling and administrative expenses—are divided equally among the organization's products.

In many situations, however, the traditional approach to costing no longer reflects the modern realities of doing business. The relationship between labor and overhead has changed. Increased automation has resulted in less labor. Total product costs are driven to a degree by higher overhead costs for setup, distribution, and maintenance of sophisticated machinery and information systems. Furthermore, the traditional approach does not always show the results of efforts to improve quality. Reliable quality should reduce the time spent resolving problems and redoing work, but these changes often are buried in overhead figures. Managers therefore need a way to monitor the costs of everything the organization does to get high-quality products to satisfied customers.

The solution at a growing number of organizations has been **activity-based costing (ABC),** which identifies various activities needed to provide a product and determines the cost of each of those activities. For example, an ABC system might list the costs associated with processing orders for a particular product, scheduling production for that product, producing it, shipping it, and resolving problems with it. The manager might discover that the production cost is within budget but that problems with scheduling and quality control were making the product unprofitable. Therefore, the manager can work with employees to improve engineering and production planning. Managers can also evaluate whether most costs go to activities that add value for customers (meeting customer deadlines, achieving high quality) or to activities that do not add value (processing internal paperwork). The organization can focus on reducing or eliminating expenditures for non-value-added activities.[37]

activity-based costing (ABC)
A control system that identifies the various activities needed to provide a product and determines the cost of those activities.

Qtron Inc., which provides manufacturing services to the electronics industry, uses ABC to control its pricing decisions, so that the company sets prices according to true costs. This, in turn, educates customers. For example, customers can see that when they make changes in product design after manufacturing has begun, the product quickly becomes more expensive. Customers therefore plan their product needs more carefully and avoid last-minute changes. Qtron passes along the efficiency-related savings, thereby attracting more business.[38]

If the ABC system measures important activities, it can provide a more useful reflection of costs than traditional accounting systems. It can clarify for managers how efforts to improve the quality of various work processes support the organization's financial performance. ABC also can help employees in many functions and product lines understand how they contribute to the organization's overall profitability. An ABC system showed Koehler Manufacturing Company that lead-acid batteries were not solidly profitable, as its managers had thought, but highly unprofitable. Compared with other products, the batteries required extensive paperwork related to handling of the hazardous by-products of the manufacturing processes. When the company's paperwork activity was attributed to specific products, profits from batteries fell by almost one-third.[39] ABC systems are complex, but computer software is making this approach feasible for more companies.

Qualities of Effective Control Systems

Properly used, controls help managers respond to unforeseen developments and achieve strategic plans. Improperly designed management control systems can lead a company into bankruptcy. Exhibit 20.7 lists indicators of the need for a more effective control approach or revised management control systems. When such problems signal that control systems are not working properly, management must examine them for possible clarification, revision, or overhaul.

Whether organizational control focuses on feedforward or feedback measurement or emphasizes the bureaucratic or decentralized approach, certain characteristics should be present. In general, for organizational controls to be effective, they should be tailored to the organization's needs and facilitate the accomplishment of its tasks. More specifically, effective controls share the following traits:

1. *Linkage to strategy.* The control system should not simply measure what was important in the past or be tailored to current operations. It should reflect where the organization is going and adapt to new strategies. Moreover, the organization should focus on activities that are relevant for strategic goals. If the dominant competitive issue facing a company is to reduce cycle time, the control system should not emphasize raw materials cost, which is unrelated.

2. *Understandable measures.* Organizations depend on employees to carry out work according to standards. An effective control system ensures that employees know and understand what is expected. In addition, managers must understand what is being measured—an obvious but important criterion in these days of new and sometimes complex control systems such as ABC and EVA. A highly sophisticated analysis of a department's performance is wasted if the manager cannot interpret whether, or where, problems exist.

- Deadlines missed frequently.
- Poor quality of goods and services.
- Declining or stagnant sales or profits.
- Loss of leadership position or market share within the industry.
- Inability to obtain data necessary to evaluate employee or departmental performance.
- Low employee morale and high absenteeism.
- Insufficient employee involvement and management-employee communications.
- Excessive company debts, uncertain cash flow, or unpredictable borrowing requirements.
- Inefficient use of human and material resources, equipment, and facilities.
- Unethical or illegal activities.

Exhibit
20.7
Indicators of the Need for More Effective Control

3. *Acceptance by employees.* The more committed employees are to control standards, the more successful the control system will be. The control system should motivate rather than demotivate. This is most likely when it includes standards that are understandable and reasonable, when employees understand the reason for the control system, and when they do not perceive the measurement process as overly intrusive.

4. *Balance of objective and subjective data.* Managers can be misled when control system data are either completely numeric or based solely on subjective opinion. Control should be perceived as objective, but quantitative information tells only part of the story. Managers should balance quantitative and qualitative performance indicators to provide a well-rounded picture of performance.

5. *Accuracy.* Upward communication, especially about performance, often is influenced by what employees believe management wants to hear. However, the control system should encourage accurate information in order to detect deviations.

6. *Flexibility.* Internal goals and strategies must be responsive to changes in the environment and the control system should be flexible enough to adapt as needed. Managers who rely too heavily on existing controls, especially feedback controls, will find themselves out of synchronization with changing events.

7. *Timeliness.* The control system should provide information soon enough to permit a management response. Corrective action is of no value if performed too late.

8. *Support of action.* Control goes beyond monitoring performance to taking corrective action. Managers therefore need a system that helps them focus on performance areas in which change is needed. The control system should highlight variances, and managers should focus on these variances, diagnosing the cause of each variance and using judgment to decide when intervention is required.

Summary and Management Solution

This chapter introduced a number of important concepts about organizational control. Organizational control is the systematic process through which managers regulate organizational activities to meet planned goals and standards of performance. The focus of the control system may include feedforward control to prevent problems, concurrent control to monitor ongoing activities, and feedback control to evaluate past performance. Well-designed control systems include four key steps: establish standards, measure performance, compare performance to standards, and make corrections as necessary.

Budget and financial controls ensure that expenditures and sales are in line with the organization's objectives. Financial analysis focuses on ratios, and budgets are an important control system for comparing actual cash flows with planned amounts.

The philosophy of controlling has shifted to reflect changes in leadership methods. Traditional bureaucratic controls emphasized establishing rules and procedures, then monitoring employee behavior to make sure the rules and procedures have been followed. With decentralized control, employees assume responsibility for monitoring their own performance.

Besides monitoring financial results, organizations control the quality of their goods and services. They may do this by adopting total quality management (TQM) techniques such as quality circles, empowerment, benchmarking, outsourcing, reduced cycle time, and continuous improvement. Other trends in controlling include the use of international quality standards, open-book management, economic value added (EVA) systems, and activity-based costing.

Control systems generally succeed when they match an organization's strategy, have understandable and reasonable standards, use a variety of performance standards, provide accurate information, are flexible, and focus on areas in which action is required.

The story of Dell Computer Corporation at the beginning of the chapter demonstrates the importance of financial control, as well as the importance of aligning control systems with an organization's strategy. As we learned in this chapter, managers should carefully assess and define the indicators they will measure. Some years ago,

Dell began to suffer because managers focused entirely on measuring growth and failed to look at other key factors that determine organizational success. Dell's top managers, including Michael Dell himself, knew they had to make some changes in management structure and financial controls in order for their company to survive. First, Dell refocused the company's financial control strategy on a cash conversion cycle, which is made up of inventory, payables, receivables, and cash flow from operations. The pay of the company's top managers also was adjusted to reflect the return on invested capital as well as growth. For the first time, managers were actually invested in the success of the company. Then Dell made sure that training videos, newsletters, and other information packages were distributed to all employees, so they became part of the financial information loop through open-book management. Dell also brought in experienced managers, including Morton L. Topfer, a 23-year veteran of Motorola, to implement the systems needed to control a large corporation. As vice chairman of Dell, Topfer pulled the company out of retail sales to allow managers to focus on improving their direct sales efforts. Topfer also reorganized the company from a centralized, functional structure to a decentralized structure based on geographic divisions. Topfer recognized the change in structure as one way to shift to a more decentralized approach to control. Kevin Rollins, senior vice president and general manager of Dell Americas, says the company's managers are expected to communicate constantly with each other, with employees, with customers—in fact, with everyone. "You have to talk, you have to listen, and all of a sudden, you'll realize you are in the loop," he explains. Ironically, by attacking its previous singular focus on growth, Dell is in fact growing. But it is growing in a stronger, more focused manner. Today, the company is known as one of the best in the industry at rapidly responding to changes in the volatile PC market.

Discussion Questions

1. Why is it important for managers to understand the process of organizational control?
2. How might a public school system use feedforward control to identify the best candidates for its teaching positions?
3. How might the manager of a family-style restaurant use concurrent controls to ensure that the restaurant is providing customers with the highest quality food and service? What feedback controls could be useful?
4. What standards of performance has your professor established for this class? How will your actual performance be measured? How will your performance be compared to the standards? Do you think the standards and methods of measurement are fair? Why or why not?
5. What is the difference between budgeting and financial analysis? Why is each type of control important to a company?

6. Imagine that you are going to be the manager of a new Wal-Mart being built in your area. What items might be listed in your capital budget? What items might be listed in your expense budget?

7. In what ways could a university benefit from bureaucratic control? In what ways might it benefit from decentralized control? Overall, which approach do you think would be best at your college or university? Why?

8. If you were managing a local video rental store, which company would you choose to benchmark one aspect of your store's performance against? Why?

9. Would you like to work for a company that uses open-book management? Would you like to be a manager in the company? Why or why not?

10. Why is it important for an organization's control system to be linked to its overall strategy?

Management in Practice: Experiential Exercise

Is Your Budget in Control?

By the time you are in college, you are in charge of at least some of your own finances. How well you manage your personal budget may indicate how well you will manage your company's budget on the job. Respond to the following statements to evaluate your own budgeting habits. If the statement doesn't apply directly to you, respond the way you think you would behave in a similar situation.

1. I spend all my money as soon as I get it.   Yes   No
2. At the beginning of each week (or month, or term), I write down all my fixed expenses.   Yes   No
3. I never seem to have any money left over at the end of the week (or month).   Yes   No
4. I pay all my expenses, but I never seem to have any money left over for fun.   Yes   No
5. I am not putting any money away in savings right now; I'll wait until after I graduate from college.   Yes   No
6. I can't pay all my bills.   Yes   No
7. I have a credit card, but I pay the balance in full each month.   Yes   No

8. I take cash advances on my credit card.   Yes   No
9. I know how much I can spend on eating out, movies, and other entertainment each week.   Yes   No
10. I pay cash for everything.   Yes   No
11. When I buy something, I look for value and determine the best buy.   Yes   No
12. I lend money to friends whenever they ask, even if it leaves me short of cash.   Yes   No
13. I never borrow money from friends.   Yes   No
14. I am putting aside money each month to save for something that I really need.   Yes   No

Yes responses to statements 2, 9, 10, 13, and 14 point to the most disciplined budgeting habits; *yes* responses to 4, 5, 7, and 11 reveal adequate budgeting habits; *yes* responses to 1, 3, 6, 8, and 12 indicate the poorest budgeting habits. If you have answered honestly, chances are you'll have a combination of all three. Look to see where you can improve your budgeting.

Management in Practice: Ethical Dilemma

Go Along to Get Along?

Rhonda Gilchrist became a nurse because she wanted to help people. As the home health care industry began to take off, she was presented with what she thought she was a terrific opportunity: a start-up home health care agency offered her a position managing its staff of visiting nurses. She supported home health care because patients were treated in the relaxed, comfortable atmosphere of their homes; home visits gave patients and nurses more independence; and home visits were intended to be much cheaper than hospital stays or doctor's office visits. Therefore, Rhonda eagerly accepted the job.

Most of the patients treated by Gilchrist's nurses were elderly, with a variety of complaints ranging from diabetes to hip injuries. At first, Gilchrist encouraged her staff to make their visits efficient and productive so that patients could be weaned from care in a timely manner. She assumed this was what the

head of the agency wanted. However, when she reported that one patient had recovered enough from a heart attack that he no longer needed three visits a week, the agency owner replied, "You should be looking for ways to increase the number of visits, not decrease them!" Gilchrist was shocked, but she soon understood that the only way to keep her job—and her nurses' jobs—was to go along with her company's wishes. Those extra visits, paid for by Medicare, were paying her salary.

Meanwhile, Gilchrist did some research on her own. She learned that the average home-care patient now gets 80 visits per year (nearly four times the number of a decade ago), for which Medicare pays up to $90 per visit. In 1995, Medicare spent $16 billion on home care. Although lawmakers eagerly embraced the idea of home health care in the 1980s, believing that the shift would save insurance companies, Medicare, and even average citizens a huge sum, the savings haven't materialized. In fact, the opposite has happened. Rhonda knows home health care is extremely important to many patients, but she also realizes it is being abused by others, as well as by the agencies. As she learned in her research, people who want to start up home health agencies don't even need any type of special training. One local doctor told her in confidence that the owner of her own agency, an engineer by training, simply wanted to open his own business, so he chose between retail clothing and home health care. The latter, with its guaranteed payments from Medicare, was a sure bet.

As she drove to the office, Rhonda considered her alternatives. She knew that some of her clients no longer needed care. But she also knew that she needed a job, and most patients were lonely and looked forward to the nurses' visits.

She wondered if there was a better way to control costs and deliver the best care to her patients.

What Do You Do?
1. Go along with the status quo and forget about the abuses of the system—that's your boss's problem. Besides, Medicare has deep pockets.
2. Look for another job as soon as possible. You don't want to be associated with unethical, and potentially illegal, practices.
3. Approach the owner of the agency and suggest other ways the agency might make a profit and deliver high-quality care, such as innovative ways to attract new clients to replace those that leave the roster in better health.

SOURCE: Based on George Anders and Laurie McGinley, "Medical Morass: How Do You Tame a Wild U.S. Program?" *The Wall Street Journal,* March 6, 1997, A1, A8.

Surf the Net

1. **Benchmarking.** Assume your boss is interested in adding benchmarking to your company's recently-instituted TQM program and has asked you to locate benchmarking information on the Internet. He told you that at the conference he attended last week he heard about a Web site called "The Benchmark Exchange" (**www.benchnet. com**). Your job is to report back to your boss with a complete report on what the Web site is all about, what the benefits of subscribing are, how much it costs to join, and the reasons for or against your company subscribing.

2. **ISO 9000.** Visit a site such as **www.connect.ab.ca/ ~praxiom/** or find another where you can locate the following information about ISO 9000, the international standards for quality management. (a) Briefly describe the kind of company that would use each of the three sets of standards: ISO 9001, ISO 9002, and ISO 9003. (b) Select one of the guidelines sections—ISO 9000, ISO 9004, ISO

10011, or ISO 10012—and tell how many sections it has and what the section titles are. (c) At the site listed above, go to page **www.connect.ab.ca/~praxiom/concepts.htm**, briefly read the "Theoretical Overview of ISO 9000," and describe your impressions of the process.

3. **Economic Value Added (EVA) Systems.** Go to **www.sternstewart.com** to supplement the text information on EVA Systems. At this site select one of the following activities: (a) View the video showing what corporate executives have to say about EVA and submit a summary of their comments; (b) Go to the "Performance Rankings" section and check out the United States and one other country of interest. Submit a comparison summary of what you learned about the two countries; or (c) Choose another category of information available at the site and submit a summary of your findings.

Case for Critical Analysis

Lincoln Electric

Imagine having a management system that is so successful people refer to it with capital letters—the Lincoln Management System—and other businesses benchmark their own systems by it. That is the situation of Ohio-based Lincoln Electric. For a number of years, other companies have tried to figure out Lincoln Electric's secret—how management coaxes maximum productivity and quality from its workers, even during difficult financial times.

Lincoln Electric is a leading manufacturer of welding products, welding equipment, and electric motors, with more than

$1 billion in sales and six thousand workers worldwide. The company's products are used for cutting, manufacturing, and repairing other metal products. Although it is now a publicly traded company, members of the Lincoln family still own more than 60 percent of the stock.

Lincoln uses a diverse control approach. Tasks are rigidly defined, and individual employees must meet strict measurable standards of performance. However, the Lincoln system succeeds largely because of an organizational culture based on openness and trust, shared control, and an egalitarian spirit.

Although the line between managers and workers at Lincoln is firmly drawn, managers respect the expertise of production workers and value their contributions to many aspects of the business. The company has an open-door policy for all top executives, middle managers, and production workers, and regular face-to-face communication is encouraged. Workers are expected to challenge management if they believe practices or compensation rates are unfair. Most workers are hired right out of high school, then trained and cross-trained to perform different jobs. Some eventually are promoted to executive positions, because Lincoln believes in promoting from within. Many Lincoln workers stay with the company for life.

One of Lincoln's founders felt that organizations should be based on certain values, including honesty, trustworthiness, openness, self-management, loyalty, accountability, and cooperativeness. These values continue to form the core of Lincoln's culture, and management regularly rewards employees who manifest them. Because Lincoln so effectively socializes employees, they exercise a great degree of self-control on the job. Production workers are paid on a piece-rate system, plus merit pay based on performance. Employees also are eligible for annual bonuses which fluctuate according to the company's fortunes, and they participate in stock purchase plans. Bonuses are based on a number of factors, such as productivity, quality, dependability, and cooperation with others. Factory workers at Lincoln have been known to earn more than $100,000 a year, and the average compensation in 1996 was $62,000. However, there also are other, less tangible rewards. Pride of workmanship and feelings of involvement, contribution, and esprit de corps are intrinsic rewards that flourish at Lincoln Electric. Cross-functional teams, empowered to make decisions, take responsibility for product planning, development, and marketing. Information about the company's operations and financial performance is openly shared with workers throughout the company.

Lincoln places emphasis on anticipating and solving customer problems. Sales representatives are given the technical training they need to understand customer needs, help customers understand and use Lincoln's products, and solve problems. This customer focus is backed up by attention to the production process through the use of strict accountability standards and formal measurements for productivity, quality, and innovation for all employees. In addition, a software program called Rhythm is used to streamline the flow of goods and materials in the production process.

Lincoln's system has worked extremely well in the United States. The cultural values, open communication, and formal control and reward systems interact to align the goals of managers, workers, and the organization as well as encourage learning and growth. Now Lincoln is discovering whether its system can hold up overseas. Although most of Lincoln's profits come from domestic operations, and a foreign venture in the 1990s lost a lot of money for the company, top managers want to expand globally because foreign markets are growing much more rapidly than domestic markets. Thus far, Lincoln managers have not developed a strategic control plan for global operations, relying instead on duplicating the domestic Lincoln system.

Questions

1. What types of control—feedforward, concurrent, or feedback—are illustrated in this case? Explain.
2. Based on what you've just read, what do you think makes the Lincoln System so successful?
3. What changes might Lincoln managers have to make to adapt their management system to overseas operations?

SOURCE: Joseph Maciariello, "A Pattern of Success: Can This Company Be Duplicated?" *Drucker Management 1*, no. 1 (spring 1997) 7–11.

Endnotes

1. Lawrence M. Fisher, "Inside Dell Computer Corporation," *Strategy and Business*, Issue 10, first quarter 1998, 68–75.
2. "Quality. The Soul of Productivity, the Key to Future Business Growth," *Interview*, Inter-City Gas Corporation, vol. 3 (autumn 1988), 3–5. The story was originally related by Patrick Lush in *The (Toronto) Globe & Mail*, June 15, 1988.
3. Douglas S. Sherwin, "The Meaning of Control," *Dunn's Business Review*, January 1956.
4. Jeannie Cameron, "Death of Traditional Accounting Will Prove to Be a Boon," *The Asian Wall Street Journal*, April 27, 1998, 16.
5. Anna Wilde Mathews, "New Gadgets Trace Truckers' Every Move," *The Wall Street Journal*, July 14, 1997, pp. B1, B10.
6. Steve Stecklow, "Kentucky's Teachers Get Bonuses, but Some Are Caught Cheating," *The Wall Street Journal*, September 2, 1997, p. A1, A5.
7. Cathy Lazere, "All Together Now," *CFO*, February 1998, pp. 28–34, 36.
8. George Anders and Laurie McGinley, "How Do You Tame a Wild U.S. Program? Slowly and Reluctantly," *The Wall Street Journal*, March 6, 1997, pp. A1, A8.
9. Anders and McGinley, "How Do You Tame a Wild U.S. Program?"
10. Leslie Scism and Scot J. Paltrow, "Prudential's Auditors Gave Early Warnings about Sales Abuses," *The Wall Street Journal*, August 7, 1997, pp. A1, A4.
11. Fisher, "Inside Dell Computer Corporation: Managing Working Capital."
12. Norm Brodsky, "Forget Spreadsheets," *Inc.*, November 1997, pp. 27–28.
13. Robin Goldwyn Blumenthal, "'Tis the Gift to Be Simple," *CFO*, January 1998, pp. 61–63.

14. Sumantra Ghoshal, *Strategic Control* (St. Paul, Minnesota: West, 1986), Chapter 4; and Robert N. Anthony, John Dearden, and Norton M. Bedford, *Management Control Systems,* 5th ed. (Homewood, Illinois: Irwin, 1984).

15. John A. Boquist, Todd T. Milbourn, and Anjan V. Thakor, "How Do You Win the Capital Allocation Game?" *Sloan Management Review,* winter 1998, pp. 59–71.

16. See Boquist, Milbourn, and Thakor, "How Do You Win the Capital Allocation Game?"

17. Anthony, Dearden, and Bedford, *Management Control Systems.*

18. Participation in budget setting is described in a number of studies, including Neil C. Churchill, "Budget Choice: Planning versus Control," *Harvard Business Review* (July–August 1984), 150–164; Peter Brownell, "Leadership Style, Budgetary Participation, and Managerial Behavior," *Accounting Organizations and Society* 8 (1983), 307–321; and Paul J. Carruth and Thurrell O. McClandon, "How Supervisors React to 'Meeting the Budget' Pressure," *Management Accounting* 66 (November 1984), 50–54.

19. William G. Ouchi, "Markets, Bureaucracies, and Clans," *Administrative Science Quarterly* 25 (1980), 129–141; and B. R. Baligia and Alfred M. Jaeger, "Multinational Corporations: Control Systems and Delegation Issues," *Journal of International Business Studies,* fall 1984, 25–40.

20. Sherwin, "The Meaning of Control."

21. Mathews, "New Gadgets Trace Truckers' Every Move," p. B10.

22. John Case, "Keeping Score," *Inc.,* June 1998, pp. 81–82+.

23. Case, "Keeping Score," p. 84.

24. A. V. Feigenbaum, *Total Quality Control: Engineering and Management* (New York: McGraw-Hill, 1961); John Lorinc, "Dr. Deming's Traveling Quality Show," *Canadian Business,* September 1990, 38–42; Mary Walton, *The Deming Management Method* (New York: Dodd-Meade & Co., 1986); and J. M. Juran and Frank M. Gryna, eds., *Juran's Quality Control Handbook,* 4th ed. (New York: McGraw-Hill, 1988).

25. Edward E. Lawler III and Susan A. Mohrman, "Quality

Circles after the Fad," *Harvard Business Review,* January–February 1985, 65–71; and Philip C. Thompson, *Quality Circles: How to Make Them Work in America* (New York: AMACOM, 1982).

26. Howard Rothman, "You Need Not Be Big to Benchmark," *Nation's Business,* December 1992, 64–65.

27. Christopher Farrell, "America's New Watchword: If It Moves, Privatize It," *Business Week,* December 12, 1994, 39.

28. Philip R. Thomas, Larry J. Gallace, and Kenneth R. Martin, *Quality Alone Is Not Enough (AMA Management Briefing),* New York: American Management Association, August 1992.

29. Kate Kane, "L. L. Bean Delivers the Goods," *Fast Company,* August/September 1997, 104–113.

30. Robert W. Haney and Charles D. Beaman, Jr., "Management Leadership Critical to CQI Success," *Hospitals,* July 20, 1992, 64.

31. Web site of the International Organization for Standardization, www.iso.ch, accessed January 19, 1999.

32. Mustafa V. Uzumeri, "ISO 9000 and the Other Metastandards: Principles for Management Practice?" *Academy of Management Executive,* 11(no. 1) (1997), 21–36.

33. Perry Pascarella, "Open the Books to Unleash Your People," *Management Review,* May 1998, 58–60.

34. Don L. Bohl, Fred Luthans, John W. Slocum Jr., and Richard M. Hodgetts, "Ideas That Will Shape the Future of Management Practice," *Organizational Dynamics,* summer 1996, 7–14.

35. Israel Shaked, Allen Michel, and Pierre Leroy, "Creating Value through E.V.A.: Myth or Reality?" *Strategy and Business,* Fourth Quarter 1997, 41–52.

36. Randy Myers, "Sure for Ure," *CFO,* November 1997, 4–46+.

37. Bohl et al., "Ideas That Will Shape the Future of Management Practice."

38. Srikumar S. Rao, "ABCs of Cost Control," *Inc. Technology,* June 15, 1997, 79–81.

39. Rao, "ABCs of Cost Control," 79.

Chapter 21

LEARNING OBJECTIVES

After studying this chapter, you should be able to

- Describe the importance of information technology for organizations and the attributes of quality information.

- Explain how networks are transforming the way companies operate and the services they offer.

- Identify different types of information systems.

- Tell how information systems support daily operations and decision making.

- Summarize the impact of information technology on competitive strategy.

- Identify specific management implications of information technology.

- List criteria for evaluating IT system success.

Information Systems and Technology

MANAGEMENT PROBLEM

Over the past decade, Cementos Mexicanos (Cemex) has gone from a sleepy company in Mexico to the world's third-largest cement company. Its 20,000 employees, 486 plants, and thousands of vehicles and freight ships move more than 50 million tons of cement annually in 60 countries. Cemex specializes in places that don't have highly developed road systems and solid telephone networks, places where equipment breakdowns are common and workers often can't get to the work site—in other words, where anything can, and usually does, go wrong. To illustrate the problems Cemex faces, consider how the cement business typically has worked in Guadalajara, Mexico's second-largest city: A builder calls in an order and specifies a delivery time. He knows, though, that delivery time depends on an endless array of variables, such as weather, traffic conditions, a missing receipt, whether the truck's walkie-talkies conked out, or the number of other orders the plant is trying to fill that day. Builders are lucky to get their delivery on the right day, let alone at the right hour. From the cement company's standpoint, things aren't so great either. Despite penalties, on delivery day about half of the customers cancel or reschedule their orders, leaving tons of costly cement rumbling around town with nowhere to go. Cemex CEO Lorenzo Zambrano knows if he doesn't stay competitive in these complex, difficult locations, foreign corporations will come in and eat Cemex's lunch. To prevent that, Zambrano wants to find a way to help alleviate the uncertainty his customers deal with daily.[1]

Can information technology play a role in helping Cemex deal with complexity and keep its commitments to customers? If you were an IT consultant, what type of systems would you recommend to Zambrano?

Today, almost every company uses some form of information technology. At Cemex, executives have long used basic information technology systems to maintain control of a growing global business. However, they are now searching for ways to adapt global technology to the essentially limitless range of local problems that can occur in developing areas of the world.

The strategic use of information technology may be one of the defining aspects of organizational success today. It is thus important to develop some understanding of the types of information technology systems and the changes IT brings to organizations. Managing information technology is all about managing change and uncertainty, particularly under time duress. The problem at Cemex is an IT consultant's dream, providing the challenge of applying information technology to bring order to situations in which complexity—even chaos—is the defining characteristic.

In order to understand the challenges managers and organizations face today, let us begin by developing an understanding of information technology and the attributes of quality information.

Information Technology

information technology
The hardware, software, telecommunications, database management, and other technologies used to store, process, and distribute information.

An organization's **information technology** consists of the hardware, software, telecommunications, database management, and other technologies it uses to store data and make them available in the form of information for organizational decision making. These technologies give the organization's managers and employees access to complex databases of customer and organizational information. The greater availability and lower costs of information technology pressure organizations to invest in new hardware, software, and other information-processing technologies lest they lose their market position.

By providing managers with more information more quickly than ever before, modern information technology improves efficiency and effectiveness at each stage of the strategic decision-making process. Whether through computer-aided manufacturing, information sharing with customers, or international inventory control, information technology aids operational processes and decision making. Consider the case of American Greetings Corporation, which sells greeting cards in about 35,000 retail locations in the United States. The company uses information technology to gather and analyze data to test the popularity of new card designs, automate production of cards, identify which kinds of cards will sell best at particular stores, fill orders, and report to retailers on the performance of American Greetings' displays in their stores. For example, the company once had hundreds of workers filling orders by hand. Today, practically the entire order-filling process has been automated, enabling American Greetings to cut labor costs. By combining efficiency through automation with a precisely targeted and well-tested product line, American Greetings stays profitable and helps its customers, the retailers, to be profitable as well.[2]

Data versus Information

data
Raw, unsummarized, and unanalyzed facts and figures.

The ability to generate more information with technology presents a serious challenge to information technicians, managers, and other users of information. They must sort through overwhelming amounts of data to identify only that information necessary for a particular purpose. **Data** are raw facts and figures that in and of themselves may not be useful. To be useful, data must be processed into finished **information**—that is, data that have been converted into a meaningful and useful context for specific users. An increasing challenge for managers is being able to effectively identify and access useful information. American Greetings, for example, might gather *data* about demographics in various parts of the country. These data are then translated into *information;* for example, stores in Florida require an enormous assortment of greeting cards directed at grandson, granddaughter, niece, and nephew, while stores in some other parts of the country might need a larger percentage of slightly irreverent, youth-oriented products.

The magnitude of the job of transforming data into useful information is reflected in organizations' introduction of the chief information officer (CIO) position. CIOs are responsible for managing organizational databases and implementing new information technology. As they make decisions involving the adoption and management of new technologies, CIOs integrate old and new technology to support organizational decision making, operations, and communication. The purchase options in hardware, software, networking, and telecommunications products can be overwhelming to information officers. The enormous amount of data that combinations of this technology can produce is equally overwhelming. Despite these challenges, the CIO manages the infrastructure so that it will place the necessary information in the right place at the right time. Ideally, this means the CIO combines knowledge of information technology (IT) with the ability to help managers and employees identify their information needs as well as ways the organization can use its IT capabilities in support of its strategy. Through a variety of technologies described in this chapter, the CIO can empower managers and employees to use shared information to meet customer needs in ways that in the past would have been impossible.

Characteristics of Useful Information

Organizations depend on high-quality information to develop strategic plans, identify problems, and interact with other organizations. Information is of high quality if it has characteristics that make it useful for these tasks. The characteristics of useful information fall into three broad categories, as illustrated in Exhibit 21.1.

1. Time—Information should be available when needed, up-to-date, provided when needed, and related to the appropriate time period (past, present, or future).

2. Content—Useful information is error free, suited to the user's needs, complete, concise, relevant (that is, it excludes unnecessary data), and an accurate measure of performance.

3. Form—The information should be provided in a form that is easy for the user to understand and meets the user's needs for the level of detail. The presentation should be ordered and use the combination of words, numbers, and diagrams that is most helpful to the user. Also, information should be presented in a useful medium (printed documents, video display, sound).

Computer Networks

Modern information technology recognizes that most organizational activities involve groups of people—the organization's employees, suppliers, and customers. For these people to cooperate, agree on solutions to problems, and

information
Data that have been converted into a meaningful and useful context for the receiver.

You may live in the United States, but it is possible for you to access your financial information at this Citibank facility in Budapest, Hungary. Due to advances in information technology, the banking industry has developed complex databases to provide financial information globally, and it is estimated that by the year 2010, four to five billion people worldwide will be active users of a vast range of financial products and services. Citibank realizes this enormous potential market. At Citibank's corporate offices, located in New York City, the "objective is to build a company that serves consumers around the world." Today, Citibank's business is as much information and communications as financial services. "Executing our global growth strategy relies heavily on state-of-the-art technology."

Exhibit *21.1*

Characteristics of High-Quality Information

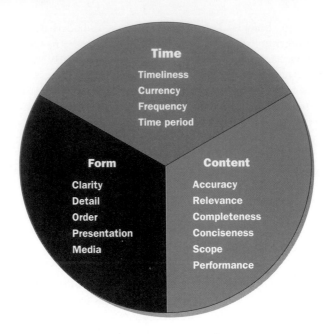

SOURCE: Adapted from James A. O'Brien, *Introduction to Information Systems,* 8th ed. (Burr Ridge, IL: Irwin, 1997), 284–285.

network
A system that links people and departments within or among organizations for the purpose of sharing information resources.

meet one another's needs, they must be able to share information. Thus, many companies use information technology that offers the ability for people to use their computers to share information.

Networks are systems that link people and departments within a particular building or across corporate offices. They may also allow company representatives to interact globally with one another and with customers. A network can be thought of as multiple brains connected to help expand the mindpower of the organization. Networks play a critical role in the shift to the learning organization because they expand the capacity for learning in fast-changing companies. They support the broad sharing of information that is an essential component of the learning organization, as described in Chapter 2. Networks also work in concert with other changes impacting today's organizations, such as the empowerment of workers, geographical dispersion of the workforce, decentralized decision making, team-based structures, and the trend toward collaboration with other organizations.

In the past, when only large mainframe computers could handle complex tasks, employees typically used terminals to send data to the mainframe or to retrieve information. Employees could not use these systems to share information directly with one another. However, as personal computers became more sophisticated, organizations began linking them with cables and software, thereby establishing networks for communication among employees. They created local area networks (LANs) by wiring together users at a single location and wide area networks (WANs) by using modems to link people at different locations via telephone.

As organizations created networks, they faced the challenge of how to enable different kinds of computers to communicate with one another. One solution has been to use a category of software called *middleware,* which mediates among myriad types of hardware and software. Even a single company may have many sizes and brands of computers and software, and middleware helps these varied components communicate on a network.

The Internet, Intranets, and Extranets. Today, widespread use of the Internet offers another way to link people in networks. Unlike other kinds of networking, the Internet enables any computer with Internet capabilities to share information with others on the Internet. Government agencies, publishers, and other service providers offer access to a mind-boggling array of data and news stories. The Internet also provides a conduit for individuals to share information via E-mail and in discussion groups. Salestar, which markets software customized for telephone companies, uses the Internet to recruit employees. The company has found this to be the most cost-effective way to reach people with experience at phone companies, because they tend to be widely scattered.[3] The Manager's Shoptalk box lists some do's and don'ts for businesses using the Internet.

The wide accessibility of the Internet can also be its major downside for businesses, however. Most organizations want to limit access to certain details of their activities. Also, they need to protect their employees' privacy by not disclosing personal information about them. Consequently, many organizations use the technology of the Internet to create networks that may be used only by authorized persons. The software that limits access is called a *firewall.* One type of such networks is an **intranet,** a network that uses Internet technology but limits access to all or some of the organization's employees. At the University of Central Florida, for example, faculty and administrators use an intranet called Polaris to look up information ranging from class rolls to departmental accounts and personnel data. Students can use Polaris to look up personal and academic data about themselves. Middleware allows the university's older mainframes to share with the intranet. Ford Motor Company's intranet connects some 120,000 workstations at offices and factories around the world to thousands of Ford Web sites offering proprietary information such as market research, analyses of competitors' components, and product development. The product-development system, for example, which

intranet
A computer network that uses Internet technology but limits access to all or some of the organization's employees.

Internet, intranet, and extranet information technology advances provide companies with the ability to have employees dispersed geographically—working at home. Anne Britt is a mortgage banker, who converted a 10 × 10 storage closet into her home office. Anne works for Norwest from her home in Houston, Texas. Her computer, linking her to Norwest database information, a separate business line, and an answering service provide her with the ability to conduct business as if she were located at Norwest headquarters.

Shoptalk

Internet Etiquette

Throughout the 1970s and 1980s, the Internet and business were incompatible notions. However, over the past several years, the Internet has opened up more and more to commercial activity. Despite this increased commercial use, many Internet users still cherish the noncommercial culture of the past. Managers who wish to promote their business in cyberspace can avoid incurring the wrath of these users by following some basic rules of Internet etiquette:

1. Don't send mass electronic mailings. Businesses that send unsolicited E-mail to individuals or newsgroups do so at their own risk. Some users will respond immediately with vitriolic messages known as "flames. "In some cases, the volume of incoming flames has overloaded the server of the offending company's Internet service provider, resulting in the cancellation of the company's account.

2. Provide information in a timely manner to those who request it. Sending E-mail about your company's products or services to people who have expressed an interest is an inexpensive, fast, and convenient way to reach potential new customers. In addition, certain newsgroups allow advertising by businesses.

3. Don't violate the sanctity of the chat room. Many users consider it especially offensive for businesses to post unrelated questions or comments in discussion areas such as chat rooms, newsgroups, and mailing lists. Businesses can participate in these areas when they have something pertinent to say about the subject matter under discussion,

but they should not use chat rooms to promote their products. It's okay, however, to give advice in areas in which you and your company can offer expertise.

4. Another acceptable approach is to "lurk" in a discussion area to become familiar with the subject matter and post any relevant messages. Read the group's frequently asked questions (FAQ) to understand what is acceptable.

5. Don't type entire messages in capital letters. This is the on-line equivalent of SHOUTING.

6. Keep messages short and to the point. Don't send potential customers files that take an excessively long time to download.

7. Don't overload your Web site with graphics. Although graphics are eye-catching, they can take a long time to appear on the user's computer screen, particularly for users with slower modems. The less frustration you create for Internet users, the better for your business.

Some old guard Internet users still grumble about the increasing commercialization of the Internet. However, they are outnumbered by those who believe in the potential of the Internet to bring about a better way of doing business. If businesses keep the rules of Internet etiquette in mind and conduct themselves with decorum, they will encounter less grumbling and more interest.

SOURCE: Tim McCollum, "Making the Internet Work for You," *Nation's Business,* March 1997, 6–13.

---

is updated hourly on the intranet, lets engineers, designers, and suppliers work from the same data, thus keeping the process moving and saving the company time and money.[4] Motorola also uses an intranet to help meet the pressures of ever faster product cycles.

MOTOROLA
www.mot.com

When Motorola, the big producer of communications equipment, needed a computer network, it turned to the World Wide Web for its multimedia capabilities and ready accessibility. The company was in a hurry to start producing cable modems, which would be used to link computers to the Internet at high speeds. Assembling these complex products would require extensive documentation, including drawings of each component. Instead of sending engineers to the drawing board, Motorola used a digital camera to take pictures of each component. The company set up an intranet Web site with the digitized images, along with instructions for assembly, testing, packing, and shipping of the modems. Highlighting and color coding identify new parts and instructions, as well as flagging those steps that have had high error rates. Users provide an ID number when they log on to the intranet, then use a Netscape browser and menus of choices to find what they need.

Motorola's intranet is less costly than paper documentation, was faster to set up than assembling the vast array of paper instructions workers would need to help them assemble complex devices, and enables the company to better comply with quality standards. That translates into big payoffs in quality, consistency, and cost reductions. For example, Blane McMichen, manager of production technologies for Motorola's information systems group, points out that the assembly lines that do not yet use cyber instructions require six support technicians to manage the paper. On the other hand, the intranet that serves the new cable-modem line needs the attention of only a single technician.[5]

An **extranet** also uses Internet technology but links authorized users inside the company with certain outsiders such as customers or vendors. A recent survey of 2,500 businesses by ActivMedia, a marketing research company, found that 13 percent of the companies were using extranets, and that number is growing fast.[6] One reason extranets are growing in popularity is that they enable users at a variety of locations to participate with whatever computers and operating systems they have. They are also an efficient way to create a network that links people on an international scale. Harley-Davidson uses an extranet to foster communications with motorcycle dealers. Using a Web browser, dealers can visit h-dnet.com to file warranty claims, submit financial statements, check recall status, request that technical service documents be faxed to them, and order parts and accessories. Harley-Davidson initially developed the extranet for U.S. dealers but plans to extend the network to other countries.[7]

Extranets support the trend to specialize in core competencies (what the company does best) and to outsource other activities. For example, a manufacturing company would focus on developing and producing goods and let other organizations handle such activities as inventory management, payroll, and billing. With an extranet, it can be just as easy to share data with such a service provider as with an internal department, and the service provider has an incentive to keep up with the latest technology and regulations in its area of speciality.

extranet
A computer network that uses Internet technology but links authorized users inside the company with certain outsiders such as customers or vendors.

Groupware.

To use the power of networks most effectively, organizations can design systems to take on the characteristics of face-to-face interaction, allowing people to collaborate in real time. Several users who are scattered around the world can be hooked to a network, for example, and collaborate on a project almost as easily as if they were sitting around a conference table. The technology that makes this possible is a type of software called **groupware,** which displays a document on more than one user's screen and allows all the users to see changes or comments as they are made by one person. Thus, engineers in different locations can review and discuss a drawing, or a sales team can review and comment on a proposal or marketing literature. With groupware, participants can simultaneously share the information in the documents displayed and their own knowledge and ideas about the documents. Managers from one of Marriott Corporation's large

groupware
Software that displays documents on more than one user's screen and allows all users to see changes or comments as they are made by one person.

Washington-area hotels used groupware to participate in an electronic meeting designed to find ways to improve guest satisfaction. The group generated 139 ideas in less than 30 minutes. After further "discussion" and rating of the ideas, the group emerged with a consensus of the specific types of additional training to be provided for hotel employees.[8]

Types of Information Systems

Most managers today appreciate the value of making information readily available in some kind of formal, computer-based information system. Such a system combines hardware, software, and human resources to support organizational information and communication needs. One way to distinguish among the many types of information systems is to focus on the functions they perform and the people they serve in an organization. We discuss three broad categories of information systems widely used today, as illustrated in Exhibit 21.2. Operations information systems support information-processing needs of a business's day-to-day operations as well as low-level operations management functions. Management information systems typically support the strategic decision-making needs of higher-level managers. Other organizational support systems include those designed to interpret geographic data, those that clone expert decision-making models for use by nonexpert users, and broad-scale systems that support planning for the needs of the enterprise as a whole. Most organizational information systems combine aspects of several of these categories in an integrated information system to provide decision makers with more support than could be obtained through the use of an individual technology.

Operations Information Systems

operations information system
A computer-based information system that supports a company's day-to-day operations.

A variety of systems, called **operations information systems,** support the information-processing needs related to a business's day-to-day operations. Types of operations information systems include transaction-processing systems, process control systems, and office automation systems. Each of these supports daily operations and decisions that typically are made by nonmanagement employees or lower-level managers.

Exhibit
21.2
Types of Information Systems

Operations Information Systems
- Transaction-processing systems
- Process control systems
- Office automation systems

Management Information Systems
- Information-reporting systems
- Decision support systems
- Group decision support systems
- Executive information systems

Other Organizational Support Systems
- Expert systems
- Geographic information systems
- Enterprise resource-planning (ERP) systems

Transaction-processing systems (TPSs) record and process data resulting from business operations. They include information systems that record sales to customers, purchases from suppliers, inventory changes, and wages to employees. A TPS system collects data from these transactions and stores them in a database. Employees use information from the database to produce reports and other information, such as customer statements and employee paychecks. Most of an organization's reports are generated from these databases. Transaction-processing systems identify, collect, and organize the fundamental information from which an organization operates.

transaction-processing system
A type of operations information system that records and processes data resulting from routine business transactions such as sales, purchases, and payroll.

While a transaction-processing system keeps track of the size, type, and financial consequences of the organization's transactions, companies also need information about the quantity and quality of their production activities. Therefore, they may use **process control systems** to monitor and control ongoing physical processes. For example, petroleum refineries, pulp and paper mills, food manufacturing plants, and electric power plants use process control systems with special sensing devices that monitor and record physical phenomena such as temperature or pressure change. The system relays the measurements or sensor-detected data to a computer for processing; employees and operations managers can check the data to look for problems requiring action.

process control system
A computer system that monitors and controls ongoing physical processes, such as temperature or pressure changes.

Office automation systems combine modern hardware and software such as word processors, desktop publishers, E-mail, and teleconferencing to handle the tasks of publishing and distributing information. Office automation systems also are used to transform manual accounting procedures to electronic media. Companies such as Wal-Mart, Chevron, and American Airlines send thousands of electronic payments a month to suppliers, eliminating the need for writing and mailing checks. These systems enable businesses to streamline office tasks, reduce errors, and improve customer service. In this way, office automation systems support the other kinds of information systems.

office automation systems
Systems that combine modern hardware and software to handle the tasks of publishing and distributing information.

Operations information systems aid organizational decision makers in many ways and across various settings. For example, at MDP Construction, an operations information system is an essential tool to help keep a lid on costs as the company handles contracts for the U.S. military, for which expensive last-minute changes are the norm. MDP uses a project management program to establish schedules for each construction project and to automatically compute the impact of any requested change on the schedule and budget for the project. Using the program, MDP can plan daily activities for its workers—and justify to the Pentagon the need for delays or additional costs.[9]

In the personal touch world of funeral directors, the McDonough Funeral Home has been able to serve customers better through the use of office automation. During a bereaved family's first visit, owner John McDonough uses a laptop computer to work through a list of 50 to 100 questions, entering the answers as they are provided. His assistant, using another computer on the network, watches the answers appear on her screen. She immediately begins creating an obituary and sends it to the local newspaper via modem. The system also files the data in a database, entering facts into the relevant forms, such as those for social security and veterans' benefits. Data about the funeral arrangements go into a planning program. With all the data available where and when they are needed, McDonough and his staff can ensure that funerals and the related arrangements proceed smoothly, with no details forgotten.[10]

Management Information Systems

Until the 1960s, information systems were used primarily for transaction processing, accounting, and record keeping. Then the introduction of computers using silicon chip circuitry allowed for more processing power per dollar. As computer manufacturers promoted these systems and managers began visualizing ways in which the computers could help them make important decisions, management information systems were born. A **management information system (MIS)** is a computer-based system that provides information and support for effective managerial decision making. The basic elements of a management information system are illustrated in Exhibit 21.3. The MIS is supported by the organization's operations information systems and by organizational databases (and frequently databases of external data as well). Management information systems typically include reporting systems, decision support systems, executive information systems, and group decision support systems, each of which will be explained in this section.

MISs typically support strategic decision-making needs of midlevel and top management. However, as technology becomes more widely accessible, more employees are wired into networks, and organizations push decision making downward in the hierarchy, these kinds of systems are seeing use at all levels of the organization.

When a production manager needs to make a decision about production scheduling, he or she may need data on the anticipated number of orders in the coming month, inventory levels, and availability of computers and personnel. The MIS can provide these data. In fact, **information reporting systems,** the most common form of MIS, provide managers and decision makers with reports that support day-to-day decision-making needs. These reports typically give managers prespecified information for use in making structured decisions. For example, activity-based costing software, such as NetProphet, EasyABC Plus, and HyperABC, allows managers to see all the costs associated with producing and selling particular products. Managers can monitor the costs and identify which products are profitable,

management information system (MIS)
A computer-based system that provides information and support for effective managerial decision making.

information reporting system
A system that organizes information in the form of prespecified reports that managers use in day-to-day decision making.

Exhibit *21.3*

Basic Elements of Management Information Systems

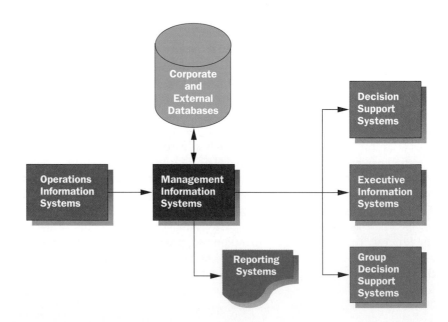

SOURCE: Adapted from Ralph M. Stair and George W. Reynolds, *Principles of Information Systems: A Managerial Approach,* 4th ed. (Cambridge, Mass.: Course Technology, 1999), 391.

which should be discontinued, and so on. After Koehler Manufacturing Company, a small business in Marlboro, Massachusetts, installed activity-based costing software, managers discovered that Koehler's best-selling product line—lead-acid batteries—was devouring company profits. This gave management the information they needed to make better decisions about future products.[11]

Decision support systems (DSSs) are interactive, computer-based information systems that rely on decision models and specialized databases to support decision makers. With electronic spreadsheets and other decision support software, users can pose a series of what-if questions to test alternatives they are considering. Based on the assumptions used in the software or specified by the user, managers can explore various alternatives and receive tentative information to help them choose the alternative with the best outcome.

Executive information systems (EISs) are management information systems to facilitate strategic decision making at the highest level of management. These systems are typically based on software that provides easy access to large amounts of complex data and can analyze and present the data in a timely fashion. EISs provide top management with quick access to relevant internal and external information and, if designed properly, can help them diagnose problems as well as develop solutions.

A **group decision support system (GDSS)** is an interactive computer-based system that facilitates group decision making. Also called *collaborative work systems*, GDSSs are designed to allow team members to interact and at the same time take advantage of computer-based support data. Participating managers may sit around a conference table equipped with a computer terminal at each position or may sit thousands of miles apart and, through live television, use team conferencing to view one another and share data displays. Such a system may employ groupware or such Internet technology as real-time discussion groups or live video or audio feeds.

A leader in the use of management information systems is retailing giant Wal-Mart. The company uses a massive database to make decisions about what to stock, how to price it, and when to reorder. The company sends store managers weekly reports of the 50 top items in terms of sales and profits. Store managers who want to boost their store's profitability can check whether they are properly promoting those 50 items. In addition, the department managers at each store keep track of which items are the top sellers in their department, then signal employees to take special care to ensure that those items are in stock. Department managers also carry scanners that allow them to check inventory levels of any item by scanning its bar code. If they run low on something, they can scan the bar code to obtain data on inventory levels at nearby stores. Back at headquarters, Wal-Mart managers and employees continuously analyze transactions data to identify relationships among purchases, looking for ways to cross-promote items that are typically purchased together.[12]

Other Organizational Support Systems

Several other types of information systems may support either operations or management applications and are used at various levels of the organization. Among the most significant support systems are geographic information systems, expert systems, and enterprise resource planning systems.

Ryder Transportation Resources uses a decision support system called RyderLinc, a cross-functional, integrated computer system that allows computers throughout the company to interact with each other as well as with those of customers and suppliers. The new information system can give customers precise information on virtually every aspect of their transportation and distribution services on a daily or even hourly basis, thus lending support to Ryder's excellent on-time, 99 percent damage-free delivery record. RyderLinc also supports sales by giving potential customers access to global data and market information and allowing them to compare the financial implications of different distribution and transportation alternatives.

decision support system (DSS)
An interactive, computer-based system that uses decision models and specialized databases to support organization decision makers.

executive information system (EIS)
A management information system designed to facilitate strategic decision making at the highest levels of management by providing executives with easy access to timely and relevant information.

group decision support system (GDSS)
An interactive computer-based system that facilitates group communication and decision making; also called collaborative work system.

geographic information system (GIS)
A type of decision support system that provides layers of information expressed visually through the use of maps.

Geographic Information Systems. A **geographic information system (GIS)** is a type of decision support system that provides users with layers of information expressed visually through maps. Users of such a system might combine maps with data to identify the areas with the greatest concentration of customers or the history of the most rainfall, for instance, or they might use a GIS to plan the most efficient routes to their customers, quickly modifying their plans as customers place or cancel orders. GISs support analytical decision making for business as well as for the management of defense troops, species management, emergency management, land use planning, redistricting, and demographics, among many other applications. In business, GISs often help perform distribution planning, site selection, trade area analysis, and regulatory compliance.[13] Exhibit 21.4 provides an example of the kind of information that can be retrieved with a GIS. This output from ArcView® software, the desktop GIS software from Environmental Systems Research Institute, shows a marketing view of the Atlanta, Georgia, market, providing a new and powerful context in which to perform comprehensive demographic, consumer, or product performance analysis. Such marketing views are created by integrating and visualizing both internal customer data and a variety of external GIS data sources. ArcView® can then be used to identify and target available customers from the lowest levels (i.e., household, block, group, sales territory) to the broadest of marketing levels (i.e., distribution market, national territory).

Germany's largest private water supply company, Gelsenwasser, uses a GIS from Cambridge, England-based Smallworld to manage water supply and

E x h i b i t 21.4 *Output from ArcView® GIS Software*

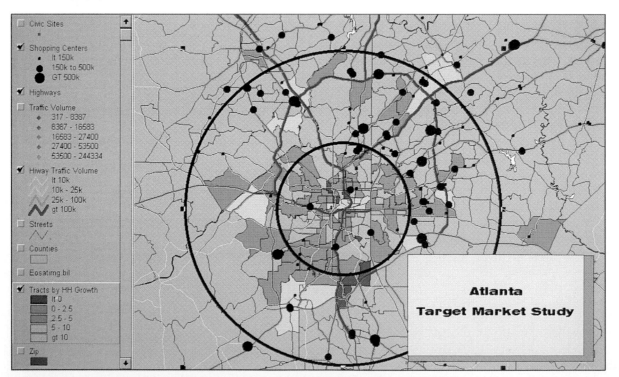

SOURCE: Reprinted courtesy of Environmental Systems Research Institute, Inc. ArcView® is a registered trademark of ESRI.

quality in its service area. Gelsenwasser created a map of its service area and divided that area into small strips, which it can analyze in detail. By combining data from meteorological reports and its tests of water samples with data about the land characteristics, employees of Gelsenwasser can keep track of water quality, identify potential problems, and determine steps they must take, such as changing the use of a parcel of land. Gelsenwasser also uses the database to inform the public about the quality of its water; it is planning to expand the GIS so that members of the public can see this information displayed on a map.[14]

Expert Systems.   An **expert system** attempts to duplicate the thinking process that managers and professionals use when making decisions. To develop this type of system, programmers codify a specialist's knowledge into decision rules and use them to write a computer program that mimics the expert's problem-solving strategy. Most expert systems address repetitive problems for specialized areas, such as diagnosing illnesses or machinery malfunctions. An expert system is the application of *artificial intelligence* (AI), a technology whose ultimate goal is to make computers gather and process data in the same way the human brain does. Cisco Systems, which sells networking software, uses AI software to help customers diagnose and fix problems with their hardware. When customers use the Troubleshooting Engine at Cisco's Web site, they answer a series of questions as the system applies each answer to narrow down and eventually pinpoint the source of the problem.[15]

Expert systems vary in complexity. An example of the simplest type is personal budgeting software you may have on your personal computer. More complex expert systems are used by businesses for strategic decision making. For example, Lincoln National's life underwriting system relies on complex medical, financial, and insurance knowledge. In addition, Lincoln National requires that an applicant's hobbies and occupation be factored into policy evaluation and pricing. The company's top four underwriters spent several years providing the knowledge to help develop this expert system.[16]

Enterprise Resource Planning (ERP) Systems.   As managers have seen how access to data can improve their decisions, they have increasingly looked for ways to pull together various kinds of data to show how a decision about one area of the business will affect the other areas of the enterprise. Fortunately, as computing power has become more affordable, information systems have been able to address that desire by taking an increasingly broad view of the organization's activities. Today, a growing number of companies are setting up a broad-scale information system called **enterprise resource planning (ERP).** An ERP system collects, processes, and provides information about an organization's entire enterprise, including orders, product design, production, purchasing, inventory, distribution, human resources, receipt of payments, and forecasting of future demand. Such a system links these areas of activity into a network, as illustrated in Exhibit 21.5. When a salesperson takes an order, the ERP system checks to see how the order impacts inventory levels, scheduling, human resources, purchasing, and distribution. Executives can use this information to evaluate operations and adjust their plans as needed to meet changing conditions.

Given the massive computing power required to run such a system, the original ERP applications were for the largest companies with powerful mainframe computers. The leading ERP system, SAP's R/3, was designed to handle

Ohio Casualty Corporation has been redesigning its information systems to provide stronger customer focus and give the company a competitive edge in a crowded marketplace. Ohio Casualty launched an expert system *in the Lexington and Louisville, Kentucky, branches as a pilot project. The knowledge-based program accepts applications for auto and homeowners' coverage and assists in making underwriting decisions. When data provided by the policyholder satisfy the criteria incorporated in the expert system, it automatically issues a policy, saving time and money because the intervention of an underwriter is not required.*

expert system (ES)
Information technology that programs a computer to duplicate an expert's decision-making and problem-solving strategies.

enterprise resource planning (ERP)
A networked information system that collects, processes, and provides information about an organization's entire enterprise, from identification of customer needs and receipt of orders to distribution of products and receipt of payments.

Exhibit 21.5   *Example of ERP Applications*

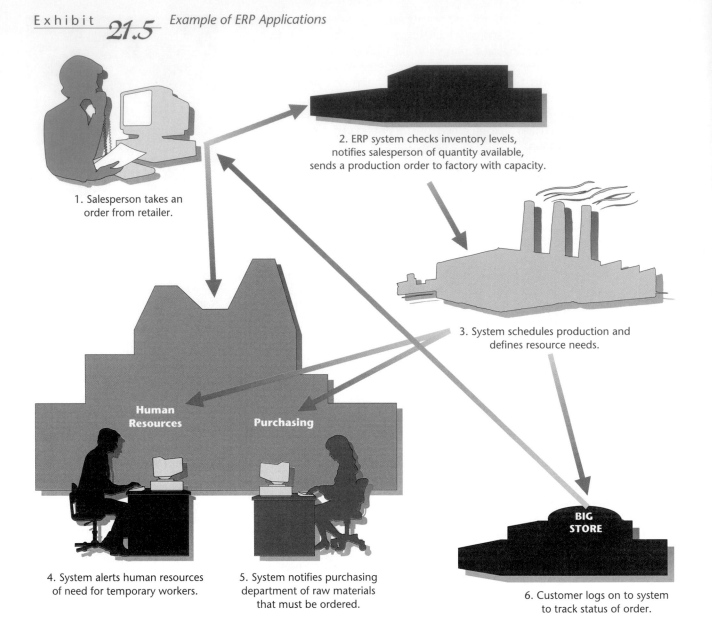

1. Salesperson takes an order from retailer.

2. ERP system checks inventory levels, notifies salesperson of quantity available, sends a production order to factory with capacity.

3. System schedules production and defines resource needs.

Human Resources

Purchasing

4. System alerts human resources of need for temporary workers.

5. System notifies purchasing department of raw materials that must be ordered.

BIG STORE

6. Customer logs on to system to track status of order.

Strategic Planning Group

7. Management uses ERP data to evaluate and adjust its strategic plan.

SOURCE: Adapted from Gail Edmondson, "Silicon Valley on the Rhine," *Business Week,* November 3, 1997, 162–166.

different currencies, languages, and legal systems, so multinational corporations can use it for the entire company. However, the growing use of networked PCs and the Internet have enabled SAP and other companies such as Oracle to offer versions of ERP that are suited for smaller organizations.

An enterprise resource planning system blurs the line dividing operations information systems from management information systems. By integrating data about all aspects of operations, ERP enables employees at every level to retrieve information to make decisions about their area of activity. A salesperson, for example, can enter an order and see what the real delivery date will be. An engineer can see how a decision about product design will affect production schedules and resource needs. Thus, the organization's ability to reap the benefits of ERP depends largely on how well it sets up organizational processes and delegates responsibility so that employees can use the information the system makes available. Hershey Foods, a $4 billion-a-year company known for its chocolate, is taking a careful approach to ensure that its ERP system will serve the needs of employees and managers.

Hershey Foods has recently embarked on a three-year, $75-million project to install an ERP system that will integrate the best finance, logistics, and sales practices from multiple business divisions. For example, the new system lets Hershey track all outstanding accounts with retailers, so it can measure payment risks and set consistent credit terms across all Hershey's divisions, large and small. In the past, a supermarket chain might negotiate credit terms with the Ronzini pasta division, then wind up having to negotiate all over again with the chocolate division.

Managers plan to have 85 percent of the company's core processes running on ERP infrastructure by 2001. The process is not an easy one, however. As Rick Bentz, Hershey's vice president for information technology, says of the undertaking: "You think that a problem is solved and then you get farther down the road and find that it's not. It's two steps forward and one step back." However, managers know that a careful, adaptive approach is the best way to ensure that the company will reap the benefits of an ERP system. They also see the implementation of ERP as an opportunity to study business practices in each of Hershey's divisions, identifying and adopting the best practices for key activities such as demand forecasting companywide.[17]

HERSHEY FOODS CORPORATION
www.hersheys.com

Strategic Use of Information Technology

Information technology is dramatically changing the processes and possibilities for doing business. Today, a minimum strategy for remaining competitive includes enabling employees, suppliers, and customers to share information over some type of computer network. Organizations adopt this technology because it allows them to improve operational efficiency and control, remain competitive in a rapidly changing environment, and tap into the knowledge of employees.

Operational Efficiency and Control

Many companies adopt information technology in an effort to speed work processes, cut costs, and improve coordination. In these ways, the appropriate use of technology can greatly increase an organization's efficiency.

Huntington Bancshares, Inc., is using cutting-edge information technology to provide customers with the most personal kind of banking. The Personal Touch two-way video system allows this customer to apply for an Instant Access Loan from a Personal Banker, in total privacy and at the customer's convenience. Information technology is improving organizational efficiency and effectiveness throughout Huntington's subsidiaries, operating in 13 states and the Cayman Islands. Early results show that Huntington's new systems can reduce expenses by as much as 65 percent, at the same time improving customer service.

Efficiency. Through investment in information systems, a company can increase its operational efficiency and lower costs. This increased efficiency better enables a company to lock in customers and broaden market reach. EZRider, a Massachusetts-based retailer of snowboards discussed in the previous chapter, has reaped numerous benefits from its investment in information technology. For example, whenever a salesperson keys in a purchase, the system makes a record of the amount of his or her sale; at the end of the pay period, EZRider's computer system automatically computes the salesperson's commission in a matter of seconds. Owner Anthony Scaturro also can check historical sales figures to identify the company's busiest periods, then schedule employees according to when they will likely be needed, rather than paying people to stand around during slow times.[18]

Many companies have realized the efficiency of information technology through the appointment of a chief information officer. CIOs are increasingly being folded into high-level strategic decision making so companies can better align their information resources with strategic needs.[19] More than anything else, CIOs must manage technological change for the organization. This may involve high-level decisions with regard to investment, product, and service.

Improved Coordination and Flexibility.   Another efficiency of information technology is the reduction of time and geographic barriers. With global networks and mobile computing, these barriers are dissolving. Time and place are becoming less and less important communication variables. A management team can work throughout the day on a project in Switzerland and, while they sleep, a team in the United States can continue where the Swiss team left off. With E-mail and voice mail, managers no longer have to arrive at 4 A.M. to communicate with personnel abroad.

Mobile computers allow employees all over the world to reach databases at any time of the day or night and to share new information. "Wired executives" can increasingly abandon the confines of corporate offices while staying on top of business through technology. Laptop computers, E-mail, cellular phones, voice mail, and faxes have freed executives to be wherever they are most needed and most productive.

Improved flexibility also means greater responsiveness to changing customer demands. State Farm Insurance uses information technology to get added value for its customers. For example, if a customer has to put his or her car in the shop after an accident, State Farm can electronically request a rental car if one is needed.[20]

Technology

LEADING THE REVOLUTION: TECHNOLOGY

Blazing a Trail Through the Internet Jungle: Amazon.com

Most of us think of bookstores as cozy old places where the floorboards creak and the stacks are jammed to the ceiling with bestsellers and obscure book titles side by side. Bookstores make us think of taking some time out during the day to browse and read, maybe even have a cup of coffee or tea if the store also has a café. Jeff Bezos understands this, but he knows that the average person does not have time to browse. He also understands how the Internet has changed commerce. So a few years ago, the former Wall Street fund manager decided to open a virtual bookstore. In order to be competitive, Bezos knew that he needed to offer three things that a "real" bookstore couldn't: convenience, low prices, and selection. Further, he knew that, in this new shopping arena, he had to get there first (before booksellers such as Borders and Barnes & Noble) in order to get ahead.

With his Wall Street background, Bezos was able to secure the venture capital to start up Amazon, as he called his new business. Based in Seattle, he had a Web site designed that was attractive and simple to use. "We had to make it a destination," explains Bezos, "the way any enjoyable store is a destination." The site does not feature elaborate graphics or animation, but consumers can easily find just about any title they want. In addition, Amazon provides descriptions of its books as well as E-mail notification to regular customers of books they might like. Because Amazon acts as a clearinghouse instead of a warehouse (Amazon directs orders to distributors, who ship the books to Amazon, who then sends them to customers), the company does not have to hold a huge inventory and can thus offer books for prices as low as 40 percent off the list price. Finally, Amazon's selection is huge; the site initially went on-line with 1 million titles and now offers more than twice that number. Theoretically, customers should be able to get any book that still is in print.

Amazon has proved to be a huge success. Within a few years, sales reached $16 million. Thus, the term *browsing* has taken on a new meaning in the bookselling business, referring now to scrolling through titles on the computer screen instead of thumbing through books in the store. But Amazon customers still can sip that cup of coffee as they browse, and they may order at as leisurely a pace as they choose. The Internet has changed yet another way in which we do business.

www.amazon.com

SOURCE: Charles C. Mann, "Volume Business," *Inc. Tech*, 1997, no. 2, 54–61.

Competitive Strategy

Because of advances in information technology, organizations are competing in a new era. The Technology box describes one organization that found a new way to offer its product—books. More and more often today, what distinguishes an organization from its competitors are its knowledge resources, such as its product ideas and ability to identify and find solutions to customers' problems. Consequently, information processing shapes many companies' strategic competitive advantage. It can shorten the distance between customers and the organization. For example, UPS and Federal Express provide customers with the exact tracking location for packages. Exhibit 21.6 provides an example of how IT can support the achievement of a company's strategy by focusing on the competitive advantages gained from transaction processing systems. For example, effective use of these systems leads to greater customer loyalty, improved service, better information gathering, and a reduction in costs.

Organizations may adopt information technology to support planned strategic change, or access to new technology may inspire a change in the organization's structure or strategy. Changes in business strategy usually precede other organizational changes, including technology adoption. For

Exhibit *21.6*

Competitive Advantages Gained from Transaction-Processing Systems: Examples

SOURCE: Adapted from Ralph M. Stair and George W. Reynolds, *Principles of Information Systems: A Managerial Approach,* 4th ed. Cambridge, MA: Course Technology, 1999, 341.

Competitive Advantage	Example
• Increase in customer loyalty	Full information about customer profile and previous requests or problems is instantly available to sales and service representatives when a customer calls.
• Superior service	Customers can track the status of their orders.
• Superior information gathering	The system can be designed to automatically configure orders to ensure they meet customers' objectives.
• Cost reduction	A warehouse management system that involves data entry with scanners and bar-coded labels can reduce labor costs and improve inventory accuracy.

example, Wal-Mart's extensive information systems support that retailer's strategic objectives for competitive pricing and operational efficiency.

Sometimes, however, adoption of information technology serves as the catalyst for change and is followed by restructuring of positions and processes. A common example today is the use of enterprise resource planning. As the technology becomes affordable at more companies, those companies' managers want to reap the benefits of sharing information. However, widespread access to information is useful only if the organization's functions are integrated as well as the software modules. According to Bruce Richardson, a vice president at Advanced Manufacturing Research, a Boston consultant specializing in ERP, "About 80 percent of the benefits [of using ERP] come from what you change in your business. The software is just an enabler."[21]

Knowledge Management

Recognizing the importance of knowledge to strategic success, a growing number of managers are seeing knowledge as an important resource to manage, just as they manage cash flow, employees, raw materials, and other resources. Rather than treating knowledge about industries, products, customers, technologies, and so on as the responsibility of individual employees, managers are seeking ways their organization can use that resource strategically. The Leadership box discusses how one manager learned how to turn data into knowledge. These efforts to systematically gather knowledge, make it widely available, and foster a culture of learning are called **knowledge management.**

Knowledge management is not a technology.[22] Rather, information technology—together with leadership that values learning, an organizational structure that supports communication, and processes for managing change—supports knowledge management. Among the existing technologies that support knowledge management are information systems, the Internet, groupware, and planning tools such as ERP systems. Two relatively new techniques are data warehousing and data mining.

Data Warehousing.   The concept of a data warehouse is not really new. Big companies have long gathered and stored what information they could. However, they tended to store billing data, accounts payable data, payroll data, and so on in separate systems. Not only are those systems unable to share data, but

Knowledge management is not new. In the late 1980s, Richard D. Fairbank and Nigel W. Morris were consultants who decided that the real value of a credit-card issuer lay in the financial information it had about its customers, which could be analyzed and used as marketing information. The idea required the building of databases and software to analyze the data. It was hard to sell, but since their first customer, Signet Banking Corp., in 1988, the business has grown at lightning speed. "We're not credit-card guys," says Morris. "The information revolution just came early to the credit-card business."

Leadership

LEADING THE REVOLUTION: LEADERSHIP

Giant Steps to Knowledge

Rishad Tobaccowala knows how to find useful information in chaotic piles of data. As the president of Giant Step, an independent operating unit of Leo Burnett, the Chicago-based advertising agency, Tobaccowala rose through the ranks of Leo Burnett largely because of his ability to make sense out of the data that came his way. When Tobaccowala first started at Leo Burnett, executives at the firm were awash in information overload; information technology had brought so much data that they couldn't figure out how to use them. So Tobaccowala went to work to find a way to turn data into information and ultimately into knowledge—the most powerful weapon in the advertising business.

Tobaccowala realized that the secret was simply in thinking the right way. "Learning to think," he says, "is more important than what you know." Tobaccowala developed intellectual "filters" to screen data to determine whether data could become useful information. Specifically, he focuses on three areas: (1) people, (2) economics, and (3) flexibility. Do the data coordinate with what he already knows about people? Do they comply with economic rules? Do they apply to changing conditions? By using his filtering technique, Tobaccowala was able to develop a creative direct-marketing campaign for Heinz; and he organized a corporate-sponsored nightly forum on America Online (the sponsor was Oldsmobile).

A few years ago, Tobaccowala met with the founders of Giant Step, a small company that produced multimedia CD-ROMs. At the time, the interactive technology was new; but Tobaccowala thought that Leo Burnett should acquire a major share in the company. He pitched the idea to Burnett executives by using his three-step filter method: (1) Eric and Adam Heneghan, Giant Step founders, meshed easily with Leo Burnett's marketing staff; (2) the Heneghan brothers' initial investment was already paying off; and (3) the Heneghans proved to be flexible in their approach. Burnett executives bought the idea and the company, making Tobaccowala president, where he continues to innovate, using his mental filters to find the information that counts.

www.giantstep.com

SOURCE: Mark Fischetti, "Masters of the (Information) Universe," *Fast Company*, August/September 1997, 181–187.

---

they typically require a specialist to create a program that will generate the reports desired. Today, however, expectations for databases have risen as the cost of processing data has plummeted. Exhibit 21.7 illustrates the phenomenal increase in computer processing speed at the same time the cost has dramatically declined. The modern meaning of **data warehousing** is the use of a huge database that combines all of a company's data and allows business users to access the data directly, create reports, and obtain answers to what-if questions.

Creation of such a system at a big company is a major undertaking that includes defining hundreds of gigabytes (billions of bytes) of data from many existing systems, providing a means of continually updating the data, making it all compatible, and linking it to business intelligence software (BIS). The BIS program allows the user to generate searches for data, perform analyses of the data, and create reports. Catalog retailer Fingerhut Corporation has over 70 million customers and offers 15,000 products. Its seven-trillion-byte database can analyze individual customers in terms of up to 2,000 variables.[23]

Data Mining. An organization with a data warehouse may offer its users access to billions or trillions of bytes of data. How can business users possibly know what to look for? A tool that can help answer this question is software for **data mining.** Data mining tools use sophisticated decision-making processes to search raw data for patterns and relationships that may be significant. Users of these tools can, for example, identify sets of products that particular market segments purchase, patterns of transactions that signal possible

knowledge management
Efforts to systematically gather knowledge, make it widely available in the organization, and foster a culture of learning.

data warehousing
The use of a huge database that combines all of a company's data and allows users to access the data directly, create reports, and obtain answers to what-if questions.

data mining
Software that uses sophisticated decision-making processes to search raw data for patterns and relationships that may be significant.

687

E x h i b i t
21.7
The Evolution of Computer Processing Speed and Cost: Intel Microprocessors

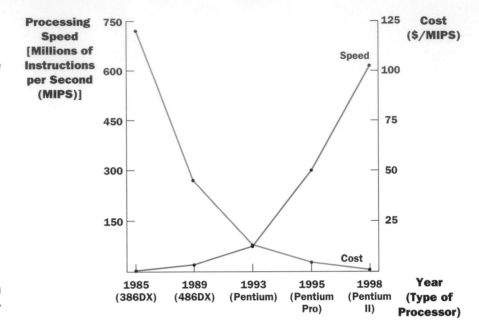

SOURCE: Adapted from Lee Gomes, "Bigger and Smaller," *The Wall Street Journal*, November 16, 1998, R6, R29.

fraud, or patterns of product performance that may indicate defects. Data mining enabled Fingerhut to learn that when customers move to a new home, they buy three times as much over the next three months. Furthermore, they purchase certain categories of products: furniture, telecommunications equipment, and decorations. Fingerhut used this information to create a new catalog tailored for movers.[24]

Data mining tools also apply to searching for information on the Internet. The World Wide Web alone contains hundreds of millions of Web pages, and the number continues to grow. Online information services such as Dialog, Dow Jones, and Lexis-Nexis offer billions more records. Managers looking for information on the Internet can use search engines such as Yahoo! or Excite. Each search engine uses different criteria, so it is important to investigate which criteria will be most useful for a particular kind of search. Also, the more specific the query, the better. A general request for information on an industry can easily generate over a million hits.

Management Implications of Information Technology

Information technology can enable managers to be better connected with employees, the environment, and each other. In general, information technology has positive implications for the practice of management, although it can also present problems. Some specific implications of information technology for managers include improved employee effectiveness, empowered employees, information overload, and organizational learning.

Improved Employee Effectiveness.   Computer technology can be used to give employees the information they need to better perform their jobs. Information technology can provide employees with all kinds of data about their customers, competitors, markets, and service, as well as enable them to share information or insights with others. For example, several years ago a Chicago-area

MTV Networks salesperson discovered that Turner Broadcasting System was offering a special two-year, rock-bottom deal for cable operators to carry TBS's Cartoon Channel instead of MTV's Comedy Central. She shared this intelligence on the computer network so other salespeople could research pricing in their own areas. Because they had this information, salespeople were able to counterattack and close several deals that had appeared lost.[25] In general, information technology enables managers to design jobs to provide employees with more intellectual engagement and more challenging work. The availability of information technology does not guarantee increased job performance, but when implemented and used appropriately, it can have a dramatic influence on employee effectiveness. Kaiser Permanente found that careful implementation was the key to reaping the benefits of a new information system.

KAISER PERMANENTE
www.kaiserpermanente.org

The largest U.S. health maintenance organization, Kaiser Permanente, is establishing a billion-dollar national clinical information system that will give its doctors, nurses, and other care providers access to the medical records of its millions of patients. In so doing, Kaiser is building on its experience with systems that some of its regional centers previously created. And that experience tells Kaiser that one of its biggest challenges will be obtaining the support of its doctors. In Cleveland, doctors resisted the idea of performing data entry (as opposed to jotting notes on paper charts), and they worried that computers would distract them from interacting with patients. The Cleveland solution has been to provide doctors with paper forms; digital images of the forms are stored in the database. In Portland, Oregon, Kaiser had doctors try using the computers to enter data, even though they initially resisted. Physician resistance has melted as the benefits to patient care become evident. The system in Cleveland, for example, provides checklists about patients' conditions that enable the HMO to identify at-risk patients requiring additional intervention. Furthermore, the doctors appreciate being able to see a full picture of the patient's condition, based on that person's visits to every care provider in the Kaiser system. At a Kaiser clinic in Cleveland, emergency room chief Dr. Neal Kaforey credits the system with saving a patient's life. When a man was wheeled in with a heart attack, the doctor at the clinic was about to inject a medication but first looked up the patient's records in Kaiser's database. The patient was severely allergic to the drug—knowledge that, on paper, would have been uselessly stored in some doctor's filing cabinet.[26]

Empowered Employees.   Information technology is profoundly affecting the way organizations are structured. Through implementing IT, organizations change the locus of knowledge by providing information to people who would not otherwise receive it. Low-level employees are increasingly challenged with more information and are expected to make decisions previously made by supervisors.[27]

These changes support the objectives of knowledge management by enabling decisions to be made by the employees who are in the best position to implement the decisions and see their effects. PeopleSoft gives all its employees access to its corporate database, including marketing presentations, project status reports, and competitive intelligence. At the Chesebrough-Ponds, Inc. plant in Jefferson City, Missouri, line workers routinely tap into the company's computer network to track shipments, schedule their own workloads, order production increases, and perform other functions that used to be the province of management.[28]

One would think that IT reduces the number of management jobs, and in many cases, it does. However, this is not always the rule. The effect of IT on middle management seems to relate mostly to the degree of centralization for computing decisions. When computing decisions and organizational decisions are centralized at higher levels of the organization, top management tends to use IT to reduce the number of middle managers. When these decisions are decentralized, though, middle managers may use IT to improve their own performance.[29]

Information Overload.   One problem associated with advances in technology is that the company can become a quagmire of information, with employees so overwhelmed by the sheer volume that they are unable to sort out the valuable from the useless. The problem is so pervasive that it has inspired a whole series of metaphors: infobog, infoglut, data slam, a tidal wave or a deluge or a flood of information. As employees simultaneously dry themselves off and extricate themselves from the bog, they may be unable to do the tasks that the access to information is supposed to be helping them with.

In many cases, the ability to produce data and information is outstripping employees' ability to process it. One British psychologist claims to have identified a new mental disorder caused by too much information; he has termed it Information Fatigue Syndrome.[30] Information technology is a primary culprit in contributing to this new "disease." However, managers have the ability to alleviate the problem and improve information quality. The first step is to ensure that suppliers of information technology and CIOs work closely with employees to identify the kinds of questions they must answer and the kinds of information they really need. Specialists often are enamored with the volume of data a system can produce and overlook the need to provide small amounts of quality information in a timely and useful manner for decision making. Top executives should be actively involved in setting limits by focusing the organization on key strategies and on the critical questions that must be answered to pursue those strategies.[31]

Organizational Learning.   Information technology is an important part of today's learning organizations because it contributes to more rapid identification of problems and opportunities, faster decision making, and greater learning capacity from widely shared information. Pioneer Hi-Bred International, a 70-year-old Des Moines, Iowa, company that tests and sells hybrid seeds, uses cutting edge technology to help its employees learn and make good decisions. The ability to track data from the beginning of the research process to the end sale has revolutionized the company. According to corporate vice president Tom Hanigan, making decisions based on so much information is "like having a map of all the roads in America and navigating a driver from the East to the West Coast by the fastest, most direct path."[32]

IT enables the accumulation and widespread communication of a larger volume as well as a wider range of information. For example, organizations can purchase access to hundreds of databases about industry, financial, and demographic trends in their environments, helping managers stay on top of important trends that will impact their business. Managers can provide key information to employees to help them make better decisions and continuously find ways to improve operations and customer service. In addition, when used appropriately, IT helps break down barriers and create a sense of team spirit that is essential for learning and growth.

System Quality	Performance of tasks the system was designed to do
Information Quality	Report format
	Appearance
	Timeliness
	Reliability
	Completeness
	Value to decision makers
User Penetration	Actual use by potential users
Longevity	Length of time system remains in use
User Satisfaction	Reactions to system operation
	Reactions to system output
Impact	Degree to which use of system affects users' behavior
	Effect of system use on organizational performance

Exhibit 21.8

Management Criteria for Information System Success

SOURCE: Adapted from W. Delone and E. McLean, "Information System Success: The Quest for the Dependent Variable," *Information Systems Research* 3, no. 1 (March 1992), 60–95.

Criteria for IT System Success

Many companies measure performance of information technology systems by asking employees and customers for feedback. Others use traditional return-on-investment or cost-benefit calculations to justify investments in IT. For example, Monsanto Company deems its investment in an enterprise resource planning system successful because the system helped the company halve the time required for production planning, cut back on inventory and working capital, and gain greater bargaining power with suppliers. These achievements save Monsanto $200 million annually.[33]

Exhibit 21.8 lists a number of criteria managers use to determine the success of an information system. These six criteria address the attributes of quality information outlined earlier in the chapter. *System quality* means the degree to which the system performs the tasks it was designed for, including generating information that is accurate, timely, reliable, and complete. *Information quality* refers to the quality of the output, such as format, appearance, information value to decision makers, and so forth. In addition, to be considered successful, the system must actually be used by employees. *User penetration* means the degree to which potential users become actual users of the system. *Longevity* means the length of time over which a system remains in use. With rapid advances in technology, most organizations today have systems that are continually evolving. *User satisfaction* relates to how positively users react to the operation of the system and its output. Finally, the *impact* of the system on the behavior of individual employees and on the performance of the organization should be taken into consideration.

Summary and Management Solution

Organizations are evolving into information cultures in which managers and employees alike can share information, and in which routine decision making can be automated through the use of expert models. Thanks to networks and communications technology, these emerging information cultures are not bound by physical space. Information technology allows companies to generate new services and products but also creates demand for quality, low cost, and speedy delivery.

Modern information technology gathers huge amounts of data and transforms them into useful information for decision makers. The systems that use this technology should be designed to generate information with appropriate time, content, and form attributes. The array of information systems available and the multitude of data they produce can be overwhelming. Many organizations hire a chief information officer to help manage decisions regarding investment and integration of old and new information system products. Often, the systems link employees and others in networks, including the Internet, intranets, and extranets.

Information systems combine hardware, software, and human resources to organize information and make it readily available. Operations information systems, including transaction-processing systems, process control systems, and office automation systems, support daily business operations and the needs of low-level managers. Management information systems, including information reporting systems, decision support systems, and executive information systems, typically support the decision-making needs of middle and upper-level managers. Other types of information systems, including expert systems, geographic information systems, and enterprise resource planning systems, may support either operations or management applications and are used at various levels of the organization.

Organizations use information technology to improve operational efficiency and control, carry out strategy, and manage their knowledge resources. Knowledge management is an increasingly important aspect of using information technology, particularly in today's learning organizations. Two new techniques that support knowledge management are data warehousing and data mining. Information technology has a number of specific implications for managers and organizations, including greater employee effectiveness, empowered employees, information overload, and increased potential for organizational learning. Managers often evaluate the success of information technology systems by considering system quality, information quality, use of the system (including user penetration and longevity), user satisfaction, and impact (both on the individual and the organization).

Recall the opening case of Cementos Mexicanos (Cemex), which needs greater flexibility to better serve customers in developing regions of the world. In Guadalajara as well as many other regions, Cemex routinely contends with traffic tie-ups, cancellations by cash-strapped customers, and bad weather. To cope with these challenges, Cemex installed sophisticated information technology systems that are designed to keep all options open, enabling Cemex to respond to unexpected problems and interruptions. The foundation of the system is business process software combined with expert programs that were painstakingly constructed based on information gleaned during more than 40 meetings with Cemex employees. Over a period of about a year, a team of specialists grilled the Guadalajara crew on the realities of their jobs and then put together "a world of judgments, not a world of facts." Continuously fed with streams of day-to-day data on customer orders, production schedules, traffic problems, roadwork in progress, weather conditions, and so forth, the system actually gets "smarter" the more it is used. In addition, the business process and expert systems are connected to a global positioning system and on-board computers in Cemex trucks. Now, Cemex trucks head out every morning to cruise the streets. When a customer calls in an order, an employee checks their credit status, locates a nearby truck, and relays directions for making the delivery. Whenever an order is cancelled, the system automatically directs the plant to scale back production. Information technology has enabled Cemex to serve developing areas of the world with a level of service that was previously out of the question.[34]

Discussion Questions

1. Why is it important for managers to understand the difference between data and information?

2. In what ways would the role of the CIO of a hospital be important?

3. What types of information technology do you use as a student on a regular basis? How might your life be different if you did not have this technology available to you?

4. How might the organizers of an upcoming Olympics use an extranet to get all the elements of the event up and running on schedule?

5. How might groupware be useful to a worldwide restaurant chain such as McDonald's?

6. In what ways might access to an MIS change the way decisions are made at a large package-delivery company?

7. Do you think that a geographic information system would be beneficial to a large mail-order company such as L. L. Bean or Spiegel? Why or why not?

8. Why is knowledge management an important consideration in the use of information technology?

9. Do you believe information overload is a problem for today's students? For employees? Discuss.

10. How is information technology affecting the way organizations are structured and the way jobs are designed?

Management in Practice: Experiential Exercise

What Is Your MIS Style?
Following are 14 statements. Circle the number that indicates how much you agree that each statement is characteristic of you. The questions refer to how you use information and make decisions.

	Disagree Strongly				Agree Strongly

1. I like to wait until all relevant information is examined before deciding something. — 1 2 3 4 5
2. I prefer information that can be interpreted in several ways and leads to different but acceptable solutions. — 1 2 3 4 5
3. I like to keep gathering data until an excellent solution emerges. — 1 2 3 4 5
4. To make decisions, I often use information that means different things to different people. — 1 2 3 4 5
5. I want just enough data to make a decision quickly. — 5 4 3 2 1
6. I act on logical analysis of the situation rather than on my "gut feelings" about the best alternative. — 5 4 3 2 1
7. I seek information sources or people that will provide me with many ideas and details. — 1 2 3 4 5
8. I try to generate more than one satisfactory solution for the problem faced. — 1 2 3 4 5
9. When reading something, I confine my thoughts to what is written rather than search for additional understanding. — 5 4 3 2 1
10. When working on a project, I try to narrow, not broaden, the scope so it is clearly defined. — 5 4 3 2 1
11. I typically acquire all possible information before making a final decision. — 1 2 3 4 5
12. I like to work on something I've done before rather than take on a complicated problem. — 5 4 3 2 1
13. I prefer clear, precise data. — 5 4 3 2 1
14. When working on a project, I like to explore various options rather than maintain a narrow focus. — 1 2 3 4 5

Total Score _____

Your information-processing style determines the extent to which you will benefit from computer-based information systems.

The *odd-numbered* questions pertain to the "amount of information" you like to use. A score of 28 or more suggests you prefer a large amount. A score of 14 or less indicates you like a small amount of information.

The *even-numbered* questions pertain to the "focus of information" you prefer. A score of 28 or more suggests you are comfortable with ambiguous, multifocused information, while a score of 14 or less suggests you like clear, unifocused data.

If you are a person who likes a large amount of information and clear, focused data, you will tend to make effective use of management information systems. You could be expected to benefit greatly from an EIS or MIS in your company. If you are a person who prefers a small amount of data and data that are multifocused, you would probably not get the information you need to make decisions through formal information systems. You probably won't utilize EIS or MIS to a great extent, preferring instead to get decision data from other convenient sources, including face-to-face discussions.

SOURCES: This questionnaire is adapted from Richard L. Daft and Norman B. Macintosh, "A Tentative Exploration into the Amount and Equivocality of Information Processing in Organizational Work Units," *Administrative Science Quarterly* 26 (1981), 207–224; and Dorothy Marcic, *Organizational Behavior: Experiences and Cases,* 4th ed. (St. Paul, Minn.: West, 1995).

Management in Practice: Ethical Dilemma

Manipulative or Not?
As head of the marketing department for Butter Crisp Snack Foods, fifty-five-year-old Frank Bellows has been forced to learn a lot about the Internet in recent years. Although he initially resisted the new technology, Frank has gradually come to appreciate the potential of the Internet for serving existing

customers and reaching potential new ones. In fact, he has been one of the biggest supporters of the company's increasing use of the Internet to stay in touch with customers.

However, something about this new plan just doesn't feel right. At this morning's meeting, Keith Deakins, Butter Crisp's CEO, announced that the company would soon be launching a Web site geared specifically to children. Although Deakins has the authority to approve the site on his own, he has asked all department heads to review the site and give their approval for its launch. He then turned the meeting over to the Information Technology team that developed the new site, which will offer games and interactive educational activities. The team pointed out that although it will be clear that Butter Crisp is the sponsor of the site, there will be no advertising of Butter Crisp products. So far, so good, Frank thinks. However, he knows that two of the young hot-shot employees in his department have been helping to develop the site and that they provided a list of questions that children will be asked to answer on-line. Just to enter the Web site, for example, a user must provide name, address, gender, E-mail address, and favorite TV show. In return, users receive "Crisp Cash," a form of virtual money that they can turn in for toys, games, Butter Crisp samples, and other prizes. After they enter the site, children can earn more Crisp Cash by providing other information about themselves and their families.

Frank watched the demonstration and agreed that the Web site does indeed have solid educational content. However, he is concerned about the tactics for gathering information from children that will almost certainly be used for marketing purposes. So far, it seems that the other department heads are solidly in favor of launching the Web site. Frank is wondering if he can sign his approval with a clear conscience. He also knows that several groups, including the national PTA and the Center for Media Education, are calling for stricter governmental controls regarding collecting information from children via the Internet.

What Do You Do?
1. Stop worrying about it. There's nothing illegal about what Butter Crisp is proposing to do, and any personal information gathered will be closely guarded by the company. Children can't be harmed in any way by using the new Web site.
2. Begin talking with other managers and try to build a coalition in support of some stricter controls, such as requiring parental permission to enter areas of the site that offer Crisp Cash in exchange for personal information.
3. Contact the Center for Media Education and tell them you suspect Butter Crisp intends to use the Web site to conduct marketing research. The Center might be able to apply pressure that would make it uncomfortable enough for Deakins to pull the plug on the new kid's Web site.

SOURCE: Based on Denise Gellene, "Internet Marketing to Kids Is Seen as a Web of Deceit," *Los Angeles Times,* March 29, 1996, A1, A20.

Surf the Net

1. **Decision Support Systems.** Visit the Web site of a company, such as SAS Institute, Inc., listed below, that creates software designed to aid in the decision-making process. If the site you visit provides information about client companies that have successfully used SAS software products, then provide a brief summary of what the company used the product for and how it helped improve the company's decision-making process. If no examples are provided, then briefly describe one SAS DSS product—its function, as well as examples of who might use the product.
   www.sas.com—company profiles available at **www.sas.com/corporate/profiles/intro.html**
2. **Knowledge Management.** The WWW Virtual Library on Knowledge Management—Forums, Articles, Magazines, Events, Resources, Analyses, and News—is located at **www.brint.com/km.**
   Review comments of this Web site include:
   "Largest Collection of Knowledge Management Literature" (*The Wall Street Journal*)
   "Best Sources for Knowledge Management and Intellectual Capital" (*Fast Company*)

"Tool for Raising Your Company's IQ" (*Forbes*)
"The Best Web site on the topic of Knowledge Management" (*InfoWorld*)
"Superb Collection on Knowledge Management and Intellectual Capital" (Tom Stewart, *Fortune*)
Visit several sections of this virtual library to familiarize yourself with its contents, select one item you found most interesting, print it out, and bring it to class so that you may contribute your findings during a classroom discussion on knowledge management.
3. **Data Warehousing.** Microsoft provides many resources for corporate IT professionals. The Web site at **www. microsoft.com/technet** is constantly being updated to reflect the rapidly-changing needs of its users. Go to the site, look over what's available, and then use the search feature on TechNet's home page or go to **www.microsoft.com/ technet/dataware/default.htm** to locate information on data warehousing. Access any of the articles, case studies, white papers, or Web site links available at Microsoft TechNet, and write a 1 to 2 page paper outlining your most significant findings.

Case for Critical Analysis
Clarklift/FIT

Wayne Reece, head of Clarklift/FIT, which owns several central Florida forklift dealerships, tried computers a decade ago. He didn't like them, and he didn't think he needed information technology to run his business. But as his company began to grow, he realized that he had taken on more debt than he was comfortable with, so he recruited a chief financial officer named Ken Daley. Reece also got back into the technology game, investing $100,000 in a proprietary inventory and accounting system developed by Fetner Associates. Daley began to look for better financing for the company and approached Citicorp's Global Equipment Finance Division. Surprisingly, it seemed that Citicorp was more interested in Clarklift's information technology capacity than it was in how many forklifts the company had sold. David B. Hilton explains why. "The theory goes that if you can trust the computer systems, you can trust the company's numbers."

Clarklift wanted to borrow a significant amount of money, so Citicorp sent CMS Management Services Co., an Indiana-based technology consulting firm, to evaluate Clarklift's existing systems. Hilton explains further, "If clients don't have the proper systems to automatically generate the sorts of financial reports we need on a monthly basis, this sort of loan would overwhelm them." Reece was already on the right track with the inventory and accounting system. Thus, the necessary data were there in the system; but as Reece, Daley, and CMS learned, it was difficult to turn the data into quality information. For instance, if someone wanted a list of accounts receivable that were past due, the database would output about 500 pages of indecipherable codes and numbers. "None of the answers just popped out of the computer," recalls Daley.

So Daley began using a software program called Monarch (ironically, already installed on the computer) to turn the data into information printed on neat, readable spreadsheets. In the process, Clarklift not only qualified for a $5 million loan from Citicorp but also discovered some of its own poor business practices. For example, Reece and Daley discovered over $100,000 worth of unused parts that could be returned to manufacturers. As Clarklift's ability to turn data into quality information has increased, Reece and Daley can see at a moment's notice how the company is performing. For instance, they can see which forklifts are being rented or sold and which are not—and on which sales lots. "It only takes me a second to know who to congratulate and who needs a good talking to," says Reece. In addition, salespeople, who now carry laptops, can enter sales figures directly into a customer's file in the contract-management software program ACT!, which Reece can access at any time. When a salesperson gives a quote to a client, he or she E-mails the quote to Reece. When Reece opens the E-mail message, the quote is automatically deposited in a central database for later reference. Finally, when customers' invoices are generated each month, the computer also produces a list of those customers who are past due and even prints out appropriate collection letters—instead of 500 pages of unintelligible numbers.

Questions

1. With its newfound reliance on information technology, do you think that Clarklift/FIT might fall into an information overload trap? Why or why not?
2. How does information technology contribute to Clarklift's knowledge management? What other strategic advantages does IT provide?
3. What steps might Clarklift/FIT take to evaluate the success of its information technology systems?

SOURCE: Joshua Macht, "The Accidental Automator," *Inc. Tech.,* 1997, no. 2, 66–71.

Endnotes

1. Peter Katel, "Bordering on Chaos," *Wired,* July 1997, 98–107.
2. Derek Slater, "Chain Commanders," *CIO Enterprise,* August 15, 1998, 29–30+.
3. Roberta Maynard, "Casting the Net for Job Seekers," *Nation's Business,* March 1997, 28–29.
4. Michael J. Major, "Working Smart: The University of Central Florida's Intranet-Based Administration Application," *CIO,* April 15, 1998, 80; and Mary J. Cronin, "Ford's Intranet Success," *Fortune,* March 30, 1998, 158.
5. Mary J. Cronin, "Intranets Reach the Factory Floor," *Fortune,* August 18, 1997, 208.
6. Jenny C. McCune, "The In's and Out's of Extranets," *Management Review,* July/August 1998, 23–25; and Sari Kalin, "The Fast Lane," *CIO Web Business,* April 1, 1998, sec. 2, 28, 32–35.
7. Sari Kalin, "The Fast Lane."
8. G. Beekman, *Computer Currents: Navigating Tomorrow's Technology* (Reading, Mass.: Addison-Wesley, 1994).

9. Christopher Caggiano, "Thriving on Bureaucracy," *Inc. Technology,* 1997, no. 1, 62–66.

10. Sarah Schafer, "Mourning Becomes Electric," *Inc. Technology,* 1997, no. 3, 64–67+.

11. Srikumar S. Rao, "ABCs of Cost Control," *Inc. Technology,* 1997, no. 2, 79–81.

12. Christopher Palmeri, "Believe in Yourself, Believe in the Merchandise," *Continental,* December 1997, 49–51.

13. ESRI Map Book, vol. 10, "Creating a New World," Environmental Systems Research Institute, Inc., 1995.

14. Smallworld Web site, www.smallworld-us.com, accessed on December 7, 1998.

15. Eric Matson, "Two Billion Reasons Cisco's Sold on the Net," *Fast Company,* February–March 1997, 34, 36.

16. Don Hellriegel, Susan E. Jackson, and John W. Slocum, Jr., *Management,* 8th ed. (Cincinnati, Ohio: South-Western College Publishing, 1999), 693.

17. Michael H. Martin, "Smart Managing: Best Practices, Careers, and Ideas," *Fortune,* February 2, 1998, 149–151.

18. Anthony Scaturro, "All in the Family," *Inc. Technology,* 1998, no. 1, 25–26.

19. Gail Dutton, "Are You Technologically Competent?" *Management Review,* November 1997, 54–58.

20. Slater, "Chain Commanders."

21. Martin, "Smart Managing," 150.

22. Karyl Scott, "Knowledge Management Is a State of Mind," *InformationWeek Online,* November 9, 1998, accessed at www. informationweek.com.

23. David Pearson, "Marketing for Survival," *CIO,* April 15, 1998, 44–48.

24. Pearson, "Marketing for Survival."

25. John R. Wilke, "Computer Links Erode Hierarchical Nature of Workplace Culture," *The Wall Street Journal,* December 9, 1993, A1, A10.

26. Erick Schonfeld, "Can Computers Cure Health Care?" *Fortune,* March 30, 1998, 111–116; and Sari Kalin, "Preventive Medicine," *CIO Web Business,* Section 2, May 1, 1998, 42–47.

27. Liz Thach and Richard W. Woodman, "Organizational Change and Information Technology: Managing on the Edge of Cyberspace," *Organizational Dynamics,* summer 1994, 30–46.

28. Paul Roberts, "Humane Technology: PeopleSoft," *Fast Company,* April–May 1998, 122–128; and James B. Treece, "Breaking the Chains of Command," *Business Week/The Information Revolution,* 112–114.

29. Alain Pinsonneault and Kenneth L. Kraemer, "The Impact of Information Technology on Middle Managers," *MIS Quarterly* 17, no. 3 (September 1993), 271–292.

30. Joseph McCafferty, "Coping with Infoglut," *CFO,* September 1998, 101–102.

31. Leonard M. Fuld, "The Danger of Data Slam," *CIO Enterprise,* Section 2, September 15, 1998, 28–33.

32. Jeremy Main, "The Shape of Things to Come," *Working Woman,* October 1998, 60–63.

33. Gail Edmondson, "Silicon Valley on the Rhine," *Business Week,* November 3, 1997, 162–166.

34. Peter Katel, "Bordering on Chaos."

Chapter 22

LEARNING OBJECTIVES

After studying this chapter, you should be able to

◉ Define *operations management* and describe its application within manufacturing and service organizations.

◉ Explain the role of operations management strategy in the company's overall competitive strategy.

◉ Summarize considerations in designing an operations system, including the relative advantages of process, product, cellular, and fixed-position layouts.

◉ Explain why small inventories are preferred by most organizations.

◉ Discuss major techniques for the management of materials and inventory.

◉ Define productivity and explain why and how managers seek to improve it.

Operations and Service Management

MANAGEMENT PROBLEM

Boeing made the planes that carry more than three quarters of all airborne travelers every day and is building most of the commercial airliners that will enter service in the near future. However, over the past few years, Boeing has stumbled badly and earnings have plummeted. After Boeing bought McDonnell Douglas, Boeing managers cut costs and aggressively sought new business in an effort to dominate the market against the company's only remaining commercial-airline competitor, Airbus Industrie. But the plan backfired when Boeing's inefficient production system could not handle the hundreds of new orders. A labor-intensive, paper-dependent design system is slow as well as extremely costly. Also, the company has evolved using 400 separate computer systems that aren't linked, leading to errors and delays. Due to earlier downsizing, Boeing had to hire thousands of mostly inexperienced new assembly workers, but the combination of inexperience and haste led to mistakes and mounting bottlenecks. Adding to the problem was an inability to obtain needed supplies in a timely manner. Parts were often rushed in by taxicab, and one worker tells of spending a frantic weekend chasing parts stockpiles all over Seattle trying to find rubber seals for jetliner doors. A securities analyst who follows the company said of Boeing: "It's been like an episode of *I Love Lucy*, the one in the chocolate factory where the assembly line becomes chaotic." Eventually, the chaos led to the shutdown of two Boeing production lines and a $1.6 billion charge against earnings.[1]

If you were a manager at Boeing, what would you do to solve Boeing's production and performance problems? How can an understanding of operations management help Boeing managers turn things around?

Like Boeing, many companies find themselves caught with out-of-date, inefficient production systems that contribute to performance problems. Strategic success is contingent on efficient operations. Operational concerns such as designing new products and services, updating production technology, and obtaining parts and supplies take on even greater importance in today's competitive and cost-conscious environment. Production costs are a major expense for organizations, especially for manufacturers. Organizations therefore try to limit costs and increase quality by improving how they obtain materials, set up production facilities, and produce goods and services. Likewise, companies are seeking a strategic advantage in the ways they deliver products and services to consumers.

In a service industry, Wal-Mart's emergence as a retail giant is largely due to the company's use of sophisticated electronics to run a huge supply and distribution network. In the manufacturing sector, the efficiency of Toyota's automobile production is legendary. Manufacturing and service operations such as these are important because they represent the company's basic purpose—indeed, its reason for existence. Without the ability to produce products and services that are competitive in the global marketplace, companies cannot expect to succeed.

This chapter describes techniques for the planning and control of manufacturing and service operations. Whereas the two preceding chapters described overall control concepts, including management information systems, this chapter will focus on the management and control of production operations. First we define operations management. Then we look at how some companies bring operations into strategic decision making. Finally, we consider specific operational design issues such as plant layout, location planning, inventory management, manufacturing productivity, and structure of the operations management function.

Organizations as Production Systems

technical core
The heart of the organization's production of its product or service.

In Chapter 1, the organization was described as a system used for transforming inputs into outputs. At the center of this transformation process is the **technical core,** which is the heart of the organization's production of its product or service.[2] In an automobile company, the technical core includes the plants that manufacture automobiles. In a university, the technical core includes the academic activities of teaching and research. Inputs into the technical core include human resources, land, equipment, buildings, and technology. Outputs from the technical core include the goods and services that are provided for customers and clients. Operations strategy and control feedback shape the quality of outputs and the efficiency of operations within the technical core.

operations management
The field of management that specializes in the physical production of goods or services and uses quantitative techniques for solving manufacturing problems.

The topic of operations management pertains to the day-to-day management of the technical core, as illustrated in Exhibit 22.1. **Operations management** is formally defined as the field of management that specializes in the production of goods and services and uses special tools and techniques for solving manufacturing problems. In essence, operating managers are concerned with all production activities within the organization. This includes decisions about where to locate facilities and what equipment to install in them. However, as with all areas of management, operations management also requires the ability to lead people. For example, Toyota's operations are admired worldwide as a model of quality and efficiency, but this success is

Exhibit *22.1*   *The Organization as an Operations Management System*

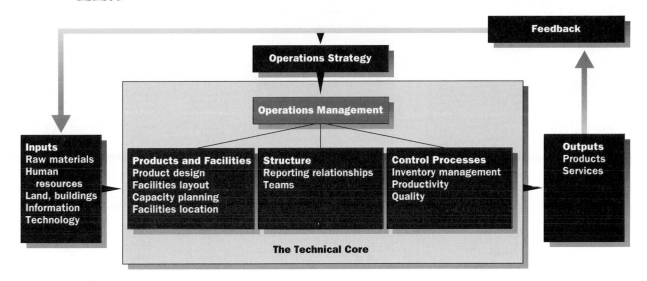

not merely a result of using the right machines or setting the right standards. According to Mike DaPrile, manager of Toyota's Kentucky assembly facilities, the Toyota Production System combines techniques, systems, and philosophy, such as a commitment to employee empowerment and total quality management. Besides installing the methodology for running an efficient assembly line, such as devices that let an individual worker shut down a line where a problem is occurring, managers must instill the necessary attitudes, such as concern for quality and a desire to innovate.[3]

Manufacturing and Service Operations

Although terms such as *production* and *operations* seem to imply manufacturing organizations, operations management applies to all organizations. The service sector has increased three times as fast as the manufacturing sector in the North American economy. Today more than one-half of all businesses are service organizations. Operations management tools and techniques apply to services as well as manufacturing. Exhibit 22.2 shows differences between manufacturing and service organizations.

Manufacturing organizations are those that produce physical goods. Ford Motor Company, which produces automobiles, and Levi Strauss, which makes clothing, are both manufacturing companies. In contrast, **service organizations** produce nonphysical outputs, such as medical, educational, or transportation services provided for customers. Airlines, doctors, consultants, and the local barber all provide services. Services also include the sale of merchandise. Although merchandise is a physical good, the service company does not manufacture it but merely sells it as a service to the customer. Retail stores such as Sears and McDonald's are service organizations.

Services differ from manufactured products in two ways. First, the service customer is involved in the actual production process.[4] The patient actually visits the doctor to receive the service, and it's difficult to imagine a barber or a hairstylist providing services without direct customer contact. The same

manufacturing organization
An organization that produces physical goods.

service organization
An organization that produces nonphysical outputs that require customer involvement and cannot be stored in inventory.

SOURCE: Based on Richard L. Daft, *Organization Theory and Design* (Cincinnati, OH: South-Western College Publishing, 1998), 130; and Byron J. Finch and Richard L. Luebbe, *Operations Management* (Fort Worth, Texas: The Dryden Press, 1995), 50.

Exhibit
22.2

Differences between Manufacturing and Service Organizations

Manufacturing Organizations	Service Organizations
Produce physical goods	Produce nonphysical outputs
Goods inventoried for later consumption	Simultaneous production and consumption
Quality measured directly	Quality perceived and difficult to measure
Standardized output	Customized output
Production process removed from consumer	Consumer participates in production process
Facilities site moderately important to business success	Facilities site crucial to success of firm
Capital intensive	Labor intensive
Examples:	*Examples:*
Automobile manufacturers	Airlines
Steel companies	Hotels
Soft-drink companies	Law firms

is true for hospitals, restaurants, and banks. Second, manufactured goods can be placed in inventory, whereas service outputs, being intangible, cannot be stored. Manufactured products such as clothes, food, cars, and VCRs all can be put in warehouses and sold at a later date. However, a hairstylist cannot wash, cut, and set hair in advance and leave it on the shelf for the customer's arrival, nor can a doctor place examinations in inventory. The service must be created and provided for the customer exactly when he or she wants it.

Despite the differences between manufacturing and service firms, they face similar operational problems. First, each kind of organization needs to be concerned with scheduling. A medical clinic must schedule appointments so that doctors' and patients' time will be used efficiently. Second, both manufacturing and service organizations must obtain materials and supplies. Third, both types of organizations should be concerned with quality and productivity. Because many operational problems are similar, operations management tools and techniques can and should be applied to service organizations as readily as they are to manufacturing operations.

Operations Strategy

Many operations managers are involved in day-to-day problem solving and lose sight of the fact that the best way to control operations is through strategic planning. The more operations managers become enmeshed in operational details, the less likely they are to see the big picture with respect to inventory buildups, parts shortages, and seasonal fluctuations. Indeed, one reason suggested for the success of Japanese companies is the direct involvement of operations managers in strategic management. To manage operations effectively, managers must understand operations strategy.

operations strategy
The recognition of the importance of operations to the firm's success and the involvement of operations managers in the organization's strategic planning.

Operations strategy is the recognition of the important role of operations in organizational success and the involvement of operations managers in the organization's strategic planning.[5] Exhibit 22.3 illustrates four stages in the evolution of operations strategy.

Many companies are at Stage 1, in which business strategy is set without considering the capability of operations. The operations department is con-

Exhibit 22.3 — Four Stages of Operations Strategy

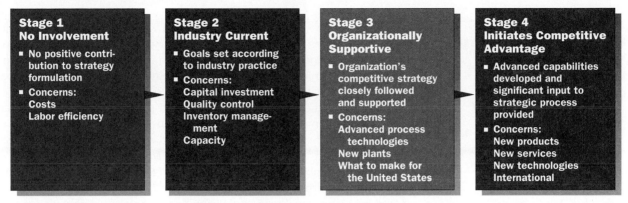

Stage 1 No Involvement	Stage 2 Industry Current	Stage 3 Organizationally Supportive	Stage 4 Initiates Competitive Advantage
■ No positive contribution to strategy formulation ■ Concerns: Costs Labor efficiency	■ Goals set according to industry practice ■ Concerns: Capital investment Quality control Inventory management Capacity	■ Organization's competitive strategy closely followed and supported ■ Concerns: Advanced process technologies New plants What to make for the United States	■ Advanced capabilities developed and significant input to strategic process provided ■ Concerns: New products New services New technologies International

SOURCE: Based on R. H. Hayes and S. C. Wheelwright, *Restoring Our Competitive Edge: Competing through Manufacturing* (New York: Wiley, 1984).

cerned only with labor costs and operational efficiency. For example, a major electronics instrument producer experienced a serious mismatch between strategy and the ability of operations to manufacture products. Because of fast-paced technological changes, the company was changing its products and developing new ones. The manufacturer had installed a materials-handling system in the operations department that was efficient, but it could not handle diversity and change of this magnitude. Operations managers were blamed for the company's failure to achieve strategic goals even though the operations department's capacity had never been considered during strategy formulation.

At Stage 2, the operations department sets goals according to industry practice. The organization tries to be current with respect to operations management techniques and views capital investment in plant and equipment, quality control, or inventory management as ways to be competitive.

At Stage 3, operations managers are more strategically active. Operations strategy is in concert with company strategy, and the operations department will seek new operational techniques and technologies to enhance competitiveness. For example, computer-based business operating systems and work flow automation help employees coordinate activities across functional and geographical boundaries and pinpoint bottlenecks or outdated procedures that slow production and increase costs.

At the highest level of operations strategy, Stage 4, operations managers may pursue new technologies on their own in order to do the best possible job of delivering the product or service. At Stage 4, operations can be a genuine competitive weapon.[6] Operations departments develop new strategic concepts themselves. With the use of new technologies, operations management becomes a major force in overall company strategic planning. Operations can originate new products and processes that will add to or change company strategy.

A company that operates at Stage 3 or 4 will be more competitive than those that rely on marketing and financial strategies because customer orders are won through better price, quality, performance, delivery, or responsiveness to customer demand, and all these factors are affected by operations. For example, improvements in operations strategy have helped Deere & Company improve its competitive standing in a difficult environment.

DEERE & COMPANY
www.deere.com

The demand for agricultural machines, Deere & Company's major product line, has been weak, even declining in recent years. How can a company that made its name in plows and tractors survive in such an economy? For Deere, the solution includes expanding its product mix and rethinking its operations strategy.

The company charges teams of employees with studying all its processes, looking for ways to do them more efficiently and to produce better quality. For example, a tool-and-die maker spent two months studying how workers changed the dies on punch presses. His observations inspired a two-year project to redesign the processes using the dies. Ultimately, the team on that project figured out how to cut the number of dies used from 100 to 5, which not only saves money but allows the company to fill orders faster.

More important than speed, such improved processes, coupled with modern technology, have opened up new markets by making Deere's operations more flexible and better able to meet precise needs. In the past, Deere mass-produced equipment for farmers and left it to smaller companies to adapt the equipment to each customer's specialized requirements, such as the number of crop rows to be planted and the spacing of those rows. Today, the company has redesigned its manufacturing so that it can affordably make custom attachments with electronic-controlled machinery. A farmer with a particular need discusses it with a Deere salesperson, who can sort through millions of possible configurations to design just the planter, combine, or other equipment the farmer needs, then send electronic orders to the factory. The farmer purchases the customized equipment when the need arises, rather than tinkering with mass-produced equipment until it wears out after a decade's use.

This flexibility also helps Deere tailor the product mix to its dealers' needs. The company used to deliver orders once a year to its U.S. dealers, who then hoped they had forecast farmers' needs accurately. Now Deere makes deliveries weekly, and dealers can adjust their orders if, say, variations in the weather affect demand.[7]

Supply Chain Management

As operations managers adopt a strategic approach, they appreciate that their operations are not independent of other activities. To operate efficiently and produce high-quality items that meet customers' needs, the organization must have reliable deliveries of high-quality, reasonably priced supplies and materials. It also requires an efficient and reliable system for distributing finished products, making them readily accessible to customers. Operations managers with a strategic focus therefore recognize that they need to manage the entire supply chain. **Supply chain management** is the term for managing the sequence of suppliers and purchasers, covering all stages of processing from obtaining raw materials to distributing finished goods to final consumers.[8]

supply chain management
Managing the sequence of suppliers and purchasers, covering all stages of processing from obtaining raw materials to distributing finished goods to final consumers.

Supply chain management techniques are being applied to the cattle industry, where each animal typically has several owners from the time it is born until it is sold as meat. Participants in the supply chain usually join an alliance such as Beef Advantage, which establishes criteria for sharing data and information technology. When calves are born at a ranch, they are tagged with microchips that function like bar codes. Whenever the ranch records data such as the calf's birthdate and weight, it uses the chip to transmit identification

Thiokol Propulsion, the world's largest producer of solid rocket motors for space, is an important part of the supply chain for NASA's Space Shuttle program. Built and tested to NASA's exacting specifications, Thiokol's reusable solid rocket motors (RSRMs) have been used for every space shuttle launch since 1988. Components of the RSRMs are exhaustively checked on one of the largest coordinate measuring machines in the world (photo). Thiokol test-fires an RSRM approximately every eighteen months, or as required by NASA, in its northern Utah test-fire facility.

data about the calf to a computer. Stockers/growers such as Capitol Land and Livestock buy calves when they are weaned; as they feed the calves, they scan the microchips when they record data about weight gain, medical treatments, and so on. Feed-yard operators such as Friona Industries then buy animals and continue the data collection process. The operators combine data on the cattle with data from packing plants to determine what conditions will most efficiently produce the best beef. The sharing of data helps each company in the process avoid duplicating medical treatments and helps it make decisions about the animals' diet. Data sharing also helps with the diagnosis and correction of problems such as diseased or overweight animals.[9]

An important component of supply chain management is managing relationships with suppliers. Managers set up procedures for identifying desirable suppliers, negotiating favorable prices, and monitoring the quality of parts, supplies, and other purchases. For example, before Toyota started buying exhaust systems and suspension components from Arvin Industries, it sent two engineers to the supplier's Indiana facility to get Arvin ready to support Toyota's production strategy. The engineers spent seven months helping Arvin improve work processes, materials management, and quality.[10]

Because supply chain management involves supplier relationships, it relies heavily on the activities known as **logistics** the various activities required to physically move materials into the company's operations facility and to move finished products to customers. Logistics is not merely a matter of transporting goods, but includes those activities along with managing the relationships needed to move goods in a timely and efficient fashion consistent with the company's strategy.[11]

The supplier relationships of many organizations involve an *arm's-length* approach, in which an organization spreads purchases among many suppliers, encouraging them to compete with one another to provide the best quality at the lowest price. Other organizations use *partnering*, cultivating relationships with selected suppliers and collaborating with them to coordinate tasks and help the suppliers meet the organization's unique needs. A study of U.S., Japanese, and Korean automakers found that U.S. companies tended to use the arm's-length approach even with suppliers they called "partners,"

logistics
The activities required to physically move materials into the company's operations facility and to move finished products to customers.

whereas Korean firms tended to use partnering. The Japanese firms, in contrast, varied the type of supplier relationship, using partnering with selected suppliers and a more arm's-length approach with companies providing components that are essentially commodities (for example, batteries and spark plugs). Because they segment suppliers, the Japanese automakers can enjoy the strategic benefits of collaboration with suppliers that produce components that can help them differentiate their products, while also enjoying the low prices that competition stimulates for commodities.[12] This study suggests that, as part of supply chain management, companies can benefit from strategically managing supplier relationships, identifying and cultivating the kind of relationship that is most advantageous for each kind of purchase.

Designing Operations Management Systems

Every organization must design its production system. This process starts with the design of the product or service to be produced. A restaurant designs the food items on the menu. An automobile manufacturer designs the cars it produces. A management consulting firm designs the various types of services it will offer to clients. Once products and services have been designed, the organization turns to other design considerations, including process reengineering, facilities layout, production technology, facilities location, and capacity planning.

Product and Service Design

The way a product or service is designed affects its appeal for customers; it also affects how easy or expensive operations will be. Some product designs are difficult to execute properly. When Volant began making an unconventional type of skis from steel, skiers began snapping them up, delighted with their flexibility and tight grip of the snow. However, producing the skis turned out to be more difficult than anyone at Volant had expected, and many pairs had to be scrapped or reworked. Expenses mounted, and the company failed to meet promised delivery dates. Eventually, Volant hired Mark Soderberg, an engineer with experience at Boeing. Soderberg made a small design change that allowed more generous manufacturing tolerances (variances from the design specifications). After the tooling was adjusted to accommodate the design change, Volant began producing the modified skis—and forecast its first year of operating in the black.[13]

To prevent such problems in the first place, a growing number of businesses are using *design for manufacturability and assembly* (DFMA). Engineering designers have long fashioned products with disdain for how they would be produced. Elegant designs nearly always had too many parts. Thus the watchword is *simplicity,* making the product easy and inexpensive to manufacture. Toyota, for example, slashed the cost of the engine used in its Corolla by cutting the number of parts used by 25 percent. The revamped 120-horsepower engine is also 10 percent lighter and 10 percent more fuel-efficient—features that appeal to consumers as well as Toyota.[14]

Using DFMA is extremely inexpensive. DFMA often requires restructuring operations, creating teams of designers, manufacturers, and assemblers to work together. They collaborate on achieving four objectives of product design:

1. *Producibility* is the degree to which a product or service can actually be produced for the customer within the firm's existing operational capacity.

2. *Cost* simply means the sum of the materials, labor, design, transportation, and overhead expense associated with a product or service. Striving for simplicity and few parts keeps product and service designs within reasonable costs.

3. *Quality* is the excellence of the product or service—the serviceability and value that customers gain by purchasing the product. In recent years, product design has moved toward consumer-friendly products, and companies are taking the time to ask questions such as "How do people use this product?" and "How can we make this product more user friendly?"

4. *Reliability* is the degree to which the customer can count on the product or service to fulfill its intended function. The product should function as designed for a reasonable length of time. Highly complex products often have lower reliability because more things can go wrong.

Toyota takes such criteria into account in its product development process. Working in teams, employees must think not only in terms of design innovation and artistry but also consider scheduling, resources required, and product quality. When possible, groups of models share the same components, which is efficient and minimizes quality problems. Engineers designing one model are encouraged to share ideas with those designing another, thereby speeding development time and avoiding the repetition of mistakes.[15]

The design of services also should reflect producibility, cost, quality, and reliability. However, services have one additional design requirement: timing. *Timing* is the degree to which the provision of a service meets the customer's delivery requirements. Recall that a service cannot be stored in inventory and must be provided when the customer is present. If you take your friend or spouse to a restaurant for dinner, you expect the meal to be served in a timely manner. The powerful push for self-service reflects the need to provide service when the customer wants and needs it. Banking by machine, pumping your own gas, and trying on your own shoes are all ways that organizations provide timely service, which is important in today's time-pressured world.

Process Reengineering

Operations management may include **reengineering,** the reconsideration and redesign of business systems that bring together all elements of a single business process, enabling managers to eliminate waste and delays. Reengineering goes beyond mere speeding up or computerization of old processes. When a company reengineers a process, its management systems, job design, and work flow are reevaluated and changed. Computers often play a major role in reengineering, and major computer companies recognize the new market potential in providing products for reengineering systems. Reengineering can be applied to improve a single department or an entire organization.

To improve its operations as described earlier, Deere & Company uses a reengineering technique called process mapping. So that employees can see all elements of a business process and identify

reengineeing
The reconsideration and redesign of business systems that bring together all elements of a single business process to eliminate waste and delays.

Filling Ultraject® plastic single-dose syringes with X-ray contrast media at Mallinckrodt Inc. would have been a slow, labor-intensive job without the new, automated filling line, installed in 1988 and then reengineered in 1995. The producer of specialty pharmaceuticals improved its producibility, cost, quality, and reliability with the design and reengineering of this system. After reengineering, machine production increased from 8 to 60 125-milliliter syringes a minute, and cost savings were realized even after a $2 million investment. Quality has improved because there is a reduced chance for contamination, and the redesigned automated robotics filling line is 650 percent more efficient than the line it replaced. In the photo, taken at Mallinckrodt's Raleigh, North Carolina plant, the robotics unit in the foreground rotates the syringes 180 degrees in preparation for filling.

problems, they use markers, stick-on notes, and yarn on big sheets of white butcher paper to create a map of whichever process they are redesigning. The employee team studies the map to identify redundancies, quality problems, and other snags in the process that must be corrected. Ultimately, they redraw the process until it runs smoothly.[16]

Facilities Layout

Once a product or service has been designed or reengineered, the organization must plan for the actual production. The four most common types of layout are process, product, cellular, and fixed-position. Exhibit 22.4 illustrates these four layouts.

Process Layout.   As illustrated in panel (a) of Exhibit 22.4, a **process layout** is one in which all machines that perform a similar function or task are grouped together. In a machine shop, the lathes perform a similar function and are located together in one section. The grinders are in another section of the shop. Equipment that performs a similar "process" is grouped together. Service organizations also use process layouts. In a bank, the loan officers are in one area, the tellers in another, and the managers in a third.

The advantage of the process layout is that it has the potential for economies of scale and reduced costs. For example, having all painting done in one spray-painting area means that fewer machines and people are required to paint all products for the organization. In a bank, having all tellers located together in one controlled area provides increased security. Placing all operating rooms together in a hospital makes it possible to control the environment for all rooms simultaneously.

The drawback to the process layout, as illustrated in Exhibit 22.4(a), is that the actual path a product or service takes can be long and complicated. A product may need several different processes performed on it and thus must travel through many different areas before production is complete.

Product Layout.   Panel (b) of Exhibit 22.4 illustrates a **product layout**—one in which machines and tasks are arranged according to the progressive steps in producing a single product. The automobile assembly line is a classic example, because it produces a single product starting from the raw materials to the finished output. Many fast-food restaurants use the product layout, with activities arranged in sequence to produce hamburgers or fried chicken, depending on the products available. The Manager's Shoptalk box describes a new variation on product layout based on the bucket brigade that was used to extinguish fires.

The product layout is efficient when the organization produces huge volumes of identical products. Note in Exhibit 22.4(b) that two lines have paint areas. This duplication of functions can be economical only if the volume is high enough to keep each paint area busy working on specialized products.

Cellular Layout.   Illustrated in panel (c) of Exhibit 22.4 is an innovative layout, called **cellular layout,** based on group-technology principles in which machines dedicated to sequences of operations are grouped into cells. Grouping technology into cells provides some of the efficiencies of both process and product layouts. Even more important, the U-shaped cells in Exhibit 22.4(c) provide efficiencies in material and tool handling and

process layout
A facilities layout in which machines that perform the same function are grouped together in one location.

product layout
A facilities layout in which machines and tasks are arranged according to the sequence of steps in the production of a single product.

cellular layout
A facilities layout in which machines dedicated to sequences of produciton are grouped into cells in accordance with group-technology principles.

Exhibit *22.4*

Basic Production Layouts

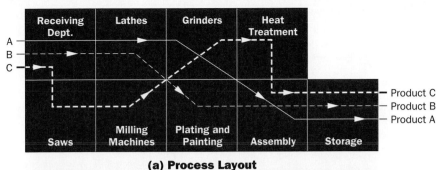

(a) Process Layout

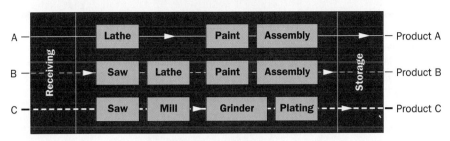

(b) Product Layout

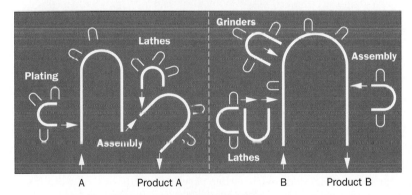

(c) Cellular Layout

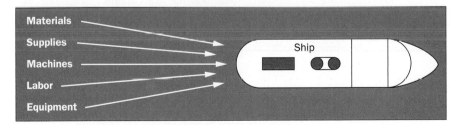

(d) Fixed-Position Layout

SOURCES: Based on J. T. Black, "Cellular Manufacturing Systems Reduce Setup Time, Make Small Lot Production Economical," *Industrial Engineering* (November 1983), 36–48: and Richard J. Schonberger, "Plant Layout Becomes Product-Oriented with Cellular, Just-in-Time Production Concepts." *Industrial Engineering* (November 1983), 66–77.

inventory movement. One advantage is that the workers work in clusters that facilitate teamwork and joint problem solving. Staffing flexibility is enhanced because one person can operate all the machines in the cell and walking distance is small.

The Bucket Brigade: An Old Name for a New Production Plan

As a manager, you probably won't find yourself standing in a real bucket brigade, handing sloshing buckets of water down a line of people toward a flaming building. But you may feel as if you are trying to put out fire after fire in your company's production plan. Two professors, Donald Eisenstein and John Bartholdi, have a plan for you to consider that may make your facility operate more efficiently. They call it the "bucket brigade."

Like the product layout (and a real bucket brigade), workers are assigned to individual tasks at workstations arranged in a sequence. But there are fewer workstations than workers, so workers must move from one task to another during production. (The stations are located near each other, in sequence.) The workers remain in the same sequence throughout the production process, handing off their completed batches of work to the next worker along the brigade and receiving their next batch from their predecessor. If this doesn't sound innovative yet, here's the twist: the slowest worker is always placed at the beginning of the production line, and the fastest at the end of the production line, with moderately paced workers stationed along the continuum. This way, according to Eisenstein and

Bartholdi, there's no bottleneck in the system; work flows continually and smoothly adjusts itself. No amount of work builds up at any single station.

Eisenstein and Bartholdi have already tested their bucket brigade plan in warehouse order picking and apparel manufacturing. They found that warehouse pickers (who actually "pick" items from stock to fill orders) on a bucket brigade became more productive because they never had to wait for work. The spontaneous self-adjustment of workload freed up managers' time, and the accuracy of order picking increased. At Champion Products, a manufacturer of active wear, bucket brigades promoted teamwork, which ultimately resulted in a streamlined production plan and compensation for workers that was based on the productivity of the team. In both cases, workers said they were more satisfied with the new plan.

The potential for the bucket brigade to foster teamwork and flexibility means that managers find themselves putting out fewer fires.

SOURCE: Donald D. Eisenstein and John J. Bartholdi III, "Bucket Brigades," *GSB Chicago*, Spring 1998, 18–20.

---

fixed-position layout
A facilities layout in which the product remains in one location and the required tasks and equipment are brought to it.

Fixed-Position Layout.   As shown in panel (d) of Exhibit 22.4, the **fixed-position layout** is one in which the product remains in one location, and tasks and equipment are brought to it. The fixed-position layout is used to create a product or service that is either very large or is one-of-a-kind, such as aircraft, ships, and buildings. The product cannot be moved from function to function or along an assembly line; rather, the people, materials, and machines all come to the fixed-position site for assembly and processing. This layout is not good for high volume, but it is necessary for large, bulky products and custom orders.

Production Technology

One goal of many operations management departments is to move toward more sophisticated technologies for producing products and services. New technology is sometimes called the "factory of the future." Extremely sophisticated systems that can work almost unaided by employees are being designed. General Motors' newest auto plants use modern production technology, along with other elements of effective operations management.

GENERAL MOTORS
www.gm.com

To expand worldwide, General Motors is taking high-tech manufacturing to its international markets. It is simultaneously building modern assembly plants in four locations: Argentina, Poland, China, and Thailand. The factories include high-tech equipment such as a modern stamping machine that operates faster than comparable machines already in use in GM plants. However, the use of automation is tailored to local conditions. For example, in contrast to GM's high-tech factory in Eisenach, Germany, which is 95 percent automated, automation in Rosario, Brazil, is just 45 percent, to keep start-up costs down in an area in which initial demand is not great and labor costs are low.

The four-plant strategy achieves efficiencies in several ways. By applying the same technology at all four locations, GM enables operations personnel to share knowledge more efficiently. For example, if one plant experiences a problem with a robot, the solution may already have been discovered at another facility. The company has also obtained better prices for bulk purchases of factory equipment. In addition, the design of each factory contributes to efficiency; each layout is shaped like a U, providing many points at which preassembled parts may be delivered.

The designers for these facilities work in teams of employees from Brazil and Germany. They are building on the expertise GM acquired in Eisenach, Germany, where it first applied what it learned about efficiency from joint ventures with Toyota, widely regarded as a leader in manufacturing productivity. In fact, the very notion of building four factories at once comes from Toyota's practice of building nearly identical manufacturing facilities, so that changes in a car's design can be made worldwide with the same adjustments in manufacturing processes.[17]

GM has discovered that automated technology is the most efficient way to expand its manufacturing operations. Two types of production technologies that are widely used in operations management are flexible manufacturing systems and CAD/CAM.

Flexible Manufacturing Systems. The use of automated production lines that can be adapted to produce more than one kind of product is called a **flexible manufacturing system.**[18] The machinery uses computers to coordinate and integrate the machines. Automated functions include loading, unloading, storing parts, changing tools, and machining. The computer can instruct the machines to change parts, machining, and tools when a new product must be produced. This is a breakthrough compared with the product layout, in which a single line is restricted to a single product. With a flexible manufacturing system, a single production line can be readily readapted to small batches of different products based on computer instructions.

Companies often adopt flexible manufacturing to support a strategy of mass customization, that is, quickly adapting products to the specific needs of individual customers, as in the earlier example of Deere & Company. When a company uses mass customization, a customer may order a computer with a particular configuration of components or six pairs of jeans with individually tailored dimensions. Particularly for this application, flexible manufacturing requires skillful management of logistics. In the past, operations managers have viewed logistics as a support function, but companies that use flexible manufacturing coordinate logistics and production activities, recognizing the ways in which

AMETEK is a leading manufacturer of electronic motors and electronic instruments in North America, Europe, and Asia. To achieve earnings per share growth from continuing operations, one of the company's four strategies is "Operational Excellence." AMETEK states that a true test of Operational Excellence is taking the best and making it better. This was done at the AMETEK Lamb Electric motor manufacturing plant in Racine, Wisconsin, which was redesigned to incorporate flow manufacturing techniques. The company's 5-year growth strategy includes the expansion of its flexible manufacturing systems to achieve world-class manufacturing at all of its operations.

Rubbermaid uses a wide range of advanced technologies to create a compelling global competitive edge. This photo shows Stacy Wolff, a lead designer in the Home Products Division's R&D facility, using computer-aided design (CAD) *in product development. The new product concept moves on to* computer-aided manufacturing (CAM), *where final production process tooling is generated. By integrating the CAD and CAM technologies, Rubbermaid can bring new products to market faster than ever before.*

flexible manufacturing system
A small- or medium-sized automated production line that can be adapted to produce more than one product line.

CAD
A production technology in which computers perform new-product design.

CAM
A production technology in which computers help guide and control the manufacturing system.

they are interrelated.[19] Thus, a company using flexible manufacturing will need to share information with its suppliers, so that when it receives an order, the suppliers will be ready to deliver whatever items are needed to fill the order.

CAD/CAM. Operations management in most businesses today employs computers for the design of products, and often for their manufacture as well. **CAD** (computer-aided design) enables engineers to develop new-product designs in about half the time required with traditional methods. Computers provide a visual display for the engineer and illustrate the implications of any design change.

CAM (computer-aided manufacturing) uses computers to direct manufacturing processes, as in flexible manufacturing systems. Typically, the CAM system is linked to CAD, so that the product specifications drive the manufacturing specifications. The computer system thus guides and controls the manufacturing process. For example, a sportswear manufacturer can use computers to mechanize the entire sequence of manufacturing operations—pattern scaling, layout, and printing. Computer-controlled cutting tables are installed. Once the computer has mathematically defined the geometry, it guides the cutting blade, eliminating the need for paper patterns. Computer programs also can direct fabric requisitions, production orders for cutting and sewing operations, and sewing line work.

The first applications of CAD/CAM involved computer-driven machine tools, which can cut and grind materials. However, many modern products are produced using molds, which have been machined by hand at great expense. Engineers extended the use of CAD/CAM to modernize this technology. An application called rapid prototyping (RP) uses CAD to create prototypes (models of a product) through a variety of methods, most of which involve using lasers to cut and bind slices of the object made from layers of plastic or paper. Other RP devices create prototypes by binding layers shaped from powdered steel, ceramics, or starch. For example, Specific Surface, a Franklin, Massachusetts, company, used CAD drawings to make pollution control filters for use in industrial plants. A machine working from the CAD specifications sprayed jets of a binder on layers of powdered ceramics, creating a variety of shapes that together formed the filters. As in this example, the most advanced applications of this technology involve rapid manufacturing: using the lasers to create not just prototypes, but reusable molds or even finished products.[20]

Facility Location

At some point, almost every organization must decide on the location of facilities. A bank needs to open a new branch office, Wendy's needs to find locations for the 100 or so new restaurants opened each year, or a manufacturer needs to build a warehouse. When these decisions are made unwisely, they are expensive and troublesome for the organization. But when they are made well, they can even surpass expectations, as the Leadership box illustrates.

The most common approach to selecting a site for a new location is to do a cost-benefit analysis. For example, managers at bank headquarters may identify four possible locations. The costs associated with each location are the land (purchase or lease); moving from the current facility; and construction, including zoning laws, building codes, land features, and size of the

The "Green Dean" Designs Environmentally Friendly Facilities

Imagine an architect actually creating wetlands—which are protected by law—around a manufacturing facility. That's what William McDonough, president of his own architectural design firm and dean of the University of Virginia's School of Architecture, did with the Miller SQA factory in Zeeland, Michigan. Usually, architects and builders try to stay away from the legal tangle that building near wetlands often causes, but McDonough has a different attitude. He believes in what he calls "eco-effectiveness," meaning that businesses as well as individuals must measure our legacy in terms of its impact on the environment. So, when he designs facilities for companies, including the Gap in California, Miller in Michigan, and Nike in the Netherlands, he takes a truly "green" approach.

McDonough describes the three principles on which he bases his "environmentally intelligent design: Remember that waste equals food. Use current solar income. Respect diversity." McDonough and his team located the Miller SQA facility near a field where they were able to *create* a series of wetlands. Why? To purify waste runoff from the factory. The building's wastewater travels through the wetlands, which naturally purify it. By the time this water reaches the nearby Black River, it is clean, equaling "food." McDonough designed the factory with roof monitors, skylights, and sloped glazing to make maximum use of "solar income" for heat and light, reducing the use of other types of energy and saving the company money. Finally, he created a unique design for the building to fit the local environment. He does not like what he views as the worldwide homogenization of design, in which the same building appears everywhere around the world.

McDonough does not confine himself to design matters related to facility location, however. He also designs layouts and manufacturing processes. When DesignTex Inc. of Switzerland asked him to come up with an organic, environmentally safe fabric, he did that—and went several steps further, designing the process to make the fabric. The process was so eco-effectively designed that government water inspectors thought their testing equipment was broken when they came to monitor the wastewater from the plant. The waste leaving the plant was actually cleaner than the water that entered the plant. "That's revolution," says McDonough proudly.

McDonough encourages all managers to change the way they think about the design of their facilities and products. "If your product is toxic, then stop making it! Don't just make it less toxic—redesign it. Start thinking about good design rather than just green design." Of course, this may mean redesigning manufacturing processes as well as facilities themselves. But in the long run, says McDonough, everyone benefits. "We've got to stop tyrannizing future generations with our bad design," he warns. He believes that it can be done, and he proves it each time he designs a new building.

www.mcdonough.com and www.mbdc.com

SOURCE: Anna Muoio, "This Green Dean Has a Blueprint for Sustainability," *Fast Company,* June/July 1998, 70, 72.

parking lot. Taxes, utilities, rents, and maintenance are other cost factors to be considered in advance. Each possible bank location also will have certain benefits. Benefits to be evaluated are accessibility of customers, location of major competitors, general quality of working conditions, and nearness to restaurants and shops, which would be desirable for both employees and customers. Once the bank managers have evaluated the worth of each benefit, they can divide total benefits by total costs for each location, then select the location with the highest ratio.

Selecting facility location is an important and complex consideration for global corporations, which must take into account cost-based variables such as transportation, exchange rates, and cost of labor. The skill levels of potential workers and the development of regional infrastructure and markets are also important considerations in selecting a location for overseas facilities.[21]

Computer-aided decision support systems and geographic information systems, described in Chapter 21, are often used to aid managers in making a location decision. As described earlier, General Motors is locating more of its facilities near the markets where it expects sales growth. Low wage rates once drove such decisions; however, GM also is increasingly enjoying the talents

Harley-Davidson Motor Company is using capacity planning to keep pace with the growing, worldwide demand for its high-quality motorcycles. As the only major American-based motorcycle manufacturer, Harley-Davidson has brand names that are among the best known in the industry. All three of the company's manufacturing facilities have been extensively redesigned and reconfigured to improve productivity, workflow, product quality, and the environment. Facilities such as this recently completed touring-motorcycle assembly line in York, Pennsylvania, have put Harley-Davidson a full year ahead in its production schedule, and the company plans to have the capacity to produce 115,000 units a year.

capacity planning
The determination and adjustment of the organization's ability to produce products and services to match customer demand.

of local engineers and marketing experts. These people help the company design and build cars that satisfy its growing foreign markets. For example, in designing its four new factories, GM used Brazilian engineers' design of the body shop because of their record in producing many different kinds of vehicles at a single factory. German engineers' success with efficiency gave them great input into the design of the assembly lines. Other conditions of foreign locations may also be favorable. For example, unions in other countries have not established work rules that interfere with such desired innovations as cell layouts and involvement of assembly workers in maintenance.[22]

Capacity Planning

Capacity planning is the determination and adjustment of an organization's ability to produce products or services to match demand. For example, if a bank anticipates a customer increase of 20 percent over the next year, capacity planning is the procedure whereby it will ensure that it has sufficient capacity to service that demand.

Organizations can do several things to increase capacity. One is to create additional shifts and hire people to work on them. A second is to ask existing people to work overtime to add to capacity. A third is to outsource or subcontract extra work to other firms, as described in Chapter 20. A fourth is to expand a plant and add more equipment. Each of these techniques will increase the organization's ability to meet demand without risk of major excess capacity.

The biggest problem for most organizations, however, is excess capacity. When misjudgments occur, transportation companies have oil tankers sitting empty in the harbor, oil companies have refineries sitting idle, semiconductor companies have plants shuttered, developers have office buildings half full, and the service industry may have hotels or amusement parks operating at partial capacity. The challenge is for managers to add capacity as needed without excess.

Inventory Management

inventory
The goods that the organization keeps on hand for use in the production process up to the point of selling the final products to customers.

finished-goods inventory
Inventory consisting of items that have passed through the complete production process but have yet to be sold.

A large portion of the operations manager's job consists of inventory management. **Inventory** is the goods the organization keeps on hand for use in the production process. The Technology box discusses one manager's use of computer systems to track and control hospital supplies. Most organizations have three types of inventory: finished goods prior to shipment, work in process, and raw materials.

Finished-goods inventory includes items that have passed through the entire production process but have not been sold. This is highly visible inventory. The new cars parked in the storage lot of an automobile factory

Hospitals Stock Their Supplies Supermarket-Style

Frank Kilzer had a brainstorm when he was shopping at the supermarket: if grocery clerks could check the store's inventory with a hand scanner, why couldn't hospitals? A decade later, he convinced St. Alexius, the hospital where Kilzer is now director of material resources, to install a similar system for $50,000. The system was a failure—but St. Alexius's computer staff understood its value and designed their own inventory tracking system that used a personal computer and a barcode scanner.

Meanwhile, Mitch Cooper was pressuring Pentagon officials to buy supplies for its military hospitals only from vendors that used bar codes on their products. In many hospitals, supplies were restocked from distributors who would repackage bulk units in smaller packages, which then received different identification numbers at each stop along the supply chain. This outdated method was costing hospitals tens of thousands of unnecessary dollars, and, most of the time, hospital officials didn't know what they had in inventory, or how much.

Now the two men have united to wage a nationwide campaign to revolutionize the health-care product supply chain. The main reasons are cost and time. For instance, if a nurse removes a pair of bar-coded surgical gloves from stock, a reorder from the manufacturer could be automatically triggered, avoiding the cost and extra time it takes for ordering to be processed through a distributor. "It looks like there's 6 percent to 10 percent of cost that could be taken out by buying directly from manufacturers," predicts Jerry W. Rayburn, senior director of resource management at Tenet Healthcare Corp, a large hospital company. At St. Alexius, Kilzer's hospital, before bar-coding was instituted managers could not account for 20 percent of the hospital's costs. Now that number has decreased to 1 percent in some departments. Inventory costs at St. Alexius have dropped 48 percent over the four years that the new system has been in place.

Instituting bar coding has not been a smooth process, however. At Cooper's military hospitals, they got the coding in place, but manufacturers were slow in applying bar codes to their products. "We backed up about ten or fifteen years because we couldn't use equipment we had in place to use bar codes," Cooper recalls. And, as mentioned above, St. Alexius also began with a flop. But hospitals and manufacturers now are beginning to work together, and progress is noticeable. St. Alexius is the nationwide leader of health-care facilities in bar coding. According to the hospital's new procedure, when products arrive, hospital workers apply tiny bar-coded stickers to each item. In the hospital pharmacy, a machine drops pills into single-dose, bar-coded packets. When a nurse is ready to give a patient a dose of medication, he or she just waves a wand scanner across the packet. "It's like having three hundred cash registers," comments Kilzer. Other scanning systems track supplies in the operating room, dialysis center, print shop, and warehouse.

Because of pressure from Kilzer and Cooper, about 40 percent of medical supplies are now bar coded, with the likelihood that that percentage will increase each year. How does the new system stack up with the employees who implement it? "It's a heck of a lot better than it used to be," notes John Davis, who works in the St. Alexius warehouse. His job, which used to be entirely manual, is now accomplished with the wave of a wand.

SOURCE: Rhonda L. Rundle, "Doctors' Orders," *The Wall Street Journal,* June 10, 1997, A1, A8.

---

are finished-goods inventory, as are the hamburgers and french fries stacked under the heat lamps at a McDonald's restaurant. Finished-goods inventory is expensive, because the organization has invested labor and other costs to make the finished product.

Work-in-process inventory includes the materials moving through the stages of the production process that are not completed products. Work-in-process inventory in an automobile plant includes engines, wheel and tire assemblies, and dashboards waiting to be installed. In a fast-food restaurant, the french fries in the fryer and hamburgers on the grill are work-in-process inventory.

Raw materials inventory includes the basic inputs to the organization's production process. This inventory is cheapest, because the organization has not yet invested labor in it. Steel, wire, glass, and paint are raw materials inventory for an auto plant. Meat patties, buns, and raw potatoes are the raw materials inventory in a fast-food restaurant.

work-in-process inventory
Inventory composed of the materials that still are moving through the stages of the production process.

raw materials inventory
Inventory consisting of the basic inputs to the organization's production process.

The Importance of Inventory

Inventory management is vitally important to organizations, because inventory sitting idly on the shop floor or in the warehouse costs money. Many years ago, a firm's wealth was measured by its inventory. Today inventory is recognized as an unproductive asset in cost-conscious firms. Dollars not tied up in inventory can be used in other productive ventures. Keeping inventory low is especially important for high-tech firms, because so many of their products lose value quickly, as they are replaced by more innovative or lower-cost models. For example, the value of a completed personal computer falls about 1 percent a week; even if shelf space for PCs were free, a company would lose money on its PC inventory.[23]

Retail giants such as Wal-Mart, Toys 'R' Us, Home Depot, and Circuit City understand that efficient inventory management is essential to competitive pricing. State-of-the-art information systems allow tight inventory control with the capacity to meet customer needs. The companies schedule orders to eliminate excess inventory. Their suppliers have refined their delivery systems so that the stores receive only the products needed to meet customer purchases. Another company that recently updated its inventory management system to enjoy these benefits is Office Depot.

OFFICE DEPOT
www.officedepot.com

For a retailer like office products superstore Office Depot, inventory is the heart of the business. Success depends on having what customers want, when they want it—but at a low price, which means the company can't afford to keep too much merchandise sitting around. Thus, Office Depot's management thought it a prudent investment to spend $25 million to upgrade the company's computers and inventory management systems.

Inventory management at Office Depot begins with demand forecasting; each store needs to have just what customers will want. The company prepares forecasts based on past sales by store, by item, and by week. They consider the past three years' demand, adjusting for seasonal variations such as tax preparation season and the start of the school year. When possible, the company uses actual demand—for example, asking school districts how much paper they will order for the next year.

The next aspect of inventory management involves minimizing inventory costs by cutting the time between when an order is placed and when items are delivered. When this lead time is short, stores don't need as much safety stock (supplies kept on hand in case of an unexpected order). Office Depot uses electronic data interchange (EDI) for most purchase orders, allowing its purchase orders to go directly to suppliers' order entry systems. Office Depot encourages participation in the EDI system by giving participating suppliers something of value: detailed weekly sales data about their products. In part because of efficiencies achieved through EDI, most of Office Depot's suppliers deliver products within a week or two from the order date.

Office Depot's inventory management system also efficiently handles goods that stores have ordered. When goods arrive at the warehouse, the company's computer checks to see that the stores' actual needs match what was anticipated, then adjusts the distribution of the orders if necessary. In deciding how many of an item to route to a particular store, the system evaluates not only the order quantity but also such factors as the number of items that make the most effective shelf display in the store. Finally, Office Depot has arranged for a company called a freight optimizing service to monitor its orders and arrange for vendors to ship orders together when that is most efficient. Together, these elements of the inventory control system make Office Depot a tough contender in the office products business.[24]

Many companies, such as Office Depot, are recognizing the critical role of inventory management in organizational success. The Japanese analogy of rocks and water describes the current thinking about the importance of inventory.[25] As illustrated in Exhibit 22.5, the water in the stream is the inventory in the organization. The higher the water, the less managers have to worry about the rocks, which represent problems. In operations management, these problems apply to scheduling, plant layout, product design, and quality. When the water level goes down, managers see the rocks and must deal with them. When inventories are reduced, the problems of a poorly designed and managed production process also are revealed. The problems then must be solved. When inventory can be kept at an absolute minimum, operations management is considered excellent. Recognizing this, companies in recent years have reduced inventory levels. In 1982, companies held $167 in inventory for every $100 in sales; in 1997, the ratio had fallen to $136 for every $100 in sales.[26]

We now consider specific techniques for inventory management. Four important ones are economic order quantity, materials requirement planning, manufacturing resource planning, and just-in-time inventory systems.

Economic Order Quantity

Two basic decisions that can help minimize inventory are how much raw materials to order and when to order from outside suppliers. Ordering the minimum amounts at the right time keeps the raw materials, work-in-process, and finished-goods inventories at low levels. One popular technique is **economic order quantity (EOQ),** which is designed to minimize the total of ordering costs and holding costs for inventory items. *Ordering costs* are the costs associated with actually placing the order, such as postage, receiving, and inspection. *Holding costs* are costs associated with keeping the item on hand, such as storage space charges, finance charges, and materials-handling expenses.

economic order quantity (EOQ)
An inventory management technique designed to minimize the total of ordering and holding costs for inventory items.

Exhibit  *Large Inventories Hide Operations Management Problems*

SOURCE: R. J. Schonberger, *Japanese Manufacturing Techniques: Nine Hidden Lessons in Simplicity* (New York: The Free Press, 1982).

The EOQ calculation indicates the order quantity size that will minimize holding and ordering costs based on the organization's use of inventory. The EOQ formula includes ordering costs (C), holding costs (H), and annual demand (D). For example, consider a hospital's need to order surgical dressings. Based on hospital records, the ordering costs for surgical dressings are $15, the annual holding cost is $6, and the annual demand for dressings is 605. The following is the formula for the economic order quantity:

$$EOQ = \sqrt{\frac{2DC}{H}} = \sqrt{\frac{2(605)\,(15)}{6}} = 55$$

The EOQ formula tells us that the best quantity to order is 55.

The next question is when to make the order. For this decision, a different formula, called **reorder point (ROP),** is used. ROP is calculated by the following formula, which assumes that it takes three days to receive the order after the hospital has placed it:

$$ROP = \frac{D}{Time}\,(Lead\ time) = \frac{605}{365}\,(3) = 4.97,\ or\ 5$$

The reorder point tells us that because it takes three days to receive the order, at least 5 dressings should be on hand when the order is placed. As nurses use surgical dressings, operations managers will know that when the level reaches the point of 5, the new order should be placed for a quantity of 55.

This relationship is illustrated in Exhibit 22.6. Whenever the reorder point of 5 dressings is reached, the new order is initiated, and the 55 arrive just as the inventory is depleted. In a typical hospital, however, some variability in lead time and use of surgical dressings will occur. Thus, a few extra items of inventory, called *safety stock,* are used to ensure that the hospital does not run out of surgical dressings. In general, companies keep more safety stock when demand for items is highly variable. When demand is easy to predict, the safety stock may be lower. However, a careful inventory manager may take into account other criteria as well. A sizable price

reorder point (ROP)
The most economical level at which an inventory item should be reordered.

Exhibit **22.6**

Inventory Control of Surgical Dressings by EOQ

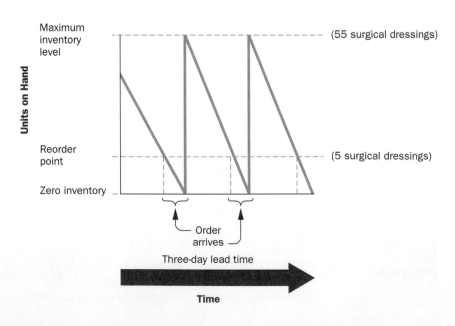

cut or volume discount may make a large purchase economically more attractive, especially in the case of a product the company is almost certain to need in the future.[27]

Materials Requirement Planning

The EOQ formula works well when inventory items are not dependent on one another. For example, in a restaurant the demand for hamburgers is independent of the demand for milkshakes; thus, an economic order quantity is calculated for each item. A more complicated inventory problem occurs with **dependent demand inventory,** meaning that item demand is related to the demand for other inventory items. For example, if Ford Motor Company decides to make 100,000 cars, it will also need 400,000 tires, 400,000 rims, and 400,000 hubcaps. The demand for tires is dependent on the demand for cars.

The most common inventory control system used for handling dependent demand inventory is **materials requirement planning (MRP).** MRP is a dependent demand inventory planning and control system that schedules the exact amount of all materials required to support the desired end product. MRP is computer based and requires sophisticated calculations to coordinate information on inventory location, bill of materials, purchasing, production planning, invoicing, and order entry. Unlike with EOQ, inventory levels are not based on past consumption; rather, they are based on precise estimates of future orders. With MRP, inventory costs can be cut dramatically.

For example, consider the hospital described earlier. Using an MRP approach, the hospital would set up the surgical schedule for the coming week—the equivalent of a master production schedule. For each scheduled surgery, a bill of materials would be issued listing the dressings and other needed items. The inventory status file would show how many surgical dressings the hospital has on hand. Now assume that the master production schedule shows that 20 surgeries will be performed next week, and the inventory status file shows 5 surgical dressings on hand. MRP would then calculate that the hospital needs 20 surgical dressings, less the 5 on hand; thus, 15 would be ordered. They arrive, are used in the 20 operations, and the entire inventory is used up. There are no extra inventory carrying costs and no risk of needing to scrap excess or obsolete inventory. In the meantime, the schedule of surgeries for the following week has been fed into the MRP system, the need for surgical dressings identified, and the inventory-ordered. Inventory flows into the hospital as it is needed, thereby minimizing inventory storage and handling costs.

Manufacturing Resource Planning

Manufacturing resource planning, called **MRP II,** represents a major development beyond MRP. MRP is a technique for managing inventory; MRP II reaches into every company operation to control all resources. MRP II creates a model of the overall business that allows senior managers to control production scheduling, cash flow, human resource planning, capacity planning, inventory, distribution, and materials purchasing. MRP II also supports marketing and engineering and provides financial information. It unites business functions by translating all operations into financial data and provides the entire company with access to the same set of numbers. In the ideal application, it is a computer-based model of the company's operations.

dependent demand inventory
Inventory in which item demand is related to the demand for other inventory items.

materials requirement planning (MRP)
A dependent demand inventory planning and control system that schedules the precise amount of all materials required to support the production of desired end products.

manufacturing resource planning (MRP II)
An extension of MRP to include the control of resources pertaining to all operations of the organization.

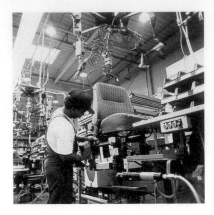

Lear Seating Corporation, the largest independent supplier of automotive seats in the world, pioneered the just-in-time (JIT) *concept in the seating industry and has now taken the concept to a higher level with its Sequential Parts Delivery system. Seat assembly is performed in modules by dedicated, highly skilled teams, and the overall operation is computer driven. Seat system orders are broadcast from the customer's assembly plant, usually as the vehicle leaves the paint department. The order is received by Lear's computers, and completed seat systems are then assembled and automatically sequenced and loaded for transport. Delivery to the customer's plant can occur within as little as 90 minutes.*

just-in-time (JIT) inventory system
An inventory control system that schedules materials to arrive precisely when they are needed on a production line.

Although MRP II evolved from MRP, it supports more of a strategic planning role for senior managers. The hardware and software for MRP II are sophisticated and complex and typically used only in larger companies. Under MRP II, the entire company's efforts are analyzed, and the computer produces corporate plans and solves corporate problems. MRP II starts with the company's business plan, which is translated into sales goals by product line. Sales goals, in turn, are translated into forecasts of materials requirements, inventory needs, and production schedules.

Just-in-Time Inventory

Just-in-time (JIT) inventory systems are designed to reduce the level of an organization's inventory to zero. Sometimes these systems are referred to as *stockless systems, zero inventory systems,* or *Kanban systems.* Each system centers on the concept that suppliers deliver materials only at the exact moment needed, thereby reducing raw material inventories to zero. Moreover, work-in-process inventories are kept to a minimum because goods are produced only as needed to service the next stage of production. Finished-goods inventories are minimized by matching them exactly to sales demand. Just-in-time systems have tremendous advantages. In particular, the reduced inventory level frees productive capital for other company uses.

Just-in-time inventory requires that the production system be simple and well coordinated, as illustrated in Exhibit 22.7. Each part of the production process produces and moves goods forward only when the next stage requires them. JIT is called a *demand-pull* system because each workstation produces its product only when the next workstation says it is ready to receive more input. This is in contrast to the traditional *batch-push system,* in which parts are made in large, supposedly efficient batches and pushed to the next operation on a fixed schedule, where they sit until used. In a push system, each workstation produces at a constant rate regardless of the actual requirement of the next workstation. The demand-pull system can result in reduced inventories, improved quality, and better responsiveness, but it requires excellent coordination among all parts of the production sequence.

Recall the analogy of the rocks and the water. To reduce inventory levels to zero means that all management and coordination problems will surface and must be resolved. Scheduling must be scrupulously precise and logistics tightly coordinated. For example, follow the movement of a shipment of odometers and speedometers from a supplier in Winchester, Virginia, to a GM Saturn plant in Spring Hill, Tennessee.

Thursday, 9 A.M.   A Ryder truck arrives at the supplier. As workers load the parts, drivers check on-board computers for destination, route, and estimated time of arrival (ETA) data.

Friday, 3 A.M.   The truck arrives at Spring Hill, Tennessee, and approaches a switching yard two miles from the Saturn plant, parking in a computer-assigned spot. The driver downloads a key-shaped floppy disk from the on-board computer into Ryder's mainframe, which relays the performance report directly to Saturn.

Friday, 12:50 P.M.   The trailer leaves the switching yard at a designated time and arrives at a predetermined receiving dock at the Saturn plant, where Saturn workers unload the parts and send them to the production line just in time.[28]

Exhibit **22.7** *Just-in-Time Inventory System versus Batch-Push System*

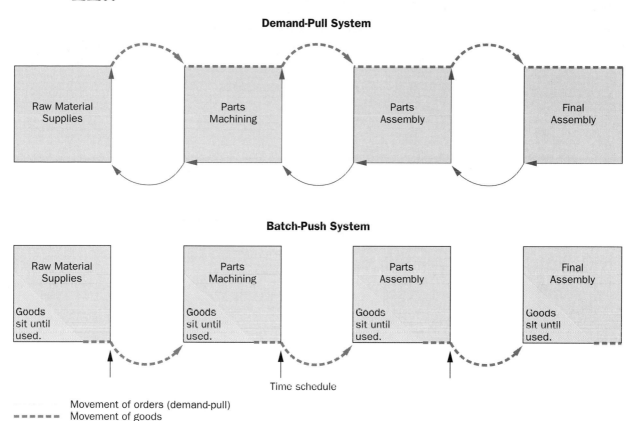

Demand-Pull System

Raw Material Supplies — Parts Machining — Parts Assembly — Final Assembly

Batch-Push System

Raw Material Supplies / Goods sit until used. — Parts Machining / Goods sit until used. — Parts Assembly / Goods sit until used. — Final Assembly / Goods sit until used.

Time schedule

——— Movement of orders (demand-pull)
- - - - - - Movement of goods

When the timing of deliveries—and shipments in the case of companies whose customers also use JIT—must be so precise, logistics expertise becomes a potential source of competitive advantage. Companies want to work with suppliers who reliably meet precise delivery times and dates; they may even pay a premium for this reliability or at least commit to a long-term relationship with reliable suppliers. Some companies develop the necessary logistics expertise in house; others contract with a growing number of contract logistics firms, such as Ryder Systems, Caliber Systems, Inc., and Emery Global Logistics. For example, Emery's services include supply chain management, inventory control, warehousing, distribution and transportation management, and order fulfillment, among others. Robert V. Delaney, vice president of Cass Information Systems, has estimated that 6 percent of logistics activities were outsourced by the mid-1990s and that the share would reach 10 percent by 2000.[29]

General Motors has seen benefits from outsourcing since it contracted with Penske Logistics to handle logistics for its 30 U.S. assembly plants. Based on an analysis of the company's distribution activities, Penske set up a distribution center (a sophisticated warehouse) in Cleveland to receive inventory and distribute it as needed to GM's factories. Penske also operates a fleet of trucks devoted to picking up and delivering the materials as scheduled by its transportation software for maximum efficiency and timely deliveries. Because the trucks pick up inventory for all GM's plants, then consolidate shipments so that inventory from several suppliers goes to each GM factory, the system reduces trucking costs.[30]

The coordination required by JIT demands that information be shared among everyone in the supply chain. In today's fast-paced business environment, communication between only adjoining links in the supply chain is too slow. Rather, coordination requires a kind of information web, in which members of the supply chain share information simultaneously with all other participants.[31] As described in Chapter 21, modern information technology permits this degree of information sharing via extranets and other computer networks.

One reason for using a contract logistics firm is to take advantage of the information technology in which these firms routinely invest. For example, GM's arrangement with Penske Logistics includes an EDI link in which GM gives Penske access to data about its production needs. Based on these data, Penske schedules pickups and deliveries, making adjustments if necessary through satellite communication between truck drivers and dispatchers.[32]

Just-in-time inventory systems also require excellent employee motivation and cooperation. Workers are expected to perform at their best because they are entrusted with the responsibility and authority to make the zero inventory system work. Employees must help one another when they fall behind and must be capable of doing different jobs. Workers experience the satisfaction of being in charge of the system and making useful improvements in the company's operations.[33]

Managing Productivity

During the 1980s, globalization and increased competition from Japan and Europe created a sense of urgency among Americans regarding U.S. growth and productivity. Productivity is significant because it influences the well-being of the entire society as well as of individual companies. The only way to increase the output of goods and services to society is to increase organizational productivity.

Measuring Productivity

productivity
The organization's output of products and services divided by its inputs.

What is productivity, and how is it measured? In simple terms, **productivity** is the organization's output of goods and services divided by its inputs. This means that productivity can be improved by either increasing the amount of output using the same level of inputs or reducing the number of inputs required to produce the output. Sometimes a company can even do both. Ruggieri & Sons, for example, invested in mapping software to help it plan deliveries of heating fuel. The software plans the most efficient routes based on the locations of customers and fuel reloading terminals, as well as the amount of fuel each customer needs. When Ruggieri switched from planning routes by hand to using the software, its drivers began driving fewer miles but making 7 percent more stops each day—in others words, burning less fuel in order to sell more fuel.[34]

total factor productivity
The ratio of total outputs to the inputs from labor, capital, materials, and energy.

The accurate measure of productivity can be complex. Two approaches for measuring productivity are total factor productivity and partial productivity. **Total factor productivity** is the ratio of total outputs to the inputs from labor, capital, materials, and energy:

$$\text{Total factor productivity} = \frac{Output}{Labor + Capital + Materials + Energy}$$

Total factor productivity represents the best measure of how the organization is doing. Often, however, managers need to know about productivity with respect to certain inputs. **Partial productivity** is the ratio of total outputs to a major category of inputs. For example, many organizations are interested in labor productivity, which would be measured as follows:

partial productivity
The ratio of total outputs to the inputs from a single major input category.

$$Productivity = \frac{Output}{Labor\ dollars}$$

Calculating this formula for labor, capital, or materials provides information on whether improvements in each element are occurring. However, managers often are criticized for relying too heavily on partial productivity measures, especially direct labor.[35] Measuring direct labor misses the valuable improvements in materials, manufacturing processes, and work quality. Labor productivity is easily measured, but may show an increase as a result of capital improvements. Thus, managers will misinterpret the reason for productivity increases.

Total Quality Management

Recall from Chapter 20 that total quality management (TQM) improves quality and productivity by striving to perfect the entire manufacturing process. Under TQM, employees are encouraged to participate in the improvement of quality. Quality and productivity teams are created. Training budgets are increased. Statistical techniques are used to assist in spotting defects and correcting them. Moreover, TQM stresses coordination with other departments, especially product design, purchasing, sales, and service, so that all groups are working together to enhance manufacturing quality and productivity.

In the United States, operations managers traditionally have resisted spending money to improve quality, believing that productivity would suffer. TQM, in contrast, recognizes that improvements in quality have a positive impact on productivity. One reason is that dollars spent on improved quality dramatically reduce waste. Poor quality causes huge delayed costs, such as the cost to rework defective products, make repairs, replace dissatisfied customers who do not buy additional products, and deal with dissatisfied customers and returned products.

When implemented properly, TQM can improve operations management. However, many companies have not experienced success. One recent study tried to determine the factors that distinguish companies that enjoy operations improvements from those that see no reduction in defects. The researchers found that companies that experienced success were those at which management viewed TQM as a means to make their companies one of the best and to achieve growth by attracting new customers. Thus, these managers saw TQM not merely as a means to solve current problems but as a way to position the company for the future. These managers viewed the various TQM techniques as being interrelated, and they saw their customers as partners, rather than as adversaries.[36]

Statistical Quality Control

Quality is not just an abstract concept. It must be measured if a TQM system is to be successful. One operations management technique for improving quality and productivity is statistical process control. But measurement is by workers, not top managers or formal control systems. Workers must be given the training and tools to use statistical techniques to evaluate their tasks and make improvements as needed. The use of statistical measurements is a powerful weapon in the drive to improve qualtiy.

Statistical quality control refers to the application of statistical techniques to the control of quality. The best known is called **statistical process control (SPC),** the application of statistical techniques to the control of work processes to detect production of defective items. In addition, workers often are trained in traditional statistical concepts such as frequency distributions, regression and correlation, acceptance sampling, and tests of significance. These techniques are widely used in manufacturing departments, because production activities can be measured and analyzed.

For example, employees can be trained to use charts as graphic representations of work processes. A statistical process control chart measures a specific characteristic, as illustrated in Exhibit 22.8. In this particular chart, workers take a sample of 5 parts each hour, where the production rate is approximately 100 per hour. The diameters of the 5 parts are measured, and the sample mean is calculated and plotted on the chart. If the upper control limit or lower control limit is exceeded, the variation is too great and is not due to chance alone. If either limit is exceeded, the operation is stopped and the cause determined. In the case illustrated in Exhibit 22.8, the tool had become loose, and so it was reset.

Procedures have been developed for implementing statistical quality control, which include the following steps.

1. *Define the characteristics of a high-quality output.* The output can be a hamburger produced by a Wendy's restaurant, a job description written by an employee in the human resource department of AT&T, or a radial tire produced at a Firestone plant. The supervisor must provide an exact definition of a high-quality output or service.

2. *Decompose the work activities into the discrete elements required for producing a high-quality output.* For making a hamburger, one discrete element is forming the raw hamburger patty, a second is cooking it, and a third is garnishing it. The quality associated with each discrete element must be defined.

statistical quality control
The application of statistical techniques to the control of quality.

statistical process control (SPC)
A type of managerial control that employs carefully gathered data and statistical analysis to evaluate the quality and productivity of employee activities.

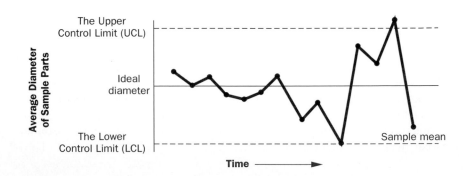

Exhibit **22.8**

A Process Control Chart

SOURCE: Ross Johnson and William O. Winchell, "Management and Quality" (Milwaukee Wis.: American Society for Quality Control, 1989), 7.

3. *Have a standard for each work element that is current and reasonable.* If standards for work elements are not already available, they must be developed. The standard is the basis for comparison of worker performance.

4. *Discuss specific performance expectations for every job with workers.* Each worker must understand what is expected with respect to his or her work elements and quality outputs. Workers should participate in decisions about how their performances will be measured.

5. *Make checksheets, and collect data for each task element.* Written documents must be developed that reflect performance, and machine operators must be taught to collect data and assess whether their performances are up to standard. Likewise, supervisors can monitor departmental performance by gathering data on team outputs.

6. *Evaluate employee progress against standards at frequent intervals.* In some manufacturing situations, the output records should be checked for every worker several times during the day. If employees are involved in running several different batches of material, different standards will apply. If planned quality standards are not met, adjustments can be made before the end of the work period.

Improving Productivity

When an organization decides that improving productivity is important, there are three places to look: technological productivity, worker productivity, and managerial productivity.

Increased *technological productivity* refers to the use of more efficient machines, robots, computers, and other technologies to increase outputs. The flexible manufacturing and CAD/CAM systems described earlier in this chapter are technological improvements that enhance productivity. Robots are another example. One reason that outsourcing can increase productivity is that a specialized firm can afford to invest in the most modern technology related to the service it provides. NationsBank, for example, arranged for Pitney Bowes Management Services (PBMS) to handle its mail services, in part because PBMS has the computer applications to handle the task. Therefore, NationsBank doesn't have to incur the cost of new technology needed to set up a modern mailing system for its 60 mail centers spread out over 16 states and the District of Columbia.[37]

Increased *worker productivity* means having workers produce more output in the same time period. Companies can improve worker productivity by establishing the means for existing employees to do more by working harder or improving work processes. Employees may simply need more knowledge, more resources, or improved task or workplace design. The company may also decide to hire employees with greater expertise or to outsource certain operations to a firm with expertise in that area, as NationsBank did to obtain the knowledge of PBMS. Improving worker productivity can be a real challenge for American companies, because too often workers have an antagonistic relationship with management. Thus, increasing employee productivity often requires improving that relationship. Many of the leadership and management approaches described in this book can enhance worker productivity by motivating and inspiring employees.

Increased *managerial productivity* simply means that managers do a better job of running the business. Leading experts in productivity and quality often have stated that the real reason for productivity problems in the United States is poor management.[38] One of these authorities, W. Edwards Deming, proposed specific points for telling management how to improve productivity. These points are listed in Exhibit 22.9

Management productivity improves when managers emphasize quality over quantity, break down barriers and empower their employees, and do not overmanage using numbers. Managers can learn to use reward systems, employee involvement, teamwork, and other management techniques that have been described throughout this book. However, it is important for managers to consider the linkage between these techniques and the company's strategy—not just to blindly insert a technique into the organization's activities. For example, although many managers have tried to create learning organizations by encouraging their employees to share knowledge, their efforts often fail because employees see no benefits and they lose interest. In contrast, creation of a learning organization tends to succeed when managers

Exhibit
22.9

Condensation of the 14 Points for Management

1. Create constancy of purpose toward improvement of product and service, with the aim to become competitive and to stay in business, and to provide jobs.
2. Adopt the new philosophy. We are in a new economic age. Western management must awaken to the challenge, must learn their responsibilities, and take on leadership for change.
3. Cease dependence on inspection to achieve quality. Eliminate the need for inspection on a mass basis by building quality into the product in the first place.
4. End the practice of awarding business on the basis of price tag. Instead, minimize total cost. Move toward a single supplier for any one item, on a long-term relationship of loyalty and trust.
5. Improve constantly and forever the system of production and service, to improve quality and productivity, and thus constantly decrease costs.
6. Institute training on the job.
7. Institute leadership (see Point 12). The aim of supervision should be to help people and machines and gadgets to do a better job. Supervision of management is in need of overhaul as well as supervision of production workers.
8. Drive out fear, so that everyone may work effectively for the company.
9. Break down barriers between departments. People in research, design, sales, and production must work as a team, to foresee problems of production and in use that may be encountered with the product or service.
10. Eliminate slogans, exhortations, and targets for the workforce asking for zero defects and new levels of productivity. Such exhortations only create adversarial relationships, as the bulk of the causes of low quality and low productivity belong to the system and thus lie beyond the power of the workforce.
11. a. Eliminate work standards (quotas) on the factory floor. Substitute leadership.
    b. Eliminate management by objective. Eliminate management by numbers, numerical goals. Substitute leadership.
12. a. Remove barriers that rob the hourly worker of his right to pride of workmanship. The responsibility of supervisors must be changed from sheer numbers to quality.
    b. Remove barriers that rob people in management and in engineering of their right to pride of workmanship. This means, *inter alia,* abolishment of the annual merit rating and of management by objective.
13. Institute a vigorous program of education and self-improvement.
14. Put everybody in the company to work to accomplish the transformation. The transformation is everybody's job.

SOURCE: Reprinted from *Out of the Crisis,* by W. Edwards Deming by permission of MIT and The W. Edwards Deming Institute. Published by MIT, Center for Advanced Educational Services, Cambridge, MA 02139. Copyright 1986 by The W. Edwards Deming Institute.

establish a strategy-related focus for what information is to be shared, then measure the results. At General Electric, for example, employees focused on learning about how to improve response time. Management had determined that improvements in this area would significantly improve the company's performance. When GE instituted its knowledge management program, managers looked for—and found—improvements in such performance measures as sales per employee.[39] The difference can be attributed to better management, not to specific techniques.

Summary and Management Solution

This chapter described several points about operations management. Operations management pertains to the tools and techniques used to manage the organization's core production process. These techniques apply to both manufacturing and service organizations. Operations management has a great impact when it influences competitive strategy, applying strategic tools such as supply chain management. Areas of operations management described in the chapter include product and service design, process reengineering, location of facilities, facilities layout, capacity planning, and the use of new technologies.

The chapter also discussed inventory management. Three types of inventory are raw materials, work in process, and finished goods. Economic order quantity, materials requirement planning, and just-in-time inventory are techniques for minimizing inventory levels.

Another important concept is that operations management can enhance organizational productivity. Total factor productivity is the best measurement of organizational productivity. Total quality management is an approach to improving quality and productivity of operations. Managers can improve both quality and productivity through statistical process control and through improvements in technology, management, and the workforce.

Boeing, described in the chapter opening, is refocusing its operations management by tackling operations problems from several angles. The company has launched a $1 billion program to modernize and better computerize production (so that it will no longer be using hundreds of unconnected computer systems) and is training managers and workers in the new technology. The automated production technology should speed up the production process, helping to prevent delays and eliminate bottlenecks. However, Boeing still is struggling with supply chain management—in particular, working out better supplier arrangements to be sure it gets parts when they are needed to keep the production process running smoothly. Another change under consideration is to outsource the manufacture of certain components, gradually focusing more and more on Boeing's core competence of design.

In addition to new techniques and technology, CEO Phil Condit and President Harry Stonecipher are changing management philosophy to make Boeing a more performance-oriented company. In particular, they are establishing rigorous production standards and instilling a team-oriented culture. The chief of the commercial airliner division and several of his top managers were let go because they did not want to go along with the new ideas. Stonecipher, who runs the production overhaul day-to-day, hopes to eliminate what he calls "crutches" that lead to production bottlenecks—particularly the use of expediters who are called to the line to fix problems. He also wants to do away with the so-called green and blue assembly lines, separate areas in which planes are reworked because parts were unavailable or were installed incorrectly originally. Each Boeing jetliner has up to four million discrete parts; one mistake means undoing and redoing lots of perfect work to get at the problem. Stonecipher and Condit believe a commitment to quality should be a part of the entire production process. "The automobile guys used to roll cars off to the side to fix things they didn't get right on the assembly line," Condit says. "Go look at production lines at Ford or Toyota now—that doesn't happen anymore." Boeing managers want to be able to say that about aircraft manufacturers as well.

Discussion Questions

1. What are the major differences between manufacturing and service organizations? Give examples of each type.
2. In what ways might a long-distance telephone company be more competitive if it operates at Stage 3 or Stage 4 of operations strategy?
3. What is meant by supply chain management? Does supply chain management apply to service organizations even though they do not produce physical goods? Discuss.
4. What type of production layout do you think would work best in a car dealership? What type would work best for a company that produces handmade pottery? Discuss reasons for your answers.
5. If you were asked to identify a location for a new resort catering to retirees, what steps would you take? How would you plan for the new resort's capacity?
6. What are the three types of inventory? Which of these is most likely to be affected by the just-in-time inventory system? Explain.
7. What is materials requirement planning? How does it differ from economic order quantity to reduce inventory?
8. Imagine you are the manager of a gourmet pizza restaurant. Identify one specific item or process for each of the six steps of implementing statistical quality control in your restaurant.
9. If you were a consultant to a local manufacturing plant that wants to improve productivity, what advice would you give managers?
10. Do you believe operations management can influence competitive strategy? Discuss.

Management in Practice: Experiential Exercise

What is Your Attitude Toward Productivity?

Complete the following questions based on how you think and act in a typical work situation. For each item circle the number that best describes you.

	Disagree Strongly				Agree Strongly
1. I spend time developing new ways of approaching old problems.	1	2	3	4	5
2. As long as things are done correctly and efficiently, I prefer not to take on the hassle of changing them.	5	4	3	2	1
3. I always believe the "effort" to improve something should be rewarded, even if the final improvement is disappointing.	1	2	3	4	5
4. A single change that improves things 30 percent is much better than 30 improvements of 1 percent each.	5	4	3	2	1
5. I frequently compliment others on changes they have made.	1	2	3	4	5
6. I let people know in a variety of ways that I like to be left alone to do my job efficiently.	5	4	3	2	1
7. I am personally involved in several improvement projects at one time.	1	2	3	4	5
8. I try to be a good listener and be patient with what people say, except when it is a "stupid" idea.	5	4	3	2	1
9. I am always proposing unconventional techniques and ideas.	1	2	3	4	5
10. I usually do *not* take risks that would create a problem for me if the idea failed.	5	4	3	2	1

Total Score _____

This scale indicates the extent to which your orientation toward productivity is based on "efficiency" or "continuous improvement." Efficeincy sometimes can be maximized by eliminating change. This may be appropriate in a stable organizational environment. Continuous improvement is an attitude that productivity can always get better and you take personal responsibility to improve it. This attitude is appropriate for a quality-conscious company experiencing frequent change.

A score of 40 or higher indicates that you take personal responsibility for improving productivity and frequently initiate change. A score of 20 or less indicates you make contributions through efficient work in a stable environment. Discuss the pros and cons of the efficiency versus continuous improvement orientations for organizations and employees.

Management in Practice: Ethical Dilemma

A Friend for Life?

Priscilla Dennis has always loved her job as president of Smallworld, a small company that produces and markets toys for young children. As a mother, Priscilla appreciates the care that goes into producing safe, high-quality toys. Late last year, Smallworld's designer invented a small cuddly talking bear. Called the Binky-Bear, the toy was made of soft brown simulated fur and had a tape inside that played 50 messages. To see what kind of appeal the Binky-Bear might have, Smallworld produced 50 of the toys and placed them in kindergartens and nurseries. Results were better than managers had hoped, with many of the kindergartens reporting that the toy quickly became the most popular in the school.

Based on these results, Smallworld decided to produce 1,000 of the bears, and they developed a catchy marketing slogan: "A Friend for Life." The bear was marketed as a toy that children could play with for years and years, and perhaps still have around as a keepsake when they had long outgrown toys. The first batch sold out within a week, so the company scheduled another production run of 25,000. However, during the run, the production manager discovered a problem. In the excitement over the new product, the designer and managers had failed to carefully look at manufacturing considerations. It turned out that the process needed to make Binky-Bear's soft fur was much more expensive than anticipated. Using the original fur will cost the company $4.98 per bear, but the manufacturing department can produce a substitute that will cut the cost to only $2.75 per bear. However, as compared with the original fur, which should last approximately 8 years, the alternate, less-expensive fur will last for only 8 months.

In an emergency meeting to discuss the problem, Smallworld's managers are considering two options: absorb the extra cost, or use the cheaper substitute fur that will not last nearly as long. Many of the managers emphasize that children aren't interested in playing with toys for more than a few months—or even weeks—anyway, so substituting the less-expensive fur shouldn't be a problem. Others, including the production manager, believe the company's reputation for quality will be severely damaged. "We're going to have complaints within 8 months, and we will rue the day we agreed to a cheaper substitute," the production manager said. The vice president for manufacturing agreed, asking, "What are we going to do about our slogan—change it to "A Friend for Eight Months"? The marketing and sales managers forcefully argued the opposite viewpoint, pointing out that Smallworld already had a fortune tied up in the bear. "If you stop production now or continue with the expensive fur, we'll lose our shirts," the marketing manager said. "The bear looks the same. I say we substitute the cheaper fur and no one will ever know the difference."

The final decision about how to handle the problem rests with Priscilla Dennis. She knows Smallworld can't afford to absorb the extra production costs, but can it afford to lose its reputation for quality? Also, she wonders if she can look her young daughter in the eye if she goes along with what the marketing manager is suggesting.

What Do You Do?

1. Substitute the less expensive fur but insist on a revised marketing campaign and advise buyers about the change in the production process.
2. Substitute the less expensive fur and wait to see what happens. The company would not be doing anything illegal, and most customers probably will never notice that the fur wears out so quickly.
3. Absorb the extra production costs. It's the ethical thing to do, and besides, the company's reputation for quality is too important to risk.

SOURCE: Based on "A Friend for Life," in Donald F. Kuratko and Richard M. Hodgetts, *Entrepreneurship: A Contemporary Approach*, 4th ed. (Fort Worth: The Dryden Press, 1998), 172–173.

Surf the Net

1. **Supply Chain Management.** Use your search engine to locate, visit, and write a review of three supply chain management resource Web sites. For example, the Stanford Global Supply Chain Management Forum **www.stanford. edu/group/scforum** "is a program in partnership with industry and the School of Engineering and Graduate School of Business at Stanford University that advances the theory and practice of excellence in global supply chain management." Another resource site can be found at **www.createcom.com/supply-chain.html.** You may review any three sites you choose to explain what is available at each site and which site you would rate as most helpful to a student group preparing a classroom presentation on supply chain management.

2. **CAD/CAM.** Visit a Web site, such as the following, that provides information about CAD and CAM software applications.

   www.cam.org/~flamy/cadcam.html

   Prepare a list of three software products in each category. For each product listed, include as much information as you can find about it from the list that follows: (a) name, (b) manufacturer, (c) price, (d) main use, (e) review comments of the product, (f) miscellaneous information, such as a Web site address that provides downloadable demos of the product

3. **Inventory Management and MRP.** Use your search engine to find Web sites, such as the one listed below, that provide information on inventory management and scheduling systems:

cadlab.mit.edu/~krish/15.566/home.html

Contribute your findings during class discussions on inventory management.

Case for Critical Analysis

Intel

The old adage used to be that fish, newspapers, and house-guests went stale after a day; these days, we could add computer microprocessors to the list. The management at Intel, which constantly manufactures new chips, knows this fact. In order to stay ahead of the competition, Intel has had to juggle its supply chain and its customers' just-in-time inventory demands with supreme skill.

Today, PC manufacturers such as Dell Computer Corp. specialize in build-to-order manufacturing, which means that they expect no slack in the supply chain, holding little or no inventory of finished product or even components. This means that Intel must coordinate its own supply levels, inventory, and manufacturing capacity to meet customers' needs and at the same time demand the same thing from its own suppliers. "All of our [customers] are trying to operate with essentially zero inventory," explains Alan Baldwin, vice president of Intel's planning and logistics group. "They need just-in-time delivery from us and real-time feedback from the marketplace." To accomplish this, Intel set up an extranet to transmit real-time inventory levels and demand to both its suppliers and its customers. Intel also put in place an enterprise resource planning system to improve inventory control, product delivery, and business integration, with an intranet designed to accelerate procurement cycles. But before Intel could actually satisfy its customers' demands, managers had to adjust production capacity so that it could fluctuate when necessary. This meant Intel managers had to analyze suppliers' abilities to provide high-quality materials and equipment.

To help suppliers develop the materials Intel needed, Intel set up Web-based tools that allow suppliers to study new products as Intel designers work on them. Intel maintains strict requirements of its suppliers. "We say to our suppliers, we're going to help you understand our needs, and your responsibility is to keep the bins stocked," notes Mary Murphy-Hoye, manager of strategic programs. Because it is in Intel's best interest to have healthy suppliers, managers work with suppliers to help them improve their own inventory and demand-forecasting methods. "You're only as good as your supply chain," notes Murphy-Hoye.

Intel's focus on its supply chain has paid off. The company used to take 24 hours to confirm orders; now, deliveries can be confirmed as soon as orders are placed. Alan Baldwin asserts that customer satisfaction has increased dramatically.

Intel redesigns its products constantly, overhauling the whole product line about every eighteen months, so manufacturing plants must be flexible. To be flexible, however, management has discovered that instituting identical architecture and applications support for ordering and production planning at every manufacturing site actually speeds up the process. According to Louis Burns, Intel's vice president and director of IT, this system allows the company to make changes and upgrades much more quickly than it could if each site were operated differently. In an industry in which products become obsolete as rapidly as fish or newspapers, speed is everything.

Questions

1. What type of facilities layout do you think would work best at Intel's plants? Why?
2. How might Intel managers use MRP II to control the company's resources?
3. Imagine that you are a manager at one of Intel's manufacturing plants. What steps might you take to ensure that workers are as productive as possible?

SOURCE: Peter Fabris, "Intel Outside," *CIO*, Section 1, August 15, 1998, 64–69.

Endnotes

1. Kenneth Labich, "Boeing Finally Hatches a Plan," *Fortune*, March 1, 1999, 100–106; and Frederic M. Biddle and John Helyar, "Behind Boeing's Woes: Clunky Assembly Line, Price War with Airbus," *The Wall Street Journal*, April 24, 1998, A1.

2. James D. Thompson, *Organizations in Action* (New York: McGraw-Hill, 1967).

3. Alex Taylor III, "How Toyota Defies Gravity," *Fortune*, December 8, 1997, 100–104+.

4. Gregory B. Northcraft and Richard B. Chase, "Managing Service Demand at the Point of Delivery," *Academy of Management Review* 10 (1985), 66–75; and Richard B. Chase and David A. Tanski, "The Customer Contact Model for

Organization Design," *Management Science* 29 (1983), 1037–1050.

5. Everett E. Adam Jr. and Paul M. Swamidass, "Assessing Operations Management from a Strategic Perspective," *Journal of Management* 15 (1989), 181–203.

6. R. H. Hayes and S. C. Wheelwright, *Restoring Our Competitive Edge: Competing through Manufacturing* (New York: Wiley, 1984).

7. Anita Lienert, "Plowing Ahead in Uncertain Times," *Management Review,* downloaded from American Management Association Web site, www. amanet.org, January 6, 1999.

8. Definition based on Steven A. Melnyk and David R. Denzler, *Operations Management: A Value-Driven Approach* (Burr Ridge, Ill.: Richard D. Irwin, 1996), 613.

9. Leigh Buchanan, "From Steer to Eternity," *Inc. Technology,* March 15, 1998, 66–68+.

10. Taylor, "How Toyota Defies Gravity," 108.

11. "Logistics, Logistics, Logistics, Logistics, Logistics," *Canadian Business,* advertising supplement, November 28, 1997, 139–140+.

12. Jeffrey H. Dyer, Dong Sung Cho, and Wujin Chu, "Strategic Supplier Segmentation: The Next 'Best Practice' in Supply Chain Management," *California Management Review* 40 no. 2 (winter 1998), 57–77.

13. Thomas Petzinger Jr., "How a Ski Maker on a Slippery Slope Regained Control," *The Wall Street Journal,* October 3, 1997, B1.

14. Taylor, "How Toyota Defies Gravity."

15. Taylor, "How Toyota Defies Gravity," 103–104.

16. Lienert, "Plowing Ahead in Uncertain Times."

17. Rebecca Blumenstein, "GM Is Building Plants in Developing Nations to Woo New Markets," *The Wall Street Journal,* August 4, 1997, A1, A5.

18. Sumer C. Aggarwal, "MRP, JIT, OPT, FMS?" *Harvard Business Review* 63 (September–October 1985), 8–16; and Paul Ranky, *The Design and Operation of Flexible Manufacturing Systems* (New York: Elsevier, 1983).

19. Noel P. Greis and John D. Kasarda, "Enterprise Logistics in the Information Era," *California Management Review* 39(4) (summer 1997), 55–78.

20. Gene Bylinsky, "Industry's Amazing Instant Prototypes," *Fortune,* January 12, 1998, 120[B]–120[D].

21. Alan David MacCormack, Lawrence James Newman III, and Donald B. Rosenfield, "The New Dynamics of Global Manufacturing Site Location," *Sloan Management Review* (summer 1994), 69–80.

22. Blumenstein, "GM Is Building Plants in Developing Nations."

23. Evan Ramstad, "Compaq Stumbles Amid New Pressures on PCs," *The Wall Street Journal,* March 9, 1998, B1, B8.

24. Malcom Wheatley, "The Next Wave," *CIO,* August 15, 1998, 75–76+.

25. R. J. Schonberger, *Japanese Manufacturing Techniques: Nine Hidden Lessons in Simplicity* (New York: Free Press, 1982).

26. Cathy Lazere, "Taking Stock of Inventory: Beyond Mean and Lean," *CFO,* November 1, 1997, 95–97.

27. Lazere, "Taking Stock of Inventory," 96.

28. Ronald Henkoff, "Delivering the Goods," *Fortune,* November 28, 1994, 64–78.

29. Francis J. Quinn, "Logistics' New Customer Focus," *Business Week* special advertising section, March 10, 1997.

30. Quinn, "Logistics' New Customer Focus."

31. Greis and Kasarda, "Enterprise Logistics in the Information Era."

32. Quinn, "Logistics' New Customer Focus."

33. "Kanban: The Just-in-Time Japanese Inventory System," *Small Business Report* (February 1984), 69–71; and Richard C. Walleigh, "What's Your Excuse for Not Using JIT?" *Harvard Business Review* 64 (March–April 1986), 38–54.

34. Emily Esterson, "First-Class Delivery," *Inc. Technology,* September 15, 1998, 89.

35. W. Bouce Chew, "No-Nonsense Guide to Measuring Productivity," *Harvard Business Review* (January–February 1988), 110–118.

36. Thomas Y. Choi and Orlando C. Behling, "Top Managers and TQM Success: One More Look after All These Years," *Academy of Management Executives* 11(1) (1997), 37–47.

37. The Outsourcing Institute, "Outsourcing: The New Midas Touch," *Business Week,* December 15, 1997, special advertising section.

38. W. E. Deming, *Quality, Productivity, and Competitive Position* (Cambridge, Mass.: Center for Advanced Engineering Study, MIT, 1982); and P. B. Crosby, *Quality is Free* (New York: McGraw-Hill, 1979).

39. Charles E. Lucier and Janet D. Torsilieri, "Why Knowledge Programs Fail: A.C.E.O.'s Guide to Managing Learning," *Strategy and Business,* Fourth Quarter 1997, 14–16, 21–27.

Video Case

How Pier 1 Keeps Everything under Control

It seems like a manager's nightmare, where everything is out of control: 750 stores, 12,500 associates, 4,500 merchandise items, vendors from 40 countries. In a way, it is. But that's the way Pier 1 Imports conducts its business, and so far, the nightmare has actually been a dream come true. The huge retailer sells over $700 million each year in decorative home furnishings, dinnerware, casual clothing, and unique gift items.

A retailer that purchases 85 percent of its merchandise, much of it handmade, from international vendors located in developing countries around the world needs to have a variety of controls in place for its processes and its products. Pier 1 employs a kind of cafeteria-style control focus, using a combination of feedforward, concurrent, and feedback controls whenever they suit the situation. The company also relies on both bureaucratic and decentralized controls. In short, Pier 1 chooses control methods the way it selects merchandise for its customers. "Our corporate values have really been based on relationships," observes Jim Prucha, vice president, merchandise shelf goods. "Since we have this tremendous network of agents and manufacturers throughout the world, we depend on their continuity to give us great product year after year." Thus, Pier 1 practices feedforward control by hiring the best agents and contracting with the best manufacturers and uses decentralized control by empowering these agents and manufacturers, who are located around the world, to make decisions. "Our buyers may come and go," notes Prucha, "but our manufacturers and agents stay the same. They in turn help educate the buyers and help keep the buyers from making mistakes. . . . Normally we've got an agent for each major country that we buy from, and that person is pretty much in charge of representing us in each of these countries, whether it be quality control of facilitating a buy or actually going out and finding product for us."

Control actually comes home to a more bureaucratic approach when merchandise samples are transported back to Pier 1's corporate headquarters in Fort Worth, Texas, to be evaluated for quality. "One of the things that we need to do when we're evaluating quality standards for products at Pier 1 is first set what the standards will be," notes Steve Woodward, vice president, merchandise furniture. "We do that here in the sample room by first bringing the goods in from around the world and having the buyer set the standards here in the sample room. . . . After we sign off on the final standard, that standard becomes the rule." Then control becomes decentralized once again, returned to the agent and manufacturer, who engage in concurrent controls. "We constantly compare [the standard] with the production that's coming off the line," remarks Woodward.

"Once the order is placed, it is up to the agent and his staff to actually monitor the manufacturing of this product to make sure that all quality standards are maintained, that the colors are exactly the same colors that we buy, that the size is the correct size, that there's no issue of poor quality," notes Jim Prucha. Practicing concurrent controls over processes is easier said than done because most of Pier 1's products are handmade and raw materials may be passing through several factories before a finished product emerges. So Pier 1 managers adapt. Steve Woodward explains, "We've got one factory in China, for example, that has over 15,000 employees, and it is a logistical nightmare for them to have all the goods come together like we expect them. So we have to sit down with them on a constant basis reevaluating the flow of goods and what's coming and pushing back orders and moving up orders to help them with their production."

Feedforward and concurrent controls aren't enough to maintain Pier 1's high quality standards, so feedback controls are in place as well, with employees trained and empowered to identify problems and resolve them. "Sometimes we don't catch all the issues and we can catch it at our distribution center as merchandise arrives," says Prucha. "If it's not caught at the distribution center, certainly it will be caught at a store level as our store employees are unpacking merchandise." When that happens, Pier 1 notifies all company stores within 24 hours. Of course, if all else fails, customers will inform Pier 1 of any quality problems. When this happens, explains Prucha, "Our manufacturers do a very good job in reimbursing us. And we, of course, reimburse the customer for any quality problems."

Because Pier 1 believes in monitoring quality every step of the way, the organization is able to control not only the quality of its products, but the quality of its processes as well. In this way, the store can offer shoppers high-quality, crafted pieces that look as though they are one of a kind.

Questions

1. Pier 1 produces low-tech products—handcrafted items made one at a time. How might company managers use high technology to implement process controls?
2. Why doesn't feedforward control completely prevent quality problems at Pier 1?
3. Why is it especially important for Pier 1 managers to establish standards of performance when products are brought to the sampling room in Texas?
4. Would you describe Pier 1 as a learning organization? Why or why not?

SOURCE: "Welcome to Pier 1," accessed March 26, 1999, at www.pier1.com.

732

Human Genome Sciences Uses IT to Find Cures

Half a millennium ago, Leonardo da Vinci sketched the human body in such detail that for centuries, scientists and artists relied on his interpretation of human anatomy for their work. Today, his drawings—as beautiful and complex as they are—have been replaced by computers. Human Genome Sciences is one company that is using state-of-the-art information technology to probe the mysteries of human genetic makeup in order to find cures for all kinds of diseases worldwide. Human Genome Sciences is a pharmaceutical company based in Rockville, Maryland, that employs about 350 scientists, doctors, and other staff in nearly 170,000 square feet of research facilities. The thing that sets HGS apart from other, much larger and older pharmaceutical companies is its heavy reliance on information technology for drug discovery. In fact, while the organization is engaged in researching its own drugs, it is earning substantial revenues by offering other pharmaceutical companies access to its technology.

It's one thing to gather vast amounts of data—it's another to turn that data into information. That's what Human Genome Sciences is good at. "[It's] our ability to go from large numbers of experimental results—on the order of several million over the last five years—and be able to make inferences about those experimental results using computational methods," comments Mike Fannon, vice president and chief information officer of HGS. HGS technology is able to automate the process of identifying and characterizing genes, involving information systems at every level, according to Fannon. "We capture information about human tissues, the source of the tissue, the organ system it came from . . . any diseases that are associated with that. That goes into the database. Then our scientists make extracts of the DNA that's in those cells. All of that information gets captured in the database, and we track these samples through a production process that involves a variety of biological and chemical processing steps." If this seems complicated, it's just the beginning. "This is a very demanding computational requirement as well as a rather demanding data management requirement that's involved here," notes Fannon.

By now, you may be wishing that you could just take a peek at da Vinci's sketches and be done with it; there's way too much data here. But the key to HGS's success with its IT is that it meets the criteria that determine how well the system is functioning. The system quality and information quality are high. "We have integrated things to the point where the instruments can talk directly to databases so that there's really very little chance that information is going to get entered incorrectly," explains Fannon. Scientists who work at HGS all use the system in some fashion. "In the downstream analysis we have our own scientists who are contributing data to the database for helping us understand characterization of the genes, results of various experiments that they might perform," continues Fannon. From an organizational standpoint, the system allows HGS to achieve its mission of finding cures or preventing human disease, first by understanding how problems can occur. "We're helping our pharmaceutical partners and ourselves by characterizing these genes and filing for patents on the composition of the sequence and we speculate about the possible utilities that that might be good for," says Fannon.

Human Genome Sciences conducts its highly sensitive research with strategic partners, who have access to certain information through an extranet that is secure. "All of the connections between us and our partners are typically dedicated connections with hardware encryption devices so that anybody snooping on the network wouldn't be able to, to get anything of use," Fannon explains. "We use Internet firewalls to drastically limit the number of circuits that can come into HGS. So we enable our scientists to go out to the Internet for their own research purposes, but we've established a standard that none of our sequence data gets transmitted across the net. We use cryptographic authentication devices." If this sounds extreme, it is also necessary in a very competitive industry in which companies routinely spend millions of dollars to research and develop new products. Companies like HGS live and die by the currency and quality of their information, so they will protect it any way they can.

Although many of HGS's processes have become automated through information systems, top management has not lost sight of the human factor in scientific research. "We view automation as a way to enhance the way people do the work, rather than to replace the way people work," claims Mike Fannon. "And especially in a research environment where really our biggest asset is our scientists' intuition and their ability to make inferences about the results of these experiments. Our emphasis has been on delivering information systems that don't get in their way." It makes you wonder whether, if he had had access to the same kind of information, da Vinci's drawings would have been different.

Questions

1. Why is it so important for managers at HGS to maintain the distinction between data and information?
2. How might HGS use knowledge management to enhance its competitiveness?
3. In what ways other than those described might HGS make strategic use of information technology?

SOURCE: Human Genome Sciences Web site, accessed March 29, 1999, at www.hgsi.com.

Video Case

Drew Pearson Scores Touchdowns with His Own Company

Lots of former athletes try to go into business for themselves once they retire from professional sports. Lots of them fail. They get bad advice, they don't understand how to run a business, they leave too much of the operations side of the company to others. Drew Pearson is different. A former wide receiver for the Dallas Cowboys, Pearson founded his own headwear company in 1986. After a few fumbles along the way, the company now launches about 60 new baseball-style caps each year and has more than 37 licensing agreements with such organizations as the National Football League, National Basketball Association, Major League Baseball, Warner Brothers, and—perhaps the greatest merchandiser of all—Disney. Drew Pearson Companies earns $60 million a year alone by selling 30 million hats, and that isn't counting the other items it manufactures by itself or through alliances.

None of this could happen without skilled management of operations at Drew Pearson Companies. In just fifteen years, the company has progressed to stage 4 of operations strategy, in which operations enjoys advanced capabilities with significant input to strategic processes and is constantly concerned with new products, new technologies, and expanding into the international market. Here's how the company does it.

First, Drew Pearson Companies is constantly coming up with new designs for its headwear products. "What's really set us apart from our competitors is we come up with innovative designs," notes Pearson. "Our creative services department is made up of three people, and they're very young. And we did that for a reason. They bring new, fresh ideas—and it's not just one every six months, but it's a continuous flow of fresh ideas."

Second, the new ideas Pearson talks about include ways to differentiate DPC products from those of the competition, as well as ways to differentiate among product lines within DPC as part of supply chain management. Because the company's products are sold through different distribution channels to various types of retailers, each distributor and retailer wants a unique product for its customers. Mike Russell, executive vice president of marketing, explains, "DPC's marketing strategy focuses on diversification of product lines . . . unique exclusives that we may have in the marketplace, and then offering exact product differences between channels of distribution. . . . There has to be a differentiation among product lines. If you don't, you won't be selling the department store chain product very long." This commitment to product differentiation led Drew Pearson Companies to expand beyond sports cap licensing. "Our vision right from the start was to have a dual vision in retail America," notes Ken Shead, president of DPC. "Meaning that we could look at sports licensing and mature that—at the same time bring together a well-thought-out strategy for character licensing." Enter Disney and Warner Brothers. Now, "we are the only headwear company that has rights with the Walt Disney Company worldwide," boasts Mike Russell.

Which brings us to the third factor in DPC's advance to stage four of operations strategy: its international expansion. Mike Russell shrugs it off as a natural progression. "From the standpoint of developing products to sell internationally, we're somewhat unique in our industry, I guess, since Mickey Mouse doesn't change whether he's sold in the United States or whether he's sold in the far East or Central America or wherever. . . . We have a definitive line of products that transcend international markets as well. And the demand for American products, or American marks, if you will, is continually growing internationally." But the move to expand internationally took a great deal of planning on the part of operations. Dave Briskie, chief financial officer, explains that the international group stages its product introductions about six months behind the domestic market, managing its inventory carefully. "We're hoping to take our inventory and move it into our warehouses overseas—keep the product flowing that way. Then we've got to be very careful with our purchases because we're overseas. That's our last line of defense. If it doesn't sell there, we're left with a liquidation situation." Planning capacity also crosses international boundaries. In one staff meeting Briskie notes, "We've got 9,438 caps pre-booked out 90 days. What we're looking to do is triple our production in Jagged Edge [a style of cap] from the overseas factories, which we can do."

Finally, company managers focus on production technology such as computer-aided design. Ken Shead describes how "the cut-up cap separated us from our competition. We were able to bring together in our creative services area the first computer that generated art that could show variation in design—three dimensional, forward looks, backward looks—things that our competition had no clue as to how we were generating these looks. While they were trying to figure out the technology, we were gaining market share."

Drew Pearson has managed to achieve far beyond his football career. "It has been a hard process," he muses, "a long time to get to where we are—but it has definitely been a worthwhile process."

Questions

1. What type of production layout do you think would work best for Drew Pearson Companies' products? Why?
2. What types of special challenges might operations managers face with regard to inventory management in any of the DPC's overseas facilities?
3. Would you describe Drew Pearson Companies as a learning organization? Why or why not?

Source: "Introduction," *Sports in Black America*, accessed March 26, 1999, at www.urbansportsnetwork.com; "Drew Pearson Cos.," accessed March 26, 1999, at www.hoovers.com.

Continuing Case

Part Six: Apple Is Back in the Black

Few companies have survived as much upheaval in the first two decades of their existence and come back on top as Apple has. But by 1999, the company was again rolling out hot new products, some of which were winning industry awards.

How did the company manage such a comeback? The media seems to love crediting the return of Steve Jobs as interim CEO—it makes a great story—but Jobs himself, though not generally considered modest, objects. "This is not a one-man show," he explains. It's much more complicated, involving more people. First was the issue of quality control and productivity. For several years, Apple products had failed in the marketplace. Their technology didn't meet customers' needs, they were too expensive, or they didn't live up to expectations. Much of the feedback that Apple received, from customers, industry reviewers, and others, was negative. Apple also seemed to lose its confidence and focus on innovation. With profits down and layoffs looming, productivity declined as well. "There's a lot of really talented people in this company who listened to the world tell them they were losers for a couple of years, and some of them were on the verge of starting to believe it themselves," notes Jobs. "But they're not losers. What they didn't have was a good set of coaches, a good plan. A good senior management team. But they have that now."

If one product launched the company twenty years ago, it could be said that one product helped turn it around—the iMac. Apple managers used their own information technology system to obtain customer feedback about Apple products as they began to develop the iMac. "We have a lot of customers, and we have a lot of research into our installed base," says Jobs. "We also watch industry trends pretty carefully. But in the end, for something this complicated, it's really hard to design products by focus groups." So Apple designers had to implement feedforward controls to minimize the risks of failure of their new product. "A lot of times, people don't know what they want until you show it to them," notes Jobs. "That's why a lot of people at Apple get paid a lot of money, because they're supposed to be on top of these things." The result is that the iMac is a competitively priced computer that gives customers what they want. It is easy to set up and operate, comes Internet ready, is speedy and powerful, and most of all fun—with its rounded translucent case, ergonomic mouse, and its rainbow of colors. Apple seems to have recaptured its early drive to create what Jobs called "insanely great" products for customers.

In addition to addressing problems of product quality, Apple managers began to address problems of quality within their processes, starting with feedback from software developers. "The real problem is that a lot of [software] developers have had a really tough time dealing with Apple over the last few years," admits Jobs. "I talked to these folks. It wasn't even about the volume of Mac sales declining—it was problems in dealing with Apple. We fixed almost all of that. The developers are coming back, and it feels really good. We haven't brought everybody back yet, but a lot of them." Improvement in product and process quality has led Apple to innovate again. "Apple is back to its roots, starting to innovate again, and people are sensing that, seeing it concretely, and really feeling good about it," says Jobs proudly. In addition, Jobs says that streamlining the organization has helped improve company processes. "The organization is clean and simple to understand and very accountable. Everything just got simpler. That's been one of my mantras—focus and simplicity. Simple can be harder than complex: You have to work hard to get your thinking clean to make it simple. But it's worth it in the end because once you get there, you can move mountains."

The world is taking notice of Apple's turnaround. In addition to its new G3 line of computers and QuickTime media software that allows multimedia presentations to play as they are being downloaded from the Internet, Network Computing awarded Apple's WebObjects 4.0 its Software Product of the Year. Network Computing reviews IT and networking products each year, then gives awards to the 50 products it considers to be the best. WebObjects is a network product that simplifies development of Internet, intranet, and extranet applications. Plus, it can run on many different network systems, among them Windows NT and UNIX, as well as Mac OS X. According to Network Computing, "WebObjects makes development of Internet and e-commerce applications fast, efficient, and scalable. . . . Objects created in WebObjects are easily maintained and fully reusable. Along with substantial power and flexibility, WebObjects brings an ease of development rarely seen in industrial-strength development environments." High praise in a competitive industry. But Apple has set its sights squarely on the future of computing and on making complex technology simple to use. In some respects, Jobs and his company have come full circle—the winner's circle. Jobs is pleased. He likes to win.

Questions

1. In what ways might Jobs's "simplicity" mantra have a positive effect on product and service design at Apple?
2. In what ways might Apple use information technology as part of knowledge management?
3. Do you think Jobs should stay on as CEO of Apple permanently? Why or why not?
4. Would you want to work at Apple as a manager now? Why or why not?

SOURCES: Art Wittmann, "The 50 Best Products of the Year," Network Computing, May 17, 1999, accessed at www.networkcomputing.com, "Steve Jobs: 'There's Sanity Returning,'" Business Week, May 25, 1998, accessed at www.businessweek.com.
iMac photo: Courtesy of Apple Computer, Inc.

Glossary

accommodative response A response to social demands in which the organization accepts—often under pressure—social responsibility for its actions to comply with the public interest.

accountability The fact that the people with authority and responsibility are subject to reporting and justifying task outcomes to those above them in the chain of command.

activity-based costing (ABC) A control system that identifies the various activities needed to provide a product or service, determines the cost of those activities, and allocates financial resources according to the true cost of each product or service.

activity ratio A ratio that measures the organization's internal performance with respect to key activities defined by management.

adjourning The stage of team development in which members prepare for the team's disbandment.

administrative model A decision-making model that describes how managers actually make decisions in situations characterized by nonprogrammed decisions, uncertainty, and ambiguity.

administrative principles A subfield of the classical management perspective that focused on the total organization rather than the individual worker, delineating the management functions of planning, organizing, commanding, coordinating, and controlling.

affirmative action A policy requiring employers to take positive steps to guarantee equal employment opportunities for people within protected groups.

ambiguity The goal to be achieved or the problem to be solved is unclear, alternatives are difficult to define, and information about outcomes is unavailable.

application form A device for collecting information about an applicant's education, previous job experience, and other background characteristics.

assessment center A technique for selecting individuals with high managerial potential based on their performance on a series of simulated managerial tasks.

attitude A cognitive and affective evaluation that predisposes a person to act in a certain way.

attributions Judgments about what caused a person's behavior—either characteristics of the person or of the situation.

authoritarianism The belief that power and status differences should exists within the organization.

authority The formal and legitimate right of a manager to make decisions, issue orders, and allocate resources to achieve organizationally desired outcomes.

autocratic leader A leader who tends to centralize authority and rely on legitimate, reward, and coercive power to manage subordinates.

BCG matrix A concept developed by the Boston Consulting Group that evaluates SBUs with respect to the dimensions of business growth rate and market share.

behaviorally anchored rating scale (BARS) A rating technique that relates an employee's performance to specific job related incidents.

behavioral sciences approach A subfield of the humanistic management perspective that applies social science in an organizational context, drawing from economics, psychology, sociology, and other disciplines.

behavior modification The set of techniques by which reinforcement theory is used to modify human behavior.

benchmarking The continuous process of measuring products, services, and practices against major competitors or industry leaders.

biculturalism The sociocultural skills and attitudes used by racial minorities to move back and forth between the dominant culture and their own ethnic or racial culture.

bottom-up budgeting A budgeting process in which lower-level managers budget their departments' resource needs and pass them up to top management for approval.

boundary-spanning roles Roles assumed by people and/or departments that link and coordinate the organization with key elements in the external environment.

bounded rationality The concept that people have the time and cognitive ability to process only a limited amount of information on which to base decisions.

brainstorming A decision-making technique in which group members present spontaneous suggestions for problem solution, regardless of their likelihood of implementation, in order to promote freer, more creative thinking within the group.

bureaucratic control The use of rules, policies, hierarchy of authority, reward systems, and other formal devices to influence employee behavior and assess performance.

bureaucratic organizations A subfield of the classical management perspective that emphasized management on an impersonal, rational basis through such elements as clearly defined authority and responsibility, formal recordkeeping, and separation of management and ownership.

business incubator An innovation that provides shared office space, management support services, and management advice to entrepreneurs.

business-level strategy The level of strategy concerned with the question "How do we compete?" Pertains to each business unit or product line within the organization.

business plan A document specifying the business details prepared by an entrepreneur in preparation for opening a new business.

CAD A production technology in which computers perform new-product design.

CAM A production technology in which computers help guide and control the manufacturing system.

capacity planning The determination and adjustment of the organization's ability to produce products and services to match customer demand.

capital budget A budget that plans and reports investments in major assets to be depreciated over several years.

cash budget A budget that estimates and reports cash flows on a daily or weekly basis to ensure that the company has sufficient cash to meet its obligations.

cellular layout A facilities layout in which machines dedicated to sequences of production are grouped into cells in accordance with group-technology principles.

centralization The location of decision authority near top organizational levels.

centralized network A team communication structure in which team members communicate through a single individual to solve problems or make decisions.

central planning department A group of planning specialists who develop plans for the organization as a whole and its major divisions and departments and typically report to the president or CEO.

ceremony A planned activity that makes up a special event and is conducted for the benefit of an audience.

certainty All the information the decision maker needs is fully available.

chain of command An unbroken line of authority that links all individuals in the organization and specifies who reports to whom.

change agent An OD specialist who contracts with an organization to facilitate change.

changing A step in the intervention stage of organizational development in which individuals experiment with new workplace behavior.

channel The carrier of a communication.

channel richness The amount of information that can be transmitted during a communication episode.

charismatic leader A leader who has the ability to motivate subordinates to transcend their expected performance.

classical model A decision-making model based on the assumption that managers should make logical decisions that will be in the organization's best economic interests.

classical perspective A management perspective that emerged during the nineteenth and early twentieth centuries that emphasized a rational, scientific approach to the study of management and sought to make organizations efficient operating machines.

closed system A system that does not interact with the external environment.

coalition An informal alliance among managers who support a specific goal.

code of ethics A formal statement of the organization's values regarding ethics and social issues.

coercive power Power that stems from the authority to punish or recommend punishment.

cognitive dissonance A condition in which two attitudes or a behavior and an attitude conflict.

collectivism A preference for a tightly knit social framework in which individuals look after one another and organizations protect their members' interests.

committee A long-lasting, sometimes permanent team in the organization structure created to deal with tasks that recur regularly.

communication The process by which information is exchanged and understood by two or more people, usually with the intent to motivate or influence behavior.

compensation Monetary payments (wages, salaries) and nonmonetary goods/commodities (benefits, vacations) used to reward employees.

compensatory justice The concept that individuals should be compensated for the cost of their injuries by the party responsible and also that individuals should not be held responsible for mat-

ters over which they have no control.

competitors Other organizations in the same industry or type of business that provide goods or services to the same set of customers.

conceptual skill The cognitive ability to see the organization as a whole and the relationship among its parts.

concurrent control Control that consists of monitoring ongoing activities to ensure their consistency with established standards.

conflict Antagonistic interaction in which one party attempts to thwart the intentions or goals of another.

consideration A type of leader behavior that describes the extent to which a leader is sensitive to subordinates, respects their ideas and feelings, and establishes mutual trust.

content theories A group of theories that emphasize the needs that motivate people.

contingency approach A model of leadership that describes the relationship between leadership styles and specific organizational situations.

contingency plans Plans that define company responses to specific situations, such as emergencies or setbacks.

contingency view An extension of the humanistic perspective in which the successful resolution of organizational problems is thought to depend on managers' identification of key variables in the situation at hand.

continuous improvement The implementation of a large number of small, incremental improvements in all areas of the organization on an ongoing basis.

continuous process production A type of technology involving mechanization of the entire work flow and nonstop production.

continuous reinforcement schedule A schedule in which every occurrence of the desired behavior is reinforced.

controlling The management function concerned with monitoring employees' activities, keeping the organization on track toward its goals, and making corrections as needed.

coordination The quality of collaboration across departments.

coordination costs The time and energy needed to coordinate the activities of a team to enable it to perform its task.

core competence A business activity that an organization does particularly well in comparison to competitors.

corporate-level strategy The level of strategy concerned with the question "What business are we in?" Pertains to the organization as a whole and the combination of business units and product lines that make it up.

corporation An artificial entity created by the state and existing apart from its owners.

cost leadership A type of competitive strategy with which the organization aggressively seeks efficient facilities, cuts costs, and employs tight cost controls to be more efficient than competitors.

countertrade The barter of products for other products rather than their sale for currency.

creativity The generation of novel ideas that may meet perceived needs or offer opportunities for the organization.

cross-functional team A group of employees assigned to a functional department that meets as a team to resolve mutual problems.

culture The set of key values, beliefs, understandings, and norms that members of a society or an organization share.

culture gap The difference between an organization's desired cultural norms and values and actual norms and values.

culture/people change A change in employees' values, norms, attitudes, beliefs, and behavior.

customers People and organizations in the environment who acquire goods or services from the organization.

cycle time The steps taken to complete a company process.

data Raw, unsummarized, and unanalyzed facts and figures.

data mining Software that uses sophisticated decision-making processes to search raw data for patterns and relationships that may be significant.

data warehousing The use of a huge database that combines all of a company's data and allows users to access the data directly, create reports, and obtain answers to what-if questions.

debt financing Borrowing money that has to be repaid at a later date in order to start a business.

decentralization The location of decision authority near lower organizational levels.

decentralized control The use of organization culture, group norms, and a focus on goals, rather than rules and procedures, to foster compliance with organizational goals.

decentralized network A team communication structure in which team members freely communicate with one another and arrive at decisions together.

decentralized planning staff A group of planning specialists assigned to major departments and divisions to help managers develop their own strategic plans.

decision A choice made from available alternatives.

decision making The process of identifying problems and opportunities and then resolving them.

decision style Differences among people with respect to how they perceive problems and make decisions.

decision support system (DSS) An interactive, computer-based system that uses decision models and specialized databases to support organization decision makers.

decode To translate the symbols used in a message for the purpose of interpreting its meaning.

defensive response A response to social demands in which the organization admits to some errors of commission or omission but does not act obstructively.

delegation The process managers use to transfer authority and responsibility to positions below them in the hierarchy.

democratic leader A leader who delegates authority to others, encourages participation, and relies on expert and referent power to manage subordinates.

departmentalization The basis on which individuals are grouped into departments and departments into total organizations.

dependent demand inventory Inventory in which item demand is related to the demand for other inventory items.

descriptive An approach that describes how managers actually make decisions rather than how they should.

devil's advocate A decision-making technique in which an individual is assigned the role of challenging the assumptions and assertions made by the group to prevent premature consensus.

diagnosis The step in the decision-making process in which managers analyze underlying causal factors associated with the decision situation.

dialogue A group communication process aimed at creating a culture based on collaboration, fluidity, trust, and commitment to shared goals.

differentiation A type of competitive strategy with which the organization seeks to distinguish its products or services from competitors'.

direct investing An entry strategy in which the organization is involved in managing its production facilities in a foreign country.

discretionary responsibility Organizational responsibility that is voluntary and guided by the organization's desire to make social contributions not mandated by economics, law, or ethics.

discrimination The hiring or promoting of applicants based on criteria that are not job relevant.

distributive justice The concept that different treatment of people should not be based on arbitrary characteristics. In the case of substantive differences, people should be treated differently in proportion to the differences among them.

diversity awareness training Special training designed to make people aware of their own prejudices and stereotypes.

divisional structure An organization structure in which departments are grouped based on similar organizational outputs.

downward communication Messages sent from top management down to subordinates.

dual role A role in which the individual both contributes to the team's task and supports members' emotional needs.

E → P expectancy Expectancy that putting effort into a given task will lead to high performance.

economic dimension The dimension of the general environment representing the overall economic health of the country or region in which the organization functions.

economic forces Forces that affect the availability, production, and distribution of a society's resources among competing users.

economic order quantity (EOQ) An inventory management technique designed to minimize the total of ordering and holding costs for inventory items.

economic value-added (EVA) system A control system that measures performance in terms of after-tax profits minus the cost of capital invested in tangible assets.

effectiveness The degree to which the organization achieves a stated goal.

efficiency The use of minimal resources—raw materials, money, and people—to produce a desired volume of output.

empowerment The delegation of power and authority to subordinates.

encode To select symbols with which to compose a message.

enterprise resource planning (ERP) A networked information system that collects, processes, and provides information about an organization's entire enterprise, from identification of customer needs and receipt of orders to distribution of products and receipt of payments.

entrepreneur Someone who recognizes a viable idea for a business product or service and carries it out.

entrepreneurship The process of initiating a business venture, organizing the necessary resources, and assuming the associated risks and rewards.

entropy The tendency for a system to run down and die.

equity A situation that exists when the ratio of one person's outcomes to inputs equals that of another's.

equity financing Financing that consists of funds that are invested in exchange for ownership in the company.

equity theory A process theory that focuses on individuals' perceptions of how fairly they are treated relative to others.

ERG theory A modification of the needs hierarchy theory that proposes three categories of needs: existence, relatedness, and growth.

ethical dilemma A situation that arises when all alternative choices or behaviors have been deemed undesirable because of potentially negative ethical consequences, making it difficult to distinguish right from wrong.

ethics The code of moral principles and values that govern the behaviors of a person or group with respect to what is right or wrong.

ethics committee A group of executives assigned to oversee the organization's ethics by ruling on questionable issues and disciplining violators.

ethics ombudsman An official given the responsibility of corporate conscience who hears and investigates ethics complaints and points out potential ethical failures to top management.

ethnocentrism The belief that one's own group or subculture is inherently superior to other groups or cultures.

ethnorelativism The belief that groups and subcultures are inherently equal.

euro The single European currency that will replace up to 15 national currencies.

executive information system (EIS) A management information system designed to facilitate strategic decision making at the highest level of management by providing executives with easy access to timely and relevant information.

exit interview An interview conducted with departing employees to determine the reasons for their termination.

expatriates Employees who live and work in a country other than their own.

expectancy theory A process theory that proposes that motivation depends on individuals' expectations about their ability to perform tasks and receive desired rewards.

expense budget A budget that outlines the anticipated and actual expenses for each responsibility center.

expert power Power that stems from special knowledge of or skill in the tasks performed by subordinates.

expert system (ES) Information technology that programs a computer to duplicate an expert's decision-making and problem-solving strategies.

exporting An entry strategy in which the organization maintains its production facilities within its home country and transfers its products for sale in foreign markets.

external locus of control The belief by individuals that their future is not within their control but rather is influenced by external forces.

extranet A computer network that uses Internet technology but links authorized users inside the company with certain outsiders such as customers or vendors.

extrinsic reward A reward given by another person.

feedback A response by the receiver to the sender's communication.

feedback control Control that focuses on the organization's outputs; also called *postaction* or *output control*.

feedforward control Control that focuses on human, material, and financial resources flowing into the organization; also called *preliminary* or *preventive quality control*.

femininity A cultural preference for cooperation, group decision making, and quality of life.

figure-ground The tendency to perceive the sensory data one is most attentive to as standing out against the background of other sensory data.

finished-goods inventory Inventory consisting of items that have passed through the complete production process but have yet to be sold.

first-line manager A manager who is at the first or second management level and is directly responsible for the production of goods and services.

fixed-position layout A facilities layout in which the product remains in one location and the required tasks and equipment are brought to it.

flat structure A management structure characterized by an overall broad span of control and relatively few hierarchical levels.

flexible manufacturing A manufacturing technology using computers to automate and integrate manufacturing components such as robots, machines, product design, and engineering analysis.

focus A type of competitive strategy that emphasizes concentration on a specific regional market or buyer group.

force field analysis The process of determining which forces drive and which resist a proposed change.

formal communication channel A communication channel that flows within the chain of command or task responsibility defined by the organization.

formalization The written documentation used to direct and control employees.

formal team A team created by the organization as part of the formal organization structure.

forming The stage of team development characterized by orientation and acquaintance.

franchising A form of licensing in which an organization provides its foreign franchisees with a complete assortment of materials and services; an arrangement by which the owner of a product or service allows others to purchase the right to distribute the product or service with help from the owner.

free rider A person who benefits from team membership but does not make a proportionate contribution to the team's work.

frustration-regression principle The idea that failure to meet a high-order need may cause a regression to an already satisfied lower-order need.

functional-level strategy The level of strategy concerned with the question "How do we support the business-level strategy?" Pertains to all of the organization's major departments.

functional manager A manager who is responsible for a department that performs a single functional task and has employees with similar training and skills.

functional structure An organization structure in which positions are grouped into departments based on similar skills, expertise, and resource use.

fundamental attribution error The tendency to underestimate the influence of external factors on another's behavior and to overestimate the influence on internal factors.

general adaptation syndrome (GAS) The physiological response to a stressor, beginning with an alarm response, continuing to resistance, and sometimes ending in exhaustion if the stressor continues beyond the person's ability to cope.

general environment The layer of the external environment that affects the organization indirectly.

general manager A manager who is responsible for several departments that perform different functions.

geographic information system (GIS) A type of decision support system that provides layers of information expressed visually through the use of maps; used for distribution planning, site selection, and trade area analysis.

glass ceiling Invisible barrier that separates women and minorities from top management positions.

global outsourcing Engaging in the international division of labor so as to obtain the cheapest sources of labor and supplies, regardless of country; also called *global sourcing*.

globalization The standardization of product design and advertising strategies throughout the world.

goal A desired future state that the organization attempts to realize.

grand strategy The general plan of major action by which an organization intends to achieve its long-term goals.

grapevine An informal, person-to-person communication network of employees that is not officially sanctioned by the organization.

Greenfield venture The most risky type of direct investment, whereby a company builds a subsidiary from scratch in a foreign country.

group decision support system (GDSS) An interactive computer-based system that facilitates group communication and decision making; also called *collaborative work system*.

groupthink A phenomenon in which group members are so committed to the group that they are reluctant to express contrary opinions.

groupware Software that enables employees on a network to interact with one another; the most common form of groupware is e-mail.

halo effect An overall impression of a person or situation based on one attribute, either favorable or unfavorable.

halo error A type of rating error that occurs when an employee receives the same rating on all dimensions regardless of his or her performance on individual ones.

Hawthorne studies A series of experiments on worker productivity begun in 1924 at the Hawthorne plant of Western Electric Company in Illinois; attributed employees' increased output to managers' better treatment of them during the study.

hero A figure who exemplifies the deeds, character, and attributes of a corporate culture.

hierarchy of needs theory A content theory that proposes that people are motivated by five categories of needs—physiological, safety, belongingness, esteem, and self-actualization—that exist in a hierarchical order.

high-context culture A culture in which communication is used to enhance personal relationships.

homogeneity A type of rating error that occurs when a rater gives all employees a similar rating regardless of their individual performances.

horizontal communication The lateral or diagonal exchange of messages among peers or coworkers.

horizontal linkage model An approach to product change that emphasizes shared development of innovations among several departments.

horizontal team A formal team composed of employees from about the same hierarchical level but from different areas of expertise.

human relations movement A movement in management thinking and practice that emphasized satisfaction of employees' basic needs as the key to increased worker productivity.

human resource management (HRM) Activities undertaken to attract, develop, and maintain an effective workforce within an organization.

human resource planning The forecasting of human resource needs and the projected matching of individuals with expected job vacancies.

human resources perspective A management perspective that suggests jobs should be designed to meet higher-level needs by allowing workers to use their full potential.

human skill The ability to work with and through other people and to work effectively as a group member.

humanistic perspective A management perspective that emerged around the late nineteenth century that emphasized understanding human behavior, needs, and attitudes in the workplace.

hygiene factors Factors that involve the presence or absence of job dissatisfiers, including working conditions, pay, company policies, and interpersonal relationships.

idea champion A person who sees the need for and champions productive

change within the organization.

implementation The step in the decision-making process that involves using managerial, administrative, and persuasive abilities to translate the chosen alternative into action.

individualism A preference for a loosely knit social framework in which individuals are expected to take care of themselves.

individualism approach The ethical concept that acts are moral when they promote the individual's best long-term interests, which ultimately leads to the greater good.

informal communication channel A communication channel that exists outside formally authorized channels without regard for the organization's hierarchy of authority.

information Data that has been converted into a meaningful and useful context for the receiver.

information reporting system A system that organizes information in the form of prespecified reports that managers use in day-to-day decision making.

information technology The hardware, software, telecommunications, database management, and other technologies used to store, process, and distribute information.

infrastructure A country's physical facilities that support economic activities.

initiating structure A type of leader behavior that describes the extent to which a leader is task oriented and directs subordinates' work activities toward goal achievement.

interdependence The extent to which departments depend on each other for resources or materials to accomplish their tasks.

internal environment The environment within the organization's boundaries.

internal locus of control The belief by individuals that their future is within their control and that external forces will have little influence.

international dimension Portion of the external environment that represents events originating in foreign countries

as well as opportunities for American companies in other countries.

international management The management of business operations conducted in more than one country.

intranet A computer network that uses Internet technology but limits access to all or some of the organization's employees.

intrapreneurship The process of recognizing the need for innovation and promoting it within an organization.

intrinsic reward The satisfaction received in the process of performing an action.

intuition The immediate comprehension of a decision situation based on past experience but without conscious thought.

inventory The goods that the organization keeps on hand for use in the production process up to the point of selling the final products to customers.

ISO 9000 A set of international standards for quality management, setting uniform guidelines for processes to ensure that products conform to customer requirements.

job characteristics model A model of job design that comprises core job dimensions, critical psychological states, and employee growth-need strength.

job description A listing of duties as well as desirable qualifications for a particular job.

job design The application of motivational theories to the structure of work for improving productivity and satisfaction.

job enlargement A job design that combines a series of tasks into one new, broader job to give employees variety and challenge.

job enrichment A job design that incorporates achievement, recognition, and other high-level motivators into the work.

job evaluation The process of determining the value of jobs within an organization through an examination of job content.

job rotation A job design that systematically moves employees from one job to another to provide them with variety and stimulation.

job satisfaction A positive attitude toward one's job.

job simplification A job design whose purpose is to improve task efficiency by reducing the number of tasks a single person must perform.

joint venture A strategic alliance or program by two or more organizations; a variation of direct investment in which an organization shares costs and risks with another firm to build a manufacturing facility, develop new products, or set up a sales and distribution network.

justice approach The ethical concept that moral decisions must be based on standards of equity, fairness, and impartiality.

just-in-time (JIT) inventory systems An inventory control system that schedules materials to arrive precisely when they are needed on a production line.

knowledge management Efforts to systematically gather knowledge, make it widely available in the organization, and foster a culture of learning.

labor market The people available for hire by the organization.

large-group intervention An approach that brings together participants from all parts of the organization (and may include key outside stakeholders as well) to discuss problems or opportunities and plan for major change.

law of effect The assumption that positively reinforced behavior tends to be repeated and unreinforced or negatively reinforced behavior tends to be inhibited.

leadership The ability to influence people toward the attainment of organizational goals.

leadership grid A two-dimensional leadership theory that measures a leader's concern for people and concern for production.

leading The management function that involves the use of influence to motivate employees to achieve the organization's goals.

learning A change in behavior or performance as a result of experience.

learning organization An organization in which everyone is engaged in identifying and solving problems, enabling the organization to continuously experiment, improve, and increase its capability.

legal-political dimension The dimension of the general environment that includes federal, state, and local government regulations and political activities designed to control company behavior.

legitimate power Power that stems from a formal management position in an organization and the authority granted to it.

licensing An entry strategy in which an organization in one country makes certain resources available to companies in another in order to participate in the production and sale of its products abroad.

line authority A form of authority in which individuals in management positions have the formal power to direct and control immediate subordinates.

liquidity ratio A financial ratio that indicates the organization's ability to meet its current debt obligations.

listening The skill of receiving messages to accurately grasp facts and feelings to interpret the genuine meaning.

locus of control The tendency to place the primary responsibility for one's success or failure either within oneself (internally) or on outside forces (externally).

logistics The activities required to physically move materials into the company's operations facility and to move finished products to customers.

low-context culture A culture in which communication is used to exchange facts and information.

LPC scale A questionnaire designed to measure relationship-oriented versus task-oriented leadership style according to the leader's choice of adjectives for describing the "least preferred coworker."

Machiavellianism The tendency to direct much of one's behavior toward the acquisition of power and the manipulation of others for personal gain.

management The attainment of organizational goals in an effective and efficient manner through planning, organizing, leading, and controlling organizational resources.

management by objectives A method of management whereby managers and employees define goals for every department, project, and person and use them to monitor subsequent performance.

management by wandering around (MBWA) A communication technique in which managers interact directly with workers to exchange information.

management information system (MIS) A computer-based system that provides information and support for effective managerial decision making

management science perspective A management perspective that emerged after World War II and applied mathematics, statistics, and other quantitative techniques to managerial problems.

manufacturing organization An organization that produces physical goods.

manufacturing resource planning (MRP II) An extension of MRP to include the control of resources pertaining to all operations of the organization.

market entry strategy An organizational strategy for entering a foreign market.

masculinity A cultural preference for achievement, heroism, assertiveness, work centrality, and material success.

mass production A type of technology characterized by the production of a large volume of products with the same specifications.

matching model An employee selection approach in which the organization and the applicant attempt to match each other's needs, interests, and values.

materials requirement planning (MRP) A dependent demand inventory planning and control system that schedules the precise amount of all materials required to support the production of desired end products.

matrix approach An organization structure that utilizes functional and divisional chains of command simultaneously in the same part of the organization.

matrix boss A product or functional boss, responsible for one side of the matrix.

mechanistic structure An organizational structure characterized by rigidly defined tasks, many rules and regulations, little teamwork, and centralized decision making.

mediation The process of using a third party to settle a dispute.

merger The combination of two or more organizations into one.

middle manager A manager who works at the middle levels of the organization and is responsible for major departments.

mission The organization's reason for existence.

mission statement A broadly stated definition of the organization's basic business scope and operations that distinguishes it from similar types of organizations.

monoculture A culture that accepts only one way of doing things and one set of values and beliefs.

moral-rights approach The ethical concept that moral decisions are those that best maintain the rights of those people affected by them.

most favored nation A term describing a GATT clause that calls for member countries to grant other member countries the most favorable treatment they accord any country concerning imports and exports.

motivation The arousal, direction, and persistence of behavior.

motivators Factors that influence job satisfaction based on fulfillment of high-level needs such as achievement, recognition, responsibility, and opportunity for growth.

multidomestic strategy The modification of product design and advertising strategies to suit the specific needs of individual countries.

multinational corporation (MNC) An organization that receives more than 25 percent of its total sales revenues from operations outside the parent company's home country; also called *global corporation* or *transnational corporation.*

multiple advocacy A decision-making technique that involves several advocates and presentation of multiple points of view, including minority and unpopular opinions.

need to achieve A human quality linked to entrepreneurship in which people are motivated to excel and pick situations in which success is likely.

network A system that links together people and departments within or among organizations for the purpose of sharing information resources.

network structure An organization structure that disaggregates major functions into separate companies that are brokered by a small headquarters organization.

neutralizer A situational variable that counteracts a leadership style and prevents the leader from displaying certain behaviors.

new-venture fund A fund providing resources from which individuals and groups draw to develop new ideas, products, or businesses.

new-venture team A unit separate from the mainstream of the organization that is responsible for developing and initiating innovations.

nonparticipator role A role in which the individual contributes little to either the task or members' socioemotional needs.

nonprogrammed decision A decision made in response to a situation that is unique, is poorly defined and largely unstructured, and has important consequences for the organization.

nonverbal communication A communication transmitted through actions and behaviors rather than through words.

norm A standard of conduct that is shared by team members and guides their behavior.

normative An approach that defines how a decision maker should make decisions and provides guidelines for reaching an ideal outcome for the organization.

norming The stage of team development in which conflicts developed dur-

ing the storming stage are resolved and team harmony and unity emerge.

obstructive response A response to social demands in which the organization denies responsibility, claims that evidence of misconduct is misleading or distorted, and attempts to obstruct investigation.

office automation systems Systems such as word processors, desktop publishing, and e-mail that transform manual procedures to electronic media.

on-the-job training (OJT) A type of training in which an experienced employee "adopts" a new employee to teach him or her how to perform job duties.

open-book management Sharing financial information and results with all employees in the organization.

open communication Sharing all types of information throughout the company, across functional and hierarchical levels.

open system A system that interacts with the external environment.

operational goals Specific, measurable results expected from departments, work groups, and individuals within the organization.

operational plans Plans developed at the organization's lower levels that specify action steps toward achieving operational goals and that support tactical planning activities.

operations information system A computer-based information system that supports a company's day-to-day operations.

operations management The field of management that specializes in the physical production of goods or services and uses quantitative techniques for solving manufacturing problems.

operations strategy The recognition of the importance of operations to the firm's success and the involvement of operations managers in the organization's strategic planning.

opportunity A situation in which managers see potential organizational accomplishments that exceed current goals.

organic structure An organizational structure that is free flowing, has few rules and regulations, encourages employee teamwork, and decentralizes decision making to employees doing the job.

organization A social entity that is goal directed and deliberately structured.

organization chart The visual representation of an organization's structure.

organization structure The framework in which the organization defines how tasks are divided, resources are deployed, and departments are coordinated.

organizational behavior An interdisciplinary field dedicated to the study of how individuals and groups tend to act in organizations.

organizational change The adoption of a new idea or behavior by an organization.

organizational citizenship Work behavior that goes beyond job requirements and contributes as needed to the organization's success.

organizational commitment Loyalty to and heavy involvement in one's organization.

organizational control The systematic process through which managers regulate organizational activities to make them consistent with expectations established in plans, targets, and standards of performance.

organizational development (OD) The application of behavioral science techniques to improve an organization's health and effectiveness through its ability to cope with environmental changes, improve internal relationships, and increase problem-solving capabilities.

organizational environment All elements existing outside the organization's boundaries that have the potential to affect the organization.

organizing The management function concerned with assigning tasks, grouping tasks into departments, and allocating resources to departments; the deployment of organizational resources to achieve strategic goals.

outsourcing The contracting out of a company's in-house function to a preferred vendor.

P → O expectancy Expectancy that successful performance of a task will lead to the desired outcome.

paper-and-pencil test A written test designed to measure a particular attribute such as intelligence or aptitude.

paradigm A mind-set that presents a fundamental way of thinking about, perceiving, and understanding the world.

partial productivity The ratio of total outputs to the inputs from a single major input category.

partial reinforcement schedule A schedule in which only some occurrences of the desired behavior are reinforced.

partnership An unincorporated business owned by two or more people.

path-goal theory A contingency approach to leadership specifying that the leader's responsibility is to increase subordinates' motivation by clarifying the behaviors necessary for task accomplishment and rewards.

pay survey A study of what other companies pay employees in jobs that correspond to a sample of key positions selected by the organization.

pay-trend line A graph that shows the relationship between pay and total job point values for determining the worth of a given job.

perception The process people use to make sense out of the environment, by selecting, organizing, and interpreting information from the environment.

perceptual defense The tendency of perceivers to protect themselves by disregarding ideas, objects, or people that are threatening to them.

perceptual distortions Errors in perceptual judgment that arise from inaccuracies in any part of the perception process.

perceptual grouping The organizing of sensory data into patterns.

perceptual organization The categorization of an object or stimulus according to one's frame of reference.

perceptual selectivity The screening and selection of objects and stimuli that compete for one's attention.

performance The organization's ability to attain its goals by using resources in an efficient and effective manner.

performance appraisal The process of observing and evaluating an employee's performance, recording the assessment, and providing feedback to the employee.

performance gap A disparity between existing and desired performance levels.

performing The stage of team development in which members focus on problem solving and accomplishing the team's assigned task.

permanent team A group of participants from several functions who are permanently assigned to solve ongoing problems of common interest.

person-job fit The extent to which a person's ability and personality match the requirements of a job.

personality The set of characteristics that underlie a relatively stable pattern of behavior in response to ideas, objects, or people in the environment.

plan A blueprint specifying the resource allocations, schedules, and other actions necessary for attaining goals.

planning The management function concerned with defining goals for future organizational performance and deciding on the tasks and resource use needed to attain them; the act of determining the organization's goals and the means for achieving them.

planning task force A temporary group consisting of line managers responsible for developing strategic plans.

pluralism The organization accommodates several subcultures, including employees who would otherwise feel isolated and ignored.

point system A job evaluation system that assigns a predetermined point value to each compensable job factor in order to determine the worth of a given job.

political activity Organizational attempts, such as lobbying, to influence government legislation and regulation.

political forces The influence of political and legal institutions on people and organizations.

political risk A company's risk of loss of assets, earning power, or managerial control due to politically based events or actions by host governments.

portfolio strategy A type of corporate-level strategy that pertains to the organization's mix of SBUs and product lines that fit together in such a way as to provide the corporation with synergy and competitive advantage.

power The potential ability to influence others' behavior.

power distance The degree to which people accept inequality in power among institutions, organizations, and people.

pressure group An interest group that works within the legal-political framework to influence companies to behave in socially responsible ways.

proactive response A response to social demands in which the organization seeks to learn what is in its constituencies' interest and to respond without pressure from them.

problem A situation in which organizational accomplishments have failed to meet established goals.

problem-solving team Typically 5 to 12 hourly employees from the same department who meet to discuss ways of improving quality, efficiency, and the work environment.

procedural justice The concept that rules should be clearly stated and consistently and impartially enforced.

process control system A computer system that monitors and controls ongoing physical processes, such as temperature or pressure changes.

process layout A facilities layout in which machines that perform the same function are grouped together in one location.

process theories A group of theories that explain how employees select behaviors with which to meet their needs and determine whether their choices were successful.

product change A change in the orga-

nization's product or service output.

product layout A facilities layout in which machines and tasks are arranged according to the sequence of steps in the production of a single product.

productivity The organization's output of products and services divided by its inputs.

profitability ratio A financial ratio that describes the firm's profits (for example, sales or total assets).

programmed decision A decision made in response to a situation that has occurred often enough to enable decision rules to be developed and applied in the future.

projection The tendency to see one's own personal traits in other people.

project manager A manager responsible for a temporary work project that involves the participation of other people at a similar level in the organization.

proprietorship An unincorporated business owned by an individual for profit.

quality circle (QC) A group of 6 to 12 volunteer employees who meet regularly to discuss and solve problems affecting the quality of their work.

raw materials inventory Inventory consisting of the basic inputs to the organization's production process.

realistic job preview (RJP) A recruiting approach that gives applicants all pertinent and realistic information about the job and the organization.

recruiting The activities or practices that define the desired characteristics of applicants for specific jobs.

reengineering The radical redesign of business processes to achieve dramatic improvements in cost, quality, service, and speed; bringing together all elements of a single business process to eliminate waste and delays.

referent power Power that results from characteristics that command subordinates' identification with, respect and admiration for, and desire to emulate the leader.

refreezing A step in the reinforcement stage of organizational development in which individuals acquire a desired new

skill or attitude and are rewarded for it by the organization.

reinforcement Anything that causes a given behavior to be repeated or inhibited.

reinforcement theory A motivation theory based on the relationship between a given behavior and its consequences.

reorder point (ROP) The most economical level at which an inventory item should be reordered.

responsibility The duty to perform the task or activity an employee has been assigned.

responsibility center An organizational unit under the supervision of a single individual who is responsible for its activity.

revenue budget A budget that identifies the forecasted and actual revenues of the organization.

reward power Power that results from the authority to reward others.

risk A decision has clear-cut goals, and good information is available, but the future outcomes associated with each alternative are subject to chance.

risk propensity The willingness to undertake risk with the opportunity of gaining an increased payoff.

role A set of expectations for one's behavior.

role ambiguity Uncertainty about what behaviors are expected of a person in a particular role.

role conflict Incompatible demands of different roles.

satisfice To choose the first solution alternative that satisfies minimal decision criteria regardless of whether better solutions are presumed to exist.

schedule of reinforcement The frequency with which and intervals over which reinforcement occurs.

scientific management A subfield of the classical management perspective that emphasized scientifically determined changes in management practices as the solution to improving labor productivity.

search The process of learning about

current developments inside or outside the organization that can be used to meet a perceived need for change.

selection The process of determining the skills, abilities, and other attributes a person needs to perform a particular job.

self-directed team A team consisting of 5 to 20 multiskilled workers who rotate jobs to produce an entire product or service, often supervised by an elected member.

self-serving bias The tendency to overestimate the contribution of internal factors to one's successes and the contribution of external factors to one's failures.

semantics The meaning of words and the way they are used.

servant leader A leader who works to fulfill subordinates' needs and goals as well as to achieve the organization's larger mission.

service organization An organization that produces nonphysical outputs that require customer involvement and cannot be stored in inventory.

service technology Technology characterized by intangible outputs and direct contact between employees and customers.

Shewhart Cycle A planning cycle used in companies that have instituted quality management; also called PDCA— plan, do, check, act—Cycle.

single-use plans Plans that are developed to achieve a set of goals that are unlikely to be repeated in the future.

situational theory A contingency approach to leadership that links the leader's behavioral style with the task readiness of subordinates.

situation analysis Analysis of the strengths, weaknesses, opportunities, and threats (SWOT) that affect organizational performance.

slogan A phrase or sentence that succinctly expresses a key corporate value.

small batch production A type of technology that involves the production of goods in batches of one or a few products designed to customer specifications.

social facilitation The tendency for the presence of others to influence an individual's motivation and performance.

social forces The aspects of a culture that guide and influence relationships among people—their values, needs, and standards of behavior.

social responsibility The obligation of organization management to make decisions and take actions that will enhance the welfare and interests of society as well as the organization.

sociocultural dimension The dimension of the general environment representing the demographic characteristics, norms, customs, and values of the population within which the organization operates.

socioemotional role A role in which the individual provides support for team members' emotional needs and social unity.

span of management The number of employees who report to a supervisor; also called span of control.

special-purpose team A team created outside the formal organization to undertake a project of special importance or creativity.

spin-off An independent company producing a product or service similar to that produced by the entrepreneur's former employer.

staff authority A form of authority granted to staff specialists in their areas of expertise.

stakeholder Any group within or outside the organization that has a stake in the organization's performance.

standing plans Ongoing plans used to provide guidance for tasks performed repeatedly within the organization.

statistical process control (SPC) A type of managerial control that employs carefully gathered data and statistical analysis to evaluate the quality and productivity of employee activities.

statistical quality control The application of statistical techniques to the control of quality.

stereotyping The tendency to assign an individual to a group or broad category and then attribute generalizations about

the group to the individual.

storming The stage of team development in which individual personalities and roles, and resulting conflicts, emerge.

story A narrative based on true events that is repeated frequently and shared by organizational employees.

strategic business unit (SBU) A division of the organization that has a unique business mission, product line, competitors, and markets relative to other SBUs in the same corporation.

strategic goals Broad statements of where the organization wants to be in the future; pertain to the organization as a whole rather than to specific divisions or departments.

strategic management The set of decisions and actions used to formulate and implement strategies that will provide a competitively superior fit between the organization and its environment so as to achieve organizational goals.

strategic plans The action steps by which an organization intends to attain its strategic goals.

strategy The plan of action that prescribes resource allocation and other activities for dealing with the environment and helping the organization attain its goals.

strategy formulation The stage of strategic management that involves the planning and decision making that lead to the establishment of the organization's goals and of a specific strategic plan.

strategy implementation The stage of strategic management that involves the use of managerial and organizational tools to direct resources toward achieving strategic outcomes.

stress A physiological and emotional response to stimuli that place physical or psychological demands on an individual.

structural change Any change in the way in which the organization is designed and managed.

substitute A situational variable that makes a leadership style redundant or unnecessary.

subsystems Parts of a system that depend on one another for their functioning.

superordinate goal A goal that cannot be reached by a single party.

suppliers People and organizations who provide the raw materials the organization uses to produce its output.

supply chain management Managing the sequence of suppliers and purchasers, covering all stages of processing from obtaining raw materials to distributing finished goods to final customers.

survey feedback A type of OD intervention in which questionnaires on organizational climate and other factors are distributed among employees and the results reported back to them by a change agent.

symbol An object, act, or event that conveys meaning to others.

symbolic leader A manager who defines and uses signals and symbols to influence corporate culture.

synergy The condition that exists when the organization's parts interact to produce a joint effect that is greater than the sum of the parts acting alone; the concept that the whole is greater than the sum of its parts.

system A set of interrelated parts that function as a whole to achieve a common purpose.

systems theory An extension of the humanistic perspective that describes organizations as open systems that are characterized by entropy, synergy, and subsystem interdependence.

tactical goals Goals that define the outcomes that major divisions and departments must achieve in order for the organization to reach its overall goals.

tactical plans Plans designed to help execute major strategic plans and to accomplish a specific part of the company's strategy.

tall structure A management structure characterized by an overall narrow span of management and a relatively large number of hierarchical levels.

task environment The layer of the external environment that directly influences the organization's operations and performance.

task force A temporary team or committee formed to solve a specific short-term problem involving several departments.

task specialist role A role in which the individual devotes personal time and energy to helping the team accomplish its task.

team A group of participants from several departments who meet regularly to solve ongoing problems of common interest; a unit of two or more people who interact and coordinate their work to accomplish a specific goal.

team building A type of OD intervention that enhances the cohesiveness of departments by helping members learn to function as a team.

team cohesiveness The extent to which team members are attracted to the team and motivated to remain in it.

technical complexity The degree to which complex machinery is involved in the production process to the exclusion of people.

technical core The heart of the organization's production of its product or service.

technical skill The understanding of, and proficiency in, the performance of specific tasks.

technological dimension The dimension of the general environment that includes scientific and technological advancements in the industry and society at large.

technology The knowledge, tools, techniques, and activities used to transform the organization's inputs into outputs.

technology change A change that pertains to the organization's production process.

telecommuting Using computers and telecommunications equipment to perform work from home or another remote location.

Theory Z A management perspective that incorporates techniques from both Japanese and North American management practices.

360-degree feedback A process that uses multiple raters, including self-rating, to appraise employee performance and guide development.

time-based competition A strategy of competition based on the ability to deliver products and services faster than competitors.

tolerance for ambiguity The psychological characteristic that allows a person to be untroubled by disorder and uncertainty.

top-down budgeting A budgeting process in which middle and lower-level managers set departmental budget targets in accordance with overall company revenues and expenditures specified by top managment.

top leader The overseer of both the product and the functional chains of command, responsible for the entire matrix.

top manager A manager who is at the top of the organizational hierarchy and is responsible for the entire organization.

total factor productivity The ratio of total outputs to the inputs from labor, capital, materials, and energy.

total quality management (TQM) A concept that focuses on managing the total organization to deliver quality to customers. Four significant elements of TQM are employee involvement, focus on the customer, benchmarking, and continuous improvement.

trade association An association made up of organizations with similar interests for the purpose of influencing the environment.

traits Distinguishing personal characteristics, such as intelligence, values, and appearance.

transactional leader A leader who clarifies subordinates' role and task requirements, initiates structure, provides rewards, and displays consideration for subordinates.

transaction processing system A type

of operations information system that records and processes the organization's routinely occurring transactions, such as daily sales or purchases of supplies.

transformational leader A leader distinguished by a special ability to bring about innovation and change.

transnational strategy A strategy that combines global coordination to attain efficiency with flexibility to meet specific needs in various countries.

two-boss employee An employee who reports to two supervisors simultaneously.

type A behavior Behavior pattern characterized by extreme competitiveness, impatience, aggressiveness, and devotion to work.

type B behavior Behavior pattern that lacks Type A characteristics and includes a more balanced, relaxed lifestyle.

uncertainty Managers know what goal they wish to achieve, but information about alternatives and future events is incomplete.

uncertainty avoidance A value characterized by people's intolerance for uncertainty and ambiguity and resulting support for beliefs that promise certainty and conformity.

unfreezing A step in the diagnosis stage of organizational development in which participants are made aware of problems in order to increase their willingness to change their behavior.

upward communication Messages transmitted from the lower to the higher level in the organization's hierarchy.

utilitarian approach The ethical concept that moral behaviors produce the greatest good for the greatest number.

valence The value or attraction an individual has for an outcome.

validity The relationship between an applicant's score on a selection device and his or her future job performance.

venture capital firm A group of companies or individuals that invests money in new or expanding businesses for ownership and potential profits.

vertical team A formal team composed of a manager and his or her subordinates in the organization's formal chain of command.

virtual team A team that uses computer technology and groupware so that geographically distant members can collaborate on projects and reach common goals.

Vroom-Jago model A model designed to help managers gauge the amount of subordinate participation in decision making.

whistle-blowing The disclosure by an employee of illegal, immoral, or illegitimate practices by the organization.

wholly owned foreign affiliate A foreign subsidiary over which an organization has complete control.

workforce diversity Hiring people with different human qualities who belong to various cultural groups.

work-in-process inventory Inventory composed of the materials that still are moving through the stages of the production process.

work redesign The altering of jobs to increase both the quality of employees' work experience and their productivity.

work specialization The degree to which organizational tasks are subdivided into individual jobs; also called division of labor.

Photo Credits

Part Openers

Information contained in the part openers was obtained from the official Whitbread Round the World Race Web site accessed at the time of writing at www.whitbread.quokka.com. Part opener photos ©Kurt Lowman.

Icon in Technology boxes is Courtesy of Magellan; icon in the Apple Continuing Case is Courtesy of Apple Computers, Inc.

Chapter 1

Page 6 © Ann States/SABA. Page 9 © Kristine Larsen. Page 12 © Josef Astor. Page 14 © Doug Menuez/SABA. Page 22 © Gerry Gropp. Page 26 © Terry Doyle/Outline Press.

Chapter 2

Page 42 Courtesy of Maytag Appliances. Page 46 Frederick W. Taylor Collection, S.C. Williams Library, Stevens Institute of Technology. Page 46 Courtesy of Ford Motor Company. Page 47 © Corbis-Bettmann. Page 49 Courtesy of German Information Center. Page 49 Courtesy of Ronald G. Greenwood. Page 50 National Archives. Page 51 Western Electric Photographic Services. Page 55 Courtesy of Weirton Steel Corporation. Page 56 Ray Crowell/Courtesy of United Steel Workers of America.

Chapter 3

Page 75 © Harriet Logan/Network. Page 76 © Douglas Levere. Page 83 Courtesy of Campbell Soup. Page 85 Courtesy of HI TECH. Page 87 © Robbie McClaren/SABA. Page 94 Courtesy of Southwest Airlines.

Chapter 4

Page 104 © Jean-Marc Loubat-Allsport/Vandystadt. Page 105 © Munshi Ahmed. Page 110 © Gamma Liaison. Page 111 © Lara Jo Regan/Gamma Liaison. Page 118 © Chris Brown/SABA. Page 122 © Graham Trott.

Chapter 5

Page 134 © Maggie Hallahan—hallahan@networkimages.com. Page 138 © Ann States/SABA. Page 146 Courtesy of A&P Supermarkets. Page 148 © Todd France. Page 152 © Alfred Ojwang, Pied Crow Magazine, CARE Kenya. Page 156 © Alcoa.

Chapter 6

Page 166 © Austin MacRae. Page 169 © Marc Longwood. Page 173 © Erica Freudenstein/SABA. Page 180 © 1999 Brian Smith. Page 186 © Kim Kulish/SABA. Page 189 © Ronald Robinson.

Chapter 7

Page 208 © 1998 Forest McMullin, Courtesy of Agrilink Foods. Page 211 Courtesy of Owens Corning. Page 214 © Steve Niedorf. Page 221 Photo by Michael Mauney, Courtesy of Walgreen Co. Page 222 Courtesy of AMETEK, Inc. Page 226 © George Simian.

Chapter 8

Page 235 © Peter Hince. Page 239 © Munshi Ahmed. Page 243 Courtesy of Merck & Co., Inc., Photographer William Taufic. Page 245 © Alan Levenson. Page 255 Courtesy of Amtran. Page 258 © Tony Baker.

Chapter 9

Page 270 © 1999 David E. Quinney, Jr. Page 274 Courtesy of Hudson Corporation. Page 275 © Stan Godlewski. Page 278 Reprinted with permission Gateway 2000, Inc. © 1998. Page 286 Courtesy of Monsanto Global Seed Group. Page 290 © 1994 Ron Chapple.

Chapter 10

Page 306 © John Madere. Page 309 Jay Rusovich for Andarko. Page 312 Courtesy of Synovus Financial Corp. Page 316 Courtesy Merck & Co., Inc. Page 325 Courtesy of Avery Dennison Corp.

Chapter 11

Page 341 Courtesy Rohm and Haas Company. Page 345 © Kathy Tarantola. Page 349 Tres Watson, Photographer for Ensearch Corporation. Page 352 © Ted Rice. Page 353 Courtesy of Dana Corporation. Page 354 © Duane Hall.

Chapter 12

Page 367 © Karl H. Nemecok, MetLife. Page 368 © Marc Royce. Page 376 © 1994 Bill Albrecht. Page 378 The Boeing Company. Page 381 © Ted Quinn/SABA. Page 383 © Daniel Levin.

Chapter 13

Page 394 Photo by Michael Mauney, Courtesy of Walgreen Co. Page 400 © 1994 Jamie Tanaka. Page 401 © Rex Rystedt. Page 404 © Robert Holmgren. Page 411 Courtesy of Dillard's, Inc. Page 413 © Fritz Hoffmann.

Chapter 14

Page 429 © Mark Peterson/SABA. Page 436 © Steve Mellon. Page 440 © Rocky Thies. Page 443 Courtesy of Colgate-Palmolive Company. Page 448 Courtesy of Texas Instruments. Page 450 © Paul F. Gero.

Chapter 15

Page 469 © Paul Elledge. **Page 471** © Peter Charlesworth/SABA. **Page 474** Ann States/SABA. **Page 484** © William Mercer McLeod. **Page 489** CMF&Z Advertising, Des Moines, Iowa, used with permission by the Iowa Department of Economic Development. **Page 494** © Gus Gustovich.

Chapter 16

Page 504 © Alan Levenson. **Page 507** © Amy Cantrell. **Page 512** © Alan Levenson. **Page 518** © Scott Peterson/Gamma Liaison. **Page 523** © Alan Levenson. **Page 525** © 1998 Emmett Martin.

Chapter 17

Page 535 © Gregory Foster. **Page 538** Georgia-Pacific Corp./Jim Robinson. **Page 543** © Daniel Sheehan/The Liaison Agency. **Page 544** © Barbara Laing. **Page 552** © Jeff Zaruba. **Page 555** © Suzanne Opton.

Chapter 18

Page 566 © Chris Schrameck. **Page 570** Courtesy of Ford Motor Company. **Page 579** © Brian Coats. **Page 581** Courtesy of Valassis Communications. **Page 584** © Peter Sibbald, 1998. **Page 589** © 1998 David Zadig.

Chapter 19

Page 599 Courtesy of TRINOVA Corporation. **Page 604** © Marc Hauser. **Page 610** © Robbie McClaran. **Page 612**

Courtesy of Gilbane Building Company. **Page 618** © Mike Malone. **Page 621** Michael Hart Photography for Cooper Industries.

Chapter 20

Page 638 © Thomas Broening. **Page 641** Courtesy of Honeywell Inc. **Page 645** Courtesy of Baldor Electric Company, Fort Smith, Arkansas. **Page 648** People Weekly © 1998 Todd France. **Page 651** Courtesy of General Electric. **Page 655** Courtesy of Emerson Electric Co.

Chapter 21

Page 671 Photo used with permission of Citibank, a member of Citigroup Inc. **Page 673** © Rocky Kneten. **Page 679** Courtesy of Ryder Systems, Inc. **Page 681** Courtesy of Ohio Casualty Insurance Company. **Page 684** Reprinted with permission from Huntington Bancshares Incorporated, 1986. **Page 686** © Manuello Paganelli.

Chapter 22

Page 705 Courtesy of Cordant Technologies. **Page 707** © Mark Joseph Photography, Inc. **Page 711** Courtesy of Ametek, Inc. **Page 712** © 1993 Rubbermaid Incorporated, Wooster, Ohio. Used with permission. **Page 714** © James Schnepf. **Page 720** Courtesy of Lear Seating Corporation.

Name Index

Company Index

Subject Index